Dictionary of
Food

Dictionary of
Food

International Food and Cooking
Terms from A to Z

Second Edition

Charles Sinclair

A & C Black • London

www.acblack.com

Contributors
Alyson Cole, Eri Eguchi, Magda Hughes, Sarah Lusznat,
Diane Nicholls, Helen Szirtes, Maureen Teulier

Text Production and Proofreading
Katy McAdam, Joel Adams, Heather Bateman, Emma Harris

First edition published 1998
as *International Dictionary of Food and Cooking*
Reprinted 1999

Second edition published 2004
as *A Cook's Dictionary*

This paperback edition published 2005
Reprinted 2008

A & C Black Publishers Ltd
37 Soho Square, London W1D 3QZ

A CIP record for this book is available from the British Library.

ISBN 978 0 7136 7500 9

A & C Black uses paper produced with elemental chlorine-free pulp,
harvested from managed sustainable forests.

Text processed and typeset by A & C Black
Printed and bound in Spain by Graphycems

Preface

The language of English cuisine is unusual in that it uses many words of foreign origin, often in their original spelling. The purpose of this dictionary is to give short definitions of these words so that both the practising chef and the amateur enthusiast, the gastronome and the student may quickly determine the meaning. It is not a recipe book or a repertoire, but it does give the ingredients of classic and well-known dishes, together with a brief summary of the cooking processes. A picture of a chef's hat indicates dishes that the professional or amateur cook could, after a little experimentation, roughly reproduce.

As in all dictionaries, the compiler has had to be selective in the words chosen for inclusion. Even so, the dictionary lists over 24,000 words, of which very few are not in current use somewhere in the English-speaking world. Some entries have been included for historical reasons and the browser will find much of interest. Classic dishes, ingredients, cooking processes, cooking implements and equipment, descriptions of function and details of service are included as well as scientific, botanical, medical, technological, hygienic and nutritional terms. Many single words appertaining to the catering industry from the countries of the European Union are translated, and the dictionary is of use in translating menu items not included. Drinks, wines and spirits are not included except where they are used as flavourings in food and food preparation.

Order of entries
All words are listed in strict alphabetical order, ignoring spaces or hyphens. Thus *à point* comes after *apog* and *S-Gebäck* after *sformata*. Numbers come before letters, so E-numbers such as *E101* and *E483* come before *earth almond* and *earth nut*. Accented characters are assumed to follow the unaccented characters which they resemble. Thus *o* comes before *ó* or *ô*, for example.

Verbs are listed as *blend, to* and *roast, to*, for example.

The names of many items in the French repertoire have been taken over wholesale into the English language. For example, *sauce béchamel* is known as *béchamel sauce*, often retaining the French acute accent, and for this reason – and to avoid making the entries too repetitious – this type of entry is listed in reverse order of the words in the dictionary. Thus *sauce béchamel* would appear under the heading *béchamel, sauce*; other examples are *supreme, sauce* and *aurora, sauce*. Similar examples occur with whole classes of French names such as *beurre* (butter), *garniture* (garnish), *salade*, *potage* (soup), *consommé*, *soufflé* etc. Phrases from French and other European languages beginning with *à la*, *al*, *alla*, *en*, etc. are also listed in reverse order:

diable *France* **1.** An unglazed earthenware cooking pot in two symmetrical halves which when put together resembles a ball with two flat sides and a long handle. Used for cooking chestnuts and vegetables without water either in the oven or on top of the stove. Can be shaken and turned over for even cooking. **2.** Kidneys or poussins, split, flattened, grilled and served with sauce diable

diable, à la *France* Strongly flavoured with a selection of Worcestershire and Tabasco sauces, mustard, cayenne pepper and vinegar. Also called **devilled**

diable, sauce *England, France* A reduction of chopped shallots, white wine, vinegar, cayenne pepper and mignonette pepper simmered with demi-glace, strained and seasoned. Served with fried or grilled fish or meat. Also called **devilled sauce**

diable de mer *France see* **monkfish**

diablo, en *Mexico, Spain* Devilled, hot and spicy

diablotins *France* **1.** Cheese-flavoured croûtons **2.** Christmas crackers

Regional and national dishes

The country or region of origin of words or phrases, if important or not obvious from the definition, is given immediately after the entry. Where a dish is of some regional origin within a country, the region will usually be indicated in the text, whereas the name of the country will be given after the entry:

> **figgy pastry** *England* A shortcrust pastry incorporating an amount of dried vine fruits equal in weight to the fat, often used for meat or bird pies (NOTE: *Figgy* is the West Country term for dried vine fruits)

Similarly, where a country is contained within a larger grouping such as Central Europe or West Africa, the text will indicate the country of origin. This style is only used where there are relatively few entries for the country. An exception is made for the original four kingdoms which made up the British Isles: these are treated as separate countries, i.e. England, Scotland, Wales and Ireland.

Terms from French and other cuisines which are also used in English cookery are labelled *England,*

Acknowledgements

Every compiler of a dictionary is indebted to so many written sources that it would be impossible to list them all. Most of the extant dictionaries and encyclopedias of food have been consulted and many hundreds of cookbooks trawled. Quite a few errors in the published literature have been spotted and corrected but it is inevitable that some will not have been detected and it is hoped that correspondents will point these out.

I am eternally indebted to those persons who first inspired me to undertake this work and to those who have given so freely of their time to correct the spellings and definitions of foreign terms. In chronological order, these are Gareth Burgess, at that time Head of the Catering and Hospitality Department of City College, Manchester, whose encouragement and practical help were given freely when it was most needed, and my agent, Chelsey Fox, whose efforts on my behalf were most welcome. The publisher of the first edition, Peter Collin, was a tower of strength and his continuous guidance, help and assistance eased the long path from first to last draft. Faye Carney, the editor for the second edition, and her staff have been extremely helpful and Faye Carney in particular has made many suggestions for improving the dictionary. Lecturing staff and former lecturing staff at the City College, Manchester, in particular Gordon Fotheringham, Mary Cork and Anthony Fallon, have been unstinting in giving me the benefit of their knowledge and experience.

I wish to pay tribute to those students and friends at UMIST and from all over the world who have corrected the entries in their respective mother tongues. Without their help the errors in this dictionary would have been legion; as it is, the ones that remain are solely my responsibility.

In alphabetical order of surname, they are:

Norhafizah Abdullah, Lee Abrams, Cornelia Allen, Christine Biermann, Bao-Dong Chen, Jan Cilliers, George Devarkos, Rosa Maria Dominguez, Tom Dyskowska, Amer El-Hamouz, Claudia Aguilar Garcia, Vipa Jayranaiwachira, Dilys Jones, Brahim and Mrs H. Khalfaoui, Jiri Klemes, Claudia Konscaq, Joan and Bjorn Kristiansen, Asher Kyperstock, Gen Larssen, Nityamo Lian, Emma Marigliano, Ferda Mavituna, David Miller, Gunnar Munksgaard, Mehdi Nemati, Claire O'Beirne, Severino Pandiella, Megan Sinclair, Amita Sitomurni (Adji), David Webb

And finally to my good lady bed companion, Pamela Davis, for whose tolerance and support over the many years that it took to compile, check and type this dictionary I owe an irredeemable debt of gratitude.

Abbreviations

° deg	degree centigrade (Celsius)	lb	pound weight
		m	metre
cm	centimetre	mm	millimetre
deg	degree Fahrenheit	oz	ounce
e.g.	for example	spp.	species
esp.	especially	subsp.	subspecies (in botanical names)
f	form (in botanical names)	var.	variety (in botanical names)
g	gram		
GM	gas mark	x	botanical cross
i.e.	that is to say	>	greater than
kg	kilogram	<	less than

ABCDEFG

AA See **arachidonic acid**

aachar *Indonesia, South Asia* Shredded cabbage and other vegetables. See also **acar**

aahaar *Nepal* Food

aal *Netherlands* Eel

Aal *Germany* Eel

Aalquappe *Germany* Eel pout

Aalsuppe *Germany* Eel soup

aam *South Asia* Ripe mango

aamchur *South Asia* A flavouring similar made from unripe mango. See also **amchoor**

aam ka achar *South Asia* A type of **mango pickle**. Halved unripe mangoes are mixed with fenugreek, turmeric, asafoetida, dried red chillies and salt, allowed to rest, then covered with warm mustard oil and kept warm until matured.

aara *South Asia* Wholewheat flour

aardappel *Netherlands* Potato

aardbei *Netherlands* Strawberry

aarey *South Asia* A semi-hard, scalded-curd, rindless cheese similar to Gouda, made in India from buffalo milk

abacate *Portugal* Avocado

abacaxi *Portugal* Pineapple

abadejo *Spain* Fresh codfish

abaissage *France* The process of rolling out pastry, etc.

abaisse *France* Thinly rolled out pastry used as a base for other foods

abaisser *France* To roll out

abalone A bivalve mollusc, *Haliotis tuberculata*, and other species of the genus *Haliotis*, found in warm sea water worldwide. It is larger than the oyster (up to 13 cm). The edible part is the foot; the frilly mantle is discarded. Abalone may be eaten raw if very young, but normally must be tenderized before being braised or sautéed lightly (less than 1 minute). See also **blacklip abalone**, **greenlip abalone**, **paua**, **ormer**, **mutton fish**. Also called **sea ormer**, **sea ear**, **earshell**

abalone mushroom Oyster mushroom

abats *France* Offal, internal organs and other edible parts of an animal from its extremities

abatte *France* A thick, broad, double-edged knife used to flatten meat

abattis *France* Poultry offal or giblets

abattis à la bourguignonne *France* Poultry giblets, excluding livers, which are reserved, are fried in butter with chopped onions and added flour, before being cooked with red wine, stock, bouquet garni and garlic in the oven. The mixture is then drained and placed in a clean pan with fried diced bacon, cooked button onions, the raw sliced livers and the strained reduced cooking liquor, and finished.

abattis aux navets *France* As **abattis à la bourguignonne**, but omitting red wine from the stock and small turned pieces of turnip sautéed in butter added with the other ingredients at the final stage

abattis chipolata *France* As **abattis à la bourguignonne**, but with white wine replacing red and with grilled chipolata sausage, cooked chestnuts and fried diced salt belly of pork added at the final stage

abattis de volaille aux champignons *France* Poultry giblets are cut in pieces, browned in butter, and cooked in a moderate oven with flour, stock, seasoning, skinned tomatoes and bouquet garni for 1 hour. Mushrooms are then added and cooking continues until everything is tender. The cooking liquor is thickened and the dish is served with chopped parsley.

abattis printanier *France* As **abattis à la bourguignonne**, but garnished **à la printanière** with the raw livers replacing the diced bacon and button onions

abattoir A slaughter house, a place where live food animals are killed, desanguinated, gutted, skinned and prepared for sale to the trade

abba *Sri Lanka* Black mustard seed

1

abbacchio *Italy* **1.** Milk-fed lamb **2.** Young unweaned lamb

abboccato *Italy* Slightly sweet. Used of wine.

abborre *Sweden* Perch

abbrühen *Germany* To scald

abbrustolito *Italy* Toasted

Abelmoschus esculentus *Botanical name* Okra

abelmosk See **abelmusk**

abelmusk A seed of a plant of the marrow family, *Hibiscus abelmoschus,* which has a musk-like flavour. Also called **abelmosk**

Abendessen *Germany* A light evening meal or supper

Aberdeen Angus A breed of prime, Scottish beef cattle renowned for the flavour, texture and tenderness of its meat (NOTE: Because of lax English law, the amount of meat advertised as Aberdeen Angus sold, far exceeds the number of cattle raised for slaughter.)

Aberdeen buttery *Scotland* A yeast-raised croissant made from a knocked-back strong flour and water dough, interleaved with a mixture of butter and lard (2:1) with a flour fat ratio of (4:3) using the rough puff pastry method with 3 threefold turns. The dough is cut in ovals, allowed to prove and baked at 200°C for 20 to 25 minutes.

Aberdeen crulla *Scotland* A sweet, deep-fried cake made from a stiff dough of creamed butter and sugar, eggs and flour, rolled into rectangles, each rectangle partially cut into three lengths, these plaited, deep-fried, drained and sprinkled with sugar

Aberdeen fillet *Scotland* A single, lightly smoked, unskinned fillet of haddock noted for its use in **Arnold Bennett omelette**. Also called **smoked fillet**

Aberdeen nips *Scotland* Cooked smoked haddock and egg yolk, blended into a hot **béchamel sauce**, served on fried bread or toast and garnished with parsley and paprika

Aberdeen preserved apples *Scotland* Peeled and cored hard eating apples are completely submerged in buttermilk for 2 days. The apples are then removed, rinsed and put in a cold sugar syrup made from water, sugar and peeled chopped ginger root (16:8:1). The syrup is slowly heated to a simmer and the apples are cooked until just soft. They are then bottled with the syrup and ginger and will keep for several months. About 2 litres of syrup per kg of apples are required.

Aberdeen roll *Scotland* Equal quantities of beef, bacon and onion are minced and mixed with rolled oats (equal to one third the weight of the beef), flavoured with mustard and Worcestershire sauce and brought together with beaten egg. This mixture is then packed in a tin with a foil cover, and baked in the oven in a bain-marie at 180°C for an hour. It may then be eaten hot immediately or, if to be eaten cold, soaked while hot in as much beef stock as it will absorb, cooled in the refrigerator, turned out and sliced.

Aberdeen rowies *Scotland* A type of croissant made from a yeast-raised strong dough in the manner of puff pastry interleaved with butter mixed with a little lard using two triple folds, made into rounds, proven a second time and baked at 200°C

Aberdeen sausage *Scotland* A slicing sausage (about 30 cm long by 10 cm diameter) made from 2 parts minced beef, 1 part fat bacon and 1 part fine oatmeal with spices and seasoning. The mixture is wrapped in a cloth and boiled. After unwrapping it is cooled and glazed or coated with breadcrumbs. (NOTE: Some sources give it as being made from minced mutton.)

Aberdeen sole *Scotland* Witch sole, a flatfish similar to the lemon sole

Aberffrau cakes *Wales* Small cakes made from flour, butter and caster sugar (3:2:1) made up by the creaming method, baked for 15 minutes at 190°C in greased deep scallop shells and sprinkled with sugar

Abernethy biscuit *Scotland* A Scottish caraway-flavoured sweet biscuit (NOTE: Named after Dr John Abernethy (1764–1831) of Bart's Hospital.)

Abgesottener *Austria* An acid-curdled cheese made from skimmed cows' milk, cooked to produce a soft, golden yellow, round cheese weighing between 0.2 and 1 kg. Contains 70% water, 10% fat and 16% protein.

A.B. Goods *United States* Sweets of the gum, jelly and marshmallow type (NOTE: The origin of the term is unknown.)

abgusht *Central Asia* An Iranian dish generally of browned meat and onions with beans, fruit, vegetables and flavourings, simmered very slowly for several hours in a slow cooker or otherwise. It may be thick or thin and served as two courses or one. Typical flavourings are tomato purée, **limu omani**, turmeric or lemon juice. (NOTE: Literally 'water of the meat'.)

abgushte miveh *Central Asia* An abgusht made with cubed lamb or beef stew meat, plus bones if available, simmered in water with a **limu omani**. After 90 minutes the bones and limu omani are removed and onions browned in ghee with turmeric are added, together with dried apricots and peaches and pitted prunes. All are then simmered for a further 30 minutes. Before serving, sugar and lemon juice are added to taste.

abi See **abiu**

abish *East Africa* An Ethiopian dish of minced beef fried with chopped onions, garlic, tomatoes and grated ginger, and brought together with beaten egg. Turmeric, chopped parsley, butter and grated goats' cheese are added and the mixture used to stuff peppers or potatoes or the like.

abiu A bright yellow, round fruit with white sweet caramel-flavoured flesh from a South American tree, *Pouteria caimito*, now grown commercially in Florida and Australia. It can only be used when fully ripe.

abji l'amid *Turkey* Potato soup flavoured with lemon juice

abklären *Germany* To clarify, to clear

abkochen *Germany* To blanch

ablémamu *West Africa* A thickening agent from Ghana made by grinding dry-roasted maize to a powder

abóbora *Portugal* Pumpkin

abodabo *Philippines* A method of cooking meat by frying pieces with garlic until browned then adding a little stock and vinegar to make a sauce

abon *Indonesia* A method of preserving meat, in which the meat is cooked in water until it is tender and all the water has evaporated, at which point the flesh is shredded and deep-fried until crisp

aborinha *Portugal* Courgette

aboyeur *France* The person responsible for shouting out the customer's order to the various kitchen departments (NOTE: Literally 'barker'.)

abraysha kabaub *Central Asia* A dessert from Afghanistan of lightly beaten eggs. The beaten eggs (about one egg per person) are poured through a moving funnel or using the fingers into hot fat so as to make a lacy open-textured omelette. This is cooked on both sides, drained, soaked in a lemon-flavoured heavy sugar syrup, rolled up and cut in slices.

abricot *France* Apricot

abricots à la parisienne *France* Halved apricots poached in vanilla-flavoured syrup, cooled, reformed around vanilla ice cream, placed on a large flat macaroon, covered in a cone shape with vanilla-flavoured crème chantilly and sprinkled with fine hazelnut praline

abricots à la royale *France* Halved apricots poached in vanilla-flavoured syrup, placed in tartlet moulds, filled with kirsch-flavoured jelly and cooled to set. When demoulded, the apricot halves are placed around the top of a **genoese** ring, that has been cooked to the soft-ball stage and glazed with redcurrant jelly. The centre of ring is filled with chopped anisette-flavoured jelly.

abricots Bourdaloue *France* Halved apricots poached in vanilla-flavoured syrup, placed on frangipane cream, covered with same, sprinkled with crushed macaroons and glazed quickly. The dish may be made up in a baked pastry flan or a **timbale**, or contained in a ring of dessert rice or genoise coated with apricot jam.

abricots Colbert *France* Poached apricots with the stones removed, filled with dessert rice, panéed and deep-fried, and served with apricot sauce

abricots Condé *France* Apricots poached in sugar syrup, arranged on a ring of dessert rice mixed with diced crystallized fruits macerated in kirsch, the whole decorated with crystallized fruits and coated with a kirsch-flavoured apricot syrup

abricots Cussy *France* The flat side of a soft macaroon covered with a finely cut **salpicon** of fruit mixed with apricot purée, half a poached apricot placed on top, the whole coated with Italian meringue, dried in the oven without colour and served with kirsch-flavoured apricot sauce

abricots gratinés *France* Halved apricots poached in sugar syrup, placed on a 2-cm-thick layer of sweetened apple purée or dessert semolina, covered with royal icing praline, dredged with icing sugar and placed in a moderate oven to colour the praline

abricots meringués *France* Halves of poached apricot placed on top of a layer of dessert rice, covered with meringue and decorated with same, dredged with icing sugar, coloured in a warm oven and served with a garnish of redcurrant and apricot jams

abricots mireille *France* Peeled and halved ripe apricots, mixed with skinned apricot kernels, sprinkled with sugar and cooled to 0°C. Prior to serving, sprinkled with kirsch, covered with vanilla-flavoured whipped cream and decorated with crystallized flowers.

abricots sultane *France* A ring-baked **genoese** stuck to a base of short pastry with apricot jam, the outside coated and top decorated with meringue, baked to a colour, the centre filled with dessert rice mixed with frangipane cream and chopped pistachios, the filling covered with poached apricots and sprinkled with chopped pistachios

abrikoos *Netherlands* Apricot

abrikos (*plural* **abrikosi**) *Russia* Apricot

Abruzzese, all' *Italy* In the style of Abruzzo, i.e. with green or red peppers

abschäumen *Germany* To skim

absorption method A method of cooking rice. The exact amount of water needed to cook the rice without leaving free water is placed, with the rice, in a heavy pan with a tight fitting lid. The pan is placed on a heat source for some time then removed to allow the rice to dry out. Precise proportions and times depend on the rice type. (NOTE: Rice cooked in this way is also known as steamed rice.)

abulón *Spain* Abalone

abura *Japan* Oil

abura-age *Japan* Soya bean pouches made by deep-frying slices of strained and pressed bean curd and splitting them open from one side to form pouches which may be stuffed

abura-kiri *Japan* A type of colander which fits inside a receptacle. Used for draining oil from fried food.

abutilon A plant of the marrow family, *Abutilon esculentum,* whose leaves are used in the same way as spinach. Also called **raughi**

acacia flower fritters Flower fritters

acacia gum See **gum arabic**

açafrão *Portugal* Saffron

açafrão-da-índia *Portugal* Turmeric

acajou Cashew nut

Acanthosicyos horrida *Botanical name* Nara nut

acar *Indonesia, South Asia* Shredded cabbage, carrots, cauliflower and other vegetables parboiled in spiced vinegar with turmeric and left to mature for a week. Also called **aachar, achar, achards, atjar**

acar bening *Indonesia* A mixed-vegetable sweet pickle, containing an assortment of cucumber, onion, pineapple, green pepper and tomato in vinegar, water, brown sugar and salt

acar ikan *Southeast Asia* The Malaysian version is a sweet-and-sour cold dish made from suitable whole fish, fried in oil until brown, then cooked in vinegar, water, brown sugar and a fried pounded spice mixture (chillies, ginger, onions, garlic, turmeric and macadamia nuts), decorated with slices of onion and chicken and served cold. The Indonesian version is similar but with the addition of lemon grass, **laos**, bay leaves and lime leaves to the pounded spice mixture and with shallots, spring onions and tomatoes added towards the end.

acarje *Burma* An appetizer made from a processed mixture of black-eyed beans and dried shrimps, made into balls, fried in oil and served with a spicy shrimp sauce

acar kuning *Southeast Asia* A highly spiced mixed-vegetable dish which can be served hot or cold. Onions, carrots, French beans, cauliflower, sweet peppers and cucumber, all cut to the size of a quartered French bean, are fried progressively in oil in the order given, with a fried spice mixture of pounded shallots, garlic, candlenuts, turmeric, ginger and red chillies. Water and vinegar are added progressively, and sugar, mustard and cucumber last of all. The mixture is cooked until al dente.

acar timun *Malaysia* A vegetable pickle made from salted and drained cucumber heated gently in vinegar, water, brown sugar and tomato sauce and mixed with a fried pounded spice mixture of garlic, chillies, turmeric and ginger

accartocciato *Italy* Twisted or wrapped, e.g. in spirals

accelerated freeze-drying Freeze-drying in which the rate of temperature drop between 0 and −5°C is very rapid, thus preventing the growth of ice crystals which would disrupt the cells and destroy the texture of the food, and in which heat is supplied to the food whilst under high vacuum and at a low temperature to remove the free and combined water

acciughe *Italy* Salted anchovies (NOTE: The singular is acciuga. Fresh anchovies are alici.)

acciughe alla carabiniera *Italy* Anchovies with potato salad

acciughe alla contadina *Italy* Anchovy salad with capers, onions and olives

acciughe in salsa verde *Italy* Anchovies in green sauce, made by alternating in a jar layers of drained anchovies with a mixture of chopped parsley, garlic, red chillies and white of bread soaked in vinegar. The layers are covered with olive oil. The finished dish is refrigerated until required.

acciughe marinate *Italy* Cleaned and filleted fresh anchovies marinated in olive oil, lemon juice, garlic, parsley, red chillies and seasoning for at least 4 hours

acciughe ripiene al forno *Italy* A dish made with cleaned fresh anchovies with heads and tails off and backbone removed leaving two fillets joined kipper-style. Two anchovies are put together like a sandwich, skin side out, with a filling of chopped herbs, garlic, pine nuts or walnuts and olive oil. The 'sandwich' is sprinkled with breadcrumbs and olive oil and baked for 10 minutes in a 220°C oven.

accompaniments Items offered separately with a main dish of food

accra *Caribbean* A yeasted doughnut mixture containing pounded salt cod and chillies, deep-fried and eaten hot with **floats**

acedera *Spain* Sorrel

aceite *Spain* Oil

aceituna *Spain* Olive

aceitunas rellenas *Spain* Stuffed olives (e.g. with anchovy)

acelga *Spain* Spinach beet

acepipes variados *Portugal* Assorted hors d'oeuvres

acerola The large dark cherry-like fruit of a tree *Malpighia glabra*, originating in Brazil but now grown in the Caribbean and Australia. It is the richest natural source of vitamin C, and primarily used as a health food. Also called **Brazilian cherry, Barbados cherry, West Indian cherry**

Acer saccharum *Botanical name* Sugar maple tree

acescence The slight vinegar smell of wine and fortified wine that has undergone some acetification particularly through being aged in wood. Not necessarily unpleasant.

acesulfame K See **acesulfame potassium**

acesulfame potassium An artificial sweetener, roughly 150 times as sweet as sucrose, used in canned foods, soft drinks and table top sugar substitutes. Also called **acesulfame K**

acetic acid The acid contained in vinegar which at 3.5% concentration will ensure the stability of pickles, etc. It is obtained by biological oxidation of alcohol in wine, ale and other fermented beverages. Very cheap vinegars are made from a chemically produced acetic acid. See also **E260**

acetini *Italy* Pickles

aceto *Italy* Vinegar

Acetobacter Any of a group of microorganisms associated with rot and browning in apples, but more importantly used for the production of vinegar from wines and ales by oxidation of alcohol to acetic acid

aceto balsamico *Italy* Balsamic vinegar

aceto-dolce *Italy* **1.** Sweetened vinegar (sometimes with honey as the sweetener) **2.** Pickles prepared with sweetened vinegar

acetoglyceride A fat containing one or more acetic acid side chains instead of the normal longer-chain fatty acids, thus giving a much lower melting point. It is used in the compounding of shortenings.

acetosa *Italy* Garden sorrel

acetosella *Italy* Wood sorrel

acha *West Africa* A hardy cereal plant. See also **fonio**

achar Shredded cabbage and other vegetables. See also **acar**

achards *France, South Asia* A **macédoine** of vegetables preserved in vinegar with spices. Escoffier gives mustard, Alexander Dumas suggested salt, saffron, chilli pepper and ginger root. See also **acar**

achee Vegetable used in Caribbean cooking. See also **akee**

achiar *Southeast Asia* A bamboo pickle made from vinegar and young green bamboo shoots

Achillea millefolium *Botanical name* Yarrow

achiote Annatto seed

Achras sapota *Botanical name* Sapodilla

achtarmige poliep *Netherlands* Octopus

achtfüssiger Tintenfisch *Germany* Octopus

acid A substance containing an excess of hydrogen ions when compared with pure water, which contains equal amounts of hydrogen ions *(acid forming)* and hydroxyl ions *(alkali forming)*. This excess causes the characteristic sour taste response. See also **acidity, alkali, alkalinity**

acid brilliant green BS A synthetic green food colouring which maintains its colour in acid conditions. See also **E142**

acid calcium phosphate The acid ingredient in some baking powders

acid cherry A cherry, *Prunus cerasus*, that is much smaller than the sweet cherry, and prized for jam making and culinary use. The two well-known varieties are the Morello and the Montmorency. Also called **sour cherry, pie cherry**

acidification The process of adding acids to, or causing acids to be produced in, foods for preservation – as in pickles, sauerkraut, soused herrings, mayonnaise, etc. The usual acids are acetic, citric and lactic. Benzoic acid is effective at low concentrations.

acidify, to To add an acid (e.g. lemon juice, vinegar or a permitted additive) to a mixture to reduce its pH to below 7. Also called **acidulate, to**

acidity Acidity is a measure of the strength of an acid measured on the scale of pH which goes from 1 *(very acid)* through 2 *(acidity of lemon juice)*, 3 *(apple juice)* to 7 *(neither acid nor alkaline)*, the pH of pure water. pH values greater than 7 refer to alkalis. Very few food-spoiling organisms will grow at a pH equal to or less than 2.

acidless orange A type of sweet orange rarely found in Europe or North America. Grown mainly in Egypt and Brazil, it has very low acid levels and is highly appreciated where grown. Some believe it to have special therapeutic and prophylactic properties. It is not suitable for processing. Also called **succari orange**, **sugar orange**

acido *Italy* Acid, pickled, sour, sharp

acidophilus milk Milk soured with a pure culture of *Lactobacillus acidophilus* at 37°C to give a lactic acid content of 0.6 to 0.8%. It is refreshing and easily digested and considered to be a health food.

acid potassium tartrate See **cream of tartar**

acidulate, to To acidify

acidulated cream Cream to which lemon juice is added in the proportions of 1 to 8

acini *Italy* Tiny pasta shapes similar to rice, used for soups. Also called **acini de pepe**

acini de pepe See **acini**

acitron A candied cactus, *Echino cactus grandis* from Mexico. Used as an ingredient of a meat stuffing.

ackara *West Africa* A Gambian christening food made of ground white beans mixed to a stiff paste with water, shaped into balls, deep-fried and served with a tomato, sweet pepper and onion sauce flavoured with garlic and chillies

ackee Vegetable used in Caribbean cooking. See also **akee**

Ackersalat *Germany* Lamb's lettuce

ackra fritters *Caribbean* Jamaican deep-fried fritters made from a mixture of cooked and mashed black-eyed beans with chopped chillies

açorda *Portugal* Bread soup made from pounded herbs, salt, garlic and water mixed with olive oil and cubed stale bread onto which boiling water is poured until the bread softens. It can be garnished with poached egg.

açorda de mariscos *Portugal* An açorda flavoured with shellfish and coriander

acorn squash *United States* Table queen squash

Acorus calamus *Botanical name* Calamus

acqua *Italy* Water

acqua cotta *Italy* A mushroom soup made from a mixture of varieties of fresh and soaked dried mushrooms, sautéed with chopped garlic for 15 minutes, boiled with canned plum tomatoes and their juice, stock, and any available mushroom-steeping liquor, finished with chopped basil and served over toast with grated Parmesan cheese (NOTE: The name, literally 'cooked water', is also used of many vegetable soups.)

acra lamori *Caribbean* Fried salt-cod fish cakes

acrolein The acrid smelling chemical produced from the thermal decomposition of overheated fat which causes eye and throat irritation

Actinidia deliciosa *Botanical name* The kiwi fruit or Chinese gooseberry

activated dough development A method of speeding up the primary proving of dough by adding small quantities of chemicals such as ascorbic acid, cysteine, bromates, etc., which modify the properties of the gluten

açúcar *Portugal* Sugar

açúcar granulado *Portugal* Granulated sugar

adalu *West Africa* Soaked dried cow peas boiled in water until almost cooked then simmered with fresh maize kernels until they begin to disintegrate. Often seasoned with baking soda or potash and pepper. Dried shrimps or pieces of smoked fish may be added to make it into a main dish. Also called **niébé et maïs**

Adamsapfel *Germany* Pummelo

adam's fig Plantain

Adam's needle *United States* See **yucca 2**

adaptation The process by which the senses become less sensitive to and less stimulated by particular odours or flavours with repeated contact, thus accounting for acquired tastes and the tolerance of high levels of spices, garlic and chillies, etc. in some cultures

adas *Indonesia, Malaysia* Fennel seed

adas cina *Indonesia* Dill

adas manis *Indonesia* Dill seed

added kit *Scotland* Sweetened curds. See also **hatted kit**

addition *France* The bill (in a restaurant)

additive A substance added to food to improve its properties such as keeping quality, health value, flavour, texture, colour, acidity, stability, tendency to oxidize or dry out, sweetness, cooking properties, viscosity, stickiness and the like. All additives must be listed on packaging either by an **E number** in the European Union or by name or both unless they are natural materials not required to be listed by any law, regulation or directive. See also **E number**

Adelaide cake A cake made from a Victoria sponge mixture with added corn flour (1:2 ratio to flour), chopped glacé cherries and chopped almonds

Ädelost A soft to semi-hard Swedish blue cheese made from whole cows' milk and cast in large rounds. Contains 44% water, 28% fat and 25% protein.

aderezo *Spain* Salad dressing

adianto *Italy* Maidenhair fern

Adiantum capillus-veneris *Botanical name* Maidenhair fern

adipic acid See **E355**

adley *Philippines* Job's tears

adobada sauce *Mexico* A Mexican sauce used in making tamales, consisting of pounded or liquidized garlic, onion and cinnamon, fried in oil until dry then simmered with tomato purée, chicken stock, chocolate, sugar and powdered dry chillies or chilli powder. Also called **adobo 1**

adobo **1.** *Mexico* Adobada sauce **2.** *Philippines* A pork, poultry or fish stew with sweet peppers, garlic, soya sauce, vinegar and coconut milk. The pieces of meat are first crisp-fried before being combined with the sauce.

adrak *South Asia* Ginger

adriatica, al *Italy* In the Adriatic style, i.e. fish grilled over wood or charcoal

adschempilavi *North Africa* Pickled meat stewed with rice

aduki bean See **adzuki bean**

adulterant A cheaper substance added to food in order to increase its weight without changing its appearance and thus increase the profit margin. Some are legal, e.g. water and phosphates in chickens, or extenders added to chilli powder.

adulterate, to To add adulterants to food

adzuki bean, azuki bean A type of small flattened oval-shaped reddish-brown bean with a white hilum, *Phaseolus angularis*, from Japan and China, used as a pulse or ground into flour. It contains more sugar than most beans and is sometimes used as confectionery. It can also be sprouted. Also called **aduki bean**, **azuki bean**

æbleflæsk *Denmark* Fried diced bacon and chopped apples

æblekage *Denmark* An individual dessert made from layers of sweetened apple purée and breadcrumbs which have been fried in butter and mixed with sugar, the whole being decorated appropriately

æbler *Denmark* Apples

æbleskiver *Denmark* A non-yeasted type of doughnut with a light texture filled with apple purée and cooked in a special pan with indentations

æg *Denmark* Egg

æggekage *Denmark* A thick omelette topped with fried bacon and served in wedges

aegletree fruit Wood apple

aemono *Japan* A highly decorative mixed salad, usually of chicken, seafood or vegetables dressed with various sauces one of which is made from **miso**, mashed tofu or egg yolk, vinegar and seasoning. Often served as an appetizer.

aerate, to To incorporate finely divided air into a liquid or powder mixture, by e.g. sieving flour, whisking or beating eggs, or beating air into a cake mixture

aerated bread Bread made from dough which has been mechanically mixed with carbon dioxide without using yeast

aerated flour *United States* Self-raising flour

aerial yam An orange-coloured yam, *Dioscorea bulbifera*, which produces several growths, or 'bulbils', resembling small tubers about the size of a large thumb above ground. These are very tasty. The underground tuber is edible but not used. The plant is cultivated in Africa, Asia and the Caribbean. Also called **air potato**, **potato yam**

Aerobacter Any of a group of bacteria used to oxidize alcohol to acetic acid in vinegar production

aerobe The term is applied to microorganisms which require oxygen from the air in order to grow and reproduce. See also **anaerobe**

Aeromonas hydrophilia A food poisoning bacterium which will grow at temperatures below 10°C

ærter *Denmark* Peas

afang *West Africa* The leaves of a forest plant, *Gnetum africanum*, from southern Nigeria and Cameroon, eaten as a vegetable. Also called **okasi**, **ukasi**

afang soup *West Africa* A soup/stew from southern Nigeria made with meat or offal of any kind which is simmered with onion, chilli pepper, winkles or other snails, stockfish, dried shrimp, red palm oil and a large quantity of chopped afang leaves and waterleaf. Served with fufu or mashed yams.

afelia *Greece* Tender pork, cubed and browned in olive oil, then simmered in white wine with coriander seeds and seasoning until the meat is tender

affettato *Italy* Sliced. Used of ham or sausage.

affogato *Italy* Poached, steamed or plunged

affumicare *Italy* To smoke

affumicato *Italy* Smoked

afiorata *Italy* The finest grade of olive oil made from the cream which rises to the top of the first cold pressing. It is skimmed off and bottled separately and contains a maximum of 1% free oleic acid.

aflata *West Africa* Fermented maize flour dough boiled with an equal quantity of water and used to make **kenkey** in Ghana

aflatoxin A toxin produced by certain moulds which grow on stored grains and nuts in tropical areas. The toxin tends to cause low-grade illness and reduced food absorption and growth and is thus not easily noticed unless specially tested for. It is most serious in animal feeds.

áfonya *Hungary* Blueberries

Aframomum korarima *Botanical name* Ethiopian cardamom

Aframomum melegueta *Botanical name* Grains of paradise

africaine, à l' *France* In the African style, i.e. garnished with aubergines, tomatoes, mushrooms and potatoes

africains *France* Small dessert biscuits

African horned melon Kiwano

African hot sauce *Central Africa* An all-purpose hot sauce made from deseeded chilli peppers, green sweet pepper, garlic, onion, tomato purée, vinegar, sugar and salt, processed and simmered until smooth, then bottled

African spinach See **amaranth** 1

afronchemoyle *Scotland* A form of haggis consisting of whole eggs, white breadcrumbs, finely diced soft interior fat of lamb, pepper and saffron, mixed and stuffed into a sheep's stomach (honeycomb tripe stomach) and steamed or boiled. The first written record is from 1390 A.D.

afternoon tea *United Kingdom* Cakes, biscuits, scones and dainty sandwiches served with tea in the mid-afternoon

afters *United Kingdom* The dessert course of a meal (*colloquial*) See also **starter**

agachadiza *Spain* Snipe

agami *South America* A popular game bird, *Guiana agami,* used in soups, stews and braised dishes. Also called **trumpeter**

agar-agar *Southeast Asia* A natural gelling agent made from seaweed of the Gelidum, Eucheuma or Gracilaria species, sometimes used instead of gelatine. The gel has a very high melting point and it will only dissolve in boiling water. Also called **seaweed gelatine, seaweed jelly, Japanese gelatine, macassar gum**. See also **E406** (NOTE: Suitable for vegetarians.)

agar-agar dengan serikaya *Southeast Asia* A sweet sugar and agar-agar jelly served with a type of sweetened egg custard made with eggs beaten with brown sugar (e.g. muscovado) and coconut cream until fluffy then cooked over a bain-marie until thick

agar-agar noodles Fine strips of agar-agar soaked in boiling water until just tender and appropriately flavoured. They are used to bulk out cold appetizers. (NOTE: Not to be confused with cellophane noodles.)

agaric A family of fungi, some edible, some deadly poisonous

Agaricus arvensis *Botanical name* Horse mushroom

Agaricus bisporus *Botanical name* Cultivated mushroom

Agaricus campestris *Botanical name* Common field mushroom

agate ware Enamel-lined metal kitchen ware

agbono *West Africa* Ogbono

age *Japan* **1.** Deep-fried tofu, cut into pouches, used to make **inari** by stuffing with sushi rice and flavourings prior to braising in a mixture of **dashi**, sugar, soya sauce and sake **2.** In recipes. See also **agemono**

agedofu *Japan* Fried bean curd

ageing The process of leaving foods to age or artificially ageing them using chemicals, e.g. hanging meat and game to improve the flavour and tenderness, adding oxidizing agents to flour to produce a stronger dough

agemono *Japan* Deep-fried food, also the coating, batter or pané used. Always done in vegetable oil, vegetables at 160°C and meat and fish at 170°C. (NOTE: Abbreviated to age in recipes.)

agemono-nabe *Japan* Pan for deep-frying

agemono no dogu *Japan* Agemono-nabe

agerhøne *Denmark* Partridge

ägg *Sweden* Egg

ägg à la Lena *Sweden* A cocotte dish with a little liver pâté on the base, a trimmed poached egg on top and all surrounded with a sherry-flavoured setting consommé, garnished with a ring of sweet pepper and cooled until set

aggiada *Italy* A garlic soup from the northwest Mediterranean region

äggkulor *Sweden* Egg balls, made from hard-boiled egg yolks, seasoned, mashed with soft butter and paprika, cooled, formed into small balls and rolled in diced truffles, truffle oil or chopped wild mushrooms. Used as garnish for soup.

agliata, all' *Italy* With garlic sauce

aglio *Italy* Garlic

aglio e olio *Italy* Sauce or dressing composed of garlic and oil pounded together

agliota *Italy* A sauce made by pounding garlic with bread and vinegar

aglycone An antibacterial agent in olives, which inhibits lactic acid fermentation and which is removed by treatment with lye (a caustic soda solution)

agneau *France* Lamb

agneau à la hongroise *France* Hungarian-style lamb made from breast of lamb, defatted and cut into small pieces, browned, added to a roux made from sliced onions browned in butter and flour, paprika added and stock as required, simmered for 1 to 1½ hours

agneau de lait *France* Unweaned milk-fed lamb

agneau de Pauillac *France* A small milk-fed lamb, usually roasted

agneau de pré-salé *France* Young lamb fed on sea-washed pastures (salt marshes or meadows)

agneau pascal *France* Spring lamb

agnelet *France* Milk-fed lamb

agnello *Italy* Lamb

agnello al forno *Italy* A saddle of lamb larded with onions and garlic, sprinkled with salt and chopped rosemary, roasted in lard and served with potatoes roasted in the same dish

agnello al latte *Italy* Milk-fed lamb

agnello con cicoria *Italy* Pieces of boned leg of lamb are casseroled with sliced onions, olive oil, tomatoes, salt and red chillies in the oven at 200°C for 1 hour. Chicory, endive or blanched dandelion leaves are then placed over the lamb, and it is cooked for a further 30 minutes.

agnello con olive all'abbruzzese *Italy* Floured steaks of boned leg of lamb, browned in olive oil, salted, defatted and heated briefly with stoned black olives (4:1 ratio), oregano, chopped green peppers and finally dressed with lemon juice

agnello in fricassea *Italy* Lamb chops are browned in lard with chopped onions and strips of pancetta (or smoked bacon); nutmeg, seasoning and brown stock are added and evaporated, then the chops are braised in white wine. To finish, the pan juices are defatted and mixed off heat with beaten egg yolks and lemon juice, the mixture being served as a coating on the chops.

agneshka kebab *Bulgaria* A casserole of lamb, including its kidneys and sweetbreads with onions, wine, lemon juice, chillies, herbs and seasoning, thickened with eggs and accompanied with boiled rice

Agnès Sorel, garnish Chopped fried mushrooms, small rounds of cooked tongue and chicken mousse or pâté

agnolini *Italy* Stuffed pasta from Lombardy similar to tortellini

agnolotti *Italy* A half-moon-shaped ravioli stuffed with minced lamb and onion sautéed in butter mixed with boiled rice or spinach, cheese and seasoning. Served after cooking in standard fashion, sometimes tossed in meat pan juices. Also called **pazlache**

agnostinele *Italy* Tiny red mullet passed through seasoned flour and fried

agoni *Italy* Small flat freshwater fish found in the Italian lakes, often salted and dried. See also **misoltini**

Agostano *Italy* Parmesan cheese made in July or August. See also **Parmigiano Reggiano**

agouti *Caribbean* A rabbit-sized humpbacked rodent, *Dasyprocta antillensis*, widespread throughout the Caribbean and Central and South America. Its firm, white, tender meat is highly prized.

Agrafa *Greece* A hard, scalded-curd, ewes' milk cheese similar to Gruyère with a few holes and a dry rind

agraz *Spain* The juice of immature grapes from which verjuice is made

agrazada *Spain* Verjuice

agresto *Italy* Verjuice from grapes

agridulce *Spain* Sweet-and-sour sauce

agrini A small, soft, acid curdled Swiss cheese made from cows' or goats' milk with a slightly sour fresh taste, 40 to 60 g in weight

agrio *Spain* Sour

agriões *Portugal* Watercress

agro, all' *Italy* Dressed with oil and lemon, also soured with lemon juice

agrodolce *Italy* Bittersweet

agua *Portugal, Spain* Water

aguacate *Spain* Avocado

aguacates rellenos de atun *Mexico* Halved avocado pears, filled with a mixture of tuna, tomato sauce, soured cream, Worcestershire sauce and seasoning, and garnished with chiffonade of lettuce and radish, used as a hors d'oeuvre

aguado *Spain* Liquid

aguaturma *Spain* Jerusalem artichoke

aguglia *Italy* Garfish

aguinaldo honey *Mexico* A very pale honey from Mexico

aguja *Spain* Garfish

agulat *Spain* Rock salmon

agurk *Denmark, Norway* Cucumber

agurksalat *Denmark, Norway* Cucumber salad. Generally slices of cucumber, salted and drained for an hour, dried, dressed with pepper, sugar and vinegar, chilled, drained and garnished with chopped parsley or dill.

agusi *West Africa* The seeds of pumpkins, gourds and other plants belonging to the family *Cucurbitaceae*. See also **egusi**

ah moi's mee *Malaysia* A Malaysian dish of stir-fried noodles with soaked Chinese mushrooms, prawns, cooked chicken, greens, garlic, onion, ginger, egg and soya sauce, garnished with crabmeat, shredded omelette and spring onion

ah moi's rendang *Malaysia* A chicken curry made with sugared chicken pieces, onions, garlic, ginger, **laos**, lemon grass, coconut milk, desiccated coconut and pandan leaves

Ahornsaft *Germany* Maple syrup

ahumado *Spain* Smoked

ahumar *Spain* To smoke

ahven *Finland* Perch

aiglefin *France* Haddock

aïgo bouïdo *France* A simple soup of garlic and sage, possibly plus thyme and bay, boiled in water with olive oil, strained and poured over dried French bread

aïgo bouïdo à la ménagère *France* A Provençale soup made from sliced onions and leeks, fried in olive oil, crushed garlic, potatoes, fennel and mixed herbs boiled in saffron-flavoured water with orange zest. The strained soup is served over French bread and the potatoes served separately with poached egg and chopped parsley.

aïgo saou *France* A fish and garlic soup made from pieces of fish, sliced onions, potatoes, bouquet garni, seasoning and garlic boiled in water. The soup is eaten with French bread dressed with olive oil and the fish is eaten separately.

aigre *France* Sour, sharp, acid

aigre doux *France* Bittersweet

aigrette *England, France* A savoury fritter made from cheese-flavoured choux pastry, served as an appetizer

aïgroissade *France* Cooked solid vegetables, e.g. roots, tubers, sweet peppers, aubergine, courgettes and the like, served warm with a mayonnaise and garlic sauce

aiguillat *France* Rock salmon

aiguille *France* **Needlefish** or **garfish** from the Mediterranean with green bones which become mauve when cooked. Also called **orphie**

aiguille à brider *France* A trussing needle

aiguille à piquer *France* A larding needle used for small cuts, e.g. filet mignon or rack of hare

aiguillette *France* A long thin cut of beef from the extreme top of the rump, extending from the sirloin to the tail stump and about one quarter way down the animal. Used for braising and boeuf à la mode.

aiguillettes *France* Long thin slices, usually of duck breast

ai gwa *China* Aubergine

ail *France* Garlic (NOTE: The plural form is **ails** or **aulx**.)

ail, à l' Flavoured with garlic

aile *France* A wing e.g. of poultry or of a game bird

aileron *France* **1.** A wing, strictly a wing tip, of a bird **2.** A fin of a fish

ailerons de poulet carmelite *France* Breasts and wing bones of poached chicken removed as two pieces, skinned, coated in aspic, placed on a layer of crayfish mousse in a **timbale**, interspersed with cooked and shelled crayfish tails, covered in aspic jelly, refrigerated and served cold

ailerons de volaille dorés *France* Large chicken or turkey winglets fried in butter to a colour and set aside. Sliced carrots and onions browned in same butter, placed in oven dish with seasoning and herbs. Winglets placed on top and cooked in a slow oven, then removed. Remainder cooked with white stock for 10 minutes, reduced, strained and poured over winglets.

ailerons de volaille farcis chipolata *France* Boned winglets of large chicken or turkey stuffed with sausage meat, braised and decorated with chipolata garnish 15 minutes before finishing

ailerons de volaille farcis grillés *France* Boned winglets of a large chicken or turkey stuffed with sausage meat, braised, coated with sausage meat, covered with caul fat, dipped in melted butter and breadcrumbs, grilled and served with sauce Périgueux

ailerons de volaille Lady Winter *France* Breasts and wing bones of poached chicken removed as two pieces, skinned, coated in aspic placed with the points uppermost around a cone of set mousse made from the flesh of the chicken legs and decorated with chopped truffle and red ox tongue

aillade *France* A garlic and nut emulsion sauce made with skinned hazelnuts pounded with garlic and egg yolk, to which a mixed nut and olive or sunflower oil is added as for mayonnaise

aillade toulousaine As **aillade**, but with walnuts

ailloli *France* An emulsion sauce, made from white crustless bread soaked in milk, squeezed and mixed with pounded garlic (and possibly egg yolk), to which olive oil is added as in making mayonnaise. The final mixture is let down with lemon juice or wine vinegar to taste. Sometimes ground almonds are added. Also called **beurre de Provence**

ailloli garni *France* A Provençal dish of salt cod and vegetables garnished with snails

aioli 1. *Italy* Garlic pounded with egg yolk and salt then made into a mayonnaise in standard fashion **2.** *France* An alternative spelling for **ailloli**

aipo *Portugal* Celery

air-dry, to To hang foodstuffs on hangers or racks in sheds or cages or in open sunlight in cold climates where there is a reasonable flow of fresh air over them. Used for hams, fish, etc.

airelle *France* **1.** Bilberry or whortleberry **2.** Blueberry

airelle rouge *France* Cranberry

air potato Aerial yam

ajam panggang *Netherlands* Grilled chicken flavoured with ginger, garlic, chilli peppers and saffron (NOTE: This dish originates from Indonesia.)

aji, aji no tataki *Japan* Horse mackerel, used in sushi

ají *Spain* Chilli peppers

ajiaceite *Spain* Garlic-flavoured mayonnaise. See also **alioli**

ajiaco *South America* A thick soup or thin stew from Colombia, made of chicken cooked in stock with sweetcorn and sausages, each serving garnished with sliced hard-boiled eggs and cream

ajiaco cubano *Cuba* A soup made from salt pork, pickled pork and pork flesh with chick peas, garlic, aubergine, sweet corn, pumpkin and potatoes, seasoned and flavoured with saffron

ajiaco de papas *South America* A potato stew from Peru made from cubed boiled potatoes mixed with chopped and fried garlic, onion and jalapeno chillies all fried to a colour, milk or cream, chopped hard-boiled eggs and crumbled cheese

aji-li-mojili sauce *Caribbean* A hot vinaigrette made with olive oil, vinegar and lime juice (2:1:1) into which processed garlic and chilli pepper are mixed together with salt and pepper

ajillo, al *Mexico* Fried with ajillo chilli

aji-mirin *Japan* A mixture of **mirin**, sugar syrup and salt used in the same way as mirin

aji-no-moto *Japan* A trademark for **monosodium glutamate**

ajlouke *North Africa* Appetizers, hors d'oeuvres, from Tunisia

ajo *Spain* Garlic

ajo blanco *Spain* **1.** A basic bread, garlic, oil and vinegar gazpacho with added pounded or liquidized skinned almonds, garnished with peeled and deseeded grapes **2.** A cold soup made from garlic and almonds pounded with olive oil to a thick paste, mixed with water and seasoning and served with **sippets**

ajomba *Central Africa* A method of cooking meat or fish in banana leaves. See also **liboké**

ajonjoli *Spain* Sesame seeds

ajowan A plant of the caraway family, *Carum ajowan*, whose seeds are used as a spice and as a source of ajowan oil and thymol. It has a strong thyme-like flavour, and is used in Indian cooking often in conjunction with starch foods and pulses. Also called **lovage 2, ajwain, carom, bishop's weed**

ajula *Italy* The North Italian name for striped sea bream

ajwain See **ajowan**

akadashi, akadashi-miso *Japan* A **miso** similar to **hatcho-miso**. Also called **aka-miso**

akagai *Japan* Ark shell, a type of clam about 10 cm in diameter. This is one of the few shellfish which use haemoglobin to transport oxygen and is thus red in colour. It is usually available cooked, and used in preparing sushi.

akami *Japan* A dark red meat from around the spine of the tuna fish, used as a separate cut in sushi

aka-miso *Japan* Akadashi

akara *West Africa* Black-eyed beans, soaked overnight and skinned, then processed with chillies, onions, salt and egg so as to incorporate air. The bean mixture is then formed into small balls and deep-fried in oil until browned. Served hot or cold. Also called **koosé** (NOTE: Also known as *akkra* in Jamaica, *acra* in Trinidad and *calas* in New Orleans)

akee The fruit of a small African tree, *Blighia sapida*, introduced to the Caribbean by Captain Bligh and now extensively grown there. The soft creamy flesh of the ripe fruit is used as a vegetable e.g. in akee and saltfish. The outer pink skin is poisonous. Also called **achee, ackee**

akee and saltfish *Caribbean* A traditional breakfast dish of Jamaica consisting of akee fried with onions, sweet peppers, chillies, tomatoes and flaked salt cod. It looks like piperade or scrambled eggs.

åkerärter *Sweden* Field peas which are yellow when dried. Used in the Swedish national soup **gula ärter med fläsk**.

akilt-b-dabbo *East Africa* An Ethiopian vegetarian dish of vegetables with bread

akni *South Asia* A court bouillon, used in Indian cooking, made by simmering herbs, spices and other flavourings in water to aromatize it. Used for steaming rice and vegetables. Typical flavourings are fried onion, coriander seed, fennel seed, chopped sweet pepper, garlic and fresh ginger.

akoho sy vanio *South Africa* A dish from Madagascar made from chicken pieces marinated in lemon juice, lemon zest, salt

11

and pepper which are then sautéed with previously sautéed onions and garlic. Tomatoes and finely chopped ginger are then added to the mixture, and finally all is simmered in coconut milk until cooked through. Served with rice.

akpith *West Africa* Maize meal and soya flour (4:1) sieved with baking powder (50g per kg of flour mixture) plus chilli powder, salt, pepper and sugar to taste. Half the mixture is cooked with twice its weight of water over a low heat, then the rest added and mixed to a stiff dough which is formed into small balls, deep-fried and eaten hot as a snack.

akudjura *Australia* Ground dried bush tomato used as a flavouring. It has a tamarillo/caramel flavour.

akureyri *Iceland* A blue cheese made from ewes' milk

ak yaw *Burma* A crisp accompaniment made from a batter of rice flour, turmeric and water, shallow-fried in spoonfuls in oil and scattered with yellow and green split peas before the fritters are turned over in the oil

ål *Denmark, Norway, Sweden* Eel

al'-, all'-, alla- *Italy* In the style of

à la *France* In the style of, in the manner of, with (NOTE: Used before feminine French nouns.)

alaccia *Italy* **1.** A large variety of sardine **2.** Celery (*Naples*)

alalonga *Italy* Albacore

alamang *Philippines* The tiny shrimp (up to 1 cm) used to make Filipino shrimp paste (**bagoong**)

alanine A non-essential amino acid

alaria A seaweed, *Alaria esculenta*, found in the North Atlantic; similar to the Japanese **wakame**. Also called **murlins**, **brown ribweed**, **ribweed**, **wing kelp**

Alaska See **baked Alaska**

Alaska black cod See **black cod**

Alaska Dungeness crab See **Dungeness crab**

Alaskan king crab A very large crab from the northern Pacific, *Paralithodes camtschatica*, weighing up to 10 kg and with a leg span of 3 m. Its excellent meat is usually processed or canned.

Alaska pollack A variety of the seawater fish pollack, *Theragra chalcogramma*, found in the northwest Pacific. It is of the cod family, weighs around 1 kg and has an olive green to brown upper skin. The lean white flesh may be cooked in any way, but is usually salted and dried or pickled. The roe is also salted for the Japanese market. Also called **Alaska pollock**, **walleye pollack**, **walleye pollock** (NOTE: The name *walleye pollack/pollock* comes from its distinctive appearance.)

Alaska pollock See **Alaska pollack**

Alba, al modo d' *Italy* In the Alban style, i.e. with truffles

albacore A small variety of tuna, *Thunnus alalunga,* up to 1 m in length with a soft white flesh, not recommended for poaching, but can be eaten raw e.g. for sashimi or baked or grilled. Also called **long fin tuna**

albahaca *Spain* Basil

albaricoque *Spain* Apricot

albedo *United States* The white inner pith of the citrus fruit skin

albergínia (*plural* **albergínies**) *Catalonia* Aubergine(s)

Albert, sauce *England, France* Grated horseradish simmered in white bouillon for 20 minutes; butter, sauce, cream and breadcrumbs added; thickened by reduction; sieved, thickened again with egg yolks and finished with seasoning, English mustard, vinegar and chopped parsley

Albert oranges *Canada* Rose hips

albicocca *Italy* Apricot

albillos *Spain* White grapes

albóndigas *Mexico, Spain* Meatballs or meat patties made from finely chopped tenderloin of pork and fat bacon combined with chopped garlic and red pepper, seasoning and bound with whole egg; fried, then braised in a suitable sauce

albóndigas con chipotle *Mexico* Minced pork, beef, bread, vinegar, sugar and seasoning, formed into balls; shallow-fried in oil until brown, then baked in the oven with **salsa de chile chipotle**, and garnished with flaked almonds

albóndigas con guisantes *Spain* Meat patties made from chopped beef, onions and seasoning; formed, browned on both sides in butter, simmered in **demi-glace** with tomato purée and garlic paste and served with the sauce and green peas

albondiguillas *Spain* Small patties made from minced cooked meat mixed with breadcrumbs, egg, white wine, chopped parsley, seasoning and herbs; panéed, shallow-fried in oil and served with tomato sauce

albondiguillas a la criolla *Spain* Albondiguillas served with a tomato sauce mixed with chopped sweet pepper sweated in butter and a separate saffron-flavoured and coloured rice pilaff

albondiguitas *Mexico* Small fried meatballs made from pork. beef, bread, vinegar, sugar and seasoning, usually served on sticks as a cocktail snack.

albricoque *Portugal* Apricot

albufera, sauce *England, France* **Sauce suprême** mixed with meat glaze and pimento butter

albumen The white of egg, the nutritive material surrounding the yolk of the eggs of higher animals, which also contains various anti-bacterial substances. Hens' egg albumen consists of the protein albumin (9 – 12%) and water (84 – 87%), in total about 58% of the weight of the egg. It forms a very stable emulsion with air and hence is used in a variety of air-raised dishes. It may be dried to a powder for reconstituting or deep-frozen.

albumen index A measure of egg quality equal to the ratio of the height of a mass of egg white to its diameter as it sits on a flat surface. A higher index indicates higher quality.

albumin A mixture of water soluble proteins found in egg white, blood and other foods. Like all proteins, these denature and coagulate when heated or treated with various chemicals e.g. alcohol. See also **ovalbumin**

alcachofa *Spain* Globe artichoke

alcachôfra *Portugal* Globe artichoke

alcahual *Mexico* A delicately flavoured amber-coloured honey from Mexico

alcaparra *Spain* Caper

alcaravea *Spain* Caraway

alcaravia *Portugal* Caraway

alce *Italy* Elk

Alchemilla vulgaris *Botanical name* Lady's mantle

Alcobaça *Portugal* A semi-hard cheese made from ewes' milk with a white smooth paste and thin dry rind, cast in small rounds (about 220 g). Contains 45% water, 30% fat and 20% protein.

alcohol The generic name for a class of chemical compounds which includes ethanol, the commonest mood-altering substance used in all cultures. Most are toxic, particularly methanol which is found in methylated and surgical spirits and many household liquids. Propanol and butanol, the other common alcohols, are used as solvents and in cleaning agents.

al cuarto de hora *Spain* Mussel soup made from chopped onions, parsley, diced ham and rice all sweated in butter, mixed with water and the liquor from the cooking of the mussels, seasoned and cooked, served with the mussels and garnished with chopped hard-boiled eggs (NOTE: The name indicates that it can be made in 15 minutes.)

al dente *Italy* Cooked to be firm to the bite. Used of pasta or vegetables. Dried commercial pasta is al dente when the whitish centre of the paste just disappears. (NOTE: Literally 'to the tooth'.)

aldoxime An artificial zero-calorie sweetener, 450 times sweeter than sucrose

ale An alcoholic drink made from top fermented extract of malted grains. The name is generally nowadays applied only to crystal (lightly coloured) malts. Ale may be flavoured e.g. with hops.

ale berry See **ale gruel**

alecost Costmary

alecrim *Portugal* Rosemary

ale flip *England* Beer heated with mace, cloves and butter, poured into separately beaten egg yolk let down with cold beer and egg white (1 egg per litre)

alegar Ale vinegar

ale gruel *England* A Yorkshire drink made from a very thin gruel of porridge oats and water mixed, when hot, with an equal part of beer, to which is added grated ginger root, nutmeg, cinnamon and sugar to taste

ale jelly *England* A jelly made from ale, sugar, cinnamon and lemon juice, boiled together, clarified with egg white and set with gelatine

alemtejo *Portugal* A soft, round cheese made from ewes' milk with added thistle-type flowers

alentejana, à *Portugal* In the style of Alentejo, i.e. with garlic, olive oil and paprika

Aleppo nut Pistachio nut

alesandre salami A variety of Italian salami

aletria *Portugal* Vermicelli

aletta *Italy* 1. A wing of a bird 2. A fin of a fish

Aleurites moluccana *Botanical name* Candlenut tree

Aleurobius acaras *Botanical name* A mite sometimes found in old, poorly stored flour. If seriously infested, the flour has a purplish tinge.

alewife *United States* A member of the herring family, *Alosa pseudoharengus*, similar to the true herring but with a deeper body. It is found off the east coast of North America and may be baked, fried or grilled.

alewife caviar *United States* The female roe of the alewife, processed to resemble caviar

alexanders A hardy biennial herb, *Smyrnium olusatrum*, with a celery-type flavour resembling lovage and angelica. Its roots can be boiled or candied, its young stems braised, its leaves and flower buds used in salad or as a pot herb and its seeds used for flavouring. Also called **black lovage**

alface *Portugal* Lettuce

alfalfa A variety of lucerne, *Medicago sativa*, a leguminous plant normally used as cattle fodder. The seeds are sprouted to give a crisp plant stem about 4 cm long, used in salads or for stir-frying as a vegetable.

alfóncigo *Spain* Pistachio nut

alfóstigo *Portugal* Pistachio nut

alfredo, all' *Italy* Tossed in cream and butter. Used e.g. of pasta.

alga *Italy, Spain* Seaweed, algae

algae Non-self-supporting vegetable-like organisms which flourish in fresh or salt water, generally greenish in colour, ranging in size from the microscopic to enormous (e.g. with 100-metre-long fronds). Of culinary importance are the microscopic Chlorella and Spirulina, which are used as health foods, and the larger seaweeds, used either as vegetables or as a source of various food-thickening agents. See also **agar-agar, alginic acid, carragheen, laver bread, nori**

alga mar An edible seaweed, *Durvillea antarctica*, exported to the USA from Chile

algarroba *Spain* Carob

Alge *Germany* Seaweed, algae

Algerian clementine *United States* Fina

algérienne, à l' *France* In the Algerian style, i.e. garnished with small croquettes of sweet potato and small empty tomatoes, seasoned and braised in oil

algin *United States* Alginates used for thickening. See also **alginic acid**

alginates Salts and esters of **alginic acid**

alginic acid A carbohydrate acid, E400, obtained from various seaweeds and used as a thickening and gelling agent in commercial ice cream and convenience foods. It is also supplied as the sodium salt, sodium alginate, E401, used mainly in ice cream, the potassium salt, E402, and the calcium salt, E404, which forms a much stiffer gel than the other salts. It is also available as an ester, propane 2-diol alginate, E405.

algue *France* Seaweed, algae

algue rouge *France* Dulse

alheira *Portugal* A sausage made with smoked ham, garlic and nuts

alho *Portugal* Garlic

alho frances *Portugal* Leek. Also called **alho-porros**

alholva *Spain* Fenugreek

alho-porro *Portugal* Leek

Alicante *Spain* A fresh, white, rindless cheese made from goat' milk, curdled with rennet and stored in weak brine or water. Contains 60% water, 15% fat and 20% protein.

alice *Italy* Fresh anchovy

aligi *Philippines* Tomalley

aligot de marinette *France* A purée of potatoes beaten vigorously with crushed garlic, bacon fat and half its weight of Laguiole cheese in a bain-marie until just smooth and elastic

alimentação *Portugal* **1.** Food **2.** Nourishment

alimentari *Italy* **1.** Groceries **2.** Grocery shop

alimentary pastes Pastas, noodles and similar foodstuffs made from dough

aliñado *Spain* Seasoned

aliño *Spain* **1.** Seasoning **2.** Salad dressing

alioli *Spain* Garlic-flavoured mayonnaise. Also called **ajiaceite**

alitán *Spain* Larger spotted dogfish

alkali An alkali is a substance containing a deficiency of hydrogen ions (or an excess of hydroxyl ions) compared with pure water. An alkali (e.g. sodium hydroxide) will combine with an acid (e.g. alginic acid) to form a neutral salt (e.g. sodium alginate). The most common culinary alkalis are sodium bicarbonate and ammonium carbonate both of which liberate carbon dioxide gas when heated or combined with an acid such as tartaric acid.

alkalinity A measure of the strength of an alkali on the scale of pH which goes from 7 (neutral) through 7.7 to 9.2 (egg white), 8.4 (sodium bicarbonate or baking soda), 11.9 (household ammonia) to 14 (highest value of alkalinity). Strong alkalis such as sodium hydroxide react with fat in the skin to form soaps which give a characteristic slimy feel.

alkaloids The components of plants responsible in most cases for their bitter taste and therapeutic effects. Typical examples are quinine used in tonic water and caffeine and theobromine found in coffee beans. Other well known alkaloids are cocaine, strychnine, atropine and morphine.

alkanet A Mediterranean plant of the borage family, *Anchusa tinctora,* whose roots provide a red or blue (depending on pH) food dye similar to henna. Also called **alkanna**

alkanna Alkanet

all *Catalonia* Garlic (NOTE: The plural is **grans d'all**.)

allache *France* A large sardine

allemande *France* The term applied to dishes garnished with German specialities such as sauerkraut, smoked sausage, pickled pork, potato dumpling, etc.

allemande, à l' *France* In the German style, i.e. garnished with noodles and mashed potatoes

allergens Compounds, either proteins or smaller chemicals, which react with the proteins of the skin and mucous membranes (eyes, nose, lungs, gut, etc.) of some persons to elicit the immune response of the body causing rashes, irritation, asthma, etc.

Typical food allergies occur with strawberries, eggs, milk, cereal, fish, peas, and nuts. The response should not be confused with that produced by enzyme deficiencies as e.g. with the inability to metabolize lactose, found in most Chinese, and the inability to metabolize gluten, which is fairly common in the West.

Allgäuer Bergkäse *Germany* A hard cows' milk cheese similar to Emmental

Allgäuer Rahmkäse *Germany* A soft, mild, Limburger-type cheese

Allgewürz *Germany* Allspice

Alliaria petiolata *Botanical name* Garlic mustard

allicin The chemical compound in garlic which gives it its characteristic smell and taste

alligator A large carnivorous amphibian found in the swamps and rivers of the southern USA and the Yangtze river in China. The meat, especially the tail meat, is eaten during the hunting season and is a speciality of Cajun cuisine.

alligator pear Avocado

allioli *Catalonia* A thick emulsion of garlic, salt and olive oil either pounded together or prepared in a mechanical blender. Served cold as an accompaniment to fish, meat or vegetables. (NOTE: From the Catalan *all* meaning 'garlic'.)

allipebre d'anguiles *Catalonia* A spicy eel stew, flavoured with paprika, peppers, garlic and saffron

allis shad See **shad**

Allium The botanical name for the important family of plants, including onions and spring onions *Allium cepa*, shallots *Allium cepa* Aggregatum group, Welsh or bunching onions (**ciboule**) *Allium fistulosum*, Egyptian onion or tree onion *Allium cepa* var. *proliferum*, leeks *Allium porum*, garlic *Allium sativum*, giant garlic (rocambole) *Allium scorodoprasum*, chives *Allium schoenoprasum* and Chinese chives *Allium tuberosum*.

Allium ascalonicum *Botanical name* Shallot

Allium cepa *Botanical name* **1.** Onion **2.** Spring onion

Allium cepa var. **proliferum** *Botanical name* Egyptian onion

Allium fistulosum *Botanical name* Welsh onion

Allium porrum *Botanical name* Leek

Allium ramosum *Botanical name* Asian leek

Allium sativum *Botanical name* Garlic

Allium schoenoprasum *Botanical name* Chives

Allium scorodoprasum *Botanical name* Giant garlic

Allium tuberosum *Botanical name* Chinese chives

allodola *Italy* Lark, the bird

alloro *Italy* Bay tree

all-purpose flour *United States* Plain white flour blended from hard and soft wheat flours

allspice The dried, green, unripe berry of a tree, *Pimenta dioca or P. officinalis*, which grows exclusively in the Caribbean and South America. It has a flavour of cinnamon, nutmeg, and cloves combined. Used in cakes, in food manufacture and extensively in Jamaican meat dishes. Also called **Jamaican pepper, pimento 1, myrtle pepper**

allumettes *France* Matchsticks e.g. pommes allumettes = straw potatoes; allumettes au fromage = cheese straws

allumettes aux anchois *France* Rectangles of puff pastry coated with a thin layer of fish forcemeat flavoured with anchovy essence and garnished with fillets of anchovy prior to baking

allumettes aux crevettes *France* As **allumettes aux anchois**, but with a forcemeat of whiting and shrimp butter containing cooked and sliced shrimps

allumettes caprice *France* As **allumettes aux anchois**, but with a forcemeat of chicken and cream with chopped ox tongue and truffle

allumettes pour hors d'oeuvres *France* Rectangles of 8 mm puff pastry used as a base for hors d'oeuvres, generally covered with a thin layer of forcemeat flavoured with cayenne pepper and cut into 7 cm by 2.5 cm rectangles prior to baking. They are decorated as appropriate.

alma-ata plov *Central Asia* A Central Asian rice **pilaf**, made with chicken stock and containing cubed lamb, julienned carrots, sliced onions, chopped apples, dried raisins, dried apricots and almonds, flavoured with orange juice and zest

al macc *Italy* A northern soup of milk with chestnuts and rice. Also called **mach**

almaciga *Spain* Mastic

almamártás *Hungary* Apple sauce

almás palacsinta *Hungary* Pancake with chopped apples

almavica *Italy* A dessert similar to semolina pudding

almeja *Spain* Clam, carpet shell and similar bivalve molluscs

almejas marineras *Spain* Clams in a sauce based on garlic and olive oil

almejas palourdes *Spain* Carpet shell clams

almejón brillante *Spain* Venus shell clam

almendra *Spain* Almond

almendrado *Spain* Macaroon

almendras garapiñadas *Spain* Sugared almonds

almôço *Portugal* Lunch (taken between 13.30 and 15.00 hrs)

almond The kernel (nut) of the fruit of the almond tree. The sweet variety, *Prunus dulcis* var. *dulcis*, is used whole, split, flaked, chopped or ground in cookery. The bitter variety, *Prunus dulcis* var. *amara*, is used for the production of almond essence and almond oil and very occasionally in cooking.

almond biscuits Ground almonds and caster sugar folded into stiffly beaten egg white, piped onto rice paper, decorated and baked at 180°C

almond butter A compound butter made from freshly shelled sweet almonds pounded to a fine paste with twice their weight of butter and passed through a fine sieve. Also called **amandine butter**

almond cream A sweet made from a mixture of ground almonds with egg yolks and orange flower water, thickened in a bain-marie and garnished with almond praline

almôndêga *Portugal* Meatball

almond essence An alcoholic extract of fermented bitter almonds, used to give an almond flavour to cakes, etc. Some almond essences are made from apricot kernels

almond flakes Dehusked almonds separated into two halves. Also called **flaked almonds**

almond flavouring A synthetic chemical product with an almond flavour and smell, much cheaper than almond essence and commonly used as a substitute

almond milk *England* A medieval substitute for milk during Lent, made by pounding sweet almonds plus a few bitter almonds with water, then mixing with barley water and sugar and boiling to a creamy consistency

almond nibs Evenly chopped blanched almonds about 2 to 3 mm in diameter used as a decoration

almond oil An oil with a very delicate flavour obtained by pressing or solvent extraction from bitter almonds. Used in confectionery and for oiling dessert moulds.

almond paste See **marzipan**

almond potatoes Pommes amandine

almond powder *United States* Very finely ground almonds used in desserts

almond sauce 1. Sweetened milk, thickened with corn flour and flavoured with almond essence **2.** *Scotland* Milk, eggs, caster sugar and ground almonds (6:2:1:1) mixed and flavoured with orange flower water and heated over a double boiler until it thickens (85°C). Served with steamed puddings.

almond slice An individual cake made from a rectangle of pastry covered with a thick almond topping similar to frangipane and decorated with flaked almonds

almuerzo 1. *Mexico* Brunch **2.** *Spain* Lunch

Alnwick stew *England* A casserole from Northumberland of cubed bacon layered with onions and potatoes, seasoned with pepper and mustard and simmered with water and bay leaf for about 2 hours

aloco *West Africa* A popular dish in the Cote d'Ivoire, consisting of plantains fried in palm oil, reserved and drained, together with chopped onions, chilli pepper and tomatoes fried in the same oil and simmered with a little water to make a chunky sauce. The sauce is poured over the plantains. Aloco is used as an accompaniment to grilled fish.

aloo *South Asia* Potato

aloo bhurta *South Asia* Boiled potatoes mashed with 3 tbsp per kilogram of minced red peppers, chopped chives and molten butter, 2 tbsp of chopped parsley or coriander leaves and a little powdered bay plus salt and pepper. Served hot or cold.

aloo bokhara *South Asia* Sour prunes

aloo chat *South Asia* A spiced potato dish made from large diced potatoes, fried in ghee until coloured, mixed with minced onions and garlic, chat masala, chilli powder, seasoning, crumbled bay leaf, chopped red chilli and chopped fresh coriander leaves, then cooked until tender in a covered pan with a little water if necessary

alootikka *South Asia* A potato and chickpea rissole served with yoghurt and tamarind sauce. Also called **alutikka**

alosa *Italy* Shad

alose *France* Shad

alose à la provençale *France* Alternate layers of sorrel mixed with chopped onions and slices of shad, finishing with a sorrel layer, are placed in a garlic-flavoured pan or casserole with a tight fitting lid. The top is sprinkled with thyme, oil, seasoning and marc or brandy, the lid sealed on and the whole cooked over a very low heat or in a slow oven for 7 hours.

alose à la tomate et au vin *France* A whole shad placed on a bed of **tomato concassée**, butter and chopped garlic in a flame-proof casserole, covered with **tomato concassée**, chopped onions, chopped mushrooms, white wine and melted butter, covered, cooked on top of the stove for 3 minutes and finished in a moderate oven for 20 to 25 minutes

alose de la Loire à l'oseille *France* An incised and seasoned whole shad, oiled and grilled for 2.5 minutes per side, finished in the oven on a bed of sorrel purée mixed with butter and lemon juice and served with the purée, wedges of hard-boiled egg and slices of lemon

alose farcie *France* A whole shad, stuffed with a forcemeat of soft roes, white bread moistened with milk, seasoning, nutmeg, chives, parsley, chervil, egg and egg yolks, is incised, wrapped in oiled paper, baked for 35–40 minutes and served accompanied by sauce Bercy

alose feinte *France* Twaite shad

alose grillée *France* Shad, incised whole or cut into **darnes**, marinated in oil, lemon juice and herbs, grilled over moderate heat until cooked through, served with lemon slices and either parsley or anchovy butter and sauce Bercy

alose grillée à l'oseille *France* Grilled shad accompanied by sorrel, stewed in butter then braised; the whole presented in a deep dish and served with melted butter, presented separately. See also **alose grillée**

alouette *France* Lark, a small bird. Once used in cooking but now protected in the EU.

alouette sans tête *France* A beef olive, also made with veal

aloyau de boeuf *France* Sirloin of beef on the bone, usually including the fillet and prepared especially for top-class roasting

aloyau de boeuf froid *France* Cold roast sirloin of beef including the fillet, on the bone and coated with aspic jelly

Aloysia triphylla *Botanical name* Lemon verbena

Alpbergkäse A cooked-curd, dense German cheese made from whole cows' milk with a dense dry rind and a few holes, cast into large rounds weighing 20 to 30 kg. Contains 40% water, 27% fat and 25% protein.

alp cheese A hard, pale yellow mountain cheese. See also **Berg**

Alpenkäse A hard, pale yellow mountain cheese. See also **Berg**

Alpenklüber *Switzerland* A **Rohwurst** made of lean pork, beef and pork fat, air-dried and eaten raw

Alpenschneehuhn *Germany* Ptarmigan

alpha-linolenic acid A fatty acid found in ester form in high proportion in walnut oil, purslane and soya oil (NOTE: It is said to be the reason why Cretans and Japanese have a low incidence of heart attacks, since it has protective effects esp. against repeat heart attacks.)

Alpin *France* A soft rindless cheese made from cows' milk curdled with rennet and made into small rounds similar to **Vacherin**

Mont d'Or. It is dry-salted and ripened for a week or more. It contains 55% water, 21% fat and 21% protein.

Alpine cheese A hard, pale yellow mountain cheese. See also **Berg**

alpine hare See **Scottish hare**

Alpine pepper *Australia* The fruit of a bush, *Tasmannia xerophila*, which is the hottest of the Australian peppers. It is unrelated to the common peppercorn, *Piper nigrum*. See also **mountain pepper**

alpine strawberry A small, delicately flavoured strawberry, *Fragaria vesca sempiflorens, F. alpina* which fruits constantly from June to October in the UK.

Alpinia galanga *Botanical name* Greater galangal

Alpinia officinarum *Botanical name* Lesser galangal

alpino *United States* A variety of salami

alsacien(ne) *France* From Alsace, usually garnished with sauerkraut and/or ham, smoked sausage and peas

alsacienne, à l' In the Alsace style, i.e. garnished with small tartlet cases filled with braised sauerkraut and topped with a round slice of lean ham

al-salooq *Persian Gulf* A sweetmeat or dessert made from a flour, milk and molten butter dough (12:5:5) flavoured with cardamon and with 2 dsp of baking powder per kg of flour. Walnut-sized balls are shaped into crescents, deep-fried at 190°C for 5 minutes until brown, then drained and coated in icing sugar.

Alse *Germany* Shad

ålsoppa *Sweden* A thick soup or thin stew made from pieces of skinned eel boiled in salted water with some mixed peppercorns for 25 minutes. The eel is then removed and replaced with floury potatoes and leeks, which are cooked until the potatoes fall and the whole is like thin mashed potatoes. The eel is then added back, and the dish is seasoned and its consistency adjusted with milk.

Altaiski See **Altay**

Altay *Russia* A hard cheese with a dry rind and medium-sized holes cast into large rounds weighing about 12 to 20 kg. Contains 42% water, 30% fat and 24% protein. Also called **Altaiski**, **Altaysky**

Altaysky See **Altay**

altea *Italy* Marshmallow

Altenburger (Ziegenkäse) A variable-fat-content small, round, soft cheese, similar to **Camembert**, made in eastern Germany from goats' and cows' milk. It contains 66 to 56%

water, 7 to 20% fat and 25 to 20% protein for the half-fat to full-fat versions.

Althaea officinalis *Botanical name* Marshmallow

altitude effects The temperature at which water boils depends upon the pressure to which it is subjected, which in an open vessel depends upon the altitude. The boiling point of water drops by approximately 1°C for every 900 feet (290 m) rise, hence the need for pressure cookers at high altitudes.

alt Kuhkäse *Germany* Hard cheese

alubia *Spain* Kidney bean

alum See **aluminium potassium sulphate**

alumbeberas *Philippines* Pomfret, the fish

aluminium An extremely thin aluminium foil, which may be used as food decoration. It has no nutritional value and may be harmful. See also **E173**

aluminium calcium silicate See **E556**

aluminium foil Aluminium metal rolled until very thin and flexible. Because it is relatively inert and does not easily corrode, it is useful as a wrapping for food or for cooking. Also called **cooking foil**

aluminium potassium sulphate A firming agent used in e.g. chocolate-coated cherries. It is also used as a preservative and firming agent for pickles in Southeast Asian cooking. Also called **alum**

aluminium sodium silicate See **E554**

alutikka *South Asia* A potato and chickpea rissole. See also **alootikka**

alveograph The instrument which measures the strength of dough prior to baking by injecting air into it at a fixed depth and flow rate through a nozzle and recording the pressure at which the resulting bubble bursts

Alvorca *Portugal* A hard, dense, grating cheese made with ewes' milk in 200 to 300g rounds with a dry brown rind. Contains 25% water, 37% fat and 33% protein.

alya *Middle East* Fat from the tails of lamb and mutton much used in Iraq

amaebi *Japan* A sweet tasting shrimp about 12 cm long used in sushi

amahong *Philippines* Asian mussel

amai *Japan* Sweet

Amalfi lemon *Italy* A prized variety of lemon from the south of Naples, which is allowed to ripen on the tree and is thus less acid. It is larger than normal with a rough knobbly skin and a very fine flavour and aroma.

Amalfi salad Cleaned and prepared mussels and small clams are boiled to open with dry white wine and chopped shallots. The sound meat is reserved. Meat from opened scallops is sliced and sautéed in butter for a few seconds. The clam and mussel liquor is reduced by half and finished with single cream to form a sauce. The salad is assembled from sliced cold waxy potatoes topped with the cooked shell fish. The sauce is poured over and the whole is garnished with chopped parsley and served warm.

amalgamer *France* To mix, amalgamate or blend

amalu *North Africa* A delicious Moroccan spread made from argan oil, almond paste and honey

amande *France* Almond

amandel *Netherlands* Almond

amandes, fish aux Fish meunière with coarsely chopped almonds added to the **beurre noisette**. Also called **poisson meunière aux amandes**

amandine *France* A name given to certain almond-flavoured French pastries and sponges

amandine butter See **almond butter**

amanida catalana *Catalonia* A salad of cooked vegetables and any of cured meat, cheese, fish or seafood, or hard-boiled eggs with lettuce and tomatoes

amanida verda *Catalonia* Green salad

amaranth 1. A widely distributed tropical and subtropical plant of the genus *Amaranthus*, whose leaves are used as a vegetable, supplied fresh or canned. There are two popular types: one is green and mild, and the other is red. It is generally lightly cooked by steaming. A variety of names are used for the local species, i.e. callaloo, bhaji, elephant's ear, sag, sagaloo, African spinach, Chinese spinach, Indian spinach, and Surinam amaranth. (NOTE: Amaranth is often credited with magical powers.) **2.** E123, a synthetic yellow food colouring banned in the USA

Amaranthus *Botanical name* Amaranth

Amaranthus caudatus *Botanical name* One of the amaranths with pale green leaves and vivid red tassel-like flowers. Often grown as an ornamental plant.

Amaranthus cruentus *Botanical name* The most commonly grown amaranth, with oval, light green leaves and long spiky flowers

Amaranthus tricolor *Botanical name* Chinese spinach

amardine *Middle East* Sheets of dried apricot paste used for flavouring drinks or desserts or as a constituent of certain Middle East lamb stews

amarelle *United States* A sour red variety of cherry with a colourless juice, used for cherry pie and liqueurs

amarena *Italy* Morello cherry

amaretti *Italy* Small sweet meringue-like macaroons made from ground almonds, sugar and stiffly whipped egg whites (3:5:1), alternatively (2:3:1), blended to a stiff paste, possibly with almond essence, piped onto parchment paper and baked at 175°C. They may be decorated with almond flakes before baking. They are usually shop-bought. See also **almond biscuits**

amasar *Spain* To knead

amassada *Portugal* Mashed

amatriciana, all' *Italy* In the style of the town of Amatrice, i.e. used of dishes with a sauce made of tomatoes, onions and salt pork or bacon

amayuela *Spain* Golden carpet shell clam

amazushoga *Japan* Red-coloured wafer-thin slices of pickled ginger. See also **benishoga**

amberjack A large round brightly coloured fish, *Seriola dumerili* and other species of *Seriola*, found in tropical and subtropical waters

amb halad *South Asia* Zedoary

ambrosia *Italy* A dessert made from layers of thinly sliced oranges, sliced bananas, fresh pineapple, desiccated coconut and caster sugar

ambrosía *Mexico* A very sweet scented herb whose leaves are used in cold drinks in the same way as mint

amchar See **amchoor**

amchoor *South Asia* A flavouring similar to tamarind made by drying slices of unripe mango, *Magnifera indica*. It is also supplied in powdered form and is used for souring and tenderizing. Also called **aamchur, amchar, amchor, amchur, mango powder**

amchor, amchur See **amchoor**

ame *Japan* A sweet jelly made from boiled millet used to flavour fish dishes

ame hnat *Burma* A dish of braised beef with fried chopped onions, garlic, ginger, chilli powder, lemon zest, etc. garnished with crisp fried onions

amêijoas *Portugal* Small, thin shelled and very sweet clams

ameixa *Portugal* 1. Plum 2. Prune

Amelanchier canadensis *Botanical name* Juneberry

amêndoa *Portugal* Almond

amendoim *Portugal* Peanut

américaine, garnish à l' Slices of lobster tails which have been fried then cooked in white wine, fish stock, brandy, meat glaze, **demi-glace** sauce, chopped shallots, **tomato concassée**, chopped parsley and cayenne pepper

américaine, sauce *France* The cooking liquor from **garnish à l'américaine** or **homard à l'américaine**, reduced, mixed with the lobster coral and cream from its head plus butter, strained and finished with chopped parsley

American broccoli Calabrese

American brown shrimp See **American shrimp**

American burbot A freshwater non-oily relative of the cod, *Lota maculosa*, found in the Great Lakes of Canada and North America. Cooked like cod.

American crayfish The small common crayfish, *Procambarus clarkii*, of North American rivers

American cress Land cress

American frosting *United States* A cake icing, hard on the outside but soft inside, made from sugar and water boiled to 120°C with a little cream of tartar, then slightly cooled and whisked into stiffly beaten egg white. Also called **boiled frosting, boiled icing, frosting**

American fudge cake See **fudge cake**

American grape A more cold-tolerant grape, *Vitus labrusca or V. rotundifolia*, which has been hybridized with the European grape, *Vitus vinifera*, to produce a wide range of cooler-climate cultivars. American grapes are considered to be inferior to the European varieties, *V. rotundifolia* having a foxy flavour.

American long-grain rice A long thin white rice from which the husk, bran and germ have been removed. Stays separate when cooked. Also called **regular milled white rice**

American meringue *United States* The type of meringue used for a Pavlova, made by mixing corn flour and acid with **meringue Suisse** and baking at a higher temperature than normal for a shorter period to give a crisp outside with a soft sticky centre

American mustard A sweet, mild variety of mustard made from ground, dehusked white mustard seeds coloured with turmeric and mixed with vinegar, etc. Used as a condiment particularly with hot dogs and hamburgers

American navy bean See **navy bean**

American oyster A variety of oyster, *Crassostrea virginica*, reaching 17 cm in length and found on the American side of the Atlantic. Usually cooked. Also called **eastern oyster**

American persimmon A variety of persimmon, *Diospyros virginiana*, about 4 cm in diameter and with redder skin and flesh

American pink shrimp See **American shrimp**

American plaice A large flatfish, *Hippoglossoides platesoides*, similar to, but with less definite markings than, the European plaice. Also called **Canadian plaice**, **sand dab**

American relishes Hors d'oeuvres consisting of aceto-dolce pickles flavoured with cinnamon and cayenne and accompanied by small cinnamon biscuits

American service A method of serving food in a restaurant by dividing it amongst individual plates in the kitchen rather than serving from a platter at the table

American shad A variety of shad, *Alosa sapidissima*, more popular in the USA than shad is in Europe

American shrimp A large shrimp of the genus *Penaeus* (up to 15 cm) fished south of the Carolinas and closely related to the king prawn. There are three varieties: the brown *P. aztecus aztecus*, the pink *P. duorarum duorarum* and the white *P. setiferus*.

American veal cuts *United States* Veal cuts

American whelk A variety of whelk, *Busycon carica*, which can reach 30 cm in length

American white shrimp See **American shrimp**

a-mer-tha-hin *Burma* A mild beef curry made from fried pieces of stewing beef and a fried, pounded spice mixture (onions, garlic, fresh ginger, salt, turmeric and chilli powder) cooked in beef stock and thick soy sauce. Other recipes include vinegar, bay leaves, fish sauce and cinnamon. Also called **amé-thà-hin**

amé-thà-hin *Burma* A-mer-tha-hin

ametlles *Catalonia* Almonds

amido *Italy* Starch

amigdala alatismena *Greece* Salted (45 g per kg), unskinned, shelled almonds which have been marinated in lemon juice or citric acid solution and drained, then baked for 30 minutes at 180°C. Eaten as an appetizer.

amilbar de arce *Spain* Maple syrup

amino acid An organic acid which is a building block of proteins. The sequence of amino acids in a protein determines its properties. 20 amino acids are incorporated in human tissue. Of these 12, or 11 in the case of rapidly growing infants, can be synthesized in the body; the remaining 8 or 9 (essential amino acids) must be obtained from food. High-class proteins contain the essential amino acids. They are in alphabetical order: alanine, arginine, aspartic acid, cysteine, cystine, glutamic acid, glycine, histidine, isoleucine, leucine, lysine, methionine, norleucine, ornithine, phenylalanine, serine, threonine, tryptophan, tyrosine and valine.

amiral, à l' *France* In the admiral's style, i.e. garnished with a mixture of sliced truffles, mussels, lobster meat, oysters and crayfish tails

ami-shakushi *Japan* A fine wire mesh skimmer for cleaning deep-fat-frying oil or removing foam from soup

ammantato *Italy* Covered with another ingredients such as cheese, sauce, etc.; napped

ammiraglia, all' *Italy* In the admiral's style i.e. containing fish or shellfish

ammollicato *Italy* Soaked and softened

ammonia A pungent irritating gas used in water solution as a cleaner and bleach. Often smelled on rotting fish and overripe cheese.

ammonium bicarbonate An old-fashioned raising agent which releases carbon dioxide on heating or reaction with acid. Not in general use. Also called **salts of hartshorn**

ammonium carbonate See **E503**

ammonium chloride See **E510**

ammonium ferric citrate See **E381**

ammonium phosphatides Food additives used as emulsifiers and stabilizers for cocoa and chocolate products

ammonium polyphosphate See **E545**

ammonium sulphate The ammonium salt of sulphuric acid used as a yeast food

Amomum globosum *Botanical name* Chinese cardamom

Amomum melegueta *Botanical name* Grains of paradise

Amomum subulatum *Botanical name* Nepal cardamom

amoras *Portugal* Berries

Amorphophallus campanulatus *Botanical name* Elephant's foot

Amorphophallus konjac *Botanical name* Devil's taro, used for preparing black bean curd

amorphous sugar *United States* Non-crystalline sugar made by melting sucrose and cooling it rapidly to form a transparent glass-like material

amouille *France* Beestings

amourettes *France* The spinal marrow of veal and lamb, prepared by thorough cleaning followed by poaching for 30 minutes in a boiling vinegar court bouillon (NOTE: Literally 'passing fancies'.)

amourettes de veau Tosca *France* Short lengths of cooked amourettes of veal mixed with macaroni, butter, grated Parmesan cheese and coulis of crayfish tails, carefully heated in a timbale, covered with *coulis d'écrevisses* (crayfish coulis) and garnished with amourettes

ampalaya *Philippines* Bitter gourd

ampil khui *Cambodia* Tamarind

ampil tum *Cambodia* Unripe tamarind

amriti *South Asia* A sweetmeat made from a **besan** batter deep-fried in the shape of small rings and soaked in a flavoured sugar syrup

amsamgelugor Tamarind

amsoh galbi kui *Korea* Marinated and grilled short ribs of beef

amsterdamse korstjes *Netherlands* Spice cakes

amuse-gueule *France* Small appetizers usually served before or while the menu choice is being made (NOTE: Literally 'mouth-pleasers'.)

amydated pectin A synthetic derivative of pectin which is more stable than the parent product. See also **E440(ii)**

amyl acetate An ester formed from amyl alcohol and acetic acid used to flavour the confectionery item, pear drops (NOTE: Some say it has a banana flavour.)

amylase An enzyme (a naturally occurring catalyst of chemical reactions) found in saliva and gastric juices which breaks down starch (a polysaccharide) into smaller subunits which are further broken down by other enzymes or which can be directly absorbed, usually as glucose, into the blood stream. Strains obtained commercially by fermentation from *Aspergillus niger* and *Bacillus subtilis* are used in the manufacture of syrups, in the brewing industry and generally in food manufacturing. Also called **diastase**

amyl butyrate An ester formed from amyl alcohol and butyric acid used as an artificial flavouring

amylolytic enzyme Any of an important class of enzymes that degrade starch to mono-, di- and polysaccharides. Important in bread-making.

amylopectin The main and more easily digested component of starch

amylose The minor and less easily digested constituent of starch

amyl valeriate An ester formed from amyl alcohol and valerianic acid with an apple-like flavour

an *Japan* A sweetened smooth or crunchy paste of ground adzuki beans

Anacardium occidentale *Botanical name* The cashew nut tree

anadama bread *United States* A yeast-raised bread containing cornmeal and molasses or black treacle

anadromous Used to describe fish which are born in a river, migrate to the sea to grow and return to their birth river to spawn. The salmon is a common example. (NOTE: The opposite is **catadromous**)

anaerobe A microorganism which will grow and reproduce in the absence of air. Facultative anaerobes will grow with or without air. Strict (i.e. non-facultative) anaerobes are poisoned by the oxygen in the air. See also **aerobe**

anago *Japan* Conger or seawater eel; thin slices are used raw in sushi

anaheim chilli A fairly hot, long, green to yellow chilli pepper which is never dried. Also called **guero**, **Californian chilli**, **California pepper**

analcolico *Italy* Non-alcoholic drink

ananá *South America, Spain* Pineapple

ananas *Denmark, France, Germany, Netherlands, Norway, Russia, Sweden* Pineapple

ananâs *Portugal* Pineapple

Ananas *Germany* Pineapple

ananas à la créole *France* Peeled and cored pineapple is cooked in kirsch-flavoured sugar syrup and cut into thin semicircles, which are used to line a dome-shaped mould. The centre of the mould is filled with a layer of vanilla dessert rice followed by diced custard apple, pineapple and banana cooked in syrup to complete. The whole is chilled until set, demoulded, decorated with angelica and surrounded with poached bananas.

ananas à la royale *France* Pineapple prepared as for **ananas georgette**, but filled with fresh fruit salad flavoured with kirsch. The base of the pineapple is surrounded with alternate poached peaches and strawberries macerated in kirsch.

Ananas comosus *Botanical name* Pineapple

ananas Condé *France* Pineapple poached and served on dessert rice with a fruit syrup

ananas georgette *France* The top of a large whole pineapple is removed and reserved. The centre of the pineapple is scooped out, chopped finely and mixed with an iced fruit mousse mixture made from cold syrup (35°Be, 1.86 kg per litre of water), pineapple purée, and crème chantilly. This mixture is replaced in the pineapple, covered with the top and the whole is allowed to set in the refrigerator.

Ananaskaltschale *Germany* A cold pineapple soup made from crushed pineapple boiled in a light sugar syrup, allowed to cool and stand, pushed through a strainer, mixed with white wine, chilled and garnished with a **macédoine** of pineapple steeped in sugar and lemon juice

ananas Ninon *France* A soufflé mould is filled with vanilla ice cream and a conical depression made from the centre to the outer edges. The depression is lined with overlapping slices of pineapple, and the centre heaped with wild strawberries covered with a purée of raspberries and sprinkled with chopped pistachios.

ananasso *Italy* Pineapple

ananas Virginie *France* Pineapple prepared as for **ananas georgette**, but with a strawberry mousse mixed with the diced flesh of the pineapple as filling

ananász *Hungary* Pineapple

anar *South Asia* Pomegranate

anara *Italy* Duck

anardana *South Asia* The ground dried seeds of sour pomegranates used in North India as a souring agent in chutneys and curries, in fillings for bread and savoury pasties, and with braised vegetables and pulses

Anari A soft, white, unripened curd cheese from Cyprus, made from ewes' milk. It has a slightly sweetish flavour and moist texture similar to the Greek **Mizithra** or Italian **Ricotta** and is eaten as a dessert.

anatra *Italy* Duck

anatra arrosto *Italy* Duck, blanched for 5 minutes, dried with paper then hot air (e.g. with a hair dryer), rubbed with ground rosemary, sage, salt and black pepper, stuffed with the same herbs mixed with chopped liver, roasted and served with sauce made from pan juices and the stuffing

anatra ripiena *Italy* Duck braised with a stuffing of meat, sausage, mushrooms and pistachio nuts

anatrino *Italy* Duckling

anatto See **annatto**

anchoa *Spain* Anchovy

anchoïade *France* An anchovy paste from Provence, made with anchovies pounded or processed with olive oil and possibly garlic to make a dip for canapés

anchois *France* Anchovy

anchois, beurre d' See **anchovy butter**

anchois, canapé d' *France* Canapé with anchovy butter

anchois, sauce *France* Anchovy sauce

anchois à la parisienne *France* Fillets of desalted anchovies arranged in a multi-diamond pattern in the centre of a plate covered with a little vinaigrette mixed with soy sauce. The centre of the diamonds and the border are filled with separately chopped hard-boiled egg yolk, hard-boiled egg white and green herbs to give a pleasing pattern.

anchois aux poivrons *France* A hors d'oeuvre of anchovy fillets marinated in oil, alternating with strips of sweet pepper and decorated with chopped hard-boiled egg, parsley and capers

anchois de Norvège *France* Norwegian anchovies, preserved in brine

anchois des tamarins *France* A hors d'oeuvre composed of anchovy **paupiettes**, each topped with a black olive, arranged around a centre of grated warm potatoes seasoned with oil and vinegar and sprinkled with chopped fines herbes

anchois frais marinés *France* A hors d'oeuvre made from fresh anchovies salted for 2 hours, drained, plunged into hot fat to stiffen, then marinaded in oil with a little acid (lemon or vinegar) for 2 days. Served with a little of the marinade.

ancho pepper A mild, richly flavoured variety of pepper, *Capsicum frutescens,* usually dried for use in Latin American cooking

anchouiada *France* Anchovy fillets pounded with garlic, shallots, thyme and olive oil with a little vinegar, used as a flavouring or dip. Similar to **bagna cauda**.

anchovas *Portugal* Anchovies. Also called **enchovas**

Anchovis *Germany* Anchovy

anchovy A small Mediterranean fish of the herring family, *Engraulis encrasicolus,* up to 20 cm in length and fished in the Mediterranean and the bay of Biscay between January and September. Usually salted whole and used as a garnish or for flavouring. A similar fish, *Stolephorus heterolobus,* is found throughout Southeast Asia and used fresh, salted or dried and is one of the fish fermented to produce fish pastes and sauces.

anchovy butter A compound butter made from butter and anchovy fillets pounded together and sieved

anchovy essence A liquid extract of cured and salted anchovies used for flavouring

anchovy fingers See **allumettes aux anchois**

anchovy paste Salted anchovies, vinegar, spices and water pounded together

anchovy paupiettes A hors d'oeuvre of flattened anchovy fillets, spread with a purée of cooked fish mixed with mayonnaise seasoned with cayenne, rolled into paupiettes and decorated with anchovy butter

anchovy sauce A rich fish **velouté**, thickened with egg yolk and cream or **sauce normande** without the butter and flavoured with anchovy; alternatively, a **béchamel sauce** with 2 tablespoons of anchovy essence per litre. It may be finished with diced, dried and desalted anchovy fillets, and is used with fish.

anchovy toast *England* A savoury or appetizer made from rounds of bread fried to a pale straw, covered with anchovies and topped with chilled Devonshire or whipped cream and served immediately

an chun *China* Quail

an chun dan *China* Quail egg

Anchusa tinctora *Botanical name* Alkanet

ancidda *Italy* Eel (*Sardinia*)

ancien impérial *France* A soft mild cheese cast in squares. May be eaten fresh or ripened.

ancienne, à l' *France* In the old style, i.e. with boiled rice, **béchamel sauce** and mushrooms

ancient egg Chinese preserved eggs

ancono *Italy* A soup made with fish, shellfish and tomatoes

and *Denmark, Norway* Duck

andaa *Nepal* Egg

andalouse, à l' *France* In the Andalusian style, i.e. garnished with halves of grilled red pepper filled with rice cooked à la Grecque and slices of aubergine, 4 cm thick, with the centre hollowed out and filled with tomatoes sautéed in oil

andalouse, sauce *England, France* Mayonnaise mixed with tomato purée and garnished with julienned red sweet pepper

andalouse mayonnaise Mayonnaise mixed with tomato purée and the finely chopped flesh of skinned and cooked sweet red peppers. Served with roast veal, poultry and hard-boiled eggs.

Andalusian sauce See **andalouse, sauce**

ande *South Asia* Egg

andijvie *Netherlands* Endive

andouille *France* A large, black, pig-based sausage boiled in water then grilled, which may be served hot or cold, usually in thin slices and garnished with mashed potato. It is generally made from pork, tripe, pork chitterlings, calf mesentery, pepper, wine, onions and spices, depending on region. It may be white through various shades of brown to black and may be dried (sechée) or smoked (**fumée**).

andouille bretonne *France* Pig tripe and chitterlings, cut into strips a little shorter than the sausage, dry-cured in salt, pepper and spices or marinated in wine and herbs, mixed with half their combined weight of similar strips of hard pork fat, placed regularly or jumbled up in beef runners, tied, salted for a week, smoked for 3 days over apple wood, brushed off, floured and boiled in water for 2 hours before serving

andouille de Cambrai *France* A tripe sausage dating from 1767

andouille de campagne *France* The typical andouille containing about 50% pork shoulder meat, the remainder being chitterlings, tripe and seasonings

andouille de Nancy *France* Equal parts of calf mesentery and belly pork cut in 20-cm-long strips, treated with salt, pepper and spice or marinated in wine and herbs, drained, seasoned, possibly mixed with chopped onions and mushrooms sweated in lard, moistened with Madeira or white wine, stuffed into beef runners and tied. Cooked by pricking and simmering in water with aromatic vegetables and a bouquet garni, then left to cool in the cooking liquor.

andouille de Vire *France* As **andouille bretonne** but with fat bacon replacing the pork fat, chopped onion, shallots and parsley added and the whole seasoned and moistened with white wine. The strips are formed in bundles and placed neatly in beef runners with each bundle tied in place. The andouille may be salted in brine and/or smoked, but in all cases it is finally simmered in a bouillon for 3 hours.

andouille pur porc *France* Andouille made with seasoned pork shoulder meat and fat

andouillette *France* A small version of the **andouille** but usually containing only coarsely chopped chitterlings and tripe and purchased in the cooked state. Generally lightly slashed and grilled or fried and served hot with fried potatoes, mustard and onions.

andouillette à la lyonnaise *France* Andouillettes cut into 1 cm. slices, sautéed in very hot butter until browned, sliced onion added and coloured, seasoned, mixed well and finished with chopped parsley and a little vinegar.

andouillette à la strasbourgeoise *France* Grilled or fried andouillette served on a bed of sauerkraut accompanied by boiled potatoes

andouillette (à la) bourguignonne *France* Andouillettes cut into 1 cm. slices, sautéed in hot butter and lard until browned, fat drained off, and andouillettes served with melted well-seasoned snail butter.

andouillette de Savoie *France* An andouillette containing pork chitterlings, tripe and calf mesentery flavoured with cumin

andouillette de Troyes *France* An andouillette containing calf mesentery, udder, egg yolks, shallots, parsley, seasoning and nutmeg, moistened with white wine

andouillette fine de porc *France* Calf mesentery and lean bacon cut in pieces, simmered in stock with herbs and an onion clouté for 2 hours, removed, coarsely chopped and combined with the strained reduced cooking liquor, egg yolks and chopped shallots, mushrooms and parsley, sweated in lard, filled into casings and tied to form small sausages. May be brined and/or smoked before simmering in a bouillon.

andouille vigneronne *France* Soaked haricot beans put in a casserole with diced fat bacon and pork rind, carrots, onions, a bouquet garni and seasoning, covered with water and boiled with some wine for an hour, a previously cooked pork andouille added and the whole braised in the oven for 2 hours. The meat and beans are served separately.

ànec amb naps *Catalonia* Duck with turnips

añejo 1. *Mexico* A cheese made from cows' or goats' milk, well matured with a strong salty flavour **2.** *Spain* Meat from 14 to 15 month old beef cattle

anelli *Italy* Rings of pasta cut from a tube about 1 cm. in diameter.

anellini *Italy* Tiny pasta rings used for soup, a smaller version of anelli

anémona de mar *Spain* Sea anemone

anémone de mer *France* Sea anemone

anemone di mare *Italy* Sea anemone

aneth *France* Dill

Anethum graveolens *Botanical name* Dill

Anethum sowa *Botanical name* Indian dill

aneto *Italy* Dill

aneurin See **vitamin B1**

ange de mer *France* Angel fish

angel cake *United States* A fat-and-egg-yolk-free light sponge made by folding very low gluten cake flour sieved with cream of tartar and caster sugar into stiffly beaten egg whites. Usually baked in a ring mould. Also called **angel food cake**

angel fish A type of shark, *Squatina squatina*, with large pectoral fins which can be treated as skate wings. The tail is also thick and meaty with a few soft flexible bones. Also called **angel shark**, **fiddle fish**

angel flake coconut A much wider cut of desiccated coconut like large flakes

angel food cake See **angel cake**

angelica A tall parsley-like plant, *Angelica archangelica* or *A. officinalis*. The blanched, peeled and boiled stalks and leaf ribs are candied for use as a decoration.

Angelica archangelica *Botanical name* Angelica

Angelica officinalis *Botanical name* Angelica

Angelica sinensis *Botanical name* Dang gui. Also called **Chinese angelica**

angélique *France* Angelica

angelitter Schnüss *Germany* A soup made from bacon, young beans and milk

angelot *France* Angel fish

angelote *Spain* Angel fish

angel's farts See **fritole di lino**

angel's hair A very fine and thin noodle wrapped in skeins like wool. Also called **vermicellini**

angel shark See **angel fish**

angels on horseback A savoury consisting of oysters wrapped in streaky bacon, grilled and served on buttered toast

anges à cheval *France* Angels on horseback

angevine, à l' *France* In the Anjou style, i.e. with the addition of local wine

anghiti *South Asia* A charcoal-burning brazier rather like a modern barbecue

angkak *Philippines* Dried and ground rice which has been coloured red/purple by fermentation with *Monascus purpureus*. Used to colour and flavour foods prepared from fish and cheese and to produce red rice wine.

anglaise, à l' *France* In the English style, i.e. plain-cooked or, if deep-fried, coated with flour, egg and breadcrumbs (i.e. panéed)

anglaise, fish à l' Fillets of fish, panéed, deep-fried at 185°C, drained and garnished with lemon wedges and a sprig of parsley and served with tartare sauce

anglaise, sauce *England, France* Crème à l'Anglaise

anglaise, sauce à l' *France* Egg custard sauce

angled loofah The fruit of a climbing vine, *Luffa acutangula*, which grows to 3 m. It has a dull green skin with 10 longitudinal ridges and is harvested at up to 50 cm. It is slightly bitter and has a similar taste and texture to okra. It is peeled before use and may be steamed, fried or braised. See also **loofah**, **club gourd**. Also called **Chinese okra**, **ridged gourd**, **ridged melon**, **pleated squash**, **angled luffa**

angler fish *United States* Monkfish

Anglesey cake *Wales* Flour, butter, sugar and eggs (3:2:2:1) with 4 tbsp of baking powder per kg of flour and a little dried vine fruit are combined by the rubbing-in method and brought together with a little milk to form a stiff paste, then baked at 190°C in thinnish layers for 30 to 40 minutes. Each cake is sliced in half and eaten hot as a jam sandwich.

Anglesey eggs *Wales* Hard-boiled eggs mixed with cooked leeks and potatoes in a cheese sauce

angola *Spain* Sour milk

angoori petha *South Asia* A petha made with small green pumpkins the size of large grapes

anguidda *Italy* Eel (*Sicily*)

anguila *Spain* Eel

anguila ahumada *Spain* Smoked eel

anguilla *Italy* Eel

anguilla alla fiorentina *Italy* Eels rolled in seasoned breadcrumbs and baked

anguilla alla griglia *Italy* Boned eels, cut in 10 cm pieces, seasoned, floured, oiled and grilled over charcoal until slightly charred

anguilla alla marinara *Italy* Eel in vinegar sauce

anguilla alla veneziana *Italy* Eel with tuna and lemon sauce

anguilla argentina *Italy* A silvery coloured eel, *Anguilla anguilla*

anguilla gialla *Italy* The common eel

anguilla in carpione *Italy* A hors d'oeuvre of pieces of eel. salted and oiled, grilled over charcoal until cooked and marinated in a mixture of oil, vinegar, bay leaves, garlic and seasoning for a minimum of 24 hours.

anguilla in teglia al pisello *Italy* Fried eel with tomato sauce and peas

anguille *France* Eel

anguille à la Beaucaire *France* Skinned boned eel stuffed with whiting and chopped mushroom forcemeat, sewn up, formed into an oval, then braised in white wine with chopped shallots, mushrooms, glazed button onions and brandy. Served from the cooking dish.

anguille à la ménagère *France* Cleaned and skinned eel cut into 8 cm. pieces, incised on each side, seasoned, grilled and served with a border of gherkins, accompanied with softened parsley butter mixed with a small amount of prepared mustard.

anguille à la meunière *France* Cleaned and skinned eels, cut in pieces, passed through seasoned flour, shallow-fried in butter, and finished with **beurre noisette**

anguille à la romaine *France* Cleaned and skinned eels cut into 5 cm pieces, stiffened in hot butter then stewed gently with peas, shredded lettuce and white wine, thickened with **beurre manié** and served immediately

anguille à la rouennaise *France* A cleaned and skinned eel is incised both sides, formed into a ring and poached with a **mirepoix** of aromatic vegetables. When cooked, it is glazed by basting with the cooking liquor. It is served with a centre garnish of mushrooms, poached oysters and poached soft roe, the garnish being coated with strained cooking liquor thickened with sauce espagnole, and the whole surrounded with shallow-fried smelts.

anguille à la tartare *France* Cleaned and skinned eel either whole or in portions, poached in white wine court bouillon, drained, panéed, deep-fried, garnished with fried parsley and gherkins and served with tartare sauce

anguille à l'escabèche *France* Pickled eel, fried in oil then cooled in aspic jelly

anguille au vert *France* Cleaned and skinned eels cut into 5 cm. pieces, placed on a bed of garden herbs (sorrel, nettle tops, parsley, salad burnet, sage, savory, chervil and tarragon) and butter; cooked until the flesh stiffens, then white wine, seasoning, and sage added; when cooking complete, liquor thickened with egg yolk and finished with lemon juice. Usually served cold.

anguille au vert à la flamande *France* Cleaned and skinned eels cut into 5 cm pieces, cooked in butter until flesh stiffens, then further cooked in beer and seasoning; towards the end of cooking chopped garden herbs (as in **anguille au vert**) added, and liquor thickened with arrowroot. Usually served cold.

anguille au vin blanc et paprika *France* Cleaned eels cut into 8 cm. pieces, placed in a shallow pan with sliced onions, a bouquet garni, garlic, seasoning, white wine and paprika, boiled, flamed with brandy, covered and cooked, then cooled in cooking liquor. The eel pieces are finally skinned, the fillets detached and covered with defatted and thickened cooking liquor.

anguille benoîton *France* Boned, skinned and filleted eel, cut into 10 cm. thin slices, twisted into spirals, passed through seasoned flour, deep-fried and piled up with fried parsley. Accompanied with a strained reduced red wine sauce made with shallots, parsley stalks and eel trimmings, thickened with butter.

anguille de mer *France* Conger eel

anguille en matelote *France* Cleaned skinned eel is cut in pieces, boiled with red or white wine, sliced onions, bouquet garni, garlic, and seasoning, flamed with brandy and cooked until done in a tightly closed pan. The cooking liquor is strained and, if white, reduced and thickened with a fish velouté and garnished with button onions, crayfish and croûtons (*marinière*); if red, it is thickened with **beurre manié** and garnished with crayfish and croûtons.

anguille frite *France* Fried eel. Small skinned eels, incised both sides, folded into figures of eight and skewered, deep-fried and garnished with fried parsley.

anguille frite à l'anglaise *France* Cleaned, skinned, boned and filleted eel cut into thin slices, marinated with seasoning, chopped parsley, oil and lemon juice, panéed and deep-fried, finished with anchovy butter and served immediately accompanied with **sauce bâtarde**

anguille fumée *France* Smoked eel, served with skin and bone removed and cut into sections

anguille in salsa *Italy* Small fried fish marinated in vinegar

anguille pompadour *France* Cleaned and skinned eel, incised both sides, formed into a ring, cooked in white wine court bouillon and cooled in the cooking liquor; then drained, dried, coated with a mixture of **Villeroi** and **Soubise** sauce, panéed and deep-fried until heated through and browned. Served with fried parsley and croquettes of **pommes dauphine**, accompanied with tomato-flavoured **béarnaise sauce**.

anguillette *France* Small eel, a speciality of the Basque country

anguria *Italy* Water melon

Angus fish soup *Scotland* A soup made from fresh haddock heads, boiled, skinned then simmered with aromatic vegetables, turnips, parsley and seasoning for 20 minutes, strained onto a white roux and finished with milk, thyme, chopped parsley and a liaison of eggs and cream

Angus potatoes *Scotland* A dish of baked potatoes from which the cooked interiors have been removed and mixed with flaked **Arbroath smokie** flesh, butter, milk and seasoning, before being returned to the cases. These are then heated through in the oven.

anho *Portugal* Lamb

anhydrate, to *United States* To dehydrate

anice *Italy* Anice (NOTE: Semi di anice is aniseed.)

Anice stellato *Italy* Star anise

anicini *Italy* Aniseed biscuits from Sardinia

anijs *Netherlands* Anise

animelle *Italy* Sweetbreads

animelle con limone e capperi *Italy* Poached calf's sweetbreads, sliced, seasoned and floured, sautéed in butter until golden, mixed with capers and lemon juice and served with the pan juices and chopped parsley

animelles *France* Testicles, usually of oxen or sheep, the latter also being known as sheep's fry. Prepared by scalding, skinning and soaking in running water, then marinated and deep-fried or treated as kidneys. Also called **frivolités**

anis *France, Philippines* Aniseed

anise A half-hardy annual umbelliferous plant, *Pimpinella anisum*, related to the plants which produce cumin, dill and fennel. It grows erect or prostrate to about 45 cm. The seeds are known as aniseed. The flowers and fresh leaves may be used in salads and as a garnish. The plant is sometimes known as aniseed.

aniseed The aromatic, oval seeds of the anise plant with a sweet liquorice-like flavour. Used in cakes, for liqueurs and in Indian cookery and as a general flavouring. First mentioned in the written literature in 1500 BC by the Egyptians. Also called **anise**

aniseed myrtle *Australia* The leaves of this native myrtle, *Backhousia anisata*, have a strong aniseed flavour with a eucalyptus aftertaste. It is related to the lemon myrtle and grows in the coastal rain forest. The leaves are used either fresh or dried, whole or ground in meat dishes, desserts and baked goods. Since the essential oils are volatile, it is usually added just before service. The essential oil can be bought separately.

anise fern Sweet cicely

anise pepper A Chinese spice made from the ground dried red berries of the feathery-leaved prickly ash tree, *Xanthoxylum piperitum*. It has a pronounced spicy-woody smell and a numbing taste and is one of the constituents of five-spice powder much used in Chinese cooking. See also **sansho**. Also called **Sichuan pepper**, **Szechuan pepper**, **Chinese pepper**, **Chinese aromatic pepper**, **Japanese pepper**, **xanthoxylum**, **fagara**

anithi *South Asia* Dill seed

anitra *Italy* Duck

anka *Sweden* Duck

ankerias *Finland* Eel

anko *Japan* A sweet bean paste made from adzuki beans, blanched and simmered for 1 to 1.5 hours until soft and passed though a sieve into a little water. This water is removed by squeezing in muslin, and the paste, combined with sugar, equal in weight to the original dried beans, and a little salt, is worked over a low heat until glossy and thick.

annanas *South Asia* Pineapple

annatto A bright orange permitted food colour, E160(b), made from the fruit pulp of a South American tree, *Bixa orellana*, like bixin and norbixin. Must be acidified before use. Also called **anatto**

annatto lard Red coloured lard used in Filipino cooking. Made by frying annatto seeds in the lard then discarding them.

annatto seed The seeds of the annatto fruits of *Bixa orellana*, usually fried in oil or lard to impart a subtle flavour and red colour to food. After cooking the seeds are discarded.

annegato *Italy* Simmered in wine

annona Custard apple

Annot *France* A ewes' or goats' milk cheese from Provence

anolini *Italy* Small, half-circle-shaped, stuffed pasta similar to ravioli. The stuffing always contains meat and is often a well reduced and sieved meat stew.

anona Custard apple

Anona cherimolia Botanical name Cherimoya

Anona diversifolia Botanical name Ilama

Anona muricata Botanical name Soursop

Anona purpurea Botanical name Soncoya

Anona reticulata Botanical name Bullock's heart

Anona spp. Botanical name Custard apples and related fruits

Anona squamosa Botanical name Sweet sop

anone *France* Custard apple

ansarino *Spain* Gosling

Anschovis *Germany* Anchovy

Ansgar *Germany* A milder variety of Tilsit cheese made in the west of Germany

ansjos *Norway* Anchovy

ansjovis *Netherlands, Sweden* Anchovy

anthocyanin, anthocyan A glucoside plant pigment extracted from grape skins which is red in acid and blue in alkaline conditions. It forms coloured complexes with metals e.g. grey with iron, green with aluminium and blue with tin, hence the off colours in e.g. canned pears where its reaction with tin gives the pears a pink colour. See also **E163**

anthoxanthan A colouring compound in potatoes and onions which is colourless in acid and yellow in alkaline conditions

Anthriscus cerefolium Botanical name Chervil

antibiotics Chemicals produced by various moulds which can kill or prevent the growth of microorganisms. As they are often incorporated in animal feeds, residues may occur in the milk or flesh of the animal. The limits of these residues are strictly controlled as continuous ingestion could develop antibiotic-resistant microorganisms in the human gut.

antiboise, à l' *France* In the Antibes style, i.e. garnished with garlic, cheese and sometimes sardines

antica, all' *Italy* In the old-fashioned, classic style

anticaking agent A compound added to powdered foods to prevent their particles sticking together. E numbers 530 to 578 are anticaking agents.

anticuchos *South America* Kebabs made from marinated ox hearts brushed with a hot chilli sauce and grilled. Common in Peru.

antimycotic Referring to the action of compounds which kill, slow down or prevent the growth of moulds, e.g. calcium propionate

antin, fish d' Poached white fish in a sauce. See also **bréval, fish**

antioxidant A chemical compound of synthetic or natural origin which retards the rate of reaction of the oxygen in the air with foods, thus slowing down the development of off flavours in fats and the colouring of cut fruit, etc. E numbers 300 to 321. Typical examples are vitamin E (from soya beans), vitamin C (from citrus fruit or made synthetically), BHT *(butylated hydroxytoluene)*, BHA *(butylated hydroxyanisole)* and propyl gallate. The last three are synthetic.

antipasti almagro *Italy* Seafood salad

antipasti assortiti *Italy* Mixed antipasti of ham, salami, anchovies, olives, fruit, etc.

antipasto *Italy* Starter, hors d'oeuvre, first course of a meal (NOTE: The plural is **antipasti**.)

antipasto alla genovese *Italy* Young broad beans with sausage

antispattering agent A compound such as lecithin which, when added to fat, prevents spattering due to water droplets

antistaling agent A compound such as sucrose stearate or glycerol which apparently slows down the staling of baked goods by softening the crumb of the bread

antojitos *Mexico* Small portions of classical Mexican dishes served as snack food for street eating or as appetizers or starters (NOTE: Literally 'what you fancy'.)

añu A South American knobbly yellow tuber from a perennial climbing plant. See also **ysaño**

anversoise, à l' *France* In the Antwerp (Anvers) style, i.e. garnished with hop shoots in cream

anxove *Catalonia* Anchovy

Anzac biscuits *Australia* Biscuits made with rolled oats, self-raising flour, sugar, butter and golden syrup (2:2:2:2:1) and a little bicarbonate of soda dissolved in water. All the ingredients are melted together, sometimes with dessicated coconut added.

AOC See **appellation d'origine contrôlée**

aojiso *Japan* See **green shiso**

aole *Italy* A fresh water fish

aonegi *Japan* Spring onions

aonori *Japan* Green flaked or shredded **nori** used as a seasoning

aoshiso *Japan* See **green shiso**

aotogarashi *Japan* A small green hot pepper

aoyagi *Japan* **1.** A round clam used raw or lightly cooked for sushi **2.** A large clam, *Mactra chinensis*, about 4 cm by 8 cm and 5 cm thick, used throughout Japan for **sashimi**, **sunomono** and **kakiage**. Also called **bakagai**

aoyose *Japan* A natural green food colouring extracted from spinach leaves

apaz onion *United States* An edible, small wild onion

apee *United States* A biscuit (cookie) whose distinguishing feature is the use of sour cream in the batter (NOTE: The biscuit is named from the initials of its creator, Ann Page.)

apelsin *Sweden* Orange, the fruit

apem *West Africa* The Ghanaian name for baby plantain

aperitif An alcoholic drink taken before a meal

Apfel *Germany* Apple

Apfelbettelmann *Germany* Chopped, peeled and cored apples, well sprinkled with sugar, layered alternately in an ovenproof dish with a mixture of fine pumpernickel crumbs, sugar, butter and chopped nuts (3:3:2:1) flavoured with cinnamon and lemon zest, starting and finishing with a breadcrumb mixture layer, topped with butter and baked at 175°C until apples are soft

Apfelbröisi *Germany* A bread pudding containing apples

Apfelkaltschale *Germany* As **Ananaskaltschale**, but with cooked apples rubbed through the strainer and garnished with diced apples and sultanas simmered in a light syrup

Apfelkren *Austria* Apple and horseradish sauce made from cooking apples simmered with sugar and lemon juice, mashed and mixed with shredded horseradish from the outer part of the root. Served with Viennese boiled beef (**Tafelspitz**).

Apfelkuchen *Germany* An open apple tart made with a slightly sweetened pastry flavoured with lemon zest and brought together with egg yolks. The base is coated with breadcrumbs mixed with melted butter, followed by sliced cooking apples and topped with currants soaked in rum. This is baked at 175°C for 10 minutes, then filled with a sweetened egg custard made with cream, sprinkled with sugar and butter and baked until the custard is set and browned.

Apfelmus *Germany* Stewed apple

Apfelpfannkuchen *Germany* A pancake with an apple filling

Apfelschmarren *Austria* Pancake batter mixed with diced apple, cooked (about 1 cm thick) until brown on both sides, broken up and sprinkled with caster sugar

Apfelschnitze *Germany* Apple fritter

Apfelsine *Germany* Orange, the fruit

Apfelstrudel *Austria* Strudel (filo) pastry rolled around a mixture of chopped raw cooking apples, sultanas, caster sugar and chopped nuts, sealed and baked. The pastry may be covered on the inside with grated nuts or fried dry white breadcrumbs. Also called **apple strudel**

Apfeltorte *Germany* Apple cake

apielsiny v romye z pryanostyami *Russia* Oranges with spiced rum. Peeled, depithed and sliced oranges, marinated and served in a sugar syrup flavoured with cloves and rum.

apio 1. Arracacha **2.** *Spain* Celery

apio-nabo *Spain* Celeriac

Apios tuberosa Botanical name Arracacha

Apium graveolens Botanical name Wild celery

Apium graveolens **var.** *dulce* Botanical name Celery

Apium graveolens **var.** *rapaceum* Botanical name Celeriac

apog *Philippines* Lime (calcium hydroxide)

à point *France* Medium rare, a degree of cooking meat or fish so that protein at the centre of the piece is coagulated but not discoloured or hardened

apon *West Africa* The kernels of the wild mango tree used, crushed, as a thickener. See also **ogbono**

appa *South Asia, Sri Lanka* Soft spongy breads made from a ground rice, rice flour and coconut milk batter or dough, raised using the fermenting sap of the coconut palm (although yeast may be substituted) and cooked in small, greased and covered wok-like pans. Eaten for breakfast. See also **string hoppers**

apparecchiato *Italy* **1.** Prepared. Used of food. **2.** Laid. Used of the table.

appareil *France* Food mixture or items for preparing a dish, e.g. *appareil à crêpes* 'pancake batter'

appel *Netherlands* Apple

appelbeignet *Netherlands* Apple fritter

äppel-fläsk *Sweden* Panéed strips of derinded pork belly, fried until brown, layered in a casserole with sweated sliced onions and raw, cored but unpeeled, slices of apple, seasoned, moistened with pan juices and water, and simmered with a lid on for 30 minutes. Served with boiled potatoes.

appellation d'origine *France* The French certificate of origin for foodstuffs, especially wine and cheese. There are only 27 French cheeses entitled to this certificate. See also **cheese certification** (NOTE: Literally 'label of origin'.)

appellation d'origine contrôlée *France* The French designation that a wine or cheese has an appellation d'origine which guarantees the origin of the grapes and the yield. Also called **AOC**

appelmoes *Netherlands* Apple sauce

äppelmos *Sweden* Apple sauce

appelsiini *Finland* Orange, the fruit

appelsin *Denmark, Norway* Orange, the fruit

appeltaart *Netherlands* Apple cake

Appenzell *Switzerland* Appenzeller

Appenzeller *Switzerland* A strong, slightly bitter, semi-hard, scalded-curd cheese made from whole cows' milk. It is cast in large rounds (6 to 8 kg), and matured in brine with wine and spices for 3 to 6 months to give it its characteristic flavour. It contains 43% water, 28% fat and 26% protein. Also called **Appenzell**

Appenzellerli *Switzerland* A spiced sausage from Appenzell. See also **Knackerli**

appertization The term for the heat-processing of foods at temperatures above 120°C, in particular, retorting and high temperature short time (HTST) processing. This process does not guarantee complete sterility but any spores present should be non-pathogenic and unable to grow in the processed food environment.

appertize, to To subject to heat treatment by retorting (121°C) or high temperature short time (HTST) processing (132°C and above)

appetite The desire for food evoked by hunger and the taste, smell or appearance of various foodstuffs

appetitost *Denmark* A sour buttermilk cheese

appetizer A general name given to small items of food served before or at the beginning of a meal or at cocktail parties

apple The fruit of the apple tree, *Malus sylvestris* var. *domestica*, which requires cool winters to fruit. There are thousands of varieties but only about fifty are commercially available. Dessert varieties are sweetish, sometimes combined with acid, used for eating raw, and, since they keep their shape on cooking, also used for tarts and in other cases where the shape of the cut fruit is important. Cooking varieties are generally acid and become soft and mushy when boiled, stewed or baked.

äpple *Sweden* Apple

apple amber *England* An 18th-century dish consisting of peeled chopped apples boiled in water with sugar, lemon juice and lemon zest. After cooking the apples are mixed with whole beaten eggs and baked in the oven with a puff pastry cover.

apple amber pudding *England* A shortcrust pastry case filled with a sweetened apple purée mixed with lemon juice and lemon zest, topped with meringue and baked

apple banana The small sweet fruit of a tropical herb of the genus *Musa* with a flavour similar to a mixture of pineapple and apple

appleberry *Australia* The green/yellow fruit of a creeper, *Billardiera cymosa* and *B. scandiens*. It is cylindrical, about 2–3 cm long, and has a fuzzy skin containing numerous seeds dispersed through the pulpy flesh. The ripe fruits which fall off the creeper have a mild aniseed flavour and can be eaten fresh or used in sauces and baked desserts.

apple bread *England* A Derbyshire bread made from dough kneaded with sweetened apple purée prior to proving

apple brown Betty *United States* Stewed apple layered with toasted butter-soaked cake crumbs

apple butter See **apple cheese**

apple cake See **Norfolk apple cake**

apple charlotte A dessert made from apples cooked in butter and sugar flavoured with grated lemon zest and ground cinnamon, placed in a mould lined with stale bread soaked in melted butter or with browned bread crumbs, covered in same, baked in the oven and served with apricot or custard sauce

apple cheese *England* Whole apples cut so as to break open the pips, cooked until soft in cider, passed through a coarse sieve to allow the pip kernels to pass through, then cooked with an equal amount of sugar and a clove until of coating consistency. Also called **apple butter**

apple corer The tube-shaped implement used to remove the core from apples

apple cream bun *England* A large choux pastry spherical bun filled with whipped cream into which slices of apple poached in syrup have been folded

apple crumble Apples, prepared as for apple charlotte, with a crumble topping baked in the oven

apple cucumber A distinctive variety of almost spherical cucumber, up to the size of an orange

apple curd A fruit curd flavoured with puréed unsweetened apples, lemon juice and lemon zest

apple dumpling Cored apples filled with a mixture of butter, caster sugar and possibly dried fruit, cinnamon, etc., are enclosed in short pastry. The tops are decorated and egg-washed. The pastry is pierced and the dumplings are baked in a hot oven for 15 minutes.

apple flan The base of a cooked flan case is covered with apples cooked as for apple charlotte and finished in a variety of ways e.g. by being covered with other fruits, nuts or a purée or mousse of candied chestnuts, by being glazed either with apricot syrup or melted redcurrant jelly, or by being covered with meringue or dredged with icing sugar. (In the latter two cases, the flan is cooked in the oven to brown.).

apple fritters As for apricot fritters but substituting peeled, cored and sliced apple

apple frushie *Scotland* A plate pie made with shortcrust pastry and a lattice top. For the filling cooking apples are peeled, cored and sliced and laid evenly over the base, sprinkled with rose water and covered evenly with honey. The pie is baked at 200°C for 25 to 30 minutes, dredged with caster sugar and served hot with cream.

apple hedgehog *England* An old Dorset dessert of peeled and cored apples which are cooked in a pan with three quarters of their weight in sugar and a little water until the sugar forms caramel. They are then poured into a buttered mould, turned out and, when set, stuck with almond flakes and served with cream or custard.

apple mayonnaise *Scandinavia* Equal quantities of mayonnaise and slightly sweetened apple purée flavoured with horseradish sauce

applemint One of the common culinary varieties of mint, *Mentha suaveolens*, with hairy apple-scented bright green leaves, used for making mint sauce, mint jelly, stuffings, salads, etc. and as a general flavouring herb. Also called **Egyptian mint**

äpplen *Sweden* Apples

apple of the Orient Persimmon

apple pandowdy *United States* An apple pie made in a dish with spiced sliced apples, covered in a pastry crust

apple pudding A suet-pastry-lined basin filled with sliced apples mixed with sugar, ground cinnamon, grated lemon zest, sealed with more suet pastry, covered with a cloth or lid and steamed or boiled for approximately 2 hours

apple sauce Peeled, cored and chopped apples, sweated in butter and a little water, possibly with ground cinnamon and then sieved, liquidized or whisked to a smooth sauce

apple sauce cake 1. *England* A Somerset cake made from a spiced cake mixture using brown sugar to which unsweetened apple sauce is added prior to folding in the flour, spices, salt and dried fruit. Topped with vanilla butter icing. Also called **Somerset apple cake 2.** *United States* A cake containing mixed dried fruit, nuts and apple sauce

apple schnitz *United States* Dried apple slices used in Pennsylvanian cooking originated by German immigrants

apple slim *Ireland* A griddle-cooked double-crust apple tart

apple snow Apple pulp or purée mixed with meringue

apple soup *England* Chopped whole apples simmered in mutton broth passed through a strainer and seasoned with ginger and salt. May be reheated with pearl barley until the barley is soft.

apple strudel See **Apfelstrudel**

apple turnover Rounds of 3 mm puff pastry, egg-washed, one half of each round heaped with a mixture of finely sliced apples, sugar and cinnamon, other half folded over and sealed, egg-washed, baked and glazed with icing sugar just before finishing

Applewood *England* A medium-flavoured Cheddar cheese from Somerset, flavoured with an extract of applewood smoke or smoked over applewood and coated with paprika

aprapransa *West Africa* A thick palm nut stew from Ghana containing cooked cow peas, palm butter or peanut butter, tomatoes, toasted maize flour and lemon juice. Usually served on special occasions with smoked herrings

apricot A round, orange-coloured fruit with a rich aromatic flavour from a tree, *Prunus armeniaca*, of the plum family. Suitable for stewing, for sorbets and for jam-making; often preserved by drying.

apricot flan Flan ring lined with sugar paste, pierced, sugared, filled with neatly arranged half apricots, sugared, baked at 210°C, ring removed, rebaked and glazed as for apple flan

apricot fritters Firm but not overripe halved apricots, sprinkled with sugar and macerated with kirsch, brandy or rum, dried, dipped in batter and deep-fried, drained, dredged with icing sugar and glazed

apricot glaze Sugar syrup boiled to 115°C, mixed with approximately half its quantity of apricot purée, reboiled to 110°C and sieved

apricot ice cream Bombe andalouse

apricot kernel The small flat kernels of the apricot stone which must be blanched in boiling water and dried in a warm oven to detoxify them. Used in Chinese cooking. Also called **Chinese almond**

apricot marmalade See **apricot glaze**

apricot sauce Apricot jam boiled with water and lemon juice, thickened as required with corn flour and strained. Alternatively, very ripe or drained stewed apricots sieved and thinned with sugar syrup (28°Be, 1.1 kg sugar per litre water) and reduced to a coating consistency.

apricot stuffing United Kingdom Roughly chopped destoned apricots mixed with an equal quantity of fine white breadcrumbs seasoned and moistened with water if required. Used for stuffing hams before they are covered in pastry.

aprikos Sweden Apricot

aprikose Denmark, Norway Apricot

Aprikose Germany Apricot

Aprikosenkaltschale Germany As Ananas Kaltschale but with ripe apricots and ground, skinned apricot kernels pushed through the strainer and garnished with slices of skinned destoned apricots

aprikos och appel soppa Scandinavia Apricot and apple soup consisting of apricots (fresh or reconstituted dried), cooking apples, celery, parsley and bay leaf, simmered in a light stock, celery and herbs discarded, the whole then liquidized or passed through a sieve, cream added and garnished with toasted almonds

apu lapu Philippines Garoupa, the fish

apulid Philippines Water chestnut

ap yeung cheung China A sausage from Hong Kong containing lean and fat pork, preserved duck livers, sugar, soya sauce and rice wine

Arabica coffee A type of coffee from the bush Coffea arabica, with a finer flavour than the higher yielding robusta varieties

arachide France, Italy Peanut

arachidonic acid A polyunsaturated fatty acid which cannot be synthesized by the human body and is therefore one of the

essential fatty acids (EFA's). It is found in egg yolks and fish oils. Its lack in infant milk formulae is thought to cause retarded brain development in new born infants. Also called **AA**

Arachis hypogaea Botanical name The groundnut plant whose seed pods, which grow underground, are the source of peanuts

arachis oil Peanut oil

Aragackij A round, scalded-curd, semi-hard, slicing cheese from Armenia made with ewes' and goats' milk matured for 2 months and with a thin dark bluish rind. Contains 40% water, 30% fat and 25% water.

Aragón Spain A semi-hard, firm cheese made with goats' and/or ewes' milk curdled with rennet, shaped into cones, dry-salted and the firm paste containing a few holes ripened for 1 week. Also called **Tronchón**

aragosta Italy Lobster (NOTE: Also used of langouste, rock lobster, spiny lobster, crayfish and most species of the genus Palinurus.)

aragosta alla fra diavolo Italy Lobster baked with a spicy tomato sauce

aragosta alla griglia con burro Italy Grilled lobster with melted butter

aragosta americana Italy Florida lobster

aragosta atlantica Italy Large pink spiny lobster of the genus Palinurus

aragosta bollita Italy Cold boiled lobster served with a vegetable salad

aragosta mediterranea Italy Spiny lobster

araignée de mer France Spider crab

Aralar A smoked ewes' milk cheese from the Basque country. See also **Idiazabal**

arame Japan A brown variety of seaweed from Japan, Eisenia bicyclis, which is similar to wakame. It is dried, cut into strips and used as a vegetable, in soup or for flavouring. Also called **sea oak**

arance caramellate Italy A dessert of peeled, depithed and sliced oranges coated with sugar syrup and decorated with caramelized orange peel

arancia Italy Orange, the fruit

arancia cardinale Italy Peeled and segmented oranges dressed with salt and olive oil

arancini Italy Croquettes made of savoury rice with butter and saffron wrapped around a filling e.g. meat and tomatoes, chicken liver and tomatoes, mozzarella cheese and tomatoes or ham and peas, and then fried

arancio amaro Italy Seville orange

arándano Spain Bilberry

arándano agrio Spain Cranberry

aranygaluska *Hungary* A sweet dumpling

araruta Arrowroot

Araucaria A genus of pine trees which are the source of **pine nuts**

araw *West Africa* A type of couscous made from millet. See also **karaw**

arbi *Malaysia, South Asia* Yam

arborio rice A medium-grain, superfino, pearly rice grown in northern Italy, used in Italian cooking and for making risotto. It cooks in 20 minutes and absorbs five times its weight of liquid. Starch is released during cooking and makes the grains creamy.

Arbroath fillet See **Arbroath smokie**

Arbroath smokie *Scotland* The original gutted, deheaded haddock or whiting, salted for 2 hours, hot smoked in less than an hour over oak and about 250 g in weight. Can be eaten cold or hot and does not need recooking. Also called **Arbroath fillet**

Arbroath-style lobster *Scotland* A dish of sliced, precooked lobster flesh, mussels and shrimps cooked in butter. These are bound with a reduced wine- and velouté-based sauce, seasoned, flavoured with lemon juice, placed in lobster shells lined with fried mushroom slices, covered with sauce and grated cheese, then glazed and garnished with parsley, anchovies and poached turned mushrooms.

arbutus The fruit of the strawberry tree, *Arbutus unedo*, used in preserves and to make an alcoholic drink. Not suitable for dessert purposes.

Arbutus unedo *Botanical name* Arbutus

arbuz *Russia* Watermelon

arca di noe *Italy* A small shell fish

archangels on horseback *United Kingdom* As **angels on horseback** but substituting scallops for oysters

Archestratus The Greek author of the oldest surviving cookbook, 'The Life of Luxury', dating from 300 BC

archiduc, à l' *France* In the Archduke's style, i.e. coated with a paprika-flavoured white sauce

archimede A pasta shape. See also **fusilli**

arctic char A type of trout, *Salvelinus alpinus*, found in both fresh and sea water in the northern hemisphere. It is better tasting than trout and is best simply baked and served with butter. See also **potted char**

Arctium lappa *Botanical name* Burdock

Arctostaphylos uva-ursi *Botanical name* Bearberry

ard bhoona *South Asia* A dry pot roast employing butter only. The meat is first seared then placed in a heavy casserole with a tight-fitting lid with enough butter to cover the meat. Cooking is completed in the oven and more butter is added at intervals. Particularly suitable for white meats.

ardennaise, à l' *France* In the Ardennes style, i.e. including juniper berries

Ardennes ham A high-quality cured Belgian ham ranked alongside Parma, York and Bayonne hams. Eaten raw.

ardilla *Spain* Squirrel

ardisone rice *Italy* A moderately priced semi-fino oval and slightly sticky rice suitable for minestrone

Areca catechu *Botanical name* Betel nut palm

areca nut Betel nut

areganato *Italy* With oregano

Arekanuss *Germany* Betel nut

Arenga pinnata *Botanical name* Sugar palm

Arenga sacchifera *Botanical name* Sugar palm

arenque *Spain* Herring

arenque en escabeche *Spain* Pickled herring

arepa *Central America* A common street food on Margarita island, Venezuela, made from white corn meal, salt and water to form a soft moist dough. This can be deep-fried in small balls stuffed with cheese, meat, fish or beans, or formed into 2.5 cm thick patties and fried on an unoiled griddle until crusted on either side, then finished in the oven at 180°C for about 20 minutes until hollow. When hollow, they are served hot with butter or jam.

arequipe *South America* A dessert made from a caramelized milk and sugar mixture, best made by boiling a tin of sweetened condensed milk for 2 hours. Also called **doce de leite**, **dulce de leche**, **cajeta de celaya**, **manjar blanco**, **natillas piuranas** (NOTE: This dessert was quite common in the UK during World War II. Its name derives either from the Peruvian town of Arequipa or from *arequipe*, the Andalusian word for rice pudding.)

arête *France* Fish bone

argan *North Africa* The plum-sized fruit of the argan tree, *Arganta sideroxylon*, which grows in the south of Morocco. These fruits are pressed for a highly prized oil, which can be used for cooking, but is more often used in the way that Westerners would use the finest olive oil. See also **amalu**

argenteuil, à l' *France* In the Argenteuil style, i.e. garnished with asparagus

argentina *Italy* Argentine, a small fish similar to a sardine

argentine A small silvery fish similar in appearance to a sardine or a smelt but from a different family. The three varieties of commerce are the lesser, the larger and the deep sea argentine, which latter comes from Japan. They may be grilled or fried.

Argentinian jujube A species of jujube which is used for the Bolivian drink chicha. Also called **mistol jujube**

arginine One of the non-essential amino acids

arhar *South Asia* Pigeon peas

arhrot *South Asia* Walnut

ariégeoise, à l' *France* In the Ariège style, i.e. containing salt pork, kidney beans, cabbage and potatoes

arigusta *Italy* Crawfish, crayfish

aringa *Italy* Herring (NOTE: The plural is **aringhe**.)

aringa alla casalinga *Italy* A hors d'oeuvre of sliced pickled herrings mixed with slices of salad onions, cooking apples and boiled waxy potatoes, bound with cream and chopped parsley

aringhe *Italy* Herrings

arisi pori *South Asia* Puffed rice

arista *Italy* Loin of pork

arkshell Cockle

arlésienne, à l' *France* In the Arles style, i.e. garnished with 1-cm-thick aubergine slices seasoned, floured and fried in oil, onion rings floured and deep-fried and peeled tomatoes sautéed in butter

Arles salami A variety of French salami

Armada *Spain* A semi-hard, sharp-tasting cheese made from cows' **colostrum** and matured for two months. Also called **Calostro, Sobado**

armadillo sausage *United States* A Texan speciality sausage made from 4 parts armadillo meat to 1 part breadcrumbs flavoured with allspice, sage, crushed black peppercorns and salt

armagnac *France* A brandy from the Southern Bordeaux region, used for flavouring

Armenian bole Very finely powdered ferric oxide (iron oxide) used to colour food orange or red. See also **E172**

Armenian bread A standard bread containing sesame and toasted sunflower seeds made into flat loaves and spread with a paste of grated Parmesan cheese, eggs, cumin, chopped walnuts and pepper before baking but after proving

Armenian cucumber *United States* A sweetish cucumber which grows in a coiled shape 25 to 50 cm long

Armenian wax pepper chilli *United States* A long waxy-skinned yellow chilli pepper with a relatively mild sweet taste

arme Ritter *Germany* French toast, pain perdue

Armillaria edodes *Botanical name* Matsutake

Armillaria mellea *Botanical name* Honey fungus

armleti *Italy* Savoury dumplings from Tuscany

Armoracia rusticana *Botanical name* Horseradish

armoricaine, à l' *France* In the Armorican style, i.e. with brandy, white wine, onions and tomatoes (NOTE: Armorica is the old name for Brittany.)

armotte *France* Maize flour cooked and mixed with goose fat; similar to **polenta** and eaten as a staple carbohydrate in Gascony

armyanski manny pudding *Russia* A pudding made from semolina boiled until cooked in white wine and water (2:3, 120 g semolina per litre of liquid) sweetened and flavoured with sugar, orange juice and zest and lemon zest. Egg yolks are then mixed in off the heat followed by stiffly beaten egg whites, which are folded in. The whole is then baked in a mould in a bain-marie at 170°C for 1 hour, cooled slightly, demoulded and served with lemon-juice-flavoured syrup and chopped pistachio nuts.

arni palikari *Greece* Fried lamb chump chops with fried chopped onions and garlic, cooked **en papillote** after layering with tomato slices and oregano, potato slices, seasoning and Faseri or Gruyère cheese slices before wrapping. Papillotes brushed with oil and baked for 1.5 hours at 180°C.

arni se lathoharto *Greece* Small steaks from boned leg of lamb, larded with garlic and cooked **en papillote** for 3 hours in the oven with olive oil, red wine, seasoning, chopped fresh marjoram and dried oregano

arni yiouvetsi *Greece* A trimmed leg of lamb is piquéed with sliced garlic, rubbed with lemon juice, oregano and seasoning, and roasted with chopped onion. The lamb is reserved. The defatted pan juices are mixed with tomato purée, seasoning and cooked pasta, sprinkled with grated Parmesan or Kefalotiri cheese, and reheated in the oven, before being served around the roast lamb.

Arnold Bennett omelette An omelette covered with flaked smoked haddock mixed with grated Parmesan cheese, cooked one side, top side dressed with cream and grilled, served unfolded (NOTE: The dish was named after the novelist Arnold Bennett and created for him at the Savoy.)

aroma The pleasant fragrance of food caused by a complex mixture of volatile chemicals released during, or produced by, the cooking process, but lost by evaporation and steam distillation; hence the necessity for careful control of the time and temperature of the cooking process. The aroma of food has important effects on both the feeling of well-being and on the digestive system.

aromate *France* Aromatic material, e.g. herbs, spices, etc.

aromatic With a fragrant, slightly spicy and slightly pungent smell. Used of herbs, spices and vegetables which impart flavour and aroma to a dish.

aromatic sauce White bouillon, boiled and infused with thyme, savory, marjoram, chives, chopped shallots, peppercorns and grated nutmeg for 10 minutes, strained, thickened with a blond roux, cooked out and finished with lemon juice and chopped and blanched tarragon and chervil

aromatic vegetables Carrots, leeks, onions and celery. Used for flavouring stocks, sauces, soups, etc.

aromatize, to To add flavours and aromas to an aqueous or oily liquid by respectively boiling or frying herbs and spices in it and then removing them

Arômes de Lyon *France* A strong-tasting cheese made from goats' and/or cows' milk, ripened in white wine for a month, dried for a month and wrapped in chestnut or plane leaves

aromi *Italy* Culinary herbs

Aroserli *Switzerland* Pork and beef-paste sausages. See also **saucisses d'Arosa**

arpajonnaise, à l' *France* In the Arpajon style, i.e. including haricot beans

arracacha 1. A leguminous plant, *Apios tuberosa*, from North America whose roots can be cooked liked potatoes and also used in desserts. Also called **apio 1 2.** The Peruvian carrot, *Arracacia xanthorrhiza*, a native of Colombia whose roots are used like potatoes or turned into a flour used for bread and pancakes

Arracacia xanthorrhiza *Botanical name* Arracacha, the Peruvian carrot

arracanato *Italy* With oregano

arraia *Portugal* Skate

Arran cheese *Scotland* A hard, moist, close-textured, rindless cheese made on the Scottish island of Arran from whole cows' milk. The usual size is just less than 1 kg.

Arran potato salad *Scotland* Cooked and cubed waxy potatoes and beetroot mixed with finely chopped shallot and chopped herbs and dressed with a vinaigrette. Cooked peas or broad beans are arranged around the edge of the bowl.

arrayán *Spain* 1. Myrtle 2. Bog myrtle

arricchito *Italy* Enriched, e.g. with cream

arròs a banda *Catalonia* Rice cooked in a fish broth

arròs a la cubana *Catalonia* Boiled rice with tomato sauce, egg and banana

arroser *France* 1. To baste 2. To sprinkle with a liquid

arròs negre *Catalonia* The famous Catalan dish of cooked rice, squid, monkfish, shellfish, onions, garlic and tomatoes with fish stock, olive oil and squid ink (NOTE: Literally 'black rice'.)

arrosticini all'abruzzese *Italy* Skewers of lamb, marinated in olive oil with seasoning, marjoram and garlic and grilled over charcoal

arrostino annegato alla milanese *Italy* Boned loin of veal, rolled around calves' liver, tied or skewered, cut into thick slices, slices sprinkled with chopped sage, rosemary and salt, floured, fried both sides in oil, stewed in the oven in white wine, lemon juice and brown stock, glazed to finish and served with risotto and the reduced, thickened and strained cooking liquor

arrostire *Italy* To roast

arrostiti *Italy* Roasted

arrosto *Italy* 1. Roasted 2. Roast meat or anything baked in the oven, e.g. arrosto-di bue, roast beef; arrosto-di castrato, roast mutton; arrosto-d'agnello, roast lamb; anguilla-arrosta, grilled eels

arrosto di maiale *Italy* Scored leg of pork, salted, oiled, sealed in the oven at 220°C for 25 minutes, then basted with a mixture of white wine, finely chopped carrots, garlic and pepper. Cooking continues in this basting liquor at 190°C until done. Served with red cabbage and mashed potatoes.

arrosto di maiale ubriaco *Italy* A tied, boned pork loin larded with carrots, floured, browned in butter, braised slowly in grappa (or brandy), red wine, nutmeg, bay leaves and seasoning until tender and served sliced with the cooking liquor (NOTE: Literally 'tipsy pork'.)

arrotolato *Italy* Rolled up

arrowhead A water plant, *Sagittaria sagittifolia*, with arrow-shaped leaves. Both the leaves and roots are used in Chinese cooking.

arrowroot *England, France* A starch powder obtained from the root of a West Indian plant, *Maranta arundinacea*, used for thickening where a clear, glossy glaze is required. Also called **araruta** (NOTE: It loses its thickening power if overcooked.)

arroz *Philippines, Portugal, Spain* Rice

arroz abanda *Spain* Fish stew served on rice

arroz a la alicantina *Spain* A fish stew made with additions of pepper, garlic, artichoke hearts and saffron, served on rice

arroz blanco 1. *Spain* White rice **2.** *Mexico* Long-grain rice fried in garlic-flavoured oil until white, cooked slowly with 2.5 times its weight of water or chicken stock and finely chopped onion, carrot, chilli and parsley or coriander

arroz con camaron seco *Mexico* Rice with dried fish. Same as **arroz con pollo** but with dried shrimps reconstituted in boiling water and tinned tuna fish substituted for the poached chicken.

arroz con frijoles *Mexico* Rice with beans, the staple dish of Mexicans. Long-grain rice fried in garlic-flavoured oil until golden, the oil discarded and the rice simmered with a green chilli, chicken stock, chopped onion and parsley, tomato purée and cooked beans plus the bean cooking liquor until all the liquid is absorbed.

arroz con leche *Spain* Rice pudding

arroz con pimenton *Mexico* Rice with sweet red pepper. As **arroz con frijoles** but with liquidized sweet red peppers and julienned peppers substituted for the beans and their cooking liquor.

arroz con pollo *Mexico* A Mexican variant of paella made with rice fried until pale yellow in garlic-flavoured oil and simmered in chicken stock until all the liquid is absorbed, together with: a whole onion and chilli which are later discarded; sealed and poached chicken meat; tomato purée; a **macédoine** of carrots and potatoes, peas, shredded cabbage, runner beans and red sweet pepper. The whole is garnished with chopped parsley.

arroz con rajas *Mexico* An oven-baked dish of layers of **arroz blanco**, sliced sweet peppers, sour and single cream, sliced Cheddar-type cheese and seasoning, topped with cheese

arroz con verduras *Mexico* **Arroz blanco** with sweet corn, peas and **macédoine** of carrots added prior to cooking in water or stock

arroz de grano largo *Spain* Long-grain rice

arroz doce *Portugal* Rice pudding

arroz parillada *Spain* Chicken, sausage, pork, onions, tomatoes, string beans and artichoke hearts fried together and served in a mould with rice

arroz refogado *Portugal* Savoury rice with an onion and tomato sauce

arroz valenciana *Spain* Rice pilaff made with chopped chicken meat, ham, red and green sweet peppers and boletus edible fungi, served with a tomato-flavoured **demi-glace** sauce

arrurruz *Spain* Arrowroot

arsekka *Italy* Mussel (*colloquial*)

arselle *Italy* Scallop

arsuma *Italy* An uncooked custard similar to **zabaglione** made with whole eggs whipped with sugar and dry white wine

Artemisia dracunculoides *Botanical name* Russian tarragon

Artemisia dracunculus *Botanical name* Tarragon

Artemisia lactiflora *Botanical name* White mugwort

Artemisia vulgaris *Botanical name* Mugwort

ärter *Sweden* Peas. Also called **ärtor**

ärter med fläsk *Sweden* The Swedish national soup of split yellow peas and pork. See also **gula ärter med fläsk**. Also called **ärter och fläsk**

ärter och fläsk *Sweden* Ärter med fläsk

artichaut *France* Artichoke

artichauts, purée d' *France* Artichoke soup

artichauts à la barigoule *France* Trimmed and blanched globe artichokes from which the choke has been removed, filled with **duxelles** enriched with chopped ham and herbs, wrapped in salt pork fat, braised in white wine or brown stock then the fat discarded, and served with a reduced brown sauce made with the cooking liquor

artichauts à la grecque *France* Globe artichoke hearts cooked **à la grecque**

artichauts à la provençale *France* Small trimmed artichokes placed in hot oil, seasoned, covered and cooked for 10 minutes, fresh peas and shredded lettuce added, and the whole tightly sealed and cooked slowly in the juices from the vegetables

artichauts Cavour *France* Small tender artichokes, trimmed to egg shape, cooked in white bouillon, drained, dipped in melted butter and coated with a mixture of grated Parmesan and Gruyère cheeses, coloured in the oven and served with chopped hard-boiled egg fried in butter and mixed with anchovy essence and chopped parsley

artichauts Clamart *France* Trimmed and divided artichokes with choke removed, cooked slowly in the oven in water with diced carrots, fresh peas, bouquet garni and salt; when cooked, bouquet garni removed, cooking liquor thickened with **beurre manié** and the whole served in same dish. A simpler alternative has cooked artichoke bottoms filled with a sieved purée of the bases of the sepals and piled with cooked young new peas (**petits pois**).

artichauts de Jerusalem *France* See **Jerusalem artichoke**

artichauts Grand Duc *France* Trimmed medium-sized artichokes cooked in salt water, drained, and arranged in a circle on a dish coated with cream sauce; napped with same, sprinkled with grated Parmesan cheese and melted butter and glazed. Served with buttered asparagus tips in the centre, and a slice of warm truffle and melted meat glaze on each artichoke.

artichauts grosse horloge *France* Cooked artichoke bottoms covered with mussels and cockles and topped with a **béarnaise sauce** flavoured with reduced shellfish cooking liquor

artichauts Stanley *France* Small trimmed artichokes or artichoke bottoms cooked over a layer of sliced, blanched onions and raw ham with white wine and thin **béchamel sauce**; cooking liquor reduced, sieved and finished with butter, then poured over the cooked artichokes; the whole sprinkled with a brunoise of ham

artichoke A plant of the thistle family, *Cynara scolymus,* whose unopened flower buds are used in cooking, particularly the base of the bracts and the base of the immature flower. The choke consisting of the immature petals and stamens, etc. is removed. See also **Jerusalem artichoke**, **Chinese artichoke**, **Japanese artichoke**. Also called **globe artichoke, French artichoke**

artichoke, Jerusalem See **Jerusalem artichoke**

artichoke bottom The flower base of the globe artichoke after the choke and bracts have been removed. Often used to hold garnishes.

artichoke heart A small immature globe artichoke with the tips of the bracts cut off. The choke has not formed at this stage.

artichokes Greek style See **artichauts à la grecque**

artichoke soup Basic soup made with artichokes. Also called **artichauts, purée d'**

artificial sweeteners Chemical and natural products other than those containing sugars used to sweeten food and drink

Artischocke *Germany* Artichoke

artisjok *Netherlands* Artichoke

Artocarpus communis *Botanical name* Breadfruit tree

Artocarpus heterophyllus *Botanical name* Jackfruit tree

ärtor *Sweden* Peas. Also called **ärter**

ärtsoppa *Sweden* Pea soup. See also **gula ärter med fläsk**

arugula Rocket

arum root Snake palm plant

Arundel mullets *England* A 17th-century Sussex dish made from small, cleaned and washed mullets, simmered in a court bouillon for 10–15 minutes, served with a reduced sauce made from the cooking liquor, sweated onions, lemon juice, white wine, herbs, chopped anchovies, seasoning and nutmeg

arval cake A cake given to mourners at funerals in the north of England (NOTE: The name is derived from the Old English word *arfwol* 'inheritance ale', used to designate the feast given by the heir of a deceased king.)

arvi *Indonesia* Yam

arvi leaf Dasheen leaf

arwa chawal *South Asia* Long-grain rice

asadero *Mexico* A cooking cheese made from cows' milk (NOTE: Literally 'good for roasting'.)

asado 1. *Mexico, Spain* Grilled or roasted, often with garlic, ham, red pepper and saffron **2.** *Argentina* An outdoor barbecue **3.** *Philippines* A method of cooking meat by simmering in soya sauce with bay, onion, tomato and peppercorns

asados *South America* Spit-roasted meat from Uruguay

asadura *Spain* Offal

asafoetida A rather unpleasant hard resin obtained from the root or stem latex of some species of Ferula, *F. asafoetida, F. narthex,* which grow in Afghanistan and Iran. The powdered form is used sparingly in Indian cookery, and the taste improves when it is briefly fried in hot oil. Also known as devil's dung for obvious reasons. The related garden plant is highly poisonous. Also called **hing**

asam *Indonesia* Tamarind

asam gelugor *Malaysia* Dried slices of tamarind

asam java *Malaysia* Tamarind

asam jawa *Indonesia, Malaysia* Dried slices of tamarind pulp

asam koh *China* Tamarind paste

asam pedas *Indonesia* Fish or meat cooked in a hot (chilli hot) and sour sauce or cooking liquor

asar 1. *Mexico, Spain* To roast **2.** *Spain* To grill

asar a la parrilla *Spain* To grill

asarijiru *Japan* Cleaned and debearded mussels, simmered in **dashi** until open; unopened mussels discarded; **mirin** added and all simmered for a further 5 minutes; mussels removed and kept warm whilst the soup is seasoned and flavoured with soya sauce and **shichimi togarashi**; mussels served in their shells with the soup

asatsuki *Japan* Spring onion

asa wat *East Africa* Freshwater fish served in a hot berbere sauce from Ethiopia

asciutto *Italy* Dry or drained. Used only of items such as pasta, gnocchi, rice, etc. which could otherwise be served in stock.

ascorbates Salts and esters of L-ascorbic acid (vitamin C) used as antioxidants. Sodium, E301, calcium, E302 and 6 ortho-palmitoyl, E304 are used in the food industry.

ascorbic acid Vitamin C used to prevent oxidation and thus browning reactions and colour changes in foods. Also used as a flour improver. See also **E300** (NOTE: Strictly, this should be known as L-ascorbic acid, the biologically active laevo-form.)

ascorbyl palmitate A chemical compound derived from ascorbic and palmitic acids used as an agent to prevent staling

ascorbyl stearate A chemical compound derived from ascorbic and stearic acids used as an antioxidant

a-sein thanat sohn *Burma* A hors d'oeuvre consisting of blanched vegetables and spring onion pieces with a sauce of tomato concassée mixed with finely chopped green chillies, salt and sugar

asepsis The prevention of contamination of a sterile or appertized food with organisms that can cause spoilage

aseptic packaging Packaging of food to ensure asepsis either by filling in unsterilized containers at 124°C, closing and leaving at temperature until all contaminants are inactivated, or by filling the food in sterilized containers in an apparatus which is itself sterilized where they can be sealed. The second method is generally used only where large numbers of containers are to be packed.

Ashburton open pasty *England* A Derbyshire pasty made from a large rectangle of puff pastry 1 cm thick, covered with stewed fruit, soaked dried fruit, mincemeat or jam to 3 cm. from edges, edges turned to centre and baked at 220°C for 20 minutes.

Ashdown partridge pudding *England* A Sussex dish consisting of a savoury suet pastry pudding filled with joints of old partridge, sliced rump steak, mushrooms, herbs, seasoning, moistened with red wine and stock. Steamed for 3 hours.

ashe anar *Central Asia* A thick Iranian soup made with lamb shanks, yellow split peas, beetroot, onion and spinach, flavoured with coriander leaves, Persian leek, spring onions, lemon juice and about one fifth its volume of pomegranate juice. The bones are removed and the meat chopped before it is finished with **nano dok**.

ashe reste *Iran* Meatballs possibly flavoured with cinnamon, boiled in water or stock with kidney beans, lentils, fine noodles, seasoning, chopped parsley, spinach and Persian leek, finished with dried mint and fried garlic

ashet *Scotland* A dish in which meat is roasted or cooked

ash gourd Wax gourd

Ashley bread *United States* A type of bread from the south made from a rice flour bread mix and cooked in a casserole

Asiago d'allevo *Italy* A hard, granular, semi-fat, sharp, grating cheese from the northwest. It is made from a mixture of skimmed and full cream milk, curdled with lactobacillus and scalded, and cast into large rounds (8 to 12 kg). It can be aged up to 2 years and becomes sharper with aging. The minimum fat content is 24% of dry matter.

Asiago grasso di monte *Italy* A semi-soft cooked curd, mellow summer cheese made in the northwest from raw whole cows' milk with numerous holes and a delicate flavour

Asiago pressato *Italy* A white, scalded-curd, mild-tasting cheese from the northwest, cast in large rounds (11 to 15 kg) with a white to pale straw paste containing a few irregular holes and a thin elastic rind. It is matured for 20 to 40 days. It contains 37% water, 23% fat and 33% protein.

Asian leek A variety of small thin leek, *Allium ramosum*, grown in China and Japan. The central white part is used in cooked dishes and the green leaves are used as a garnish.

Asian mussel A greenish-black shelled mussel, *Perna virides*, commonly found and cooked in Southeast Asia. The flesh is sometimes dried or deep-fried as a snack food.

Asian pear The crisp, white, pear-flavoured fruit of a Japanese tree, *Pyrus pyrofolia or P. ussuriensis,* now also cultivated in New Zealand. The shape varies from apple to pear. The juicy semi-sweet flesh has a fragrant flavour and is enclosed in a golden skin rather like a russet apple. It is eaten raw or as a garnish e.g. with game. Also called **Japanese pear, Beijing pear, Peking pear, snow pear, nashi**

Asiatic yam A very heavy yam, *Dioscorea alata,* (up to 10 kg) grown in Southeast Asia. The plant is distinguished by the winged petioles of the leaves. Also called **winged yam, greater yam**

asida *North Africa* Cooked semolina served in Morocco with honey

asier *Denmark* Sweet pickled cucumber used as a garnish

Asimina triloba *Botanical name* Papaw

asino *Italy* Donkey

asparagi alla Fiorentina *Italy* Boiled asparagus browned in butter and garnished with a fried egg

asparagi al Parmigiano *Italy* Tender, cooked asparagus with grated Parmesan cheese and melted butter

asparagi e funghi al burro *Italy* Diagonally cut 25 mm pieces of asparagus and similar sized pieces of mushrooms, sautéed (asparagus first) in butter with seasoning until dry and al dente, served immediately

asparagi pasticciati con uova *Italy* Peeled asparagus stalks cut into 5 cm lengths, boiled until tender, drained and mixed with sliced onion cooked to transparency in butter; beaten eggs with seasoning and grated Parmesan cheese added while the mixture is hot and stirred until scrambled; cream added and the whole served immediately with the cooked asparagus tips as a garnish

asparago *Italy* Asparagus

asparagus A perennial plant of the lily family, *Asparagus officinalis*. The young shoots are removed in spring. White asparagus is cut below ground when the tips protrude about 5 cm above ground. Green asparagus is cut at ground level when the shoots are about 15cm long. Asparagus should be used as fresh as possible, scraped, carefully washed and cooked in plenty of boiling salted water. See also **sprue**

asparagus bean A long (up to 40 cm) green bean, *Dolichos sesquipedalis*, with a frill down four sides, which can be cooked whole when young in the same way as French beans. The dried ripe beans of some varieties are sold as black-eyed beans. Also called **yard long bean**, **long bean**, **yard bean**

Asparagus officinalis *Botanical name* Asparagus

asparagus pea A leguminous plant from southern Europe, *Lotus tetragonolobus or Psophocarpus tetragonolobus*, with a flower rather like a small sweet pea with smooth brown seeds and grown extensively in Southeast Asia. The pods can be eaten like a mangetout when not longer than 6 cm and preferably 3 cm. Also called **Goa bean**, **winged pea** (NOTE: Not to be confused with the **asparagus bean**.)

asparagus royale Half-cooked asparagus tips, cold **béchamel sauce**, cream, green spinach for colouring and egg yolk, mixed, sieved and poached as a **royale**

asparagus sauce Cooked asparagus, liquidized with white stock and white wine, strained, seasoned and cream added

asparagus soup Basic soup without leek and using chicken stock and fresh asparagus trimmings or a tin of asparagus, finished with cream or milk. Also called **crème d'asperges**

asparges *Denmark, Norway* Asparagus

aspargesbønner *Norway* French beans, the pods

aspartame A dipeptide made from the two amino acids, aspartic acid and the methyl ester of phenylalanine, used as an artificial sweetener with roughly 180 times the sweetening power of sucrose. It is a risk to persons suffering from phenylketonuria (1 in 15,000 Europeans), and a warning to this effect should be on all containers. Used in soft drinks, yoghurts, drink mixes and sweetening tablets.

aspartic acid A non-essential amino acid

asperge *France, Netherlands* Asparagus

asperges à la flamande *France* Cooked asparagus served with a sauce made from hard-boiled yolk of egg combined with melted butter. The sauce may be made at the table by each guest from individually served portions of hot hard-boiled egg and melted butter.

asperges à la milanaise *France* Cooked asparagus laid in rows on a buttered dish which has been sprinkled with grated Parmesan cheese; points sprinkled with same; the whole coated with brown butter and glazed lightly. Also called **asperges à l'italienne**

asperges à la polonaise *France* Cooked asparagus arranged in rows, the tips sprinkled with a mixture of chopped hard-boiled yolk of egg and parsley, the whole coated with brown butter and fine white breadcrumbs which have been fried to a golden brown in butter

asperges à l'italienne *France* Asperges à la milanaise

asperges au gratin *France* Cooked asparagus arranged in rows, tips and one third of remaining stalk coated in Mornay sauce, uncoated stalk protected with buttered paper, sauce sprinkled with grated Parmesan cheese and the whole glazed. Also called **asperges Mornay**

asperges Mornay *France* Asperges au gratin

aspergesoep *Netherlands* Asparagus soup

Aspergillus flavus *Botanical name* The mould which produces aflatoxin. It is a strict aerobe.

Aspergillus niger *Botanical name* One of the principal moulds used in the production of food-grade citric acid, and for the production of enzymes such as glucose oxidase and pectinase

Aspergillus oryzae *Botanical name* A fungus or mould used to ferment rice in the first stage of soya sauce and **miso** production

Aspergillus parasiticus A mould which grows on cereals, potatoes and onions and produces aflatoxin

Aspergillus sojae One of the moulds used to ferment soybeans and rice to make **miso**

asperula *Italy* Sweet woodruff

aspérula olorosa *Spain* Sweet woodruff

aspic *England, France, Italy, Spain* A savoury jelly made with the appropriate clarified stock (meat, chicken or fish) flavoured with vegetables, herbs, sherry, etc. with added gelatine if required, mainly used for decorative larder work (NOTE: Nowadays instant aspic granules at 70 g per litre of water are usually used.)

aspic de bécasses *France* The leg flesh and intestines of roast woodcock pounded together with brandy and aspic jelly and sieved, piled onto slices of breast, cooled, covered with a brown chaud-froid sauce, placed breast uppermost in an aspic-lined mould, filled with aspic jelly and demoulded when set

aspic de volaille à l'italienne *France* An aspic-lined mould is decorated with slices of truffle and filled with alternate layers of **julienne** of cooked chicken breast, slices of cooked red ox tongue and truffle, each layer separated by cool aspic jelly. The whole is filled with aspic jelly and served with salade italienne and sauce remoulade.

aspic de volaille gauloise *France* An aspic-lined mould is decorated with slices of truffle, then filled with alternate layers of slices of chicken, cockscombs coated with brown chaud-froid sauce, chicken kidneys coated with white chaud-froid sauce and slices of ox tongue. All are cooked, each layer being separated with aspic jelly. The whole is demoulded when set.

aspic d'ortolans *France* Cold roast whole buntings (not boned out) placed breast side down in a border mould coated with aspic, filled with aspic jelly and demoulded when set (NOTE: Buntings are no longer served as food in the EU.)

aspic mould A decoratively-shaped mould, usually metal, used for aspic-bound and coated foods

aspic of fillets of sole A fish-aspic-lined mould, decorated and filled with either cooled and aspic-coated poached and trimmed fillets of sole or paupiettes of sole stuffed with a fish forcemeat and truffle and

cut in slices; the whole filled with aspic jelly and demoulded when set

aspic of foie gras An aspic-lined mould decorated with truffle and cooked egg white, filled with slices or scoops of cooked foie gras, each coated with cool aspic; the whole filled with aspic and demoulded when set

Aspik *Germany* Aspic

assad *South Asia* Cubed pork shoulder, coated with a paste of ginger, garlic, turmeric and seasoning, fried in ghee until coloured, then simmered with water, cinnamon stick, cloves, dried chillies and mace until tender

assadeiro *Portugal* A large, shallow roasting pan

assado *Portugal* Roasted

assaisoner *France* To season

assam jawa *Southeast Asia* Tamarind

assam tea A high-quality tea from Assam in northeast India

assiette *France* Plate

assiette anglaise *France* A plate of assorted sliced cold meats and sausages

assiette de charcuterie *France* A plate of assorted sliced sausages

assonza *Italy* Lard flavoured with hot pepper and fennel seeds, spread on toast

assorted hors d'oeuvres A variety of hors d'oeuvres served separately in **raviers** or similar dishes, e.g. potato salad, niçoise salad, egg mayonnaise, rice salad, anchovies, cauliflower à la grecque, tomato salad, Russian salad. The assortment should have contrast of colour, taste and texture.

assorti *France* Assorted

assortito *Italy* Assorted

ast, a l' *Catalonia* Spit-roasted

astaco *Italy* The crayfish, *Astacus fluviatilis*, also the popular name for lobster

astaco americano *Italy* True lobster

astakos me latholemono *Greece* Lobster flesh, dressed with a mixture of olive oil, lemon juice, chopped marjoram and seasoning, piled in the pregrilled half lobster shells, brushed with more dressing, grilled for 8 minutes and served immediately

astaxanthin The pink colouring in a small shrimp-like creature which gives the pink colour to the flesh of salmon. Now fed to farmed salmon which are generally pinker than wild.

astice *Italy* Plural of astaco

astringent A liquid such as lemon juice or a solution of tannin which tightens up the skin or mucous membranes of the mouth

asukal *Philippines* Sugar

asupara *Japan* Asparagus

ata A wholemeal flour used for making unleavened breads. See also **atta**

atap chee *Malaysia* Palm nut

atemoya A hybrid variety of **custard apple**, genus *Anona*, derived from the cherimoya and the sweet sop

athénienne, à l' *France* In the Athenian style, i.e. garnished with onion, aubergine, tomato and sweet red pepper, all fried in oil

atherine A small silvery fish similar in appearance to the lesser argentine, usually grilled or fried

Atherton raspberry *Australia* One of the wild raspberries available commercially in Queensland. As it deteriorates quickly it is usually only available frozen. See also **wild raspberry**

athol brose *Scotland* A dish consisting of a gruel made by pouring boiling water over oatmeal with whisky and honey added for flavour. Sometimes most of the oatmeal is omitted.

atis *Philippines* Rose apple

atjar Shredded cabbage and other vegetables. See also **acar**

Atlantic blue crab See **blue crab**

Atlantic butterfish See **butterfish 1**

Atlantic catfish Catfish

Atlantic cod The name given in North America to cod caught in the North Atlantic Ocean

Atlantic croaker A seawater fish, *Micropogonia undulatus*, found off the North American coast, up to 1 kg in weight and with lean delicately flavoured flesh

Atlantic deep sea scallop A large North Atlantic scallop, *Placopecten magellanicus*, fished off the American coast

Atlantic mackerel Mackerel

Atlantic salmon The wild salmon of the Atlantic, *Salmo salar,* with medium oily pink flesh and a mild flavour, which can weigh up to 18 kg. It can be distinguished from farmed salmon by signs of wear especially on the tail fin. Cooked in any way and often smoked.

Atlantic silverside A slender round oily seawater fish, *Menidia menidia*, 13 to 15 cm long with a translucent green back and silver bands lengthways along the sides. It is caught on the Atlantic coast and in the estuaries of North America, and usually fried or grilled.

Atlantic squid *Loligo forbesi*, a slightly larger variety of squid than the Mediterranean, but otherwise similar

Atlantic sturgeon Common sturgeon

Atlantic thread herring See **thread herring**

atmospheric steamer A device used to cook foods in live steam at atmospheric pressure, Condensation of steam on the surface of the food or its container gives the highest rate of heat transfer available with the exception of high-temperature radiant heat. The food temperature is limited to 100°C.

atole *Mexico* A thin porridge or thick gruel of maize flour (**masa harina**) or corn flour, boiled with water, milk, cinnamon, sugar and puréed fresh fruit. Served hot for breakfast.

atole de arroz *Mexico* As **atole**, but made with rice or rice flour and flavoured with cinnamon

Atriplex hortensis *Botanical name* Orach

atsu-age *Japan* Lightly fried bean curd

atta *South Asia* A wholemeal flour used for making unleavened breads such as chapatis, puri and paratha. Also called **ata**

attar *Middle East* A spice shop in Arab countries

attelette *France* The small silver skewer used to present **attereaux** after cooking or for certain garnishes

atterato *Italy* A method of serving vermicelli with butter, pine nuts and chocolate

attereaux *France* Hors d'oeuvres consisting of thin slices of various cooked (e.g. meats) or raw (e.g. vegetables) ingredients on a skewer, coated in a reduced sauce, panéed and deep-fried just before serving, garnished with fried parsley and possibly presented on a mound of rice (**socle**) or on fried bread

attereaux à la florentine *France* Attereaux au Parmesan

attereaux à la genevoise *France* Attereaux of chicken livers, lambs sweetbreads, brains, mushrooms, truffles, artichoke hearts coated with a well-reduced **duxelles sauce**, when cool covered with a forcemeat mixed with beaten egg, panéed, deep-fried and served immediately

attereaux à la princesse *France* Attereaux au Parmesan

attereaux à la royale *France* Attereaux au Parmesan

attereaux au Parmesan *France* Semolina cooked in just sufficient white bouillon, mixed with grated Parmesan cheese and butter, spread out 0.5 cm thick to cool into a stiff paste, cut into 2.5 cm rounds and alternated with similar slices of Gruyère cheese on a skewer, panéed, deep-fried and served immediately. Also called **attereaux à la florentine**, **attereaux à la princesse**, **attereaux à la royale**

attereaux d'huitres à la Villeroy *France* Attereaux of oysters alternating with slices of cooked mushrooms on a skewer coated with sauce Villeroy reduced with juices from the oysters, panéed, deep-fried and served immediately

attereaux Villeroy *France* **Attereaux** coated with sauce Villeroy

ättika *Sweden* Vinegar

attorta *Italy* An S-shaped cake from Umbria made from flour, ground almonds, sugar and lemon zest

atum *Portugal* Tuna fish

atún *Spain* Tuna fish

au *France* In the style of; used before masculine French nouns (NOTE: Also means 'with' or 'in'.)

aubergine *England, France, Italy* The purple fruit of an East Indian annual plant, *Solanum melongena*, of the same family as the tomato and deadly nightshade. Generally violet to deep purple in Europe and North America and up to 30 cm long, but can be white or deep yellow streaked with purple and the size of a hen's egg. The bitter taste of some varieties is removed by sprinkling with salt and allowing to drain. Also called **eggplant**, **garden egg**, **Guinea squash**

aubergines à la bordelaise *France* Salted and drained slices of aubergine, seasoned, floured and sautéed in olive oil with finely chopped shallots, white breadcrumbs used to absorb the excess oil, the whole served with lemon juice and chopped parsley or grilled with olive oil and coated with bordelaise sauce

aubergines à la crème *France* Aubergines cut in 0.5 cm slices, salted and drained for 1 hour, dried, cooked in butter and mixed with cream sauce

aubergines à la napolitaine *France* Peeled aubergines, cut lengthwise in slices, seasoned, floured, deep-fried, reformed with tomato purée flavoured with Parmesan cheese between the slices, arranged in a dish coated with tomato sauce, sprinkled with grated Parmesan cheese, oiled and buttered and baked

aubergines à la parisienne *France* As for **aubergines à l'égyptienne** but filled with a mixture of chopped aubergine flesh, white meat, marrow or bacon fat, egg yolks, stale breadcrumbs, nutmeg and seasoning, then baked in the oven

aubergines à la provençale *France* As for **aubergines à l'égyptienne**, but filled with a mixture of aubergine flesh, onions and tomato flesh, all coarsely chopped and cooked in oil, fresh breadcrumbs, chopped parsley, seasoning; flavoured with garlic, gratinéed and served with tomato sauce

aubergines à la serbe *France* As for **aubergines à l'égyptienne** but filled with a mixture of chopped cooked mutton, tomato flesh and onions chopped and cooked in butter, plain boiled rice, crumbed and gratinéed and served with tomato sauce and chopped parsley. Also called **aubergines à la turque**

aubergines à la turque *France* Aubergines à la serbe

aubergines à l'égyptienne *France* Aubergines cut in half lengthwise, flesh cut away from edges and scored, aubergines deep-fried, then the flesh removed from skins. Skins arranged in a buttered dish, filled with a mixture of chopped flesh and chopped onions cooked in oil, oiled, baked for 15 minutes and served topped with sautéed sliced tomato and chopped parsley.

aubergines à l'orientale *France* Peeled aubergines cut lengthwise into slices, seasoned, floured, deep-fried, made into sandwiches with a filling of chopped fried aubergine and tomato flesh, white breadcrumbs, seasoning and garlic flavouring. Filled aubergines placed in an oiled dish, sprinkled with oil and baked for 30 minutes. Served hot or cold.

aubergines au gratin *France* As for **aubergines à l'égyptienne** but filled with a mixture of chopped aubergine flesh and **duxelles**, arranged in a dish, sprinkled with white breadcrumbs and oil, baked and served with tomato sauce

aubergines frites *France* Aubergines cut in thin round slices, seasoned, battered or panéed, deep-fried and served immediately

Auflauf *Germany* **1.** Omelette **2.** Baked soufflé

Aufschnitt *Germany* Cold meat

Aufschnittwurst *Switzerland* A scalded sausage (**Brühwurst**) made with pork and beef

Augsburgerwurst *Germany* A lightly smoked cooking sausage made with chopped lean pork and back fat, flavoured with cinnamon, cloves, nutmeg, seasoning and a little saltpetre, filled into beef runners and air-dried for 4 days before being smoked

augurk *Netherlands* Gherkin

augurken *Netherlands* Pickles

Auld Reekie plum cake *Scotland* A rich fruit cake flavoured with whisky (added at the flour folding stage) and chopped preserved ginger

aumônières surprise *France* A dessert made from thin sweet pancakes or crêpes with a centre filling of fruit salad, ice cream, etc., pulled up into a bag or purse shape and tied with a blanched strip of angelica or liquorice, and served on a coulis of fruits

Aunus *France* A small triangular-shaped cheese from Charente made with ewes' milk

Aura *Finland* A semi-soft, blue-veined cheese made from whole cows' milk, cast in 2.5 kg rounds. Contains 45% water, 28% fat and 24% protein.

Auricularia auricula *Botanical name* Jew's ear

Auricularia polytricha *Botanical name* Chinese mushroom

aurin *France* Grey mullet

aurore, sauce *England, France* Suprême sauce, lightly flavoured with either tomato purée or sieved **tomato concassée** and finished with butter. Used for boiled chicken, poached eggs, etc.

aurore maigre, sauce *France* As **sauce aurore** but using fish stock to make the velouté base. Used for fish.

Ausbackteig *Germany* Dough or flour-based paste or pâte

aush *Central Asia* A dish from Afghanistan of noodles made with a flour and water dough, boiled and mixed with cooked spinach, yellow split peas and **chakah**. Served with **keema**.

aushak *Central Asia* A type of ravioli from Afghanistan, filled with a mixture of chopped leeks, chilli peppers, salt and oil, and poached in the usual way. Served in **chakah**, sprinkled with rubbed dried mint and topped with **keema**.

Auster *Germany* Oyster, originally the European flat oyster

Austerpilz *Germany* Oyster mushroom

Australian barracuda Snoek

Australian black bream *Australia* A typical bream-shaped fish, *Acanthopagrus butcheri*, quite common in Victorian waters. Generally 0.5 to 1.5 kg in weight, they have white, delicately flavoured flesh. The upper body is green to blackish, and the belly and chin are white. Also called **southern bream**

Australian fondant icing See **plastic icing**

Australian oyster An oyster, *Crassostrea commercialis*, grown off the coasts of Australia and New Zealand

australique *Australia* Ortanique

Austrian pancakes A type of sweet soufflé omelette. See also **Salzburger Nockerln**

Austro/Malaysian laksa *Australia* A Malaysian **laksa** flavoured with lemon aspen and lemon myrtle

autoclave A high-pressure-steamed and steam-heated chamber which cooks food very rapidly and which is also used to sterilize canned and bottled food

autocondimentor A person who seasons any meal placed in front of them, whatever it is and regardless of how much seasoning it has already had and of how it tastes

autolysed yeast Yeast cells which have been subjected to limited and controlled autolysis to liberate cell contents and change their flavour. The result which looks like thick molasses in appearance is used in vegetarian cooking and as a sandwich spread.

autolysis The process by which cells are broken down by their own enzymes or acid products when dead. In the early stages cell contents are released adding to flavour but later the material becomes putrid. The process occurs when meat is hung or when fish goes bad.

automatic boiler A boiler with an automatic water feed designed to produce fresh boiling water on demand

autrichienne, à l' In the Austrian style, i.e. including soured cream, paprika, onions and fennel

autumn partridge pot *England* A Norfolk dish of jointed older partridges passed through seasoned oatmeal and slowly casseroled between diced bacon and mushrooms, onions and tomatoes with stock and red wine flavoured with cloves, bay, thyme and seasoning

autumn pudding *England* As **summer pudding**, but using stewed autumn fruits such as apples, plums and blackberries, etc.

autumn vegetable soup *England* A variety of diced vegetables, sweated in butter and cooked in vegetable stock with a bouquet garni until just tender

available nutrients Nutrients in food which can be digested and absorbed in the body. Some become unavailable when bound to another compound, e.g. avidin in raw egg whites binds biotin to make it unavailable. Cooking frees the biotin.

avaisances *Belgium* Meat-filled pastries

avanzi *Italy* Leftovers

avdrakla *Greece* Purslane

aveia *Portugal* Oatmeal

aveline *France* Filbert

avella *Italy* Hazelnut

avellanas *Spain* Hazelnuts

ave maria *Italy* Short tubes of pasta used in soups. See also **cannolicchi**

avena *Italy, Spain* Oats

avena a medio moler *Spain* 1. Oat grits 2. Coarse oatmeal

avern *Scotland* Wild strawberry

aves *Portugal, Spain* Poultry

aves de corral *Mexico* Poultry

avgolemono *Greece* A sauce made by combining egg yolks or whole eggs with lemon juice and stock then cooking in a double boiler until thick. Alternatively a reduced velouté sauce thickened with a mixture of egg yolks and lemon juice. Also called **saltsa avgolemono**

avgolemono soupa *Greece* A soup made with chicken stock and rice with eggs, lemon juice and seasoning

avgotarabo The salted and dried roe of grey mullet used as an appetizer and for making taramasalata. Also called **botargo** (NOTE: Recorded as being eaten by Samuel Pepys on the 5th June 1661.)

avidin A component of egg white which impairs the uptake and utilization of the vitamin biotin in the body. One of a number of protective chemicals in the white whose function is to prevent bacterial attack of the yolk. It is inactivated by heat.

avocado The pear-shaped fruit of a species of subtropical laurel, *Persea americana*, with a rough, thick, green to dark brown skin, a creamy yellow flesh and a large single stone, usually eaten as a starter or salad, but also used as an ingredient of guacamole. The flesh mixed with grated nutmeg is said to be a male aphrodisiac. Also called **avocado pear**, **alligator pear**

avocado mousse Purée of avocado flesh, mixed with lemon juice, icing sugar, and hot gelatine solution, cooled, whipped cream folded in, moulded, set and demoulded

avocado oil Cooking oil extracted from the pulp of damaged avocados. Contains about 20% saturated, 65% monounsaturated and 15% polyunsaturated fats.

avocado pear See **avocado**

avocado soup See **sopa de aguacate**

avocat *France* Avocado

avocat épicure *France* The diced flesh of halved avocados, mixed with diced gherkins, walnuts, mayonnaise and paprika, replaced in the empty half skins, garnished with pickled walnut and served on crisp lettuce

avocat Singapour *France* The diced flesh of halved avocados, sprinkled with vinegar, mixed with crab meat, mayonnaise, cream and lemon juice, replaced in the empty half skins and served on crushed ice with crisp lettuce and lemon slices

avoine *France* Oats

avron *Scotland* Cloudberry

awabi *Japan* Abalone

awasi *East Africa* A type of Ethiopian mustard sauce

awayukikan *Japan* A dessert made from agar-agar and caster sugar dissolved in boiling water (1:50:60) cooled to less than 60°C, beaten into stiffly beaten egg whites (one fifth of the weight of the sugar) and poured into a mould or dish and decorated

awenda bread *United States* A bread of Amerindian origin made from hominy grits

ayam *Indonesia, Malaysia* Chicken

ayam bakar *Malaysia* Chicken pieces coated with a paste of pounded garlic, lemon grass, **laos**, turmeric and salt, left for 50 minutes, boiled in water with bay leaves, soya sauce and butter for 30 minutes until the cooking liquor is reduced to coating consistency, then grilled to finish

ayam goreng jawa *Indonesia* A dish of chicken cut in pieces, simmered until tender in water, with chopped shallots, garlic, coriander powder, **laos powder**, lemon grass, grated nutmeg, cinnamon, bay leaves, brown sugar and salt until most of the liquid is absorbed, drained, cooled and deep-fried until golden brown

ayam kecap *Indonesia* A dish of poached chicken pieces, tossed with a fried pounded spice mixture of onion, garlic and deseeded red chillies, simmered with chicken stock, nutmeg, cloves, strained tamarind purée and soya sauce until tender

ayam opor *Indonesia* A dish of chicken pieces fried in a pounded spice mixture (garlic, onion, macadamia nuts and coriander seeds), stewed with coconut milk, **laos**, lemon grass, lime leaves, bay leaves, salt and sugar until tender and garnished with crisp fried onions

ayam panggang kecap *Southeast Asia* Roasted chicken cut into four pieces, flattened, marinated with dark soya sauce, chopped shallots, garlic, chilli powder, lemon or lime juice and sesame seed oil for 1 hour then reheated under the grill

Aylesbury duck *England* One of the 2 standard duck breeds, the other being **pekin**. It matures in about 7 weeks and contains a lot of fat.

Aylesbury game pie *England* A Buckinghamshire terrine made in a dish lined with bacon from alternating layers of seasoned forcemeat (pork fat, leg meat, liver, etc.) and diced meat from hare, chicken and pheasant previously marinated in brandy, thyme, bay and seasoning, covered with marinade and bacon, sealed and oven-cooked in a bain-marie for 3 hours. May be served hot or cold and demoulded.

ayran *Middle East* A yoghurt-based drink similar to **lassi**, but flavoured with cardamom seeds (two pods per 100 ml of yoghurt)

Ayrshire bacon *Scotland* Bacon from Ayrshire which has its rind removed after curing and is tightly rolled and secured with string

Ayrshire galantine *Scotland* A **galantine** of minced bacon and beef shoulder steak mixed with breadcrumbs, nutmeg, mace and seasoning, bound with egg and stock, rolled in a cloth, simmered in water with aromatic vegetables, removed from the cloth, pressed until set, glazed with aspic jelly and served cold

Ayrshire gigot *Scotland* A boned, rolled and tied gammon joint

Ayrshire meat roll *Scotland* A mixture of minced **Ayrshire bacon**, minced stewing steak, finely chopped onions, eggs, white breadcrumbs, nutmeg and pepper, rolled and wrapped in a floured cloth, simmered for two hours, removed from the cloth and coated with toasted breadcrumbs

Ayrshire roll Back bacon, skinned, rolled and tied. Available in Scotland.

Ayrshire shortbread *Scotland* A Scottish shortbread using less butter than the standard recipe but enriched with egg and cream

ayu *Japan* Freshwater trout

ayurveda *South Asia* A science of living which offers guidance on food, menus, cooking techniques and conditions in which food should be eaten. In brief it recommends fresh vegetarian food but definitely not red meat and that a balanced meal should contain a little of each taste and quality. Six tastes are distinguished, sweet, salt, sour, bitter, pungent and astringent and six qualities, light, heavy, oily, dry, hot and cold. Eating should be a leisurely activity and a period of quiet after a meal should also be observed. Steaming is considered the best method of cooking, and the attitude of the cook, who should be serene and tranquil, is important.

azafrán *Spain* Saffron

azarole The Naples medlar, *Crataegus azarolus,* a native of the Mediterranean with a crisp fruit the size of a crab apple containing 3 or 4 hard seeds. It is eaten fresh or used for jam making. Also called **Naples medlar, Mediterranean medlar**

azêda *Portugal* Sorrel

azêdo *Portugal* Sour

azeitão *Portugal* A soft, mild, ewes' milk cheese made in cylinders (up to 250 g) with a creamy fine textured tangy flavoured paste and a yellow rind. Eaten with a spoon.

azeite *Portugal* Olive oil

azeitonas *Portugal* Olives

azijn *Netherlands* Vinegar

azodicarbonamide See **E927**

azorubine Carmoisine

azúcar *Spain* Sugar

azúcar de pilón *Spain* Sugar lump

azúcar en cortadillo *Spain* Cube sugar

azúcar en cuadrillo *Spain* Sugar lumps

azúcar en polvo *Spain* Granulated or caster sugar

azuki bean See **adzuki bean**

azul A nondescript, dense, strong-tasting blue cheese made in Latin America from pasteurized and homogenized cows' milk, similar to the equally nondescript Danish blue. Contains 43% water, 31% fat, 22% protein.

azyme *France* Unleavened

baak dau gok *China* The light green variety of long bean

baak kwo *China* Ginkgo nut

baars *Netherlands* **1.** Perch **2.** Bass

baba 1. *Poland* A Polish cake resembling a long gathered skirt (NOTE: Literally 'an old woman'.) **2.** *France* A light-textured cake made from a sweetened yeast-raised dough, often baked in small or large ring moulds or in dariole moulds. May be soaked in syrup flavoured with rum or liqueur and/or filled with cream. Served hot or cold.

baba au kirsch *France* A baked baba cake soaked in kirsch-flavoured sugar syrup

baba au rhum *France* A baba cake baked in a small ring mould, soaked in rum-flavoured syrup and the centre filled with whipped cream

babaco A hybrid of the paw paw, *Carica papaya,* which when cut across resembles a five pointed star. The soft pulp has a pleasant mixed-fruit taste. Originally from Ecuador but now grown in New Zealand. Also called **star fruit**

babaghanouji An Armenian aubergine pâté; the same as **baklazhannaia ikra** except that parsley is substituted for coriander and pomegranate seeds are added at the same time as the parsley

babaofan *China* Glutinous rice pudding with eight ingredients. Also called **eight treasure rice**

babassu The Brazilian palm, *Orbignija speciosa or O. martiana,* whose nuts yield a valuable oil.

babbelaar *Netherlands* Butter cake

babelutten *Belgium* A caramel biscuit

babeurre *France* Buttermilk

babi guling *Indonesia* Roast pork

babi lemak *Southeast Asia* A pork stew from Singapore made with coconut milk, onions, **blachan**, herbs and spices

baboy letsonin *Philippines* Roast sucking pig

baby beef *United States* Meat from a beef animal between 14 and 52 weeks old, no longer veal, but not yet true beef

baby bel *France* A small, soft, whole cows' milk cheese similar to Edam and covered in red wax

baby corn See **miniature corn**

baby's head *England* Steak and kidney pudding (*colloquial*; *navy*)

bacalaitos *Caribbean* Puerto Rican fried fish cakes made with cod

bacalao *Spain* Dried cod, salt cod, cod or ling

bacalao a la ajo arriero *Spain* Cod cooked in a garlicky sauce with parsley and pepper

bacalao a la vizcaína *Spain* Poached salt cod, boned, floured and browned in oil; bread cubes, raw ham, garlic, chopped onions, bay leaf and ñoras added and sweated until tender; pimenton and poaching liquor added and cooked for 10 minutes; fish reserved; cooking liquor liquidized, sieved, seasoned and sugared, and its consistency adjusted, then poured over salt cod and all heated through

bacalao al pil-pil *Spain* Cod cooked in olive oil, from the Basque region

bacalao seco *Spain* Stockfish

bacalhau *Portugal* Dried salt cod used as a staple protein food in Portugal

bacalhau à portuguêsa *Portugal* Casseroled salt cod with tomatoes, onions, potatoes and sweet peppers

bacalhau cozido *Portugal* Salt cod boiled with vegetables

bacalhau fresco à portuguêsa *Portugal* Cod steaks fried in oil with aubergines, tomatoes, onions and garlic. Served with rice.

bacallà *Catalonia* Salt fish, also cod

bacca *Italy* Berry (NOTE: The plural is **bacche**.)

baccalà *Italy* Salt cod

baccalà alla bolognese *Italy* Salt cod cooked in butter and oil with garlic and pepper

baccalà alla cappuccina *Italy* Salt cod cooked with oil, vinegar, parsley and garlic

baccalà alla genovese *Italy* Salt cod grilled and served with oil, lemon juice and boiled potatoes

baccalà alla napoletana *Italy* Salt cod, fried in oil then stewed in a sauce of tomatoes, garlic, oil and capers

baccalà alla veneziana *Italy* Salt cod browned in oil with onion and stewed in a thick anchovy sauce

bacche *Italy* Berries

bac cua *Vietnam* Ginkgo nut

bachelor's button *United States* A round sweet biscuit with a cherry in the centre

Bachforelle *Germany* Brown trout

bacile *France* Samphire, *C. maritimum.*

Bacillus cereus A bacterium which grows on rice, usually found in temperate countries in spore form. The spore will germinate after cooking and lead to growth of the vegetative form which can cause food poisoning. There are 2 strains, one has an incubation period of 1 – 5 hours, a duration of 6 – 24 hours and the symptoms are nausea and vomiting and occasionally diarrhoea; the other has an incubation period of 8 – 16 hours, a duration of 12 – 24 hours and the symptoms are abdominal pain, diarrhoea and occasionally nausea.

Bacillus licheniformis Bacteria which can produce a toxin causing diarrhoea and vomiting. The incubation period is 4 – 8 hours.

Bacillus subtilis Bacteria which can produce a toxin causing vomiting, abdominal pain and diarrhoea. The incubation period is 2 – 18 hours.

back bacon That part of the side of bacon which, if uncured, would be pork loin or shoulder chop

backen *Germany* To bake

Bäckerei *Germany* 1. Pastries 2. Patisserie

back fat Hard fat from the back of the pig, usually specified for high-quality sausage making

Backhendl *Austria* Panéed chicken fried in lard or oil

Backhuhn *Germany* Panéed and fried chicken

Backobst *Germany* Dried fruit

Backobstkompott *Germany* Mixed dried fruit, soaked overnight then simmered in a sugar water syrup (4:5) with a cinnamon stick and lemon rind until the fruit is all tender, then drained and covered with the reduced cooking liquor. Served hot or cold and possibly flavoured with liqueur or spirits.

Backpflaume *Germany* Prune

Backpulver *Germany* Baking powder

Backstein *Germany* The Bavarian version of **Limburger** cheese

Backteig *Germany* Batter for deep-frying

Backwerk *Germany* 1. Cakes 2. Pastries

bacon *England, France, Spain* The flesh of pork, divided in two halves along the backbone, then dried and preserved by treatment with salt, saltpetre and spices. These remove water from the meat and have some antibacterial action. Commercial curing methods leave more water in the flesh by including polyphosphates and do not give a bacon which keeps as well as the traditionally cured or dry-cured variety. Bacon may be smoked after curing to enhance the flavour. It is usually sold after boning.

baconer A pig bred for bacon to give a high yield of back bacon, generally long with little fat and small head and legs

bacon froise *England* A plain flour, egg and milk batter into which whisked egg white is folded, half added to a buttered fry pan and cooked until set, crisp bacon pieces added, the remaining batter added, cooked and turned to brown both sides

bacon rasher A thin slice cut at right angles to the backbone from a side of bacon. Also called **rasher**

bacon strip *United States* Bacon rasher

bacoreta *Spain* Little tunny

bacteria The plural form of **bacterium**. Important in the food industries are *Salmonella, Bacillus cereus, Campylobacter, Staphylococcus, Listeria*, all of which are food poisoning organisms and *Lactobacillus* spp. and *Streptococcus* spp., etc. which are used in the production of various foodstuffs. See under each heading. See also **food poisoning bacteria**

bacterial count The number of bacteria per unit weight or volume of a foodstuff, which is indicative of food quality in some cases

bactericide A chemical which kills actively growing bacteria

bacterium A single-celled micro-organism which replicates by growth and then division. Some are beneficial, some harmful. See examples under entry **bacteria**.

badaam *South Asia* Almond

badasco *France* The Provençal name for the fish, **rascasse**, used in fish soups and bouillabaisse

badèche *France* Sea bass

Badischer Hecht *Germany* Pike fillets with button onions, covered in sour cream half baked in the oven then finished by gratinating with breadcrumbs and grated cheese

baecheoffe *Switzerland* Baked potato

baechu *Korea* Chinese leaves

baeckoffe *France* A meat and potato hotpot from the Alsace region of France made from boneless stewing meat marinaded in Alsace Riesling wine with chopped onions, garlic and herbs, layered with potatoes and onions, covered in the marinade; the pot then sealed and cooked in the oven for up to 4 hours at 175°C (NOTE: Literally 'baking oven'.)

bagaceira *Portugal* The Portuguese equivalent of marc or grappa, a type of rum made with sugar cane residues

bagel A Jewish bread roll made by forming the dough into a ring, then briefly boiling after proving and prior to baking

baggiana *Italy* A bean, tomato and basil soup from Umbria

baghar *South Asia* A mixture of sliced onions and possibly other vegetables, flavoured with chopped garlic, chillies and whole spices, fried in ghee or clarified butter and used as a topping for **dhal**

baghlava *Iran* Baklava

baghrir *North Africa* A fine semolina and flour pancake from Morocco usually eaten at breakfast. It is cooked on one side only and has a distinctive honeycombed appearance. Often served with butter and honey or **khli'**.

bagna 1. *France* A small Niçoise salad served on a round bun with the centre scooped out, eaten as street food (*colloquial; Provence*) **2.** *Italy* A regional name for sauce

bagna cauda *Italy* A mixture of melted butter or olive oil, chopped anchovies, garlic, and basil, served hot with raw or cooked vegetables

Bagnes et conches *Switzerland* A hard delicately flavoured cheese

bagnet *Italy* The name for sauce in Piedmont

bagnomaria *Italy* See **bain-marie**

bagolan *Philippines* Cuttlefish

bagoong *Philippines* Salted shrimps or small fish fermented in a closed jar for several weeks and used as a flavouring or condiment. The liquid which is drawn off is used as a fish sauce known as **patis**.

Bagozzo *Italy* A cooked-curd, grana-type cheese with a very hard yellow paste containing fine holes. It has a sharp flavour and a red rind, and is often sliced and grilled.

Bagration *Russia* A veal and chicken consommé flavoured with bay, thyme and dill and served hot over cooked asparagus tips and garnished with sour cream (NOTE: Named after General Bagration who was killed at the battle of Borodino in 1812 and has various dishes named after him.)

baguette *France* Long, thin, crusty French bread, about 250 g weight and formed on a cloth. Not baked in a tin. The top is slashed in a characteristic diagonal pattern before baking. (NOTE: The form originated in Paris in the middle of the 19th century, where it was introduced from Vienna by the Austrian embassy. It rapidly became popular throughout France.)

baharat *Middle East* A spice mix from the Persian Gulf consisting of nutmeg, black peppercorns, coriander seeds, cumin seeds, cloves, green cardamom, paprika and cayenne pepper and used with meat and vegetables

Bahia Washington

bai cai *China* Pak choy

baie *France* Berry

baie de ronce *France* Wild blackberry

baigan *South Asia* A long thin aubergine

bai guo *China* Gingko nut

bai horapa *Thailand* Basil

bai karee *Thailand* Curry leaf

bai krapow *Thailand* Purple basil

bai magrut *Thailand* Makrut lime leaves

bai mak nao *Cambodia* Lemon grass

baingan *South Asia* Aubergine

bainiku *Japan* Puréed umeboshi plums added to dips and sauces to give a tart flavour

bain-marie *England, France* A dish to contain boiling or hot water in which other dishes are stood for cooking or to keep them warm at temperatures below boiling. May be specially made with appropriate containers.

bain-marie, au *France* Method of cooking an item in a container placed in a pan of water so as to prevent it reaching too high a temperature

bairm breac *Ireland* Barm brack

bai sa ra neh *Thailand* Mint

baiser *France* Two meringue shells sandwiched together with whipped cream (NOTE: Literally 'a kiss'.)

bai toey hom *Thailand* Screwpine

bajai halászlé *Hungary* A fish and potato soup from Baja

bajoue *France* Pig's cheek

bajra *South Asia* Bulrush millet

bakagai *Japan* A type of large clam. See also **aoyagi** (NOTE: The name is sometimes incorrectly used for **mirugai** which is a different species.)

bake 1. *United States* A North American term for a social gathering at which baked or barbecued food is served, e.g. 'clam bake' **2.**

Caribbean A type of biscuit from Trinidad made from plain flour, butter and baking powder (25:6:1) by the rubbing-in method, brought together with coconut milk and either baked, griddled or fried

bake, to To cook in an oven with dry heat. Heat is transferred by radiation from the hot metal surfaces or by convection from natural or forced circulation of hot air or gas-combustion products. Sometimes steam may be added to increase the relative humidity and reduce the loss of weight by evaporation of water. Baked goods are usually brown on the outside.

bake and shark *Caribbean* A local snack food from Trinidad and Tobago consisting of shark meat marinated in lime juice, then coated in seasoned flour, fried and placed between two fried bakes

bakeapples Cloudberries

bake blind, to To bake an unfilled pastry case in a tin by lining the inside with foil or greaseproof paper and filling this with dried beans or grain so as to prevent the case losing its shape. After the pastry has set, the filling is removed and the pastry case is finished in the oven.

baked Alaska Very cold ice cream placed on a sponge cake, covered with meringue and baked in a hot oven so that the meringue is browned whilst the ice cream remains solid. Also called **Norwegian omelette**, **omelette soufflée surprise**, **omelette norvégienne**

baked apple *United Kingdom* A cored apple with skin on, stuffed with sultanas, brown sugar and cinnamon powder and baked in the oven as a dessert

baked bananas Peeled bananas, halved, baked with rum, brown sugar, lemon juice and butter and served with whipped cream or ice cream

baked batter pudding *England* A Yorkshire pudding batter baked in the oven with sweet or savoury solid additions

baked beans Cooked navy beans *(from the USA)* in a tomato sauce. The tinned variety are an important source of protein and fibre in Europe and North America, especially for children. The navy bean is now being replaced in some brands by European varieties of the haricot bean.

baked custard *United States* Crème renversée

baked egg custard An egg custard mix of eggs, sugar, milk and flavourings, baked in the oven until set and browned, sometimes in a pastry case. (4 to 5 eggs per litre).

baked pudding *United Kingdom* As **steamed pudding** but cooked uncovered at 180°C in an oven for about an hour until well risen

bakelse *Sweden* A sweet pastry or small cake

bake pan *United States* A large rectangular straight-sided shallow pan without a cover, used for oven-baking

baker's cheese *United States* A soft, smooth type of cottage cheese made from a pasteurized skimmed milk with a lactic starter culture. Extensively used in the bakery trade. Contains 74% water, 0.2% fat and 19% protein.

baker's dozen Thirteen of anything, a bonus of one over the regular dozen

baker's yeast A particular strain of the yeast *Saccharomyces cerevisiae*, suitable for bread making. Sold as a beige, crumbly, solid cake, usually containing about 75 to 80% free water. Must be used fresh.

bakery An establishment where cakes and bread are baked, often with a shop attached

Bakewell pudding *England* A thickish irregular puff pastry case lined with jam and filled with an almond-flavoured egg, butter and sugar mixture, eaten hot or cold (NOTE: So called from the town of Bakewell in Derbyshire.)

Bakewell tart *England* A shortcrust pastry case lined with jam and filled with an almond cake mixture, baked and finished with icing (NOTE: So called from the town of Bakewell in Derbyshire.)

baking chocolate Unsweetened or bitter chocolate used in cooking. See also **bitter chocolate**

baking powder A chemical raising agent made from a finely ground mixture of two parts cream of tartar to one part bicarbonate of soda which liberates carbon dioxide gas on heating. Domestic baking powders replace some of the cream of tartar with an acid phosphate which is slower to act and gives more time for preparation and cooking.

baking sheet A heavy steel sheet, usually rectangular with raised edges on 3 sides, on which rolls, biscuits, etc. are cooked in the oven. The unraised edge is to facilitate sliding the baked goods onto a cooling rack. See also **baking tray**

baking soda See **bicarbonate of soda**

baking tray A steel sheet with a raised edge all around or on three sides for use in an oven. Various shapes are available for pizzas, tarts, etc., or a rectangular tray can be used as a base for flan rings and smaller containers. See also **baking sheet**

baklava, **baklaoua** A Middle Eastern, Armenian and Greek dessert made from layers of filo pastry interspersed with chopped nuts, ground almonds, breadcrumbs, sugar, spice, butter, etc.; after baking at 170°C for 50 minutes, soaked in sugar syrup or honey, cooled and cut into squares or diamonds. The Armenian version is usually baked in a round pan and prescored in a diamond pattern and cut into diamonds after baking.

baklazhannaia ikra *Southwest Asia* A Georgian pâté made from the flesh of roasted aubergines, simmered with chopped and sweated spring onions and green sweet peppers, skinned tomatoes and cayenne pepper until all cooked and thick, mixed with chopped coriander and lemon juice and cooled

bakonyi betyárleves *Hungary* A thick soup of chicken, beef, noodles, mushrooms and vegetables. Also called **outlaw soup**

bakonyi gombamártás *Hungary* A mushroom sauce from Bakony

bakudai *Japan* A type of pea used as a garnish for sashimi and salads. The pods are steeped in tepid tea to make them open and the seeds are removed and washed prior to use.

balabusky *Eastern Europe* A yeast-raised Ukrainian bread made from rye flour, wheat flour and sour cream (1:2:1). Water, sugar and yeast are used to form the slightly sticky dough which is mixed with caraway seeds, shaped into rolls, sprinkled with more caraway seeds, proved and baked at 200°C.

balacan *Malaysia* A strong-smelling dried paste made from small crustaceans. See also **blachan**

balachaung *Burma* Chopped garlic, spring onion and ginger root fried in oil until golden, reserved; finely chopped dried shrimps fried with turmeric in the same oil, mixed with the garlic, etc.; softened shrimp paste added and all cooked over a low heat to form a smelly but tasty concoction. Used as a side dish.

balachong *South Asia* A South Indian relish of minced prawns, fried with minced onion, mango and tomatoes or similar plus spices, then pounded with salt and vinegar to an acceptable taste and consistency. Also called **balachow, balichow**

balachow *South Asia* Balachong

balantier *France* Wild pomegranate

Balaton *Hungary* A semi-hard, scalded-curd, cows' milk cheese with a buttery, aromatic flavoured paste with holes. Contains 42% water, 20% fat and 25% protein.

balcalhao di kismur *South Asia* A seafood salad from Goa made of salt cod soaked in diluted palm vinegar, flaked and mixed with fried sliced onions, green and red chillies, sweet green peppers, ginger, garlic and spices and finished with dried shrimp powder and lemon juice

baleron *Poland* A popular smoked pork sausage

balichow *South Asia* A South Indian relish of minced prawns. See also **balachong**

balik *Turkey* Fish

ballach *Ireland* Wrasse, the fish

Ballater scones *Scotland* Flour, butter and buttermilk (8:1:5) with 1 dsp of salt, 1 dsp of bicarbonate of soda and 2 dsp of cream of tartar per kg of flour, dry ingredients mixed, butter rubbed in, and all brought together with the buttermilk. Formed into rounds by hand, cut in quarters, docked and baked at 220°C for 10 to 15 minutes. Eaten warm.

baller A food preparation implement consisting of half a hollow sphere with sharp edges on the end of a handle. Used for cutting out balls from melons, cucumbers, root vegetables, ice cream, cheese, cooked gizzards, etc. Made in various sizes.

ball garlic Bulb garlic

ballon *France* A boned joint of meat tied into a ball shape prior to cooking

balloon whisk The professional chef's whisk which consists of about 12 teardrop-shaped pieces of stainless steel wire, the two ends of each secured around the circumference of a stout circular handle about 2 cm diameter by 15 cm long. The whole forms a 3 dimensional tear drop shape which fits easily the contours of a basin. They come in various sizes.

ballottine *France* 1. A roll of boned and stuffed poultry, meat or fish 2. Meat loaf

ballottine de volaille *France* A chicken boned from the inside, lined with pâté, stuffed with forcemeat made from the leg meat, cooked, cooled and coated with aspic jelly

Ballymaloe *Ireland* A wholemeal, yeast-raised bread, the yeast activated with treacle in place of sugar

balm Lemon balm

balmain bug *Australia* Sand lobster

balmoral loaf tin A corrugated cylindrical metal loaf tin somewhat like a bellows, which produces a ridged loaf or cake easily cut into slices. Also called **ribbed loaf tin, toast rack tin**

Balmoral shortbread *Scotland* Queen Victoria's favourite shortbread made from flour, butter and sugar (3:2:1) pressed out very thin (4 mm) and cooked at 180°C for 30 minutes

Balmoral tripe *Scotland* Veal tripe cut in 8 cm squares, bacon slightly smaller laid over each square which is then peppered, rolled up and packed seam side down over bay leaves in a saucepan, seasoned and covered with chopped onions, parsley and veal stock. It is simmered for 2 hours until tender adding sliced mushrooms 10 minutes before the end. Finished with cream before serving.

balnamoon skink *Ireland* Chicken broth finished with egg yolks and milk and garnished with green peas, shredded lettuce and diced celeriac

baloney *United States* Bologna sausage

balsam apple Kantola

balsamella *Italy* Béchamel sauce

balsamic vinegar A highly fragrant, sweetish vinegar from Italy, made from concentrated grape juice and aged in wood for at least 10 years

Balsamita major *Botanical name* Costmary

balsam pear Bitter gourd

balti A style of cheap Indian fast food, which originated in Birmingham, UK, in the 1970s, consisting of marinated and spiced ingredients stir-fried and served in a **karahi**. Balti is Hindi for bucket, and there is no suggestion that there is an authentic Indian balti cooking style.

Baltic herring A small species of herring, *Opisthonema oglinum*, found in the Baltic Sea

balut *Philippines* Fertilized duck eggs containing an intact embryo duck. Thought to increase male potency when eaten.

Bambara groundnut *West Africa* One of the original peanuts from the Bambara region of Mali, probably taken to Africa by the Spaniards from Latin America via the Phillipines and Asia

bamboo Any large tropical woody grass of the genus *Bambusa*, normally used as a construction material. The leaves and shoots of some species are used in cooking.

bamboo fungus A very expensive fungus fruiting body, *Dictyophora phalloidea*, which grows in China on a certain kind of bamboo. It is light in colour, looks like a small lacy purse and has a musty earthy taste and crunchy texture. Also called **staghorn fungus**

bamboo leaf The blanched and softened leaves of certain species of bamboo used as a food wrapping for grilling, steaming, boiling, etc.

bamboo mustard cabbage See **chuk gaai choy**

bamboo shoots The immature shoots of the bamboo, used either fresh, salted, pickled, dried or canned in Chinese and Southeast Asian cooking. Fresh shoots must be parboiled to remove toxins. Dried shoots are the most tasty but require long soaking and cooking. Tinned are the most convenient.

bambú *Italy, Spain* Bamboo

Bambusa *Botanical name* Bamboo

Bambusa vulgaris *Botanical name* Cultivated bamboo shoots

Bambusprosse *Germany* Bamboo shoot

ba mee *Thailand* Egg noodle

bamee *Malaysia* A thin white noodle made from wheat flour

bami *Netherlands* A spicy dish of noodles with all or some of pork, shrimp, eggs, onions and various vegetables. Brought from Indonesia.

bamieh *Middle East* Okra

bamiya *Middle East* Okra

bammy *Caribbean* A Jamaican bread made from cassava flour, soaked in milk or water then fried or steamed

bamya *Egypt, North Africa* A stew of minced lamb, okra, tomato, onion, green pepper, lemon juice, and herbs

banaan *Netherlands* Banana

bana caldo *Italy* Olive oil mixed with chopped anchovies, chopped garlic and seasoning simmered in butter for 10 minutes. Used as a dip.

banak *Philippines* Grey mullet

banán *Hungary* Banana

banana *England, Italy, Japan, Portugal* The fruit of a giant herb, genus *Musa*, (all sterile hybrids without exact species names, but sometimes named *M.sapientum*), grown in hot climates throughout the world. The individual fruits 7 – 24 cm long grow in bunches from a central stalk and are usually picked green for transportation and ripened to yellow prior to sale. The flesh is soft and cream coloured and when underripe a source of useful low-digestibility starch, said to reduce the chance of bowel cancer. The skin is thick and easily removed. Dessert bananas when ripe have a sugar content of 17 to 19%. Unripe bananas and some which would never reach a high sugar content are eaten as a staple food and known as plantain. After fruiting the stem of the plant dies back and new suckers grow from the base.

banana chilli A yellow and rather mild sweet chilli pepper

banana fig *United States* Sun-dried slices of banana which are dark and sticky and resemble figs

banana flour A flour made from plantains which have been dried and ground. Also called **pisang starch, plantain flour**

banana flower The fat red to purple pointed group of male flowers which forms in the initial stages at the tip of a bunch of bananas. Used like the globe artichoke in Indian and Southeast Asian cooking.

banana fritters See **fruit fritters**

banana heart The pith at the centre of the trunk of a banana plant. It is sliced and soaked in salted water for several hours and used in Burmese cooking. The sap must not be allowed to contact the clothes or body.

banana leaf The leaves of bananas sometimes used as disposable table cloths or plates in Indian and Southeast Asian restaurants or as a substitute for greaseproof paper when cooking **en papillote**

banana pepper *United States* A mild yellow-green pepper up to 10 cm long used in salads and as a stuffed vegetable

banana prawn A yellowish beige variety of king prawn, *Penaeus merguiensis*

bananas Foster *United States* A New Orleans speciality of fried bananas, spiced, sugared, flamed with rum and served with whipped cream

banana shoot The shoots which grow from the base of the banana plant are forced by excluding light and become long thick white spikes rather like asparagus. Cooked in hot ashes or baked.

banana split A longitudinally split banana filled with ice cream and finished with whipped cream and chopped nuts

banana squash A winter squash shaped like a banana

banane *France* Banana

Banane *Germany* Banana

banane des antilles *France* Plantain. Also called **banane plantain**

banane plantain *France* Plantain

bananer *Denmark, Norway, Sweden* Bananas

bananes baronnet *France* Bananas served with cream and kirsch

bananes Beauharnais *France* Bananas served with sugar, rum and macaroons

bananes pesées *Caribbean* A Haitian dish of green plantains soaked in salted water for an hour, drained, sautéed in oil until tender, then flattened with a fish slice or similar until half their original thickness and fried until golden brown and crisp on the outside. Served with **sauce ti-malice**.

Banbury cake *England* An oval-shaped Oxfordshire cake made from puff pastry filled with dried vine fruits, sugar, butter, spices, flour and rum, prior to baking, finished with an egg white and caster sugar glaze just before removing from the oven

banda *Indonesia* Yam

bandal *South Asia* A rich cream cheese made from cows' or buffaloes' milk

bandeng *Indonesia* Bangus

bangers *England* Cooked English sausages (*colloquial*)

bangers and mash *England* A simple meal of fried English sausages, mashed potatoes and gravy (*colloquial*)

bangkwang *Malaysia* Yam bean

bangus A farmed round fish, *Chanos chanos* and *C. Salmoneus,* which is very popular in the Phillipines and Indonesia. It grows up to 1.5 m and has a greenish grey skin and delicate flesh. Also called **milkfish**

banh cuon *Vietnam* Cellophane noodles

banh hoi *Vietnam* Rice vermicelli

banh mi *Vietnam* Bread

banh pho *Vietnam* White rice noodles about 3 mm wide. They cook very quickly and are used with the popular Hanoi soup called pho. Also called **nu tieu**

banh phong tom *Vietnam* Prawn crackers

banh trang *Vietnam* Dried thin and almost transparent pancakes made from cassava, water and salt. Moistened to soften before use in wrapping food prior to cooking as in e.g. spring rolls.

banh uot *Vietnam* Freshly made thin pancake wrappers similar to **banh trang** but made with a mixture of wheat, tapioca and corn flours with peanut oil, water and salt

banh xeo *Vietnam* Fried pancake

banira *Japan* Vanilla

banitza susu sirene *Bulgaria* A pie made of layers of pastry interlayered with a mixture of egg, cheese and yoghurt

bankebiff *Norway* Beef, browned in butter and simmered in stock

bankekød *Denmark* Stewed beef

banket letter *Netherlands* Flaky pastry (**millefeuille**) cakes filled with almond paste

banku *West Africa* A Ghanaian staple made from a maize meal dough which has been allowed to ferment for 2 to 3 days and is then boiled with water for about 20 minutes to make a very stiff cooked porridge. This is formed into tennis-ball-sized portions for serving. Sometimes equal parts of maize meal and grated cassava root are used.

bannock *Scotland* 1. A circular scone made from barley flour, oatmeal or barley meal and cooked on a griddle. Various types are produced for breakfast and high tea. 2. A biscuit resembling shortbread but containing chopped mixed peel and almonds. Also called **Pithcaithly bannock**

bannock fluke Turbot

Banon *France* A small Provençal cream cheese sprinkled with savory, wrapped in vine leaves and presented on a slice of wood

banquet A formal meal with many courses served to a large gathering of people

bantam A small, more primitive type of domestic fowl or chicken usually with brightly coloured feathers producing small eggs

bantam eggs Eggs from the bantam fowl, sometimes used of the very small eggs first laid by chickens. See also **pullet eggs**

banteng A small cow-like animal from Southeast Asia and domesticated in Indonesia. The flesh is reputed to be very tasty.

bao *China* 1. Blanching and refreshing 2. Aubergine

baobab The fruit of the African baobab tree, *Adansonia digitata*. The fruit is large and pulpy. Also called **monkey bread**

bao zi *China* Steamed bread bun, sometimes stuffed

bap *United Kingdom* A small, flat round white bread with a soft crust and generally dusted with flour

baptist cake *United States* A deep-fried enriched yeast dough bun from New England. Also called **hustler, holy poke, huff juff**

bar 1. *France* Bass, the fish. Also called **badèche, bézuche, cernier, loup de mer** 2. *England, France* An establishment which serves drinks and light snacks 3. A unit of pressure; 1 bar roughly equals the pressure exerted by the atmosphere

bär *Sweden* Berry

bara bread *Caribbean* Split pea flour, plain flour and butter (4:2:1) with 8 teaspoons of baking powder per kg of combined flours, flavoured with cumin, turmeric, minced garlic and minced seeded chilli pepper and brought together with warm water to form a firm dough, rested, then rolled out to 3 cm thick and fried both sides. Eaten hot, usually as a sandwich with **channa** and a hot sauce. (NOTE: From Trinidad)

bara brith *Wales* A Welsh sweet bread made from a yeasted dough with caraway seeds and a high proportion of dried vine fruits soaked in tea (NOTE: Literally 'speckled bread'.)

bara ceirch *Wales* The traditional UK oatcake but made with bacon fat. See also **oatcake**

bara claddu *Wales* A simple cake made from plain flour, sugar, dried vine fruits and egg (4:4:4:1) with a little baking powder and mixed spice. The dry ingredients are well mixed and brought together with the beaten egg and a little milk to a cake consistency, then baked in a buttered loaf tin at 160°C for about an hour. Served sliced with butter.

bara jheenga *South Asia* Lobster

bara lawr *Wales* Laver bread

baranina *Russia* Lamb

bárányhús *Hungary* Lamb

báránypaprikás *Hungary* Diced lamb fried in lard with diced lean bacon, chopped onions and paprika then all simmered with water, tomato purée, thinly sliced sweet green peppers and seasoning until cooked and finished with sour cream. Served with rice, **tarhonya**, dumplings.

bárányporkolt *Hungary* Diced lamb fried in lard with chopped onions, diced bacon and paprika and all simmered in seasoned brown stock and tomato purée until cooked. Served with **tarhonya**.

bara sem *South Asia* 1. Jack bean 2. Sword bean

barbabietola *Italy* Beetroot

barbada *Spain* Brill

barbadine *France* Passion fruit

Barbados cherry Acerola

Barbados sugar Muscovado sugar

Barbarakraut *Germany* Land cress

Barbarea verna *Botanical name* Land cress

Barbarea vulgaris *Botanical name* Winter cress

barbari *Central Asia* A yeast-raised Iranian white bread mixed for 15 minutes, proved, shaped into rectangles 30 by 12 by 1 cm, proved again, indented along its length to look like a Lilo mattress and baked at 220°C for about 15 minutes

barbary duck A fleshy, well-flavoured, slightly gamey lean duck, *Cairina moschata,* with musky-flavoured flesh, originally from South America but now bred in France and elsewhere and very popular in Australia. It is slaughtered at up to 3 months old and should be cooked more slowly than duckling and barded and basted. Also called **muscovy duck**

barbary pear Prickly pear

Barbe *Germany* Barbel, the fish

barbeau *France* Barbel, the fish

barbecue 1. A method of cooking food similar to grilling, generally in the open air over smouldering charcoal or some other form of radiant heat. The meats are often treated with spice mixture. Also called **barbeque 2.** The equipment used to cook meat in this way (NOTE: Derived from the French *barbe à queue* 'beard to tail', referring to the barbecueing of the whole animal.)

barbecue sauce The general term for any spicy sauce served with barbecued food. e.g. a mixture of soya sauce, rice wine or vinegar, spring onions, garlic, chilli sauce and ground toasted sesame seeds or peanuts blended in a food processor.

barbecue spice mix A medium hot blend of ground spices rubbed on to meat before grilling, made from black peppercorns, celery seeds, cayenne pepper, dried thyme, dried marjoram, paprika, mustard powder, salt and soft brown sugar

barbeel *Netherlands* Barbel, the fish

barbeen *Middle East* A salad green rather like watercress

barbel The coarse European freshwater fish, *Barbus barbus*, related to the carp. Can grow up to 45 cm in length.

barbeque See **barbecue**

Barberey *France* A soft cheese made from partially skimmed cows' milk formed into a disc (250 g), covered with wood ash and ripened for a month. Also called **Troyes**

barberon *France* The Provençal name for **salsify**

barberry The fruit of the bush *Berberis vulgaris*, generally used for preserves if at all

barbo *Italy, Norway, Portugal, Spain* Barbel, the fish

barbot Eel pout

barbotine *France* Tansy

barbounia *Greece* Red mullet

barbue *France* Brill

barbue Brancas *France* Brill baked with vegetables in a tomato sauce

Barcelona nut Hazelnut

barchetta *Italy* Barquette, a small boat-shaped tartlet

bar clam See **surf clam**

bard, to To cover meat with thin layers of fat or fatty bacon to prevent it drying out during roasting whilst other parts of the meat are cooking. Often used to protect the breast meat of birds and chicken.

bardatte *France* Cabbage stuffed with hare

barde *France* A layer of fat or fatty bacon used to bard meat

bardé *France* Wrapped or covered in a thin solid sheet of fat or fatty bacon, used in roasting to protect parts from the heat

barder *France* To bard

barfi *South Asia* A sweet resembling fudge. See also **burfi**

barista *South Asia* Sliced onions fried until crisp. Used to finish savoury dishes.

bark gor *China* Ginkgo nut

barley One of the oldest cultivated cereals, *Hordeum vulgare,* with a seed of similar size to rice. Not suitable on its own for making leavened bread since it contains little gluten. Sometimes used in soups (as an addition to broth), occasionally to make a flour or meal, but predominantly either as animal feed or for conversion to malt (by sprouting) for fermentation in the beer and spirit industries. See also **pot barley, pearl barley**

barley broth *Scotland* Scotch broth but made with a mutton stock

barley flakes Partially cooked barley, flattened and dried. Used as one constituent of muesli, also for puddings and toppings.

barley flour Ground barley used as a thickening agent, for making unleavened bread, or as a substitute for some of the wheat flour in leavened bread

barley meal Coarsely ground pot barley used to make a kind of porridge or gruel and bannocks

barley pudding *Scotland* A Lothian dish of barley cooked in the oven at 150°C with 6 to 7 times its weight of water for 2 hours, currants are added for the last 20 minutes. Served with sugar and cream.

barley sugar A transparent, caramel-coloured and lemon-flavoured brittle sweet now made from sugar and water, originally from sugar and barley water

barley syrup See **malt**

barley water A drink made from the water in which pearl barley has been cooked. Once thought to have medicinal properties.

barm Yeast

barm brack *Ireland* A sweet bread made from yeasted dough mixed with dried vine fruits and chopped candied peel, possibly previously soaked in tea to rehydrate, and caraway seeds. Popular at Christmas and Hallowe'en. Also called **bairm breac**

barm cake *England* A soft bread roll in the shape of a circle often split and filled for use as a sandwich

Bärme *Germany* Yeast (*North Germany*)

barnacle A cylindrical stalk-like crustacean, *Pollicipes cornucopia,* up to 15 cm long, which is found on sea-washed rocks around the Atlantic coast. The foot with which it attaches itself to the rock and the tough papery skin covered in small scales are discarded. May be eaten raw or cooked. Popular in Spain and Portugal. Also called **goose barnacle, goose-necked barnacle**

barnacle goose Brent goose

Barnstaple fair pears *England* Large Comice pears, peeled with the stalk on, piquéed with blanched halved almonds, poached in red wine with sugar and cloves for 15 minutes

53

and served with the strained reduced cooking liquor and clotted cream

barnyard millet A type of millet, *Echinochloa crusgalli,* grown mainly as a fodder crop in the east and now an escaped wild plant in the UK and the USA

baron d'agneau *France* Fillet end (top half) of a leg of lamb used for roasting

baron of beef *England* A large beef joint consisting of two sirloins, connected by the backbone. Roasted for celebratory occasions.

baron of lamb The saddle and two legs of lamb in one piece

barquette *France* **1.** Small boat-shaped tartlet **2.** The small tin in which a barquette is baked

barquillo *Spain* Wafer

barracouta Snoek

barracuda A slender round-bodied ferocious seawater game fish of the genus *Sphyraena* found in warm water worldwide. Barracudas are generally eaten at around 2.5 kg and have lean firm flesh. Very large Caribbean barracudas over 1 m long have poisonous flesh which causes joint pains, trembling and vomiting.

barralax *Australia* **Gravlax** made with barramundi fillets, cold cured and flavoured with a dusting of lemon myrtle instead of dill weed

barramundi, barramunda *Australia* The edible Australian lungfish, Lates calcarifer. Also called **lungfish**

barrel 1. A wooden cask with specially shaped wooden staves forming the sides which are held together with iron hoops which when knocked down from either end compress all the staves together to make the sides watertight. Used for wine, beer, salted herrings, olives and the like. **2.** A liquid measure equivalent to 159 litres, 42 US gallons or 35 imperial gallons

barrel bread A cylindrical loaf baked in a ridged tin so that it can easily be cut into uniform slices. Also called **crinkled musket, landlady's loaf, lodger's loaf, pistol, piston, rasp**

barrinaire *Italy* Sand eel

barrogog bis basela *North Africa* A lamb stew with prunes

Barsch *Germany* **1.** Perch **2.** Bass

barszcz *Poland* A Polish version of **borscht** made from fermented sour beet juice, traditionally served on Easter day

barszcz zimny *Poland* Cold soup made from the juice of pickled beetroot and cucumbers, thickened with semolina, finished with egg

yolks and sour cream, seasoned, chilled and served with slices of hard-boiled egg

barya a jagnjetinom *Balkans* A lamb and okra casserole from Serbia

barzotte *Italy* Soft-boiled, as of eggs

basal mahshi *Persian Gulf* Stuffed onion made by making a radial slit from root to tip, boiling the onion and separating the layers. These are then stuffed as with cabbage rolls using a meat and rice filling and baked with a water and tamarind pulp mixture.

basal metabolic rate The rate at which the resting body uses energy. For the average healthy adult this is 1700 K cal per day equal to 7100 kJ per day.

bas de carré *France* The top part of the shoulder of veal, equivalent to scrag end of lamb

base 1. The chemical term for a substance which reacts with an acid to form a salt **2.** The major component of a dish which is the main determinant of its properties as e.g. stock is the base of soups and sauces. Also called **fond**

Basella alba *Botanical name* Ceylon spinach

bashan *Middle East* A smoked cheese from Israel made with ewes' and goats' milk. The rind is a glossy red and the paste has a sharp flavour.

bashit *Scotland* Mashed, as in bashit neeps (*colloquial*)

basic cake mixture Flour, butter, caster sugar and eggs in the proportions by weight of 8:5:5:5 with 1 level teaspoon of baking powder per 8 oz of flour (16 g per kg flour)

basic foods Seven classes of food are considered necessary for a balanced daily diet: green and yellow vegetables, starchy tubers, fruits, milk products, meat including fish or eggs, cereals and fats and oils. Vegetarians would substitute pulses for the meat products.

basic soup A **mirepoix** of onions, leek and celery plus twice the quantity of the vegetable after which the soup is named, sweated in butter, flour added and cooked out without colour; a bouquet garni and white stock added; the soup simmered and skimmed for 1 hour; the bouquet garni removed; the soup liquidized, seasoned and consistency adjusted, creamed if required and garnished as appropriate. See also **cream soup**

basil A tender annual herb, *Ocimum basilicum,* with an aromatic flavour reminiscent of mint and cloves used in salads, pesto and Italian cooking, and added at the last minute to cooked dishes. See also **bush basil, holy basil, lemon basil, hairy**

basil, purple basil, kemangi. Also called **sweet basil**

basilic *France* Basil

basilico *Italy* Basil

Basilienkraut *Germany* Basil

basin A wide flattish dish

basket A steel mesh utensil (about 8 to 12 mm pitch) with a handle, which fits in a deep-fat fryer and is used to lower damp foods, especially potato chips, into the fat slowly so that the boiling off of the water does not cause the fat or oil to boil over. It is also used for blanching vegetables in boiling water.

Basler Leckerli *Switzerland* A Christmas biscuit containing candied peel, almonds, honey, hazelnuts, cinnamon and kirsch baked in relief-carved wooden moulds depicting traditional scenes. See also **Tirggel, Züritirggel**

basmati rice A dense thin long-grain rice with an aromatic and nutty flavour, more expensive than American long-grain rice, used in Indian cooking for biryani and pilau. Best boiled without salt for about 10 minutes, or in lots of boiling water for 8 minutes then drained, covered and finished on a very low heat for a further 10 minutes. (NOTE: The name means fragrant, and the rice is grown in the foothills of the Himalayas.)

basquaise, à la *France* In the Basque manner, i.e. with ham, tomatoes and red peppers

bass A prized silvery grey round non-oily fish, *Dicentrarchus labrax*, up to 1 m in length which lives in saltwater lakes, estuaries and around some European coasts. The flesh is white and is cooked in any way. Also called **salmon dace, salmon bass, common bass**

bassia fat *South Asia* A soft yellow oil extracted from the seeds of the Indian butter tree. See also **mowra butter**

bastani *Iran* Ice cream

bastard saffron Safflower

baste to To spoon melted fat over food during cooking either to prevent drying out or to aid heat transfer

bastilla *North Africa* Layers of crisp-fried **warkha pastry** interleaved in the savoury version with pigeon meat, chicken or fish, almonds, spices and lemon-flavoured eggs, or, in the sweet version, with a milky almond sauce to make a kind of pie. Both types are liberally dusted with icing sugar. It was introduced from Portugal by the Moors. Also called **b'stilla, pastilla, bisteeya**

basting brush A brush used to spread fat or other liquids over food prior to and during cooking

bastoncini *Italy* Small stick-shaped biscuits

batagur *Malaysia* A species of turtle now endangered due to excessive exploitation. Even though local consumption is forbidden by the Muslim religion, they have been exported in quantity.

batakh *South Asia* Duck

batangas *Philippines* A type of mandarin orange. See also **ponkan mandarin**

bâtarde, sauce *France* Salted water thickened with a white roux then reheated with a liaison of egg yolks and cream and a little lemon juice, strained and about 30% of its weight in butter added just before service. Served with asparagus or poached fish. Also called **beurre, sauce au**

batata 1. *Portugal* Potato, usually firm waxy types 2. *Spain* Sweet potato

batata charp *Middle East* An Iraqi patty of duchesse potatoes surrounding a filling made from sweated chopped onion fried with garlic and minced meat until dry. The filling is then simmered with **baharat, tomato concassée** and chopped parsley, flattened into cakes, floured and fried on each side until brown. A fried vegetable filling may be used instead of meat.

batata frita *Portugal* Potato chips

Batate *Germany* Sweet potato

batavia *France* 1. Batavian endive. Also called **scarole** 2. Curly lettuce, e.g. Webb's

batavian endive A variety of winter endive, *Cichorium endivia*, with larger flatter leaves than true endive. Used as a salad green. Also called **plain-leaved escarole**

batch loaf *United Kingdom* A loaf which has been baked close to others on a tray so that the dough touches and partially joins. After baking they are split apart to reveal soft sides.

batelière, à la *France* In the boatman's style, i.e. garnished with some or all of fried eggs, mushrooms, button onions, and crayfish, or, with small pastry shells with a rich fish filling

Bath asparagus *England* The flowerhead and stem of the spiked star of Bethlehem plant, *Ornithogalum pyrenaicum*, which grows wild around Bath. It tastes rather like asparagus and is boiled or steamed.

Bath bun *England* A sweet, yeast-raised bun containing mixed peel and sultanas originating in Bath, Somerset; egg-washed and topped with coarse white sugar crystals before baking

Bath chap Pig's cheek

Bath Oliver A plain flat biscuit (NOTE: It was invented by Dr Oliver of Bath in the 1700s, and at that time supposed to have slimming properties.)

batir *Spain* To whip or whisk

bâton 1. *England, France* A long baguette-type French loaf or bread roll tapering at either end and baked on a flat tray **2.** A type of cut for root vegetables, roughly 6mm x 6mm x 25mm

bâton de manioc *Central Africa* Cassava tubers treated to remove cyanide compounds, processed to a smooth paste, wrapped in softened banana leaves in cylinders between 2 cm and 10 cm in diameter and 30 cm long, then steamed for between 4 and 8 hours. Eaten warm as the staple carbohydrate source with soups and stews. They will keep in their wrappings for several days. Also called **bobolo**, **chikwangue**, **kwanga**, **mintuba**, **placali**

bâtons royaux *France* Small patties of minced chicken and game

bat out, to To flatten pieces of raw meat with a cutlet bat and thus reduce cooking time

batsoa *Italy* Pig's trotters, panéed and deep-fried. See also **piedini di maiale alla piemontese**

Battelmatt *Austria, Italy, Switzerland* A soft cooked-curd cheese made from cows' milk with a springy tender texture and delicate taste and numerous small holes. The curd is pressed in variously-sized cylindrical moulds, salted in brine or dry salt and ripened for 3 to 4 months.

Battenberg A rectangular long oblong sponge made in two different colours arranged lengthwise in a 2x2 checkerboard pattern and covered all round with a marzipan coating

batter 1. A basic mixture of flour, milk and eggs with possible added flavourings, made either to pouring consistency for pancakes, drop scones, Yorkshire pudding, etc. or to coating (i.e. more viscous) consistency for fritters, **cromesquis**, **bhajias**, etc (NOTE: From the French *battre*, 'to beat'.) **2.** *United States* A general term used in North America for any soft mixture made from flour including cake and scone mixes, etc. as well as batter proper

batter, to To coat with batter

batter bread *United States* An unsweetened bread or pudding made with white cornmeal from dent corn raised with well-beaten eggs. Also called **spoon bread** (NOTE: From the southern states.)

batter dip *United States* Frying batter

battre *France* To whip, especially eggs

battuto *Italy* A mixture of chopped onion, garlic, celery and herbs, sweated in oil and used as a base or flavouring ingredient for soups and stews

batu giling *Indonesia* A granite slab and rolling pin used for grinding spices or crushing flavourings such as ginger, onions, garlic, chillies, etc. Also called **batu lesong**

batu lesong *Indonesia, Malaysia* Batu giling

bau dau gok *China* A light coloured variety of long bean

baudroie *France* Monkfish

bauern *Germany* Country-style

Bauernbratwurst *Switzerland* A country-style scalded sausage, made for grilling or frying

Bauernbrot *Germany* Peasant bread, rye bread

Bauernfrühstuck *Germany* Fried potatoes topped with scrambled eggs, ham and cucumber. Served at lunch. (NOTE: Literally 'farmer's or peasant's breakfast'.)

Bauernomelett *Germany* A bacon and onion filled omelette

Bauernschmaus *Austria* A dish of sauerkraut, pork sausages and dumplings

Bauernsuppe *Germany* A country soup of beans, bacon and vegetables

bauletti *Italy* Paupiettes of veal

Baumé scale A complicated scale of density originally based on brine and equivalent to the percentage by weight of salt in a salt and water solution at 15.5°C. Also used for sugar syrups but this has no simple relationship to sugar concentration. Written °B or °Bé. The relationship between °Bé and specific gravity is °Bé = 145 − (145/specific gravity), e.g. a 50% sugar solution, specific gravity 1.23, is 27°Bé.

Baumkuchen *Germany* A Christmas cake shaped like a tree and iced with chocolate to resemble bark

Baumwollöl *Germany* Cottonseed oil

baunilha *Portugal* Vanilla

Bavarian cream See **bavarois**

Bavarian sausage Very well trimmed lean pork and veal, finely minced with back fat, shallots and garlic, mixed with a little coriander, sugar, seasoning and saltpetre, packed in sheep casings, linked, air-dried and smoked until golden brown

bavarois *France* A dessert made from either a vanilla-flavoured egg custard or a fruit purée both containing gelatine, let down with sugar syrup, combined when beginning to thicken, with whipped cream and sugar. Cooled in a mould, which is either oiled or lined with caramel, demoulded when fully set and decorated if required. Also called **crème bavaroise, Bavarian cream**

bavarois au marasquin *France* A cherry-flavoured bavarois

bavaroise *France* A hot drink made with milk, tea, eggs and sugar, flavoured with vanilla or liqueur (NOTE: Not to be confused with **bavarois**.)

bavaroise, sauce *England, France* Hollandaise sauce flavoured with grated horseradish

bavette 1. *France* Flank or skirt of beef **2.** *Italy* Long thin strips of pasta noodles with an oval cross section, available fresh or dried

baveuse *France* Moist or runny. Used for the just runny top of an omelette which becomes the interior when it is folded.

bavosa *Italy* Soft in the centre, as of omelettes and frittatas. See also **baveuse**

bavose *Italy* Blenny, the fish

bawal puteh *Malaysia* White pomfret, the fish

bawal putih *Indonesia* Pomfret, the fish

bawang bakung *Malaysia* Asian leek

bawang besar *Malaysia* Onion

bawang bombay *Indonesia* Onion

bawang daun *Indonesia, Malaysia* Spring onion

bawang merah *Indonesia, Malaysia* Shallots

bawang putih *Indonesia, Malaysia* Garlic

bawd *Scotland* Hare, rabbit (*colloquial*)

bawd bree *Scotland* A rich soup made from a jointed hare browned in lard with bacon and winter vegetables, simmered in water with minced shin beef, bay, cloves and peppercorns until all soft, strained, and the puréed vegetables and finely shredded hare meat returned. The soup is thickened without boiling using a little of the acidulated hare's blood and finished with redcurrant jelly, lemon juice and port. Served with dumplings made with hare's liver, onions and breadcrumbs.

ba-wel *Burma* Squid

bay An evergreen laurel-like shrub, *Laurus nobilis*, whose fresh or dried leaves are used for flavouring, especially in a bouquet garni, marinades, **béchamel sauce**, milk puddings and fish. Also called **sweet bay, laurel**

bayam *Indonesia, Malaysia* Amaranth

bay boletus An edible fungus, *Boletus badius*, with a 5 to 15 cm diameter smooth brown cap and a short slender stem and with pores rather than gills under the cap. It grows profusely under spruce and pine trees and occasionally on the wood or pine cones.

bay bug Sand lobster

Bayerische Leberknödel *Germany* Liver dumplings made with raw chopped calves' liver, sieved and mixed with egg, chopped bacon fat, onions, fried bread crumbs, seasoning and flour to stiffen, formed into tangerine-sized dumplings, poached and served with **beurre noisette** and sauerkraut

bayleaf See **bay**

bay lobster Sand lobster

bayonnaise, à la *France* In the Bayonne style, i.e. containing Bayonne ham

Bayonne ham *France* A dry-cured lightly smoked ham similar to Parma and eaten raw

bay salt Salt produced by the natural solar evaporation of seawater, usually in large crystals of up to 5 mm. See also **sea salt**

bay scallop A small bivalve scallop, *Argopecten irradians*, up to 7.5 cm diameter with an off-white to black shell. Found off the east coast of North America, it has a very delicate flavour and can be eaten raw when fresh.

bay trout *Australia* See **salmon 2**

bazilik *Russia* Basil

BBB See **bleu-blanc Belge**

beadlet A **sea anemone**, *Actinia equina*, eaten in France, generally brown to green in colour but occasionally red. Also called **tomate de mer**

beakie *Australia* Southern sea garfish

bean A leguminous plant characterized by a long pod containing a string of separated seeds. Both the young immature pods and seeds and fresh or dried mature seeds are used for a variety of culinary purposes. The principal vegetable varieties in Europe and North America are broad, dwarf French, climbing French and runner, but many others e.g. mung, soya, lima, etc. are in widespread use.

bean clam A small American clam of the genus *Donax*, similar to the wedge shell clam

bean curd A rather flavourless, textureless but nutritious coagulated soya bean protein made by treating boiled soya bean milk with various coagulants such as flaked sea salt (**nigari**), Epsom salts, vinegar, etc. and separating off the curd as for cheese. It can be soft and jelly-like or have the water content progressively reduced to form finally a cheese-like substance. It may be boiled, fried, etc. and is a most important source of first-class protein, minerals and vitamins in Chinese and Japanese cuisine and for vegans. Also called **tofu, soya bean curd, bean custard, soya bean cake**

bean curd brains A cream coloured lightly coagulated bean curd which has a soft lumpy appearance

bean curd cheese Bean curd fermented with brine or rice wine and spices and mixed with red food colouring and sometimes cereal extenders. It has a strong flavour of cheese and is served as a side dish or condiment, or used as flavouring. Also called **Chinese cheese**, **pickled bean curd**, **red bean curd**, **soya bean cheese**, **fermented bean curd**

bean curd noodles Thin strips of dried bean curd used in the same way as noodles but not normally fried after boiling. More nutritious than starch-based noodles. Also called **soya noodles**, **soya vermicelli**

bean curd sheets See **bean curd skin**

bean curd skin The skin which forms on the surface of hot soya bean milk if allowed to stand. It is lifted off and dried. When softened it is used for wrapping food prior to cooking. Also called **bean curd sheets**

bean curd sticks Bean curd skins rolled into stick-like quills before drying. After softening they are cut in pieces and used in cooked dishes as is or after deep-frying. Also called **rolled bean curd**, **second bamboo**

bean paste A variety of seasonings made from yellow or black dried soya beans, softened, fermented with an added culture, salted and dried or mixed with brine. Sometimes other grains or pulses are added. They keep well, are strongly flavoured and are used in Japanese, Chinese and Southeast Asian cuisines. The important ones are yellow bean sauce, black bean sauce, chilli bean paste, **Hoisin sauce**, hot black bean sauce, **Dhwenjang**, soya bean paste, sweet bean paste and **miso**.

bean sauce A bean paste let down with brine or oil to give a softer consistency

bean sprouts The young shoots of the mung bean, *Phaseolus aureus*, or adzuki bean, used as a vegetable in Chinese and Japanese cooking. Other seeds that may be sprouted include soya beans, lentils, wheat, rye, mustard seed and cress. Also called **green gram**, **moyashi**, **tu ya ts'ai**

bean thread noodles Cellophane noodles

bean threads *United States* Cellophane noodles

bear 1. A large omnivorous animal of the *Ursidae* family. Black bears and polar bears are confined to the Northern Hemisphere and brown bears are found worldwide. The meat, which tastes like strong-flavoured beef, is very rare as the species is becoming endangered. 2. See **bere**

bearberry The red fruit of a plant from northern moors, *Arctostaphylos uva-ursi*, similar to the cranberry and picked from the wild

beard The gills of an oyster or the fibrous threads by which mussels attach themselves to rocks

beard, to To remove the frilly gill parts or beards of certain shellfish such as oysters and the threads from mussels which attach them to the rocks

bear grass *United States* See **yucca 2**

béarnaise sauce *England, France* A hollandaise sauce, but with chopped tarragon stalks in the initial reduction and finished after straining with chopped tarragon and chervil. More egg yolks are used than for hollandaise to give a thicker sauce. Served warm with grilled meat and fish.

béarnaise tomatée, sauce *France* Choron, sauce

bearnässås *Sweden* See **béarnaise sauce**

bearss lime Persian lime

beastlyns Beestings

beat, to To incorporate air into a mixture and to intimately combine the ingredients by vigorous agitation with a spoon, whisk, fork or mechanical or electric mixer

beater A general term for any implement used for beating

Beaufort *France* A hard cooked-curd cows' milk cheese from Haute Savoie with AOC status. It is ripened for 3 months and has a firm springy paste with a thin rind. It is similar to Gruyère but with a higher fat content and fruitier aroma. Also called **Gruyère de Beaufort**

Beaumont *France* A semi-hard cheese made with cows' milk in the Haute Savoie using the same techniques as Toma. It has a springy texture without holes and is cast in 20-cm-diameter thin rounds.

bebek *Indonesia* Duck

becada amb cóc *Catalonia* Cooked woodcock in a bread roll

becado *Spain* Woodcock

bécasse *France* Woodcock

becasseau *France* Young woodcock

bécassine *France* Snipe

beccaccia *Italy* Woodcock

beccaccia alla norcina *Italy* Woodcock stuffed with a mixture of its entrails, herbs and truffle

beccacino *Italy* Snipe

beccafico *Italy* Game bird

beccute *Italy* Maize flour cakes containing pine nuts and sultanas

béchamel, sauce *England, France* A basic white sauce made from a white roux and seasoned milk flavoured with an onion clouté using 100g of flour per litre. The onion is removed and the sauce strained after simmering for at least 30 minutes. A very important base and often referred to simply as béchamel.

bêche-de-mer *France* Sea cucumber (NOTE: Literally 'spade of the sea'.)

beckasin *Sweden* Snipe

bécsi heringsaláta *Hungary* Herring salad with vinegar

Beda *Egypt* A soft scalded-curd cheese made from buffalos' or cows' milk. The unbroken salted curd is drained in cheese cloth and may be eaten fresh or ripened for up to 3 months. Contains 53% water, 21% fat and 19% protein. Also called **domiati**

bedeu *France* The Provençal name for **tripe**

bee balm Bergamot

beechmast Beech nut

beech nut A small nut from the beech tree, genus *Fagus* and *Nothofagus*, similar in flavour to a hazelnut but not commonly used. A flavoursome oil can be extracted from them. Also called **beechmast**

beechwheat Buckwheat

beef The meat of the animal known as a cow (female) or bull (male) (NOTE: The Anglo-saxon name 'Ox' is still used for some of what were once the less desirable parts e.g. oxtail, ox liver)

beef bourguignonne See **boeuf à la bourguignonne**

beefburger A mixture of lean minced beef, chopped onions and seasoning formed into a thin patty. Usually grilled and served as fast food on a soft white bread bun with a variety of garnishes. Also called **hamburger**

beef cervelat *England* A variety of smoked red-dyed sausages made with lean beef, possibly bullock heart, fat pork, seasoning and a little saltpetre, sometimes with ground spices. The mixture is left to cure then sometimes packed in beef middles, tied and smoked for 12 hours at 50°C, or, dried for eight days and cool-smoked for 6 days.

beef cotto *United States* A low-fat coarse cut beef salami containing whole peppercorns

beef dripping The fat collected after roasting beef or rendered from beef suet. A less flavoursome variety is made by boiling up beef scraps and separating off the fat which collects on the surface.

beef grading *United States* The standard government-recognized grades are prime, choice, good, standard and commercial. Prime is rarely available in retail markets.

beef hare *England* Strips of chuck steak passed through seasoned flour flavoured with nutmeg, packed in an ovenproof dish

with celery seeds, topped with onion and parsnip, moistened with red wine, stood for 2 hours and baked with a tight fitting lid at 170°C until tender

beef herbs The principal herbs used with beef are basil, bay, caraway, chervil, lovage, marjoram, mint, oregano, parsley, peppermint, rosemary, sage, savory, tarragon and thyme

beef middles Beef casings for salami, **Knackwurst**, cervelat and similar sausages about 4.5 to 5.5 cm diameter taken from the middle of the beef intestine

beef olive A thin slice of topside of beef rolled around a savoury stuffing, tied and braised in the oven

beef runners Beef casings for black puddings, Bolognese sausage, etc. about 3.5 to 4.5 cm in diameter, made from the first part of the beef intestine

beef sausage *Scotland* A sausage of lean beef, bullock heart, suet, chopped onions and seasoning chopped very fine (cheaper varieties adulterated with bread and meal) packed into pig casings and possibly smoked

beefsteak *United States* Steak, as in beefsteak and kidney pie

beefsteak fungus *United Kingdom* A bright red edible fungus, *Fistulina hepatica*, shaped rather like a thick tongue which grows on trees. Treat as mushroom. Also called **poor man's beefsteak**

beefsteak plant Shiso

beefsteak tagalog *Philippines* Trimmed rump steaks marinated with sliced onion, soya sauce, lime juice and pepper for 2 hours, removed, dried, fried in oil with sliced onion and bacon and served with a sauce made from the deglazed pan juices and the marinade accompanied by garlic-flavoured rice

beef Stroganoff Strips of fillet steak or other tender cut of beef, shallow-fried in butter and mixed with sweated chopped shallots, reduced white wine, cream, lemon juice and seasoning, possibly finished with soured cream

beef suet The hard granular fat interspersed with membranes from around the kidneys of cattle

beef tataki *Australia* Fillet steak or similar served tataki-style, i.e. seared briefly on all sides under a hot grill then thinly sliced and presented to show the brown exterior and pink interior

beef tea A clear consommé of beef

beef tenderloin *United States* Fillet of beef

beef tomato A very large fleshy tomato up to 10 cm in diameter often stuffed as an individual dish

beef Wellington A part-roasted fillet of beef spread with **duxelles** and liver pâté, wrapped in puff pastry, egg-washed and baked in the oven. The meat and pastry should finish cooking simultaneously. Served sliced.

Beenleigh blue *England* A ewes' milk cheese made in Devon similar to Roquefort

beer Fermented malt extract flavoured with hops, sometimes used as a cooking liquor

beer sausage Bierwurst

bees sting Bienenstich

beesting pudding Colostrum from the cow and sugar baked slowly in the oven

beestings The first milk (**colostrum**) from the cow after giving birth. It is very rich and creamy and is used for puddings and sweets. (NOTE: Also frozen to preserve it for use as a restorative for newly born lambs.)

beestings curd A curd made by mixing cows' **colostrum** with fresh milk and water, heating to 37°C, cooking and straining

beeswax The wax excreted by bees to construct honeycomb. Used as a glazing agent in sugar and chocolate confectionery. See also **E901**

beet 1. The generic name for members of the *Beta* family including beetroot, Swiss chard, spinach beet and sugar beet, which latter is the main source of sugar in Europe **2.** *United States* Beetroot

Beetensuppe *Germany* Borscht

beetroot A biennial plant, *Beta vulgaris vulgaris*, grown as an annual for the swollen root which grows at ground level. Most are deep red but there are pink and yellow varieties. The roots contain a high proportion of sugar and as the red colour easily leaches out they are boiled in their skins as a vegetable. They are also used for soup (**borscht**) and pickled in vinegar. The young leaves may be used as a vegetable.

beetroot consommé Grated beetroot, onion and carrot simmered with a bay leaf and chicken stock for 40 minutes, strained, simmered with egg white for 15 minutes to clarify, strained and finished with lemon juice and sour cream

beetroot red E162, a red food colouring extracted from beetroot. Also called **betanin**

beetroot soup Shredded beetroot and onion sweated in butter, flour added and cooked out, stock added, simmered and skimmed for 30 minutes, seasoned, consistency adjusted and finished with lemon juice and cream or sour cream

beet sugar Sugar produced from sugar beet. Chemically it is identical to cane sugar (both contain sucrose).

beetwortel *Netherlands* Beetroot

bef stroganov *Russia* Beef Stroganoff traditionally made with sliced onions sweated for at least 30 minutes with sliced mushrooms added towards the end, combined in the pan with sautéed strips of fillet steak, English mustard, sugar and sour cream, all warmed through and served with straw potatoes and chopped parsley

begendi *Turkey* A smooth paste made from a mixture of thick **béchamel sauce** and a purée of cooked aubergine flesh. Used as a starter.

begiessen *Germany* **1.** To baste **2.** To sprinkle with liquid

beg wat *East Africa* As **doro wat**, but made with red meat

beh *Central Asia* The Iranian name for **quince**

beid hamine *Middle East* Hard-boiled eggs, the shells coloured with onion skins or ground coffee. They are simmered for 5 to 6 hours in water with the colourant and are served as an appetizer with salt and ground cumin.

beid mahshi *Middle East* Hard-boiled eggs, halved lengthways; yolks mashed with finely chopped onion and parsley, olive oil, cinnamon and seasoning, made into balls and replaced in the egg whites; filled whites laid on lettuce leaves, sprinkled with paprika or chilli powder, dressed with vinaigrette or yoghurt sauce and garnished with chopped parsley

beigel Bagel

beignet *France* **1.** Fritter, a food item coated in batter and deep-fried. Also called **French fritter 2.** A ball of yeast-raised sweetened dough or flavoured choux pastry, deep-fried and served hot with a dusting of sugar and possibly jam or fruit sauce. Rather like a doughnut. Also called **French puff**

beignet de fleurs *France* Flower fritters, e.g. of acacia

beignet soufflé *France* A light deep-fried sweet fritter. See also **pet de nonne**

Beijing cabbage Chinese leaves

Beijing duck Peking duck

beijing kao ya *China* Peking duck

Beijing pear Asian pear

Beilagen *Germany* Accompaniments to a meal

Bein *Germany* Leg; of an animal, etc.

Beinfleisch *Austria* Boiled beef

Beja *Portugal* A ewes' milk cheese from the Alentajo weighing about 2 kg. It can be eaten fresh or after ripening into a semi-hard cheese for from 1 to 2 years.

bejel *Spain* Tub gurnard

Bekassine *Germany* Snipe

bekon *Japan, Russia* Bacon

bekutak *Indonesia* Cuttlefish

bel *Nepal* Wood apple

beladi *Middle East* The common orange

belan *South Asia* Rolling pin

belangah *Malaysia* A terracotta cooking pot similar to an Indian chatty. Also called **blangah**

belarno *Italy* A hard, rich cheese

belegte Brote *Germany* Open sandwiches on rye bread

Belfast ham *Ireland, Scotland* A dry-salted ham smoked over peat. Also found on the West coast of Scotland.

Belfermière *Luxembourg* A semi-hard cows' milk cheese cast in squat cylinders *(1.8 kg)*. Similar to **Port-Salut**.

Belgian chicory A perennial dandelion-like plant, *Cichorium intybus*, with bitter green leaves. The conical roots are trimmed and have the leaves cut off 2 cm above the crown and are then forced to produce white, yellow-tipped, compact, leafy shoots up to 15 cm long by 5 cm diameter, known as chicons, which are in season from January to March. They can be cooked as a vegetable or eaten raw in salads. The roots have been used as a coffee substitute and when young can be boiled as a root vegetable. The flowers and seedlings of the unforced plant can be used in salads. Also called **Witloof chicory**, **succory**, **Belgian endive**, **endive**

Belgium endive *United States* Belgian chicory

beliashi *Russia* A shallow-fried pastry made with a wheat-flour unleavened dough containing a variety of fillings

belimbing *Malaysia* The fruit of a relative of the carambola, *Averrhoa bilimbi*, about 8 cm long, light green and acidic. Used for souring food. Also called **sour finger carambola**, **cucumber tree fruit**

belimbing manis *Indonesia* Carambola

belimbing wuluh *Indonesia* Belimbing, the fruit

belinjo *Indonesia* A small red fruit. See also **melinjo**

belle dijonnaise, à la *France* With blackcurrants

Belle-Hélène *France* Served with ice cream and chocolate sauce, as in pear Belle-Hélène

Bellelay *France* An alpine semi-hard unpasteurized cows' milk cheese. See also **Tête de Moine**

belle meunière, fish Fish meunière dressed with one grilled mushroom, one slice of peeled tomato and one floured and shallow-fried soft herring roe

bellevue, à la *France* Coated in transparent aspic jelly (NOTE: Literally 'in full view'.)

Bellos *Spain* A hard cheese made from ewes' and/or goats' milk with a strong pungent close-textured paste and a dry rind. Usually cast in smallish cylinders (700 g). Contains 27% water, 36% fat and 27% protein. Also called **Queso de Los Bellos**, **Bellusco**

bell pepper *United States* Sweet pepper

Bellusco *Spain* Bellos

belly fat Soft fat from the belly of a pig with specific uses in sausage, pâté and pastry making

belly of pork See **pork belly**

belly pork See **pork belly**

belon *France* A particular size of oyster from Brittany

Bel Paese *Italy* A rich, mild, quick-ripened creamy cheese made on an industrial scale since 1906 from whole cows' milk, weighing about 2.5 kg and coated with a yellow wax rind (NOTE: Literally 'beautiful country'.)

beluga caviar *Russia* The light grey caviar from the roe of the female beluga, the largest of the sturgeon family. Usually served as a hors d'oeuvre.

beluga sturgeon One of the largest fish, *Acipenser huso or Huso huso*, in the sturgeon family from the Black Sea, the Caspian Sea and the rivers that flow into them. It can live up to 100 years and weigh up to 1600 kg, but is normally caught much younger and produces up to 20 kg of caviar of the same name. (NOTE: Should not be confused with the beluga whale.)

beluge *Iran* Beluga caviar

Belval *France* A firm mild cheese from Picardy with a shiny rind

belyashi *Russia* A deep-fried meat pasty

bem passado *Portugal* Well done. Used e.g. of meat.

benachin *West Africa* A one-pot meal in which ingredients are added in order of cooking time but usually starting with onions and garlic fried in oil followed by water or stock then the ingredients which usually include meat or fish, vegetables, tomato paste, seasonings but always rice. Occasionally the rice is steamed in a colander rested over the simmering liquid in the pot and when cooked stirred into the stew.

Benalty pie *Scotland* Teviotdale pie

ben cotta *Italy* Well done. Used of steaks.

benfri gädda *Sweden* Boneless pike. A whole pike, head on, cleaned but not scaled, boiled in salted water then allowed to cool before gently easing the flesh from the skin and bones. The flesh is ideal for filling vol-au-vents when combined with a béchamel and/or velouté sauce. Often served with an egg or horseradish sauce.

Bengal gram *South Asia* A small variety of chick pea. See also **channa 1**

Bengal rice A small-grain white rice with a fine flavour from Bengal in the east of India

Benicasa hispida *Botanical name* Fuzzy melon

benishoga *Japan* Red-coloured wafer-thin slices of pickled ginger rhizome used as an accompaniment to Japanese dishes especially sushi. Also called **gari**, **amazushoga**

benløse fugler *Norway* Beef olives (**paupiettes**) stuffed with pork and onion and served with a spiced gravy

benne seed Sesame seed

benniseed *West Africa* Sesame seed

benoil tree Drumstick pod

benoiton, à la *France* Fish served with a reduced red wine sauce flavoured with shallots

bento *Japan* Different cold foods served in a **bento bako** at lunchtime. Also called **obento**

bento bako *Japan* The partitioned lacquered lunch box used by Japanese office workers to hold their midday meal

bento box See **bento bako**

bentonite See **E558**

bento no tomo *Japan* A trade name for a seasoning made from a mixture of dried fish, salt, soya sauce, seaweed and monosodium glutamate, pounded or processed to a paste

ben tree Drumstick pod

benzoates Salts of benzoic acid used as food preservatives. Those used in the food industry are, sodium E211, potassium E212 and calcium benzoate E213.

benzoic acid A naturally occurring acid found in most berries and in large concentrations in gum benzoin, now made synthetically for use as the food preservative E210

berawecka *France* A spiced bread roll from Alsace, containing dried vine fruits and flavoured with kirsch. Also called **bireweck**

berbere A ground spice mix from Ethiopia, used in stews and in panés. Made from dry-fried deseeded red chillies, coriander seeds, cloves, green cardamom, ajowan, allspice, black peppercorns, fenugreek seeds, cinnamon and dry ginger.

berberecho *Spain* Cockle

berberetxo *Catalonia* Cockle

Berberis vulgaris *Botanical name* Barberry

berbigão *Portugal* **1.** Cockle **2.** Mussel

Bercy *France* With sauce Bercy or beurre Bercy

Bercy, fish White fish, shallow-poached in fish stock, white wine, lemon juice with chopped parsley and sweated chopped shallots. The cooking liquor is strained, mixed with fish velouté, and seasoned, its consistency is adjusted, then it is finished with butter, lightly whipped cream and a **sabayon**. The reserved and dried fish is coated with this sauce, glazed under the grill and garnished with chopped parsley. (NOTE: A popular example is filets de sole bercy.)

Bercy, sauce *England, France* Chopped shallots sweated in butter, white wine and fish stock added and reduced, fish velouté added, seasoning and consistency adjusted and the sauce finished with butter and chopped parsley

Bercy butter See **beurre Bercy**

bere A type of primitive barley first recorded in 4000 BC, still grown in the Orkneys and said to be an acquired taste. Also called **bear**

bere bannock *Scotland* A brown round scone-like cake made in the Orkneys with the flour ground from bere

berenjena *Spain* Aubergine

Beresford pudding *England* A steamed pudding made from a Victoria sponge mixture flavoured with grated orange zest

berffro cakes *Wales* Flour, butter and sugar (4:2:1) made into a stiff biscuit mixture by rubbing in or melting and the dough rolled out and cut into rounds. Each round is marked with the impression of a scallop shell, the emblem of the pilgrims to the shrine of St James, and baked at 170°C until coloured. Also called **James' cakes**, **cacennau lago** (NOTE: *Berffro* is a shortened form of *Aberffraw* in Anglesey, where the cakes come from)

Berg *Germany* A hard, pale yellow mountain cheese made from full-fat cows' milk resembling Emmental but cast in smaller rounds. Also called **alp cheese**, **Alpenkäse**, **Alpine cheese**, **mountain cheese**

Bergader *Germany* A soft blue-green veined cows' milk cheese with a cracked but smooth strong-flavoured paste and a wrinkled light brown rind

bergamot 1. A citrus hybrid, probably of Seville orange and sweet lime, *Citrus bergamia*, used only for its highly perfumed rind oil which amongst other uses is sprayed on tea to produce Earl Grey **2.** A perennial lemon-scented herb, *Monarda didyma*, used in salads, summer drinks and with pork. Also called **bee balm**

Bergen bread Bread enriched with plant oestrogens obtained from linseed and soya oil. Said to reduce menopausal symptoms.

bergère, à la *France* In the shepherdess' style, i.e. garnished with fried sliced mushrooms and straw potatoes

Bergkäse A generic name for many different types of cooked-curd, pressed semi-hard cows' milk cheeses from the Alps such as Berg, Gruyère, Fontina, Montasio, Walliser and the like. Also called **mountain cheese**

Bergues *France* A soft cows' milk cheese similar to **Saint-Paulin** made near Dunkirk. It has a dense supple paste with a thin washed rind covered in blue-black mould and is cast in thin rounds (2 kg).

berinjela *Portugal* Aubergine

berkoush *North Africa* Moroccan rice pudding made with milk

Berkswell lemon chicken *England* A young chicken, jointed and browned in a seasoned mixture of lemon juice and molten butter, put in a covered dish with chicken stock and baked at 160°C or simmered for an hour. The chicken is reserved and served with a sauce made from the thickened cooking liquor and extra chicken stock.

Berliner *Germany* A jam filled doughnut from Berlin (NOTE: Made unintentionally famous by President Kennedy who, when visiting Berlin and speaking near the Berlin Wall, said 'Ich bin ein Berliner' He should have said 'Ich bin Berliner' or 'Ich komme aus Berlin'.)

Berliner Hühnerfrikasse *Germany* Diced chicken flesh, diced calf's tongue, sweetbreads, prawns, sliced asparagus and diced mushrooms (8:2:2:2:2:1), all previously cooked, mixed with a chicken velouté with added egg yolks (2 per litre) and lemon juice, heated to boiling and served. The velouté is normally made with the chicken cooking liquor.

Berliner Luft *Germany* A light mousse of egg yolks, creamed with sugar and lemon juice, flavoured with lemon zest, mixed with softened gelatine leaves and strained; stiffly beaten egg whites folded in; all placed in a mould to set, demoulded and served with a border of raspberry syrup

Berliner Pfannküchen *Germany* A thick puffy pancake with jam

Berliner Riesenbratwurst *Germany* A very large **Bratwurst**

Berliner Rotwurst *Germany* A type of black pudding made with pig's blood, coarsely chopped meat and diced bacon with salt and black pepper, coloured dark red

Berliner Torte *Germany* Short pastry flavoured with cinnamon and lemon zest, mixed with finely chopped hazelnuts and baked in 4 circles which are filled when cool with 3 layers of redcurrant jelly and covered with vanilla-flavoured fondant

berlingozzo *Italy* Cream cake

Bermuda onion *United States* Spanish onion

bernard-l'ermite *France* Hermit crab

bernard-l'hermite *France* Hermit crab

Berner Platte *Switzerland* A dish of smoked pork ribs, beef, tongue or sausage, lean bacon, ham, salted tongue and roasted marrow bone arranged on a bed of sauerkraut or beans

berrichonne, à la *France* Garnished with cabbage, bacon, onions and chestnuts for large joints of meat

berro *Spain* Watercress

berry A small fruit with pulpy flesh enclosing one or more seeds or an assembly of small sacs of juice each enclosing one seed within it or on its surface

berry sugar *United States* Sugar finer than granulated similar to caster sugar

Bertholletia excelsa *Botanical name* Brazil nut tree

bertorella *Spain* Three-bearded rockling, the fish

berza *Spain* A pork stew made with chopped aromatic vegetables and garlic browned in olive oil, 5cm cubes of floured and browned pork, soaked haricot beans and chick peas; stock added and all simmered until almost cooked; French beans and sliced roasted sweet red peppers added and cooked 15 minutes; finally sliced black pudding and seasoning added for a further 10 minutes of cooking

berza marina *Spain* Sea kale

besan *South Asia* Ground chick pea flour, more aromatic and less starchy than wheat flour, excellent for batter and for coating fish. Used extensively in Indian cookery. Also called **besan flour**, **gram flour**, **bessan**

besan flour See **besan**

beschuit *Netherlands* A well toasted dry rusk

beschuittaart *Netherlands* A cake made with rusks

besciamella *Italy* See **béchamel, sauce**

beskidzka *Poland* A very common hard sausage made from pork and beef

bessan See **besan**

bessara *North Africa* A Moroccan dip made from cooked broad beans and red sweet peppers, ground cumin seeds, oil and lemon juice, all processed to a smooth paste

best-before date Date mark used on packaged food which has a shelf life of 6 weeks to 3 months after packing (NOTE: Under UK regulations this date can be changed by the manufacturer after the first date has expired. Such relabelled foods tend to enter the market and discount shop trade.)

best-before-end date Date mark giving only the month and year. Used on packaged food which will stay in good condition for longer than 3 months (usually not more than 18 months). (NOTE: Under UK regulations this date can be changed by the manufacturer after the first date has expired. Such relabelled foods tend to enter the market and discount shop trade.)

best end of lamb The vertebrae and first six rib bones counting from the rear of the lamb, cut down the centre of the back bone. The ribs are shortened to about 10 cm. Usually skinned and chined and the ends of the ribs scraped before cooking.

best end of veal *United Kingdom* The ribs of the animal extending about half way down its side from the backbone and from the loin to the shoulder. Corresponds to the best end of lamb. Usually roasted, fried or grilled.

besugo *Spain* See **bream 1**

beta-apo-8'-carotenal (C30) An orange carotene compound extracted from fruit and vegetables used as a food colouring. See also **E160(e)** (NOTE: The more fat soluble ethyl ester, E160(f), is also available.)

betacyanin One of the red colours in beetroot, less susceptible to colour change than **anthocyanin**

beta-jio *Japan* A method of salting food by sprinkling it with salt for an hour then rinsing off the salt. This leaves the surface layer lightly salted. Used for fatty fish.

betanin See **beetroot red**

betasuppe *Norway* Mutton broth

***Beta vulgaris* Cicla group** *Botanical name* Swiss chard, spinach beet

Beta vulgaris maritima *Botanical name* Sea beet

Beta vulgaris vulgaris *Botanical name* Beetroot

betel leaf The leaf of the betel pepper, *Piper betle*, used in Indian cooking and as a wrapping for **pan**

betel nut The hard nut of a palm tree, *Areca catechu*, with stimulating properties, ground and mixed with lime and other spices and wrapped in a betel leaf to make pan. The green unripe nuts are known as chikni and

are shelled and boiled before drying. The orange to scarlet ripe nuts are known as chali and are dried in the husk and shelled. Also called **areca nut**

beterraba *Portugal* Beetroot

Bethmale *France* A hard cows' milk cheese from Touraine with a spicy flavour

Bethmännchen *Germany* A marzipan biscuit from Frankfurt

bette *France* **1.** Chinese cabbage or Chinese leaves **2.** Swiss chard

betterave rouge *France* Beetroot

beurre *France* Butter

beurre, au *France* Cooked in or served with butter

beurre, sauce au *France* Bâtarde, sauce

beurre à la meunière Nut-brown butter. See also **beurre noisette**

beurre à la polonaise *France* Butter cooked until nut brown, one quarter its weight of very fine fresh white breadcrumbs added and cooked until golden brown

beurre Bercy *France* White wine reduced by one half with chopped shallots, cooled, mixed with softened butter, diced, poached and drained bone marrow, chopped parsley, seasoning and lemon juice. Used as a garnish with steaks and chops.

beurre blanc *France* Reduced white wine and vinegar flavoured with shallots, strained, sufficient cold butter beaten in in stages over a low heat until the sauce is of coating consistency. Served warm with fish and vegetables.

beurre Chivry *France* Ravigote butter

beurre Colbert *France* **Beurre maître d'hôtel** mixed with melted meat glaze and chopped tarragon

beurre composé *France* Compound butter

beurre d'ail *France* A compound butter made from equal quantities of blanched peeled cloves of garlic and butter, processed and passed through a sieve

beurre d'amandes *France* Almond butter

beurre d'anchois *France* Anchovy butter

beurre d'aveline *France* Hazelnut butter

beurre de caviar Caviar butter

beurre d'échalotes *France* A compound butter made of equal quantities of chopped shallots and butter, the shallots blanched, refreshed and squeezed dry through a cloth, then all pounded together and sieved

beurre de crevettes *France* A compound butter made from equal quantities of cooked shrimps and butter, pounded together and sieved. Alternatively it can be made by pounding together butter and shrimp remains, shells, etc. and sieving.

beurre d'écrevisses *France* A compound butter made from the remains of crayfish cooked for some other purpose, pounded with an equal quantity of butter and sieved

beurre de hareng *France* Herring butter

beurre de laitance *France* A compound butter made with poached soft roes pounded with twice their weight in butter, flavoured with mustard and sieved

beurre de Montpellier *France* A mixture of blanched, refreshed and drained watercress, parsley, chervil, tarragon, chives and spinach leaves with blanched chopped shallots, gherkins, capers, garlic and anchovy fillets processed to a fine paste, mixed with three times its weight of butter, raw and hard-boiled egg yolks mixed in and one fifth the combined weight of olive oil whisked in, seasoned and finished with a little cayenne pepper. Used to coat fish for cold buffets.

beurre de moutarde *France* Mustard butter

beurre de noisettes *France* Hazelnut butter

beurre de paprika A compound butter made from softened butter mixed with chopped onions, which have been sweated in butter, and paprika powder, and all sieved

beurre de piments *France* A compound butter made from braised sweet red pepper pounded with twice its weight in butter and sieved

beurre de Provence *France* An emulsion sauce made with bread soaked in milk and crushed garlic. See also **allioli**

beurre de raifort *France* Horseradish butter

beurre de saumon fumé *France* Smoked salmon butter

beurre d'estragon *France* Tarragon butter

beurre de truffes *France* Truffle butter

beurre fondu *France* Butter and a small amount of water or wine, boiled until combined then strained through double muslin or a tammy cloth. Served hot with boiled fish and some vegetables. Also called **melted butter sauce**

beurre (à la) maître d'hôtel *France* A compound butter made with lemon juice, seasoning and finely chopped parsley. Formed into rolls, refrigerated and cut into 0.5-cm thick slices. Served with grilled meat and grilled or fried fish.

beurre manié *France* A well-kneaded mixture of equal quantities of flour and butter, small quantities of which are used to progressively thicken liquids and sauces

beurre marchand de vins *France* Red wine reduced with chopped shallots, seasoned, then mixed with a little melted meat glaze and softened butter equal in weight to the original wine, lemon juice and chopped parsley. Used with grilled sirloin steaks.

beurre monté *France* Monter au beurre

beurre noir *France* Butter browned in the frying pan, passed through a fine strainer and mixed when lukewarm with a reduction of vinegar and coarsely ground pepper. This may be kept molten until used when fried chopped parsley and chopped capers are sprinkled over the food to be coated with the butter.

beurre noisette *France* Nut-brown butter prepared by melting butter over heat and adding lemon juice after it has melted and foamed and just before it burns, used with **fish meunière**. Also called **beurre à la meunière**

beurre printanier *France* A compound butter made from vegetables appropriate to the dish being garnished, cooked, pounded with an equal weight of butter and sieved

beurre ravigote *France* Ravigote butter

beurre vert *France* Ravigote butter

Beuschel *Austria, Germany* Stewed calves' lungs with vinegar and sugar. Served with dumplings.

Beutelmelone *Germany* Melon

beyainatu *East Africa* A small portion of every dish on the menu (NOTE: Literally 'of every type'.)

beyaz peynir *Turkey* A soft white freshly eaten cheese made from ewes' milk, possibly mixed with goats' milk. It may be ripened in brine.

bézuque *France* Bar, the fish

BG See **bouquet garni**

BHA E320, butylated hydroxyanisole, a controversial antioxidant allowed only for use in fats, oils and essential oils

bhaatmas *Nepal* Soya beans

bhagoni *South Asia* A tinned brass cooking pot. See also **degchi**

bhaji 1. See **amaranth 1 2.** See **bhajia**

bhajia An Indian vegetable fritter, usually onion, served as a starter or as an accompaniment to a meal. See also **pakora**. Also called **bhaji**

bharta *South Asia* Cooked and puréed, especially vegetables

bharti *South Asia* Barnyard millet

bhat *Nepal* Rice

bhatoora, bhatura *South Asia* A deep-fried chapati. See also **puri**

bhedaa *Nepal* Lamb, sheep

bhel puri *South Asia* Puffed rice and peanuts mixed with cooked and dried lentils, chopped onion and coriander leaves. Served with a spicy sauce as a snack.

bhindi *South Asia* Okra

bhogar *South Asia* The process of basting meat in a casserole, either by shaking with a sideways and downward motion to cover the meat with the cooking juices, or by adding the cooking liquor to aromatized ghee in a separate pan, reducing it to the right consistency then adding it back to the meat

bhojia *South Asia* Spiced stir-fried vegetables

bhoona 1. Indian frying which covers sautéing (**sukha bhoona**), pot roasting (**dummed bhoona**) and a type of braising in ghee in a closed container (**ard bhoona**) **2.** another spelling of **bhuna 2**

bhoona pursindah *South Asia* Flattened deboned lamb or pork chops, marinaded in a mixture of yoghurt, minced chillies and sweet pepper, black pepper and ground cloves for 6 hours, then fried in butter which has been aromatized with cinnamon and sweet nim leaves, until cooked and dry

bhorji *South Asia* Scrambled. Used of eggs.

BHT Butylated hydroxytoluene, a controversial antioxidant allowed only for use in fats, oils and essential oils. See also **E321**

bhuna 1. another spelling of **bhoona 1 2.** A dry curry dish made with fried meat

bhuni khichhari *South Asia* A dry version of **khichhari**

bianchetti *Italy* Very tiny fish fry, so small that they are transparent. Generally mixed with egg and made into an omelette or used in soup. Also called **gianchetti**

bianco, in *Italy* Served with oil, melted butter and lemon juice. Used usually of fish.

bianco di Spagna *Italy* A large tender and commonly used white bean

bianco d'uovo *Italy* White of egg

bian dou *China* Beans

biarrotte, à la *France* In the Biarritz style, i.e. garnished with ceps and potato cakes

bias cut An oblique cut or one at an angle to the grain of the food

bibb lettuce *United States* A variety of butterhead lettuce considered to be one of the finest

biber *Turkey* Sweet peppers

biber dolmasi *Turkey* Sweet peppers stuffed with a mixture of chopped onions, raisins, pine nuts, cooked rice, herbs and seasoning, baked in the oven and served cold

bibliothèque internationale de gastronomie International Library of Gastronomy

bicarbonate of potash See **E501**

bicarbonate of soda Sodium bicarbonate, a mild alkali which gives off carbon dioxide when heated or mixed with acid. It is one of the ingredients of baking powder and also used as a mild cleansing agent. Also called **sodium bicarbonate, baking soda**. See also **E500**

bicchiere *Italy* A glass or tumbler, also a measuring cup

biefstuk *Netherlands* A cut of beef equivalent to sirloin or round steak (USA)

biefstuk van de haas *Netherlands* Filet mignon of beef

bien cuit *France* Well done; in the case of meat, all pinkness gone

Bienenstich *Austria, Germany* A yeasted pastry with an almond topping similar to an almond slice. Also called **bee sting**

bien padado *Spain* Well done. Used of meat, steak, etc.

Bier *Germany* Beer

bière *France* Beer

Bierkaltschale *Germany* Cold beer soup

Bierkäse *Germany* A rectangular-shaped sharp-tasting semi-hard cows' milk cheese. See also **Weisslacker**

Bierplinsen *Germany* Cooked meat or sausages, coated in frying batter made with beer and deep-fried

Bierschinken *Germany* A **Brühwurst** made with 2 parts lean shoulder pork, 1 part belly pork, minced very fine with seasoning, spices and containing chunks of cooked ham fat and sometimes pistachio nuts. Usually eaten cold.

Biersuppe *Germany* Lager, boiled and thickened with a brown roux, flavoured with cinnamon stick, cardamom seeds and lemon zest plus salt and sugar, strained and served with croûtons

Bierwurst *Germany* A coarse-textured dried slicing sausage made from spiced pork or pork and beef, and garlic. Also called **beer sausage** (NOTE: Once made from ham marinated in beer; hence the name.)

Biestmilch *Germany* Beestings

biet *Netherlands* Beetroot

biete *Italy* Swiss chard

bietola *Italy* **1.** Swiss chard **2.** Spinach beet

bietola da coste *Italy* Spinach beet

bietoline *Italy* A leaf vegetable. See also **erbette**

bife *Portugal* Steak of beef, pork, lamb, fish, etc.

biff *Norway, Sweden* Beef

biff à la Lindstrom *Sweden* Raw minced fillet steak mixed with diced cold boiled potatoes, double cream, diced pickled beetroot, grated onion, capers, egg yolk and seasoning, formed into egg-sized balls and shallow-fried so as to remain pink in the middle. Served hot with fried onions.

biff med lök *Sweden* Fried rump steak served with fried onions and boiled potatoes

biffstek *Sweden* Beef steak

Bifidobacterium A bacterium used for the fermentation of milk

Bifidobacterium plantarum One of the microorganisms used as starter culture for fermented milk products especially in Japan

bifschteks *Russia* Beef steak

bifteck *France* General name for steak suitable for frying or grilling

bifteck américaine *Belgium* Chopped raw beef with mayonnaise, seasoning and spices

bifteck Bercy au père François *France* Beef steak with a sauce based on red wine, shallots and parsley

bifteck haché *France* 1. Minced beef 2. Hamburger or beefburger

bifteck tartare *France* Steak tartare

biftek *Spain* Beef steak. Also called **bistec**

bifuteki *Japan* Beef steak

biga *Italy* A starter for bread made from plain flour, water and fresh yeast (32:12:1) mixed to a slack dough and left to work for at least 12 hours

bigarade *France* Seville orange

bigarade, à la *France* Served with orange or an orange-based sauce using Seville oranges if available

bigarade, sauce *France* Sauce made from the cooking liquor or deglazed pan residues of duck with Seville orange, if available, and lemon juice and finished with a **julienne** of blanched lemon and orange zest. Also called **orange sauce**

bigarro *Spain* Winkle

bigatan *Philippines* Ridged sand clam

bigoli *Italy* Thick home-made spaghetti from Venice

bigorneau *France* A small gastropod mollusc, *Nassa mutabilis*, similar in shape to a winkle and treated in the same way. Very common in Brittany.

bigos *Poland* A typical winter stew made from cabbage, sauerkraut, chopped pork, gammon, smoked sausage, dried mushrooms, onions, lard, tomato purée, garlic, paprika and seasoning, cooked in advance and reheated. Sometimes prunes, plum tomatoes and red wine are added.

bigoudine, à la *France* In the Bigouden style, i.e. with baked slices of scrubbed potatoes with the skin left on (NOTE: Bigouden is a village in Pont d'Abbé, Brittany.)

bihun *Indonesia, Malaysia* Rice vermicelli

bijan *Malaysia* Sesame seed

bijane *France* A cold soup made from sweetened red wine thickened with fresh breadcrumbs

bijeni sir *Balkans, Greece* A soft cooked-curd cheese with holes from the Former Yugoslav Republic of Macedonia. It is made from ewes' or a mixture of ewes' and cows' milk.

biji sawi *Malaysia* Black mustard seed

bikini *Catalonia* A toasted cheese and ham sandwich, similar to a croque-monsieur

biko *Philippines* A dessert made from glutinous rice, sugar and coconut milk. Served with latik.

biksemad *Denmark* Beef hash, served with a fried egg

bilberry The dark-blue-bloomed berry of a low-growing wild bush, *Vaccinium myrtillus*, that grows on acid moorland. Harvested with a large-toothed curved comb. Slightly acid and used for pies or jam. Also called **whortleberry**, **huckleberry**, **blaeberry**, **whimberry**, **windberry**

billeri *Italy* Lady's smock

billy bi *France* A mussel soup made from fish stock, mussel liquor and a little cream, flavoured with lemon zest or lemon grass and garnished with shelled mussels

biltong *South Africa* Dried strips of game meat or beef which will keep for years. Tough and leathery, it requires cutting into very thin strips before eating raw or cooking. Venison makes the best biltong but beef is the most usual. Also called **jerky**, **jerked beef**, **jerked meat** (NOTE: Literally 'bull tongue'.)

bind, to To bring together dry or crumbly ingredients with a binding agent such as egg, flour paste, thick sauces or even water, etc. so as to make a cohesive mass which can be shaped prior to, and which will hold its shape during, cooking

bindae duk *Korea* Fritters made with a mung bean flour batter

bindi *South Asia* Okra

bing cherry *United States* A round, plump red to purple, and very juicy cherry

bing ji ling *China* Ice cream

bingleberry A variety of dewberry

bin tong *China* Lump sugar (3)

biocide The general name for any chemical substance which destroys microorganisms and other forms of life

biocoli *Italy* Toasted sweet bread

bioflavonoids A complex family of chemicals including rutin and hesperidin which are widely distributed in fresh raw fruits and vegetables. It is thought that they have protective effects on vitamin C stores in the body and are involved in the strength of capillaries. They have no known toxicity.

biotin A very stable vitamin necessary for yeast and bacterial reproduction. Its presence in bread dough is essential. Its absence, in an active form, in egg white is responsible for the preservation of the egg against bacterial attack. It is widely distributed in all animal and plant tissues, with high concentrations in yeast, liver and kidney. It is also synthesized by intestinal bacteria and easily absorbed in the gut. It is required for the metabolism of carbohydrates and has no known toxicity. Raw egg white taken in excessive quantities whilst under antibiotic treatment could lead to a deficiency state which would appear as skin disease. Currently this affects only a few babies and is easily cured. Also called **vitamin H**

biphenyl See **E230, diphenyl**

bird A feathered and winged animal, not necessarily having the ability to fly. Either domesticated e.g. chicken, duck, goose, turkey, guinea fowl, etc. or wild e.g. duck, pheasant, partridge, etc.

bird cherry *United States* A native cherry, *Prunus pennsylvanica*, used to make a jelly-type conserve. Also called **pin cherry**

birdseye chilli A small (max. 2 cm long) chilli from Thailand, blisteringly hot and varying in colour from green to red

bird's nest 1. The nest of a small species of swallow found on the coasts of Southeast Asia. The birds, which consume a lot of seaweed, secrete a gelatinous saliva which they use to construct the nest. This is used to make a soup which is more renowned for its texture than its flavour but is regarded as a health food by the Chinese to prevent brittle bones in old age. There may be some scientific justification for this. **2.** *United States* A nest made from raw straw potatoes deep-fried between nesting frying baskets

bird's nest soup A delicately flavoured soup made by cooking cleaned birds' nests in a sweet or savoury consommé

bireweck *France* A spiced bread roll from Alsace. See also **berawecka**

Birkhuhn *Germany* Grouse

Birne *Germany* Pear

Birnenbrot *Germany* A sweetened fruit loaf

biroldo *Italy* A Tuscan blood pudding containing pine nuts and raisins or cheese

birthday cake An iced and decorated cake to celebrate a birthday. Often baked in special tins to give shapes appropriate to the occasion and recipient. Usually with as many candles as the age and some piped greeting.

biryani *South Asia* A vividly coloured and aromatic pilau-type dish of rice and fish or meat. The meat or fish, precooked with spices, is mixed with uncooked, parboiled or cooked rice previously fried with spices as for risotto, caramelized onions, and possibly almonds, and then steamed in a tightly sealed container. The colour is derived from saffron or turmeric. Spices and herbs are selected from parsley, bay, mint, lovage, coriander leaves, garlic, fresh ginger root, chillies, cardamom, cloves, coriander seed, peppercorns, cumin, fennel, anise, cinnamon or cayenne pepper. Vegetables incorporated include carrots, green peppers and onions. Additional ingredients include butter and yoghurt.

bis(e) *France* Wholemeal (flour or bread)

Bischofsbrot *Germany* A Christmas cake containing dried vine fruits, nuts and chocolate drops (NOTE: Literally 'bishop's bread'.)

biscocho *Philippines* Crumbled dried toast used for thickening sauces and stews

biscoito *Portugal* Biscuit

biscote *Spain* Rusk

biscotte *France* **1.** Rusk **2.** Melba toast

biscotti *Italy* **1.** Biscuits **2.** Rusks

biscotti da tè *Italy* **1.** Tea cakes **2.** Petits fours

biscotti di prato *Italy* A hard sweet biscuit containing almond pieces

biscuit 1. A crisp, dry, small, flat, baked, sweet or savoury cake (NOTE: Literally 'twice cooked'. See biscuit production methods.) **2.** *United States* An English scone. Also called **hot biscuit 3.** *France* Sponge cake

biscuit à la cuiller *France* Sponge finger (UK), lady finger (USA)

biscuit crust pastry Flan pastry

biscuit cutter A light metal or plastic outline shape used to cut individual biscuits from rolled-out dough. Also called **cookie cutter**

biscuit de Reims *France* A type of macaroon

biscuit press A large syringe with variously shaped attachments at the end remote from the plunger. It is filled with biscuit dough which is pressed out to form the various shapes. Also called **cookie press**

biscuit production methods The five methods are sugar batter, flour batter, blending, foaming and rubbing in. See under each name for method.

biscuit sec *France* Plain biscuit (UK), cookie (USA)

biscuit tortini *United States* A frozen dessert made with cream, eggs and crushed macaroons

biscuit turner A small broad spatula with an offset blade, used to lift and turn small items on the baking tray

bishara *North Africa* A thick purée of cooked beans from Morocco flavoured with cumin and paprika, used as a dip or thinned out as a soup

bishop's cake *United States* A light sponge cake with raisins and almonds

bishop's weed Ajowan

Biskotte *Germany* Langue de chat

biskvit *Russia* Sponge cake

bismalva *Italy* Marshmallow

Bismark filler *United States* A large plain nozzle used with a piping bag for filling pastries etc.

Bismark herrings Flat fillets of herring interspersed with sliced onion and marinated in spiced vinegar

bisque *England, France* A soup made from shellfish or crustaceans in a way similar to lobster sauce but using a white meat stock instead of fish stock, omitting the garlic and finishing with diced shellfish or crustacean flesh and cream

bisque de homard *France* A **bisque**, made either with live lobster, halved, cleaned and claws cracked, or, cooked lobster shell excluding the claws. Also called **lobster bisque**

bisquit tortoni *Italy* A frozen dessert of cream, nuts and fruit sprinkled with crushed macaroons

bistec *Spain* Beef steak

bistecca *Italy* Beef steak

bistecca alla pizzaiola *Italy* Beef steak with a sauce of sweet peppers, tomatoes and garlic flavoured with oregano and spices

bistecca fiorentina *Italy* Beef steak grilled over charcoal and served rare with a little olive oil

bistecchina *Italy* A thin steak

bisteeya A type of filled pastry. See also **bastilla**

bistro *England, France* A small restaurant, with a bar, serving snacks and full meals (NOTE: The word was taken over from Russian by Napoleon's troops during the invasion of Russia. It means 'quick' and was used jocularly of the slow service in that country's inns.)

biswa tulsi *South Asia* Basil

bitki *Russia* See **bitok 2**

bitochki *Russia* Small meatballs, fried and served with a piquant sauce enriched with soured cream

bitok 1. *France* The French name for a Russian meat loaf served with soured cream

2. bitok (*plural* **bitki**) *Russia* A minced pork or beef patty with breadcrumbs and sweated chopped onions bound with egg, panéed, fried in chicken fat or lard and served with lingonberry or cranberry sauce or the pan residues deglazed with sour cream

bittara appa *South Asia, Sri Lanka* A popular breakfast food made from **appa** batter or **string hoppers**, cooked very slowly with a whole shelled egg in the centre

bitter almond The kernel of the nut of the bitter almond tree, *Prunus dulcis* var. *amara*, used for the production of almond essence and almond oil. Toxic if the kernel is consumed in quantity. Used occasionally as a flavouring in some classic European dishes. The oil is not available in the USA.

bitterballen *Netherlands* Minced ham bound with a thick white sauce containing gelatine. Formed into balls, panéed and deep-fried. Eaten as an appetizer. (NOTE: Probably derived from the old nautical term, bitter, meaning 'the end of a cable'.)

bitter chocolate Chocolate containing 5 to 20% sugar used for baking and confectionery rather than for eating directly. Also called **baking chocolate**

bitter cucumber See **bitter gourd**

bitter gourd An Indian vegetable, *Momordica charantia*, found also in China and Southeast Asia, which looks like a small green warty cucumber. It is usually sliced, its seeds discarded and soaked in salt water to remove the bitter taste. It is usually braised or steamed and combined with strong flavours. It can be pickled, and in Indonesia it is eaten raw in salads. Also called **balsam pear**, **bitter cucumber**, **bitter melon**

bitterkoekjes *Netherlands* Macaroons

bitter melon See **bitter gourd**

bitter orange See **Seville orange**

bittersweet Tasting both bitter and sweet at the same time

bitto *Italy* A hard cooked-curd cheese cast and pressed in cylinders weighing 15 to 25 kg. After moulding, the cheese is repeatedly dry-salted and then ripened and dried for 2 to 6 months for the table version and 2 to 3 years for the grating version. The paste of the young cheese has a buttery texture with a few holes and a delicate taste. It becomes denser and more crumbly with age. Used especially in **polenta**, **polenta taragna** and **sciatti**.

bivalve Any shellfish of the mollusc family with two shells hinged together enclosing the animal. Examples are mussels, oysters, cockles, clams and scallops.

biwa *Japan* Loquats

Bixa orellana Botanical name The plant which bears **annatto seeds**

bixin A golden yellow food colouring obtained from the seeds of achiote. See also **annatto**

bizcocho Spain 1. Biscuit 2. Sponge cake

bizcochos borrachos Spain Sponge cake dredged with sugar and cinnamon and splashed with wine

bjano sirene Bulgaria A soft ewes' milk cheese cast like a small brick (1 kg). The salty, acid paste is dense and covered with a thin rind. Contains 50% water, 25% fat and 20% protein.

björnbär Sweden Blackberry

bjørnebær Norway Blackberry

blåbær Norway 1. Blueberry 2. Bilberry

blåbär Sweden Blueberry

blacan See **blachan**

blachan A strong-smelling dried paste from East Asia made from salted and fermented small crustaceans and sold in small blocks. Used for flavouring. Also called **blacan**, **blakhan**, **kapi**, **terasi**, **balachan**, **trasi**

black back salmon Australia See **salmon 2**

black bass United States A small freshwater fish of the genus *Micropterus*, with a firm delicate white flesh found in North American rivers. The skin must be removed before cooking to avoid off flavours.

black bean 1. A type of French bean, *Phaseolus vulgaris*, widely cultivated in South America and East Asia. The dried bean has a black skin and white flesh and can be used as kidney beans. It must be boiled vigorously for 15 minutes. Also called **black kidney bean**, **Mexican black bean**, **Mexican bean 2.** Fermented soya beans made by cooking, salting and fermenting until they become almost black. Used as flavouring in made up dishes or to produce various pastes and sauces. See also **black bean sauce**

black bean curd A dirty grey, spongy curd made from the tuber of a taro-like snake palm, *Amorphophallus konjac*, by peeling, pounding, boiling then precipitating the curd with lime. Can be flavoured or deep-frozen (**snowed**) to give it a different texture. Added to soups, braised dishes and the like. See also **konnyaku**. Also called **devil's taro**, **devils' tongue**

black bean sauce Black fermented soya beans flavoured with garlic and star anise and let down with brine. Used as flavouring, dressing or dip.

blackberry A dark red to black soft fruit, *Rubus fruticosus*, which grows on long rambling canes in late summer. The berries consist of a large number of individual sacs of juice each containing a seed and all gathered in an elongated sphere. Available wild or cultivated they are used for pies, jam or stewed fruit, often teamed with apples. Also called **bramble**

black bottom pie United States A custard pie with a layer of dark chocolate custard on the bottom

black bread Pumpernickel

black bream One of the seawater bream, *Spondiyliosona cantharus*, with an excellent flavour; found from the Mediterranean to the North Sea. Also called **old wife**. See also **Australian black bream**

black bun Scotland A rich, spiced, dark fruit cake encased in pastry and eaten in Scotland on New Year's eve. Often well matured. Also called **Scotch bun**, **Scotch black bun**

black butter See **beurre noisette**

black cap pudding England A pudding made from basic steamed pudding mixture, poured into a greased basin whose base is covered with currants or blackcurrant jam. When turned out it has a black cap. Served with a sweet jam or syrup sauce.

blackcock See **black grouse**

black cod A round bodied fish, *Anoplopoma fimbria*, from the North Pacific which has a grey-black to black upper surface and weighs about 2.5 kg. It is not a member of the cod family and has a rich oily flesh. Available fresh or preserved. Also called **blue cod**, **Alaska black cod**

black crowdie Scotland Crowdie cheese combined with cream and coated with oatmeal and crushed black pepper

black cumin A variety of **cumin** with a very dark seed and a sweeter smell than ordinary cumin, found in Northern India and Iran. Used in North Indian and Moghul cooking. Also called **sweet cumin** (NOTE: Sometimes the name is used incorrectly for **nigella**.)

blackcurrant The fruit of a low growing bush, *Ribes nigrum*, which looks like a small black grape. The berries can be combed off the stalks with a fork. They have a rich, slightly sour flavour and are used to flavour liqueurs, in pies, to make jam and occasionally to make a sauce similar to redcurrant sauce.

black drum See **sea drum**

black duck United States A highly prized wild duck, *Anas rupripes*, shot for the table. The domesticated version is the **Cayuga duck**.

blackened United States A term used in Cajun cooking for searing meat or fish in a very hot cast iron skillet to give the aroma of barbecued or charcoal grilled meat or fish

black-eyed bean 1. See **black-eyed pea 1 2.** *United Kingdom* Cow pea

black-eyed pea 1. A legume, *Vigna catjang*, related to other species of the genus *Vigna* (**cow pea** and **long bean**) from South America but now grown also in India and Southeast Asia. The pods grow up to 60 cm long and the beans when mature are yellow-brown to red in colour with a dark eye and similar in size and and shape to a kidney bean. To confuse matters it is sometimes referred to as asparagus bean which is a completely different species. Also called **black-eyed bean**, **catjang bean 2.** *United States* Cow pea

black-eyed susan *United States* Cow pea

blackfish *Australia* A commercial fish from New South Wales available all the year round but particularly in autumn. Suitable for all types of cooking, it is easily skinned and deboned.

Black Forest cherry cake See **Black Forest gateau**

Black Forest gateau A layered chocolate sponge partially soaked in kirsch-flavoured sugar syrup, with whipped cream and black cherries between the layers, the whole decorated with whipped cream, cherries and grated chocolate or caraque. Also called **Black Forest cherry cake**

Black Forest ham A smoked and air-dried ham from southern Germany with a strong flavour. Served with potato salad.

black forest mushroom See **shiitake mushroom**

black fungus Cloud ear fungus

black game See **black grouse**

black gram A legume, *Phaseolus mungo*, grown mainly for its dry seeds (the young pods can be eaten as a vegetable), found in India and the Caribbean. The plant and pods are very hairy and look somewhat like the dwarf French bean. The small seeds are black or dark green with a white interior and prominent white hilum. They require long boiling and are very important in Indian cooking. It is one of the most expensive pulses but widely used. The ground bean is used in idlis, dosas and poppadoms. Also called **urd bean**, **urad dal**, **black lentil**, **mash**, **woolly pyrol**, **uluthan**

black grouse A game bird, *Lyrurus tetrix*. Shooting season in the UK 20th August (1st of September in parts of the south) to the 10th of December. Hanging time 3 to 10 days. Drawn and trussed and roasted like chicken for about 1 hour. Sometimes called moorfowl, moorgame and moorcock in England adding to the confusion. Also called **black game**, **blackcock**, **greyhen**

black halibut Greenland halibut

black kidney bean See **black bean**

black-leg chicken A traditional French breed of chicken with firm flesh, superior in quality to the normal roasting chicken. Needs slightly slower cooking.

black lentil See **black gram**

blacklip abalone One of the main species of abalone, *Haliotis ruber*, with a red corrugated shell. It lives in crevices in rocks and reefs. (NOTE: So called because of its black mantle.)

black lovage Alexanders

black Mike *United States* A meat and vegetable stew (*colloquial*; Forestry workers)

black moss Hair vegetable

black mustard seed A strong, pungent variety of mustard, *Brassica nigra*, from Southern Europe and India not grown for international trade and only available locally. Used in curries.

black olive Olive

black pepper Made from whole green unripe berries of the vine, *Piper nigrum*, dried in the sun. Usually freshly ground, it has a hot pungent flavour. See also **peppercorn**

black PN A synthetic black food colouring. See also **E151**

black pomfret A greyish-brown skinned variety of **pomfret** with not as fine a flavour as white pomfret

black pots *England* A Cornish speciality of **gerty meat pudding** with added pig's blood

black pudding *United Kingdom* Groats boiled in muslin until cooked, mixed with diced pork leaf or back fat, a little finely chopped onion, seasoning, herbs and spices and mancu. Pig's blood is added to the warm mixture (roughly 2/3rds the dry weight of the groats), the whole thickened with fine oatmeal. Filled into beef runners or wide hog casings tied in smallish links, plaited and boiled gently for 20 minutes. Preservative is added to commercial varieties. The spices and herbs added vary according to region. See under Bury, North Staffordshire, Stretford, Yorkshire and Welsh blood pudding. See also **Scottish black pudding**. Also called **blood pudding**, **blood sausage**

black rice 1. A type of glutinous rice from Indonesia and the Phillipines. It resemble wild rice in appearance but is a true rice. Its nutty flavour is appreciated in puddings and cakes. **2.** *Mexico* Rice cooked in the cooking liquor obtained after boiling black beans

black salsify Scorzonera

black sea bass A deep-bodied seawater game fish, *Centropistes striatus*, also caught commercially. It has a grey to black upper skin surmounted by a very sharp fin and weighs between 0.5 and 2 kg. It has firm white flesh and may be cooked in any way. Found in deep water off the eastern coast of the USA.

black sesame seeds A black coloured sesame seed used as a garnish in desserts and puddings and, when ground, in soup or to make **gomasio**

black soya bean A smaller variety of soya bean than the yellow. Served as a salad or, when puréed and sweetened, as a cake and bun filling.

blackstrap molasses The darkest variety of molasses being that black mixture of invert sugars and other compounds remaining after crystallization of raw sugar from sugar cane juice

black treacle A mixture of molasses and invert sugar syrup used as a general sweetener but particularly for treacle toffee and treacle tart

black tree fungus Cloud ear fungus

black trumpet Horn of plenty

black turnip A large black-skinned turnip from Italy with a sharp, pungent, white and crisp flesh

black vinegar A dark, mild and sweetish vinegar similar to balsamic vinegar but made from fermented glutinous rice or sorghum. Presumably made in a similar way. Commonly added to many dishes as a flavouring in north and central China.

black walnut *United States* A variety of walnut tree with black coloured walnuts

bladder cherry Chinese lantern

blade bone *United Kingdom* A large beef joint from the top of the forequarter between the ribs and the neck and clod. Usually boned and sold as blade steak or chuck steak.

blade mace The one-piece outer lacy covering, the aril, of a nutmeg. See also **mace**

blade of pork *United Kingdom* The shoulder blade and surrounding muscle. Can be roasted or boned out and roasted or cut up for braising or stewing.

blade steak *United Kingdom* Blade bone

blaeberry Bilberry

Blakeney fritters *England* Small balls of dough made from flour, butter, sugar and egg yolk, put on a baking sheet and a hole pressed into the centre of each. After the fritters have been glazed and baked at 180°C for 30 minutes, jam is put in the hole.

blakhan *South Asia* A strong-smelling dried paste made from small crustaceans. See also **blachan**

blanc 1. *France* White **2.** *France* A cooking liquor consisting of water, lemon juice, flour and salt **3.** See **blanc de poulet**

blanc, au *France* White in colour e.g. chicken or veal, or cooked in white stock

blanc de poulet *France* White meat or breast of chicken

blanc de volaille *France* Breast of chicken

blanc d'oeuf *France* White of egg

blanch, to 1. To plunge items into boiling salted water or to bring to the boil in same and cook for 2 to 5 minutes, in order to part cook, retain colour and nutrients, to inactivate enzymes that cause changes in colour, flavour or nutritive properties during storage or, for a shorter time, to loosen tomato, almond and other skins prior to removing. Usually followed by refresh. **2.** To partially cook chipped potatoes in the deep-fryer, in order to prevent discolouring and to improve the texture, also to have them prepared ready for quick cooking

blanchaille *France* Young fish, similar to whitebait, but of sardines with possibly a few anchovies. Cooked as whitebait.

blanched almonds Almond kernels with the skin removed

blanchir *France* To blanch or scald

blancmange *United Kingdom* A sweet, semi-solid dessert made with milk, sugar, flavourings and colour, thickened with corn flour, poured into a mould and demoulded when set. Originally a medieval dish made with almonds. (NOTE: Literally 'white eats'.)

blancmange mould same as **jelly mould**

blanco *South America* A cows' milk cheese similar to Ricotta

blandade grönsaker *Sweden* A large white cauliflower cooked al dente and cored, placed at the centre of a dish, decoratively surrounded by small carrots, young beetroot, mangetout peas, spinach, petit pois and spring onions all cooked al dente plus hard-boiled eggs, sliced tomatoes and sliced cucumber, all sprinkled with chopped parsley. Served with mousseline sauce or melted butter.

blandad frukt *Sweden* Mixed fruit

blangah *Malaysia* A terracotta cooking pot. See also **belangah**

blanket tripe A smooth tripe from the first stomach of the cow or ox. Considered to be the finest. Also called **plain tripe**

blanquette *France* A white stew of meat cooked in stock with onions and mushrooms, the cooking liquor then made into a sauce with a liaison of egg yolks and cream

blanquette de veau *France* Veal stewed in a lemon-flavoured white sauce

Blarney *Ireland* A firm, semi-hard pale-coloured mild cows' milk cheese with a few scattered large holes which resembles the Danish Samsø. The yellow paste is enclosed in a red rind. Contains 39% water, 29% fat and 24% protein. Also called **Irish Swiss cheese**

blast-freeze, to To rapidly freeze food items by subjecting then to a blast of air at –28°C

Blätterteigpastete *Germany* Vol-au-vent

blau *Germany* Very rare. Used of meat. See also **bleu**

Blaubeere *Germany* Blueberry

Blaufelchen *Germany* Pollan, the fish

blawn whiting *Scotland* Freshly caught whiting, cleaned and eyes removed, dipped in salt, which is immediately shaken off and the fish hung in a drying wind for 1 to 3 days depending on size, by passing string through the eye sockets. The fish are cooked by coating with molten butter and grilling on each side. Also called **wind-blown whiting**

blé *France* 1. Wheat 2. Corn

bleaching agent Any compound used to whiten flour or other food commodity, such as chlorine or chlorine dioxide

bleak A small freshwater fish of the carp family found in European rivers. Cooked like sprats.

bleeding bread Bread infested with *Serratia marcescens*, which causes red staining. In warm damp conditions this can occur overnight, and in medieval times there were reported cases of it being interpreted as a miracle and causing religious riots.

blended flour *United States* Two or more types of flour blended for making specific items, e.g. pretzels, cookies

blender 1. An electric machine consisting of a glass or plastic vessel with a fast rotating steel blade directly coupled to an electric motor below. This pulverizes, mixes, blends or emulsifies the contents of the vessel which can be wet or dry. **2.** A hand-held electric machine with a fast rotating shrouded metal blade at the end of an extension on the motor, used for wet mixtures e.g. for making purées or emulsions such as mayonnaise. Also called **liquidizer**

blending method for biscuits A method of making biscuits by simply blending or mixing all the ingredients together, e.g. brandy snaps

blend to To mix into a homogeneous mass

blenny A small slimy fish found both in the sea and in rivers in Europe and North America, treated like whitebait

blé noir *France* Buckwheat flour

blette *France* Bette

bletted Very over-ripe, soft and almost disintegrating (fruit)

bleu *France* 1. Describes meat that is very underdone, the surface only being quickly browned 2. Describes cheese that is blue-veined because of penicillium moulds grown within the paste, usually along cracks or needle holes (NOTE: Literally 'blue'.)

bleu, au *France* A method of cooking fish or shellfish by plunging them alive into boiling water or court bouillon

bleu-blanc Belge *Belgium* A breed of cattle with a high yield of hindquarter, bred for its beef. Also called **BBB**

Bleu d'Auvergne *France* A soft blue-veined unpressed cows' milk cheese made in small (up to 1 kg) and larger (up to 3 kg) cylinders. The starter is a spore suspension of *Penicillium glaucum* and the moulded cheese is dry-salted for 5 to 6 days and ripened at high humidity for 2 to 4 weeks. The paste is white and creamy with evenly distributed veining and a pleasant but distinctive taste. Used as a dessert cheese. Made in the Massif Central and has Appellation d'Origine status.

Bleu de Bresse *France* A heavily promoted, modern French semi-hard, blue-veined cheese made from pasteurized cows' milk and sold in small short cylinders. Also called **Bresse bleu**

Bleu de Corse *France* A soft ewes' milk cheese with a firm buttery texture, a strong flavour and a few blue-veined cracks. The best are ripened in the Rochefort caves.

Bleu de Gex *France* A semi-hard blue-veined cheese with AOC status, made from cows' milk, cast into 7 to 8 kg rounds, pressed, dry-salted and ripened for 3 to 4 months. Contains 31% water, 33% fat and 30 % protein.

Bleu de Haut-Jura *France* The official name for cheese made in the Haut-Jura region. The most well known are **Bleu de Gex** and **Bleu de Septmoncel**, both of which have AOC status.

Bleu de Laqueuille *France* A cheese similar to **Bleu d'Auvergne** but with a milder taste and dryer rind

Bleu de Quercy *France* A soft blue cheese made in Aquitaine from cows' milk. It has a strong flavour and a greyish-green natural rind. It has Appellation d'Origine status.

Bleu de Sainte Foy *France* A strong-tasting blue-veined cows' milk cheese from Savoie

Bleu de Sassenage *France* A semi-hard blue cheese from near Grenoble, similar to **Bleu**

de Gex with slightly more water and less fat. Also called **Sassenage**

Bleu des Causses *France* A soft blue-veined cheese made from the milk of cows pastured on Les Causses (high limestone pastures) in southern France. The paste is firm, rich and evenly veined. It has Appellation d'Origine status.

Bleu de Septmoncel A blue cheese similar to **Bleu de Gex** but with a slightly smoother rind. It has AOC status.

Bleu de Thiézac *France* A blue-veined cows' milk cheese very similar to **Bleu d'Auvergne**

Bleu de Tigne *France* A blue-veined cows' milk cheese from Savoie

blewit, blewits A variety of edible fungus, *Tricholoma saevum*, with a short stem with a blueish appearance thickening at the base and a 6 to 15 cm diameter, and a dirty yellow to greyish ochre smooth cap rather like a field mushroom. The flesh has a pleasant scent but should be thoroughly cooked. It grows in grass and pasture land along the edges of woods especially in warm areas.

Blighia sapida *Botanical name* Akee

blind-cook, to To cook an open pie or tart casing without the filling, usually by lining it with aluminium foil and filling it with dry beans so that it keeps its shape while cooking. The base is usually docked.

blinde vinken *Netherlands* A stuffed piece of veal or beef, especially a beef olive

Blindhuhn *Germany* A bean and bacon casserole with dried apples and vegetables from Hanover

blindjo *Indonesia* A small red fruit. See also **melinjo**

blind scouse Lobscouse without meat, eaten in very hard times

blini *Russia* Small pancakes made from a yeast-raised batter of buckwheat flour and milk, which is rested overnight, mixed with milk, plain flour, melted butter, egg yolks and salt, proved, has stiffly beaten egg whites folded in, and is then browned either side in 10 cm circles on a buttered griddle. May be kept for up to 2 days. Traditionally served with melted butter but may be garnished with various fillings. Also called **bliny**

blintzes A Jewish speciality of small pancakes made into turnovers with a sweetened cream cheese filling, sealed and fried in butter, sprinkled with cinnamon and served with soured cream

bliny See **blini**

bloater A whole herring, still containing the gut, which is lightly salted and cold-smoked. Has a gamey flavour. Sometimes gutted

herring that have been similarly treated are sold as bloaters. Grilled or fried.

block roux Roux made in large quantities, cast into blocks and portioned for use as required

block sausage Diced streaky pork mixed with finely chopped garlic, cardamom and seasoning, moistened with rum, packed into ox casings, air-dried, salted and cold-smoked

blodfersk *Norway* Blood fresh. Used of very fresh fish or meat.

blødkogt *Denmark* Soft-boiled, as of eggs

blodkorv *Sweden* Swedish blood sausage

blódmor *Iceland* Blood sausage

blodpudding *Sweden* Black pudding

bloedpens *Belgium* Boudin noir

bloedworst *Netherlands* A blood sausage containing raisins, oat bran and pork fat

bloemkool *Netherlands* Cauliflower

blomkål *Denmark, Norway, Sweden* Cauliflower

blomkålsgratang *Sweden* Cauliflower au gratin

blommer *Denmark* Plums

blondir *France* To sweat (esp. onions) in fat or oil until they start to take a hint of colour

blond roux A mixture of equal parts of fat (dripping, clarified butter, etc.) and flour cooked to a sandy texture for slightly longer than a white roux with no more than a hint of colour. Used for thickening liquids, soups, veloutés, sauces, etc. Also called **roux blond**

blood The red oxygenating liquid that circulates around the body of animals, usually drained after killing and used as a commercial raw material. Pig's blood is used for making black puddings, hare's blood in jugged hare and chicken's blood in coq au vin. It adds flavour and can be used in the same way as and with the same precautions as egg for thickening sauces. It is often sold in a coagulated cooked state for use in various dishes. When blood is not drained from the animal, the meat is very dark.

blood heat See **lukewarm**

blood orange Pigmented orange

blood pudding Black pudding

blood sausage Black pudding

bloom 1. The white coating on some fruits such as plums, grapes and peaches which is said to consist of wild yeasts **2.** A white coating which appears on the surface of chocolate after variations in temperature over some time. Probably recrystallized fat and sugar.

bloomer A large loaf made from a roll of proven dough baked on a flat tray, diagonally slashed and glazed with beaten egg or salt water

blotched mackerel *Australia* Queensland school mackerel

bløtkake *Norway* A cream filled sandwich sponge sometimes coated with marzipan

bløtkokt *Norway* Soft-boiled, as of an egg

blower dryer The last stage of a continuous dishwasher where the rinsed dishes are dried by blasts of hot air

blu, al *Italy* Plunged alive into boiling water. See also **bleu, au**

blubber The subcutaneous fat of the whale, seal and other marine mammals

blue 1. When applied to meat means the surface just seared brown whilst the interior is still raw **2.** When applied to cheese means inoculated with various species of *Penicillium* using needles, to encourage the growth of the blue-green fungus within the cheese

blueberry 1. The highbush blueberry, from *Vaccinium corymbosum*, has been bred from the American wild blueberry. The purple fruits with a grey bloom are produced in clusters on 1.5 to 2 m high bushes and are similar to bilberries. **2.** Rabbit-eye blueberries, from *Vaccinia ashei*, are smaller and grittier than the highbush varieties. Both cultivated and wild varieties are used to make the well-known American blueberry pie.

blueberry muffin *United States* A slightly sweetened muffin mixture containing blueberries which have been washed, drained and added to the other dry ingredients. Baked at 200°C in muffin tins for 18 minutes.

bluebonnet rice A type of long-grain rice

blue cheese dressing Soured cream, blue cheese, vinegar, pepper and crushed garlic combined with mayonnaise

blue Cheshire *England* A blue-veined Cheshire cheese made in 8 kg cylinders and ripened for up to 6 months. It has a strong-flavoured warm yellow paste.

blue cod Black cod

blue crab A mottled blue crab, *Callinectes sapidus*, up to 20 cm across, with blue claws and a very fine flavour often eaten just after it has shed its shell. Very popular in North America and caught off the southeastern coast of the USA, mainly in Chesapeake Bay, and in the eastern Mediterranean where it has been recently introduced. Also called **Atlantic blue crab, blue manna crab, sand crab**

blue Dorset *England* A white, crumbly, blue cheese from Dorset with a brown, crusty rind

made with skimmed cows' milk. It has a strong flavour similar to Stilton. The blue mould is evenly distributed through the paste and is not in veins. Also called **Dorset blue, blue vinny, blue vinney**

blue drawers *Caribbean* Duckanoo

bluefin tuna The tasty but very rare variety of tuna, *Thunnus thynnus*, growing to 2 m long and 150 kg. It migrates over wide reaches of the southern oceans and was once very common in the Mediterranean. Now a threatened species.

bluefish A medium-sized (up to 3 kg), oily seawater fish, *Pomatomus saltarix*, with a grey to greenish blue upper skin with firm, white flesh found in the warmer waters of the Atlantic and in the Mediterranean. It leaves the deep water for the coast during summer and is sometimes fished for sport. It can be poached, baked or grilled.

blue garoupa See **garoupa**

bluegill A freshwater fish, *Leponis macrochirus*, found in North America and farmed in the USA and Japan. Generally blue with dark blue gill covers and a firm moist flesh, weighing up to 0.5 kg. Usually shallow-fried or partly poached, skinned, battered and deep-fried.

blue ginger Ginger shoots

blue hare See **Scottish hare**

blue manna crab See **blue crab**

blue meat *United States* The meat of a suckling calf

blue melilot A Turkish melilot, *Melilotus coeruleus*, with blue flowers, now predominantly used to flavour the curds used for Sapsago cheese

blue mould Species which grow as surface moulds on e.g. bread and jam. See also **mould**
'Penicillium'

bluemouth A type of deepwater scorpion fish, *Sebastes dactilpterus*, with red skin mottled with black and with a blue flash on the gill covers. Used in bouillabaisse.

blue mussel The European mussel, *Mytilus galloprovincialis*, very similar to the common mussel

bluepoint *United States* A popular type of oyster found and farmed off the coast of Long Island

blue sausage *Switzerland* Sausages containing horsemeat which are dyed blue

blue shark A common European shark, *Prionace glauca*, sometimes passed off as tuna

blue Shropshire *England* A blue-veined cheese similar to Stilton but with a milder flavour and made in Leicestershire. Also called **Shropshire blue**

blue Stilton See **Stilton**

blue trout Forelle blau

blue velvet swimming crab A gourmet crab from Spain

blue vinney See **blue Dorset**

blue vinny See **blue Dorset**

blue Wensleydale *England* A blue-veined version of Wensleydale cheese. Very rare.

Blumenkohl *Germany* Cauliflower

Blumenkohlsuppe *Germany* Cream of cauliflower soup

Blut *Germany* Blood

Blut Schwartenmagen *France* A type of black pudding from Alsace. See also **schwartenmagen**

Blutwurst *Germany* A raw sausage made from pig's blood with a variety of meat, bacon or offal additions, possibly onions, together with herbs and spices. May be poached or fried and eaten hot or cold.

BMR See **basal metabolic rate**

bo *Vietnam* Beef

boar A species of wild pig, *Sus scrofa and others*, still hunted in parts of Europe and Asia. It is not bled after killing so has a very dark meat. Also called **wild boar**

boar's head The head of a boar, almost exclusively used for decoration in the same way as a pig's head

bob (*plural* **bobi**) *Russia* Bean

bo bay mon *Vietnam* An elaborate and costly meal of seven different beef dishes, starting with a beef fondue with vinegar and ending with a kind of gruel (**chao thit bo**). See also **fondue chinoise** (NOTE: Literally 'beef in seven dishes'.)

bobe *Italy* A type of sea bream

bobolo *Central Africa* Treated cassava tubers. See also **bâton de manioc**

bobotee *United States* A pudding-like dish of almonds, onions and breadcrumbs in a seasoned white sauce

bobotie *South Africa* Cooked minced beef or lamb, mixed with milk-soaked bread, raisins, almonds, sweated chopped onions, vinegar or lemon juice, spices and seasonings, placed in a dish, covered in an egg custard and baked until set

bocas de la isla *Spain* A speciality of Cadiz made from the claw of the fiddler crab

bocca di dama *Italy* Fruit and nut cake

bocca negra *Italy* Dogfish

bocconcino *Italy* Thin slices of ham, veal and cheese, panéed and fried

böckling *Sweden* Buckling

böckling-låda *Sweden* Buckling pie, made with cleaned and filleted buckling placed in a dish and covered with a rich seasoned egg custard mix sprinkled with chopped chives and cooked in the oven until set

böckling och purjolökslåda *Sweden* Cleaned and filleted buckling laid in the base of a greased ovenproof dish, covered with alternate stripes of chopped hard-boiled egg yolk, egg white and raw leeks, seasoned, dotted with butter and baked in a moderate oven for 15 minutes adding double cream half way through

Bocksbart *Germany* Salsify

Bockshornklee *Germany* Fenugreek

bockwurst *United States* As the German variety of **Bockwurst**, but with the addition of eggs and sometimes milk and flavoured with leeks or chives

Bockwurst *Germany* Similar in appearance to a long frankfurter but made from finely minced veal or beef together with pork, back fat, and seasoning, flavoured with nutmeg, coriander, ginger and garlic, packed into sheep casings, smoked and scalded. Poached in water. See also **Frankfurter**

boczek *Poland* Hard, smoked pork meat

body mass index A measure of obesity in human beings equal to a person's weight in kilograms divided by the square of their height in metres. If between 25 and 30, then the person is considered overweight, if over 30 they are obese. (Example weight 75 kg (168 lb), height 1.7 m (5 ft 7 in), body mass index = $75/(1.7 \times 1.7)$ = 25.95, hence overweight).

body skirt *United Kingdom* The less muscular part of the diaphragm of beef cattle

boeren *Netherlands* Farm (NOTE: Printed on the rind of genuine Dutch farmhouse cheeses.)

boerenkool *Netherlands* 1. Kale 2. Broccoli

boerenkool met worst *Netherlands* Broccoli or kale and mashed potatoes with sausage

boerewors *South Africa* Pork or lamb sausages made from the principal meat mixed with other meats and bacon or pork fat, seasoned, flavoured with coriander and other spices and herbs, moistened with vinegar or wine and packed after standing into hog casings. Usually grilled. Also called **wors**

boeuf *France* Beef or ox

boeuf, estouffade de *France* Braised beef, similar to **boeuf en daube** and enriched with pigs' trotters

boeuf à la bourguignonne *France* A piece of beef, usually topside, larded and marinated in red wine and brandy for 12 hours, drained, sealed, browned and braised in the marinade and brown stock to half-cover. Served with a sauce made from the degreased, strained and reduced cooking liquor and garnished with glazed button mushrooms and onions, fried diced bacon and heart-shaped croûtons.

boeuf à la ficelle *France* A fine, trimmed, boneless piece of fillet, rump or sirloin of beef, suspended in seasoned and boiling water with a **mirepoix** of aromatic vegetables, a bouquet garni and an onion clouté so that it does not touch the base of the pan and simmered very slowly at 35 minutes per kg. Served sliced with watercress, mustard, horseradish and pickles.

boeuf à la mode *France* **Aiguillette** of beef, larded, marinated and braised in red wine, served with vegetables

boeuf de Constance *France* Specially selected beef carcasses from animals that have been finished on yeasty beer with their fodder without exercise for the last three months to make their muscles tender and massaged daily during this period to push surface fat into the back muscles (NOTE: The technique was copied from the Japanese.)

boeuf en daube *France* Marinated and larded beef braised with the marinade and a bouquet garni in a **daubière** lined with salt pork for at least 4 hours and served as is. See also **daube** (NOTE: Sometimes used incorrectly of beef braised with wine, onion, vegetables and garlic.)

boeuf miroton *France* A dish of boiled beef. See also **miroton**

boeuf salé *France* Smoked brisket of beef. Also called **pikefleisch**

bøf *Denmark* Beef

bofu *Japan* The thin red stems from parsnips, split in four lengthwise using a skewer, curled in ice water and used as a garnish for sushi and sashimi

boga *Italy, Spain* Bogue, the fish

bogavante *Spain* Large clawed lobster

bog butter *Scotland* A strong-flavoured butter made by burying firkins of butter in a bog to ripen it

boghe *Italy* Bogue, the fish

bog myrtle An aromatic bush, *Myrica gale*, with a flavour like bay which grows wild on boggy moors. Also called **sweet gale** (NOTE: The oil is said to be the best repellent for the ferocious Scottish midges.)

bogrács gulyás *Hungary* Hungarian goulash

bogue *England, France* A small (up to 1 kg) round seawater fish, *Boops boops*, with a silvery yellow skin, interchangeable with bream

Bohemian pheasant Guinea fowl

bohémienne *France* A very simple ratatouille made from tomatoes and aubergines, separately cooked in olive oil before combining

bohémienne, à la *France* In the gypsy style, i.e. garnished with tomatoes, rice, fried onions and possibly sweet red peppers and paprika

bohémienne, sauce A cold sauce made like mayonnaise using a base of thick cold **béchamel sauce**, egg yolks, seasoning and a little vinegar into which olive oil and tarragon vinegar are whipped. Finished with mustard.

Böhmische Dalken *Austria* An egg yolk and sugar enriched yeast-raised dough, mixed with stiffly beaten egg whites before proving, made into a circular shape which has the centre indented after proving and served hot with red jam in the centre after baking

Bohnen *Germany* Beans

Bohnenkraut *Germany* Savory

boil, to To cook in water or a water-based liquid at its boiling point and with sufficient heat input to generate bubbles of steam which agitate and stir the mixture

boiled beef and carrots *England* A famous traditional London dish, the subject of a popular song. Made from soaked salted silverside or brisket simmered with an onion clouté, turnips, celery, leeks and small carrots until tender and served with the defatted and reduced cooking liquor.

boiled custard *United States* Custard made on top of the stove

boiled egg An egg cooked by boiling in its shell in water

boiled frosting *United States* American frosting

boiled icing *United States* American frosting

boiled sweets Hard translucent sweets made by boiling sugar, glucose, acid and flavourings to 149°C

boiler onions *United States* Small white mild onions used whole in soups, stews, etc. or may be puréed

boiling fowl Chickens older than 18 months weighing between 2 to 3.5 kg not suitable for roasting, grilling or frying. Usually a hen which has had 1 or 2 laying seasons. Used to produce a highly flavoured stock.

boissons *France* Drinks (NOTE: *Boissons incluses* means *drinks included*.)

bok choi Pak choy

bok-choy Pak choy

bokking *Netherlands* Bloater

bokko ko maasu *Nepal* Goat

bokkoms *South Africa* Salted fish, a west coast speciality

boko-boko *East Africa* A type of porridge made from shredded meat, **burghul** and spices (cinnamon, cumin, turmeric and the like) cooked in a closed pot very slowly and for a long time in the cooking liquor in which the meat was boiled. When finished, butter and flavourings are stirred in to give a smooth porridge. Popular amongst the Swahili and introduced by the Arabs.

bolacha *Portugal* Crackers, the biscuits

boles de picolat *Catalonia* Meatballs in tomato sauce

Boletaceae A family or subgroup genus of the fungi of which *Boletus edulis* or cep is the most well known. All varieties are characterized by close-packed tubular structures under the cap in place of the more common gills and only one variety, the bitter boletus, is poisonous and is distinguished from the cep by its bitter taste. Of the others, the white boletus, *B. albidus*, the devil's boletus, *B. satanus*, the red-stalked boletus, *B. erthropus*, and the yellow boletus, *B. calopus*, are inedible. All the other 23 varieties are edible. However all pickers should be trained by an expert.

bolet bronze *France* A variety of cep found in vineyards. See also **cèpe de vendage**

Boletus badius Bay boletus

Boletus edulis Cep

bolinhos *Portugal* Small balls (of meat, fish, etc.)

boller *Denmark* Balls, as in fish or meatballs

bollicina *Italy* Whelk

bollito *Italy* Boiled

bollito misto *Italy* A rich stew made by simmering boned pig's head, flank of beef with bones in, shin beef, boiling fowl, tongue, sausage, sweated carrots, onions and celery, with seasoning in water for 4 hours. The boiling fowl and sausage are added towards the end. It is usually served from a special trolley with the meats carved at the table and presented with a sharp sauce. Used as a test of a good restaurant.

bollo *Spain* 1. A small loaf 2. A bread roll

bôlo *Portugal* 1. Ball 2. Cake 3. Pie

bôlo de anjo *Portugal* Angel cake

bologi *West Africa* Waterleaf

bolognaise, sauce *France* Bolognese sauce

Bologna sausage Salsiccia di Bologna

Bolognese sauce A sauce made from fine-minced beef fried in olive oil with chopped onions, garlic and skinned tomatoes, mixed with herbs and seasonings and simmered with stock or wine and/or tomato juice and possibly thickened with flour. Served with spaghetti. Also called **bolognaise, sauce**

bolony *United States* Bologna sausage

bomba di riso *Italy* A dish of cooked rice moulded around a filling of cooked minced meat, herbs and seasoning, chopped mushrooms and diced cheese or ham

Bombay duck *South Asia* Sun-dried pieces of the bummaloe fish, *Harpodon nehereus*, found in Indian waters. It has a very strong smell and a not particularly pleasant taste. Served with curry. Also called **bombil**

bombe 1. *France* An ice cream speciality of different flavours in a near spherical or conical shape, often made by lining a bombe mould with one ice cream and filling the centre with another, possibly mixed with nuts, glacé fruits or liqueurs **2.** *Italy* A breakfast roll

bombe glacée *France* A mixture of ice creams and flavoured ices

bombe mould A special mould for making ice cream bombes

bombil *South Asia* Bombay duck

bombolette *Italy* Fritters

bomeloe Bummaloe

bonalay Ale flip

bonavista bean Hyacinth bean

bonbon *France* Sweet, item of confectionery

bondail A bondon type cheese flavoured with garlic

Bondard See **Bondon**

Bondart See **Bondon**

bondas *South Asia* Spiced balls of mashed potatoes coated in a **besan** batter and deep-fried

Bonde See **Bondon**

bondelle *France* Houting, the fish

bondepige med slør *Denmark* A traditional dessert made from layers of crumbled rye bread, sweetened apple purée and molten red jam, finished with a whipped cream and red jam topping

Bondon *France* A small bun-shaped, soft, whole cows' milk cheese made in Normandy. Also called **Bondard, Bondart, Bonde**

bone, to To remove bones from animal carcasses and fish, generally with as little damage to the flesh as possible

boneless With any bones having been removed

boneless steak *United States* A steak without bone cut from the **sirloin**

bone marrow See **marrow**

bone marrow sauce See **moelle, sauce**

bonen *Netherlands* Beans

bones The skeletons of animals and fishes together with connective tissue, gristle, etc.

Used to make stock by long simmering (4 hours plus) with water, aromatic vegetables and a bouquet garni to release flavour and gelatine. The simmering stock is repeatedly skimmed to remove fat and scum (coagulated protein and dirt). Bones are either browned or blanched before simmering. They are sometimes put in the bottom of a pan to prevent food sticking to the base and to add flavour to the dish.

bone taint A fault which can occur in meat on the bone preserved by surface salting, due to growth of species of *Clostridium* and *Streptococcus* around the bone which is furthest from the salt and the last part to become salted. Particularly noticeable if the meat is not correctly chilled. See also **cold shortening**

boniato *Central America, Spain* Sweet potato

boning knife A thick, non-pliable, sharp knife used for boning animals or a thin, pliable sharp knife for boning fish

bonita *Italy* Bonito

bonite *France* Bonito

bonito 1. A fish, *Katsuwonus pelamis*, more correctly called Pacific bonito, whose dried flesh is used as a base for all Japanese broths and stocks. The dried flesh is grey black with a light grey coating of mould and is sold either in blocks (**katsuo-kezuriki**) or as very thin shavings (**hana katsuo** or **kezuri-bushi**). It is also ground and agglomerated into granules for making dashi. Also called **frigate mackerel 2.** See **little tunny, skipjack tuna**

bonito flakes Dried shavings or flakes of Pacific bonito used in Japanese cooking especially for making **dashi**. Removed from the dish after the flavour has been extracted.

Bonitol *Germany* Little tunny, the fish

boniton *France* Little tunny, the fish

bonnachen *Scotland* A sausage from the Highland region made from 2 parts lean beef to 1 part suet with seasoning, saltpetre, sugar, ground ginger and cloves

bonne bouchée *France* A canapé or savoury food item served as an appetizer or at the end of a meal (NOTE: Literally 'a good mouthful'.)

bonne femme *France* Simple; involving little or no complication. Used of cooking.

bonne femme, à la *France* In the housewife's style, i.e. cooked with mushrooms, potatoes, onions and sometimes fried bacon

bonne femme, fish As for **fish Bercy** with the addition of sliced button mushrooms to the cooking liquor. The mushrooms are separated after poaching and used as a garnish.

bonnefoy, sauce *France* A white **bordelaise sauce** made with dry white instead of red wine and a white velouté instead of **espagnole sauce**. Finished with a little chopped tarragon. Also called **bordelaise au vin blanc, sauce**

bønner *Denmark* Beans

bönor *Sweden* Beans

Boodles' orange fool *England* A type of syllabub made with filtered orange juice replacing the alcoholic liquid. Alternatively a bowl lined with slices of trifle sponge and filled with a type of fool made from sweetened orange and lemon juice with grated zest and whipped cream, allowed to soak, refrigerated and decorated with orange slices. Named after Boodle's club.

Boodles' stuffing Mashed ripe bananas mixed with an equal volume of wholemeal breadcrumbs, finely chopped onion, chopped tarragon and seasoning. Used to stuff quails, small birds or chicken breasts.

bookmaker sandwich An underdone minute steak between two slices of hot buttered toast

bookweeten janhinnerk *Netherlands* Buckwheat pancake with bacon

boolawnee *Central Asia* Pastry turnovers with a leek and chilli filling. From Afghanistan.

boomla *South Asia* Bummaloe, the fish

boontjie sop *South Africa* Bean soup made from stock and dry beans (3 or 4:1), the beans soaked overnight and simmered in the stock with a chilli until soft, then all passed through a sieve

boova shenkel *United States* A meat stew with dumplings, originating with the Dutch immigrants to Pennsylvania

boquerones *Spain* Fresh anchovy fillets, pickled in salt and vinegar or crisp fried

borage A hardy annual herb, *Borago officinalis*, with hairy, cucumber-flavoured leaves and intense blue flowers. Used to flavour drinks and rarely in salads. The leaves can be cooked as spinach. The flowers may be crystallized for decoration.

Borago officinalis *Botanical name* Borage

borani *Central Asia* An Iranian salad of various cooked vegetables with garlic and nuts etc. dressed with drained yoghurt

borani esfanaj *Central Asia* An Iranian salad consisting of sautéed onion and garlic which has been cooked with chopped spinach until it has wilted, allowed to cool, seasoned and dressed with yoghurt

borassus palm Palmyra palm

borda *Hungary* Chop

Bordeaux mustard A dark coloured, slightly sweet, prepared mustard often flavoured with herbs and milder than Dijon mustard

bordelaise, à la *France* Incorporating wine sauce, bone marrow, ceps or a garnish of artichokes and potatoes

bordelaise, sauce *England, France* A brown sauce made from a reduction of red wine, shallots, thyme, bay leaf and mignonette pepper, simmered with **demi-glace** for 30 minutes and strained. Finished with meat glaze and lemon juice and garnished with diced poached bone marrow if available. Used with steak.

bordelaise au vin blanc, sauce *France* A white **bordelaise sauce**. See also **bonnefoy, sauce**

border See **bordure**

border mould See **ring mould**

bordetto *Italy* A fish stew in tomato sauce from the north of Italy

bordure *France* A ring or border, usually of cooked rice or vegetables around the edge of a plate, used to contain other foods in the centre

borecole A flat-leaved variety of kale

boreg See **börek**

börek *Turkey* A puff pastry or filo pastry pasty, sometimes filled with honey and nuts and soaked in a sugar syrup, or alternatively with a meat or cheese filling. The sweet variety is similar to the Greek **bourekakia**. Also called **boreg**

boretto *Italy* A saffron-flavoured fish stew. See also **brodetto**

borgmästarfläta *Sweden* Rectangles of Danish pastry, 40 cm by 8 cm, spread with cinnamon-flavoured butter cream followed by almond paste, rolled into long cylinders, 3 cylinders plaited, proved for 45 minutes, egg washed, sprinkled with flaked almonds and baked at 230°C for 15 to 20 minutes

borjú *Hungary* Veal

borjúpaprikás *Hungary* As **paprikás csirke** but substituting veal for chicken

borjúpörkölt *Hungary* Diced veal fried in lard with chopped onions, paprika and garlic then simmered with water, tomatoes or tomato purée and seasoning until cooked

bornholmeræggekage *Denmark* An omelette filled with smoked herring, radish and chives

bornholmere *Denmark* Buckling

borowik szlachetny *Poland* Cep, *Boletus edulis*

borragine *Italy* Borage

borrêgo *Portugal* Lamb

borride *France* A Provençal fish soup. See also **bourride**

bors *Hungary* Pepper

borscht *Poland* Borshch

bors de fasole *Romania* A broth made with haricot beans, raw beetroot, onions, celery, spinach, tomatoes, oil, vinegar and seasoning

borshch *Russia* See **bortsch**

borshchok *Russia* A clear beetroot soup made by simmering beef or game stock with grated raw beetroot for 10 minutes and straining. The beetroot is acidified with vinegar or lemon juice before adding the hot stock ro preserve its colour. Served with croûtons. Also called **bortschchock**

borststuk *Netherlands* Brisket of beef

bortsch *Russia* A generic name for various soups based on beetroot, e.g. beetroot soup, beetroot consommé, borszcz, borshchok. Also called **borshch**

bortschchock *Russia* Borshchok

bosanske cufte *Balkans* A Bosnian speciality of meatballs made from seasoned minced lamb or beef, bound with egg and flour, baked in the oven and served reheated with an egg and yoghurt sauce flavoured with caraway seeds

bosanske lonac *Balkans* A rich casserole from Bosnia based on diced pork, lamb and beef cooked in wine with vegetables and seasoning, given body with a calf's foot and flavoured with vinegar

bosbessen *Netherlands* 1. Blueberries 2. Bilberries

boscaiolo, al' (It) In the style of the forester, i.e. with mushrooms

bosega *Italy* Grey mullet

bossons macérés *France* A strong-tasting goats' milk cheese from Languedoc soaked in olive oil, white wine and brandy

Boston baked beans *United States* White beans casseroled with salt pork, an onion clouté, mustard, sugar or treacle and salt for a long time until tender. Served with Boston brown bread.

Boston bean Navy bean

Boston blue fish Coley

Boston brown bread *United States* A steamed, yeast-raised bread containing white and brown flour, fine cornmeal or semolina and treacle

Boston cracker *United States* A large, thin and slightly sweet cracker

Boston cream pie *United States* A sandwich sponge filled with crème pâtissière and coated with chocolate icing

Boston lettuce *United States* A small variety of butterhead lettuce

bot *Netherlands* Flounder, the fish

Botany Bay greens *Australia* Warrigal greens

botargo *England, Italy* The salted, pressed and dried roe of the female tuna fish or grey mullet, which latter is often coated with a preservative wax. A popular delicacy or hors d'oeuvre in Italy, Greece and Egypt. Also called **bottarga**

boter *Netherlands* Butter

boterham *Netherlands* Cold sliced meats, assiette anglaise

boterhammenworst *Netherlands* A boiled sausage made from minced fatty veal and pork back fat cured with a mixture of salt, sugar and saltpetre (6:2:1) for 2 days using 1 part of the curing mixture per 30 parts of meat mixture, this then mixed with flour, ground pepper, ginger, nutmeg and mace, packed into ox bungs, hot smoked and simmered in water

boterhammetje *Netherlands* Sandwich

boterkoek *Netherlands* Butter cake, similar to Scottish shortbread

bot gao *Vietnam* Rice flour

botifarra *Catalonia* A small firm sausage made with minced pork loin and belly, moistened with white wine, seasoned and flavoured with garlic, cinnamon and powdered cloves, air-dried for 2 days, boiled in salted water and air-dried again. Called butifarra in Spanish.

botifarra amb mongetes *Catalonia* Grilled white or black sausage with haricot beans

botifarra blanca *Catalonia* A cooked white sausage containing pork tripe and pine nuts

botifarra negre *Catalonia* A cooked black sausage made with pig's blood, minced pork belly and spices

boti kabab *South Asia* Small pieces of very tender meat, marinated for several hours, skewered and grilled under intense heat whilst being basted with ghee

bôt mì *Vietnam* Corn flour

bot nep *Vietnam* Glutinous rice flour

bot ngot *Vietnam* Monosodium glutamate

bottagio *Italy* Pork stew

bottarga *England, Italy* The salted, pressed and dried roe of the female tuna fish or grey mullet. See also **botargo**

bottatrice *Italy* Eel pout

bottle, to To preserve food, usually fruit but sometimes vegetables, in sealed sterilized bottles. Prevention of bacterial spoilage is by heating to 130°C for 30 minutes, or by addition of acid, salt or sugar, all of which inhibit bacterial growth. Apart from fruit, most food is too difficult to bottle under domestic conditions.

bottle gourd Although often scooped out and dried for ornamental use, this fruit of the plant *Lageneria siceraria* is used when young as a somewhat bland vegetable after removing the large seeds. It looks like a smooth cucumber with a bulge at the flower end. Used to make **kampyo**. Also called **trumpet gourd**, **calabash** (when inedible), **dudhi** (when edible)

bottom round *United States* The bottom of the hindquarter of beef adjacent to shin beef

Botton *England* A semi-hard Cheddar-like cheese made from unpasteurized cows' milk in Danby, Yorkshire

botulism Food poisoning caused by the toxin excreted by *Clostridium botulinum*, which is a strict spore-forming anaerobe. It can therefore only grow in sealed cans and jars from which air is excluded or rarely in the centre of cooked food. Used to be responsible for deaths when home-bottling of vegetables was common. The toxin is destroyed and made harmless by boiling for a few minutes. See also *Clostridium botulinum*

botvinya *Eastern Europe* A celebratory summer soup from the Ukraine made with white wine mixed with pickled beetroot juice, spinach and sorrel leaves, beetroot tops, pickled cucumber, shrimps, sturgeon, herbs, vinegar and seasoning, all cooled with crushed ice

bot xa xiu *Vietnam* Roast pork spices

bou a l'adoba *Catalonia* A peasant beef casserole

boucan *Caribbean* A wooden grid on which meat is sun-dried and smoked (boucanned) to preserve it

bouchée *France* A small filled vol-au-vent or puff-pastry shell made by cutting virgin puff pastry in a round and half-cutting the centre, cooking and scooping out the middle prior to filling. When half-risen in the oven it should be pressed down flat to give an even rise. (NOTE: Literally 'a mouthful'.)

bouchées à la reine *France* Chicken-filled bouchées

bouchées de fruits de mer *France* Bouchées filled with diced mushrooms cooked in butter, which have been sweated with mixed shellfish, bound with sauce vin blanc and garnished with picked parsley

bou de Fagne *Belgium* A small soft brick-shaped cheese made from cows' milk. The paste has a pleasant taste and aroma with a few holes. The rind is orange-yellow with a slight bloom.

boudin 1. *France* Sausage or pudding as in black or white pudding, **boudin noir** or **boudin**

blanc 2. *United States* A Creole sausage mixture made from pork liver, cooked pork and rice, spring onions and seasoning

boudin à la crème *Belgium, France* A simple boudin noir mix of 2 parts pigs blood to 1 part cream with egg, butter, chopped onion and seasoning

boudin à la Flamande *Belgium* A boudin noir mix with a large amount of onion, dried vine fruits and chopped parsley instead of spices

boudin Asturien *France* Morcilla

boudin blanc *France* A white cooked sausage made from finely ground white meat (chicken, rabbit, veal, pork), cream, egg, onions, starchy material, spices, herbs and seasoning. It is then boiled and may be eaten cold or cooked in the usual manner. Popular at French Christmas celebrations.

boudin blanc à l'ancienne *France* A boudin blanc made from raw fish, chicken breast, sweetbreads or carp roes pounded one by one with bread boiled in milk, butter, cooked cows' udder, boiled rice, onion purée and egg yolks, seasoned and flavoured with nutmeg and mixed with cream before being filled into casings and simmered in milk

boudin blanc de Paris *France* A mixture of finely processed raw poultry breast meat, pork loin, flare and back fat, sweated chopped onions, softened breadcrumbs, eggs, cream, seasoning and quatre-épices, filled loosely into beef runners, linked and simmered in milk and water for 20 minutes, cooled and grilled or fried

boudin blanc d'Ourville *France* A **panada** made with milk, mixed with chopped pork fat, sweated chopped onions, butter, cream, egg yolks, seasoning and quatre-épices, packed into pieces of casing tied either end leaving room for expansion, simmered in water then grilled

boudin blanc rennais *France* A mixture of chopped poultry breast meat and fat pork with onions boiled in milk flavoured with cloves and chervil, fine breadcrumbs, eggs and seasoning, filled loosely into beef runners, linked and simmered for 45 minutes, cooled then fried

boudin Breton *France* A boudin noir mix using a mixture of pigs' and calf's blood

boudin creole *United States* A boudin noir mix of blood, milk-soaked bread, pork back fat, garlic, parsley, chives, seasoning, quatre-épices and rum

boudin d'Auvergne *France* A boudin noir mix with added milk and hard pork back fat and flare fat

boudin de Brest *France* A boudin noir mix with higher proportions of blood and cream

and boiled onion instead of sweated chopped onion. Made into long 20-cm links.

boudin de Lyon *France* A boudin noir mix flavoured with paprika, chives, thyme, parsley and brandy

boudin du Languedoc *France* A boudin noir mix including lean neck and spare rib of pork, flavoured with caraway seeds or aniseed

boudin du Poitou aux épinards *France* A boudin noir mixture of blood, chopped spinach, pork flare fat and gin, flavoured with orange flower water, thyme, quatre-épices and salt. Cooked as boudin noir.

boudin noir *France* A black pudding made with pigs' blood, pork, kidney fat, cream, onions, salt and spices. The chopped pork fat and onions are sweated in lard, mixed with the other ingredients, poured into casings, linked, and simmered at 90°C until the blood solidifies and the boudins rise in the water. There are many variations.

boudin noir à l'ail *France* A boudin noir mix with chopped garlic instead of spice

boudin noir à l'anglaise *France* A boudin noir mix with the addition of boiled rice or pearl barley

boudin noir à la normande *France* Sliced boudin noir and peeled and sliced dessert apples sautéed in butter until slightly browned. Served as is or with a reduction of cider and pan juices or flamed with calvados.

boudin noir alsacien *France* A boudin noir mix with chopped apple

boudins entre ciel et terre *France* A dish of mashed potatoes, enriched with egg yolks and butter, and apple purée placed in a serving dish, warmed, well-grilled boudins placed on top and all napped with melted butter

bouffi *France* A type of bloater, lightly salted and smoked, eaten cooked or raw. Also called **craquelots**, **demi-doux**

bouillabaisse *France* A Mediterranean soup made with firm white fish and shellfish, with tomatoes, garlic, saffron, herbs and olive oil boiled 10 minutes before adding soft fish. Served with slices of French bread.

bouilli 1. *France* Boiled; past participle of *bouillir* 'to boil' **2.** *United States* A classic Cajun soup made with beef offal

bouillie *France* **1.** A thick porridge from Brittany made with buckwheat flour and resembling **polenta 2.** Baby cereal **3.** Gruel **4.** Porridge **5.** Pulp

bouillinade *France* A fish stew with onions, potatoes, garlic and sweet peppers from Roussillon

bouillir *France* To boil

bouillir à petit feu *France* To simmer

bouillon 1. *France* A stock specifically made for soup, not especially clarified **2.** *England* A pasty mixture of salt, MSG, vegetable and/or meat extracts and flavourings; sold commercially in large tubs for making convenience stocks

bouillon cube See **stock cube**

boula *United States* A green turtle soup with green peas, flavoured with sherry, garnished with grated cheese and sometimes with whipped cream

boulangère, à la *France* In the baker's wife's style, i.e. cooked in the oven with sliced onions, potatoes and stock

boule *France* The flat ball-shaped traditional bread loaf with a rough crust, weighing up to 12 kg. Sometimes made by the sourdough method. (NOTE: **Boule** is the origin of the French word *boulangerie*, meaning baker's shop.)

boule de Bâle *Switzerland* A pork meat, beef and fat pork sausage, smoked over beech wood, scalded and cooled. Served hot.

boule de macreuse *France* A forequarter cut of beef extending down from the middle of the shoulder to the top of the leg and including parts of English chuck, leg of mutton cut and brisket. Used for braising and stewing.

boule de neige *France* A sponge or ice cream dessert topped with whipped cream

boulette 1. *France* Rissole, meatball or meat croquette **2.** *France* A small shortcrust or puff pastry pasty with a cooked meat or poultry filling, panéed and deep-fried **3.** *Belgium* A small strong-flavoured cheese made in a variety of shapes, often flavoured with herbs

boulette d'Avesnes *France* A soft, cooked and kneaded-curd cheese made from buttermilk in northern France. It is seasoned with salt, herbs and spices and ripened for 3 months.

boulettes creole *West Africa* Highly spiced minced meatballs from Gambia simmered with onions, green sweet peppers, tomatoes, ginger and chillies in oil and stock

bounceberry Cranberry

bouquet *France* Common prawn

bouquet de Moines *Belgium* A soft cows' milk cheese with a smooth even-textured delicately flavoured paste covered in a brown rind and made in 400 g cylinders

bouquet garni *France* Herbs tied in a bundle, or wrapped in muslin or a blanched leek leaf, usually consisting of thyme, parsley stalks, celery leaves, bayleaf and possibly peppercorns. Abbreviation **BG**

bouquetière, à la *France* In the florist's style, i.e. a method of presentation of hot cooked food, usually steaks or chops or the like on a platter surrounded by alternating small piles of individual servings of vegetables. The number of each variety corresponding to the number of servings of meat, etc.

bouquette *Belgium* A pancake made with a buckwheat batter containing raisins

bouranee baunjaun *Central Asia* Aubergine slices salted and drained, browned on both sides in oil then layered in a pan with sweated onions, sliced raw green peppers and tomatoes with a little chilli powder, covered in water and simmered until tender. Served in a dish with the Afghanistan sauce (**chakah**) below and above the vegetables.

bourani esfenaj *Iran* A mixture of cooked spinach, yoghurt and chopped garlic, served as a starter

Bourbon biscuit Two rectangular chocolate-flavoured biscuits, sandwiched together with a chocolate cream filling

bourdaine *France* A dessert from Anjou consisting of an apple dumpling with jam

bourdaloue *France* Poached fruit served in a vanilla syrup

bourekakia *Greece* **1.** A small sweet cake made from nuts and honey surrounded by layers of filo pastry or puff pastry like a sausage roll, baked, cooled and soaked in sugar syrup (NOTE: Similar cakes are common throughout the Middle East.) **2.** A savoury pasty made with filo pastry filled with cheese, poultry, vegetables or meat, fried or baked and eaten hot or cold

bourgeoise, à la *France* Domestic in nature and usually without a set recipe, often garnished with carrots, onions and bacon

bourgouri *Middle East* Powdered wheat. See also **burghul**

bourguignonne, à la *France* In the Burgundy style, i.e. with red Burgundy wine, shallots, mushrooms and bacon

bourguignonne, sauce *England, France* Red wine flavoured with chopped shallots or onions, mushrooms, parsley, thyme and bay leaf, reduced, strained and thickened with **beurre manié**. Served with grilled or roast beef. Also called **Burgundy sauce**

bouride *France* Strongly garlic-flavoured

bourride *France* A Provençal fish soup made with small pieces of sea fish sautéed with onions, celery, and garlic, boiled in white wine, water, herbs and seasoning and garnished with diced boiled potatoes. Served with mayonnaise and bread.

boursin *France* A commercial fresh cream cheese flavoured with garlic and herbs or rolled in crushed peppercorns

boursotto *France* A rice, anchovy, vegetable and cheese pasty from Nice

boutefas *Switzerland* A large smoked sausage from the Vaudois made of 4 parts pork to 1 part beef

bovine somatotrophin A genetically engineered growth hormone given to cows to increase their milk production but leading to their discomfort and an increased incidence of udder troubles

bovine spongiform encephalopathy The so-called mad cow disease caused by an infective agent *(prion)* which causes scrapie in sheep and which has been passed on to cattle by feeding them with sheep offal. It has now been shown that the agent can be transmitted to other animals and there is a strong presumption that it can cause a new type of Creutzfeldt-Jacob disease in humans especially amongst those who consumed the cheaper types of manufactured beef products in the 1980s. There is considerable evidence that the incubation period depends on the amount of the agent ingested. It has led to a decrease in the consumption of beef and the banning of the sale of certain parts of the beef carcass. Also called **BSE**

Bovril *United Kingdom* A proprietary meat extract made from hydrolysed meat protein and extractives used for flavouring or as a drink when diluted with hot water

bowara *East Africa* Pumpkin leaves, eaten fresh or after drying and reconstituting. From Zimbabwe.

bowl A vessel of roughly hemispherical shape, sometimes with a flat base, used in the kitchen to mix, weigh and prepare the **mise en place**

Bowles' mint The common mint type, *Mentha x villosa 'Alopecuroides'*, with large roundish hairy leaves, mid-green in colour and with a mixed apple/spearmint aroma

box crab A small pink crab, *Calappa granulata*, with red claws which fit over its face and jaw parts so that it looks like an irregular ball. Found off Spanish coasts.

boxthorn A plant, *Lycium chinense*, of the tomato family with small deep-green, oval leaves used in Cantonese cooking to flavour soup

boxty *Ireland* Mashed cooked potatoes mixed with grated raw potatoes, flour, baking powder, fat and seasoning, formed into cakes, baked, split and eaten hot with butter

boxty bread *Ireland* A potato bread from Northern Ireland made of equal parts of mashed potatoes, grated raw potatoes and self-raising flour with a little extra baking powder, brought together into a stiff dough and baked at 200°C

boysenberry A hybrid of raspberry, strawberry, dewberry and blackberry, similar to a blackberry but dark red and with a rather acid taste

bra *Italy* A soft or hard cows' milk cheese from Piedmont, cast in wheel shapes (6 to 8 kg). The cheese is moulded, pressed, salted and ripened 45 days for the soft version or 6 months for the hard version. The paste is pale cream changing to a dense yellow with minute holes as it ages.

braadkip *Netherlands* 1. Chicken 2. Broiler

braai *South Africa* Barbecue

braaivleis *South Africa* Barbecue

brabançonne, à la *France* In the Brabant (Belgium) style, i.e. garnished with Brussels sprouts, hops or chicory

bracchiolini *Italy* A giant **beef olive** from Sicily made with a stuffing of hard-boiled eggs, pork fat, parsley, cheese and chopped onions. This is then fried in oil and brandy, stewed in a tomato sauce flavoured with cinnamon and herbs and cut in slices for serving.

brace of pheasants Two pheasants, one the brightly plumaged cock and the other the hen, the better eater

Brachsenmakrele *Germany* Pomfret, the fish

bracie, alla *Italy* Charcoal-grilled

braciola *Italy* Cutlet, chop

braciola di maiale *Italy* Pork chop

braciolette ripiene *Italy* Veal olives (**paupiettes**)

bracioline *Italy* Small cutlets of lamb

bräckkorv *Sweden* A sausage made from finely minced beef, lean pork and fat bacon, mixed with mashed potatoes, milk, seasoning, sugar, saltpetre and allspice, diced bacon added, the whole filled into casings, linked, dry-salted for 1 day and possibly smoked

bradan *Ireland* Salmon

bradan rost *Scotland* Salmon roasted in a hot smoke kiln at around 105°C for a short period

Bradenham ham *England* A west country ham cured with dry salt or brined for a month, pickled in molasses, salt and saltpetre for a month and smoked over applewood and oak. This turns the skin black and the meat red and sweet. To cook, it is soaked in water to remove salt and then boiled.

brændende kærlighed *Denmark* Mashed potato and bacon (NOTE: Literally 'burning love'.)

bragance, à la *France* In the Braganza (Portugal) style, i.e. garnished with stuffed tomatoes and potato croquettes

Braganza cabbage Portuguese cabbage

Brägenwurst *Germany* A lightly smoked thin sausage made from pigs' brains, oats and flour

braid cheese See **string cheese**

brains The brains of animals are classed as offal and are a delicacy in Italy, France and other countries. Their use is falling out of favour due to problems with the agent responsible for scrapie and BSE, which affects the brains of sheep and cows. If used they should be plump, fresh and covered with an easily removed membrane. They are soaked in salted water, the membrane and blood vessels removed and the brains poached in acidulated water.

brains sausage *United States* Casings filled with a mixture of chopped brains, pork and pork fat with grated onions and seasoning, linked, boiled for a few minutes and cooled. Served fried in butter.

braise, to To cook previously browned food in just enough liquid to cover it in a pan with a very tight fitting lid which reduces evaporation. The cooking is very slow and the meat is usually placed on a **mirepoix** of vegetables. Braising is often finished in the oven after the meat and liquid have been brought to the boil on top of the stove.

braisé(e) *France* Braised; past participle of *braiser*, 'to braise'

braised rice Rice pilaff

braiser *France* To braise

bramble Blackberry

bramble jelly 1. *United Kingdom* Wild blackberry jelly 2. *United States* Crab apple and blackberry jelly (a clear jam without seeds)

bramborová polévka *Czech Republic* Beef stock, thickened with a brown roux and simmered with garlic, marjoram and seasoning, strained and garnished with diced carrots and celeriac and shredded cabbage previously sweated in butter plus diced boiled potatoes, mushrooms and fried salt pork

Bramley's Seedling *United Kingdom* A large green sour cooking apple, ideal for purées, sauces, baking and most culinary uses. Available all year round.

bran The outer layer of cereal grains composed mainly of cellulose, which is left in wholemeal flour. When removed by sifting the flour, it is used as an animal feed or for high-fibre breakfast cereals.

branche, en *France* Served whole; especially of vegetables, e.g. celery, spinach

branco *Portugal* White

Brand *Germany* A hard cheese made from naturally soured milk mixed with beer

brandade de morue *France* Poached salt cod, skinned, boned and fried in oil with garlic, then pounded with oil, milk and seasonings to a fine paste, put in a baking dish and glazed

brandade de thon *France* A dish from Brittany of canned or cooked tuna chunks mixed with cooked haricot beans and dressed

branding griddle A cast-iron plate with raised parallel ribs used to give the desirable brown lines on grilled steaks or fish. It has a gutter round the edges to collect fat.

brandon puff *United States* A muffin made with a mixture of cornmeal and flour

brandy A high-alcohol spirit distilled from wine and matured. Used for flavouring and flambéing or flaming food. Similar spirits are grappa and marc. Also called **cognac, armagnac**

brandy butter A mixture of softened butter, caster sugar, brandy and possibly spice, served when cool with hot puddings or mince pies usually at Christmas. Also called **hard sauce**

brandy sauce *United Kingdom* A sweetened **béchamel sauce**, flavoured with brandy. Served with Christmas pudding or mince pies.

brandy snap A crisp biscuit made with a thin mixture of butter, icing sugar, egg whites, soft flour and flavouring dropped in spoonfuls onto a baking tray, cooked at 240°C until lacy and brown, immediately rolled into a tube and left to cool. Generally filled with whipped cream.

Brandza See **Brynza**

bran flour *United States* Wheat bran finely ground

brank Buckwheat

Brânză de burduf A ewes' milk cheese stronger than Brynza which is matured in a special leather bag (**burduf**). Sometimes flavoured by bringing into contact with fir tree bark.

Branzi *Italy* A semi-hard scalded-curd slicing cheese from Bergamo cast in wheel shapes (up to 15 kg). The moulded and pressed curd is salted in brine and ripened for 3 to 5 months. The paste has a soft supple texture with small evenly distributed holes. If kept, it will harden and may be used as a grating cheese.

branzino *Italy* Bass

brasa, a la *Catalonia* Cooked over open flames, e.g. barbecued or char-grilled

brasare *Italy* To braise

brasas, nas *Portugal* Charcoal-grilled

brasato *Italy* Braised

braskartofler *Denmark* Fried potatoes

brasserie 1. *France* A brewery **2.** *England, France* An informal eating house or pub which supplies à la carte cooked dishes at all hours. They tend to be rather more pretentious and expensive in the UK.

brassica The most important class of leafy vegetables, belonging to the genus *Brassica* and grown throughout the world in a variety of forms. Generally classified as western brassicas, such as kale, cauliflower, cabbage, Brussels sprouts, calabrese, broccoli raab, kohlrabi, swedes and turnips, or oriental brassicas, such as mizuna greens, komatsuna, Chinese cabbage, pak choy and Chinese broccoli. The oriental brassicas are mainly cultivated for the leaves and leafy stems. See individual items for details.

Brassica hirta Mustard (for sprouting and salads)

Brassica juncea *Botanical name* Brown mustard and oriental mustard

Brassica napus *Botanical name* Rape and salad rape

Brassica napus Napobrassica Group *Botanical name* Swede

Brassica nigra *Botanical name* Black mustard

Brassica oleracea Acephala Group *Botanical name* Kale

Brassica oleracea Botrytis Group *Botanical name* Cauliflower

Brassica oleracea Capitata Group *Botanical name* Cabbage

Brassica oleracea Gemmifera Group *Botanical name* Brussels sprouts

Brassica oleracea Gongylodes Group *Botanical name* Kohlrabi

Brassica oleracea Italica group *Botanical name* Calabrese and sprouting broccoli

Brassica oleracea var. tronchuda *Botanical name* Portuguese cabbage

Brassica rapaa Utilis Group *Botanical name* Broccoli raab

Brassica rapa Rapifera group *Botanical name* Turnip and turnip tops

Brassica rapa var. alboglabra *Botanical name* Chinese broccoli

Brassica rapa var. chinensis *Botanical name* Pak choy

Brassica rapa var. nipposinica *Botanical name* Mizuna greens

Brassica rapa var. parachinensis *Botanical name* Choy sum

Brassica rapa var. pekinensis *Botanical name* Chinese leaves

Brassica rapa var. perviridis *Botanical name* Komatsuna

Brassica rapa var. rosularis *Botanical name* Chinese flat cabbage

Brat *Switzerland* A grilling cheese made from cows' milk

Bratapfel *Germany* Baked apple

braten *Germany* To roast

Braten *Germany* Roast meat

Bratenbrühe *Germany* Gravy

Bratenfett *Germany* Dripping

Bratfisch *Germany* Fried fish

Brathendl *Austria* Roast chicken

Bratheringe *Germany* A type of **escabeche** made from filleted herrings, floured and fried then marinated in vinegar with onion, bay leaf, peppercorns and mustard seed. Served cold.

Brathuhn *Germany* Roast chicken

Bratkartoffeln *Germany* Fried potatoes

Bratrollmops *Germany* Rollmop herrings made up and fried before pickling

bratt pan A large versatile rectangular tilting pan used in commercial kitchens, heated by gas or electricity and mainly used for shallow- or deep-frying, boiling, braising and stewing. A typical installation can process 200 portions per hour.

Bratwurst *Germany* A pale-coloured raw sausage, made from finely ground pork or veal, sweated chopped onion, seasoning and ground mace. Sometimes smoked and/or lightly scalded and grilled or fried before serving.

Braudost *Iceland* A cows' milk cheese similar to Edam (NOTE: Literally 'bread cheese'.)

braune Ecke *Germany* A crisp and crusty rye bread roll

braune Tunke *Germany* Brown sauce

Braunschweiger Cervelat *Germany* A **cervelat** mix containing sugar, packed into beef middles, air-dried for 3 weeks and cool-smoked over oak and beech with juniper berries

Braunschweiger Kohl *Germany* Common cabbage

Braunschweiger Kuchen *Germany* Brunswick cake

Braunschweiger Mettwurst *Germany* A **Mettwurst** speciality from Brunswick

Braunschweigerwurst *Germany* Speciality sausages from Brunswick known by their type, e.g. Braunschweiger Mettwurst or Schlackwurst, etc. See under type names

brawn Meat from the head, generally of pigs but sometimes calves, sheep or cows, etc. stewed on the bone with the usual flavourings, deboned, defatted, put in a mould and covered with reduced, defatted and strained cooking liquor, demoulded when set and served thinly sliced. Also called **head cheese**

Brazilian cherry Acerola

Brazilian guava Feijoa

brazil nut A large hard-shelled nut from the fruit of a tall tropical tree, *Bertholletia excelsa*. The nuts in their shells are shaped liked the segments of an orange and are grouped together inside the round fruit. Usually sold shelled, except at Christmas. Also called **cream nut**, **para nut**

brazo de gitano *Spain* Gypsy's arm

breac geal *Ireland* **1.** Salmon trout **2.** Brown trout

bread A staple food made from a mixture of ground grains or seeds (flour), salt and water, baked, grilled or fried to a solid mass. Now usually refers to wheat or rye flours but other grains are used in small quantities and ground legumes in India. Bread is either unleavened, i.e. no raising agent is used, or leavened, i.e. raised by the action of a chemical raising agent or a yeast fermentation of part of the flour. Leavening introduces small bubbles of gas into the flour-water matrix, giving the bread a lighter texture.

bread, to *United States* To pané

bread and butter pudding *United Kingdom* A dessert made from slices of white crustless bread well soaked in an egg custard mixture, layered or arranged in an oven-proof dish with dried vine fruits and spices and baked in the oven until crisp and brown on top

bread and butter sausage *England* Finely chopped veal and pork, mixed with ground cloves, ginger, saltpetre, seasoning and small pieces of scalded lean bacon, packed into ox casings, smoked until red, boiled and cooled. Possibly eaten with bread and butter.

breadcrumbs Crustless bread reduced to a fine particle size generally less than 3 mm in diameter. Used either fresh, dried, fried or toasted in various dishes and coatings.

bread flour The type of flour made from hard wheat used in the West for making bread. It generally, though not necessarily, contains a high proportion of protein (greater than 12%), the gluten content of which aids, after kneading, the rising of the dough and the stabilization of the texture on baking.

breadfruit The large, heavy, 20 cm diameter fruit of *Artocarpus communis*, mostly starch

with a thick yellow to green and brown rind. Introduced into the Caribbean from the Pacific islands by Captain Bligh of mutiny fame. Used as a staple food, baked, boiled or fried like yam.

bread herbs The principal herbs used in bread are aniseed, basil, caraway, chives, dill, fennel, lovage seed, poppy seed, rosemary, sunflower seed and thyme

bread knife A long non-tapering knife with a serrated edge used for cutting bread, cakes and other friable dryish foods. Also called **serrated knife**

breadnut A variety of breadfruit which contains large 2.5 cm long seeds which may be roasted or boiled and eaten as nuts

bread pudding *United Kingdom* A baked pudding made from white crustless bread mixed with milk, eggs, sugar, dried vine fruits, flour, butter, jam or marmalade and spices and baked in the oven. Eaten hot or cold.

bread sauce A thick sauce made from white crustless bread mixed with milk which has been simmered with an onion clouté, chopped sweated onions, butter, spices and seasoning. Served with roast poultry and game.

bread saw A knife with a serrated edge used to cut cleanly bread, cakes and other dry crumbly goods

bread sticks See grissini

breakfast The first meal of the day. See also **English breakfast**, **continental breakfast**

breakfast cereals Breakfast food other than bread or cake made from cereal grains, principally, maize, rice, wheat, or oats. Some are cooked as needed, e.g. porridge, boiled rice and congé, others are commercially processed by precooking, pressing, drying and coating, e.g. cornflakes and rice crispies. Yet others use only a part of the cereal, e.g. bran flakes, and others are used raw such as rolled oats in muesli. Generally eaten with milk and sugar, possibly fruit and other flavourings.

breakfast cream *United States* Light cream

breakfast sausage Equal parts of finely chopped beef and lean pork, mixed with breadcrumbs, 1 cm dice of pork back fat, ground mace, nutmeg and seasoning, packed into weasands, smoked, then boiled. May be eaten cold or heated using any cooking method.

bream 1. A round, red-backed, deep-bodied seawater fish of the genera *Pagellus* and *Spondyliosoma*, with a silver underside and red fins weighing up to 1 kg and with a firm, mild-tasting, white flesh. Found in the North

East Atlantic. Also called **red bream 2.** A yellowish similarly shaped freshwater fish, *Abramis brama*, of the carp family of little importance

breast of lamb A cheap cut of lamb consisting of the rib cage and belly, composed of layers of fat, connective tissue and muscle. Usually boned, stuffed, rolled and braised or roasted but can be chopped on the bone and stewed or barbecued.

breast of veal The rib cage of the calf cooked like breast of lamb

brécol, brecoli *Spain* Broccoli

brêdes *South Africa* Boiled greens as served with rice in Madagascar

bredie *South Africa* A meat and vegetable stew

bree *Scotland* Soup (*colloquial*)

Breitling *Germany* Sprat

breka *Spain* Pandora, the fish

brème *France* Bream

brème de mer *France* Pomfret, the fish

Bremer Klaben *Germany* A raisin and citron cake

Bremer Kükenragout *Germany* Stewed chicken and vegetables in a cream sauce

Brennsuppe *Germany* A brown soup in which the flour is browned by dry-roasting or frying. Usually contains onions and wine.

Brenten *Germany* Almond pastry from Frankfurt, flavoured with rose water and rum

Brent goose A small, dark, wild goose, *Branta bernicla* and other species of *Branta*, that breeds in the Arctic. Also called **barnacle goose**

bresaola *Italy* Cured air-dried beef, matured for several months, cut in wafer thin slices, marinated and served as a hors d'oeuvre

bresi Air-dried beef from the Haute Savoie on the French Italian border; similar to **bresaola** from the contiguous Italian region

Bressan *France* A mild goats' milk cheese from Bresse

bressane, à la *France* In the Bresse style (NOTE: Bresse is a town in eastern France.)

Bresse bleu *France* A type of blue cheese. See also **Bleu de Bresse**

Bresse chicken A famous free-range chicken from north of Lyon, France. It is considered to have the finest-flavoured flesh of any chicken and is correspondingly expensive. It is the only poultry with an Appellation d'Origine.

bretonne, à la *France* 1. In the Brittany style, i.e. with whole or puréed white beans 2. Coated in sauce bretonne. Used of eggs or fish.

bretonne, fish Fish meunière dressed with a few picked shrimps and sweated sliced mushrooms

bretonne, garnish Shrimps, capers and gherkins for fish and haricot beans for meat

bretonne, sauce *France* 1. For cooked haricot beans: chopped onions fried in butter until light brown, white wine added and reduced by half, **espagnole sauce**, a little tomato sauce and chopped garlic added, simmered 8 minutes and finished with chopped parsley 2. For fish: fish **velouté** mixed with a fine **julienne** of leek, celery, onion and mushrooms sweated in butter, simmered and skimmed and finished with cream and butter

bretonneau *France* Turbot

Breton sauce Sauce bretonne

brettone *Spain* Brussels sprouts

bretzel *France* Pretzel

bréval, fish As for **fish Bercy** with the addition of sliced button mushrooms and **tomato concassée** to the cooking liquor. These are reserved after poaching and used as a garnish. Also called **antin, fish d'**

Brevibacterium linens A microorganism associated with the ripening of Brick cheeses

brewer's yeast See yeast

breyani *South Africa* A Cape Malay dish of rice and lentils with lamb or chicken and flavoured with coriander

Brezel *Germany* Pretzel

briciola *Italy* Crumb, of bread, etc.

briciolone *Italy* Small pieces, e.g. of dried porcini (NOTE: Literally 'broken bits'.)

Brick *United States* A brick-shaped, yellow, medium-soft, slicing cheese with a lot of small holes, created in Wisconsin. It has a lactic starter and is surface-ripened with *Brevibacterium linens*. It is ripened for 15 days at high humidity and then under cooler conditions whilst the rind, which develops a red colour, is washed at intervals until the cheese is ready to be wrapped. The paste has a sweet and spicy nutty flavour, similar to Münster, Saint Paulin and Tilsit.

brider *France* To truss

bride's bonn *Scotland* A flat cake made with self-raising flour, butter and caster sugar (5:2:1) by the rubbing in method, brought together with milk and flavoured with caraway seeds. Cooked on a hot griddle on the wedding day and traditionally broken over the bride's head as she entered her new Shetland house.

bridge rolls Small finger rolls of soft white bread about 8 by 3 cm, the dough often enriched with egg, usually filled and served as open or closed sandwiches at buffets and functions

bridie *Scotland, England* A meat pasty from Scotland and Northumberland

Brie *England, France* A soft, smooth, full-fat cows' milk cheese, formed into a large wheel shape with a surface fungus used to develop its flavour. It matures in about 6–8 weeks when the centre should be soft but not runny with a faint mushroom aroma and a mild piquant, aromatic and slightly acid taste. Usually sold in wedges, sometimes flavoured with herbs, etc. and now available in a blue-veined version. Contains 46% water, 30% fat and 22% protein.

Brie de Coulommiers *France* A milder and smaller version of Brie. Also called **Coulommiers**

Brie de Meaux *France* A Brie cheese with AOC status, produced from unpasteurized cows' milk in the area surrounding Paris

Brie de Melun *France* The original Brie (13th century) made from unpasteurized cows' milk with an orange-red rind and a strong flavour. It is sold on straw mats and has AOC status.

brigade A team of people working in a restaurant, generally divided into the kitchen brigade and the restaurant brigade

Brighton sandwich *England* Self-raising flour, butter, caster sugar and egg (4:2:2:1) brought together by the rubbing-in method, the dough then divided in two and one half rolled into a circle and covered with sieved apricot jam, the other half placed on top. The top is painted with apricot jam and covered with flaked almonds. Baked at 180°C for 15 minutes then at 160°C for a further 20 minutes.

brigidini *Italy* Aniseed-flavoured biscuits

brik *North Africa* A large deep-fried pasty made from filo pastry with a filling of raw egg, vegetables and tuna fish, served hot

brill A firm-fleshed flatfish, *Schopthalmus rhombus* or *Rhombus laevis*, from the shallow waters of the North Atlantic and Mediterranean. About 30–40 cm long with a freckled grey or brown upper surface. At best in autumn and winter, and cooked on the bone.

Brillat-Savarin 1. A 19th-century French epicure who had an important influence on classic French cooking **2.** *France* A triple-cream, cows' milk cheese from Normandy similar to Brie **3.** A garnish of small tartlets filled with foie gras, asparagus tips, truffles, etc.

brilliant black PN A synthetic black food colouring. See also **E151**

brilliant blue FCF A synthetic blue food dye, licensed for use in the UK but not in the EU generally. Used in canned vegetables. See also **E133**

brin *France* A sprig, of a herb

Brin d'amour *France* A soft goats' milk cheese from Corsica, flavoured with, and its grey surface coated with, herbs. Presented in small squares which have been matured for three months. Also called **fleur de maquis**

brine A solution of salt in water used to preserve food. Preservation occurs by diffusion of salt from the brine into the food and of water from the food into the brine. On a small scale this can make the brine too dilute. Brines should be between 80 and 100% saturation i.e. between 290 and 360g of salt per litre of water. Eggs and potatoes will float in such a brine. However 200g of salt per litre of water is sufficient to inhibit bacterial growth.

brine, pickling A solution of salt, saltpetre and herbs and spices in water used to preserve raw meats and sometimes vegetables by soaking

brine, to To soak a foodstuff in brine

bringa *Sweden* **1.** Brisket (of beef) **2.** Breast (of lamb)

bringebær *Norway* Raspberry

brinjal *South Africa, South Asia* A long thin aubergine extensively used in Indian cuisine

brinjal kassaundi *South Asia* A hot spicy pickle made from brinjal aubergines

brinjela *Portugal* Aubergine

Brinza 1. *Middle East* A soft rindless ewes' milk cheese with irregular holes made in Israel. Contains 60% water. 18% fat and 20% protein. **2.** A cheese similar to Feta. See also **Brynza**

brioche *France* A yeast-raised bread enriched with eggs and butter, often eaten warm, and sometimes filled

brioche à tête *France* A small brioche made with a ball of the same dough on top

brioche loaf A large brioche which is sliced like bread

Briol *Belgium* A Limburger-type cheese

brionne Choko

brioscia *Italy* Brioche

briouats *North Africa* A type of sweet triangular samosa from Morocco filled normally with date or almond paste, but other fillings are also used. Deep-fried until crisp.

brique à l'oeuf *North Africa* An egg deep-fried in a filo pastry packet

Briquette Neufchâtel

briser *France* To break, of bones

brisket *United Kingdom, United States* A coarse fatty cut of beef from the lower part of the shoulder. Usually boned and rolled for boiling, braising or pot-roasting. May be salted or pickled and sold cold.

brisler *Denmark* Sweetbreads

brisling Small sprats similar to sardines, usually canned in oil. Also called **Swedish anchovies**

brit *United States* **1.** Young herring **2.** Young mackerel

brittle See **praline**

briwat *North Africa* Small Moroccan pasties made in a triangular shape with flaky pastry and various fillings and deep-fried in oil

Brix scale A scale of density based on sugar syrups and measured in degrees. The degree Brix, °Brix, is the percentage by weight of sugar in a sugar water solution at 20°C. Thus 100°Brix is pure sugar, 50°Brix is equal weights of sugar and water i.e. 1 kg of sugar per litre of water. Some hydrometers are calibrated in °Brix.

broa 1. *Portugal* A very popular yeast-raised large flat bread from Minho made with various flours **2.** *Spain* Cornmeal bread

broach A spit, for roasting meat, etc.

broad bean The seed of a legume, *Vicia faba*, eaten as the whole pod when very young (up to 8 cm) or as green unripe oval-shaped beans from more mature pods (up to 30 cm). Usually boiled but uncooked beans are eaten as a snack food in the eastern Mediterranean. The dried bean, which is creamy in colour, is used as a pulse or canned. It was one of the first legumes to be harvested in Europe. It is a direct descendant of the field bean or horse bean which has been cultivated in Europe since the Stone Age. Also called **fava bean**, **flava bean**, **Windsor bean**, **shell bean**, **Scotch bean**

broad bean sauce A thick brown sauce made from fermented ground broad beans and flavoured with garlic, chillies and spices. Used in Szechuan, China instead of soya bean sauces.

broad leaf sage See **sage**

broad leaf sorrel See **sorrel**

broad leaf thyme A bushy shrub, *Thymus pulegioides*, growing to 40 cm. with large leaves and a stronger flavour than garden thyme.

Broccio *France* A ewes' or goats' milk unsalted curd cheese from Corsica, similar to the Italian Ricotta. Eaten as soon as made. Also called **Brocciu cheese**

Brocciu cheese See **Broccio**

broccoletti *Italy* Broccoli raab

broccoli *England, Italy* A brassica related to cauliflower which exists in two forms, the heading or **calabrese** type and the sprouting type, *Brassica oleraceae* var. *italica*. The sprouting varieties are harvested in spring after overwintering and consist of small immature purple or green tight clusters of miniature flowers which branch from a thick 1 m tall main stem. They are cut repeatedly for use as a vegetable or salad item until they become too small to be of use. Eaten raw, boiled, steamed, cold or hot.

broccoli raab The leaves of a turnip-type plant, *Brassica rapa* (Utilis Group), used in the same way as **turnip tops**

broccoli rabe *Italy* Broccoli

broccoli rape Rape

broccolo *Italy* Broccoli

brochain *Scotland* Broth

brochan *Scotland* Porridge or gruel

broche *France* A spit, for roasting of meats, etc.

broché(e) *France* Trussed (NOTE: past participle of *brocher*, 'to truss')

broche à la *France* Spit-roasted

brochet *France* Pike

brocheta *Mexico, Spain* **1.** Skewer **2.** Brochette

brochet de mer *France* Barracuda

brochette *France* **1.** A skewer, used for kebabs **2.** Pieces of meat, etc. on a skewer and cooked

brochette of lamb See **shish kebab**

brochettes *North Africa* Kebabs of marinated offal, lamb or mutton and fat

brochettes de Parme *France* Hors d'oeuvre on a skewer. See also **attereaux au Parmesan**

brocoli *France* Broccoli

brócoli *Spain* Broccoli

bróculi *Spain* Broccoli

bröd *Sweden* Bread

brød *Denmark, Norway* Bread

brodetto *Italy* **1.** A sauce made from broth with beaten eggs and lemon juice **2.** A saffron-flavoured fish stew similar to bouillabaisse. It has many local variations. Also called **boreta**, **broeta**

brodetto alla romana *Italy* An Easter stew of beef and lamb finished with egg yolks, lemon juice and grated Parmesan

brodino, al *Italy* Finished with egg yolks and lemon juice, especially of lamb stews

brodo *Italy* Broth, stock

brodo di manzo *Italy* A clear beef broth, usually containing pastini

brodo ristretto *Italy* Consommé

broeto *Italy* A saffron-flavoured fish stew. See also **brodetto 2**

broil, to To grill

broiler *United States* A young chicken weighing just over 1 kg

broit *Ireland* Brill, the fish

brokkoli *Norway* Broccoli

Brombeere *Germany* Blackberry

bromelain See **bromelin**

bromelin A protease used in beer production to remove protein haze and also to solubilize soya protein. Can be used to convert topside into a much softer meat resembling fillet steak. Also called **bromelain**

brönies *Scotland* A spiced beefburger from the Shetland isles made from equal quantities of sassermaet and plain minced beef plus some finely chopped onions and a few breadcrumbs brought together with egg, formed into rounds, floured and fried

bronze turkey A breed of turkey usually hung to improve its flavour. It has an excellent taste and a plump breast. It is more slow growing than the whiter breeds and the white meat is darker. Also called **Cambridge bronze**

bronzino *Italy* Sea bass

brood 1. *Netherlands* Bread 2. *Belgium* A cows' milk cheese similar to Edam, shaped like a loaf and coated with a yellow wax

broodje *Netherlands* A longish bread roll used to make a sandwich

broodpap *Netherlands* Bread pudding

broom corn Common millet

Bröschen *Germany* Sweetbreads

brose See **athol brose**

Brot *Germany* Bread

brotchan *Ireland* A broth made with leeks, potatoes and onions

Brötchen *Germany* Small bread roll

broth 1. The liquid in which meat or fish had been boiled together with herbs, vegetables and spices (NOTE: This is the original meaning.) 2. Stock, brunoise vegetables and either barley or rice simmered with a bouquet garni and seasoning and finished with chopped parsley

Brotkock *Germany* Bread pudding

Brotkrümmel *Germany* Breadcrumbs

Brotsuppe *Germany* Bread soup made with meat stock and bread and flavoured with nutmeg

Brotwurzel *Germany* Cassava

broufado *France* A Provençal beef stew with vinegar, anchovies and capers

brouillade *France* A stew using oil (NOTE: Literally 'a fog'.)

brouillade périgourdine *France* Scrambled eggs flavoured with truffles

brouillé(e) *France* Scrambled, as in *oeufs brouillés*, scrambled eggs

brousse du Rôve *France* A ewes' milk curd cheese from Provence similar to Ricotta

brown Partially or wholly untreated e.g. brown rice, brown sugar

brown, to To bake grill or roast in the oven so that the outer surface of the food turns a golden brown due to caramelization or Maillard reactions

brown and serve *United States* Convenience food, usually bread, cooked to a state where it just needs to be browned before serving

brown bean sauce See **yellow bean sauce**

brown beef stock Chopped beef bones, roasted in the oven until brown and the fat poured off. The bones, deglazed pan juices, chopped aromatic vegetables browned in fat and a bouquet garni are added to water, simmered for 8 hours, skimmed continuously and strained (proportions: bones 4, vegetables 1, water 10). Also called **fond brun**, **estouffade**

brown betty *United States* A pudding made from layers of sugar, breadcrumbs, butter, sliced apples, spices and lemon zest baked until brown

brown braising The sealing of meat in oil by browning on all sides prior to braising on a bed of chopped root vegetables

brown bread A general term for bread made from a brown low-extraction flour such as wholemeal. Now also applied to artificially coloured white breads.

brown bread ice cream *United Kingdom* A vanilla-flavoured ice cream containing brown breadcrumbs

brown butter sauce See **beurre noisette**

brown cap mushroom A derivative of the cultivated white mushroom more like its wild counterpart with a lightly feathered effect above the rim. They have a lower water content than the white mushroom and keep their shape better when cooked. They do not need peeling.

brown chaud-froid sauce Demi-glace thickened with 75 g of gelatine per litre

brown chicken stock As for **brown beef stock**, but with chicken bones substituted for beef bones. Also called **fond brun de volaille**

browned flour *United States* Flour which has been browned or dry-roasted to give it a nutty baked flavour. Used for thickening stews and sauces.

brown FK A synthetic brown food dye, licensed for use in the UK but not in the EU generally. Used to dye kippers. See also **E154**

brown flour Wheat flour containing between 80 and 90% of the dehusked grain. Part of the bran is removed but the wheat germ remains. Also called **wheatmeal flour**

brown fungus Cloud ear fungus

brown hare Common hare

brownie *United States* A slightly underbaked rich chocolate sponge, soft in the middle, possibly with nuts and/or iced with chocolate, made in a square tin and cut into square or rectangular individual pieces

brown lamb stew See **navarin**

brown long-grain rice An unpolished long-grain rice which, when boiled, has a nutty flavour with a chewy texture. Requires about 30 minutes boiling. See also **brown rice**

brown mustard seed The hot and bitter brown seed of an annual, *Brassica juncea*, native to India. Used whole in Indian cooking or ground and mixed with white mustard in the various mustard-based condiments and flavourings available. Also called **Indian mustard**

brown mutton stock As for **brown beef stock**, but with mutton or lamb bones substituted for beef bones. Also called **fond brun de mouton**

brown onion sauce See **lyonnaise, sauce**

brown onion soup Finely sliced onion and garlic well browned in butter, flour added and cooked to a brown roux; brown stock added, simmered for 15 minutes, strained and seasoned. The soup is served in bowls with the top covered with toasted French bread slices and the whole sprinkled with cheese and browned under a fierce heat. Also called **French onion soup**

brown oyster sauce Any of the European oyster sauces with the milk and cream replaced with brown stock. Used for grills and meat puddings.

brown ribweed Alaria

brown rice Unprocessed rice from *Oryza sativa*, from which only the husk is removed. More flavoured and chewy than polished rice.

brown roux Four parts of fat (clarified butter, dripping or vegetable oil) cooked slowly but not overcooked with 5 parts of soft plain flour until the flour is light brown in colour. Used for **espagnole sauce** and soups and as a general thickening agent.

brown sauce See **espagnole, sauce**

brown shrimp One of the common European varieties, *Crangon crangon*, of shallow water shrimp up to 6 cm long found on sandy shores. It has the ability to vary its colour for camouflage.

brown stock Stock made with bones and/or vegetables which have been browned in the oven. See also **brown beef stock**

brown sugar Unrefined or partially refined sugar, dark brown to fawn in colour with varying crystal sizes and varying amounts of entrapped molasses. See also **demerara sugar**, **muscovado sugar**

brown trout A golden brown game fish, *Salmo trutta*, with white flesh found in the upper reaches of unpolluted rivers. It has a better flavour than rainbow trout. It is best shallow-fried, but may be grilled, poached or baked **en papillote**. Also called **river trout**

brown veal stock As for **brown beef stock**, but substituting veal bone for beef bones. Also called **fond brun de veau**

brown vegetable stock Chopped aromatic vegetables browned in oil, simmered with water, tomatoes, mushroom trimmings, peppercorns and yeast extract for 1 hour and strained (proportions vegetables 1, water 3 and 4 g yeast extract per litre)

broyé(e) *France* Bruised or ground

Brucialepre *Italy* A soft surface-ripened cows' milk cheese from Piedmont with a white creamy mild paste and a thin soft rind. Made in thin circles (300 g).

brugnon *France* Nectarine

Brühe *Germany* 1. Broth 2. Gravy

Brühwurst *Germany* A group of sausages including Frankfurters, Bockwurst and Bierschinken made from finely minced pork or beef with spices and bacon, filled into casings and generally lightly smoked before being scalded at 80°C to seal in the flavour. Not suitable for keeping.

bruin brood *Netherlands* Wholewheat bread

bruine bonen *Netherlands* Kidney beans

bruinkaalssupe *Netherlands* Brown cabbage soup

bruiss *United States* Pobs (boiled milk and bread.)

brûlé(e) *France* Caramelized, browned. Usually applied to dishes with a crisp caramelized sugar topping as in *crème brûlée*.

brûler *France* 1. To burn 2. To brown or caramelize

bruna bönor *Sweden* 1. Brown beans 2. A national dish of soaked brown beans, simmered until tender, drained and mixed with salt, vinegar and dark brown sugar. Eaten with fried pork.

brunch A combination of breakfast and lunch eaten any time between 10.00 and 15.00 hrs

brunede kartofler *Denmark* New potatoes fried in butter and sugar until golden brown and tender

brune kager *Denmark* Brown spiced biscuits

brun fisksuppe *Norway* Fish soup thickened with a brown roux

Brunnenkresse *Germany* Watercress

brunnies *Scotland* A wholemeal bannock from the Shetland isles made with buttermilk and a greater than normal proportion of chemical raising agent. The name comes from the Norwegian 'brun' meaning brown.

brunoise *France* **1.** Small 2mm-cubed dice of vegetables, etc. **2.** The procedure of cutting vegetables, etc into small dice

brunoster *Norway* A sweet cheese, the colour of brown sugar, from the north of Norway

Brunswick cake A rich cake with dried fruit and almonds

Brunswick salad Strips of slicing sausage mixed with finely chopped pickled cucumber, sliced tomato, grated apple and cooked French green beans, all dressed with a vinaigrette made from the cucumber pickle juice and finished with chopped parsley

Brunswick stew *United States* A stew made from chicken and/or squirrels, vegetables, garlic, tomatoes, sweetcorn and seasoning, sometimes thickened with okra

bruschetta *Italy* Lightly toasted thick slices of bread rubbed with cut garlic cloves and cut ripe tomatoes, sprinkled with olive oil and salt and eaten as an accompaniment to a meal or as a snack. Also called **fettunta**, **fett'unta**, **fregolotta**

bruscion *Switzerland* A soft goats' milk cheese eaten very fresh

brusco *Italy* Sharp, sour

brush, to To cover or coat foods before, during or after cooking with milk, fat, oil, beaten egg, sieved jam or sugar syrup or the like, using a small brush

brush roast *United States* Oysters cooked over a barbecue or wood fire, served with mustard pickle, butter and corn bread

brusselkaas *Belgium* A type of low-fat, rindless cheese. See also **fromage de Bruxelles**

Brussels lof *Netherlands* **1.** Endive **2.** Cooked endive rolled in ham with cheese

Brussels mosaic A sausage attributed to Belgium consisting of finely minced pickled pork and veal flavoured with ground pepper, ginger and cardamom, this paste mixed with largish chunks of ox tongue, liver sausage, bacon fat and frankfurter to give a mosaic appearance when cut, packed into middles or bungs, smoked, simmered and resmoked

Brussels sprouts A member of the *Brassica* family, *Brassica oleraceae* (Gemmifera Group), consisting of small (up to 4 cm diameter), usually tight, basal leaf buds distributed evenly along a thick vertical stalk, harvested in autumn and winter and said to taste better after being frosted. Usually boiled or steamed but may be braised.

Brust *Germany* Breast (of meat)

brut(e) *France* Raw

Bruxelles *Belgium* A soft fermented skimmed cows' milk cheese

bruxelloise, à la *France* In the Brussels style, i.e. with a garnish of Brussels sprouts, braised chicory and roast turned potatoes

brylépudding *Sweden* Crème caramel

Bryndza See **Brynza**

brynt smör *Sweden* Beurre noisette

Brynza A Central European and Balkan semi-hard ewes' and goats' milk white cheese similar to Feta. Also called **Brandza**, **Brinza**, **Bryndza**

brysselkål *Sweden* Brussels sprouts

BSE See **bovine spongiform encephalopathy**

B'soffner Kapuziner *Austria* An almond and raisin pastry (NOTE: Literally 'drunk monk'.)

BST See **bovine somatotrophin**

b'stilla *North Africa* A type of filled pastry. See also **bastilla**

buab *Thailand* Angled loofah

buah keloh *Malaysia* Drumstick vegetable

buah keras *Malaysia* Candlenut

buah pala *Malaysia* Nutmeg

buah pelaga *Malaysia* Cardamom

bubble and squeak *England* A southeastern dish of leftover mashed potatoes and chopped cooked cabbage, fried in dripping or lard and stirred until the crisp brown bits are well distributed throughout the mixture. May have chopped cooked beef, fish or other protein source added. Once a dish of the poor.

bubbly jock *Scotland* Turkey (*colloquial*)

bucaniere, al' *Italy* In the style of the pirate, i.e. with seafood and tomato sauce

bucati *Italy* A type of macaroni (NOTE: From *bucare*, 'to pierce'.)

bucatini *Italy* A smaller version of bucati. Also called **perciatelli**, **perciatelloni**

buccellato *Italy* Aniseed-flavoured cake containing currants

buccin *France* Whelk

buccino *Italy, Spain* Whelk

bûche de chèvre *France* A soft goats' milk cheese rather like **Sainte-Maure**. Made in a log shape (900 g).

bûche de Noël *France* Yule log. The traditional French Christmas cake made like a Swiss roll and decorated with a chocolate cream to simulate the bark of a tree and dusted with icing sugar to simulate snow.

Buchweizen *Germany* Buckwheat

Buckinghamshire mutton pie *England* A small double shortcrust pastry pie filled with diced cooked mutton or lamb plus half the meat's weight in diced cold potatoes with a little chopped onion, chopped parsley and rosemary to flavour and a little stock to moisten. Baked at 220°C for 15 to 20 minutes.

buckler leaf sorrel A hardy perennial, *Rumex scutulatus*, of the sorrel family. It has light green silver-patched leaves with a mild lemony flavour and is less acid than sorrel. Preferred by the French for sorrel soup.

buckling A whole hot smoked herring ready for eating. Traditionally smoked over juniper twigs, especially in Scandinavia.

buck rarebit Welsh rarebit topped with a poached egg

buck venison See **venison**

buckwheat The seed of a plant, *Fagopyrum esculentum*, of the dock family native to Russia. After dehusking the grain may be toasted and/or ground to a flour and used in the same way as other cereal grains. Has a pleasant nutty flavour. Also called **beechwheat, saracen corn, kasha, brank**

buckwheat flour A flour made from buckwheat, used in making **kasha**, Russian **blini**, Breton **galettes**, and pancakes of various kinds

buckwheat noodles See **soba, cha-soba**

Buddha's hand citron A type of citron in which the fruit is split down its length into many finger-like section each with its own skin. Mainly used for perfuming rooms and clothing in Japan and China. Also called **fingered citron**

budding *Denmark* Pudding

budduzze *Italy* A Sicilian dish of meatballs simmered in tomato sauce

budelli *Italy* Intestines, entrails, guts

budelline *Italy* Giblets

bu ding *China* Pudding

budino *Italy* 1. Pudding 2. A small black pudding or **boudin noir** from Aosta

budino di ricotta *Italy* Cheese pudding

budino torinese *Italy* Chestnut pudding

bue *Italy* Old beef

buey *Spain* Meat from old bulls, rather tough

buey del mar *Spain* The common crab of Northern Europe (NOTE: Literally 'ox of the sea'.)

bufala *Italy* Buffalo

buffalo The meat of the draught animal, the water buffalo, used in Southeast Asia in place of beef

buffalo wings *United States* Deep-fried chicken wings brushed with a hot chilli sauce

buffet A meal consisting of large tables laid out with a selection of hot and/or cold foods and drinks from which guests make a selection. May be self-service or served. Usually for large formal or small informal gatherings.

buffet Russe A buffet of assorted Russian foods, blini, caviar etc.

buglosa *Spain* Sweet violet

bugloss *Spain* Viper's bugloss

bugne lyonnaise *France* A sweet fritter from Lyon

buisson *France* A cluster, of small fish, langoustines, etc (NOTE: Literally 'a bush'.)

buko *Philippines* A young coconut. Also called **maprao, narijal**

bulavesa *Catalonia* A fish soup similar to bouillabaisse

bulb baster An implement resembling a large eye dropper used for basting or for collecting fat-free gravy etc. Also called **turkey baster**

bulb garlic A rounded mild garlic resembling a button onion from Szechuan province in China. Also called **ball garlic**

bulfahf *North Africa* Grilled sheeps' or lambs' liver. One of the dishes made from the animal killed for the Eid festival in Morocco.

bulgar *Middle East* Powdered wheat. See also **burghul**

bulgogi *Korea* A circular metal hotplate over a heat source used to grill or cook food at the table

bulgogi wa sajeog gui *Korea* Slices of beef marinated in soy sauce, rice wine, onions, garlic, ginger, sesame oil, spices and seasoning, then grilled or barbecued

bulgur *Middle East* Powdered wheat. See also **burghul**

buljol *Caribbean* A salad from Trinidad consisting of saltfish which has been desalted and shredded, mixed with onions, tomatoes, chives and fresh thyme, then dressed with lemon juice and oil

buljong *Norway* Beef broth

bull 1. An uncastrated male of the bovine species, usually used as a source of semen for impregnating cows 2. *Catalonia* Various meats stuffed into pig casings (NOTE: From bullit, 'boiled'.)

bullabesa *Spain* A fish soup similar to bouillabaisse

bullace A small wild blue-black plum, *Prunus insititia*, with a tart flavour used for jam making

bullas *Caribbean* A flat heavy ginger cake from Jamaica

bullock A young bull less than a year old

bullock's heart A type of custard apple, *Anona reticulata*, with a more solid granular flesh than usual. It is heart-shaped with a reddish brown skin. Also called **ramphal**

bulls *Catalonia* Various meats stuffed into pig casings (from bullit meaning boiled)

bully beef Corned beef

bul'on *Russia* Broth

bulrush *Australia* Cumbungi

bulrush millet An important staple millet, *Pennisetum typhoideum*, from Africa and India which grows quickly, will stand drought and is used for making flour and unleavened bread. Also called **reedmace, cat tail**

bulviv desros *Lithuania* A cheap peasant sausage made from grated potatoes, a little sweated diced bacon and chopped onion, bound together with eggs and water, filled into casings, linked and baked for 2 hours, basting as necessary with water. Served with sauerkraut.

bummaloe A predatory fish with easily perishable flesh, *Harpodon nehereus*, up to 40 cm long and found off the west coast of India. When salted and dried, it is known as Bombay duck, because of the ease of catching it during the monsoon. Also called **bomeloe, bummalow**

bummalow See **bummaloe**

bun A small round, oval or cylindrical baked shape made from sweetened, yeast-raised dough with flavourings and spices usually containing dried vine fruits

Bundenfleisch *Switzerland* Bünderfleisch

Bünderfleisch *Switzerland* Cured and dried beef similar to **bresaola**. Also called **Bundenfleisch, Bündnerfleisch**

Bundkuchen *Germany* A type of cake. See also **Gugelhopf**

Bündnerfleisch *Switzerland* Bünderfleisch

Bündnerplat *Switzerland* A dish of cured and dried beef

Bündnerwurst *Switzerland* Minced pork and diced pork fat, seasoned and flavoured with ground cloves, packed into a pig's bladder, smoked then boiled. Served hot or cold.

bundt pan *United States* A cake pan or mould with a vertical tube in the centre and scalloped edges, used to provide a decorative shape to the cake or mould

bung The sausage casing made from the large intestine being, about 50 mm in diameter from a pig (**hog bung**) or 75 to 100 mm in diameter from beef (**ox bung**). Used for large diameter sausages, e.g. Bologna, liver sausage, haggis, etc. Also called **fat end**

bunga *Philippines* Pigeon pea

bunga cingkeh *Malaysia* Cloves

bunga kantan *Malaysia* Ginger buds

bunga lawang *Indonesia, Malaysia* Star anise

bunga pala *Malaysia* Mace

bunga siantan *Malaysia* Ginger buds

bun loaf A sweet, yeast-raised loaf with flavourings and spices possibly containing dried vine fruits

bunny chow *South Africa* A type of trencher made from a loaf cut in half horizontally, the soft centre removed and the halves filled with curry. Eaten using the bread scooped out to mop up the curry. The true trencherman eats the container last of all.

buntan *Japan* Pummelo

bun tau *Vietnam* Cellophane noodles

Bunter Hans *Germany* A large bread-based dumpling, cooked in a cloth then cut up and served with cooked vegetables or stewed fruit

bun tin Individual round tins either in trays or single, used for baking small cakes, buns, tartlets, Yorkshire puddings, popovers, etc. See also **barquette**. Also called **patty tin**

buñuelos *Mexico, Spain* Light and puffed up fritters made from a biscuit dough, sprinkled with icing sugar and cinnamon and served as soon as cooked

bunya nut *Australia* A large almond-shaped nut from the pine cone (up to 10 kg) of the 80-metre Queensland bunya bunya pine, *Araucaria bidwillii*. The nut is encased in an elongated woody shell, and the meat is beige in colour with a waxy texture tasting like an earthy chestnut. Bunya nuts are supplied fresh (January to March) or frozen, and can be eaten raw or cooked. When frozen, they should be boiled to loosen the shell. Use like chestnuts or as a potato substitute.

bunyols de bacallà *Catalonia* Salt cod fritters served as tapas

buost *Sweden* A firm, low-fat, slightly pungent cows' milk cheese rather like **Tilsit**

bu qi *China* See **water chestnut**

burbot Eel pout

burdock The widely distributed, dock-like plant, *Arctium lappa*, popular in China and Japan, whose young spade-like leaves are eaten like spinach and whose long thin roots are used as a vegetable. Once used in the UK to flavour the drink dandelion and burdock. Also called **gobo**

Burenwurst *Germany* A Brunswick sausage containing beef and bacon fat bound with a little **fécule**

burfi *South Asia* A sweetmeat made from a mixture of sugar syrup and ground almonds or pistachios resembling fudge. Also called **barfi**

Burgenländisch Hauswürstel *Austria* A famous sausage from Burgenland adjacent to the Hungarian border containing roughly 2 parts lean pork to 1 part pork back fat and 1 part beef

burger See **beefburger**

burghul *Middle East* Wheat which has been dehusked, parboiled, dried then cracked into a coarse powder prior to sale. It is easily reconstituted with boiling water and may be used for made up dishes or to accompany a main dish. Also called **bulgur, bulgar, bourgouri, pourgouri**

burgonya *Hungary* Potatoes. Also called **krumpli**

burgonyakrémleves *Hungary* Cream of potato soup

burgoo *United States* A meat and vegetable stew thickened with okra. Also called **mulligan stew**

Burgos *Spain* A soft mild scalded-curd cheese made from ewes' milk around the town of the same name. It has an even textured paste without holes and is cast in 1 to 2 kg discs. Often sweetened and used as a dessert. Contains 65% water.

Burgundy beef See **boeuf à la bourguignonne**

Burgundy sauce See **bourguignonne, sauce**

buri *Japan* Yellowtail, the fish

burida *Italy* Fish stew with garlic, oil, tomatoes, dried mushrooms, onions, celery and saffron

Burmeister *United States* A cows' milk cheese from Wisconsin similar to Brick

burnet See **salad burnet**

burnt cream *England* A version of **crème brûlée**, as served at Trinity College, Cambridge. Also called **Cambridge burnt cream**

buro *Philippines* Salt

burong dalag *Philippines* Mudfish cured by layering it in an earthenware dish with salt, soft-boiled rice and angkak colouring

burong mustasa *Philippines* Pickled mustard greens which are red in colour

burpless cucumber *United States* Long cucumber

burrida *Italy* A fish soup made from available seafood in Sardinia

burrie *Portugal* Winkle

burrino *Italy* A small, mild, spun curd pear-shaped cheese made from a cows' milk and moulded around a centre of butter. Eaten young (3–4 weeks) and sometimes waxed. Also called **butirro, burro, manteca**

burritos *Mexico, Spain* Rolled pancakes filled with pork, ham and melted cheese or other savoury filling possibly coated with cheese sauce, gratinated with cheese and browned in the oven, or served with guacamole and a sour cream topping

burro *Italy* 1. Butter 2. A small, mild, pear-shaped cheese with a butter centre. See also **burrino**

burro, al *Italy* With butter only. Used of pasta.

burro banana *United States* A flat, square-shaped banana with a lemony flavour from Texas. Also called **chunky banana**

burro e formaggio *Italy* A sauce or dressing of melted butter and grated cheese

burro e parmigiano *Italy* A sauce or dressing of melted butter and grated Parmesan cheese, used with pasta

burro fuso *Italy* Melted butter

burro nero *Italy* Beurre noisette

Bury black pudding *England* The most famous of the UK black puddings, flavoured with marjoram, thyme, mint, penny royal and celery seed. Also called **Bury pudding**

Bury pudding See **Bury black pudding**

busecca *Italy, Sweden* A thick tripe soup made with onions and usually with beans

bush basil A compact, tiny-leaved and very hardy variety of basil, *Occimum basilicum* var. *minimum*, with a medium flavour, which originated in South America. Also called **Greek basil**

bush cucumber *Australia* A type of melon, *Cucumis melo ssp. agrestis*, 2–5 cm in length with a speckled or striped bitter green skin. The flesh has a sweet, minty, cucumber flavour and is used in salsas and relishes.

bushel A volume measure equal to 8 gallons in either imperial or USA measure

bushetta *Australia* Mountain pepper bread, toasted, spread with a mixture of bush tomato chutney, **tomato concassée** and torn basil leaves, topped with a mixture of akudjura and Parmesan cheese and cut into convenient sizes

bushman's silverside *Australia* A piece of silverside rolled in a mixture of wattleseed and akudjura to form a crust, then roasted until the crust is black and the meat done. Served with a sauce of finely chopped muntries, onions and shiitake mushrooms all sweated in oil and brought together with stock.

bush tomato *Australia* A general name for many species of *Solanum*. The most important is the small fruit (10–13 mm diameter) of a bush *Solanum centrale*, from the centre of the continent. They are toxic when fresh, but this toxicity is removed by drying. The dried berries have an intense spicy flavour. When ground they are used as a thickening agent and a dry seasoning; they are often used with tomatoes to intensify the flavour. Also called **desert raisin**

bushukan *Japan* Citron, the fruit

Busserl *Germany* Small pastries (NOTE: Literally 'kisses'.)

buss-up shut *Caribbean* An extremely large roti flatbread made with flour and butter (3:1) and baking powder at 4 teaspoons per kg of flour, all brought together with water. The dough is flattened and fried both sides on a large griddle, then torn into strips. (NOTE: Literally 'burst-up, i.e. torn, shirt')

bustard A large game bird of the family *Otididae* from Asia, Africa and Australasia

bustard plover Plover

buster *United States* The name for a crab which has just shed its shell

buta *Japan* Pork

butaniku *Japan* Pork

butarega *Italy* The salted, pressed and dried roe of the female tuna fish or grey mullet. See also **botargo**

butcher A person who prepares slaughtered and dressed meat for sale. Sometimes also slaughters the animals and dresses the carcasses.

Bute herrings *Scotland* Herring fillets, salted and sugared for several hours, dried and rolled up and baked in the oven at 180°C in water and lemon juice for an hour, drained and served cold with a sauce of sour cream with grated cucumber and chopped herbs

buterbrod *Russia* Otkrytyi buterbrod

butifarra *Spain* A small firm pork sausage. See also **botifarra**

butifarra negra *Spain* Butifarra with added pigs' blood and chopped mint

butifarrón sabroso *Caribbean* A meat loaf or giant rissole containing minced beef and salt pork, chillies, sweet pepper, onion, coriander and oregano and cooked in a large heavy frying pan

butirro *Italy* A small, mild, pear-shaped cheese with a butter centre. See also **burrino**

buttariga *Italy* The salted, pressed and dried roe of the female tuna fish or grey mullet. See also **botargo**

butter 1. The emulsion of milk in fat produced by churning (i.e. mechanically mixing) cream and containing about 80% fat and 17% water. There are roughly 1 billion separate liquid globules per gram. A variety of types of butter are produced depending on, the type of animal, the method of production, the season, added salt or acidification of the cream prior to churning.
2. A name given to various soft butter-like preserves made from fruits. Similar to fruit cheeses.

Butter *Germany* Butter

butter-basted poultry Ready basted **poultry** in which the fat part of the injected material contains butterfat

butter bean The butter-coloured, kidney-shaped seed of the legumes *Phaseolus lunatus* and *P. limensis*, grown worldwide in warm climates. May be eaten like broad beans in the country of cultivation but usually ripened and dried for export. Must be boiled for 15 minutes to destroy protease inhibitors. Also called **lima bean**, **Madagascar bean**

butter clam *United States* Two varieties of clam of the genus *Saxidomus*, found on the Pacific coast

butter cream A cake filling or coating made by whisking butter with an equal part of icing or caster sugar. It can be made less rich by replacing some of the butter with milk or coffee.

buttercrunch lettuce *United States* A variety of butterhead lettuce

buttercup squash A winter squash common in the USA with a deep green striped skin and a medium-sweet creamy and mild orange flesh. It is in the shape of a turban surmounted with a pale cap.

butterfat The fat found in milk which forms the main part (82 percent) of butter. It contains about 40% saturated, and less than 4% unsaturated fats.

butterfish 1. A small oily seawater fish, *Peprillus tricanthus*, with white tender flesh and a bluish upper surface, weighing up to 200 g and found on the Atlantic coast of the USA. May be baked or fried. **2.** A small eel-like seawater fish, *Pholis gunnellus*. Also called **gunnel 3.** A deep-bodied freshwater fish, *Eupomotis gibbosus*, with greyish skin changing to golden yellow on the underside **4.** *Australia* Mulloway

butterfly cakes Small sponge cakes from the top of which a hemispherical section is removed, cut in half and replaced like wings on top of the depression which is filled with cream, butter cream, mashed fruit or the like

butterfly chop A thick chop cut through until almost separated, opened out and flattened to look like a pair of butterfly wings prior to cooking

butterfly cut A type of cut in which any piece of meat, chop, prawn or the like is cut through until almost separated then flattened out to look like a butterfly

butterhead lettuce A type of lettuce with smooth soft leaves forming a rounded compact head. Also called **flat lettuce, round lettuce, cabbage lettuce**

Butterkäse *Germany* A soft rich, cows' milk cheese with a close-textured elastic paste with no holes and a delicate buttery taste and smell. The thin rind is covered with mould. Sometimes flavoured with caraway seeds. Contains about 60% water, 18% fat and 17% protein. Also called **Damenkäse, ladies' cheese**

Buttermilch *Germany* Buttermilk

Buttermilchquark *Germany* A **quark** made from a mixture of buttermilk and skimmed milk

buttermilk The liquid remaining after the conversion of cream into butter. If made from raw cream, it will thicken naturally from the naturally present lactobacillus. Used as a drink or for scones and soda bread.

butternut 1. The edible oily nuts of the tree *Juglans cinerea*, a member of the walnut family found in the USA **2.** Nara nut

butternut squash A bulbous, pear-shaped, pale yellow winter squash, *Cucurbita maxima*, with orange flesh, common in the USA; the flesh is used as a vegetable or for savoury dishes

butter pat A small pat of butter

butter pit Nara nut

butter sauce Sauce bâtarde thickened with white roux only and with no egg yolks

Butterschmalz *Germany* Melted butter

butter swirls *United States* The process known as **monter au beurre**, i.e. adding cold butter to a sauce or soup at the last moment before service to give it a sheen

Butterteig *Germany* Puff pastry

buttock steak *United Kingdom* Topside

button mushroom A small immature mushroom in which the gills are not visible

button onion Small onions less than 2.5 cm diameter used for pickling and in boeuf bourguignonne. Best peeled after blanching. Also called **pickling onion, pearl onion**

button quail A small ground living bird of the *Turnicidae* family from the warmer parts of Africa, Europe and Asia

butty *England* A slang name for a sandwich, mainly used in the North especially Liverpool (*colloquial*)

butylated hydroxyanisole See **BHA**

butylated hydroxytoluene See **BHT**

butyl stearate The ester formed from butanol and stearic acid used as a release agent

butyric acid A fatty acid which when in ester form is a constituent of butter fat. The free fatty acid is liberated by oxidation of the butter and is responsible for the rancid flavour and smell.

Butyrospermum parkii *Botanical name* Shea tree

buz *Turkey* Ice

byssus The beard of tough fibres with which a mussel attaches itself to solid objects

cá *Vietnam* Fish: the following word indicates the type or state of the fish

caakiri *West Africa* A sweet dessert, nowadays made with couscous, but which can be made with any grains. The couscous softened and heated with butter and salt, then mixed with sugar, vanilla, extract and possibly nutmeg and any of sour cream, evaporated milk, yoghurt or other milk product added to taste. Served warm or chilled. Also called **chakrey**, **thiakry**

cabai *Indonesia* Pepper, *Piper nigrum*

cabai hijau *Indonesia* Green chilli

cabai merah *Indonesia* Red chilli

cabai rawit *Indonesia* Bird's eye chilli

caballa *Spain* Mackerel

cabanos *Poland* See **kabanos**

cá bass *Vietnam* Bass

cabassol(les) *France* A dish of lamb offal cooked with ham and vegetables from Languedoc

cabbage The most common member of the *Brassica* family, *Brassica oleracea* (Capitata Group), which consists of green, white or reddish leaves springing from a central stalk either loosely as in spring cabbage or in a tight pointed or round mass of layered leaves with some open outer leaves. The white varieties are often eaten raw or fermented but all may be pickled, fermented, boiled, stewed, braised or fried. The coarser outer green leaves are a major source of folic acid essential to prevent some birth defects.

cabbage lettuce Butterhead lettuce

cabbage palm Palmetto

cabbage rolls A very common North and Eastern European dish made from blanched and trimmed cabbage leaves made into a parcel-like roll with the sides tucked in using a variety of fillings and baked generally in a tomato sauce. Taken to North America by immigrants. Also called **pigs in blankets**

cabbage turnip Kohlrabi

Cabeça de velha *Portugal* One of the finest of the Quiejo da Serra cheeses (NOTE: Literally 'old lady's head'.)

cabécou *France* A small highly flavoured cheese made from ewes' or goats' milk in Aquitaine

cabello de ángel *Spain* A dessert made from a squash

cabeza *Spain* Head, of an animal or of e.g. garlic

cabichou A small, white, cone-shaped goats' milk cheese. See also **chabichou**

cabidela *Portugal* A blood-thickened sauce

cabillaud *France* Cod

cabillaud à la boulangère *France* Fresh cod baked in butter with potatoes and chopped parsley

cabillaud à la flamande *France* Cod, poached in white wine with chopped shallots and served with lemon wedges

cabillaud à la portugaise *France* Sliced cod, cooked with wine, tomatoes and garlic and served with rice

cabinet pudding A simple moulded pudding made from bread and butter or sponge cake with chopped glacé cherries and dried vine fruits soaked in egg custard (6 to 8 eggs per litre of milk) cooked in the oven in a bain-marie and served hot accompanied with egg custard sauce or apricot sauce. Also called **pouding de cabinet**

cabliaud *France* Cod

caboc *Scotland* A mild, smooth cheese made from full-cream cows' milk with added cream, coated with fine oatmeal

cá bo lò *Vietnam* Baked fish

cabot *France* Chub, the fish (NOTE: Literally 'dog or cur'.)

ca bo uang *Cambodia* Yellowfin tuna

caboul sauce Mayonnaise flavoured with curry powder. Used with cold meats.

cabra *Portugal, Spain* Goat

cabracho *Spain* Scorpion fish

Cabrales *Spain* A distinctive, strong-flavoured, smooth, semi-hard cheese made from cows' milk in Asturia, sometimes blue-veined and sometimes wrapped in leaves. Ripened for 5 to 6 months in limestone caverns. Contains 30 to 35% water, 31% fat and 28 to 30% protein. Also called **Cabraliego**, **Picón**

Cabraliego *Spain* Cabrales

Cabreiro *Portugal* A white, strong-flavoured cheese made from a mixture of goats' and ewes' milk eaten either young or after maturing in brine

cabrichiu *France* A small, white, cone-shaped goats' milk cheese. See also **chabichou**

cabrito *Portugal* Kid or young goat

cabrito asado *Mexico* Roast baby kid flavoured with garlic and chillies

cabrón *Spain* Goat

cabus *France* White cabbage

caça *Portugal* Game

cacahouette *France* Peanut

cacahué *Spain* Peanut

cacahuete *Spain* Peanut

cacah(o)uète *France* Peanut

cacao *France, Italy, Spain* Cocoa

cacao bean Cocoa bean

cacao butter Cocoa butter

cacau *Portugal* Cocoa

cacciagione *Italy* Wild game

caccia Torino Small salami, weighing about 200 g, made of pork and beef and, being small, maturing quicker than the normal size

cacennau lago *Wales* Berffro cakes

cacerola *Mexico* Casserole

cachalot *France* Sperm whale

cachat *France* A strong-flavoured ewes' milk cheese from Provence, often ripened in vinegar

cá chep *Vietnam* Carp

cachet *France* A soft, white, creamy farm cheese made from ewes' milk in Provence (NOTE: Literally 'tablet'.)

ca chim den *Vietnam* Black pomfret, the fish

ca chim mi *Vietnam* White pomfret, the fish

ca chim trang *Vietnam* White pomfret, the fish

Cacietto *Italy* A smaller version of Cacio Cavallo

cacik *Turkey* A mixture of chopped cucumber, garlic and lettuce in yoghurt, similar to **tsatsiki**

cacio *Italy* Cheese

Cacio Cavallo *Italy* A semi-hard, mild-flavoured, pale yellow, pear-shaped cheese from Sicily with a shiny yellow rind and made from spun curd similar to Provolone. It is ripened 2 to 3 months for slicing and 6 to 12 months for grating.

Caciofiore *Italy* A hard ewes' milk cheese with a high fat content, a tender paste and no rind, suitable for the table or for cooking

Cacioricotta *Italy* A ewes' milk cheese from central and southern Italy and Sardinia made in 2 versions. The soft version is made by a lactic coagulation and may be eaten fresh or salted and ripened for 2 to 3 months for use as a dessert or grating cheese. The hard version is coagulated with rennet or fig juice and the curd is moulded, salted and ripened for 3 to 4 months.

Caciotta *Italy* A small soft mild slicing cheese made from a variety of pasteurized milks with a lactic starter. Usually contains 50% water, 32% fat and 22% protein.

Caciotta di Pecora *Italy* A soft ewes' milk cheese shaped like a small drum, 14 cm diameter by 7 cm with a mild-tasting dense paste and a smooth soft rind. Contains 50% water, 26% fat and 23% protein.

caciucco *Italy* A highly seasoned fish soup served with pieces of garlic-flavoured toast

ca com *Vietnam* A small fish similar to an anchovy prepared like **ikan bilis**

cactus leaf Nopal

cactus pear Prickly pear

cadan *Ireland* Herring

Cádiz *Spain* A soft goats' milk cheese made in 1.5 kg discs and eaten after a few day's ripening

cadju *Sri Lanka* Cashew nut

cadog *Ireland* Haddock

caecum A blind, sac-like extension to the intestine of an animal which after cleaning is used as a type of sausage skin

Caerphilly *United Kingdom* A moist, mild, crumbly cheese made from cows' milk. Originating in Wales it is now more generally in the UK. It is slightly acidic from the lactic starter and matured for less than 2 weeks. May be substituted for feta cheese. Also called **new cheese**

Caesar salad *United States* A mixture of crisp lettuce, anchovies, garlic-flavoured croutons and grated Parmesan cheese, tossed with a dressing of raw or coddled egg, seasoning, oil and vinegar

caesar's mushrooms Ovoli

café 1. *France* Coffee **2.** *England, France* The name given to a place selling drinks and snacks but not formal meals

café au lait *France* Coffee mixed with hot milk

café brûlot *France* Hot black coffee, sometimes with added spices (e.g. cardamom), flamed with brandy

Café Konditorei *Austria* A coffee shop which sells cakes and sweets for consumption both on and off the premises

café liégeois *France* Iced coffee served in a glass with whipped cream or ice cream

café renversé *Switzerland* Café au lait

cafetière A straight sided glass pot with a lip into which a tight fitting plunger with a fine wire mesh is fitted. Ground coffee and boiling water are put in the pot, the plunger is placed on top and when the coffee has infused, the plunger is depressed to filter the coffee extract which is then poured out.

caffeine The alkaloid found in tea (2–4% by weight) and coffee (1–2% by weight) and in cola drinks, responsible for some of their stimulating properties

caglio *Italy* Rennet

caidan *China* Menu

cai juan *China* See **spring roll**

caille *France* Quail

caillé *France* Curds

caillebotte *France* A white, soft, creamy curd cheese made from a variety of milks, usually sold in small wickerwork baskets or earthenware pots (NOTE: Literally 'curdled bale or bunch'.)

cailleteau *France* Young quail

caillette *France* 1. The fourth stomach of the calf, used as a source of rennet 2. A package of flavoured chopped meat and offal wrapped in pig's caul or wafer-thin sheets of pork fat 3. The Provençal name for a **crépinette**, but the crépinette does not usually contain offal

caillettes de foie de porc *France* Strips of pigs' liver and bacon and chopped pigs' sweetbreads marinated for 24 hours with chopped garlic, parsley and seasoning, formed into thin cylinders and wrapped in pig's caul, tied, roasted in a medium oven for 1 to 2 hours, cooled in the pan juices and served cold in slices

caillettes provençales *France* Chopped lean pork, pork belly and liver mixed with chopped cooked spinach, sweated chopped shallots, garlic, parsley, thyme and seasoning, the whole lightly fried, bound with egg, made into balls, each ball wrapped in pig's caul and all baked in a moderate oven with skinned and deseeded tomatoes, chopped parsley and garlic. Served hot.

caimo A yellow fruit of South American origin. See also **abiu**

caisse *France* A small French oblong container not greater than 6 cm long, used to hold hot food. It may be made of ceramic, paper or dough. (NOTE: Literally 'box'.)

Caithness cheese *Scotland* A mild, pale yellow, creamy cheese made from cows' milk

cajan pea Pigeon pea

Cajanus cajan *Botanical name* The pigeon pea plant

cajeta de celaya *South America* A dessert made from a caramelized milk and sugar mixture. See also **arequipe**

caju *Portugal* Cashew nut

Cajun (*Louisiana*) A style of cooking based on rice, okra and crayfish, developed by the French Canadians who settled during the 18th century in Southern USA. See also **Créole cuisine**

Cajun-blacken, to To sear, on an extremely hot cast iron frying pan or griddle, batted out or thin tender cuts of meat, fish or poultry which have been dipped in molten butter and sprinkled with Cajun spice mix

Cajun spice mix A mixture of ground spices from Louisiana used in Cajun and Créole cooking consisting of paprika, black pepper, cumin seeds, mustard seeds, cayenne pepper, dried thyme, dried oregano and salt. Usually blended with garlic and onion and rubbed on meat or fish prior to cooking.

cake 1. A baked or fried mixture of generally fat, flour, eggs and sugar with flavourings and raising agents to lighten and aerate the mixture. May also incorporate root vegetables, principally carrot. **2.** *Netherlands* Cake

cake flour *United States* A very high-extraction low-protein white flour used for making very light-textured cakes such as angel cake

cake mixtures The five important cake mixtures are basic, Victoria sponge, Genoese, pound and fatless. The first two use a chemical raising agent; the last three rely on air beaten into the egg for raising. See under the name for proportions. See also **cake production methods**

cake production methods The five methods are: rubbing in, creaming, fatless whisking, whisking and melting. See under each name for details.

cake rack A wire grid used to support hot baked goods, cakes or bread while they cool so as to prevent their bases becoming damp

cake stand 1. A round platform which can rotate on which a cake is placed for icing and decoration **2.** A round platform on a pedestal for displaying a cake. By having it on a pedestal more room is available on the table.

ca khoai *Vietnam* Bummaloe, the fish

calabacín *Spain* Marrow, courgette

calabacita *Spain* Courgette

calabash Bottle gourd

calabaza A member of the squash family found in Spain and popular in the Carribean. Very large with yellow flesh and used in savoury dishes.

calabrese A variety of broccoli, *Brassica oleracea* (Italica Group), originally from Calabria in Sicily but now widely grown. The immature compact central flower heads, about 10 cm across, and their stems, and young side shoots are harvested in summer and cooked as a vegetable. See also **broccoli**. Also called **American broccoli**, **Italian broccoli**

calaloo *Caribbean* A soup made from dasheen leaves, okra, crabmeat, salt pork, etc. See also **callaloo soup**

calamar *Spain* Squid

calamares en su tinta *Spain* Squid, stuffed and fried, served with a sauce made from their ink

calamaretti *Italy* Small squid

calamari *Italy* Squid (pl.)

calamaro *Italy* Squid

calamars a la romana *Catalonia* Fried squid rings served as tapas

calamento *Spain* Catmint

calaminta *Spain* Catmint

calamondin A small mandarin and kumquat hybrid, *Citrofortunella microcarpa*, up to 4 cm diameter, rather like a small thin-skinned orange. Used for marmalade and pickles. Also called **China orange**, **Panama orange**

calamus A wild marsh plant, *Acorus calamus*, whose roots used to be candied. Used as a flavouring, mostly in liqueurs. Also called **sweet flag**

Calamus rotang Botanical name Rattan palm

calas *United States* A breakfast dish from New Orleans consisting of a mixture of cooked rice, flour, spices and sugar, spoonfuls of which are deep-fried

calawissa onion Egyptian onion

Calcagno *Italy* A hard ewes' milk cheese aged for at least 6 months and moulded in wicker baskets so that it has an uneven rind

calciferol See **vitamin D**

calcionetti *Italy* Apple and almond fritters

calcium An essential element for health used in the formation of bones and for the transmission of nerve impulses as well as in other metabolic processes. Requires vitamin D for absorption. Available from milk products, pulses and cereals as well as from inorganic sources such as hard water, chalk and lime.

calcium acetate The calcium salt of acetic acid (vinegar) used as a preservative and firming agent. See also **E263**

calcium carbonate A natural mineral source of calcium produced from limestone. Used in a very finely ground form as an acidity regulator and as a source of calcium in processed foods, especially manufactured bread in the UK. Also called **chalk**, **ground chalk**, **precipitated chalk**. See also **E170**

calcium chloride See **E509**

calcium dihydrogen di-L-glutamate See **E623**

calcium disodium EDTA See **E385**

calcium formate The calcium salt of formic acid used in the same way as the acid. See also **E238**

calcium gluconate See **E578**

calcium glutamate See **E623**

calcium heptonate A food additive used as a firming agent and sequestering agent in prepared food and vegetables

calcium hydrogen malate See **E352**

calcium hydroxide See **E529**

calcium lactate See **E327**

calcium malate See **E352**

calcium phytate A sequestering agent used in wine

calcium polyphosphate See **E544**

calcium saccharin The calcium salt of saccharin used as saccharin

calcium silicate See **E552**

calcium stearoyl-2-lactate A calcium salt corresponding to the sodium salt **sodium stearoyl-2-lactate** and with the same uses. See also **E482**

calcium sulphate See **E516**

calçots *Catalonia* A spring-season speciality of Tarragona, consisting of green-leek-sized onions, roasted on an open fire and served with a spicy tomato sauce dip

caldeirada de peixe *Portugal* A fish and/or shellfish stew similar to **bouillabaisse**. The ingredients depend on what is available locally and may include potatoes.

caldereta *Spain* A thick fish stew

caldereta asturiana *Spain* Fish stewed with onions, pepper and spices

caldillo de congrio *South America* A fish soup from Chile made from the local fish, congrio

caldo 1. *Italy, Spain* Hot **2.** *Portugal, Spain* A clear soup or broth

caldo de carne *Portugal* Meat stock

caldo de gallina *Spain* Chicken broth

caldo de perro gaditano *Spain* A fish stew made from sliced white fish salted for 1 hour, drained, added to fried onions and garlic, water, seasoning and Seville orange juice and cooked until tender

caldo de pescado *Spain* Fish soup

caldo de pimentón *Spain* A fish stew with potatoes, tomatoes, garlic and paprika

caldo gallego *Spain* A thin stew or soup of beans, ham, chicken, beef, cabbage, potatoes, turnips and onions, from Galicia

caldo verde *Portugal* Potato and cabbage soup. The national soup of Portugal, made with potatoes, olive oil and finely shredded green Portuguese cabbage.

Caledonian cream *Scotland* An excellent dessert made from finely minced Dundee marmalade, caster sugar, lemon juice, brandy and cream (1:1:1:1:4), the first four ingredients well mixed and the half-whipped cream whisked in. Served in a bowl decorated with some pieces of peel from the marmalade.

calendola *Italy* Marigold

caléndula *Spain* Marigold

Calendula officinalis *Botanical name* Marigold

calf The young of some of the larger herbivores, principally used of young cows or beef cattle (NOTE: The plural is **calves**.)

calf's foot The foot of the calf which when boiled is a useful source of gelatine for aspic and other jellies or to give body to a stew

calf's foot jelly The jelly made by boiling a calf's foot with aromatic vegetables and herbs, straining and clarifying then cooling. Once thought to be beneficial for invalids.

calf's head The head of a calf usually boiled and the flesh used for brawn or pies. Not generally available during the BSE scare because of the danger of infection from brain tissue.

calf's tongue The tongue of a calf usually boiled, skinned and then either eaten hot or pressed in a mould with a setting jelly, cooled, demoulded and sliced

caliente *Spain* Hot

California bonito Skipjack tuna

California dry chilli *United States* A long red chilli pepper that has been left to dry on the bush

Californian chilli *United States* Anaheim chilli

Californian halibut A sinistral flatfish, *Paralichthys californicus*, related to the brill and turbot but not to the halibut

Californian mussel *United States* A mussel, *Mytilus californianus*, found along the west coast and very similar to the common mussel

California pepper *United States* Anaheim chilli

California roll *United States* A cone of **nori**, filled with sushi rice and pieces of crab meat and avocado pear

California whiting *United States Merluccius undulatus*, a similar fish to North Atlantic whiting

Calimyrna fig *United States* A small sweet nutty-flavoured fig with an amber skin. Used fresh, in fruit salads and chutney and in cooked meat dishes.

calipash The fatty, gelatinous, dull-green, edible lining of the upper shell of a turtle

calissons *France* Lozenge-shaped almond biscuits or confections

callaloo 1. See **amaranth 1 2.** *Caribbean* In spite of its name, a stew made with dasheen leaves, okra, aubergines, tomatoes, onions and garlic with meat or crab, all cooked in coconut milk and flavoured with herbs and spices. Also called **kallaloo, calaloo, callau, callilu**

callaloo soup *Caribbean* A soup made from dasheen leaves, okra, crabmeat, salt pork, onions, garlic and sometimes coconut

callau, callilu See **callaloo**

callos *Spain* Tripe, usually served in a stew with chick peas

calmar *France* Squid and flying squid, a speciality of Aix en Provence

Calocarpum mammosum *Botanical name* Sapote

Calocarpum viride *Botanical name* Green sapote

calorie The outdated measure of the energy content of foods, still used in popular parlance to estimate the fattening potentiality of food (since if not used for energy, food is usually stored as fat). The Calorie *(capital C)* or kilocalorie used in nutrition has 1000 times the value of the calorie *(small c)* used in science and is the energy required to heat 1 kg of water by 1°C. See also **joule**

calorific value The amount of heat produced when 1 g (small calorie) or 1 kg (large Calorie or kilocalorie) of food is completely burned or metabolized to carbon dioxide and water by oxygen

calostro *Spain* **1.** A semi-hard, sharp-tasting cheese. See also **Armada 2.** Beestings

calrose rice A type of slightly glutinous white rice with a higher starch content than normal making it easier to eat with chopsticks

caltrops A very similar fruit to **water caltrop** of the related species, *Trapa natans*. It too has been used as a food source since Neolithic times and is still grown and eaten in central Europe and Asia. It has a floury texture and an agreeable flavour and may be eaten raw, roasted or boiled like a chestnut. Also called

Jesuit's nut (NOTE: It also is often called a water chestnut, but it is not the canned water chestnut familiar in the West.)

cá luôc *Vietnam* Boiled fish

calvados *France* An alcoholic spirit made by distilling cider, much used for flavouring dishes from Normandy

calves' kidneys Light coloured, tender and delicately flavoured kidney of young cattle, grilled or fried

calves' liver A golden brown, smooth and delicate liver much used in Italian cooking. Requires very little cooking.

calzone *Italy* A yeasted, white bread dough, rolled out thinly, formed into a pocket and filled with cheese or salami and cheese (in Naples) or with onions, olives, anchovies, capers and cheese, rather like a large pizza. Baked in the oven or if small sometimes fried. Also called **calzuncieddi**

cá ma-cá-ren *Vietnam* Mackerel

ca mang *Vietnam* Bangus, the fish

camarão *Portugal* Common prawn

Camargue *France* A soft, creamy cheese made from ewes' milk and flavoured with fresh thyme and bay

Camargue red rice A natural hybrid between short-grain rice and the wild red rice of the Camargue discovered in 1980. It has the red colour and subtle taste of its wild parent but does not shed its grain on ripening.

camarón *Spain* Common prawn

camaroon *Philippines* Large shrimp or prawn

Cambazola A dull, fat, soft, blue-veined German cheese with a white Camembert-type rind

Cambridge bronze Bronze turkey

Cambridge burnt cream *England* Burnt cream

Cambridge cheese York cheese

Cambridge sauce *England* A processed mixture of hard-boiled egg yolks, anchovy fillets, capers, mustard, tarragon, chervil and chives, made into a thick emulsion sauce with oil and vinegar and finished with chopped parsley. Served with cold meat.

Cambridge sausage *England* A lean pork frying sausage flavoured with sage, cayenne pepper, ground mace, nutmeg and seasoning

camel A large domesticated animal from arid regions with either one hump, *Camelus dromedarius*, or two, *C. bactrianus*, used both as a draught animal and as a source of meat and milk. The fat in the milk is very finely dispersed and cream cannot be separated from it.

Camembert *France* A soft, small, wheel-shaped cheese about 250 g in weight made from full cream cows' milk, dry-salted to 3% salt, surface-ripened for 10 to 14 days with *Penicillium candidum* and *P.camembertii*, which forms a white fungus on the rind, then wrapped in paper and boxed. Contains 57% water, 21% fat and 20% protein, half of which is hydrolysed by the fungus. Originating in Normandy but now widely produced.

Camembert de Normandie *France* The traditional Camembert cheese from Normandy made with unpasteurized milk and specially licensed with Appellation d'Origine status

Camerano *Spain* A soft goats' milk cheese, moulded in wicker baskets and eaten within one day of draining and salting

camicia, in *Italy* **1.** Poached. Used of eggs. **2.** Baked in their jackets. Used of potatoes. (NOTE: Literally 'in a shirt'.)

camoscio *Italy* Chamois, a small goat-like mammal, *Rupicapra rupicapra*, famous for its leather, but the meat is eaten in Italy, usually marinated and stewed

camotes *Philippines, Spain* Sweet potatoes

campagnola, alla *Italy* Country-style

camp coffee A liquid extract of coffee and chicory once used as an instant coffee

campden tablets A mixture of sodium metabisulphite, E223, and potassium benzoate, E212, used as a food and wine preservative

campo, di *Italy* Wild. Used of e.g. mushrooms, asparagus, etc. (NOTE: Literally 'of the field'.)

Campylobacter A genus of food-poisoning bacteria found in raw meat and poultry which cause diarrhoea, vomiting and fever

Campylobacter jejuni A food-poisoning bacteria found in chicken and milk which is a major cause of gastroenteritis. The incubation period is 2 to 10 days and the duration of the often severe illness, which is flu-like with abdominal pain and fever followed by diarrhoea, is 5 to 10 days.

ca muc *Cambodia* Cuttlefish

ca mu cham *Vietnam* Garoupa, the fish

cá muoi *Vietnam* Salt fish

can *United States* Any metal container used for keeping or preserving food, hermetically sealed if used for preservation

can, to To preserve food in a sealed, tin-plated steel or aluminium can by heating after sealing to cook and sterilize the contents

Canadian bacon See **Canadian-style bacon**

Canadian Cheddar A Cheddar-type cheese made in Canada

Canadian plaice See **American plaice**

Canadian service A variation on English service in which the host or hostess apportions the food on a plate and passes it to a guest

Canadian-style bacon A quick-cured mild bacon with more sugar and less salt than normal in the curing liquid

canalons a la barcalonesa *Catalonia* A type of stuffed cannelloni. See also **canelons a la barcalonesa**

caña medular *Spain* Marrow bone

canapé *England, France* Small biscuits or pieces of toast covered with various savoury items and decorated. Served at buffets, cocktail parties and with drinks. (NOTE: Literally 'couch or settee'.)

canard *France* Duck

canard à la presse *France* Breasts of lightly roasted (20 minutes) Rouen duck sliced and warmed at the table in a mixture of brandy and the blood and juices obtained by crushing in a press the remainder of the carcass less the legs. Sometimes flambéed with brandy. Also called **canard rouennais à la presse**

canard à l'orange *France* Duck with orange. Roast mallard (200°C, 40 min.) or widgeon or teal (220°C, 25 min.), previously seasoned and flavoured, served with sauce made from defatted pan residues, red wine, stock and Seville orange juice thickened with **fécule** or arrowroot. Garnished with wedges of sweet orange and watercress.

canardeau *France* A duckling (slightly older than a caneton)

canard rouennais *France* A specially bred duck from the Rouen district, usually filled with a stuffing made from its own liver, roasted and served with a red wine sauce

canard rouennais à la presse *France* See **canard à la presse**

canard sauvage *France* Wild duck, usually mallard duck

Canary pudding *England* A basic steamed pudding mixture with half the flour replaced with fresh breadcrumbs, a third to a half of the milk with Madeira, and flavoured with grated lemon zest

Canavalia ensiformis Botanical name Jack bean

Canavalia gladiata Botanical name Sword bean

cancalaise, à la *France* In the Cancale (Brittany) style, i.e. with a fish sauce made from white wine with mussels, prawns and oysters

canch mexicana *Mexico* A chicken broth containing chopped onions and tomatoes sweated in butter, rice, diced chicken meat and chopped mint

candied fruit Pieces of fruit soaked in a heavy sugar syrup until all the water is replaced with the syrup, then dried so that the surface is covered with crystalline sugar unlike glacé fruit. Used as a confectionery item and for decoration. Also called **crystallized fruit**, **preserved fruit**

candied peel Citrons, halved, pulp removed, immersed in brine or sea water for 1 month to ferment then washed, dried and candied with sugar syrup. Usually candied in the country where used. Sometimes used as a confectionery item but more usually chopped and used in cakes.

canditi *Italy* Candied fruit

candle, to To examine eggs in front of an intense light to see if they are fresh and to assess their quality

candle fruit A North African variety of aubergine, shaped like a small banana with ivory coloured skin

candlenut The macadamia-shaped nut of a tree, *Aleurites moluccana*, grown in Southeast Asia. When ground, used as a thickening agent in Malaysian cooking. It must be cooked before consumption to detoxify it. The kernel is removed by charring the outer shell so that it can be cracked. (NOTE: So called because the nuts were once ground to a paste with copra and cotton to make candles)

cane *France* A female duck

canel *Caribbean* Cinnamon

canela *Central America, Portugal, Spain* Cinnamon (NOTE: Cinnamon is the most important spice used in Portugal.)

canela em pau *Portugal* Cinnamon quill

canelle knife A small knife shaped so that thin narrow strips of skin may be cut from the skin of citrus fruit, cucumbers, etc.

canellini *Italy* A generic name for all types of white beans

canelones *Spain* Minced meat

canelons a la barcalonesa *Catalonia* Cannelloni stuffed with a cooked chicken liver and pork meat filling

canesca *Italy* A variety of shark

Canestrato *Italy* A semi-hard scalded-curd Sicilian cheese made from ewes' milk and matured in a wicker basket to give it a distinctive surface pattern. Also called **Incanestrato**, **Pecorino**, **Pecorino canestrato**, **rigato**, **Siciliano**

canestrelli *Italy* 1. Small scallops 2. Sweet scallop-shaped pastries from the northwest

cane syrup *United States* The concentrated juice from sugar cane used in place of golden syrup or molasses

caneton *France* A small duck or duckling

caneton à la rouennaise *France* A Rouen duck strangled, plucked whilst warm, liver less the gall bladder returned to the cavity, spit-roasted for 15 to 30 minutes and skinned. Legs removed and thigh bones excised, brushed with butter, grilled and salted, wing removed, panéed and grilled and all, together with the sliced breast, served with a sauce made with juices pressed from the carcass, red wine, shallots and the sieved liver.

caneton rouennais *France* A specially bred duckling from the Rouen district, generally pot-roasted or roasted but may be braised if to be served cold

cangrejo *Spain* Crab

cangrejo de mar *Spain* Shore crab

cangrejo de rio *Spain* Freshwater crayfish

cangrejo moruno *Spain* A small furry crab, *Eriphia verrucosa*, found in the Mediterranean and used particularly in the paella of the Balearic islands

canh ga *Vietnam* Chicken wing

canistel *United States* An egg-shaped fruit, *Pucheria campechiana*, with a thin glossy skin and a yellowish, creamy and slightly sweet flesh. Used in fruit salads.

canja *Portugal* A clear chicken soup with rice, shreds of chicken breast, mint and lemon juice

canja de galinha *Portugal* Chicken broth with chicken livers and rice

can measure *United States* North American recipes sometimes use USA can sizes as a volume measure. They are approximately: buffet, 236 ml; picnic, 295 ml; no. 300, 413 ml; no. 1 tall and no. 303, 472 ml; no. 2, 590 ml; no. 21/2, 826 ml; no. 3 cylinder, 1375 ml and no. 10, 2830 to 3060 ml. See also **liquid measure, dry measure, cup measure, market measure, volume measure**

canneberge *France* A cranberry

canned food Food preserved in cans or tins

cannella *Italy* Cinnamon

cannelle *France* Cinnamon

cannellino bean A variety of haricot bean, *Phaseolus vulgaris*, slightly larger than normal, now extensively grown and used in Italy. Also called **fazolia bean**

cannelloni *Italy* Large squares of thin pasta which are first poached, then rolled around a stuffing to form tubes which are placed in a dish, covered in a sauce, possible gratinated with cheese and baked in the oven

cannelon *France* A small puff pastry roll, filled with meat, fish, poultry or game

cannocchia *Italy* Mantis shrimp

cannoli *Italy* Horn-shaped pastries filled with cream cheese, whipped cream, custard, chocolate cream or similar

cannolicchi *Italy* Short and fairly thick tubes of pasta used in soups. Also called **ave maria**

cannolichio *Italy* Razor shell, mollusc

canola Rapeseed

can opener An implement for removing the tops from sealed cans of food

canotière, à la *France* In the boatman's style, i.e. freshwater fish cooked with shallots, mushrooms and white wine

canotière, sauce *France* The lightly salted cooking liquor from poached freshwater fish reduced by two thirds, thickened with **beurre manié**, simmered 5 minutes, strained and finished with butter and a little cayenne pepper

Cantal *France* A large (up to 50 kg) semi-hard cheese made from cows' milk and matured from 3 to 5 months. The rind is grey with red streaks and has a powdery surface, and the paste is firm, full of bite and has a nutty flavour. It has been made for at least 2000 years and is protected by an Appellation d'Origine. Contains 44% water, 26% fat and 23% protein. Also called **Fourme de Cantal**, **Fourme de Salers, Salers**

Cantalon *France* A smaller version of Cantal cheese

cantaloup *England, France* Cantaloupe melon

cantaloupe melon 1. A variety of sweet melon, *Cucumis melo*, developed in Cantelupo, central Italy. It has a grey-green rough skin with deep longitudinal grooves, the flesh is orange-yellow, very sweet and fragrant, and individual fruits weigh up to 750 g. It is ripe when there is a slight give at the stalk end under gentle pressure. The principle types in Europe are the charentais, ogen, tiger and sweetheart. Also called **rock melon 2.** *United States* Musk melon

canterellen *Netherlands* Chanterelle mushrooms

canthaxanthin See **E161(g)**

Cantonese cooking The style of cooking from southeast China, including stir-frying of meat and vegetables with the addition of corn flour-thickened chicken stock, sweet-and-sour dishes, and steamed sweet and savoury delicacies known as **dim sum**

Cantonese onion Chinese chive

cantucci *Italy* Small hard, sweet biscuits containing almond pieces. Traditionally dunked in Vin (or Vino) Santo, a rich sherry-like wine from Tuscany. Also called **cantuccini**

cantuccini *Italy* Cantucci

canvas back *United States* A wild duck, *Aythya valisineria*, with a distinctly flavoured flesh due to its diet of wild celery shoots

cao gu *China* Straw mushroom

cao mei *China* See **strawberry**

capão *Portugal* Capon

caparon *Italy* Shellfish

capeado *Spain* Battered and deep-fried

cape gooseberry A cherry-sized, yellow-fleshed, slightly sour fruit of a plant *Physalis peruviana* originally from Peru but now grown in Egypt, Colombia and South Africa. It is loosely enclosed in a segmented, papery, fawn husk which looks like a Chinese lantern. Used in fruit salads and for decoration. Also called **physalis**, **goldenberry**

capelan See **capelin**

capelin *United States* A medium oily fish, *Mallotus villosus*, similar to smelt and up to 25 cm in length. It is greenish on top and white underneath and found in the North Atlantic. Also called **capelan**, **caplin**

capelli d'angelo *Italy* Angel's hair

capellini *Italy* A very thin spaghetti

capelvenere *Italy* Maidenhead fern

caper The flower bud of a small Mediterranean bush, *Capparis spinosa* or *C. inermis*, which is pickled in brine for use in sauces and on pizzas.

capercaillie A large game bird, *Tetrao urogallus*, about the size of a turkey, common in Scandinavia, northern Russia and the alps and recently reintroduced to Scotland. In season 1st October to 31st January; hanging time 7 to 14 days. Also called **capercailzie**, **wood grouse**

capercailze See **capercaillie**

caperizzoli *Italy* Molluscs

caper mayonnaise Chopped capers, chopped sweet red peppers and tarragon vinegar mixed with mayonnaise

caper sauce A velouté sauce made from mutton stock flavoured with chopped capers, served with boiled leg of mutton. See also **câpres, sauce aux**

capillaire commun *France* Maidenhair fern

capillaire syrup A thick mucilaginous liquid extracted from the maidenhead fern and flavoured with orange flower water or other

capillari *Italy* Tiny eels

capilotade *France* Boned-out leftovers of chicken or game birds sliced and reheated in **sauce italienne** with some sweated sliced mushrooms, garnished with chopped

parsley and accompanied by heart-shaped croûtons

capilotade, en *France* In crumbs, squashed to a pulp or to bits. Used of a cake.

capirotada *Mexico* Bread pudding

capitaine *Central Africa* The Nile perch, *Lates niloticus*, which is prized throughout Africa for its eating qualities. It is found in the Nile, Lake Chad, Lake Victoria and the Congo and Niger rivers. Usually grilled or fried and served with hot sauce, e.g. pili-pili sauce. Also called **Nile perch**, **mbuta**

capitone *Italy* Conger eel

caplin See **capelin**

capocollo *Italy* Boned out, skinned, cured and cooked pork shank, rolled in ground spices and pepper and served in thin slices

capon A castrated male domestic fowl which grows larger and is more tender than the intact bird

caponata *Italy* A salad of fried aubergines and onions with tomatoes, anchovies, capers and olives served on a large dry biscuit or toasted bread. Other fruits and vegetables may be included together with some sugar and vinegar and the whole mixture may be reduced to a thick chutney-like consistency.

caponatine *Italy* A salad of pickled vegetables

capone gallinella *Italy* Tub gurnard

capozzella *Italy* Roasted lamb's head

cappa *Italy* Razor shell, mussel, various shellfish generally

cappa ai ferri *Italy* Grilled scallops

cappa liscia *Italy* Venus shell clam

cappalletti *Italy* Small ravioli made in the shape of a three cornered hat, usually stuffed with a **mousseline** of fish or shellfish

Capparis inermis Botanical name Caper bush, spineless variety

Capparis spinosa Botanical name Caper bush, spiny variety

cappelle di fungo *Italy* Mushroom caps

cappello *Italy* Hat. Used of foods shaped like a hat, either conical or like an Italian priest's, e.g. pies or boned-out hams, etc.

capperi *Italy* Capers

cappone *Italy* 1. Capon 2. Gurnard, the fish

cappone in galera *Italy* A salad of anchovies and capers

capponi *Italy* Small red mullet

cappon magro *Italy* A mixed salad of cooked vegetables, anchovies, fish, lobster and garlic-flavoured rusks

cappuccino *Italy* 1. Espresso coffee mixed with milk that has been boiled and foamed by steam injection, served with a sprinkling of ground spice such as cinnamon, nutmeg or cocoa 2. Nasturtium leaves

cappuccio, a *Italy* Round, as in round lettuce (NOTE: Literally 'like a hood or cap'.)

cappucina *Italy* Lettuce

capra *Italy* **1.** Goat **2.** A freshwater lake fish similar to trout

capra di mare *Italy* Spider crab

câpre *France* Caper

câpres, sauce aux *France* Butter sauce with the addition of 120 g of capers per litre at the last moment. Served with boiled fish.

capretto *Italy* Kid, young goat

caprice, fish As **fish Saint Germain**, but topped with a lengthways slice of banana passed through seasoned flour and shallow-fried. Served with Robert sauce.

Caprice des Dieux *France* An oval-shaped, mild, soft cheese from the Champagne region made from cows' milk with added cream and sold in a small box

capricorn *England* A goats' milk cheese from Somerset with a relatively mild flavour and cast in cylinders

caprini *Italy* Small goats' milk cheeses

caprino di pasta cruda *Italy* A soft cheese made from unpasteurized goats' milk and ripened for 3 months

caprino semicotto *Italy* A hard scalded-curd goats' milk cheese from Sardinia made in a drum shape. The cheese is brined, dry-salted and ripened for at least 3 months.

capriolo *Italy* Deer, roebuck

caprylic acid A fatty acid which when esterified is a constituent of goats' milk fat, butter fat and coconut oil. When liberated by oxidation it has a rancid goaty smell.

capsaicin The hot flavouring component of chilli peppers and cayenne peppers

capsanthin A peppery flavouring and pink food colouring obtained from paprika. Also called **capsorubin**. See also **E160(c)**

Capsella bursa-pastoris *Botanical name* Shepherd's purse

capsicum The general name for the hollow seed pods of plants of the genus *Capsicum* which are relatives of the tomato. They range from green, yellow or red sweet peppers to the very hot chilli and cayenne peppers, not to be confused with the spice pepper *Piper nigrum*. See also **sweet pepper**, **chilli peppers**, **cayenne pepper**

Capsicum annuum **Grossum Group** *Botanical name* Sweet peppers

Capsicum annuum **Longum Group** *Botanical name* Chilli peppers

Capsicum frutescens *Botanical name* Cayenne peppers

capsorubin See **capsanthin**

capuchina *Spain* Nasturtium

capucine *France* Nasturtium

caquelon *Switzerland* A wide-based pot with a short stubby handle to one side in which cheese fondue is prepared and kept hot and molten over a spirit lamp or candle

carabasso arrebossat *Catalonia* Deep-fried battered courgettes. See also **carbasó arrebossat**

carabinero *Spain* A large king prawn. See also **crevette rouge**

caracóis *Portugal* Snails

caracoles *Spain* Snails

caracol gris *Spain* Winkle

carafe An open-topped glass container with a bulbous or conical shape used to serve wine or water (with a narrow-flared top) or coffee (with a wide-flared top and a handle) at meals

caraili sauce *Caribbean* A hot sauce from St Vincent made from chilli peppers deseeded and finely sliced, bitter gourds boiled in salt water drained and seeds removed and the flesh thinly sliced, finely chopped onions, Caribbean cilantro, sliced raw carrot, chives, parsley and finely chopped garlic marinated in vinegar, lime juice and oil with salt and pepper. Used with fish etc.

carajay *Philippines* Wok

carambola The fruit of a small evergreen tree, *Averrhoa carambola*, from Southeast Asia which, when cut across its axis, has the appearance of a five-pointed star. The crisp yellow flesh has an acid, sweet and aromatic flavour and it is often used for decoration. The flavour and colour are improved by poaching it in a little light syrup. It can also be used for jam and chutney. Also called **star fruit**

caramel *England, France* The golden-brown distinctly flavoured compound formed when sugar is heated to 182°C. Used for colouring, as an ingredient in its own right and to flavour the confectionery called caramel. (NOTE: In its darker form it is the permitted food colouring E150.)

caramel cream Crème caramel

caramel custard *England* Crème caramel

caramelize, to To cause sugars to break down into brown flavoured compounds by heating to around 180–185°C. Caramelizing is responsible for some of the brown colour developed by baking, frying, roasting or grilling sugar-containing foods.

caramelized potatoes See **brunede kartofler**

caramella *Italy* Caramel

caramellato *Italy* Caramelized, candied or glazed

caramelo *Spain* Caramel

caramel sauce *England* A hot sauce made with caramel, water and butter (3:2:2), whisked together

caramel stage See **sugar cooking**

caramote *France* A transverse-striped king prawn, *Penaeus kerathurus*, from the Mediterranean. It is brown with reddish tints becoming pink when cooked and is up to 22 cm long. It is considered to be the finest crustacean flesh in the world. Also called **crevette royale, grosse crevette**

caramujo *Spain* Winkle

cá rán *Vietnam* Fried fish

caranguejo *Portugal* Crab

carapace The hard upper shell of crustaceans, tortoises or turtles

carapau *Portugal* A small seawater fish between a sardine and smelt in size

carapulca *South America* A Peruvian stew made from meat, papa seca, tomatoes, onions and garlic

caraque A form of flaked chocolate made by coating a thin layer of chocolate on marble or on a steel tray, allowing it to set and cool, then removing it with a scraper as though stripping paint

caraway The plant from which **caraway seeds** are obtained. The young leaves may be used in salads and soups and the roots can be cooked as a vegetable.

caraway mint Sprouted caraway seeds used as a herb in Vietnamese cooking

caraway seeds The small brown seeds of a biennial European plant, *Carvum carvi*, with a sweet aromatic flavour. Used to flavour rye bread, cakes, cheese and other foods and is the principal flavouring in Kümmel liqueur.

carbasó arrebossat *Catalonia* Deep-fried battered courgettes

carbohydrates The principal energy sources in human food which are simple sugars (*monosaccharides*) or chains of repeated sugar units (*disaccharides, trisaccharides and polysaccharides*). The polysaccharides have many repeated sugar units and are starches or various types of cellulose. They are all with the exception of cellulose and a few starches broken down in the gut into absorbable monosaccharides either by acids and enzymes in the gastric juices or by the action of microorganisms. See also **monosaccharide, cellulose, dietary fibre**

carbonade *France* Meat grilled over charcoal but now often used of very dark-coloured braised beef. Also called **carbonnade**

carbonade of beef See **carbonade à la flamande**

carbonado *Argentina* Beef stew with apples, pears, potatoes, tomatoes and onions

carbonara *Italy* The sauce or dressing used with **spaghetti alla carbonara**

carbonata *Italy* A dish from the northwest of beef or salt beef stewed in red wine. Often served with polenta.

carbonate, to To dissolve carbon dioxide gas in a liquid as in the production of soft drinks or some sparkling wines

carbonated water Water in which carbon dioxide has been dissolved. Sometimes stored under pressure. The gas is released when the pressure is reduced or when the water is warmed up or on contact with the mouth. Also called **soda water, mineral water**

carbon black A very finely divided form of carbon used as a food colouring. Also called **vegetable carbon**. See also **E153**

carbon dioxide The gas produced when the carbon in foods is oxidized either by the action of yeasts and other microorganisms, by combustion or by cellular processes in the body, or when chemical raising agents are heated or react in water. The gas is responsible for the raising of bread, cakes, etc. See also **E290**

carbonnade *France* Charcoal-grilled meat or beef braised dark brown. See also **carbonade**

carbonnade à la flamande *Belgium* A stew made from beef, onions, garlic and dark beer, thickened with slices of bread coated in French mustard (NOTE: So called because of its dark ('carbonated') colour.)

carborundum stone A hard stone made from finely powdered silicon carbide fused together. Used for sharpening knives; often shaped like a steel and used in the same way. Causes more wear than a conventional steel.

carboxymethyl cellulose A non-nutritive cellulose derivative used for thickening and stabilizing ice cream and jellies. It is also used as wallpaper paste.

carcass The body of a slaughtered animal, prepared for use as meat

carcasse *France* A carcass, e.g. of chicken

carcass of chicken The remains of plucked and dressed chicken after the legs, breasts and wings have been removed. Cut into 3 pieces for chicken sauté so as to add flavour to the pan residues or used for stock.

carciofi alla romana *Italy* Artichokes boiled in oil with herbs

carciofini *Italy* Artichoke hearts

carciofo *Italy* Artichoke

carciofo alla giudea *Italy* Jerusalem artichoke

cardamine *France, Italy, Spain* Lady's smock

Cardamine pratensis *Botanical name* Lady's smock

cardamom The dried fruit of a perennial bush, *Elettaria cardamomum*, belonging to the ginger family, consisting of green or bleached pods (5 to 10 mm long) containing loose black seeds with an aromatic flavour and smell. Larger pods are in general brown to black and their seeds are of a lower quality and used in pickles and chutneys. Cardamom is used to flavour coffee in the Middle East as well as being common in Indian, Eastern and Scandinavian cuisines. Young cardamom leaves are used as a food wrapping and to flavour food in Southeast Asian cuisines. Cheap cardamom substitutes are Nepal cardamom, Chinese cardamom, Javanese winged cardamom and Ethiopian cardamom. Also called **cardamon**, **cardamum**

cardamome *France* Cardamom

cardamomo *Italy, Spain* Cardamom

cardamon, cardamum Cardamom

cardeau *France* A sardine

cardi *Italy* A relative of the globe artichoke. See also **cardoon**

cardinal *France* A term used to describe the pinky-red colour of food by analogy with the colour of a cardinal's robes

cardinal, sauce *France* A pink sauce based on lobster and truffles, served with fish

cardinal fish The large red mullet of the Mediterranean. Considered to be the finest quality.

cardinal suppe *Norway* A cream soup containing chopped ham and noodles

cardine *France* Megrim, the fish

cardon *France* A cardoon

cardone *Italy* A cardoon

cardoni *United States* A thistle-like plant resembling celery with an artichoke flavour. Used cooked or raw in salads.

cardoon *Scolymus cardunculus*, a relative of the globe artichoke, which can grow to a height of 2 or more metres. The thick celery-like stems are blanched whilst growing in the autumn to reduce bitterness and used as a vegetable. They need long slow cooking. The leaves, roots and buds can also be used.

cardo silvestre *Spain* Cardoon

Carême, Antonin (1784 – 1833) A famous French chef who worked for George IV, Napoleon and Czar Alexander amongst others, originated the classic French repertoire of cooking, 'La Grande Cuisine', and developed the organization of the brigade of chefs into specialities

cargol *Catalonia* Snail

cargo rice A dark rice which has only been dehusked, rich in bran, protein, vitamins, etc.

cari *France, Spain* Curry

Caribbean banana bread *Caribbean* Pain fig banane

Caribbean black pudding *Caribbean* An exotic black pudding made with chopped spring onions, sweet red peppers, grated sweet potato or boiled rice, pig's blood, butter, seasoning and marjoram, well mixed, packed into hog casings leaving room for expansion, tied in circles, simmered for 20 minutes, pricked, cooked for a further 30 minutes and served hot

caribou Moose

Carica papaya *Botanical name* The papaya tree

caril *Portugal* Curry powder

carlins *England* Soaked and boiled pigeon peas which are drained, fried in butter and sweetened with brown sugar and possibly a little rum. From Northumberland.

Carlsbad prune A large dessert prune meant to be eaten at the end of a meal

Carlton salad dressing Pineapple juice thickened with a **sabayon** whilst whisking vigorously, cooled, a well-rubbed mixture of hard-boiled yolk of egg, raw yolk of egg, French mustard and vinegar whisked in and all finished with slightly whipped double cream

carmarguaise, à la *France* In the Carmargue style, i.e. cooked with tomatoes, garlic, orange peel, olives, herbs and wine or brandy

carmine See **cochineal**

carmoisine E122, a synthetic red food colouring. Also called **azorubine**

carn *Catalonia* Meat

cârnăcior *Romania* A grilling sausage made with ground lamb, garlic and spices

carnaroli riso The best superfino Italian risotto rice from Piedmont, well rounded and extremely absorbent

carnauba A Brazilian palm, *Copernicia cerifera*, with an edible starchy root. Also the source of carnauba wax. Also called **wax palm**

carnauba wax The wax from the Brazilian palm used in the food industry as a glazing agent in sugar and chocolate confectionery. See also **E903**

carne *Italy, Portugal, Spain* Meat, e.g. carne de porco is pork in Portuguese, carne di maiale is the same in Italian and so on

carne a la castellana *Spain* Meat served with tomatoes, potato croquettes and onion rings

carne asada a la parilla *Spain* Boiled meat

carne asada al horno *Spain* Baked or roasted meat

carne de boi *Portugal* Beef

carne de cerdo *Spain* Pork

carne de cordero *Spain* Lamb

carne de membrillo *Spain* Quince jelly, reduced to a thick paste, usually eaten with cheese

carne de porco à algarvia *Portugal* Fried pork and clams

carne de ternera *Spain* Veal

carne de vaca *Portugal, Spain* Beef

carne de veado *Portugal* Venison

carne de venado *Spain* Venison

carne de vinha de alhos *Portugal* Pickled pork

carne di maiale *Italy* Pork

carne ensopada *Brazil* A pot roast of beef, bacon, ham, garlic, onions, butter and seasoning

carne in umido *Italy* Stewed beef

carneiro *Portugal* Mutton

carne lessa *Italy* Boiled beef

carne mechada *Central America* A stuffed beef roll, boiled and served sliced with its puréed cooking liquor

carne picada *Portugal* Chopped or minced meat

carne picardo *Spain* Minced meat

carnero *Spain* Mutton

carne secca *Italy* The Tuscan name for bacon

carnes frias *Portugal* Cold meats sliced and presented as in assiette anglaise

carne tritata *Italy* Minced meat

Carnia *Italy* A semi-hard scalded-curd cows' milk cheese, similar to Montasio, from Friuli

carn i olla *Catalonia* The meat and vegetable part of the traditional Catalan hotpot. See also **escudella i carn d'olla**

carnitine A chemical widely distributed in plant and animal tissues and in particularly high amounts in muscle. No vitamin function has been ascribed to it but it may be involved in fatty acid transport in muscle cells. (NOTE: It has been suggested that carnitine may be connected with the medical condition myalgic encephalopathy (ME, chronic fatigue syndrome).)

carob The fruit of a leguminous evergreen tree, *Ceratonia siliqua*, from the Mediterranean. The brown, ripe seed pods (20 by 2.5 cm) contain an edible sweet pulp and hard inedible seeds. The pulp is dried and ground into a powder resembling and used as a substitute for cocoa and chocolate powder especially by those who required stimulant-free confectionery and drinks. Also called **locust bean**

carob flour See **carob powder**

carob powder The powdered dried inner pulp of the carob bean, used in place of cocoa powder in cakes and drinks. Also called **carob flour, St John's bread**

Carolina duck *United States* A highly prized wild duck, *Aix sponsa*, shot for the table. Also called **wood duck**

Carolina rice A round short-grain rice from South Carolina which, when cooked, is sticky, but not as sticky as Italian rice. Used for puddings, Italian-style risotto and as a staple carbohydrate in China and Japan. The seed was originally introduced into the USA from Italy by Thomas Jefferson.

Carolina whiting *United States Merluccius americanus* or *Merluccius undulatus*, a similar fish to the North Atlantic whiting

caroline *France* 1. A small eclair made from choux pastry, often filled with a savoury stuffing as a hors d'oeuvres 2. Chicken consommé with rice and chervil

carom Ajowan

carota *Italy* Carrot

carotenes Various yellow/orange pigments in carrots and other yellow and green vegetables and fruit. It is converted into the antioxidant vitamin A in the body and used as a permitted orange food colouring E160(a). Lycopene in tomatoes and beta-carotene in carrots are two well-known examples. Also called **carotenoids, provitamin A**

carotenoids See **carotenes**

carotte *France* Carrot

carottes, purée de *France* Carrot soup

carottes vichy *France* Vichy carrots

caroube *France* Carob

carp A medium-oily, variously coloured, freshwater fish, *Cyprinus carpio*, which is found worldwide both in the wild and farmed, harvested at 30 – 60 cm long (1.5 – 2.5 kg) but can grow much bigger. A common feast dish in Central Europe and highly regarded in Asia.

carpa *Italy, Spain* Carp

carpaccio *Italy* Raw fillet of beef, sliced paper thin and served with a mustard sauce or oil and lemon juice

carp caviar *United States* Female carp roe, treated to resemble and used as a substitute for caviar

carpe *France* Carp

carpe à la juive *France* Baked carp stuffed with raisins, chopped almonds, herbs and spices, originates in the Alsace region of France

carpeau *France* A young carp

carpet bag steak A thick beef steak (**sirloin** or **fillet**) into which a pocket is cut and filled with oysters, then grilled. Popular in Australia and North America, but originated in the UK when oysters were very cheap.

carpet shell A small European bivalve mollusc, *Tapes decussatus,* with a dark grey shell, similar to various small clams

carpet shell clam A white to light brown clam, *Venerupis decussata,* with dark brown radial markings and up to 8 cm in diameter. It is found around Britain and in the Mediterranean and can be eaten raw like an oyster.

carpion *France* A type of trout

carpione *Italy* Carp

carragahen *Spain* See **carragheen**

carrageen See **carragheen**

carragheen *Ireland, France* An extract of the seaweeds *Chondrus crispus* and *Gigantina stellata*. These are rinsed, kept damp and bleached in the open air until creamy white, dried and used as a thickening agent. Used in Jamaica as the basis of a punch called Irish moss. Also called **Irish moss**, **sea moss, pearl moss, carrageen**. See also **E407**

carré *France* Best end (of lamb, carré d'agneau; of veal, carré de veau)

carré de Bray *France* A small, square, soft, creamy cows' milk cheese from Normandy sold on rush mats

carré de l'est *France* A small, square, soft and rather salty Camembert-type cheese made in Lorraine and Champagne from cows' milk. Contains 52% water, 25% fat and 20% protein.

carré de porc *France* The equivalent of the best end of lamb cut from the front of the loin of pork

carrelet *France* Plaice

carrello *Italy* A trolley of desserts or hors d'oeuvre brought to the table in a restaurant

carrettes *United States* Small immature carrots. Also called **French carrots**

carrot An orange-coloured, tubular root vegetable from a biennial plant, *Daucus carota,* common all over the world. One of the aromatic vegetables used for its flavour but also eaten raw when young or cooked as a vegetable.

carrot cake 1. *United States* A cake made with grated raw carrots, oil, sometimes crushed pineapple, flour, sugar, etc. with a cream- cheese-based topping. Also called **paradise cake, passion cake 2.** Various cake recipes found in many countries containing grated young raw carrots in part substitution for or in addition to the flour

carrot soup Basic soup with carrots and a small amount of tomato purée. Served accompanied with croûtons. Also called **carottes, purée de**

carruba *Italy* Carob

carry *France* Curry

çarsi kebabi *Turkey* Cubes of lamb or mutton marinated in vinegar with chopped onions and seasoning, skewered and grilled. Served with a sprinkling of roasted almond slivers and sour cream.

carta cinese *Italy* Rice paper

carta de musica *Italy* A paper-thin crisp bread. Also called **fresa pistocco**

cártamo *Italy, Spain* Safflower

carte *France* A menu in a restaurant

carte, à la *France* Dishes prepared to order and individually priced on the menu, usually more expensive than a fixed menu *(formule)* or a plat du jour

carte du jour *France* The menu of the day, usually cheaper than the à la carte menu, similar to table d'hôte in more prestigious restaurants

carthame *France* Safflower

Carthamus tinctorus *Botanical name* Safflower

cartilage Dense elastic connective tissue in the body which is especially prominent around joints. The younger the animal, the softer and more gelatinous it is. It is solubilized by long slow cooking and adds body to a cooking liquor, hence the use of calves' feet in stews.

cartoccio, al *Italy* En papillote

cartouche *England, France* A circle of buttered greaseproof paper place over the liquid contents in a dish to exclude air and to prevent a skin forming whilst it is cooking or being kept hot

Carum carvi *Botanical name* Caraway

carve, to To cut slices of cooked meat from a large joint for serving or any similar operation. Meat that is roasted is usually left to rest for 10 – 20 minutes to improve its texture for carving.

carvery A restaurant or section of a restaurant where roast or baked joints of meat or poultry are sliced to order and served. Sometimes self-service or at least with customer participation.

carvi *France, Italy* Caraway seed

Carya illionensis *Botanical name* The hickory tree which produces pecan nuts

casa, di *Italy* Home-made

casaba melon Winter melon

casalinga *Italy* Home-made

Casanova *Germany* A soft surface-ripened cows' milk cheese which is creamy and delicate when young but becomes sharper with age. Contains 55% water, 22% fat and 19% protein.

casatella *Italy* A soft fresh rindless cows' milk cheese from Lombardy

cascabel *Mexico* Chilli cascabel

cascadura *Caribbean* A mud-dwelling fish much prized in Trinidad. It must be thoroughly cleaned in fresh water or else the flavour is too strong. It may be curried, made into a Creole stew or barbecued.

cascia, alla maniera di *Italy* In the style of Cascia, i.e. with anchovies, tomatoes and truffles, especially of pasta

casein The main protein found in milk and in cheese

casein mark A mark placed on the rind of a cheese which usually gives the date of manufacture, the geographical source of the cheese and other special quality designations

caseiro *Portugal* Home-made

caserta *Italy* A pepperoni sausage containing chilli

Cashel blue *Ireland* A semi-soft, sharp-flavoured, blue-veined cheese made from unpasteurized milk

cashew apple The fruit associated with the cashew nut. It is eaten raw in Indonesia but generally is only suitable for making jam.

cashew leaves The young leaves of the cashew are used to flavour rice in Java, Indonesia

cashew nut The slightly curved nut from the fruit of a tropical tree, *Anacardium occidentale*, originally from South America but now grown worldwide. The nut and shell hang below the fruit, and the shells contain a skin irritant and are removed before exporting the nuts. See also **cashew leaves**, **cashew apple**. Also called **acajou**

casia *Spain* Cassia

casings The name given to all parts of the alimentary canal from the gullet to the rectum used, after cleaning and treatment, to enclose meat mixtures as in sausages, salamis, puddings, etc. Nowadays casings are often made of plastic. See also **ox casings, hog casings, sheep casings, bung, runner, weasand**

cá sông *Vietnam* Raw fish

casow *Philippines* Cashew nut

cassaba The variety of melon, *Cucumis melo inodorus*, from which various sweet melons, e.g. honeydew, have been bred

cassareep The reduced sweetened spicy juice made from a bitter variety of cassava. Used as a condiment in Caribbean cooking.

cassata *Italy* A compound ice cream made from layers of at least three different flavours and colours containing chopped nuts and chopped glacé fruits. Also called **Neapolitan ice cream**

cassata alla siciliana *Italy* A many-layered chocolate cake from Sicily, soaked in liqueur, filled with Ricotta cheese and decorated with nuts and glacé fruits. Sometimes layered with ice cream.

cassatedde di Ricotta A deep-fried, crescent-shaped pasty filled with chocolate and sweetened Ricotta cheese, the baking powder raised pastry for which is made with flour, wine, butter, lard and sugar

cassava *England, Italy* A tropical, virtually pure starch tuber up to 30 cm long of a plant, *Manihot utilissima*, which is grown in hot countries and used as a major carbohydrate source in South America, Africa and other countries. The roots of some varieties have to be grated and boiled in several changes of water, or partially fermented, to remove toxic cyanide compounds which are in the plant cells and are broken down by enzymes in the sap. The leaves are also edible and do not contain toxic compounds and are cooked as a vegetable or used as a food wrapping. Many people are permanently crippled by the poison especially in Africa. Also called **manioc, tapioca, yuca, yucca**

casse *France* Cassia

casse-croûte *France* A sandwich made by slicing a small crusty French bread (pistolet, flute or baguette) lengthways, then buttering and filling

casser *France* To break, e.g. bones, eggs

casser la croûte *France* To eat

casserole *England, France* 1. A heavy metal, glass or earthenware dish with a tightly fitting lid used for slow cooking of meat, vegetables, etc. 2. Any food cooked in a casserole 3. The trade description for one-dish, in-flight meals prepared by commercial companies for airlines

casserole, en *France* Cooked in a saucepan on top of the stove

casserole, to To cook slowly a selection of ingredients, meat, vegetables, etc., usually in the oven but possibly on the stove in a dish with a tightly closed lid. The food is normally served from the casserole dish.

casserolette A small casserole dish in which food may be heated and/or served

casseruola *Italy* Casserole

cassette *Belgium* A soft, pale, creamy, rectangular cows' milk cheese, seasoned, wrapped in walnut leaves and sold in small willow baskets

cassettine siciliane *Italy* Sweet almond pastries

cassia *England, Italy* A spice which is the inner bark of a tropical evergreen tree, *Cinnamomum cassia*, grown in China and the East. It has a similar aroma to cinnamon but is not as delicate. One of the constituents of five spice powder.

cassia buds The dried unripe fruits of the cassia tree used as a flavouring and as a substitute for curry leaves. The fresh buds and leaves are used as a vegetable.

cassis *France* 1. Blackcurrant 2. A liqueur flavoured with blackcurrant (**crème de cassis**)

cassol *France* The clay cooking pot from Languedoc in which cassoulet is traditionally made

cassola *Italy* Fish soup from Sardinia with chillies and tomatoes. Served with a garlic toast.

cassola de peix *Catalonia* A fish casserole

cassolette *France* A small portion-sized dish or casserole used for presenting small entrées, hors d'oeuvres or entremets, made of pleated paper, silver or china

cassonade *France* Soft brown sugar

cassoni *Italy* Pasties filled with green vegetables and fried

cassoulet *France* A rich stew from Languedoc consisting of haricot beans which have been simmered in a flavoured bouillon, layered in an earthenware pot with lamb or fresh and smoked pork, smoked sausages, possibly **confit d'oie**, onions, carrots and a pig's foot for its gelatine content. Cooked slowly in a casserole in the oven, the lid being removed towards the end to develop a crust on the surface.

castagna *Italy* Chestnut

castagnacci *Italy* Fritters or waffles made with a chestnut flour batter

castagnaccio *Italy* A sort of cake made from a chestnut flour/water paste mixed with pine nuts, fennel seeds and plumped and dried currants or sultanas, placed in a greased baking tray dribbled with olive oil and baked until a crust forms

castagne all'ubriaca *Italy* Peeled roasted chestnuts covered with a cloth soaked in red wine and kept warm for 30 minutes. Eaten as is or with honey.

castaña *Spain* Chestnut

castañas con mantequilla *Spain* Peeled chestnuts simmered in water with celery, salt and sugar for 40 minutes, celery removed, drained and served very hot with butter

Castanea crenata *Botanical name* Japanese chestnut

Castanea sativa *Botanical name* Sweet chestnut

castanha *Portugal* 1. Chestnut 2. Cashew nut

Castelmagno *Italy* A soft blue-veined cows' milk cheese from Cuneo which is ripened in cool damp conditions. It resembles a milder version of Gorgonzola.

Castelo Branco *Portugal* A smooth, white, semi-hard cheese from the town of the same name, made with a mixture of cows' milk and ewes' or goats' milk. and cast in a disc shape. The paste has no holes and no rind. It is delicately flavoured when young but develops a strong flavour after 3–4 weeks.

caster sugar Refined white sugar *(sucrose)* intermediate in size between granulated and icing sugar, used in cake and dessert making because it dissolves easily without forming lumps. Also called **castor sugar**

Castigliano *Spain* A hard ewes' milk cheese with a strong flavour, a pale cream paste and brown rind shaped in a thin disc

castle cheese Schlosskäse

castle pudding A small steamed or baked pudding made from a Victoria sponge mixture flavoured with vanilla and lemon zest cooked in individual dariole moulds and served with jam sauce

castor sugar See **caster sugar**

castradina *Italy* 1. Mutton 2. Smoked and dried mutton from Venice. Usually boiled with rice.

castrato *Italy* Mutton

casuela criola *Caribbean* A typical casserole from Cuba using offal or cheap cuts of meat sautéed in oil. This is then stewed with tomatoes, beans and whatever vegetables are to hand, flavoured with oregano and bay and finally thickened with corn flour. Vegetables are added according to cooking time.

casuelita *Caribbean* A rich Cuban seafood stew made by sweating onions, garlic, tomatoes and chives then adding lobster meat, peeled prawns, white fish goujons and sundry shellfish. This is all cooked gently then let down with hot stock and white wine, seasoned and served hot with a garnish of chopped almonds and parsley.

casu marzu A Sardinian delicacy which was discovered by accident when a pecorino cheese was left outside to ripen and became infested with fly maggots. The maggots caused enzymatic ripening of the cheese by modifying the fats and proteins, making it pungent and runny. (NOTE: Literally 'rotten cheese'. It is said that the maggots can get into a person's eyes, so the cheese is always eaten enclosed in bread.)

cata *France* Dogfish

catabolism The chemical breakdown of food in the mouth, stomach and gut to form simpler compounds (sugars, amino acids, fatty acids etc.) which can be absorbed into the bloodstream

catadromous (Fish) which are born at sea, migrate to brackish or fresh water to grow and then return to the estuaries or the sea to spawn. The eel is a common example. (NOTE: The opposite is **anadromous**.)

cataire *France* Catmint

catalane, à la *France* In the Catalan style, i.e. with tomatoes and rice and possibly olives and aubergine

cataplana *Portugal* A hinged metal cooking container shaped like a giant clam, or two woks, which has a very good seal for use on top of the stove

catchup Ketchup

cater to To provide prepared food for large or small groups usually as part of a business or public enterprise

catfish A medium-oily, white-fleshed, blunt-headed seawater fish, *Anarchis lupus*, with a long dorsal fin and whiskers. It is greenish grey with darker stripes and is found in the North Atlantic. Also called **Atlantic catfish, wolf fish**, **sea cat**, **sea wolf**

catjang bean See **black-eyed pea 1**

catmint A sprawling aromatic hardy perennial plant, *Nepeta cataria*, which may be used as a flavouring for meat or as a tea and the young shoots may be used in salads. If grown in the open the plant will be destroyed by cats who are inordinately attracted to it. Also called **catnip**

catnip Catmint

cat's tongues See **langues de chat**

catsup *United States* Ketchup (usually tomato)

cat tail Bulrush millet

cattle The plural collective English term for all ages and sexes of the bovine species

cattley Strawberry guava

cá tuoi *Vietnam* Fresh fish

Caucasian pilaff A rice pilaff containing chopped lamb and onion which is first fried in lard then simmered in stock with bay and seasoning

cauchoise, à la *France* In the style of Caux in Normandy, i.e. cooked with apples, cream and calvados. Usually refers to meat.

caudière *France* Caudrée

caudle *England* A mixture of freshly soured cream and beaten eggs added to pies and casseroles in Cornwall about 15 minutes before the end of the cooking period (*colloquial*)

caudrée *France* A one-pot meal of vegetables and fish from the north rather like a **potée**, i.e. the liquor is used as the soup course and followed by fish plus vegetables as the main course. Also called **caudière**

caul The lace-like fatty membrane which lines the abdominal cavity of sheep, pigs, etc. Used for covering joints of meat, wrapping stuffed meats, faggots and other foods, where string or casing could be used, to hold their shape during cooking. It has the advantage of adding fat to baste the food and being edible. Also called **lard net**

cauliflower A vegetable, *Brassica olereacea* (Botrytis Group), consisting of a short thick central stalk topped with a white hemispherical head of closely packed immature flowers, 10–15 cm in diameter surrounded with long green leaves. Usually eaten raw, steamed, boiled or pickled.

cauliflower au gratin *United Kingdom* Cauliflower cheese

cauliflower bellevue A steamed whole head of cored cauliflower presented on a plate which has been covered with chopped cooked spinach sautéed in butter with garlic until fairly dry and the cauliflower surrounded decoratively with steamed carrot slices which have been sautéed in butter

cauliflower cheese *United Kingdom* Cooked sprigs of cauliflower coated with a cheese sauce, gratinated with cheese and browned under the grill. Also called **cauliflower au gratin**

cauliflower soup Basic soup with cauliflower, garnished with small cooked florets of cauliflower. Also called **chou-fleur, purée de**

caustic soda See **sodium hydroxide**

cavallucci di Siena *Italy* Small honey cakes containing candied fruit peel and nuts shaped in the form of a horse

cavatieddi *Italy* Pasta curls served with sauces or cheese. Also called **mignuic, mignule**

caveach A method of preserving fish by first frying it then pickling it in vinegar. See also **escabeche**. Also called **pickled fish**

cavedano *Italy* Chub

caviale *Italy* Caviar or substitutes

caviar 1. *England, France, Spain* The very expensive prepared roe of the female **sturgeon** found in the wild in Russia, the Mediterranean, the eastern Atlantic and the western Pacific but now being farmed. The main varieties are beluga, sevruga and osciotre caviar. The colour can vary from white to black and gold to orange brown, but different colours are not mixed. It is prepared from freshly caught fish within 2 hours. The roes are removed carefully and rubbed through a string sieve to remove membranes and then drained. The eggs are mixed with 50 to 80 g of fine salt per kg and preservative according to destination. It is not sterilized and must therefore be kept under refrigeration. It is at its best after 3 days and thereafter develops a fish flavour. **2.** A general term used for prepared fish roe where the eggs are separated so as to resemble sturgeon caviar, e.g. lumpfish roe. See also **imitation caviar**

caviar blanc *France* Mullet roe

caviar butter Butter and caviar (4:1) pounded together and passed through a fine sieve

caviar d'aubergine *France* Poor man's caviar (aubergine purée)

caviar de saumon *France* Salmon roe

caviar niçois *France* A paste made from anchovies, olives and herbs processed with olive oil

caviar pearls See **ikura**

caviar rouge *France* Salmon roe. Also called **caviar de saumon**

caviglione *Italy* Small gurnard

cavolata *Italy* A pork, cabbage and potato soup from Sardinia

cavolfiore *Italy* Cauliflower

cavolfiore alla romana *Italy* Cauliflower browned in oil and served with a tomato sauce gratinated with cheese

cavolfiore alla vastedda *Italy* Cauliflower florets dipped in anchovy butter and deep-fried

cavolfiore alla villeroy *Italy* Cauliflower with lemon sauce

cavolfiore indorato e fritto *Italy* Cauliflower panéed and fried

cavolini di Bruxelles *Italy* Brussels sprouts

cavolo *Italy* Cabbage

cavolo broccoluto *Italy* Broccoli

cavolo marino Sea kale

cavolo nero *Italy* Black cabbage, a type of kale

cavolo rapa *Italy* Kohlrabi

cavolo riccio *Italy* Kale

cavolo verza *Italy* Savoy cabbage

cavroman *Italy* A mutton or lamb stew with potatoes, sweet peppers and onions

cawl *Wales* A basic country soup made of meat and vegetables as available, cooked together in a large pot or cauldron. Bacon or mutton were traditionally the meat used and potatoes, leeks and onions the vegetables. Other ingredients and herbs were at the cook's discretion.

cawl cennin *Wales* A Welsh leek, onion and celery purée soup made with chicken stock. Occasionally a piece of bacon is added. Garnished with chopped chives.

cawl pen lletwad *Wales* A vegetable soup made with whatever vegetables are available but no meat

cawl sir benfro *Wales* Pembrokeshire broth

caws Aberteifi *Wales* A tasty cheese made in Cardigan

caws pobi *Wales* Roasted cheese

çay *Turkey* Strong tea usually served in glasses with sugar but without milk

cayenne chilli A long, thin, red chilli pepper which is extremely hot-flavoured and used to make cayenne pepper

cayenne pepper 1. *also* **cayenne** The dried and finely ground spice made from a variety of cayenne peppers. Used sparingly as a seasoning in Europe and the USA. **2.** The very pungent fruit of a branching perennial bush, *Capsicum frutescens*, which may be yellow, orange or red and is similar in shape to a chilli pepper. May be used sparingly as a flavouring and in sauces. Also called **hot pepper**

cay hoy *Vietnam* Star anise

Cayuga duck The domesticated version of the wild black duck of North America

cay vi *Vietnam* Aniseed

caza *Spain* Game

cazón *Spain* **1.** Smooth hound, the fish **2.** Brown sugar

cazuela *Spain* An earthenware casserole glazed on the inside

cazuela a la catalana *Spain* Minced meat browned in olive oil and reserved; carrots and onions fried until golden in same oil; flour, tomatoes, stock and reserved mincemeat added; all simmered for 45 minutes, then topped with slices of **butifarra** and baked or grilled until piping hot

cazuela de cordero *South America* A lamb and vegetable stew from Chile, containing pumpkin and thickened with beaten egg

cazuela de habas verdes a la granadilla *Spain* French green beans and artichokes with poached eggs

ceba (*plural* **cebes**) *Catalonia* Onion

cebada *Spain* Barley

cebada perlada *Spain* Pearl barley

cebiche A dish of marinated white fish. See also **ceviche**

cebola *Portugal* Onion

cebolado *Portugal* A soft brown paste made by first frying onions and possibly garlic in olive oil until golden brown then covering and sweating until soft and able to be mashed

cebolinha verde *Portugal* Spring onion

cebolinho *Portugal* Chive

cebolla *Spain* Onion

cebolleta *Spain* Shallot

cebollino *Spain* Chive

Cebrero *Spain* A hard, cooked-curd, full-flavoured, firm, mountain cheese made from cows' milk and shaped like a malformed mushroom. Also called **Piedrafita**

cece *Italy* Chick pea (NOTE: The plural form is *ceci.*)

cecenielli *Italy* Deep-fried tiny anchovies and sardines

ceche *Italy* Elvers, fried with garlic and sage, bound with egg and flour and refried as small loose pancakes

ceci *Italy* Chick peas (NOTE: The plural form is *ceci.*)

Cecil A spun curd cows' and/or ewes' milk cheese with no rind from Armenia in which the curd is twisted into a spiral shape to give a 4 kg cheese. Eaten fresh.

cedioli *Italy* Tiny eels

cedoaria *Spain* Zedoary

cédrat *France* Citron, the fruit

cédrat de corse *France* Corsican citron

cedro *Italy* Citron, the fruit

cedro di diamante *Italy* Diamante citron

cedrone *Italy* Capercaillie, the bird

ceebu jën *West Africa* A classic fish dish from Senegal made from whole or filleted fish, slashed and stuffed with **roof**, placed on a bed of onions and smoked fish which have previously been fried in oil, then simmered in water with tomato purée, root vegetables, green vegetables and a chilli pepper until all cooked. When the fish is cooked, it and the vegetables are removed and kept warm; a little of the broth is kept aside, and short-grained rice is cooked in the remainder, (1:2) on liquid, until it has absorbed all the liquid. The rice including the crust at the bottom is turned out on to a large platter and the fish and vegetables are arranged around and on the rice, garnished with parsley and slices of lime and served with the excess broth in a separate dish. Also called **thiebu djen**

cefalo *Italy* Grey mullet

celan *France* Sardine

céleri *France* Celery

céleri, purée de *France* Celery soup

celeriac The thickened globular upper root of a plant, *Apium graveolens* var. *rapaceum*, with a pronounced celery flavour. Much used

as a winter root vegetable in central Europe. Also called **knob celery**

céleri-rave *France* Celeriac

céleri remoulade *France* Grated celeriac in mayonnaise sauce

celery *Apium graveolens* var. *dulce*, one of the aromatic vegetables used for flavouring and also eaten braised or raw. It grows as a cluster of green, ridged crisp stalks about 30 cm long, closely packed and white in the centre with feathery leaves. The whole may be grown in a paper collar to whiten all the stalks. The leaves are used in a bouquet garni. There are other strong-flavoured varieties grown for their seeds or for drying and grinding. See also **wild celery**

celery cabbage Chinese leaves

celery salt A mixture of table salt and dried and ground celery from a strong-tasting variety or a mixture of salt and the essential oil of celery, both used for flavouring

celery sauce Celery hearts simmered with white bouillon, a bouquet garni and an onion clouté until tender, the celery passed through a fine sieve and mixed with an equal quantity of cream sauce and a little of the reduced celery cooking liquor

celery seeds The small brown seeds of a wild celery plant, *Apium graveolens*, native to southern Europe, used as a flavouring in pickles, tomato ketchup and tomato juice. Used by Scandinavians and Russians in soups and sauces.

celery soup Basic soup with celery, garnished with a fine **julienne** of celery cooked in salted water. Also called **céleri, purée de**

celestine *France* A garnish for consommé of strips of fried pancake

cellentani *Italy* Pasta made from short pieces of ridged macaroni shaped in a helix

cellophane noodles Thin dried noodles made from seaweed and mung bean flour which are translucent. Used in Chinese and Japanese cooking. They can be boiled and become soft, slippery and gelatinous, cooked as a stir-fry or deep-fried. Also called **bean thread noodles**, **transparent noodles**, **jelly noodles**, **transparent vermicelli**

cellulose Long-chain polysaccharides grouped into bundles cemented together with other compounds, which form the structural support of all plants and plant parts. Not digested by humans but provides roughage or fibre which swells in the gut and is a necessary component of a healthy diet for correct operation of the bowels.

cellulose derivatives Various derivatives made by adding side chains to cellulose used as bulking and thickening agents. The principal ones used in food manufacture are methyl cellulose, E461, hydroxypropyl-, E463, hydroxypropyl methyl-, E464 and ethyl methyl cellulose, E465.

Celsius scale The scale of temperature in which the freezing point of water is 0 and the boiling point 100, written 0°C and 100°C. Also called **centigrade scale**

celtuce *United States* A lettuce grown for the stalk only which is eaten raw or sliced and braised. Also called **stem lettuce**

cena *Italy* Dinner

cenci *Italy* A Venetian snack of crisp, wafer-thin, deep-fried strips of pastry. See also **galani**

cendawan *Malaysia* Shiitake mushroom

cendré(e) *France* General term for small, strong-flavoured, cows' milk cheeses in a variety of shapes which have been matured in wood ash (NOTE: Literally 'ash-coloured'.)

cengkeh *Indonesia* Cloves

cenoura *Portugal* Carrot

centeio *Portugal* Rye

centeno *Spain* Rye

centigrade scale See **Celsius scale**

centilitre One hundredth of a litre, 10 millilitres. Abbreviation **cl**

centola *Spain* Spider crab

centralized service The service of food in an establishment where trays or plates of food are completely prepared and laid out in the main kitchen and dispatched from there

century egg Chinese preserved egg

cep An edible group of the Boletaceae family, the most common of which is *Boletus edulis*. All are characterized by very fat stems, a round sometimes shiny cap and spongy flesh with tiny pinholes. The edible varieties are fawn to brown with white to brown flesh. They are common in Europe under beech, oak and pine and are slightly phosphorescent at night. They can grow to 1 kg in weight, have a meaty taste and dry well. Used in all mushroom dishes. Also called **penny bun**

cèpe *France* Cep

cèpe de chêne *France* A variety of cep which grows under oak trees and is said to have a finer flavour than the cèpe de pin

cèpe de pin *France* A variety of cep which grows under pine trees

cèpe de vendage *France* A darker variety of cep which grows in vineyards. Also called **tête-de-nègre**, **bolet bronzé**

cèpes à la bordelaise Sliced ceps fried in butter with chopped shallots and parsley or in oil with garlic

cephalopod The subgroup of molluscs such as squid, octopus, cuttlefish with a soft body, tentacles growing from around the head and gut parts and in some a hard internal shell. All have a sac of dark brown or black ink in their body cavity which they can squirt out to provide a protective screen. (NOTE: Literally 'head-footed'.)

cepumi *Latvia* Biscuits made from creamed butter and sugar with caraway seeds, orange juice and orange zest, made into a dough with self-raising flour and salt, rolled to a diameter of 5 cm, chilled, sliced and baked at 180°C until browned

cerdo *Spain* Pork

cereal The edible grains of monocotyledons such as wheat, rice, barley, maize, oats, etc. which may be eaten whole or ground into flour. Together with starchy roots they are the main source of energy carbohydrates for humans.

cereal cream *United States* Half-and-half

cereales *Spain* Cereal plants

céréales *France* Cereal plants

cereali *Italy* Cereal plants

cerebro *Spain* Brains

cereja *Portugal* **1.** Cherry **2.** Ripe coffee bean

cereza *Spain* Cherry

cerf *France* Stag, male deer

cerfeuil *France* Chervil

cerfeuil musqué *France* Sweet cicely

cerfoglio *Italy* Chervil

ceriman The fruit of a tropical tree. See also **monstera deliciosa**

cerise *France* Cherry

cerises, sauce aux *France* Cherry sauce

cerises jubilées *France* Hot cherries flambéed with kirsch

çerkez tavugu *Turkey* Chicken poached in water with sliced onion browned in oil, drained, cooled and disjointed and served covered with a sauce made from soaked bread crusts pounded with hazelnuts, let down with seasoned chicken stock and flavoured with paprika. The dish is sprinkled with a mixture of hot oil and paprika.

cerneau *France* Unripe or half-shelled walnut

cernia *Italy* Mediterranean grouper

cernier *France* Bar, the fish

certosa *Italy* A mild and creamy Stracchino type cheese made from cows' milk

certosino *Italy* A small version of Certosa

cervelas *France* A large, thick, smooth sausage usually made from pork flavoured with garlic and in a red casing. It is boiled then smoked before sale. Also called **saveloy** (NOTE: So called because originally made from brains (*cervelle* in French).)

cervelas de poisson *France* A fish loaf from Champagne made with pike flesh

cervelas maigre à la bénédictine *France* A sausage made from eel and carp flesh, minced together with onions, garlic and shallots sweated in butter, spices and seasoning, bound with egg and packed in cleaned fish intestines. Smoked for 3 days before poaching in white wine. Used by the monks as a substitute for pork sausages during Lent.

cervelat *Europe* The general European name for a large thick-linked sausage made of various meats, mainly lean pork and beef and pork fat, usually packed in beef middles, dried, smoked and dyed red or yellow. The meat is chopped or minced finely and incorporates saltpetre, seasoning and flavourings but not garlic. Served cold in slices.

cervellata *Italy* A pork sausage from Northern Italy flavoured with Parmesan cheese, saffron and spices

cervelle *France* Brains

cervello *Italy* Brains

cervo *Italy* Venison

Cetraria islandica *Botanical name* Iceland moss

cetriolini *Italy* Gherkins

cetriolo *Italy* Cucumber

ceun chai *China* Chinese celery

cevada *Portugal* Barley

cevapcici *Balkans* Grilled mincemeat balls from Serbia

cévenole, à la *France* In the Cévennes style, i.e. with chestnuts and mushrooms

ceviche *South America* A dish of cubed, raw, white fish marinated in lime juice, lemon juice, garlic, onions, chillies, chopped coriander leaves and seasoning, and served with chopped skinned tomatoes and avocado. Originally from Peru, now widely available. Does not need further cooking. Also called **seviche**, **cebiche**

Ceylon moss Agar-agar

Ceylon spinach A short-lived tropical and subtropical twining perennial, *Basella alba*, with large green or red leaves which can grow to 4 m. The leaves are grown as a vegetable. Also called **Indian spinach**, **vine spinach**

Ceylon tea A black tea produced in Sri Lanka

cha See **char**

chá *Portugal* Tea

chã *Portugal* Round of beef

chaamal *Nepal* Uncooked rice

chaat *South Asia* A mixture of diced fruit, vegetables, etc. with dressing. See also **chat**

chaat masala *South Asia* An Indian spice and herb mixture for fruit and vegetable salads. See also **chat masala**

chaat murgh *South Asia* Lettuce with a mixed topping. See also **chat murgh**

chabai *Malaysia* Bird's eye chilli

chabi Chabichou

chabichou *France* A small, white, firm, soft cone-shaped goats' milk cheese from Poitou with a strong goaty flavour ripened for 15 to 20 days. Also called **cabichou**, **cabrichiu**, **chabi**

chablisienne, à la *France* Cooked in the white wine Chablis or served with a sauce based on the wine

chabyor *Russia* Savory, the herb

chado The traditional Japanese tea ceremony. Also called **cha no yu**

chadon beni *Caribbean* A coriander-like herb

chadon beni sauce *Caribbean* A herb mix from Trinidad made from finely minced cilantro, garlic, deseeded chilli peppers, parsley, thyme and basil mixed with vinegar, lime juice and oil. Used in stews and curries. Also called **shadow bennie sauce**

Chaenomeles speciosa *Botanical name* Japonica

chafing dish 1. A dish with a spirit lamp or candles beneath, placed on the table in front of guests and used to keep food warm 2. A small portable bain-marie for use at the table 3. A shallow metal dish heated by a flame or an electric heater, used for cooking or holding hot foods beside the table or on a buffet table. Also called **hot plate**

chagga coffee A full-bodied coffee from the slopes of Mount Kilimanjaro in Tanzania, named after the Wachagga people who grow and process it

cha gio *Vietnam* Rice paper rolls filled with pork, fish, vegetables and noodles which are deep-fried until crisp

cha giò viet nam *Vietnam* Vietnamese spring rolls

cha gwa *China* Cucumber

cha gwoo *China* Straw mushroom

chahr ziu *China* Chinese honey-roast pork. See also **char siu**

chai *Russia* Tea

chair blanche *France* White meat, as of breast of chicken

chair noire *France* Dark meat, as of chicken

chakah *Central Asia* A very common sauce from Afghanistan made from drained yoghurt combined with crushed garlic and salt. The drained yoghurt is rather like cream cheese.

chakchouka *North Africa* **1.** Seasoned sweet peppers, onions and skinned tomatoes sliced and sautéed in olive oil with harissa until soft and blended. Formed into patties, a hollow made in each and a raw egg put in and cooked until set. **2.** A vegetable stew from Morocco similar to **ratatouille**, sometimes with eggs added to resemble a piperade. Also called **thetchouka**

chakhokbili *Southwest Asia* A Georgian meat and potato stew made with lamb or chicken pieces browned in oil, chopped onions and tomatoes added and softened, cubed potatoes and seasoning added and all simmered or braised until tender. Chopped garlic, coriander leaves, parsley and basil added, simmered 10 minutes with stirring then rested a few minutes before serving.

chakin-zushi A sushi rolled in a thin pancake or crêpe instead of **nori**. Also called **fukusa-zushi**

chakla *South Asia* A wooden board with a smooth side for rolling out dough and a recessed side for kneading dough

chakrey *West Africa* A sweet dessert made with couscous. See also **caakiri**

chal *Central Asia* A fermented camel's milk from Central Asia rather like a strong-smelling yoghurt

chalau *Central Asia* Long-grain rice, fried in oil then cooked in twice its weight of water in a tightly closed pan. From Afghanistan.

chali *South Asia* The orange to scarlet ripe nuts of betel

chalk See **calcium carbonate**

challa, challah A plaited bread covered in poppy seeds made from yeast-raised dough enriched with eggs and used on the Jewish Sabbath. Also called **challah**, **cholla**

chalota *Portugal* Shallot

chalote *Spain* Shallot

chalupa *Mexico* A filled oval piece of tortilla dough, raised at the edges and cooked and garnished with black beans, diced fresh cheese and nopales

chamak *South Asia* A style of finishing in Indian cookery. See also **tarka**

Chambarand *France* A small, creamy, delicately flavoured cheese with a pink/orange rind made from cows' milk by Trappist monks. Also called **Trappiste de Chambarand**

Chamberat *France* A cows' milk cheese similar to **Saint-Paulin**

chambourcy *France* A commercial version of cream cheese

chamois d'or *France* A soft cheese made with cows' milk enriched with cream and shaped rather like a thick Brie

champ *Ireland* Rich mashed potatoes mixed with chopped spring onions. Served with melted butter for dipping.

champignon *Denmark, France, Germany, Netherlands* Mushroom

champignons, aux *France* Cooked or garnished with mushrooms or coated with a mushroom sauce

champignons, crème de *France* Mushroom soup

champignons, sauce aux *France* Mushroom sauce

champignons marinés *France* Pickled mushrooms

champinjoner *Sweden* Mushrooms. Also called **svamp**

champiñón *Mexico* Mushroom

champorado *Philippines* Chocolate-flavoured glutinous rice eaten as a snack

chamsur *Nepal, South Asia* Watercress

chana *South Asia* A small variety of chick pea. See also **channa**

chandagar *Burma* See **lump sugar 3**

chandi ka barakh, chandi ka warq *South Asia* Silver leaf

chane jar garam *South Asia* Dry-roasted chick peas, seasoned with amchoor, chilli and cumin. Eaten as a snack.

chanfaina *Spain* A liver and giblets stew

chanfana *Portugal* A leg of lamb or goat browned in oil with sliced onion and garlic, seasoned and floured, covered with red wine, flavoured with cloves and bay and simmered or braised in the oven in a closed dish for 3 to 4 hours, topping up with wine as required

chang *China* Sausage

chan ga *Vietnam* Chicken legs

chang hau *China* Asian mussel

changr *China* Sausage

chanh *Vietnam* Lemon

channa *South Asia* **1.** A small variety of chick pea and the most common pulse used in India. When dehusked and split into dal, it is oval and yellow as opposed to the split pea which is round. Also called **Bengal gram**, **chana**, **gram 2.** Curds made from boiling milk acidified with lemon juice. See also **paneer**

channa ki dal *South Asia* Dehusked, split and polished chick pea

channel catfish A freshwater catfish, *Ictaluris natalis*, with the usual whiskers around the mouth and a very black skin, white on the underside

Channel Islands milk *United Kingdom* Milk from Jersey, Guernsey or South Devon cows' with a minimum butterfat content of 4%. but averaging 4.8%. Also called **Jersey milk**, **gold top**

cha no yu *Japan* The traditional Japanese tea ceremony. Also called **chado**

chanquetes *Spain* Young fish similar to whitebait but of sardines and other local fish varieties. Cooked as whitebait.

chantelle *United States* A cows' milk cheese similar to **Bel Paese**

chanterelle *France* An edible mushroom, *Cantharellus cibarius*, deep yellow and smelling of apricots, shaped like the upturned horn of a trumpet with wavy edges on a short stalk. Much prized in French cuisine. Also called **girolle**

chantilly, crème *France* Crème chantilly

chantilly, sauce *France* A mayonnaise made very thick and using lemon juice instead of vinegar. Stiffly whipped cream added at the last moment. Sometimes used for sauce mousseline, which is a warm butter emulsion sauce. Also called **mayonnaise chantilly**

chantilly cream A sweetened whipped cream flavoured with vanilla or brandy which is often substituted for plain whipped cream

chantilly mayonnaise A mixture of mayonnaise and whipped cream served with cold foods

chao 1. *China* To stir-fry or sauté **2.** *Vietnam* A type of wok but smaller and shallower than the Chinese type

cháo *Vietnam* A stew or thick soup

chao dou fu *China* Fried bean curd

chao fan *China* Fried rice

chao ji dan *China* Scrambled eggs

chao mian *China* Chow mein

chao pai *Vietnam* Dried and possibly salted fish

chao shao bao *China* A steamed bun filled with roast pork

chao thit bo *Vietnam* A thin stew or thick soup based on rice, diced beef, fried noodles and peanuts

Chaource *France* A soft, cows' milk cheese shaped like a small drum (600 g) which can be eaten fresh or after ripening for a month, when the rind becomes covered in a mould and the interior breaks up into small cracks. Contains 63% water, 19% fat and 15% protein. It has AOC status.

chao yulanpian donggu *China* Sliced **hoshi-shiitake** mushrooms sautéed with sliced bamboo shoots

chap The lower part of a pig's cheek. See also **pig's cheek**

chapan *France* A crust of bread rubbed with raw cut garlic to absorb the flavour. This is then tossed with a salad to give it a garlic flavour.

chapathi See **chapati**

chapati *South Asia* An unleavened bread made from a wholemeal dough shaped like a pancake and dry cooked on a hot griddle or flat slightly dished pan. Also called **chapathi**, **chapatti**, **phulka**

chapatti See **chapati**

chapelure *France* Sieved breadcrumbs made from crushed oven dried bread

chapon *France* **1.** Capon **2.** The end of a loaf of bread rubbed with garlic and dressed with oil and vinegar. Eaten with or added to salad.

char 1. A fresh water fish of the salmon family with firm white to pink flesh found in unpolluted rivers and lakes in Europe **2.** See **arctic char 3.** Colloquial name for tea from the Cantonese word *chai*, e.g. 'char and a wad' – tea and bun (NOTE: The name 'tea' comes from the Chinese province of Amoy, where it is called t'e.)

charbon de bois, au *France* Grilled over charcoal

charcuterie *France* **1.** Cooked and ready-prepared pork products, e.g. sausages, hams, rillettes **2.** A shop which makes and sells charcuterie and other delicatessen items

charcutier, -ière *France* Pork butcher, delicatessen dealer (NOTE: From *chair cuitier*, 'flesh cooker'.)

charcutière, sauce *England, France* As for **Robert sauce**, but finished with a **julienne** of gherkins

chard See **Swiss chard**

chard cabbage *United States* Chinese leaves

char dou fu *China* Fried bean curd

charentais melon A French variety of cantaloupe melon with a greenish yellow skin and a sweet, juicy, orange and highly scented flesh

charhearth broiler *United States* A gas or electrically heated barbecue generally using ceramic coals. The food is cooked on a grill over the red hot coals and drips from the food catch fire to give the characteristic charcoal-grilled flavour to the food.

charlotte *England, France* **1.** Apple charlotte (NOTE: The dish also be made on the same principle with other fruit.) **2.** A variety of salad potato

charlotte moscovite A charlotte russe but with the base of the mould filled with red jelly

charlotte mould A straight or sloping-sided round mould used for making charlotte desserts

charlotte royale *France* A charlotte mould lined with slices of jam-filled Swiss rolls and filled with a charlotte mixture or **bavarois**

charlotte russe *France* A charlotte mould, sides lined with sponge finger biscuits, base layered with fan-shaped pieces of finger biscuit and filled with a vanilla **bavarois**. When set, demoulded and decorated.

charlotte sibérienne *France* A cake with the centre removed to form a bowl and filled with fruit and cream

charlottka *Russia* See **sharlotka**

char masala *Central Asia* A simple spice mix from Afghanistan used to flavour rice dishes. Made from equal parts of cinnamon, cloves, cumin seed and black cardamom seed.

charn *China* The curved spoon-shaped spatula which fits the curve of a wok and is used to manipulate the food in the wok

charni *South Asia* Chutney

Charnwood *United Kingdom* A smoked Cheddar cheese coated with paprika

charolais *France* **1.** A very large breed of French cattle famous for its meat **2.** A small, soft, strong-flavoured, hard, cylindrical cheese made from cows' and/or goats' milk which is ripened for 2 to 3 weeks. The paste has a delicate texture with a few small cracks and the greyish blue rind is thin and unblemished. Contains 58% water, 24% fat and 21% protein.

charoli nut Small round nut about the size of a pine nut, used to garnish Indian sweetmeats. Also called **chironju**

charoset, charoseth A condiment made from chopped apples and walnuts flavoured with cinnamon and moistened with a sweet dessert wine. Used at the Jewish Passover feast. Also called **charoseth**

charqui *United States* Smoked and sun-dried strips of beef or venison. Also called **jerked beef, chipped beef, jerky, jerked meat**

char siu *China* Chinese honey roast pork made from skinned and deboned pork shoulder or fillet, marinaded in salt, sugar, **hoisin sauce**, yellow bean sauce, red bean curd, chopped garlic, light soy sauce and dry sherry, roasted and basted with the marinade until a rich dark brown, removed from the oven and brushed with honey. Excess marinade can be reduced for use as a dipping sauce. Also called **chahr ziu, cha siew, red pork**

char siu bow *China* Bread dough formed into small balls around a filling of finely chopped stir-fried char siu, reconstituted black mushrooms and spring onion mixed with **hoisin sauce**, oyster sauce and a little sugar and thickened with corn flour and stock. The balls are allowed to rise then cooked by steaming for 15 minutes.

char siu jeung *China* See **roast pork spice**

char siu powder See **roast pork spice**

chartreuse ragoût *Denmark* A decoratively arranged casserole of meat or poultry with colourful vegetables

cha shao bao *China* A steamed bun filled with roast pork

cha siew *China* Char siu

chasni *South Asia* A sweet and sometimes sour syrup used to glaze food which is being grilled or roasted. Usually for meat or poultry.

chasnidarh *South Asia* A style of Indian dish made with young meat or fish in a sweet-and-sour sauce, possibly with fruits and vegetables

cha-soba *Japan* Buckwheat noodles containing powdered green tea. They have a distinctive colour and smell.

chasseur, (à la) *France* In the hunter's style, i.e. with a selection of onions, shallots, sliced mushrooms, tomatoes and white wine and/or brandy

chasseur, sauce Chopped shallots, garlic and mushrooms sweated in butter, fat removed, reduced with red wine, skimmed, deseeded tomatoes and **demi-glace** added, simmered, seasoned and finished with parsley and tarragon

chat *South Asia* A mixture of diced fruit, vegetables, possibly with meat and shrimps and with a spicy, sour dressing

châtaigne *France* Sweet chestnut

châtaigne d'eau *France* Water chestnut

chateaubriand *England, France* A large steak cut from the thickest part of a fillet of beef. Generally grilled to serve two persons or the whole thick end roasted.

chateaubriand, sauce *England, France* White wine with chopped shallots, thyme, bayleaf and mushroom trimmings reduced by two thirds, an amount of brown veal stock equal to the original wine added and all reduced by half, strained and finished with **beurre maître d'hôtel** and chopped tarragon. Used with red meat.

chateaubriand cheese A cream cheese from Normandy made with cows' milk and added cream

château potatoes 1. *United Kingdom* Roast turned potatoes **2.** *United States* Long thin strips of potatoes cooked in butter

châtelaine, à la *France* Garnished with artichoke hearts, chestnuts and puréed onions and served with a cream sauce

chat masala *South Asia* An Indian spice and herb mixture for fruit and vegetable salads with a fresh sour taste containing cumin seeds, black peppercorns, ajowan seeds, anardana seeds, salt, asafoetida, chilli powder, amchoor, dried mint and dried ginger. Also called **chaat masala**

chat murgh *South Asia* Lettuce, topped with a mixture of sliced tomatoes, eggs and onion, deseeded and finely chopped green chillies and shredded chicken, sprinkled with salt, sugar and chat masala and dressed with lemon juice. Allowed to stand for 10 minutes before serving.

chatnee *Caribbean* A hot spice mix from St Lucia made from freshly grated turmeric, chives, thyme, seeded chilli peppers and salt and pepper all processed in a blender or with a mortar and pestle. Traditionally added to cooked rice.

chatni gashneez *Central Asia* A smooth chutney from Afghanistan made from equal weights of walnuts and coriander leaves processed with a green chilli and lemon juice or vinegar to make a spreadable paste

chattak *South Asia* A unit of weight equal to 5 tolas, approximately 56 g or 2 oz. Also called **chitak**

chatti *Sri Lanka* A terracotta cooking pot similar to an Indian chatty

chatty *South Asia* An unglazed clay cooking pot. Because the clay absorbs flavours from the food, separate pots are used for different classes of food, e.g. fish, meat, vegetables, etc.

chatui *South Asia* Sambal-like side dishes

chaud(e) *France* Hot

chaudeau *France* Sweet pudding sauce

chaudeu *France* An orange-flavoured tart from Nice in Provence

chaud-froid, sauce A coating sauce made from equal parts of warmed béchamel or velouté sauce and aspic jelly, or either sauce thickened with gelatine. Used to coat salmon, chicken, turkey, hams, etc. for cold buffets. See also **brown chaud-froid sauce**

chaudin *France* The large intestine (colon) used in sausage making

chaudrée *France* A dish from Bordeaux of conger eel and other white fish cooked with potatoes, garlic and white wine, a type of chowder or fish soup

chaudron *France* Cauldron

chauna A sour cows' milk cheese. See also **chhana**

chaunk gobhi *South Asia* Brussels sprouts

chaurice *United States* A Creole version of chorizo containing chopped onions and parsley, thyme, bay leaves and allspice

chausson *France* A round flat light pastry turnover usually filled

chaussons aux pommes *France* Apple turnover

chaussons aux queues de langoustines *France* A pastry turnover filled with lobster meat from the tail

chávena *Portugal* Teacup, used as a fluid measure

Chavignol *France* A small, hard, goats' milk cheese. See also **Crottin de Chavignol**

chawal *South Asia* Rice

chawan *Japan* A straight-sided porcelain or glazed pot dish about the size of a teacup with a conical lid. Used for steaming egg custards.

chawan mushi *Japan* A savoury steamed custard made with 7 eggs per litre of **ichiban dashi**, flavoured with **mirin** and salt and contains a few pieces of chicken breast meat, prawn and mushroom marinaded in soya sauce and sake. It is steamed for 15 minutes, garnished and served in the chawan.

chawara *South Asia* Date

chay *Vietnam* Vegetarian

chayote Choko

chebeh rubyan *Persian Gulf* Prawn paste balls with a filling of sweated chopped onions that have been flavoured with **baharat** and **loomi** powder and simmered in a sweet-and-sour sauce. The prawn paste is made from processed shelled prawns and coriander leaves mixed with ground rice, turmeric and loomi powder to a cohering mass.

checkerberry *United States* Wintergreen

cheddam *Australia* A combination of Cheddar and Edam-type cheeses

cheddar, to To repeatedly cut and stack blocks of milk curd turning between operations so as to drain off as much whey as possible

Cheddar *England* The renowned English cheese from the Cheddar Gorge area now made all over the world. It is a hard, scalded-curd, full-fat cows' milk cheese made with a lactic starter and traditionally cloth bound. The paste is firm and yellow with a very pleasant flavour ranging from mild to sharp (tasty) depending on maturity (3–12 months). It is available in farmhouse (5–12 kg rounds) and commercial versions of indeterminate size. An excellent dessert and cooking cheese. Contains 36% water, 34% fat and 29% protein.

Cheedham *Australia* A cows' milk cheese similar to Cheddar and Edam

cheegay *Korea* A thin stew or thick soup of various ingredients. Crabs, fish and bean curd are often cooked in this way.

chee mah *China* Sesame seed

chee mah jee mah *China* White sesame seeds

cheena chatti *Sri Lanka* A slightly dished circular pan like a shallow wok used for cooking bread especially atta

cheese 1. A solid derivative of milk made by coagulating most of the protein matter (**casein**) in the milk into curds and draining off the remaining watery constituents of the milk (**whey**). The processing combines a variety of the following processes: separating or adding cream, souring the milk with a lactobacillus, heating or boiling it, coagulating the protein content with rennet or other coagulant, breaking up the curd and draining off the whey, salting the curd, heating the curd, milling the curd, adding cultures of microorganisms, pressing the curd to a paste, needling the paste and maturing it. The type of cheese depends on the source of the milk, the treatment, the amount of water removed from the curd, the butterfat left in the curd, the microorganisms that grow in it or on the surface and the length of time and the conditions under which it matures. Cheese is a major source of protein and fat for humans. **2.** See **fruit cheese**

cheese cake *Central Europe, United States* A crushed biscuit or pastry base covered with a processed mixture of cream, cottage or curd cheese mixed with eggs, sugar, butter and/or cream, lemon juice, grated lemon zest, vanilla and corn flour and baked in the oven

cheese certification Cheeses may be certified by type or by origin as detailed in the 1951 Stresa convention. Typical type certifications are Cheddar, Camembert, Brie, Gruyère, Gouda, Fynbo and Adelost. Typical origin certifications are Gorgonzola, Parmesan, Pont l'Evêque, Roquefort and Bleu d'Auvergne. Type certified cheeses may be made in any country, e.g. Canadian Cheddar, but origin certified may only be made in designated geographical areas.

cheesecloth Loosely woven cloth originally used for pressing curds into cheese but also for draining and filtering any foods

cheese fondue *Switzerland* A coating-consistency mixture of Emmental or Gruyère cheese melted with garlic, white wine, corn flour and kirsch in a pot (**caquelon**), kept hot on the centre of the table and eaten immediately, used to coat cubes of bread impaled on fondue forks

cheese herbs The principal herbs used in cheese are basil, caraway, chervil, chives, dill, fennel, marjoram, mint, rosemary, sage, savory, tarragon and thyme

cheese layer cake *United States* A three layered cheese made from a white cheddar, one layer of which is flavoured with pistachios and one with pink champagne, the whole coated with almonds

cheese pastry Shortcrust pastry flavoured with cheese and seasoning used as a basis for savouries and sometimes in the UK for apple pie

cheese plate Several varieties of cheese arranged on a plate and shown to customers or guests who make a selection from them

cheese sauce A boiling **béchamel sauce** into which grated melting cheese (Cheddar, Gruyère, Emmental, etc.) and egg yolks are incorporated off the heat, the whole strained and reheated but not boiled. Used for fish or vegetables. Also called **Mornay, sauce**

cheese spread A rather nondescript cheese preparation made by combining mild cheese with milk and emulsifiers, used for spreading on bread or biscuits and appreciated by children

cheese straws Cheese pastry cut into narrow finger length strips and baked. Used as a snack food.

chef *England, France* A generic name for a restaurant cook, e.g. chef de partie, sous chef, etc.

chef de cuisine *England, France* Head chef in the kitchen

chef de partie *England, France* Chef in charge of a section of the kitchen e.g. vegetables, sauces, meat cooking, larder, etc. Usually given the name of the section

chef de rang *France* A high-ranking chef or principal waiter in a restaurant

chef de station *France* Waiter who serves a particular group of tables. Also called **station waiter**

chef écailler *France* Oyster opener

chefe de mesa *Portugal* Head waiter, maître d'hôtel

chef entremétier *France* Vegetable chef

chef garde-manger *France* Larder chef who is concerned with cold dishes, salads and preparation of meat and fish for cooking by others

chef pâtissier *France* Pastry chef

chef poissonier *France* Fish chef

chef potager *France* Soup chef

chef restaurateur *France* Chef in charge of the à la carte menu

chef rôtisseur *France* Roast chef

chef saucier *France* Sauce chef

chef's salad An over the top, large salad combining vegetables, salad vegetables, meats, cheeses, eggs, etc.

chef tournant *France* A chef who helps out in any section of the kitchen (NOTE: Literally 'rotating chef'.)

chef traiteur *France* Chef in charge of outside functions, buffets, etc.

che hau sauce *China* A spicier version of hoisin sauce

chelou *Central Asia* Basmati rice boiled 5 minutes and drained. Equal parts of butter and water (butter 1:8 on original rice) are boiled, then half placed in a pan to coat the parboiled rice which is made into a mound covering the base of the pan; the remaining butter water mixture is poured on top. It is then cooked on a low heat with a tight-fitting lid until fluffy.

chelou kabab *Iran* A kebab of lamb fillet, marinated in lemon juice with chopped onion and spearmint, grilled over charcoal and served with rice

chelou kebab *Central Asia* An Iranian kebab made from the eye of the lamb loin stripped out and trimmed of all fat and gristle, flattened, slit lengthways in three and cut into 20-cm pieces. These are marinated in raw onion juice and lemon juice for 12 hours, skewered lengthways, brushed with clarified butter and barbecued for about 5 minutes. Served with grilled tomatoes and hot **chelou**, into which diners mix raw egg yolk then butter, seasoning, sumac and yoghurt as desired.

Chelsea bun *England* A bun made by taking a rectangle of egg-enriched yeast-raised dough, covering it with melted butter, currants and sugar, rolling it up, slicing it, then packing these into a buttered tray so that the spiral is visible prior to baking and glazing (NOTE: Chelsea buns were much liked by King George III and Queen Charlotte in the 18th century.)

chemise, en *France* Used of food wrapped or left in its natural skin prior to cooking. Wrappings include pastry, pané, batter, vine leaves, etc. (NOTE: Literally 'in a shirt'.)

chemiser *France* To coat the inside of a mould with aspic or other coating so that when the whole is demoulded it is **en chemise**

chenelline *Italy* Tiny dumplings used to garnish soup

chenette *Caribbean* A small round fruit like a grape. See also **genip**

cheng mein *China* Wheat starch

chenna *South Asia* Curds made from boiling milk acidified with lemon juice. See also **paneer**

Chenopodium album *Botanical name* Fat hen

Chenopodium bonus-henricus *Botanical name* Good King Henry

Chenopodium quinoa *Botanical name* Quinoa

cheong *China* Sausage

cheppia *Italy* Twaite shad, the fish

cherimoya *South America* One of the most common custard apples, *Anona cherimolia*, with a pineapple-type flavour. From Peru, now grown in Spain and Israel. Also called **cherimoyer**

cherimoyer See **cherimoya**

chermoula *North Africa* A processed mixture from Morocco of some or all of finely chopped onion, garlic, parsley, coriander leaves, red chillies, ground cumin, paprika, cayenne pepper, lemon juice, vinegar, oil and salt, used as a marinade and flavouring. Often used on fish before frying. Also called **sharmoola**

cherries jubilee *United States* Vanilla ice cream topped with a sweet cherry sauce and flambéed at the table

cherry The fruits of various members of the genus *Prunus*, 1 – 2.5 cm in diameter, generally spherical with a slight depression where they are attached to the stalk, with a central stone (up to 5mm diameter) surrounded by a plum-like flesh and a smooth shiny outer skin. The colours range from white to deep purple/black and the flavours from sweet to acid. Used in sweet and savoury dishes. The kernels are used to flavour some liqueurs. Classified as sweet cherries and acid or sour cherries.

cherry cake A rich sponge cake containing glacé cherries

cherry plum A small variety of plum, *Prunus cerasifera*, from western Asia, common in China. It is sometimes used as a windbreak in the UK. The rather tasteless flesh improves with cooking.

cherry salmon A Pacific salmon, *Oncorhynchus masu*, found off the coast of Japan

cherry sauce Port wine reduced with a little mixed spice and grated orange zest, redcurrant jelly and orange juice added and dissolved then finished with stoned cherries which have been poached in syrup. Used with venison and duck.

cherrystone *United States* Quahog clam

cherry tomato A very small (up to 2 cm diameter) tomato, used principally for decoration

chervil A herb of the carrot family, *Anthriscus cerefolium*, with flat parsley-like leaves and a slightly pungent mild parsley flavour. It loses its flavour on boiling and is usually added to hot dishes just before serving.

Cheshire black pudding *England* Black pudding flavoured with coriander, pimento and caraway seeds

Cheshire cheese *England* A crumbly, mellow, slightly salty cows' milk cheese which is matured from 1 to 15 months (farmhouse types usually for over 9 months) suitable for dessert or culinary use, manufactured in a similar way to Cheddar. There is a white variety and a red one coloured with annatto. It is the oldest known English cheese dating from at least Roman times.

Cheshire onion pie *England* A shortcrust pastry quiche with sweated onions as the vegetable. The custard is flavoured with nutmeg.

Cheshire potted cheese *England* Grated Cheshire cheese, mixed with softened butter, ground mace and sweet sherry or Madeira into a smooth paste, placed in pots and covered with melted butter. Used as a spread with celery or for canapés, etc.

Cheshire potted pigeon *England* A dish of pigeons which are boiled until the meat falls off the bones, with the meat then being processed with seasoning and Worcestershire sauce plus some of the reduced cooking liquor to make a soft paste. This is pressed into ramekins and covered with molten butter.

Cheshire soup *England* A soup made from pork stock, diced potatoes, grated carrots and chopped leeks with pinhead oatmeal added at 50g per litre after the vegetables have softened. It is simmered until thick and finished with 50g per litre of grated Cheshire cheese. It is served hot, sprinkled with an equal amount of grated cheese.

chesnok *Russia* Garlic

chessel A vat or mould used in cheese making. Also called **chessit**

chessit Chessel

chess pie *United States* A pastry case filled with a mixture of walnuts or pecans, fruit juice or sweet sherry, butter, eggs and cream

Chester *France* A hard, scalded-curd cows' milk cheese made with a lactic starter on a large commercial scale in blocks or rounds of 30 kg. It has a mild tasting smooth paste and a thin rind. Contains 39% water, 31% fat and 24% protein.

chestnut The edible fruit (up to 4 cm diameter) of the sweet chestnut tree, *Castanea sativa*, a native of southern Europe. It has a hard woody skin and a cream-coloured interior containing more starch and less protein and fat than most nuts. Also called **Spanish chestnut**, **sweet chestnut**

chestnut purée Chestnuts incised with a cross at the top, boiled for 15 minutes and the outer and inner skin removed. Boiled in stock with a sprig of celery for 45 minutes, rubbed through a sieve, warmed and mixed with cream, butter, salt and sugar to taste.

chetha si biyan *Burma* A chicken stew flavoured with onions, garlic, turmeric, fresh ginger, coriander leaves, lemon and salt

cheung *China* Sausage

cheu yuan *China* Citron, the fruit

chevaine *France* Chub, the fish

chevesne *France* Chub, the fish

cheveu d'ange *France* Angel's hair

cheveux de vénus adiante *France* Maidenhair fern

Cheviot cheese *England* A Cheddar cheese flavoured with chopped chives

chèvre *France* 1. Goat 2. Goats' milk cheese. Also called **fromage de chèvre**, **mi-chèvre**

chevreau *France* Kid, the young of the goat

chevreton *France* A strong goats' milk cheese with a hard rind and soft runny interior

chevrette *France* 1. Kid, a young goat 2. Doe, female deer 3. A metal tripod

chevreuil *France* 1. Male deer 2. Venison

chevreuil, sauce *England, France* As **sauce poivrade**, but with bacon or game trimmings added to the **mirepoix** and with red wine added after straining. Finished with a little sugar and cayenne pepper. Served with game.

chevreuse *France* A small goose liver tart

chevron *United States* A young goat

Chevrotin des Aravis *France* A semi-hard goats' or goats' and cows' milk cheese from Savoie with a typical goaty smell and taste

Chevru *France* A cows' milk cheese from the region surrounding Paris, similar to **Brie de Coulommiers**

chewing betel Pan

chezzarella *United States* A coarse mixture of Cheddar and Mozzarella cheeses to give a marbled effect

chhana *South Asia* A sour cows' milk cheese. Also called **chauna**

chhanna *South Asia* Pomfret, the fish

chhas *South Asia* Buttermilk

chhena *South Asia* Curds made from boiling milk acidified with lemon juice. See also **paneer**

chi *China* Chicken

chiarificare *Italy* To clarify

chícharo *Mexico* Pea

chicharro *Spain* Mackerel

chicharrón *Middle East, Spain* Pork crackling

Chichester pudding *England* A soufflé made with milk, coarse white breadcrumbs, eggs and caster sugar (9:7:4:1). All the ingredients except the egg whites are well mixed with a flavouring of lemon zest and juice. The egg whites are whisked to a stiff peak and folded into the mixture and all baked in a well-buttered soufflé dish at 180°C for about 30 minutes until well risen and browned. It must be served immediately.

chichinda *South Asia* Snake gourd

chicken The common domestic fowl, *Gallus gallus*, bred for its meat and eggs. Generally known as poultry.

chicken à la king *United States* Diced cooked chicken, fried chopped onions, mushrooms and green and red peppers in a **béchamel sauce**. Sometime flavoured with sherry. Served with rice.

chicken breasts Bellinger *Australia* Suprêmes of chicken stuffed with a **salpicon** of avocado and banana, sautéed and served in a sauce of the same ingredients as the stuffing flavoured with orange zest and garnished with orange segments

chicken brick An unglazed terracotta dish in two halves shaped to take a whole chicken and used to cook a chicken in the oven without added fat. Dates back to Roman times. Also called **Roman pot**, **Römertopf**

chicken broth Blanched boiling fowl simmered in water with constant skimming for 1 hour, **brunoise** of celery, turnip, carrot and leek and a bouquet garni added, simmered until almost cooked, washed rice added, cooked chicken and bouquet garni removed, diced lean chicken meat returned, the whole skimmed, seasoned and served with chopped parsley

chicken cacciatora See **pollo alla cacciatora**

chicken demi-deuil Chicken stuffed with truffle and poached with aromatic vegetables, jointed, slices of truffle inserted between the skin and flesh and served with the vegetables and strained reduced cooking liquor (NOTE: Literally 'chicken half mourning', because of the black and white contrast.)

chicken fat A soft fat used as a substitute for butter in Jewish cooking, since meat and milk products cannot be used together. It contains about 35% saturated, 50% monounsaturated and 15% polyunsaturated fat. Also called **Schmalz**

chicken feet The feet of chickens, not usually sold with the carcass, are blanched, descaled and used to add flavour and gelatine to stocks and sauces

chicken fried steak *United States* Good-quality frying steak, floured, coated with an egg-based batter, floured again, then deep-fried and served with a white gravy

chicken gumbo Portioned chicken and diced smoked ham (2.5 mm cubes) browned in oil; sliced onion, **tomato concassée** and sliced okra added and fried for 5 minutes; then all simmered in water with salt, cayenne pepper, dried red chilli and a faggot of herbs for 1.5 hours skimming as necessary; faggot removed, shelled oysters added and cooked 2 minutes; seasoning adjusted and finished with a little **filé** powder. Served with rice.

chicken halibut A small immature halibut

chicken Kiev *Russia* A pocketed chicken suprême filled with a pounded mixture of garlic butter and chopped parsley, opening secured, panéed and shallow-fried and cooked through until golden

chicken liver Small delicately flavoured and very tender livers used for pâtés, terrines, etc.

chicken Marengo See **poulet sauté Marengo**

chicken Maryland *United States* Panéed chicken portions deep-fried in oil, served with corn fritters, fried bananas and gravy

chicken of the woods A rare fan-shaped fungus which grows on old oak trees often in inaccessible places. The flesh is white to salmon and the surface skin is orange to yellow. It must always be cooked.

chicken paprika See **paprikás csirke**

chicken piri-piri Charcoal grilled chicken basted with a mixture of **piri-piri sauce**, olive oil, garlic, tomato purée, Worcestershire sauce and salt both before and during cooking

chicken soup A **mirepoix** of onion, leek and celery sweated in butter, flour added and cooked out without colour, chicken stock and a bouquet garni added, simmered and skimmed for 1 hour, bouquet garni removed, liquidized, strained and finished with cream. Garnished with diced cooked chicken meat. Also called **crème reine**, **crème de volaille**

chicken spatchcock See **spatchcock**

chicken steak *United States* Thin small portions of chuck steak with the characteristic line of white connective tissue down the middles

chicken stock *China* A most important stock in Chinese cooking made by simmering chicken carcasses with onions and ginger. See also **white chicken stock**, **brown chicken stock**

chicken tetrazzini *United States* Cooked chicken pieces in a velouté sauce over cooked pasta, gratinated with breadcrumbs and Parmesan cheese and browned under the grill. Served with broccoli.

chicken tikka masala *United Kingdom* Small marinated pieces (a **tikka**) of chicken with a spice mixture (**masala**) of ground cumin and coriander seeds plus chilli powder and powdered amchoor in the yoghurt marinade. After frying, the chicken is mixed with caramelized onions and garlic plus the marinade and stock, then simmered until all is cooked and the sauce is thick. (NOTE: Said to be the most popular dish in the UK)

chicken turbot A small immature turbot

chicken yassa *West Africa* Poulet yassa

chickling vetch Lath

chickpea A legume, *Cicer arietinum*, with 2 or 3 brown or yellow peas per pod, usually used as a dried pulse or ground to make **besan**, but may be used like broad beans. Common around the Mediterranean in the Middle East and India. See also **channa**. Also called **garbanzo, garbanzo pea, ram's-head pea**

chickweed A vigorous creeping annual, *Stellaria media*, usually classed as a weed but may be eaten raw in salads or boiled as a vegetable

chicle The coagulated sap or latex of the sapodilla tree used in the production of chewing gum

chico Sapodilla

chicon *England, France* The white, yellow-tipped, compact and pointed rosette of leaves produced by forcing the trimmed roots of **Belgian chicory**

chicorée *France* Endive

chicorée frisée *France* Endive

chicorées au jambon *Belgium* A Belgium dish of cooked heads of chicory, wrapped in ham, reheated in cheese sauce and served with boiled potatoes

chicory A group of plants, *Cichorium intybus*, grown for their leaves which all have a distinctive slightly bitter flavour. They include **Belgian chicory** whose roots are forced to produce the well-known white compact chicons commonly known as chicory, red chicory also known as radicchio and sugar loaf chicory.

chicory escarole *United States* Batavian endive

chicory root The root of the chicory plant which, when dried, ground and roasted, can be used as a substitute for or as an extender or adulterant of coffee

chicosapote, chicozapote *Spain* Sapodilla

chieh *China* Mandarin orange

chien *Vietnam* Fried

chifferoni *Italy* Curved pasta tubes, elbow macaroni

chiffonade *France* **1.** A garnish or base for other foods made from a very finely sliced roll of lettuce or sorrel leaves (not chopped) **2.** A soup of finely shredded herb leaves

chiffon cake A cake similar to angel cake but enriched with oil

chiffon pie *United States* A baked pastry case filled with a fruit-based mousse and decorated

chiftele *Romania* Croquettes of minced cooked beef mixed with minced lean pork, seasoned, flavoured with paprika and marjoram, panéed and deep-fried. Served with a tomato sauce.

chih mah *China* Sesame seeds of either colour

chikhirtma A sour chicken soup from Georgia, made by simmering a whole chicken with onion, celery, saffron, peppercorns and cayenne pepper for 90 minutes, skimming as necessary and straining. The stock is thickened with a roux made with onions fried until coloured, and finished with beaten eggs, egg yolks, lemon juice and chopped fresh mint, parsley and coriander.

chikku Sapodilla

chikni *South Asia* The green unripe nuts of betel

chiko Sapodilla

chiko roll *Australia* A concoction of chicken and vegetables, covered in dough and breadcrumbs and deep-fried

chiku Sapodilla

chikuwa *Japan* A fish cake formed in a cylindrical shape around a sliver of bamboo. After steaming it is usually grilled. See also **kamaboko**

chikwangue *Central Africa* Treated cassava tubers. See also **bâton de manioc**

chila *Portugal* A gourd with long thin stranded flesh similar to vegetable spaghetti. Also called **gila**

chilaquiles *Mexico* Strips of cornmeal tortilla, fried until crisp and reheated with tomato sauce. May have cooked meat added. Garnished with grated cheese, chopped onions, chillies and cream.

chile See **chilli peppers**

chile guajillo *Mexico* A long thin reddish brown and very hot chilli, smooth with a pointed end and often dried

chile peppers See **chilli peppers**

Chile saltpetre Sodium nitrate which can be used instead of saltpetre. As it contains more nitrate radical per gram than saltpetre it is roughly one sixth more effective in weight terms.

chiles en nagada *Mexico* As **chiles rellenos**, but stuffed with minced beef, fruits (apricots, apples, plums), napped with a sweet sauce made of nuts and cream and garnished with grenadine seeds to resemble the Mexican flag

chiles rellenos *Mexico* Sweet peppers stuffed with a cheese filling, deep-fried and topped with cheese

chili *United States* The term used for the fruit of all capsicum species whether hot or sweet

chili con carne *United States* As **chilli con carne**, but need not include beans

chili con queso *United States* Molten cheese flavoured with minced or finely chopped chillies and served hot with tortilla chips

chilienne, à la *France* In the Chilean manner, i.e. with rice and red peppers

chilindron *Spain* A meat casserole from Aragon made without water from either split game birds, chicken, pork chops or lamb chops, sautéed in olive oil until brown, added to a mixture of sweated chopped onion and garlic with diced ham, saffron, paprika, red peppers and skinned tomatoes, and simmered in a covered pan until cooked

chill, to To reduce the temperature of cooked food to between 0 and 5°C in a refrigerator or cold room. An initial cooling may be done in cold water if suitable and will be quicker.

chilled food Food, usually cooked, kept at a temperature between 0 and 5°C so that it only needs reheating prior to serving

chilli See **chilli peppers**

chilli arbol Very small hot chilli peppers used in Mexico and the East

chilli bean Red kidney bean

chilli bean paste Yellow or black bean sauce left thick and mixed with chopped dried chillies and other spices. Recipes vary with the manufacturer. Also called **hot bean paste**, **Sichuan hot bean paste**

chilli California A variety of chilli pepper grown in California. It is large, fairly mild and deep red, and resembles the Kashmiri chilli. Roasting intensifies the flavour.

chilli cascabel A round dried variety of hot chilli pepper whose seeds rattle inside, from the Spanish for rattle

chilli con carne A dish adapted from Mexico and the southern United States and now adopted in many countries. It contains stewed minced beef and cooked red kidney beans in a sauce made of onions, garlic, chilli powder, tomatoes, spices, seasonings and stock.

chillies The fruits of the genus *Capsicum* (NOTE: This name is usually confined to the hot varieties.)

chilli flakes Dried and crushed chillies used as a flavouring

chilli flower A garnish made by slicing a long chilli into 7 or 8 segments from the base to the tip leaving them attached at the base and not disturbing the inner pith and seeds. It is then placed in iced water to make the petals curl back on themselves.

chilli oil A red-coloured, hot-tasting oil made by infusing crushed dried chillies in hot vegetable oil. Used as a flavouring or condiment.

chilli peppers The fruit of the annual bush, *Capsicum annuum* Longum Group, related to the sweet pepper but thinner and and up to 9 cm long. They mature from green to red becoming hotter as they mature. The main sources of the capsaicin and other hot-flavouring compounds are the seeds and internal white pith which can be discarded. They are used for flavouring and as an appetizer. If eaten raw or cooked they can be intensely irritating to the mucous membranes unless the person is habituated to them, and hands should be thoroughly washed after handling. Much used in Indian, Mexican and other highly spiced cuisines. See under individual names, Anaheim chilli, banana chilli, chilli arbol, chilli California, chilli cascabel, chilli pequin, chilli poblano, Fresno chilli, guajillo, guero chilli, habanero chilli, jalapeno chilli, New Mexico chilli, serrano chilli, etc. Also called **chile peppers**, **chillis**

chilli pequin A very small hot green chilli pepper used in Mexico and East Asia

chilli poblano A chocolate brown variety of the hot chilli pepper used in Mexico to make a sauce, mole poblano, with unsweetened chocolate, as well as for general cooking

chilli powder The name of various mixtures of dried ground chillies with other dried herbs and spices. The pure chilli powder is very hot, but milder blends contain ground, dried sweet red peppers, oregano, and garlic amongst other things. Some are quite mild but all should be tested by adding to a known quantity of the cooked food and tasting before use.

chilli sauce A hot, commercially prepared, cold sauce or ketchup made from chilli peppers and used for flavouring other dishes

chill storage A method of preserving foods by storing at temperatures between –1°C and +4°C. Not suitable for all foods.

chilogrammo *Italy* Kilogram, unit of weight, abbreviated kg

chimichangas *Mexico* Fried stuffed tacos made from wheat flour tortillas, filled with cooked minced beef, accompanied by shredded lettuce, grated cheese, radishes and spring onions (NOTE: From Sonora state.)

chimichurri *Argentina* A sauce for meat and poultry made from, oil, vinegar, garlic, chopped onions, cayenne pepper and seasonings blended together

china cap strainer *United States* A conical metal strainer. See also **chinois 1**

China orange Calamondin

chinchin *West Africa* Small balls of a raised dough from Nigeria made from equal quantities of self-raising flour, plain flour and sugar with dried yeast and baking powder, deep-fried in oil so as to cook through and brown

chine, to To cut through the ribs of a joint of meat close to the back bone so as to make the meat easier to carve or preparatory to removing the backbone. Usually done with lamb and pork.

chine bone A joint of meat consisting of the vertebrae (backbone) of an animal with some of the surrounding muscle. Usually stewed or braised.

chine of beef Forerib of beef

chine of pork The term used for a saddle, i.e. two undivided loins from a small pig

Chinese anise *United States* Star anise

Chinese apple Pomegranate

Chinese aromatic pepper Anise pepper

Chinese artichoke The pale, short, tapering tuber of a plant, *Stachys sieboldii*, which has concentric segments and resembles a Jerusalem artichoke, although more regular in shape. Also called **chorogi**, **crosnes**, **Japanese artichoke**, **stachys**

Chinese bean Cow pea

Chinese black bean A fermented and salted soya bean used for flavouring and for making sauces

Chinese broccoli See **Chinese kale**

Chinese cabbage Chinese leaves

Chinese cardamom A dark brown, rather hairy cardamom substitute from the plant *Amomum globosum*. Usually available in Chinese food stores.

Chinese celery A variety of celery with narrow deep green stems and a strong flavour

Chinese cheese See **bean curd cheese**

Chinese cherry Lychee

Chinese chive A vegetable of the onion family, *Allium tuberosum*, like a very large chive. Sold in three forms, dark green leaves, blanched leaves known as yellow chives and the round fairly stiff flowering stem with a pointed flower bud at the tip known as flowering chive. The taste varies from mild to strong according to the variety. See also **garlic chive**. Also called **Chinese onion**, **Chinese leek**, **Cantonese onion**

Chinese cinnabar melon *United States* A deep red coloured melon with sweet smooth-textured flesh

Chinese date Mauritanian jujube

Chinese dried black mushroom Shiitake mushroom

Chinese egg roll See **spring roll**

Chinese flat cabbage A low-growing brassica, *Brassica rapa* var. *rosularis*, with white stems and small rounded white-veined deep green leaves. Resistant to frost. Also called **flat cabbage**

Chinese gooseberry Kiwi fruit

Chinese green cabbage See **jiu la choy**

Chinese honey orange Ponkan mandarin

Chinese kale An annual leaf vegetable, *Brassica rapa* var. *alboglabra*, growing to 45 cm. The soft green leaves, green stems and white flower buds are used like broccoli. Also called **Chinese broccoli**

Chinese keys A reddish brown root vegetable from the ginger family that looks like a misshapen bunch of keys. Used in Thai and Indonesian curries and pickles.

Chinese lantern A type of physalis, *Physalis alkekengi*, grown mainly for its decorative red papery husk. Edible varieties are light brown. See also **cape gooseberry**. Also called **bladder cherry**

Chinese leaves The large, generally close-packed, very pale green heads of an oriental brassica, *Brassica rapa* var. *pekinensis*. Loose-leaved varieties are available. Grown widely, Chinese leaves originated in China, have a mild flavour and are often pickled. Used in stir fries. Also called **Chinese cabbage**, **Nappa cabbage**, **Shantung cabbage**, **Korean cabbage**, **celery cabbage**, **Beijing cabbage**

Chinese leek See **Chinese chive**

Chinese mushrooms Whole dried mushrooms from China which when reconstituted are used to flavour Chinese dishes

Chinese mustard cabbage A leaf vegetable with long stalks and small leaves with a strong mustard flavour used in soup or salads, cooked like spinach, or pickled like sauerkraut

Chinese nuts Dried lychees

Chinese okra A large (up to 30 cm) variety of okra grown in the USA, originally by Chinese market gardeners

Chinese olive seed Kernels of the small Chinese kanari fruit, *Canarium album*, similar in size to a pine nut and used in the same way

Chinese onion See **Chinese chive**

Chinese parsley Coriander

Chinese pea Mangetout

Chinese pepper Anise pepper

Chinese plum A variety of red-gold apricot, *Prunus armeniaca*, grown in China and Japan since records were kept. They are dried and candied or salted.

Chinese plum sauce See **plum sauce**

Chinese preserved eggs Hen and duck eggs preserved by coating them in a mixture of lime, wood ash, salt and rice husks and packing them into earthenware tubs for 3 to 4 months. The yolk becomes a greyish green and the white a pale amber and translucent. They are served shelled as an appetizer. Variously known with characteristic modesty as 1000 year old eggs, 100 year old eggs, century eggs, Ming dynasty eggs and ancient eggs. See also **salted duck eggs**

Chinese red date Jujube

Chinese red stew *United States* Red cooked meat. See also **red cooking**

Chinese sausage See **lap cheong**

Chinese spinach One of the amaranths, *Amaranthus tricolor*, with red, yellow and green leaves. Also called **spineless amaranth**

Chinese truffle A truffle, *Tuber himalayense*, indistinguishable from the French black truffle except by taste and smell, but being imported into Europe and, since it is much cheaper than the French truffle, in some cases being substituted for the genuine article

Chinese vegetable marrow Wax gourd

Chinese water chestnut See **water chestnut**

Chinese water lily Lotus

Chinese water spinach Swamp cabbage

Chinese yam A scaly-skinned variety of yam with white flesh, *Dioscorea esculenta*. The plant produces several small tubers instead of the more usual single tuber.

ching chao ming xia *China* Sautéed prawns

ch'ing ts'ai *China* Pak choy

chini *South Asia* Sugar

chinois *France* 1. A conical metal strainer with one handle usually about 15 cm deep and 12 cm across either of perforated metal or fine wire mesh (NOTE: So called because of its resemblance to a Chinese coolie hat) 2. A candied small green kumquat

chinonaise, à la *France* In the Chinon style, i.e. with a garnish of potatoes and cabbage filled with sausage

chinook salmon The largest of the Pacific salmon, *Oncorhynchus tshawytscha*, weighing between 4 and 22 kg with a flaky, oily flesh. Also called **king salmon**, **royal chinook**, **spring salmon**

chinquapin *United States* Pine nut

chiocciola di mare *Italy* Winkle

chiocciole *Italy* 1. Snails 2. Small pasta shells used in soup

chiodi di garofano *Italy* Cloves

chip See **chips**

chip basket A wide, 1 cm mesh, woven wire metal basket used to hold food for deep-frying or blanching. Also called **frying basket**

chip butty *England* A sandwich containing fried potato chips popularized in Liverpool humour (*colloquial*)

chi po *Thailand* Preserved finely chopped turnip used in Thai cooking

chipolata garnish A garnish of brown glazed button onions, chipolata sausages, chestnuts poached in white stock, glazed turned carrots (olive size) and diced belly of salt pork fried to a light brown colour

chipolata sausages Small pork or beef sausages cooked and served whole (NOTE: From the Italian *cipolla* meaning 'onion', although it contains no onion. A typical recipe might contain seasoned lean and fat pork, a little rusk and ground rice, coriander, paprika, nutmeg, cayenne pepper and thyme, all packed in sheep casings and made into small links)

chipotle chilli A dried and smoked chilli widely used in Mexican cooking. See also **jalapeño chile**

chipped beef Flakes of **charqui** used as a flavouring

chipples *England* The Cornish name for chopped spring onion or shallot tops

chips 1. Batons of potato deep-fried until brown and soft (UK) or golden and crisp (USA, Fr and elsewhere) 2. A generic name for thin slices of potato or other starchy product or mixture, deep-fried until crisp and brown

chiqueter *France* To flute the edge

chirashi-zushi *Japan* A plate or lacquered box of sushi-meshi rice scattered with various fillings

chirongi nut A round nut the size of a small pea with a musky flavour. Used in the Hyderabad state of India.

chironju *South Asia* Charoli nut

chitak *South Asia* A unit of weight equal to 5 tolas, approximately 56 g or 2 oz. Also called **chattak**

chitcharon *Philippines* A dry snack made from pork crackling or fried chitterlings. Also called **sitsaron**

chitterlings 1. The cleaned middle portion of pig gut about 18 m from the stomach, generally boiled before sale. May be fried. Often chopped and incorporated into sausage fillings. **2.** *United States* Odd pieces of newly killed pigs, cut into squares and simmered in broth

chive A small invasive perennial plant of the onion family, *Allium schoenoprasim,* with thin tubular leaves and purple flowers. The chopped leaves have a mild onion flavour and are used as a garnish or for flavouring but not with prolonged cooking. The flowers are used for decorating dishes.

Chivry, sauce *France* White wine boiled and infused with chervil, parsley, tarragon, chopped shallots and fresh young salad burnet for 10 minutes, squeezed out, mixed with 5 times its volume of velouté sauce and finished with **ravigote butter**. Served with boiled and poached chicken.

chi yu *China* Chicken fat

chi zhi *China* Black bean sauce

chłodnik *Poland* A cold soup similar to **chotodziec**, but containing blanched young beetroot tops and an additional garnish of diced fresh cucumber, lemon slices and occasionally cold sturgeon

chłodnik litewski *Poland* A chilled summer soup originating in Lithuania, made from beetroot, cucumber, dill, chives, milk or yoghurt, lemon juice and soured cream processed with water or chicken stock. Served with quartered hard-boiled eggs and sliced radishes.

chlorine A highly irritant gas liberated when bleach reacts with organic matter and acids. Can be dangerous if some cleaning agents are used improperly. Used as a flour improver. See also **E925**

chlorine dioxide See **E926**

chlorophyll The green colouring matter in plants which is a part of the system which turns carbon dioxide into carbohydrates using the energy from the sun. Also used as a permitted green food colouring E140, together with its copper complex E141.

chnang phleung *Cambodia* Steamboat

chocart *France* A Breton pastry tart filled with a spice and lemon mixture. Also called **choquart**

chochon rouci *Caribbean* A meat stew from St Lucia containing pork, onions, leeks, celery, cabbage, carrots, tomatoes, cucumber, garlic and seasonings

chocola *Netherlands* Chocolate

chocolade *Netherlands* Chocolate

chocolat *France* Chocolate

chocolate 1. *England, Spain* A bitter dark brown solid mixture of cocoa butter and cocoa bean solids, made from the fermented pods of the cacao tree from which the seeds are removed, and which are dehusked, roasted and shelled, then ground into a paste which is worked between rollers until the correct smooth physical form is achieved. This chocolate is then further processed to make cocoa solids, cocoa butter, cocoa powder, chocolates *(confectionery),* cooking chocolate, couverture, etc. **2.** A confectionery item made by mixing chocolate and cocoa butter to give about 35% fat content then flavouring with almond, vanilla and/or other spices and sweetening to taste. In the UK, chocolates are adulterated with vegetable fat, butter fat and milk solids.

chocolate cake A cake flavoured and coloured with chocolate or cocoa powder

chocolate chip cookies *United States* Biscuits containing small recognizable pieces of chocolate and possibly chopped nuts. Also called **Maryland cookies**

chocolate crackles *Australia* A children's party biscuit made from a mixture of rice bubbles, icing sugar, desiccated coconut and cocoa powder bound together with copha

chocolate fudge sauce A thick pouring sauce made from melted chocolate, brown sugar, butter, vanilla essence and milk, served hot with ice cream

chocolate log A cake consisting of a Swiss roll coated with chocolate or chocolate butter cream, the coating made to resemble bark using a fork or other implement. Also called **yule log**

chocolate pudding *United Kingdom* Basic steamed pudding flavoured with cocoa or grated chocolate

chocolate sauce 1. A sweetened white sauce flavoured with chocolate or cocoa powder used with baked or steamed puddings **2.** Molten chocolate mixed with sugar, butter and vanilla essence used to coat profiteroles, cakes, ice cream, etc. Solid when cold

chocolate up and over pudding *England* A type of sponge pudding where the uncooked sauce is put on top of the uncooked sponge and ends up after cooking below the sponge. The Victoria sponge mixture has one quarter of the flour replaced by cocoa and the sauce is made by sprinkling demerara sugar, chopped nuts and cocoa over the sponge and covering with strong black coffee containing 200 g of demerara sugar per litre. It is baked in a well-buttered pudding dish for 1 hour at 180°C.

chocolate vermicelli Short fine strands of extruded chocolate 1mm by 3 mm approximately. Used for decoration.

chocolat liégeois *France* As **café liégeois**, but with chocolate

choi *Central Asia* Black tea from Afghanistan, often flavoured with cardamom and sweetened

choice *England* A rump and sirloin of beef not disjointed

choice beef *United States* A high-quality tender and well-flavoured beef with less marbling than prime quality

choix, au *France* At the choice of the customer, choose at will

cho kanjang *Korea* Tahini

choke The central hairy part of an artichoke consisting of immature petals and stamens which is removed when cooked before serving or using

chokecherry *United States* A small astringent native cherry, *Prunus virginiana*, used to make a jelly-type conserve

choklad *Sweden* Chocolate

chokladglass *Sweden* Chocolate ice cream

choko A green pear-shaped squash similar in size to the avocado which grows on a rampant vine, *Sechium edule*. Originally from South America, it is now grown in Australia, the Caribbean and the USA. The flesh is fairly tasteless and must be cooked before eating. The central seed may be eaten when very young and the young leaves and shoots and fleshy roots are also edible. Also called **brionne**, **christophine**, **custard marrow**, **mango squash**, **chayote**, **mirliton**, **pepinello**, **vegetable pear**, **xoxo**, **chow-chow**

chokolade *Denmark* Chocolate

chokoreto *Japan* Chocolate flavour

cholecalciferol See **vitamin D3**

cholent A Jewish casserole made from beef brisket, beans, vegetables and barley which is cooked slowly for 24 hours in flavoured stock so that it can be prepared and started the day before the Sabbath

cholent simmes A cholent based on a mixture of minced turkey meat and onions bound with egg and matzo meal, used in one piece instead of brisket, together with beans and possibly dried fruits, casseroled in a lemon, honey and chicken stock

cholesterol A complex alcohol (**sterol**) found in most body tissues and many foods. It is a high-molecular-weight alcohol normally synthesized by the liver, a constituent of cell membranes and a precursor of steroid hormones. There is a total of about 140 g in the body most of which is synthesized in the body. There is no evidence that dietary cholesterol influences the amount of body cholesterol. The concentration in blood is thought to be an indicator of other problems predisposing to heart and vascular system disease.

choline A water-soluble compound which is needed for B vitamin action and is important for brain function and fat metabolism. It can be synthesized in the body by healthy humans when adequate methionine is present in the diet and is not strictly a vitamin. It is found in high concentration in most animal tissues and egg yolk is the richest source. Deficiency may cause fatty liver and a predisposition to cirrhosis of the liver. It has no known toxicity.

cholla 1. A plaited bread covered in poppy seeds. See also **challa 2.** Chick pea

cholodyetz A Jewish appetizer made from calf's foot jelly. See also **petcha**

chompoo *Thailand* Rose apple

chondroitin A polysaccharide component of cartilage and bone

chongos *Spain* A lemon and cinnamon-flavoured custard

chop A slice of meat cut across the back about 1 to 3 cm thick consisting of a part of the spinal column, the muscles surrounding it and part of the rib cage or belly extending to at most 15 cm. either side. Usually halved through the spinal cord, but sometimes complete, e.g. Barnsley chop. Usually from a lamb, pig or goat.

chop, to To divide food into pieces of varying size using a knife or cleaver on a chopping board

chopa *Spain* Black bream

chop kebab *Bulgaria* Cubes of lamb and peeled marrow, threaded on skewers, marinated in tomato juice, seasoned and grilled

chopped egg and onion A Jewish appetizer made with chopped hard-boiled eggs, onions and seasoning bound together with molten chicken fat

chopped herring A Jewish appetizer of chopped salted herring fillets mixed with white bread, grated sour apples, chopped onion and hard-boiled egg white, vinegar and seasonings. Served on lettuce and garnished with sieved hard-boiled egg yolk.

chopped liver A Jewish appetizer made from cooked liver, onions and hard-boiled egg yolks all chopped, seasoned, bound with molten chicken fat, served on lettuce and garnished with chopped hard-boiled egg white

chopping board A thick board of hard wood or plastic used to protect the edge of the knife and the surface of the table when chopping food. Different coloured plastics are now recommended for different types of food in commercial establishments in order to reduce cross-contamination, i.e. red for raw meat, blue for fish, brown for vegetables, green for salads and fruit, yellow for cooked meats and white for dairy products. See also **cutting board**

chop sticks Two slender tapering wood, plastic or ivory sticks about 30 cm long used in the East for eating solid food. The technique for use requires some practice.

chop suey A Western version of Chinese food invented to use up scraps of meat, consisting of shredded meat or poultry, chopped or sliced mushrooms, onions and bamboo shoots, bean sprouts, seasoning, etc. in a corn flour thickened chicken stock laced with MSG. Served with rice and soya sauce.

chop suey greens Garland chrysanthemum

choquart *France* A Breton pastry tart. See also **chocart**

choriceros chilli A mild and piquant hot chilli from Spain

chorizo *Middle East, Spain* A type of sausage made from pork, beef, olive oil, red peppers, garlic and seasoning, stuffed in hog casings. Often scalded, dried and left to mature for 2 to 3 months when it develops a surface mould. Sometimes cold-smoked. Served as an appetizer or with chick peas as a main course.

chorizo basquais *France, Spain* A softer and less highly spiced version of chorizo

chorizo canton *Philippines* Lap cheong, Chinese sausage

chorizo de Catimpalos *Spain* A chorizo containing large chunks of ham

chorizo de Estremadura *Spain* A highly spiced expensive chorizo made with finely processed pork fillet and pig's liver flavoured with the usual sweet red pepper, but including crushed juniper berries, tomato purée, cayenne pepper and other spices, packed in beef casings and cold-smoked for a week or more with juniper berries added to the fire

chorizo de lomo *Spain* A chorizo sausage made with large pieces of pork loin

chorizo de Salamanca *Spain* A coarse-textured chorizo

chorizo picante *Mexico* A pork chorizo made without fat, seasoned, flavoured with garlic, chilli powder and ground cumin seed and preserved with added vinegar. When dried will keep for several weeks.

chorizos combinados *Spain* Mixed sliced sausages

Chorley cake *England* A parcel of shortcrust pastry with a filling of currants, brown sugar and melted butter in the centre, rolled flat until the currants show through the pastry, egg washed, slit and baked at 190°C

Chorleywood process *United Kingdom* A method of making bread developed at the British Baking Industries Research Association, Chorleywood, (now the Flour Milling and Baking Research Association), which cuts down on the time necessary to knead and prove the dough. In essence it uses intensive mixing of the flour, water, salt, yeast, vitamin C and fat for from 3 to 5 minutes imparting 11 watt-hours of energy per kg of the dough in that time and raising its temperature to 30°C. Double the normal amounts of yeast and improvers are also added. The dough can then be immediately divided into tins. The whole bread-making process takes less than 3.5 hours from flour to bread and produces a very cheap loaf without character suitable only for use as a loss leader and for feeding ducks.

chorlito *Spain* Plover

chorogi Chinese artichoke

choron, sauce *England, France* A **béarnaise sauce** combined with tomato purée. Also called **béarnaise tomatée, sauce**

chota piaz *South Asia* Shallot

chotenn bigoudenn *France* A pig's head roasted with garlic

choti elaichi *South Asia* Bleached or green cardamom

chotodziec *Poland* A cold soup made from the juice of pickled cucumbers blended with sour milk, strained and garnished with diced beetroot, slices of hard-boiled egg, crayfish tails, chopped chives and chopped dill. Served on a plate with an ice cube.

chou *France* Cabbage

chou à la crème *France* Cream puff

chou blanc *France* White cabbage

chou brocoli *France* Broccoli

chou cabus *France* White cabbage

choucroute *France* Sauerkraut or pickled cabbage

choucroute aux poissons *France* Poached freshwater fish served on a bed of pickled cabbage with a wine-based cream sauce

choucroute garnie à l'alsacienne *France* Pickled cabbage topped with sausages, pork chops and knuckles of ham. Served with mustard and horseradish sauce.

chou de mer *France* Seakale

chou farci *France* Stuffed cabbage

chou-fleur *France* Cauliflower

chou frisé *France* Kale

chou marin *France* Seakale

chou navet *France* Swede

chou palmiste *France* Heart of palm

chou pomme *France* White cabbage

chou-rave *France* Kohlrabi

chouriço *Portugal* A chorizo-type sausage made with pork cured in brine, seasoned, flavoured with garlic and paprika and moistened with red wine, packed into casings, smoked and preserved in olive oil

chouriço de sangue *Portugal* Black pudding, boudin noir

chou rouge *France* Red cabbage

chou vert *France* Green cabbage

choux de Bruxelles *France* Brussels sprouts

choux pastry Pastry made by melting 4 parts butter and 10 parts water, beating in 5 parts strong flour and 8 parts of egg over heat until the paste leaves the side of the pan, piping onto baking trays and baking until dry

chow chow 1. Choko **2.** See **chow chow preserve**

chow chow preserve 1. A Chinese preserve of ginger, fruits and peel in a heavy syrup **2.** Chopped mixed vegetables in a mustard flavoured pickle sauce

chowder *United States* The name for fish soups generally based on a mixture of fish stock and milk with sweated chopped vegetables usually including potatoes and sweet corn, pieces of fish and/or shellfish added towards the end so as not to overcook and occasionally thickened with corn flour, a similar starch or **beurre manié**. In the USA, meat, salt pork and bread or crackers may be included.

chow fun *China* Wide flat rice noodles

chow mein As chop suey but served with boiled or fried noodles. Also called **chao mian**

choy pin *China* Turnip

choy sum *China* A leaf vegetable, *Brassica rapa* var. *parachinensis*, resembling pak choy but with slightly bitter stems which are the part usually eaten. It occasionally shows small yellow flowers. Also called **flowering white cabbage**

chrain A Jewish relish made from grated horseradish mixed with chopped beetroot. Served with gefilte fish or cold fried fish.

christening cake A rich fruit cake covered with marzipan and white icing with appropriate decorations to be served after a christening

Christmas cake A very rich moist cake with a high proportion of dried vine fruits, chopped nuts and candied peel, often with added brandy or rum, covered with almond paste and icing and appropriately decorated. The cake itself before covering is often matured for several months.

Christmas melon *United States* A small smooth melon with a mottled green and yellow rind and pale green flesh. it is similar in taste to the honeydew. Also called **Santa Claus melon**

Christmas pudding A steamed or boiled pudding made from flour, suet, sugar, dried vine fruits, spices, milk and sometimes breadcrumbs, cooked, matured and reheated for serving. Traditionally a small coin was inserted into the pudding as a token of good fortune for the receiver. Also called **plum pudding**

christophine Choko

christstollen A yeasted, egg-enriched and sweetened fruit bread incorporating almond flakes, rum soaked dried vine fruits, candied peel, glacé cherries and chopped angelica and flavoured with lemon zest and almond essence

Christstollen *Germany* An enriched sweetened Christmas bread. See also **Stollen**

chromium A trace element required by the body for health, found in fish, nuts, whole grains, yeast and seaweed

chrysanthemum Particular types of chrysanthemum plants are grown for their edible flowers, petals and leaves in China and Japan. There are two types grown for leaves and one for flowers. See also **garland chrysanthemum**

Chrysanthemum coronarium *Botanical name* Garland chrysanthemum

chrysanthemum cut A Japanese method of cutting turnip or other root vegetables by standing the piece between two parallel chopsticks, cutting down at right angles to the chopsticks in very thin slices joined at the base, rotating the piece through 90 degrees and repeating. This gives fine strands springing from a solid base like the centre of any daisy-like flower.

chrysanthemum greens Garland chrysanthemum

chtapothi *Greece* Octopus

chub A freshwater fish, *Leuciscus cephalus*, which is a relative of the carp. Rarely used for food on account of the numerous small bones and the somewhat muddy flavour.

Braised chub's head is a popular dish in China.

chuck *United States* The name of a large part of the forequarter of beef extending to the brisket and excluding only the foreribs and part of the middle ribs. It is cut in a number of different ways which depend on the locality but are mainly self explanatory, e.g. chuck roll, chuck steak, blade steak, chuck tender, shoulder steak, chuck short ribs, arm steak, etc.

chuck ribs of beef *United Kingdom* The first two ribs of beef counting from the head end, the meat of which is generally used off the bone for stewing and braising

chuck roll *United States* A rolled joint of beef from the ribs of the chuck

chuck steak 1. *United Kingdom* Blade bone **2.** *United States* A cut of beef from between the neck and shoulder used for stewing

chuck wagon stew *Canada* A stew from Alberta made from beef fried in fat, water, potatoes, carrots, apples, small onions, herbs and seasonings thickened with corn flour

chucruta *Spain* Sauerkraut

chufa *Spain* Tiger nut

chui kan *China* Kumquat

chu ju *China* Mandarin orange

chuka-nabe *Japan* Wok

chukandar *South Asia* Beetroot

chuk gaai choy *China* One of the oriental mustards with ribbed green stalks and serrated leaves growing to 30 cm. The strong flavour is reduced by parboiling. Also called **bamboo mustard cabbage**

chuk surn *China* Bamboo shoot

chuleta a la vienesa *Spain* Veal cutlet

chuleta de cordero *Spain* Lamb chop

chuleta de ternera *Spain* Veal cutlet

chump chops *United Kingdom* Chops cut from the top of a leg of lamb and the rear of the loin including parts of the pelvis but not any vertebrae except the coccyx

chump end of loin of lamb *United Kingdom* The end of the loin nearest the tail or pelvis

chump of pork *United Kingdom* The top of the pork leg and the rear of the loin including parts of the pelvis but not any vertebrae except the coccyx. Usually sold as a piece and not as chops.

chum salmon See **Siberian salmon**

chung *China* Scallion

chung choy *China* Turnip

chung tau *China* Shallots

chun juan *China* Spring roll

chunky banana *United States* Burro banana

chuño blanco *South America* A preserved form of bitter potato from the Andean region of Peru made by freezing raw potatoes, removing the skins, squeezing out the released liquid, washing in running water and drying. Used as a basis of stews, soups and cheese dishes and with fruit and molasses as a dessert (**mazamorra**).

chuño negro *South America* A preserved form of potato similarly processed to chuño blanco but with the skins left on and not washed in running water. Dark brown in colour it is usually soaked in water for one to two days before cooking to remove strong flavours.

chuoi *Vietnam* Banana

chupe de camarones *South America* A thick soup from Peru containing prawns, fried onions, garlic, tomatoes, peppers, potatoes, peas, sweet corn, eggs, cream, parsley or coriander and seasoning

churek *Russia* A yeast-raised bread from the Caucasus enriched with milk and melted butter, flavoured with ground anise (aniseed), glazed with egg and sprinkled with sesame seeds

churn 1. A tall almost cylindrical metal vessel with a deep rimmed lid used in the olden days to keep milk for sale or further processing **2.** A vessel of moderate size, often made of wood in which cream was converted to butter by agitation, now superseded by machinery

churn, to To agitate cream with a regular motion to convert it into butter and buttermilk

churrasco *Portugal* Charcoal grilled meat or chicken, usually on a skewer

churrasco a gaucha *Brazil* A barbecue usually featuring beef or chicken

churros *Spain* Banana-shaped fritters squeezed through a nozzle into deep fat, fried, sprinkled with sugar and eaten for breakfast often by dunking in a hot cinnamon drink

chutney A mixture of chopped apples, onion and garlic with possibly other vegetables and/or fruits cooked in a vinegar, sugar and spice mixture to a thick consistency, used as a relish. Also called **sweet pickle**

chutoro *Japan* The very highly prized middle section of tuna belly (**toro**). See also **otoro**

chyet-thon-phew *Burma* Garlic

chymosin A protease used in cheese making

chymotripsin One of the proteases found in the human digestive system. The seeds of some legumes contain chymotrypsin inhibitors which prevent its digestive action.

For this reason these seeds must be well cooked before consumption.

ciabatta *Italy* An oval-shaped bread made from a very slack dough of flour, water and fresh yeast (20:14:1) with dried milk powder, salt and olive oil and some sour dough or biga. The batter is beaten then kneaded until silky (1000 movements suggested), proved 2 to 3 hours at 26 to 30°C, shaped on a flat tray, proved again until doubled in volume and baked 20 to 25 minutes at 230°C. (NOTE: Literally 'slipper'.)

ciafotta *Italy* Ciambotta

cialda *Italy* Waffle, wafer

cialledda del massaro *Italy* A country soup made with slices of bread covered with vegetables

ciambelle *Italy* 1. Ring-shaped cakes or pastries with nuts and candied fruit. Also called **panafracchi 2.** Bread loaves (*Tuscany and Sardinia*)

ciambotta *Italy* A type of Spanish omelette made with potatoes, sweet green peppers, tomatoes and aubergines cooked in olive oil. Also called **ciamotta**, **cianfotta**

ciammotte ammuccate *Italy* Snails seasoned with pepper, mint and herbs

ciamotta *Italy* Ciambotta

cianfotta *Italy* Ciambotta

ciaronciedi moena *Italy* A potato-based ravioli from the Dolomite region of Italy, stuffed with a filling based on figs or dried pears and finished with melted butter and poppy seeds

ciasto *Poland* Cake

ciboule *France* 1. Spring onion 2. Chive

ciboulette *France* Chives

cibreo *Italy* Cooked cockscombs and sweetbreads served with a vegetable **timbale**. The dish is said to date from Roman times.

cicala *Italy* A flat Mediterranean lobster-like crustacean. See also **cigarra**

ciccioli *Italy* Pork scratchings, crackling

cicely See **sweet cicely**

Cicer arietinum *Botanical name* Chick pea

cicerchia *Italy* A large pebble-like pea

cicerelle *France* Sand eel

cicerello *Italy* Sand eel

cichorel *Netherlands* Chicory, endive

Cichorium endivia *Botanical name* Endive

Cichorium intybus *Botanical name* Chicory

cicoria *Italy* Chicory, the leaf

cicoria spadona *Italy* Sword-leaved green chicory

cicoriella *Italy* Wild chicory

cider The fermented juice of apples, often used as a cooking liquor in Southern England and Northern France. Can be distilled to a strong spirit sometimes used for flavouring.

cider cake A chemically raised basic cake mixture made by the creaming method containing sultanas equal in weight to the flour which have been soaked in dry cider (8:5) for at least 12 hours. Baked at 180°C until cooked.

cider vinegar A vinegar made by the oxidation of the alcohol in cider to acetic acid

cidra *Spain* Citron, the fruit

cidre *France* Cider

ciernikis *Poland* An appetizer made from a cottage cheese, butter and flour dough, seasoned and flavoured with nutmeg, rolled out, cut in squares, boiled, drained and served sprinkled with grated cheese and breadcrumbs which have been browned in butter

ciervo *Spain* Venison

cigala *Spain* Dublin bay prawn

cigalle *France* Dublin bay prawn

cigarra *Spain* A flat Mediterranean lobster-like crustacean, *Scyllarides latus,* very similar to a slipper lobster and with small claws. Large ones are treated like lobster; small ones are used in paella.

cilantro 1. *Spain, United States* Coriander leaves. See also **chadon beni 2.** *Caribbean* A herb, *Eryngium foetidum,* from Costa Rica, Dominica and Mexico with a similar flavour to coriander, very common in Trinidad

ciliegia *Italy* Cherry

cili padi *Malaysia* Bird's eye chilli

cima di vitello *Italy* Veal in aspic

cima ripiena *Italy* Breast of veal with a pocket cut into it and filled with various stuffings

cimbopogone *Italy* Lemon grass

cime di rapa *Italy* Broccoli raab

cimeter *United States* A knife with a curved pointed blade for accurate cutting of steaks etc.

cincho *South America* A ewes' milk cheese from Venezuela similar to Villalon

cinghiale *Italy* Wild boar

Cinnamomum cassia *Botanical name* Cassia

Cinnamomum zeylanicum *Botanical name* Cinnamon

cinnamon A very popular spice made from the dried bark of a tree of the laurel family, *Cinnamomum zeylanicum,* which is either ground or rolled up into small curls called 'quills'. Extensively used for sweet and savoury items.

cinnamon basil *Italy* A variety of basil with a cinnamon aroma

cinnamon sugar A mixture of caster sugar and ground cinnamon used for baking, principally in Central and Northern Europe

cioccolata *Italy* Chocolate

cioppino *United States* A mixed seafood stew from the west coast similar to bouillabaisse, i.e. with wine, olive oil, garlic, onions, tomatoes, green sweet peppers, spices, herbs and seasoning

cipolla *Italy* Onion

cipollette *Italy* Spring onions

cipolline *Italy* Small silverskin onions, pearl onions

Circassian sauce See **satsivi**

ciriole *Italy* 1. Tiny eels 2. Crusty round bread rolls (*Rome*)

ciruela *Spain* Plum

ciruela damascena *Spain* Damson

ciruela pasa, ciruela seca *Spain* Prune

cisco Lake herring

ciseler *France* 1. To shred or cut in julienne strips 2. To incise

citrange A hybrid of the sweet orange and a poncirus citrus, developed in the USA to withstand cool climates. The flesh is sharp tasting.

citrates and dihydrogen citrates Salts of citric acid used for the same purposes as citric acid. The ones used are sodium, E331, potassium, E332 and calcium, E333. See also **E330**

citric acid The commonest food acid originally extracted from citrus fruits where it is in high concentration but now made by a fungal fermentation. Also found in gooseberries, raspberries, etc. See **E330** for uses.

citroen *Netherlands* Lemon

citrom *Hungary* Lemon

citron 1. A citrus fruit from an evergreen tree, *Citrus medica*, native to East Asia. It is shaped like a lemon up to 20 cm long by 13 cm diameter with a knobbly skin. It is grown for its skin which is used to make candied peel, as a flavouring and after carving as a garnish. The flesh is very sour. 2. *Denmark, France, Sweden* Lemon

citronella Lemon grass

Citronella microcarpa *Botanical name* Calamondin

citron fromage *Denmark* A lemon-flavoured dessert

citronkräm *Sweden* A lemon-flavoured dessert

citronnat *France* Candied lemon peel

citron peel The peel, including the zest and pith, of the citron which is brined, dried, soaked in a strong sugar syrup, then dried and chopped

citron vert *France* Lime, the fruit. Also called **lime**

citrouille *France* Pumpkin

citroxanthin The yellow pigment found in citrus peel

Citrullus lanatus *Botanical name* Watermelon

Citrullus vulgaris *Botanical name* Watermelon

Citrullus vulgaris var. fistulosus *Botanical name* Tinda

citrus The most important tree fruit crop in the world (around 70% of all fruit grown) which will grow within 40 degrees of latitude on either side of the equator. There are six genera of which three are of commercial importance, i.e. Poncirus (*trifoliate orange*), Fortunella (*kumquat*) and Citrus (eight important species). All three will hybridize with each other and most *Citrus* species are cross-fertile, hence the increasing number of varieties. See also **Citrus**

Citrus The 8 most important Citrus species are sweet orange *C. sinensis*, mandarin *C. reticulata*, grapefruit *C. paradisi*, pummelo *C. grandis*, lemon *C. limon*, lime *C. aurantifolia*, citron *C. medica* and sour orange *C. aurantium*. All of these varieties will cross-fertilize and it is thought that the sweet orange may be a pummelo x mandarin cross, the grapefruit a pummelo x sweet orange cross and the lemon a lime x citron x pummelo cross. See also **citrus fruits**

Citrus aurantifolia *Botanical name* West Indian lime

Citrus aurantium *Botanical name* Seville orange

Citrus bergamia *Botanical name* Bergamot, the fruit

Citrus deliciosa *Botanical name* Mediterranean mandarin

citrus fruits Fruits of the genus Citrus which have been cultivated for 2000 years and known in Europe since the 16th century. They all have a two-layered separable green, yellow or orange skin, the outer layer (zest) being rich in essential oils, the inner (pith or albedo) being white and soft, all enclosing a segmented fruit containing juice sacs and seeds (pips). The juices contain sugar, flavours, aromas and citric acid. The relative proportions of these determine the palatability and uses of the fruit. (NOTE: Examples of citrus fruits are: orange, lemon, lime, cumquat, grapefruit, mandarin, tangerine and clementine.)

Citrus grandis *Botanical name* Pummelo

Citrus hystrix *Botanical name* Makrut lime

Citrus junos *Botanical name* Yuzu
Citrus latifolia *Botanical name* Persian lime
Citrus limettiodes *Botanical name* Sweet lime
Citrus limon *Botanical name* Lemon
Citrus medica *Botanical name* Citron
Citrus nobilis *Botanical name* King mandarin
Citrus paradisi *Botanical name* Grapefruit
Citrus reticulata *Botanical name* Common mandarin
Citrus sinensis *Botanical name* Sweet orange
Citrus sphaerocarpa *Botanical name* Kabosa
Citrus sudachi *Botanical name* Sudachi
Citrus unshui *Botanical name* Satsuma mandarin
city chicken *United States* Diced veal from the lean part of the shoulder cooked on a skewer
ciuppin *Italy* A fish stew
cive *France* Chives
civet *England, France* A dark brown stew made from wild rabbit, hare or other game animal, thickened with its blood
civet de lièvre *France* Jugged hare
civette *France* Chives
clabber *United States* Milk soured almost to the point of separating into curds and whey, something like junket. Eaten plain or flavoured.
clafoutis *France* Black cherries baked in a thick creamy batter until golden brown, sprinkled with sugar and served warm with cream, often at harvest time
claire *France* A fattened oyster. Also called **huître de clair**
clam A bivalve shellfish found worldwide with lean flesh which can be eaten raw, poached, steamed, baked or fried. All must be live when purchased and consumed as soon as possible after being allowed to clean themselves in water with a little oatmeal for 24 hours and subsequently well scrubbed. There is considerable confusion in the naming and classification of clams for culinary purposes. See amongst others, bean, carpet shell, golden carpet shell, little neck, quahog, sand, soft shell, surf, venus shell, warty venus and wedge shell.
clamart *England, France* A garnish of globe artichoke hearts filled with petit pois
clam bake *United States* A social gathering at the beach in which food (clams, chicken, corn on the cob, potatoes, etc.) is steamed in a pit in the beach by means of heated rocks using damp seaweed to provide the steam
clam chowder *United States* A famous USA soup made from small clams cooked over a high heat with dry white wine and water until all open. The sound clams are reserved and the cooking liquor is strained off to make a broth with fried diced bacon, leeks and celery and chopped potatoes. Towards the end of the cooking period, milk, cream, seasoning and the reserved clams are added, simmered for 5 minutes, finished with chopped parsley and served with croûtons.
clam knife A short-bladed sharp knife used to open shellfish
clapper cut Hyoshi-giri
clapshot *Scotland* A vegetable accompaniment of potatoes and swedes boiled in salted water until soft and mashed with seasoning, butter and chopped chives
claquebitou *France* A goats' milk cheese flavoured with herbs from Burgundy
clara *Portugal* Egg white
clarificar *Spain* To clarify
clarified butter Pure butter fat without any solids, liquid or foam. It should be transparent when molten.
clarifier *France* To clarify, e.g. butter, consommé
clarify, to To remove all solids and immiscible fluids from a liquid by skimming, filtering, by entrapping the impurities in coagulated egg whites or isinglass, by solubilizing with enzymes, etc. to leave a perfectly clear liquid e.g. for bouillon
clarifying agent A substance that removes suspended impurities in liquids. Egg white is the most common in food preparation, e.g. for consommés.
clary sage A biennial herb, *Salvia sclarea*, belonging to the mint family. It has a flavour similar to sage. Famous for its very expensive essential oil. Also called **clear eye**
clavelado *France* Skate, the fish
claviari *Italy* A type of fungus
clavo *Mexico* Clove
claytonia Winter purslane
clear, to 1. What happens to dough during the later phases of kneading when it becomes elastic, smooth and silky **2.** To clarify
clear eye See **clary sage**
clear oxtail soup As **thick oxtail soup** but omitting the flour and slightly thickening before garnishing using arrowroot and cooking until clear. Also called **queue de boeuf clair**
clear soup See **consommé**
cleaver An instrument with a wide rectangular heavy blade used in the West for chopping through small bones and cartilage. but increasingly, following East Asian practice, as a precision-slicing knife.

clementine A hybrid citrus fruit of the mandarin and Seville orange. One of the common mandarins, *Citrus reticulata*, said to have been grown accidentally in 1902 by a Father Clément. It is small, sweet, round and juicy with a thin skin and few pips. See common mandarin.

clipfish Klipfish

cloche, sous *France* Describes a dish of food served under a domed cover with a handle on the top

clod *England* A cut of beef from the neck between the head and the blade bone suitable only for mincing or long slow stewing or braising

cloïsses *Catalonia* Clams

clonorchis A species of fluke with a similar mode of transmission, prevalence and effects as **opisthorchis**

cloot *Scotland* A large square of muslin or linen used to contain boiled puddings

clootie dumpling *Scotland* A spiced pudding similar to Christmas pudding and boiled in a cloot. Sometimes eaten cold like cake. Also called **cloutie dumpling**

Clostridium botulinum The bacterium found in home canned and bottled vegetables which causes **botulism**. The spores of this organism are not killed by cooking at normal temperatures. The incubation period is 18 to 36 hours and death occurs in 1 to 8 days or there is a slow recovery lasting 6 to 8 months. The symptoms are disturbance of vision, dry mucous membranes of the mouth, tongue and pharynx, which cause difficulty in speaking and swallowing, and progressive weakness and respiratory failure. Immediate medical attention should be sought if there is any suspicion of the condition.

Clostridium perfringens A food-poisoning bacterium found in cooked and reheated meats and meat products. The incubation period is 8 to 12 hours, the duration 12 to 24 hours and the symptoms are diarrhoea, abdominal pain and nausea. There is rarely vomiting and no fever.

clot, to To coagulate

clotted cream *England* A thick, yellow, pasteurized cream with a minimum fat content of 48% from Devon or Cornwall. It is made by heating full cream milk slowly and skimming off the cream from the surface. Used with jam as a spread on scones for the traditional Devon cream tea. Also called **clouted cream**

cloudberry A wild berry from a creeping plant, *Rubus chamaemorus*, similar to a blackberry and found in Northern Europe and North America. It is a deep golden colour with a baked apple/honey taste. Used to flavour a liqueur.

cloud ear fungus An edible fungus, *Auricularia polytricha*, grown in China on oak logs and available as small, black, brittle dried pieces which expand 5 times in volume when reconstituted. Used in Chinese dishes. Also called **wood ear**, **wood fungus**, **tree fungus**, **brown fungus**, **black fungus**, **black tree fungus**, **rat's ear**, **tree ear**

clou de girofle *France* Clove

clouté(e) *France* Studded, as in onion clouté. See also **piquer**

clouted cream See **clotted cream**

cloutie dumpling See **clootie dumpling**

clovas de comer *Philippines* Cloves

clove basil A variety of basil with a slight clove aroma and flavour

cloverleaf roll *United States* Three balls of yeasted and proven dough placed on a baking tin so that when risen and baked they stick together and resemble the three parts of a cloverleaf

cloves The dried unopened flower buds of an evergreen tree, *Eugenia caryophyllus*, with a strong, sweet, aromatic smell and flavour. The tree is a native of Indonesia but now grown in East Africa. Cloves are used whole or ground in desserts and savoury dishes. Ground cloves are mixed with tobacco to make the Indonesian kretek cigarette which has a soporific effect on the smoker.

clovisse *France* **1.** Carpet shell clam **2.** Golden carpet shell clam

club gourd Angled loofah

club sandwich A sandwich made from two slices of toasted bread filled with lettuce, sliced chicken, sliced tomatoes, crisp fried bacon and mayonnaise, garnished with chutney, pickles or olives

club steak *United States* A beef steak cut from the small end (rib end) of the short loin with no fillet

cluck and grunt *United States* Eggs and bacon (*colloquial*; Wild West)

cluster bean Guar bean

coagulate, to The process by which liquids or some of the soluble components of liquids, usually proteins, become solid, e.g. when white of egg or blood solidifies or milk curdles. Also called **clot, to**

coalfish Coley

coarse salt *United States* Sea salt

coat, to To cover pieces of cooked or uncooked food with a liquid which sticks to the surface, e.g. sauce, batter, melted butter or a glaze, or a combination of liquid and solid, e.g. egg and breadcrumbs, either to seal in flavour, to add flavour or to improve the appearance

coating batter A thick, viscous mixture of flour, water or milk, with possibly egg, cream or sugar, and seasoning used to coat items of food, generally prior to frying, deep-frying, or baking

coating consistency (A liquid) with sufficient body or viscosity such that when it coats a solid it will not drain off. Tested by inverting a spoonful of the mixture which should not leave the spoon.

coating sauce A thick sauce of coating consistency used to cover foods to improve their appearance and flavour

cob A round, hemispherical, white or brown loaf baked on a flat tray, sometimes with a cross incised on the top before baking

cobalamin See **vitamin B12**

cobalt A trace element necessary for health which is a constituent of vitamin B12 (cobalamin). Found in meat, eggs, dairy products and yeast extract.

cobbler *England* Any sweet or savoury cooked food mixture covered or part covered with uncooked scones (sweet or savoury as appropriate), egg- or milk-washed, possibly cheese gratinated and baked at 220°C until the scones rise and are browned. See e.g. fish cobbler, cobbler pudding.

cobbler pudding A cold stewed fruit mixture covered with round scones, brushed with beaten egg and baked until brown

cobek *Indonesia* A ceramic mortar used with a ceramic pestle (**uleg-uleg**). Also called **tjobek**

Coblenz sausage Koblenz sausage

cobnut Hazelnut

Coburg cake A small, spiced sponge cake soaked in flavoured sugar syrup

coca 1. *Catalonia* A crisp pastry base often used as the base for snacks and tapas **2.** The American shrub, *Erythroxylon coca*, from whose leaves an extract is obtained which was once used used in cola drinks

cocada *Spain* A coconut-flavoured custard

coca de Sant Joan *Catalonia* A yeast-raised cake, sprinkled with candied fruits and pine nuts, served on St John's night (Midsummer's Eve) throughout Catalonia

cocciole *Italy* Cockles, shellfish

cocer al vapor *Spain* To steam

cocer en cazuela con poco agua *Spain* To braise

cochineal A deep red food colouring. Originally extracted from and contained in the fat and egg yolks of an insect, *Coccus*

cacti, found in Mexico and Brazil, but now made synthetically. Also called **carmine**

cochineal red See **ponceau 4R**

cochinillo *Spain* Suckling pig

cochinillo asado *Spain* Spit-roasted suckling pig

cochinita pibil *Mexico* Minced pork mixed with annatto seeds ground to an oily paste and pork fat, wrapped in banana leaves and baked in the oven. Served with black beans, tortillas and chopped onions in vinegar. Also called **pibil pork**

cochino *Spain* Pig

cochon *France* Pig

cochon de lait *France* Sucking pig

cocido *Spain* **1.** A stew. See also **olla podrida** **2.** Cooked

cocido a la madrileña *Spain* A slowly cooked casserole containing meat, fowl, sausages, vegetables and chickpeas

cock The adult uncastrated male of the domestic fowl *Gallus gallus*. Also used of other males e.g. crabs, fish, wild birds.

cock-a-leekie *Scotland* A soup made with equal parts of chicken and veal stock garnished with a **julienne** of prunes, cooked white chicken meat and leeks

cockle A bivalve shellfish, *Cerastaderma edule* (UK), *C. glaucum* (Mediterranean) and *Cardium edule*, with ribbed, grey to brown, pink or even dark blue, almost circular shell from 2.5 to 10 cm diameter found on most sea coasts and with over 200 varieties worldwide. May be eaten raw or cooked for 6 minutes, but usually sold cooked. Treat like mussels. See also **cuore rossa**, **dog cockle**, **prickly cockle**, **spiny cockle**. Also called **arkshell**

cockle cakes *Wales* Cockle cakes are made by mixing fresh cleaned cockles in a thick batter and frying them a spoonful at a time in oil. The batter is made from flour, beaten egg and molten butter (4:2:1). Also called **teisennau cocos**

cockle pie *Wales* An open pie made with shortcrust pastry layered with fresh cockle meat, chopped spring onions and chopped bacon alternately in that order until the pie is full. The liquid from the shucked cockles is poured in, the top decorated with strips of pastry in a lattice and all baked at 200°C for 30 minutes. Served hot or cold. Also called **pastai cocos**

cockles pen-clawdd *Wales* Chopped spring onions and breadcrumbs fried in butter until the breadcrumbs are crisp, well-cleaned cockles in their shells added to the pan and shaken over the heat with a lid on until the cockles are open and heated through.

Served with a generous sprinkling of chopped parsley.

cock paddle Lumpfish

cocktail avocado *United States* A small seedless fruit of the Fuerte avocado with the characteristic buttery flavour and used in the same way

cocktail sauce Mayonnaise flavoured with tomato purée, horseradish sauce, Worcestershire sauce and Tabasco, used with prawns, crab and lobster

coco *France, Middle East, Portugal* Coconut

cocoa bean The seed of a tree, *Theobroma cacao*, originally from South America but now grown in West Africa. Used as the source of chocolate and cocoa.

cocoa butter The highly saturated white or yellow fat pressed out of cocoa beans, mainly used for chocolate manufacture

cocoa powder Defatted cocoa beans treated with an alkali, further processed, dried and ground to a fine powder for use as a flavouring or to make drinks

cocomero *Italy* Watermelon

coconut 1. The oval fruit (up to 20 cm long) of a tropical palm, *Cocus nucifera*, with an outer fibrous covering, an inner hard shell lined with a white crisp flesh about 6 mm thick and containing a white, sweet, translucent liquid **2.** The inner lining of the coconut often shredded, grated and/or dried. See also **desiccated coconut, makapuno**

coconut crab A large edible land crab, *Birgus latro*, which lives in burrows and is found on islands in the Indian and Pacific oceans

coconut cream A thick creamy liquid made either by mixing coconut milk with sufficient dried coconut milk powder or puréeing coconut flesh with coconut milk. Used to add body and flavour to stews, etc.

coconut grater A hemispherical grater with a handle used for removing the flesh from fresh coconuts

coconut milk 1. The liquid obtained by soaking grated or desiccated coconut in water and straining off the solid particles. Used in Indian and Eastern dishes. Available as a dried powder for reconstituting. **2.** The white translucent liquid inside a coconut used as a refreshing drink or as flavouring. Also called **coconut water**

coconut oil The highly saturated oil extracted from dried coconut (**copra**), used in the food-manufacturing industry and in Asian cooking as well as for soap and cosmetics. It contains about 75% saturated fat and is solid at ambient temperatures in temperate climates.

coconut pudding *United Kingdom* Basic steamed pudding mixture with 1 part in 6 of the flour replaced by desiccated coconut

coconut sugar Palm sugar

coconut syrup A clear viscous sweet syrupy sap extracted from the trunk of the coconut palm

coconut vinegar A mild vinegar made from coconut wine. See also **suka**

coconut water See **coconut milk 2**

coconut wine The fermented sap of the coconut palm from India. Used as a beverage and as the ferment for **appa** bread. Also called **toddy**

coco quemado *Caribbean* A type of enriched thick custard from Cuba made with plain milk, sugar, egg yolks and plain flour (10:10:5:2) flavoured with coconut cream to taste and when cooled sprinkled with toasted grated coconut flesh

cocotte *France* A shallow earthenware, cast iron or porcelain dish with a lid, a casserole

cocotte, en *France* A method of cooking eggs in a small cocotte, ramekin or soufflé dish which is placed in rapidly boiling water. Various food items may be put under the egg before cooking or over it after cooking.

cocotte minute *France* A domestic pressure cooker

cocoyam Taro

cocozelle squash *United States* A small summer squash resembling the courgette

cocum The fruit of an Indian tree. See also **kokum**

cod A round, non-oily sea water fish, *Gadus morrhua*, from the northern oceans up to 40 kg in weight with a white flaky flesh and a grey green skin. Used to be cheap and common in the northern hemisphere. Dried and salted it is a major item in international trade as a protein source.

coda di bue *Italy* Oxtail

coddes *United States* A Maryland speciality of codfish fish cakes panéed and deep-fried

coddle *Ireland* A rich stew of any of, meat, cured meat, beans, vegetables and herbs

coddle, to A way of cooking eggs by putting them into boiling water which is then covered and removed from the source of heat. The white is usually just set.

coddled eggs Eggs cooked by coddling, i.e. by being placed in boiling water which is not further heated

codling A young, immature cod

cod liver oil Oil extracted from cod livers used as a major natural source of vitamins A and D and EFAs

codorniz *Portugal, Spain* Quail

cod roe The eggs of the cod fish, available fresh, canned or smoked. It has a mild fishy flavour and a creamy grainy texture. Used to make cheaper versions of taramasalata instead of grey mullet roe.

coelho *Portugal* Domesticated rabbit

coelho bravo *Portugal* Wild rabbit

coeliac disease A metabolic disease in which the sufferer must not eat foods containing gluten

coentro *Portugal* Coriander leaves

coeur *France* 1. Heart 2. Neufchâtel

coeur à la crème *France* A dessert made from a curd or cream cheese allowed to drain in a perforated heart-shaped mould, turned out onto a plate and decorated with summer fruits and sprinkled with sugar. Also called **fromage à la crème**

coeur d'artichaut *France* Artichoke heart

coeur de filet *France* The trimmed eye of the fillet of beef

coeur de palmier *France* Heart of palm

coeurs d'artichauts *France* Artichoke hearts, small, tender and trimmed artichokes. See also **artichauts Clamart**, **artichauts Grand Duc**

coffee The water extract of ground, roasted coffee beans used as a beverage and for flavouring

coffee bean The fruit of an evergreen bush, *Coffea arabica* or *C. canephora*, native to Ethiopia but now widely grown in high-altitude tropical regions. The red fruit, which contains two almost hemispherical green seeds, is first fermented, the pulp removed and the seeds dried prior to roasting at or near their point of sale. After roasting they contain about 50% water soluble material including caffeine and flavours. The two main varieties are robusta and arabica but they are often identified by their place of origin.

coffee cake *United States* A plain sponge cake usually served warm with coffee

coffee cream *United States* Pasteurized cream from cows' milk containing 18 to 30% butterfat for adding to coffee. Also called **light cream**, **table cream**

coffee grinder A mechanically, electrically or hand-operated grinder for roasted coffee beans with an arrangement for adjusting the particle size, very fine for espresso, fine for filters, Turkish and cona, medium for cafetières and percolators and coarse for jug infusion

coffee kisses Small drop cakes or biscuits containing ground nuts, sandwiched together with coffee-flavoured butter cream

coffee sugar Coarse crystals, to 3 mm, of translucent, usually amber-coloured sugar but these may be mixed with crystals of other colours

cognac *France* Brandy from the Cognac region, used as a flavouring and for flambéing

cogombre *Catalonia* Cucumber

cogumelos *Portugal* Mushrooms

cohombrillo *Spain* Gherkin

coho salmon An important commercial variety of Pacific salmon, *Oncorhynchus kisutch*, up to 4.5 kg in weight with an oily, deep pink to red flesh. Now in danger of extinction due to degradation of the coastal streams where the salmon spawn. Also called **silver salmon**

coiblide *Ireland* Champ

coiled wire whisk The normal domestic whisk consisting of a loose coil of stainless steel wire wrapped around a single loop of stiff wire held in a suitable handle

coing *France* Quince

Coix lachryma-jobi *Botanical name* Job's tears

col *Spain* Cabbage

cola bean The nut of a West African tree, *Cola acuminata* or *C. nitida*, now also grown in the Caribbean and South America, which yields a red extract containing caffeine and other stimulants and flavours used to make cola type drinks. Also called **cola nut**, **kola nut**

colache *Mexico* Diced squash mixed with chopped onions fried in butter, **tomato concassée**, sweet corn kernels and seasoning and baked in a slow oven in a covered dish without added water

colander A perforated bowl used to drain liquids from solid food. Usually with handles and sometimes with a flat base.

cola nut See **cola bean**

colazione *Italy* Breakfast

colbert, (à la) *France* Containing small pieces of vegetables and poached egg. Used of a clear soup. See also **sole Colbert**

colbert butter A compound butter containing parsley, lemon juice, tarragon and meat extract, refrigerated in the shape of a cylinder and cut into 5 mm thick rounds to garnish grilled fish, steaks and rare roast beef

colbert sauce A sauce flavoured with parsley, spices, lemon and Madeira wine, served with vegetables

Colbi *Middle East* An Israeli cows' milk cheese resembling Gouda cheese. Also called **kolbee**

Colby *United States* An orange-coloured scalded-curd hard Cheddar-like cheese but slightly softer and with a more open texture from Colby, Wisconsin. Made from whole cows' milk. It has a dark brown rind and is not cheddared.

colcannon *Ireland* Potato mashed with onion flavoured milk and butter to which are added chopped and poached spring onions and (savoy) cabbage seasoned with nutmeg. Sometimes topped with grilled bacon rashers. Also called **kolcannon**

colcasia *Indonesia* Yam

Colchester *England* A famous oyster from the town of the same name

cold collation A meal consisting of a selection of cold foods

col de Bruselas *Spain* Brussels sprouts

cold-pressed A term used of oil which has been produced by direct pressure on the cold untreated fruit, nut or seed. This usually gives a more distinctive flavour than hot pressing or solvent extraction.

cold room A refrigerated room used to store perishable foods

cold shortening The process by which carcass meat becomes tough if chilled too rapidly after slaughter, especially with beef and sheep. The chilling rate should not lead to temperatures in any part of the carcass below 10°C in 10 hours or less after slaughter.

cold-smoke, to To lightly smoke food at a temperature not greater than 33°C so as not to cook the flesh but usually in the range 20°C to 30°C. Used mainly for salmon, kippers, gammon and some sausages. The weight loss should be about 18% for salmon, 12 to 14% for haddock and 25% for cod roes. With the exception of things like cheese and hard-boiled eggs, the goods are first lightly brined.

cold soufflé A gelatine-based mousse put in a soufflé dish with a paper collar extending about 8 cm vertically above the rim, this being removed when the mousse has set so as to resemble a soufflé

cold-store bacteria Bacteria which can grow at temperatures down to –8°C and survive in deep-freezers

cold table See **smörgåsbord**

cole An old English word used for members of the cabbage family, now only surviving in borecole, coleslaw and the corrupted forms kale and cauliflower

colère, fish en Long round fish, skinned, degutted, gills and eyes removed, tails fixed in mouth, panéed and deep-fried, stuffed olives put in eye sockets and served with remoulade or tartare sauce

coleseed Rape

coleslaw Finely shredded white hearts of cabbage bound together with various dressings such as mayonnaise, soured cream, yoghurt, French dressing, possibly in combination, and with other possible additions such as nuts, grated carrots, chopped and vinegared onions, celery, apples, etc. A very popular salad item. Also called **slaw**

coleweed Rape

coley A cheap fish, *Pollachius virens*, of the cod family up to 6.5 kg in weight but with a darker skin and a brownish flesh which whitens on cooking. Found in the North Atlantic. Also called **saithe**, **coalfish**, **pollock**, **Boston bluefish**

col fermentada *Spain* Sauerkraut

coliflor *Spain* Cauliflower

colimaçon *France* A variety of snail

colin *France* **1.** Hake **2.** Coley

colinabo *Spain* Turnip

colineau *France* Codling

colin mayonnaise *France* Cold poached hake, served with mayonnaise

colinot *France* Codling

collagen One of the constituents of connective tissue (the supporting structure of the body). It is a fairly soft protein which breaks down into gelatine on prolonged boiling or cooking at low temperatures.

collar bacon The top front section of a side of bacon cut into bacon joints or sliced into rather rectangular-shaped rashers

collard See **collard greens**

collard greens The edible green leaves from non-hearting brassicas including root vegetables

collé(e) *France* With added gelatine (NOTE: From *coller*, 'to glue'.)

college cake A spiced fruit cake containing caraway seeds

college pudding *England* A steamed or baked pudding made from fresh breadcrumbs, shredded beef suet or softened butter, caster sugar and eggs (4:3:2:2) with 15 g (4.5 teaspoons) of baking powder per kg of breadcrumbs, the same weight of mixed sultanas and raisins as breadcrumbs and generously flavoured with ground cinnamon, cloves and nutmeg. Baked in dariole moulds at 180°C for 45 minutes.

coller, to To add body to a mixture by dissolving gelatine in it

collet *France* Neck of lamb or veal. Also called **collier**

colli di polli ripieni *Italy* The skin of a chicken's neck stuffed loosely with a mixture of finely processed lean beef, egg, cheese, lemon zest, lemon juice and breadcrumbs, tied either end and poached in stock until cooked. Served cold and sliced.

collier *France* Collet

collo *Italy* Neck (of lamb, etc.)

colloids Very finely divided particles of any phase, gas, liquid or solid, which are dispersed in another phase without settling by surface forces alone. Food examples are milk solids in milk and oil droplets in mayonnaise.

collop 1. *United Kingdom* A small slice of meat like an escalope (*colloquial*) **2.** *Scotland* A minced beef stew **3.** Egg fried with bacon

collop, to To cut into small pieces

colmenilla *Spain* Morel

Colocasia esculenta *Botanical name* The taro plant

colocassa A Mediterranean tuber of the genus *Colocasia*, similar in size to a small pointed swede, up to 2 kg in weight, with a rough, light brown skin and a starchy, bland, white flesh. Used in stews or fried. Also called **cologassi, kolocassi**

colo de castra *Italy* A Venetian dish of mutton, stewed with celery and onions and served with rice and peas

cologassi See **colocassa**

colomba *Italy* Dove-shaped Easter cake

colombaccio *Italy* Wood pigeon

colombian coffee A smooth strong coffee from Colombia

colombière *France* A soft cows' milk cheese from Savoie cast in the shape of a dish with a mild smooth paste

colombo *Italy* Wood pigeon

colombo de giraumon *Caribbean* A Martinique dish of pumpkin cubes cooked with sweated onions and garlic, fried spices, chopped tomatoes, sultanas and seasoning. Used as a vegetable accompaniment to meat etc.

colon The large intestine of an animal used as a casing for sausages

colonne *United States* A cylindrical instrument with a metal tube used to core fruits or cut solids into cylindrical shapes. See also **apple corer** (NOTE: From the French word for *column*.)

colorau *Portugal* Dried and powdered red pepper made from a reasonably hot variety of capsicum

colorau-doce *Portugal* Paprika

colostro *Italy* Colostrum, beestings

colostrum The first liquid obtained from the mammary gland after an animal has given birth. It is extremely nutritious and health-promoting and is used by farmers as a miracle cure for new born animals in difficulty. See also **beestings**

colour, to To give colour to food by the addition of natural or artificial food colourings or by heating to produce a brown colour by caramelization or Maillard reactions

col rizado *Spain* Kale

coltsfoot The green stalks of the coltsfoot plant, *Tussilago farfara*, are rinsed, dry-salted for 10 minutes to draw out the juices, rinsed, the outer fibrous covering stripped off and eaten as rhubarb, generally only in the East. Also called **bog rhubarb**

Colwick *England* A soft, white, creamy, slightly acid cows' milk cheese

colza *France, Italy, Spain* Oilseed rape, *Brassica napus*, used for its leaves and young shoots or for the oil from its seeds

colza oil Rapeseed oil

com *Vietnam* Cooked rice

comal *Mexico* The terracotta griddle on which tortillas are baked

combava *France* Makrut lime, the fruit

comber 1. A seawater fish of the perch family, *Serranus cabrilla*. Also called **sea perch 2.** *Ireland* A very sweet, fine potato from Ireland which when new can be eaten as a dish in its own right

combination menu A menu in which popular items are repeated each day and others changed on a cyclical or irregular basis

combination oven A standard fan-assisted electric oven combined with a microwave energy source to give very fast cooking together with the surface browning and hardening of a conventional oven

combine, to To mix ingredients together

comfrey A hardy herbaceous perennial herb, *Symphytum officinale*, rarely used nowadays. The young leaves can be used in salads and the stems blanched and cooked like asparagus. The leaves contain more protein than any other known member of the vegetable kingdom and are commonly used as an organic fertilizer.

comida *Spain* Lunch

comino *Italy, Mexico, Spain* Cumin

comino dei prati *Italy* Caraway seed

çömlek kebabi *Turkey* A lamb and mixed vegetable casserole served with boiled potatoes or rice pilaf

commercial beef *United States* Beef from old animal used for manufacturing. More flavoursome than standard grade. Also called **utility beef**

commis chef A junior chef, assistant to the chef de partie

commis de rang *France* Assistant waiter

commis waiter An assistant to a station waiter

common crab The common decapod crustacean, *Cancer pagurus*, found from Norway to Spain in the North Atlantic. It has a generally mottled brownish red shell with ten legs, two of which have developed into muscular claws, and a tail which is tucked underneath the body. It is up to 20 cm. in diameter. The shell is shed periodically to allow the animal to grow. The edible parts, which must be cooked in salted water (35 g salt per litre), consist of white muscular tissue and a soft brown tissue. The grey feather-like gills (dead man's fingers), the mouth and the stomach bag and all its green to grey-white contents are discarded. Often served in the shell. It is illegal to sell juvenile crabs (less than 13 cm across) or gravid females in the UK. Also called **edible crab**

common eel Eel

common flounder Winter flounder

common hare A hare, *Lepus europaeus*, distributed across the whole of Europe through to eastern Asia. Also called **brown hare**

common jack Crevalle jack

common ling Ling

common mandarin A large group of mandarin oranges, *Citrus reticulata*, of which the clementine is perhaps the best known. They are grown extensively in Spain and Morocco and seedless varieties have been developed. See also **satsuma**

common marjoram Oregano

common millet A millet of temperate climates, *Panicum miliaceum*, mainly used as bird seed and animal feed in the West but can be made into an unleavened bread. Also called **broom corn**, **hog millet**, **proso**, **Indian millet**

common morel Morel

common mushroom The most common cultivated mushroom, *Agaricus bisporus*, also found in the wild. It has a light creamy coloured top with a definite skin and brown gills underneath the cap. Sold as button (completely closed cap with no gills showing), cup (half open cap) and flat (fully mature open cap).

common mussel The usually dark blue to black crescent-shaped bivalve, *Mytilus edulis*, with orange flesh grown extensively around the Atlantic coast in unpolluted seawater. They are also found in the wild but these are suspect because of pollution. If they are purchased live, the shells should be tightly closed or close when tapped, and only those which open when heated should be used.

common orange A type of sweet orange which comprises a large and diverse group with a wide range of qualities but generally paler than navels and with many seeds. Usually suitable for processing into juice. The best known of this group is the Valencia although the Shamouti *(Jaffa or Cyprus)* is quite common and there are at least 20 varieties traded widely.

common otter shell clam A white to light yellow clam with a long shell up to 12.5 cm

common prawn The main British and Western European prawn, *Palaemon serratus*, fished extensively from Norway down to Spain. It reaches a maximum length of 9 cm and is translucent when alive.

common puffball The edible pear-shaped or pestle-like fruiting body of a fungus, *Lycoperdon perlatum*, which when young is densely covered with spines or loose cone-shaped warts which leave their marks on the older fungus. Grows profusely up to 8 cm tall and 5 cm diameter Eaten when young before the centre becomes full of spores.

common purslane See **summer purslane**

common skate A European skate, *Raja batis*, with a long pointed snout and smooth greenish brown skin with spots. The eyes are on the upper side with the mouth and gills on the lower. The medium-oily white flesh which is taken from the wings has a good flavour and may be cooked in any way. Also called **tinker skate**

common snook A pike-like game fish, *Centropus undecimalis*, caught off the coast of Florida, USA

common sturgeon A large sturgeon, *Acipenser sturio*, which can grow to 60 kg and is found in the Caspian Sea, Black Sea, Mediterranean and the western Atlantic. It has a firm white to pink flesh which may be baked, grilled or smoked. The roe, which may amount to up to 22 kg from a single female, is processed into caviar mainly in Russia and Iran. The Atlantic sturgeon is now only found in the Gironde estuary and is currently an endangered species. Captive breeding is being attempted.

composé(e) *France* Arranged with several elements as for e.g. in salade composée

composta *Italy* Compote of fruit, stewed fruit

composto *Italy* Composed, compound. Used of a salad, etc.

compota *Portugal, Spain* Jam and stewed fruits

compote *England, France* **1.** Stewed fruit **2.** A stew made from game birds such as pigeon or partridge, cooked until the meat is very tender

compote d'abricots à la minute *France* Halved apricots boiled in sugar syrup for 3 minutes, skimmed and orange juice added

compotier *France* A large shallow glass dish on a raised stem and base, used to serve fruit compotes and other desserts

compound butter Butter flavoured by pounding it with herbs, shells, spices, etc. then sieving out any inedible or unwanted bits. Usually formed into a roll, refrigerated and cut in slices to finish hot dishes for presentation. usually written as beurre followed by the name of the flavouring e.g. beurre d'amande, beurre de paprika. All are listed under **beurre** and/or the English name of the flavouring.

compressed yeast *United States* Small greyish cakes of compressed live yeast weighing about 18 g, used in baking

Comté *France* A hard, cooked-curd Gruyère type cheese produced from cows' milk in Franche-Comté, with AOC status. It has an aromatic nutty-flavoured soft paste with medium-sized holes. Used as a cooking cheese or for dessert. Also called **Gruyère de Comté**

Comuna *Spain* A variety of orange

comune *Italy* Common orange

conalbumin One of the proteins in white of egg. It reacts with iron to give a pink colour.

concassé(e) *France* Chopped or crushed as in tomates concassées; past participle of *concasser*, 'to crush or grind'

conch A large sea snail with a spirally coiled shell found on the Central American and Florida coast. The tough flesh requires tenderizing.

concha *Spain* Mussel, scallop

concha de peregrino *Spain* Scallop

concha peregrina *Spain* Scallop

conchiglia *Italy* **1.** Shellfish **2.** Shell-shaped pasta

conchiglia di San Giacomo *Italy* See **coquille Saint Jacques**

conchiglie *Italy* **1.** Shells, especially scallop shells, used as containers for hot dishes **2.** Pasta shaped like a half shell (not the conch shell) **3.** Small shell-shaped citron-flavoured cakes from Sicily

conchigliette *Italy* Small pasta shells used in soup

con chom chom *Vietnam* Sea urchin

concombre *France* Cucumber

concombre salé *France* Pickled cucumber

Condé *France* A dessert made from individual portions of dessert rice or pastry topped with canned or poached fruit, glazed with jam and decorated with whipped cream. See also **condés au fromage**

condensed milk Milk from which about 85 to 90% of the water has been removed to leave an evaporated milk containing 45 to 50% water, to this is added about 70 g of sugar per 100 g of evaporated milk to give a thick sticky liquid containing about 55% sugar including lactose, and 28% water which is thus resistant to bacterial contamination. Available in both full cream and skimmed versions. the skimmed version containing about 60% sugar in the resulting mixture.

condés au fromage *France* Puff pastry rectangles, covered with an egg-enriched **béchamel sauce**, seasoned with Cayenne pepper and mixed with finely diced cheese and baked in a hot oven

condiment *England, France* A seasoning, usually salt, pepper, nutmeg, various pasty or dry mixtures of herbs and/or spices, sometimes pickles, individually added to food by the eater after it is served

condimento *Italy, Spain* Seasoning, condiment

condiment set A decorative carrier holding two or more small bottles or pots for condiments such as oil, vinegar, salt, pepper, ground cumin etc. and sometimes toothpicks

condition, to To subject a substance, principally meat, cheese and alcoholic beverages, to the process of ageing at a controlled temperature to improve quality. With meat this process occurs naturally after slaughter. Sometimes, with game birds, the innards are left in to assist conditioning.

condito *Italy* Seasoned or dressed

cone See **cornet**

conejo *Spain* Rabbit

conejo a la gallega *Spain* Rabbit fried with onions and tomatoes

conejo frito a la catalina *Spain* Rabbit, marinated in vinegar and white wine then fried

coney **1.** *England* Rabbit (*colloquial*) **2.** *United States* A hot dog

confectioner's custard See **crème pâtissière**

confectioner's sugar *United States* Icing sugar containing a little corn flour. Also called **powdered sugar**

confeitado *Portugal* Candied. Also called **conservado**

confetti sugar *United States* Large sugar crystals dyed different colours for decorative purposes

confettura *Italy* Jam

confit(e) *France* **1.** Well-cooked meat, particularly duck, goose or pork, preserved in its own fat **2.** Fruits cooked and preserved in brandy or a sweetened liquor; vegetables preserved in vinegar or pickled

confit d'oie *France* Slices of cooked goose breast preserved in goose fat

confiture *France* Jam or marmalade

confiture d'abricots *France* Apricot jam

confiture d'oranges *France* Orange marmalade

cong *China* Scallion or spring onion

cong bao yang rou *China* Stir-fried lamb and spring onions

congeal, to To become stiff or jelly-like owing to a drop in temperature

congee The standard breakfast dish of the Chinese consisting of a gruel of well-soaked rice boiled with salt and water, flavoured by sprinkling sweet or savoury ingredients over the surface. Also called **rice gruel**, **rice soup**

congelato *Italy* Frozen

congeler *France* **1.** To freeze **2.** To deep-freeze

conger eel A seawater eel, *Conger conger*, which grows up to 2 metres long. It has an oily, coarse, well-flavoured firm flesh, usually sold in steaks.

conger pie *United Kingdom* Conger eel poached in a seasoned stock and red wine, skinned, deboned and laid in a buttered ovenproof dish over a bed of sweated onions and garlic, and covered with the poaching liquor, thickened if required. It is then topped with potatoes creamed with milk and egg yolks and lightened with stiffly beaten white of egg. The whole gratinated with grated Cheddar cheese and baked in a 200°C oven for 20 minutes.

congou Black tea from China sometimes used in blended tea

congre *France* Conger eel

congress tart A small pastry tart spread with jam and filled with a mixture of ground almonds, sugar and egg prior to baking

congrio *Spain* Conger eel

congro *Portugal* Conger eel

cong tou *China* Onion

coniglio *Italy* Rabbit

coniglio alla reggiana *Italy* Jointed rabbit browned in oil and lard or bacon fat, reserved; chopped onion browned in the same fat; chopped and crushed garlic, chopped celery and **tomato concassée** added and simmered, followed by dry white wine and the reserved rabbit; seasoned and all simmered until the rabbit is tender. Finished with chopped chervil or parsley.

conill amb xocolata *Catalonia* Rabbit with garlic, liver, almonds, fried bread, chocolate and old wine

conkies *Caribbean* Two parts of a mixture of grated coconut, pumpkin, sweet potato and brown sugar (6:3:2:3) are combined with one part of a mixture of corn flour, milk, wheat flour and molten shortening (4:2:1:1) to make a stiff dough. This mixture is flavoured with cinnamon, nutmeg, almond essence and raisins and a few tablespoons of it wrapped and tied in a banana leaf prior to steaming. Also called **paimi** (NOTE: Conkies are traditionally made in Barbados on the 5th of November, Guy Fawkes Day)

connective tissue The structural material of the animal body normally seen as cartilage, sinew or gristle in meat but also present in bone and as the inner layer of skin, etc. It consists mainly of proteins principally collagen fibres interlaced with elastin fibres embedded in a gel. The more elastin the less soluble is the tissue.

con poy *China* Dried slices of a type of scallop with a distinctive flavour. Very expensive and used like truffles in Western cooking.

conserva *Italy* **1.** Preserve or jam made from fruit or vegetables **2.** Tinned

conserva de fruta *Portugal* Jam

conserva di frutta *Italy* Jam

conservado *Portugal* Candied. Also called **confeitado**

conservare in scatola *Italy* To can

conserve Fruits preserved in sugar, usually as a jellied mixture which may or may not contain distinct pieces of fruit. The jelling properties come from pectin, the vegetable equivalent of gelatine. Jam and marmalade are examples.

conserve, en *France* In a tin, canned

conserve, petit-pois en *France* Tinned peas

conserves *United States* Elaborate jams with additions such as nuts, raisins, liqueurs, etc.

conserves au vinaigre *France* Pickles

consistency The property of a mixture which determines its flow or cutting properties. The word is usually qualified as e.g. coating consistency, dropping consistency, thick consistency, jam-like consistency, buttery consistency, etc.

consistency of cheese Cheeses are classified as soft, semi-hard or hard according to their consistency

consommé *England, France* A transparent clear soup made from a well-flavoured meat, fish, chicken or vegetable stock, simmered without stirring or disturbance with the appropriate minced flesh and/or vegetables mixed with egg whites for 2 hours and carefully strained. Will usually set when cold and as such is sometimes chopped and used as a garnish. Also called **clear soup**

consommé à la royale *England, France* A hot consommé garnished with **royale** shapes

consommé aux profiteroles *England, France* A hot consommé with unsweetened choux paste piped into pea-sized pieces, baked and added to it at the last moment

consommé brunoise *England, France* As consommé julienne with the same vegetables cut as a **brunoise**

consommé celestine *England, France* Hot consommé with the addition at the last moment of a **julienne** of pancake, the pancake seasoned and flavoured with chopped parsley, tarragon and chervil

consommé des viveurs *France* A strong-flavoured bouillon or consommé. See also **viveur en tasse**

consommé en tasse *England, France* Cold consommé served lightly jellied in a cup. If there is not sufficient natural gelatine, more may be added.

consommé julienne *England, France* A hot consommé garnished at the last moment with a **julienne** of carrot, turnip and leek previously cooked in salted water and refreshed

consommé madrilène *England, France* A basic consommé well-flavoured with tomato and celery and garnished with a brunoise of skinned and deseeded tomato flesh just before serving

consommé vermicelle *England, France* Hot consommé with cooked and refreshed vermicelli added at the last moment

conta *Portugal* The bill in a restaurant

contamination The ingress of impurities, either microorganisms or compounds such as detergents, bleach, dust etc. into a foodstuff, usually by contact with surfaces or other foods

conti, à la *France* Garnished with a bacon and lentil purée, usually used of joints of meat

continental breakfast A small breakfast consisting of bread rolls, croissants or toast with butter and jam or marmalade plus a hot drink of coffee, chocolate or tea

continental sausage Sausages usually made from 100% meat which are traditionally preserved by the addition of small amounts of glucose on which species of *Lactobacillus* grow and reduce the pH by producing lactic acid. They are also ripened by the surface growth of aspergillus and penicillium moulds.

continuous grill A grill in which food is loaded on a conveyor and cooks on both sides as it travels to the unloading position, e.g. in burger bars

continuous phase That phase in a two or more phase mixture which is continuously interconnected, e.g. vinegar is the continuous phase in mayonnaise and **hollandaise sauce**s, butterfat in butter and milk in cream. See also **dispersed phase**, **emulsion**

contiser *France* To make small incisions in food in which to insert small pieces of solid flavouring as e.g. garlic slivers, truffle, tongue, etc. See also **piquer**

conto *Italy* The bill in a restaurant

contorno *Italy* Vegetable dish or side dish, vegetable garnish

contre-filet *France* Sirloin off the bone. Also called **faux-filet**

controfiletto di bue *Italy* Sirloin of beef

convection oven An oven in which heated air is circulated by a fan over the food to be baked or cooked. Also called **forced convection oven**

convenience food Food which allegedly needs little preparation prior to serving. It may be a chilled, non-sterile cooked meal or a vacuum-packed fully cooked meal. Other forms require the addition of eggs, milk, water, etc. or elaborate mixing, heating and stirring, often taking as long to prepare as the same dish cooked with fresh ingredients purchased in semi-processed form.

converted rice Rice which has been soaked and steamed before being hulled. This preserves more of the nutrients from the outer coat in the polished grain which is yellow but whitens on cooking. The process does not shorten the cooking time. Also called **parboiled rice**

con vich *Vietnam* Turtle

coocoo *Caribbean* Cornmeal cooked with seven times its weight of salted water and a fair quantity of butter to make a stiff paste. It is then shaped into balls and, in Trinidad, served in a buttered dish garnished with vegetables and salads to taste.

coo-coo *Caribbean* A cooked paste of cornmeal or breadfruit, okra and water, served with fish especially in Barbados. Also called **cou-cou**

cook A person who prepares food for eating

cook, to To make food flavoursome, edible and digestible usually, but not necessarily, by subjecting it to heat

cook-and-hold oven An oven that cooks for a preset time at a selected temperature, then reduces the temperature and sometimes adjusts the humidity to values where the food can be kept warm for a long period. Often used in carveries for roast meat.

cooked cheese Cheese made from curdled milk which has been cooked before the whey is separated from the curds

cooked curd Curd for cheese which has been heated to temperatures greater than 48°C. See also **scalded curd**

cooker An appliance for cooking food by the application of heat or other type of energy, usually self contained

cookie 1. *United States* A biscuit **2.** *Scotland* A glazed bread roll made from enriched yeast dough containing dried vine fruits

cookie cutter *United States* Biscuit cutter

cookie press *United States* Biscuit press

cooking apple *United Kingdom* A variety of apple such as Bramley's Seedling, generally with a tart flavour and usually large, which softens when cooked and is particularly suitable for stewing and baking

cooking chocolate Unsweetened chocolate available in block form or as chips (NOTE: Not to be confused with the cheap, brown chocolate-flavoured substance often sold under this name.)

cooking fat Normally a white, hard and tasteless unsalted fat made by hydrogenation of deodorized vegetable or fish oils

cooking foil See **aluminium foil**

cooking liquor The liquid in which food has been cooked, often used as the basis of a sauce to go with the food

cook out, to To completely finish the cooking process so that no suggestion of the uncooked food remains. Used especially of starch-thickened sauces, soups, etc.

cook's knife A heavy, easily sharpened, well-balanced, steel-bladed knife with a substantial handle, sharpened on one edge, broad near the handle and tapering to a point and with a convex curve to the blade so that it can be used for chopping with a rocking motion

cool, to To reduce the temperature of food by a variety of means e.g. placing in a refrigerator, plunging in cold water, adding ice cubes, standing a container in cold water, etc.

coon *United States* A strong-tasting Cheddar-type cheese made from cows' milk

Cootamundra bush bread *Australia* Bread flavoured with ground wattleseed

copeau *France* Pastry twist (NOTE: Literally 'shaving'.)

copeaux de chocolat *France* Chocolate shavings used for decoration

coperto *Italy* **1.** Cover charge in a restaurant **2.** Covered with some ingredient e.g. a slice of cheese

copha *Australia* A white shortening made from hardened vegetable oils

copocolla *Italy* A sausage made from chunks of mildly cured shoulder pork, sometimes air-dried before being mixed with finely minced fat pork, red sweet peppers, seasoning and spices and packed in beef casings

copollotto The boiled bulbs of grape hyacinth served in a sweet-and-sour sauce. Also called **lambascione**

copos de avena *Spain* Rolled oats

coppa 1. A salted pork slicing sausage, dried and smoked with herbs; from Corsica **2.** *Italy* A rather fatty ham cut from the shoulder **3.** A large sausage containing distinct pieces of shoulder pork and pork fat obtained from pigs fed on chestnuts **4.** *Italy* Bowl or cup

coppa cotta *Italy* A type of brawn made from the meat of pig's heads and tongues, pressed until set into a solid mass

coppa di Corse *Italy* Smoked ham produced in Corsica

coppa gelata *Italy* Mixed ice creams

copper A trace element necessary for health. Sufficient is usually obtained from water that has been delivered via copper pipes.

copper pan The type of pan generally used in high-class kitchens made of thick copper with a tin lining. The copper makes for even and quick distribution of heat and uniformity of temperature.

copra The white inner meat of the coconut. Used fresh or grated and dried in cooking. The dried copra is traded internationally as a source of oil and animal feed.

Coprinus comatus *Botanical name* Shaggy ink cap

coq *France* Male of a bird, especially of a chicken, cockerel

coq à la bière *France* As **coq au vin**, but cooked in beer and flavoured with juniper berries (NOTE: From the north)

coq au vin *France* Chicken, possibly previously marinated, simmered in red wine with brandy, onions, carrots, garlic and bouquet garni and sometimes bacon, garnished with glazed button onions, glazed button mushrooms and croûtons

coq au vin jaune *France* Chicken stewed with edible fungi, cream and the local white wine from Arbois

coq de bruyère *France* Grand *(large)* capercaillie or petit *(small)* black grouse

coq en pâte *France* Chicken pie

coque 1. *France* Shell of an egg **2.** *France* Cockle **3.** An Easter cake made from a brioche dough flavoured with citron

coque, à la *France* Cooked in its shell. Used especially of an egg.

coquelet *France* A young cock chicken around 1 kg

coquetier *France* Egg cup

coquillage *France* Shellfish

coquille *France* Shell of an egg, nut, mollusc, etc.

coquille, en *France* Cooked in a scallop shell

coquille Saint Jacques *England, France* **1.** The commonest European scallop, *Pecten jacobaeus*. Also called **pilgrim scallop 2.** Halved scallops, poached in seasoned milk, reserved, a thick velouté sauce made with sliced mushrooms and the cooking liquor, cooked out, scallops and sherry added and the mixture spooned onto scallop shells and gratinated with a mixture of breadcrumbs, grated cheese and dry mustard. Garnished with lemon twists and picked parsley.

coquimol *Caribbean* A Haitian sweet pouring cream made from heavy sugar syrup (3:1) into which roughly equal volumes of coconut cream and egg yolks are beaten. This is then brought to the consistency of double cream by heating over hot water. It is finally flavoured with vanilla essence, white rum and a sprinkling of nutmeg.

coquina 1. *Spain* Wedge shell clam **2.** *United States* Winkle, the shellfish

coquito nut *South America* Small immature coconuts which are eaten whole

corail *France* **Coral**, eggs of shellfish and crustaceans

coral The ovaries and eggs of the female lobster which turn a brilliant red when cooked and are used in the sauce to accompany lobster dishes

corallo *Italy* Lobster coral

coratella *Italy* Offal, also a stew of lambs' lungs, liver and heart

coratella di agnello alla sarda *Italy* Lamb offal interspersed with slices of ham, threaded on a skewer, wrapped in pig's caul or intestine and grilled

corazón *Spain* Heart

çorba *Turkey* Soup

corbeille de fruits *France* Basket of fruit

corbina *United States* A fish of the drum family. Also called **corvina**

Corchorus olitorius *Botanical name* The meloukhia plant

cordeiro *Portugal* Lamb

cordero *Spain* Lamb

cordero al ajillo *Spain* Lamb fried with garlic, pepper and saffron

cordero asado *Spain* Roast lamb

cordero lechazo *Spain* Suckling lamb

cordero manchego *Spain* Lamb casseroled in wine and garlic, served with fried sweet peppers and garnished with chopped parsley

cordon *England, France* A line of sauce or gravy poured around an item of food on a dish

cordon bleu 1. *France* A style of cooking based on classic French cooking taught by some French and English cookery schools or a description of a person so trained. Often part of the 'finishing' education of children of the wealthy. **2.** See **escalope cordon bleu**

core, to 1. To remove the inedible centre of fruits such as apples and pears which contain seeds rather than single stones, using a cylindrical corer and without damaging the edible part of the fruit **2.** To remove the central blood vessels and tubes from a kidney

coregone bondella *Italy* Houting, the fish

coregone laverello *Italy* Pollan, the fish

coriander An annual plant, *Coriandrum sativum*, cultivated worldwide for its leaves, seeds and roots. The leaves look like flat parsley and have a slightly soapy herb-like flavour and are used as a herb. The small, brown, round seeds (3 to 4 mm diameter) have a mild sweet spicy flavour quite different to the leaves with a hint of pepper and aniseed and are used extensively throughout the world as a whole or ground spice. The roots are used as a vegetable and also as a flavouring in Thai cooking. Also called **Chinese parsley** (leaves only), **cilantro**

coriandre *France* Coriander

coriandro *Spain* Coriander

Coriandrum sativum *Botanical name* Coriander

corindolo *Italy* Coriander

corkscrew greens Fiddlehead fern

corn A general term once used of all grains such as wheat, oats, barley, rye, maize, etc. but now used only of wheat in Europe and of maize in the USA

corn bread *United States* A deep yellow coloured bread made with a mixture of cornmeal from flint corn and flour

corn chips Tortilla chips

corncrake A small game bird, *Crex crex*, which migrates from Northern Europe to Africa during the winter

corn dog *United States* A Frankfurter dipped in a cornmeal batter, deep-fried until crisp and presented on a stick

corne *France* A horn-shaped brioche from Nantes

corned beef Beef that has been cooked and preserved in salt together with some sodium nitrite to give it a pink colour. Usually sold in tins. Also called **bully beef** (NOTE: So called from the corns (small crystals) of salt used in the curing.)

corned beef hash *United States* A mixture of coarsely mashed potatoes, chopped corned beef and cooked chopped onion formed into a cake and shallow-fried on each side until browned. Topped with a poached egg and served with toast and chilli sauce.

corned bief *Netherlands* Corned beef

corne grecque *France* Okra

Cornell bread *United States* A high protein bread developed at Cornell university containing soya bean flour, wheat germ and dried skimmed milk solids

corner of gammon A triangular piece of meat cut from a gammon

cornes de gazelle *North Africa* Croissant-like pastries filled with honey and almonds. Also called **kaab el ghzal, ka'b ghzahi**

cornet A large cone shape (up to 12 cm by 4 cm diameter) made with a wafer mixture in which ice cream is served so that it can be eaten as a snack. Also called **cone**

cornetti *Italy* **1.** Sweet breakfast bread rolls **2.** Pastry horns usually filled with cream

corn-fed chicken Chicken fed principally on yellow maize which gives its skin and flesh a yellow colour

corn flakes A popular breakfast cereal made from small blobs of cooked and flavoured maize porridge, flattened, crisped and toasted to a golden colour

corn flour 1. *United Kingdom* Pure starch powder extracted from maize kernels. It blends easily with water without forming lumps and thickens into a translucent paste. Used for blancmange, English custard, for thickening sauces and gravies and to give a lighter shorter texture to some cakes and biscuits. It is a common thickening agent and source of starch in Chinese cooking. Also called **corn starch 2.** *United States* Ground corn which can be white or yellow. When used in baking it must be used with gluten-rich flours.

corn fritter *United States* Sweet corn kernels bound in batter and deep-fried. Served hot with chicken Maryland.

cornichon *France* Gherkin

Cornish fairings *England* Crisp and spicy biscuits from Cornwall enriched with butter and sweetened with brown sugar and golden syrup

Cornish heavy cake *England* A cake from Cornwall made from a lard-based puff pastry containing currants. Also called **heavy cake**

Cornish hog pudding *England* Hog pudding

Cornish kiddley broth *England* A type of fish soup similar to the **cotriade** of Brittany, made with fish stock and whatever fish and vegetables were available and said to be garnished in the old days with chipples and marigold petals (NOTE: *Kiddley* is Cornish for 'soup kettle'.)

Cornish pasty *England* A pasty made from a rolled out circle of short pastry, preferably made with strong flour filled with diced raw skirt steak and vegetables (turnips, potatoes and onions), the opposite edges of the circle brought together over the filling, sealed, fluted and the whole then baked (NOTE: Originally used by Cornish miners as a complete meal. It is said that a genuine Cornish pasty can be dropped down a mine shaft and not break.)

Cornish saffron cake *England* A fruited yeast-raised cake flavoured with saffron, baked in a deep round tin, sliced and buttered when cold. Also called **saffron cake**

Cornish sly cake *England* Currants, chopped mixed peel, spices and sugar sandwiched between layers of flaky pastry, the whole rolled out until the currants just show, sprinkled with caster sugar, cut into fancy shapes and baked. Also called **sly cake, fig sly cake**

Cornish splits *England* Small milk bread rolls about 8cm in diameter, either yeast or baking powder raised and enriched with butter and sugar at the rate of about 60g per kg of flour, baked at 220°C for 10 to 15 minutes and either eaten hot, split and buttered, or cold with jam and clotted cream

Cornish squab cake *England* A single-crust pastry pie, baked blind, filled with cooked potatoes which have been seasoned and mashed with cream, covered with strips of pickled pork and baked at 200°C until browned

Cornish yarg *England* A creamy mild-flavoured cheese made from cows' milk and generally covered with nettles

cornmeal *United States* White, yellow or rarely blue, dried maize kernels ground to varying degrees of fineness

corn oil A light delicately flavoured vegetable oil extracted from the germ of maize kernels. Contains 15% saturated, 35%

monounsaturated and 50% polyunsaturated fat. Also called **maize oil**

corn on the cob A complete cob of sweet corn, (a variety of maize), boiled, leaves removed and kernels eaten with salt and butter. Also called **sweet corn**

corn pone *United States* An unleavened cornmeal bread made from dent corn, fried or baked

corn salad Lamb's lettuce

corn starch *United States* Corn flour

corn sugar *United States* Sugar, principally glucose, crystallized from acid hydrolysed corn flour. Less sweet than sucrose.

corn syrup 1. Hydrolysed maize starch consisting mainly of glucose. Used as a general liquid sweetener in drinks and manufactured foods. **2.** *United States* Golden syrup

corona, alla *Italy* Ring-shaped

coronation chicken A cold dish made from diced, cooked chicken meat mixed with mayonnaise, chopped tomatoes, onions and apricots, whipped cream and flavoured with curry powder, lemon and bay

corps, qui a du *France* With body. Used of sauces and soups.

correlet *France* Dab, the fish

Corsican citron A citron lacking acidity with a very rough and bumpy ridged skin

Corsican mint A type of mint, *Mentha requiena*, with tiny peppermint-scented bright green leaves and tiny flowers. Grows only to 3 cm.

corvina *United States* Corbina

corvino *Portugal* Croaker, the fish

Corylus avellana *Botanical name* Hazelnut

Corylus colurna *Botanical name* Turkish hazelnut

Corylus maxima *Botanical name* Filbert

coscetta *Italy* Leg of lamb or poultry

coscia *Italy* Haunch (of venison), leg (of lamb, goat, etc.)

coscia di montone *Italy* Leg of lamb

cosciotto *Italy* Leg of lamb

cos lettuce A type of lettuce with long, substantial and well-flavoured leaves and with a fairly loose heart. Also called **romaine lettuce**

costalame di bue *Italy* Ribs of beef

costata *Italy* Rib chop

costeleta *Portugal* Cutlet or boned out chop

costeleta de carne *Portugal* Chop, of an animal

costeletas de carneiro *Portugal* Mutton chops

costeletas de porco *Portugal* Pork chops

costelles de cabrit rostides *Catalonia* Roast cutlets of young goat

costillas *Spain* Chops, ribs

costmary A bitter mint-flavoured herb, *Tanacetum balsamita*, resembling tansy, once used in beer making. Can be used sparingly as a culinary herb. Also called **alecost**

costole *Italy* Ribs

costoletta *Italy* Cutlet

côt dua *Vietnam* Coconut milk

côte *France* **1.** Rib (beef) **2.** Cutlet (veal, lamb) **3.** Chop (mutton, pork)

cotechino *Italy* A large cooking sausage made with lean and fat pork, white wine, spices and seasoning, usually simmered and served with polenta, mashed potatoes or lentils. Used in **bollito misto**.

côte d'agneau *France* Lamb chop

côte de boeuf *France* Rib of beef

côte de porc bruxelloise *Belgium* Pork chop served with a large amount of endive

côte de porc fumée *France* Smoked bacon

coteghino *Italy* A stew made with pork skin

côtelette *France* **1.** Chop **2.** Cutlet

côtelettes decouvertes *France* The ribs between the best end of lamb or veal and the neck which are hidden behind the shoulder blade cut into cutlets. Equivalent of scrag end.

côtelettes premières *France* Fem. The first four ribs of lamb or veal counting from the rear of the animal equivalent to the best end, divided into cutlets.

côte première *France* Loin chop

côtes couvertes *France* Rolled rib of beef from the middle and chuck rib end. Usually slow roasted or braised.

côtes premières *France* Best end of lamb or veal used for roasting in the piece

côtes secondes *France* The four ribs next to the best end of lamb or veal used for roasting in the piece

Cotherstone *England* A white loose-textured cheese with a clean fresh flavour, made in Yorkshire from unpasteurized cows' milk

cotiche *Italy* Pork rind

cotignac *France* A thick quince and apple jelly eaten as a confectionery item

cotochinjos *Brazil* Parboiled chicken legs, coated in a paste of tapioca cooked in stock, deep-fried and served with a tomato sauce

cotogno *Italy* Quince

cotolette *Italy* **1.** Chops **2.** Cutlets

cotriade *France* A fish stew from Brittany using a fish stock made from wine, water, sweated finely chopped onions, a bouquet garni and the fish heads and trimmings, all strained through a coarse colander; sliced or whole potatoes simmered in the stock for 30 minutes; pieces of various fish added and simmered a further 12 minutes; the broth then separated, finished with cream and served over toasted bread; the fish and potatoes served as a separate course

Cotswold cheese *England* A type of **double Gloucester** cheese flavoured with chopped chives and/or onions

cottage cheese A low-fat, very loose-textured, soft mild cheese made of small white curds which have been repeatedly washed and drained and not pressed or matured. Popular in the USA and Europe. Contains 75 to 80% water, 3 to 5% fat and 15 to 16% protein.

cottage loaf A white yeasted bread made from a large sphere of dough on which is placed and secured a small sphere, the whole proven and baked on a flat baking tray

cottage pie Stewed minced beef and onions in a thick gravy placed in a basin, topped with a layer of mashed potatoes whose surface is roughened with a fork, the whole then baked in the oven until browned

cottage potatoes *United States* Cold cooked potatoes, diced or sliced, fried in butter without stirring until brown on one side, then turned over and browned on the other side. Also called **country fried potatoes**

cottage pudding *United States* Plain cake covered with a hot sweet pudding sauce

cotto 1. *United States* A type of salami containing pork and peppercorns. Abbreviated from salame cotto ('cooked salami'). **2.** *Italy* Cooked

cotton bean curd See **momendofu**

cottonseed flour A high-protein flour (about 40%) often used to enrich bread

cottonseed oil Oil extracted from cotton seeds used in the fish canning industry

cotton thistle The true Scottish thistle, a hardy biennial, *Onopordum acanthium*, which can grow to 2.5 m. The young stems may be blanched, peeled and used like asparagus. The large flower heads may be cooked like globe artichokes.

cotufa *Spain* Jerusalem artichoke

coturnice *Italy* Partridge

cou *France* **1.** Neck, of chicken, etc. **2.** Scrag end of lamb or veal, not the neck

couche-couche *United States* A Cajun dish of fried corn dough served with jam and milk or cane syrup

cou-cou A cooked paste served with fish. See also **coo-coo**

coudenac *France* A pork sausage from the Basque country. Eaten hot.

cou d'oie *France* A boned neck of goose with intact skin stuffed with a mixture of goose flesh, goose liver and truffles, cooked and preserved in goose fat. Eaten cold as a hors d'oeuvres.

Couhé Vérac *France* A goats' milk cheese from Poitou which is wrapped in leaves

coulibiac *France* A fish pie, originally from Russia, of brioche or puff pastry filled with salmon or sturgeon, butter, mushrooms, rice or buckwheat and cream and possibly chopped hard-boiled eggs. Also called **koulibiac**

coulis *England, France* A purée or strongly flavoured thick sauce prepared without starch, of vegetables, tomatoes, meat, fish, etc. but more often of liquidized and sieved fruit, possibly with added sugar, acid or liqueur, consistency adjusted with fruit juice

coulis of shellfish The pounded remains of prawn or crawfish shells, eggs, coral and other remains of lobster or crawfish, mixed with cream and passed through a very fine sieve

Coulommiers *France* A mild soft creamy cheese made from cows' milk, similar to Brie but cast in smaller (500 g) rounds. Also called **Brie de Coulommiers**

counter guard A transparent glass or plastic shield at and/or below face level used to protect unwrapped food on display from the coughs, sneezes and other contaminants emitted by customers. Also called **sneeze guard**

counter service The method of service where customers sit at a counter from behind which food is served and possibly cooked

country captain 1. *South Asia* A west Bengal Anglo-Indian dish of skinned chicken pieces, browned in oil with sweated onion slices and mixed with a paste blended from fresh ginger, onion, garlic and water together with cayenne pepper, salt, sugar and white vinegar and all cooked until tender **2.** *United States* A chicken stew adapted from the Indian version with green pepper, onion, garlic, curry powder, herbs, raisins, tomatoes, almonds and seasoning

country fried potatoes *United States* Cottage potatoes

country ham *United States* Dry cured and highly salted ham

cou nu *France* A breed of chicken with a well-flavoured flesh not suitable for factory farming. Usually free-range and maize fed. (NOTE: Literally 'bare neck'.)

coupe *England, France* An individual dish of ice cream, decorated and garnished with fruit sauces, fresh and preserved fruit, nuts, whipped cream, crystallized flowers, chopped jelly, etc.

coupé-coupé *Central Africa* The Central African version of the barbecue in which a large piece of beef (brisket, flank, shoulder or the like), previously marinaded, is slow cooked over a hardwood or charcoal grill with plenty of smoke. The meat is basted every so often to keep it moist using the marinade and will normally take 4 to 5 hours to cook. As street food it would then be sliced and served in bread.

coupe dish A small, goblet-shaped glass or metal dish in which cold desserts are assembled and served

coupe glacée *France* Ice cream sundae

coupe Jacques *England, France* Strawberry and lemon ice cream topped with kirsch-soaked fruit and decorated

coupe-oursin *France* A special tool for cutting sea urchins in half

coupe Saint-Jacques *France* Fruit salad topped with vanilla ice cream

couques *Belgium* A heavy, very sweet gingerbread

courge *France* Squash or gourd

courge à la moelle *France* Vegetable marrow

courgette *England, France* The small juvenile version of the vegetable marrow (summer squash, *Cucurbita pepo*) up to 15 cm in length, usually green but yellow cultivars exist. Cooked whole or sliced, boiled, stewed, roasted or fried, used as a raw salad vegetable when very young. Also called **zucchini**

courgette flowers The large, yellow, male flowers of pumpkins, squash and marrows. Must be used very fresh and are often stuffed with flavoured meat or served as fritters. Also called **squash blossoms**, **zucchini flowers**

couronne *France* A baguette formed into a circle or torus

couronne, en *France* In the shape of a ring or torus

couronne de côtelettes d'agneau rôties *France* Crown roast of lamb made from two best ends

course An individual stage in a meal, particularly in the West, where different classes of food, e.g. soup, meat, desserts, hors d'oeuvres, savouries, cheese, fruit, etc. are served separately

court bouillon *England, France* A cooking liquor for deep-poaching fish consisting of water, vinegar, lemon juice, white wine, a bouquet garni and seasoning for the white variety, and malt vinegar, a bouquet garni and aromatic vegetables for the brown variety. Brown court bouillon should be cooked and strained before use. Other types are available, e.g. plain court bouillon, white wine court bouillon, red wine court bouillon and salted water. Fish served cold are allowed to cool in the CB.

courting cake *England* A Victoria sponge cake in three layers with strawberries and whipped cream filling and sprinkled with icing sugar. Once made in the north of England as evidence of the bride-to-be's pastry skills.

couscous *North Africa* **1.** A cereal made from fine semolina agglomerated with a little water to form grains about 3 mm across which are coated with fine wheat flour and dried **2.** The name of the dish made from couscous which has been moistened with water to make it swell, then steamed, heaped on a plate and covered with steamed vegetables, mutton or chicken, with possibly chickpeas and/or onions glazed in honey

couscousière *France* An open steamer used for cooking couscous over a pan of stew as it simmers

couscous kedra *North Africa* Couscous with chicken, raisins and chickpeas

couscous royale *North Africa* Couscous with vegetables and grilled meats or kebabs, all served in separate dishes accompanied with harissa and individually self served by guests

couteau *France* **1.** Knife, as e.g. couteau de cuisine, kitchen knife **2.** Razor shell (UK), Razor shell clam (USA)

couve *Portugal* Cabbage and various species of *Brassica*

couve de bruxelas *Portugal* Brussels sprouts

couve-flor *Portugal* Cauliflower

couve gallego Portuguese cabbage

couve lombarda *Portugal* **1.** Collard greens **2.** Kale

couvert *France* Cover, place setting

couverture A high-quality chocolate with added cocoa butter to give a high gloss and various proportions of sugar, used for coating confectionery items and cakes and for making caraque. Milk solids are added to milk chocolate couverture.

couve tronchuda Portuguese cabbage

Coventry cakes *England* Oven-baked pastry triangles filled with jam and glazed with sugar

Coventry god cakes *England* Oven-baked puff pastry triangles filled with fruit mincemeat and glazed with sugar. Eaten at Christmas.

cover 1. A place setting for one person in a dining area. Capacities or quantities are often measured in covers. **2.** A lid of a dish or pan, etc.

cover charge A charge made in a restaurant on a per-capita basis, supposedly to cover the cost of preparing the table for the customer

cow A female of the bovine species, usually used for milking and reproduction and then for cheap beef or manufactured beef products

cowberry Large, tart, dark red berries similar to cranberries, from a shrub, *Vaccinium vitisidaea*, which grows in the colder high-altitude regions of Europe and North America. Popular in Germany and Scandinavia. Also called **lingonberry**, **mountain cranberry**

cow cod soup *Caribbean* A Jamaican soup made with a bull's genitals

cowfoot *Caribbean* A thick and gelatinous stew from Jamaica made with calves' or cows' feet

cow heel The foot of a cow which, because of the large amount of collagen in the connective tissue is used to add gelatine to stocks or stews when boiled with them

cow pea An important erect legume, *Vigna unguiculata*, with pods to 15 cm which originated in Africa where it is grown for the dried seeds which can be black through to white or coloured. Now also grown in the Caribbean and the USA. It can be sprouted or, rarely, cooked in the pod when young. The leaves are sometimes eaten as a vegetable. The **long bean** which is common in southern China and Southeast Asia, has been bred from it. Also called **black-eyed bean**, **black-eyed pea**, **black-eyed susie**, **Chinese bean**, **southern pea**

cowslip A hardy herbaceous perennial, *Primula veris*, with yellow flowers and a rosette of primrose-type leaves. The flowers may be used in jams, pickles or for flavouring desserts. The leaves may be used in salads or for meat stuffings.

cows' udder Elder

cozido 1. A Brazilian meat stew **2.** *Portugal* Boiled

cozido à portuguesa *Portugal* A Portuguese national dish, being a stew made from brisket or similar cut of beef, bacon, sausage, yams, vegetables, cabbage, haricot beans and rice. The cooking liquor serves as both soup and sauce. The sausage is usually bland e.g. farinheira, but white or black pudding may be substituted. Pigs' ears, tails and trotters are sometimes included. Also called **Portuguese boiled dinner**

cozinha *Portugal* Kitchen

cozze *Italy* The southern Italian name for mussels

cozzula *Italy* A type of bread from Sardinia

crab A short-tailed decapod (10-legged) crustacean which yields 38 to 50% of its weight in edible meat. Varieties include: blue crab, jonah crab, mud crab, red crab, rock crab, shore crab, snow crab, southern stone crab, spanner crab and spider crab. See also **common crab**

crab apple The wild version of the apple, *Malus pumila*, with generally small (up to 3 cm diameter) tart and crisp fruits. Used for making jams and preserves.

crab au gratin *United States* A Louisiana dish of cooked crab meat bound together with a **béchamel sauce** mixed with sour cream and seasoning, gratinated with cheese and browned in the oven

crab backs *Caribbean* A dish of cooked crab meat mixed with fried onions, fried skinned tomatoes, Worcestershire sauce, vinegar and seasoning, served on a crab shell, sprinkled with breadcrumbs and butter and browned in the oven

crab bisque *United States* A Louisiana bisque made from a white roux thickened milk base with fried onions, cooked crab meat, sweet corn kernels, Tabasco and Worcestershire sauces and seasoning

crab boil *United States* A social occasion at which crabs are boiled in water flavoured with the following whole spices in a bouquet garni, black peppercorns, mustard seed, dill seed, coriander seed, cloves, allspice, dried ginger and bay leaf, and then served with accompaniments

crab butter The yellow-white fat which lines the upper shell of the crab. Used in dressings and sauces.

crab claws The two large pincer-like claws on either side of the mouth parts. The meat is considered to be the best from the crab.

crabe *France* Crab

crabe froid à l'anglaise *France* Dressed crab

crabe vert *France* Shore crab

crab legs. *United States* The legs of the Alaskan king crab which are large enough to be eaten on their own. They do not include the claws.

crab Louis *United States* A Californian salad of crab meat on a chiffonade of lettuce, coated with Louis sauce and garnished with hard-boiled egg and black olives

crab yolk Tomalley

cracked wheat Coarsely crushed grains of wheat, dry cooked for 25 minutes. Served hot as a breakfast cereal, served as an accompaniment to other dishes or sprinkled on rolls or bread prior to baking. Also called **kibbled wheat**

cracked wheat flour *United States* A coarse flour rather like oatmeal which has been cut from the wheat rather than ground and hence does not release starch very readily

cracker *United States* The general name given to any type of plain or salted hard biscuit

cracker flour *United States* A soft wheat flour with a low water absorption ability

crackling The skin of a pork, bacon or ham joint which has been scored to 3 or 4 mm with a sharp knife in strips or a diamond pattern prior to roasting and which becomes crisp and golden brown if basted with water; it is served as an accompaniment to the roast

cracklins *United States* Crackling

cracknel *United States* A type of hard crisp plain biscuit made of a paste which is boiled before being baked causing it to puff up

crackseed *United States* The bruised and squashed seeds of various fruits which are preserved in salt and sugar (NOTE: From Hawaii)

crakeberry Crowberry

crake herring *Ireland* The northern name for scad

Crambe maritima *Botanical name* Seakale

cranachan 1. *Ireland* A dessert made from stiffly whipped cream into which honey and whisky (6:1:1) are folded, followed by toasted and chopped almonds and toasted rolled oats, flavoured with lemon juice and garnished with orange slices **2.** *Scotland* Crannochan

cranberry The hard ripe fruits (diameter to 2 cm) of a wild or cultivated evergreen shrub, *Vaccinium macrocarpum*, which grows in cool regions of the northern hemisphere. They are deep red in colour, very tart and used in sweet and savoury dishes, the most famous of which is as a sauce accompaniment to turkey. Also called **bounceberry, craneberry**

cranberry juice The juice of cranberries containing compounds which prevent even antibiotic-resistant bacteria from attaching to the urinary tract lining and causing urinary tract infections.The effect occurs after 2 hours and remains for up to 12 hours. It should not be taken in conjunction with blood-thinning drugs such as warfarin.

cranberry sauce Cranberries stewed with water and sugar, liquidized and sieved. Traditionally served with turkey. Also called **airelles, sauce**

craneberry See **cranberry**

crannochan *Scotland* A dessert made from raspberries, cream, toasted oatmeal, whisky

liqueur and heather honey. Also called **cranachan**

cranshaw melon *United States* A hybrid of the Persian and the winter melon

crapaud *Caribbean* An edible toad, *Leprodactylus fallax*, found in Dominica and Montserrat. Also called **mountain chicken**

crapaudine, à la *France* Cut horizontally from below the point of the breast over the top of the legs to the wing joints, back bone broken and the whole flattened so that the breast points forward, the legs back and the wings are folded in the centre. It is then grilled and with imagination resembles a toad. Also called **spatchcock** (NOTE: Literally 'toad-like'.)

crappit *Scotland* Stuffed, filled

crappit heids *Scotland* Cleaned haddock heads stuffed with a mixture of oatmeal, suet and onions, then boiled

crappit muggies *Scotland* Cod stomachs stuffed with a mixture of minced cod liver, oatmeal and finely chopped and sautéed onions. From the northern islands.

craquelet *Switzerland* Seasoned pork and beef, processed to a very fine creamy paste, packed into casings, smoked and cooked. Eaten hot or cold.

craquelot *France* A type of bloater. See also **bouffi**

Crataegus azarolus *Botanical name* Azarole

Craterellus cornucopioides *Botanical name* Horn of plenty

crauti *Italy* Sauerkraut

cravo *Portugal* Clove

cravo-de-india *Portugal* Clove

crawfish 1. Spiny lobster **2.** *United States* The Créole name for freshwater crayfish

crayfish 1. A freshwater crustacean resembling the lobster, found in unpolluted streams and lakes but now generally farmed. Crayfish breed in autumn and are best caught in summer. Cooked as lobster. The European variety, *Astacus fluviatilis*, is about the size of a Dublin Bay prawn. Some Australian varieties can weigh up to 6 kg. Most make excellent eating. Also called **crawfish**. See also **signal crayfish, yabbie, marron 2.** The name is often used indiscriminately for crayfish, crawfish and similar crustaceans with or without claws, especially in the USA

crayfish, Scandinavian cooking Cleaned live crayfish immersed in just sufficient salted boiling water flavoured with dill flowers to completely cover them, the water brought back to the boil and the crayfish boiled for exactly 3 minutes, drained, refreshed and then left in the cooled cooking liquor for 24 hours

crayfish butter Beurre d'écrevisses

crayfish sauce Hollandaise sauce or **sauce vin blanc** mixed with **beurre d'écrevisses**

creachan *Scotland* A north Scottish haggis-type pudding made with the entrails of calves

cream The globules of butter fat which rise to the top of milk entrapping larger or smaller amounts of milk. The type is determined by the butterfat content. See half cream, single cream, whipping cream, double cream, extra thick double cream, clotted cream, Jersey cream, etc.

cream, to To beat one or a mixture of ingredients vigorously so as to give it or them the consistency of whipped cream and incorporate air, especially fat and sugar in cake making

cream bun See **cream puff**

cream caramel See **crème caramel**

cream cheese A soft, acid curdled spreading cheese made from a mixture of cows' milk and cream. The curds are spun off and milled with stabilizers and preservatives prior to packaging for immediate sale and consumption. Contains between 45% and 65% butter fat. Also called **Philadelphia cream cheese**

cream crackers Light, fawn-coloured, square unsweetened biscuits made from flour, fat, water and salt. Usually eaten with cheese. Nothing to do with cream.

cream-crowdie *Scotland* Crannokan

creamed cakes Cakes made by the creaming method with high proportions of fat, sugar and eggs to flour. Usually require little if any raising agent due to the amounts of air incorporated during preparation. Examples are Madeira cake, rich fruit cake, Victoria sponge. Also called **rich cakes**

creamed coconut See **coconut cream**

creamer 1. A dry white powder made from glucose and vegetable fats used as a substitute for cream or milk in coffee **2.** An implement for separating cream from milk

cream horns Cones made from overlapping strips of puff pastry wrapped around conical metal moulds, baked in the oven, cooled, removed from the mould and filled with jam and whipped cream

creaming method of making cakes The method of making cakes by vigorously beating together fat and sugar to incorporate air and give a soft, light, fluffy texture, incorporating well beaten eggs slowly with continuous beating to form a stable emulsion, then gently folding in flour and other dry ingredients to avoid losing air. The trapped air expands with steam during the baking and setting process. e.g. Victoria sandwich, fruit cake.

creaming quality The ability of fats to absorb air when mixed or beaten

cream nut Brazil nut

cream of artichoke soup See **Palestine, crème**

cream of green pea soup See **Saint Germain, crème**

cream of tartar Acid potassium tartrate (potassium hydrogen tartrate), a crystalline substance which is precipitated from wine as it ages. Now made synthetically and combined with sodium bicarbonate to make the raising agent baking powder.

cream of tomato soup See **tomates, crème de**

cream of vegetable soup Vegetable soup with added cream, milk or **béchamel sauce**

cream puff 1. A round bun of cooked choux pastry, split, centre scooped out if soft, the halves filled with whipped cream or crème pâtissière and sandwiched together then dusted with icing sugar or coated with coffee or chocolate-flavoured soft icing. Also called **cream bun 2.** *United States* Profiterole

cream puff pastry *United States* Choux pastry

cream sauce Béchamel sauce with the addition of cream, natural yoghurt or fromage blanc. Used for poached fish and boiled vegetables. Also called **crème, sauce**

cream slices Baked rectangles of puff pastry divided into two rectangles of the same area which are sandwiched together with jam and whipped cream or crème pâtissière and the top covered with soft icing. Also called **millefeuilles**

cream soup 1. A soup made from a vegetable purée soup with added cream, milk or yoghurt **2.** A vegetable purée type of soup mixed with **béchamel sauce 3.** A velouté soup with added cream, milk or yoghurt

cream tea *England* An afternoon snack or meal consisting of scones, whipped or clotted cream and jam served with tea. Popular in Devon and Cornwall and country district tourist areas.

crecchietto *Italy* A type of pasta from Apulia

crécy, (à la) *France* In the Crécy style, i.e. garnished with or containing carrots

crédioux aux noix *France* A soft, cooked-curd cows' milk cheese coated with walnut pieces

cree'd wheat Frumenty wheat

crema 1. *Italy, Spain* Cream **2.** *Italy* Custard, custard cream, dessert **3.** *Italy* Cream soup

crema batida *Spain* Whipped cream

crema catalana *Catalonia* Crème brûlée flavoured with cinnamon and lemon and served very cold

crema di pollo *Italy* Cream of chicken soup

crema di verdura *Italy* Puréed vegetables possibly including potatoes or cooked rice and finished with cream

crema española *Spain* A dessert made with flavoured and sweetened milk and eggs set with gelatine

crema fritta *Italy* Fried sweet or savoury egg custard cut in diamond shapes

crema pasticceria *Italy* Crème pâtissière, confectioner's custard

crema rovesciata *Italy* Baked egg custard

cremat *Catalonia* 1. Crisp-fried 2. Caramelized

creme *Portugal* 1. Cream 2. Cream soup

crème *France* Cream

crème, à la *France* With or containing cream

crème Agnés Sorel *France* A cream of chicken soup garnished with mushroom slices and **julienne** of tongue

crème aigre *France* Sour cream

crème à l'anglaise *France* A thick egg custard made with 16 egg yolks and 500 g of sugar per litre of milk, flavoured as required with vanilla, lemon zest or, after cooling, with liqueur. The sugar and egg are whisked to the ribbon stage and boiling milk added, whisked, and heated to a coating consistency. Must not be boiled. Strained and served hot or cold. Also called **sauce anglaise**, **crème anglaise**, **English egg custard**

crème à la vanille *France* A vanilla-flavoured baked egg custard

crème anglaise *France* Crème à l'anglaise

crème au beurre *France* Crème beurre

crème bachique *France* Cinnamon and sauternes-flavoured custard

crème bavaroise *France* A dessert made from vanilla-flavoured egg custard or fruit purée. See also **bavarois**

crème beurre *France* A butter cream for filling or covering cakes made by combining hot sugar syrup with egg yolks, cooling the mixture then whisking it into well-creamed butter with flavourings such as chocolate, coffee, vanilla and fruit purée. Also called **crème au beurre**

crème brûlée *France* A thick, rich egg custard baked in individual portions in ramekins, cooled, sprinkled with brown sugar and caramelized under the grill or with a blow torch until crisp

crème caramel *France* Individual sized ramekins, with a base layer of, or lined with, caramel, filled with egg custard, baked in a bain-marie in the oven, cooled, demoulded on to a plate so that the caramel is on top and decorated or left plain. Sometimes made in a large dish and portioned. Also called **cream caramel**, **caramel cream**, **caramel custard**, **French flan**, **flan**

crème chantilly *France* Sweetened whipped cream

crème crécy *France* Creamed carrot soup garnished with plain boiled rice

crème d'amandes *France* Almond cream

crème de riz *France* White soup coloured and thickened with powdered rice

crème d'orge *France* Soup made with fine barley

crème fleurette *France* Unsweetened whipping cream

crème fouettée *France* Whipped cream

crème fraîche *France* A lactobacillus culture of cream with a fresh sour taste. It may be used as cream, keeps better and does not separate on boiling.

crème frite *France* A custard, stiffened with thick flour and egg yolk, flavoured and sweetened, then spread 1.5 cm thick, cooled and chilled, cut in shapes, battered or panéed and deep-fried. If panéed sprinkled with caster sugar, if battered dredged with icing sugar and glazed under the grill.

crème glacée *France* 1. Ice cream 2. Ice cream sundae

crème moulée *France* Baked egg custard served cold either in a dish or demoulded

crème patisserie See **crème pâtissière**

crème pâtissière *England, France* Confectioner's custard. An egg and flour-thickened custard made with sweetened milk flavoured with vanilla (4 eggs and 200 g flour per litre). Used as a filling for flans, cakes, pastries, tarts, etc. The flour prevents the egg from curdling.

crème pralinée *France* Crème pâtissière flavoured with powdered praline

crème renversée *France* A demoulded crème caramel. Also called **cup custard**

Crémet Nantais *France* A soft white unsalted cream cheese from Brittany made with cows' milk

crémeux (euse) *France* Creamy

cremona mustard See **mostarda di Cremona**

crempog *Wales* Welsh pancake

crempog las *Wales* Pancake omelette

crenata *United States* Pine nut

créole, à la *France* In the Creole style, i.e. with rice and possibly tomatoes and sweet peppers

Créole *United States* A style of cooking developed by the settlers of part French descent from Louisiana using tomatoes, peppers, onions and spices. See also **Créole cuisine**

Créole cheese *United States* A New Orleans speciality cheese consisting of cottage cheese with double cream

Créole Christmas cake *Caribbean* A dark, rich fruit cake from Trinidad, well flavoured with rum, brandy, port and liqueur. Also called **gateau noir**

Créole crab *United States* The meat from freshly boiled crab (10 minutes) fried gently in olive oil, a little water, chopped onion and garlic, lemon juice, seasoning, thyme, bay leaf and a chilli pepper added, then simmered slowly for 30 minutes. Served with boiled rice after discarding the bay, thyme, bouquet garni and chilli pepper.

Créole cuisine *United States* A cooking style developed in the Southern USA combining Caribbean, French, African and Spanish cooking based on shellfish, rice, okra and filé powder

Créole mustard *United States* A hot whole grain mustard seed macerated in vinegar

crepe *Italy, Portugal* Pancake

crêpe *France* A large thin pancake made with white flour

crêpe dentelle *France* A very thin pancake from Brittany

crêperie *France* A restaurant or shop usually with a connection with Brittany which specializes in filled sweet and savoury crêpes and pancakes

crepes do céu *Portugal* Pancakes filled with whipped cream and candied fruit (NOTE: Literally 'Heavenly crêpes'.)

crêpes Parmentier *France* Potato-based pancakes

crêpes Suzette *France* Small pancakes folded in quarters, simmered in a buttery orange sauce, flamed with brandy and served as a dessert

crépine *France* Pig's caul

crépinette *France* 1. A croquette wrapped in grilled or fried bacon 2. A ball of seasoned and flavoured minced meat, wrapped in pig's caul or very thin slices of salt pork fat, possibly coated with melted butter and breadcrumbs and baked, grilled or fried. Also called **caillette 3**

crépinettes d'agneau *France* Crépinettes filled with a mixture of chopped lamb and **duxelles** bound with **espagnole sauce**

crépinettes d'agneau à la liégeoise *Belgium* Crépinettes filled with a mixture of chopped lamb, breadcrumbs moistened with milk, sweated chopped onions, seasoning and crushed juniper berries

crépinettes de foie de porc à la vauclusienne *France* Crépinettes filled with a seasoned mixture of chopped pig's liver, bacon, spinach, onion and stoned black olives, flavoured with chopped parsley and nutmeg, tied and baked in the oven

crépinettes de volaille *France* Crépinettes filled with chopped chicken and mushroom, possibly with truffles, bound in a chicken velouté sauce

crépinettes Reine Jeanne *France* Crépinettes filled with chopped blanched sheeps' or calves' brains, **duxelles** and truffles, bound with a thick **béchamel sauce**, panéed with egg white and breadcrumbs, fried and served hot with lemon wedges

crèque *France* Bullace, the fruit

crescent *United States* Croissant

crescente *Italy* Dough made with flour, sodium bicarbonate raising agent, salt and milk, rested, rolled into very thin discs which are fried both sides in hot olive oil until they bubble, drained and served hot with a savoury topping

crescentina *Italy* Flat bread made from dough containing pieces of bacon

crescenza *Italy* A soft cows' milk cheese with a buttery texture and no rind from Northern Italy and similar to **Stracchino**. Contains 57% water, 22% fat and 20% protein.

crescione *Italy* Deep-fried pasta triangles filled with spinach and cream

crescione dei prati *Italy* Lady's smock

crescione di fonte *Italy* Watercress

crescione di giardino *Italy* Cress

crespella *Italy* A thin stuffed crêpe

crespone *Italy* A salami from Milan made with approximately equal amounts of lean pork, lean beef and pork fat, seasoned and flavoured with garlic and moistened with white wine, packed in fat ends or beef middles, dry-salted and air-dried

cress A small plant, *Lepidium sativum*, from Iran. The seeds are grown to the two leaf stage on a 6 cm stalk, generally together with mustard and used in salads or for garnishing. It may be grown for the young true leaves, which are harvested continuously. Also called **garden cress, curly cress, peppercress, peppergrass**

cresson alénois *France* Land cress

cresson cultivé *France* Cress

cresson de fontaine *France* Watercress

cresson de prés *France* Lady's smock

cresson de ruisseau *France* Watercress

cresson d'Inde *France* Nasturtium

cressonnière, purée *France* A **purée Parmentier** with watercress added with the potatoes, and garnished with blanched and refreshed watercress leaves

cretons 1. *France* Crackling **2.** *Canada* A type of **rillette** from Quebec made from crisped bacon rind simmered with pork, onions, spices and seasoning until soft, thickened with bread crumbs and allowed to set in a mould. Usually served on bread.

crevalle See **crevalle jack**

crevalle jack An oily tropical and warm water sea fish of the genus *Caranx* with a deep body, bluish green on top, silver underneath, weighing 1 to 3 kg. Also called **crevalle**, **jack**, **common jack**

crevette *France* Brown shrimp

crevette grise *France* Shrimp

crevette nordique *France* Deepwater prawn

crevette rose *France* Common prawn

crevette rose du large *France* A large pink king prawn, *Parapenaeus longirostris*, caught off Spain, Portugal and in the Mediterranean and up to 16 cm long. Also called **red prawn**

crevette rouge *France* A large king prawn found in the Mediterranean which is either, *Aristeus antennatus*, up to 20 cm long with a light red body and a mauve head or, *Aristeomorphia foliacea*, up to 30 cm and blood red in colour

crevette royale *France* A Mediterranean king prawn. See also **caramote**

crevettes, sauce aux *France* Boiling fish velouté, consistency adjusted using fish stock or cream, seasoned, strained and finished with picked shrimps

criadilla de tierra *Spain* Truffle, the fungus

criadillas *Spain* **1.** Sweetbreads **2.** Testicles

crimp, to To pinch together, successively along the edges of pastry where two layers meet, as in a covered pie or pasty, so as to seal the pastry and for decoration. See also **scallop, to**

crinkled musket Barrel bread

criolla, a la *Spain* In the South American style

crisp, to To make food brittle and firm e.g. by chilling vegetables, by drying off biscuits or bread in the oven, by soaking in water or commercially with a variety of firming agents

crispbread A, usually rectangular, crisp, light biscuit made from crushed rye or wheat, salt and water, often with a pattern of depressions. Thought to be non-fattening but if buttered, the depressions hold more butter that the equivalent flat biscuit.

crisphead lettuce A type of lettuce with very crisp leaves forming a tight solid ball. Called iceberg when the outer leaves are removed.

crispito *Mexico* A tightly rolled tortilla, fried or deep-fried and eaten with dipping sauces

crisps Thin slices of raw potato deep-fried in hot oil until brown and crisp. Nowadays often made with processed potatoes so as to have a regular shape. May be flavoured and seasoned. Also called **potato crisps**, **game chips**

Crithmum maritimum *Botanical name* Samphire

critical moisture content The percentage of water in a food item or substance at which it becomes unsuitable for sale or use

critmo *Italy* Samphire, *Crithmum maritimum*

croaker The general term for any of over 200 species of fish which make croaking noises e.g. the Atlantic croaker

croccante *Italy* Praline

crocche *Italy* Croquette

crocchetta *Italy* Croquette

crocette *Italy* Small cone-shaped shellfish

crockery Plates, dishes, cups, etc. and all types of domestic pots, usually of ceramic materials, used at meals

Crocus sativus *Botanical name* Saffron

croissant *France* A light, flaky, crescent-shaped breakfast roll made from white, yeast-raised dough interleaved with butter in the same way as puff pastry. Cut in triangular shape, rolled with a point on the outside and bent into a crescent shape before baking.

cromesquis *France* A small cylindrical croquette of minced meat bound with a thick sauce, wrapped in bacon or pig's caul, coated with fritter batter and deep-fried. Served as a hors d'oeuvre or light main course. Also called **kromeski**, **kromesky** (NOTE: Cromesquis are a 19th-century French adaptation of a Polish dish)

crookneck squash A yellow or orange summer squash with a neck bent into a hook, common in the USA. Also called **yellow squash**

crop A chamber at the bottom of a bird's throat in which food is stored prior to it being passed on to the gizzard for processing

croquant 1. *France* Crunchy **2.** A type of crisp biscuit

croque au sel, à la *France* **1.** With salt and nothing else **2.** With a sprinkling of salt

croque-madame *France* As **croque-monsieur**, but with cooked chicken replacing the ham

croquembouche *France* A tall pyramid made of cream-filled choux pastry spheres coated with caramel and decorated. Traditionally served at French weddings.

croque-monsieur *France* Popular French fast food consisting of a sandwich filled with ham and Gruyère cheese, crust removed, cut into decorative shapes, dipped in beaten egg and shallow-fried until golden. Sometimes only toasted. Eaten hot.

croquesignole *United States* A round or square holeless Cajun doughnut

croqueta *Spain* 1. Croquette 2. Meatball

croquetes *Portugal* Croquettes

croquetes de camarão *Portugal* Shrimp croquettes eaten as an appetizer or hors d'oeuvres

croquetjes *Netherlands* Croquettes

croquette *England, France* Any mixture of minced cooked meat, etc. combined with mashed potatoes and/or breadcrumbs, herbs, onions, seasonings and egg or stock to form a stiff paste which is shaped into cylinders, spheres, rounds, ovals etc., panéed and deep-fried

crosnes *France* Chinese artichoke (NOTE: So called from the French town where they were first introduced.)

crosnes du Japon *France* Japanese artichoke

crosse de boeuf *France* Knuckle of beef, also used of calf's foot

crosta *Italy* Crust, e.g. of bread

crostacei *Italy* Crustaceans

crostata *Italy* Pie

crostata di fragole *Italy* Strawberry pie

crostatina *Italy* Tart

crostato *Italy* 1. Browned 2. With a crust

crostini *Italy* 1. A piece of good bread, toasted over charcoal or on a griddle, rubbed with a cut clove of fresh garlic, spread with olive oil or butter and topped with a variety of savoury items such as sliced tomatoes, capers, olives, anchovies, cheese, avocado or prawns, i.e. bruschetta with a topping. Eaten as a starter. Also called **crostoncini** 2. Croûtons or toasted bread

crostini alla fiorentina *Italy* A crostini spread with a chicken liver pâté

crostini alla napoletana *Italy* A crostini spread with tomatoes and anchovies

crostini alla parmigiana *Italy* A crostini spread with grated Parmesan and anchovies

crostini di mare *Italy* A crostini spread with minced shellfish

crostoncini *Italy* Crostini

crostoni *Italy* A large crostini eaten as a light meal

crostoni, sul *Italy* On toast

Crotonese *Italy* A hard, scalded-curd, ewes' milk cheese cast in wicker basket moulds in 2 kg discs. It has a dry rough orange/yellow rind with a cream coloured paste and the odd hole or crack. Used for slicing or grating depending upon age.

Crottin *France* Crottin de Chavignol

Crottin de Chavignol *France* A small, hard, goats' milk cheese with a strong flavour from the Berry region.I has AOC status. Often deep-fried or grilled and served with lettuce as a starter. Also called **Crottin**, **Chavignol** (NOTE: Literally 'droppings', because of its appearance.)

croupion *France* Parson's nose

croustade *France* A hollowed out piece of bread, deep-fried until crisp, or a baked pastry case used to serve cooked meats, vegetables, etc. bound in a savoury sauce

croustade d'oeufs de caille Maintenon *France* Poached quails' eggs laid on a bed of **duxelles** and **hollandaise sauce** in a pastry **barquette**

croustillant *France* Crunchy, crisp or crusty

croustilles *France* Potato crisps

croûte 1. *France* Crust, rind or toast 2. *France* A circle or rectangle of fried or toasted bread on which game or other dishes and savouries are served 3. A small pastry crust, usually crescent-shaped, served with savoury dishes

croûte, en *France* Enclosed in pastry then baked e.g. of fish or meat

croûte anchois *France* Anchovy toast

croûte au pot *France* A beef and vegetable soup each serving topped with toasted bread and cheese

croûte aux morilles *France* Morels on toast

croûtons *England, France* Small (8mm) cubes of bread fried until crisp and golden in clarified butter and served as an accompaniment to purée soups

crow *England* Mesentery

crowberry The black skinned fruit of a shrub, *Empetrum nigrum*, which grows in hilly areas of Northern Europe, similar to and can be substituted for the cranberry. Also called **crakeberry**

crowdie *Scotland* 1. A gruel made from oatmeal once used as a staple food in Scotland 2. A mild-flavoured cottage cheese made from rennet-curdled, skimmed, unpasteurized cows' milk. Eaten fresh usually with an admixture of cream. Also called **crowdy**

crowdie cream *Scotland* A celebratory crowdie from Skye consisting of cream beaten until stiff, toasted medium oatmeal, caster sugar and a good single malt whisky. Each person is given a bowl of the cream and adds the other ingredients according to his or her taste.

crowdy See **crowdie**

crown roast of lamb Two best ends of lamb, chined and with scraped ribs, joined in a circle so that the ribs curve outwards like a crown. Roasted and served with cutlet frills on the ends of the ribs. The centre may be filled with stuffing before cooking.

cru *Portugal* Raw

cru(e) *France* Raw

crubeens Pig's trotters simmered with herbs and aromatic vegetables for about 3 hours

crucetta *Italy* A Calabrian dish of roasted figs stuffed with nuts

cruchade *France* A sweet cornmeal fritter

crucian carp A silver-coloured type of carp similar to bream in appearance

crudan *Ireland* Gurnard, the fish

crudités *France* A selection of crisp vegetables suitable for eating raw, cut into long strips or batons and often served with a dipping sauce such as mayonnaise, soured cream or other cold sauce, usually as a hors d'oeuvre or appetizers

crudo *Italy, Spain* Raw, fresh

cruet A set of pots, shakers and grinders for serving condiments, usually on a small tray

crulla *Scotland* Flour, eggs, caster sugar and butter (6:2:1:1) with 2 dsp of baking powder per kg of flour, made into a soft dough by the creaming method, rolled out and cut into narrow 15-cm-long strips. These are plaited in threes, deep-fried until brown, drained and sprinkled with caster sugar.

crullers *United States* A sweetened egg-enriched pastry made with butter, cut into strips, deep-fried and dusted with icing sugar. Eaten warm. Also a popular snack in China and often sliced and served with **congee** or soup.

crumb, to *United States* To pané or cover with crumbs

crumb crust A mixture of crushed biscuits combined with sugar and melted butter which is often substituted for pastry, e.g. in cheese cakes and in the USA for tarts and flans where Graham crackers are the biscuit of choice

crumber A device used by a waiter to remove crumbs from a table, either a small dustpan and brush or small carpet sweeper

crumble A compote of fruit topped with a mixture of fat, flour and sugar, sometimes with oatflakes and/or white of egg, baked in the oven until the topping is crisp and crumbly

crumble, to To rub a dry solid between the fingers or otherwise so as to reduce it to crumbs

crumbs Small irregularly shaped particles made from large friable pieces, e.g. of cake, bread, biscuits

crumpets A yeasted flour liquid batter (3:4) made with equal parts of milk and water and a little oil, allowed to froth, baking powder added at the rate of 5 g per kg of flour, left 40 minutes to rest then cooked in rings on a greased griddle to form small, circular, flat buns with a honeycombed top surface. Usually served toasted with butter.

crusca *Italy* Bran

crush, to To squeeze or press a solid so as to extract liquid, to turn it into a semi-solid or to reduce it to smaller particles

crust 1. The outer hard golden brown surface of bread or cakes or other mixtures which are baked or fried **2.** The pastry top on a filled sweet or savoury pie or dish not necessarily having a pastry base

crustacean A class of aquatic animals with a hard external segmented shell (exoskeleton) containing a soft body, usually with muscular legs, tail and possibly claws, such as lobster, prawn, crab, etc.

crustáceos *Spain* Crustaceans

crustacés *France* **1.** Shellfish **2.** Crustaceans **3.** Seafood

cryptoxanthin See **E161(c)**

crystallized flowers Small flowers or flower petals soaked in sugar syrup and dried, often artificially coloured, used for decoration. Traditionally violets.

crystallized fruit See **candied fruit**

Csabai *Hungary* A well-flavoured spicy sausage containing chilli pepper and paprika

császárkörte *Hungary* A type of pear, white butter pear

csemege *Hungary* Dessert

cseresznye *Hungary* Cherries

csipetke *Hungary* Tiny dumplings made by cooking pieces of egg noodle dough in simmering water until al dente, draining and tossing in lard. Served with soups and stews.

csirke *Hungary* Chicken

csirkegulyás szegedi módra *Hungary* Jointed chicken simmered in white stock with thinly sliced green sweet peppers, diced potatoes, tomatoes, sweated celeriac, onions, carrots and Hamburg parsley and served with boiled **csipetke** tossed in butter

csuka *Hungary* Pike, the fish

cu *China* Vinegar

cuajada 1. *Spain* Curds **2.** *South America* A soft, creamy, cows' milk cheese from Venezuela often wrapped in banana leaf

cuajo *Spain* Rennet

cuan *China* Simmering of meat or vegetables e.g. in a steamboat

cuaresmeño *Mexico* A dark green round chilli

cubeb The dried, dark brown, unripe fruits of a plant, *Piper cubeba*, native to Indonesia and about the size of a peppercorn with a stalk. They have a warm, somewhat bitter, flavour close to allspice with a hint of turpentine and were one of the spices used to flavour hippocras. Used in Indonesian cooking. Also called **tailed pepper**

cube sugar White or brown crystals of sugar compressed into small cubes (about 15 mm edge). Also called **sugar lump, loaf sugar**

cu cai tau *Vietnam* Mooli

cucchiaino *Italy* Teaspoon, also used as a volume measure equal to 5 ml

cucchiaio da tavola *Italy* Tablespoon, also used as a volume measure equal to 15 ml

cuchara *Spain* 1. Spoon 2. Ladle

cucharada *Spain* Tablespoonful used as a volume measure equal to 15 ml

cucharadita *Spain* Teaspoonful used as a volume measure equal to 5 ml

cuchay Chinese chive

cucina *Italy* 1. Cooking, cuisine 2. Kitchen

cuckoo flower Lady's smock

cucumber A fruit of a member of the Cucurbitaceae family, *Cucumis sativus,*, introduced to the UK from India in 1573 and harvested in the unripe green stage between 5 and 35 cm in length and 1.5 to 5 cm in diameter. The smaller ones are usually pickled in flavoured brine or vinegar, the larger are generally eaten raw as a salad vegetable or deseeded, salted, drained and diced combined with herbs and yoghurt or used as a bulking agent in various mixtures. See also **dill pickles, gherkin, Japanese cucumber, yellow cucumber, ridge cucumber, long cucumber**

cucumber mayonnaise Finely chopped cucumber and salt mixed with mayonnaise

cucumber sauce See **doria, sauce**

cucumber tree fruit Belimbing

Cucumeropsis spp. *Botanical name* Egusi melon

Cucumis anguria *Botanical name* Gherkin

Cucumis melo *Botanical name* The vine from which the sweet melons, mush melon, canteloupe and honeydew melon are obtained

Cucumis sativus *Botanical name* Cucumber

Cucurbitaceae The botanical family name for a group of vine plants whose fruits include cucumbers and melons, watermelons, summer squash including marrows and courgettes, winter squash, pumpkins, chokos, etc.

Cucurbita maxima The botanical name of the American vine from which some varieties of winter squash are obtained. Distinguished by soft hairs on the stems, a swollen almost smooth stem and leaves which are not deeply lobed.

Cucurbita moschata The botanical name of the American vine from which some varieties of winter squash are obtained especially the cushaw and crookneck

Cucurbita pepo The botanical name of the vine from which pumpkins, marrows and summer squash are obtained. Distinguished by roughly bristled stems, short ridged fruit stalks and deeply lobed leaves.

cu hành *Vietnam* Onion

cuiller à bouche *France* Tablespoon, also used as a volume measure equal to 15 ml

cuiller à café *France* Coffee spoon = teaspoon, also used as a volume measure equal to 5 ml

cuiller à dessert *France* Dessertspoon

cuillerée à café *France* Teaspoonful

cuillerée à soupe *France* Tablespoonful

cuina volcànica *Catalonia* Cuisine based on local produce in the La Garrotxa region ranging from potatoes and beans to wild boar and truffles (NOTE: Literally 'volcanic cuisine'.)

cuipi ji *China* Chicken cooked so that the skin is crisp

cuire *France* To cook

cuire à la vapeur *France* To steam

cuisine *France* 1. Kitchen 2. Cooking, cookery, the art of cookery 3. Kitchen or catering staff

cuisine au jus *France* A style of cooking avoiding cream, butter and flour for sauces but instead relying on the natural cooking juices

cuisine bourgeoise *France* Plain cooking

cuisine de terroir *France* Regional cooking

cuisine du soleil *France* The modern haute cuisine of the French Riviera based on fresh fruit and vegetables, olive oil, garlic and the herbs of Provence such as thyme, fennel, sage, etc.

cuisine épicée *France* Hot or spicy dishes or food

cuisine ménagère *France* The cooking of the ordinary household

cuisine minceur *France* A low-calorie style of cooking developed in France, with little or no fat or starch

cuisse *France* Thigh

cuisseau *France* Haunch (of veal)

cuisse de mouton *France* Leg of mutton

cuisse de poulet *France* Chicken leg, divided into drumstick (**pilon de cuisse**) and thigh (**gras de cuisse**)

cuisses de grenouilles *France* Frogs' legs, usually sautéed with butter, chopped garlic and parsley or served in a cream sauce

cuisson *France* Cooking

cuissot *France* Haunch of venison or wild boar

cuit(e) *France* Cooked; past participle of *cuire*, as in *bien cuit*, 'well cooked'

cuixa de xai al forn *Catalonia* Roast leg of lamb

cuka *Malaysia* Rice vinegar

cukor *Hungary* Sugar

culaccio *Italy* Rump of beef

culantrillo *Spain* Maidenhair fern

culatella *Italy* A smoked raw ham made from lean pork cut from the leg, similar to Parma ham. Sometimes soaked in wine before maturing. Very expensive, used for hors d'oeuvres. Also called **culatella di Parma**, **culatella di Zibello**

culatella di Parma, culatella di Zibello See **culatella**

cul de veau *France* Chump chop

culinaire *France* Culinary, relating to cookery

cullen skink *Scotland* A fish stew or soup made from onions sweated in butter, mixed with flour to make a roux, chopped potatoes and milk added, simmered, then 10 minutes before serving flaked smoked haddock or smoked cod added and the whole diluted with stock to the right consistency

cullis A misspelling or anglicized transliteration of the French word **coulis**

culotte de boeuf *France* Rump steak of beef

cultivated mushroom See **common mushroom**

cultivateur, à la *France* In the farmer's style, i.e. with mixed vegetables and pork or bacon

culture A large quantity of bacteria, yeast, fungal mycelium or fungal spores grown in a nutrient medium and used to start fermentation as in the production of wine, cheese, yoghurt, etc. Also called **ferment**

cultured buttermilk Buttermilk which has been fermented with a species of *Lactobacillus*. May be sweetened and flavoured for use as a drink or may be substituted for milk or buttermilk in recipes.

cultured milk Milk soured with various species of *Lactobacillus* at 20°C to give 0.45 to 0.6% lactic acid concentrations It has a refreshing acid taste

Cumberland ham *England* A large, traditional, strong-tasting ham, cured with salt, saltpetre and brown sugar, matured in air for 3 months. Usually boiled or baked.

Cumberland herb pudding *England* A dish of pearl barley, spring cabbage, onion, leeks, butter and egg. The vegetables and barley are fully cooked then mixed with egg and butter and baked in a pie dish at 180°C for 10 to 15 minutes.

Cumberland rum nicky *England* A rich double-crust tart filled with a sticky mixture of chopped stoned dates, soft brown sugar and stem ginger soaked in rum

Cumberland sand cake *England* A cake of eggs, caster sugar, corn flour, butter and flour (4:4:4:2:1) with 2 tbsp of baking powder per kg of flour, flavoured with nutmeg and lemon juice and made by the creaming method. Baked at 180°C for about 30 minutes. Originally served with sherry.

Cumberland sauce *England* A mixture of warmed redcurrant jelly, blanched and refreshed chopped shallots, lemon juice, orange juice, port and a little English mustard, finished with a blanched and refreshed fine **julienne** of orange zest. Served with cold ham.

Cumberland sausage *England* A sausage made of coarsely chopped pork with seasoning and nutmeg in a natural casing. Not linked but sold from a large coil. Now often modified with the addition of rusk and cereal.

cumbungi *Australia* A water plant, *Typhus domingensis* or *T orientalis*, from the northern river systems. The new shoots and the base of the more mature stems, after stripping them of their outer layers, are cooked like leeks. They have a flavour reminiscent of young artichokes or heart of palm. Also called **bulrush**

cumi-cumi *Indonesia* Squid

cumin 1. *England, France* The seeds of an annual plant, *Cuminum cyminum*, grown around the Mediterranean and through to East Asia. It has a strong pungent flavour and is much used in Arab, Indian and Spanish cooking. Also called **white cumin 2.** *France* Caraway

cumin des prés *France* Caraway seed

cumino *Italy* Cumin

Cuminum cyminum *Botanical name* Cumin

cumquat Kumquat

cu nang *Vietnam* Water chestnut

cuoccio *Italy* Gurnard, the fish

cuocere alla graticola *Italy* To grill

cuocere a vapore *Italy* To steam

cuocere in umido *Italy* To stew

cuore *Italy* Heart

cuore edule *Italy* Cockle

cuore rossa *Italy* A cockle used in Italian cooking with bright red flesh when alive

cuoriccini *Italy* Sicilian heart-shaped biscuits traditionally served at weddings

cup cakes Small sponge cakes cooked in individual bun tins or paper cases (NOTE: So called because originally baked in cups)

cup custard *United States* Crème renversée

cup leaf Daun mangkok

cup measure A volumetric method of measuring out ingredients now only used in the US and Australia, but once used in the UK. 1 US standard cup = 236 ml volume (8 US fluid oz.) and will hold 145 grams of plain flour, 200 grams of dry rice and 220 grams of caster sugar. The British standard cup was 285 ml (10 fluid oz.). See also **liquid measure**, **dry measure**, **can measure**, **market measure**, **volume measure**

curaçao The generic name for various orange-flavoured liqueurs used to flavour cakes and desserts

curcuma *France* Turmeric

cúrcuma *Spain* Turmeric

Curcuma longa *Botanical name* Turmeric

Curcuma zedoaria *Botanical name* Zedoary

Curcuma zerumbet *Botanical name* Zedoary

Curcumin A natural yellow food colouring obtained from turmeric. See also **E100**

curcumina *Italy* Turmeric

curd The solid which separates from milk or soya milk which has been coagulated and cut or stirred. Used to make curds and whey, cheese, or soya bean curd.

curd cheese A soft white cheese made from the curds which separate from a lactic acid fermentation and coagulation of milk. It is not pressed and is slightly sour tasting. often used for making cheesecake.

curd cheese pastry *Central Europe* Pastry made from equal parts of curd cheese, butter and flour. It resembles flaky pastry when cooked.

curdle, to To separate into visible immiscible solid and/or liquid phases as in the production of curds and whey from coagulated milk, or when mayonnaise breaks down into oil droplets and vinegar or when a cooked egg mixture separates

cure, to To preserve meat, game, poultry, fish or any flesh by smoking, salting or treating with salt, saltpetre, sodium nitrite or sugar or with brine or any combination of these. The purpose is to remove water from the flesh and to inhibit bacterial action. The nitrite accentuates the pink colour of haemoglobin. See also **dry-salt, to**, **pickling brine**

curled octopus A species of octopus, *Eledone cirrosa*, with a maximum length of 40 cm and curled tentacles with a single row of suckers. Not as fine a quality as the common octopus but often served braised in tomato sauce and sometimes canned. Also called **white octopus**

curly algae Wakame

curly cress See **cress**

curly endive See **endive**

curly kale Kale

curly parsley Parsley

curly seaweed Wakame

currant 1. Dried grape of the small black Corinth variety from Greece now grown elsewhere. More tart and with less sugar than the sultana and raisin. Also called **currant raisins 2.** The small, round berry of a variety of shrubs from Northern Europe and North Africa. See also **redcurrant**, **blackcurrant**, **white currant**

currant pasty A mixture of currants, brown sugar, spices, apple and pork scratchings sandwiched between 2 layers of pastry, baked and cut into squares

currant raisin *United States* Currant

currant tomato A tiny tomato, *Lycopersicon pimpinelli folium*, 1 cm in diameter and used for decoration

currie, sauce *France* Curry sauce made with white bouillon

currie à l'indienne, sauce *France* Finely sliced onion sweated in butter with a bouquet garni, mace and a cinnamon stick, sprinkled with curry powder, fried, then a mixture of equal parts of coconut milk and veal or fish stock added, simmered, strained and finished with cream and lemon juice. Also called **indienne, sauce**

curry 1. *England, France* A general term for highly spiced cooked dishes of meat, vegetables, fish, pulses, etc. originating from India and Southeast Asia, popular in the West, often containing varying proportions of hot chillies (NOTE: Curry means 'mixture' in Hindi and the dish got its name when foreigners asked what was being cooked and were told a mixture.) **2.** *South Asia* A stew with a pungent aromatic sauce made by browning onion in ghee, separating, adding meat which has been defatted and degristled to the fat, searing this, adding aromatics and frying over medium heat until the fat separates, then adding salt, water and chillies or sweet peppers, simmering for a long period adding water as necessary and finally adding onions and other vegetables towards the end. Also called **turrcarri**

curry butter A compound butter flavoured with curry powder, cayenne pepper, ginger and lemon juice, refrigerated as a roll and cut into 5 mm slices for use as a garnish

curry-flavoured oil Peanut oil flavoured with curry powder

curry leaf The leaves of a small tree, *Murraya koenigii*, from hilly regions of India which give off a spicy odour when bruised. Fresh leaves are used to add flavour to many Indian dishes. The dried leaves lose much of their flavour.

curry mayonnaise See **caboul sauce**

curry paste Ground spices and flavouring agents processed with garlic, chilli peppers and fresh ginger to a thick paste and fried in oil until the oil separates (about 10 minutes) and then mixed with a little salt. This will keep for a considerable time. Vinegar is added for vindaloo curry paste.

curry plant A shrub, *Helichrysum angustifolium*, of the daisy family from Southern Europe with silvery needle-like leaves which impart a mild curry (Indian spice mix) flavour to cooked dishes. Use like rosemary. (NOTE: Not to be confused with **curry leaf**.)

curry powder A mixture of ground spices used for making curry especially in the West. Made from a selection of coriander seeds, cumin seeds, mustard seeds, black peppercorns, fenugreek seeds and chillies to produce varying degrees of hotness, all of which are dry-roasted, together with unroasted dried ginger, turmeric, cinnamon and cloves. There are many variations, e.g. Madras and West Indian curry powder. Rarely used in Indian cooking, but useful for those not wishing to stock individual spices.

curry sauce Chopped onions and garlic cooked in fat without colour, flour and curry powder added and the roux cooked without browning the flour, tomato purée and stock added to form a smooth sauce, chopped apples, chutney, desiccated coconut, sultanas, grated fresh ginger and salt added, simmered and skimmed for 30 minutes. Served with meat, fish, eggs, etc.

currysill *Sweden* A typical smörgåsbord dish of sliced matjes herring, diced cold boiled potatoes and chopped hard-boiled eggs mixed and bound with a curry-flavoured mayonnaise and served cold

curuba A type of elongated passion fruit, *Passiflora maliformis*, from South America with a yellow green skin and a taste similar to, but slightly more acid, than passion fruit

Curworthy *England* A semi-hard cheese made with unpasteurized cows' milk from Devon and Cornwall. It is matured for 6 weeks and has a creamy buttery taste.

cuscinetti *Italy* Fried cheese sandwich (NOTE: Literally 'small cushion'.)

cush *United States* A cornmeal pancake

cushaw *United States* A large variety of crookneck squash

cush cush yam A red skinned yam from a plant, *Dioscorea trifida*, native to South America which produces several small tubers instead of the more normal single large tuber

cushion A cut of lamb, veal or beef from the inside top of the rear leg

cushion of veal *United Kingdom* The thick longitudinal muscle at the rear inside of the leg of veal, equivalent to topside of beef. Used for escalopes, roasting, braising and sautéing. Also called **nut**

cusk Tusk

cussy, à la *France* Garnished with large mushrooms, chestnuts, cock's kidneys and truffles, usually of steaks and roast chicken

custard 1. A general term for various sweetened milk-based sauces, flavoured with vanilla and thickened with flour and/or eggs **2.** *United Kingdom* English custard

custard apple The general name for a group of tropical fruits of the genus *Anona*, including atemoyas, cherimoyas, sweet sops and sour sops which generally have a scaly skin and a soft custard-like flesh tasting variously of combinations of pineapple, strawberry, banana, etc. Also called **annona**, **anona**

custard banana The fruit of a tree, *Asimina tribloa*, from the Southeast of the USA and Mexico. It looks and tastes something like a small vanilla-flavoured banana but has a thin skin and numerous seeds in the flesh.

custard cream See **crème pâtissière**

custard fritters Crème frites which have been battered

custard marrow 1. Patty pan squash **2.** Choko

custard powder *United Kingdom* A mixture of corn flour, sometimes yellow colouring, and artificial vanilla flavouring very popular in England for thickening sweetened milk to make English custard

custard sauce English custard

cut, to To use a knife or scissors to divide solid foods into smaller pieces

cut and fold, to To mix dry ingredients into a batter or foamed mixture by gently sprinkling them on the surface and very carefully incorporating them by slowly turning over the mixture with a metal spoon, spatula or knife

cut in, to To combine hard fat with dry ingredients by repeatedly cutting the fat with one or two knives beneath the surface of the the dry ingredients until it is reduced to small uniform pieces each coated with dry ingredients

cutlet A transverse section from the rib cage of an animal containing part of the vertebrae and ribs with accompanying flesh. Usually of lamb, veal or pork.

cutlet bat A heavy metal implement with a flat face about 10 cm by 7 cm and a handle used to thin out pieces of meat, fish, etc. by striking the food, usually contained between two pieces of polythene, on a solid work surface. See also **bat out, to**

cutlet frill A small piece of frilled white paper shaped like a chef's hat which is used to cover the end of the bare, scraped rib bone on a cutlet or roast joint after it has been cooked. Also called **frill**, **paper frill**

cutters See **pastry cutters**

cutting board A flat-surfaced board, usually wood, hard plastic or glass on which food is cut or chopped. Plastic boards are of different colours for different classes of food, but have been shown to be less hygienic than hardwood boards. See also **chopping board**

cuttlefish A cephalopod, *Sepia officinalis*, from the Mediterranean and eastern Atlantic with an oval body and head from which two long and eight short tentacles spring, in all about 25 cm long. It has one internal stiffening bone (**cuttlebone**). The guts which together with the parrot-like beak must be removed before cooking include the ink sac, the contents of which can be used in an accompanying sauce. Cooked like squid or octopus. Sometimes eaten in East Asia as a snack food when in its dried form. See also **little cuttlefish**

cuu *Vietnam* Lamb

cwt Abbreviation for hundredweight, a unit of weight still used in the USA

Cyamopsis psoraloides *Botanical name* Guar bean

cyanocobalamin Vitamin B12

cyclamate An artificial sweetener about 30 times as sweet as sugar, now banned in many countries

Cydonia oblonga *Botanical name* Quince

cygne *France* A swan-shaped pastry filled with chantilly cream

Cymbopogan citratus *Botanical name* Lemon grass

cymling Patty pan squash

Cynara scolymus *Botanical name* The globe artichoke

Cyperus esculentus *Botanical name* Tiger nut

Cyphomandra betacea *Botanical name* Tamarillo

cyprus oval Shamouti

cysteine hydrochloride See **E920**

Cystophyllum fusiforme *Botanical name* Hiziki

DEFGHIJK

daai dau nga choy *China* Soya bean sprouts

daai gaai choy *China* One of the oriental mustards with a rounded lettuce-type head, curly pale green leaves and thick grooved stems. It has a slightly astringent taste and is usually pickled or salted. Also called **Swatow mustard cabbage**

daam *China* Sea urchin

daanti *South Asia* A ceramic pestle used with a matching mortar (**imamdusta**) for grinding soft grains and spices

daarim *Nepal* Pomegranate

dab A small flatfish, *Limanda limanda*, up to 25 cm long, from North West European coastal waters, white below and brown with greenish spots above. Cooked as plaice.

da bai cai *China* Chinese cabbage

dabo *East Africa* The Ethiopian name for bread

dabo fir fir *East Africa* An Ethiopian snack of bread with butter and berbere

dabo kolo *East Africa* An Ethiopian snack made from whole wheat flour mixed with berbere spice mix to taste (approx. 8 tbsp per kg of flour), sugar (4 tbsp per kg) and salt (2 tsp per kg) and sufficient water to make a thick dough. This is kneaded, rested, then 250 g softened butter per kg of flour is incorporated and the dough is rolled and cut into small cylinders and baked at 180°C for 30 minutes until browned on all sides. Cooled and stored in an airtight container.

dabulamanzi salad *Caribbean* A St Vincent salad made from finely chopped carrot, ginger, cabbage and garlic, lightly sautéed in sesame oil then poured over washed and dried lettuce leaves followed by chopped avocado flesh

Dacca *South Asia* A cheese made from cow or buffalo milk, ripened for 2 to 3 weeks in wicker baskets, then smoked

dace A bony freshwater fish, *Leuciscus leuciscus*, resembling in shape a small haddock. Steamed, baked or fried. Also called **dare**, **dart**

dacquoise *France* A speciality of Dax consisting of layers of meringue containing toasted and coarsely ground nuts interspersed with whipped cream and soft fruits such as raspberries and strawberries, the whole decorated and circular in shape. Cut in wedges for serving.

dadarisi *Netherlands* An omelette stuffed with a spicy Indonesian filling

dadels *Netherlands* Dates

dadi *Italy* Dice, of vegetables, etc.

dadlar *Sweden* Dates

dadler *Denmark, Norway* Dates

da dou *China* Soya beans

daging kambing *Indonesia, Malaysia* Lamb

daging kerbau *Indonesia* Buffalo meat

daging smor *Netherlands* Stewed meat, Indonesian style

dagwood sandwich *United States* A multi-layered sandwich with a variety of fillings in between each layer

dahchini *South Asia* **1.** Cinnamon **2.** Cassia

dahi *Nepal, South Asia* Yoghurt

dahi balle *South Asia* Fried bean cakes served in a herb and spice-flavoured yoghurt sauce

dahl See **dhal**

dahorpt *Balkans* Diced mutton simmered with onions and herbs until tender, reserved, rice cooked in the strained cooking liquor with chopped sweet green peppers, mixed with the meat and lightly vinegared. See also **kissela dahorp**

-dai *Japan* Red sea bream, as in **kinmedai**

dai choy goh *China* Agar agar

daidai *Japan* Seville orange

daikon *Japan* A shorter and rounder variety of **mooli** used in the same way

daikon no nimono *Japan* 4 cm pieces of daikon boiled in salted water until tender and

169

simmered in **dashi** with a little soya sauce and **mirin** and covered with an **otoshibuta** for about 30 minutes

daikon oroshi *Japan* Finely grated daikon or mooli used as a marinade especially for octopus and to mask or remove strong fishy smells

daikon shreds *Japan* Very fine almost hair-like shreds of mooli made by cutting a long thin ribbon like a wide potato peeling, rolling it up and cutting it across in very thin slices. Used as a garnish for sushi.

daing *Philippines* Cleaned fish which have been salted and dried in the sun

dai rau song *Vietnam* A platter of mixed herbs, salad leaves, raw vegetables cut in strips and cooked rice or noodles served with meals as a side dish

dairy The buildings in which milk is removed from the animals and further processed into cream, butter, cheese and other milk products. Nowadays removal and processing are usually carried out at different locations.

dairy products Milk and all other products derived directly from it such as cheese, butter, cream, yoghurt, etc.

dai suen *China* Asian leek

daizu *Japan* Dried soya beans

daktyla *Greece* A long loaf of bread, topped with sesame seeds and made up of several sections easily pulled apart

dal See **dhal**

dalchini *South Asia* Cinnamon and cassia bark

Dalia *Romania* A cows' milk cheese similar to **Kashkaval**

dalle *France* A thin slice or escalope of round fish cut across the bone (NOTE: Literally 'slab'.)

damaschina *Italy* Damson

damasco *Portugal* Apricot

damask cream *England* A junket made with sweetened single cream flavoured with nutmeg and brandy, set with rennet at 37°C for 2 to 3 hours, and carefully decorated with a mixture of clotted cream and rose water. Also called **Devonshire junket**

Damaszenerpflaume *Germany* Damson

dame *Italy* Small raisin cakes

dame blanche *France* A common Belgian and northern French dessert of white ice cream, whipped cream and chocolate sauce

Damenkäse *Germany* A soft rich, cows' milk cheese. See also **Butterkäse**

damper *Australia* Unleavened bread made from flour, salt and water cooked on a griddle, barbecue or in hot wood fire ashes

Dampfbraten *Germany* Beef stew

Dampfnudeln *Germany* Sweetened yeast-raised, flour-based dumplings or noodles, steamed or poached in milk and served with custard, stewed fruit or jam

Dampfwürstel *Austria* A mild sausage containing beef and bacon fat bound with a little **fécule**, lightly scalded and possibly smoked

damson A small blue black plum with a yellow green flesh from a Middle Eastern tree, *Prunus damascena* or *P. insititia*, with a greyish yeast bloom. Rather acid but excellent in preserves and cooked dishes.

damson and apple tansy *England* Cooked apples and stoned damsons fried in butter with sugar until soft, mixed with ground cloves and cinnamon followed by stiffly beaten egg whites. Cooked over a low heat until set, sprinkled with sugar and browned under the grill. Originally flavoured with tansy.

dan *China* Egg

dana *Turkey* Veal

Danablu Danish blue

Danbo *Denmark* A hard cows' milk cheese which is salted in brine and matured for 5 months, often waxed and with internal holes like Emmental. Fairly mild in flavour and often contains caraway seeds. Contains 45% water, 24% fat and 29% protein.

Dancy tangerine *United States* The traditional Christmas tangerine is an old (1867) variety of mandarin grown from seed by Colonel Dancy. It has a deep orange-red thin skin with a tender well-flavoured flesh. They tend to decay rapidly.

dandelion A common European wild plant, *Taraxacum officinale*. The young and/or garden blanched leaves are used in salads and the ground and roasted roots are used to make a coffee substitute.

dan gao *China* Cake

danger zone The range of temperatures most suitable for bacterial growth, 7 to 60°C (45 to 140°F). Food should not be kept in this range for any length of time.

dang gui *China* The dried root of a relative of angelica, *Angelica sinensis*, used to flavour soup and reputed to have medicinal properties

dang noi *Thailand* Cassava

dango *Japan* Dumpling

Danish *United States* A Danish pastry

Danish blue *Denmark* A blue-veined white and crumbly cooked-curd cows' milk cheese made commercially in large quantities. It is inoculated with *Penicillium roquefortii* spores to produce the blue veining. It is dry-salted, ripened for 3 months and held in a cold store for a further 2 months. The flavour is sharp and somewhat salty. Marketed aggressively.

Danish blue brie *Denmark* A Danish version of a blue-veined Brie cheese

Danish mellow blue *Denmark* A more mellow and creamier textured version of Danish blue cheese

Danish open sandwich See **smørrebrød**

Danish pastries Sweet cakes and buns made with **Danish pastry** usually filled with fruit, custard, jam or the like. Examples are spandauer, wienerlangd, kammar and borgmästarfläta, all strangely enough from Sweden.

Danish pastry A yeasted, egg and sugar-enriched, strong flour dough (2 eggs per kg of flour) brought together with cold milk, layered with 0.6 times the weight of flour in butter, using the English puff pastry method with 3 threefold turns, resting between turns as usual. The pastry is rolled out to the appropriate thickness, garnished appropriately, proved and then baked at 230°C.

Danish salami A type of salami made with a mixture of pork, beef or veal and a high proportion of pork fat, coloured red to resemble meat, dry-salted or brined, air-dried and possibly smoked. Eaten raw in thin slices and not suitable for cooking.

dansk fläskkotlett *Sweden* Danish pork chops made from seasoned chops rubbed with curry powder, fried quickly in butter, soured cream added and all simmered for 10 minutes. Garnished with diced ham and apple and sliced onion sweated in butter.

dansk leverpostej *Denmark* A pâté made from calf's liver, flour, cream, butter, eggs, onions, spices and seasoning served warm with boiled potatoes or cold with open sandwiches, etc.

dansk potatis *Sweden* Large potatoes baked with the skin on at 200°C for 45 minutes, rolled between the hand and a board to soften the inside, opened and topped with chopped prawns in creamed butter

dansk wienerbrød *Denmark* Danish pastry (NOTE: Literally 'Danish Vienna bread'.)

darang *Philippines* Dried smoked fish which develop a characteristic deep red colour

darchini *South Asia* Cinnamon

dare Dace

dare oh *Burma* A rounded deep pan similar to a wok made of brass or cast iron with a handle at either side

dariole *France* A small pastry with custard cooked in a dariole mould

dariole mould A small bucket-shaped mould used to make individual desserts such as crème caramel, madeleines, etc.

Dariworld *United States* A semi-hard cooked-curd cows' milk cheese, salted in brine then ripened in plastic packs. Contains 45% water, 27% fat and 23% protein.

darjeeling An expensive unblended black tea with a very fine flavour from the foothills of the Himalayas. Often drunk without milk or sugar.

dark brown sugar *United States* Muscovado sugar

dark soya sauce A less salty version of soya sauce used to colour food as well as for its full-bodied flavour

dark sugar General term for the various types of **brown sugar**

darn *China* Hen's egg

darne *France* A thick slice or steak of fish cut across the backbone and including the bone. See also **fish steak**

dart Dace

dartois *France* 1. A garnish of celery, carrots, turnips and potatoes used with meat dishes 2. Two pieces of sweet or savoury puff pastry sandwiched together with a sweet or savoury filling and baked

dasheen *Caribbean* A tropical and subtropical plant, *Colocasia esculenta* var. *antiquorum*, brought from Southeast Asia to the Caribbean as a staple food for slaves. The leaves are edible and the tubers of the plant (referred to as **taro** or **cocoyam**) may be boiled, baked or roasted. See also **taro**, **cocoyam** (NOTE: The name dasheen is a corruption of *de Chine*, meaning 'from China'.)

dasheen leaf The fan-like leaf of taro and similar tubers of species of *Colocasia*, used as a vegetable and in **callaloo soup**. Also called **arvi leaf**, **patra**

dashi *Japan* A fish stock made from dried seaweed (**kelp** or **kombu**), dried Pacific bonito flakes and other flavourings. The first infusion of the raw materials is called **ichiban dashi** and is used for soups, whilst the second, **niban dashi**, is used as a stock or cooking liquor. See also **katsuodashi**, **Hondashi**

date The fruit of the date palm, *Phoenix dactylifera*, with a yellow skin and brown sweet flesh enclosing a single elongated stone, the whole about 4 cm by 2 cm, which grow in clusters arranged in two rows along a central stalk. Usually traded in the dried form which is sweet and sticky. Popular at Christmas in Europe as a snack and also used to sweeten and flavour cakes.

date mark A date stamped on a packaged food item indicating either the use-by date, best-before date, best-before-end date or **display-until date**

date mussel See **sea date**

date shell See **sea date**

dátil (*plural* **dátiles**) *Spain* Date

dátil de mar *Spain* Sea date

datolya *Hungary* Dates

datte *France* A date

datte de mer *France* A sea date

Datteln *Germany* Dates

datteri *Italy* Dates

datteri farciti *Italy* Stuffed dates

dattero di mare *Italy* Sea date

daub, to To lard

daube *France* A rich casserole made from previously marinated meat with a selection of vegetables, wine, garlic, onions and seasonings according to region. Cooked slowly in a sealed pot and traditionally served with boiled potatoes or pasta.

daube disef An egg stew from Mauritius, made with hard-boiled eggs and new potatoes boiled in their skins, both fried until brown, mixed with a sauce made from chopped onions, garlic, green chillies, ginger, parsley and thyme all sweated in oil, chopped skinned tomatoes, tomato purée, sugar, seasoning and water and finished with chopped coriander and petit pois

daubière *France* An earthenware casserole with a tight-fitting lid used to cook daubes. Originally they had a deep lid in which burning charcoal could be put.

Daucus carota *Botanical name* Carrot

dau gok *China* A dark green variety of long bean

dau hao *Vietnam* Oyster sauce

dau hu *Vietnam* Bean curd

dau hu chien *Vietnam* Fried bean curd

dau hu chung *Vietnam* Bean curd

dau hu ki *Vietnam* Dried bean curd

dauil nakhud *Central Asia* Yellow split peas

dau me *Vietnam* Sesame seed oil

dau mil, dau miu *China* 1. Pea leaf 2. Pea shoot

daum kesom *Indonesia, Malaysia* Vietnamese mint

daumont, à la *France* Garnished with mushrooms, soft fish roe, crayfish tails and sometimes fish quenelles. Used for fish.

daun bawang *Indonesia, Malaysia* Scallion or spring onion

daun jeruk purut *Indonesia* Makrut lime leaves

daun kari *Indonesia* Curry leaf

daun kari pla *Malaysia* Curry leaf

daun kemangi *Indonesia* The most commonly used basil

daun ketumbar *Indonesia, Malaysia* Coriander leaves

daun limau purut *Malaysia* Makrut lime

daun mangkok *South Asia* A shrub, *Polyscias scutellarium*, whose aromatic young leaves are used as a green vegetable, usually shredded. The whole leaves are also used to hold food.

daun pandan *Indonesia, Malaysia* Screwpine

daun pudina *Malaysia* Mint

dauphin *France* A dolphin

Dauphin *France* A cows' milk cheese from the near the Belgian border, flavoured with herbs and spices and formed into decorative shapes. The cheese itself is similar to **Maroilles**.

dauphine, à la *France* With pommes dauphine

dau phong *Vietnam* Peanut

dau phong rang *Vietnam* Roasted peanuts used as a garnish and for flavouring

daurade *France* Gilt-head bream

daurade commune *France* See **bream 1**

dau see *China* See **black bean 2**

dau xanth *Vietnam* Mung bean or bean sprout

Davidson's plum *Australia* A very sharp sloe-like fruit with an intense acid flavour about 5 cm long which comes from a 12-metre northern tree, *Davidsonia pruriens*. It is used in small quantities in jams, dressings and desserts. It can be used as a substitute for **tamarind**.

da xia *China* Prawn

dayap *Philippines* A small lime (up to 1.5 cm diameter) used as a souring agent

DeArbol chilli A small long and thin, very hot dried chilli pepper with a bright shiny skin. Should be used with care.

deauvillaise, à la *France* In the style of Deauville in Normandy. Used especially of sole poached with cream and chopped onions.

dębowiecka *Poland* A firm medium-sized slicing sausage from Poznan, made with pork containing only a little fat

debrecen *Hungary* A spicy sausage made of 2 parts lean pork, 1 part pork fat and 1 part beef, seasoned and flavoured with spices. Used in various stews.

debrecener rohwurst *Hungary* A hard **Rohwurst** made entirely of pork

debrecziner *Hungary* A spicy coarse-textured sausage similar in size to the Frankfurter

decaffeinated coffee Coffee made in the usual way from green beans which have been solvent treated to selectively remove the caffeine. It has a similar flavour to, but is not as stimulating as coffee.

decant, to To gently pour off the clear liquid from the top of a mixture of liquid and heavier particles, where the latter have settled to the bottom. Usually applied to wine to separate it from the crystals of tartaric acid which are precipitated on long standing.

decanter A glass container with a stopper, often decorated, in which decanted wine or other drinks are kept for serving

decentralized service Service where food is prepared in bulk and sent to to serving points where it is placed onto dishes or trays for onward dispatch, e.g. in hospitals

dechi *Nepal, South Asia* A tinned brass cooking pot. See also **degchi**

decilitre One tenth of a litre, 100 millilitres. Abbreviation **dl**

decompose, to To undergo a process of bacterial, fungal or enzymic attack which causes food to break down into usually strong-smelling and often toxic components. Some decomposition enhances flavour and texture e.g. in game, cheese and many fermented foods, but these can easily go bad as the process of decomposition has started.

decorate, to To make pleasing to the eye by adding shapes, colours and textures to a dish, e.g. to cakes, desserts, cold buffet items, sandwiches, salads, etc.

decorated eggs Painted and decorated hard-boiled eggs in their shells. Often used at Easter as symbols of resurrection or of fertility.

decorating bag *United States* Piping bag

decorating comb A flat plate or spatula with serrated edges used to make ridged surfaces on cake icing. Different edges may have different profiles.

découper *France* To carve, joint or cut in pieces

dee la *Thailand* Sesame seed

deem sum *China* Dim sum

deep-dish pizza *United States* A North American style pizza made in a dish with sides like a flan or tart tin. Used so that more filling than is usual with a traditional pizza may be cooked with the dough. Also called **deep-pan pizza**

deep fat Hot fat or oil of sufficient depth to completely cover the item being fried. Usually held in a special cooking utensil designed to prevent accidents.

deep-freeze An insulated and refrigerated cabinet or chest for freezing and storing frozen food at temperatures below −20°C

deep-freeze, to To cool food below −20°C so as to prevent deterioration

deep-freezing A method of preserving food by storing at temperatures below −10°C, usually around −18°C to −20°C

deep-fry, to To cook food by immersing it in and covering it with hot fat or oil at a temperature between 175 and 195°C. The food is quickly sealed, crisped and cooked if not too thick.

deep-fryer The cooking utensil which contains sufficient depth of fat and a means of heating it, used for deep-frying. It should have a cool zone below the heating element and hot fat, to collect burnt fragments of food, and a thermometer and/or thermostat to control the temperature.

deep-poaching, fish Large cuts of fish or whole fish cooked in simmering court bouillon or acidulated and salted water until cooked. Cooking is finished when the flesh leaves the bone. Usually garnished with picked parsley, plain boiled potatoes, slices of blanched aromatic vegetables and a little cooking liquor and served separately with a suitable sauce.

deep sea argentine See **argentine**

deepwater prawn A large prawn, *Pandalus borealis*, up to 13 cm long, red when live and found from Greenland to the UK, large quantities being fished in Norwegian waters. Also called **northern prawn**, **deepwater shrimp**

deepwater shrimp See **deepwater prawn**

deer A family of herbivores, *Cervidae,* found throughout the world. Most of the males have bony antlers which are shed and regrown annually throughout life. They range in size from 55 cm high at the shoulder to 2.4 m. The important meat varieties are red, fallow and roe deer in Europe, the white-tailed mule deer and moose in North America and the caribou and reindeer of Arctic regions. The meat is known as venison.

defrost, to 1. To thaw or warm up deep-frozen food to room temperature in readiness for cooking or eating. Usually done by slow application of heat to avoid cooking part of the food, often in a microwave oven. **2.** To warm up a refrigerator or deep-freeze so as to remove ice and snow encrusted on the internal surfaces

degchi *South Asia* A tinned brass cooking pot with a heavy base, straight sides and no handles used for cooking over charcoal or wood. Also called **bhagoni**, **dechi**, **patila**

degh *Central Asia* The narrow-necked conical cooking pot of Afghanistan

degh fasli *South Asia* A type of cassoulet made with any variety of beans and breast of lamb cut in cubes and marinated in processed and liquefied onions. After all are simmered together with tomatoes, sweet peppers and aromatic spices and herbs the meat is removed and fried in butter, the separated cooking liquor is defattted and reduced by half, then all is recombined and flavoured with ground mace and bay leaves.

deghi mirch *South Asia* Kashmiri chilli

déglaçage *France* **1.** The process of deglazing **2.** Defrosting

déglacer *France* **1.** To deglaze **2.** To defrost

deglaze, to To dissolve and loosen coagulated meat juices which stick to the bottom of a roasting dish or frying pan using water, stock or wine. The resulting solution or suspension is sometimes reduced in volume by boiling and is used to add flavour to sauce or stock.

degorge, to See **dégorger, faire**

dégorger, faire 1. *France* To soak in water to remove impurities before cooking; used of e.g. fish, offal, meat, etc. **2.** To remove water and sometimes bitter flavours from a food by chopping, covering with salt, allowing to drain for some time then rinsing and drying. Used with cucumbers, aubergines, courgettes, kantolas and karellas.

dégraisser 1. *France* To skim off fat and scum from the top of a simmering liquid as in the preparation of stocks and sauces **2.** To remove fat from meat

degrease, to To remove fat from the surface of a liquid, either by skimming, decanting or soaking it into paper

degree Celsius The divisions of the Celsius scale of temperature of which there are 100 between the freezing point and the boiling point of water, 0°C and 100°C respectively. Written °C. Also called **degree Centigrade**

degree Centigrade See **degree Celsius**

degree Fahrenheit The divisions of the Fahrenheit scale of temperature of which there are 180 between the freezing point and the boiling point of water, 32°F and 212°F respectively. Written °F.

degue *West Africa* Millet porridge (**tô**) mixed with soured milk and honey

dégustation *France* Tasting or sampling e.g. of wine, oysters, etc.

dehumidify, to To remove water vapour from air, either by passing the air over a chemical which absorbs water or a cold surface which condenses it. Used in humid areas.

dehydrate, to To remove water from a food product generally to improve its keeping quality. Food may be dehydrated by sun or air drying, heating, salting or applying a vacuum whilst adding heat.

deipnon The first part of a formal meal in ancient Greece when the food was served. See also **symposium**

déjeuner *France* Lunch

deli *United States* A delicatessen where food can also be eaten on the premises

delicatessen A shop or area within a shop selling ready-to-eat savoury items such as preserved meats and fish, cheese, slicing sausages, salads, pâtés, dips, etc.

délice *England, France* A thin fillet of fish with the two ends folded underneath to form a rectangular parcel. Usually poached. (NOTE: Literally 'a delight'.)

Délice de Saint Cyr *France* A rich, triple-cream cheese made from cows' milk in the area surrounding Paris

Delikatessaufschnitt *Germany* Assorted cold meats, assiette anglaise

deliquescent The description of a substance that absorbs water from the atmosphere and dissolves in it, e.g. pure salt without additives will cake and eventually dissolve

delizie *Italy* **1.** Appetizers **2.** Delicacies

della rice A type of long-grain rice

Delmonico potatoes *United States* Potato balls, boiled then dressed with butter, lemon juice, chopped parsley and seasoning

Delmonico steak *United States* A boneless beef steak 2.5 to 5 cm thick, cut from the wing and fore rib with all bone fat and coarse meat removed. Treat like fillet steak. Also called **spencer steak**

dem à la Saint Louisienne *West Africa* A Senegalese dish of stuffed fish in the French style. See also **mulet farci à la Saint-Louisienne**

Demeltorte *Austria* A pastry filled with candied fruit

demerara sugar A light brown sugar with coarse crystals originally from Demerara in British Guiana but now produced widely from raw cane sugar. Used for coffee and various desserts. Less moist than muscovado.

demersal Which live near or on the sea bed. Used of e.g. flatfish.

demi *France* Half

demi-deuil *France* With black and white ingredients, usually poached chicken, sweetbreads, eggs, shellfish, etc. for white and truffles for black, and served with suprême sauce (NOTE: Literally 'half-mourning'.)

demi-deuil salad A salad of sliced boiled waxy potatoes, seasoned, mixed with real truffle shavings and dressed with a mixture of olive oil, vinegar, French mustard and single cream

demi-doux *France* A type of bloater. See also **bouffi**

demi-glace, sauce *England, France* A mixture of equal parts of **espagnole sauce** and brown stock reduced by simmering to a half quantity, skimming as necessary, and finally strained. Used as a basis for other sauces.

demi-loaf *United States* A small individual-sized loaf

demi-sel *France* **1.** Slightly salted, as of butter, cheese, etc. **2.** A moist, white, salted curd cheese made from cows' milk and with 40% butterfat content. It has a mild, slightly sour flavour.

demi-suisse *France, Switzerland* A 30 g Suisse cheese. Also called **petit-suisse**

demi-tasse *France, United States* A half cup or a small cup usually used to serve coffee

demoiselles de Cherbourg *France* Small lobsters

denature, to To change the properties of protein, usually by heat or chemical action. Generally denaturing reduces the solubility and changes the colour and appearance of protein, e.g. as when heating egg white or blood.

dendang *Indonesia* Surf clam

dénerver *France* To remove tendons, gristle, arteries, veins and membranes from meat and muscle

dengaku *Japan* Grilled, skewered and coated with a sweetened **miso**. See also **miso-dengaku**

dengu *East Africa* A Kenyan dish of cooked mung dal mixed with sautéed onions and coconut milk, brought to the boil and flavoured with paprika. Served with rice, chapatis or mashed sweet potatoes.

dénoyauter *France* To stone or pit a fruit

density **1.** Mass or weight per unit volume. e.g. water has a density of 1 kg per litre, saturated brine about 1.22 kg per litre and vegetable oil about 0.8 kg per litre. **2.** The quality of hardness, thickness, opacity, etc. of something. See also **specific gravity**

dent corn *United States* A common tall form of maize, *Zea mays* var. *indentata*, with yellow or white kernels in which the hard coat covers only the sides so that they are indented at the top.

dent-de-lion *France* Dandelion

dente, al *Italy* Al dente

denté *France* Dentex, the fish (NOTE: Literally 'toothed'.)

dentex The general species name of a group of Mediterranean fish, *Dentex dentex*, similar to sea bream with a firm flesh and up to 1 m in length. Baked or grilled.

dentice *Italy* Dentex, the fish

dentón *Spain* Dentex, the fish

Denver sandwich *United States* Western sandwich

deodorize, to To remove or mask the smell of cooking food, e.g. with herbs or spices

dépecer *France* **1.** To joint **2.** To carve

dépouiller *France* **1.** To skim fat, scum and similar from the surface of stock, soup, sauce and the like **2.** To remove the skin of an animal

Derby *England* A pale yellow, hard but flaky textured cheese made from cows' milk. Mild when young but matures over 6 months to develop a fuller flavour.

Derby sage parsnips *England* Parsnips peeled and cut in smallish pieces, parboiled, dried, coated in a mixture of flour and finely grated sage Derby (2:1) and seasoning and then roasted in the oven using dripping or oil, basting occasionally

Derby sauce *England* A proprietary sauce invented by Escoffier. Worcestershire sauce is used as a substitute.

derek tibs *East Africa* Fried meat from Ethiopia served 'derek', i.e. without sauce

derere *East Africa* The Tanzanian name for **okra**

derrynaflan *Ireland* A semi-soft Irish cheese

dés, en *France* Diced

desayuno *Mexico, Spain* Breakfast

Desenchildkröte *Germany* Terrapin

desert raisin *Australia* Bush tomato

deshebrar *Spain* To shred

déshydrater *France* To dehydrate

desiccate, to To dry or remove water from substances, as in desiccated coconut

desiccated coconut The grated or shredded white inner lining of the coconut, vacuum-dried at 70°C and used as an ingredient in sweet and savoury dishes and as a decoration

desnatar *Spain* To skim

désossé Boned, without bones

dessaler *France* To desalt by soaking in water

dessert *Denmark, England, France, Norway* The pudding, ice cream, fruit or other sweet item served at or towards the end of meal

dessert apple A normally sweet apple suitable for eating raw. Because they do not lose their shape on cooking, dessert apples are used to make uncovered decorative apple tarts.

dessert cream Mixtures of cream with custard and/or fruit purée, often set with gelatine and with a smooth creamy texture. Used as the basis of many desserts.

dessert grape Special grape varieties selected for eating raw. Classed as: sweetwater – the earliest ripening; muscat – the second to ripen and having the finest flavour; and vinous, which have less flavour but are strong-growing and mature late in the season.

dessert herbs The principal herbs used in desserts, custards, fruit salads, compotes and the like are angelica, aniseed, bay (custard only), bergamot, dill, elderflower, lemon balm, lemon thyme (custard only), lemon verbena, mint, rosemary, rose petals, scented geraniums and sweet cicely

dessert rice Rice prepared for compounded sweets, puddings and desserts, etc. Long-grain rice is washed and blanched twice, cooked with boiling milk, sugar, butter, salt, and vanilla or orange zest flavouring in the oven without stirring, when cooked removed from the oven and enriched with egg yolks. Nowadays dessert rice more often made with short-grain rice cooked in sweetened milk, drained and sweetening adjusted.

dessertspoon A standard volume measure, 10 ml in the UK and 12 ml in Australia, not defined in the USA. Abbreviation **dsp**

destone, to To stone

détrempe *France* A slack mixture of flour and water

devein, to To remove the large vein which runs along the back of the tail meat of a shrimp or prawn

Deventer koek *Netherlands* Deventer cake, a spice cake from Deventer

devil butter A compound butter flavoured with cayenne pepper, vinegar, Worcestershire and Tabasco sauces, refrigerated in a roll and cut into 5 mm slices for garnishing meat and fish dishes

devilled Strongly flavoured with a selection of Worcestershire and Tabasco sauces, mustard, cayenne pepper and vinegar. See also **diable, à la**

devilled kidneys Peeled, cored and chopped kidneys, sautéed in butter, drained and mixed off the heat with boiling sauce diable. Usually served on toast.

devilled sauce See **diable, sauce**

devilled sausages Sausages baked in the oven, basted at intervals with a mixture of mustard, chutney, anchovy essence, oil and cayenne pepper. Served with mashed potatoes.

devilling Application of a selection from Worcestershire sauce, Tabasco sauce, mustard, cayenne pepper, vinegar and other highly flavoured condiments to the surface of meat, fish, etc. prior to panéing and frying. See also **diable, à la**

devil's dung Asafoetida

devil's food cake *United States* A rich, sweet and dark brown chocolate cake

devils on horseback As angels on horseback but with prunes instead of oysters

devil's taro Black bean curd

devil's tongue 1. Snake palm plant **2.** Black bean curd

Devon flat *England* A flat biscuit made with self-raising flour, caster sugar, clotted cream and egg (4:2:2:1), brought together with a little milk and baked at 220°C

Devon garland *England* A cows' milk cheese from North Devon flavoured with fresh herbs

Devon sausage *Australia* A rather cheap slicing sausage made of manufacturing meat, principally pork and mutton. Also called **devon** (NOTE: Named after a breed of Australian cattle)

Devonshire chudleighs *England* A smaller version of **Cornish splits**

Devonshire cream Clotted cream

Devonshire hog pudding *England* Hog pudding

Devonshire junket *England* Damask cream

Devonshire pie *England* Layers of pork chops, sliced apples which have been peeled and cored, and sliced onions in alternate layers in a pie dish with sugar and allspice on each layer of chops. Covered with gravy and topped with flaky pastry. Baked at 220°C for 10 minutes and then at 180°C for 90 minutes.

Devonshire split *England* A sweet yeasted bun, split open and filled with jam and whipped cream

Devonshire squab pie *England* A deep pie filled with lamb, apples, onions and seasoning and covered in a pastry crust prior to baking

dewberry An early ripening soft fruit hybrid of the blackberry of the genus *Rubus*, similar to, but larger and juicier that a blackberry and with a more trailing habit. Cook or use as blackberry.

dewcup Lady's mantle

dewwahra *North Africa* Lamb's tripe in a coriander and garlic sauce eaten during Eid in Morocco

dextral Term used of a flatfish in which the eye on the left of the juvenile form moves to join that on the right which becomes the uppermost side of the adult fish

dextrin A polysaccharide made by reducing the number of repeating glucose units in starch. Used in commercial food preparations and when dissolved in water as a glaze for bread and rolls.

dextrose See **glucose**

d-glucono-1,5-lactone See **E575**

DHA See **docosahexaenoic acid**

dhal *South Asia* **1.** Term used for dehusked and split pigeon peas, lentils or similar small pulses (NOTE: From the Hindi word meaning 'to split'.) **2.** A thin gruel-like dish of cooked dehusked split pulses with aromatic flavourings and spice, onions and other vegetables, very commonly served at Indian meals. Also called **dal**, **dahl**, **dholl**

dhania *South Asia* Coriander seed

dhania-jeera, **dhania-jira** *South Asia* Mixed coriander and cumin seeds (2:1), dry-roasted to bring out the flavour and ground

dhaniya *South Asia* Coriander seed

dhansak *South Asia* A mild lamb or chicken stew with vegetables, lentils and spices topped with fried onion rings. Originally brought from Iran to India by the Parsees.

dhansak masala *South Asia* A mixture of ground coriander and cumin seeds

dholl See **dhal**

dhuli urd *South Asia* Dehusked black gram from which all traces of black have been washed out

dhwen-jang *Korea* A strong-flavoured salty bean paste similar to **hatcho-miso**

diabetic food Food with reduced sugar and carbohydrate suitable for diabetic persons, especially jams, marmalades, soft drinks, biscuits, cakes and confectionery items

diable *France* **1.** An unglazed earthenware cooking pot in two symmetrical halves which when put together resembles a ball with two flat sides and a long handle. Used for cooking chestnuts and vegetables without water either in the oven or on top of the stove. Can be shaken and turned over for even cooking. **2.** Kidneys or poussins, split, flattened, grilled and served with sauce diable

diable, à la *France* Strongly flavoured with a selection of Worcestershire and Tabasco sauces, mustard, cayenne pepper and vinegar

diable, sauce *England, France* A reduction of chopped shallots, white wine, vinegar, cayenne pepper and mignonette pepper simmered with **demi-glace**, strained and seasoned. Served with fried or grilled fish or meat. Also called **devilled sauce**

diable de mer *France* Monkfish

diablo, en *Mexico, Spain* Devilled, hot and spicy

diablotins *France* **1.** Cheese-flavoured croûtons **2.** Christmas crackers

diacetin See **glycerol di-acetate**

diamante citron The principal Italian citron grown in Calabria with a very thick, yellow smooth and slightly ridged skin

diamant noir *France* French black truffle

diane, sauce *England, France* A poivrade sauce enriched with cream

diaphragm The muscular partition separating the lung and abdominal cavity in mammals. Not usually traded separately except in beef cattle.

diastase See **amylase**

diavola, alla *Italy* Devilled, served with a spicy sauce, often of a chicken, split, flattened and grilled

diavolini *Italy* Small fried spicy rice cakes

dibs *Middle East* A sugar syrup made from the sugar in sweet grapes, raisins or carob beans by expression, extraction and concentration. Used as a sweetener.

dicalcium diphosphate See **E540**

dice, to To cut into small cubes with sides between 5 and 15 mm

di centro *Italy* Parmesan cheese made in July and August. See also **Parmigiano Reggiano**

dick *Germany* Thick

Dictyophoria phalloidea *Botanical name* Bamboo fungus

dienone A breakdown product of ptaquiloside found in bracken and a potent carcinogen

diente *Spain* A clove of garlic

dieppoise, à la *France* In the Dieppe style. Used of any dish containing or garnished with shrimps or served with a shrimp sauce.

diepvries *Netherlands* Deep-frozen

diet, to To control the intake of food in general or of particular types of food usually with a view to losing weight but sometimes for other medical or health reasons, e.g. for coeliac disease and diabetes

dietary fibre Long-chain carbohydrates which are not digested in the gut but which add to the bulk of bowel contents, reducing constipation and decreasing the transit time of waste matter thus thought to reduce the incidence of bowel cancer. Also called **roughage**

dietetics The science and study of nutrition and diet

diethyl ether An organic solvent used in some flavourings and food colours

dietician A person trained in dietetics, nutrition and food related illness who advises on these topics usually in relation to illness and health

digester The original name of the pressure cooker

digestibility A measure of the degree to which food can be converted to nutrients which can be used in metabolism. Generally measured subjectively in humans though animal measurement techniques could be used.

digestif An alcoholic drink such as brandy, taken after a meal to aid digestion

digestion The processes which take place in the stomach and bowels whereby food is broken down into small molecules which can be absorbed into the blood and transported round the body for use. The process makes use of acid, enzymes and emulsifying agents secreted into the mouth, stomach and bowel and of microorganisms in the gut which convert food into other compounds necessary for health.

digestive Any item of food or drink thought to aid digestion

digestive biscuit *United Kingdom* A crumbly slightly sweet biscuit made from wholemeal flour

Digitaria exilis *Botanical name* Hungry rice

dihydrogen citrates See **citrates and dihydrogen citrates**

dijaj ala timman *Middle East* Iraqi roast chicken with a stuffing based on rice, onion, pine nuts, chopped walnuts and sultanas, flavoured with **baharat**

Dijon mustard A pale, smooth and clean-tasting prepared French mustard made with brown mustard seed, salt, spices, water and white wine or, more traditionally, verjuice. The most common mustard used in cooking.

dijonnaise, à la *France* In the Dijon style, i.e. with mustard or blackcurrants and blackcurrant liqueur

dika *West Africa* The seeds of the wild mango tree. See also **etima**

dilaw *Philippines* Turmeric

dilis *Philippines* A small fish similar to anchovy prepared like **ikan bilis**

dill A tall, hardy annual, *Anethum graveolens*, from the Mediterranean and southern Russia with feathery leaves and clusters of tiny brown seeds reminiscent of aniseed and caraway. Used in bread and cakes, with fish and in pickled cucumbers. See also **Indian dill** (NOTE: From the Norse *dilla* 'to lull or induce sleep'.)

Dill *Germany* Dill

dillilammas *Finland* Boiled mutton in dill sauce

dillisk *Ireland* Dulse

dillkött *Sweden* Best end or scrag end of lamb, blanched and simmered in stock with dill weed, parsley, salt and peppercorns until tender (about 1 hour). Served with dill sauce.

dill pickles Small cucumbers (gherkins) pickled in vinegar flavoured with dill seed or dill weed as well as garlic, spices and salt. The best undergo a lactic fermentation.

dillsås *Sweden* Dill sauce

dill sauce *Sweden* A white velouté sauce flavoured with white wine vinegar, sugar and dried dill, finished with a liaison of egg and cream and garnished with fresh dill

dill weed The leaves of the dill plant used in salads and to flavour pickled cucumbers and fish. Also called **Laotian coriander**

dilute, to To make less concentrated by adding e.g. water to sugar syrup or vinegar to prepared mustard

dimbula *Sri Lanka* A mellow and smooth unblended black tea from Sri Lanka

dimethylpolysiloxane See **E900**

dim sum *China* Steamed or deep-fried sweet or savoury snacks served at lunch or in the afternoon before a Chinese meal or with Chinese tea. If steamed, often served in characteristic woven split cane baskets. (NOTE: Literally 'heart warmers'.)

dinar *Catalonia* Lunch

dinca fala *Wales* Tinker's apple cake

dinde *France* Hen turkey

dindon *France* Cock turkey

dindonneau *France* Young turkey, poult

diner *France, Netherlands* Dinner

dinner The main meal of the day usually of two or more courses containing meat, fish, cheese or other high protein foods as well as carbohydrates. Served in the evening or around noon, depending on working patterns, region or country, or social class.

dió *Hungary* Walnuts

Dioscorea The group of plants from which the starchy tuber yam is obtained. See under **yam** for varieties.

Dioscorea alata *Botanical name* Asiatic yam

Dioscorea bulbifera *Botanical name* Aerial yam

Dioscorea cayenensis *Botanical name* Guinea yam

Dioscorea elephantipes *Botanical name* Elephant's foot (2)

Dioscorea esculenta *Botanical name* Chinese yam

Dioscorea japonica *Botanical name* Mountain yam

Dioscorea rotundata *Botanical name* White yam

Dioscorea trifida *Botanical name* Cush-cush yam

diósmetélt *Hungary* Freshly cooked egg noodles mixed with lard, finely chopped walnuts and sugar, served as a dessert

Diospyros discolor *Botanical name* Mabalo

Diospyros kaki *Botanical name* Kaki fruit, persimmon

Diospyros spp. *Botanical name* Persimmon, American persimmon, kaki, sharon fruit

Diospyros virginiana *Botanical name* American persimmon

diot *France* A fresh sausage containing root vegetables, turnips, beetroot and carrots according to season

dip A soft savoury, usually cold, sauce into which pieces of food such as raw vegetables, crisps, biscuits, etc. are dipped prior to eating

dip, to To fully or partially immerse a solid material or food into liquid or semi-liquid, either to coat the solid or to absorb some of the liquid into it

diphenyl A potent fungicide permitted for use in the wrappings of and in packing cases for oranges and tomatoes. Also called **biphenyl**, **phenylbenzene**. See also **E230**

diphenylamine A food additive with no E number or UK number used as an antioxidant

diplomate, sauce *France* Sauce normande with 75 g per litre of lobster butter, garnished with truffles and diced lobster meat. Served with whole large fish.

diplomatico *Italy* A chocolate cake flavoured with rum and coffee

diplomat pudding As cabinet pudding but served cold with redcurrant, raspberry, apricot or vanilla sauce. Also called **pouding diplomate**

diplomat sauce See **diplomate, sauce**

dipper A large ladle with a long handle used for transferring small quantities of liquid from a large container

dirty rice *United States* A Louisiana dish consisting of a mixture of fried chopped onions, celery, sweet peppers, garlic and minced beef cooked with long-grain rice in a seasoned stock (NOTE: So called because of its appearance)

disaccharide A sugar consisting of two simple sugars such as glucose, fructose or galactose chemically bonded together. The most common is sucrose, ordinary beet or cane sugar, which consists of glucose and fructose.

dishwasher rinse Water at around 82°C used for the final rinse cycle

disinfectant A chemical which kills growing bacteria, yeasts etc but not necessarily spores

disjoint To cut carcass meat, game or poultry into pieces by severing the joints between bones

disodium dihydrogen EDTA See **disodium dihydrogen ethylenediamine-NNN'N'-tetra acetate**

disodium dihydrogen ethylenediamine-NNN'N'-tetra acetate A salt of EDTA used as a sequestering agent. Also called **disodium dihydrogen EDTA**

disossato *Italy* Boned, without bones

dispersed phase That phase in a two or more phase mixture which consists of separate and unconnected globules, droplets, particles or bubbles, e.g. oil is the dispersed phase in mayonnaise and hollandaise sauce, buttermilk in butter and air is the dispersed phase in whipped white of egg. See also **continuous phase**

display-until date A date mark used on packaged food for stock control purposes and not an indication of shelf life

dissolve, to To mix a solid with a liquid so that the individual molecules of the solid are separately dispersed in the liquid and cannot be seen. The colour but not the transparency of the liquid may be changed. Not all solids dissolve in all or any liquids.

disznóhús *Hungary* Pork

ditali *Italy* Thimble-sized tubes of pasta

ditalini *Italy* A small version of **ditali** used in soup

di testa *Italy* Parmesan cheese made between April and June. See also **Parmigiano Reggiano**

ditini *Italy* Cinnamon biscuits from Sicily

divinity A type of fudge made with egg whites, sugar and ground nuts

djej *North Africa* Chicken

djej bil loz *North Africa* A Moroccan dish of chicken stewed with blanched almonds and spices, the sauce thickened with mashed chicken liver

djej matisha mesla *North Africa* A Moroccan dish of chicken stewed in oil with onion, garlic, tomatoes, spices and seasoning until very tender, the chicken reserved and the juices reduced, flavoured with honey and served with the chicken garnished with fried or dry-fried almonds and sesame seeds

djej mqualli *North Africa* A Moroccan dish of chicken stewed with preserved lemons and olives, the sauce thickened with mashed chicken liver

djuvec *Balkans* A casserole of meat and rice with tomatoes, aubergines, peppers, courgettes, celery, onions and garlic

djuvec od praziluka *Balkans* A vegetarian casserole of leeks, tomatoes, chillies and rice from the Former Yugoslav Republic of Macedonia

doan gwa *China* Wax gourd

Döbel *Germany* Chub

Doboschtorte *Germany* A tall 10-layer sponge cake with a mocha filling

dobostorta *Hungary* A layered cake filled with and sides coated with chocolate cream, top covered with caramel which is divided before it sets to facilitate serving

dobrada *Portugal* Tripe

dobrada a modo de porto *Portugal* Cooked chick peas, pieces of honeycomb tripe cooked in water, black pepper, bay leaf, cumin parsley, onions and garlic browned in oil and cooked tomatoes all combined in a casserole and simmered or baked for 1 hour

dobrada com feijão branco *Portugal* Stewed tripe, sausages and white beans

dobrogea A Romanian ewes' milk cheese. See also **Penteleu**

doce *Portugal* Sweet

doce de amendos *Portugal* A sweet almond-flavoured dessert with almonds

doce de chila *Portugal* The tough threads of **chila** or vegetable spaghetti, separated, refrigerated in water overnight, drained, blanched, drained and cooked over medium heat with an equal weight of sugar, drained, the syrup boiled with a cinnamon stick to 116°C and added back to the strands off the heat. Cooled and bottled. Used in sweets and in place of marmalade or jam.

doce de leite *Brazil, Portugal* A dessert made from a caramelized milk and sugar mixture. See also **arequipe**

dock, to To make a number of closely spaced holes in rolled-out pastry either with a fork, a hand roller with many short spines or an industrial scale machine. The purpose is to allow any air bubbles in the pastry to collapse and thus prevent irregularities when baked.

docono *West Africa* A semolina milk pudding from Guinea flavoured with vanilla and cinnamon and mixed with sliced banana

docosahexanoic acid A polyunsaturated essential fatty acid (EFA) found in egg yolk and fish oils. Its lack in the food of newborn children raised on breast milk substitutes is thought to cause retarded brain development. Also called **DHA**

doddy Bottle gourd

dodine *France* Boned poultry stuffed with pâté, simmered in wine and served with deglazed pan juices

dodol *Malaysia* A dark sweet dessert made from cooked rice and mangosteen

doe Female deer

dog cockle A variety of cockle, *Glycmeris glycmeris*, found throughout the Mediterranean. It has a distinctive patterned shell, yellow with red to brown circles which appear as though feathered.

dogfish A white-fleshed, slightly oily, round-bodied fish of various species of the shark family with a flexible cartilaginous skeleton up to 1 m in length and usually bought skinned. Common in European waters. See e.g. larger spotted dogfish, lesser spotted dogfish, rock salmon and smooth hound. Also called **huss**, **rock eel**, **flake**, **rigg**

dogh *Iran* A type of **lassi** made from yoghurt, dried peppermint or spearmint, salt and water

dog rose See **rose**

dog salmon See **Siberian salmon**

doh peeazah A variation of **korma** in which two additions of onions are made (2 parts onion to 1 part meat). The first half are browned and then cooked with the meat, the second half are grated or processed and added to the meat near the end of the cooking process. Also called **do piaaza**, **dopiaza**

doily A small circular placemat of cloth, plastic or paper often embossed and pierced, placed under or on top of plates to protect or beautify. Often used under cup cakes, petit fours, chocolates and the like.

dok jun *Thailand* Mace

dok mali *Thailand* Jasmine essence

dolce *Italy* 1. Sweet 2. Mild 3. Soft 4. Fresh

dolceforte *Italy* Sweet and strong as applied to dishes with these characteristics

Dolce Latte *Italy* A soft creamy and mild blue-veined cheese made from cows' milk (NOTE: Literally 'sweet milk'.)

dolci *Italy* Sweets or desserts, usually eaten in a pastry shop, not with a meal

dolichos bean Hyacinth bean

Dolichos biflorus Botanical name Horse gram

Dolichos sesquipedalis Botanical name The asparagus bean. Also named *Vigna sesquipedalis*.

dolma 1. *Turkey* Blanched vine, fig, cabbage or other edible leaves wrapped around a filling of minced lamb and rice or other savoury mixture then braised. Served hot or cold. **2.** *Middle East* Stuffed aubergines or courgettes

dolmades *Greece* Vine leaves, wrapped around a filling of fried onions, rice, parsley, seasonings and either currants and nuts, or, fried minced beef or veal, the parcels simmered in water and lemon juice and served cold as an appetizer. See also **dolma**. Also called **dolmathes**

dolmathes See **dolmades**

Dolmeh *Central Asia* Stuffed, as e.g. of vine leaves, cabbage leaves, apples, tomatoes, quinces etc. usually with a meat filling. The common meaning is stuffed vine leaves. The Greek *dolmades* comes from the same root.

dolphin fish A warm seawater round fish of the genus *Coryphaena*, found worldwide with a bright silvery gold colour and very tender flesh. Up to 7.5 kg in weight. Poached, baked, fried or grilled. Also called **dorado**

domasni nadenizi-na furna *Bulgaria* A mixture of chopped onions, minced meat, fat and a little raw rice, seasoned and flavoured with paprika, packed into sheep's casings and baked in the oven in water and fat with frequent basting

domates dolmasi *Turkey* Tomatoes stuffed with a mixture of fried onions, raisins, pine nuts, rice, herbs and seasoning, baked in the oven and served cold

domiati *Egypt* A soft scalded-curd cheese made from buffalos' or cows' milk. See also **Beda**

Dominican masked duck *United States* A highly prized wild duck, *Nomonyx dominicus*, from the south, shot for the table

domoda *West Africa* A Gambian meat stew generally with lemon juice, chilli pepper, onions, garlic, aubergine and tomatoes but always with peanut butter equal in weight to the meat in the cooking liquor. The meat is normally browned before stewing and the peanut butter is added for the last ten minutes.

domsiah *Iran* The finest quality rice

domuz *Turkey* Pork

dòn *Vietnam* Crisp

dôn *Vietnam* **1.** Stuffed **2.** Assembled or put together

donabe *Japan* An earthenware casserole used for one-pot meals (**nabemono**) cooked at the table

Donaukarpfen *Germany* Carp from the river Danube

donburi *Japan* **1.** A big rice bowl **2.** A dish of cooked rice topped with some or all of meat, fish, egg, vegetables and garnishes all arranged in a decorative manner and served with spicy sauces, the typical fast food of Japan

dondurma *Turkey* Ice cream

doner kebab Thin slices of raw lamb meat with fat and seasoning built up on a spit to make a cylinder 20 cm diameter and 60 – 80 cm long, spit-roasted while rotating in front of a source of radiant heat and thin slices

carved from the surface as it is cooked. Served with a meal or as takeaway food in a pocketed hot pitta bread with salad. A cheaper version made from minced lamb, fat and other ingredients is common in the UK. Also called **döner kebabi**

döner kebabi *Turkey* The authentic Turkish version of **doner kebab**

dong *Thailand* Pickle

dongde *China* Frozen

dong gu *China* Dried **hoshi-shiitake** mushrooms harvested in winter

dong guei *China* The dried root of a relative of angelica, *Angelica sinensis*. See also **dang gui**

dong gwa *China* Wax gourd

dong gwa jong *China* A rich broth served in the elaborately carved skin of a wax gourd

dongo-dongo *Central Africa* A soup/stew of dried, salted or smoked fish in an okra-thickened stock with sautéed onions, garlic and chilli peppers. A large amount of chopped okra is used and a pinch of baking powder and tomato purée are also added.

do'nut *United States* The American spelling of the doughnut, a version of the similar European bun which is made in the form of a torus after its inventor observed that the centre of the European version was sometimes not cooked

donzella *Italy* Wrasse, the fish

doodh *South Asia* Milk

doodhi Bottle gourd

dooren *Malaysia* Durian

doperwtjes *Netherlands* Green peas

do piaaza, dopiaza *South Asia* A variation of **korma**. See also **doh peeazah**

Doppelrahmstufe *Germany* An official category of double cream cheeses with a fat content of 60 to 85% (based on dry matter)

doppio *Italy* **1.** Strong **2.** Concentrated

doppskov *Denmark* Diced leftovers of meat, fried in butter with chopped onion, simmered in cream sauce until heated though, mixed with diced boiled potatoes and served topped with a fried egg

dorada *Spain* Gilt-head bream

dorade *France* Gilt-head bream

dorado **1.** Dolphin fish **2.** A freshwater fish from South American rivers

dorata *Italy* Gilt-head bream

dorato *Italy* Dipped in an egg batter and fried to a light golden colour

doré *France* **1.** Egg-washed with beaten egg yolks **2.** Golden brown

dorée *France* John Dory, the fish

dorer, faire *France* To brown slightly

doresshingu *Japan* A salad dressing

doria *France* Containing cooked cucumber

doria, fish Fish **meunière**, dressed with small turned pieces of cucumber sweated in butter or blanched

doria, sauce *England, France* A **béchamel sauce** enriched with cream and flavoured with cooked, chopped cucumber and grated nutmeg. Served with fish.

dormeur *France* Common crab

dorogobuski, dogorobouski *Russia* A strong-flavoured cows' milk cheese matured for 6 weeks with an orange red rind. Sold in small squares.

doro wat *East Africa* A dish of chicken pieces and hard-boiled eggs simmered in a thick sauce made from onions caramelized in ghee or butter, tomato paste, garlic, cardamom and berbere or finely chopped chillies. Served with rice or injera. Considered to be the best of the Ethiopian wat dishes.

Dorsch *Germany* Cod

Dorset apple cake *England* Flour, chopped apples, sugar and lard (2:2:1:1) plus 3 dsp of baking powder per kg of flour, the lard rubbed into the flour and all the rest brought together to a firm dough with milk. Made into a flat cake 2 cm thick, baked at 190°C for about 1 hour, cut in half, well buttered and eaten hot.

Dorset blue See **blue Dorset**

dorso *Italy* Back, of a rabbit, hare, etc.

dorure *France* Beaten egg for egg-washing and glazing

dory A seawater fish, *Zeus taber*, from the Mediterranean and the Bay of Biscay, famous for St Peter's thumbprint (a large black spot ringed with yellow) behind both gill covers. The head takes up nearly half its length (up to 60 cm female, 45 cm male). The fish is a sandy colour tinged with yellow and blue and has a very fine-flavoured white flesh. Also called **John Dory**

dosa *South Asia* A dish of fried pancakes for which the partially fermented thick pouring batter is made from ground rice and ground **urad dal** in water. Often stuffed with cooked vegetables e.g. mashed potato.

dot, to To put small pieces of butter, etc. over the surface of food so that when grilled or heated it will cover it

Dotterkäse *Germany* A cheese made from skimmed cows' milk and egg yolks

dou *China* Pulse

douara *North Africa* A casserole of marinated lambs' tripe, liver and heart

double-acting baking powder A chemical raising agent which releases carbon dioxide firstly on being moistened and secondly on being heated

double boiler Two saucepans which fit together one on the other. The top one contains the food to be cooked and the lower one which is directly on the heat contains boiling or hot water. Used to limit the temperature of the food being cooked and to prevent burning especially when melting chocolate, thickening with egg yolk, etc. Also called **double saucepan**

double cream 1. A thick cream with a minimum butterfat content of 55%. Sometimes used for whipping but should be diluted with 10% milk. **2.** *United States* Soft cream cheese made from milk enriched with extra cream

double cream cheese A cream cheese with a high fat content made from cream. Generally used for spreading on bread or as a constituent of desserts.

double-crème *France* Soft cream cheese

double-crust Describes a pie or food dish with a pastry crust below and above the filling, usually in one continuous sheet

double-crust pie A pie with both a pastry base and top

double-decker sandwich *United States* A sandwich made with 3 slices of bread and 2 fillings

double Gloucester *England* A hard orange-coloured cows' milk cheese with a rich mellow flavour suitable for cooking and as a dessert. Double refers to its size.

double grid A wire mesh with handle which opens to enclose fish, beef burgers, patties or the like, allowing them to be turned over on the grill or barbecue without damage

doubles *Caribbean* A popular fast food consisting of curried chickpeas between two small, fried and seasoned batter pancakes

double saucepan See **double boiler**

douce *France* Sweet or mild, used before feminine words

douce-amère *France* Sweet-and-sour

dou fu *China* Bean curd

dou fu nao *China* Bean curd brains

dou fu pok *China* Fried bean curd

dough A mixture of flour, liquid and possibly yeast and other ingredients which after kneading has a firm, pliable and sometimes elastic consistency rather like putty. Used for making bread, buns, scones, etc.

doughboy *United States* Dumpling

dough cake *England* A white bread dough enriched with eggs and butter containing sugar, spices and dried vine fruits and baked in a cake or loaf tin

dough hook A hook-shaped heavy metal arm used in mixing machines for mixing and kneading bread doughs etc.

doughnut A ball of slightly sweetened yeasted or chemically raised dough, deep-fried, drained and coated with caster sugar often with jam in the middle. The ring doughnut was the original form made by wrapping the dough around a stick which was suspended in hot oil, the ball form followed but was in turn generally superseded by a ring formed by extrusion because of the difficulty of cooking the centre of the ball without overcooking the surface.

douille *France* Piping nozzle or tube

dou jiang *China* Soya bean milk

dou sha *China* Adzuki bean paste

dou sha bao *China* Sweet buns made from bean flour

doux *France* Sweet or mild, used before masculine words

dou zhi *China* Black soya beans

Dover sole One of the finest seawater flatfish, *Solea solea* and *S. vulgaris*, up to 50 cm long and caught around North West Europe and in the Mediterranean. It is much prized for its lean white flesh. The upper surface is a mud colour and the lower is white. It is very slimy when fresh. Also called **sole**

dovi *East Africa* The Tanzanian name for **peanut**

dow foo *China* Bean curd

dow ghok *China* Asparagus bean

dow see *China* Fermented and salted black soya beans

drabantost *Sweden* A semi-hard scalded-curd cows' milk cheese. The paste has a bland flavour and is springy with occasional holes.

Drachenkopf *Germany* Bluemouth, the fish

dragées *France* 1. Sugared almonds 2. Small silver-coloured sugar balls and small chocolate hemispheres used for cake decoration

dragoncello *Italy* Tarragon

dragon's eye Longan

drain, to To allow liquid to fall away from a solid by holding it in a colander, chinois or similar item or by laying the solid on absorbent paper. The liquid is usually either water, fat or cooking liquor.

dranken *Netherlands* Drinks, beverages

drappit eggs *Scotland* Poached eggs

draw, to To remove the innards (heart, lungs, intestines, etc.) of birds and poultry, and sometimes the leg sinews

drawn butter 1. *United States* Clarified butter **2.** Melted butter used as a dressing for vegetables, sometimes emulsified with water or vinegar

drawn butter sauce *United Kingdom* A sauce made from a white roux and flavoured water, traditionally served with vegetables or, with the addition of lemon juice, with steamed or poached fish

dredge, to To lightly sprinkle with flour or sugar or other fine powder using a dredger or sieve

dredger A cylindrical metal can with either a removable perforated top or a mesh base used for sprinkling flour, sugar or other fine powders on food items prior to or whilst cooking

Dresden dressing *United States* A condiment sauce made from hard-boiled egg, onions, mustard and other flavourings and seasonings. Used with meat.

Dresdener Stollen *Germany* A variety of **Stollen** from Dresden

dress, to 1. To add a dressing, e.g. of oil and vinegar, to a salad prior to tossing the salad **2.** To garnish a dish **3.** To arrange a food item which has been cooked, as in to dress a crab **4.** To prepare poultry or game for cooking by plucking, drawing and trussing

dressé(e) *France* Garnished

dressed crab Seasoned white and dark crab meat, the latter mixed with breadcrumbs, placed in the upturned cleaned crab shell and garnished or decorated with sieved egg yolk, chopped egg white and chopped parsley arranged in rows across the surface

dressed tripe Bleached and partially cooked tripe

dressieren *Germany* To truss

dressing 1. A mixture of oil and vinegar with various flavourings used to dress salads **2.** *United States* Stuffing or forcemeat

dreux A soft surface-ripened cheese made in Normandy. See also **feuille de Dreux**

dried The adjective applied to any edible material from which all or most of the water has been removed so as to improve its keeping quality and inhibit bacterial, fungal and insect attack as e.g. applied to fruit, milk, mushrooms, pasta, yeast, egg, tomatoes, peas, pulses, etc.

dried beef *United States* Round beef cured with salt and sugar, sliced paper thin, then smoked and pressed. Also called **smoked beef**, **sliced beef**

dried duck See **pressed duck**

dried fruit Fruit that has had the water content reduced by solar or other drying methods to give a hard almost leathery texture and to reduce the water activity so that it is not degraded by microorganisms.

Apricots, peaches, apples, bananas, grapes, tomatoes, plums and similar can all be dried.

dried gourd strips See **kampyo**

dried grapes See **dried vine fruits**

dried lychees The dried fruit which looks like a raisin and is eaten as a confection or added to desserts

dried mushrooms Completely dehydrated fungi of various types, used extensively in Chinese and Japanese cooking

dried shrimp Whole or ground dried shrimps used extensively in Southeast Asian cooking. Also called **shrimp floss**

dried vine fruits Dried grapes especially currants, sultanas and raisins

drikker *Norway* Drinks, beverages

drinde Dehydrated pork rind, ground and formed into granules for incorporation in cheap English sausages. Up to 10% of the required meat content of sausages may be drinde under UK law.

dripping The fat which is extracted from fatty animal tissue and bones by heating or boiling. Originally referred only to the fat from roast meat or bird which had a fine flavour.

dripping cake *England* A spiced fruit cake with beef dripping substituted for butter

dripping pan A shallow rectangular metal dish placed under roasting food to catch any dropping juices. A Yorkshire pudding used to fulfil this function.

drisheen *Ireland* A black pudding made with 2 parts blood to 1 part cream and 1 part breadcrumbs, seasoned and flavoured with tansy and other chopped herbs, filled into 4 cm casings, knotted and boiled for 20 or so minutes. The blood used depends on the supply. Sheep, pig, goose, turkey and hare blood have all been used. The original from Limerick uses sheep's blood.

drizzle, to A vogue word for to sprinkle or perhaps with the connotation of a thin stream rather than individual droplets of a liquid

droëwors *South Africa* Dried sausage looking rather like a dog chew

dronningsuppe *Norway* Chicken broth finished with sherry and a liaison of egg yolks and cream and garnished with small forcemeat balls

drop flower tube *United States* A piping bag nozzle with a star-shaped opening, used to make flower shapes or swirls

drop lid A floating wooden pan lid. See also **otoshibuta**

dropped scone See **drop scone**

dropping consistency The consistency of a cake or pudding mixture such that a spoonful of the mixture held upside down should drop off the spoon in more than 1 and less than 5 seconds

drop scone *United Kingdom* A flat cake made from a thick coating batter of flour, water, sugar, eggs and cream or butter and a raising agent, dropped on to a hot greased griddle and cooked on both sides. Served with butter and jam. Also called **dropped scone**, **Scottish pancake**, **Scotch pancake**, **flapjack scone**, **griddle cake**

druer *Norway* Grapes

druif *Netherlands* Grape

druiven *Netherlands* Grapes

drum The general class of fish which make drumming noises using their air bladders. Similar to croaker.

Drumlanrig pudding *Scotland* A type of summer pudding made with alternate layers of white crustless bread and cooked rhubarb, sweetened to taste, in a pudding basin, put under a weight for 24 hours, turned out and served with sour cream and sugar (NOTE: Named after the castle in Dumfriesshire.)

drumstick The lower part of a chicken or other fowl's leg below the thigh

drumstick bean See **drumstick pod**

drumstick pod The green-skinned slightly peppery tasting seed pod of a tree, *Moringa oleifera*, which is very thin and up to 40 cm long with small cream-coloured seeds. The young pods can be used as a vegetable or when older, boiled and the centre scooped out for use in soup. The mature beans only are used in Indian cooking. Originally from India it is now grown in the Caribbean, Africa and Southern USA. Also called **drumstick bean, benoil tree, bentree, susumber**

drumstick vegetable The pods of a relative of the drumstick tree, *Moringa pterygosperma*, which grows in India and has the taste and texture of a vegetable marrow. Cut in lengths and cooked like asparagus. The roots of the tree can be grated as a substitute for horseradish.

drunken chicken Boiled chicken pieces drained and marinated for 12 to 24 hours with a mixture of salt, sugar and yellow rice wine or dry sherry, drained and garnished with chopped coriander leaf

drupe The name for any fleshy or pulpy fruit enclosing a single stone

druvor *Sweden* Grapes

dry, to 1. To remove superficial or surface moisture from food **2.** To remove superficial and bound water from edible products to produce e.g. dried fruit, dried beans, etc.

dry-fry, to To heat and cook food in a frying pan without oil or fat. Suitable for fatty foods or for non fatty foods using, with care, a non-stick frying pan. Often used to prepare spices.

dry goods Any dry foods that can be stored for long periods without deterioration

dry goose *Scotland* The southern name for **fitless cock**

dry ice Solid carbon dioxide which exists at –79°C. Can be used for very rapid freezing or to produce a fine fog or mist.

dry jack *United States* A 6-month-old **Monterey Jack** with a distinctive flavour. Suitable for grating.

dry measure Cup measure

dry mustard *United Kingdom* Ground dried yellow mustard seeds used as a spice and flavouring agent or when mixed with water as an English condiment

dry-roast, to A method of bringing out the flavours of spices and other flavouring agents by subjecting them to dry heat (180°C) in an oven for a few minutes. Pastes, etc. should be wrapped in foil prior to dry-roasting.

dry-salt, to To preserve food by covering with, immersing in or rubbing on a mixture of coarse dry salt, saltpetre and sugar and possibly spices in the absence of light and leaving it until the food is dehydrated and brine runs off; the first 3 usually in the proportions 50:2:1. Can be used for meat, fish, vegetables, nuts, etc.

dry shell bean *United States* Haricot bean

dua nao *Vietnam* Freshly grated young coconut (**kelapa**)

dua nao kho *Vietnam* Desiccated coconut

Dubarry, à la *France* Containing or garnished with cauliflower

Dubarry, crème *France* Creamed cauliflower soup garnished with small, cooked florets of cauliflower

dubbele boterham *Netherlands* An English-type sandwich with two pieces of buttered bread and a filling

dubbelsmörgås *Sweden* An English-type sandwich with two pieces of buttered bread and a filling

Dublin bay prawn A type of lobster, *Nephrops norvegicus*, up to 25 cm long (excluding the claws) and rose grey to pink in colour, fished from the western Mediterranean through to Iceland. It is not a prawn. The shelled tail meat is known in the UK as scampi, although monkfish is a cheaper version often substituted for it. Also called **scampi**, **Norway lobster**

Dublin coddle *Ireland* A casserole of onions, bacon, potatoes and pork sausage traditionally served with soda bread

Dublin lawyer *Ireland* Diced lobster meat and its coral, lightly sautéed in garlic butter, flambéed with whisky and heated with cream. Served on the shell with the pan juices poured over.

ducana *Caribbean* A dish from Antigua similar to duckanoo but also containing grated sweet potatoes, raisins and vanilla essence

duchesse, à la *France* 1. Garnished or served with duchesse potatoes 2. A dish of tongue and mushrooms in a **béchamel sauce** 3. (*of pastries*) Containing an almond mixture

duchesse, sauce *England, France* Tomato and hollandaise sauces combined with chopped ham and white wine

duchesse potatoes Seasoned, riced or mashed potatoes mixed with butter and egg yolks and piped into assorted shapes then baked in the oven until browned. Often egg-glazed after an initial drying period in the oven. Also called **pommes duchesse**

duck The general name for a family of swimming birds *Anatidae* with webbed feet and a broad flat beak, some wild, others domesticated, common in French and Chinese cuisines. See also **canard**, **Peking duck**

duckanoo *Caribbean* A Jamaican dessert of African origin made from corn flour, sugar and nutmeg wrapped in a banana leaf and steamed. Also called **blue drawers**

duck eggs The eggs of ducks, which are about twice the weight of a hen's egg, and are usually pale blue in colour with an almost translucent white when set. See also **salted duck eggs**, **Chinese preserved eggs**, **thousand year egg**

duck feet A Chinese delicacy. They are deboned and softened by slow braising. Sometimes stuffed. Also called **duck webs**

duckling A young duck

duck press A press consisting of a perforated cylinder into which the duck is put. It is then squeezed with a screw-operated piston to extract the juices.

duck sauce 1. See **hoisin sauce** 2. The sauce used with Peking duck consisting of sweet bean paste, sugar and sesame seed oil processed together, let down with water and simmered until thick

duck skin When cooked to a crisp texture, the most prized part of a roast duck in Chinese cuisine

duck webs See **duck feet**

dudhi Bottle gourd

dudi Bottle gourd

due *Denmark* 1. Pigeon 2. Squab

dug *Central Asia* A diluted yoghurt drink from Afghanistan

Dugléré, fish As for **fish Bercy**, with **tomato concassée** added to the cooking liquor. Cooking liquor strained, reduced, mixed with fish velouté and butter, consistency adjusted, seasoned and served over the fish with some of the strained shallots and tomatoes.

dügün çorbasi *Turkey* A beef broth thickened with flour and garnished with diced beef. Paprika butter is added just before serving

dügün eti *Turkey* A dish of cubed mutton fried in mutton fat with quartered onions, then stewed in tomato purée and water flavoured with lemon juice

duhay *Philippines* Pomfret, the fish

duja *Italy* A special pot for the preservation of a type of salami, **salamin d'la duja**

duke cherry A hybrid of sweet and acid cherries, originating in France where they are known as *royale*

dukka *Egypt* A ground spice mix used as a condiment especially to flavour bread dipped in olive oil. It is made from sesame seeds, skinned hazelnuts or chick peas, coriander seeds, cumin seeds, all dry-roasted, with salt, black pepper and dried thyme or mint.

dukkah *Egypt* A dry mixture of dry-roasted sesame seeds, coriander seeds, walnuts and cooked and dried chick peas. See also **zahtar 2**

dukkous al-badinjan *Persian Gulf* Baked aubergine flesh puréed with garlic, chilli pepper and paprika

dukkous al-tamat *Persian Gulf* A tomato sauce made from tomatoes, garlic and oil flavoured with **baharat**

dukuna *Caribbean* A variant of **ducana** from Antigua, made from cornmeal, grated or desiccated coconut, mashed sweet potatoes, raisins and sugar, wrapped in leaves or in a cloth and steamed. Also called **paymi**

dulce *Mexico, Spain* Sweet

dulce de leche *Mexico, Spain* A dessert made from a caramelized milk and sugar mixture. See also **arequipe**

dulces *Spain* Sweets, desserts

dulet *East Africa* An Ethiopian dish of minced tripe, liver and lean meat fried in butter with chopped onions, chillies, cardamom and pepper

dulse A purple-coloured seaweed, *Palmaria palmata* or *Rhodymenia palmata*, from the intertidal zone in Ireland and the coastal regions of the North Atlantic, eaten raw or cooked and then dried for use as a snack food or health food. Also called **dillisk**

dum, to To steam in the Indian way, for meat usually on a trivet standing clear of the liquid in a pan with a tight-fitting lid, for vegetables by chopping them and browning in a little ghee then heating in a closed pan with a little water or **akni**

dummed Steamed Indian-fashion. See to dum.

dummed bhoona *South Asia* Pot-roasting in Indian cuisine. See also **bhoona**

dumpling 1. A round ball of sweet or savoury dough or pastry sometimes made with suet or dripping or other fat, cooked in soups and stews to accompany them, or, if sweet, steamed, boiled or baked as a pudding. Sometimes used to coat a piece of fruit as in apple dumpling. 2. In Asia a dumpling is often a savoury or sweet filling surrounded with a thin dough sheet similar to ravioli and steamed or boiled

dumpling wrappers *Southeast Asia* Wrappers for filled dumplings consisting of a wheat flour dough made with egg yolks and warm water, salt and baking powder, kneaded until silky, rested and rolled out thinly and cut in squares or circles. They are normally filled and the edges brought together like a purse.

dun 1. *China* Braising of food in its own juices in a tightly sealed casserole. Also called **wei** 2. A brown mould which grows on salted fish

Dundee biscuit *Scotland* A rich short biscuit made with plain flour, caster sugar and butter (4:2:1) bound with egg yolk, glazed with egg white and sprinkled with chopped almonds

Dundee cake *Scotland* A fruit cake made by the creaming method from pound cake mixture containing about 25% more flour than normal and using soft brown sugar with an equal amount of dried vine fruits, candied peel and chopped almonds; flavoured with grated lemon and orange zest and topped with rings of split blanched almonds before baking

Dundee marmalade *Scotland* A dark, rich orange marmalade with coarsely cut peel

dundu See **dun dun**

dun dun *Africa* Slices of yam or sweet potato, floured, egged and deep-fried. Served hot with omelettes. Also called **dundu**

Dunesslin pudding *Scotland* A thick flour and egg custard made from milk, eggs, flour, butter and sugar (12:4:2:1:1), flavoured with vanilla or lemon juice and zest poured over jam or stewed fruit in the bottom of a pudding basin then browned in the oven at 180°C for 20 minutes

Dungeness crab *United States* The most popular crab, *Cancer magister*, caught off the shores of the North Pacific Ocean and weighing up to 1 kg. The legs are often as meaty as the claws. Also called **market crab**, **Alaska Dungeness crab**

dunk, to To dip a solid cake or biscuit into a hot drink before eating it

Dunlop *Scotland* A mild, hard cows' milk cheese made in the same way as Cheddar except that the curd is not cheddared and the cheese is consequently moister. Originally Irish but introduced to Scotland by religious refugees.

Dunmow flitch *England* The name given to the flitch which is awarded annually in Great Dunmow to any married couple who can prove that they have not quarrelled during the preceding year

dünsten *Germany* 1. To steam 2. To stew

duo *United States* A pasteurized and processed Emmental-type cheese filled with walnuts, herbs, spices, black pepper and a salami or smoked salmon forcemeat

duong cuc vang *Vietnam* Palm sugar

dur *France* Hard, as in *oeuf dur*, hard-boiled egg

durchgebraten *Germany* Well done

Durham lamb cutlets *England* Minced cold cooked lamb mixed with an equal amount of mashed potatoes and some minced onion and cooking apple, flavoured with chopped parsley and tomato purée then formed into cutlet shapes, panéed and shallow-fried

durian *England, Indonesia, Malaysia* The fruit of a Malaysian tree, *Durio zibethinus*, cultivated all over Southeast Asia, which has an offensive odour but pleasant taste. It has a green to yellow spiky thick rind, is shaped like a rugby ball and weighs up to 4.5 kg. The segmented flesh is a yellowy soft pulp containing brown inedible seeds. Eaten raw or in both sweet and savoury dishes. The flesh may be canned and the peel is used to smoke fish.

duro *Italy* Hard as in a hard crust

durra Great millet

Dürrerund *Austria* A medium-sized brown skinned sausage similar to Brunswick sausage

durum wheat A hard, high-protein wheat, *Triticum durum*, used for the production of semolina and pasta. Grown in Italy, Spain and North and South America.

Durvillea antarctica *Botanical name* Alga mar

Duse, à la *France* Garnished with tomatoes, French beans and potatoes, particularly of joints of meat

dusky flathead *Australia* See **flathead**

dust, to To sprinkle lightly with finely ground powder such as icing sugar, cocoa, flour, ground nuts, etc.

Dutch cabbage Savoy cabbage

Dutch cheese *United States* Cottage cheese

dutch oven A heavy pot with a domed tight-fitting lid used for slow cooking and pot roasts etc.

Dutch sauce Béchamel sauce enriched with egg yolks and cream and flavoured with lemon juice. Served with fish, chicken and vegetables.

duva *Sweden* Pigeon

duvor i kompott *Sweden* Braised pigeons made by frying a little diced pork in pork fat, adding pigeons to brown followed by mushroom and covering with seasoned stock flavoured with parsley, chives and tarragon. This is then simmered with a lid on until the pigeons are tender and served with thickened cooking liquor and garnished with the pork and mushrooms.

duxelles Chopped shallots or onions and mushrooms, sautéed in butter until quite dry. Used in many other dishes for flavour and bulk.

duxelles, sauce *England, France* Equal volumes of white wine and mushroom cooking liquor with chopped shallots, reduced by two thirds then simmered with **demi-glace** sauce, tomato purée and duxelles for 5 minutes and finished with chopped parsley. Used for gratinated dishes.

D value The number of minutes of heat required to reduce the number of viable organisms in a sample of food by a factor of 10. This depends on the temperature and the microorganisms, e.g. 12D minutes of heat treatment are required for canning where D is determined by the treatment temperature and conditions for *Clostridium botulinum*.

dwaeji galbi kui *Korea* Marinated and grilled pork spare ribs

dwarf bean French bean

dwarf cape gooseberry A smaller version of the cape gooseberry, *Physalis pruinosa*, with a similar structure and found in the USA. It grows wild in Hawaii. Also called **ground cherry**, **strawberry tomato**, **poha**

dybfrossen *Denmark* Deep-frozen

dynia, dynya *Russia* Melon

dyrerya *Denmark* Saddle of venison

dyrerygg *Norway* Previously marinated venison cooked in sour cream

dyrestek *Norway* Roast venison

dyrlægens natmad *Denmark* A Danish open sandwich spread with spiced lard, liver pâté, veal and jellied consommé (NOTE: Literally 'vet's midnight snack'.)

dzhazh msharmal *North Africa* A chicken **tagine** from Morocco with olives and preserved lemons and flavoured with ginger, saffron and pepper

E F G H I J K L

E100 Curcumin, the natural colouring obtained from turmeric, used in cakes and margarine

E101 Riboflavin and riboflavin-5'phosphate, vitamin B2 used as a food colouring

E102 Tartrazine, a synthetic dye used as a food colouring in soft drinks but suspected of possibly causing allergies and hyperactivity in children

E104 Quinoline yellow, a synthetic food colouring

E110 Sunset yellow FCF or orange yellow S, synthetic food colourings used in biscuits

E120 Cochineal, the red food colouring extracted from an insect

E122 Carmoisine or azorubine, synthetic red food colourings

E123 Amaranth, a synthetic yellow food colouring banned in the USA, used in alcoholic drinks

E124 Ponceau 4R, a synthetic red food colouring used in dessert mixes

E127 Erythrosine BS, a synthetic red food colouring used in glacé cherries

E128 *United Kingdom* Red 2G, a synthetic dye. Used to colour sausages. (*not licensed for use throughout the EU*)

E131 Patent blue V, a synthetic food colouring

E132 Indigo carmine or indigotine, a synthetic blue food colouring

E133 *United Kingdom* Brilliant blue FCF, a synthetic food dye used in conjunction with yellows to colour canned vegetables (*not licensed for use throughout the EU*)

E140 Chlorophyll, the green food colour made from plants

E141 Copper complexes of chlorophyll used as food colourings

E142 Green S, acid brilliant green BS and lissamine green, synthetic green food colourings

E150 Caramel, the dark brown food colouring made from sugar. Used in beer, soft drinks, sauces and gravy browning.

E151 Black PN or brilliant black PN, synthetic black food colourings

E153 Carbon black or vegetable carbon, very finely divided carbon used as a food colouring in e.g. liquorice

E154 *United Kingdom* Brown FK, a synthetic food dye used on kippers (*not licensed for use throughout the EU*)

E155 *United Kingdom* Brown HT, a synthetic food dye used for chocolate cake (*not licensed for use throughout the EU*)

E160(a) Carotenes, orange food colourings from plants, also precursors of vitamin A

E160(b) Annatto, bixin and norbixin, golden yellow food colourings obtained from the seeds of achiote. Used on crisps.

E160(c) Capsanthin or capsorubin, peppery-flavoured and pink food colouring obtained from paprika

E160(d) Lycopene, a natural red food colour, one of the carotenoids extracted from ripe fruit especially tomatoes

E160(e) Beta-apo-8'-carotenal (C30), an orange carotene compound extracted from fruit and vegetables

E160(f) The ethyl ester of E160(e), an orange food colouring

E161(a) Flavoxanthin, a natural carotenoid yellow food colouring

E161(b) Lutein, a natural carotenoid yellow/red food colouring extracted from flower petals. Also called **xanthophyll**

E161(c) Cryptoxanthin, a natural yellow carotenoid food colouring with some vitamin A activity extracted from petals and berries of *Physalis* spp

E161(d) Rubixanthin, a natural carotenoid yellow food colouring, isomeric with E161(c) extracted from rose hips

E161(e) Violaxanthin, a natural carotenoid yellow/brown food colouring

E161(f) Rhodoxanthin, a natural carotenoid violet food colouring

E161(g) Canthaxanthin, a natural orange food colouring extracted from shellfish and used in fish food to give colour to farmed salmon

E162 Beetroot red or betanin, a red food colouring extracted from beetroot. Used for ice cream and liquorice.

E163 Anthocyanins, red, violet or blue vegetable food colours extracted from grape skins. Used in yoghurt.

E170 Calcium carbonate used as an acidity regulator, obtained from limestone. Used as a firming agent, release agent and diluent.

E171 Titanium dioxide, an inert white pigment, usually used in high-quality white paints, but also in sweets

E172 Iron oxide and hydroxides, natural red, brown, yellow and black food colourings and pigments

E173 Aluminium, a silvery metal sometimes used in very thin films as a food decoration

E174 Silver, sometimes used in very thin films or layers as a food decoration

E175 Gold, sometimes used as gold leaf, a very thin film for decoration of cakes and dragees

E180 Pigment rubine or lithol rubine BK, a synthetic red colour restricted to colouring the rind of hard cheeses

E200 Sorbic acid, used as a preservative in baked and fruit products, soft drinks and processed cheese slices

E201 Sodium sorbate, the sodium salt of sorbic acid used as a preservative in frozen pizzas and flour confectionery

E202 Potassium sorbate, the potassium salt of sorbic acid, used as E201

E203 Calcium sorbate, the calcium salt of sorbic acid, used as E201

E210 Benzoic acid, a naturally occurring organic acid also made synthetically, used as a preservative in beer, jam, salad cream, soft drinks, fruit products and marinated fish

E211 Sodium benzoate, the sodium salt of benzoic acid, used as E210

E212 Potassium benzoate, the potassium salt of benzoic acid, used as E210

E213 Calcium benzoate, the calcium salt of benzoic acid, used as E210

E214 Ethyl 4-hydroxybenzoate, a synthetic derivative of benzoic acid used as a food preservative

E215 Sodium ethyl 4-hydroxybenzoate, the sodium salt of E214, used as E210

E216 Propyl 4-hydroxybenzoate, a synthetic derivative of benzoic acid, used as E210

E217 Sodium propyl 4-hydroxybenzoate, the sodium salt of E216, used as E210

E218 Methyl 4-hydroxybenzoate, a synthetic derivative of benzoic acid, used as E210

E219 Sodium methyl 4-hydroxybenzoate, the sodium salt of E218, used as E210

E220 Sulphur dioxide, a pungent and irritating gas which is one of the most common preservatives used in food. Used in dried fruit, dehydrated vegetables, fruit products, juices and syrups, sausages, cider, beer and wine, to prevent the browning of peeled potatoes and to condition biscuit doughs.

E221 Sodium sulphite, a compound formed from caustic soda and sulphur dioxide, used as E220

E222 Sodium hydrogen sulphite, a similar food preservative to E221, but containing a higher proportion of sulphur dioxide

E223 Sodium metabisulphite, a compound which contains twice as much sulphur dioxide as E221

E224 Potassium metabisulphite, a similar compound to E223

E226 Calcium sulphite, a food preservative similar to E221

E227 Calcium hydrogen sulphite, a food preservative similar to E222

E228 Potassium bisulphite, a food preservative used in wines

E230 Diphenyl, a fungicide which may be used on the wrappings of oranges and bananas or in their packing cases. Also called **biphenyl**, **phenyl benzene**

E231 2-hydroxy diphenol, a synthetic compound used in the same way as E230. Also called **orthophenyl phenol**

E232 Sodium diphenyl-2-yl oxide, a synthetic compound used in the same way as E230. Also called **sodium orthophenylphenate**

E233 2–(thiazol-4-yl) benzimidazole, a synthetic compound used in the same way as E230. Also called **thiabendazole**

E234 *United Kingdom* Nisin, a food preservative licensed for use in the UK but not generally in the EU. Used in cheese and clotted cream. (*not licensed for use throughout the EU*)

E236 Formic acid, a natural chemical found in some fruit but made synthetically for use as a flavour enhancer

E237 Sodium formate, the sodium salt of formic acid, used as a flavour enhancer

E238 Calcium formate, the calcium salt of formic acid, used as a flavour enhancer

E239 Hexamine, a synthetic chemical used as a preservative, restricted to preserved fish and Provolone cheese

E249 Potassium nitrite, the potassium salt of nitrous acid, used to maintain the pink colour of cured meats and in some cheeses

E250 Sodium nitrite, the sodium salt of nitrous acid, used to maintain the pink colour of cured meat by reacting with the haemoglobin

E251 Sodium nitrate, the sodium salt of nitric acid, used for curing and preserving meat

E252 Potassium nitrate the potassium salt of nitric acid, used for curing and preserving meat. Also called **saltpetre**

E260 Acetic acid, the acid component of vinegar, used as an acidity regulator, as a flavouring and to prevent mould growth

E261 Potassium acetate, the potassium salt of acetic acid, used as a preservative and firming agent

E262 1. *United Kingdom* Sodium acetate used in the same way as potassium acetate, E261. Licensed for use in the UK but not generally in the EU. **2.** Sodium hydrogen diacetate, a sodium salt similar in effect to E261, used as a preservative and firming agent (*not licensed for use throughout the EU*)

E263 Calcium acetate, the calcium salt of acetic acid used as a firming agent and as a calcium source in quick-setting jelly mixes

E270 Lactic acid, one of the products of anaerobic metabolism of some microorganisms and animal muscle, widely used as an acidifying agent, flavouring and as a protection against mould growth in e.g. salad dressings and soft margarine

E280 Proprionic acid, a simple fatty acid naturally occurring in dairy products but also synthesized for use as a flour improver and preservative

E281 Sodium proprionate, the sodium salt of proprionic acid, used as a flour improver and preservative

E282 Calcium proprionate, the calcium salt of proprionic acid, used as a flour improver and preservative

E283 Potassium proprionate, the potassium salt of proprionic acid, used as a flour improver and preservative

E290 Carbon dioxide, the gas produced when sugar and many other food items are metabolized in the body and by microorganisms. Provides the gas for raising yeasted goods, for use as a propellant, as the gas in sealed packs where oxygen must be excluded and in fizzy drinks.

E296 *United Kingdom* Malic acid, an acid found in fruit and also produced synthetically, used as a flavouring in soft drinks, biscuits, dessert mixes and pie fillings (*not licensed for use throughout the EU*)

E297 *United Kingdom* Fumaric acid used as E296 (*not licensed for use throughout the EU*)

E300 L-ascorbic acid, vitamin C, used to prevent oxidation and thus browning reactions and colour changes in food. Also used as a flour improver.

E301 Sodium L-ascorbate, the sodium salt of ascorbic acid, used for the same purposes as E300

E302 Calcium L-ascorbate, the calcium salt of L-ascorbic acid, used for the same purposes as E300

E304 6-o-palmitoyl L-ascorbic acid, an oil soluble ester of ascorbic acid, used for the same purposes as E300 and especially in Scotch eggs

E306 Extracts of natural substances rich in tocopherols, i.e. vitamin E, used as vitamin additive to foods and as an antioxidant especially in vegetable oils

E307 Synthetic alpha-tocopherol, one of the tocopherols, used an antioxidant in cereal-based baby foods

E308 Synthetic gamma-tocopherol, one of the tocopherols, used as E306

E309 Synthetic delta-tocopherol, one of the tocopherols, used as E306

E310 Propyl gallate, the propyl ester of gallic acid, allowed for use as an antioxidant in oils, fats and essential oils only

E311 Octyl gallate, the octyl ester of gallic acid, allowed for use as an antioxidant in oils, fats and essential oils only

E312 Dodecyl gallate, the dodecyl ester of gallic acid, allowed for use as an antioxidant in oils, fats and essential oils only

E320 BHA, butylated hydroxyanisole, a controversial antioxidant, allowed for used in fats, oils and essential oils only

E321 BHT, butylated hydroxytoluene, a controversial antioxidant, allowed for use in fats, oil, essential oils and chewing gum

E322 Lecithin, a natural substance found in egg yolk, used as an emulsifier and antioxidant, e.g. in low-fat spreads

E325 Sodium lactate, the sodium salt of lactic acid, used as a buffer i.e. to maintain near constant pH in foods and as a humectant in jams, preserves and flour confectionery

E326 Potassium lactate, the potassium salt of lactic acid, used as a buffer in foods such as jams, preserves and jellies

E327 Calcium lactate, the calcium salt of lactic acid, used as a buffer and as a firming agent in canned fruits and pie fillings

E330 Citric acid, the acid present in citrus and other fruit and in animals, used as an acidifying agent, as an emulsifier, as a flavour enhancer, to increase the effects of preservatives, to inhibit bacterial action, as a buffer and as a sequestrant to protect foods from reaction with metals in e.g. soft drinks, biscuit fillings, jams, dessert mixes and processed cheeses

E331 Sodium dihydrogen citrate, disodium citrate, trisodium citrate, sodium salts of citric acid with the same uses as E330

E332 Potassium dihydrogen citrate, tripotassium citrate, potassium salts of citric acid with the same uses as E330

E333 Calcium citrate, dicalcium citrate, tricalcium citrate, calcium salts of citric acid used in the same way as E330 and also as a firming agent

E334 Tartaric acid, an acid naturally present in many fruits with the same uses as citric aid, E330

E335 Monosodium and disodium tartrate, sodium salts of tartaric acid, used as E334

E336 Potassium tartrate and potassium hydrogen tartrate, potassium salts of tartaric acid used in the same way as E334, the latter is the cream of tartar used as a constituent of baking powder

E337 Potassium sodium tartrate, a mixed salt of tartaric acid, used in the same way as E334

E338 Orthophosphoric acid, an inorganic acid used as an acidity regulator in soft drinks and cocoa

E339(a) Sodium dihydrogen orthophosphate, a sodium salt of orthophosphoric acid, used as a buffer, sequestrant and emulsifying agent

E339(b) Disodium hydrogen orthophosphate, used as E339(a)

E339(c) Trisodium orthophosphate, used as E339(a) but not as a buffer

E340(a) Potassium dihydrogen orthophosphate, a potassium salt of orthophosphoric acid with the same uses as E339(a)

E340(b) Dipotassium hydrogen orthophosphate with the same uses as E339(a)

E340(c) Tripotassium orthophosphate with the same uses as E339(a) but not as a buffer

E341(a) Calcium tetrahydrogen diorthophosphate, a calcium salt of orthophosphoric acid used as a firming agent, anti-caking agent and raising agent

E341(b) Calcium hydrogen orthophosphate with the same uses as E341(a)

E341(c) Tricalcium orthophosphate with the same uses as E341(a)

E350 *United Kingdom* Sodium malate and sodium hydrogen malate, sodium salts of malic acid used as buffers and humectants in sweets, cakes and biscuits (*not licensed for use throughout the EU*)

E351 *United Kingdom* Potassium malate used as E350 (*not licensed for use throughout the EU*)

E352 Calcium malate and calcium hydrogen malate, calcium salts of malic acid E296, used as firming agents in processed fruit and vegetables (*not licensed for use throughout the EU*)

E353 Metatartaric acid, a sequestering agent used in wine (*not licensed for use throughout the EU*)

E355 Adipic acid, an organic acid used as a buffer and flavouring in sweets and synthetic cream desserts (*not licensed for use throughout the EU*)

E363 Succinic acid, an organic acid used as a buffer and flavouring in dry foods and beverage mixes (*not licensed for use throughout the EU*)

E370 1,4-heptanolactone, used as an acid and sequestering agent in dried soups and instant desserts (*not licensed for use throughout the EU*)

E375 Nicotinic acid used as a colour stabilizer in bread, flour and breakfast cereals (*not licensed for use throughout the EU*) Also called **vitamin B3**

E380 Triammonium citrate, an ammonium salt of citric acid used as a buffer and emulsifier in processed cheese (*not licensed for use throughout the EU*)

E381 Ammonium ferric citrate, used as an iron supplement in bread (*not licensed for use throughout the EU*)

E385 Calcium disodium EDTA, used as a sequestering agent in canned shellfish (*not licensed for use throughout the EU*)

E400 Alginic acid, a water-loving carbohydrate acid extracted from seaweeds in the form of mixed sodium, potassium and magnesium salts, capable of absorbing 200 to 300 times its weight in water. Used for thickening and gelling, e.g. in ice cream and soft cheeses.

E401 Sodium alginate, the sodium salt of alginic acid used as an emulsifier and stabilizer in cake mixes and in ice cream to provide a creamy texture and to prevent the formation of ice crystals

E402 Potassium alginate, the potassium salt of alginic acid used as a thickener and stabilizer

E403 Ammonium alginate, the ammonium salt of alginic acid used as a more soluble thickener and stabilizer

E404 Calcium alginate, the calcium salt of alginic acid which gives a much more solid gel than the other alginates

E405 Propane-1, 2-diol alginate, an ester of alginic acid which is more miscible with fats and oils than simple salts. Used in salad dressings and cottage cheese.

E406 Agar-agar, a polysaccharide extracted from certain seaweeds, used for thickening, gelling and stabilizing purposes. Soluble only in hot water. Used in ice cream and vegetarian jellies.

E407 Carrageenan, a polysaccharide extracted from certain seaweeds consisting of galactose units several of which are sulphated. Used as an emulsifier for oil water mixtures and for gelling and thickening. Used in quick setting jelly mixes and in milk shakes.

E410 Locust bean gum, a plant gum used as a thickener or gelling agent, e.g. in salad cream

E412 Guar gum, a plant gum used as a thickener or gelling agent in packet soups and meringue mixes

E413 Gum tragacanth, a plant gum used as a thickener or gelling agent in e.g. salad dressings and processed cheese

E414 Gum arabic, a plant gum used as a thickener or gelling agent especially in confectionery. Also called **acacia gum**

E415 Xanthan gum, a thickener and gelling agent used in sweet pickles and coleslaw

E416 *United Kingdom* Karaya gum used as an emulsifier and stabilizer in e.g. soft cheeses and brown condiment sauce (*not licensed for use throughout the EU*)

E420(i) Sorbitol, a compound found in many berries and fruits, generally synthesized from glucose. Used as a humectant and as a sweetening agent for diabetics.

E420(ii) Sorbitol syrup, a water solution of sorbitol

E421 Mannitol, found in many plants and plant exudates, now synthesized from sucrose. Used as a humectant and in sugar-free confectionery.

E422 Glycerol, the alcohol which occurs in nature as the other component of fatty acid esters in fats and oils. Used as a humectant in cake icing and confectionery.

E432 – 436 A group of polyoxyethylene (20) sorbitan esters of fatty acids, used as emulsifiers and stabilizers in bakery products and confectionery creams. They are polyoxyethylene (20) sorbitan monolaurate (432), monooleate (433) monopalmitate (434), monostearate (435) and tristearate (436). (*not licensed for use throughout the EU*)

E440(i) Pectin, a natural plant polysaccharide used as a gelling agent or thickener

E440(ii) Amydated pectin, a synthetic derivative of pectin more stable than the parent product

E450(a) Disodium dihydrogen diphosphate, tetrasodium diphosphate, tetrapotassium diphosphate, trisodium diphosphate, salts of phosphoric acid used for flavouring, as stabilizers, buffers, sequestrants, emulsifiers, texturizers and raising agents in fish and meat products, whipping cream, bread, canned vegetables, processed cheese and the like

E450(b) Pentasodium triphosphate and pentapotassium triphosphate, used as E450(a)

E450(c) Sodium polyphosphates and potassium polyphosphates, mixtures of phosphoric acid salts used as E450(a) and to stabilize added water in poultry, ham, bacon and other similar meat products where it appears as a white exudate on cooking

E460(i) Microcrystalline cellulose, a bulking agent used to add bulk and to stabilize slimming foods, convenience foods, desserts and the like and also in grated cheese

E460(ii) Powdered cellulose, as E460(i)

E461 Methyl cellulose, a methyl derivative of cellulose used as a thickener, e.g. in low-fat spreads

E463 Hydroxypropyl cellulose, a derivative of cellulose, used as E461

E464 Hydroxypropylmethyl cellulose, a mixed derivative of cellulose, used as a thickener in ice cream

E465 Ethylmethyl cellulose, a mixed derivative of cellulose, used as a thickener in gateaux

E466 Sodium carboxymethyl cellulose, the sodium salt of a derivative of cellulose, used as a thickener and bulking agent in jellies and gateaux but mainly used for wallpaper paste

E470 Sodium, potassium and calcium salts of fatty acids, edible soaps used for emulsification of cake mixes

E471 Mono and di-glycerides of fatty acids, manufactured synthetic fats used in place of fats and oils in baked goods, desserts, etc. to improve keeping qualities and to soften and stabilize them

E472(a) Acetic acid esters of mono and di-glycerides of fatty acids, manufactured synthetic fats and oils used as E471

E472(b) Lactic acid esters of mono and di-glycerides of fatty acids, manufactured synthetic fats and oils used as E471 and in convenience toppings

E472(c) Citric acid esters of mono and di-glycerides of fatty acids, manufactured synthetic fats and oils used as E471 and in continental sausages

E472(d) Tartaric acid esters of mono and di-glycerides of fatty acids, manufactured synthetic fats and oils used as E471

E472(e) Diacetyl tartaric acid esters of mono and di-glycerides of fatty acids, manufactured synthetic fats and oils used as E471, especially in bread and frozen pizzas

E472(f) Mixed acetic and tartaric esters of mono and di-glycerides of fatty acids used as E471

E473 Sucrose esters of fatty acids, manufactured synthetic fats and oils used as E471

E474 Sucroglycerides, manufactured synthetic fats and oils used as E471, especially in ice creams

E475 Polyglycerol esters of fatty acids, manufactured synthetic fats and oils used as E471, especially in cakes and gateaux

E476 Polyglycerol esters of polycondensed fatty acids of castor oil, used in chocolate-flavoured coatings for cakes

E477 Propane-1, 2-diol esters of fatty acids, manufactured synthetic fats and oils used as E471, especially for instant desserts

E481 Sodium stearoyl-2-lactylate, the sodium salt of a derivative of lactic and stearic acids, used to stabilize doughs, emulsions and whipped products

E482 Calcium stearoyl-2-lactylate, the calcium salt corresponding to E481. Used in gravy granules.

E483 Stearyl tartrate, a derivative of stearic and tartaric acids, used in cake mixes

E491 – 495 *United Kingdom* Sorbitan monostearate (491), tristearate (492), monolaurate (493), monooleate (494) and monopalmitate (495), fatty acid esters of sorbitol used in cake mixes (*not licensed for use throughout the EU*)

E500 Sodium carbonate, sodium hydrogen carbonate (**bicarbonate of soda**) and sodium sesquicarbonate, used as bases, aerating agents and diluents in jams, jellies, self-raising flour, wine, cocoa and the like (*not licensed for use throughout the EU*)

E501 Potassium carbonate and potassium hydrogen carbonate (bicarbonate of potash) used as E500 (*not licensed for use throughout the EU*)

E503 Ammonium carbonate and ammonium hydrogen carbonate, used as buffers and aerating agents in cocoa and biscuits (*not licensed for use throughout the EU*)

E504 Magnesium carbonate, used as a base and anti-caking agent in wafer biscuits and icing sugar (*not licensed for use throughout the EU*)

E507 Hydrochloric acid (*not licensed for use throughout the EU*)

E508 Potassium chloride, used as a gelling agent and as a substitute for salt (**sodium chloride**) (*not licensed for use throughout the EU*)

E509 Calcium chloride, used as a firming agent in canned fruit and vegetables (*not licensed for use throughout the EU*)

E510 Ammonium chloride, used as a yeast nutrient in bread making (*not licensed for use throughout the EU*)

E513 Sulphuric acid, a common industrial acid used for neutralizing alkaline mixes. It produces sulphates on reaction which are mostly harmless. (*not licensed for use throughout the EU*)

E514 Sodium sulphate, used as a diluent for food colours (*not licensed for use throughout the EU*)

E515 Potassium sulphate, used as a substitute for salt (**sodium chloride**) (*not licensed for use throughout the EU*)

E516 Calcium sulphate, used as a firming agent and as a yeast food in bread making (*not licensed for use throughout the EU*)

E518 Magnesium sulphate, used as a firming agent (*not licensed for use throughout the EU*) Also called **Epsom salts**

E524 Sodium hydroxide, a very strong base used to adjust acidity in cocoa, jams and sweets (*not licensed for use throughout the EU*)

E525 Potassium hydroxide, a very strong base used to adjust acidity in sweets (*not licensed for use throughout the EU*)

E526 Calcium hydroxide, a weak base used as a firming agent in sweets (*not licensed for use throughout the EU*)

E527 Ammonium hydroxide, a weak base used as a diluent and solvent for food colours and as an acidity regulator for cocoa (*not licensed for use throughout the EU*)

E528 Magnesium hydroxide, a weak base used to regulate acidity in sweets (*not licensed for use throughout the EU*)

E529 Calcium oxide, a weak base used to regulate acidity in sweets (*not licensed for use throughout the EU*)

E530 Magnesium oxide, a fine white powder used as an anti-caking agent in cocoa products (*not licensed for use throughout the EU*)

E535 Sodium ferrocyanide, used as an anti-caking agent in salt and used in winemaking (*not licensed for use throughout the EU*)

E536 Potassium ferrocyanide, used as an anti-caking agent in salt and used in winemaking (*not licensed for use throughout the EU*)

E540 Dicalcium diphosphate, a calcium salt of phosphoric acid, used as a buffer and neutralizing agent in cheese (*not licensed for use throughout the EU*)

E541 Sodium aluminium phosphate, used as an acid and raising agent in cake mixes, self-raising flour and biscuits (*not licensed for use throughout the EU*)

E542 Edible bone phosphate, a fine powder made from boiled dried and ground bones, used as an anti-caking agent (*not licensed for use throughout the EU*)

E544 Calcium polyphosphate, used as an emulsifier in processed cheese (*not licensed for use throughout the EU*)

E545 Ammonium polyphosphate, used as an emulsifier, a texturizer and to help retain water in frozen chickens without drip on thawing (*not licensed for use throughout the EU*)

E551 Silicon dioxide, very finely powdered purified sand, used as an anti-caking agent in skimmed milk powder and sweeteners (*not licensed for use throughout the EU*)

E552 Calcium silicate, used as an anti-caking agent in icing sugar and as a release agent in sweets (*not licensed for use throughout the EU*)

E553(a) Magnesium silicate and magnesium trisilicate, used as anti-caking agents and in sugar confectionery (*not licensed for use throughout the EU*)

E553(b) Talc, a very finely ground natural mineral with a slippery feel, used as a releasing agent in tableted confectionery (*not licensed for use throughout the EU*)

E554 Aluminium sodium silicate, used as an anti-caking agent (*not licensed for use throughout the EU*)

E556 Aluminium calcium silicate, used as an anti-caking agent (*not licensed for use throughout the EU*)

E558 Bentonite, a very fine white clay-like mineral used as an anti-caking agent (*not licensed for use throughout the EU*)

E559 Kaolin, a very fine white clay used in dry powder form as an anti-caking agent (*not licensed for use throughout the EU*)

E572 Magnesium stearate, a type of soap used as an emulsifier and releasing agent (*not licensed for use throughout the EU*)

E575 D-glucono-1,5-lactone, an acid and sequestering agent used in cake mixes and continental-style sausages (*not licensed for use throughout the EU*) Also called **glucono delta-lactone**

E576 Sodium gluconate, used as a sequestering agent (*not licensed for use throughout the EU*)

E577 Potassium gluconate, used as a sequestering agent (*not licensed for use throughout the EU*)

E578 Calcium gluconate, used as a buffer, firming agent and sequestering agent in jams and dessert mixes (*not licensed for use throughout the EU*)

E620 Glutamic acid

E621 Sodium hydrogen L-glutamate, the sodium salt of glutamic acid, used as a flavour enhancer (*not licensed for use throughout the EU*) Also called **monosodium glutamate, MSG**

E622 Potassium hydrogen L-glutamate, similar to E621 (*not licensed for use throughout the EU*) Also called **monopotassium glutamate**

E623 Calcium dihydrogen di-L-glutamate, similar to E621 (*not licensed for use throughout the EU*) Also called **calcium glutamate**

E627 Guanosine 5'-disodium phosphate, a breakdown product of the nucleus (genetic material) of cells, used as a flavour enhancer in savoury foods, snacks, soups, sauces and meat products (*not licensed for use throughout the EU*) Also called **sodium guanylate**

E631 Inosine 5'-disodium phosphate, a flavour enhancer similar to E627 (*not licensed for use throughout the EU*) Also called **sodium inosinate**

E635 Sodium 5'-ribonucleotide, a flavour enhancer similar to E627 (*not licensed for use throughout the EU*)

E900 Dimethylpolysiloxane, used as and anti-foaming agent in liquid foodstuffs and ingredients (*not licensed for use throughout the EU*)

E901 Beeswax (*not licensed for use throughout the EU*)

E903 Carnauba wax (*not licensed for use throughout the EU*)

E904 Shellac (*not licensed for use throughout the EU*)

E905 Mineral hydrocarbons, highly purified mineral oils used to prevent dried vine fruits sticking together and as a glazing and release agent (*not licensed for use throughout the EU*)

E907 Refined microcrystalline wax derived from crude oil, a soft amorphous looking wax used as a release agent and in chewing gum (*not licensed for use throughout the EU*)

E920 Cysteine hydrochloride, the acid salt of the amino acid cysteine used as a flour improver (*not licensed for use throughout the EU*) Also called **L-cysteine hydrochloride**

E925 Chlorine (*not licensed for use throughout the EU*)

E926 Chlorine dioxide, used as a flour improver (*not licensed for use throughout the EU*)

E927 Azodicarbonamide, used as a flour improver (*not licensed for use throughout the EU*)

ear A tight cluster of seeds or grains at the top of a stalk as in wheat, rye, etc.

early flowering yellow rocket Land cress

earshell Abalone

earth almond Tiger nut

earthenware Dishes and pots made from baked and vitrified clay, sometimes porous and sometimes glazed, i.e. coated with a glass-like substance to avoid absorption of water and flavours. Sometimes heat resistant. See also **stoneware**

earth nut Tiger nut

eascu *Ireland* **1.** Conger eel **2.** Common eel

Easter biscuit *England* A rich biscuit from the West Country once eaten at Easter. It is made with plain flour, caster sugar, butter and egg yolk (7:3:4:0.6) by the creaming method and flavoured with mixed spice, cinnamon, currants and chopped peel. Glazed with egg white and sugar.

Easter cake Simnel cake

Easter egg 1. A hollow egg-shaped chocolate confection given as a gift at Easter **2.** A hard-boiled egg with the shell painted and decorated, regarded as a symbol of fertility or resurrection according to beliefs and given as a gift at Easter. In the UK, rolled down hills by children until broken.

eastern king prawn A variety of king prawn, *Penaeus plebegus*, found in the East

easternola *United States* A mild pork sausage seasoned and flavoured with garlic

eastern oyster See **American oyster**

eastern rock lobster *Australia* A type of spiny lobster, *Jasus verreausci*, coloured olive green and found in eastern Australia. Also called **crayfish**

eastern surf clam See **surf clam**

eau *France* Water

eau-de-Cologne mint A herb of the mint family, *Mentha piperata* var. *citrata*, with smooth bergamot-scented purple-tinged dark green leaves and a distinct eau de Cologne smell, suitable for drinks but not used in cooking.

eba *West Africa* A thick porridge made from **gari** and served with soups and stews as the carbohydrate component

ébarber *France* **1.** To remove the beard from shellfish **2.** To trim

Eberesche *Germany* Rowanberry

ebi *Japan* Shrimp or prawn, often eaten raw in sushi

ebi no kimini *Japan* Glazed shrimps made from large prawns with the tail shell left on, passed through corn flour, boiled 10 seconds in water then placed in a small amount of boiling **dashi**, sake, sugar and salt, brought back to the boil, beaten egg yolk poured slowly over the prawns, simmered 2 minutes without stirring, removed from the heat and rested for a further 2 minutes

ebi no suimono *Japan* A clear soup with shrimps

ebi oboro *Japan* Shrimp paste

écarlate, à l' *France* A description of salted and pickled meat, usually tongue (NOTE: Literally 'scarlet'.)

Ecclefechan tart *Scotland* A tart filled with a mixture of butter, dried vine fruits and walnuts

Eccles cake *England* A filled puff pastry case similar to the **Banbury cake** (NOTE: Originated in Eccles, now a suburb of Manchester.)

ecet *Hungary* Vinegar

ecetestorma *Hungary* Horseradish sauce

échalote *France* Shallot

échauder *France* **1.** To heat a liquid such as milk to just below its boiling point **2.** To heat by pouring boiling water over

échine *France* The top part of the forequarter of pork, the spare rib joint (NOTE: Literally 'backbone'.)

Echinochloa colona *Botanical name* Shama millet

Echinochloa crusgalli *Botanical name* Barnyard millet

Echinochloa frumentacea *Botanical name* Japanese millet

Echium vulgare *Botanical name* Viper's bugloss

Echourgnac *France* A small, pale yellow, delicately flavoured cows' milk cheese from Aquitaine. It has brown rind and the cheese contains small holes.

Echtermainzkäse *Germany* A soft Handkäse-type cows' milk cheese with a yellow rind and white paste. The flavour varies from mild to sharp depending on age.

éclair *England, France* A finger length of choux pastry piped on a tray, baked, cooled, split in half lengthways and filled with Chantilly cream or crème pâtissière, the top coated with coffee or chocolate glacé icing

éclanche *France* Shoulder of mutton

Ecole Supérieure de Cuisine Française de Paris A prestigious private cookery school for grands chefs cuisiniers

écossaise, à l' In the Scottish style, i.e. with barley and root vegetables

écossaise, sauce Cream sauce mixed with a **brunoise** of carrot, celery, onion and French beans which have been stewed in butter and white bouillon until almost dry. Served with eggs and poultry.

écrevisse *France* Crayfish

écrevisse à pattes rouges *France* Freshwater crayfish

ecuelle *France* A deep dish used to serve vegetables

écumer *France* To skim

écureuil *France* Squirrel

Edam *Netherlands* A semi-hard, ball-shaped, yellow cheese made from partially skimmed cows' milk using a lactic starter. It dates from at least the 8th century. After shaping, it is dry-salted or brined, ripened for a few weeks and coated with a red wax. Rather mild and bland but easily sliced. Contains 45% water, 25% fat and 28% protein. Also called **Manbollen, Katzenkopt, Moor's head**

edamame *Japan* Fresh soya beans

Edamer *Germany* The German version of Edam cheese

eddik *Norway* Vinegar

eddike *Denmark* Vinegar

eddo See **eddoe**

eddoe A roundish scaly underground stem from a plant, *Colocasia esculenta*, similar to but smaller than *taro* and used as a starchy staple food in African and Caribbean cuisine

Edelblankkäse *Germany* A soft surface-ripened cows' milk cheese with white veining. The flavour is mild when young but becomes sharper with age.

Edelkastanie *Germany* Chestnut

Edelpilzkäse *Germany* A blue-veined cheese. See also **Pilz**

édeskömény *Hungary* Caraway seeds

edesseg *Hungary* Sweet things

edible bone phosphate See **E542**

edible chrysanthemum See **garland chrysanthemum**

edible crab Common crab

edible sea urchin A large sea urchin, *Echinus esculentus*, up to 8 cm across but not as flavoursome as the small varieties. Found from Norway to Portugal.

Edinburgh fog *Scotland* Sweetened whipped cream flavoured with vanilla and mixed with chopped almonds and crushed macaroons

Edinburgh stuffing *Scotland* Sausage meat, finely chopped chicken liver, dry breadcrumbs with seasoning, dried herbs and grated nutmeg brought together with beaten egg. Used for stuffing chicken.

Edinburgh tart *Scotland* A single-crust puff pastry tart filled with equal quantities of molten butter, sugar, candied peel and sultanas, mixed with beaten egg three times the weight of the butter. Baked at 230°C for 15 to 20 minutes.

EDTA See **ethylenediamine-NNN'N'-tetra-acetate**

eel A long, smooth, round, catadromous fish of the genus *Anguilla* up to 130 cm long and weighing to 8 kg, usually without scales and with no pelvic fins. The flesh is dense and fatty and the bones are a good source of gelatine. Usually killed immediately before cooking. Often smoked and served with horseradish. Popular in Japan and Chinese coastal regions. See also **elver**

eel pie island pie *England* A pie of skinned and boned eel pieces brought to the boil in water with nutmeg, sherry, chopped parsley and sweated chopped onions and immediately removed. The eel pieces are placed in a pie dish with some coarsely chopped hard-boiled eggs. The cooking liquor is thickened with **beurre manié**, seasoned and acidulated with lemon juice, then poured over the eel. The top covered with puff pastry, egg-washed, and the whole is baked at 220°C for 15 minutes then at 190°C for a further 30 minutes. (NOTE: Named after Eel Pie Island in the Thames at Twickenham.)

eel pout A freshwater, non-oily fish, *Lota lota*, a relative of the cod found in Northern Europe. Resembles and is cooked like eel. Also called **barbot, burbot, lote**

een choy *China* Chinese spinach

eend *Netherlands* Duck

EFA Essential fatty acid

effervesce To bubble vigorously or foam, not by boiling

efterrätt *Sweden* Dessert

e-fu noodles Flat yellow-coloured egg noodles from China which have been fried until crisp before sale. They can be eaten as is or softened by blanching.

egg *England, Norway* A most important food item both for its nutritive and texturizing properties. Most eggs have a hard shell made of calcium carbonate, an inner membrane, an air pocket at one end between the membrane and the shell, a central yellow to orange yolk supported by two filaments and a surrounding transparent white. In fertilized eggs the embryo is seen as a small blood spot at the edge of the yolk. Hen's eggs are the most common food item, but duck eggs and quail's eggs are available. See also **egg white**, **egg yolk**, **egg sizes**

eggah An Arabic version of the omelette. See also **eggeh**

egg and butter sauce Melted butter, seasoned, flavoured with lemon juice and chopped parsley and mixed with diced hard-boiled eggs at the rate of 12 per kg of butter. Used for whole poached fish.

egg and crumb, to *United States* To pané

egg beater See **rotary beater**

egg-bread *East Africa* A light wheat flour pancake. See also **mkate mayai**

egg coagulation Separated white of egg coagulates between 60 and 65°C and the yolk between 62 and 70°C. These temperatures are raised when eggs are mixed into liquids with other additions. Coagulation and thickening of an egg, milk and sugar mixture, as in custard, will take place between 80 and 85°C and it will start to curdle at 88 to 90°C. Also called **egg setting**

egg cup A small container shaped like a goblet used to hold a soft-boiled egg in its shell for ease of opening and eating

egg custard A mixture of egg (whole or yolk), sweetened milk and flavouring cooked over a bain-marie or in a double boiler until the egg has set (80 to 85°C). The consistency depends on the proportions of egg to milk.

egg custard sauce A thin pouring sauce similar to crème à l'anglaise but with only 8 to 10 egg yolks per litre of milk. Also called **fresh egg custard sauce**, **sauce à l'anglaise**

eggeh *Middle East* The Arabic version of the omelette in which precooked vegetables together with seasonings, herbs and spices are bound into a stiff mixture with the egg prior to cooking by frying on both sides. May be cooked as one large circle or in tablespoonfuls. Probably the origin of the Spanish tortilla.

eggeh beythat *Middle East* Hard-boiled eggs with the shell removed, pricked through to the yolk in several places, deep-fried in olive oil until brown, then rolled in a mixture of cinnamon, turmeric, ground cumin and coriander and seasoning. Served hot or cold.

eggerøre *Norway* Scrambled egg

egg foo yung *China* An omelette filled with a mixture of shredded cooked meat, shellfish and cooked vegetables flavoured with soya sauce, garlic, chopped spring onions and sherry or rice wine

egg herbs The principal herbs used with eggs are basil, chervil, chives, dill, marjoram, oregano and rosemary

eggkake *Norway* Omelette

egg mayonnaise A hors d'oeuvre consisting of shelled, hard-boiled eggs, halved lengthwise, placed on a plate, cut side down, coated with mayonnaise and garnished

egg noodles Narrow ribbons of pasta containing eggs, sometimes made from eggs, flour and salt only. Available fresh or dried. Common in Italy, Southeast Asia, Japan and China. Chinese egg noodles are sometimes flavoured to suit the dish they will be served with.

egg pasta See **pasta all'uovo**

eggplant Aubergine

egg poacher A type of miniature **bain-marie** with an upper dish containing hemispherical indentations each sized to hold an egg. Used to poach eggs.

egg roll See **spring roll**

eggs à la russe Hard-boiled eggs, halved, the yolks removed and seasoned and mashed with mayonnaise, Dijon mustard, a little dry English mustard, finely chopped gherkins and spring onions. This mixture is returned to the halved whites and each decorated with paprika (tapped through a coffee strainer) and a caper. See also **iaitsa po-russki**

egg sauce Béchamel sauce flavoured with nutmeg with the addition of diced hard-boiled eggs (6 eggs per litre). Used for poached or boiled fish and smoked haddock. See also **Scotch egg sauce**

eggs Benedict *United States* A muffin or slice of toast covered with grilled Canadian-style bacon, topped with a poached egg, coated with **hollandaise sauce** and garnished with a slice of truffle

egg separator An implement shaped like a large spoon or small ladle with a slot or holes to allow the white of an egg to pass through leaving the yolk in the spoon

egg setting See **egg coagulation**

egg sizes 1. *United Kingdom* A numerical system for sizing eggs originally ranging from size 1 (greater than 70 g) to size 7 (less than 45 g). The standard egg used in recipes is size 3, weighing 60 to 65 g (2 oz). The system in the UK has recently been changed to small (minimum weight 45 g); medium (minimum weight 55 g); large (minimum weight 65 g); and extra large (minimum weight 90 g). The standard 65g (2 oz) egg size in this system is medium. **2.** *United States* US egg sizes are jumbo, extra large, large, medium and small

egg slicer A small implement rather like a cheese slice but with a hollow base to hold a hard-boiled and shelled egg, and multiple wires on a hinged frame which cut through the egg and into slots in the base

eggs Sardou *United States* Poached eggs served with artichoke hearts, anchovies, chopped ham and truffle and accompanied with **hollandaise sauce**

egg thread net A lacy crêpe made by allowing beaten and strained eggs to drip off the fingers into hot fat in an omelette pan to form a lacy pattern which is cooked until firm enough to handle. Used as a food wrapping or garnish in Southeast Asia.

egg timer An apparatus for timing the boiling of eggs, traditionally a sand-filled hour glass which measured only the three minutes necessary to soft-boil an egg

egg-wash, to To brush beaten egg over bread rolls, pastry, duchesse potatoes and similar foods prior to cooking in order to glaze them and give them a pleasant brown colour. They may be partially baked to harden the surface prior to egg-washing.

egg wedger As egg slicer but with the wires arranged to cut the egg into wedges

egg whey *Wales* A light custard made with 6 eggs per litre of milk flavoured with a little nutmeg, ginger and sugar, poured over broken bread and set either in the oven in a bain-marie or over hot water on top of the stove. See also **egg custard**

egg white The transparent gel surrounding the yolk of an egg which amounts to about 60% of the weight of a hen's egg. When fresh the egg white is viscous and stands high on a plate, as it ages it becomes thinner and is better for whisking. See also **albumen**

eggy bread *England* Unsweetened and unflavoured **pain perdu** topped with grated Caerphilly cheese and chopped pickled onion mixture and grilled until brown. Served immediately.

egg yolk The central part of the egg usually light yellow to orange, semi-liquid and held separate within a fragile membrane. It contains about 16% protein mainly lecithin, 33% fat including cholesterol plus vitamins, trace elements and water. It represents about 30% of the total weight of a hen's egg.

eglantine Rose

églefin *France* Haddock

eglefino *Italy* Haddock

Egon Ronay's Guide *United Kingdom* One of the restaurant guides to which complaints or experiences may be sent. Address: 73 Ulverdale Rd. London SW10 0SW. Others are the Good Food and Michelin Guides.

egres *Hungary* Gooseberries

egushi *West Africa* The Ghanaian name for **pumpkin seeds**. See also **egusi**

egusi *West Africa* The seeds of species of *Cucurbitaceae*, which include gourds, melons, pumpkins etc. used when ground as thickeners. The name is also used for the fruits themselves in West Africa. Also called **agusi**

egusi melon A melon of the genus *Cucumeropsis*, especially *C. edulis*, grown in west Africa for its oil-bearing seeds.

egusi sauce *Central Africa* Onions, tomatoes and chilli pepper sweated until cooked then liquidized, let down with a little water and thickened to a smooth sauce with egusi which has been roasted and ground to a fine powder. Served with staples or with grilled meats and fish.

egusi soup *West Africa* A soup/stew made by browning meat in palm oil or peanut oil transferring it to the cooking liquor, then frying onion, chilli pepper, tomatoes and okra in the same pan, when these are soft, tomato purée, dried shrimp and ground egusi seeds are added, heated through and all mixed in the stew. Finally chopped greens and seasoning are added and all cooked until done.

Egyptian bean Hyacinth bean

Egyptian lentils Masoor

Egyptian lotus The Nile plant, *Nymphaea lotus*, used in the same way as the true lotus

Egyptian mint Applemint

Egyptian onion A member of the onion family, *Allium cepa* var. *proliferum*, which produces a cluster of small bulbs at the flower instead of seeds. These are often too small to be of culinary interest. Also called **tree onion, calawissa onion**

égyptienne, à l' *France* In the Egyptian style, i.e. with lentils.

égyptienne, purée *France* As **purée Saint Germain**, but substituting yellow split peas for the peas and leaving out the carrot. Also called **yellow pea soup**

ei *Netherlands* Egg

Ei *Germany* Egg

Eichhörnchen *Germany* Squirrel

Eidotter *Germany* Yolk of egg

eierenpannekoeken *Netherlands* Pancakes

Eierfrucht *Germany* Aubergine

Eierhaber *Switzerland* A type of omelette made with eggs, milk, seasoning and a little flour, cooked then cut in small pieces

Eierkuchen *Germany* Pancake

Eierpflanze *Germany* Aubergine

Eierrösti *Switzerland* Diced bread soaked in milk then mixed with beaten eggs and cooked in butter

Eierteigwaren *Germany* Egg noodles and egg-based pasta

ei gebakken *Netherlands* Fried egg

eindosen *Germany* To can

eingemacht *Germany* Preserved, as of fruits, etc.

Eingemachte *Germany* 1. Jam 2. Marmalade 3. Preserves

Eingepökelte *Germany* Pickles

Einkorn A variety of wheat, *Triticum monococcum*, grown on poor soil in Central Europe, containing a single column of grains along the ear

Einsiedlerkrebs *Germany* Hermit crab

Eintopf *Germany* A meat and vegetable stew from the mining areas using fairly tender cuts of meat served with the unthickened cooking liquor (NOTE: Literally 'one pot'.)

Eis *Germany* 1. Ice 2. Ice cream

Eisbein *Germany* Boiled pickled pig's knuckle, usually served with sauerkraut, puréed peas and potatoes

Eisenia bicyclis *Botanical name* Arame

Eiweiss *Germany* White of egg

ejotes *Mexico* Green beans

ekmek *Turkey* Bread

ekmek kadayifi *Turkey* Honey-soaked bread or cake topped with buffalo milk cream

eksili çorba *Turkey* Mutton broth thickened with a mixture of flour, eggs, lemon juice and water and garnished with diced fatty mutton

eksili köfte *Turkey* Meatballs made from a mixture of chopped raw beef, eggs, chopped parsley, moistened breadcrumbs and seasoning, cooked in a sauce of water, tomato purée and sweated chopped onions, finished just before service with crushed garlic, cinnamon and vinegar

ekte mysöst Real **Mysost**, i.e. made from pure goats' milk

Elaeis guineensis *Botanical name* The oil palm from which palm oil and palm kernel oil are extracted

elaichi *South Asia* Cardamom

elastin One of the proteins which make up connective tissue, predominating in sinews and gristle. It does not break down into gelatine on cooking.

Elbo *Denmark* A hard, mild, slightly acidic tasting cheese similar to **Danbo**, made from cows' milk and cast in bricks of up to 5 kg. The slightly acid-tasting paste contains a few holes and the smooth brown rind is usually covered in red wax.

elbow macaroni *United States* Short pieces of macaroni curved into a right angle bend

elder *United Kingdom* Cooked and pressed cows' udder. Now rare.

elderberry The fruit of a tree, *Sambucus niger* (EU & USA), *S. canadensis* (eastern USA) and *S. caerula* (western USA), which consist of clusters of spherical shiny black fruits to 5 mm in diameter each containing a single seed. The eastern and western USA varieties are larger than the European, may be red or golden and are commercially cultivated as a fruit.

elderflower The white creamy flowers of the elderberry tree which grow in clusters. Used for decoration and sometimes deep-fried as fritters.

élédone *France* Curled octopus

eleesh *South Asia* A rather oily river fish from the Hooghly

elefante di mare *Italy* Lobster

Elefantenlaus *Germany* Cashew nut

elenolic acid One of the antibacterial agents in olives which inhibit lactic acid fermentation. It is removed by treatment with dilute caustic soda solution (**lye**) or by daily soaking in fresh water for 2 to 3 weeks.

Eleocharis dulcis *Botanical name* Water chestnut

Eleocharis tuberosa *Botanical name* Water chestnut

elephant apple Wood apple

elephant garlic *United States* A very large garlic-looking vegetable with a very mild garlic flavour. The cloves may be cooked as any tuber, or may be used raw in salads.

elephant's ears See **amaranth 1**

elephant's foot 1. A plant, *Amorphophallus campanulatus*, from India grown for its white to pink fleshed tubers which keep extremely well. The higher yielding type is rather acrid and requires long boiling. Also called **suram** 2. An African species of yam, *Dioscorea elephantipes*, with clusters of tubers which grow above ground

Elettaria cardamomum *Botanical name* Cardamom

Eleusine caracana *Botanical name* Ragi

elevenses *United Kingdom* A mid-morning drink and possibly snack (*colloquial*)

elft *Netherlands* Shad

el ful *Egypt* A dish made with brown beans. See also **ful medames 2**

elg *Norway* Elk

eliche *Italy* Pasta twists rather like fusilli

Ellendale *Australia* An important mandarin from Australia with a very juicy high-quality flesh which is sweet and tasty. Now also grown in South America.

elmo *United States* A semi-soft creamy-textured cows' milk cheese with a hickory nut flavour

elöétel *Hungary* Hors d'oeuvres

elöételek *Hungary* Appetizers

elote *Mexico* Fresh corn

elver A young eel considered a delicacy in France and Spain, usually stewed in garlic, sautéed or deep-fried

emblanquecer *Spain* To blanch

embotits *Catalonia* A platter of cold meats (assiette anglaise)

embuchado de lomo *Spain* A cured loin of pork (eye of loin only) enclosed in a skin like a long straight sausage and kept in olive oil. Eaten raw.

embutido *Spain* Cold slicing sausage

emek *Middle East* A popular Israeli cheese resembling Edam

émincé *France* Cut into thin slices or shredded with a knife or mandolin or in a food processor

émincer *France* To slice thinly, to cut into slivers or thin slices

émissole lisse *France* Smooth hound, the fish

Emmental *Switzerland* A hard cooked-curd cows' milk cheese from the Emmental valley with a sweet, nutty-flavoured glossy paste containing random holes. Both lactic and propionic acid starters are used and, after forming into a large wheel (up to 80 kg) wrapped in cheesecloth, it is salted in brine and ripened for 5 to 7 months. Copied worldwide. Used to make fondue. Contains 35% water, 37% fat and 27% protein. Also called **Emmenthal**, **Emmentaler**

Emmentaler *Switzerland* **1.** Emmental **2.** A regional **Brühwurst**-type sausage

Emmental grand cru de l'Est *France* A French Emmental cheese with a regionally administered Appellation d'Origine

Emmenthal *Switzerland* Emmental

émoudre *France* To grind

empada *Portugal* Pie, patty

empadinha *Portugal* Small pie or tart

empadinha de camarão *Portugal* Small shrimp pie

empanadas *Mexico, South America* Pasties made from a yeast-raised dough containing sweet or savoury fillings, baked or shallow-fried and eaten hot

empanadillas *South America, Spain* Small semicircular pasties made with a well-rested flour and butter pastry (8:5), rolled very thin, filled with a savoury mixture and deep-fried until golden

empanaditas *Mexico, South America* Small **empanadas** eaten as snacks or appetizers

empanado *Spain* Coated in breadcrumbs

empedrat *Catalonia* A salad of salt cod and white beans, normally a starter

emperor's omelette An Austrian dessert of shallow-fied batter containing sultanas or raisins. See also **Kaiserschmarren**

Empetrum nigrum *Botanical name* Crowberry

emping melinjo *Indonesia* The kernel and horny covering around the fruit of the melinjo tree. It is rolled flat and sun-dried for use as a snack or garnish.

emshmel *North Africa* Chicken with lemon and olives from Khemisset in Morocco

emulsifier A compound which aids the dispersion of one liquid or semi-solid in another with which it is immiscible, e.g. oil and vinegar to make mayonnaise, butter with milk and sugar in cake mixes. The emulsifier is usually a long-chain molecule, one end of which dissolves in water and the other end in fat. Egg yolk and French mustard are culinary emulsifiers but many others, synthetic as well as natural, are used in commercial made-up dishes and mixes.

emulsion 1. A mixture of two or more immiscible liquids or semi-solids in which one is divided into very small droplets (less than 0.01 mm diameter) dispersed in the other(s). Mayonnaise, hollandaise sauce and cake batters are typical examples. See also **emulsifier, homogenize, to, dispersed phase, continuous phase 2.** Butter whisked into salted boiling water, used for reheating vegetables just before service to give a pleasing sheen

en *France* In, as in *en croûte*, 'in a crust'; *en papillote*, 'in paper or foil'

enamel A glass-like covering for steel sometimes used for trays, saucepans, casseroles, etc. The enamel can be chipped, crazed by temperature shock or scratched with harsh cleansers or metal spoons, etc.

enasal *Sri Lanka* Cardamom

encarnada *Portugal* Red

enchaud *France* A dish from Périgord of pork and pigs' trotters piquéed with garlic, baked and flavoured with truffles

enchilada *Mexico* A thin **masa harina** tortilla fried both sides, brushed with chilli or tomato sauce, rolled around a filling of cooked meat or poultry or grated cheese, coated with more sauce and eaten hot with guacamole and/or refried beans

enchilado *Mexico* A white, salty and crumbly cows' milk cheese made in a block and sometimes coloured on the outside with chilli powder or annatto. Used for cooking especially enchillada.

enchovas *Portugal* Anchovies. Also called **anchovas**

encornet *France* Squid

encre *France* The black ink from squid or octopus used in sauces for same

encurtidos *Spain* Pickles

endive 1. A bitter salad plant, *Cichorium endivia*, with curly ragged leaves all springing from the base without a heart. Originally from Southeast Asia and introduced by the Dutch in the 16th century and subsequently developed. It can be blanched by excluding light when it is growing to remove the bitterness. Known as chicorée in France and escarole in the USA. Unfortunately (Belgian) chicory is known as *endive* in France, causing much confusion. See also **escarole**, **batavian endive**. Also called **moss curled endive**, **staghorn endive**, **curly endive**, **winter frisée 2.** *France* Belgian chicory

endiver *Sweden* Chicory or chicon

endives à l'étuvée *France* Braised chicons of Belgian chicory

endives au jambon *France* Braised chicons of Belgian chicory wrapped in a slice of ham

Endiviensalat *Germany* Endive salad

endomame *Japan* A type of pea

endosperm The white 80% to 90% inner portion of the wheat grain consisting of spherical starch granules surrounded by a protein matrix and some cell wall material which remain after the bran and wheat germ have been removed

endrina *Spain* Sloe, the fruit

endrina grande *Spain* Bullace, the fruit

endura *Sri Lanka* Dill seed

enebro *Spain* Juniper

eneldo *Spain* Dill

engelsk bøf *Denmark* Fillet steak (NOTE: Literally 'English beef'.)

English breakfast *United Kingdom* A substantial meal of fruit juice, fruit and/or cereals followed by a selection of bacon, sausages, kidneys, eggs, tomatoes, mushrooms and bread, all grilled or fried, or kedgeree or kippers followed by toast, butter, jam and/or marmalade and tea or coffee. Often called Scottish breakfast and Irish breakfast but never British breakfast.

English custard *United Kingdom* Sweetened milk thickened with custard powder (corn flour and vanilla flavouring) and served as a sweet pouring sauce. Sometimes coloured yellow. Also called **custard**, **custard sauce**

English egg custard *United Kingdom* Crème à l'anglaise

English muffin *United States* See **muffin 1**

English mustard A mixture of dehusked and ground brown and white mustard seeds mixed with wheat flour and turmeric, sold dry or mixed with water and preservatives. Used for flavouring or as a condiment.

English puff pastry method Roll out dough into a rectangle 20 cm x 30 cm, cover two thirds (20 x 20) with an even layer of the remaining fat, fold in three to give three layers of dough interleaved with two layers of fat, roll out to the original size repeat the fold, rest the dough then proceed as for **puff pastry**

English sausage *England* Apart from regional and speciality sausages, a rather revolting mixture of ground meat (which includes fat, **drinde**, mechanically recovered meat and other parts of the animal not generally considered to be meat) with rusk, extenders, binders and flavourings packed in casings. By law, pork sausage must contain 65% meat (of which 10% may be drinde), whilst pork and beef sausage need only contain 50% meat.

English service A style of service, usually at private parties, where the host apportions food onto plates which are then distributed by a waiter

English truffle A truffle, *Tuber aestivum*, found in Wiltshire, UK, growing in the root area of beech trees, but not generally available

enguia *Portugal* Eel

enkulat tibs *East Africa* A type of Spanish omelette made with eggs, green and red sweet peppers and sometimes onions served with bread for breakfast in Ethiopia

enlatar *Spain* To can

enlever *France* To remove

enoki *Japan* Enokitake

enokitake *Japan* A small delicately flavoured mushroom, *Flammulina velutipes*, which grows in clumps at the base of the Chinese hackberry tree. They have slender stalks (up to 8 cm long) with a white gold cap. Sold in clumps for use as a garnish or in Japanese salads such as **aemono** and **sunomono**. Available fresh or dried. Also called **enoki**

enrich, to 1. To add some or all of butter, milk, sugar and eggs to a bread dough to produce buns, etc. or to add butter or cream to a batter or sauce, or similar additions **2.** To add back vitamins, trace elements or minerals to processed foods such as white flour, cereals, margarine, fruit juice, etc., sometimes to replace losses in processing, sometimes as a matter of public health policy

enriched rice *United States* Rice, enriched with vitamins and minerals to make up for some of the losses in milling

enrollado *Mexico* Rolled

ensaimada *Spain* A stuffed savoury or sweet bread similar to an empanada

ensalada *Spain* Salad

ensalada andaluza *Spain* A salad of sweet peppers, tomatoes, olives, rice and garlic

ensalada de arroz *Spain* Rice salad

ensalada de pepino *Spain* Cucumber salad

ensalada de San Isidro *Spain* Lettuce and tuna salad

ensalada de verano *Spain* A salad of baked aubergine, tomatoes, sweet peppers and onions with an oil and lemon juice dressing

ensalada variada *Spain* Mixed green salad

ensaladilla *Spain* Salad

enset *East Africa* A relative, *Ensete ventricosum*, of the banana whose corms and stems are used as a food and fibre source in Ethiopia. The tree is very resistant to drought and supports some of the densest populations in Africa. It could be grown in western and southern Africa.

ensopada *Portugal* A meat or fish and vegetable soup thickened with bread

Ente *Germany* Duck

Entenbrüstchen *Germany* Duck breast

Entenmuschel *Germany* Barnacle

Entenweissauer *Germany* Duck in aspic

entosensal *Philippines* Caul

entrahmte Milch *Germany* Skimmed milk

Entrammes *France* The cheese from Entrammes in Brittany made by the monks who originally made **Port-Salut** but who sold the name to commercial interests. Very similar to **Port-Salut**.

entrecot *Spain* Entrecôte steak

entrecôte 1. A steak cut from the middle part of a sirloin of beef **2.** *France, Italy* A thick juicy well-marbled beef steak cut from the wing ribs

entrecôte al ferri *Italy* Grilled fillet or entrecôte steak of beef

entrée *England, France* **1.** The main course or courses of a dinner consisting usually of a proteinaceous part such as meat, game, fish or pulses, with or without accompaniments, but complete with one of the classic white or brown sauces and garnish. Served hot or cold but if there are two dishes, the hot is served first. **2.** Traditionally, a dish forming a complete course in itself without

accompaniments, served between the fish course and the roast

entrée, en *France* A method of trussing a bird in which the drumstick is put through an incision in the skin

entremeses *Spain* Hors d'oeuvres

entremétier *England, France* Vegetable cook

entremets *France* Sweet or dessert, the course following the cheese at a French dinner. Originally any dish served after the main course.

entrocosta *Portugal* Entrecôte steak

E number A three-figure number, currently in the range 100 to 500 and prefixed by a capital E, which is used on packaging to identify all food additives accepted as safe throughout the EU. These do not cover all the additives allowed in the UK or other countries of the EU. Many of these have numbers, and those legal in the UK but not generally throughout the EU are followed by a note saying 'not licensed for use throughout the EU'.

enzymatic browning Browning of fruit and vegetables that occurs when cut surfaces are exposed to air. This is inhibited by acids, e.g. lemon juice or vinegar.

enzyme A natural protein which speeds up the rate of chemical reaction under moderate conditions of temperature, such as oxidation, browning of apples, decolorizing of vegetables, etc. They are easily inactivated by extremes of pH, high concentrations of salt, addition of alcohol or most importantly by temperatures of 80°C or above

épaule *France* Shoulder, usually of lamb or veal, as in *épaule d'agneau*, *épaule de veau*

epazote A strong-flavoured herb used in Mexican cooking and to make an infused tea. Also called **Mexican tea**, **wormseed**

eper *Hungary* Strawberries

éperlan *France* Smelt

epicarp The outer peel of citrus fruit

épice *France* Spice

épices composées *France* A classic spice mix of dried and ground thyme, basil, bay and sage plus coriander seeds, mace and black peppercorns all ground. Also called **spice Parisienne**

epicure A person who appreciates fine food

épicurienne, sauce *France* Mayonnaise flavoured with gherkins and smooth chutney. Served with cold meat, eggs, poultry and fish.

épigramme *France* Slices of boiled breast of lamb, panéed and fried in butter

épinard *France* Spinach

épine *France* Loin of meat (NOTE: Literally 'backbone'.)

épis de maïs *France* Sweetcorn

eple *Norway* Apple

eplesnø *Norway* Apple snow

éplucher *France* To peel

Epoisses *France* A soft strong-flavoured cows' milk cheese from Burgundy, formed into 300 to 400 g discs and washed in brine or local eau-de-vie. Sometimes wrapped in vine leaves or flavoured with spices. Normally has a scored orange crust.

éponger *France* To dry using an absorbent material such as kitchen paper

Epping sausage *England* A skinless frying sausage made of equal parts of pork meat and beef suet, finely minced, seasoned, flavoured with nutmeg, sage and a little bacon and bound with egg

Epsom salts See **E518**

équille *France* Sand eel

erba *Italy* Herb

erba cipollina *Italy* Chive

erba gatta *Italy* Catmint

erbaggi *Italy* 1. Pot herbs 2. Green vegetables 3. Salads

erba riccia *Italy* Lamb's lettuce

erbette *Italy* A spinach or beet-like leaf vegetable. Also called **bietoline**

Erbsen *Germany* Peas

Erbsenbrei *Germany* Puréed peas

Erbsensuppe *Germany* Pea soup

Erdapfel *Austria* Potato

Erdapfelnudeln *Austria* Very small potato dumplings rolled in fried breadcrumbs

Erdartischocke *Germany* Jerusalem artichoke

Erdbeere *Germany* Strawberry

Erdbeerkaltschale *Germany* A cold strawberry soup made from pulped wild strawberries mixed with sugar and white wine, passed though a sieve and garnished with whole wild strawberries dipped in sugar

Erdnuss *Germany* Peanut

ergo *East Africa* The Ethiopian name for a type of yoghurt

ergocalciferol See **vitamin D2**

Erimis peynir *Turkey* A semi-hard spun-curd cheese made from ewes' or goats' milk and eaten fresh

Eriobotrya japonica *Botanical name* Loquat

eriphie *France* A type of small furry crab. See also **cangrejo moruno**

erizo de mar *Spain* Sea urchin

Erkentaler *Germany* An Emmental-type cheese

ermek kaimaksi *Southwest Asia* A bread pudding from Armenia made from slices of crustless heavy bread toasted in the oven at 170°C until golden, overlapped in a shallow dish, moistened with a little milk and then soaked in a sugar syrup (2 kg per litre) and baked at 180°C until brown and puffy. Served covered with a type of clotted cream (**kaimak**).

ermitaño *Spain* Hermit crab

Ermite *Canada* A semi-hard blue-veined cows' milk cheese from Quebec

erter *Norway* Peas

ertersuppe *Norway* Pea soup

Eruca vesicaria *Botanical name* Rocket

erucic acid A fatty acid once a significant constituent of rapeseed oil and considered a potential danger to health in large quantities. Varieties of rape which contain only low concentrations have now been developed for oil production.

erugala Rocket

ervanço *Portugal* Chick peas

ervilhas *Portugal* Peas

erwentensoep *Netherlands* A thick puréed soup made from split green peas and vegetables in a meat stock. It is refrigerated after cooking then reheated with Frankfurter sausages. A national dish of Holland.

erwten *Netherlands* Peas

erythrosine BS A synthetic red food colouring, used for glacé cherries. See also **E127**

ésaü *France* Containing lentils (NOTE: From the Bible story.)

escabeche *Spain* 1. Pickled 2. Cooked small whole fish marinated in a spiced oil and vinegar mixture and served cold in the marinade 3. The marinade used in 2 above

escalfado *Portugal* Poached

escalfados Poached eggs

escalfar *Spain* To poach

escalivada *Catalonia* Roasted aubergines, onions, tomatoes, sweet peppers and black olives dressed with olive oil. Called escalibada elsewhere in Spain.

escalopado *Mexico* Made into escalopes

escalope *England, France* A thin slice of meat cut from a large muscle without bone, gristle or sinews, often from the top of the leg or the fillet, and beaten out until very thin prior to frying

escalope cordon bleu Two escalopes of pork or veal, made into a sandwich with 1 slice of Gruyère cheese and 1 slice of ham, edges dampened to seal, panéed, marked with a diamond pattern on the presentation side, shallow-fried and served with a rondel of lemon and chopped parsley

escalope de veau *France* A veal escalope usually panéed and fried or coated with flour, seared and simmered in stock or wine

escalope normande, vallée d'Auge *France* An escalope of veal or chicken breast served with a calvados-flavoured cream sauce and sautéed apples

escamarlà (*plural* **escamarlans**) *Catalonia* **1.** Dublin bay prawn(s) **2.** Scampi

escargot *France* Edible snail

escargot clamp A small pair of metal tongues used to hold a snail shell while the snail meat is extracted

escargot de mer *France* Whelk (NOTE: Literally 'sea snail'.)

escargot fork A small fork with two long tines, used to extract snail meat from its shell

escargotière *France* Dish on which snails are served

escargots à la bourguignonne *France* Snails with garlic butter and chopped parsley

escarola *Spain* Endive

escarole *Italy, United States* A variety of slightly bitter broad-leaved endive, *Cichorium endivia*, used in salads. Usually blanched in the garden. Also called **scarola**

Escherichia coli A human gut bacteria whose presence in food indicates poor food hygiene. Some strains found in meat can cause food poisoning. The incubation period in 12 to 72 hours, the duration is 1 to 7 days and the symptoms are either cholera-like illness with watery diarrhoea and pain or prolonged diarrhoea with blood and mucous.

Escoffier Auguste Escoffier 1846 – 1935, apprentice chef at age 13, worked until 1920, took charge of the Savoy Hotel (London) kitchens in 1890, opened the Carlton and the Paris Ritz in the late 1890s, wrote and published Le Guide Culinaire in 1903 which contains over 5000 recipes and is still a classic reference book. Famous for his instruction to chefs – *faites simple* – 'keep it simple'.

escopinyes *Catalonia* Cockles

escovitch *Caribbean* Escabeche

escudella *Catalonia* A plain broth with rice or pasta

escudella i carn d'olla *Catalonia* The soup part of the traditional Catalan hotpot

escupina grabada, escupina gravada *Spain* Warty venus clam

eshkaneh *Central Asia* A meatless soup from Iran based on onion and a souring agent with various additions of vegetables or chopped nuts, fruit etc. Eggs, either beaten and dribbled in or poached, are used to finish the soup

Eskdale *England* A Camembert type cheese from Yorkshire

esmorzar *Catalonia* Breakfast

espadín *Spain* Sprat

espadon *France* Swordfish

espagnole, à l' *France* In the Spanish style, i.e. with sweet peppers, tomatoes, garlic and onions

espagnole, sauce *England, France* Brown sauce, one of the three classic basic sauces made from a brown roux mixed with tomato purée and brown stock. It is flavoured with defatted browned aromatic vegetables and simmered from 4 to 6 hours, skimmed as necessary and finally strained. Also called **brown sauce, Spanish sauce**

espaguetis *Italy* Spaghetti

espargo bravo *Portugal* Wild asparagus

espargos *Portugal* Asparagus

espárrago *Spain* Asparagus

espàrrecs *Catalonia* Asparagus

especia *Spain* Spice

espetar *Spain* To truss

espinaca *Spain* Spinach

espinacs a la catalana *Catalonia* Cooked spinach with pine nuts, raisins and anchovies, often used as a starter

espinafre *Portugal* Spinach

espresso *England, Italy* Coffee made with dark-roasted finely ground coffee through which superheated water (water under pressure at a temperature greater than 100°C) is forced. This extracts a high proportion of coffee solubles plus bitter components not normally found in conventionally brewed coffee.

esprot *France* Sprat

esqueixada 1. *Spain* Fish salad from Galicia **2.** *Catalonia* A salt cod, onion and sweet pepper salad

esquexada *Catalonia* A salt cod, onion and sweet pepper salad

esquinade *France* Spider crab

Esrom *Denmark* A semi-hard soft cheese with irregularly-shaped holes ripened for 1 to 3 weeks. It is cast in 500 g to 1 kg bricks and has a mild piquant flavour and a thin yellow to orange coloured rind. Contains 50% water, 23% fat and 22% protein.

essbare Muschel *Germany* Clam

essence An extract of flavouring compounds usually from fruit or vegetable matter but occasionally from meat. The extractant is usually alcohol.

essential amino acids Amino acids which are necessary for health and cannot be synthesized in the body and must therefore be obtained from food. They are: isoleucine, leucine, lysine, methionine, phenylalanine, threonine, tryptophan and valine, plus histidine which is required by growing infants and may be required by adults.

essential fatty acids Fatty acids which cannot be synthesized in the body and must be obtained from food sources. The important ones are: linolenic, linoleic, arachidonic (AA), gamma linolenic (GLA) and eicosopentanoic acid (EPA). All are involved in the synthesis of prostaglandins which have a variety of important bodily functions and in the construction of the myelin sheaths around nerve fibres and the synthesis of cell walls. Also called **vitamin F, EFA**

essential oil The oily compounds secreted by or extracted from plants, flowers and fruit which have a concentrated aroma. Used in flavourings.

essenza *Italy* A meat or fish glaze

Essig *Germany* Vinegar

Essiggurke *Germany* Pickled gherkins

Essigkren *Germany* Horseradish sauce, grated horseradish in vinegar with sugar and spices

Essigpilze *Germany* Pickled mushroom

estanboli polou *Central Asia* An Iranian rice-based dish (**polou**) made with cubed lamb or beef and chopped onion, simmered after frying with cinnamon, paprika and tomato purée. The pan or dish may be lined when assembling with slices of potato coated in clarified butter and the whole cooked dish turned out like a cake.

ester The general name for the compound produced by reacting an alcohol with an acid. Most esters have pleasant fruity flavours and aromas. Some are extracted from fruits but many are now made synthetically.

esterase An enzyme which breaks down esters into their component acids and alcohols, thus destroying or modifying the flavour or aroma

Esterhazy Rostbraten *Austria* Roast stuffed fillet of beef basted with Madeira wine

Esterházy rostélyos *Hungary* Thin slices of seasoned sirloin steak browned in lard and casseroled with sliced onion, carrots, Hamburg parsley and flour, browned in the same fat, seasoned stock, slices of lemon and capers until cooked. The steak is removed and transferred to a dish on a bed of julienned carrots and Hamburg parsley previously fried in butter and simmered in stock. The strained juices from the casserole

are poured over, sour cream added and all simmered for a few minutes. Served with rice or noodles.

estofado *Spain* Beef or veal pieces simmered with sliced onions, strips of green pepper, chopped tomatoes, the flesh of charred garlic, olive oil, lemon juice, wine, paprika, bay, parsley and thyme for about 2 hours or until cooked adding a minimum of water as required. See also **humba**

estofado de rabo *Spain* Oxtail stew with garlic, tomato and anchovy paste

estofar *Spain* To stew

estofat *Catalonia* Stewed

estofat de bou *Catalonia* A rich beef stew with sausages and potatoes, flavoured with herbs and sometimes with chocolate

estofat de porc senglar amb bolets *Catalonia* Wild boar casserole with wild mushrooms

estofat de quaresma *Catalonia* A Lenten vegetable stew

estomac *France* Stomach

Estonkij See **Estonski**

Estonski A semi-hard cows' milk cheese from Estonia which uses a complex mixed culture as a starter to give it a mildly acid aromatic flavour. Contains 45% water, 25% fat and 23% protein. Also called **Estonkij**

estouffade 1. *England, France* Brown beef stock **2.** *France* A beef or pork pot roast with vegetables or beans, herbs, seasoning and stock or wine. Also called **étouffat**

estragon *France, Russia* Tarragon

estragon, à l' *France* Flavoured with tarragon

estragon, sauce *England, France* A velouté sauce based on fish stock flavoured with tarragon. Served with fish.

estragón *Spain* Tarragon

Estragon *Germany* Tarragon

estrella *Spain* A hard ewes' milk cheese from Toledo. See also **Oropesa**

estrellado *Spain* Fried (egg)

esturgeon *France* Sturgeon

esturión *Spain* Sturgeon

et *Turkey* Meat

étamine *France* Muslin, cheesecloth or tammy cloth for straining

ethanol The alcohol produced by the fermentation of sugars which is responsible for the intoxicating effects of alcoholic drinks. It disappears from boiling liquid after some time. Used as a solvent for food colourings and flavourings. Also called **ethyl alcohol**

Ethiopian cardamom The seed pods of a bush, *Aframomum korarima*, from Ethiopia used as a cheap substitute for green cardamom. Has a more camphor-like flavour than the true cardamom.

ethoxyquin A chemical used to prevent discoloration (**scald**) on apples and pears

ethrog See **etrog**

ethyl acetate An ester of ethanol and acetic acid used as a solvent for food colours and flavourings

ethyl alcohol See **ethanol**

ethylene A gas given off by ripening fruit which also accelerates ripening. An overripe banana is often used in an enclosed space to provide this gas.

ethylenediamine-NNN'N'-tetra-acetate A very common and powerful sequestering agent both as is and as its salts. Abbreviated to EDTA.

etikkasilli *Finland* Pickled herring

etima *West Africa* The name given to the seeds of the wild mango tree in Gabon and Cameroon. Also called **odika**, **dika**

étolaj *Hungary* Cooking oil

Eton mess *England* Chopped strawberries macerated in kirsch (5:1 by weight) then mixed with cream whipped to a trail and crushed meringue and served immediately in individual dishes decorated with strawberries and mint leaves

étouffat *France* A beef or pork pot roast with vegetables or beans, herbs, seasoning and stock or wine. See also **estouffade**

étouffée *France* A pot with a very tight-fitting lid used for steaming or braising

étouffée, à l' *France* Cooked in a pot with a tight-fitting lid and with very little liquid over a low heat

étouffe of beef *United States* A Creole pot roast from Louisiana containing beef, onions, green peppers, tomatoes, garlic and seasonings. Also called **smothered beef**

étrille *France* Velvet swimming crab

etrog A citron smaller than most varieties with a smooth firm and yellow to yellow orange skin with deep ridges. Used in the Jewish feast of the tabernacles. Also called **ethrog**

etto *Italy* Hectogram equal to one tenth of a kilogram, 100 g

étuvée, à l' *France* Braised

eucalyptus oil *Australia* A very distinctive tasting oil extracted from eucalyptus leaves. 2 to 4 drops per litre is adequate flavouring for use in desserts or savoury sauces. Also called **gumleaf oil**

Euda *United States* A low-fat semi-hard cows' milk cheese which is salted, moulded and ripened for 3 months

Eugenia caryophyllus *Botanical name* Cloves

Eugenia uniflora *Botanical name* Surinam cherry

europäischer Flusskrebs *Germany* Freshwater crayfish

European edible frog See **frog**

European flat oyster The original oyster of European waters, *Ostrea edulis*. Considered to have the best flavour, with the English native being the most prized. They are found from Norway down to Morocco and the Mediterranean and are best served raw with a squeeze of lemon. See also **oyster**

European grape The original European grape variety, *Vitis vinifera*. See also **grape**

European sand smelt See **sand smelt**

European Welsh onion See **Welsh onion**

eustis A variety of **limequat**

Euter *Germany* Udder

evaporated milk Homogenized cows' milk from which 60 to 65% of the water has been removed under a vacuum at not more than 66°C. Sold sterilized in cans. Use as a cream substitute.

evening primrose A hardy biennial plant, *Oenothera biennis*, growing to 2 m with large yellow flowers. The seeds are the source of evening primrose oil which contains a high proportion of gamma linoleic acid, a precursor of many important body chemicals and used as a health supplement and prophylactic. The leaves and stems were once used as a popular food by North Native Americans. The root may be boiled and eaten either pickled or as a salad vegetable.

Eve's darning needle *United States* See **yucca 2**

Eve's pudding *England* A pudding made in a dish with alternating layers of sliced apples and sugar, topped with a basic steamed pudding mix or Victoria sponge mixture and baked

eviscerate, to To remove the internal organs from a carcass. Most animals are now eviscerated at the abbatoir but fish, poultry and game birds often need eviscerating after purchase.

Evora *Portugal* A pale yellow mountain cheese made from a mixture of ewes' and cows' milk. It is well salted with a full flavour and has a crumbly texture. Eaten either fresh when creamy and piquant or fully ripe when firm and biting.

ewe A female sheep

Excelsior *France* A mild double cream cows' milk cheese from Normandy shaped like a small cylinder

Exeter stew *England* Chuck steak, cubed, floured and browned with chopped onions, carrots and turnips and simmered in brown stock for 2 to 3 hours. Served with savoury dumplings cooked in the stew for the last half hour.

exocet *France* Flying fish

explorateur *France* A small cylindrical-shaped triple-cream cows' milk cheese from the Paris region with a delicate flavour and a Camembert-type rind

extended life See **ultra-heat treated**

extender A substance added to food to increase its bulk as e.g. flour with ground spices or gelatine, water and sugar with whipped cream

extract, to To remove and preserve flavour, colour or aroma from a foodstuff by a variety of means, e.g. simmering in water, macerating in alcohol, with oil, steam distillation, squeezing, pressing or absorbing onto a solid or fat

extraction 1. The process of extracting one component from a mixture **2.** The percentage of flour which is obtained from the original dehusked wheat grain. For white flours this is normally around 80%. Above this figure the bran content starts to increase giving a brown appearance.

extractives The flavouring components in meat and browned vegetables which dissolve in the cooking liquor to give it flavour

extracts Flavourings, aromas and colours in concentrated form produced by extraction

extra vergine *Italy* Extra virgin olive oil

extra virgin olive oil The first cold pressing of stoned and skinned ripe olives with a free oleic acid content of less than 1% The term

has nothing to do with quality and there is no regulation to prevent manufacturers reducing the acidity by chemical means

Extrawurst *Austria, Germany* A moist, light coloured **Brühwurst** made from a well-spiced mixture of beef and pork or bacon fat. Used for slicing and sandwiches, in salads, or cooked in stews and casseroles. Also called **Fleischwurst**

extrude, to To force a paste or semi-solid through variously shaped holes under high pressure as e.g. in the production of spaghetti, macaroni and the like

eye 1. The term for the circular or oval shape formed from the cross section of a single muscle cut out from a chop or slice of meat **2.** The dark spot on a potato from which the next year's shoots would sprout

eyeballs Eyeballs of sheep removed from the head after cooking are eaten as a delicacy in some Middle Eastern countries

Eyemouth fish pie *Scotland* Pieces of white fish simmered in milk with chopped shallots for 5 minutes, reserved then added to a roux-thickened sauce made with the cooking liquor and some white wine. This mixture is layered with sliced hard-boiled eggs and tomatoes in a pie dish, topped with mashed potatoes and gratinated with cheese and breadcrumbs and browned under the grill.

eye of round *United States* The round muscle in the centre of the top of the hindquarter (rear leg) of beef. Part of the topside in the English cuts.

FGHIJKLM

faa jiu *China* Anise pepper

faan *China* Rice

faan sue *China* Sweet potato

faarn woon *China* The small individual rice bowl from which Chinese meals are eaten

faat sau gwa *China* Choko

fabada *Spain* A Spanish **cassoulet** from Asturia made with butter beans, sausage and smoked ham

façon de, à la *France* In the style or manner of

fadge Irish potato cakes

fagara Anise pepper

fågel *Sweden* Poultry or game

fågelbo *Sweden* As **solöga**, but with a ring of chopped cold boiled potatoes added (NOTE: Literally 'bird's nest'.)

fågelsås *Sweden* Game sauce made from game bones browned with aromatic vegetables, simmered in stock for 20 minutes, skimmed, strained, thickened with **beurre manié** and finished with cream

faggot 1. The name applied to a bunch of herbs tied with string and used as a bouquet garni **2.** *Wales, England* A pâté of liver, salt pork or bacon, herbs, spices, seasoning, minced onion and extender such as breadcrumbs, oatmeal or mashed potato, formed into a tennis-ball size and covered with pig's caul. Traditionally made with liver, lungs, spleen, pork scraps and fat. Simmered or baked. Also called **savoury duck, poor man's goose, Welsh faggot**

fagianella *Italy* Pheasant

fagiano *Italy* Pheasant

fagioli *Italy* Dried beans

fagioli asciaboli *Italy* Butter beans

fagioli assoluti *Italy* Cooked bean fried with garlic in oil

fagioli borlotto An Italian bean of the same family as French beans with a pinkish skin when dried. Also called **rose cocoa bean**

fagioli di lima *Italy* Butter beans

fagiolini *Italy* French green beans

fagiolini all'aretina *Italy* French beans stewed with oil, tomatoes and sage

fa goo *China* Shiitake mushroom

fagot *United States* Faggot (of herbs)

fagottino *Italy* Pastry

fagylaltot *Hungary* Ice cream

fah chiu *China* Hot seasoning pepper

Fahrenheit scale The scale of temperature in which the freezing point of water is 32 and the boiling point 212 written 32°F and 212°F. Once used in the UK and found in old recipes, still in use in the USA.

faht choy *China* A marine alga made up of fine hair-like strands, probably the same as **nori**

fai chee *China* Chopsticks

fai gee *China* Large chopsticks (30 to 50 cm), used in cooking

faire lever *France* To leaven or raise with yeast or chemical raising agent

faire revenir *France* To brown (vegetables, meat, etc.)

fair maids A Cornish name for smoked pilchards (*colloquial*)

fairy cakes Small individual cakes made from a sponge mixture with currants, baked in a bun tin or paper case and decorated

fairy ring mushroom An edible mushroom, *Marasmius oreades*, which grows in circular rings on grass land, the rings becoming larger each year. It has a small fawn hump backed cap on a slender stem.

faisan *France* Cock pheasant

faisán *Spain* Cock pheasant

faisandeau *France* Young pheasant

faisander *France* To hang game

faisane *France* Hen pheasant

faisão *Portugal* Pheasant

faisinjan Fried chicken or duck cooked in a pomegranate and crushed walnut sauce. See also **fesenjan**

fajita *Mexico* A soft tortilla filled and rolled with some or all of grilled meat, grated cheese, chopped lettuce, tomatoes and spring onions. Served warm with sour cream.

fak *Thailand* Wax gourd

falafel *Middle East* A common street food made from soaked chick peas, onions, garlic, fresh parsley or coriander leaves, ground cumin and coriander seed, cayenne pepper, salt and baking powder processed to a fine cohering paste, formed into small flattened balls and deep-fried for 3 to 4 minutes. See also **ta'amia**. Also called **felafel**

faloode *Iran* An Iranian version of ice cream made from starch noodles, herb extract, rose water and sugar

falscher Hase *Germany* Mock hare made with chopped beef, pork and veal mixed with sweated chopped onions, capers, lemon juice and seasoning, bound with eggs, formed into a roll, panéed and roasted in butter. Served with pan residues deglazed with cream.

falscher Wildschweinbraten *Germany* Mock boar made from a skinned and trimmed leg of pork, marinated in red wine and vinegar (4:1) with grated onions, juniper berries, lemon zest, bay leaves, tarragon, ground cloves, allspice, ginger and black pepper for 2 days then roasted at 160°C in the usual way

falsk hollandäs *Sweden* Mock **hollandaise sauce**, not based on béchamel as is Dutch sauce but on a fish velouté enriched with egg yolks into which butter and lemon juice are whisked over a low heat until thick and creamy

falukorv *Sweden* A sausage from Falun made of beef, lean pork and pork back fat, hot smoked and eaten hot either as is or as a made up dish

familiario *Italy* In a simple, homely style

fan *China* Rice

fanchette, fanchonnette *France* A tiny tart made of puff pastry filled with crème pâtissière and covered with meringue. Also called **fanchonnette**

fanesca A Lenten soup from Ecuador made from salt cod, vegetables, peanuts, cheese, milk, cream, stock and seasonings

fan kua *China* A heavy metal pan used for cooking rice by the absorption method

fan mussel One of the largest British mussels, *Pinna fragilis* or *P. pectinata*, up to 35 cm long with a yellow brown shell which it buries in the sand. Cooked like a scallop. Also called **pen shell**, **sea wing**

faoitin *Ireland* Whiting, the fish

faqqas *North Africa* A hard crunchy biscuit from Morocco flavoured with aniseed and sesame seeds or almonds and raisins

faqqus *North Africa* A variety of Moroccan cucumber, often grated and mixed with sugar, orange-blossom water and thyme as a salad

far *France* A rum-flavoured tart or flan from Brittany

får *Sweden* Mutton

faraona *Italy* Guinea fowl, often covered in damp clay before roasting

Färberbaum *Germany* Sumac

farce *England, France* A stuffing or forcemeat

farce, to To stuff

farce de gibier *France* Game livers quickly browned with chopped onion in butter (4:1:1), plus thyme and bay leaf, leaving the centre of the livers underdone; then sieved, seasoned and mixed with butter equal in quantity to that used for frying

farci(e) *France* Filled with a savoury stuffing or forcemeat

farcima A type of ancient Roman sausage thought to be the origin of the words 'farce' and 'forcemeat'

farci niçois *France* Stuffed courgettes, aubergines, tomatoes and onions braised slowly in olive oil

farcir *France* To stuff

farcit *Catalonia* Stuffed

farcito *Italy* Stuffed

farçon au cerfeuil *France* Riced potatoes, mixed with beaten eggs, milk, fried diced bacon, onions and shallots, raisins, grated cheese, seasoning and chervil and baked in a greased dish at 220°C until golden

fare bollire *Italy* To boil

fåre frikassée *Norway* Fricassée of lamb or mutton

fårekjøtt *Norway* Mutton

fåre kød *Denmark* Mutton

fårekotelett *Norway* Mutton chop

fårepølse *Norway* A sausage made with a mixture of mutton, beef, goats' meat and sugar, seasoned and moistened with alcohol of some kind

fårestek *Norway* Roast leg of lamb or mutton

farfalle *Italy* Small pasta pieces made in the shape of a bow tie or butterfly

farfallini A small version of farfalle

farfel A small diamond- or pellet-shaped Jewish pasta

fårgryta med linser *Sweden* A casserole of middle neck of lamb browned in dripping, laid in a heavy pot on a bed of sweated onions, covered with water or stock plus a bouquet garni and seasoning, simmered and skimmed for an hour, soaked lentils added and simmered until cooked, bouquet garni removed and the whole finished with a little soya sauce and chopped parsley

får i kål *Sweden* A lamb and cabbage casserole consisting of blanched and possibly parboiled breast of lamb or shoulder of lamb, trimmed, defatted and cut in pieces, layered with cabbage in a large pan with a few peppercorns, salt and flour between each layer, covered in stock and simmered 1.5 to 2 hours. Served garnished with chopped parsley. It may be reheated.

farina *England, Italy* The name given to various types of flours made from wheat, nuts or root vegetables

farinaceous Containing a high proportion of starch

farina di granturco *Italy* Corn flour

farinata alla contadina *Italy* Polenta, wheat flour and milk boiled to a gruel with poppy seeds and sweetened. Also called **mus**

farinata alla ligure *Italy* A fried cake of chick pea flour

farine *France* Flour

farine de blé *France* Wheat flour

farine de froment *France* Wheat flour

farine de maïs *France* Corn flour

farinha de avêa *Portugal* Oatmeal

farinha de mandioca *Portugal* A flour made from cassava much used in Brazil

fårkött *Sweden* Mutton

farl 1. *Ireland, Scotland* Small thin triangular-shaped biscuits or cakes made with wheat flour or oatmeal. Usually baked in the round and scored for quarters. (NOTE: Literally 'fourth part'.) **2.** *Scotland* A quarter, e.g. of an oatcake

farmed salmon Salmon grown in cages in sea lochs or inlets in Scotland, Norway and other suitable locations. Distinguishable from wild salmon by their pinker flesh and perfect tail fins.

Farmers' *United States* Cottage cheese made from cultured cows' milk with added cream, salted and sold in tubs

farmhouse Cheddar *England* The traditional Cheddar cheese made in small dairies, always matured in cloths for 1 to 2 years and having a superb flavour

farmhouse loaf A white bread dough raised in an oblong loaf tin, dusted with flour and the top slit or slashed lengthwise so that the slit opens out as it bakes

farofa *Brazil* A bland mealy flour made from cassava, often toasted before use

farricello *Italy* Barley

far sang *China* Peanut

farsh *Russia* Stuffing

farshi *Nepal* Winter squash

farshirovannyi perets (*plural* **farshirovannie pertsy**) *Russia* Stuffed sweet peppers, usually with a cooked spicy mixture of minced lamb, onions, rice and sultanas with tomato purée, eggs and honey and all baked at 190°C for 40 minutes. Also called **perets farshirovanny**

Färsk getost *Sweden* A semi-hard goats' milk cheese made in a brick shape (up to 1.2 kg) and ripened for up to 1 week

färsk sill *Sweden* Fresh herring

fårstek *Sweden* Leg of mutton

far sung yau *China* Peanut oil

fasan *Denmark, Norway, Sweden* Pheasant

Fasan *Germany* Pheasant

faschierter Braten *Germany* Meat loaf

fasciola A species of fluke infecting cattle and sheep worldwide, transmitted to humans by watercress and other aquatic plants which act as host to the larvae, and causes liver damage for which no satisfactory cure yet exists

faséole *France* Kidney bean

fasnacht *United States* A yeast-raised potato dough, rolled out, cut in diamond shapes, proved and fried. Traditionally eaten on Shrove Tuesday by the descendants of Pennsylvania Dutch immigrants.

fasol (*plural* **fasoli**) *Russia* **1.** French beans in the pod **2.** Flageolet beans **3.** Haricot beans

fasolaro *Italy* Venus shell clam. Also called **cappa liscia**

fassolatha *Greece* A meatless soup made with parboiled (15 minutes) haricot beans drained then fried with chopped onions and garlic in olive oil, all boiled in water with tomato purée, **tomato concassée**, bay and oregano until the beans are tender, seasoned and finished with chopped parsley

fast food Food which can be cooked very quickly while the customers wait, e.g. fish and chips, hamburgers, doner and shish kebabs and Chinese stir-fry dishes

fast-freeze, to To freeze food very rapidly so as to prevent the formation of large ice crystals within the cell which would disrupt them and cause the contents to leak out on thawing, thus destroying the structure of the food

fasulya *Turkey* Beans

fasulya plâki *Turkey* A salad made from cooked haricot beans, chopped onions, tomatoes and sweet peppers, dressed with olive oil, flavoured with seasonings and chopped parsley or dill

fat An ester of fatty acids and glycerol formed in the bodies of animals or plants as a long term energy store, and in the case of animals as a source of energy for their young prior to weaning and as an essential component of cell walls. May be heated to high temperatures without decomposition and generally adds flavour, texture and succulence to most foods and dishes. Oils are fats with low melting points. Also called **lipid**

fatányéros *Hungary* A mixed grill of 3 or 4 kinds of meat and offal, served on a wooden platter and accompanied by chips and pickles

fat choy *China* Hair vegetable

fat content of cheese The fat content is expressed as a percent by weight of the dry matter, so that a soft high-fat cheese could contain a lower overall percentage of fat than a hard low-fat cheese

fat end See **bung**

fat extenders Food additives that allow the fat content of food to be reduced without affecting the texture

fathead Sheepshead fish

fat hen A hardy perennial herb, *Chenopodium album*, similar to **Good King Henry**, whose seeds, which are rich in fat and protein, have been used since Neolithic times and may be ground into a flour

fatia *Portugal* Slice

fatias frias *Portugal* Sliced meats, assiette anglaise

fatira *East Africa* Ethiopian savoury pasties

fatless cake mixture Equal parts by weight of flour, caster sugar and eggs without raising agent, made up using the fatless whisking method

fatless sponge A light sponge cake made without fat and which goes dry and stale very quickly. Angel food cake is an example.

fatless whisking method A method of making cakes by combining eggs and sugar with a balloon whisk over hot water until light, creamy and doubled in volume and at the ribbon stage, removing from the heat and continuing to whisk until cool, then carefully folding in the dry ingredients. The job may be done in a mechanical mixer without heat.

fat mouse Various varieties of short-tailed mice of the genus *Steatomys*, which are eaten as a delicacy in South America

fa ts'ai *China* Hair vegetable

fattiga riddare *Sweden* Pain perdu, French toast

fatto in casa *Italy* Made on the premises, home-made

fattoosh *Middle East* Fattoush

fattore, alla maniere del, al modo di *Italy* In farmhouse style, i.e. crisply fried with gherkins and mustard sauce

fattoush *Middle East* A Syrian and Lebanese salad of chopped cucumber, tomatoes, spring onions and sweet green peppers with shredded lettuce heart, chopped mint, parsley and coriander leaves, all seasoned and dressed with olive oil and lemon juice. The salad is chilled and just before serving, cubes of thin crisply toasted bread are added. Also called **fattoosh**

fatty acid A long-chain hydrocarbon with an acid group at one end. This combines with an alcohol such as glycerine by the esterification reaction to form natural fats and oils, or with a metal such as sodium to form a soap. They are also esterified with a variety of higher alcohols for use in convenience foods. Generally produced from natural fats and oils, and they are the initial breakdown product of fats in the body.

fatty acid salts Sodium, potassium and calcium salts of fatty acids which form edible soaps used as emulsifying agents. See also **E470**

fatty cutties *Scotland* The same as the Northumberland **singing hinny**

Faubonne *France* A puréed vegetable soup flavoured with herbs

fausse limande *France* Scald, the fish

fausse tortue *France* Mock turtle

faux-filet *France* A cut of beef steak from the top of the sirloin. Also called **contre-filet**

fava *Italy, Portugal* Broad bean

fava bean Broad bean

favata *Italy* A rich stew of dried beans, pork, fennel, cabbage and tomatoes

fave *Italy* Broad beans

fave dei morti *Italy* Almond and pine nut biscuits, traditionally baked in Lombardy for All Soul's day

faverolles *France* A Provençal name for haricot beans

faves a la catalana *Catalonia* A stew made of broad beans, black pudding, bacon, onions and garlic

favollo *Italy* A type of small furry crab. See also **cangrejo moruno**

favorite, à la *France* Garnished with asparagus tips, pâté de foie gras and truffles (steaks), or artichoke hearts, potatoes and celery (roasts)

fazan *Russia* Pheasant

fazan po-gruzinsky *Southwest Asia* Georgian-style pheasant braised in green tea, grape juice, orange juice and zest, chopped walnuts and sweet fortified wine for

50 minutes. The drained pheasant is portioned, browned in the oven at 220°C and served with the strained cooking liquor reduced to a syrupy consistency and accompanied with quince jelly.

fazolia bean Cannellino bean

feather beef steak A frying or braising steak cut from between the neck and fore rib of beef. It is oval in shape with a feathery line of gristle running down the centre.

feather fowlie *Scotland* A good chicken stock made by boiling a chicken with bacon and aromatic vegetables, straining and thickening the liquid with a liaison of egg yolks and cream, and adding back the minced chicken flesh (NOTE: The name is said to be a corruption of the French *velouté de volaille*)

febras de porco *Portugal* A boned-out leg of pork cooked in red wine and flavoured with brandy, cloves, garlic and cumin

fechun *France* Cabbage rolls stuffed with pork from Franche-Comté

fécula *Spain* Starch

fécule Starch; particularly potato starch which is made by grinding raw potatoes and washing away the solubles with water, leaving a pure starch similar in properties to corn flour and arrowroot. Also called **potato starch**, **potato flour**

fedelini *Italy* Very thin pasta noodles used in soup

Federwild *Germany* Game birds

fegatelli *Italy* Small cubes or slices of pig's liver threaded on skewers then grilled or baked in various ways

fegatini *Italy* Chicken livers

fegato *Italy* Liver

fegato alla Veneziana *Italy* Liver and onions

fegato di maiale *Italy* Pork liver

fegato d'oca *Italy* Goose liver

fehérhagyma mártás *Hungary* Onion sauce

Feige *Germany* Fig

feijão 1. *Portugal* Bean **2.** *Brazil* Butter bean, lima bean

feijão branco *Portugal* White bean

feijão de frade *Portugal* Black-eyed pea

feijão de vaca *Portugal* Black-eyed pea or cow pea

feijão de vagem *Portugal* Feijão verde

feijão encarnado *Portugal* Red bean

feijão manteiga *Portugal* Butter bean

feijão preto *Portugal* Black bean

feijão verde *Portugal* Green beans, runner or French. Also called **feijão de vagem**, **vagem**

feijoa The fruit of an evergreen shrub, *Feijoa sellowiana*, a native of South America but now grown in Australia and the southern

USA. It is about 5 cm long with a reddish green inedible skin and whitish to green flesh which surrounds a core of soft seed-filled pulp. Tastes like guava with a hint of pineapple. Also called **Brazilian guava**, **pineapple guava**

feijoada completa *Brazil, Portugal* A stew of black beans, dried and salted beef, fresh beef, tongue, bacon, sausage, pig's trotters, ears and tails, onions, garlic, tomatoes, parsley, bay leaves chillies and seasoning. A national dish of Brazil accompanied with white rice, **farofa**, orange and green vegetables.

Feijoa sellowiana *Botanical name* Feijoa

feine Extrawurst *Austria* Extrawurst in which the filling is very finely minced

feine Mettwurst *Germany* Fine-textured Mettwurst

feiner Zucker *Germany* Granulated or caster sugar

Feingebäck *Germany* Pastry

feingemischter Aufschnitt *Germany* Mixed sliced cold meats

fejessaláta *Hungary* Lettuce

felafel A common street food made from soaked chick peas, onions and garlic with herbs and spices, deep-fried in balls. See also **falafel**

Felchen *Germany* A type of freshwater trout

felisówka *Poland* Soured buttermilk which has been allowed to ferment slightly and is slightly alcoholic

fenalår *Norway* Smoked leg of mutton

Fenchel *Germany* Fennel

fen chiew *China* Red girl wine

fennel 1. See **Florence fennel 2.** A herb, *Foeniculum vulgare*, indigenous to the Mediterranean with an aniseed flavour. The dried seeds are used as a spice or may be sprouted for winter salads and the feathery leaves are used to flavour fish dishes or in salads. Also called **sweet cumin**

fennel sauce Butter sauce, mixed with blanched chopped fennel at the rate of 20 ml per litre

fennel spice mix A blend of flavours suitable for coating fish prior to barbecueing. Made from fresh garlic, grated lemon zest and ground black peppercorns, coriander seeds, fennel seeds and dried thyme pounded together.

fenogreco *Spain* Fenugreek

fenouil *France* Florence fennel

fenouil de mer *France* Samphire, *Crithmum maritimum*

fen si *China* Cellophane noodles

fenugrec *France* Fenugreek

fenugreek A herb, *Trigonella foenum-graecum*, with 10-cm-long seed pods containing irregular yellow seeds about 4 mm long. The seeds are cooked or roasted (but not too much), before use, to develop the flavour, and they have an aromatic smell. They are ground for use as a spice especially in commercial curry powders and other spice mixtures and can be sprouted for salad purposes. The leaves, known as methis, are used as a vegetable and lose their bitterness on cooking. Dried fenugreek leaves are used as a flavouring and in marinades.

ferchuse *France* A Burgundian dish of pig's heart and lights, possibly with other offal, cooked in red wine with onions and potatoes

ferment See **culture**

ferment, to To carry out the process of fermentation

fermentation The process whereby a microorganism such as a yeast, fungi, lactobacillus, etc. breaks down an energy source (starch, sugar, protein, etc.) in the absence of air, into smaller molecules such as alcohol, acetic acid, lactic acid, etc. thus gaining the energy necessary for growth and reproduction. The process is important in the production of many foods such as yoghurt, cheese, soya sauce, tempeh, vinegar, sauerkraut, etc.

fermented Which has been subjected to the process of fermentation

fermented bean curd See **bean curd cheese**

fermented black bean See **black bean 2**

fermented red rice The yeasty rice grains (brewer's grains) left after making rice wine, coloured red. Alternatively cooked rice fermented with *Monascus purpureus*. This latter is sold in Chinese stores as a mixed culture called wine balls or cubes. Used mainly in northern China. Also called **red rice**, **red mash**

Fermier *France* Farmhouse cheese, usually made from unpasteurized milk (NOTE: Literally 'farmer'.)

fermière, à la *France* In the farmer's wife's style, i.e. with carrots, onions, celery and turnips

ferri, ai *Italy* Grilled over a barbecue or open fire

ferritu *Italy* An instrument used for making pasta cylinders

fersken *Denmark, Norway* Peach

fersk røget laks *Denmark* Freshly smoked salmon

Ferula asafoetida *Botanical name* Asafoetida

Ferula narthex *Botanical name* Asafoetida

ferulic acid An acid which concentrates in the bran fraction of wheat and can be used to measure the bran content of flour

fesa *Italy* Leg of veal

fesenjan *Iran* Fried chicken or duck cooked in a pomegranate and crushed walnut sauce and served with rice. Also called **faisinjan**

festen Preisen, zu *Germany* At fixed prices

festival *Caribbean* A light, sweet, fried dumpling from Jamaica

feta *Greece* A white, dry, crumbly cheese made from cows', ewes' or goats' milk, cut in blocks (*fetes* is the word for block or slice) and matured in brine to give it a sharp acidic and salty taste. Widely used throughout the Balkans and now made in Western Europe. Contains 46% water, 27% fat and 21% protein. Also called **fetta**

fetta 1. *Greece* Feta **2.** *Italy* A slice

Fettsuppe *Germany* A rich soup

fettuccine *Italy* Flat narrow ribbon noodles made from an egg-based pasta dough, available fresh or dried

fettuccine al burro *Italy* Fettuccine with butter and grated Parmesan cheese

fettuccine alla papolina *Italy* Fettuccine with ham and butter

fettuccine alla trota *Italy* Fettucine pasta cooked al dente and mixed with sweated chopped onions and garlic, flaked smoked trout, seasoning, mace and cream, heated for 1 minute and garnished with chopped parsley and red lumpfish roe

fettunta *Italy* Lightly toasted bread rubbed with garlic and tomato. See also **bruschetta**

feuille de chêne *France* Oak leaf lettuce

feuille de Dreux *France* A soft surface-ripened cheese made in Normandy from partially skimmed cows' milk and cast in 300 to 500 g discs. Contains 55% water, 14% fat and 26% protein.

feuille de vigne *France* Vine leaf

feuilletage *France* Puff pastry

feuilleté(e) 1. *France* Flaky as in *pâte feuilletée*, meaning flaky pastry, puff pastry **2.** Danish pastry

feuilleté de poularde riviera *France* Chicken pie

feuilleter de la pâte *France* To turn and roll flaky or puff pastry

fève *France* Broad bean

fèves d'Espagne *France* Runner beans

ffagod sir benfro *Wales* A type of faggot from Pembrokeshire made with minced pigs' liver and onions mixed with suet and breadcrumbs, seasoned and flavoured with chopped sage

fiambre *Portugal* **1.** Ham **2.** Cold cooked meat

fiambre de bonito *Spain* Tuna fish balls cooked in a white wine sauce

fiambres *Spain* Cold cooked meats

fiamma, alla *Italy* Flamed, flambéed

fiasco, al *Italy* Cooked in a sealed flask, especially beans

fibre Non-digestible carbohydrates of vegetable origin which add bulk to the bowel contents causing a more rapid transit through the body, curing constipation and reducing the incidence of bowel cancer. Available from most whole unprocessed natural vegetables, seeds and fruit and in processed form from the bran by-products of grain milling.

fica *Italy* Pomfret, the fish

ficelle *France* A short very thin French bread similar in construction to the baguette

fichi *Italy* Figs

fichi indiani *Italy* Prickly pears

fichi secchi *Italy* Dried figs

fico *Italy* Fig

fico d'India *Italy* Prickly pear

Ficus carica *Botanical name* Fig

fiddle fish Angel fish

fiddlehead fern *United States* The tightly-curled young fronds of the oyster fern, *Matteuccia struthiopteris*, used either as a salad vegetable or cooked like spinach. Grown in the northeast of the USA, it becomes toxic when the fronds begin to open. Also called **corkscrew greens**

fidegela *Switzerland* A sausage made with pigs' liver and rind flavoured with fennel

fideos *Spain* **1.** Noodles **2.** Spaghetti

fideos gordos *Spain* Thick spaghetti

fideus a la cassola *Catalonia* Fideus (a kind of noodle) garnished with red sweet peppers, pork chops or pork fillet and sausages

fidget pie *England* A pie made in a dish from chopped back bacon, onion, cooking apples and chopped parsley combined with cider and flour (for thickening) covered with short pastry and baked at 190°C until brown. Originally used as a food for the harvest workers.

field bean A hardy legume, *Vicia faba*, related to, but a more primitive form of, the broad bean. It is grown all over Europe and Asia often on poor soils. The beans may be used fresh or dried but must be boiled before eating to destroy toxic compounds. In Western Europe used for animal food and as the principal component in the production of quorn. Also called **horse bean**

field lettuce *United States* Lamb's lettuce

field mushroom An edible wild mushroom, *Agaricus campestris*, with a white cap and pink to brown gills found in late summer on rough grassland

fieno greco *Italy* Fenugreek

fieto *Italy* Pomfret, the fish

Fife broth *Scotland* Pork ribs simmered with potatoes and barley for 2 hours, removed and deboned, the meat chopped small and returned, all seasoned and garnished with chopped parsley

fig The fruit of a tree, *Ficus carica*, which grows in warm and semi-tropical regions. The fruit, which varies from round to pear shape, has a soft skin varying from green to purple filled with a red to purple sticky seed filled pulp. They may be eaten raw for dessert, are easily skinned if required, but are commonly dried or canned and used for desserts, snacks, in cakes and biscuits and sometimes with meat and game.

figa *Italy* **1.** Pomfret, the fish **2.** A Venetian word for liver

figadini con l'uva *Italy* Sautéed chicken livers with grapes

figado *Portugal* Liver

figa garbo e dolce *Italy* Panéed and fried calves' liver with vinegar and sugar

figatelli *France* A pigs' or lambs' liver sausage from Corsica

figgy pastry *England* A shortcrust pastry incorporating an amount of dried vine fruits equal in weight to the fat, often used for meat or bird pies (NOTE: *Figgy* is the West Country term for dried vine fruits)

figgy pudding *England* A steamed suet pudding filled with minced apples and figs. Served at Christmas.

figner *Denmark* Figs

figos *Portugal* Figs

fig sly cake *England* A sugar pastry brought together with water instead of egg and made into a sandwich with a filling of chopped dried figs, currants, raisins and walnut pieces all cooked in water and reduced to a thick paste. Baked at 190°C until brown and cut in squares. See also **Cornish sly cake**

figue *France* Fig

figue de barbarie *France* Prickly pear

figue de mer *France* Violet, the seafood

fijn brood *Netherlands* Fine bread

fikener *Norway* Figs

fikon *Sweden* Figs

filato *Italy* In strands or threads

filbert The fruit of a small deciduous tree, *Corylus maxima*, very similar to the hazelnut but with a husk that is longer than the nut and often completely encloses it. Also called **Kentish cob**

filbunke *Sweden* Soured milk or junket

filé *Hungary, Portugal* Fillet of beef, pork, etc.

filé powder Dried and ground sassafras leaves used as a flavouring in Creole cooking. Also called **gumbo filé**, **filet powder**

filet *Catalonia* Sirloin

filet de boeuf *France* 1. The whole fillet of beef, often roasted whole 2. A boneless piece of tender frying- or grilling-quality beef

filet de porc *France* The centre part of the pork loin to which the kidney is attached, a prime roasting joint which may or may not included the fillet (**pointe de filet**)

filete *Spain* Fillet of beef, pork or lamb. See also **tenderloin**

filete de vaca *Spain* Fillet of beef

filet mignon *England, France* A steak cut from the thin end of a fillet of beef. Grilled, fried or used for beef stroganoff, stir fries, steak tartare or the like. (NOTE: Literally 'dainty fillet'.)

filet powder See **filé powder**

filetto *Italy* Fillet (of pork, beef, etc.)

filfil soodani *Middle East* Sudanese pepper

filhó *Portugal* Fritter or pancake

Filipendula ulmaria *Botanical name* Meadowsweet

filipino red A thin sausage made of dried raw pork minced with garlic and mixed with saltpetre, brown sugar, MSG, seasoning and a red dye and packed into narrow hog casings

fillet 1. A piece of fish removed from the bone and running the whole length of the fish 2. Various cuts of meat and poultry

fillet, to To cut away from the bone the flesh of fish, meat or poultry

fillet end of leg of lamb The upper half of a hind leg of lamb

fillet of beef The muscle which runs along the lower portion of the backbone on the inside of the ribs. As it is very little used by the animal it is very tender and is the most expensive cut of beef. It is cut into fillet steak, filet mignon, chateaubriand and tournedos.

fillet of fish The flesh of fish free from skin and bone. Two fillets are usually obtained from a round fish and four from a flatfish.

fillet of lamb *United Kingdom* The top half of a leg of lamb

fillet of pork *United Kingdom* The top half of a leg of pork

fillet of veal *United Kingdom* The equivalent of sirloin and rump in beef usually cut into thin slices for escalopes

fillet steak A transverse slice through the centre part of a fillet of beef

filling 1. A food item contained within a case as e.g. jam in a doughnut, cream in an eclair,

stuffing in a chicken 2. Which leaves the consumer feeling satiated

filmjölk *Sweden* A sour-tasting yoghurt

film yeasts The yeasts that form a whitish scum on the surface of pickles and pickling brines. They are non-toxic.

filo pastry A pastry rolled out so thin that it is translucent, usually sold ready prepared in layers of several rectangular sheets. It originated in Turkey and travelled into central Europe during the spread of the Ottoman empire. Used for many Balkan and Middle Eastern specialities. Also called **phyllo pastry**

filosoof *Netherlands* A type of cottage pie (NOTE: Literally 'philosopher'.)

filter, to To strain through fine muslin, paper or a tammy cloth so as to remove suspended solids from a liquid

filter coffee Coffee made by letting near boiling water flow through ground coffee held in a filter paper supported on a metal or plastic mesh or perforated container

filtrate The liquid that flows through a filter

Fina A variety of common mandarin originating in Algeria and widely grown in Spain. It has a very pleasant flesh but the fruit tend to be small. Also called **Algerian clementine**

financière, à la *France* In the financier's style, i.e. garnished with cockscombs, kidneys, slices of truffle, mushrooms and olives

financière, sauce *France* Madeira sauce reduced by 25%, a little truffle essence added and all strained. Served with dishes garnished *à la financière*.

finanziere *Italy* Cooked cockscombs and sweetbreads served with a vegetable **timbale**. See also **cibreo**

Fin de siècle *France* A double-cream cows' milk cheese from Normandy

findik köftesi *Turkey* Small meatballs made from a mixture of chopped mutton, chopped and sweated onions, flour, eggs, butter and seasoning, fried in butter then simmered in mutton stock with chopped fresh mint

Findon fish pudding *Scotland* Aberdeen fillet baked at 180°C in a covered dish with butter and milk for 20 minutes, then skinned, deboned and flaked and mixed with potatoes mashed with the fish cooking liquor, put in a dish covered with sliced tomatoes and grated cheese and browned in the oven

Findon haddock *Scotland* Finnan haddock

fine marineret sild *Denmark* Fine-quality pickled herrings

fine olive oil Oil pressed from the olive pulp after the second cold pressing and after heating the pulp with water. The free oleic acid content must not be more than 3.3%. This oil is also referred to as refined olive oil.

fines herbes *France* A classic herb mixture, usually chopped chervil, chives, parsley and tarragon, although other similar herbs may be substituted. Used particularly in omelettes.

fines herbes, sauce aux *France* Boiling white wine infused with fines herbes for 20 minutes, strained, mixed with twice its amount of **demi-glace** sauce if required brown, or with white velouté sauce if white, and finished with chopped fines herbes and lemon juice just before serving

finger A strip of food usually a rectangular piece of toast or a white bread roll about 10 cm by 2–3 cm

finger bowl A small bowl filled with lemon-flavoured water, used by guests to clean their fingers after eating messy foods

finger buffet A buffet consisting of only those items which can be eaten with the fingers and do not require the use of a knife, fork or spoon

fingered citron Buddha's hand citron

finger food Food served at a buffet or stand-up meal which can be eaten with the fingers

finger kombu *United States* Sea girdle

fingerling A small fish of any species under 1 year old

finger millet Ragi

finik (*plural* **finiki**) *Russia* Date

finlabong *Philippines* Bamboo shoot

finnan haddie *Scotland* Finnan haddock

finnan haddock *Scotland* Haddock which has been split, soaked briefly in brine and cold-smoked for 6 hours over oak to a pale straw colour. Originally from Findon near Aberdeen. Also called **finnan haddie**, **Findon haddock**

finnisk far-stuvning *Finland* Breast of lamb cut in pieces, fried in butter and stewed with stock, carrots, turnips and potatoes

finnlandskaia *Finland* A strong-flavoured beef broth served with slices of sour cream pancakes mixed with Hamburg parsley on toast topped with cheese and grilled until brown

fino *Italy* 1. Fine olive oil 2. A grade of rice which is long and tapering and requires about 16 minutes to cook but will stand long cooking without losing structure. Used for risotto.

finocchio *Italy* Fennel

finocchio marino *Italy* Samphire, *Crithmum maritimum*

finocchiona *Italy* A type of salami flavoured with fennel which cannot be kept for any length of time

Finte *Germany* Twaite shad

fiocchi d'avena *Italy* Oatmeal

fiocchi di granturco *Italy* Cornflakes

fiochetti *Italy* Small bow-shaped pieces of pasta

Fior di latte *Italy* A soft, spun-curd cows' milk cheese made in the same way as Mozzarella using a lactic starter or citric acid addition before coagulation and formed into various shapes. Contains 61% water, 18% fat and 17% protein. Used as a cheaper substitute for Mozzarella in the pizza trade.

fiore di sambuco *Italy* Small pasta stars used in soup (NOTE: Literally 'elder flowers'.)

fiore di zucchine ripiene *Italy* Stuffed courgette flowers

fiorentina *Italy* A grilled fillet steak with no sauce

fiorentina, alla *Italy* In the Florentine style, i.e. with oil, garlic, ham, parsley and pepper

Fiore Sardo *Italy* A hard ewes' milk cheese from Sardinia made in the shape of two cones joined at their bases. It is salted in brine, dry-salted and may be ripened for 3 to 4 months. It has a sharp tasting paste with a dry brown rind. Eaten when young as a dessert cheese, when mature after 6 months, it is used for grating and cooking. Contains 26% water, 35% fat and 30% protein.

fiori di zucca *Italy* Pumpkin or squash flowers

fire point The lowest temperature at which a liquid will take fire and burn continuously when a small flame is passed over its free surface. It is around 340°C for cooking oils.

firm ball stage *United States* Sugar cooking

firming agent A chemical compound used to maintain crispness in canned and bottled vegetables

firnee *Central Asia* A setting custard from Afghanistan made with milk, sugar and corn flour and flavoured with ground cardamom seeds and powdered saffron. It is poured before setting into a large dish or individual dishes and when set, decorated with shelled pistachio nuts.

firni *South Asia* A milk pudding made with ground rice and almonds

firstings Beestings

Fisch *Germany* Fish

Fischbeuschlsuppe *Austria* A thick well-flavoured soup made with the gills of freshwater fish

Fischbrut *Germany* **1.** Fish fry **2.** Small fish **3.** Whitebait

Fischcrouton *Germany* Fish balls

Fischhackbraten *Germany* Baked fish loaf

Fischlaich *Germany* Soft fish roe

Fisch mit feinen Kräutern *Austria* Fish with chopped mixed herbs

Fischrogen *Germany* Hard fish roe

Fischschüssel *Germany* Fish and bacon terrine

fish Cold-blooded, free-swimming vertebrate animals with flat or spindle-shaped streamlined bodies which live either in fresh or seawater and obtain oxygen for respiration by circulating water over gills from which mammalian vertebrate lungs evolved. They have fins instead of limbs and their skin is usually covered with scales. Classified as freshwater, seawater, anadromous or catadromous, flat or round, oily or white and if flat, dextral or sinistral.

fish and chips *United Kingdom* A national dish consisting of deep-fried battered fish fillet and potato chips usually served with salt and vinegar (NOTE: Reputedly invented in the 17th century in the Meuse valley when the newly arrived potato, which was viewed with some suspicion, was cut to resemble small fishes and deep-fried with them.)

fish cake A circular patty made from a mixture of mashed potato, cooked fish and seasoning, panéed and usually fried

fish cobbler *England* A savoury **cobbler** made with sweated chopped onion and garlic with sliced carrots, courgettes and celery, cooked for 10 minutes, chopped tomatoes, fresh herbs and stock added, simmered, seasoned and small pieces of white fish added and cooked for a maximum of 2 minutes then finished as a cobbler

fish cooking methods The principal methods are shallow-poaching, deep-poaching, grilling, shallow-frying, steaming and baking **en papillote**. Stewing is only used for fish soups. See under each name for details.

fish cutlet A slice of fish cut across the backbone anywhere from the head to the vent so that a cross section of the gut space is shown

fish fillet See **fillet of fish**

fish finger A rectangular piece of compressed white fish flesh with a breadcrumb coating. Usually sold frozen. The fish flesh is usually mechanically recovered from all the bones and skin and there is no waste and often little taste. Popular with children.

fish glaze Fish stock reduced by boiling until a sticky consistency. Used as a base for sauces and to improve their flavour. Also called **glace de poisson**

fish gravy Nuoc mam

fish herbs The principal herbs used with fish are alexanders, basil, bay, caraway, chervil, chives, dill, fennel, lemon balm, lemon thyme, lovage, marjoram, mint, parsley, rosemary, sage and savory

fish kettle A long (up to 60 cm), deep and narrow pan especially made for poaching a large whole round fish. It has an internal perforated plate with handles on which the fish rests and with which it is lifted out without damage.

fish maw The buoyancy bladder of a fish similar in appearance to the mammalian lung. The maw of the conger pike is used in Chinese cooking and is usually sold in dried form which needs reconstituting for about 3 hours and treating with vinegar. It has little flavour of its own but absorbs flavours and is prized for its spongy texture.

fish muddle *United States* Fish stew

fish oil Oil obtained from fish, principally from the livers of cod and halibut, which contains essential fatty acids (EFAs) as well as vitamins A and D which are all necessary for health. Often sold in gelatine capsules as a vitamin supplement, but the required amounts can be obtained by eating oily fish once a week. Oily fish can contain up to 30% fat of which about 20% is saturated.

fish paste Fish preserved either by salting or fermenting or both, sometimes with added grain, and processed to make a paste of variable consistency with a fishy salty flavour. The liquid which drains off is fish sauce. It is made all over Asia, especially in Southeast Asia.

fish pie *United Kingdom* Sliced parboiled potatoes layered in the base of a greased casserole, covered with a mixture of flaked smoked haddock, sliced mushrooms, chopped tomatoes and soured cream, covered with another layer of sliced potatoes, gratinated with grated Cheddar cheese and butter and baked at 180°C for 30 minutes

fish pudding *Scotland* White fish fillets, minced twice and flavoured with allspice and seasoning, combined with thin cream, butter, eggs and flour (8:10:2:2:1), adding the cream last of all in a food processor. Tested by dropping a teaspoonful into boiling water and adjusting the consistency with milk or egg white. The mixture is put in a cake tin which has been buttered and sprinkled with breadcrumbs and this is cooked in a slow oven in a bain-marie for 1 to 1.5 hours. Allowed to rest then demoulded and served with a sauce.

fish puffs *England* Flaked fish (fresh or smoked) mixed with a batter into which lemon juice and egg whites, whisked to a peak, have been folded. This mixture is deep-fried a dsp at a time for about 3 minutes until golden. The puffs are then drained and served with a piquant sauce with a milk or fish-stock base.

fish sauce The salty fishy tasting liquid which drains off fermented and/or salted fish. It is a popular flavouring agent in Southeast Asia and is used in the same way as soya sauce. **Nuoc mam** is the commonest example in the West.

fish sausage A sausage made with 80% fish flesh, free of skin and bone, blended to a fine paste with suet and **fécule** or corn flour, seasoned, flavoured with mace and cayenne pepper, filled into narrow casings and linked

fish slice A flat oblong slatted sheet of metal on a long handle used in the domestic kitchen for handling flat items of food such as fish fillets, fried eggs, rissoles and hamburgers in shallow frying or poaching pans. Professional chefs use a palette knife for fish fillets.

fish soup *United Kingdom* Strained fish stock thickened with a white roux and enriched with cream or milk, flaked cooked fish added and chopped parsley sprinkled on the surface

fish steak A slice of fish cut across the back bone anywhere from the vent to the tail of a round fish

fish stew See under individual entries for: **bouillabaisse, bourride, chaudrée, cotriade, matelote, meurette, pochouse** and **waterzooi**

fish stick *United States* Fish finger

fish stock Stock made from the bones of white fish sweated with onions and lemon juice in butter, simmered for 30 minutes with water (0.4 kg bones, per litre), skimmed continuously then strained. Also called **fond de poisson, fumet de poisson**

fish velouté A velouté sauce made with fish stock and used as a base for many fish sauces

fisk *Denmark, Norway, Sweden* Fish

fiskbullar *Sweden* Fish balls

fiskeballer *Norway* Fish balls made with processed fish and cooked potatoes

fiskeboller *Norway* A mixture of minced raw cod and/or haddock, bread crumbs, egg, cream and seasonings formed into balls, poached in fish stock and served with a wine or cheese sauce

fiskefärs *Denmark* Minced fish

fiskefrikadellar *Denmark* Fish balls

fiskegrateng *Norway* Skinned and flaked boiled cod covered with a cream and egg yolk enriched white sauce, gratinated with cheese and baked in the oven until brown

fiskekaker *Norway* Fishcakes made from chilled raw haddock, corn flour, cream and milk processed in a blender then fried in butter and oil

fiskepudding *Norway* Fish pudding

fiskesuppe *Norway* A strong fish stock made with bones, fins, cleaned fish heads, a bouquet garni and an onion clouté just covered with water, simmered for 30 minutes, skimmed and strained, mixed with half its volume of milk thickened with a blond roux, cooked out, seasoned, finished with sour cream and lemon juice and garnished with chopped parsley

fiskfärs *Sweden* Fish pudding

fiskgryta *Sweden* **Paupiettes** made from plaice or sole fillets rubbed with salt and filled with a mixture of chopped onion, grated cheese and **tomato concassée**, packed tightly and poached in a dish moistened with lemon juice or wine, dotted with butter and baked in a moderate oven for 30 minutes. Served from the dish.

fiskkaggen *Norway* A fish loaf made with boiled white fish processed with butter, egg yolks, breadcrumbs, nutmeg and seasoning, stiffly beaten egg whites folded in and all baked in a mould as a soufflé, cooled, demoulded and eaten cold

fiskkroketter *Sweden* Fish cakes or croquettes

fisk med fyllning *Sweden* Stuffed fish

fisk og skalldyr *Norway* Seafood

fisk på fat *Norway* Fish fried then baked in a sauce (NOTE: Literally 'fish on a platter'.)

fisksoppa *Sweden* Fish soup. First a stock is made from roughly chopped small cleaned fish with their gills removed, covered with roughly 2 to 3 times their weight in water with salt, sliced onion and white peppercorns and simmered for 30 minutes. The skimmed and strained stock is then mixed with sweated chopped onions, sliced leek and mushrooms, skinned and cored tomatoes, saffron, rosemary, basil, garlic and seasoning, simmered until all cooked, then prawns and mussels added for the last minute.

fisnoga A Jewish appetizer made from calf's foot jelly. See also **petcha**

Fistulina hepatica *Botanical name* Beefsteak fungus

fitless cock *Scotland* Oatmeal, shredded suet and finely chopped onion (2:1:1) brought together with beaten egg, shaped in the form of a chicken, wrapped in a floured cloth and boiled for two hours. Also called **dry goose** (NOTE: Fitless cock was traditionally eaten on Shrove Tuesday)

five-spice powder *China* A blend of five spices, star anise, anise pepper, cassia or cinnamon, fennel seed and cloves ground together. May include two from cardamom, dried ginger or dried liquorice root. Used to flavour marinades and to season roast meat and poultry. Also called **Chinese five spices**

fjærkre *Norway* Poultry

fjordland *Norway* A semi-skimmed cows' milk cheese resembling **Emmental** or **Jarlsberg**

Fladen *Switzerland* A flat fruit cake made with pears, nuts and marzipan

fläderbär *Sweden* Elderberries

flæsk *Denmark* Pork or bacon. Also called **svinekød**

flæskesteg *Denmark* Roast pork

flageolet *France* Flageolet bean

flageolet bean An 8 to 10 mm long light green oval bean from semi-mature French bean pods after the pod has become stringy but before it dries off. Eaten fresh or dried. Also called **green shell bean**

Flageolett *Germany* Flageolet bean

flake 1. Thin slivers or slices of food such as is obtained when a cooked fish is gently broken with a fork or as in corn flakes, almond flakes, etc. **2.** The flesh of certain small Australian sharks **3.** Dogfish

flake, to To form or make into flakes

flaked almonds See **almond flakes**

flaked rice See **rice flakes**

flake salt *United States* A flaked form of salt used for pickling

flaky pastry A pastry similar to puff pastry made with a lower ratio of fat to flour (3 to 4) and folded, rolled and turned only three times. The lift is not as great as with puff pastry.

flam *Catalonia* Crème caramel

flamande, à la *France* In the Flemish style, i.e. with a garnish of braised vegetables and bacon or small pork sausages; usually for joints of meat

flambé, to To add an alcoholic spirit to a dish and set it alight either before (in the ladle or spoon) or after adding it. This may be done in the kitchen during cooking or when presenting the dish to the customer. Used to add the flavour of brandy, whisky or rum to a dish and for the visual effect. Also called **flame, to**

flamber *France* To flambé

flame, to To flambé

flameado *Spain* Flamed, flambéed

flamiche *Belgium* A deep shell or case of bread dough baked with a filling of egg and cheese

Flammulina velutipes Botanical name Enokitake mushroom

flan 1. An open, cylindrical and straight-sided tart, either sweet or savoury, and either in a blind prebaked pastry case or with a sponge or biscuit crumb base with fillings that require little if any cooking **2.** *France* Custard tart **3.** *Portugal, Spain* Crème caramel

flan brioche aux fruits confits *France* A dessert similar to bread and butter pudding

flanchet *France* Breast of veal

flank A cut of beef or veal. See also **thick flank**, **thin flank**

flank of lamb Lamb flank

flank steak *United States* A narrow flat cut of beef from below the short loin, fried or grilled. Also called **London broil**

flan pastry A rather brittle **shortcrust pastry** in which beaten egg instead of water is used to bind the fat and flour. Caster sugar (4 g per 100 g of flour) may be used for sweet tarts and flans. Also called **biscuit crust pastry**, **sweet crust pastry**

flan ring A plain or fluted ring of metal placed on a flat baking tray and used to form flan pastry cases for blind or other baking

flapjack 1. *England* A type of biscuit made from fat, sugar, rolled oats and golden syrup, baked in a shallow tray and cut into rectangles or squares **2.** *United States* A thick pancake cooked on a griddle

flapjack scone Drop scone

flare fat A sheet of soft fat from the inner lower part of a pig's abdominal cavity

flash, to To brown the surface of a cooked dish very quickly under a very hot grill or in a very hot oven

flash-fry steak Minute steak

flash point The lowest temperature at which the vapour over hot oil will burn but will not sustain combustion of the liquid. It is around 290°C to 330°C for cooking oils.

fläsk *Sweden* Pork

fläskgryta med jordärtscockor *Sweden* Cubed pork fillet browned and seasoned, sprinkled with flour, then stock, tomato purée and cream added, simmered until cooked, mixed with cooked Jerusalem artichokes and finished with sherry

fläsk i form *Sweden* A type of pork pie made from alternate layers of seasoned sliced potatoes and onions covered in milk and topped with slices of rindless salted pork belly, sprinkled with powdered rosemary and baked in a hot oven until the pork is crisp and all cooked

fläskkorv *Sweden* A sausage made from lean pork and fat bacon (3:1), minced twice, bound with **fécule** and ham stock, seasoned, flavoured with ginger, loosely filled into casings, linked, dried and dry-salted for a day. May be stored in brine.

fläskkorvsstuvning *Sweden* Thick slices of pork sausage cooked in pork stock with sliced onions and diced potatoes

flat A flat dish, usually oval, on which food is presented to the customer in a restaurant

flatbone steak *United States* A steak cut from the **sirloin**

flatbread Unleavened bread made without yeast such as chapati, paratha, tortilla, matzo and crispbread

flatfish A fish which, as it matures, changes shape so that both eyes and the mouth are on one side which becomes the upper part when swimming or lying on the sea bottom. See also **dextral**, **sinistral**

flathead *Australia* Any fish of the genus *Platycephalus* found in southern Australian waters. They are usual caught commercially as a by-catch, but are very popular with recreational fishermen. All are long and thin with a flat head and weigh from 1 to 3 kg, though they can reach 6 kg.The sand flathead, *P. bassensis*, is caught in Victorian and Tasmanian waters and is distinguished from other varieties by the spines in front of the gill cover and a large black blotch on the tail. The dusky flathead, *P. fuscus*, is found as far as up southern Queensland. They are considered excellent eating and they taste better the bigger they are. Generally prepared as oblique slices from fillets. They can be eaten as sushi.

flat-leaved parsley See **flat parsley**

flat lettuce Butterhead lettuce

flat lobster Slipper lobster

flat mushroom A fully mature mushroom in which the cap is fully open so that all the gills are exposed on one side

flat parsley A variety of parsley, *P. crispum Neapolitanum*, in which the leaves are flat rather than curled. It is said to have a superior flavour. It is the commonest form in continental Europe.

flat sours *United States* Spoilage bacteria that do not produce a gas, thus leaving the ends of cans in which they are growing flat instead of domed and hence giving no sign of their presence

flattbrød *Norway* A thin crisp flat biscuit made of wheat, rye and barley flours. See also **crispbread**

flauta *Mexico* A large tortilla filled and rolled (NOTE: Literally 'a flute'.)

flava bean Broad bean

flavour The blend of taste and smell sensation experienced when food and drink are placed in the mouth. Taste is a direct nervous transmission from the tongue and is the same for all humans comprising salt, sweet, sour and bitter. Smell is far more complex, involves the nose and a large area of the cerebral cortex and is to some extent culturally determined.

flavoured crisps Crisps with added flavour usually artificial and sprayed on as they are being cooled, e.g. cheese and onion, smoky bacon, salt and vinegar, etc.

flavour enhancer A substance which having little or no flavour of its own intensifies other flavours with which it is combined. Monosodium glutamate is the most common and is used to enhance the flavour of vegetables and meat, especially in Chinese cooking. Flavour enhancers are common in processed and convenience foods.

flavourings Ingredients in cookery which add flavour to a dish made principally from other ingredients. They can be of natural origin and add little bulk, such as herbs, spices, seasoning, extracts, essences, etc., or those which also add bulk, such as aromatic vegetables and meats. Others, particularly fruit flavours, are purely synthetic in origin. Processed and convenience foods generally contain mixtures of natural and synthetic flavours.

flavoxanthin A natural carotenoid yellow food colouring. See also **E161(a)**

Flavr Savr *United States* A genetically engineered tomato designed to maintain its flavour over an extended shelf life. It is now on sale in the USA. It contains anti-ripening genes and does not need to be labelled under current UK rules.

flead *England* Mesenteric fat from veal or beef

Flecke *Germany* Tripe

Fleisch *Germany* Meat

Fleischbrühe *Germany* A consommé based on meat stock

Fleischgerichte *Germany* Meat dishes

Fleischkäse *Germany* Meat loaf

Fleischklösse *Germany* Meatballs

Fleischkuchen *Germany* Meat pies

Fleischschnitte *Germany* Slice of meat

Fleischwurst *Germany* Extrawurst

fleishig A Jewish term describing food containing or derived from meat or meat products, or equipment used in preparing such food. See also **milchig**

flensje *Netherlands* Thin pancakes

flesh The name for edible muscular parts of animals, for some other tissues of shellfish and crustaceans and for the edible parts of fruits

fleshy Succulent and slightly resistant to the bite

fleske pannekaker *Norway* Pancakes filled with a pork stuffing

fleskepølse *Norway* Very fatty pork sausages

flet *France* Flounder, the fish

flétan *France* Halibut

fleur de maquis *France* A soft goats' milk cheese from Corsica. See also **Brin d'amour**

fleur de muscade *France* Mace

fleuriste, à la *France* In the florist's style, i.e. with a garnish of potatoes and tomatoes stuffed with mixed vegetables

fleuron *England, France* A small crescent-shaped piece of flaky or puff pastry which after cooking is used as a garnish

Fliederkaltschale *Germany* A cold soup made from hot milk infused with elder blossoms, vanilla and cinnamon, strained, sweetened and thickened with egg yolks, cooled and served sprinkled with crushed macaroons

flies' cemeteries *England* Eccles cakes or similar currant cakes and biscuits (*colloquial*)

flint corn *United States* An early maturing variety of maize, *Zea mays* var. *indurata*, in which the small kernels are completely covered by a flinty hard skin. Not as widely grown as dent.

flipper pie *Canada* A pie from Newfoundland made from the flippers of young harp seals together with vegetables during the annual cull (April/May)

flippit *United Kingdom* A small pancake made from a seasoned self-raising flour and egg (2:1) batter with just enough water to make it a thick dropping consistency, cooked in oil for 2 minutes then flipped over and cooked until it bubbles and rises slightly. Served immediately with a savoury topping.

flitch A complete side of pork (half a pig), salted and cured

floating islands See **îles flottantes**

floats *Caribbean* Yeasted bread from Trinidad, cut into thin rounds and fried. Served hot with accra.

floddies *England* Potato and onions grated, seasoned and mixed with a little flour, chopped herbs and chopped cured or cooked meat, brought together with egg and deep-fried in tablespoonfuls (NOTE: Floddies are traditional to the northern English towns of Gateshead and Durham)

fløde *Denmark* Cream

flødekage *Denmark* A layered cream sponge cake

flødeost *Denmark* Cream cheese

flødeskum *Denmark* Whipped cream

Flohkraut *Germany* Pennyroyal, the herb

flondre *France* Flounder, the fish

flor de Jamaica *Jamaica* flower

Florence fennel The swollen bases of the leaves of a variety of plant, *Foeniculum vulgare* var. *dulce*, which form a tight bulb-like crisp vegetable with a pleasant mild aniseed flavour. Eaten raw or cooked. Also called **fennel**, **sweet anise**

florentine A biscuit containing a high proportion of chopped dried vine fruits, candied peel and nuts and coated with chocolate on one side

florentine, à la *France* In the Florentine style, i.e. served with spinach, sometimes napped with cheese sauce. Usually used of fish or eggs.

florentine, fish As for **fish Mornay**, but with the fish placed on a bed of cooked spinach prior to coating with sauce

florid lobster *United States* A large spiny lobster, *Palinurus argus*, with a purple/brown shell and a yellow band across the tail

flory *Scotland* A double-crust puff pastry tart filled with a corn flour thickened and sweetened custard made with prune soaking water, plum juice or the like, flavoured with port and lemon juice and with halved or whole fruit embedded in it. The top is glazed and the tart baked at 230°C for 15 minutes and then at 200°C for a further 15 minutes or until cooked. Called after the name of the fruit e.g. plum flory.

fløte *Norway* Cream

fløtekaker *Norway* Cream cakes

fløtekarameller *Norway* Crème caramel

fløtemysost *Norway* A semi-hard cooked-curd cheese made with a mixture of cows' milk and cream. It has no rind and a smooth texture. Contains 20% water, 25% fat and 50% protein.

fløtesuppe *Norway* Cream soup

fløtevafler *Norway* Cream-based waffles

flounder 1. A flat sea fish, *Platichthys flesus*, similar to plaice but with an inferior taste and texture. Found in all coastal regions of the Atlantic Ocean. **2.** *United States* The general term for any flatfish **3.** *Australia* A small coastal flatfish, *Pseudorhombus arsius*, excellent edible quality but rather small (from 25 to 40 cm in length). Cooked in the same way as all flatfish. Also called **large-toothed flounder**

flour Finely ground cereal grains, dried pulses and dried starchy tubers, consisting mainly of starch, often treated to remove fibre and oils or modified to change its cooking or baking properties. The term is most commonly used of wheat flour.

flour, to To cover the surface of a food or cooking implement or preparation surface with flour, usually to absorb surface moisture and to prevent sticking

flour batter biscuit method A method of making biscuits by creaming half the flour with the fat, beating in the sugar and eggs previously mixed, then blending in the other dry ingredients. An example is the cookie.

flour corn See **squaw corn**

flour dredger A dredger filled with flour used to flour

floury 1. (Potatoes) which have an open soft texture when cooked as opposed to the waxy variety. See also **potato 2.** The taste of food containing flour which is undercooked

flower fu Fully cooked, dried and crushed gluten dough rather like breadcrumbs which is sprinkled directly over food. See also **kohanafu**

flowering chive The flower stem and bud of the Chinese chive used as a garnish or vegetable

flowering white cabbage Choy sum

flower pepper Anise pepper

flowers for salads See **salad flowers**

Flügel *Germany* Wing

fluid ounce A subdivision of the pint. There are 20 in the imperial pint equal in volume to 28.4 ml and 16 in the US pint equal to 29.6 ml. Abbreviated to fl oz.

fluke A long-lived parasitic flatworm which infects vertebrate (including human) livers, lungs and brains, causing a variety of diseases. The eggs are shed in faeces. The larval stages first infect snails, then pass to aquatic plants, shellfish and fish from whence they reinfect the vertebrates. Freezing kills the larvae but raw freshwater fish, shellfish and unwashed aquatic plants represent the greatest danger to both tourists and the more affluent countries which import them unfrozen.

flummery 1. *Wales* An old Welsh dessert made of sweetened and flavoured milk thickened by boiling with oatmeal, and set in a mould prior to turning out when cold. Originally a fermented and soured oatmeal gruel. **2.** *United States* Any of several sweet puddings thickened with cornflour. Usually milk- or fruit-based.

Flunder *Germany* Flounder

flundra *Sweden* Flounder

flute An indentation pressed into the edge of pie or pasty for decoration or to help seal two edges of pastry together

flute, to To scallop

flûte *France* **1.** A small French bread stick smaller than a baguette but bigger than a ficelle **2.** A transverse slice of French bread, toasted and cut in quarters and served as an accompaniment to soup especially minestrone **3.** A type of glass for drinking champagne

flying fish The name given to various species of seawater fish which have enlarged pectoral fins allowing them to glide above the surface of the water for considerable distances so as to avoid predators. Found in tropical and semi-tropical waters where they are prized as a food.

flying flusk See **flying squid**

flying lamb slices *China* A pot of flavoured stock at the table kept boiling over a heater, into which guests dip very thin slices of raw, possibly marinated, leg of lamb using chopsticks or a fondue fork. When cooked in a few seconds, they are eaten with a variety of dips and relishes. The cooking liquor remaining may have eggs and soya sauce, etc. added and is consumed by the diners.

flying squid *Todarodes sagittatus*, a relative of the common squid up to 120 cm long and with two broad, flat swimming fins which allow it to glide above the surface for short distances. Fished commercially but rather tough and needs long slow cooking. Also called **flying flusk**

flyndre *Norway* Sole, the fish

foam cake *United States* A cake which uses an egg-white foam to give it a very light texture. See also **angel cake**

foaming biscuit method A method of making biscuits by whisking egg whites with some sugar to a light meringue, then folding in the dry ingredients being extra careful with ground nuts

focaccetta *Italy* See **focaccia 2**

focaccia *Italy* **1.** A bun or cake **2.** A flour, salt and water yeast-raised dough rolled out thinly and formed into a sandwich with a cream cheese filling, sealed at the edges and baked at 230°C for 20 minutes. Also called **focaccetta**

focaccia del Venerdí Santo *Italy* A tart filled with a mixture of fennel, endive, anchovies, olives and capers. Also called **scalcione**

focaccia di vitello *Italy* Focaccia with a veal filling

focaccia ligure *Italy* A baked round of yeasted dough with many toppings including herbs, coarse salt, diced ham, onions, artichokes and cheese

foderare *Italy* To line a dish or pan, e.g. with sponge fingers, sponge cake slices, biscuits, bacon, dough, etc.

Foeniculum vulgare *Botanical name* Fennel

fofas de bacalhau *Portugal* Cod fish balls

fogas *Hungary* A type of pike-perch

foglia *Italy* Leaf

foglia di vite *Italy* Vine leaf

foglie de alloro *Italy* Bay leaves

Fogosch *Austria, Germany* A freshwater fish similar to a trout

foie *France* Liver

foie de poulet *France* Chicken liver

foie de veau *France* Calf's liver

foie de veau moissonnière *France* Calf's liver fried with onions and herbs and deglazed with red wine

foie de volaille *France* Chicken livers

foie gras *England, France* The grotesquely enlarged liver of goose or duck achieved by force-feeding with cooked maize gruel using a tube inserted down the throat of the bird. Used for savoury dishes and pâté de foie gras.

foie gras de canard *France* A pâté of duck liver made in the Dordogne. Some think it better than the goose-liver foie gras.

foie gras en croûte *France* Prepared goose liver cooked in a pastry case and very expensive

foil See **aluminium foil**

foiolo alla milanese *Italy* Tripe and onion stew with cheese

foi thong *Thailand* A dessert made by pouring beaten egg in a thin stream into hot sugar syrup. A type of **roti jala** cup is used called a foi tong cone.

fokhagymásmártás *Hungary* Garlic sauce

folares *Portugal* An Easter gift of eggs baked in scooped out bread rolls

fold in, to The procedure of combining one ingredient with a liquid or semi-solid either of which contains entrapped air bubbles, so as not to break down or release the air, usually by very gentle cutting and turning with a metal spoon or spatula as e.g. icing sugar into whisked egg white, flour into an egg/fat/sugar batter, whisked egg white into an egg milk mixture

folic acid One of the B group of vitamins found in green leaves (hence the name) and other foods. Essential for health and especially to prevent foetuses developing neural cord defects (e.g. spina bifida) and cleft palates during pregnancy. Deficiency can cause a form of anaemia (**megaloblastic**

anaemia) but excess can mask the signs of pernicious anaemia caused by vitamin B12 deficiency. Also called **vitamin Bc**

Folie de béguines *Belgium* A large loaf-shaped cows' milk cheese (up to 8 kg). The paste is strong flavoured with many small holes.

foncer *France* To line the base of a pan or dish with slices of ham or bacon

fond *France* Foundation or basis, meaning the foundation of all cooking, i.e. the stocks which are converted into soups and sauces and are used as cooking liquors. Generally reserved for meat and vegetable stocks, e.g. *fond de veau* meaning veal stock and so on. See also **fumet**

fondant Sugar syrup boiled to 116 to 118°C, i.e. between the soft and hard ball stage, used when cooled as a basis for cake icing. It must be diluted with water and used at a precise temperature. If mixed with glycerine and gums it remains temporarily malleable at room temperature and may be rolled out for covering cakes and used to mould decorations.

fondanti *Italy* Small savoury croquettes

fondant potatoes Thick sliced or turned potatoes, buttered and seasoned, half covered in white stock and cooked in the oven at 240°C until tender and all stock absorbed

fond blanc *France* White beef stock

fond blanc de veau *France* White veal stock

fond blanc de volaille *France* White chicken stock

fond brun *France* Brown beef stock

fond brun de veau *France* Brown veal stock

fond brun de volaille *France* Brown chicken stock

fond d'artichaut *France* Artichoke bottom

fond de gibier *France* Game stock

fond de marmite *France* White beef stock

fond de tarte *France* **1.** Pastry base **2.** The crème pâtissière base of a French tart

fondo *Italy* **1.** Stock **2.** Bottom or heart, e.g. of an artichoke

fondre *France* To melt

fondre, faire *France* To sweat

fonds d'artichauts aux points d'asperge *France* Artichoke bottoms cooked in butter, filled with creamed asparagus tips coated with Mornay sauce and glazed

fondue 1. *England, France, Switzerland* Cheese melted with wine and flavourings and kept hot at the table over a heater. Cubes of bread impaled on fondue forks are dipped into the molten mixture. Also called **Swiss fondue 2.** Any type of food preparation and cooking in which guests dip small or thin pieces of food into a hot liquid (oil, boiling stock or the like) which is kept hot at the table, and then consume the pieces individually **3.** *France* A vegetable cooked until it is reduced to a pulp, e.g. tomatoes

fondue au marc, fondue au raisin *France* A small round cheese made from skimmed milk and ripened in a coating of grape pips. See also **Tomme au raisin**

fondue bourguignonne *France* Oil kept hot at the table into which guests dip pieces of raw lean meat impaled on fondue forks to cook the meat prior to consuming it with various sauces and condiments

fondue chinoise *France, Switzerland* As **flying lamb slices**, but with rolls of wafer-thin slices of lean beef

fondue fork A long fork, usually with two barbed prongs at the end of a thin metal rod with a handle. Used for dipping food into hot oil, boiling stock or molten cheese at the table. See also **fondue**

fondue neufchâteloise *Switzerland* Gruyère and Emmental cheese dissolved in hot white wine with butter, pepper, cayenne pepper, kirsch and flavoured with garlic rubbed around the bowl. Eaten on cubes of bread in the usual way.

fonduta *Italy* Fontina cheese, soaked in milk for half an hour, warmed while stirring, beaten egg and butter added, whisked until thick and finished with grated truffle. Served with bread.

fong toa hu *Thailand* Bean curd sticks

fonio *West Africa* An ancient fine-tasting cereal, *Digitaria exilis* (white fonio) or *Digitaria iburua* (black fonio), grown in the West African uplands. It withstands drought, tolerates poor soil and matures very quickly. It can be boiled, dry-fried and ground to various sizes and is a useful famine crop. Also called **acha**

Fontainebleau *France* A cheese with a soft creamy texture made from cows' milk in the area around Paris. It is usually mixed with cream and served as a dessert with fruit.

Fontal *France, Italy* A smooth, semi-hard mild-flavoured cows' milk cheese similar to Fontina, made in both Italy and France. It is cast in large 20 kg wheels and has a tender, buttery, mild-tasting paste with occasional holes, and is waxed or wrapped in plastic. Suitable for melting. Contains 43% water, 27% fat and 27% protein.

Fontina *Italy* A semi-hard scalded-curd mild-flavoured slightly rubbery-textured dark yellow cheese with numerous small holes and a tough brown rind made from very fresh unpasteurized cows' milk in the Aosta valley. It is dry-salted or brine-washed intermittently for 2 months whilst being ripened in caves. Used for fondue, fonduta and as a dessert cheese. Contains in summer 38% water, 31% fat and 26% protein. The winter cheese has about 2 percentage points less fat and 2 percentage points more water.

food chopper A food processor in which the bowl revolves in the opposite direction to the rotating cutting blades, used for high volume work in commercial kitchens

food colourings Permitted dyes either of natural or synthetic origin used to colour food especially by manufacturers of processed food

food fibre See **fibre**

food grinder *United States* Mincer, mincing machine

food hygiene That science and/or craft which determines how food should be grown, picked or harvested, slaughtered if appropriate, transported, stored, handled, cooked and served to avoid contamination or deterioration which could be harmful to health, and also the design and cleaning of premises, vehicles, implements and equipment with which food is associated

food hygiene certificate A certificate of competence in food hygiene issued after appropriate training. Required for all food handlers in the EU.

food labelling Under EU rules, packaged food must be labelled with the name, the list of ingredients in descending order of weight, the net quantity, a best-before or best-before-end date, special conditions of storage or use, the name and address of the packager or seller and, under certain conditions, the particulars of the place of origin. The location of the factory or packaging centre is required in some countries.

food laws The legislation which lays down requirements for food hygiene, for the purity of food, for the description of food and for the weights and measures associated with it

food mill See **mouli 1**

food mixer An electrically operated machine that processes solids and liquids by means of various attachments to a powered head, which operate within or over a bowl. It can mix, beat, knead, whip, sieve, chop, grind, mince, liquidize etc.

food poisoning Any disease of an infectious or toxic nature caused by or thought to be caused by consumption of food or water regardless of presenting symptoms and signs (i.e. not necessarily gastrointestinal) and including illness caused by toxic chemicals associated with food but excluding illness due to known allergies or food intolerances

food poisoning bacteria The main bacteria responsible for food poisoning are, in alphabetical order: *Bacillus cereus, Campylobacter, Clostridium botulinum, Clostridium perfringens, Escherichia coli, Salmonella, Staphylococcus aureus, Vibrio parahaemolyticus* and *Yersinia enterocolitica*. See under each heading.

food poisoning by bacteria, causes The principal causes are in descending order of importance: inadequate cooling; more than 24 hours between preparation and consumption of a meal; inadequate thermal processing; inadequate hot storage; inadequate reheating; eating contaminated raw food; cross contamination; inadequate cleaning of equipment; food from unsafe sources; use of leftovers

food poisoning causative agents Agents that can cause food poisoning are: substances added during preparation, e.g. lead; substances synthesized by the commodity during growth and storage e.g. poisons in potatoes and red beans; substances formed by processing or storage under poorly controlled conditions e.g. some kinds of fish poisoning; substances stored by a commodity e.g. paralytic shellfish poisoning caused by a poison in some of the plankton or algae that they consume; allergens, e.g. strawberries; bacteria; and unidentified agents, probably viruses. See also **food poisoning bacteria**

food preservation science The study of the means used to destroy or inhibit the growth of those microorganisms with the potential to cause deterioration in food. The means involve intrinsic properties of the food, extrinsic properties of the environment and physiological properties of the microorganisms which enable them to flourish because of the interaction of the intrinsic and extrinsic properties.

food processor A kitchen appliance consisting of a cylindrical bowl with cover through which projects a vertical shaft onto which various circular cutting, slicing and beating implements may be attached. The shaft is rotated by an electric motor at varying speeds but generally lower than a **blender** Used for chopping, slicing, mixing, puréeing and pulverizing tasks for all kinds of ingredients and mixes.

food safe See **meat safe**

food slicer See **slicing machine**

food store A room or cabinet set aside for storing foods, generally with good ventilation, vermin proof and with easy clean slotted or mesh shelving

foo gwa *China* Bitter gourd

fool A purée of fruit into which whipped cream or custard is mixed. May be sieved and sometimes thickened with gelatine.

foon tiu meen *China* Wide flat noodles

foo yu *China* Bean curd cheese

foo yung *China* Omelette, often filled with cooked meat, vegetables and/or shellfish

forced convection oven See **convection oven**

forcemeat Meat, game or fish flesh, free of gristle, bone and fat, ground finely and mixed with a **panada** of flour, rice, potato or bread, possibly cream, eggs, egg yolks or egg whites, fat or suet, etc., together with seasonings and butter to a piping consistency. Used as a basis of stuffings, quenelles, mousselines, borders and bases, pies, terrines and galantines.

forcing bag See **piping bag**

forel (*plural* **foreli**) *Netherlands, Russia* Trout

foreleg of beef See **shin beef**

forell *Sweden* Trout

Forelle *Germany* Trout

Forelle blau *Austria, Germany* Freshly caught trout, possibly knocked on the head and gutted, plunged into a gently boiling white fish court bouillon. The skin turns a characteristic blue if the fish is absolutely fresh. When cooked, it is served with melted butter and boiled potatoes. Also called **blue trout**

Forellenbarsch *Germany* Largemouth black bass

foreloin of pork *United Kingdom* The rib end of the loin, equivalent to the best end of lamb. Roasted on or off the bone or cut into chops.

forequarter The front half of a meat animal usually extending to the last rib

fore rib of beef *United Kingdom* The joint of beef consisting of the 7th to the 10th rib counting from the head of the beast with the attached muscles and the half vertebrae from a side of beef but excluding the breast end of the ribs. Used for roasting on or off the bone and first class braising. Also called **standing rib roast**

foreshank *United States* Shank of beef

forestberry herb *Australia* A dried free-flowing powdered herb with a strong passion fruit flavour with hints of cumin and caraway. It is used to enhance the flavour of berry and stone fruits.

forestière, (à la) *France* In the forester's style, i.e. garnished with mushrooms, ham or bacon and fried potatoes. Usually meat or poultry.

forest mushroom Hoshi-shiitake

Forfar bridie *Scotland* A Scottish pastry turnover containing beef, suet and onions

fork An implement with 2 or more prongs and a handle conveniently grasped in the hand used for eating solid foods, carving or cooking. Carving forks usually have 2 large prongs.

fork luncheon A buffet type meal served on a plate and eaten with a fork usually while standing up

förlorade *Sweden* Poached

forloren skildpadde *Denmark* A dish supposed to resemble turtle made from the meat, tongue and brains of a calf's head, with meatballs, fish balls and hard-boiled eggs

forlorent *Norway* Poached

Formagella della Val Bavona *Switzerland* A soft cows' milk cheese with an even textured, delicately flavoured paste and a thin smooth rind

Formagella Ticinese A soft cows' milk cheese with an even textured, delicately flavoured paste from Ticino cast in 2 kg rounds

formagelle *Italy* Small farmhouse cheeses from North Italy made with any type of milk

formaggini *Italy* Small cheeses. See also **Robiolini**

formaggio *Italy* Cheese

formaggio bianco *Italy* The general term for soft unripened lightly salted cows' milk cheeses

formaggio di crema *Italy* Cream cheese

formatge *Catalonia* Cheese

formic acid The simplest organic acid found in some fruits and in the poison of ants, now made synthetically for use as a flavour enhancer. See also **E236**

forn, al *Catalonia* Cooked in the oven

forno, al *Italy* Cooked in the oven

forrett *Norway* Appetizer, hors d'oeuvre

forshmak *Russia* A three-layered dish consisting of skinned and deboned herrings soaked in milk for 3 hours, minced with caramelized onions and combined with grated cooking apple as the first layer. The second layer is crustless white bread moistened with milk and mixed with beaten eggs, and the top layer is mashed potatoes, plain or piped decoratively. Baked at 180°C for 30 minutes, brushed with butter and sprinkled with breadcrumbs for the last 5 minutes to form a crust.

fortuné *France* A miniature cake similar to a macaroon, baked and served in a small paper case, sprinkled with icing sugar and topped with half a glacé cherry (NOTE: Literally 'fortunate'.)

fortune cookie *United States* A small cake or biscuit originated by Chinese Americans containing a slip of paper on which a horoscope, proverb or joke is printed

Fortunella One of the three important genera of citrus fruit of which the kumquat and the calamondin are the most common examples

Fortunella japonica *Botanical name* Kumquat

Fortunella margarita *Botanical name* Kumquat

fouasse *France* A sweet bun

foudjou *France* A dish from Languedoc consisting of strong-flavoured pungent goats' milk cheese flavoured with garlic and brandy and served with potatoes

fouet *France* Whisk

fouetter *France* To whip or whisk, especially cream

fougasse *France* A type of bread or pastry made from yeast-raised dough, oval or ring-shaped, with a variety of fillings put between two layers of raised and knocked-back dough, proved, then baked at 200°C

fougassettes *France* A bread made with olive oil and flavoured with orange-flower water

foule medames Ful medames

four *France* Oven

four, au *France* Cooked in the oven

Fourme d'Ambert *France* A semi-hard blue-veined cows' milk cheese from the Auvergne, ripened for 2 to 3 months and with a creamy texture and full-bodied flavour. It is cast in a tall cylinder shape and has a dark rind rather like Stilton. It has AOC status. Also called **Fourme de Montbrison**, **Fourme de Pierre-sur-Haute**

Fourme de Cantal *France* A type of cheese with a red-streaked rind. See also **Cantal**

Fourme de Laguiole *France* A semi-hard pressed cows' milk cheese. See also **Laguiole**

Fourme de Montbrison *France* Fourme d'Ambert

Fourme de Pierre-sur-Haute *France* Fourme d'Ambert

Fourme de Salers *France* A type of cheese with a red-streaked rind. See also **Cantal**

fourrage *France* Stuffing or filling

fourré(e) *France* Filled

fourré à la crème *France* Filled with cream, e.g. a cake

four spices Quatre-épices

fowl An edible bird, usually applied to older or tougher poultry suitable for boiling, casseroling or making soup

fox noodles Kitsume-udon

fox tail millet A temperate climate millet, *Setaria italica*, certainly grown in China in 2700 BC, now grown in the USA for animal feed and in Russia for beer. Also called **German millet**, **Hungarian millet**, **Siberian millet**, **Italian millet**

foyot, sauce *France* **Béarnaise sauce** with added melted meat glaze whisked in slowly. Also called **valois, sauce**

fözelék *Hungary* Vegetables

fracassata *Italy* Meat stew with an egg sauce

Fragaria alpina *Botanical name* Alpine strawberry

Fragaria vesca *Botanical name* Wild strawberry

Fragaria vesca sempiflorens *Botanical name* Alpine strawberry

Fragaria x ananassa *Botanical name* Cultivated strawberry. Originally a cross between *F. virginiana* (arrived 1556 from the USA) and *F. chiloensis* (arrived 18th century).

fragole *Italy* Strawberries

fragole di bosco *Italy* Wild strawberries

fragolini *Italy* Wild strawberries

fragolini di mare *Italy* Curled octopus

fragolino *Italy* Sea bream. Also called **pagello**

fragrant mushroom Shiitake mushroom

fraîche *France* Fresh or cool, the feminine form of *frais*

frais *France* Fresh or cool; usually applied to fresh cheeses and vegetables

fraisage *France* A method of kneading dough by spreading it across the board with the heel of the hand, gathering it up into a ball and repeating the process

fraise *France* 1. Strawberry. 2. Caul, the inner fatty membrane of the abdominal cavity.

fraise de bois *France* Wild strawberry

fraises Romanoff *France* Fresh strawberries macerated in liqueur and orange juice and served with a topping of whipped cream

framboesa *Portugal* Raspberry

framboise *France* Raspberry

frambozen *Netherlands* Raspberries

frambuesa *Spain* Raspberry

française, à la *France* In the French style, i.e. with a garnish of spinach and potatoes, sometimes also cooked lettuce and asparagus

française, fish à la Fillets of fish dipped in milk and passed through seasoned flour, deep-fried at 195°C, drained, garnished with lemon wedges and picked parsley and served with sauce diable

frangipane 1. *France* Almond paste **2.** *United Kingdom* An almond-flavoured cake mixture made from butter, sugar, eggs, ground almonds and flour, used for **Bakewell tarts** and other similar items **3.** *France* A thickening agent or panada, made rather like choux pastry from flour, egg yolks, butter and milk with seasonings, for use in the manufacture of chicken and fish forcemeats **4.** *France* Confectioner's custard containing chopped or ground almonds, used as crème pâtissière

frangipane flan See **frangipane tart**

frangipane tart A 16th-century Italian tart introduced to France at that time, consisting of a blind-baked pastry case lined with jam, filled with cooked cream containing crushed ratafia biscuits, lightly browned butter, rum and lemon zest, decorated with whipped cream and chopped pistachios. Also called **frangipane flan**

frango *Portugal* A young chicken

frango com ervilhas *Portugal* Chicken cooked in olive oil and butter and served with petit pois, onions and the pan residues deglazed with port

frango guisado *Portugal* A chicken, onion and tomato stew

frank *United States* Frankfurter (*colloquial*)

frankfurter *United States* A cheap imitation of the German Frankfurter made from the cheapest pig and beef meat and offal, finely ground with water and emulsifiers, mixed with flour, onion, seasoning, spices, saltpetre, colouring and so on, packed into narrow casings and linked. Made in various lengths. Used for hot dogs.

Frankfurter *Germany* A yellowish-brown, smooth-textured, scalded and cold-smoked sausage made from finely ground pork and bacon fat. Usually poached in water to heat it up. Called Bockwurst in Frankfurt.

Frankfurter Bohnensuppe *Germany* Kidney beans previously rehydrated, boiled in water or stock with herbs until tender, finished with butter and garnished with sliced frankfurters

Frankfurter Kranz *Germany* A rich cake made by the creaming method from sugar, corn flour, plain flour, butter and eggs (4:3:2:3:3) with 8 teaspoonfuls of baking powder (6 g) per kg of total flour and flavoured with lemon zest and rum, baked at 160°C, cut in 3 horizontal slices, filled with a rum flavoured and egg yolk enriched butter cream and the top and sides covered with crushed almond praline

Frankfurter Würtschen *Germany* Pale boiled sausages for which Frankfurt is famous, containing finely ground meat products

Frankfurt tongue sausage *Germany* Cured pork leg meat finely minced, seasoned and flavoured with mace and cardamom, diced pork tongue and pistachio nuts added, the mixture packed into thin bullock casings, boiled until cooked then smoked over oak and juniper berries

Frankische Butterplätzchen *Germany* Biscuits made by the creaming method from half and half butter and clarified butter, sugar, eggs, and flour (4:4:3:9), flavoured with vanilla and baked at 200°C

franskbröd *Sweden* French bread, i.e. baguette, petit pain, bread roll or the like

franskbrød *Denmark* French bread, i.e. baguette, petit pain, bread roll or the like. Also called **rundstycke**

franske kartofler *Denmark* Potato chips

franske poteter *Norway* Potato chips

frappe *Italy* **Galani**, but the strips of pastry knotted

frappé(e) *France* Frozen or chilled. Used to describe dishes served on crushed ice.

frappo *France* A strong-tasting casserole of ox tripe from Languedoc

frassino di montagna *Italy* Rowanberry

Frauenhaar *Germany* Maidenhair fern

freak coconut Makapuno

fréchure *France* A casserole of pigs' lights from Vivarais

freddo *Italy* Cold

free-range eggs Eggs laid by hens which nominally have free access to open pasture. Often theoretical since the birds have only limited openings from the barn to the outside and are not bred to freedom from hatching.

freeze, to To reduce the temperature of food to below 0°C so that any free water solidifies and other materials become stiff or glass-like. Mixtures are frozen to make ice cream, sorbet, etc. At even lower temperatures below −20°C food is preserved from deterioration. See also **deep-freeze, to**

freeze-concentrate, to To concentrate fruit juice or other aqueous liquids by freezing out part of the water as crystals and removing them

freeze-dried bean curd Bean curd which has been freeze-dried. When reconstituted it retains the porous texture of the dried product.

freeze-dry, to A method of dehydrating food by subjecting it to a vacuum whilst it is frozen. This causes the frozen water to evaporate whilst preserving an open structure in the food which facilitates rehydration. Freeze-dried vegetables are used in instant soups and the technique is most widely used for instant coffee.

freezer A chest, upright cabinet or walk-in room which is kept at a temperature of − 20°C in which deep-frozen foods may be stored. Also used to deep-freeze foods.

freezer burn The discoloration which occurs on the surface of food where it comes into direct contact with a cold surface because of inadequate packaging

freezer knife A knife with a serrated or saw-like edge to its strong blade, used for cutting up frozen food

freginat *Catalonia* **1.** Fried or sautéed, with a sauce **2.** The meat used in preparing something in the freginat style

freginat de fetge *Catalonia* Liver, usually calves' liver

freginat de pollostre *Catalonia* Chicken fried or sautéed with onions and garlic

fregit *Catalonia* Fried

fregolatta *Italy* Lightly toasted bread rubbed with garlic and tomato. See also **bruschetta**

fregula *Italy* Saffron flavoured semolina dumplings cooked in broth and served with cheese. Also called **succu tundu**

Freiburger Vacherin *Germany, Switzerland* A smaller soft version of Gruyère cheese. See also **Vacherin fribourgeoise**

frejol (*plural* **frejoles**) *Spain* Beans other than broad beans. See also **haba**

frejon *West Africa* An unusual dish from Sierra Leone made from partially mashed cooked cow peas mixed with coconut milk (2:1), salt and sugar and flavoured with cocoa mixed to a paste with a little water

French artichoke See **artichoke**

French bean A South American, half-hardy annual legume, *Phaseolus vulgaris*, usually a dwarf bush but occasionally climbing, which carries 10 to 15 cm long thin fleshy pods, usually green but some yellow or purple. When immature, the whole pod is eaten as a vegetable. At a later stage when the pods become stringy the fresh green beans are known as flageolet beans and can be treated as peas, i.e. used as they are or dried. When fully mature, cream- or fawn-coloured and completely dry, the beans are known as haricot beans. They are grown extensively all over the world. Also called **dwarf bean, kidney bean, string bean, snap bean, haricot vert**

French black truffle The famous and expensive truffle, *Tuber melanosporum*, from Périgord which grows in the root area of oak and hazelnut trees. In appearance it is wrinkled and warty, dark brown to black with a strong distinctive fragrance and mild flavour. Now grown in California, New Zealand and Australia. Also called **diamant noir**, **Périgord truffle**

French bread Any of the varieties of long thin bread with a crisp brown crust and the characteristic diagonal slashes which imitate the traditional French daily bread. See also **flute**, **baguette**

French carrots *United States* Carrettes

French dressing See **vinaigrette**

French flan See **crème caramel**

French fries *United States* Potato chips

French fritters Beignet

French frying *United States* Deep-fat frying

French icing *United States* A cooked cake covering made from icing sugar, butter, eggs and flavouring

French knife *United States* Cook's knife

French marjoram Pot marjoram

French meringue 1 part egg white beaten until stiff with 2 parts of icing sugar, vanilla essence and a pinch of salt over a bain-marie for up to 30 minutes. Piped to form various shapes.

French mustard A mild flavoured mustard made from dehusked and ground, brown and black mustard seeds mixed with vinegar and water

French onion soup See **brown onion soup**

French parsley Flat parsley

French puff Beignet

French puff pastry method Dough formed into a ball, cross cut on the top, corners pulled out and rolled out to a square with a thick centre and thin corners. Fat of the same consistency as the dough placed on the centre, the corners pulled over the fat and rolled out to a rectangle to give 2 layers of dough sandwiching 1 layer of fat, folded, rolled out and rested, then turned and rolled as for **puff pastry**.

French service 1. A style of laying the table with a plate (not necessarily used), cutlery, glasses and a napkin on the plate 2. A method of serving food in which guests help themselves from food offered on a dish or flat from the left by a waiter

French sorrel A name used indiscriminately for both **sorrel** and **buckler leaf sorrel**

French stick See **French bread**

French tarragon See **tarragon**

French toast Stale bread slices dipped in an egg and milk mixture, sweetened and flavoured with vanilla for the dessert version, then fried in (clarified) butter until crisp and golden. The sweet version is served as a dessert in France and as a breakfast dish in the USA, topped with maple syrup, fruit or jam or sprinkled with cinnamon and sugar. See also **pain perdu**

French whip *United States* Balloon whisk

Freneuse, crème *France* Purée Freneuse creamed with cream, milk or thin **béchamel sauce**

Freneuse, purée *France* A basic soup with potatoes and turnips. Also called **potato and turnip soup**

fresa *Spain* Strawberry

fresa pistocco *Italy* A paper-thin crisp bread. See also **carta de musica**

fresca *Mexico* 1. Fresh 2. Cool 3. A cocktail made with tequila, grapefruit juice and soda water

fresco *Italy, Portugal, Spain* Fresh, cool

fresh egg custard sauce See **egg custard sauce**

fresh fruit salad As fruit salad but restricted to fresh fruits

fresh ham *United States* An uncured hind leg of pork

fresh pasta Freshly made soft pasta which cooks in 3 to 5 minutes. Cannot be formed into elaborate shapes like dried pasta.

freshwater bream A fish, *Abramis brama*, related to the carp family with a lot of bones and a muddy flavour. Generally caught for sport only.

freshwater drum *Alpodinotus grunniens*, the only member of the drum family of fish which lives all its life in fresh water. It is 30 to 40 cm long weighs to 500 g and is from the lakes and rivers of the Northern USA. The flesh is light coloured and mild in flavour.

freshwater shark Pike

Fresno chilli *Mexico* A small conical fairly hot chilli pepper with a green or greenish-yellow colour

fresones *Spain* Large strawberries

fresse alla cunese *Italy* Minced pork liver and beef wrapped in pig's caul and fried

fressure *France* Offal from pigs or calves

friandises *France* 1. Titbit, delicacy, sweetmeat 2. A selection of small sweets, preserved fruits, etc. served with petit fours and tea or coffee

friand sanflorain *France* A herb-flavoured pork pie from Saint Flour in the Auvergne

friar's chicken 1. *England* Soup made by cooking a small chicken cut in four pieces in veal stock until tender. The seasoned cooking liquor is thickened with egg yolks, finished with chopped parsley and served with the chicken meat. **2.** *Scotland* Chicken stock thickened with a liaison of eggs and cream to which is added finely chopped chicken meat at the rate of 150 g per litre. This is warmed to not more than 85°C to avoid curdling, garnished with parsley and served immediately.

friar's omelette A baked omelette with stewed apples

fricadelle 1. Fried small meatballs of minced beef and pork, etc. See also **frikadeller 2.** *France* Croquette

fricandeau *England, France* A slice of meat, usually cushion veal, or large fish, cut along the fibres to 4 cm thick, beaten with a cutlet bat, larded with thin strips of salt pork fat and braised slowly until tender so that it may be cut with a spoon. Served dressed with the braising liquor and suitable garnishes.

fricandó *Catalonia* Braised veal with wild mushrooms

fricassea *Italy* Fricassée, usually finished with eggs and lemon juice

fricassee *United States* A veal or poultry stew in which the meat is first lightly browned so as to give a light brown colour to the stew

fricassée *England, France* A stew of sealed white meat and/or vegetable in a velouté sauce, cooked in the oven and finished with a liaison of egg yolks and cream

fricaude *France* A rich Lyonnaise stew of pigs' offal

Fridatten *Austria* Thin strips of pancake used as a garnish

fried bean curd Cubes of bean curd deep-fried to give a golden outer skin if lightly fried, or a crisp outer skin with just a little soft bean curd in the centre

fried cream *United States* As **crèmes frites**, but panéed with crushed cake crumbs and sprinkled with sugar and rum

fried creams Crèmes frites

fried egg A shelled egg shallow-fried in hot fat. The white on the top of the egg is coloured either by basting with hot fat or by turning the egg over when almost finished. Tastes differ as to the amount of cooking required.

fried rice Cooked rice stir-fried in oil with chopped vegetables usually containing spring onions, and beaten egg which is dribbled into the mix as it is being stirred and fried. Often served in place of boiled rice in Western Chinese restaurants or as a dish on its own.

fries Plural of **fry**

friese *Netherlands* A pale strong-flavoured and very hard and dense cows' milk cheese. See also **nagelkaas**

friese Kanterkaas *Netherlands* A cheese like **nagelkaas**, but without the cumin and cloves. See also **Kanterkaas**

friese Nagelkaas *Netherlands* A pale strong-flavoured and very hard and dense cows' milk cheese. See also **nagelkaas**

frigate mackerel See **bonito 1**

friggere *Italy* To fry

frijolada *Spain* A stew made with black beans, ham shank and sausage with fried onion and sweet peppers in a chicken or beef stock flavoured with herbs and served with rice

frijoles *Spain* Beans

frijoles blancos *Spain* Haricot beans

frijoles con puerco *Mexico* Black beans cooked until soft in water, drained and cooked in the oven with cubes of pork. The beans and pork are served on top of rice cooked in the bean cooking liquor (black rice) and garnished with coriander, chopped onions, chopped radish and a well-spiced tomato and garlic sauce.

frijoles negros *Spain* Black eyed beans much used in Caribbean cooking. See also **black bean 1**

frijoles refritos *Mexico* Refried beans made from various beans boiled until tender with onions, garlic, chillies, seasoning and sometimes skinned tomatoes, drained, mashed, mixed with fried onions, reheated and served as an accompaniment or as a dip

frijoles rojos *Spain* Kidney beans

frikadeller *Denmark, Sweden* Small meatballs of minced beef and pork with grated onion, allspice, egg, seasoning and milk, deep or shallow-fried, served in tomato sauce with potatoes and cooked red cabbage or salad. Popular in Northern Europe. Also called **fricadelle**

Frikadeller *Germany* Small meatballs of minced pork, deep or shallow-fried, served in a tomato sauce and popular in northern Europe

frikkadel *South Africa* The standard German **Frikadeller**

frikkadels *Sri Lanka* An adaptation of the European frikadeller made with minced beef, desiccated coconut, garlic, etc. and flavoured with dill or mint

frill 1. See **cutlet frill 2.** Mesentery

frío *Portugal, Spain* Cold

frire *France* To fry

Frisch See **Frischkäse**

frische Leberwurst *Germany* Fresh liver sausage. See also **Leberwurst**

frischer Hering *Germany* Fresh herring

frisches Obst *Germany* Fresh fruit

frischgemachte *Germany* Freshly cooked, cooked to order

Frischkäse Fresh cheese; refers to products such as quark and cream cheese which are not left to mature. Also called **Frisch**

frisée *France* Endive (NOTE: Literally 'curly'.)

frise kaas *Netherlands* Soft cheese

frit(e) *France* Fried

fritella *Italy* A thick, yeast-raised flour and water batter mixed with chopped vegetables, etc. and deep-fried

frites *France* Potato chips, chips, usually cut thinner than the UK version

friteuse *England, France* Chip pan, deep-fryer

fritieren *Germany* To deep-fry

frito *Spain* Fried

frito de cordero *Spain* A lamb stew made with cubed lamb, onions, bay, paprika, white wine and hot chilli pepper, thickened with machado

frito de verduras *Spain* Pisto

fritole di lino *Italy* A choux pastry, teaspoonfuls of which are fried in a 2 cm depth of olive oil until the expanding ball turns itself over to complete browning taking about 2 minutes in all. When cooled filled with any thickened cream mixture and served warm.

frittata *Italy* An omelette made in the same way as a Spanish tortilla but incorporating a variety of ingredients such as cheese, prosciutto, precooked vegetables and pasta shapes

frittatine *Italy* Pancakes

frittella *Italy* Fritter, pancake

frittelli di Venezia *Italy* Balls of yeast-raised flour dough, flavoured with white wine, grated lemon zest and raisins soaked in wine, deep-fried in oil, drained and dusted with icing sugar

fritter The general name for a portion of sweet or savoury food coated with batter and deep-fried

fritter batter A thick coating batter made from a smooth mixture of flour, oil and warm water into which stiffly beaten egg whites are blended. Alternatively yeast and sugar may be used to raise the batter.

fritto *Italy* Fried

fritto composto *Italy* A mixture of fried croquettes each made from a different meat

fritto misto *Italy* Various items of boned meat and poultry, offal and vegetables, panéed or coated in batter and deep-fried

fritto misto di mare *Italy* As **fritto misto**, but with fish or shellfish. Served with lemon wedges.

frittura *Italy* Fried food

fritura *Spain* Fried food

friture **1.** *France* The process of frying **2.** *France* Fried food **3.** *France* Deep fat for frying **4.** *England* A large oval pan fitted with a wire basket used for deep-frying. Usually placed on top of the stove.

frituurvet *Netherlands* Oil or deep fat for frying

Friulano *Italy* A semi-hard scalded-curd cheese from Friuli rather like a young **Montasio** with a yellow/brown rind enclosing a firm paste containing a few small holes

frivolité *France* Small savouries served at the beginning of a formal meal or banquet

frivolités *France* Testicles, usually of oxen or sheep (*colloquial*) See also **animelles**

frizzes *United States* Dried sausages made from coarsely chopped pork and beef flavoured with peppercorns and garlic and filled into hog casings

frizzle, to To fry until very crisp and brown

frog One of a group of amphibian animals most of which are edible. The European edible frog, *Rana esculenta*, grows to 12 cm long in the body, is green and does not have black marks behind the eyes. It is generally farmed for the back legs only, although it may be stuffed and eaten whole.

frogs' legs The hind legs of frogs which when fried or stewed resemble chicken. Popular in France and the USA.

froid(e) *France* Cold

froise An old English word for fritter, still in use when qualified, e.g. apple froise

frokost **1.** *Norway* Breakfast **2.** *Denmark* Lunch

frollo *Italy* **1.** Short (of pastry) **2.** Tender or high (of meat or game)

fromage *France* Cheese

fromage affiné *France* Cheese which is fully matured and ripened

fromage à la crème *France* Cream cheese

fromage à la croûte *France* Welsh rarebit

fromage à la pie *France* A white cheese prepared with full cream milk mixed with herbs (NOTE: Said to resemble the black and white plumage of the magpie.)

fromage blanc *France* A very smooth-textured low-fat soft cheese with a fresh clean taste. Made from cows' milk with medium to low butterfat content, sometimes flavoured. Often served for dessert in place of whipped cream.

fromage de Bruxelles *Belgium* A low-fat tangy rindless cheese made from pasteurized cows' milk. Also called **brusselkaas**, **hettekees**

fromage de monsieur *France* A soft cows' milk cheese similar to, but milder than, Camembert

fromage des Pyrénées *France* A semi-hard ewes' milk cheese made in cylinders (up to 7 kg). The paste is yellowish with a strong taste and the dry rind is sometimes coloured black. Also called **fromage du pays**

fromage de tête (de porc) *France* Brawn (NOTE: Literally 'head cheese'.)

fromage de trappiste *Belgium* A semi-soft cheese made from cows' milk. Similar to **Port-Salut**.

fromage d'Italie *France* A dish made from pigs' liver

fromage du curé *France* A strong-smelling cows' milk cheese from Normandy cast in squares

fromage du pays *France* Fromage des Pyrénées

fromage fondu *France* 1. Cheese spread 2. A small skimmed-milk goats' cheese ripened in grape seeds. See also **Tomme au raisin**

fromage fort *France* A mixture of overripe dessert cheese mixed with herbs, spices, oil and spirits, sealed in pots and left to mature to the strength required. Very strong-tasting and piquant.

fromage frais *France* A soft young cultured cheese with a pleasant fresh flavour, often enriched with cream. Used as a dessert mixed or flavoured with fruit and since it does not curdle when boiled, used as a cream substitute.

fromage glacé *France* Cheese-shaped ice cream

fromager *France* To add grated cheese

fromaget *France* Cheesecake

fromez *Middle East* A mild goats' milk cheese from Israel

Froschschenkel *Germany* Frogs' legs

frossen fløde *Denmark* Frozen whipped cream, used for decoration

frost, to 1. To give items especially soft fruits and the rims of glasses or coupes a frosty appearance by dipping in lightly whipped egg white then in caster sugar and leaving to dry 2. *United States* To ice (a cake)

frosting *United States* American frosting

frozen food Particular foods, made-up or partially made-up dishes which have been frozen to –20°C and which can be stored for at least 6 weeks and generally much longer. It is generally stated that once defrosted, frozen foods cannot be refrozen but there is no justification for this rule providing the period at greater than 0°C is less than an hour. Frozen foods have generally been prepared for use prior to freezing.

frozen yoghurt A dessert similar to ice cream made from a mixture of yoghurt, sugar and flavourings

Frucht *Germany* Fruit

Frucht des Brotbaumes *Germany* Breadfruit

Fruchteis *Germany* Fruit ice

Fruchtpastete *Germany* Fruit pie or tart

Fruchtsalat *Germany* Fruit salad

fructe coapte le flamă *Romania* Fruit fritters dusted with icing sugar, sprinkled with spirits or alcohol and flamed at the table

fructose 1. One of the three common monosaccharides found in fruit and with a sweetening power greater than glucose or sucrose (cane or beet sugar). Also called **fruit sugar, laevulose, levulose** 2. One of the sugars in corn syrup

frugt *Denmark* Fruit

frugt kage *Denmark* Fruit pie

Frühlingskäse *Austria* Cottage cheese mixed with cream, caraway seeds and chopped chives and parsley

Frühlingsuppe *Germany* Spring vegetable soup based on a meat stock

Frühstück *Germany* Breakfast

Frühstückkäse *Germany* A cheese similar to **Limburger** used as a breakfast cheese

fruit *England, France, Netherlands* The seed-bearing part of any growing plant, but generally restricted to those fruits in which the seeds are unimportant and the flesh or juice sac surrounding the seeds contains, when ripe, a high proportion of sugar plus various esters which give the fruit its distinctive flavour. The natural function of such fruits is to be eaten by animals who as a result disperse the seeds. Some fruit trees and bushes have been bred to have infertile seeds with no or only vestigial seeds.

fruit and almond tartlets *Ireland* Equal quantities of butter, caster sugar and ground almonds mixed and baked in tartlet moulds at 180°C till straw-coloured. Filled before serving with fruit and whipped cream.

fruit à pain *France* Breadfruit

fruit batter pudding *England* A baked pudding mixture from Yorkshire containing pieces of fresh fruit

fruit bread Bread made from a sweetened and possibly egg and butter enriched yeast dough, containing dried vine fruits and sometimes spices, candied peel and citrus zest. Also called **fruit loaf**

fruit butter See **fruit cheese**

fruit cake 1. A generic term for cake mixes containing various amounts of dried vine fruits, glacé cherries and chopped candied peel 2. *United States* Candied fruits, dried vine fruits and nuts, bound together with just sufficient cake mixture to hold the fruit together when baking

fruit chat *South Asia* A fruit and vegetable salad served on lettuce made from boiled waxy potato, deseeded and peeled cucumber, banana, papaya, mango, pineapple and apple all cubed, and orange segments, sprinkled with chat masala and lemon juice

fruit cheese A solid preserve made by boiling a purée of fruit with sugar to form a mixture which when cooled and set can be sliced like cheese

fruit cocktail A mixture of various diced, possibly parboiled fruits, with cherries and other whole small fruit, in a sugar syrup. Used in desserts, pies, tarts, etc.

fruit crumble *United Kingdom* A dessert or pudding made from fruit and sugar in an oven proof dish, topped with a **crumble** mixture, baked in the oven and eaten hot with cream, custard or ice cream. Also called **fruit streusel**

fruit curd Mixtures of sugar and butter thickened with egg yolks over a double boiler and flavoured with various fruits. The most common is lemon curd.

fruit de la passiflore *France* Passion fruit

fruit essence An **essence** extracted from a fruit

fruit-flavoured yoghurt Yoghurt mixed with fruit juice, fruit flavouring or essences, usually sweetened, often coloured and thickened with starch

fruit fritters Largish slices or pieces of raw fruit, coated in fritter batter, deep-fried until golden brown, drained, dusted with icing sugar and eaten hot

fruit jelly 1. A gelatine-set dessert made from sweetened fruit juice or fruit flavoured water, also used in trifles **2.** A jam or preserve made from strained and clear fruit juice boiled with sugar and set with fruit pectin if necessary

fruit juice Liquid extracted from raw or cooked fruit used for flavouring, as a starter or appetizer or as a drink

fruit leather *United States* An early method of preserving fruit by mixing fruit purée with brown sugar or honey, spreading on a baking sheet and drying in a slow oven. It was then cut in strips and dusted with sugar. Also called **leather**

fruit loaf See **fruit bread**

fruit pie A pie with a base and top of pastry filled with fruit, sweetened if necessary before baking

fruit pudding *United Kingdom* Basic steamed pudding mixture with soaked dried vine fruits equal to half the weight of flour added in

fruit salad A mixture of sliced, or whole if small, fresh fruit and presoaked dried fruits in fruit juice or a plain or flavoured sugar syrup, served as a dessert often with cream, custard, yoghurt or crème fraîche

fruits cuits *France* Stewed fruit

fruits de mer *France* Seafood, i.e. shellfish, crustaceans, etc. but excluding oysters (NOTE: Literally 'fruits of the sea'.)

fruits glacés *France* Candied fruit

fruit snow Lightly sweetened fruit purée combined with egg whites which have been beaten with icing sugar

fruit soup *Central Europe, Scandinavia* A popular soup made from sweetened stewed fruit thickened with **fécule**, arrowroot, corn flour or fine semolina and flavoured with wine, lemon juice or vanilla

fruit sponge pudding A baked pudding rather like a fruit crumble but with a topping of Victoria sponge mixture

fruits rafraîchis *France* Fruit salad

fruit streusel *United States* Fruit crumble

fruit sugar See **fructose**

fruit syrup Fruit flavoured sugar syrup made from fruit juices and water, used for flavouring and as a drink base

fruit turnover As **apple turnover**, but with various fruits

fruit yoghurt Yoghurt to which has been added a sterilized mixture of suitably sized fruit pieces in a sugar syrup

frukost *Sweden* Breakfast

frukt *Norway, Russia, Sweden* Fruit

frukti *Russia* See **frukt**

frukt-kräm *Sweden* Puréed fruit

fruktpai *Norway* Fruit pie

fruktpaj *Sweden* Fruit pie

frullato *Italy* Whisked or whipped

frumento *Italy* Wheat

frumenty *United Kingdom* A medieval pudding made from frumenty wheat boiled with milk and presoftened dried vine fruits, thickened if necessary with flour, sweetened and spiced with cinnamon, allspice or nutmeg. Traditionally eaten at Christmas, Easter and in Lent. Served with butter, cream or rum. Also called **furmenty**, **fumenty**, **thrumenty**

frumenty wheat Hulled or pearled wheat, soaked in excess water and a pinch of salt for 24 hours, excess water poured off and the remaining softened wheat stirred over heat until it boils, cooled and used to make frumenty. Also called **cree'd wheat**

frushie *Scotland* Brittle or crumbly

fruta *Portugal, Spain* Fruit

fruta azucarada *Spain* Candied fruit

fruta del arbol del pan *Spain* Breadfruit

frutas del mar *Spain* Shellfish and edible crustaceans, etc.

frutas doces *Portugal* Sugar plums, i.e. plums preserved by soaking in sugar syrup then draining

frutta *Italy* Fruit

frutta candita *Italy* Candied fruit

frutti di mare *Italy* Shellfish

frutto dell'albero del pane *Italy* Breadfruit

fry The collective noun for the pair of testicles of a lamb or calf (thus lamb's fry), skinned then fried, braised or stewed. Sometimes used of other offal.

fry, to To cook food in hot fat or oil at temperatures which seal the surface rapidly. May be in shallow or deep fat or oil.

fryer 1. *United States* A young chicken suitable for frying **2.** The pan used for deep-frying

frying basket See **chip basket**

frying batter. A batter of flour and water (4:5), plus salt and/or oil and/or whole egg or stiffly beaten egg white (4 eggs per kg of flour)

frying pan A shallow circular pan with outwardly sloping sides, a heavy base and a long handle. Used for shallow frying.

fry kettle *United States* Deep-fryer

fry-up *England* An informal dish of fried assorted fresh or, more generally, leftover food

fu *Japan* Wheat gluten

fuarag *Scotland* Soured cream and toasted medium oatmeal (5:1) are mixed with sugar to taste and left for several hours to thicken. Often eaten spread on oatcakes or with stewed fruit.

fudge A confection of butter, sugar and milk which forms a soft sweet pasty mixture, used as a filling for tarts or as a sweet or candy on its own or enrobed in chocolate

fudge cake *United States* A rich, moist chocolate cake which has a fudge-like texture. Also called **American fudge cake**

fudge frosting *United States* A thick fudge-like icing usually containing chocolate or cocoa powder

fudge tart *England* A Gloucestershire tart made by pouring molten hot fudge into a blind baked pastry case where it solidifies

fuet *Catalonia* A long, dry-cured sausage

fufu *West Africa* A purée of yams, sweet potatoes or plantains served as the carbohydrate source with stews

fugath *South Asia* A style of cooking in which vegetables are fried with onions and spices

fugu *Japan* The puffer fish, *Fugu rubripes*, whose liver and blood contain a deadly nerve poison. The flesh is used in sashimi and this contains just enough of the poison to give a tingling sensation in the lips. Only licensed chefs may prepare the fish. Several deaths occur yearly in Japan from consuming incorrectly prepared fugu.

fu jook pin *China* Bean curd sticks

fuki *Japan* Coltsfoot stalks

Fukien cooking The cooking of the eastern coast province of China between Shanghai and Canton. It includes delicate soups, sucking pig, seafood, egg rolls and makes extensive use of soya sauce.

fukusa-zushi *Japan* A sushi rolled in a thin pancake. See also **chakin-zushi**

ful *Egypt* Brown beans. Also called **ful medames**

full-cream milk Pasteurized unskimmed milk with a minimum 3% butterfat content (average 3.8%). Also called **whole milk**, **silver top**

full-fat soft cheese A soft white cheese with a butterfat content between 20 and 45% made from cows' milk. Used for dessert or cooking.

Füllung *Germany* Stuffing

ful medames *Egypt* **1.** A brown dried bean similar to a broad bean. Also called **ful 2.** A dish of ful medames which have been soaked and drained then casseroled for 4 to 7 hours to soften, cooking liquor discarded and the beans dressed with lemon juice, olive oil, crushed garlic and seasoning without breaking them up then garnished with chopped hard-boiled eggs and parsley. Also called **el ful**, **foule medames**

ful nabed *Egypt* Broad beans

fumaric acid See **E297**

fumé(e) *France* Smoked

fumenty See **frumenty**

fumer *France* To smoke

fumet *France* **1.** Aroma **2.** A concentrated fish or mushroom stock used for flavouring. Made by boiling the stock with additional fish or mushrooms and aromatic vegetables, straining off the liquid and reducing it to a syrupy consistency.

fumetto *Italy* Fumet, concentrated stock

funchi *Caribbean* A pudding from the Dutch West Indies made from cornmeal or corn flour. Also called **fungee**

functional foods Foods containing additional components which provide specific medical or physiological benefits over and above those provided by the naturally occurring nutrients, including the more traditional supplemented foods such as bread, breakfast cereals etc. as well as those with a more ostensibly medicinal purpose, e.g. Benecol, Yakult, etc. Also called **nutraceuticals**, **pharma foods**. See also **probiotics**

funge *Central Africa* A fufu-like staple porridge from Angola made with maize meal or cassava meal

fungee *Caribbean* Funchi

funghi *Italy* Mushrooms, fungi

funghi porcini *Italy* Ceps. See also **porcini**

fungi The plural of **fungus**. Varieties of fungi include: blewit, boletus, cep, chanterelle, chestnut mushroom, common mushroom, field mushroom, girolle, honey fungus, horn of plenty, horse mushroom, Jew's ear, matsutake, morel, orange peel fungus, oyster mushroom, parasol mushroom, pine mushroom, puffball, shiitake, truffle and wood ear.

fungo *Italy* Mushroom

fun gor *China* Ground pork and shrimp mixed with chopped chives or spring onions and light soya sauce. Made into small turnovers with wheat starch dough circles and steamed for 12 to 15 minutes.

fungus The name given in cookery to the fruiting body of a fungus which arises from the long branching thread-like strands of mycelium which grow on decaying organic matter and is usually the only visible part of the fungus. The fruiting bodies grow extremely rapidly and carry the spores by which the fungi are dispersed. They grow in the wild or are cultivated and are generally eaten before they mature. They do not require sunlight to grow and are most colours except green. (NOTE: The plural is **fungi**.)

funkaso *West Africa* Nigerian pancakes made from a well-mixed batter of millet flour and water with a little sugar and salt which has been allowed to stand for at least 4 hours

funnel cake *United States* A cake made by running batter through a funnel into hot fat in a spiral pattern. When cooked it is served with sugar or maple syrup. Introduced by Dutch immigrants to Pennsylvania. See also **furtaies**

furi-jio *Japan* Hand-sprinkled salt used for salting vegetables, meats and fish. The food is laid on a salt-sprinkled board and sprinkled with salt from above. It is usually left about 40 to 60 minutes then rinsed and dried.

furmenty See **frumenty**

furtaies *Italy* A fried pastry dessert from the Dolomite region made from a batter of milk, flour, salt, egg yolks beaten with grappa into which is folded stiffly whipped egg whites. The batter is dribbled through a funnel into hot butter to make a spiral, fried on both sides and sugared.

fu ru *China* Bean curd cheese

furutsujusu *Japan* Fruit juice

fusilli *Italy* Pasta made into the shape of a corkscrew, hence the alternative name archimede (from Archimedes' screw pump). Also called **rotelle**, **tortiglione**, **tortiglioni**, **archimede**

fuso *Italy* **1.** Melted or clarified. Used of butter. **2.** Processed. Used of cheese.

futari *West Africa* Equal quantities of squash and yam simmered in coconut milk with fried onion, seasoned and flavoured with ground cloves and cinnamon

futomaki *Japan* Big roll, an assortment of items surounded by rice and wrapped in nori

fuzzy melon A Chinese vegetable like a dumbbell-shaped courgette, but covered with a fine down which grows on a vine, *Benincasa hispida*. It is used in its immature state as a vegetable and must be peeled before use. Steamed, stir-fried or added to soup. The mature version is known as Chinese vegetable marrow. Also called **hairy melon**, **summer melon**, **hairy brinjal**

fyldt *Denmark* **1.** Filled **2.** Stuffed

fyll *Norway* Stuffing

fyllda svamphattar *Sweden* A dish served at smörgåsbord consisting of parboiled mushroom caps marinated in French dressing and filled with a mixture of cleaned sardines, grated onion, hard-boiled egg yolk, Worcestershire sauce and mayonnaise.

Fynbo *Denmark* A semi-hard scalded-curd cows' milk cheese similar to **Samsø** from the island of Fyn. It has a lactic starter and the paste is smooth and creamy with a few large holes. The brown dry rind is usually waxed.

fytt kålhode *Norway* Stuffed cabbage

GHIJKLMN

ga *Vietnam* Chicken: the preceding word indicates which part of the chicken

gaai laan *China* Chinese kale

gaau sun *China* Wild rice shoots

Gabelfrühstück *Germany* Fork breakfast, i.e. a substantial breakfast similar to an English breakfast or brunch

gabi *Philippines* Taro

gacha *Spain* A soft pudding

gad *Middle East* A cows' milk cheese similar, to the Danish **Danbo**, with fairly large holes

gädda *Sweden* Pike

gado gado *Indonesia* A salad made from a mixture of bean sprouts and shredded or julienned vegetables, steamed until al dente, dressed with a thick spicy sauce based on onions, garlic, dry-roasted trassi, brown sugar, tamarind juice, peanut butter, coconut milk, ground cumin, dark soya sauce and ground lemon grass processed together, the whole garnished with chopped hard-boiled eggs

gaelic See **Galic**

gaeng *Thailand* Indicates liquid in a dish, therefore used as a prefix for stews, soups, etc. Also called **kaeng**, **keng**

gaeng dang *Thailand* Red curry paste

gaeng jued *Thailand* Clear soup

gaeng kaee *Thailand* A thick, slightly sweet-and-sour, shrimp soup flavoured with turmeric, citrus (peel, lemon grass or leaves) and a variety of aromatic spices. Sometimes meat or chicken are substituted for shrimps.

gaeng khiao wann *Thailand* Curry

gaeng mussaman *Thailand* A heavily spiced beef curry with coconut and peanuts said to have been introduced by Muslim civil servants from British India. Also called **Muslim curry**, **musaman curry**

gaffel *Denmark, Norway, Sweden* Fork

gaffelbitar *Sweden* Small pieces of herring

gafgeer *Central Asia* A slotted or pierced serving spoon from Afghanistan

gage A group of smaller plums, *Prunus domestica* or *P. insititia*, noted for their sweet flavour and pleasant smell. The two common varieties are the greengage and the golden mirabelle.

Gagel *Germany* Bog myrtle

gai *Thailand* Chicken

gai choy Chinese mustard cabbage

gai hoot *China* Steamed coagulated chicken blood used in soups and stews

gai larn *China* Chinese kale

gai larn tau *China* Kohlrabi

gaimer *Middle East* A type of clotted cream made from buffalo milk in Iraq

Gaisburger Marsch *Germany* A beef and vegetable broth made from cubed chuck steak (1:4 on water) and pieces of marrow bone simmered with a bouquet garni and onion clouté for 2 hours; skimmed; bouquet garni, marrow bone and onion clouté removed; marrow from bone added back and simmered with diced root vegetables and leeks for 30 minutes; garnished with small **Spätzle** dumplings

Gaiskali *Germany* A soft goats' milk cheese

gai ts'ai *China* Chinese mustard cabbage

gai yau *China* Chicken fat

gajar *South Asia* Carrot

gaji jijim *Korea* Thin slices of roast beef sandwiched between fried aubergine slices. Served with a mixture of soya sauce and vinegar.

gajjar *South Asia* Carrot

gajjar halwa *South Asia* A sweetmeat made from dried milk, carrots and spices rather like fudge. Also called **gajjar ka halva**

gajjar ka halva See **gajjar halwa**

gajus *Malaysia* Cashew nut

gal Abbreviation for gallon

galactose One of the common monosaccharides which in combination with glucose forms lactose, the sugar in milk. It is this monosaccharide liberated in the body which is responsible for lactose intolerance.

galaktoboureko *Greece* A traditional dessert made from an egg custard set in filo pastry. Also called **galatoboureko**

galamb *Hungary* Pigeon

galangal The roots of plants of the ginger family respectively **greater galangal**, **lesser galangal** and **kempferia galangal**. Greater galangal has a flavour like a mixture of ginger and pepper with a sour overtone, lesser galangal is more pungent with a hint of cardamom and eucalyptus, whilst kempferia galangal has a stronger taste and is the variety found dried and sliced in the West.

galani *Italy* A Venetian snack of crisp, wafer-thin, deep-fried strips of pastry, dusted with icing sugar. Also called **cenci**, **frappe**

galantina **1.** *Italy* Galantine (of meat) **2.** *Portugal* Aspic

galantine *England, France* Boned white meat, possibly stuffed and rolled, cooked and pressed into a symmetrical shape and glazed with aspic

galapong *Philippines* A dough made with ground rice and left standing overnight to partially ferment. Used for making sweet snacks.

galatoboureko See **galaktoboureko**

galego lime West Indian lime

galera *Spain* Mantis shrimp

galette *France* **1.** A round flat sweet or savoury cake or biscuit made from a variety of foods, e.g. puff pastry, shortbread, batter, almond paste, potatoes, etc. **2.** A buckwheat or brown flour pancake very popular in Brittany as a lunch dish with a sweet or savoury filling

galette de la chaise-dieu *France* A sweetish goats' milk cheese from the Auvergne

galette des Rois *France* A galette made from puff pastry for the twelfth night after Christmas. A single bean is baked in the galette which brings luck to the person finding it.

Galia melon A variety of musk melon with green flesh and a green to yellow skin. It is sweet, juicy and fragrant.

Galic *Scotland* A rich full cream soft cows' milk cheese. It is flavoured with the chopped leaves of wild garlic (**ransons**) and covered with rolled oats and chopped nuts. Also called **gaelic**

Galician cabbage Portuguese cabbage

gali foto *Africa* Cooked cassava flour served with fried lobster or shrimp and a sauce of fried onions, tomatoes, eggs, spices and corned beef

galil *Middle East* A blue-veined ewes' milk cheese from Israel, similar to Roquefort

galingale **1.** Tiger nut **2.** The original European name for **greater galangal**, once considered to be an aphrodisiac

galinha *Portugal* Chicken

galinha á Zambeziana *South Africa* A dish of chicken cooked in a lime juice, garlic and **piri-piri sauce**, from Mozambique

galinha recheada *Portugal* Chicken stuffed with eggs and olives

galinha salteada *Portugal* Sautéed chicken

galinhola *Portugal* **1.** Woodcock **2.** Moorhen

Galium odoratum *Botanical name* Sweet woodruff

Galium verum *Botanical name* Lady's bedstraw

gallates Esters of gallic acid used as antioxidants in oils, fats and essential oils only. Those available are propyl gallate, E310, octyl gallate, E311 and dodecyl gallate, E312.

gallera, in *Italy* Wrapped in a beef and/or ham slice

Gallert *Germany* **1.** Gelatine **2.** Jelly

galleta *Spain* Biscuit

galletta *Italy* **1.** Wafer **2.** Biscuit **3.** Hard tack **4.** Ship's biscuit

galletto *Italy* Cockerel, young cock chicken

gallina *Italy, Spain* Hen

gallinaccio *Italy* **1.** Turkey, turkey cock **2.** Chanterelle, the fungus

gallinaceous The generic description of an order of heavy-bodied ground-living birds *Galliformes* which include the domestic fowl, turkey, pheasant and grouse

gallina de Guinea *Spain* Guinea fowl

gallina di faraona *Italy* Guinea fowl

gallina pepitoria *Spain* Fried chicken served with a sauce of pounded garlic, almonds and hard-boiled egg yolks

gallinella *Italy* **1.** Hen **2.** Boiling fowl **3.** Woodcock

gallinella d'acqua *Italy* Moorhen

gallineta **1.** *Spain* Bluemouth, the fish **2.** *South America* Guinea fowl

gallino rennet A type of rennet extracted from the gizzard lining of chickens or turkeys which produces a delicate curd

gallo *Italy* Cock, rooster, male chicken

gallo cedrone *Italy* Grouse

gallo di bosque *Italy* Grouse

gallon **1.** *United Kingdom* The old imperial liquid measure still found in recipes. 1 imperial gallon equals 4.54 litre, 160 fluid oz, 8 pints or 32 gills. **2.** *United States* The liquid measure still in use in the USA. 1 US gallon equals 3.78 litres. (NOTE: Both are abbreviated gal.)

galupe *Italy* Grey mullet

galuptzes A Jewish speciality consisting of blanched cabbage leaves wrapped around a filling of meat and rice. See also **holishkes**

Galway oyster festival *Ireland* An annual festival in celebration of the oyster held annually at the end of September in this attractive Irish town

gamat *Philippines* Nori

gamba *France, Spain* A large Mediterranean prawn, especially the **crevette rose du large**

gambas a la plancha *Spain* Grilled prawns

gamberello *Italy* Common prawn

gamberetti *Italy* Small shrimps

gamberetti di mare *Italy* Prawns

gamberettino *Italy* Shrimp

gamberetto grigio *Italy* Brown shrimp

gambero *Italy* Crayfish

gambero di acqua dolce *Italy* Freshwater crayfish

gambero di mare *Italy* Lobster

gambero imperiale *Italy* A Mediterranean king prawn. See also **caramote**

gambero rosa *Italy* A large Mediterranean prawn, **crevette rose du large**

gambero rosso *Italy* A large king prawn, **crevette rouge**

gambes a la planxa *Catalonia* Prawns cooked on the griddle

gambrel The hock of an animal

game Wild birds and animals hunted for food, generally only in season at certain times of the year. Some animals and birds such as quail, rabbit and deer, which are now reared for the table in captivity, are still classed as game. The flavour of true game is supposed to be related to the intermittence of its food and its more stressful life than a domestic animal or bird. See under individual types: boar, capercaillie, deer, duck, goose, grouse, partridge, pheasant, wood pigeon, ptarmigan, quail, rabbit, snipe, teal, widgeon and woodcock.

game chips See **crisps**

gamecock The male of the wild fowl

game farce Farce de gibier

game fish Fish which are caught by rod or line for sport as well as for food, e.g. wild salmon, trout, shark, etc.

game herbs The principal herbs used with game are basil, bay, juniper, lovage, marjoram, rosemary, sage, savory and thyme

game pie *United Kingdom* A traditional raised pie with a pastry top made with hot water pastry and filled with pieces of boned game, rump steak, lean ham, pork sausage meat and seasonings, baked in a hinged oval mould and filled when cool with aspic jelly

game pie mould An oval metal mould consisting of two side pieces and a base which all clip together, often fluted. Used for raised game and pork pies.

game pudding *United Kingdom* The cooked flesh of game pounded with liver of the same animal together with bread and game stock or mashed potatoes and butter and packed into suitable casings

game sausage Trimmed flesh of game minced with lean ham, then processed with butter, seasoning, sweet red peppers and mace and packed into suitable casings

game stock As for brown beef stock but substituting game bones for beef bones. Also called **fond de gibier**

gamey Used to describe the smell and flavour of meat and game which has been hung. In meat such a smell would indicate that it had hung too long. In game this is the smell and flavour required to indicate that the meat has been sufficiently tenderized.

gamma-linoleic acid A fatty acid obtained from the seeds of the **evening primrose**, used as a medicine

Gammelost *Norway* A soft, cooked-curd, blue-veined cheese made from unpasteurized skimmed cows' milk. The natural *Streptococcus lactis* acts as a starter and the curd is inoculated with *Penicillium roquefortii* and ripened for 4 weeks at high humidity to give the blue veining and a heavy growth on the rind which give it its strong flavour.

gammiris *Sri Lanka* Peppercorn

gammon The name given to a whole hind leg cut from a side of bacon after curing. It has a lighter cure than ham and is either used as bacon or cut into thick (1 cm) gammon rashers or steaks.

gammon corner A large triangular joint of meat cut from a boned gammon

gammon hock The knuckle (foot) end of gammon containing more sinews and connective tissue than usual. Suitable for boiling, stewing and braising. The meat is often used in pies. Also called **gammon knuckle**

gammon knuckle See **gammon hock**

gammon slipper A triangular piece of lean meat cut from a gammon. It is smaller than a gammon corner and is used for boiling.

gammon steak A thick slice of bacon cut from across a boned gammon

Gamonedo *Spain* A strong, smoked, blue-veined cheese made in Asturia from a mixture of cows', goats' and ewes' milk and similar to **Cabrales**. After smoking, it is wrapped in fern leaves and matured for 2 months.

ganache *France* A chocolate-flavoured cream mixture used as a filling or topping for cakes pastries, etc., made from cream and melted chocolate with flavourings and sometimes butter. The quality depends on the quality of the chocolate.

gan bian siji dou *China* Stir-fried sliced French beans

gander The male goose

gandhmul *South Asia* Zedoary

gan dia fen *China* Corn flour

gandules *Caribbean* Pigeon peas, from Puerto Rico

ganmodoki *Japan* Fried patties of bean curd mixed with vegetables and spices

gans *Netherlands* Goose

Gans *Germany* Goose

Gänschen *Germany* Gosling

Gänsebraten *Germany* Roast goose

Gänsebrust *Germany* Breast of goose

Gänseleberpastete *Germany* Goose live pâté, pâté de foie gras

Gänseleberwurst *Germany* A fine goose liver **Kochwurst**

Gänseweisssauer *Germany* Goose cut into small pieces, simmered in water with vinegar, seasoning and herbs until tender, reserved, cooled and served covered with the strained and clarified cooking liquor cooled over ice until viscous but not set. Extra gelatine added if necessary.

ganso *Portugal, Spain* Goose

ganth gobhi *South Asia* Kohlrabi

gan zi *China* Orange

gao *Vietnam* Uncooked rice

Gaperon See **Gapron**

Gapron A dome-shaped low-fat, soft and supple cheese made in the Auvergne from skimmed cows' milk or buttermilk and flavoured with garlic. Also called **Gaperon**

gar See **garfish**

garam *Indonesia* Salt

garam masala *South Asia* A blend of ground spices with many variants meant either to be sprinkled on food just before it is served, to be added towards the end of cooking, or to be used to form an aromatic crust on foods which are bland and simple. Typically it will contain black pepper, black cumin, cinnamon, cloves, mace, cardamom, coriander seed and bay leaf, all dry-fried or roasted then dried and ground. Blends include: Moghul masala, Gujarati masala, Kashmiri masala, parsi dhansak masala, chat masala, char masala and green masala.

garbanzo *Spain* Chick pea

garbanzo pea Chick pea

garbure *France* A thick vegetable soup from Béarn containing beans, garlic, herbs, seasoning, preserved meats (duck, goose, turkey or ham), and sometimes chestnuts. Served over slices of bread.

Garcinia indica Botanical name Kokum

Garcinia mangostana Botanical name Mangosteen

garde manger *England, France* The larder area of a kitchen used for preparing cold buffets, canapés, hors d'oeuvre and the like and for preparing meat, fish and shellfish ready for cooking by others

garden cress See **cress**

garden egg Aubergine

garden orach Orach

garden pea See **pea**

garden rue See **rue**

garden thyme See **thyme**

Gardinia schomburgiana Botanical name Madun (2)

gardon *France* Roach, the freshwater fish

garfish A long (up to 60 cm) slender seawater fish, *Belone belone*, with green bones and a firm flesh, greeny-blue in colour with a silver underside and found on most European coasts. Usually skinned before cooking. Also called **gar**, **garpike**, **longnose**

garganelli *Italy* Home-made macaroni

garhi yakhni *South Asia* A highly reduced meat stock similar to glace de viande. See also **yakhni**

gari 1. A coarse flour or meal rather like coarse semolina made from dried cassava. Used as a source of carbohydrate. An instant form is made by moistening, fermenting, drying and then dry-frying the ground cassava. Also called **garri** 2. *Japan* Wafer-thin slices of pickled ginger. See also **benishoga**

garibaldi A soft, thin, rectangular biscuit consisting of a layer of minced currants between two layers of soft sweet biscuit

gari foto *West Africa* Dry-fried **gari** softened with water then folded into a type of piperade made with onions, tomatoes and eggs. Usually served in Ghana for breakfast or lunch with red beans and tomato sauce.

garithes *Greece* Prawns

garland chrysanthemum A hardy perennial, *Chrysanthemum coronarium*, whose flowers are used in Chinese cooking. The seed may also be sewn thickly like cress and the young leaves used in salads or stir-fried. Also called **chop suey greens**, **chrysanthemum greens**, **edible chrysanthemum**

garlic The cluster of small bulbs that grow at the base of a plant, *Allium sativum*, after the first season of growth. Each segment or 'bulblet' is called a clove and the whole cluster is called a 'head' of garlic. Each clove gives rise to a new head after one season. The clove consists of a white pungent, peppery flesh in a relatively tough skin. This is easily removed by squashing the clove. When raw, the smell and taste are very strong and a cut clove run around a bowl will flavour anything contained within it. When cooked it loses most of its pungency. Very widely used in cookery throughout the world. It has been considered as an aid to good health since antiquity and is now thought to have anti-cancer properties.

garlic bread A long thin French loaf cut almost through transversely at 2 to 4 cm intervals, a pat of garlic butter put in each cut and the whole, wrapped loosely in aluminium foil and baked in the oven until the butter has melted, and the outside become crisp (180°C for 15 minutes.)

garlic butter A compound butter made by processing butter, garlic, salt and chopped parsley to a smooth paste

garlic chive A type of Chinese chive with a pronounced garlic taste used as a flavouring

garlic clove An individual segment of a head of garlic, covered in a thin layer of papery skin

garlic dressing A salad dressing (French or vinaigrette), flavoured with crushed garlic

garlic head The cluster of garlic cloves that grows beneath the soil

garlic mustard An early flowering perennial or biennial wild herb, *Alliaria petiolata*, growing to 1 m. The heart-shaped indented leaves have a slight garlic flavour and may be included in salads or boiled as a vegetable. Also called **jack-by-the-hedge**

garlic powder Finely ground dried garlic flesh

garlic press A small implement rather like a lever type nut cracker with a receptacle with a perforated base on one arm to hold the clove of garlic and a piston on the other which when pressed into the receptacle pushes the flesh of the garlic though the perforations thus effectively chopping and crushing it

garlic purée Puréed garlic flesh with preservative, and possibly oil and salt. Available in tubes or jars to use for flavouring in the same way as tomato purée.

garlic salt Dried and ground garlic mixed with salt used for flavouring

garlic sausage *United Kingdom* A smooth pale-coloured slicing sausage made from pork and beef coarsely minced, cured separately (4% curing salt) in the refrigerator for 36 hours, finely minced with garlic, mixed with extenders, packed into weasands or large casings and hot smoked

garmerong *Romania* Red chilli pepper blended with a little water, olive oil, ground walnuts. See also **muhamara**

garmucia *Italy* A mixed vegetable soup from Tuscany

garmugia *Italy* Beef stewed with peas and artichokes

garnacha *Mexico* A turnover made with tortilla dough, filled with a savoury stuffing and cooked. Used as an appetizer or snack. Also called **picada**, **sope**

garnalen *Netherlands* Very small shrimps

Garnelen *Germany* Brown shrimps

garni Garnished with vegetables; past participle of *garnir*

garnir *France* To garnish

garnish A decoration, always edible, added to a savoury dish to enhance its appearance, ranging from the simple sprig of a herb, to very elaborate garnishes which are often more difficult to prepare than the main dish

garniture *France* Garnish

garofano di mare *Italy* Sea anenome

garofolato *Italy* 1. With cloves 2. A pot roast of beef with tomatoes and wine, flavoured with cloves

garotes *Catalonia* Sea urchins' eggs served raw with bread and spring onions or garlic

garoupa One of the grouper family of fish, *Plectropomous leopardus*, which is found around the coasts of China and Southeast Asia. It is up to 1 m in length and comes in two types. Red garoupa is pink with orange red spots and blue garoupa is red with blue spots. Prized in Chinese cooking.

garpike See **garfish**

garretto *Italy* 1. Shin beef 2. Knuckle or hock

garri See **gari**

Gartenkresse *Germany* See **cress**

Gartenraute *Germany* Rue, the herb

Gartensalat *Germany* Lettuce

garum Fermented fish made into a paste used by the ancient Romans as a flavouring. Probably like some of the East Asian fish pastes.

gås *Denmark, Norway, Sweden* Goose

gåsestak *Norway* Roast goose

gåsesteg *Denmark* Roast goose

gashneez *Central Asia* Coriander

gåsleverkorv *Sweden* A goose liver sausage made with minced goose liver mixed with boiled rice, sweated chopped onions, raisins, corn syrup, seasoning and chopped marjoram, loosely packed in the unbroken neck skin of the goose, tied and simmered until cooked. Served cold or in made up dishes.

gåsleverpastej *Sweden* One goose liver finely minced with one third of it weight of lean pork and one third its weight of suet, passed through a coarse sieve, mixed with ground cloves, bayleaf and nutmeg, seasoned, placed in a covered greased mould and cooked in a bain-marie in a medium oven for 30 to 40 minutes

gas mark A scale of temperature, written as GM, peculiar to gas ovens and based on an arbitrary scaling of the first oven thermostat when °F were in use. The relationship to temperature is as follows:- GM1/4 110°C, 225°F; GM1/2 130°C, 250°F; GM1 140°C, 275°F; and thereafter 25°F per unit until GM9 240°C, 475°F. Also called **regulo**

gåsöga *Sweden* As **solöga**, but with rings of anchovy, onion and dill

gaspereau Alewife

gass *Middle East* Doner kebab

gastaurello *Italy* Skipper, the fish

gastronome A connoisseur of fine food and wine

gastronomy The study and knowledge of fine food and wine

gastropod The name given to any mollusc (soft bodied invertebrates without segments or limbs) with a hard, one piece outer shell, sometimes coiled, such as the abalone, snail, whelk, winkle, etc. Also called **univalve**

gata *Philippines* Coconut

gà tây *Vietnam* Turkey

gâteau 1. *France* Cake **2.** *England, France* An elaborate cake sliced for a dessert made from layers of sponge, biscuit or pastry or a mixture of these interspersed with sweet fillings and decorated

gâteau au fromage *France* Cheesecake

gâteau aux amandes *France* Almond cake

gâteau d'anniversaire *France* Birthday cake

gâteau de patate *Caribbean* Cooked sweet potato mashed with ripe banana and sugar (12:2:3) and eggs (3 per kg of potato), flavoured with coconut milk, vanilla essence, cinnamon and nutmeg then let down to a thick pouring mixture with evaporated milk, baked in a buttered tin for 90 minutes at 180°C, turned out, cooled and served with cream or coquimol (NOTE: From Haiti)

gâteau de riz *France* Rice pudding

gâteau de semoule *France* Semolina pudding

gâteau noir *France* Créole Christmas cake

gâteau Pithiviers *France* Two layers of puff pastry with a rich cream filling containing almonds and rum (NOTE: From Pithiviers)

gâteau Saint Honoré *France* A circle of cooked shortcrust or sugar pastry, biscuit or sponge, with a circle of choux pastry piped around the edge, topped with choux buns filled with whipped cream and coated with caramel, the centre filled with crème pâtissière and the whole decorated

gâteaux à apéritif *France* Small savoury biscuits

gato marino *Spain* Lesser spotted dogfish

gato pardo *Spain* Larger spotted dogfish

gatto, gatto di patate *Italy* Seasoned mashed potatoes enriched with eggs, milk and Parmesan cheese, half of the mixture spread in a flat oven-proof dish, covered with Mozzarella and/or other cheeses or fillings, covered with the remainder of the mixture, gratinated with breadcrumbs and baked until crisp on top

gattuccio *Italy* Lesser spotted dogfish

Gätupgelter *Germany* Channel catfish

gaucho *Argentina* A rich-tasting firm cheese made from skimmed cows' milk resembling **Port-Salut**

gau choy *China* Chinese chive or garlic chive

gau choy fa Flowering chive with a mild flavour

gau choy sum *China* Flowering chive with a strong flavour

gaufres *Belgium, France* Rectangular waffles made by cooking a pancake mixture with raising agent between two hot indented metal plates (**gaufrier**) to give a large surface to volume ratio. Served with butter or sugar syrup.

gaufrette *France* Wafer

Gaultheria procumbens Botanical name Wintergreen

gaur See **guar bean**

gaur bean See **guar bean**

gau wong *China* Yellow chives, i.e. Chinese chives which have been blanched by growing them in the dark

ga xao xa ot *Vietnam* Chicken stir-fry with lemon grass and chillies

gayette *France* A small Provençal **crépinette** made with pigs' liver, fat bacon and possibly pork, diced, finely seasoned and flavoured with garlic and spice, wrapped in pig's caul and tied, baked in the oven in lard or stock. Served hot or cold.

gazpacho *Spain* A cold soup based on stale bread, garlic, oil and vinegar pounded to a paste and mixed with water, nowadays incorporating various salad ingredients such as tomatoes, sweet peppers, cucumbers, leaves and herbs. The bread is often omitted.

gdra *North Africa* The lower part of a **couscousière** in which the meat and vegetables are cooked to produce steam. See also **kskas**

ge *China* Pigeon

Gebäck *Germany* Fancy pastries, tortes, rolls, biscuits, generally eaten in the afternoons

gebacken *Germany* **1.** Fried **2.** Baked

gebackene Eier *Germany* Fried egg. Also called **Spiegeleier**

gebackene Kartoffeln *Germany* Baked potatoes

gebakjes *Netherlands* **1.** Pastries **2.** Tartlets

gebakken *Netherlands* Fried

gebonden soep *Netherlands* **1.** Cream soup **2.** Thick soup

gebraden *Netherlands* Roasted

gebraden kip *Netherlands* Roast or fried chicken

gebraten *Germany* Roasted

gebunden *Germany* Thickened (as of sauces)

gedämpfte Ente *Germany* Steamed duck

gedämpfte Rinderbrust *Germany* Beef, marinated in wine and slowly braised with onions and carrots

ge dan *China* Pigeon egg

gedünstete Gurke *Germany* Stewed cucumbers in a sour cream sauce

gedünsteter Ochsenschlepp *Germany* Braised oxtail

gee choy *China* Nori sheets

gee jook *China* Bean curd sticks

geelbeck toutjies *South Africa* A traditional Cape delicacy made by removing the head and bones from a Cape salmon (a relative of the cod) but leaving the flesh attached to the tail. The flesh is cut into 4-cm-wide strips which are salted and hung up to dry. After 5 hours the salt is washed off and the fish is resalted lightly and hung up for seven days. It is then ready to eat.

gefilte fish Fish balls of ground raw fish with seasonings, or fish cutlets stuffed with the same mixture, simmered in a court bouillon with sliced carrots and saffron. A Jewish speciality served hot or cold.

Geflügel *Germany* **1.** Poultry **2.** Fowl

Geflügelklein *Germany* Chicken giblets

Geflügelleber *Germany* Chicken livers

Geflügelragout *Austria* A chicken and chicken giblet stew

gefüllt *Germany* Stuffed

gefüllte Kartoffeln *Germany* Stuffed baked potatoes

gefüllter Gansenhals *Germany* A goose liver sausage made from chopped goose liver and pork, mixed with breadcrumbs and seasoning, bound with egg, stuffed into the intact skin of the goose's neck, tied and fried in goose fat. Eaten cold.

gefüllter Rinderbraten *Germany* Rib roast of beef stuffed with onions, celery, carrots and hard-boiled eggs

gefüllter Schöpsenrücken *Germany* Roast and stuffed saddle of mutton

gegrillt *Germany* Grilled

gehakt *Netherlands* Chopped

gehaktballetjes *Netherlands* Meatballs

Geheimratskäse *Austria, Germany* A semi-hard, scalded-curd close-textured cheese produced in Southern Germany. It has small holes and a delicate taste and is enclosed in a tender rind.

Gehirn *Germany* Brains

Gehirnwurst *Germany* A sausage made from a mixture of 2 parts pigs' brain, 1 part lean pork and 1 part pork fat, chopped, seasoned and flavoured with mace, filled into hog casings, linked in pairs, boiled for 5 minutes then cooled. Served fried in butter.

gekocht *Germany* **1.** Boiled **2.** Cooked

gekookt *Netherlands* Boiled

gekristalliseerde gember *Netherlands* Crystallized ginger

gel Jelly. Technically any liquid which is in a solid state by virtue of the network of strands of protein or carbohydrate which gives it a solid structure.

gel, to To set into a jelly

gelat *Catalonia* Ice cream

gelatin *United States* Gelatine

gelatina *Italy, Spain* **1.** Gelatine **2.** Jelly

gelatine The soluble protein obtained by boiling bones and connective tissues in water and purifying it by fractional precipitation. Produced in powder form and as a purer sheet or leaf. Used extensively for gelling and setting jellies, aspic, mousses, etc. and adding body to sauces and soups. Since proteases break down the protein and destroy the gelling action it cannot be used with raw pineapple or paw paw or other fruits used to tenderize meat. See also **leaf gelatine**

gélatine *France* Gelatine

Gelatine *Germany* Gelatine

gelato *Italy* **1.** Ice cream **2.** Iced, frozen, or chilled

Gelbe Rübe *Germany* Carrot

Gelbwurz *Germany* Turmeric

gelé *Sweden* Jelly

gelée *France* **1.** Jelly **2.** Aspic

gelée, en *France* **1.** Garnished with chopped jelly **2.** Coated in aspic jelly

geléia *Portugal* Jelly

gelinotte *France* Hazel hen

gelling agent Any substance which when dissolved in a liquid will enable it to set into a gel

gelo *Italy* Ice

gelo di melone *Italy* The diced and sieved pulp of watermelon, sweetened, thickened with arrowroot or **fécule**, flavoured with vanilla and mixed when cool with chopped bitter chocolate, candied fruit and pistachio nuts, allowed to set in moulds, demoulded and sprinkled with cinnamon

gelsomino *Italy* Jasmine

gema *Portugal* Egg yolk

gember *Netherlands* Ginger

gemeiner Dornhai *Germany* Rock salmon

gemeiner Krake *Germany* Octopus

gemeine Sepie *Germany* Cuttlefish

gemelli *Italy* Short lengths of spaghetti twisted together

gemischt *Germany* Mixed

gemischter kalter Braten *Germany* A plate of assorted sliced cold roast meats

gemischter Salat *Germany* Mixed salad

gemsenfleish *Italy* A dish of chamois cooked in vinegar and served with polenta. From the alpine region.

Gemüse *Germany* Vegetables

Gemüsesuppe *Germany* Vegetable soup

gendarme 1. *France* Popular name for red herring (**hareng saur**), often served as a hors d'oeuvre **2.** *France, Switzerland* A small flat rectangular spicy smoked sausage made with beef, pork fat, pork rind and wine. See also **Ländjäger**

genevoise, sauce *France* A fine **mirepoix** of vegetables browned in butter with parsley, thyme and bayleaf, a chopped salmon head and pepper added and stewed, the fat drained off, red wine added and reduced by half, a fish-stock-based **espagnole sauce** added, simmered 1 hour, strained, skimmed and finished with anchovy essence and butter. Served with salmon and trout.

gen furay *West Africa* A snack from the Gambia consisting of small fried fish, coated with a mixture of fried onions, tomatoes, garlic and chilli

Genghis Khan griddle Mongolian barbecue

gengibre *Portugal* Ginger

genièvre *France* Juniper berry

genip *Caribbean* A small round fruit like a grape, from the tropical American tree, *Melicoccus bijugatus*, eaten raw by removing the skin and sucking the slightly astringent pulp off the seed. Also called **Spanish lime**, **chenette**

genmai *Japan* Brown rice

genoa cake A fruit cake decorated with almonds or brazil nuts

genoese A light sponge cake made from creamed eggs and sugar into which molten butter is rapidly whisked to form a stable emulsion. Sifted flour is then folded in prior to baking. Also called **génoise**, **genoese cake**, **genoese sponge**

genoese cake, genoese sponge See **genoese**

genoese sponge mixture Flour, butter, caster sugar and eggs (2:1:2:4) without raising agent. Made up by the whisking method.

génoise *France* Genoese

génoise, à la *France* In the Genoese style, i.e. including tomato sauce

génoise, sauce *France* A purée of skinned pistachios, pine nuts and a little cold béchamel, strained then made into a mayonnaise type sauce with egg yolk, lemon juice and oil

genoise paste Flour, butter, caster sugar and eggs (2:1:3:5), made up using the whisking method and used for baked desserts. Not to be confused with **genoese**, which is a cake.

genovese, alla *Italy* In the Genoese style, i.e. with olive oil and garlic

gen stew *West Africa* A fish stew from the Gambia containing onions, green sweet peppers, tomatoes, garlic and chilli

gentleman's relish *England* A paste made from salted anchovies, tomatoes and extenders used as a relish and to spread on fingers of hot buttered toast as a savoury

geoduck A large Pacific clam, *Panope generosa*, weighing up to 1.5 kg. The flesh is usually fried.

George's bank flounder Winter flounder

gepökeltes Rindfleisch *Italy* Ham, from the alpine region

geranium See **scented geraniums**

Gerardmer Lorraine

geräuchert *Germany* Smoked

geräucherte Bratwurst *Germany* A smoked **Bratwurst** containing 6 parts of lean pork chopped fine to 1 part of fat bacon chopped coarsely

Geringium foetidum *Botanical name* See **cilantro 2**

germ That part of a seed, grain or nut from which the new plant starts to grow, equivalent to an embryo. The remainder of the seed is the food supply for the growing plant.

German chocolate *United States* A milk chocolate for cooking, flavoured with vanilla and containing additives which make it stable when heated

German coffee A mixture of kirsch and hot sweetened coffee topped with whipped cream and drunk through the cream

German garlic sausage See **Jagdwurst**

German lentils The original brown lentils used in British cooking since the Victorian era

German millet Foxtail millet

German mustard A prepared, sweetish mustard from Dusseldorf, often flavoured with herbs and spices

germano reale *Italy* Mallard, the wild duck

German pound cake A cake similar to **genoa cake** but with less fruit and no almonds or brazil nuts

German salami A hard, preserved and highly seasoned slicing sausage about 5 cm in diameter made from finely minced pork and beef, normally flavoured with garlic and peppercorns and contained in a casing. Sometimes smoked.

German sausage 1. A generic name for all sausages originating in Germany usually made from 100% meat products with spices, flavourings, garlic and seasoning, often smoked. There are three principal types: **Brühwurst**, **Rohwurst** and **Kochwurst**. **2.** *United Kingdom* Luncheon sausage

germicide A disinfectant

Géromé *France* A cows' milk cheese from Lorraine similar to Munster

Géromé anisé *France* Géromé cheese flavoured with aniseed

gerookt *Netherlands* Smoked

gerookte paling *Netherlands* Smoked eel eaten as a snack or hors d'oeuvres, garnished with lemon and gherkin slices

geroosterd brood *Netherlands* Toast

geröstet *Germany* Grilled

geröstete Kartoffeln *Germany* Fried potatoes

gerst *Netherlands* Barley

Gerste *Germany* Barley

Gerstensuppe *Germany, Italy* Barley soup containing bacon, onions and celery from the alps

gerty meat pudding *England* A type of haggis from Cornwall made from boiled pigs' offal including lungs and spleen, minced with the scallops from the fat and with groats, boiled in the cooking liquor from the offal, seasoned, packed into large casings, tied and boiled

Gervais *France* A branded soft cream cheese generally sold in 6 individually wrapped segments of a circle, but the name is also used to denote the general types of fresh cows' milk cheeses sold in small tubs

geschabt *Germany* **1.** Scraped **2.** Grated **3.** Ground

geschmort *Germany* **1.** Braised **2.** Stewed

Geschnetzeltes *Switzerland* Fried pieces of veal and fried chopped onions simmered in a sauce made from wine, stock, seasoning and cream. Usually accompanied by Rösti.

geselchtes *Austria* Smoked pork or bacon

gęsinka *Poland* A soup made from chopped carrots, onions, celeriac and mushrooms sweated in butter until tender, passed through a sieve and mixed with beef broth, seasoned, thickened with sour cream and egg yolks and finished with lemon juice and a little cooked pearl barley

gesottenes Rindfleisch *Germany* Boiled beef and vegetables, served with horseradish sauce

gestoofd *Netherlands* Stewed

Gestreifte *Germany* Red mullet, *Mullus surmuletus*

getmesost *Sweden* A Swedish version of **getost** cheese made with the whey from goats' milk cheese

getost *Sweden* A hard goats' milk cheese, dry-salted and ripened for 2 to 4 months and with a dry rind

Getreide *Germany* Cereal

getrüffelt *Germany* Flavoured with truffles

geung *China* Ginger root

gevogelte *Netherlands* Poultry

gevuld *Netherlands* Stuffed

gevulde boterkoek *Netherlands* Buttercake with a marzipan filling

gevulde broodje *Netherlands* Filled bap or bread roll

gevulde kalfsborst *Netherlands* Stuffed breast of veal

gevulde kool *Netherlands* Cabbage rolls stuffed with a meat filling

gewöhnliche Herzmuschel *Germany* Common cockle

Gewürz *Germany* Spice

Gewürzegurke *Germany* Pickled gherkin

Gewürzgurkensosse *Germany* A seasoned meat stock slightly thickened with roux, mixed with sweated chopped onions and finely chopped dill pickles (300 g per litre) and simmered 10 minutes

Gewürzkuchen *Germany* Spice cake

Gewürznelke *Germany* Clove, the spice

ghaw-be-thot *Burma* Fried cabbage flavoured with **blachan**

ghee *South Asia* Clarified unsalted butter used in Indian cooking because of its high smoke point in comparison with other oils and fats. Also called **ghi**, **usli ghee**

gherigli *Italy* Kernels of nuts, etc.

gherkin A small (up to 8 cm long) variety of prickly cucumber which grows in damp subtropical and tropical climates. The immature fruits are soaked in brine and treated with boiling vinegar. Some varieties of small ridge cucumbers are occasionally sold as gherkins.

ghi Ghee

ghiaccio *Italy* 1. Ice 2. Iced

ghiandole *Italy* Glands (thyroid, lymph, etc.) of pork

ghiotta *Italy* Dripping pan used under spit-roasts

ghiotta, al *Italy* In a delicious style, nowadays with tasty vegetables and accompaniments such as onions, tomatoes, sweet peppers, olives, capers or raisins

ghiotto *Italy* 1. Greedy 2. Delicious, appetizing

ghiottone *Italy* A gourmand

ghiozzo *Italy* Goby, the fish

ghiraybah *Persian Gulf* Shortbread biscuits made with clarified butter using the creaming method

ghisau *Italy* A beef stew from Sardinia made with red wine, tomatoes and potatoes. Also called **stuffau**

ghiu *Nepal* Ghee

ghiveci călugăresc *Romania* Fried onions stewed with potatoes, carrots, celery, aubergines, courgettes, French beans, garlic and salt. Served with roast meat and bread. Also called **monk's hotchpotch**

ghivetch 1. An Armenian vegetable stew made from garlic-flavoured olive oil and beef stock (3:8), seasoned, flavoured with bay, dried tarragon and oregano, brought to the boil, whatever mixed vegetables are available added, and the whole baked in a closed dish at 180°C for about 1 hour until all tender. Quick cooking vegetables may be added towards the end. 2. *Bulgaria* As the Armenian version but with and egg and yoghurt topping and baked without a lid

ghoriba *North Africa* A type of Moroccan macaroon made with beaten whole eggs, icing sugar and ground almonds (1:2:4), flavoured with lemon zest and vanilla but raised with baking powder (1:50 on almonds). Baked at 180°C. Also called **ghriyyba**

ghormehsabzi *Iran* Lamb chops and kidney beans in a thick sauce flavoured with parsley, Persian leek, coriander and sun-dried lemon, served with rice

ghriyyba *North Africa* Ghoriba

ghuiyan *Nepal, South Asia* Yam

gia *Vietnam* Bean sprouts

giallo *Italy* Yellow

giambonetto *Italy* A boned leg of chicken shaped and tied to resemble a ham

gianchetti *Italy* Very tiny fish fry. See also **bianchetti**

gianfottere *Italy* A vegetable stew from Calabria made with aubergines, courgettes, sweet peppers and herbs

giant garlic A mild garlic-flavoured bulb, *Allium scorodoprasum*, of the onion family with mauve flowers which develop edible aerial bulbs like the tree onion. Also called **rocambole**, **Spanish garlic**

giant granadilla A large tropical passion fruit, *Passiflora quadrangularis*, with an indifferent-tasting greenish yellow fruit. Immature fruits are sometimes baked as a vegetable.

giant puffball A spherical fruit body of a fungus, *Langermannia gigantea*, which can grow up to 30 cm in diameter but is eaten when young before the spores, which are made within the outer flesh, have formed. Normally sliced, panéed and fried.

giant saxidome A large clam, *Saxidomus gigantus*, found along the west coast of North America down to San Diego

giant shells *United States* Conchiglie, pasta shells

giant west coast clam A large clam, *Schizothaerus nuttalli*, from the west coast of the USA which lives 60 cm deep in the mud. It makes excellent chowder. Also called **Washington clam**

giant white radish Mooli

giardiniera, alla *Italy* In the gardener's style, i.e. with assorted fresh or pickled vegetables

gia vi pha lau *Vietnam* Five-spice powder

gibelotte *France* A fricassée of rabbit in wine usually with onions and potatoes

gibier *France* Game

gibier à plume *France* Game birds

gibier à poil *France* Game animals

gibier d'eau *France* Waterfowl

giblets The entrails and neck of poultry and birds comprising the neck, gizzard, liver, heart and sometimes kidneys. Used for stock or gravy, but livers and gizzards often used as the basis of separate dishes.

Gien *France* A soft creamy but firm cheese with a fine flavour made around Orleans from a mixture of goats' and cows' milk, matured in leaves or wood ash for about 3 weeks

gigginstown *Ireland* A hard, unpasteurized cheese

Gigha *Scotland* A firm cheese made from cows' milk on the island of Gigha in Scotland

gigoret *France* Pig's head cooked in blood and red wine. A dish from Poitou-Charentes.

gigot *France* Leg of lamb or deer

gigot boulangère *France* A garlic piquéed leg of lamb, roasted with butter at 200°C over a thick bed of preroasted sliced potatoes flavoured with chopped onions and herbs until the lamb is cooked, the dish then covered with foil and rested 10 minutes before serving

gigot d'agneau à la couronne d'ail *France* Sealed and browned leg of lamb, pot-roasted with 50 to 60 cloves of garlic, sweet white wine, brandy and seasoning. Served with defatted pot juices and a fresh green salad.

gigot lamb chops *England* The North of England name for chump chops of lamb

gigot of lamb *Scotland* A full leg of lamb

gigot pourri *France* A leg of lamb roasted with a large number of garlic cloves

gigue *France* Haunch (of venison, etc.)

gila *Portugal* A type of gourd. See also **chila**

Gilboa *Middle East* A cows' milk cheese from Israel similar to Edam

gild, to 1. To glaze with beaten egg before baking. Gives a rich golden colour to the goods. **2.** To coat the surface of some hard food with gold leaf for decorative purposes and to exhibit the wealth of the person serving it

gildeneh yoich Jewish chicken soup

gilead *Middle East* A ewes' milk cheese from Israel resembling **Kashkaval**

gili khichhari *South Asia* A moist version of **khichhari** for children and invalids

gill *United Kingdom* A fluid measure equal to one quarter of an imperial pint in the standard British and USA system,i.e. 142 ml and 118 ml respectively, and one eighth of a pint in Scotland. To confuse matter further a gill of beer in England is half a pint.

gilt A female pig, especially a young sow

gilt-head bream A silvery seawater bream, *Sparus aurata* and *Chrysophrys aurata*, from the Northern Mediterranean with a gold-tinged head and fine-tasting flesh, very similar to the sea bream and easily confused with it. Weighs approximately 1 kg. A related species, *Chrysophrys major*, is used in Japan for sashimi.

gin *Burma* Ginger

gindungo *Central Africa* A type of hot chilli pepper from Angola

ginepro *Italy* Juniper berry

ginestrata *Italy* A light mildly spiced soup from Tuscany made with chicken stock, egg yolks, butter and white wine

gingelly *South Asia* Light sesame seed oil

gingembre *France* Ginger

ginger The knobbly, buff-coloured, branching rhizome (creeping fleshy root) of a tropical plant, *Zingiber officinale*, with a warm aroma and hot burning taste. Available fresh, dried, preserved in sugar syrup and as a ground dried powder. Used extensively in all forms in all cuisines.

gingerbread 1. *United Kingdom* A moist fawn to dark brown cake made by the melting method, sweetened with golden syrup or treacle and flavoured with powdered ginger root. May be decorated with slices of preserved ginger. **2.** *United States* A ginger-flavoured biscuit

gingerbread man *United Kingdom* A ginger biscuit mixture rolled and cut in the shape of a man (the traditional shape) and decorated with currants to represent eyes and buttons. Baked at 190°C until brown.

ginger buds The pink buds of various types of ginger plant which are sliced and used as a garnish or eaten raw in salads. Also called **pink ginger buds**, **torch ginger**

ginger mint A mint type, *Mentha x gentilis 'variegata'*, with smooth, gold-splashed leaves and a spicy flavour. Used for flavouring.

ginger nut A small round biscuit strongly flavoured with ginger

ginger pudding *United Kingdom* Basic steamed pudding mixture flavoured with ground ginger and chopped stem ginger

ginger shoots Long thin pinkish stalks of the ginger plant which are harvested in spring. They are pickled in vinegar in Japan where they are known as hajikama shoga. Also called **blushing ginger**

ginger snap A round sweet biscuit flavoured with ginger and very crisp and crunchy

gingko See **ginkgo nut**

ginitan *Philippines* Guinataan

Ginkgo biloba *Botanical name* Maidenhair tree

ginkgo leaf cut See **icho-giri**

ginkgo nut The kernel of the fruit of the maidenhair tree, *Ginkgo biloba*. From East Asia but now grown around the Mediterranean. The flesh of the fruit is not edible but the nuts are used in Japanese cooking. May be roasted, used in sweet or savoury dishes or as a garnish or snack food.

ginnan *Japan* Ginkgo nut

ginseng The roots of various members of the genus *Panax*, found in East Asia and North

America. Besides its medicinal uses it is used to flavour soups and stews.

giorno, del *Italy* Of the day, as in dish of the day

giovane *Italy* Young, new, of vegetables, etc. Also called **giovine**

giovine *Italy* Giovane

girasol *France, Spain* Sunflower

girasole *Italy* Sunflower

girdle See **griddle**

girdle cake See **griddle cakes**

-giri *Japan* A cutting stroke of the knife, e.g. hyoshigi-giri, a baton cut for vegetables

giriama *East Africa* A Kenyan fish dish made from stir-fried onion, garlic, saffron, turmeric and cumin. Fish is added towards the end with chopped tomatoes and the whole then simmered in coconut milk until creamy.

girofle *France* Cloves

girolle *France* 1. Chanterelle 2. A special knife used to cut very thin slices of cheese and butter

gist *Netherlands* Yeast

gîte *France* Lamb shank and foot

gîte à la noix *France* Thick flank of veal, topside of beef (UK), bottom round of beef (USA). Also called **noix pâtissière**

gîte-gîte *France* Shin beef

githeri *East Africa* A Kenyan dish of equal quantities of cooked cow peas or black-eyed beans and maize kernels mixed with a kind of ratatouille of onions, sweet peppers and tomatoes. See also **nyoyo**

giuncata *Italy* 1. A soft curd cheese retaining some whey, made from cows' or ewes' milk and named after the rush container in which the curds are drained 2. Curds and whey 3. Junket

givre The powdery white crystals of vanillin found on the best quality vanilla pods

gizzadas *Caribbean* Small Jamaican tarts filled with shredded coconut flavoured with nutmeg and ginger

gizzard A thick muscular organ in a bird, often the second stomach, used to grind food

gizzard shad See **shad**

Gjetöst *Scandinavia* A sort of cheese which is an acquired taste. It is made with the whey from cheese made with goats' and cows' milk. This is reduced by boiling to a paste of caramelized lactose and whey proteins and is made in both soft, for spreading, and hard consistencies. The hard variety is eaten as shavings made with a special knife.

gjuwetch *Bulgaria* Diced mutton simmered in oil with chopped onions, sweet green peppers, aubergines, green beans, squash, okra and potatoes until cooked, most oil drained off the mixture, seasoned, covered with slices of tomatoes, oiled and baked in the oven

glaçage *France* Icing or glazing with an egg wash

glace *France* 1. Ice 2. Ice cream 3. Glaze, i.e. reduced clear meat stock 4. Royal icing

glacé(e) *France* 1. Ice cold, iced 2. Glossy

glacé cherry Candied cherries, not dried and with a glossy appearance, coloured with red or various other colours of food dye, used for decoration of cakes and desserts or sometimes in cake mixtures

glace de poisson *France* Fish glaze

glace de viande *France* A reduction of clarified meat stock which is shiny and syrupy. Used to add flavour and body to other dishes. Also called **glaze**

glacé fruit Candied fruit which has not been dried so as to retain a glossy appearance

glacé icing A simple mixture of sugar and water or strained fruit juice (100:15) of coating consistency which has a glossy appearance when spread on cakes, biscuits, etc. Possibly coloured and flavoured. Also called **water icing**

glace portative *France* Ice cream to take away as e.g. ice cream cone

glacer *France* To glaze

glacière *France* Ice box

gladde haai *Netherlands* Smooth hound, the fish. Also called **toonhaai**

Glamorgan cheese sausage, Glamorgan sausage *Wales* A skinless sausage from Wales made with a mixture of grated cheese, breadcrumbs, chopped onion, parsley, thyme or rosemary, seasoning and possibly mustard, bound with egg, shaped into cylinders and fried

Glarnerschabziger Sapsago

glas *Denmark, Sweden* 1. Glass 2. Tumbler

Glasgow magistrates *Scotland* Loch Fyne herring, the analogy is to their plumpness

Glasgow pale *Scotland* A small haddock prepared as finnan haddock but smoked more

Glasgow tripe *Scotland* Tripe is cooked in its own juices with an equal weight of chopped onions and some butter in a covered dish in the oven at 170°C for 2 hours. Half an hour before finishing some of the cooking liquor is thickened with flour and returned. The dish is finished with cream and chopped parsley and served with baked potatoes.

glasmästarsill *Sweden* Pieces of herring, marinated in vinegar and sugar for 2 days, the marinade drained off, heated and poured over the herring pieces which have been packed in a jar interspersed with slices of carrot and onion, grated horseradish, bay leaves and pickling spices. Refrigerated until eaten. Also called **glass blower's herring**

glass 1. *Sweden* Ice cream **2.** *Norway* Glass or tumbler

glassato *Italy* Glazed, iced

glass blower's herring See **glasmästarsill**

glasswort Samphire, *Salicornia europaea*

Glasur *Germany* Icing

Glattbutt *Germany* Brill

Glatthai *Germany* Smooth hound, the fish

Glattrochen *Germany* Common skate

glaze See **glace de viande**

glaze, to 1. To give a glossy coating to sweet and savoury dishes so as to produce a decorative finish. Beaten egg, milk, and lard are used with bread or buns. Sugar and fruit syrups are used with sweetened doughs and cakes. Arrowroot and sugar thickened fruit juices are used with fruit tarts, butter with vegetables, and aspic jelly is used with savoury items, canapés, etc. **2.** To brown food under a very hot grill e.g. crème brûlée and sauces containing a liaison of eggs and cream used on fish

glazuur *Netherlands* Glazed

gliadin One of the types of protein in gluten which is soluble in dilute salt solutions. This affects the plasticity of dough.

glister pudding *Scotland* A steamed pudding made from a Victoria sponge mixture flavoured with ginger, marmalade and lemon juice. Served with custard or wine sauce.

globe artichoke See **artichoke**

globe onion The common variety of spherical onion with a brown papery skin and concentric layers of white translucent crisp flesh springing from the root end. Fairly strong-flavoured and especially pungent when raw.

Glomzda *Poland* **1.** A type of cottage cheese **2.** Quark

Gloucester cheese *England* Cheese originally made from morning milk (lower fat) of the Gloucester cow. It is a hard cheese with a mild and pale-coloured paste and cast in squat cylinders. Now very rare. See also **single Gloucester, double Gloucester**

Gloucester pudding *England* A steamed suet pudding containing chopped raw apple and chopped candied mixed peel

Gloucester sauce *England* Very thick mayonnaise mixed with sour cream, lemon juice, chopped fennel and a little Worcester sauce. Served with cold meat.

Gloucester sausage *England* A pork sausage made with meat from the Gloucester old spot, a traditional breed of pig with plenty of fat

Gloucestershire pie *England* Layers of cooked and sliced lamb and thinly sliced apple and onions, both of which have been boiled for 5 minutes, placed in a greased ovenproof dish, seasoned and sprinkled with dried herbs between layers. The layers are covered with a rich gravy, topped with mashed potatoes and swedes, brushed with molten butter and baked at 190°C for an hour.

Gloucester squab pie *England* same as **Devonshire squab pie**

glucono delta-lactone See **E575**

glucose A monosaccharide which forms the building block of many starch and cellulose carbohydrates and is one of the constituents of the disaccharides sucrose (with fructose), maltose (with itself) and lactose (with galactose). It inhibits the oxidation of foods and facilitates browning in fried sausages. Often added to continental sausages to act as the substrate for a lactic acid fermentation which improves their keeping qualities. Also called **dextrose**

glucose oxidase An enzyme obtained from *Aspergillus niger*, used to remove traces of glucose from egg white that is to be dried

glucose syrup *United States* See **corn syrup 1**

gluea *Thailand* Salt

Glumse *Germany* Cottage cheese

glutamate de sodium *France* Monosodium glutamate

glutamato de sodio *Spain* Monosodium glutamate

glutamic acid One of the amino acids used by animals and humans. See also **E620**

gluten The general name given to the proteins in common wheat consisting mainly of glutenin and gliadin. These are responsible for the visco-elastic behaviour of and the baking properties of dough made from wheat flours and for the ability of the dough to entrap bubbles of carbon dioxide. It is extracted from wheat, especially in East Asia and when cooked forms a spongy soft mass which absorbs flavours and is used rather like bean curd and for making cakes.

gluten flour Dry powdered gluten made by washing the starch from high protein flour, drying and grinding

gluten-free food Food which contains no gluten. Necessary for the small fraction of people who are allergic to gluten.

glutenin One of the protein types in gluten insoluble in water or salt solution. It contains many cross linkages which are broken or rearranged during the kneading of dough and is responsible for its elasticity.

glutiminato di soda *Italy* Monosodium glutamate

glutinous rice Black or white, short- or long-grain rice which is particularly sticky when boiled and easy to handle with chopsticks. Used in Chinese and Japanese dishes especially boiled and sweetened in sushi. It should be soaked in cold water for 8 hours then cooked with an equal weight of water for about 12 minutes and left to stand covered for a further 10 minutes. See also **black rice**, **mochi-gome**, **pinipig**. Also called **sticky rice**

glutinous rice flour A fine white flour made from glutinous rice and used to make soft cakes, buns and dumplings especially in Asian and Southeast Asian cooking

glycérie *France* Sweet woodruff

glycerine A sweetish colourless oily liquid, completely miscible with water, which when esterified with fatty acids forms natural fats and oils. Used as a humectant to prevent foodstuffs drying out, especially royal icing. Also called **glycerol**. See also **E422**

glycerol See **glycerine**

glycerol di-acetate An ester of glycerol and acetic acid used as a solvent for food colours and flavourings. Also called **diacetin**

glycerol monoacetate An ester of glycerol and acetic acid used as a solvent for food colours and flavourings. Also called **monoacetin**

glycerol tri-acetate An ester of glycerol and acetic acid used as a solvent for food colours and flavourings. Also called **triacetin**

glycine An amino acid used as a sequestering agent and buffer

Glycine max *Botanical name* Soya bean

glycogen A polysaccharide produced in the animal body from glucose and stored in the liver and muscles. Very quickly broken down into glucose and thus a very important quickly available energy store. Animals that are killed after stress e.g. of the hunt or from poor handling have little or no glycogen in their muscles which are thus less flavoursome than otherwise.

Glycyrrhiza glabra *Botanical name* Liquorice

GMP See **good manufacturing practice**

gnocchetti *Italy* Tiny gnocchi used for garnishing soup

gnocchi *Italy* Small dumplings made in the form of balls, cylinders or circular slices which are poached and used as a garnish or served with a sauce. Made from semolina, choux paste or potatoes.

gnocchi alla bava *Italy* Gnocchi made with buckwheat flour, fresh cheese and cream

gnocchi dolci *Italy* Sweet dumplings

gnocculi *Italy* Potato gnocchi from Sicily served with cheese and broth or meat sauce

goa *Philippines* Goa bean

goa bean A legume, *Psophocarpus tetragonolobus*, which is a native of southern Europe but grown extensively in Southeast Asia. It has winged four-angled pods similar to the asparagus pea which are cooked whole in the same way. The roots are also edible.

goak sung *China* Bamboo fungus,

goat A horned animal, slightly bigger than a sheep, which can metabolize almost any carbohydrate source. Bred mainly for their milk in the West, they are an important source of meat in Africa, the Eastern Mediterranean, the Middle East, the Caribbean and parts of Asia. Young goats' meat is eaten in France and Italy especially in the spring.

goat fish 1. Red mullet **2.** *Australia* Redfish

goat pepper A very small chilli pepper from Indonesia dried and sold worldwide for pickling

goats' milk Goats' milk has a higher fat and protein content and a stronger flavour than cows' milk and is often made into cheese. It has something of a health food reputation in the West.

gobhi *South Asia* Cauliflower

gobhi mhaans *South Asia* Braised lamb with cauliflower, the lamb browned in butter in the usual way with onion and ginger then cooked in yoghurt with tomatoes, paprika, salt, cayenne pepper, turmeric and coriander seed. Finally the cauliflower and sweet red pepper are added with water and all cooked until the meat is tender and the cauliflower reduced to a soft sauce.

gobo *Japan* Burdock root used in sauces, stocks and braised dishes

goby A small seawater fish of the *Gobidae* family with a sucker, similar to the freshwater gudgeon. Treated as a whitebait.

gochian *South Asia* A type of black mushroom from Kashmir similar to the morel

gochujang *Korea* A chilli paste similar to sambal oelek

gochu jeon *Korea* Green sweet pepper rings and halved chilli peppers stuffed with a meat mixture, floured, dipped in beaten egg and deep-fried in sesame seed oil

godard, sauce *France* White wine reduced with a fine **mirepoix** of vegetables and ham, **demi-glace** sauce and mushroom essence added, simmered, strained and reduced

godaste färsen *Sweden* Finely minced beef and pork mixed with softened rusk, egg yolk, seasoning and a little paprika. Half of this placed in a greased oblong mould, slices of skinned tomatoes placed on top followed by the remainder of the forcemeat, topped with a mixture of French mustard, chopped onion and parsley and butter and baked in a 200°C oven for 1 hour to give a crisp crusty surface. Served from the dish. (NOTE: Literally 'the finest forcemeat'.)

godiveau *France* A forcemeat made with cushion of veal, beef kidney suet and eggs (4:4:1) with all skin, tissue, sinew, etc. removed, processed, seasoned and flavoured with nutmeg, sieved and, after resting on ice, blended with ice water or cream over ice until of the correct consistency as checked by poaching a small amount

goed doorbakken *Netherlands* Well done. Used of meat, steak, etc.

goetberg *United States* A cardamom-flavoured sausage originating in Sweden and resembling the German cervelat

Goetta *Germany* As **Scrapple**, but thickened with oats

goettinger *United States* A German-style hard sausage similar to cervelat

gofio *Spain* A flour with a nutty flavour made by grinding a variety of toasted cereal grains such as wheat, maize and barley. Originating in the Canary islands it is sold as a health food in Spain.

gogi jeon-gol *Korea* Stir-fried strips of beef with sliced onion, mushrooms and mooli, strips of fresh pear and egg

gogol-mogol *Russia* A type of **zabaglione** made by beating equal weights of egg yolk and caster sugar together until lemon-coloured and frothy. Rum is stirred in at the rate of 400 ml per kg of egg yolks and the mixture poured into wine glasses and allowed to set.

gogue *France* A **boudin noir** made with pigs blood, cream, eggs, chopped onions sweated in lard, breadcrumbs moistened in milk, beet leaves and seasoning, poached in casings and air-dried for 5 to 7 days

gohan *Japan* Cooked rice served in a Japanese-style bowl. See also **raisu**

gohanmono *Japan* The generic Japanese term for all types of cooked rice and rice dishes

Golan *Middle East* A ewes' milk cheese from Israel similar to Provolone

gold beet *United States* A golden-yellow and sweeter variety of beetroot which may be eaten raw or cooked

Goldbrassen *Germany* Gilt-head bream

golden apple betty *England* Triangles of white crustless bread soaked in a mixture of equal quantities of molten butter and brown sugar flavoured with cinnamon. One third of these are layered in the base of a pie dish, slices of cored and peeled cooking apples laid over and topped with the remaining bread. Baked at 160°C for 60 to 75 minutes until the top is crisp.

goldenberry Cape gooseberry

golden buck cheese *United States* Buck rarebit

golden carpet shell A small European bivalve mollusc, *Venus gallina*, similar to various small clams with a greyish brown shell

golden carpet shell clam Smaller versions, *Venerupis aurea* (yellow) and *V. geographica* (grey), of the carpet shell clam, without radial markings.

golden cutlets Small decapitated haddocks split, boned and smoked. A smaller version of the Arbroath smokie.

golden fillets *United Kingdom* Thin fillets of haddock or cod, lightly smoked and artificially coloured golden yellow. Also called **smoked fillets**

golden gage Mirabelle

golden gram Mung bean

golden grey mullet A variety of grey mullet, *Mugil auratus*, with golden spots on its gill covers

golden mountain oyster *United States* A light brown fan-shaped mushroom

golden mullet Red mullet

golden needles Lily buds

golden nugget A variety of squash which may be used as a potato substitute, i.e. chipped or mashed

golden oak mushroom *United States* Shiitake mushroom

golden passion fruit Yellow passion fruit

golden plover Plover

golden sweetie See **sweetie**

golden syrup An invert sugar mixture (i.e. one which will not crystallize) made either by clarifying and decolorizing the remaining uncrystallizable portion of the sugar after production of sugar crystals or by treatment of sugar syrup with acids or the enzyme invertase. Contains sucrose, glucose and fructose and is used as a sweetening agent.

golden threads Beaten and strained egg yolks piped using a very fine nozzle in a piping bag onto the surface of hot sugar syrup to form a lacy pattern. Removed and rolled up and repeated as required. See also **yemas de San Leandro**

Goldkarpfen *Germany* Gilt-head bream

gold leaf E175, gold beaten out until it is extremely thin. Occasionally used for decoration.

gold'n'rich *United States* A cows' milk cheese from Illinois similar to **Port-Salut**

gold top *United Kingdom* Channel Islands milk (NOTE: So called because in the UK the bottles have a gold-coloured foil top.)

Goliath *Middle East* A variety of **pummelo** from Israel with a pebbly greenish-yellow rind and white seedless juicy flesh (NOTE: Unfortunately it is being marketed as a **pomelo** (Spanish for 'grapefruit'))

gol mirich *South Asia* Peppercorns

golonka w piwie *Poland* Pork knuckle cooked in beer

golubtsy *Russia* Cabbage rolls made from blanched and trimmed cabbage leaves wrapped in neat parcels around a mixture of minced beef and veal, chopped onion sautéed in butter, cooked rice and seasonings, the parcels placed seam side down in a deep oven dish and covered with a thickened sauce of concassée tomatoes, beef stock and sour cream, topped with bacon and baked open-topped at 180°C for 1 hour until the rolls are slightly browned. Rested for 10 minutes before serving.

goma *Japan* Sesame seed

goma-abura *Japan* Sesame seed oil

goma arábiga *Spain* Gum arabic

goma-dare *Japan* A dipping sauce made from **dashi**, **mirin**, sake and sugar (5:2:2:1). Roasted sesame seeds roughly half the volume of the liquid are added.

gomashio See **gomasio**

gomasio 1. *Japan* A mixture of black sesame seeds and coarse salt ground together and used as a condiment on rice, raw vegetables and salads. Also called **gomashio**, **sesame salt 2.** A mixture of toasted celery seeds and salt

gombaleves *Hungary* Mushroom soup

gombás *Hungary* Mushrooms

gombo Okra

gomma arabica *Italy* Gum arabic

gomme adragante *France* Gum tragacanth

gomme arabique *France* Gum arabic

Gomolya *Czech Republic, Hungary* A ewes' milk cheese very similar to **Liptói**. Also used to make **Brynza**. Also called **Homolky**, **Hrudka**

Gomost *Scotland* A cheese made in the same way as **getost**, but with whole milk curds and whey

gong bao rou ding *China* Chopped pork cooked with hot peppers

gong bao xiaren *China* Shrimps cooked with hot peppers

gong jao lei *China* A large perforated metal skimmer used for retrieving deep-fried food from a wok and draining it

gong yiu chee *China* Con poy

Gonterser Bok *Switzerland* Hard-boiled egg, dipped in batter and fried in butter

good beef *United States* A relatively tender grade of beef with little fat but less juicy or flavoursome than choice grade beef

Good Food Guide *United Kingdom* One of the restaurant guides to whom complaints or experiences may be sent. Address: Freepost, 2 Marylebone Road, London NW1 1YN. Others are Egon Ronay and Michelin.

Good King Henry A hardy perennial herb, *Chenopodium bonus-henricus*, whose leaves have been used as a vegetable from Neolithic times. The flower spikes may be cooked like broccoli and the young shoots like asparagus. The water should be changed during cooking.

good manufacturing practice Methods used in the food industry to control contamination with food poisoning organisms, their toxins or food spoilage enzymes. See also **HACCP**. Also called **GMP**

goolab jamoon *Caribbean* A typical Indian sweet from the Caribbean made from flour and butter (2:1) rubbed together and made into a stiff dough with evaporated milk. Formed into almond-shaped pieces, deep-fried and dipped in sugar syrup before being dried.

goose A large migratory game bird of various species from the *Anser* genus. Pink footed and greylag are the common varieties. The domestic goose was bred from the greylag. Wild geese are cooked as game. Domestic geese are generally eaten when less than a year old. The points to look out for are a yellow hairless beak, yellow supple feet (red indicates an older bird) and pale yellow fat. Usually roasted. It is one of the few domesticated birds which cannot be reared intensively.

goose barnacle See **barnacle**, **percebes**

gooseberry The fruit of a bush *Ribes uva-crispa* of the same family as the blackcurrant. Generally picked when immature and around 1 to 4 cm in length. They have a firm yellowish green flesh containing several embedded seeds and a hairy, occasionally smooth, green striated skin. In this state they are used for pies, tarts and preserves. Dessert gooseberries are green to light brown and are eaten raw when ripe.

gooseberry sauce A purée of gooseberries, water or white wine and a little sugar, boiled 5 to 10 minutes, sieved and mixed with a little butter sauce. Served with mackerel, duck and goose.

goose blood pudding *Scotland* A pudding made with goose blood mixed with seasoned barley meal, stuffed into the unbroken skin of the goose's neck, tied and simmered in broth until cooked

goose egg A large egg with a taste similar to a hen's egg and cooked in the same way. It requires 7 minutes for soft boiling.

goosefish *United States* Monkfish

goose liver Foie gras

goose liver sausage *Sweden* Gåsleverkorv

goosenecked barnacle See **barnacle**

goose sausage *England* A sausage made with 2 parts of lean beef chopped with a little suet and mixed with 1 part of chopped roast lean goose meat, moistened with garlic-flavoured Madeira wine, seasoned and packed into hog casings

goose skirt *United Kingdom* Thick skirt

Goosnargh cakes *England* A Lancashire biscuit made from flour and butter (4:3) mixed with caraway seeds and ground coriander. The butter is rubbed into the dry ingredients and the dough rolled out to 6mm thick, cut in rounds, dusted with caster sugar and baked at 130°C until firm and buff-coloured.

gorchitsa *Russia* Mustard

gorda *Mexico* A cornmeal dough enriched with lard and cooked as a thick cake

gordita *Mexico* A cornmeal and potato dough mixed with cheese and fried in lard. Served with minced pork and guacamole.

Gorgonzola *Italy* The famous soft, blue-veined, creamy-textured, sharp-flavoured cheese made from pasteurized cows' milk in the Lombardy region since at least the 11th century and legally protected with a certificate of origin. A lactic starter is used and after draining and turning, it is dry-salted, drained for a further 3 to 4 days, ripened at high humidity, salted, wiped and turned then needled with *Penicillium glaucum* and ripened for 50 to 60 days in natural caves. It is well veined and internally cracked. Wrapped in foil before sale. Used as a dessert cheese or in cooking.

Gorgonzola a due paste *Italy* A Gorgonzola made from curd from an evening milking which has been exposed to mould spores. This is moulded in the shape of a cone and surrounded in a cylindrical mould by lightly drained curds made from the next morning's warm milk.

Gorgonzola bianco *Italy* A rich, soft, quick ripening cheese from south Lombardy. See also **Pannarone**

Gornoaltaysky *Russia* A hard pungent cheese made from cows' or ewes' milk. Sometimes smoked.

goroka *Sri Lanka* A tart orange fruit used for souring in the same way as tamarind e.g. in fish dishes

gorokh *Russia* Peas

gosh feel *Central Asia* Deep-fried pastries from Afghanistan made in the shape of an elephant's ear from 10 cm circles of dough. This is made from eggs, milk and flour (1:1:3) with a little sugar (1:40 on flour) and oil and flavoured with ground cardamom. After frying the pastries are sprinkled with icing sugar and chopped nuts.

goshi *South Asia* Goat or lamb

gosht *South Asia* Meat

gosling A young goose up to 6 months old

gospel green *England* A semi-hard, milled, slightly crumbly cheese made from the unpasteurized milk of Friesian cows in Sussex

gota *South Asia* A mixture of seeds, sometimes dyed. e.g. aniseed, fennel and similar served at the end of a meal as a digestive.

gothaer *United States* An air-dried German sausage similar to cervelat

Götterspeise *Germany* Chantilly cream mixed with grated chocolate and pumpernickel crumbs

Gouda *Netherlands* A large (5 kg) wheel-shaped semi-hard mild and creamy cows' milk cheese with a small number of irregular holes and a wax coating made in the same way as Edam. If matured for a year its colour darkens and the flavour becomes strong and piquant. Small Gouda cheeses are also supplied. Suitable for slicing and cooking. Very popular as a part of Dutch breakfast.

Gouds kaas *Netherlands* Gouda cheese

Gougelhopf Sponge cake or large choux pastry balls filled with whipped cream. See also **Kugelhopf**

gougère *France* A savoury dish made by piping choux pastry, sometimes cheese-flavoured, in a large or small circular tart shape on a baking tray, baking it and filling the centre with fish, chicken, mushrooms, kidneys, etc. bound in a savoury sauce. Served cold or warm as a main course or as hors d'oeuvres.

gougnette *France* A type of doughnut dredged with sugar

goujon 1. *France* Gudgeon 2. *England, France* A strip of skinned white fish, usually sole, cut on the diagonal 8 cm by 6 mm, possibly marinated, rolled in the hand, panéed or battered and deep-fried, now also used of similar sized strips of chicken (NOTE: So called from the resemblance to gudgeons, which are cooked whole in the same way.)

goujonette *England, France* A small goujon of fish 5 cm by 6 mm cooked in the same way as a goujon

goulash A rich beef stew flavoured with paprika and originally based on Hungarian gulyás, a meat and vegetable soup. Served with sour cream.

gourami See **pla ra**

gourd The name used for members of the squash family the skins of whose fruits can be used as containers or for decoration. Several of the over 500 varieties are useful as edible vegetables e.g. bottle gourd, turk's cap gourd turban gourd, towel gourd, snake gourd.

gourmand A person who eats to excess and indiscriminately (NOTE: Literally 'greedy person'.)

gourmandise *France* **1.** Sweetmeat **2.** Delicacy

gourmet A person who appreciates good food and drink

gourmet powder See **monosodium glutamate**

Gournay *France* A mild, somewhat acidic, slightly salty and rindless, soft Camembert-type cheese from Normandy

Gournay affiné *France* Gournay cheese, surface-ripened for up to 8 days in damp cellars to develop the mild flavour

gousse d'ail *France* Clove of garlic

goûter *France* To taste

govyadina *Russia* Beef

Gower fisherman's stew *Wales* A stew made from cleaned and selected cockles boiled in a large saucepan until open, the cockle meat removed and the cooking liquor strained off. White wine, a quartered onion, mace and a bouquet garni are added to this, and the whole reduced by one third. Then the onion and the bouquet garni are removed, finely chopped onion is added and the haddock and plaice fillets are poached in this liquid for about 15 minutes. Finally, the white flesh of the fillets is separated from skin and bone, the liquor thickened with a blond roux and the flaked haddock, pieces of plaice, cockle meat, crab meat, peeled shrimps, saffron and seasoning are added, simmered for 1 minute and served.

Gower oyster soup *Wales* A roux-thickened mutton broth, flavoured with onions, mace and black pepper, poured whilst simmering over shucked oysters at the rate of 30 or more oysters per litre of broth

Goya *Argentina* A cheese similar to Asiago

goyave *France* Guava

Graçay *France* A dense, soft, white goats' milk cheese from Berry, matured for 6 weeks and coated with charcoal powder. Formed into stubby cones.

Gracillaria verrucosa *Botanical name* Hair vegetable

Grádaost *Iceland* A blue cheese made from cows' milk

grädde *Sweden* Cream

Gräddost *Sweden* A semi-hard, scalded-curd cows' milk slicing cheese with a pale yellow, close-textured paste containing numerous small holes

gräddvåfflor *Sweden* Waffles made with sour cream

graellada de marisc *Catalonia* A plate of grilled shellfish and/or crustaceans served with allioli

graellada de peix *Catalonia* Mixed seafood grill

Graham bread *United States* Wholemeal bread

Graham cracker *United States* A biscuit made from Graham flour, similar to the UK digestive biscuit

Graham flour *United States* A wholemeal flour developed by the nutritionist Sylvester Graham in the early 19th century. Used to make Graham bread and Graham crackers. Graham is now added to the name of any food made from wholemeal or wholewheat flour.

Graham rusk *United States* A bread roll made from Graham flour, split in half after baking and dried slowly

grain The edible seeds of various cultivated plants usually, but not always, monocotyledons (grasses). The most common are wheat, rice, maize, barley, oats, rye and millet. Sold as whole, kibbled, cracked, ground into flour, flattened into flakes or partially cooked.

grain de cassis *France* Blackcurrant

grain de groseille *France* Redcurrant

grains of paradise A spice with a hot peppery taste made from the dried seeds of a perennial reed-like plant, *Amomum melegueta* or *Aframomum melegueta*, indigenous to West Africa and used in its cookery. Also called **Guinea pepper**, **Guinea grains**, **melegueta pepper**

graisse *France* Fat, grease

graisse de porc *France* Lard

graisse de rognon *France* Suet

graisse de rôti *France* Dripping

gram 1. Subdivision of the kilogram unit of weight, 1 kilogram equals 1000 grams. Abbreviated g. **2.** *South Asia* **Channa**, unless qualified as in black gram or green gram, etc.

gram flour Ground chick pea flour. See also **besan**

gramme *France* Gram, unit of weight

grammi *Italy* Gram (1), unit of weight

Grampian grouse pudding *Scotland* A way of using old grouse in a suet-pastry pudding. The meat from the grouse is stripped off, chopped and together with pieces of rump steak tossed in seasoned flour. A pudding basin is lined with the pastry and filled with a mixture of the meat, chopped onions and chopped mushrooms plus stock made from the grouse carcasses. It is then covered with the rest of the pastry sealed to the lining. This is then steamed with a foil cover for about 6 hours until the grouse is tender. Half way through the cooking period the stock is topped up through the lid.

gramugia *Italy* An artichoke, asparagus, bean and bacon soup from Tuscany

grana 1. *Italy* A hard, cooked-curd cows' milk cheese with a granular texture made with partially skimmed (2% butterfat) cows' milk. A lactic starter is used and the curd moulded and drained for 2 days, brined for 28 days and ripened under controlled conditions for up to 18 months. Used for cooking, grating and dessert and very popular in Italy. They are usually stamped with the type and the name of the producer when soft and have the same information printed on the rind. **2.** *Philippines* A red food colouring obtained from a local plant

grana Bagozzo *Italy* A grana cheese from Brescia where it is referred to as the 'cheese of love'

granada *Philippines, Spain* Pomegranate

granadilla *Spain* Purple passion fruit

granadillo Passion fruit

grana Emiliano *Italy* A grana cheese similar to grana **Lodigiano** with a very black rind

grana Lodigiano *Italy* A grana cheese produced near Milan. The hard smooth rind encloses a more crumbly paste than most grana cheeses and tiny scattered holes, each of which may contain a drop of clear liquid. The paste tends to turn green when cut.

grana Padano *Italy* A hard grana cheese which easily melts and dissolves in the mouth with a mellow but intense flavour which strengthens with age (of the cheese). Used both for grating and dessert.

grana Parmigiano *Italy* A fine variety of Parmesan cheese. See also **Parmigiano Reggiano**

granary bread Bread made from granary flour

granary flour A strong brown flour to which malted wheat flakes have been added

granata *Italy* Pomegranate

Granatapfel *Germany* Pomegranate

granatina *Italy* Pomegranate syrup

granceole *Italy* Large crabs served in their shells and dressed with oil and vinegar

grancevola *Italy* Spider crab

granchio *Italy* Crab

granchio comune *Italy* Shore crab

granchio di sabbia *Italy* A small crab, *Portunus holsatus*, with a dark body and pink claws and legs. The two rear legs have spade-like ends to assist it in moving over sand. (NOTE: Literally 'sand crab'.)

granciporro *Italy* Common crab

grand-duc, au *France* In the style of the Grand Duke, i.e. garnished with asparagus, truffle, crayfish tails and Mornay sauce. Used especially of chicken.

grande *Italy* Large, big

grande cigale *Spain* A Mediterranean lobster-like crustacean. See also **cigarra**

grande roussette *France* Larger spotted dogfish

grand marnier *France* An orange-flavoured liqueur used to flavour desserts especially crêpes Suzette

grand-mère, à la *France* In grandmother's style, i.e. with onions or shallots, bacon, mushrooms and diced potatoes. Also used to denote croûtons in scrambled egg and pasta in vegetable soup.

grand tétras *France* Capercaillie

grand-veneur, sauce *France* A poivrade sauce prepared with game stock, game blood added and cooked then all strained. Served with game.

granelli *Italy* **1.** Grains, seeds, pips **2.** Lambs' or calves' testicles

granelli alla maremmana *Italy* Lambs' testicles floured, egged and fried. Served with lemon wedges.

granita *Italy* A partially and slowly frozen flavoured sugar syrup which consists of an ice crystal (up to 3 mm) mush in a syrupy substrate. Used as a dessert.

granité *France* Granita

grano *Italy, Spain* **1.** Wheat **2.** Corn **3.** Grain

granola *United States* A breakfast cereal mix similar to muesli. The composition varies but is taken from rolled oats, wheat and rye flakes, seeds, nuts, wheat germ, bran, raisins, desiccated coconut and similar.

Usually lightly toasted or baked with butter and served with milk, yoghurt, fresh fruit, etc.

grano saraceno *Italy* Buckwheat

granoturco *Italy* Maize, corn

granoturco dolce *Italy* Sweet corn

granseola *Italy* Spider crab

granseola alla triestina *Italy* Spider crab baked with breadcrumbs and garlic

granulate, to To form into small particles or granules by crystallization or agglomeration

granulated sugar Standard refined white sugar (sucrose) with crystals from 0.5 mm to 1 mm across

granzeola alla veneziana *Italy* Boiled crayfish or spider crab served on the shell with lemon juice and oil

grape The fruit of a vine, *Vitis vinifera, V. labrusca* or *V. rotundifolia* and hybrids, grown worldwide where the winters are cool and summers long and hot. The berries normally grow in clusters and range from green to dark purple and from 5 to 30 mm in diameter. The flesh varies from sour to sweet and succulent and is usually relatively firm but juicy and may contain up to 3 inedible seeds. Used for wine making, as a dessert fruit for decoration and garnishing and when dried for use as dried vine fruits (raisins, currants and sultanas).

grape cheese A small round skimmed-milk cheese ripened in a coating of grape pips. See also **Tomme au raisin**

grapefrugt *Denmark* Grapefruit

grapefruit Large spherical fruits of a citrus tree, *Citrus paradisis*, which grow in clusters and are cultivated in the USA, South America and some Mediterranean countries. They are probably a cross between sweet orange and pummelo, the latter's seeds were taken to Barbados by the British. The two main types are Marsh seedless and pigmented varieties. They have a thick yellow skin, with red pigmentation in some cases, with somewhat astringent typical citrus flesh. Halved grapefruits with the flesh loosened and membranes removed are often used as a breakfast dish or starter to clear the palette. Used for marmalade and supplied as skinned segments in cans.

grapefrukt *Norway, Sweden* Grapefruit

grape hyacinth A type of lily, *Muscari comosum*, whose bulbs are boiled and eaten as a vegetable especially in Italy

grape leaves *United States* Vine leaves

grapeseed oil A delicately flavoured oil extracted from grape seeds used in the manufacture of margarine and for salad dressings

grappa *Italy* A clear alcoholic spirit distilled from the fermented remains of the grapes after they have been pressed for winemaking

grappe de raisin *France* Bunch of grapes

gras (grasse) *France* Fat

gras, au *France* Richly cooked

gras de cuisse *France* Chicken thigh

gras-double *France* Tripe

gräslök *Sweden* Chive

Grasmere gingerbread See **Grasmere shortbread**

Grasmere shortbread *England* Shortbread from Grasmere in the Lake District containing chopped mixed candied peel, sweetened with brown sugar and flavoured with ginger. Normally dusted with its own crumbs before baking. Also called **Grasmere gingerbread**

grassato *Italy* A goat or lamb stew from Sicily containing potatoes, cheese and wine

grass carp A carp with a long round body rather like a mullet

grass mushroom See **straw mushroom**

grasso *Italy* 1. Fat, grease 2. Fatty, rich, with meat

grasso d'arrosto *Italy* Dripping

grasso di bue *Italy* Suet

grass pea Lath

grate, to To shred or convert to a powder, firm textured foods such as carrots, cheese, apples, nutmegs, etc. using either a hand-operated or food processor type of grater

grater 1. A round or rectangular thin metal tube with a handle at one end, in the sides of which are pressed arrays of holes of differing sizes with sharp projections. Food rubbed against the projections is cut into fine slivers or raspings depending on the size of the holes and projections. Slivers accumulate on the inside of the tube, powder or raspings on the outside. 2. A hand-operated version of the above in which the cylinder rotates while the food is pressed against it 3. A food processor attachment consisting of a rotating circular disc containing the sharpened holes

graticola *Italy* Grill, gridiron

gratin *Denmark* Soufflé

gratin, au 1. *France* Sprinkled with grated cheese and/or breadcrumbs and browned under the grill 2. *United States* Covered with cheese sauce or grated cheese and baked

gratin, sauce *France* White wine, fish stock and chopped shallots reduced by half, **duxelles** and fish-based **demi-glace** sauce added and simmered, then finished with chopped parsley. Used for the preparation of gratinated fish.

gratinate, to To bake food so as to form a crust on the surface, now usually done by sprinkling the surface of a prepared dish of food with grated cheese and/or breadcrumbs and then browning it under the grill or in the oven

gratinato *Italy* Gratinated

gratin dauphinois *France* Thin slices of potato, layered with garlic, cheese, seasoning and cream/milk, then baked slowly until the top is golden brown and the potatoes cooked

gratin dish An oval dish used for the cooking and presentation of gratinated food

gratiné(e) *France* Gratinated or napped with a glazing sauce and browned in the oven or under the grill

gratiniert *Germany* Gratinated

gratin savoyard *France* Pommes savoyard

gratter *France* To scratch or scrape

gratterons *France* Fried diced pork and pork fat. See also **scratchings**

grattugiato *Italy* Grated

Gratz *Austria* Graz

Graupensuppe *Germany* Barley soup

gravad lax *Sweden* Gravlax

gravad makrill *Sweden* Pickled mackerel prepared in the same way as gravlax, except that the skin is not used. Very fresh mackerel is essential.

Graviera *Greece* A cheese made from cows' milk and resembling Gruyère

gravlax Two scaled, boned and surface-dried salmon fillets sandwiched skin side out with a mixture of 2 parts salt, 2 parts sugar, 1 part saltpetre (if available), and crushed white peppercorns, with a layer of dill weed also in the sandwich and laid beneath and on top. The thick part of each fillet is opposite the thin part of the other. They are then pressed together in a bowl with a board and weight and left in the refrigerator for 24 hours, turning the package a couple of times. Wash, dry and cut thin slices of the flesh for use as a hors d'oeuvre. The skin is cut in strips and dry-fried until crisp and served as a garnish with dill and lemon. Traditionally salmon blood was also rubbed into the flesh to give it a scarlet colour. Also called **gravad lax** (NOTE: Literally 'grave salmon' referring to the underground chambers where it was prepared.)

gravlax sauce *Scandinavia* A sauce made from French mustard mixed with oil, vinegar, sugar, chopped dill and seasoning. Served with gravlax and other marinated fish. Also called **Scandinavian sweet mustard sauce**

gravy 1. A sauce made from the fat-free juices, extracts and scrapings from the pan in which meat, fowl or game has been roasted, mixed with wine or stock, reduced, seasoned and possibly cream added. See also **jus (de) rôti, jus lié 2.** *United Kingdom* Juices, extracts and scrapings plus some of the fat from the pan in which meat, fowl or game has been roasted, mixed with flour to make a roux, briefly cooked, stock or water added to give the consistency required, sometimes coloured with gravy browning

gravy browning A solution of dark caramel with salt used to colour gravies, etc. Sometimes other permitted brown colouring agents are used

grayling A silvery freshwater fish of the genus *Thymallus*, belonging to the salmon family, with firm white flesh and a scent of thyme, weighing between 0.5 and 1.5 kg. Different varieties are found in Northern and Central Europe, the USA and New Zealand. Cooked like trout.

Graz *Austria* A firm and full-flavoured cheese made from cows' milk

Grazalema *Spain* A ewes' milk cheese from the Cadiz area which resembles Manchego. Contains 35% water, 33% fat and 25% protein.

grease, to To coat the surface of a tin, dish, baking sheet, paper or aluminium foil, etc. which comes into contact with food with fat or oil so as to prevent the food sticking to it during the cooking or preparation process

greasyback prawn Greentail prawn

greater galangal The root of an Indonesian lily-like plant, *Langusa galanga or Alpinia galanga*, somewhat similar to ginger in appearance and with a sour gingery/peppery taste, used extensively in Southeast Asian cooking. The flowers, buds and young shoots may also be used as a garnish or vegetable. Also called **galingale, Laos ginger, Siamese ginger, Thai ginger**

greater yam Asiatic yam

great lakes trout Lake trout

great millet The principal type of sorghum, *Sorghum vulgare*, which is a staple throughout the underdeveloped world. It comes in two varieties, white grain sorghum used for bread and the red bitter grain used for brewing beer.

great northern bean Navy bean

great scallop One of the larger scallops, *Pecten maximus*, with a pink to brown shell up to 15 cm across. The flesh weighs about 60 g. Also called **king scallop**

greaves Scallops

greca, alla *Italy* Grecque, à la

grecque, à la *France* 1. A method of cooking vegetables e.g. artichokes, button onions, cauliflower sprigs, celery, leeks, etc. for use as a cold hors d'oeuvres, in a liquor consisting of water, olive oil, lemon juice, bay, thyme, coriander seeds and seasoning **2.** In the Greek style, i.e. with olive oil, lemon, herbs and spices

Greek basil See **bush basil**

green almond Pistachio nut

green bacon *United Kingdom* Bacon which has not been smoked. See also **Wiltshire cure**. Also called **plain bacon**

green banana Plantain

green bean The immature pod of the **French bean**

green butter Ravigote butter

green cheese See **Sapsago**

green cod Pollack

green coffee bean Coffee beans which are ready to be roasted. These will keep indefinitely and some will improve with age.

green curry paste *Thailand* A paste used for curry made from dry-fried shallots, garlic, lemon grass, coriander seeds and cumin seeds blended with fresh green chillies, black peppercorns, coriander root and leaves, galangal, lime peel, **terasi** and salt

green dressing See **salsa verde**

green fig A fresh as opposed to a dried fig

greengage A sweet amber coloured plum, *Prunus domestica* or *P. insititia*, about 25 to 4 cm in diameter and with a fine flavour, introduced to England from France by Sir William Gage as an unlabelled specimen in 1724. Also called **gage**

green goddess dressing *United States* Thick mayonnaise thinned with soured cream and flavoured with garlic, anchovy, minced spring onions, parsley and lemon juice. Served with fish and shellfish.

green goddess salad *United States* An elaborate salad of chopped cos lettuce, endive and chicory, mixed with chopped anchovies, spring onion, parsley, tarragon and cloves, served in a bowl rubbed with raw garlic, dressed with mayonnaise let down with tarragon vinegar, and topped with chicken, crab meat or shrimps

green goose *United Kingdom* A young goose up to 3 months old which has been fed on pasture. Generally eaten at Michaelmas (September 29th) and less fatty than the Christmas goose.

green gram See **bean sprouts**, **mung bean**

Greenland halibut A sinistral flatfish, *Reinhardtius hippoglossoides*, found in Arctic and sub-Arctic deep water of the North Atlantic Ocean at depths of 200 to 2000 m. The skin is dark grey or brown on both sides and the flesh is dense and oily.

Often smoked. Known as turbot by Canadians who control some of its habitat. Rapidly being fished out by Canadian and EU fishing fleets. Also called **Greenland turbot**, **black halibut**, **turbot**

Greenland turbot See **Greenland halibut**

green laver See **nori**, **sea lettuce**

green leaf lettuce *United States* Loose leaf lettuce

greenlip abalone One of the most tender of the abalone, *Haliotis laevigata*, with a corrugated red shell streaked with light green. Found on open rock faces.

green-lipped mussel A large variety of mussel, *Perna canalicula*, from New Zealand with a green blue shell and a particularly rich flavour. Reputed to have medicinal and prophylactic properties.

green lollo lettuce Lollo biondo

green masala *South Asia* A mixture of fresh ginger, garlic, green chillies and fresh coriander leaves pounded together with water into a paste. Used with fish or chicken.

green mayonnaise See **verte**, **sauce**

green olive The unripe fruit of the olive tree which are treated with dilute caustic soda solution (1.5%) to remove glycosides, then repeatedly washed with water prior to placing in brine (8%) in which they are left to ferment for 1 to 6 months prior to storing in 7.5% brine

green onion See **spring onion**

green oriental radish One of the large radishes, *Raphanus sativa*, with green flesh and skin, about 20 cm by 5 cm diameter

green pea soup Soaked dried or washed fresh peas, whole carrot, chopped green leek and onion, a bouquet garni and a knuckle of ham added to white stock, simmered and skimmed until all tender, carrot and ham removed, the remainder liquidized or passed through a sieve, strained, seasoned, consistency adjusted and served hot accompanied with croûtons. See also **Saint Germain**, **purée**

green peppercorns Soft dark green and underripe peppercorns with a mild subtle flavour, usually pickled in brine or vinegar. Also sold fresh or dried, but the flavour is less piquant. Used for flavouring especially beef, game and marinades or in the ground dried version as a condiment. Also called **Madagascar green peppercorns**

green peppers *United States* Underripe sweet peppers

green plantain *United States* Plantain

green plover Plover

green purslane See **summer purslane**

greens A generic term for all types of leaf that are cooked and used as a vegetable. See e.g. spring greens.

green S E142, a synthetic green food colouring

green salad A salad of mixed raw green leaves. Occasionally sliced raw green vegetables or fruits might be added.

green sapote A fruit similar to the sapote from a deciduous tree, *Calocarpum viride*, which grows in cooler climates. It is round, green skinned and more sweet and juicy than the true sapote.

green sauce Blanched and refreshed leaves of spinach, tarragon, chervil, chives and watercress, squeezed dry, passed through a fine sieve and combined with mayonnaise. Also called **sauce verte, salsa verde**

green sea urchin A 5 cm sea urchin, *Strongylocentrus droebachiensis*, which is found on both sides of the North Atlantic

green shell bean *United States* Flageolet bean

green shiso A variety of **shiso** with wide flat deep green leaves with serrated edges. It is used as a garnish, added to sushi, battered and fried as tempura and sometimes pickled.

green snap bean *United States* The immature pod of the **French bean**

green sprouting broccoli Calabrese

green swimming crab See **shore crab**

greentail prawn A type of prawn, *Metapenaeus bennettae*, intermediate in size between the deep water and the king prawn. Found in river estuaries. Also called **greasyback prawn**

green tea Non-fermented tea, often drunk with Chinese meals

green tomatoes Underripe tomatoes sometimes used to make chutney

green turtle A large edible sea turtle, *Chelonia mydas*, found in warm seas. Now very rare and possibly an endangered species.

green walnuts Young immature walnuts picked before the shell develops. Usually pickled which causes them to turn black, but also made into jam.

greeter *United States* The male person who greets guests in a restaurant (NOTE: The female equivalent is called a hostess.)

grelhado *Portugal* Grilled

grelos *Portugal* 1. Buds 2. Sprouts

gremolada, gremolata *Italy* A mixture of chopped parsley, chopped garlic and grated lemon zest. See also **gremolata, alla**

gremolata, alla *Italy* Sprinkled with a mixture of chopped garlic, grated lemon zest and grated nutmeg

grenade *France* Pomegranate

grenadier An ugly fish found on the Hatton bank to the west of Rockall. Now being fished commercially. The name was changed from rat fish to aid marketing.

grenadilla Purple passion fruit

grenadin *England, France* A small slice or fillet of veal, usually larded and braised

grenadin de veau fermier Prince Orloff *France* A grenadin of veal stuffed with a duxelle of mushrooms and foie gras

grenadine 1. *England, France* A sweet tart red fruit syrup made from pomegranate juice. Used as a flavouring. **2.** *Italy* Grenadin of veal

grenobloise, à la *France* In the Grenoble style, i.e. used of fish which is floured, fried and served with a garnish of lemon, capers and chopped parsley

grenobloise, fish Fish meunière dressed with peeled segments of lemon and a few capers

grenouille *France* Frog

gressin *France* A long baguette-like French loaf

Gressingham duck *England* A cross between a mallard and domestic duck with lean dark and tender meat combining the advantages of both

gretski orekhi *Russia* Walnuts

Grevéost *Sweden* A commercially produced semi-hard scalded-curd cows' milk cheese with a mild flavoured paste containing very large holes

Greyerzer *Switzerland* Gruyère

grey gurnard See **gurnard**

greyhen Black grouse

greylag goose A variety of wild goose from which most of the domesticated varieties have been developed

grey-legged partridge An English native bird, *Perdrix perdrix*, which is leaner and tastier than the red-legged partridge found in France. It weighs about 450 g and is suitable for 1 serving. Roasted at 190°C for 20 to 25 minutes.

grey mullet A round seawater weed eating fish, *Liza auratus* and various species of *Mugil*, 30 to 70 cm long and 0.5 to 1 kg in weight, some of which are farmed. It has a small head with vestigial teeth and is found worldwide in many varieties in warm waters. The skin is silvery grey and the flesh is firm, white and oily but bruises easily. The skin requires thorough scaling. Suitable for all cooking methods. The roe is traditionally used to make taramasalata. The dried and salted roe is known as botargo. See also **golden grey mullet**. Also called **striped mullet**, **black mullet**

grey mullet roe See **botargo**

grey plover Plover

grey squirrel A tree-living American squirrel, *Sciurus carolinensis*, once an important item of food, now used only in Brunswick stew. Introduced into Europe in the 19th century.

grib (*plural* **griby**) *Russia* Mushroom

gribiche, sauce *England, France* Mashed hard-boiled egg yolks blended with oil and vinegar or lemon juice, flavoured with chopped capers and gherkins, tarragon, chervil and parsley, seasoned and finished with a **julienne** of egg white. Served with fish.

griblette *France* Pork chop

gribnaya ikra *Russia* A pâté from western Russia made by sautéing finely chopped wild mushrooms and other fungi with an equal quantity of finely chopped onions in butter (1:2 on mushrooms). This is then deglazed with a little dry sherry and well mixed with a curd cheese and cream cheese mixture equal to half the original weight of the mushrooms and a large quantity of finely chopped parsley, tarragon and marjoram prior to chilling. (NOTE: Literally 'mushroom caviar'.)

gribnoy ikra *Russia* See **gribnaya ikra** (NOTE: Literally 'mushroom caviar'.)

gribouis A variety of cep common in Russia and often dried

griddle A thick heavy flat metal plate which is heated either continuously or intermittently and on which drop scones, pancakes, crumpets and any item which does not need to be contained in a pan may be cooked by conduction of heat. Also called **girdle**

griddle cakes Drop scones made on a griddle. Also called **girdle cake**

griddle pan cake *United Kingdom* Drop scone

griddle scone A traditional scone mix cooked on a griddle instead of in the oven

grid iron A stout metal rack used inside a grill pan or over an open fire or barbecue

griechisches Heu *Germany* Fenugreek

Grièges *France* A log-shaped blue-veined cows' milk cheese. See also **Pipo crem'**

Griesbrie *Germany, Switzerland* Semolina pudding

griesmeelpap *Netherlands* Semolina pudding

Griessklösschen *Germany* Dumplings made from semolina boiled in milk and seasoned water with butter until thick, eggs (3:4 based on dry semolina) beaten in off the heat and

small balls poached in simmering water for 20 minutes. Served with a sweet sauce as a dessert, with butter as an accompaniment to meat or made very small as a soup garnish.

Griessmehl *Germany* Semolina

Griessnockerl *Austria, Germany* Dumplings made with a seasoned semolina, egg and butter dough, simmered in beef stock

Griessnockerlsuppe *Austria* A clear meat or chicken stock or consommé garnished with tiny Griessnockerl

Griesstorte *Germany* A layer cake similar to **Mandeltorte** but using a mixture of semolina and ground almonds (5:3) instead of ground almonds

griet *Netherlands* Brill

grifole *Italy* A type of fungus which grows on trees

griglia, alla *Italy* Cooked on the grill

grigliata mista *Italy* Mixed grill

grigliate *Italy* Grilled

grignaudes *France* Pieces of shredded pork fried until crisp. Eaten cold as a snack in the same way as pork scratchings.

gril, sur le *France* Grilled

grill A metal box-like structure with an open front and a rack on which to place food to be grilled. Elements on the underside of the top surface are heated to a red glow with either gas or electricity. Also called **salamander**

grill, to To cook food by direct radiant heat over or under a heat source, e.g. barbecue or grill. A quick method of cooking to a crisp brown finish without added fat or oil. Also called **broil, to**

grillad *Sweden* Grilled

grillade *France* A mixed grill or any food which has been grilled or a grilled slice of meat or fish

grillade à la champagneules *France* Fried ham on toast coated with a cheese and beef fondu (NOTE: From Lorraine)

grillades *United States* A Creole light stew from Louisiana of thinly sliced veal cooked with green sweet pepper, celery, onion, tomatoes and seasoning. Served with rice.

grillé(e) *France* Grilled

grilled grapefruit Half a grapefruit prepared for eating, covered with brown sugar and butter and browned under the grill. Served hot as a starter.

grilleret lammehoved *Denmark* Grilled lamb's head

grillettato *Italy* 1. Simmered 2. Braised 3. A braised dish

grilling fish Small whole fish diagonally slashed, or fillets, darnes, tronçons and suprêmes of fish, passed through seasoned flour and melted butter, possibly breadcrumbs, then grilled both sides until the flesh leaves the bone or is cooked through

grilling sauce See **barbecue sauce**

grill pan A shallow metal pan with a handle and removable metal rack used for grilling food

grilse A small 3-year-old salmon (1 to 4 kg) which returns to its birthplace to spawn after its first year at sea

grind, to 1. To reduce hard substances such as coffee beans, nuts. spices, dried roots and cereals to a fine powder using either a pestle and mortar, a food processor, an electric or hand-operated rotary grinder or a food mill. **2.** *United States* To mince meat (as in 'ground beef')

grinder *United States* Hoagie

griots *Caribbean* A Haitian pork dish made by simmering cubed shoulder pork with onion, chilli pepper, a fair amount of chopped chives, one sixth the weight of the pork of Seville or other bitter orange juice, thyme and seasoning. After 90 minutes the liquor is drained off, the pork removed and fried in very hot oil until brown and crusty then added to the other drained ingredients.

griotte *France* Morello cherry

gris de Lille *France* A strong-smelling salty cows' milk cheese from the north, cast in squares

griset *France* Black bream

grisette An edible mushroom, *Amanita vaginata*, of the generally toxic genus *Amanita*. It has a grey cap and a white stem and does not travel well. Should only be picked by experts.

grisfötter *Sweden* Pigs' feet

griskin 1. The oval-shaped lean part of a loin of bacon **2.** The meat left attached to the spine of a pig when it is separated from the sides which are to be made into bacon

griskött *Sweden* Pork

Grisoni *Switzerland* Thin square sectioned salami made with salted air-dried beef

grissini *Italy* Long thin (up to 30 cm by 1 cm) dried bread sticks served as an appetizer, snack or accompaniment to a meal. Also called **Italian bread sticks, torinese**

gristle Tough inedible connective tissue which forms tendons, the covering of individual muscles and the structures which hold joints together. It is composed of varying proportions of collagen and elastin according to function. The collagen is broken down into gelatine on prolonged boiling.

grits 1. *United States* Coarsely ground dried maize kernels, usually boiled in water until soft, traditionally served with bacon and eggs for breakfast. Also called **hominy grits 2.** Any coarsely ground dehusked grain. Also called **semolina**

grive *France* Thrush, the songbird. Like the lark can no longer be hunted in the EU. Once made into pâté.

grive del langhe *Italy* A mixture of chopped pork, liver and spices, wrapped in pigs' caul and simmered in oil

griwash *North Africa* A flour, ground sesame seed and egg-based pastry from Morocco, fried in hot honey and eaten during Ramadan

groaning cake *England* A light fruit cake given to women in labour

groats Dehusked whole oat grains. Can be used to make a coarse-textured porridge preferred by some.

grød *Denmark* Porridge

grødaertesuppe *Denmark* Green pea soup

groen haring *Netherlands* Matjes herring

groente *Netherlands* Vegetables, greens

groentesoep *Netherlands* A mixed vegetable soup containing vermicelli

gromack *Scotland* A restorative for those coming in wet and cold consisting of a tbsp each of oatmeal, honey and whisky with cream to taste stirred in and eaten from a glass

grönar bönar *Sweden* Green beans

grondin *France* Gurnard

grondin galinette *France* Gurnard

grongo *Italy* Conger eel

grønlangkål *Denmark* Creamed cabbage

grønnsaker *Norway* Vegetables

grønsagsfromage *Denmark* A vegetable soufflé

grönsaker *Sweden* Vegetables

grönsakpuré *Sweden* Thick puréed mixed vegetable soup

grönsakssoppa *Sweden* Vegetable soup

grönsallad *Sweden* Lettuce salad

grøntsager *Denmark* Vegetables

groppa *Italy* Back or rump of an animal

groseille à maquereau *France* Gooseberry

groseille blanche *France* White currant

groseille noire *France* Black currant

groseille rouge *France* Redcurrant

groseilles, sauce *France* Gooseberry sauce

groseille verte *France* Gooseberry

groselhas *Portugal* Berry fruits such as red or blackcurrants, gooseberries

groselheira *Portugal* Gooseberry

grosella blanca, grosella verde *Spain* Gooseberry

grosella colorada *Spain* Redcurrant

grosella negra *Spain* Black currant

grosert *Scotland* Gooseberry

gros Lorraine *France* Lorraine

gros mollet *France* Lumpfish

gros pain *France* A large crusty French loaf similar in construction to the baguette. Also called **pain parisien**

grosse Bohne *Germany* Broad bean

grosse crevette *France* A Mediterranean king prawn. See also **caramote**

gros sel *France* Cooking salt

grosse Mettwurst *Germany* Coarse-textured Mettwurst

grosse palourde *France* Venus shell clam

grosse pièce *France* A joint of meat

grosser Weisenkopf *Germany* Salad burnet

grossetana, alla *Italy* In the style of Grosseto, Tuscany, i.e. with mushrooms and tomato sauce, or of pasta, with butter and cheese

grossköpfige Meeräsche *Germany* Grey mullet

grosso rombo *Italy* Halibut

grösti A meat loaf with potatoes and onions from the alpine region

Gröstl *Austria* Cubes of beef fried with onion in pork fat, seasoned and served mixed with slices of fried waxy potatoes

grotebonen *Netherlands* Broad beans

ground almonds Dried sweet almonds, dehusked and ground to a soft meal

ground beef *United States* Minced beef

ground chalk See **calcium carbonate**

ground cherry Dwarf cape gooseberry

groundhog *United States* Woodchuck

ground meat *United States* Minced meat

groundnut See **peanut**

groundnut oil See **peanut oil**

ground rice Rice flour or meal available in a range of particle sizes. Used for milk puddings, as a thickener and to give a crisp texture to biscuits, shortbread and batters.

ground tomato Tomate verde

grouper A variety of warm seawater fish of various species, but all with firm white flesh. Found in the Caribbean, Mediterranean, Southeast Asia and similar warm waters. Colours vary from grey-green through blue to red and brown, often with contrasting coloured spots. Lengths are usually in the range 30 cm to 1 m and weights from 2 to 10 kg. See also **garoupa**, **Mediterranean grouper**

grouse *England, France* A small single portion wild game bird which is found on heather moors in Northern Europe, the finest of which is the red grouse found only in the UK and Ireland. The young birds which have downy feathers under their perfectly fledged wings are the best eating. The shooting season in the UK is 12th August to the 10th of December. The birds should be hung for 2 to 4 days before drawing and plucking. Barded and roasted on toast in the roasting pan at 200°C for 40 minutes, or at 230°C for 20 minutes and rested for 10. Garnished with watercress and served with jus rôti, bread sauce, fried breadcrumbs and pommes allumettes. See also **black grouse**, **red grouse**, **sage grouse**. Also called **moor fowl**, **moor game**

grouse family A family of game birds from cold regions with feathered legs and feet including grouse, ptarmigan, capercaillie and hazel hen

grovbrød *Norway* A coarse dark rye bread

gruau d'avoine *France* Oat grits, coarse oatmeal

gruel A thin porridge made by boiling fine oatmeal or barley meal in water, milk or stock. Once believed to be suitable for invalids and convalescents.

grün *Germany* Green

grüne Bohnen *Germany* Green beans

grüne Bohnen auf norddeutsche Art *Germany* Blanched French beans simmered in a thin velouté sauce with chopped parsley

grüne Erbsen *Germany* Green peas, garden peas

grüne Fisolen *Austria* Green beans flavoured with fennel

grüne Gurke *Germany* Cucumber

grüne Pflaume *Germany* Greengage

grüner Salat *Germany* A green leaf salad dressed with a herb and garlic-flavoured vinaigrette

grüne Sosse *Germany* Sauce verte mixed with finely chopped hard-boiled eggs, additional green herbs and flavourings as available, e.g. parsley, sorrel, savory, dill, onion and leek. A speciality of Frankfurt served with meat.

Grünkohl *Germany* Kale

grunt *United States* An early settlers' dessert of steamed dough mixed with berries, probably an adaptation of the English spotted dick

grusha *Russia* Pear

gruth dhu Black crowdie

Grütze *Germany* Groats, grits

Grützewurst *Germany* A sausage made from strips of pig's intestines (**chitterlings**) mixed with groats or wheatmeal previously boiled in a flavoured stock, the mixture seasoned and flavoured with grated lemon zest, packed into casings, linked, boiled for a few minutes, dried, then fried in butter. Also called **saucisson au gruau**

Gruyère *Switzerland* A sweetish, nutty-flavoured large (up to 45 kg), hard cooked-curd cheese made in Switzerland from the milk of cows grazed on Alpine pastures but now copied throughout the world. It is dry-salted or brined for 8 days and ripened for up to 3 months and eaten between 3 and 10 months old. The paste is pale yellow and contains scattered small holes. Served as a dessert or slicing cheese and used to make fondue.

Gruyère de Beaufort *France* A Gruyère type cheese from Beaufort, sometimes without holes and weighing up to 65 kg. Also called **Beaufort**

Gruyère de Comté *France* A Gruyère-type cheese produced in Franche-Comté. See also **Comté**

gruzinskaya granatovaya podlivka *Southwest Asia* A Georgian chutney made from pomegranate seeds, depithed orange segments cut in pieces, chopped spring onions and chopped chilli peppers combined with lemon or lime juice, paprika, cayenne pepper and chopped coriander leaf and matured for 12 hours

grystek *Sweden* Pot-roasted beef or reindeer with a cream enriched thickened sauce, served for Sunday lunch with boiled potatoes, vegetables and redcurrant jelly

gryta *Sweden* Stew

grzyb (*plural* **grzyby**) *Poland* Mushroom

gua *China* Melon

guacamole *Mexico* A purée of ripe avocado flesh, skinned and deseeded tomatoes, deseeded chillies, lime juice and parsley used as a dip or as a filling for tacos and tortillas

guaiva *Italy* Guava

guai wei ji *China* Sliced chicken marinated in soya sauce and garlic (NOTE: Literally 'strange tasting chicken'.)

guajolote *Mexico* Wild turkey

guanbano *Philippines* Soursop

guanciale *Italy* A cured bacon made from the jaw and cheek of the pig. Traditionally used for spaghetti alla carbonara.

guanosine 5' disodium phosphate See **E627**

guar bean A variety of green bean, *Cyamopsis psoraloides*, with long thin pods that grow in clusters. Used in India as a vegetable and in the USA as cattle fodder. The dried beans are not eaten. The beans are a source of guar gum (E412) used as a thickener and stabilizer in processed foods. Also called **gaur bean**, **cluster bean**

guard of honour Roast lamb consisting of two best ends or racks of lamb, rib bones scraped as for a crown roast and interlinked, with the vertebrae at the base and the skin side outwards so as to look like a guard of honour. The space between two joints may be filled with stuffing. The bone ends are fitted with cutlet frills before presentation.

guar gum A gum (E412) extracted from guar, used as a thickener and stabilizer in processed food

guarnecido *Portugal* Garnished

guarnito *Italy* Garnished

guatlles amb salsa de magrana *Catalonia* Quail in a pomegranite sauce

guava A round or pear-shaped tropical fruit from a tree, *Psidium guajava*, related to the myrtle and eucalyptus. It is the size of an orange, has a musky-smelling white to pink flesh containing a lot of edible seeds, and an inedible red skin which is removed before the fruit is used. It can only be eaten when ripe and does not travel well except by air freight. Made into a jelly or available tinned in the west.

guayaba *Spain* Guava

guaymas sauce Mayonnaise flavoured with fresh tomato purée and chopped stuffed olives. Served with cold meat and poultry.

gubbins sauce *England* A cold condiment sauce made by blending butter, made up English mustard, wine vinegar and Devonshire cream (1:1:1:2) with a little tarragon vinegar and seasoning

gubeen *Ireland* A semi-soft, full-fat cheese from west Cork made from pasteurized milk using a lactic starter and vegetarian rennet, moulded into 20 cm wheels, drained for 18 hours, brined for 8 hours and matured for 2 to 4 weeks

guchalpan *Korea* Stuffed pancakes. Traditionally there are 9 different stuffing ingredients.

guchi *South Asia* Cloud ear fungus

gudbrandsdalsost *Norway* A hard, cooked-curd cheese made from a mixture of the whey from cows' milk, cream and goats' milk which is coagulated by heating

gudgeon A European freshwater fish, *Gobio gobio*, of the carp family up to 20 cm long with whiskers at the corners of the mouth. Generally fried, grilled or panéed or battered and deep-fried.

guéridon *France* The pedestal table used by a waiter when cooking food such as crêpes suzette or tournedos at the customer's table

güero *Mexico* Anaheim chilli (USA)

gueyteow *Thailand* Noodles

guey teow sen lek *Thailand* Rice ribbon noodles

Gugelhopf *Switzerland* A type of cake made from a fatless sponge mixture containing lemon zest, chopped almonds, seedless raisins and milk, raised with either yeast or baking powder, baked in a deep fluted ring mould and iced when cold. See also **Kugelhopf**. Also called **Gugelhupf**

Gugelhupf *Germany* Gugelhopf

gui choy *China* Mustard greens

guimauve *France* Marshmallow

guinataan *Philippines* A cooking method in which the ingredients are simmered in coconut milk. Also called **ginitan**

guindilla chilli A long and thin mildly piquant red coloured hot chilli from Spain, usually dried

guinea corn Sorghum

guinea fowl A recently domesticated game bird, *Numida meleagris*, related to the pheasant, between 1 and 2 kg in weight with white spotted grey plumage and rather dry flesh. Cooked as chicken or pheasant but barded or larded. Also called **Bohemian pheasant**

guinea fowl eggs Small eggs hard-boiled for 5 minutes and used as a garnish

guinea grains See **grains of paradise**

guinea pepper See **grains of paradise**

guinea pig A large rodent, *Cavia porcellus*, widely used in Europe as a pet or laboratory animal, but an important source of animal protein in South America where large varieties are bred. The flesh is rather like pork.

guinea squash Aubergine

guinea yam A largish yam (up to 5kg) with distinctive yellow flesh from a plant, *Dioscorea cayenensis*, grown in the USA, Africa and the Caribbean. Also called **yellow yam**

guinep *Caribbean* A small round fruit like a grape. See also **genip**

guisado *Philippines, Portugal, Spain* A method of cooking in which meat is first sautéed then braised or simmered until done, also stew or stewed

guisantes *Spain* Green peas

guiso de dorado *South America* A fish stew from Paraguay containing dorado, a famous river fish of that country

guiso de repollo *South America* A Bolivian dish consisting of cooked cabbage mixed with tomato sauce containing onion, potatoes, chillies, coriander and seasonings. Served with grilled or fried meat and poultry.

guitare *France* Guitar fish

guitar fish A type of skate, *Rhinobatus rhinobatus*, which looks a little like an angel fish and is found in the southern Mediterranean. Moderately good to eat.

guitarra *Spain* Guitar fish

gui yu *China* Crucian carp

Guizotia abyssinica *Botanical name* The plant from which niger oil is extracted

Gujerat masala *South Asia* A hot spice mix containing in addition to those listed under garam masala, sesame seeds, fennel seeds, ajowan seeds and chillies. See also **masala**

gujjia *South Asia* A crescent-shaped sweet pasty filled with chopped nuts and grated coconut

gula *Indonesia, Malaysia* Sugar

gula ärter med fläsk *Sweden* A substantial national soup served traditionally on winter Thursdays. Made from dried yellow peas soaked overnight and cooked in the soaking water, as many pea skins as possible removed, a piece of boned pork, sliced onion or leek, marjoram or ginger and seasoning added and the whole simmered for 2 hours until peas and pork are tender. The pork is removed and served separately with mustard. The soup is served very hot. Also called **ärter med flask**, **ärtsoppa**

gulab *South Asia* Rose water

gulab jamon *South Asia* A Bengali speciality of dumplings made from dried milk and syrup, deep-fried, soaked in a sugar syrup and flavoured with rose essence and cardamom. Also called **gulab jamun**

gulab jamun See **gulab jamon**

gulai *Indonesia, Malaysia* A type of curry in which the ingredients are simmered in an excess of coconut milk or soured stock with rempah and spices and with a little jaggery

gula jawa *Indonesia* Palm sugar

gulaman *Philippines* Agar-agar

gula melaka *Malaysia* Palm sugar

gula merah *Indonesia, Malaysia* Brown sugar

Gulasch *Germany* Goulash

gule ærter *Denmark* A winter soup made from pork belly, mixed vegetables and yellow split peas similar to the Swedish gula ärter med fläsk

gulerødder *Denmark* Carrots

gullet of beef *Scotland* A western Scottish term for clod of beef

gull's eggs Eggs of various species of gulls, usually sold hard-boiled for hors d'oeuvres. Examples are turquoise blue and speckled; fawn with dark brown speckling from the common gull, brownish olive green with dark brown spots from the black-headed gull and off white with brown and blue-grey spots from the herring gull. The latter is about twice the size of a hen egg.

gully bean Pea aubergine

gulrøtter *Norway* Carrots

gulyás *Hungary* A thicker more stew-like version of gulyás le leves

Gulyas *Austria* Goulash

gulyáslé leves *Hungary* A rich meat and vegetable soup made from shin beef, onion, tomatoes, green sweet peppers and potatoes flavoured with paprika. The original goulash.

Gulyassuppe *Austria* Soup with diced meat and vegetables

gum A polysaccharide, usually obtained from plants in water solution with sticky and gelling properties. The common types of vegetable origin are gum arabic, gum tragacanth, guar gum, locust bean gum and xanthan gum.

gum arabic A polysaccharide vegetable gum obtained from the dried exudate of a Middle Eastern and Indian tree, *Acacia senegal*, used as a thickener, emulsifier and stabilizer, in the manufacture of chewing gum, marshmallows and fruit gums and as a glaze on cake decorations. Also called **gum acacia**, **acacia gum**. See also **E414**

gumbo 1. Okra **2.** *United States* A thick soup or thin stew from Louisiana made with chicken or prawns, tomatoes, rice, sweet peppers, spices, herbs and seasonings and thickened with okra. See e.g. chicken gumbo.

gumbo filé Filé powder

gum jum *China* Lily bulb

gum kum *South Asia* Lily bulb

gumleaf oil *Australia* Eucalyptus oil

Gummiarabicum *Germany* Gum arabic

gum tragacanth A vegetable gum obtained from a shrub, *Astralagus gummifer*, grown in western Asia. Used for thickening creams and jellies, to prevent crystallization of sugars in jam and ice creams and to make **pastillage**, a particularly stiff royal icing used with wedding cakes. See also **E413**

Gundel palacsinta *Hungary* A pancake filled with a creamed nut and raisin filling, flambéed at the table

gunfo *East Africa* An oat or barley flour porridge served in Ethiopia for breakfast with butter and berbere

gung 1. *Thailand* Crustaceans **2.** *Vietnam* Ginger

gunga pea Pigeon pea

gung foi, gung nang *Thailand* **1.** Shrimp **2.** Prawn

gunnel See **butterfish 2**

guo jiang *China* Jam

guo tieh *China* Fried dumpling

gur Jaggery

gurabiah *North Africa* An Algerian biscuit made from butter and icing sugar (2:1) beaten until fluffy, cake flour (1.2:1) on butter folded in to make a soft dough. Half a date pressed into each small ball of dough and all baked at 200°C until golden.

gurdakupura turcarri *South Asia* A kidney curry made with lamb or veal kidneys which have been soaked in vinegared water for 24 hours, then skinned and cored. Chopped onions are fried in a large amount of ghee until brown; sesame seeds, turmeric, cumin seed and cayenne pepper are added and fried; kidneys added and fried for 5 minutes until butter fat separates; **tomato concassée**, powdered bay leaf and mace are added with a little water and cooked until dry; more water added and cooked until dry. The whole is then fried with constant stirring until dark red, simmered with water until kidneys are tender, and kept warm for 10 minutes until served. See also **turcarri**

gurepufurutsu *Japan* Grapefruit

gurka *Sweden* Cucumber

Gurke *Germany* Cucumber

Gurkensalat *Germany* Cucumber salad

gurnard A small round seawater fish of the genus *Friglidae*, with an ugly oversized head and enormous spiny fins, highly coloured with glittering scales and found in the Mediterranean and the North East Atlantic. There are three types, grey, red and yellow. Poached or steamed, popular in France. Also called **gurnet**, **sea robin**, **tub gurnard**

gurnet See **gurnard**

gururu *East Africa* Curdled milk, similar to cottage cheese. See also **maziwa mabichi**

gus *Russia* Goose

gusano de maguey The Mexican agave worm, the larva of a butterfly, *Hipopta agavis*, which feeds on agave plants. It is traditionally found in bottles of mescal, a spirit distilled from agave in southern Mexico. The worms are also served fried in garlic and chilli as a regional delicacy.

guscio *Italy* **1.** Shell **2.** Husk **3.** Pod

guscio, al *Italy* (*of eggs*) Boiled in the shell

gush halav *Middle East* A cows' milk cheese from Israel similar to **Edam**

gus prigotovlyenny v marinadye *Eastern Europe* An Estonian dish of goose rubbed with lemon juice, salt and saltpetre, rested 1 day, then marinated in a boiled water, salt and sugar brine (120:10:3) with raw onion, carrot, garlic, peppercorns and bay for 3 days, drained, then simmered in water with the pickling vegetables, herbs and spices until cooked (100 minutes). Served with lingonberry or cranberry sauce.

Güssing *Austria* A cheese similar to **Brick** made from semi-skimmed cows' milk

gut, to To remove the entrails from an animal or fish including the gills in a fish and to clean out the abdominal cavity

gutap *Russia* Deep-fried pasties made with a wheat flour unleavened dough enriched with butter and filled with e.g. meat mixture, vegetables or set egg custards with vegetables

gutdurchgebraten *Germany* Well done. Used of steaks, meat, etc.

guts See **innards**

Gutsleberwurst *Germany* A mild-flavoured, coarse-textured liver sausage (**Kochwurst**) containing recognizable pieces of liver, pork and fat

güveç *Turkey* A casserole very similar to guvetch

guvetch *Central Europe* A type of ratatouille made from various colours of sweet pepper, onion, garlic, green beans, tomatoes, chillies and seasoning all stewed in sunflower oil. Served with rice or pasta.

gwaar ki phalli *South Asia* Guar bean

gyin sein *Burma* Ginger

gypsy herring *United Kingdom* A name used in Cornwall for pilchard (*colloquial*)

gypsy's arm *Spain* A type of Swiss roll filled with jam or strawberries and cream. Also called **brazo de gitano**

gyudon *Japan* Rice with stir-fried beef and onions and a sauce served with green tea as fast food

gyulai *Hungary* A smoked pork sausage flavoured with paprika

gyümölcs *Hungary* Fruit

gyümölcslé *Hungary* Fruit juice

gyuniku *Japan* Beef

HIJKLMNO

Haagse bluf *Netherlands* A light sorbet of whipped egg whites and redcurrant juice (NOTE: Literally 'Hague swank'.)

haam *China* Salt

haam daan *China* Salted duck egg

haar chee meen *China* Brown noodles flavoured with shrimp

haas *Netherlands* Hare

haas ko phul *Nepal* Duck egg

haba *Spain* Broad bean, fava bean

habanero chilli An extremely hot, lantern-shaped chilli from the Caribbean, with a colour varying from green to red looking rather like a small sweet pepper

habas a la montañesa *Spain* Broad beans baked with ham

habas al horno *Spain* Baked beans

habeet *Middle East* Lamb stewed with **loomi** or lemon zest, garlic and a little vinegar. From Iraq.

habichuela *Spain* Kidney bean

habichuelas verdes *Spain* Green beans

habitant pea soup *Canada* A thick soup from Quebec using dried yellow and green peas with onions, salt pork, herbs and seasonings

HACCP A system developed by NASA to ensure safe food for astronauts, now applied in industry. It consists of applying checks to possible contamination points at all stages of food processing from primary producer through slaughter houses, packers, processors, retailers and restaurants or canteens. However the adoption of this system should not be an excuse for abandoning end product testing. Full form **Hazard analysis critical control point system**

haché(e) *France* Finely chopped or minced

hachee *Netherlands* Minced meat

hachée, sauce *France* Vinegar with finely chopped onion and shallot reduced by half, court bouillon from the fish being poached added, thickened with **beurre manié**, simmered 10 minutes and finished with chopped fines herbes, capers and duxelles

hacher *France* To chop up or mince

hachis 1. *Denmark* Minced meat **2.** *France* Finely chopped cooked meat reheated in a sauce **3.** *France* Chopped vegetables

hachis Parmentier *France* Shepherd's pie

hachoir *France* A rocking chopper consisting of a curved blade with a vertical handle at each end which is used with a rocking motion. Several blades can be paralleled together for a faster chopping action.

hackad *Sweden* Chopped

hackad biff med lök *Sweden* Chopped beef and onions

Hackbraten *Germany* Meat loaf

hacken *Germany* To mince or chop up

Hackfleisch *Germany* Minced meat

haddock A common round fish, *Melanogrammus aeglefinus*, of the cod family found in the Atlantic Ocean. It is up to 60 cm long and 4 kg in weight with a greyish brown upper surface and with a dark spot behind each of the gill covers. The flesh is softer and less flaky than cod and may be cooked in any way. Often smoked.

haddock à la russe *Sweden* A large cleaned haddock with head and fins, simmered in salted water with onion, bayleaf and mixed peppercorns for 15 minutes. Flesh removed and reserved, cooking liquor strained and made into a velouté with an equal amount of thin cream, finished with butter and egg yolk and poured over the fish, reheated and garnished with crisp fried onion and chopped hard-boiled egg.

haemagglutinins See **lectins**

haemoglobin The red cells in blood responsible for the transport of oxygen from the lungs to the tissues

haew *Thailand* Water chestnut

Hafer *Germany* Oats

Haferbrei *Germany* Porridge

Hagebuttensuppe *Germany* A warm soup made from blanched rose hips simmered with breadcrumbs, cinnamon, lemon zest, sugar, a little salt and white wine, sieved, let down with white wine, thickened with egg yolks and finished with butter. Served with croûtons.

haggamuggie *Scotland* Haggis made with fish liver instead of sheep offal

haggis *Scotland* A sausage made from the minced heart, liver and lungs of a sheep mixed with oatmeal, suet, minced onion, spices, herbs and seasoning, all encased in a sheep's stomach and boiled prior to being served hot. Nowadays more commonly stuffed in a plastic casing. Traditionally served at Burns' night suppers with tatties, bashit neeps and an excess of whisky, whilst Burns' Ode to the Haggis is recited with due ceremony. (NOTE: Said to have originated with the Romans who, when campaigning, packed iron rations in a sheeps stomach.)

hagyma *Hungary* Onions

Hahn *Germany* Cock, rooster, mature male chicken

Hähnchen *Germany* Chicken

hahni *Finland* Goose

haiga-mai rice *Japan* An incompletely polished rice leaving the germ attached so that it has a nutty flavour

hairst bree *Scotland* A type of hotchpotch with as well as the usual vegetables, broad beans, shredded lettuce, cauliflower florets and chopped herbs

hair tube A piping-bag nozzle with multiple small openings to make a hair- or grass-like icing decoration

hair vegetable A black alga, *Gracilaria verrucosa*, which grows in very fine hair-like strands off the south coast of China. It is steamed as a vegetable, braised with bacon for Chinese New Year and used as a garnish or decoration. Also called **black moss**

hairy aubergine A Thai variety of aubergine with a bitter tart taste and an orange skin covered in fine hairs. It is sliced and used raw in salads or finely chopped for use in sauces.

hairy basil *Southeast Asia* One of the Southeast Asian basils, genus *Ocimum*, with lemony-peppery-flavoured narrow pale leaves and red tinged seed pods, similar to the Italian dwarf basil. The flavourless seeds are used as a thickening agent.

hairy brinjal Fuzzy melon

hairy gourd A variant of the bottle gourd, *Lageneria siceraria*, with not such a pronounced bottle shape. It is light green, covered in fine hairs and grows up to 75 cm in length.

hairy lychee Rambutan

hairy melon Fuzzy melon

hai shen *China* Sea cucumber (NOTE: Literally 'ginseng of the sea'.)

hai wei *China* Sea food

hai zhe *China* Jellyfish

hai zhe pi *China* Jellyfish

hajdú *Hungary* A cheese made from cows' milk and resembling **Kashkaval**

hajikamashoga *Japan* Pickled **ginger shoots**

hákarl *Iceland* Shark, alternatively, strips of shark flesh, tenderized by being left to ripen under stones in the open air for several weeks, then washed and air-dried. Has rather a pungent odour.

hak chih ma *China* Black sesame seeds

hake A superior tasting fish, *Merluccius merluccius*, of the cod family with a grey to bluish skin and lean white flesh. The lower jaw protrudes beyond the upper. Caught in the western part of the North Atlantic. Cooked in any manner.

hakkebøf *Denmark* Minced or chopped beef

hakket æg og sild *Denmark* Smoked herring and hard-boiled eggs minced together and used as a topping on open sandwiches

hakusai *Japan* Chinese leaves

hal *Hungary* Fish

halal 1. Slaughtered according to the rules of the Muslim religion. Used of meat. **2.** Selling such meat. Used of a butcher.

halászlé *Hungary* A fish stew made with a mixture of freshwater fish cut in pieces, simmered in water and sour cream with paprika and tomato purée, strained and the fish pieces served with cooking liquor thickened with egg yolks and lemon juice

halawch *Middle East* Halva

halba *Malaysia* Fenugreek

halb durchgebraten *Germany* Medium rare. Used of steak, meat, etc.

halber Hahn *Germany* A dark bread roll spread with ripe cheese and mustard

halbran *United States* A very young duckling

halb roh *Germany* **1.** Rare. Used of meat, steaks, etc. **2.** Al dente

haldi *South Asia* Turmeric

half-and-half *United States* Cream containing 10.5 to 18% butterfat. Also called **cereal cream**

halfatányéros *Hungary* A mixture of a variety of panéed and plain fried fish served with tartare sauce

half cream A thin cream with a minimum butterfat content of 12% used as a pouring cream

half moon cut Hangetsu giri

half-mourning *United States* Poularde demi-deuil

half pound cake *United Kingdom* Pound cake made with half quantities (225 g) sufficient to make one 20 cm round cake

halia *Malaysia* Ginger

halibut *England* A large (up to 3 m) fine-flavoured seawater fish, *Hippoglossus hippoglossus*, found in Northern waters. It has dark green to brown upper side and the flesh is firm, white and medium oily. Cooked in any way. The liver is an important source of fish oils used as a vitamin (A & D) supplement.

hälle-flundra *Sweden* Halibut

hallon *Sweden* Raspberry

halmajonéz *Hungary* Fish with mayonnaise served as a hors d'oeuvre

haloua dial jeljlane *North Africa* A Moroccan sweetmeat made from honey, sesame seeds and nuts (8:3:3). The honey is boiled to the thread stage, the sesame seeds are dry-fried until brown and the nuts, almonds or hazelnuts, are dry-fried, skinned and coarsely chopped. The mixture is boiled for 2 minutes then poured into an oiled tray.

Haloumi *Greece, Middle East* A soft or semi-hard cheese with a salty lactic flavour made from ewes' or goats' milk. It is heated in whey to boiling point, drained, salted and preserved in salted whey for up to 40 days. Known as jubna in Arabic.

halstra *Sweden* Roast

halstrad *Sweden* Grilled

Hals und Innereien *Germany* Giblets

halva *Middle East, North Africa* A sweetmeat made from crushed sesame seeds or almonds combined with boiled sugar syrup. Made in block form and sold in slices. Also called **halawch**

halvaye shir *Central Asia* An Iranian milk pudding thickened with ground rice and flavoured with ground cardamom and rose water, garnished with chopped nuts

halwa *South Asia* A type of pudding made from vegetables, lentils, nuts and fruit, cooked with sugar and ghee to a sticky consistency

halwa rghayit *North Africa* A cone-shaped honey cake from Morocco served with fresh butter on celebratory occasions

halwau-e aurd-e sujee *Central Asia* A sweet from Afghanistan made from coarse semolina cooked with an equal weight of clarified butter for 5 minutes. A hot medium sugar syrup is mixed in and cooked to absorb all the liquid. Nuts, ground cardamom seeds and rose water are added and the cooking finished over a low heat with a tight-fitting lid. The mixture is then poured into a greased tray, cooled and cut in pieces.

ham 1. *England, Netherlands* The hind leg and thigh of a pig cut from the carcass and matured separately. Sometimes incorrectly used for the hind leg and thigh cut from a side of bacon. If to be cooked it should be soaked in water until the soaking water is not salty and boiled at a temperature around 80°C or baked until the final centre temperature is 65°C. **2.** *United States* Leg of pork either cured or uncured **3.** The thigh of any animal. Occasionally used of cured beef and mutton. **4.** *Vietnam* Stewed

hamachi *Japan* The young of the yellowtail, (Japanese amberjack), *Serriola quinqueradiata*, about 40 cm long, a fish much used for sushi and sashimi and grilled as shioyaki. Also called **inada**

hamad m'rkad *North Africa* Preserved lemons

hamaguri *Japan* Clams

hamaguri sumashi-jiru *Japan* Clam and mushroom soup made from sound clean clams soaked in salt water for 3 hours, boiled in water until the shells open, unopened ones discarded, mushroom caps and watercress added to the cooking liquor, cooked 1 minute, a little soya sauce and some sake added, heated to boiling point, garnished and served

Haman's ears *Middle East* Hamantaschen

hamantaschen The Yiddish name for small sweet triangular pastries filled with a mixture of poppy seeds, chopped walnuts, syrup, raisins, butter and milk. Eaten at the Jewish festivals of Purim and Lots. Also called **Haman's ears**

hamburger See **beefburger**

Hamburger Aalsuppe *Germany* Eel pieces poached in fish stock and reserved. Peeled and quartered pears poached in white wine with a little sugar and lemon zest and reserved. The strained cooking liquors mixed with a strong beef broth, slightly thickened with a brown roux and garnished with green peas and a brunoise of carrots, leeks and Hamburg parsley and served over dumplings, the eel pieces and the pears.

Hamburger Apfelsuppe *Germany* As **Hagebuttensuppe**, with apples instead of rose hips and cider instead of white wine. Served warm.

hamburger bun A soft flat round yeast-raised bun which is used to make a sandwich with a hamburger. Standardized by some fast food chains to a tasteless uniformity.

hamburgerkött *Sweden* Smoked ox breast

Hamburger Krebssuppe *Germany* Crayfish soup made from crayfish sautéed in butter and flamed with brandy, cooked in white stock and white wine until tender, tail meat reserved; the shells pounded, sweated in butter, flour added and cooked; cooking liquor added, simmered, seasoned and strained over the crayfish tails, small dumplings and green peas

Hamburger Rauchfleisch *Germany* Very thin slices of cold-smoked brisket of beef served with horseradish sauce

hamburgerryg *Denmark* Smoked loin of pork served with a sauce made from redcurrant jelly, mustard and grated onion

Hamburg parsley A type of parsley, *Petroselinum crispum 'tuberosam'*, whose root, which has a strong celery-like flavour, is used as a vegetable in Central Europe. Also called **parsley root, turnip rooted parsley**

Hämchen *Germany* Pigs' knuckles and sauerkraut

ha mei *China* Dried shrimp

hamine eggs *Egypt* Hard-boiled eggs coloured brown with onion skins or similar

Hammel *Germany* Mutton

Hammelfleisch *Germany* Mutton

Hammelkeule *Germany* Leg of mutton

Hammelkotelett *Germany* Mutton chop

Hammelschulter *Germany* Shoulder of mutton

Hammelwürste *Germany* A sausage made of minced pork, mutton and garlic

hammerhead shark One of the better edible sharks, *Sphyrna zygaena*, found in the Atlantic and Mediterranean. Palatable when young.

hampe *France* Thin flank of beef; breast of venison

hamperilainen *Finland* Beefburger

ham sausage 1. *Germany* A scalded sausage made from finely ground pork and beef mixed with spices and garlic and interspersed with chunks of ham and lean bacon (minimum 50%) to give a marbled appearance. Used for slicing and grilling or frying or as an addition to stews, etc. **2.** *United Kingdom* A sausage made from finely chopped ham mixed with 20% coarsely chopped pork fat, moistened with stock and flavoured with white pepper, cayenne pepper, mace and ginger, packed into **weasands**, tied, simmered for an hour and cold-smoked for 10 days

hamu *Japan* Ham

hamuth heloo *Middle East* An Iraqi dish of lamb, browned in ghee then braised with onions, **noomi** and cinnamon bark, with dried fruits (apricots, dates, prunes, sultanas etc.) added together with date syrup or brown sugar halfway through the cooking process. The cinnamon and noomi are removed before serving.

hana gatsuo *Japan* Hana katsuo

hana-giri *Japan* The flower cut of root vegetables made by trimming cylinders lengthways so that when sliced transversally, they make a 5 petalled shape

hana hojiso *Japan* Small stems of the shiso plant with seed pods, used as a garnish. The seeds are also scraped from the stem into the soya dipping sauce used with sashimi. Also called **hojiso**

hana katsuo *Japan* Pacific bonito flakes or shavings. Also called **hana gatsuo**

hanatsuki kyuri *Japan* Very small cucumbers with intact flowers still attached, used as a garnish

hand *United Kingdom* Hand and spring of pork

Hand *Germany* Handkäse

hand and spring of pork *England* Name used in London and the southwest for a foreleg and shoulder of pork excluding the blade. Also called **hand of pork**

Handkäse *Germany* A variety of soft hand moulded cheeses (25 to 125 g) made from naturally soured and curdled skimmed or semi-skimmed cows' milk. Sometimes flavoured with herbs or spices and widely variable in colour, texture and flavour. Contains 50 to 55% water, 2% fat and 27 to 35% protein. Also called **Hand, Harzkäse, Sauermilchkäse**

hand of pork *United Kingdom* Hand and spring of pork

hand parer *United States* See **peeler**

hang, to To leave meat or game birds, especially the tougher old birds, to hang in a cool dry airy store for sufficient time to allow the meat fibres to be broken down by the acid conditions which develop. Animal meat is hung as complete or half carcasses for up to 2 weeks or more. Game birds with the exception of wild duck, which may be drawn, are hung by the neck without being drawn or plucked.

hangetsu giri *Japan* Half round cuts of vegetables especially carrots, bamboo shoots, radishes, etc. Also called **half moon cut**

hangibjúga *Iceland* Smoked sausage

hangikjöt *Iceland* Smoked lamb

hangop *Netherlands* Cottage cheese, curds, alternatively a thick buttermilk and sugar dessert

hangtown fry *United States* An omelette served with fried bacon and panéed and fried oysters

hanhea *Finland* Goose

hanh la *Vietnam* Spring onions

hanh tay *Vietnam* Onion

hanjuku tamago *Japan* Soft-boiled eggs

Hanoi beef soup *Vietnam* Pho

hanpen *Japan* A soft fish cake made from ground fish flesh and starch formed into squares or triangles and steamed. Eaten as is or grilled, poached or deep-fried and dipped in soya sauce.

hao you gai lan *China* Broccoli in oyster sauce

hao you niu rou *China* Beef with oyster sauce

hapankaali *Finland* Sauerkraut

har *China* **1.** Shrimp **2.** Prawn

hara dhania *South Asia* Coriander leaves

harak mas *Sri Lanka* A beef curry flavoured with onions, garlic, ginger, vinegar, spices and coconut

haram Describes food forbidden by Islamic law

hara mirich *South Asia* Green chilli

häränfile *Finland* Fillet steak

häränhäntäliemi *Finland* See **oxtail soup 1**

hara piaz *South Asia* Spring onions

harcsa *Hungary* Wels, the fish

hard Hard to the bite as applied to wheat, difficult to cut as applied to cheese, resisting penetration by a sharp object

hardal *Turkey* Mustard

hard ball stage See **sugar cooking**

hard-boil, to To boil something until it hardens, usually used of whole eggs boiled for 10 minutes until the yolk is solid

hard cheese A cheese which is difficult to cut, normally with a water content less than 40%

hard clam Quahog clam

hard crack stage A stage in sugar cooking when the sugar temperature rises to 157°C in the UK and 149°C in the USA. See also **sugar cooking**

hard dumpling See **Sussex dumpling**

hardfiskur *Iceland* Fish cleaned and split along the abdominal cavity, sometimes with bone removed, to make a triangular shape. In this form hung up to air dry in freezing conditions. When dry will keep almost indefinitely. Eaten raw.

hårdkogt *Denmark* Hard-boiled

hårdkokt *Norway, Sweden* Hard-boiled

hard-neck clam Quahog clam

hard red spring wheat flour *United States* A high gluten bread flour

hard red winter wheat flour *United States* A good bread flour made from a more flaky and thinner seed than the equivalent spring wheat flour

hard roe The eggs of female fish usually floured and fried

hard sauce See **rum, brandy butter**

hardshell clam Quahog clam

hard smoked herring Red herring

hardtack A hard biscuit made of flour, salt and water only. Also called **ship biscuit**, **sea biscuit**, **pilot biscuit**

Harduf *Middle East* An Israeli semi-soft spreading cheese made from ewes' milk to resemble Lipto

hard wheat A tough wheat which resists cracking and with the starch grains tightly bound. It contains no triabolin and it fractures across the starch grains. Durum wheat is one of the hardest.

hare *England, Norway* A wild game animal resembling a large rabbit but which does not hop nor live in burrows. There are several varieties, the common, Scottish and the Mediterranean all distinguished from rabbit by their dark flesh and powerful back legs. The blood, which is collected for **jugged hare**, is prevented from coagulating by adding 5 ml of vinegar. Hares are usually hung by the legs for 5 to 10 days before being paunched. May be roasted, braised or stewed. Shooting season in the UK is from the 1st of August to the last day of February although it is not a law. Hare is not sold from March to July.

hare channa *South Asia* Fresh or dried, green immature chick peas

hareng *France* Herring

hareng fumé *France* Kipper

hareng mariné *France* Pickled herring

hareng salé *France* Bloater

hareng saur *France* The French version of the red herring often served as a hors d'oeuvre

hareragu *Norway* Jugged hare

haresteg *Denmark* Roast hare

har gow *China* Small purses of minced shrimp made by placing the filling in the centre of a rolled out circle of wheat starch dough and pulling the edges to the centre to make it look like a string purse or bag

harhardal *South Asia* Yellow dahl

haricot à rame *France* Runner bean

haricot bean The shelled and dried mature **French bean**, usually white, about 8 to 10 mm long and oval-shaped. Sometimes coloured. Used extensively in Western cooking. See also **French bean**. Also called **dry shell bean** (NOTE: The name is derived from the Aztec *ayecotl*.)

haricot bean soup See **soissonaise, purée**

haricot beurre *France* **1.** Butter bean **2.** A type of yellow French bean

haricot de mouton *France* Stewed mutton with root vegetables

haricot de Soissons *France* Kidney bean

haricot grimpant *France* Runner bean

haricot lamb *United Kingdom* A lamb stew with haricot beans, onions and turnips

haricot rouge *France* Kidney bean

haricot sec *France* Haricot bean

haricot vert *France* The immature pod of the **French bean** or green beans

hari gobhi *South Asia* Broccoli

hari mirch *South Asia* Sweet green pepper

harina *Spain* Flour

harina de maíz *Spain* Corn flour

haring *Netherlands* Herring

haringsla *Netherlands* Herring salad

harira *North Africa* A thick Moroccan purée-type soup of chick peas, lentils and haricot beans in a mutton or chicken stock with eggs, lemon, sometimes tomatoes and various herbs such as coriander, parsley or tarragon. Often served as a starter.

harissa *North Africa* A hot chilli sauce made from softened, deseeded red chillies, garlic, salt, caraway seeds, cumin seeds, coriander seeds and dried mint leaves blended to a paste with olive oil. Some versions contain many more spices.

harrar A top-quality Ethiopian arabica coffee bean used for Turkish coffee

harslet *United Kingdom* Haslet

hart *Netherlands* Heart

hartgekocht *Germany* Hard-boiled

harusame *Japan* Cellophane noodles (NOTE: Literally 'spring rain'.)

Harvard beets *United States* Sliced, diced or julienned beetroot cooked in vinegar and sugar then thickened with corn flour

harvest pudding *England* Sage and onion stuffing, chopped cooked ham, grated cheese and eggs (5:2:1:2), the first three ingredients and the egg yolks mixed together, the stiffly beaten egg whites folded in and all then baked in an ovenproof dish at 190°C for 35 minutes

Harz, Harzer *Germany* Harzerkäse

Harzerkäse *Germany* A small, round, firm, pungent cheese made by hand from cows' milk in the Harz mountains. Often eaten with goose fat on black bread. Also called **Harz, Harzer**

Hase *Germany* Hare

Hasehendl *Germany* A name used in Frankfurt for chicken (*colloquial*)

Hase im Topf *Germany* Hare casseroled with wine and spices

Haselhuhn *Germany* Hazel hen

Haselnuss *Germany* Hazelnut

Haselnusscreme *Germany* A sweetened custard made with milk, sugar and egg yolks (10:4:1), heated to coating consistency, softened gelatine (2 g per 100 ml) and ground blanched hazelnuts (40 g per 100 ml) added, cooled but not set, then a third of its volume of cream, whipped to a soft peak, folded into the mixture which is poured into moulds to set

Haselnussmakronen *Germany* Hazelnut macaroons made in the same way as ordinary macaroons using ground skinned hazelnuts and flavouring them with cocoa powder and lemon zest

Hasenbraten *Germany* Roast hare

Hasenklein *Germany* Hare, floured and browned with bacon dice then all braised in red wine and stock with with pepper, spices, herbs, redcurrant jelly and lemon juice

hash *United Kingdom, United States* Pieces of leftover meat served in a well-seasoned gravy or brown sauce with mashed potatoes and cooked vegetables

hash, to To cut or chop food into small pieces

hash brown potatoes *United States* A southern dish of grated raw potatoes fried like a pancake in bacon fat, often served for breakfast with bacon and egg, also, diced potatoes fried with onions. Also called **hash browns, hashed brown potatoes**

hash browns See **hash brown potatoes**

hashed brown potatoes See **hash brown potatoes**

hashi *Japan* Chopsticks

ha shoga *Japan* Ginger shoots

haslet *England* An old English meat loaf, or faggot if wrapped in pig's caul, based either on pigs heart, liver, lungs and sweetbreads or pork mixed with finely chopped onion, dried bread crumbs, herbs and seasonings, cooked, sliced and served hot or cold. Sometimes wrapped in a pig's caul. Similar ingredients may also be stewed or casseroled under the same name. A more expensive version uses lean pork. Also called **harslet, pig's fry**

hassaku *Japan* A naturally occurring hybrid of *Citrus*, relatively unknown outside Japan

hasselback potatoes See **hasselbackspotatis**

hasselbackspotatis *Sweden* Medium potatoes, peeled, cut with thin parallel cuts without completely severing each slice, each slice brushed with butter and sprinkled with dried white breadcrumbs, half baked in the oven, sprinkled with cheese and baking completed (NOTE: Literally 'hazel hill potatoes'.)

hasselnöt *Sweden* Hazelnut

hasty pudding 1. *England* A thick **béchamel sauce** enriched with egg, placed in a flameproof dish, covered with butter, brown sugar and cinnamon and browned under the grill **2.** *United States* Cornmeal thickened and spiced milk sweetened with molasses. Also called **Indian pudding**

hasu *Japan* Lotus root

hatcho-miso *Japan* A very dark, salty, thick and strong-flavoured **miso** made mainly of soya beans and used in soups

hatted kit *Scotland* Soft curds made from a mixture of buttermilk and full-cream milk, double cream and caster sugar (7:4:1). The cream and sugar are whipped to a stiff peak and folded gently into the curds, which may be flavoured with nutmeg or cinnamon. The curds were made in the old days by milking a cow directly into buttermilk but they are now made with rennet, left overnight and strained through a fine sieve or tamis cloth. Also called **added kit**

hat tiêu den *Vietnam* Black pepper

hat tiêu trắng *Vietnam* White pepper

hauki *Finland* Pike

haunch The rear leg of an animal with part of the loin attached

Hauptelsalat *Austria* Lettuce

Hausfrauenart *Germany* In the style of the housewife, i.e. with sour cream and pickles

hausgemacht *Germany* Home-made

Hausmachernudeln *Germany* Home-made noodles

haute cuisine *France* Top-grade cooking

havande gädda *Sweden* A whole pike, scaled and opened up from the back and cleaned so as not to break the abdominal skin and leaving in the backbone. A salt herring is placed in the abdominal cavity and the pike is reformed, seasoned, panéed and baked, basting with milk. Served with the juices which have been thickened with crushed ginger biscuits. (NOTE: Literally 'pregnant pike'.)

Havarti *Denmark* A semi-hard scalded-curd cows' milk cheese with a pungently flavoured paste containing numerous holes. The rind may be dry or washed in which case the cheese has a better flavour. Either 45% or 60% butterfat content.

havermout *Netherlands* **1.** Oatmeal **2.** Rolled oats

havij polou *Central Asia* An Iranian rice-based dish (**polou**) made with pieces of chicken, chopped onions and carrot batons with turmeric, fried in turn, then simmered

with lemon juice, brown sugar and water. Served with **chelou**.

Haxe *Germany* Knuckle (of veal, etc.)

haybox cooking A method of slow cooking in which the food is brought to the boil in a container which is then put inside an insulated container with an insulated lid to complete cooking without further heating. Originally the insulation was hay packed in a wooden box or hole in the ground.

haymaking cheese Single Gloucester

hazel grouse See **hazel hen**

hazel hen A European woodland grouse, *Tetrastes bonasia*, mainly from Scandinavia and Russia with a white excellently flavoured and tender flesh. Also called **hazel grouse**

hazelnut A thick-shelled nut from the European or North American hazel tree, *Corylus avellana*, with an outer husk that does not completely cover the nut. The nuts are small (up to 1 cm) and pointed, with a firmly attached skin which is loosened by roasting or blanching. Grown in the UK, Italy and Spain, they have a distinctive flavour and are used in cooking, confectionery and as a dessert nut. The oil is prized for its flavour. See also **filbert**. Also called **cobnut**, **Barcelona nut**

hazelnut butter A compound butter made from skinned and roasted hazelnuts pounded with a few drops of water, mixed with softened butter and passed through a sieve

haze peper *Netherlands* A thick hare stew made from the hindquarter or the legs

HDL See **high-density lipoprotein**

head cheese Brawn

heart The muscular organ which continually pumps blood around the body (NOTE: From a young animal they are reasonably tender, but older hearts being tough require long braising or stewing)

heart cockle See **heart shell**

heart of palm The hearts, i.e. terminal buds or young shoots of various types of palm, an important leek-like vegetable grown in Brazil and Florida, now common in canned form throughout the USA and France. Also called **cabbage palm**, **palm heart**

heart of rape Rape

heart shell A bivalve mollusc, *Glossus humanus*, similar to but not a true cockle; it is heart-shaped when viewed side on. Found in the eastern Atlantic from Iceland to the Mediterranean. Also called **heart cockle**

heat, to To warm through without boiling

heat lamp A source of infra-red radiation usually suspended above a food serving or food-holding area to keep the food warm

heat treatment of curds Curds for cheese may be uncooked, i.e. not subjected to a temperature greater than 39°C, scalded, i.e. subjected to temperatures between 40 and 48°C or cooked i.e. subjected to temperatures in excess of 48°C

heavenly hash *United States* The name given to various sweet desserts

heavy cake Cornish heavy cake

heavy cream *United States* A cows' milk cream with a butterfat content of 36 to 40%. Used for whipping. Also called **heavy whipping cream**

heavy syrup See **syrup**

heavy whipping cream *United States* Heavy cream

Hebridean lobster *Scotland* Cubed cooked lobster meat, sautéed briefly in butter, flamed with Drambuie (a whisky liqueur) and cooked for a few minutes in a cheese sauce enriched with the mashed lobster coral, finished with added cream and piled into the lobster shells with a mushroom and parsley garnish. This is not a traditional dish.

hechima *Japan* Loofah

hecho See **muy hecho**, **poco hecho**

Hecht *Germany* Pike

Hechtdorsch *Germany* Hake

Hecht mit Sauerkraut *Germany* Flaked pike flesh mixed with sauerkraut, covered with cream and baked in the oven

hedelma *Finland* Fruit

hedelmäkakku *Finland* Fruit cake

hedelmäkeitto *Finland* Cold fruit soup

hedelmäslaatti *Finland* Fruit salad

hed fang *Thailand* Straw mushroom

hedgehog A small rodent-like animal with a covering of sharp retractable quills. Traditionally baked in a clay covering by country folk. The clay enables the skin and quills to be easily removed.

hedgehog mushroom *United States* A type of mushroom with a fawn-orange cap and white tooth-like projections below

hed hom *Thailand* 1. Shiitake mushroom 2. Chinese mushroom

hed hunu *Thailand* Cloud ear fungus

heet bliksem *Netherlands* A spiced mixture of pork chops, potatoes and apples (NOTE: Literally 'hot lightning'.)

Hefe *Germany* Yeast

Hefeklosse *Germany* Yeast-raised dumplings made with an egg and butter enriched flour dough (1:1:7) made with milk flavoured with nutmeg, kneaded and proved as bread and finally steamed. Served with sweet or savoury dishes.

Hefekranz *Germany* A savarin usually decorated with almonds and candied fruit

Heidelbeere *Germany* 1. Blueberry 2. Bilberry

Heidesand *Germany* Biscuits made from self-raising flour, butter and sugar (4:3:2) mixed by the blending method, flavoured with vanilla, cut into rounds as in refrigerator cookies and baked at 175°C until firm and light brown

heiko *Malaysia* A smooth dark brown shrimp paste used in Thailand and Malaysia

heilbot *Netherlands* Halibut

Heilbutt *Germany* Halibut

Heilbutt unterm Sahneberg *Germany* Fillets of halibut laid in a buttered baking dish, sprinkled with onions sweated in bacon fat and covered with parcooked lean bacon rashers, covered with a white wine court bouillon and baked at 165°C until the fish is firm. Served topped with a velouté sauce made with the cooking liquor into which whipped double cream has been folded, sprinkled with grated cheese and browned under a very hot grill. (NOTE: Literally 'halibut under a mountain of cream'.)

heimische Home-made (*Yiddish*)

heiss *Germany* Hot

heisse Biersuppe *Germany* Lager and sugar (9:1) boiled then thickened off the heat to avoid curdling, with a liaison of egg yolks and sour cream (1:7 on lager), seasoned and flavoured with a little cinnamon

heko *Philippines* The sediment from the fermented fish or shrimp paste bagoong, boiled with 3 times its weight in water for 30 minutes and then allowed to settle. Used as a mild fishy seasoning.

helado *Spain* 1. Ice cream 2. *also* **helada** Frozen

heldersoep *Netherlands* Clear soup, consommé

helgeflundra *Sweden* Halibut

Helianthus annuus *Botanical name* Sunflower

Helianthus tuberosus *Botanical name* The Jerusalem artichoke plant

Helichrysum angustifolium *Botanical name* Curry plant

hellefisk *Norway* Halibut

helleflynder *Denmark* Halibut

helstekt *Norway* Fried

Helston pudding *England* Equal quantities of raisins, currants, suet, sugar, breadcrumbs, flour and ground rice with 1 tsp of mixed spice per kg of dry ingredients plus the same quantity of bicarbonate of soda which is dissolved in the milk with which the dry ingredients are brought together. The mixture is boiled in a well-greased covered pudding basin for 2 hours.

Hemerocallis fulva *Botanical name* The day lily from which lily buds are obtained

hemicellulose A polysaccharide carbohydrate found in fruit and vegetables. Some forms known as pectin are responsible for the setting of jams.

hen The female of a bird, usually the female chicken which has been bred to lay eggs

Hendl *Austria* Chicken

Henne *Germany* Hen

hennepot *Belgium* Chicken hotpot

herb A generic name for low growing plants and shrubs but more generally reserved for those plants with flavouring and medicinal properties. See culinary herb.

herbe aux chats *France* Catmint

herbes de Provence *France* A mixture of culinary herbs usually containing thyme, marjoram, basil and oregano. Used fresh or dried.

herb salts *United States* A mixture of pure ground salt and ground dried herbs, Used as a flavouring

herbs for particular food items See under food items: beef, bread, cheese, dessert, egg, fish, game, lamb, liver, pork, poultry, salads, soup, turtle soup, vinegar. For example, herbs for beef are listed under **beef herbs**.

Hereford sausages *England* Fried sausages are simmered for 20 minutes in a sauce made from chopped bacon and onions sweated in some of the fat from the sausages. Flour is added to form a roux and finally cider and pork stock together with a bay leaf. Finally sliced mushrooms are added for the last 10 minutes.

Herefordshire cod *England* Cod fillet baked in strong cider with sliced mushrooms and tomatoes for 15 minutes at 190°C, the cooking liquor thickened with a blond roux and poured over the fish, the top gratinated with cheese and the dish browned under a grill

hergma *North Africa* **1.** Calves' feet **2.** Morrocan street food of lamb or calves trotters cooked with chickpeas and burghul

Hering *Germany* Herring

Hering Rollmop *Germany* Rollmop herring, often served with mustard, horseradish sauce or tomato sauce

Heringshai *Germany* Porbeagle shark

Heringskartoffeln *Germany* A casserole of alternate layers of herring and sliced potatoes

Herkimer *United States* A Cheddar-like factory produced cows' milk cheese from New York

herkkusienikastike *Finland* Mushroom sauce

herkkusienikeitto *Finland* Cream of mushroom soup

hermit crab An edible crab normally found in France. Also called **bernard-l'hermite**

herneet *Finland* Peas

hernekeito *Finland* Green pea soup

hero *United States* Hoagie

herrera *Spain* Striped bream

Herrgårdsost *Sweden* A hard scalded-curd factory-produced cheese made from pasteurized cows' milk using a lactic starter and resembling Emmental. The pressed cheese is salted in brine, coated in wax and ripened for 3 to 4 months. Available in skimmed milk (30% butterfat) and whole milk (45% butterfat) versions.

herring A round oily fish, *Clupea harengus*, with a wide distribution. The upper surface is steel blue and the underside silvery white. Sizes range from 20 to 40 cm in length. It has rather a lot of fine bones and may be cooked whole or filleted and is also sweet and/or sour pickled, salted and smoked. Very popular in Northern Europe and an important source of EFAs. See also **rollmop herring**, **kipper** (NOTE: The name is from the old German *heer*, meaning an army, referring to its habit of once congregating in very large shoals.)

herring butter A compound butter made from filleted, smoked salt herrings, diced and pounded with half their weight of butter and sieved

herring caviar *United States* The roe of the female alewife herring processed to resemble caviar

herring flippits *United Kingdom* Freshly cooked **flippits** spread with a little mustard, topped with a grilled herring fillet, sprinkled with black pepper and served with lemon wedges

herrings, salted Russian-style *Russia* Selodka

hertebout *Netherlands* Haunch of venison

hertevlees *Netherlands* Venison

Herve *Belgium* A soft, washed rind cows' milk cheese from north of Liège with a very strong pungent smell formed into squat 7.5 cm cubes with the typical red brown rind. Contains 51% water, 24% fat and 22% protein.

hervir *Spain* To boil

hervir a fuego lento *Spain* To simmer

Herzmuschel *Germany* Cockle

Herzogin Kartoffeln *Germany* Mashed potatoes browned in the oven, duchesse potatoes

Herzwurst *Germany* A sausage made from coarsely chopped pigs' hearts mixed with finely minced pork shoulder and belly, seasoned, flavoured with nutmeg and allspice and filled into hog casings

hesperidin One of the bioflavonoids found in high concentration in citrus fruit

Hesperis matronalis *Botanical name* Sweet rocket

hetao ren *China* Walnut

hetao zha ji pian *China* Deep-fried chicken with walnuts

hettekees A low-fat, rindless cheese. See also **fromage de Bruxelles**

heuk bone of beef *Scotland* The eastern Scottish term for rump of beef

heung mao tso *China* Lemon grass

heung nu fun *China* Five spice powder

hexamethylene tetramine See **E239**

hexamine E239, a preservative permitted only for fish and Provolone cheese

hibachi *Japan* A cast iron barbecue with a slatted iron grid

Hibiscus sabdariffa *Botanical name* Jamaica flower

hickory *France, United States* A hardwood tree *Carya* spp. commonly used for smoking food.

hickory nut *United States* The sweet edible nut of the hickory tree related to the pecan and similar to the walnut

hie *Japan* Japanese millet

hielo *Spain* Ice

hierbabuena *Spain* Mint, the herb

hierbas finas *Spain* Fine herbs, a mixture of herbs

higadillo *Spain* The liver of a small animal, particularly a bird

higadito de pollo *Spain* Chicken liver

hígado *Spain* Liver

higashi *Japan* Hard cakes mainly made of sugar and always purchased. They keep well.

highbush blueberry See **blueberry**

high country bread *Australia* Mountain pepper bread

high-density lipoprotein A specific complex of fat and protein that transports cholesterol in the blood. High levels appear to protect against heart and vascular disease. See also **cholesterol**, **low-density lipoprotein**. Abbreviation **HDL**

Highland Crowdie *Scotland* A smooth cottage type cows' or goats' milk cheese with a light fresh flavour

Highland fish sauce *Scotland* Anchovies steeped in wine vinegar for a week then mixed with red wine, chopped horseradish, onion and parsley together with lemon thyme, bay, grated nutmeg, ground mace, cloves and black pepper and all simmered together for about 30 minutes and strained and bottled. Used with a brown butter sauce at the rate of 1 tbsp per 50 g of butter as a dressing for fish.

High-Moisture Jack A young **Monterey Jack** with a mild flavour matured up to 6 weeks

high-ratio flour A very fine flour which can be combined with up to twice as much sugar as normal. Used in cake-making.

high-ratio shortening Fat with a higher proportion of mono- and diglycerides than usual which can absorb more sugar than normal

high tea *United Kingdom* A substantial afternoon meal, once popular in Scotland and the north of England, now usually found only in more traditional hotels and boarding houses. Usually an assortment of cold meats and fish, salads, sandwiches, sweets, cakes and buns with tea or coffee.

higo chumbo *Spain* Prickly pear

hiilillä paistettus silakkaa *Finland* Grilled herring

hijiki A sun-dried and coarsely shredded brown seaweed. See also **hiziki**

hikiniku *Japan* Minced beef

Hildersheimer Streichleberwurst *Germany* A spreading paste-like sausage made with pigs' liver and pork

hilloa *Finland* Jam

hilum The scar on a seed or bean where it joined its stalk

him *China* Ridged sand clam

Himbeere *Germany* Raspberry

Himbeerkaltschale *Germany* Raspberries, macerated in sugar syrup, sieved, mixed with white wine and a little lemon juice and served cold garnished with whole raspberries dipped in sugar

himmelsk lapskaus *Norway* Fresh fruit and nuts sometimes served with a brandy-flavoured egg sauce (NOTE: Literally 'heavenly potpourri'.)

Himmel und Erde *Germany* Creamed potatoes and apple purée mixed with fried chopped onions and topped with fried liver (NOTE: Literally 'heaven and earth'.)

himmeri *Finland* Lobster

hina *Japan* A 3 to 4-month-old chicken. Also called **hinadori**

hinadori *Japan* Hina

hindbær *Denmark* Raspberry

hindi *Turkey* Turkey

hind loin of pork The rear of the loin containing the kidneys and pork fillet (tenderloin). Roasted or cut into loin chops and chump chops (rear end).

hind saddle *United States* The rear end of a veal or lamb carcass cut between the 12th and 13th ribs counting from the neck end

hing *South Asia* Asafoetida

hinojo *Spain* Fennel

hinojo marino *Spain* Samphire, *Crithmum maritimum*

hin sui *China* Squid

hip The seed capsule of a flower, used especially of the rose

hip bone of beef *England* A Midlands term for beef rump

hipogloso *Spain* Halibut

Hippen *Germany* Almonds pounded with egg whites, caster sugar, a little flour and cinnamon, stiffly beaten egg whites folded in, the batter spread thinly on oiled baking sheets, baked at 220°C, taken off the sheet when hot and rolled around a thin cylinder like a brandy snap. Used for garnishing desserts. Also called **Hohlhippen**

hirame *Japan* Flounder or halibut, used raw in sushi

Hirams Söndagshöna *Sweden* Sunday chicken. A large chicken stuffed with a mixture of minced gammon and giblets, fresh white breadcrumbs, chopped and crushed garlic, seasoning and chopped parsley, stitched up, brought to the boil in water or stock flavoured with cloves, skimmed then simmered with parsnip, onions and leeks until tender. Served with a roux-thickened, strained cooking liquor finished with a cream and egg yolk liaison.

hiratake *Japan* Oyster mushroom

hira-zukuri *Japan* A type of cut for fish such as snapper or sea bass used in sashimi in which the fillets are skinned and cut across the grain in slices

hirino *Greece* Pork

Hirn *Germany* Brains

hirn-profesen *Italy* Bread slices spread with brains, dipped in batter and deep-fried (NOTE: From the alpine region of Italy.)

Hirsch *Germany* Stag

Hirschbraten Roast venison

Hirse *Germany* **1.** Millet **2.** Sorghum

hirvi *Finland* Elk

hisopo *Spain* Hyssop

hiyamugi *Japan* A somen-type noodle but even thinner. Generally served cold with a dipping sauce.

hiyashi *Japan* Chilled

hiyashi somen *Japan* A thin white noodle resembling vermicelli. See also **somen** (NOTE: Literally 'ice noodles'.)

hiyu *Japan* Amaranth

hiziki *Japan* A sun-dried and coarsely shredded brown seaweed, *Cystophyllum fusiforme* or *Hisikia fusiforme*, found in shallow coastal waters of East Asia and rich in iron and calcium. May be eaten on its own, as a garnish or in soups and stews. Also called **hijiki**

hjärta *Sweden* Heart

hjerte *Denmark, Norway* Heart

hjort *Sweden* **1.** Deer **2.** Roebuck

hjortetakk *Norway* A special doughnut made at Christmas

hjortron *Sweden* Cloudberry

hjortstek *Sweden* Venison steak. Also called **rådjursstek**

hmo *Burma* Straw mushroom

hoagie *United States* A sandwich made with a split hoagie roll filled with an assortment of meats, cheeses, salad vegetables, pickles, onions, etc. Also called **grinder**, **Italian sandwich**, **sub and submarine**

hoagie roll A flat oblong bread roll about 15 to 20 cm long, used for a hoagie

hoan jo *China* Date

hob 1. The flat metal framework on top of a cooker on which pans are placed in order to be heated or a similar surface above or beside an open fire on which food containers are put to keep hot **2.** A set of gas or electric rings set in a metal plate with controls, usually mounted in a work surface separate from the oven

hochepot *France* A soup made with salt pork, pigs' tails and ears, beef, mutton, cabbage and root vegetables (NOTE: Literally 'shaking pot'.)

hochepot flamand *Belgium* As hochepot, but the meat and most of the vegetables served separately from the soup with small boiled sausages

Hochwild *Germany* Game

hock The part of an animal between the foot and lower limb corresponding to the ankle and part of the lower calf of a human. It consists mainly of gristle and connective tissue with a little flesh. Used to provide gelatine by prolonged boiling.

hodesalat *Norway* Lettuce

hodge-podge See **hotchpotch**

hodgils *Scotland* Dumplings made like the Welsh **trollod** with added chopped chives

hoe cake *United States* A dent corn cornmeal batter pancake originally cooked on the blade of a hoe. Also called **Johnny cake**

hoen kwe *Indonesia, Malaysia* Mung bean flour

hog 1. *United States* A general term for pig **2.** *United Kingdom* A castrated male pig reared for slaughter

hog casings The cleaned and scraped intestines of pigs, being the first 18 m of pig gut measuring from the stomach with a diameter between 32 and 46 mm, classed as narrow, medium, wide and extra wide. Used for sausages and bratwursts.

hogget A sheep between 12 months and 24 months old, popular in Australia

hog millet Common millet

hog plum The plum- or egg-shaped fruit (up to 7.5 cm) of trees of the genus *Spondias*, similar to the mango. Cultivated in Southeast Asia and South America. A large stone is surrounded by yellow and flavoursome flesh and a yellow to red skin. Also called **Jamaica plum**, **otaheite apple**

hog pudding *England* A type of haggis from the southwest made with finely chopped pigs' pluck or fatty pig meat for the more expensive versions, mixed with boiled groats, seasoning and flavourings, packed into wide hog casings and boiled until cooked. The Devonshire variety is flavoured with mace, nutmeg, thyme and cayenne pepper, the Cornish one with mace, nutmeg, parsley and thyme. Also called **hog's pudding**

hog's pudding *England* Hog pudding

hoh laan dau *China* Mangetout pea

hoh laan dow *China* Mangetout pea

hohle Schokoladenhippen *Germany* Tubes made of thin chocolate, filled with whipped cream

Hohlhippen *Germany* Brandy-snap-shaped garnishes made mainly from almonds. See also **Hippen**

hoh yow *China* Oyster sauce

hoi git *China* Jellyfish

hoi sin cheung *China* Hoisin sauce

hoisin sauce *China* A sweet thick red-brown sauce made from fermented soya beans, sugar, garlic, five spices and a little chilli and coloured with annatto. Used with roast pork and poultry as a condiment or to glaze the meat as it is being roasted so as to give it a rich red chestnut colour. Also called **duck sauce**, **suan mei jiang**

hoja *Spain* Leaf

hoja de laurel *Spain* Bay leaf

hojaldre *Spain* Puff pastry

hojiso *Japan* Small stems of the shiso plant with seed pods, used as a garnish. See also **hana hojiso**

hökarepanna *Sweden* Grocer's stew made from sliced pork fillet and calves' kidney alternated in a casserole dish with seasoned sliced raw potatoes and onions, finishing with potatoes, covered with lager and dotted with butter, boiled, skimmed then simmered with a lid for 1 hour or more

hoki An important deep-water commercial fish from New Zealand. Exported to Europe as fillets.

hokkien mee noodles *China* Egg noodles

holipce See **holishkes**

holishkes A Jewish speciality consisting of blanched cabbage leaves wrapped around a filling of meat and rice and simmered in a sweet-and-sour tomato sauce. Also called **gluptzes**, **holipce**, **praakes**

hollandaise, à la 1. *France* In the Dutch style, i.e. served with **hollandaise sauce 2.** Coated with melted butter and served with boiled potatoes. Used of poached fish.

hollandaise, sauce *England, France* A reduction of crushed peppercorns and vinegar, cooled, a small amount of cold water added, egg yolks whisked in and the whole cooked to a thread over a bain-marie whilst continuing to whisk, removed from the heat and molten clarified butter poured in slowly with vigorous whisking to form a stable emulsion, seasoned and strained. Served warm with hot fish and some vegetables.

holländische Sosse *Germany* Hollandaise sauce

hollandse palingsoep *Netherlands* A soup made from sweated skinned eels poached in a stock made from the eel trimmings and white wine, eel flesh reserved, poaching liquor strained, seasoned and thickened with egg yolks and butter and poured over the eel pieces and toast and garnished with a **julienne** of sweated leek, celery and Hamburg parsley

holodny sup-salat *Russia* See **kholodny sup-salat**

Holsteinerschnitzel *Germany* A panéed and fried veal escalope topped with a fried egg and garnished with various items, usually anchovy fillets

Holsteinerwurst *Germany, United States* A sausage consisting of equal parts of cured pork and fresh beef minced finely with sugar, seasoned and strongly spiced with coriander, nutmeg and cardamom, filled into casings, linked or made into rings and smoked for a considerable time

Holstein schnitzel *United States* Holsteinerschnitzel

holubtsi *Eastern Europe* Cabbage rolls (**golubtsy**) from the Ukraine often containing chopped mushrooms instead of minced meat

holy basil An oriental variety of basil with a darker leaf than basil and a sharper, slightly aniseed flavour

holy poke *United States* Baptist cake

Holyrood pudding *Scotland* An enriched semolina pudding made by adding 4 tbsp of marmalade and 50g of egg yolks per litre of milk to the cooled pudding, folding in the associated stiffly beaten egg whites plus ratafia biscuits at the rate of 100 g per litre, then baking at 180°C until risen and browned

homard *France* Lobster

homard, sauce *France* A lobster-flavoured sauce made by sweating lobster flesh in the shell, or well-crushed cooked lobster shell, with a **mirepoix** of onion, carrot and celery in butter; flaming with brandy; adding flour and tomato purée to make a cooked-out roux; adding fish stock, white wine, a bouquet garni and garlic; simmering, removing lobster flesh if used, returning crushed shell to the sauce; simmering and straining. **Coral**, if any, should be added before straining.

homard à la bordelaise *France* Lobster prepared as for **homard à l'américaine**, up to and including flaming; reduced white wine, fish stock, tomato sauce, a bouquet garni and seasoning added; cooked 15 minutes; meat removed and sauce prepared in the same way and finished with butter, lemon juice and chopped tarragon and chervil

homard à l'américaine *France* Lobster killed with a knife; chopped lobster tail and cracked claws seasoned, lightly fried with chopped shallots and garlic in oil and butter, flamed with brandy, then white wine, fish stock, meat glaze, **demi-glace** sauce, chopped tomato flesh, parsley and cayenne pepper added; cooked 15 minutes; lobster removed and meat reserved, coral and creamy parts of head added to cooking liquor; this reduced; butter added, the sauce strained and poured over the reserved lobster meat prior to serving

homard à l'armoricaine *France* Lobster cooked in oil with shallots, tomatoes, white wine and brandy (NOTE: From Brittany. There is controversy over the attribution of the name américaine or armoricaine to these lobster dishes which are essentially the same)

homard cardinal *France* Cooked lobster flesh arranged with a **salpicon** of chopped lobster flesh, cooked mushrooms, the creamy parts from the head and chopped truffle mixed with a little sauce cardinal, either in a dish or a halved lobster shell supported by the lobster claws; coated with sauce cardinal, sprinkled with grated cheese and butter and glazed under the grill

homard thermidor The sliced flesh from a grilled half lobster laid on cream sauce mixed with a little English mustard, coated with the same and glazed lightly in the oven or under the grill. Also called **lobster thermidor**

hom horm *Thailand* Shiitake mushroom (NOTE: Literally 'good smell'.)

hominy Dehusked whole dried maize kernels with the germ removed. Usually boiled in water with 1 teaspoonful of bicarbonate of soda per litre to dehusk and soften it, prior to drying or using in cooking. Also called **hulled corn**

hominy grits *United States* Coarsely ground dehusked maize kernels used to make a kind of porridge

homity pie *England* A shortcrust pastry pie from the Lake District filled with potato, onion, cheese, garlic, herbs and seasoning then baked

hom lek *Thailand* Shallots

homo *United States* Homogenized milk

homogenize, to To break down the dispersed phase of a two-phase mixture into such small droplets that they cannot separate out under gravity and thus form a stable emulsion. Fat globules in milk are treated in this way to give homogenized milk.

homogenized milk 1. *United Kingdom* Milk which has been homogenized so that the cream does not separate out. Sold in red-topped bottles. **2.** *United States* As the UK type but with 3.25% butterfat and 8.25% other milk solids

Homolky A ewes' milk cheese very similar to **Liptói**. See also **Gomolya**

homos Hummus

hon *Japan* High-quality or pure

höna *Sweden* A boiling or large older chicken

Honan cooking A style of Chinese cooking from the inland province of Honan which is northeast of Szechuan. It is highly spiced and often contains wine. Yellow river carp is a speciality of the region. Also called **Hunan cooking**

Hondashi *Japan* A trademark for instant **dashi** granules

høne *Denmark* Chicken

høne bryst *Denmark* Chicken breast, the white meat of chicken

hønekødsuppe *Denmark* Chicken and vegetable soup

honey Flower nectar partially digested and regurgitated by the honey bee, *Apis* *mellifera*, as a thick sugary syrup with a distinctive flavour. Used by bees as a convenient food source and food storage medium. Its flavour and aroma depend to some extent on the types of flower from which the nectar was obtained. Strict vegans should not eat honey.

honey-baked ham *United Kingdom* Ham baked in the oven whilst basting with honey and possibly brown sugar

honeybun *United States* A flat yeast-raised bread roll glazed with honey before baking

honeycomb The hexagonal wax storage chambers of the honey bee which are formed in stacked tiers and in which honey is stored. Honey can still be purchased in this form.

honeycomb mould A light dessert made by folding stiffly whisked egg white into a mixture of jelly and cold egg custard sauce. If the mixture of egg custard and jelly is warm prior to folding in the egg white, then it separates into a jelly layer topped by a fluffy mousse.

honeycomb tripe Tripe from the second stomach of an ox which has a honeycomb appearance

honeydew melon A slow ripening oval, i.e. rugby ball-shaped, variety of winter melon with a thick yellow to green ridged skin and firm pale green, sweet and delicately flavoured flesh. Not as sweet as some varieties but a good keeper.

honey fungus A fungus, *Armillaria mellea*, which is a garden pest and grows on live trees causing them to wilt and die. The cap is golden brown when young, becoming lighter as it ages. The slender stem curls out from a swollen base attached to the tree trunk. Although edible it has a bitter taste and unpleasant smell and is not recommended.

honey tangerine *United States* A mandarin/orange cross developed in Florida in 1913 and propagated by C Murcott Smith and J Ward Smith. It has a rather leathery peel and tough segment walls but the juice content is very high and it is sweet and well-flavoured. It is grown in Florida and Brazil and commands a premium price. Also called **Murcott tangerine**, **Smith tangerine**

hong chee *China* Persimmon

hong dow *China* Adzuki bean

hong dow sar *China* Sweet red bean paste

hong mei *China* Red rice

hongo *Spain* Fungus

hongroise, à la *France* In the Hungarian style, i.e. in a sauce flavoured with paprika or with onions, tomatoes, paprika and soured cream

hongroise, sauce *France* A velouté sauce flavoured with lightly fried onions and paprika. Served with freshwater fish, poultry and roast veal. Also called **Hungarian sauce**

hong-shao *China* Red cooking

hong yu *China* Red snapper

hong zao *China* Red rice

Honig *Germany* Honey

Honigkuchen *Germany* Honey cake made by the melting method from self-raising flour, honey, sugar and ground almonds (5:3:2:1) flavoured with lemon zest, cocoa powder, ground spices, candied peel and almond essence, thinned with a little water to a moderately stiff dough and baked at 175°C. The top is covered with almond flakes when it is removed from the oven. Best after maturing for several days.

honiglekach A Jewish New Year cake sweetened with honey. See also **lekach**

honing *Netherlands* Honey

honingkoek *Netherlands* Honey cake

honje *Indonesia* Torch ginger

honmirin *Japan* Mirin

honning *Norway* Honey

honningkake *Norway* Honey cake

hønsekødsuppe *Denmark* Chicken and vegetable soup

hønsesuppe *Denmark, Norway* Chicken soup

honshimeji *Japan* Oyster mushroom

hönssoppa *Sweden* Chicken soup

hontarako *Japan* Codfish roe, salted and dyed red to resemble caviar. See also **tarako**

honung *Sweden* Honey

hoo pla chalarm *Thailand* Shark's fin

hop A plant, *Humulus lupulus*, of the mulberry family with long twining stems bearing catkin-like flower clusters which when dried are used to give the bitter flavour to beer. The young shoots may be used as a vegetable.

Hopfen *Germany* Hops

Hopfenkäse *Germany* A type of soft cheese wrapped in hop leaves. See also **Nieheimer**

hop jeung gwa *China* Choko

Hoppelpoppel *Germany* Scrambled eggs with bacon and/or sausages and potatoes

hopper *Sri Lanka* A type of flat bread or pancake made with rice flour and coconut milk and deep-fried until crisp. See also **string hoppers**

hopping John *United States* A mixture of cooked rice and black-eyed peas

hop shoots The tender shoots of the hop plant used as a vegetable in France and Belgium

horapa *Thailand* Basil

horchata *Mexico, Spain* A summer drink made in Spain from ground tiger nuts (**chufas**) and in Mexico from ground rice or cantaloupe melon seeds

Hordeum vulgare *Botanical name* Barley

horenso *Japan* A delicate mild-flavoured variety of spinach with pink stems

horenso no sarada *Japan* Spinach leaves washed and cooked for 5 minutes until tender, wrung out, cut into shreds and dressed with pasty mixture of soya sauce, rice vinegar, toasted and crushed sesame seeds, a little dry mustard, minced spring onions, grated fresh ginger and schichimi togarishu

hor fun *China* Rice ribbon noodles

horiatiki *Greece* A Greek salad of cucumber, tomato, olives, onions and feta cheese with an olive oil and vinegar dressing

Hörnchen *Germany* Slightly sweet crescent-shaped rolls similar to croissants

horned melon Kiwano

horno, al *Mexico, Spain* Baked or roasted in the oven

horn of plenty A funnel-shaped edible fungus, *Craterellus cornucopioides*, with a grey exterior and brownish-black gills. Grows in beech woods. Also called **black trumpet**

horoku *Japan* A large earthenware plate with a fitted lid used for baking

hors d'oeuvre *England, France, Netherlands* Single cold food items, a selection of well-seasoned cold dishes or well-seasoned hot dishes usually served at the beginning of a meal but sometimes as snacks or with a buffet or cold table

horse An animal, *Equus caballus*, whose sweet-flavoured meat is eaten in many countries and used as a substitute for beef in many recipes. Not eaten in the UK and the USA.

horse bean See **field bean, jack bean**

horse clam A large (up to 1.5 kg) clam, *Thesus nuttalli*, from the Pacific Ocean with lean light-coloured meat. Generally fried but in Japan eaten raw.

horse gram The reddish brown, white, black or mottled seed of a legume, *Dolichos biflorus*, from India, which is rather wrinkled in appearance, similar to a chick pea, and rarely split. Eaten if there is nothing else but usually the whole plant is used as green manure or animal fodder. Also called **Madras gram, kulthi bean**

horse mackerel Various large fish of the mackerel family, *Trachurus trachurus*, *Decapterus punctatus* and others found in tropical and subtropical seas; with elongated bodies and large spiky scales. They do not have so good a flavour as mackerel. Also called **scad**

horse mushroom A wild edible mushroom, *Agaricus arvensis*, similar to the field mushroom. It has a cream to yellow cap and greyish gills and turns yellow when cut or broken giving off an aniseed smell.

horse mussel A large mussel, *Modiolus modiolus*, found throughout the North Atlantic. It has a purplish yellow shell and orange flesh which is not as well-flavoured as that of the common mussel.

horseradish A hardy invasive perennial plant, *Armoracia rusticana*, whose thick roots have a hot pungent white flesh which is grated for use in horseradish sauce. The young leaves have a similar but milder flavour and may be used in salads.

horseradish butter A compound butter made from grated horseradish pounded with 5 times its weight of butter and sieved

horseradish sauce Peeled and grated horseradish, mixed with vinegar, seasoning and lightly whipped cream. Served with roast beef, smoked trout and smoked eel. See also **Albert, sauce**. Also called **sauce raifort**

hortalizas *Spain* Green leaves cooked as a vegetable

hortelã pimenta *Portugal* Peppermint

hortobágyi rostélyos *Hungary* Beef steak braised with stock and bacon bits and served with a large semolina dumpling

ho see *China* Dried oysters

hoshi-shiitake *Japan* A close relative of the shiitake mushroom, *Cortinellus shiitake*, fawn to black in colour and available fresh or dried. Also called **winter mushroom, forest mushroom, Japanese black mushroom**

hostess *United States* The female person who greets guests when they enter a restaurant (NOTE: The male equivalent is called a greeter.)

hot and sour soup *China* A Pekinese soup or broth with vegetables, mushrooms, threads of egg, soya sauce, vinegar and spices including hot chillies. Thickened with corn flour to a runny consistency.

hotategai, hotate *Japan* Scallop, served raw in sushi or fried

hot bean paste See **chilli bean paste**

hot biscuit *United States* Scone

hot black bean sauce A sauce made from cooked black soya beans mashed with chillies, sesame oil, garlic, salt and sugar. Used as a flavouring.

hotchpotch A thin stew of lamb or mutton and vegetables similar to Irish stew

hot cross bun Originally called a cross bun and could be eaten on Good Friday without breaking the fast; now consisting of a yeast-raised enriched sweet bun flavoured with spices, currants and chopped candied peel, well glazed and with a cross formed on the top using a slack flour water mixture, pastry or by cutting a cross prior to proving. Eaten at Easter.

hot dog *United States* A hot poached or steamed North American frankfurter served in a long soft white bread roll with American mustard or other relish

hôtelière, à l' *France* In the hotelier's style, i.e. garnished with **beurre maître d'hôtel** and chopped fried mushrooms. Used especially of fish.

hotel rolls White crusty rolls, the tops of which are slashed after proving so that when baked the crust opens in a cross

hot fudge *United States* A hot topping for ice cream and desserts made with chocolate, butter and sugar

hot house cucumber *United States* Long cucumber

hot pepper Cayenne pepper

hot plate 1. A cast-iron or steel plate sometimes used as a cooking surface on electric or gas ranges in a similar way to a griddle **2.** See **chafing dish**

hotpot A casserole of meat or fish and vegetables baked in the oven with a topping of either sliced potatoes which become brown and crisp when done or a pastry crust. See also **Lancashire hotpot**

hot-smoke, to To smoke food at a temperature between 40 and 105°C thus cooking it at the same time. Food is usually cold-smoked first, and fish is restricted to 80°C.

hot water pastry A strong dense pastry used for hand raised meat pies made from flour, fat and water and/or milk (2:1:1) boiled together. Moulded whilst warm.

houblon *France* Hops

hough of beef Skink of beef

hough of pork *Scotland* The knuckle half of a leg of pork (*colloquial*)

hou goo *China* Oyster mushroom

houmous Hummus

houmus Hummus

household flour See **plain flour**

house lamb *United Kingdom* Milk-fed lamb

house leek A hardy evergreen perennial succulent, *Sempervivum tectorum*, which grows in clusters of rosettes on walls and roofs. The leaves are used in salads by the Dutch.

houtic *Netherlands* Houting, the fish

houting A freshwater white fish, *Coregonus oxyrhynchus* or *C. lavaretus*, from the northern rivers of Europe and Asia.

hovdessert *Sweden* Meringues with chocolate sauce and whipped cream, sometimes with chopped bananas and/or whipped cream

Hovis The name of bread made with Hovis flour

Hovis flour Flour milled by a process which preserves the wheat germ from degradation (NOTE: The name was derived from the Latin *hominis vis*, meaning 'strength of man'.)

howtowdie *Scotland* A dish of boiled chicken with poached eggs and spinach (NOTE: From the Old French *hutaudeau*, 'a pullet'.)

hoy kwai *China* Turtle

hoy lai *Thailand* Surf clam

hoy meng phu *Thailand* Asian mussel

hoy nangrom *Thailand* Oyster

ho yo jeung *China* Oyster

hrachová polevká *Czech Republic* Beef stock thickened with a white roux, simmered with onions, garlic and marjoram, mixed with a purée of yellow split peas, strained and garnished with diced fried pigs' ears, potatoes, croûtons and chopped parsley

hramsa *Scotland* A mixture of Scottish Cabroc cheese and double cream flavoured with chopped leaves of wild garlic (**ramsons**), served as a dessert or a dip

hrira *North Africa* A thick rich soup from Morocco which can be used as a meal in itself or as a starter. Often used to break the fast during Ramadan. It contains lamb, chicken giblets, chickpeas, lentils, rice or shariyya, onions, garlic, herbs and spices. It is thickened with flour, sometimes contains eggs and is finished with lemon juice.

Hrudka A ewes' milk cheese very similar to **Liptói**. See also **Gomolya**

hsien ts'ai *China* Chinese spinach

htamin *Burma* Rice

htamin lethoke *Burma* A platter or platters of cold, cooked long-grain rice, various types of noodles and vegetables served to guests who pick up a selection with their fingers and mix them in their own bowl with small amounts of sauces, condiments and other spicy or pungent accompaniments always using their fingers (NOTE: Literally 'finger-mixed rice'.)

huachinango *Mexico* Red snapper

hua daio *China* Red girl wine

hua hom *Thailand* Onion

hua jiao *China* Sichuan peppercorn

hua jiao you *China* Sichuan pepper oil

hua juan *China* Steamed bread rolls

huang chiu *China* Red girl wine

huang gwa *China* Cucumber
huang you *China* Butter
huang yu *China* Croaker, the fish
hua pak had *Thailand* Mooli
hua sheng *China* Peanuts
hua sheng you *China* Peanut oil
hua tiao *China* Red girl wine
hubbard squash A very warty-skinned winter squash, eaten at the green unripe stage as well as in the orange mature stage. Common in the USA.
hu chiao *China* Anise pepper
huchiao *China* Peppercorn
hucho A freshwater fish found in the rivers of northern Europe. Prepared like salmon. Also called **huck**
huck See **hucho**
huckleberry 1. Bilberry **2.** *United States* The fruit of a small bush, *Gaylussacia frondosa*, related to the blueberry. It is up to 1 cm in diameter and has a sweet and juicy flesh.
hueso *Spain* Bone
hueso medular *Spain* Marrow bone
hueva *Spain* Hard fish roe
huevos *Spain* Eggs
huevos a la flamenco *Spain* Eggs baked with chopped tomatoes, onions and ham and garnished with asparagus tips, red sweet peppers and slices of pork sausage
huevos al horno *Spain* Baked eggs
huevos al nido *Spain* Egg yolks cooked in small bread rolls and covered with white of egg (NOTE: Literally 'eggs in a nest'.)
huevos al plato *Spain* Shirred eggs
huevos al trote *Spain* Hard-boiled eggs, halved lengthways, egg yolks mixed with tuna fish and mayonnaise and replaced
huevos duros *Spain* Hard-boiled eggs
huevos escalfados *Spain* Shirred eggs
huevos medio cocidos *Spain* Poached eggs
huevos pasados por agua *Spain* Soft-boiled eggs
huevos revueltos *Spain* Scrambled eggs
huffed chicken *England* An old Sussex dish of stuffed chicken wrapped in suet pastry, decorated with pastry leaves, glazed and baked at 180°C until the internal temperature as measured with a meat thermometer is 80°C and finished at 220°C to brown the pastry if necessary
huff juff *United States* Baptist cake
huffkin *England* As Kentish huffkin but formed in large oval flat loaves weighing about 750 g
Huhn *Germany* Chicken
Hühnerbein *Germany* Chicken leg
Hühnerbraten *Germany* Roast chicken

Hühnerbrühe *Germany* Chicken broth
Hühnerbrust *Germany* Chicken breast
Hühnerklein *Germany* Chicken giblets
Huhn mit Käsesauce *Switzerland* Boiled chicken with cheese sauce
hui *China* Lengthy simmering of tough foods to tenderize them
huile *France* Oil
huile, à l' *France* Served with olive oil or other oil or with a dressing made from the same
huile blanche *France* Poppy seed oil
huile de colza *France* Rapeseed oil
huile de coton *France* Cottonseed oil
huile de noix *France* Walnut oil
huile de tournesol *France* Sunflower seed oil
huile d'olive *France* Olive oil
huile vierge *France* First pressing of oil bearing berries or seeds
huitlacoche *Mexico* An edible fungus, *Ustilago maydis*, which infects green maize cobs causing the kernels to grow large, black and deformed but with a pleasant taste
huître *France* Oyster, originally the European flat oyster
huître de claire *France* A fattened oyster. Also called **claire**
huître portugaise *France* Portuguese oyster
huîtres, sauce aux *France* **Sauce normande** with the addition of poached and bearded oysters. Used for poached fish.
huîtres Dubarry *France* Oysters served in potato cases
hu jiao miar *China* Pepper
huku *East Africa* The Tanzanian name for chicken
hull, to To remove the outer inedible covering of a fruit or seed or the remains of the flower calyx and stalk from berry fruits
hulled corn Hominy
Hülsenfrüchte *Germany* Pulses
hu luo bo *China* Carrots
hu ma *China* Sesame seed
humba *Philippines* A type of Spanish **estofado** but with vinegar and possibly bean curd
humble pie *England* A meat pie made from offal. Also called **umble pie** (NOTE: The name is derived from the old French *nombles* meaning edible entrails of a deer.)
Humbolt dressing *United States* A seasoned mixture of crab butter and mayonnaise used with crab meat
hummer *Denmark, Norway, Sweden* Lobster
Hummer *Germany* Lobster
hummer-kotletter *Sweden* Lobster cutlets made from hen lobster meat, coral, egg yolk and a little egg white, anchovy essence, seasoning, sugar and nutmeg, processed,

formed into cutlet shape, panéed and shallow-fried in butter. Served with melted butter and lobster coral.

Hummerkrabben *Germany* Large prawns

hummerstuvning *Sweden* Lobster stew. Cream and the water from making lobster butter made into a velouté and cooked out. Cut-up lobster meat, seasoning, ground cloves and a little brandy added, and the whole warmed but not boiled. Served as soon as the lobster meat is cooked through. Excessive cooking toughens the meat. (NOTE: Sometimes translated as lobster Newburg.)

hummus *Middle East* 1. A purée of cooked chick peas 2. An appetizer, dip or hors d'oeuvre made from cooked chick peas puréed with olive oil mixed with tahini, garlic paste and lemon juice, dressed with olive oil and garnished with chopped parsley. Often accompanied by black olives and pitta bread. See also **hummus-bi-tahina**. Also called **homos**, **houmous**, **houmous**, **humus**

hummus-bi-tahina *Middle East* The classic hummus of Syria made from soaked chick peas boiled and skimmed until tender with a little bicarbonate of soda added to the water, puréed with garlic and mixed with tahina paste equal to two thirds of the weight of the dry chick peas, chilli powder, ground cumin, lemon juice and salt. Garnished with olive oil, lemon juice, chopped parsley and cumin and a few whole cooked chick peas.

humpback salmon Pink salmon

Humulus lupulus *Botanical name* Hop

humus See **hummus**

Hunan Chinese province north of Kwantung, with a similar style of cuisine to Cantonese

hundreds and thousands Fine (up to 1mm in diameter) multicoloured strands or balls of sugar, used as a cake decoration. Also called **nonpareille**

hundredweight A measure of weight used for large quantities of goods. Now obsolete in the UK, but still used in the USA. In the UK it is equal to 112 lb and in the USA to 100 lb. Abbreviation **cwt**

hundred year egg Chinese preserved eggs

Hundshai *Germany* Larger spotted dogfish

hung *Vietnam* A type of mint

Hungarian butter See **beurre de paprika**

Hungarian goulash An authentic Hungarian stew containing cubed beef, fried onions, green sweet peppers, tomatoes, garlic, pasta, stock and caraway seeds. Not thickened. Also called **borgrács gulyas**

Hungarian millet Foxtail millet

Hungarian salami A well-spiced lightly smoked salami made from fatty pork. It keeps well and the flavour improves with age.

Hungarian sauce See **hongroise, sauce**

hung jo *China* Jujube

hung liu *China* Five spice powder

hung que *Vietnam* Mint

hungry rice A variety of millet, *Digitaria exilis*, important as a staple in the dry areas of West Africa

hung zao *China* Jujube

hunter's sauce See **chasseur, sauce**

hunter's sausage See **Jagdwurst**

Huntingdon fidget pie *England* Fidget pie

Huntsman *England* A speciality cheese from Melton Mowbray consisting of a layer of blue Stilton between two layers of double Gloucester

hun tun *China* Won ton wrappers

hunyadi töltöt *Hungary* An escalope of sirloin steak, covered with a mixture of butter creamed with egg yolk, chopped ham, sliced macaroni and stiffly beaten egg white, rolled and tied, seasoned, browned in lard, then stewed with a little brown stock, fried onion slices, thinly sliced sweet green peppers and plenty of paprika, with sour cream added at the half cooked stage

hunza Small wild apricots from the Himalayas with a delicious flavour. Usually traded in the dried form when they are pale brown and wrinkled. Ideal soaked and poached.

huo tui *China* Ham

hure *France* Head of pig or boar

hure de sanglier *France* Boar's head

hús *Hungary* Meat

Hushållsost *Sweden* A semi-soft, scalded-curd, pale and mild creamy cows' milk cheese shaped like a cylinder. It has a slightly open texture and some holes. Sometimes flavoured with cloves and cumin and covered in wax or plastic.

hush puppies *United States* Deep-fried dumplings from the southern states of the USA made from a cornmeal batter flavoured with onions and served with fried fish. Used to be thrown to dogs to keep them quiet.

husk 1. The outer bran layer of cereals and seeds 2. The empty shell of a nut

huss Dogfish

hussaini kabab *South Asia* Nuts and raisins formed into cylinders and coated with a bound minced beef, then pan fried or grilled

hussarde, à la *France* In the hussar's style, i.e. garnished with aubergines, stuffed potatoes, grated horseradish and possibly mushrooms. Used of joints of meat.

hussarde, sauce *France* Finely sliced onions and shallots, browned in butter, white wine added and reduced by half; **demi-glace** sauce, tomato purée, white stock, garlic, a bouquet garni and a piece of raw ham added; all simmered 30 minutes, strained, ham reserved and the sauce finished with finely chopped reserved ham, a little grated horseradish and chopped parsley. Served with grilled or spit-roasted meat.

hustler *United States* Baptist cake

hutch *United States* A sideboard or cupboard used for storing plates, napkins, cutlery etc.

hu tieu *Vietnam* White rice noodles about 3 mm wide. See also **banh pho**

hutspot *Netherlands* A type of Irish stew or hotpot of meat with carrots, onions and mashed potatoes

Hüttenkäse *Germany* Cottage cheese

Hutzelbrot *Germany* Fruit bread

huzarensla *Netherlands* Russian salad, a mayonnaise bound salad of diced meat, apples, beetroot and potatoes with pickles (NOTE: Literally 'Hussar's salad'.)

hvalk kjøtt *Norway* Whale meat

hveteboller *Norway* Sweet bread rolls

hvid *Denmark* White

hvide bønner *Denmark* Kidney beans

hvidløg *Denmark* Garlic

hvidløgssmør *Denmark* Garlic butter

hvidvinssovs *Denmark* White wine sauce

hvit *Norway* White

hvitkålsalat *Norway* Coleslaw

hvitløk *Norway* Garlic

hvitting *Norway* Whiting, the fish

hyacinth bean A warm climate legume, *Lablab purpureus*, from India now cultivated worldwide. The whole pods which range in colour from green to purple may be treated as French beans when young or the dried beans which are brown with a white hilum may be used as a pulse. The beans must be well boiled before eating. They may also be sprouted in the dark for bean sprouts. Also called **Egyptian bean, lablab bean, dolichos bean, bonavista bean, black bean**

hydrochloric acid The acid secreted in the stomach which maintains the pH of the contents around 2, thus inhibiting or killing bacteria and helping with the breakdown of food. A permitted food additive, E507, in the UK.

hydrogen A highly inflammable light gas occasionally used in sealed packaging, more often for hydrogenating vegetable and fish oils in order to harden them

hydrogenated glucose syrup A modified glucose syrup used in sugar free confectionery

hydrogenation The process of chemically combining hydrogen with unsaturated oils and soft fats to make them more saturated and harder. Used to make margarine and lard substitutes from oils. Doubts are being cast on the wholesomeness of the resulting hard fats many of which have no natural analogs.

hydrogen sulphites Salts similar to the sulphites but containing a higher proportion of sulphur dioxide, used as food preservatives in the food industry. Those permitted are sodium hydrogen sulphite, E222, and calcium hydrogen sulphite, E227.

hydrolysed protein Protein which has been broken down into smaller subunits (**peptides**) by treatment with water at high temperature and pressure or other hydrolysing agents. This produces highly flavoured compounds as in yeast and meat extracts and also occurs during fermentation of proteins (soya sauce, **miso**, tempeh, etc.) and to a limited extent when cooking proteins.

hydrolysis The reaction of water molecules with other compounds, usually to break them down into smaller subunits and requiring the action of acids, enzymes or long heating. It is used e.g. to convert starch into simpler sugars and is the process which occurs when starch solutions and sauces are thinned by boiling them too long.

hydrometer A short stubby cylinder surmounted with a long graduated tube. The whole is sealed and weighted so that it floats upright in a liquid always displacing its own mass of liquid thus indicating by the depth to which it sinks the density or specific gravity of the liquid. Used for measuring alcohol, salt and sugar concentrations in solution.

hygiene The general term for those procedures and practices which prevent the transmission of disease between and to humans, the multiplication of harmful microorganisms in the body or environment and the accumulation of dirt, poisons and toxins where they could be harmful to living creatures

hygroscopic Describes a substance that absorbs water from the atmosphere without necessarily showing any signs of damp, e.g. silica gel which is used to maintain a dry atmosphere over some foods

hylderbærsuppe *Denmark* Elderberry soup

hyoshigi-giri *Japan* Baton cut for root vegetables. Also called **clapper cut**

hyphae The filaments and fungal strands which make up the main mass of fungi and from which fruiting bodies, e.g. mushrooms, sprout. Quorn is an example of a food made from hyphae.

hyse *Norway* Haddock

hysope *France* Hyssop

hyssop A hardy semi-evergreen shrub, *Hyssopus officinalis*, whose leaves can be used in small amounts to flavour game, pâtés, soups, lamb stews and fruits

Hyssopus officinalis *Botanical name* Hyssop

iabloko Apple

iablonnik *Russia* A cold apple soup made from peeled and cored finely chopped cooking apples simmered until soft with sugar and cloves, cooled, the cloves removed and the soup flavoured with vanilla extract

iachmen *Russia* Barley

iachmennyi khleb *Russia* Yeast raised barley bread made with barley flour and wheat flour (2:3), milk, a little honey and yeast, kneaded and proved in the usual way and baked at 200°C for 15 minutes reducing to 180°C until cooked

iahnie de ciuperci *Romania* Chopped onions fried lightly in oil followed by sliced mushrooms until all browned, **tomato concassée** or purée, seasoning and chopped dill added and all served cold

iahnie de fasole *Romania* Cooked navy or haricot beans mixed whilst hot with sliced fried onions, oil, lemon juice, seasoning and chopped dill and served cold

iaika minsky *Russia* Halved hard-boiled eggs filled with the yolks mashed with mayonnaise, double cream, chopped dill and parsley and paprika and mixed with chopped white of egg, the filled eggs sprinkled with breadcrumbs and grated cheese, decorated with crossed anchovy fillets and baked for 10 minutes at 200°C and served warm. Also called **jajka minsky**

iaitsa po-russki *Russia* Hard-boiled eggs, halved, the yolks blended with English and French mustard, seasoning and finely chopped gherkins and spring onion, the mixture returned to the eggs and decorated with paprika and capers. See also **eggs à la russe**

i'a lawalu Fish baked in taro leaves, a speciality of Hawaii

iarpakh dolmasy *Russia* Vine leaves stuffed with a filling of soaked bulgur, fried chopped onions and minced lamb with pine nuts, currants, chopped dried apricots, lemon juice and herbs, casseroled in chicken stock for 40 minutes and served cold with cinnamon-flavoured yoghurt and lemon wedges

iben *North Africa* The highly prized buttermilk left after making zebda

ibu roti *Malaysia* Khamir

ice Frozen water sometimes used in place of water where intense agitation or prolonged processing might overheat a mixture. The energy necessary to melt ice would heat the same mass of water by 80°C. Also used for cooling.

ice, to To cover or decorate cakes, biscuits, buns, etc. with icing

iceberg lettuce A crisphead, tightly packed ball lettuce with the outer leaves removed and with little flavour. Ideal for shredding or for a chiffonade.

icebox pie *United States* A pie with a filling which is chilled or frozen to make it firm

ice cream A flavoured, sweetened and coloured mixture of (egg) custard and cream (substitute) rapidly frozen to a stiff paste to avoid the formation of large detectable ice crystals. Used as a dessert and for many made up desserts.

ice cream sundae Individual portions of ice cream topped with canned or fresh fruit, whipped cream, chocolate or other sweet sauce and chopped nuts. Used for a dessert.

iced fancies Small sponge cakes completely covered with flavoured fondant icing and decorated

ice-glaze, to To add a thin layer of ice to frozen food by spraying with or dipping in water. It is said to preserve freshness and flavour but is usually used to increase apparent weight. Common with frozen prawns.

Iceland moss An edible lichen, *Cetraria islandica*, resembling a dark carragheen from mountainous and arctic regions. It grows to 1.2 m in length and is prepared by soaking it in boiling water with sodium bicarbonate to remove the bitter flavour, then soaking in water overnight. Used like carragheen or may be dried and ground to make a flour.

Iceland scallop A small species of scallop, *Chlamys islandica*, fished in the northern Atlantic

iceplant A sprawling succulent plant, *Mesambryanthemum crystallinum*, whose fleshy leaves and young stems may be used raw in salads or cooked like spinach

ichiban dashi *Japan* The first infusion in making dashi. See also **dashi**

ichigo *Japan* Strawberries

ichimi *Japan* Flaked red peppers

icho-giri *Japan* A quarter round cut of vegetables, especially large and tapering root vegetables. Also called **ginkgo leaf cut**

icing A paste formed from icing sugar and water with possible additions of lemon juice, egg white, glycerine, colouring and flavouring, used to coat cakes and buns, etc. for decorative purposes. See also **American frosting, glacé icing, fondant, royal icing, transparent icing**

icing bag See **piping bag**

icing sugar Very finely ground sugar with no particles larger than 0.1 mm (100 microns) used to make icing, to dredge desserts and cakes, etc. for decoration, and to make some confectionery items

ICMSF The International Commission on Microbiological Standards for Foods which sets standards for assigning foods to various classes of health hazard ranging from case 1, no health hazard and low incidence of spoilage, to case 15, severe and direct health hazard possibly influenced by conditions of handling

iç pilav *Turkey* A pilaf made from round short-grain rice, fried onions and pine nuts, chopped lamb's liver, currants, tomato, cinnamon and seasoning, braised in water in the oven in a covered dish. Also called **Turkish pilaf**

Idiazabal *Spain* A smoked ewes' milk cheese from the Basque country. It is firm with a few holes and has a mild smoky flavour. Also called **aralar, urbasa, urbia**

idli *South Asia* Small steamed cakes served with spices, coconut or other flavourings as an accompaniment to a main dish. Made from a batter of rice flour and urad dhal which has been left to ferment overnight.

iets vooraf *Netherlands* Appetizer

ifisashi *East Africa* A vegetarian greens in peanut sauce from Zambia. The sauce is made from ground peanuts or natural peanut butter, chopped onion and tomato boiled vigorously in water before adding the chopped greens and simmering until cooked.

igat *Philippines* Eel

igname *France, Italy* Yam

Igny *France* A mild cows' milk cheese made in the shape of a disc, from the abbey of the same name in Champagne

iguana A large lizard, *Iguana iguana*, up to 2 m long from Central and South America with white tender mild-flavoured meat generally more expensive than beef or fish

ijs *Netherlands* **1.** Ice **2.** Ice cream

ika *Japan* Cuttlefish and squid, used raw in sushi

ikan alu-alu *Indonesia* Barracuda

ikan bawal hitam *Indonesia* Black pomfret, the fish

ikan bawal putih *Indonesia* White pomfret, the fish

ikan berinti *Malaysia* Stuffed fish

ikan bilis *Malaysia* Small fish such as anchovy and similar, cooked, dried in the sun then deep-fried. Used as an addition to other dishes. Also called **ikan teri**

ikan karau *Indonesia* A fish similar to salmon

ikan kembung *Indonesia* A fish similar to a small bonito

ikan merah *Indonesia* Snapper or bream

ikan merah puchat *Indonesia, Malaysia* Snapper or bream

ika no surimi *Japan* Minced squid. Also called **surimi-ika**

ikan teri *Indonesia, Malaysia* Ikan bilis

ikan terubuk *Indonesia* Herring

ikra *Russia* Caviar

ikura *Japan* The large (0.5 cm diameter) orange-red eggs of salmon. Often used in sushi. Also called **caviar pearls, keta caviar, salmon caviar**

ilama A custard apple, *Anona diversifolia*, growing in lowland tropics and similar to the **cherimoya**

Ilchester *England* A beer and garlic-flavoured Cheddar cheese

îles flottantes *England, France* A thin egg custard topped with spoonfuls of poached meringue mixture and finished with a sprinkling of crushed praline or caramel. Served cold.

Ilha *Portugal* A Cheddar-type cows' milk cheese from the Azores (NOTE: Literally 'island'.)

illawara plum *Australia* The purple-black fruit of an ancient pine, *Podocarpus elatus*, grape-sized and semi-sweet with the seeds, which are easily broken off, growing on the outside. They have a rich flavour with a slightly resinous quality and a refreshing aftertaste. The slight bitterness is intensified if cooked in aluminium. May be used as fresh fruit or in desserts and with meat.

Illicium verum *Botanical name* Star anise

illipe butter *South Asia* A soft yellow oil extracted from the seeds of the Indian butter tree. See also **mowra butter**

illustrierte Salatgurke *Germany* A compound salad of sliced pickled cucumbers alternated with slices of Emmenthal and anchovy fillets garnished with ham cornets filled with capers and halved hard-boiled eggs

imam bayaldi *Middle East* A Syrian salad based on aubergines

imamdusta *South Asia* A ceramic mortar used for grinding soft grains and spices using a matching pestle (**daanti**)

imbalagha *East Africa* A fish dish accompanied with bananas from the Lake Malawi region of Tanzania

imbiancare *Italy* To blanch

Imbiss *Germany* Snack

imbottini delizia *Italy* Paupiettes of veal stuffed with ham, cheese and truffle shavings

imbottito *Italy* Stuffed

imbrecciata *Italy* A chick pea, bean and lentil soup from Umbria

imbriaco *Spain* Red mullet, *Mullus barbatus*

imitation caviar A product made from the hard female roe of some types of fish just before spawning. It is washed, sieved to remove fibre, salted (1:6 or less on roe), kept 2 to 3 days, drained, surface dried and pressed into jars. It goes under names such as lumpfish caviar, German caviar, etc.

imli *South Asia* Tamarind

impanato *Italy* Panéed or coated with bread crumbs

impastare *Italy* To knead

impastoiata *Italy* A mixture of polenta and beans from Umbria served with a tomato sauce

impératrice, à l' *France* The name given to enriched dishes and cakes, e.g. riz à l'impératrice

imperial agaric Ovoli

impériale, à l' *France* In the imperial style, i.e. used of chicken garnished with foie gras, mushrooms and cockscombs or kidneys

inada *Japan* The young of the fish yellowtail (Japanese amberjack), *Serriola quinqueradiata*. See also **hamachi**

inaka-miso *Japan* A red coloured **miso** usually made with barley as the added grain. May be sweet or salty. Used in soups and stews. Also called **sendai-miso**, **red miso**

inari *Japan* A sushi product

inari-zushi *Japan* A sushi packed into a deep-fried bean curd pouch (an **abura-age**)

Incanestrato A semi-hard scalded-curd Sicilian cheese. See also **Canestrato**

incasciata *Italy* A mixture of noodles, chopped hard-boiled eggs and shredded meat

incassettato *Italy* Encased, e.g. in pastry

incir *Turkey* Figs

incise, to To cut deep slits in raw food, e.g. to aid penetration of a marinade or tenderizer or to insert garlic, herbs or spices

inconnu *Canada, United States* A white fleshed oily freshwater fish, *Leucichthys mackenzii*, with a protruding lower jaw, from the great lakes of Canada. It has a silver grey back and white underside and weighs up to 4 kg. Use as salmon.

incubation period The time following the introduction of a microorganism into a host (i.e. food or a person) during which it establishes itself and grows without visible signs or effects

Indian bread *United States* Cornmeal bread

Indian butter tree A tree, *Madhuca indica* and *M. longifolia*, from central India. The dried flowers are used as food and the seeds are the source of **mowra butter**.

Indian corn *United States* An alternative name for the maize which is generally known in the USA as corn

Indian cress Nasturtium

Indian date Tamarind

Indian dill A plant, *Anethum sowa*, similar to the European dill but with longer and narrower seeds and a slightly different flavour

Indianerkrapfen *Austria* A light pastry dipped in chocolate and filled with whipped cream

Indian fig Prickly pear

Indian jujube Jujube

Indian lotus Lotus

Indian millet Common millet

Indian mustard Brown mustard seed

Indian nut Pine nut

Indian oyster A small rectangular-shaped oyster, *Crassostrea cucullata*, with a pink margin on its black shell, found throughout the coasts of Southeast Asia and Japan. Usually cooked by simmering, e.g. in kaki-miso, or quick frying and using in filled omelettes.

Indian pear Prickly pear

Indian pudding *United States* A traditional pudding made from cornmeal, milk, butter, treacle, eggs and spices. Similar to hasty pudding.

Indian rice Wild rice

Indian spinach See **amaranth 1**, **Ceylon spinach**

Indian sweet lime See **sweet lime**

indienne, à l' *France* In the Indian style, i.e. highly spiced, etc.

indienne, sauce *France* Currie à l'indienne, sauce

indigo carmine A synthetic blue food colouring. Also called **indigotine**. See also **E142**

indigotine See **indigo carmine**

indisches Ragoutpulver *Germany* Curry powder

indivia belga *Italy* Belgium chicory

indmad *Denmark* 1. Giblets 2. Offal

indring *Indonesia* Hairy basil

induction period The time during which foodstuffs such as fats are protected by additives such as antioxidants before they begin to deteriorate

indura bread *East Africa* A teff grain sour dough raised bread from Ethiopia made in the form of a spiral flat pancake

indyeika *Russia* Turkey

infarinata *Italy* A Tuscan dish of polenta cooked with beans, bacon and cabbage, cooled and eaten cold or sliced and fried

infiammato *Italy* Flambéed

infra-red That portion of the electromagnetic spectrum which is used in cooking to transfer heat by radiation from a hot surface to the food as in a grill, barbecue, electric or halogen hob

infuse, to To bring a liquid into contact with some food, herb or spice so as to transfer aroma, taste and soluble components to the liquid from which the solid material is strained. e.g. brewing of coffee or tea, extraction of vanilla from a pod and of aromatics from a bouquet garni

infuser A small perforated closed container which allows boiling water to come into contact with tea, herbs, spices, etc. thus extracting flavour from the solid

ingee *South Asia* Ginger

ingefaer brød *Denmark* Gingerbread

ingefära *Sweden* Ginger

ingemaakte vruchten *Netherlands* Canned fruit

ingen *Japan* Runner beans

inguru *Sri Lanka* Ginger

Ingwer *Germany* Ginger

Ingwerbrot *Germany* Gingerbread

Ingwerkuche *United States* A ginger cake introduced by Dutch immigrants to Pennsylvania

inhame *Portugal* Yam

inihaw *Philippines* Grilled on skewers over a heat source

injera *Africa* A round, sour-tasting flat bread from East Africa resembling pitta bread, made from millet flour, yeast and water using the sourdough method. It has the texture of tripe and is eaten with stews.

ink cap See **shaggy ink cap**

inkfish Squid

inkokt ål *Sweden* Boiled eel often served cold at the smörgåsbord. Made from pieces of skinned eel simmered in a white wine court bouillon for 25 minutes.

inky-pinky *Scotland* A kind of stew of leftovers made with beef stock thickened with corn flour and heated with cold roast beef which has been trimmed of all fat and gristle. Cooked carrots and cooked button onions are added together with seasoning and 25 ml of vinegar per litre of stock. Served with small squares or triangles of toast (**sippets**).

inlagd gurka *Sweden* Thinly sliced cucumber marinated in vinegar, sugar and water, drained and served with a garnish of chopped dill and parsley

inlagd sill *Sweden* Salt herring soaked in water for at least 12 hours, washed and drained, cleaned, boned and filleted and marinated in vinegar and water (5:2), sugar, white pepper, bay leaves and sliced shallots. Served with the marinade coloured with beetroot juice.

innards Internal organs of an animal especially in the abdominal cavity. Also called **guts**, **viscera**

inosine 5'-disodium phosphate See **E631**

inositol A water-soluble carbohydrate which is found in fruits and cereals either free or combined. It has a role in fat metabolism and also appears to be essential for the transmission of nerve impulses as the concentration in nerves is much higher than in the blood and is correlated with the speed of response, since both decline with age. It is also a major constituent of human semen. It has no known toxicity.

insaccati *Italy* Sausages (*colloquial*) (NOTE: Literally 'in a bag'.)

insalata *Italy* Salad

insalata alla moda d'alba *Italy* A salad of asparagus, celery and truffles

insalata capricciosa *Italy* A salad made from a **julienne** of celeriac, ham, tongue and mushrooms bound with mayonnaise

insalata composta *Italy* Salade composée

insalata cotta e cruda *Italy* A salad of mixed cooked vegetables and raw salad greens

insalata di mare *Italy* Seafood salad

insalata di rinforzo *Italy* A salad of anchovies, capers and olives, topped up daily with the same or similar items as part is consumed

insalata mista *Italy* Mixed salad

insalata paesana *Italy* A peasant salad of potatoes, eggs and vegetables, all cooked and cooled

insalata russa *Italy* Russian salad

insalata siciliana *Italy* Stuffed tomatoes with anchovies

insalata verde *Italy* Green salad, usually of only one type of leaf

insalatine *Italy* Salad greens

insalatone *Italy* A mixed salad of cooked vegetables

insolation A method of drying food by exposing it to the sun. Used for meat, fish and fruit.

instant flour *United States* Wheat flour processed to make it easily soluble in hot or cold liquids

instant food Food which has been prepared and dehydrated in such a way that it is immediately useable on adding (boiling) water. Coffee, tea, soup and noodles are typical examples.

instant rice See **precooked rice**

integrale *Italy* Wholemeal, bread, flour, etc.

integument The barrier around natural food items such as egg shell and vegetable or fruit peel, which provides a barrier to microbial invasion of the food

intercosta *Italy* A small entrecôte steak

interiora *Italy* Offal, innards

interlard, to *United States* Lard, to

international kidney Jersey royal

International Library of Gastronomy A library of over 3,500 rare books related to cooking and gastronomy from the 14th to the 19th century assembled by Arazio Bagnasco in Lugano Switzerland. Address: Bibliothèque Internationale de Gastronomie, Casella Postale 33, 6924 Soprengo (Lugano) Switzerland.

intestines That part of an animal's digestive system between the last stomach and the rectum which forms a tube or in some cases a blind sac. After cleaning, they may be used as sausage casings, eaten after preparation or incorporated into manufactured foods. See also **chitterlings, andouille, casings**

intingolo *Italy* 1. Sauce or gravy 2. Tasty dish 3. Stew

inulin A fructo-oligosaccharide added to some breakfast cereals targeted at children's parents. It is a prebiotic and is selectively metabolized by, thus encouraging the growth of, probiotic bacteria in the colon.

in umido *Italy* 1. Braised 2. Stewed

invernengo *Italy* Parmesan cheese made during the winter, from December to March. See also **Parmigiano Reggiano**

invertase An enzyme obtained from *Saccharomyces cerevisiae* that is used to prevent granulation in thick sugar syrups and fondants

invert sugar Simple sugars (**monosaccharides**) whose configuration has been changed by heat, enzyme or acid treatment so that they will not crystallize and will prevent other sugars from crystallizing

involtini *Italy* Slices of meat, ham and cheese rolled together and served in broth

involtini di vitello *Italy* Paupiettes of veal stuffed and cooked as beef olives

involtino *Italy* A roll or roulade (not bread)

iodine A trace element required for health especially of the thyroid gland, now included in iodized salt but available particularly from shell fish, seawater fish and seaweed

iodized salt Salt to which potassium iodide or iodate (a source of iodine) is added in order to overcome any deficiencies of iodine in the diet, especially in certain parts of the country where iodine is not present in the soil or drinking water

ionizing radiation Electromagnetic radiation which causes chemical changes in materials through which it passes, in particular ionization of compounds and production of short-lived free radicals which cause the death of living organisms. It is used for the sterilization of food in hermetically sealed packs, for the reduction in amount of spoilage flora on perishable foods, for the elimination of pathogens in foods, for the control of infestation in stored cereals, for the prevention of sprouting of root vegetables in storage and for retardation of the development of picked mushrooms (e.g. opening of the caps). Unfortunately there is no current legislation requiring the labelling of foods so treated.

iota *Italy* A slowly cooked soup from the northeast. See also **jota**

Ipomoea aquatica *Botanical name* Swamp cabbage

Ipomoea batatas *Botanical name* The sweet potato plant

Ipomoea reptans *Botanical name* Swamp cabbage

ippoglosso *Italy* Flounder

Iraty *France* A strong cheese from the Basque county made from a mixture of cows' and ewes' milk. The flavour depends on the proportions of each milk which in turn depends on the season.

Iraty brebis pyrénées *France* A semi-hard ewes' milk cheese from the Basque region, made in 4 to 5 kg cylinders. It is matured for 3 months and has a golden mellow tasting paste with small holes. Farm produced cheeses have AOC status.

iri dori *Japan* A chicken casserole made from pieces of skinned chicken breast, reconstituted shiitake mushroom caps, carrot and bamboo shoot, browned in oil then simmered in **dashi**, **mirin** and sugar for 10 minutes. Soya sauce is added and the cooking liquor reduced to a quarter. Peas, sliced onions, cauliflower or any other quickly cooked vegetables are added and cooked a further 3 minutes.

irio *East Africa* A Kenyan dish of beans or peas soaked and cooked then boiled with plantains or greens, potatoes and maize kernels, mashed with butter, seasoned and flavoured with herbs and/or spices. Also called **kienyegi**

Irish moss Carragheen

Irish potato cake *Ireland* A paste of mashed potatoes, flour, butter and salt rolled out to 8 – 10 mm, cut into triangles and fried until brown on both sides. Also called **fadge**

Irish soda bread See **soda bread**

Irish stew *Ireland, England* A stew or casserole of cheap cuts of lamb on the bone with waxy potatoes, onions and seasoning, once popular in the North of England and Northern Ireland

Irish Swiss cheese Blarney

irlandaise, à l' *France* In the Irish style, i.e. with potatoes

irlandisches Moos *Germany* Carragheen

iron A trace element vital for many body processes especially formation of haemoglobin in the blood. Available in meat, offal, fish, cereals, pulses and vegetables. Vitamin C ingested at the same time as iron-containing foods facilitates absorption in the gut.

iron hydroxide Various hydrated iron oxides of which ordinary rust is the common example. When finely ground they can be used as a brown food colouring. See also **E172**

iron oxide Various combinations of iron and oxygen which when finely ground have colours ranging from yellow through brown to black and are used as a food colouring and source of iron. See also **E172**

iron rations Emergency food of high calorific value for a given weight, especially high-fat, high protein, chocolate, etc. Often dehydrated or tinned so that they will keep for years for use in emergencies

irradiate, to To treat food with ionizing radiation in order to kill all microorganisms and insects in fruits, cereals, pulses, dried fruits and the like. It also prevents sprouting of roots and tubers. It does not destroy toxins or viruses and may cause chemical changes in the food. Often used to preserve sealed packs of food and to increase the shelf life of perishables. Since no laws govern the labelling of irradiated food it is impossible to know whether it has been treated in this way. Some authorities consider it a dangerous practice.

is *Denmark, Norway, Sweden* Ice

iscas *Portugal* Casserole, a typical one might be tripe with white beans and sausages in a cream sauce

iscas de figado *Portugal* Thinly sliced calves' liver marinated in oil, wine, chopped onion and garlic overnight, drained, dried and fried in small batches in oil for 2 minutes, reserved, then served with the pan residues deglazed with the marinade and reduced by half

ischiana, all' *Italy* In the style of Ischia, i.e. stewed in oil and white wine with tomatoes and herbs

Ischler biscuits Ischlertörtchen

Ischlertörtchen *Austria, Germany* Rich round buttery biscuits made with a mixture of ground almonds and flour sandwiched in pairs with red jam and covered with chocolate icing

ise ebi *Japan* Lobster

isinglass 1. An extract from the buoyancy bladders of fish used to clarify liquids especially wine. Can be used as a gelling agent. **2.** A solution of sodium silicate in water used to preserve eggs by its reaction with the shell which makes it impervious to air

iskembe çorbasi *Turkey* Tripe soup flavoured with lemon juice, garlic and vinegar and thickened with a liaison of egg yolks and cream

Islay *Scotland* A miniature Dunlop cheese suitable for melting. When mature eaten for dessert.

Islay scollops *Scotland* Scallops, cut in half if very thick, dipped in seasoned flour and fried in butter for 2 to 3 minutes per side then served with browned butter and lemon juice

isleta bread *United States* A bread shaped like a bear's paw, made by Pueblo Indians

is longus *Italy* A Sardinian dish of the grilled or spit-roasted intestines of cattle

isomalt A modified malt sugar used in sugar-free confectionery and as an extender in some foods

isopropyl alcohol A solvent used for food colours and flavourings and in glass cleaners

issopo *Italy* Hyssop

isterband *Sweden* A skinless sausage made with minced beef and pork mixed with parboiled barley and possibly mashed potato, salt-cured and air-dried. May be hot smoked. Split and fried or grilled and served with fried onion and pickled beetroot.

ita-kamaboko *Japan* A Japanese fish cake formed on a small rectangle of wood and often grilled or coloured brown. See also **kamaboko**

Italian bread sticks See **grissini**

Italian brine A sausage curing solution consisting of equal parts of water and white wine, fully saturated with salt and with 17 g of saltpetre and 8 g of bicarbonate of soda per litre

Italian broccoli Calabrese

Italian meringue mixture Sugar syrup boiled to the soft ball stage (115°C) then beaten into egg whites until soft and peaky

Italian millet Foxtail millet

Italian parsley Flat parsley

Italian red onion An oval-shaped onion somewhat smaller then the globe with a red tinge to the flesh and a mild, almost sweet flavour. It makes an attractive garnish when cut in rings. Whitens on cooking. Also called **red onion**

Italian sandwich *United States* Hoagie

Italian sauce See **italienne, sauce**

Italian sausage *United States* A type of pork sausage which may be spicy or sweet

Italian white truffle A smooth beige-pink truffle, *Tuber magnatum*, with a stronger aroma than the French black truffle. Best left uncooked.

Italico A generic term for a variety of quick ripening cheeses started with *Streptococcus thermophilus* and ripened for 20 to 30 days. **Bel Paese** is a well known example. Usually contain 51% water, 25% fat and 21% protein.

italienne, à l' *France* In the Italian style, i.e. with pasta, cheese, mushrooms, tomatoes and sometimes artichokes

italienne, sauce *France* 1. A mixture of **demi-glace**, duxelles, chopped lean ham and **tomato concassée** simmered and finished with chopped parsley, chervil and tarragon. Served with fried lamb or veal. 2. A cold sauce of poached brains, puréed, strained and mixed with a lemon juice mayonnaise, seasoning and finely chopped parsley. Served with cold meats.

Ital nut soup *Caribbean* A typical Rastafarian dish made from shelled and roasted peanuts blended with vegetable stock and coconut milk and flavoured with allspice, chilli pepper and garlic

Ital restaurant *Caribbean* A Rastafarian restaurant in which the food is completely meat free and theoretically salt free in accordance with Rastafarian teaching

Ital stew *Caribbean* A vegetarian stew made with pumpkin, yams, breadfruit, sweet potato and cassava, cut into chunks and boiled in vegetable stock and coconut milk flavoured with onion, garlic, chilli pepper, allspice, chives and thyme. Banana and plantain pieces are added just before service, and it is usually served with dumplings.

itami-udon *Japan* Soft-fried noodles. Udon noodles boiled in salted water until al dente, drained, refreshed, redrained and oiled, mixed in the frying pan with grated carrot, shredded Chinese cabbage and diced sweet pepper, which have all been fried in oil flavoured with chopped garlic and ginger, and all fried gently whilst being stirred. Seasoned and sprinkled with soya sauce before serving.

itik *Malaysia* Duck

ito *Japan* A prefix meaning 'cut in fine strips'

ito-kezuri-katsuo *Japan* Fine pink thread-like shavings of dried Pacific bonito flesh used as a garnish

ito-konnyaku *Japan* Thinly sliced **konnyaku**

ito-zukuri *Japan* A type of cut for small fish used for sashimi rather like a **julienne**, 5 cm by 3 mm square

ivoire, sauce *France* **Suprême sauce** with meat glaze added to give an ivory colour. Used with boiled chicken. Also called **ivory sauce**

ivory egg A rare variety of plum tomato with a pale golden yellow skin which contains no lycopene. This may make it suitable for those allergic to the red fruit. Available in the USA but rare in Europe due to EU regulations.

ivory sauce See **ivoire, sauce**

ivy gourd Tindoori

iwashi *Japan* Sardines

iwashi no tsumire jiru *Japan* Sardine balls made with fresh, skinned sardine fillets processed with **miso**, ginger and flour. These are poached in water until they rise then reserved, the cooking liquor strained, salted, flavoured with soya sauce, the cooked sardine balls and cooked turnip slices added and the soup served at once with a lemon peel garnish.

iyokan *Japan* A naturally occurring hybrid of *Citrus* spp. as yet relatively unknown outside Japan.

izer cookie *United States* A biscuit baked in a mould with various figures and designs embossed in it

izmir köftesi *Turkey* A mixture of chopped raw mutton, soaked white breadcrumbs, eggs, onion juice, seasoning and nutmeg, shaped into long rolls, fried in butter then simmered in tomato purée and water

J KLMNOP

ja *China* Deep-frying

jääpalanen *Finland* (Piece of) ice

jäätellö *Finland* Ice cream

jabalí *Spain* Wild boar

jabuke u rumo *Balkans* Apples poached in syrup, chilled and topped with whipped cream, glacé cherries and a little rum (NOTE: From Slovenia)

jachtschotel *Netherlands* A casserole of meat, potatoes and onions, a hunter's dish

jack 1. Crevalle jack **2.** See **Monterey Jack**

jack bean A perennial legume, *Canavalia ensiformis*, from tropical America, also grown in the southern USA. It has edible white beans which require boiling to destroy toxins and the immature pods can be eaten as a vegetable. Also called **horse bean**

jack-by-the-hedge Garlic mustard

jacket potato Washed, cleaned and dried potatoes with skin on, pricked with a fork and baked in an oven, in hot ashes or on a barbecue with or without a covering of aluminium foil until the flesh is soft. Often served cut open with some kind of filling.

jackfish Pike

jackfruit The Malaysian fruit of a tree, *Artocarpus heterophyllus* or *A. integrifolia*, which can take up to six months to ripen from picking. The fruit is large (up to 32 kg) with a yellow to brown spiky skin and yellow fibrous flesh. The juicy pulp surrounding the large white seeds is eaten and tastes like a mixture of banana and pineapple, the seeds may be dried and roasted or ground and the fibrous flesh is sometimes boiled or baked as a vegetable. The flowers and young leaf shoots are used in salads and as a vegetable. Also called **jakfruit**

Jacobean potatoes Potatoes roasted in their skins

Jacobsmuschel *Germany* Coquille Saint-Jacques. See also **Pilgermuschel**

Jaffa orange Shamouti

jagaimo *Japan* Potato

Jagdwurst *Germany* Hunter's sausage. A large **Brühwurst** of diced pork fat and finely minced lean pork. Also called **German garlic sausage, hunter's sausage**

Jägerart *Germany* In the hunter's style, i.e. with mushrooms and wine

jägert *Germany* Sautéed with onions

jagger *United States* A sharp wheel attached to a handle, used to cut pastry or pizzas

jaggery 1. *South Asia* A crude brown sugar made from the sap of coconut or palmyra palm trees, sold in round cakes or lumps. Also called **gur, palm sugar 2.** Brown cane sugar, often sold in round sticky balls

jagri *South Asia* Jaggery

jagung *Indonesia, Malaysia* Miniature corn

jahe *Indonesia* Ginger

jaiba *Mexico* A small crab with a hard shell

jaiphal *South Asia* Mace and nutmeg

jajka minsky *Russia* See **iaika minsky**

jakfruit Jackfruit

jalapeño chile *Mexico* A variety of gently tapering hot green Mexican chilli about 6 cm long. Used fresh in curries or pickled for use as a snack food.

jalea *Spain* Jelly

jalea, en *Spain* Jellied

jalebi Jelabi

jalfrezi *South Asia* A South Indian style of dry-frying meat that is cut in cubes. The normal spices, cumin seeds, chopped ginger, turmeric and curry paste are fried in ghee, the meat added and coloured and fried until almost cooked, chopped green chillies, tomatoes and sweet pepper added and stir-fried for 10 minutes followed by garam masala, coriander leaf and creamed coconut for the final stir-fry. Served with plain rice or bread and mango chutney. Also called **jhal frazi**

jälkiruokaa *Finland* Sweet, dessert

jalousie *England, France* A medieval tart consisting of a rectangular puff pastry sheet covered in a sweet filling held in by a thin strip of puff pastry around the sides, this covered with a further sheet of puff pastry cut horizontally to resemble a slatted blind

jam A fruit preserve made by mixing fruit or boiling it with sugar and water and adding extra gelling agent if required, usually pectin. The high sugar concentration inhibits but does not totally prevent proliferation of microorganisms, so jam is usually bottled hot in sterile jars with a seal, or sterilized after bottling.

Jamaica flower The red flower of a mallow bush, *Hibiscus sabdariffa*, which originated in Mexico and is now grown in the Caribbean and India, used as a flavouring, as a vegetable and as the basis of sauces. The fruit of the plant can be used to make jam and jelly. Also called **Flor de Jamaica**, **Jamaica sorrel**, **red sorrel**, **rosella**

Jamaican pepper Allspice

Jamaica plum Hog plum

Jamaica sorrel See **Jamaica flower**

Jamaika Pfeffer *Germany* Allspice

jambalaya *United States* A Creole rice dish similar to Spanish paella including any of chicken, ham, sausage, prawns and crayfish together with fried onions, celery, green pepper cooked with long-grain rice, mounded onto a plate and served with Tabasco sauce

jambalaya aux chaurices *United States* A jambalaya with chopped sausages as the principal meat

jamberry Tomate verde

jambon *France* Ham

jambon blanc *France* An unsmoked or lightly smoked French cooking ham usually boiled. Also called **jambon glacé**, **jambon de Paris**

jambon cru *France* Raw, air-dried ham

jambon cuit de Prague *France* Prague ham

jambon de Bayonne *France* Bayonne ham

jambon de campagne *France* A locally produced ham for cooking, usually sweet cured and smoked

jambon de Paris *France* Jambon blanc

jambon des Ardennes *France* Ardennes ham

jambon de Toulouse *France* An unsmoked ham that is salted and dried. Eaten raw or cooked.

jambon fumé *France* Smoked ham

jambon glacé *France* Jambon blanc

jambonneau *France* **1.** Pork hock or knuckle from either the front or hind leg **2.** A small knuckle of ham

jambonnette *France* A **saucisson sec** from Vivarais shaped to look like a ham

jambon persillé *France* The raw, lean meat from cured shoulder and leg of pork, mixed with a wine-flavoured jelly and chopped parsley, cooked in a mould, cooled until set and turned out. Also called **parsley ham**

jambos Surinam cherry

jambu air *Indonesia, Malaysia* Water apple

James' cakes *Wales* Berffro cakes

jamón *Spain* Ham

jamón serrano *Spain* A high-quality salted and air-dried ham, matured for 18 months. Eaten raw. It should be made from free-range lean black Iberian pigs and weigh between 6 and 8 kg. Fakes weigh less. It is salted for 10 days, lightly brined and hung for a least a year. Also called **mountain ham**

jam puffs Puff pastry, cut into shapes, cooked, slit in half and filled with jam and whipped cream

jam roly-poly *England* Suet-crust pastry spread with jam, rolled up, wrapped in a cloth or placed in a mould and steamed, boiled or baked

jam sauce *England* Jam boiled with lemon juice and water, thickened with arrowroot or corn flour if required, cooked out and strained. Traditionally used with steamed or baked puddings.

jam sugar Granulated sugar mixed with citric acid and pectin, used for making jam with those fruits that need extra acid and pectin

Jamswurzel *Germany* Yam

jam tart A small or large open tart made with sweet pastry filled with jam let down with a little water

jam turnover A diamond-shaped piece of pastry, half covered with jam leaving the edges free, the other half folded over, sealed at the edges, pricked and glazed with milk and caster sugar prior to baking

jamu *Japan* Jam

jamur *Indonesia, Malaysia* Straw mushroom

jamur hitam *Indonesia* Shiitake mushroom

jamur tiram *Indonesia, Malaysia* Oyster mushroom

jan coude mai marge *Caribbean* A stew of salt beef, salt pork, red kidney beans, yellow yams and other vegetables flavoured with thyme and coconut oil (NOTE: From St Lucia)

jang yau see yau *China* Dark soya sauce

jan hagel *Netherlands* Finger biscuits flavoured with cinnamon and topped with flaked almonds and sugar

jan in de zak *Netherlands* A steamed pudding with currants and raisins

janis *Finland* Hare

Janssons frestelse *Sweden* Jansson's temptation

Jansson's temptation *Sweden* A traditional casserole of grated raw potatoes, chopped onions, butter, anchovy fillets or strips of matjes herring and cream baked to a golden crust. Reputed to have tempted a religious fanatic from his vow to give up earthly pleasures of the flesh. Often served at the end of a party when it is supposed to tempt guests to stay longer.

jantar *Portugal* Dinner

jao lei *China* A wire mesh strainer or spider used to manipulate food in water or oil

Japanese artichoke Chinese artichoke

Japanese aubergine A small (up to 7 cm long) cylindrical or pear-shaped aubergine often cooked as tempura

Japanese black mushroom Hoshi-shiitake

Japanese broiled vegetables Vegetables such as leeks, courgettes, sweet peppers, aubergines and mushrooms, threaded on skewers, oiled, grilled until brown, brushed with a mixture of **miso**, sugar and **mirin** and reheated under the grill for a further 2 minutes. Served immediately.

Japanese bunching onion Oriental bunching onion

Japanese chestnut A large but inferior chestnut, *Castanea crenata*, which has replaced the native American chestnut which was lost to the blight

Japanese cucumber A small ridge cucumber with the characteristic skin. Most varieties are quite small (up to 5 cm) with very thin skin and small seeds. Slices are used as a garnish for sushi and sashimi.

Japanese fish balls Kamaboko

Japanese fish sausage Kamaboko

Japanese gelatine Agar-agar

Japanese ginger sauce Chicken glace de viande, soya sauce, grated ginger root, minced spring onions and soft brown sugar combined to give a thickish sauce adding water if necessary. Used with sukiyaki.

Japanese horse radish Wasabi

Japanese meatballs Finely minced or double minced beef, mixed with minced spring onions, grated ginger root, flour, soya sauce and egg to make a thick paste, formed into balls and normally deep-fried

Japanese medlar Loquat

Japanese millet An Asian coarse grass, *Echinocloa frumentacea*, grown for its seeds which are eaten as porridge or with rice

Japanese omelette Eggs beaten with a little **dashi** and salt, cooked in a rectangular omelette pan (**maki-yakinabe**), rolled up, and this repeated 2 more times each time rolling the omelette around the previous roll. It is then sliced. Often the egg is layered with some contrasting coloured ingredient before rolling.

Japanese oyster Pacific oyster

Japanese parsley See **mitsuba**

Japanese pear Asian pear

Japanese pepper Anise pepper

Japanese plum A small round yellow, orange or red plum from China, *Prunus salicina* or *P. triflora*. Also called **salicine plum**

Japanese quince Japonica

Japanese radish See **mooli**, **daikon**

Japanese red prawn One of the famous large prawns, *Penaeus nipponensis*, of Japan, up to 20 cm long

Japanese rice *United States* A variety of hard short-grain rice which is greyish white and translucent with a dark mark in the centre

Japanese rice vinegar A mild clear rice vinegar which is not very strong. The aroma is pleasant but quickly disappears on exposure to the air. Used as a dressing for the salads sunomono and aemono.

Japanese rice wine Sake

Japanese sherry Mirin

Japanese vegetable cuts The mundane and decorative cuts and garnishes of vegetables which have been brought to a high art by Japanese chefs. See e.g. hana giri, hangetsu giri, hyoshigi giri, icho giri, katsura muki, matsuba, matsuka nani, mijin giri, ogi giri, roppo muki, sainome giri and sen giri.

Japanese wineberry Wineberry

japonais *Switzerland* Small round almond macaroons filled with butter cream

japonaise, à la *France* Garnished with Japanese artichokes

japonica The fruit of the ornamental quince, *Chaenomeles speciosa*, which sometimes ripen on the tree but can be ripened indoors. Must not be eaten raw. Used in pies or stewed or made into a jelly. Also called **Japanese quince**

japonica rice A short-grained rice shorter and thicker than Carolina rice but with similar characteristics and uses

japuta *Spain* Pomfret, the fish

jardinière *France* A garnish of mixed spring vegetables

Jarlsberg *Norway* A hard scalded-curd cheese similar to but softer and sweeter than Emmental, shaped in a large round and coated with wax. Made from pasteurized cows' milk.

jarret *France* Shin and shank of beef or knuckle of veal

jarrete *Spain* Knuckle

jasmine Various climbing shrubs, *Jasminum sambac* and other species of *Jasminum*, of the olive family whose leaves and flowers are used to flavour Chinese and Southeast Asian dishes. The unopened buds are used as table decoration and jasmine oil and essence are extracted from the flowers.

jasmine essence An alcoholic extract of jasmine flowers used to flavour desserts, rice and other dishes especially in Thailand

jasmine fragrant rice An aromatic long-grain rice with a more subtle flavour than basmati and slightly sticky when cooked. Best cooked for 10 minutes without salt. Used in Chinese and Southeast Asian cookery. Also called **Thai fragrant rice**, **Thai jasmine rice**

jasmine oil The essential oil from jasmine flowers

Jasminum sambac *Botanical name* Jasmine

jätkän lohipotti *Finland* Laxgryta

jaune d'oeuf *France* Egg yolk

Jausenwurst *Austria* A snack sausage made with beef, lean pork and bacon fat, seasoned, flavoured and bound with **fécule**

Javaanse sla *Netherlands* A salad based on Indonesian ingredients

Java coffee A mature coffee from Indonesia with a subtle mellow flavour

javali *Portugal* Wild boar

Javanese winged cardamom A cheap cardamom substitute from a variety of *Amomum*, available in Southeast Asia

Java rice A short-grained variety of rice particularly suitable for rice pudding as 80 g will absorb a litre of milk

Java sugar Palm sugar

javitri *South Asia* Nutmeg and mace

jbane *North Africa* A Moroccan goats' milk cheese eaten fresh or after maturing on straw

jean-doré *France* John dory

jeera *South Asia* Cumin

jeera sali *South Asia* A delicate long-grain rice shaped in a crescent rather like cumin seeds. Sold in the west as basmati or pilau rice. Always cooked by the absorption method.

jelabi *South Asia* Spirals of batter formed and fried in a deep-frying pan by dribbling batter out of a funnel. Served as a dessert with rose water-flavoured sugar syrup.

jelita *Czech Republic* A small blood sausage which is boiled or fried

jellied eels *England* Portions of fresh skinned eel, simmered in water or flavoured fish stock with vinegar, allowed to cool and served as a snack

jellied mayonnaise See **mayonnaise collée**

Jello *United States* A proprietary jelly, i.e. the gelatine-based product as opposed to the clear jam

jelly 1. The name given to any sweet or savoury liquid which is converted to a solid with a small amount of a gelling agent such as gelatine or agar agar **2.** *United States* Jam

jelly bag A cloth bag used to strain fruit juice prior to making jelly from it

jelly crystals *Australia* Flavoured gelatine used to make jelly

jelly cube A concentrated jelly made from gelatine, sugar and flavouring in water, set in a rectangular shape and partially divided into cubes to be used by adding to hot water to make fruit-flavoured jelly

jellyfish The salted and sun-dried skin of the jellyfish, *Rhopilema esculenta*, is used in Chinese cooking. It is rather tasteless and either shredded or sold in a piece. It should be reconstituted, shredded if necessary and marinated but not cooked and has a crunchy texture.

jelly mould A plastic or metal container with various shapes in which jelly is set then demoulded and turned out onto a plate or dish

jelly mushroom See **straw mushroom**

jelly noodles Cellophane noodles

jelly roll *United States* Swiss roll

jemuju *Malaysia* Caraway seed

jengibre *Spain* Ginger

jerked beef Charqui

jerked meat Charqui

jerk pork *Caribbean* Pork steaks marinated in a mixture of soya sauce, sesame-flavoured oil, brown sugar, jerk seasoning, thyme, chopped spring onions and chopped apple. The drained steaks are barbecued or baked in the oven, then served with a sauce made from the marinade, tomato purée and water and garnished with apple slices fried in butter.

jerk seasoning *Caribbean* A variable Jamaican spice mixture used for coating meat prior to frying or grilling consisting of some or all of ground cayenne and black pepper, allspice, cinnamon, oregano, bay leaf, nutmeg, onion and garlic and the like, presented as a paste or powder

jerky Charqui

Jerome *Austria, Germany* A semi-hard cows' milk cheese with a mild to slightly sharp paste

Jersey milk See **Channel Islands milk**

Jersey royal One of the earliest well-flavoured new potatoes harvested in the UK on the island of Jersey and commanding a premium price. Also called **international kidney**

Jersey wonder *England* A deep-fried twist or ring of a light dough mixture, dusted with sugar and eaten warm (NOTE: From the Channel Islands.)

jeruk asem *Malaysia* Citron

jeruk bodong *Indonesia* Citron

jeruk nipis *Indonesia* Lime, the fruit

jeruk purut *Indonesia* Makrut lime

jeruk sekade *Indonesia, Malaysia* Citron

Jerusalem artichoke A knobbly brown root of a plant, *Helianthus tuberosus*, which is a relative of the sunflower with a flavour similar to the artichoke. Jerusalem is a corruption of the Italian girasole meaning sunflower. Also called **winter artichoke**

Jesuit's cress Nasturtium

Jesuit's nut Caltrops

jésus *France* A large cured dry sausage (up to 3 kg) made with coarsely chopped pork meat and pork fat and matured for a long time

jets de houblon *France* Hop shoots

jeung *China* Ginger

jewfish 1. *United States* Giant sea bream **2.** *Australia* Mulloway

Jewish chicken soup See **gildeneh yoich**

Jewish salami A kosher salami made from beef with garlic and seasonings

Jewish sausage Small sausages made of minced beef, onion and carrot extended with matzo meal and bound with egg. Served at Passover.

jew's ear An edible fungus, *Auricularia auriculajudae*, similar to and related to cloud ear fungus and available dried. This is a mistranslation from the Latin for Judas's ear and is so called because it grows on the elder tree on which he is reputed to have hanged himself. Also called **Judas's ear**

jew's mallow *Middle East* Meloukhia

jhal frazi *South Asia* Jalfrezi

jhanna *South Asia* A perforated spoon with small holes used for producing small droplets of batter to be deep-fried or boiled

jhingli *South Asia* Angled loofah

jhol *Nepal* Soup

ji *China* Shallow frying

jian *China* Shallow frying

jiang *China* Ginger root

jiang niu rou *China* Marinated beef

jiang you *China* Soya sauce

jiao zi *China* Dumpling

jibia *Spain* Cuttlefish

jicama The large turnip-like root (25 cm in diameter) of a leguminous plant, *Pachyrrhizus erosus*, from Central and South America, with a brown inedible easily separated skin and juicy white flesh which can be eaten raw or cooked. The root contains little or no protein and may be lobed. The pods and seeds of the plant are edible when young but can be poisonous when mature. Popular in Mexico and California. Also called **yam bean**, **jicana**, **Mexican yam bean**

jicana See **jicama**

ji dan *China* Hen egg

jiemo *China* Mustard

ji gan *China* Chicken liver

jigger *United States* A volume measure equal to 1 American ounce, 30 ml or 2 tbsp

jin dan *China* Meiwa kumquat

jinga *South Asia* **1.** Shrimp **2.** Prawn

jing lung *China* The round bamboo nesting steamers used for **dim sum** and other steamed foods

jintan manis *Malaysia* **1.** Aniseed **2.** Fennel seed

jinten *Indonesia* Cumin

jinten putih *Malaysia* Cumin

jiraa *Nepal* Cumin seed

ji rou *China* Chicken meat

ji tang *China* Chicken soup

jit choh *China* Red vinegar

jit gwa *China* Fuzzy melon

jitrnice *Czech Republic* A fresh offal (liver and lungs) sausage for boiling or frying

jiu la choy *China* One of the oriental mustards with thick white stems and pointed green leaves growing to 45 cm. It has a strong bitter flavour and is parboiled before stir-frying. Also called **Chinese green cabbage**, **sow cabbage**

ji you *China* Chicken fat

Job's tears A warm climate plant, *Coix lachryma-jobi*, with large seeds, eaten mainly in Southeast Asia and the Phillipines as a source of protein. The fruits are used for necklaces and it is grown as a garden plant in southern Europe.

Jochburg *Austria* A Tyrolean cheese made from cows' and goats' milk with a distinctive flavour and shaped into large thin discs

jocoque *Spain* Sour cream

jodda *Italy* The local Sicilian name for yoghurt

Joe Mazetti *United States* A split round bread bun (**balm cake**) with a filling of cooked minced beef, oregano, basil, tomato sauce and seasoning

joetkal *Korea* Dried and salted fish similar to Bombay duck. Used for flavouring or as a snack food or side dish.

joghurt *Hungary* Yoghurt

Joghurt *Germany* Yoghurt

Johannisbeere *Germany* Redcurrant

Johannisbeerkaltschale *Germany* Redcurrants cooked in sugar syrup, sieved and mixed with white wine. Served cold garnished with whole redcurrants and crushed macaroons.

Johannisbeersosse *Germany* A jus roti or similar with added redcurrant jelly

Johannisbrot *Germany* Carob bean

John Dory A seawater flatfish, *Zeus faber*, with olive brown skin, two distinguishing black thumb marks (Saint Peter's thumb) on each side below the head and very sharp spines, found in the Atlantic and Mediterranean. It is similar to sole, has firm white fillets and the bones make excellent stock.

Johnny cake *United States* A cornmeal batter pancake similar to **hoe cake** made from the less starchy flint corn. Also called **Rhode Island johnny cake**

joint A large thick portion of animal flesh often including some bone. Names of the same joint vary considerably from place to place even within one country.

joint, to To divide a carcass into manageable portions by severing a joint in the skeleton, by chopping, or by removing whole muscles or muscle groups

Joinville, sauce *France* Sauce normande finished with crayfish and shrimp butters instead of cream and butter. Used with fish.

jojutla rice A type of long-grain rice

Jókai bableves *Hungary* A fresh or dried butter bean soup with smoked pig knuckle and carrots, flavoured with garlic, paprika and parsley. Named after the author.

jollof *West Africa* A stew or casserole from Nigeria, Gambia and Senegal made of beef, chicken or mutton simmered with fried onions, tomatoes, rice and seasonings. Many other vegetables and garnishes are added according to availability.

jolly boy *United States* A fried flat cake made with cornmeal dough, split in half, buttered and served with maple syrup

Jonagold apple A hybrid of the Jonathan and Golden Delicious apples with a sweet, slightly tart, flavour used both for dessert and cooking

Jonah crab A close relative, *Cancer borealis*, of the rock crab but a little heavier (up to 500 g). It has a brick red shell and, like the rock crab, is not particularly well-flavoured although quite edible.

jonchée *France* 1. A fresh cream cheese from Poitou-Charentes 2. A type of junket

jonc odorant *France* Lemon grass

jong eendje *Netherlands* Duckling

joojeh kabab *Central Asia* An Iranian kebab of chicken pieces marinated in lemon juice, grated onion and seasoning for about 4 hours, threaded onto skewers, brushed with paprika and molten butter and then grilled or barbecued

jook *China* A gruel of well-soaked rice boiled with salt and water, flavoured by sprinkling sweet or savoury ingredients over the surface. See also **congee**

Jordan almond See **sugared almond**

jordärtskockor *Sweden* Jerusalem artichoke

jordbær *Denmark, Norway* Strawberry

jordgubbar *Sweden* Strawberries

jordnötter *Sweden* Peanuts

joshinko *Japan* Rice flour

jota *Italy* A slowly cooked soup from the northeast of potatoes, beans or polenta, turnips, bacon and sauerkraut. Also called **iota**

joue *France* Cheek (of pork)

jou kuei *China* Cinnamon

joule The scientific unit of energy, too small to be of use in nutrition. Hence the **kilojoule** equal to one thousand joules is used. (NOTE: Named after James Joule, the scientist from Manchester, UK, who investigated the equivalence of heat and other forms of energy.)

jour, du *France* Of the day as in soupe du jour, soup of the day

jowar *South Asia* Great millet, sorghum, usually the white grained seed ground for making unleavened bread

jowl The meat from the cheeks and face of a pig

ju *China* Blanching and quick-boiling for 5 minutes in plain water to release blood from meats

juan canary melon *United States* An oval melon with sweet white flesh tinged with pink near the seeds and a bright yellow skin

jubna *Middle East* Haloumi

Judas's ear Jew's ear

judd mat gaardebou'nen *Luxembourg* Smoked collar of pork cooked with broad beans and flavoured with summer savory. The national dish of Luxembourg.

judía *Spain* Kidney bean

judías blancas *Spain* Haricot beans

judías de Lima *Spain* Lima bean

judías verdes *Spain* Runner beans

judías verdes a la andaluza *Spain* Boiled green beans sautéed with chopped tomatoes and **julienne** of ham

judic, à la *France* Garnished with stuffed tomatoes, braised lettuce, potatoes and sometimes truffles and kidney

judru *France* A type of salami from Beaune made with pork only

jug, to An old-fashioned term for cooking in a heavy earthenware casserole or jug

jugged hare *United Kingdom* A jointed hare tossed in seasoned flour, browned with bacon and butter, then beef stock, port, onion clouté, marjoram and redcurrant jelly added, boiled then casseroled for 3 hours or until tender, onions removed and cooking liquor thickened with the reserved blood of the hare. Garnished with chopped parsley.

jugged kippers *Scotland* A method of cooking kippers by removing their heads and tails, packing them into a jug, covering with boiling water, leaving 8 minutes after which they are removed, dried off and served with beurre maître d'hotel

jugjug *Caribbean* A Barbadian celebratory dish of salt beef and salt pork desalted and boiled with twice their weight of pigeon peas with a faggot of thyme, marjoram and chives and some chopped onions until the meat is tender. The meat and peas are separated from the cooking liquor, any bones removed, then all minced. A stiff porridge is made with some of the cooking liquor, butter and three fifths the meat's weight of sorghum flour. The two mixtures are combined and served warm.

Juglans cinerea *Botanical name* Butternut tree

Juglans nigra *Botanical name* Walnut tree

Juglans regia *Botanical name* Walnut tree

jugo *Spain* 1. Juice 2. Gravy

jugo de naranja *Spain* Orange juice

jugurttia *Finland* Yoghurt

juhla *Finland* A sharp-flavoured Cheddar-type cheese made from cows' milk

juice The liquid expressed or released from fruits, vegetables or even meats by any of several methods, squeezing, pressing, liquidizing, freezing and thawing, heating, etc. Juice is usually strained to remove solids

juice extractor An implement for manually or mechanically extracting juice from fruits. For citrus fruits, it usually consists of a ribbed convex cone, on which half the citrus fruit is turned, above a slotted base. Other fruits are generally liquidized and strained.

jujube 1. The red, wrinkled fruit of a shrub, *Zizyphus jujuba*, of the buckthorn family which grows in the East and Provence and is partially dried, candied or made into a stiff jelly. It has the shape of an olive, is green when unripe and red to dark brown when ripe, and has a single stone and a sweet and sticky white flesh, rather like a small date. Other shrubs of the genus *Zisyphus* have similar fruits. See also **Mauritian jujube**, **Argentinian jujube**, **lotus jujube**. Also called **Chinese red date**, **Indian jujube**, **red date**, **jujube nuts 2.** Confectionery made from jellied and sweetened fruit juices

jujube nut See **jujube**

juk *China* A gruel of well-soaked rice boiled with salt and water, flavoured by sprinkling sweet or savoury ingredients over the surface. See also **congee**

julefrokest *Denmark* A Christmas cold table with a whole cooked gammon as centrepiece

julekake *Norway* Christmas cake

julienne *England, France* Cut pieces of vegetables, fruit or citrus rind measuring roughly 25 by 3 by 3 mm (smaller in the case of citrus rind). Usually used either raw, blanched or cooked as a garnish.

julskinka *Sweden* A hot or cold ham sometimes used as a centrepiece of a Christmas cold table. If cold, piped with Happy Christmas ('God Jul') in white chaud-froid sauce. The ham is prepared by simmering a whole gammon with a bouquet garni, nutmeg and an onion clouté until the internal temperature reaches 80°C. It is then cooled in the cooking liquor, removed, dried, skin stripped off, coated with a mixture of mustard and ginger followed by breadcrumbs, egg yolk and sugar and browned in the oven. Nowadays, often baked in the oven.

jumble 1. A small lemon or almond-flavoured biscuit baked in a tiny heap or an 'S', shape **2.** *United States* A biscuit flavoured with rose water and containing chopped walnuts and desiccated coconut

jumbo Larger than normal or expected, e.g. jumbo oats, jumbo burger

jumeau *France* A cut of the forequarter of beef extending down from the end of the côtes couvertes including the leaner parts of the leg of mutton cut and the brisket immediately in front of the foreleg. Used for braising.

jump baarn *China* A chopping block usually made from soapwood cut across the grain so as not to take the edge off the cleaver

juneberry *United States* The fruit of a decorative shrub, *Amelanchier canadensis*, with a red to black fruit similar to a blackcurrant. Eaten raw or cooked. Also called **serviceberry**

junges Hammelfleisch *Germany* Lamb

junges Huhn *Germany* Spring chicken

Jungeszwiebeln *Germany* Spring onions

juniper The dried berries of a shrub, *Juniperus communis*, from temperate Northern regions used to flavour gin, for marinades and as a pickling spice. The piney flavour also goes well with game and pork.

junípero *Spain* Juniper

juniper spice mix A mixture of ground spices suitable for flavouring dense textured fish, beef and lamb before barbecueing made from juniper berries, black peppercorns, allspice, cloves, dried bay leaves and salt

Juniperus communis *Botanical name* Juniper

junket *United Kingdom* Sweetened and flavoured milk mixed at blood heat (37°C) with rennet to cause it to set. Once set it must not be disturbed or it will separate into curds and whey.

junk food Food with plenty of Calories, generally in the form of cheap sugar, fat, starch and recovered protein, highly seasoned and flavoured if savoury, but with few or no vitamins or trace elements, and if the major source of energy will lead to suboptimal health

Jurawurst *Switzerland* Smoked sausage from the Jura. See also **saucisse d'Ajoie**

jus *France* Juice, either from fruit, vegetables or from meat

jus, au *France* Served only with its own roast juices

jus de bissap *West Africa* Approximately half a litre of Jamaica flowers steeped in 2 litres of boiling water, allowed to cool for ten minutes, strained and 250 to 500 g sugar added and the drink chilled. Other flavourings may be added e.g., ginger, lemon juice, orange flower water, mint etc. The national drink of Senegal. Also called **karkadé**

jus de viande *France* Gravy

jus lié *France* **Espagnole sauce** made from veal or chicken bones without flour, thickened with arrowroot or corn flour, simmered briefly, seasoned and strained. Also called **thickened gravy**

jus (de) rôti *France* Roast gravy

Jussière, garnish *France* Onions, braised lettuce, potatoes and sometimes carrots

juusto *Finland* Cheese

juustoleipä *Finland* A hand made low-fat cows' milk slicing cheese in the form of a loaf. Often sliced and toasted or dunked in coffee. Also called **leipäjuusto**

ju zi *China* Orange

juzi *China* Tangerine

KLMNOPQ

kaab el ghzal *North Africa* Croissant-like pastries filled with honey and almonds. Also called **cornes de gazelle**

kaagati *Nepal* Lemon

kaakro *West Africa* A snack food from Ghana made from mashed plantains and flour (5:1) flavoured with grated fresh ginger, onion, black pepper and paprika, all processed to a smooth paste with water, formed into small balls and deep-fried in oil. Served hot with lemon. Also called **kaklo**

kaali *Finland* Cabbage

kaalikääryle *Finland* Blanched cabbage leaves wrapped around a stuffing and baked

kaalipiiras *Finland* A cabbage filled pie served hot or cold

kaankro *Nepal* Cucumber

kaas *Netherlands* Cheese

kaassaus *Netherlands* Cheese sauce

kabab *South Asia* Kebab, usually on a wooden skewer or on iron if cooked in a tandoori oven

kabab-e murgh *Central Asia* Chicken brushed with clarified butter is roasted and basted with a thick sauce made with tomatoes, onions and butter during the final 30 minutes. It is served on bread garnished with sliced hard-boiled eggs and chopped coriander leaves. From Afghanistan.

kabachok *Russia* Squash, marrow

kabak dolmasi *Turkey* A young marrow or large courgette filled with a mixture of onions, raisins, pine nuts, chopped parsley or dill and seasoning, baked in the oven and served cold

kabak tathsi *Turkey* A dessert made from cooked pumpkin flesh, soaked in sugar syrup and sprinkled with chopped walnuts

kabanos (*plural* **kabanosy**) *Poland* A thin and hard smoked pork sausage made into links about 30 cm long

kabaragh *South Asia* Lamb chops cooked in milk with ginger and fennel

kabaub *Central Asia* The traditional kebab from Afghanistan made from cubed lamb marinated overnight with yoghurt, garlic, salt and pepper, then grilled or barbecued

Kabeljau *Germany* Cod

kabeljauw *Netherlands* Codfish

ka'b ghzahl *North Africa* Croissant-like pastries filled with honey and almonds. Also called **cornes de gazelle**

kabocha *Japan* A small winter squash similar to a small green pumpkin. Cooked like swede or marrow.

kabosu *Japan* A very acid citrus fruit, *Citrus sphaerocarpa*, grown in Japan for use as a garnish or flavouring. It has a very dark green rind which is thin and smooth and juicy flesh with several seeds.

kabu *Japan* Turnip

kabuli channa *South Asia* Yellow chick peas

kabu no tsukemono *Japan* A salad pickle made from thinly sliced turnip mixed with a little crumbled **kombu**, sliced ginger, chopped dry red chillies, chopped lemon rind, julienned carrot and salt, all pressed under a weighted board for 12 hours or more, wrung out and dressed with equal parts of soya sauce and **mirin**

kacang djong *Malaysia* Bean sprouts

kacang eeris *Malaysia* Pigeon pea

kacang goode *Indonesia* Pigeon pea

kacang ijo *Malaysia* Bean sprouts

kacang-kacang *Indonesia, Malaysia* Barracuda

kacang kedele *Indonesia* Soya bean

kacang merah *Indonesia* Black-eyed pea

kacang mete *Indonesia* Cashew nut

kacang monyet *Indonesia* Cashew nut

kacang padi *Malaysia* Bean sprouts

kacang panjang 1. *Indonesia* Black-eyed pea **2.** *Malaysia* Long bean

kacang tanah *Indonesia, Malaysia* Peanut

kachalo *Central Asia* Potato

kachauri *South Asia* A type of pitta bread made into a pocket and stuffed with a spiced bean mixture

Kachkaval A hard, scalded ewes' or ewes' and cows' milk cheese made from spun curd. See also **Kashkaval**

kachkeiss *Luxembourg* A matured and hardened curd cheese cooked with butter, sour cream, seasoning and sometimes yolk of egg, served on bread

kachoomar *South Asia* A side dish of sliced onions, tomatoes and sweet peppers dressed with lemon juice. often served before a meal as the menu choice is being made.

kachur *South Asia* Zedoary

kacsa *Hungary* Duck

kadhai *Nepal, South Asia* A small wok used for one-dish cooking. See also **karahi**

kadin budu köfte *Turkey* Chopped raw beef mixed with boiled rice, chopped parsley and salt, shaped into oval cakes, steamed or boiled, cooled, dipped in beaten egg and fried

kadin göbegi *Turkey* Small fried biscuits soaked in syrup and eaten as a dessert (NOTE: Literally 'lady's navel'.)

kadju *South Asia* Cashew nut

kadu *South Asia* Winter squash

Kaempferia galanga *Botanical name* Kempferia galangal

Kaempferia pandurata *Botanical name* Kempferia galangal

kaeng *Thailand* Indicates liquid in a dish. See also **gaeng**

kærnemælk *Denmark* Buttermilk

kærnemælkskoldskaal *Denmark* Cold buttermilk soup

kærnemælksuppe *Denmark* A cold soup made from eggs, buttermilk, sugar, vanilla and lemon sprinkled with crushed cornflakes and chopped almonds

kaffe *Denmark, Norway, Sweden* Coffee

kaffebröd *Sweden* Coffee cake

Kaffeekuchen *Germany* Coffee cake

Kaffir beer *South Africa* Beer produced from sprouted millet seed. See also **pombé**

kaffir corn A variety of millet, *Sorghum vulgare* var. *caffrorum*, from South Africa, used as millet or sorghum.

kaffir lime Makrut lime

kaga *Japan* A variety of Japanese cucumber

kage *Denmark* Cake

Kaggost *Sweden* A medium soft and mild, yellow coloured cheese made from cows' milk and sometimes flavoured with cumin

kaha bath *Sri Lanka* Turmeric coloured spiced rice used on festive occasions

kahve *Turkey* Turkish coffee

kai *Thailand* Egg or chicken

kaibashira *Japan* Scallops

kai kem *Thailand* Salted duck eggs

kail 1. See **kale 2.** *Scotland* Greens of any kind and the soups made with them, not necessarily the brassica kale, which is called lang kail

kailkenny *Scotland* A dish of mashed potatoes mixed with chopped cooked cabbage (1:1) and cream, similar to colcannon

kaimak *Russia* A type of clotted cream from Armenia made by simmering a mixture of double cream and milk (5:3) for 15 minutes whilst repeatedly incorporating air with a ladle. It is then cooled slowly for 4 hours and refrigerated for 24 hours all without agitation. The solidified cream from the top is cut in squares and lifted out with a slotted spoon. It will keep up to a week in a refrigerator.

kai pad bai krapow *Thailand* Diced chicken meat stir-fried with fresh basil leaves and bird's eye chillies, moistened with a little fish sauce and served as a side dish

kaiseki ryori *Japan* A succession of small dishes served in a formal style, ingredients change with the seasons but do not included red meat

Kaiserfleisch 1. *Germany* Smoked sucking pig **2.** Boiled bacon

Kaisergranat *Germany* Dublin bay prawn

Kaiser Koch *Germany* Rice pudding with almonds

Kaiserschmarren *Austria* A thick sweet batter containing sultanas or raisins, shallow-fried in long strips until crisp, drained and served in a heap dredged with sugar. Eaten as a dessert with stewed fruit. See also **emperor's omelette**

kai wat *East Africa* A very spicy wat

kajiki *Japan* Swordfish

kajmak *Balkans* Feta and cream cheeses beaten with butter until fluffy and served as an appetizer

kaju *South Asia* Cashew nut

kaka *Sweden* Cake

kakadu plum *Australia* The fruit of a tall slender northern tree, *Terminalia ferdinandiana*, very similar in appearance and structure to a large green olive. It has a tart gooseberry-like flavour and is best cooked and sieved to get rid of the fibrous material.The pulp is used in jams, relishes and sauces. It can be stripped of its flesh in the same way as a mango, or it can be pickled whole in sweetened vinegar. It has a very high vitamin C content (3%). Also called **wild plum**

kakao *Russia, Sweden* Cocoa

Kakao *Germany* Cocoa

kakavia *Greece* A fish soup similar to bouillabaisse. See also **psarassoupa**

kakda *South Asia* Cucumber

kake *Norway* Cake

kakee Persimmon

kakejiru soup *Japan* **Dashi**, soya sauce and mirin (10:1:1) with a little salt and sliced spring onions simmered for about 10 minutes

kaki 1. Persimmon **2.** *Japan* Oyster

kakiage *Japan* A tempura made in clumps from mixed small fish, shellfish and shrimps, also from vegetables such as carrot, burdock and onion cut small

kaki-nabe *Japan* Oysters simmered with vegetables in a **miso** and sake broth

kakitama-jiru *Japan* A soup made from **dashi** flavoured with a little salt and soya sauce, slightly thickened with corn flour. After cooking out, it is brought to a very gentle simmer and beaten egg mixed with a little dashi is dribbled from a moving ladle and allowed to set. The soup is removed from the heat and finished with juice squeezed from freshly grated ginger root and garnished with lemon rind shapes. (NOTE: Literally 'egg drop soup'.)

kakku *Finland* Cake

kaklo *West Africa* A snack food from Ghana made from mashed plantains and flour. See also **kaakro**

kakukfú *Hungary* Thyme

kaku-zukuri *Japan* A type of cut for large thick fillets of fish used in sashimi consisting of 1 cm dice

kål *Denmark, Norway, Sweden* Cabbage

kala *Finland* Fish

kalács *Hungary* A well-raised white milk-bread available as rolls or in slices

kala jeera *South Asia* **1.** Black cumin, a variety of cumin found in Kashmir, Pakistan and Iran. Used in Moghul cooking. **2.** Caraway seed

kalakakot *Finland* Fish cakes

kalakeitto *Finland* A fish, onion and potato soup with a milk and water base thickened with rye bread and corn flour and garnished with chopped fresh dill leaf

kalakukko *Finland* A hollowed-out rye loaf filled with small white fish (**muikku**), fat pork and seasoning, baked slowly until filling is cooked, then sliced and served hot

kalamansi *Philippines* The local lemon which is about the size of a small lime and has a bright green skin. Generally used as a lemon.

The rind is crystallized for use as a garnish or snack.

kalamarakia tiganita *Greece* Young squid, cleaned, sliced and floured then browned in hot oil for 3 minutes. Served as an appetizer on cocktail sticks.

kalamarossoupa me domata *Greece* A thin stew or thick soup made from sliced squid, sweated onions and garlic, **tomato concassée**, sliced mushrooms, red wine and water (1:4), all simmered for 10 minutes only, seasoned and finished with chopped parsley

kala namak *South Asia* Salt

kalassås *Sweden* A festive sauce for fish used at parties, made with double cream with 10% of uncooked egg yolk mixed in and flavoured with wine vinegar, caster sugar, French mustard and freshly ground white pepper

Kalb *Germany* Veal

Kalberwurst *Switzerland* Veal sausage

Kalbfleisch *Germany* Veal

Kalbsbeuschel *Austria* A ragout of calves' lights and hearts, once a dish of the poor but now fashionable

Kalbsbraten *Germany* Roast veal

Kalbsbratwurst *Switzerland* A white **Bratwurst** made from a mixture of veal, bacon and milk, seasoned and flavoured with spices

Kalbsbries *Germany* Calves' sweetbreads

Kalbsbrust *Germany* Breast of veal

Kalbsfüsse *Germany* Calves' feet

Kalbshaxen *Austria, Germany* A speciality of the Austrian-Bavarian border region consisting of a well roasted or fried pork or veal leg joint which is crisp, brown and tender, served with boiled potatoes and salad

Kalbskopf *Germany* Calves' head

Kalbsleber *Germany* Calves' liver

Kalbsleberwurst *Germany* A spreading sausage made from calves' liver

Kalbslende *Germany* Fillet of veal

Kalbsmilch *Switzerland* Calves' sweetbreads

Kalbsnierenbraten *Germany* Boned loin of veal with some flank, stuffed with halved, skinned and cored calves' kidneys, seasoned and sprinkled with dried thyme, rolled, tied and roasted on a **mirepoix** of vegetables at 175°C in the usual way

Kalbsrippchen *Germany* Veal chop

Kalbsrolle *Germany* Boned breast of veal covered with a stuffing containing minced beef and sausage with breadcrumbs soaked in milk, sweated chopped onion, parsley, nutmeg, lemon zest and seasoning bound with egg, rolled up, tied, browned in lard and braised in stock for about 2 hours. Served hot with the reduced cooking liquor thickened with **beurre manié** or cold with clarified and jellied cooking liquor.

Kalbsroulade *Germany* A type of meat loaf made with a pork and veal mixture containing diced pork fat and pistachio nuts

kald *Norway* Cold

Kaldaunen *Germany* Tripe

kåldolmar *Sweden* Blanched cabbage leaves wrapped around a filling of minced beef or pork, butter, rice cooked in milk until very soft and seasonings, lightly fried then baked in a covered dish with a sweetened stock. Served with the cooking liquor thickened with corn flour and soured cream, boiled potatoes and cranberry sauce.

kåldolmer *Denmark* Stuffed cabbage

kaldt kjøtt *Norway* Cold sliced meats, assiette anglaise

kale A member of the *Brassica* family, *Brassica oleracea* (Acephala Group), with a tall thick stem from which spring large curly leaves and, later, tender flower stalks. It will stand through the winter and both the leaves and the flowering stalks (in spring) can be eaten. It has a stronger flavour than cabbage and is known in northern Europe as 'peasant's cabbage'. When shredded and fried in oil it resembles fried seaweed. See also **borecole**. Also called **curly kale, kail**

kale brose *Scotland* A Scottish peasant dish of cows' heel simmered and skimmed for 4 hours, finely shredded kale and toasted oatmeal added and boiled until cooked. A more up-market version uses beef broth with beef cheek.

kaleji *South Asia* Liver

kalfsgehakt *Netherlands* Minced veal

kalfskotelet *Netherlands* Veal cutlet

kalfslapje *Netherlands* Veal steak

kalfsoester *Netherlands* Grenadin of veal

kalfsvlees *Netherlands* Veal

kalfszwezerik *Netherlands* Calves' sweetbreads

kali *South Asia* Loofah

kalia *Poland* Chicken broth flavoured with the juice of pickled cucumbers and garnished with diced chicken meat, celeriac, carrots and Hamburg parsley

kali mirch *South Asia* Black peppercorn

kali mirich *South Asia* Black peppercorn

kalkkuna *Finland* Turkey

kalkkunapaisti *Finland* Roast turkey

kalkoen *Netherlands* Turkey

kalkon *Sweden* Turkey

kalkun *Denmark, Norway* Turkey

kalkunragout *Denmark* Casserole of turkey in a sweet-and-sour sauce, served with mashed potatoes or chestnut purée

kall *Sweden* Cold

kallaloo *Caribbean* A soup made from dasheen leaves, okra, crabmeat, salt pork, etc. See also **callaloo soup**

kall citron-kyckling *Sweden* Cold lemon chicken made from boiled, skinned and deboned chicken meat covered with a sauce made from cream, egg yolk and sherry (12:1:1) stirred over heat until thick, and the whole topped with shredded lemon zest

kall tomatsoppa *Sweden* Tomatoes boiled in just sufficient water to cover them for 15 minutes, passed hot through a chinois onto grated or processed onion, seasoned and flavoured with sugar, lemon juice and Worcestershire sauce. Served cold as a soup.

Kalmar *Germany* Squid

kalocsai halászlé *Hungary* A fish soup based on red wine

kalonji *South Asia* Nigella

kalops *Sweden* Beef stewed in the old-fashioned way with onions, peppercorns, bay leaf and possibly allspice

kalt *Germany* Cold

kalte pikante Sosse *Germany* Spicy ketchup

Kalteschale *Germany* Cold fruit soup

kalte Speisen *Germany* Cold dishes

kalua puaa *United States* A Hawaiian speciality of seasoned shredded roast pork, wrapped in taro leaves and briefly roasted or barbecued

kalvbräss-stuvning *Sweden* Creamed calves' sweetbreads made from cleaned and blanched whole sweetbreads, sweated in butter with sliced onion and carrot and boiled 10 minutes with flavoured veal stock. The sweetbreads are then reserved, cooled, chopped and combined with a cream sauce. Also called **stuvad kalvbräss**

kalvebrisler *Denmark* Calves' sweetbreads

kalvekjøtt *Norway* Veal

kalvekød *Denmark* Veal

kalvemedaljong *Norway* Roast veal

kalvenyrestek *Norway* Loin of veal

kalvfilé pandora *Sweden* Seasoned escalopes of veal, fried in butter, arranged in an oven-proof dish and covered with strips of ham, sweet green pepper and sliced mushroom. This covered with the pan juices which have been deglazed with cream, topped with slices of Gruyère cheese and browned under the grill.

kalvfilet Oscar *Sweden* Flattened medallions of veal passed through seasoned flour, browned in butter, napped with **choron sauce** or **béarnaise sauce** and garnished with lobster and asparagus tips (NOTE: Named after King Oscar II of Sweden.)

kalvkött *Sweden* Veal

kalvkyckling *Sweden* Paupiettes of veal, veal birds, veal olives

kalv med fänkål *Sweden* Lightly browned veal escalopes simmered in white wine or stock in a closed dish over a bed of chopped bulb fennel for about 20 minutes and served with the reduced cooking liquor thickened with a liaison of egg and cream

kalvrulad med bacon *Sweden* Escalopes of veal covered with bacon, rolled and tied, dusted with flour and browned with chopped bacon, onions and shallots, covered with stock and a bouquet garni, seasoned and then braised with a cover for 1 to 1.5 hours, untied and served with the strained braising liquor

kalvsteck i öl *Sweden* Leg or shoulder veal browned with carrots and onions in butter then simmered in brown ale with bay, cloves and seasoning until tender

kalvstek på grönsaksbädd *Sweden* Veal shoulder rubbed with seasoning and powdered rosemary, roasted on a **mirepoix** of onions, carrots, leeks and celeriac and basted with stock from time to time. When cooked (1 to 2 hours) the veal is sliced, laid over the vegetables and served from the dish.

kama *Japan* A heavy metal pan used for cooking rice by the absorption method

kamaboko *Japan* Cooked fish cakes made with ground up white fish flesh bound with starch, egg white, **mirin** and sugar. Either steamed or dusted with corn flour and shallow-fried. They have a slightly rubbery texture and are either sliced and added to soups, noodles, etc. or served as a hors d'oeuvres with a sauce. The surface is often coloured to give an attractive appearance when sliced. See also **chikuwa, hanpen, ita-kamaboko, natto**. Also called **Japanese fish balls, Japanese fish sausage**

kamano lomi *United States* An appetizer from Hawaii made with chopped smoked or desalted salted salmon, chopped onions and salt to taste

kamasu *Japan* Saury pike

kambing *Indonesia* Goat

kamias *Philippines* Belimbing (1), the fruit

kami-jio *Japan* A method of lightly salting food especially raw fish by wrapping the food in paper and allowing it to stand for an hour immersed in salt

kamin *Thailand* Turmeric

kaminari-jiru *Japan* A soup containing bean curd and vegetables

kammar *Sweden* Cinnamon-flavoured butter cream placed over the central 10 by 32 cm strip of a rolled 32 cm square of Danish pastry, the sides folded over to give a 10 by 32 cm rectangle, cut in 4 cm pieces, each piece having 4 cuts to the centre along the long side, brushed with water, rolled in coarse sugar and almond nibs, bent to open out the cuts, proved 30 minutes and baked at 230°C for 8 minutes (NOTE: Literally 'combs'.)

Kammuschel *Germany* Scallop, the shellfish

kampyo *Japan* Thin dried strips of the flesh of bottle gourd. When softened by blanching in weak brine they are used as edible strings for tying and wrapping food or as a filling for sushi. Also called **kanpyo, dried gourd strips**

kamrakh *South Asia* Carambola, the fruit

kana *Finland* Hen

kana gushi *Japan* Short metal skewers for grilling whole or sliced fish and other foods

kananpoika *Finland* Chicken

kanari fruit The small sour fruit of a Chinese tree, *Canarium album*. The kernels from the stone are known as Chinese olive seeds.

kande *East Africa* A Tanzanian staple food of beans and maize, possibly with additional flavouring of vegetables and meat

kandierte Früchte *Germany* Candied fruit

kaneel *Netherlands* Cinnamon

kanel *Sweden* Cinnamon

kanewala choona *South Asia* Lime (calcium hydroxide)

kangaroo tail *Australia* The tail of a kangaroo cooked as oxtail

kangaroo tail soup *Australia* As **oxtail soup**, with kangaroo tail substituted for oxtail

kangkong *Philippines* Swamp cabbage

kani *Japan* Crab, used both generally and in sushi

kaniini *Finland* Rabbit

kanin *Denmark, Norway, Sweden* Rabbit

Kaninchen *Germany* Rabbit

kanin i flødepeberrod *Denmark* Jugged rabbit served with a horseradish and cream dressing, mushrooms and onions

kanjadaa *West Africa* A soup/stew from the Gambia. See also **superkanja**

kan lan *China* Kanari fruit

kanom *Thailand* Cake, dessert

kanom bang *Thailand* Bread

kanoon *Thailand* Jackfruit

kan phoo *Thailand* Cloves

kanpyo *Japan* Thin dried strips of the flesh of bottle gourd. See also **kampyo**

kanten *Japan* Agar-agar

Kanter *Netherlands* Kanterkaas

Kanterkaas *Netherlands* A cheese like **Nagelkaas**, but without the cumin and cloves. Also called **Kanter**, **Friese Kanterkaas**

kantola A small bitter gourd, *Momordica muricata*, used in the cooking of India and East Asia. It is similar to a courgette with a thick green knobbly skin. The young seeds are edible but harden with age like a marrow. It should be blanched and degorged before cooking and hard seeds removed. Also called **balsam apple**, **ucche**

Kantwurst *Austria* A rectangular-shaped **Rohwurst** made with lean pork and pork fat (2:1)

kanyah *West Africa* A sweet snack from Sierra Leone made from 2 parts of shelled and skinned peanuts, 2 parts of parched rice both crushed to small pieces but not too fine, mixed with 1 part sugar then all processed to a powder and formed into balls, pyramids or cubes

kao 1. *China* Roast **2.** *Thailand* Rice

kao liang *China* Millet

kaolin See **E559**

kao mao *Thailand* Young unhusked rice, flattened and roasted. Used as a coating for fried food.

kao mian bao *China* Toast

kaong *Philippines* Palm nut

kao pan *Thailand* A variety of Thai pummelo with a sweetish flavour and with less acid than a grapefruit

kao yang rou *China* Lamb

kapama *Bulgaria* A ragoût of floured pieces of boneless lamb, sautéed in oil with sliced onions and then simmered with paprika, seasoning and a little water until nearly cooked, mixed with plenty of chopped spring onions, simmered until all cooked, covered with blanched spinach leaves and served

Kapaun *Germany* Capon

Kapern *Germany* Capers

kaperssaus *Netherlands* Caper sauce

kapi *Thailand* A moist shrimp paste which becomes very pungent and dark brown as it matures. See also **blachan**

kapor *Malaysia* Lime (calcium hydroxide)

kapormártás *Hungary* Dill sauce

káposzta *Hungary* Cabbage

kappamaki *Japan* A **maki-sushi** made in the normal way with a centre filling of batons of cucumber and bainiku

kappan *Hungary* Capon

kapulaga *Indonesia* Cardamom

kapuśniak *Poland* A soup of sauerkraut cooked in water with marrow bones, pork and bacon pieces, pork sausage, carrots, celeriac, Hamburg parsley and onions, then strained, the liquid thickened with a roux and served with a garnish of diced pork, bacon and sausage

kapusta *Russia* Cabbage

kapustnyi rulet *Russia* Cabbage rolls stuffed with a mixture of sweated chopped onions, seasoned minced pork and veal, boiled barley, chopped gherkins and sweet peppers and meat stock, placed in a baking dish with a thickened tomato sauce mixed with sour cream, covered with a yeast-raised rye dough, proved and baked at 180°C until brown

Kapuzinerkresse *Germany* Nasturtium

kara-age *Japan* Dusted with flour and deep-fried

karabu nati *Sri Lanka* Cloves

karahi *South Asia* A small wok used in Northern Pakistan for one-dish cooking. Used to serve food in **Balti** restaurants. Also called **kadhai**, **kurhai**

Karamel *Germany* Caramel

karamelrand *Denmark* Caramel custard

karapincha *Sri Lanka* Curry leaf

karashi *South Asia* English-style mustard condiment without adulterants

karashina *Japan* A mild version of mustard greens

karasumi *Japan* The salted roe of mullet similar to caviar

karaw *West Africa* A type of couscous made from millet. Also called **araw**

karaya gum See **E416**

karbonader 1. *Denmark* Fried pork and veal rissoles **2.** *Netherlands* A spiced rolled meat ready for roasting

Kardamome *Germany* Cardamom

kardemommerkoekje *Netherlands* Cardamom-flavoured biscuits

kardi *South Asia* A spicy yoghurt-based sauce

Kardone *Germany* Cardoon

karee *Thailand* Curry

karei *Japan* Flounder or sole

kare kare *Philippines* A meat and vegetable stew thickened with ground peanuts and coloured red with burong-mustasa. The meat is usually oxtail, shin beef or tripe. Served with fried bagoong. Also called **kari kari**

karela *South Asia* Bitter gourd

Karelian hotpot See **karjalanpaisti**

Karelian open pasties *Finland* Rye dough formed into an oval boat shape, filled with a cooked savoury rice mixture, baked in the oven and served warm with a topping of chopped hard-boiled eggs and butter

karella *South Asia* Bitter gourd

Karfiol *Austria* Cauliflower

karhu *Finland* Bear

karhunkinkku *Finland* Smoked leg of bear

karhunliha *Finland* Bear meat

kari *Sri Lanka* Curry. See also **red curry, white curry**

karicollen *Belgium* Tiny steamed snails served as street food

karides güveç *Turkey* Prawns cooked in a tomato sauce and gratinated with cheese

kari kari *Philippines* A meat and vegetable stew thickened with ground peanuts. See also **kare kare**

kari patty *South Asia* Curry leaves

kari phulia *South Asia* Sweet nim leaves

karjalanpaisti *Finland* A casserole of cubed lamb, pork or beef with onions and carrots, seasoned and flavoured with bay, cooked very slowly in the oven and served with boiled potatoes and mashed swede. Also called **Karelian hotpot**

karkadé *West Africa* A chilled drink. See also **jus de bissap**

karljohanssvamp *Sweden* The boletus fungus

karlovska lukanka *Bulgaria* A large sausage made with pork, beef and bacon (4:2:1), chopped and mixed with sugar, seasoning, caraway seeds and oregano, filled into wide casings, tied in 25 cm links, pricked, air-dried, wrapped and stored in wood ash for up to a year

Karlssons frestelse *Sweden* As **Jansson's temptation**, but using buckling instead of anchovies or matjes herring

karnemelk *Netherlands* Buttermilk

karni yarik *Turkey* Aubergine flesh removed via a single incision, chopped and fried in butter with onions and minced lamb or mutton, placed back in the skin, buttered and baked in the oven until browned

kärnmjölk *Sweden* Buttermilk

Karotten *Germany* Carrots

karp *Russia* Carp

karpalo *Finland* Cranberry

karpalo kiisseli *Finland* A cranberry pudding made from the juice thickened with **fécule** or similar

karper *Netherlands* Carp

Karpfen *Germany* Carp

karry *Denmark* Curry

Kartano *Finland* A cows' milk cheese similar to Gouda

kartofel *Russia* Potato

kartofelnye pirozhki z barabinoy *Central Asia* Lamb patties from Kazakhstan made with grated potatoes, squeezed dry in a towel, mixed with grated onion and minced lamb, seasoned and flavoured with chopped parsley, coriander and ground cumin and brought together with flour and egg, made into round patties and fried in clarified butter

kartofelnye vareniki *Russia* Potato dumplings made from mashed potatoes, flour and lard (11:3:1); bound with egg yolk and kneaded to a silky dough; stuffed with sweetened chopped prunes and walnuts; poached until they float; drained and rolled in toasted breadcrumbs mixed with cinnamon and sugar. Served immediately with sour cream.

kartofelnyi salat *Russia* Potato salad, potatoes usually sliced with radishes, spring onions, gherkins and dill and dressed with Russian dressing

Kartoffel (*plural* **Kartoffeln**) *Germany* Potato

Kartoffelbrei *Germany* Puréed potatoes

Kartoffelklösse *Germany* Potato dumplings made with riced cooked potatoes, semolina and flour (8:1:1), seasoned, flavoured with nutmeg and brought together with beaten egg until the dough holds its shape in a spoon. Made into balls about 5 to 7 cm in diameter and poached in simmering water until they float and a further minute after they float. Served with butter and fried or toasted breadcrumbs. Usually stuffed with e.g. croûtons, meat or plum jam.

kartoffelmos *Denmark* Mashed potato used as a stuffing, potato puffs

Kartoffelpuffer *Germany* Large potato pancakes made from grated raw potato fried in a flour and egg batter served very hot with cold apple purée as accompaniment

Kartoffelsalat *Germany* Potato salad

Kartoffelspatzen *Germany* Cold boiled potatoes on the raw side, grated and mixed with hot milk, butter, breadcrumbs and seasoning and bound with egg, made into small dumplings and poached in water. Drained and served with melted butter.

Kartoffelsuppe *Germany* Potato soup made with diced potatoes, stock or water and cream (5:3:1) cooked in the stock or seasoned water, rubbed through a sieve (not liquidized), and mixed with cream, some milk and grated onion, and simmered 5 minutes

kartoffler *Denmark* Potato

kartofi sus sirene *Bulgaria* Sliced potatoes and cheese baked in milk

karupillam *Malaysia* Curry leaf

karvaviza *Bulgaria* A black pudding including pork from the neck and belly minced with lungs, heart and kidneys, mixed with pigs' blood, seasoned, flavoured with allspice, caraway and oregano, packed in casings, linked, dried and smoked

karvaviza drug vid *Bulgaria* A **karvaviza** which is boiled rather than air-dried

karvaviza po banski *Bulgaria* As **karvaviza** but including pigs' spleen (melt)

kasar peyniri *Turkey* A hard, cooked-curd ewes' milk cheese with a strong, pungent-flavoured and dense paste, dry-salted for 15 days and ripened for 3 months

kascher *France* Kosher

Käse *Germany* Cheese

Käsefladen *Germany* Cheese omelette

Käsekuchen *Germany* A flat cheesecake

Käserösti 1. *Germany* See **potatiskaka med ost 2.** *Switzerland* Sliced crustless white bread soaked in milk in a baking dish, topped with Swiss cheese and baked until brown. Served with a sprinkling of chopped fried onions.

Käsestangen *Germany* Cheese straws

Käseteller *Germany* Cheese plate

Käsetorte *Germany* Cheesecake

Käsewurst *Austria* A sausage made from a pork sausage mix containing an additional 15 to 35% diced Gruyère, Emmental or similar cheese

kasha *Russia* 1. Whole buckwheat groats 2. The dish made by dry-frying the buckwheat groats until they pop, then adding 1.5 to 2 times their weight in water and cooking in the oven (180°C) or in a steamer for about 45 minutes until soft

kashata *East Africa* A kind of peanut brittle snack made from dry-roasted peanuts mixed with caramelized sugar, grated coconut and flavoured with cinnamon or ground cardamom

kashia keihi *Japan* Cassia

Kashkaval A hard, scalded ewes' or ewes' and cows' milk cheese made from spun curd in the Balkans with an aromatic salty flavour and which has been ripened for 2 to 3 months. Similar to **Cacio Cavallo**. Also called **kaskaval, kachkaval**

Kashmiri chilli *South Asia* A large deep red chilli from Kashmir used throughout India for its colour and flavour rather than for its hotness. Treat as sweet red pepper.

Kashmiri mirich *South Asia* Kashmiri chilli

Kashmir masala A mild Indian spice mix containing black cumin seeds, green cardamoms, black peppercorns, cloves, cinnamon, mace and nutmeg

kashrut See **kashruth**

kashruth Orthodox Jewish dietary laws and a description of the state of a food being kosher. Also called **kashrut**

kashubha *Philippines* Saffron

kas kas *Malaysia* Poppy seeds

Kaskaval See **Kashkaval**

Kasseler Leberwurst *Germany* A dark coloured sausage made from pigs' liver and diced lean pork

Kasseler Rippchen *Germany* Smoked loin and spare rib of pork usually roasted and served with potatoes and braised red cabbage or sauerkraut

Kasseri *Greece* A hard, scalded-curd, mild and white ewes' milk cheese similar to Provolone. Often panéed and deep-fried as a hors d'oeuvres but also used for dessert or as a melting cheese on Greek pizza.

Kassie *Germany* Cassia

Kassler *Germany* A lightly salted loin of pork, mildly smoked with the smoke from juniper berries. Eaten raw, fried or roasted. Served cold in thin slices as a hors d'oeuvre or hot with creamed potatoes or noodles and pease pudding.

Kastanie *Germany* Chestnut

Kastanienreis *Austria* A dessert made from puréed chestnuts and whipped cream

kastanier *Denmark* Chestnut

kastaniesovs *Denmark* A chestnut sauce flavoured with Madeira

kastanja *Finland* Chestnuts

kastanje *Netherlands* Chestnut

kastanjepuré *Sweden* Chestnut purée

kastanjer *Sweden* Chestnuts

kastha besan *South Asia* A special frying batter made from **besan** and yoghurt (8:3) mixed and blended with ground cardamom and coriander seeds and cloves, saffron, chilli powder, black pepper and minced chives and allowed to stand for an hour

Kastlerribchen *Belgium* Smoked pork loin cooked in white wine with sauerkraut and juniper berries

kasutado *Japan* Custard

kaszanka *Poland* A popular soft sausage or black pudding made with a well-spiced mixture of pork, pigs' liver, lungs and blood, extended with boiled buckwheat, packed in casings and knotted

kaszinótojás *Hungary* Egg mayonnaise

katai *South Asia* Whitebait

katakuri-ko *Japan* A starch thickener. Once obtained from the roots of the dog tooth violet, *Erythronium dencanis*, but now usually **fécule** which is much cheaper.

katalou *Turkey* A type of vegetable stew made with coarsely chopped French beans, aubergines, sweet green peppers, tomatoes and okra simmered in oil with garlic and chopped parsley

katch *South Asia* Lamb

katchumbari *East Africa* A relish from Kenya made from chopped and/or shredded vegetables from one or more of tomatoes, onion, garlic, sweet pepper, cucumber and cabbage flavoured with chilli pepper or coriander, seasoned and dressed with lemon juice

kateh *Middle East* Plain boiled rice dried off in the oven to form a crust on the surface of the rice

Katenrauchwurst *Germany* A country-style, very large (45 cm by 10 cm) **Rohwurst** made from coarsely chopped pork containing chunks of smoked pork slowly smoked over aromatic woods such as juniper, pine, heather or beech until very dark and strongly flavoured. Often served with beer and black bread.

Katenschinken *Germany* A smoked ham baked in a rye flour dough

Katenspeck *Germany* A speciality pork product made from cured, smoked and cooked belly pork. It has a dark brown rind and may be eaten cold or used to flavour stews and soups.

Katerfisch *Germany* Fillets of sole marinated for 10 minutes with salt and lemon juice, laid in a buttered baking dish, covered with a layer of tomato purée mixed with vinegar and horseradish, scattered with sweated onion rings, dotted with butter and baked at 190°C until firm. Served from the dish.

kathal *South Asia* Jackfruit

kathal ke beej *South Asia* Jackfruit

katiem *Thailand* Garlic

katkarapu *Finland* **1.** Shrimp **2.** Prawn

katnim *South Asia* Curry leaf

katora The small metal or earthenware bowls in which individual portions of food are served at an Indian meal. The different components of a meal are served separately and not on one plate as in the West. Also called **katori**

katori *South Asia* Katora

katrinplommen *Sweden* Prunes

katsuo *Japan* Skipjack tuna. Usually referred to as bonito, strictly Pacific bonito.

katsuobushi *Japan* Blocks of boned and dried Pacific bonito (skipjack tuna) flesh used to make bonito flakes

katsuodashi *Japan* A liquid concentrate of **dashi**; instant dashi

katsuo-kezuriki *Japan* A special implement for making Pacific bonito flakes from blocks

katsura-muki *Japan* A long very thin sheet of mooli or carrot cut from a cylinder of the vegetable in one continuous motion. The sheet is as wide as the cylinder is long and can be up to 40 cm long. When rolled it is used to make very fine shreds.

katt pie *Wales* A traditional deep-pan double-crust mutton pie about 10 cm diameter, made on Templeton fair day, the 12th of November. The filling in the hot water pastry is minced mutton, nowadays generally lamb, layered with equal quantities of currants and brown sugar in that order and baked at 220°C for 20 to 30 minutes. (NOTE: As the letter 'k' does not exist in Welsh, the origin of the name is a mystery.)

katushki *Russia* Fish **quenelles** made from white fish flesh and softened white bread processed with egg, seasoning and chopped dill, consistency adjusted with flour, formed into balls (2cm diameter), chilled, then poached in fish stock, broth or consommé

Katzenjammer *Germany* Sliced cold beef and cucumber in mayonnaise

Katzenkopt *Netherlands* Edam

Katzenminze *Germany* Catmint

kau fu *China* A type of half cooked spongy gluten dough added to braised dishes

kaviaarib *Finland* Caviar

kaviar *Denmark, Norway, Sweden* Caviar

kaviár *Hungary* Caviar

Kaviar *Germany* Caviar

kavurma *Turkey* A dish of boiled, drained and chopped spinach mixed with chopped onions and minced mutton, fried in butter and served with a poached egg on top

käx *Sweden* Biscuit

kayla Plantain

kayu manis *Indonesia, Malaysia* Cinnamon

kaz *Turkey* Goose

kazunoko no agemono *Japan* Soft herring roes, blanched in salted water for 2 minutes, dried, coated in batter and deep-fried. The batter is made from flour, salt and warm water rested and, at the last minute, stiffly beaten egg white folded in.

kazy *Central Asia* A horsemeat sausage from Kyrgyzstan and Kazakhstan

k'dras *North Africa* A Moroccan chicken **tagine** cooked with onion, saffron and spices and a large amount of smen

kebab *Middle East, South Asia* Any cubed or sliced food especially meat and vegetables impaled on a skewer or brochette and cooked under the grill, over a barbecue or in a tandoori oven until lightly charred on the outside. If meat, often tenderized by marinating with an acid-based marinade and basted whilst cooking. Usually served on or off the skewer with rice and salad. Also called **kebob, shashlik**

kebabchés *Bulgaria* Meatballs

kebap *Turkey* Kebab

kebob Kebab

kecap asin *Indonesia* A thick, salty and dark coloured soya sauce used for colouring and flavour

kecap bentang manis *Indonesia* Kecap manis

kecap ikan *Indonesia* A fermented fish sauce

kecap manis *Indonesia* A sweet, thick dark aromatic soya sauce used as a seasoning and condiment and for satay. Also called **ketjap sauce, kecap bentang manis, sweet soya sauce**

kecipir *Indonesia* Goa bean

kecombrang *Indonesia* Ginger buds

kecsege *Hungary* Sterlet, a small sturgeon from the Caspian Sea

kecskeméti barackpuding *Hungary* Apricot pudding with vanilla cream

kedgeree *United Kingdom* A dish of flaked smoked haddock mixed with cooked rice, curry powder and hard-boiled egg usually served at breakfast. Adapted from the Indian dish **khichhari** (fish with rice and lentils) during the British occupation of India.

kedjenou *West Africa* A popular chicken stew from the Cote d'Ivoire made from chicken pieces, aubergines, okra, chilli pepper and tomatoes in water or stock flavoured with grated ginger, bay leaf, garlic and thyme. It is usually slow-cooked in a sealed pot which is shaken from time to time to prevent sticking.

keem *Korea* Nori

keema 1. *South Asia* Minced meat **2.** *Central Asia* A common sauce from Afghanistan rather like a bolognese, made with minced meat fried in oil and simmered with tomato purée and water

Kefalotir *Balkans* A cheese similar to **Kefalotiri**

Kefalotiri *Cyprus, Greece* A very hard scalded-curd ewes' or ewes' and goats' milk cheese similar to Parmesan and made in a cylindrical shape with a rounded top. Also called **Kefalotyri**

Kefalotyri See **Kefalotiri**

kefir *Russia, Scandinavia* A slightly alcoholic and sour drink made originally from mare's milk, now from cows' milk and cultured with mixed microorganisms in the form of kefir grains. Contains 0.6 to 0.9% lactic acid and 0.2 to 0.8% alcohol. It is used to treat gastro-intestinal problems in Russia.

kefir grains A dried agglomeration of lactic Streptococci, Leuconostocs, yeasts and dried milk, broken into small pieces, To use, they are soaked in 2 changes of water at 20 to 30°C until swollen to 3 or 4 times their original size. They are then used to ferment milk or whey for 1 day to make kefir. They may be reused until they disintegrate, if washed after each use and kept in the refrigerator.

kefta See **kefteji**

keftedakia *Greece* Small keftedes eaten as an appetizer. Also called **keftethakia**

keftedes *Greece* Keftethes

kefteji *North Africa* Fried meatballs usually of mutton or offal flavoured with coriander and cumin. Often served in a rich pepper sauce with an egg. Also called **kefta**

keftethakia *Greece* Keftedakia

keftethes *Greece* Large meatballs made from seasoned minced lamb, beef or veal, mixed with white breadcrumbs, sweated chopped onions and garlic and flavoured with ouzo and mint, floured and fried. Served with salad and bread. Also called **keftedes**

keitto *Finland* Soup

kekada *South Asia* Crab

kekel *East Africa* Ethiopian for boiled meat

kekererwten *Netherlands* Chick peas

Keks *Germany* Biscuit

keksi *Finland* Biscuit

kela *South Asia* Banana

keladi *Malaysia* Yam

kelapa *Indonesia, Malaysia* Coconut

kelapa muda *Indonesia* A young coconut about 10 months old. It has a soft gelatinous sweet flesh which is easily scraped from the shell. Used in desserts and drinks.

kelapa sayur *Malaysia* Chopped mixed vegetables cooked in coconut milk

kelapa setengah tua *Malaysia* Young coconut. See also **kelapa muda**

kelapa tua santan *Malaysia* Coconut milk

kelbimbó *Hungary* Brussels sprouts

keledek *Malaysia* Sweet potato

kelewele *West Africa* A street food from Ghana made from sliced plantains marinated in a spice mixture of grated ginger, cayenne peppers and salt in water then deep-fried. Other spices may be added to the marinade and lemon juice can be used instead of water

kelp A general name for varieties of brown seaweed of the genus *Laminaria*, common on the European coasts. Can be eaten raw or cooked.

kelt A salmon which has spawned and is thin and useless for eating

kem *Thailand* Salty

kemangi *Indonesia, Malaysia* A mild basil native to Indonesia and Malaysia

kembang kol *Indonesia* Cauliflower

kembang pala *Malaysia* Mace

kemiri *Indonesia* Candlenut

kempferia galangal Long thin roots of a plant, *Kaempferia galangal* or *K. pandurata*, which resemble dahlia tubers. Normally dried and sliced for use in East Asian dishes. It has a stronger flavour than **lesser galangal** and should be used sparingly. Also called **lesser ginger**

kenan *West Africa* A traditional Ghanaian dish made with a whole fish. See also **kyenam**

kencur *Indonesia* **1.** Powdered lesser galangal root **2.** Zedoary

keneffa *North Africa* **Warqa pastry** from Morocco layered with sugar, cinnamon and almonds

keng *Thailand* Indicates liquid in a dish. See also **gaeng**

kenkey *West Africa* Finely ground maize flour mixed to a dough with water and allowed to ferment for 2 to 3 days. After kneading, half the dough is boiled with an equal quantity of water for ten minutes and all combined with the uncooked dough, divided and wrapped in banana leaves which are then steamed for 2 to 3 hours.

Kentish cob Filbert

Kentish huffkin *England* A small oval flat yeast-raised loaf or roll with a deep indentation in the centre and a soft crust. The dough is enriched with a little sugar and butter and they weigh about 60 g each.

Kentish pudding pie *England* Kent Lent pie

Kentish sausage *England* A coarse-textured sausage containing lean pork and pork fat (2:1), seasoned and flavoured with sage, mace and nutmeg

kentjoer *Netherlands* Zedoary

Kent Lent pie *England* Short crust pastry baked blind in a flan case, filled with milk thickened with ground rice which is added into a creamed butter, sugar and egg mix flavoured with grated lemon zest, salt and nutmeg, currants sprinkled on top and the whole baked at 190°C until browned

Kentucky ham *United States* Ham made from pigs traditionally fattened on acorns, beans and clover. The ham is dry-salted and smoked over apple and hickory wood and matured for up to a year. The name refers to the method of curing.

Kenya coffee A sharp, aromatic coffee from Kenya

kenyér *Hungary* Bread

kepong beras boh *Indonesia* Galapong

kepro knedlo zelo *Czech Republic* A traditional Czech dish of roast pork with dumplings and sauerkraut

képviselöfánk *Hungary* Cream puff

keraa *Nepal* Banana

keran ka achar *South Asia* Pickled venison meat

kerapu bara *Malaysia* Garoupa, the fish

kerapu lodi *Indonesia* Garoupa, the fish

kerbau *Indonesia* Buffalo

kere *Indonesia* Ridged sand clam

kerma *Finland* Cream

kermakakku *Finland* Cream cake

kerma kastike *Finland* Cream sauce

kermes A red dye similar to cochineal from an insect, *Coccus ilicis*, which lives on the kermes oak. Referred to by Chaucer as grains of Portugal.

kernel The edible, usually central, part of a nut or stone of a fruit

Kernhem *Netherlands* A soft sticky cows' milk cheese with 60% butterfat. Initially rindless, it can be ripened for 30 days in a cool damp atmosphere to give a rich full flavour and an orange-brown rind.

kern milk *Scotland* The Scottish term for buttermilk

kerrie *Netherlands* Curry

kerrierijst *Netherlands* Curried rice

kers *Netherlands* Cherry

kerupuk *Indonesia* A large deep-fried crisp pancake flavoured with dried prawns. See also **krupuk**

kerupuk singkong *Indonesia* A type of poppadom made from tapioca starch and cassava chips

kesäkeitto *Finland* Summer vegetable soup (NOTE: Literally 'summer soup'.)

kesar *South Asia* Saffron

keshar *Nepal* Saffron

keshy yena *Caribbean* Edam cheese stuffed and baked with various mixtures of poultry, fish, shellfish, meat, etc (NOTE: From the Dutch East Indies)

kesksou *North Africa* The Berber name for **couscous**

keskülü fukara *Turkey* A sweetened milk pudding thickened with rice flour and flavoured with liquidized almonds or almond essence and chopped almonds and topped with chopped pistachio nuts and desiccated coconut. Served chilled.

kesong puti *Philippines* Cottage cheese made from water buffalo milk. Also called **quesong puti**

kesra *North Africa* A type of Arab bread made with strong flour containing about 10% cornmeal in the usual way using a sourdough starter equal to approximately one third of the previous batch. Also called **kisra**, **khobz**

kesram *South Asia* Saffron

kesti *Finland* A cheese similar to Tilsit, flavoured with caraway seeds

keta *Russia* Siberian salmon

keta caviar 1. Ikura **2.** Ketovaia

ketan *Indonesia* A glutinous rice served as a dessert with desiccated coconut and a brown sugar syrup

ketchup A commercially produced sauce sold in bottles to be used cold as a condiment. Usually of one particular flavour, e.g. tomato, mushroom, etc. See also **Pontac ketchup**. Also called **catsup**, **catchup** (NOTE: The name is derived from the Indonesian word for sauce, 'kecap')

ketela pohon *Indonesia* Cassava

ketelkoek *Netherlands* Steamed pudding

ketimun *Indonesia* Cucumber

ketjap *Netherlands* Ketchup

ketjap sauce Kecap manis

ketola *Malaysia* Angled loofah

ketola ular *Malaysia* Snake gourd

ketovaia *Russia* The large red and almost transparent eggs of Siberian salmon. It is more salty then true caviar and has a different flavour. Also called **red caviar**, **keta caviar**

ketumbar *Indonesia, Malaysia* Coriander seeds

ketumbar jinten *Indonesia, Malaysia* A mixture of ground cumin and coriander seeds

Keule *Germany* Saddle, haunch or leg (of meat)

Keulenrochen *Germany* Thornback ray

kevada *Nepal* Screwpine

kewra Screwpine

kewra essence An extract of the flowers of screwpine used in India to flavour meat, poultry and rice dishes

kex *Sweden* An unsweetened cracker biscuit

key lime West Indian lime

key lime pie A blind baked pastry or Graham cracker case filled with a mixture of sweetened condensed milk, lime juice and egg yolks which have been cooked out over a bain-marie. Served cold or topped with meringue and browned in the oven.

kezuri-bushi *Japan* Flakes or shavings of dried Pacific bonito

kg The abbreviation for kilogram in any language

kha *Thailand* Greater galangal

khabli palau *Central Asia* An elaborate lamb pilaff from Afghanistan made with browned almond slices and a **julienne** of carrots and raisins, and flavoured with garam masala, ground cardamom and ground coriander. The meat, cooked with onions and the spices, is mixed with the carrots, raisins and almonds and put on top of the half-cooked rice before being finished in the oven or on top of the stove.

khachapuri *Southwest Asia* A Georgian yeasted flour and water dough incorporating melted butter (25% of flour). It is kneaded and allowed to rise, rolled out and cut into squares. Grated Haloumi cheese mixed with egg is piled in the middle of each square, and the corners pulled into the centre. The breads are egg-washed and the filling sprinkled with chopped herbs, then the breads baked at 190°C for 25 minutes or until the cheese is browned.

khagina *South Asia* Eggs and yoghurt (6:1) beaten with (**besan**) at the rate of 5 tbsp besan for 6 eggs and flavoured with ground coriander and cardamom seed, grated onion, chopped chives and salt to taste. The dish is then cooked as a rather thick omelette in the usual way and served by cutting thick slanted slices from the folded omelette.

khajur *South Asia* Date

kha kho *Vietnam* Shallots

khal *Nepal* A stone mortar used for grinding grains and spices

khalia *South Asia* A brass or cast iron mortar used for grinding hard grains and spices using a matching pestle (**musaria**)

kha mar *Burma* Oyster

kha-min *Thailand* Turmeric

kha min khao *Thailand* Zedoary

khamir *South Asia* A natural yeast used for making soft bread. It is propagated in sourdough fashion with flour and yoghurt.

khanom chine *Thailand* Small bundles of cooked rice noodles sold as instant food. Usually resteamed and served with a savoury sauce or curry.

khanom jeen *Thailand* **1.** Fast food **2.** Instant food

khao *Thailand* Rice

khao chair *Thailand* Ice-cold cooked long-grain rice served with a selection of small snacks and appetizers

khao niew *Thailand* Sticky rice

khao pad *Thailand* Fried rice

khao phod *Thailand* Sweet corn

khao phoune *Laos* Cooked rice vermicelli topped with bean sprouts, salad leaves, chopped banana heart and flower and covered with a creamy coconut milk sauce flavoured with chillies and peanuts and containing chopped fish, meat or poultry. Often served for breakfast.

khao tom gung *Thailand* **Congee** flavoured with fish sauce. Eaten for breakfast.

khara korma *South Asia* A korma made with whole instead of ground spices. The meat is simmered first with yoghurt and cinnamon until dry, then with a water extract of garlic until dry, then fried in butter until cooked and crusty. It is then mixed with the previously soaked spices and herbs and their marinating liquor: typically chilli peppers, fennel, cinnamon, cloves, cumin, bay leaves, peppercorns marinated in lime juice, nigella and cardamom seeds, plus a little asafoetida and ground ginger. All is then cooked in butter until dry and the fat separates.

khas khas 1. *South Asia* Poppy seeds **2.** An aromatic grass, *Vetiveria zizanioides*, used as a flavouring in Indian cooking. Grown in India and the south of the USA. Also called **vetiver**

khas syrup A sweetened extract of the aromatic grass, khas khas

khas water An extract of the aromatic grass, khas khas

kha-wel *Burma* Cuttlefish

kha-ya-nyo *Burma* Asian mussel

kheer *South Asia* A dessert made from rice cooked in milk until it is completely disintegrated> Then sugar, raisins, chopped dried apricots, bruised cardamom seeds and cinnamon stick are added and the whole cooked for 1.5 hours. Almond slivers are added towards the end. The mixture is then cooled and thinned with a little rose water until a thick pouring consistency, put in individual bowls, chilled and decorated. Also called **sheer**

kheera *South Asia* Cucumber

khesari *South Asia* Lath

khichhari *South Asia* A dish of cooked rice mixed with a variety of ingredients from a few sprouted seeds or lentils to an elaborate mixture of spices, nuts and raisins. The origin of kedgeree. Also called **kichardi, kitcheri, khichri**

khichri *South Asia* Khichhari

khing *Thailand* Ginger

khing dong *Thailand* Chow chow preserve

khleb *Russia* Bread

khleb i sol *Russia* Bread and salt, the traditional words of welcome in Russia. The two commodities are often offered to guests when arriving for a celebratory meal.

khli' *North Africa* Marinated and dried strips of meat which are then cooked and preserved in fat

khnehey *Cambodia* Ginger

khoa *South Asia* Milk dehydrated by stirring over a low heat until it becomes a thick paste which is pressed into cakes. See also **khoya**

khoai mon *Vietnam* Taro

khobz *North Africa* Bread

khobz bishemar *North Africa* **1.** A savoury turnover or similar made from pastry wrapped around a filling or from a stuffed pitta-type bread **2.** Bread dough made into parcels filled with a mixture of beef suet, red chilli peppers, and fresh parsley, all finely chopped with ground cumin and paprika. Allowed to prove then docked and fried in butter until crisp and golden. Served hot.

kholodny sup-salat A cold soup made from chopped red onion, radishes, tomatoes, cucumbers and garlic seasoned and dressed with a little Tabasco sauce plus oil and lemon juice, mixed with chilled chicken consommé just before serving accompanied by garlic-flavoured croûtons

khoobani *South Asia* Apricot

khoresh *Central Asia* An Iranian dish which literally means 'sauce' but contains meat browned in clarified butter with onions and spices, then simmered with vegetables and/or fruit often with the addition of lemon juice and brown sugar. Always served with a rice dish such as **chelou**.

khoreshe alu *Central Asia* A khoresh of cubed lamb or beef flavoured with turmeric and cinnamon. Prunes, lemon juice and brown sugar are added for the last 45 minutes of simmering.

khouzi *Middle East* A festive dish from Iraq consisting of a whole lamb steam-roasted whole, head down, in a tannour oven over a dish of saffron rice (**timman z'affaran**). The top is sealed with palm leaves and clay and the fat from the tail end bastes the lamb as it slowly cooks, with the juices being absorbed by the rice. Palm-leaf ribs are used to skewer the lamb and these impart their own flavour.

khoya *South Asia* Milk dehydrated by stirring over a low heat until it becomes a thick paste which is pressed into cakes. It is used for making sweetmeats and Indian cakes and to enrich sweet or savoury dishes. A different texture is obtained by coagulating the milk with lemon juice before dehydrating. Also called **khoa**

khren *Russia* Horseradish

khtim baraing *Cambodia* Onion

khtim kraham *Cambodia* Shallots

khtim slek *Cambodia* Spring onion or scallion

khubz *North Africa* Morrocan bread cooked in a circular glazed terracotta dish. It is proved but not knocked back.

khubz-tanou *Middle East* A very thin bread from the Lebanon

khum *South Asia* Cloud ear fungus

khurma po-samarkandski *Russia* Blanched persimmons, skinned, cut in sections and fanned on a plate, covered with a sauce made with corn flour-thickened orange juice, flavoured with lemon juice and zest, and scattered with pomegranate seeds

khus-khus *South Asia* Poppy seed

khuwa *Nepal* Milk dehydrated by stirring over a low heat until it becomes a thick paste which is pressed into cakes. See also **khoya**

khvorost *Russia* Deep-fried biscuits made from egg yolk, egg and icing sugar, creamed, flavoured with rum and vanilla and mixed with salted plain flour to make a stiff paste; kneaded 10 minutes, rolled out very thin and cut into 12 by 5 cm rectangles; a longitudinal slit made at one end and the other end threaded through this; deep-fried in hot oil, drained and sprinkled with cinnamon and icing sugar. A very traditional biscuit.

kibbeh *Middle East* **1.** Made with **burghul 2.** Lean lamb and **burghul** (1:2), the burghul washed and water squeezed out, the lamb double minced, mixed with finely chopped onion and seasoning and kneaded for 10 to 15 minutes with wet hands until a smooth paste results

kibbeh nayeh *Middle East* Kibbeh niya

kibbeh niya *Middle East* Kibbeh made with fine **burghul**, spread on a plate, covered with olive oil and sprinkled with chilli powder and pine nuts. Served with lettuce and raw onion. Also called **kibbeh nayeh**

kibbeh tarablousieh *Middle East* Minced lamb fried in oil for 15 minutes, chopped onion, seasoning and allspice added and fried 20 minutes, then roasted or fried pine nuts and parsley added to form a stuffing. Kibbeh in egg-sized balls made into long oval purses between the index finger and thumb, stuffing added, the package closed, rolled into an oval shape and deep-fried. Served with lemon wedges.

kibble, to To grind or chop coarsely

kibbled wheat Cracked wheat

kicap cair *Malaysia* Light soya sauce

kicap hitam *Malaysia* A sweet dark soya sauce similar to **kecap manis**

kicap pekat *Malaysia* Dark soya sauce

kichardi *South Asia* A dish of cooked rice mixed with a variety of ingredients. See also **khichhari**

Kichererbsen *Germany* Chickpeas

kickshaw *United Kingdom* An old-fashioned term for a food delicacy or fancy dish

kid A young goat, a popular meat in Mediterranean countries

Kidderminster plum cake *England* A type of **Eccles cake** with a filling made from mixed dried fruits, flour, soft brown sugar, butter and egg (4:1:1:1:1), well mixed and flavoured with ground mixed spice. Before baking at 200°C, the tops of the cakes are docked and brushed with a mixture of water and granulated sugar.

kidney The internal organ of an animal which filters out breakdown products of metabolism from the blood and delivers them in water solution to the bladder. The main bulk is a uniform brownish-red tissue arranged around blood vessels and tubes. Generally prized as tender and tasty offal. The kidneys of smaller animals are grilled or fried after removing the hard core, outer membrane and fat. The kidneys of larger animals are generally stewed.

kidney bean A type of kidney-shaped dried **French bean** ranging in colour from white to black. See also **red kidney bean**

kidney fat See **suet**

kidney soup A brown roux and tomato purée boiled with brown stock; chopped ox kidney, carrot and onion lightly browned in fat and a bouquet garni added; all simmered and skimmed for 2 hours; bouquet garni removed, and the remainder liquidized, strained, seasoned, consistency adjusted and garnished with diced cooked kidney. Also called **soupe aux rognons**

kiełbasa *Poland* A boiling sausage formed in a ring containing beef, pork, garlic, seasoning and spices

Kieler Sprotten *Germany* Salted and smoked sprats

kieli *Finland* Tongue

kienyeji *East Africa* A Kenyan dish of beans or peas. See also **irio**

kiev A method of pocketing, stuffing and cooking chicken breasts. See also **chicken Kiev**

kieve *Ireland* A large mash tun used for brewing

kikka-kabu *Japan* Baby turnips, peeled and trimmed top and bottom, cut with a chrysanthemum cut, stood in salted water for 30 minutes to soften, dried and sprinkled with a mixture of caster sugar and salt and garnished with sweet pepper rings or with grated lemon to resemble red or yellow chrysanthemums. Stood in individual bowls lined with chrysanthemum leaves.

kiku *Japan* Chrysanthemum flowers and leaves used as a garnish. Also called **kikuna**

kikuna *Japan* Kiku

kikurage *Japan* Cloud ear fungus

kilawin *Philippines* A method of preparing fish for consumption without heating it by marinating in coconut vinegar, lime juice or kalamansi juice until it becomes translucent

kilic kebap *Turkey* A kebab of swordfish pieces, onion, tomatoes and bay leaves dressed with lemon and grilled over charcoal

kilkis *Scandinavia* Norwegian anchovies, preserved in brine. See also **anchois de Norvège**

Killarney *Ireland* Irish Cheddar cheese

Kilmeny kail *Scotland* A young rabbit chopped in convenient pieces and a piece of bacon of about the same weight simmered in water for 2 to 3 hours. When the meat is cooked it is removed and finely chopped cabbage or kale, equal in weight to the rabbit, is added and cooked a further 15 minutes. Some of the meat is diced and returned to the soup, which is served with oatcakes; the rest is served separately as a main course.

Kilner jar *United Kingdom* A strong glass jar with a separate glass lid sealed to the jar with a rubber ring and held on by a metal closure. Used for preserving fruit and vegetables. (NOTE: Named after Kilner's Bridge, a village in South Yorkshire)

kilocalorie The old unit of energy equivalent to 1000 calories. Often referred to as Calorie with a capital C and now replaced by the kilojoule. It is the energy necessary to heat 1 kg of water by 1°C.

kilogram The common measure of weight approximately equal to 2.2 lbs, divided in grams (g) (1000 g per kg). 1 lb is approximately 454 g and 1 oz approximately 28 g. Abbreviation **kg**

kilogramme *France* Kilogram

kilojoule The unit of energy used in nutrition which has replaced the kilocalorie or Calorie. 4.2 kilojoules equals 1 Calorie. Abbreviation **kJ**

kim *Korea* Toasted **nori** eaten as a snack or crumbled over food

kim cham *Vietnam* Lily buds

kimchi *Korea* Fermented cabbage (usually Chinese leaves) or other vegetables, flavoured with salt, garlic and chillies. An acquired taste which provides most of the vegetable nutrients in the Korean diet. A Western substitute can be obtained by mixing chopped Chinese leaves which have been salted to remove excess liquid with minced spring onions, garlic, ginger, chillies,

a little sugar, soya sauce and vinegar and storing in a closed jar in the refrigerator for at least 24 hours. Also called **Korean pickled cabbage**

kimini *Japan* A dish of braised shrimps. See also **ebi no kimini**

kinako *Japan* Soya bean flour

kinchay *Philippines* Chinese celery

king *Thailand* Ginger

king, à la *England, France* Served in a rich cream sauce with mushrooms and green sweet peppers

king crab A large light-brown crab, *Paralithodes camtschatica*, with long legs and weighing up to 3.5 kg, found on the coasts of Alaska

King George whiting *Australia* A fish, *Sillaginodes punctatus*, which is found only in Australian waters, mainly in South Australia, and is considered one of the finest fish for eating. It can grow to 70 cm in length and up to 4 kg in weight. The body is light to dark brown, the underside is silver below and there is a row of small dark spots along the sides. Also called **spotted whiting**

king mandarin An important mandarin, *Citrus nobilis*, probably a mandarin/orange hybrid, from Southeast Asia and Japan. The Japanese variety is smaller and has a smoother rind than that from Southeast Asia but is slightly bitter.

king prawn A large prawn of the *Penaeidae* family, found in the Mediterranean, off the Spanish and Portuguese coasts and elsewhere in the world. Generally a dirty greyish-brown when raw, and pink to red when cooked. Varieties include crevette royale, crevette rouge, eastern king prawn, western king prawn, banana prawn and tiger prawn.

kings acre berry A hybrid blackberry of the genus *Rubus*

king salmon See **chinook salmon**

king scallop Great scallop

kinkan *Japan* Kumquat

kinkku *Finland* Ham

kinmedai *Japan* A commonly used type of red sea bream (**tai**)

kinoko *Japan* Mushroom

kinome *Japan* Young shoots of the anise pepper tree, *Xanthoxylum piperitum*, used as a garnish

kinpira *Japan* A method of cooking burdock roots or carrots or both together by cutting into small batons or matchsticks, shallow frying and seasoning with sugar, chilli pepper, sake and soya sauce

kinugoshi tofu *Japan* Silk bean curd

kip *Netherlands* Chicken

kip aan't spit *Netherlands* Grilled chicken

kippelever *Netherlands* Chicken liver

kipper A gutted herring, split and flattened from the belly side, lightly brined and then cold-smoked

kipper, to To preserve fish by salting then smoking

kipper sausage *Scotland* A sausage made with kipper flesh without bones or skin, probably mixed with suet and breadcrumbs

kippesoep *Netherlands* Chicken broth

kiri bath *Sri Lanka* A thick mixture of cooked soft rice and coconut cream, shaped into flat diamonds and served with jaggery at festivals

kiriboshi daikon *Japan* Sun-dried strips of mooli. Added to soups and stews.

kirkeen *Ireland* Carpet shell clam

kirsch A strong alcoholic infusion of cherry and cherry kernels used as a flavouring in e.g. black forest gateau

Kirschen *Germany* Cherries

Kirschenkaltschale *Germany* Morello cherries and the cracked kernels cooked in sugar syrup, strained, mixed with white wine and served cold, garnished with whole pitted cherries

Kirschwasser *Germany* Kirsch, the liqueur

kirsebær *Denmark* Cherries

kirsikka *Finland* Cherries

kisel *Russia* Kissel

kishk *Middle East* A fermented mixture of bulgar, milk and yoghurt, dried, powdered and used to make a kind of porridge

kishka *Hungary, Russia* A sausage rather like haggis made from chopped beef suet, onion, flour or rice and seasonings, stuffed in beef intestines, tied and simmered over a low heat with onions. Served hot with horseradish sauce as an appetizer. Also called **stuffed derma**

kisra *North Africa* A type of Arab bread. See also **kesra**

kissel An East European dessert of puréed red berries and/or fruit juice, thickened with gelatine, corn flour or arrowroot and served with cream. Sometimes used in the same way as redcurrant jelly in savoury sauces.

kissela dahorp *Balkans* Diced mutton simmered with herbs, separated and mixed with half cooked rice, fried chopped onions, paprika, a little vinegar and sufficient of the cooking liquor to be absorbed by the rice and all baked in the oven until the rice is cooked

kisu *Japan* A small white fish

kiszka kaszana *Poland* A cooked sausage made with blood and dehusked buckwheat

kitcheri *South Asia* A dish of cooked rice mixed with a variety of ingredients. See also **khichhari**

kited fillet *United States* A boned and filleted round fish in which a cut is made along the top of the fish to expose the main bones and viscera which are removed leaving the two halves joined by the abdominal flesh at the bottom of the fish

kitfo *East Africa* A type of steak tartare from Ethiopia, possibly warmed slightly in a frying pan, seasoned with chopped onion, lemon juice, hot chilli sauce or any of chopped chillies, cumin, cinnamon, coriander, rosemary and garlic. Made into small balls or patties and served with a variety of chopped salad vegetables.

kitha neem *South Asia* Curry leaf

kitsune-udon *Japan* Udon noodles cooked until al dente, topped with **abura-age**, simmered in **dashi**, soya sauce, **mirin** and sugar until they have absorbed most of the liquid and served with **kakejiru soup**

kiwano A large egg-shaped fruit with a reddish-yellow warty skin enclosing a sweet green watery and rather insipid flesh and large cucumber-like seeds. Eaten like passion fruit. Grown in Africa and New Zealand. Also called **horned melon**

kiwi fruit A small egg-shaped fruit up to 10 cm long from a trailing climber, *Actinidia chinensis* or *A. deliciosa*. It has a light-brown hairy skin containing a sweet bright-green flesh tasting of melons and strawberries and with symmetrically arranged black seeds. It is often peeled and sliced for decoration or used in tarts and salads. As the fruit contains proteases it can be used to tenderize meat, but will degrade gelatine and prevent jellies from setting. Originally from China, but now mainly grown and exported from New Zealand. Also called **Chinese gooseberry**

kjeks *Norway* 1. Dry crackers 2. Biscuits

kjøtt *Norway* Meat

kjøttbolle *Norway* Meatball

kjøttedeig *Norway* Minced meat

kjøttfarse *Norway* Hamburger meat, minced meat

kjøttpudding *Norway* Meat loaf

kjøttsuppe *Norway* Meat broth, bouillon

Klaben *Germany* A white fruit bread with nuts and dried vine fruits

klaicha *Middle East* A sweet pastry from Iraq made with water instead of eggs and filled with pitted dates sweated in butter. They can be in the form of balls pressed into a decorated mould, in rolls like a sausage roll or flat like a Chorley cake. They are baked at 170°C for 30 minutes.

klarbär *Sweden* Sour cherry (**amarelle**)

klare Fleischbrühe *Germany* Clear beef broth, consommé

klare Rindsuppe *Austria* Clear beef broth

klatkager *Denmark* Rice fritters

Kleie *Germany* Bran

kleine gevlekte hondshaai *Netherlands* Dogfish

kleingefleckter Katzenhai *Germany* Dogfish

Kleist *Germany* Brill

klejner *Denmark* Crullers

kletskoppen *Netherlands* Ginger snaps

Kliesche *Germany* Dab, the fish

klimatofilla *Greece* Vine leaves

klimp *Sweden* A traditional product of dumplings made from a very thick roux-based white sauce with added egg yolk and variously flavoured with grated bitter almonds, crushed cardamom seeds, or grated cheese, poured into moulds, chilled, turned out and nowadays usually sliced for use as a consommé garnish

klipkous *South Africa* Abalone

klippfisk *Norway* Cod that is salted and spread out on stones and rocks to dry. Also called **clipfish**

klobas *Czech Republic, Hungary* A juicy sausage made from smoked pork or veal mixed with wine, filled into casings and formed into a continuous spiral like a Cumberland sausage

Kloepfer *Switzerland* Klöpfer

Klöpfer *Switzerland* A cervelas sausage from Basle made of beef, pork, bacon and pork rind, seasoned and lightly spiced, packed in medium or narrow hog casings, tied into 10 cm lengths and lightly smoked. Also called **Kloepfer**

Klopse *Germany* Meatballs made with a mixture of meats

Klösse *Germany* Dumplings made from potatoes and flour mixed with milk, fat and sometimes bacon. Breadcrumbs and semolina may be incorporated. Boiled and served as an accompaniment to sweet or savoury dishes. Also called **Knödel**

Klosterkäse *Germany* A soft, surface-ripened cheese made in block form from semi-skimmed cows' milk. Similar to Romadur. Contains 52% water, 19% fat and 24% protein.

kluay *Thailand* Banana

klyukva *Russia* Cranberries

Knackerli *Switzerland* A spiced sausage from Appenzell made from beef, pork and veal. Also called **Appenzellerli**

Knackwurst *Germany* A short fat variety of Frankfurter made from a seasoned mixture of lean pork, beef, pork fat and saltpetre, flavoured with garlic and cumin, filled into beef runners, dried and smoked. Served hot after poaching.

knaidlech Very popular Jewish dumplings made with crushed unleavened matzos, eggs, water, salt and molten fat or oil, boiled and served with soup. Suitable for Passover since made with matzo meal. Also called **knedlach**

knakworst *Netherlands* Sausage, Frankfurter

Knaost Pultost

knead, to To mix a stiff dough by repeatedly compressing it and folding in or over; this may be done manually or mechanically by using a dough hook at slow speed. In the case of bread doughs made from strong flour, kneading is used to develop sheets of gluten in the mixture and to incorporate air. The air acts as nuclei for the formation of bubbles of carbon dioxide during rising and proving; the gluten sheets facilitate their retention in the cooking dough.

kneaded butter Beurre manié

knedlach See **knaidlech**

knedlíky *Czech Republic* Huge soft dumplings made from flour and/or semolina, eggs, fat and water, boiled and served with soup or if sweetened as a dessert

Knepfle Small dumplings from Alsace made with semolina or mashed potatoes and flour, mixed with chopped parsley, chopped leek and egg yolks

kneten *Germany* To knead

knickerbocker glory Alternate layers of jelly, fruit, ice cream and whipped cream assembled in a tall sundae glass

Kniestück *Germany* Knuckle of veal

knife A thin steel blade, one edge of which is sharpened, the whole fitted with a handle. They come in various thicknesses and profiles and sometimes with a serrated or saw edge, for various types of work.

knishes Semicircular Jewish pastry turnovers with a variety of fillings, some specific to particular festivals

kniv *Denmark, Norway, Sweden* Knife

knob celery Celeriac

Knoblauch *Germany* Garlic

Knoblauchwurst *Germany* A sausage made from a seasoned mixture of lean pork and pork fat, spiced and heavily flavoured with garlic and formed in a ring

knoblaugh *United States* Knoblauchwurst

Knochen *Germany* Bones

knock back, to To lightly knead a yeast-raised dough which has risen once in order to eliminate large gas bubbles and help further develop the gluten. This is done prior to shaping the dough. Also called **knock down, to**

knock down, to To knock back

knockit corn *Scotland* Groats made from bere, the original domesticated barley from the Orkneys

knockpølse *Denmark* A Danish version of knackwurst made from a mixture of finely chopped beef, pork and veal with about 10% diced pork back fat, seasoning and saltpetre, flavoured with nutmeg, cinnamon, ginger and garlic, packed into hog casings, linked (12 cm), air-dried and hot smoked

knockwurst *United States* A version of Knackwurst made with smoked beef and pork

Knödel *Austria, Germany* Dumpling

knödel alla tirolese in brodo *Italy* Bread and bacon dumplings served in beef broth

knoflook *Netherlands* Garlic

knol *Netherlands* Turnip

knol-kohl *South Asia* Kohlrabi

knolle *Italy* Large boiled dumplings from the northwest

Knollensellerie *Germany* Celeriac

knotted marjoram See **marjoram**

knuckle The lower parts (shin) of a leg of veal, pork or lamb, extending down to the hock

knuckle of lamb See **shank end of lamb**

knuckle of veal The lower part of a leg of veal below the thick part of the muscle usually cut into rounds for **ossobuco**

knusprige Kruste *Germany* Pork crackling

kobegyu, kobeushi *Japan* Steaks from a type of beef cattle reared or finished on beer and brewer's grains and massaged daily to produce tender back meat marbled with fat. The technique has now been introduced into France. See also **boeuf de Constance**

Koblenz sausage A thin sausage made from veal and pork which has been pickled in brine for several days, minced with onions and garlic, flavoured with pepper, packed loosely in narrow hog casings, linked, air-dried and smoked over oak and beech. Served hot. Also called **Coblenz sausage**

koblihy *Czech Republic* Jam doughnut

kochujang *Korea* Chilli bean paste

Kochwurst *Austria, Germany* A group of German/Austrian slicing or spreading sausages such as **Leberwurst**, **Zungenwurst** and **Berliner Rotwurst** which are steamed or boiled for a considerable time. They do not keep.

kød *Denmark* Meat

kødboller *Denmark* Meatballs

kødfars *Denmark* Meat stuffing, forcemeat

koek *Netherlands* 1. Cake 2. Biscuit (NOTE: The plural is **koekjes**.)

koeksister *South Africa* A twisted or plaited doughnut, deep-fried in oil and dipped into cold sugar syrup and then possibly in desiccated coconut

kofta 1. *Middle East* Cylinders of a spiced minced meat mix formed around skewers brushed with oil, and grilled over charcoal. A typical mix might contain double minced lamb, chopped onion, chopped parsley, ground allspice, fenugreek, red pepper and salt. Also called **kofte**, **kufta 2.** *South Asia* Finely ground meat sometimes blended with finely chopped aromatics, seasoning and herbs, bound with egg and formed into balls, sometimes over sweet-sour plums or a paste of dried apricots and herbs. May be braised, curried or grilled on skewers. See also **nargisi**

kofte See **kofta**

köfte *Turkey* Meatballs shaped like small rolls and fried in mutton fat. Usually made from chopped raw lamb or mutton, mixed with water, soaked breadcrumbs, eggs, garlic, cinnamon and salt.

kogt *Denmark* Cooked or boiled

kohada *Japan* Fillets of a small spotted sardine, the gizzard shad, *Clupanodon punctatus*, used in sushi etc. Also called **konoshiro** (NOTE: The larger fish called konoshiru grows up to 25 cm but is difficult to eat because of the many small bones.)

kohanafu *Japan* Fully cooked, dried and crushed gluten dough rather like breadcrumbs which is sprinkled directly over food. Also called **flower fu**

kohitsuji *Japan* Lamb

Kohl *Germany* Cabbage

Kohlenhydrat *Germany* Starch

kohlrabi The thickened turnip-like lower stem of a member of the *Brassica* family, *Brassica oleraceae* (Gongylodes Group), from which the rather sparse leaves spring. It is generally green to red, and grows above ground. The flesh is crisp, has a mild flavour and is eaten raw or cooked. Popular in Germany.

Kohlrabi *Germany* Kohlrabi

Kohlroulade *Germany* Blanched cabbage leaves wrapped around minced meat, fried then braised

Kohl und Pinkel *Germany* Cabbage and sausage

koi-kuchi shoyu *Japan* Dark soya sauce

koki *Central Africa* A bean paste similar to **moyin-moyin**

koko *Central Africa* The name given to **afang**, *Gnetum africanum*, in the Central African Republic. The leaves are usually prepared for sale as a chiffonade to make cooking easier. Also called **mfumbwa**

kokoska u unaku od slacice *Balkans* A Croatian speciality of roast chicken coated with a thick sauce made from seasoned chicken stock and vinegar thickened with egg yolks and soured cream. Served with dumplings.

kokosnoot *Netherlands* Coconut

kokosnøtt *Norway* Coconut

koksalt *Norway* Salt

kokt *Norway, Sweden* Boiled

kokt torsk *Sweden* Thick slices of poached cod served with egg sauce or melted butter and accompanied by boiled potatoes

kokum The fruit of an Indian tree, *Garcinia indica*, of the same family as the mangosteen. The flesh is dried and used as a souring agent. A semisolid fat, kokum butter, is extracted from the large seeds. The dried fruits resemble sour prunes. Also called **cocum**

koláce *Czech Republic* A fruit-filled bun

kola nut See **cola bean**

kolbasa *Russia* Smoked ham sausage common in the western Russian republics

kolbász *Hungary* Sausage

kol-bee An Israeli cheese resembling Gouda. See also **Colbi**

kolcannon See **colcannon**

koldtbord *Norway* Fork supper (buffet), cold collation, similar to smörgåsbord

koldt kød *Denmark* Cold sliced cooked meats

kołduny *Poland* A type of ravioli

kolja *Sweden* Haddock

kolje *Norway* Haddock

Kölle *Germany* Savory, the herb

kolo *East Africa* Roasted barley eaten as a snack in Ethiopia

kolocassi See **colocassa**

kolokythaki *Greece* Courgettes

kolska *Poland* A firm pork sausage from Poznań and Lublin

komatsuna A diverse group of oriental brassicas, *Brassica rapa* var. *perviridis*. The loose leaves which form a plant up to 30 cm by 18 cm have a flavour between cabbage and spinach. They are eaten cooked as a vegetable or sliced raw in salads. Also called **spinach mustard**

kombu *Japan* A type of broad leafed kelp, genus *Laminaria*, which is available as dried thick dark-green strips (30 cm long and folded) or in powdered form. Used to make stock, to make a tea or eaten as a vegetable after boiling for 30 minutes. On storage it develops a white surface covering which should be wiped off before use. It is soaked

to soften and then scored with a knife to release the flavour and may be used twice or more before before all the flavour is extracted. See also **oboru kombu**, **tororo kombu**, **shiraita kombu**. Also called **sea kelp**, **tangle kelp**

kome *Japan* Uncooked rice

Komijnekass *Netherlands* A hard cheese flavoured with caraway seeds and cloves

komkommer *Netherlands* Cucumber

komló *Hungary* Hops

kompot *Russia* Compote, often made with a mixture of diced fruit and nuts, sweetened with honey

Kompott *Germany* Compote, fruit stewed in a sugar syrup

Konfitüre *Germany* Jam

kong syin tsai *China* Swamp cabbage

Königinpastete *Germany* A savoury filled pasty, usually meat and mushrooms

Königinsuppe *Germany* A chicken soup thickened with a liaison of cream and eggs

Königsberger Klopse *Germany* Meatballs simmered in good stock and served with the thickened cooking liquor flavoured with capers and boiled rice

Königskuchen *Germany* A rum-flavoured cake made by the creaming method from flour, sugar, butter, separated eggs and ground almonds (2:3:2:4:1) with 8 teaspoonfuls (6 g) of baking powder per kg of flour, creaming with egg whites and folding in the stiffly beaten egg whites after the flour. The cake is flavoured with lemon zest and rum-soaked dried vine fruits and baked at roughly 175°C. (NOTE: Literally 'king's cake'.)

Königwurst *Germany* A sausage made from equal parts of chicken and partridge meat mixed with chopped mushrooms, truffle shavings, seasoning and mace, moistened with wine, packed into casings, tied and braised. Eaten cold. (NOTE: Literally 'king's sausage'.)

konijn *Netherlands* Rabbit

koninginne groente *Netherlands* The thick white asparagus much liked by the Dutch and in season during May and June (NOTE: Literally 'queen of vegetables'.)

konjac Gum extracted from the tubers of the snake palm plant, *Amorphophallus konjac*, which has gelling properties and is used in making black bean curd

konjak *Sweden* Brandy

konjakk *Norway* Brandy

konnyaku *Japan* A low-calorie, virtually tasteless, complex oligosaccharide produced from the tubers of the snake palm plant, *Amorphophallus konjac*. It is mainly used to to form translucent gelatinous bricks (see **black bean curd**) but the dry powder is used as a low-calorie substitute for gelling starch in confectionery, drinks, edible films etc. In the brick form it is used like bean curd. It may be sliced thinly for use as a vegetarian sashimi. See also **ito-konnyaku**, **shirataki noodles**

konoshiro *Japan* Fillets from a small sardine which are used in sushi. See also **kohada**

konservirovannye tomati po-bakinski *Southwest Asia* A Georgian tomato chutney made with chopped red and yellow sweet peppers, chillies, chopped onions and tomatoes all combined in their raw state with sugar, salt and a little wine vinegar and left for at least 24 hours before using

konservirovannye yabloki *Russia* Apple preserve made from peeled, cored and chopped dessert apples stewed in dry cider with light brown sugar, finely chopped onion, garlic, peeled ginger and sweet red pepper, flavoured with lemon zest, lemon juice and cayenne pepper and matured for at least 3 days. Served with pork.

kontomiré *West Africa* Ghanaian for the **dasheen leaves** used as a vegetable

kookoo Eggah

kool *Netherlands* Cabbage

koolraap *Netherlands* Turnip

koosé *West Africa* A black-eyed bean mixture formed into small balls. See also **akara**

koosmali *South Asia* A side dish made with grated raw carrots and fried black mustard seeds

kop *Denmark* Cup

Kopanisti *Greece* A semi-hard creamy strong-tasting blue cheese from the Aegean islands. It is salted and placed in pots to ripen for 1 to 2 months.

Kopenhagener *Germany* Danish pastries

Kopfsalat *Germany* Lettuce

Kopfsalatherzen *Germany* Lettuce hearts

Kopfsalatsuppe *Germany* Lettuce soup

kopi luwak *Indonesia* An Indonesian coffee bean, very rare, very expensive and said to have a fine distinctive flavour. The luwak, a nocturnal civet, eats wild ripe coffee fruits and the beans, still encased in their protective endocarp, are collected from the animal droppings. They are washed and treated in the usual way.

kopp *Norway, Sweden* Cup

koprivstenska lukanka *Bulgaria* A keeping sausage made from neck or spare rib of pork and leg of beef (2:1), chopped, drained, minced, seasoned, mixed with sugar and caraway seeds, allowed to mature for 12

hours then packed in ox casings, made into long links and air-dried for 3 months

kopvoorn *Netherlands* Chub, the fish

kop yop *Indonesia* Makapuno

Korbkäse *Germany* A soft acid-curdled cows' milk cheese with a smooth texture and thin rind weighing to 125 g

Korean cabbage Chinese leaves

Korean pickled cabbage Fermented cabbage (usually Chinese leaves) or other vegetables, flavoured with salt, garlic and chillies. See also **kimchi**

koriandr *Russia* Coriander

korinkake *Norway* Currant cake

Korinthen *Germany* Currants, from dried grapes

koritsa *Russia* Cinnamon

koriyenda *Japan* Coriander leaves

korma 1. *South Asia* Braising of meat or vegetables with some or all of water, stock, yoghurt or cream. Styles vary, with some cooked to a thick sauce, some to almost dry and others to a flaky crust. Only the best young meat is used. The early parts of the braising process often involve dry cooking, i.e. using a heavy pan over a fierce heat, searing the meat, then adding cooking liquor gradually so as to maintain dry but not burnt conditions. See also **doh peeazah**, **shikar korma 2.** *Central Asia* The basic Afghan stew of cubed meat browned in oil with onion and garlic, then simmered with pulses and/or vegetables plus flavourings, typically chillies, pepper, cumin and coriander. The standard korma has yellow split peas. The name after korma indicates the vegetable used, e.g. *korma shulgun* 'turnip korma'.

korma powder *South Asia* A mild spice mix used in korma cooking with white pepper instead of chilli powder

korma sadah *South Asia* A relatively simple dish by Indian standards of braised mutton. Pieces of mutton are rubbed with a paste of shallots, garlic, cloves, coriander leaves, salt and a little butter, and fried in butter until dry. Yoghurt and some basil leaves are added and the mixture is again stirred and boiled until dry, more butter, mace and chopped chives are added and the dish slowly cooked until well browned. A little water may be added to ensure that the meat is cooked through. Finally paprika is added and the dish finished in a slow oven for about 30 minutes.

Korn *Germany* **1.** Cereals **2.** Grain

koromo *Japan* Batter for tempura. See also **soya batter**

körsbär *Sweden* Cherries

körte *Hungary* Pear

korv *Sweden* Sausage
korv och bröd *Sweden* Sausage in a roll
korv Stroganoff *Sweden* A sausage stroganoff made with strips of skinned Vienna-type sausage (Frankfurter, Falukorv, etc.), fried in butter with chopped onions until brown then simmered in a closed pan for 10 minutes with acidulated cream and tomato purée
Koscher *Germany* Kosher
kosher Food slaughtered and/or prepared according to the strict Jewish dietary laws
kosheri *Egypt* A street food consisting of layers of cooked lentils and rice topped with caramelized onions and a tomato sauce. Sometimes a layer of pasta is placed between the rice and the onions. Generally served with a hot chilli pepper sauce. The Egyptian version of the Indian **khichhari**.
kosher salt *United States* Sea salt
koshi-an *Japan* A smooth sweet red bean paste
kosho *Japan* 1. Peppercorn 2. Pepper, the spice
kosie *West Africa* A snack food from northern Ghana made from mashed cooked beans blended with half their volume of finely sliced onion, processed with a little chilli, eggs (4 per kg of cooked beans), plus salt and water until frothy then shallow-fried in spoonfuls and served with a dip
Kossuth cake *United States* Iced sponge cake filled with whipped cream or ice cream
Kostromskoi *Russia* A cows' milk cheese similar to Gouda
kota kapama *Greece* Portioned chicken, browned in olive oil and butter, reserved; chopped onions, garlic and celery browned in the same fat; then all combined with tomato purée, chopped or canned tomatoes and red wine, flavoured with a cinnamon stick and simmered 45 minutes; cinnamon removed and the chicken served with the reduced cooking sauce
kotcho *East Africa* Bread made from the starch extracted from the Ethiopian domesticated **enset** plant. This is scraped from the leaf bases and obtained from the stem and the swelling at the base of the plant, it is then fermented in pits lined with enset leaves and will keep in this state for long periods. The enset plant can be harvested at any season and is drought resistant.
kotelet *Denmark, Netherlands* Cutlet, chop
kotelett *Norway* Chop
Kotelett *Germany* Cutlet, chop
kotlett *Sweden* Chop, cutlet
kotlety *Russia* Minced beef and pork, milk-soaked breadcrumbs, egg and seasoning formed into round or oval patties, panéed and fried. Served with a béchamel or tomato sauce and vegetables.
kotlety iz rybi *Russia* As **kotlety**, but made with minced cod or pike flesh and butter. Served coated with melted butter and with vegetables in a **béchamel sauce**.
kotlety pojarski *Russia* Minced chicken, veal or pork processed with breadcrumbs, butter and cream and flavoured with nutmeg, chilled, panéed, rechilled then fried and served with an appropriate sauce
kotlety po-kievski *Russia* Chicken kiev. The stuffing is traditionally unsalted butter, lemon juice, lemon zest and chopped tarragon. Deep-fried at 190°C.
kotopitta *Greece* A double-crust chicken pie using layers of buttered filo pastry as the container filled with diced cooked chicken bound with a chicken velouté flavoured with chopped coriander and walnuts and enriched with egg
kött *Sweden* Meat
köttbullar *Sweden* Minced beef meatballs fried and served with creamed potatoes and cranberry sauce
köttfärs *Sweden* 1. Minced meat 2. Meat loaf
koud *Netherlands* Cold
koud vlees *Netherlands* Assorted sliced cold cooked meats
koulibiac Coulibiac
koumiss A thick slightly alcoholic and sour drink originally made from ass or camel's milk now made from fresh mare's milk. It is similar to but more alcoholic than **kefir** and rather like a gassy alcoholic yoghurt. Used to treat gastro-intestinal problems in Russia. Also called **kumiss**, **kumyis**
kou mou *China* A white irregularly shaped mushroom similar to an oyster mushroom, grown and used in northern China. Possibly the same species as St George's mushroom.
kouneli *Greece* Rabbit
kourabi *Sweden* A sweet biscuit served with coffee
kourabiedes *Greece* A crisp crescent-shaped biscuit flavoured with almond and aniseed
kovo *South Africa* A large-leaved vegetable similar to spring cabbage but sweeter and lighter in texture
koyadofu, koyatofu *Japan* Freeze-dried bean curd
koyun *Turkey* Mutton
krab *Russia* Crab
krabba *Sweden* Crab
krabbe *Norway* Crab
Krabbe *Germany* Shrimp

krabbesalat *Norway* Crab meat on lettuce, celery and dill with a mustard dressing

krabbetjes *Netherlands* Pork spareribs

krachai *Thailand* Kempferia galangal

kra dook *Thailand* Spare ribs

kräfta *Sweden* Crayfish

Kraftbrühe *Germany* Beef consommé

kraftor *Sweden* Crayfish

Kraftsuppe *Germany* Beef and vegetable soup

Kraine *Austria* A sausage similar to **Burgenländisch Hauswürstel**

krajana *Poland* A firm smoked sausage from Poznan knotted in links

Krakauer *Austria* A sausage similar to Polish **krakowska** but containing visible chunks of lean meat

Krake *Germany* Octopus

krakelingen *Netherlands* 1. Crackers 2. Pretzels

krakowska *Poland* A slicing sausage made from a very firmly consolidated mixture of seasoned chopped lean beef, lean pork and pork fat packed in beef middles and smoked. Common throughout the country.

kranjska kobasica *Balkans* A smoked sausage made from diced pork and bacon (6:1), kneaded with sodium nitrate, garlic and seasoning for about 30 minutes, filled into small casings, linked in pairs and smoked for 3 days if to be eaten immediately or longer if to be kept

kransekage *Denmark* Almond pastry ring

Kranzkuchen *Germany* A braided sweet cake

Krapfen 1. *Germany, Italy* Sweet fritters 2. *Switzerland* A rich fruit cake with pears, nuts and marzipan

Krapfenchen *Germany* Special doughnuts or fritters served on Shrove Tuesday (Mardi Gras)

krapivnyi shchi *Russia* A soup made from seasoned meat or vegetable stock, with young nettles, sorrel, sausages and chopped onions. Served with soured cream.

krapow *Thailand* Purple basil

krappe *Denmark* Crab

krasnyi perets *Russia* Paprika

kra-thin *Thailand* Cassia

kratiem *Thailand* Garlic

kratiem dong *Thailand* Pickled garlic

krauch soeuch *Cambodia* Kaffir lime

Krauskohl *Germany* Kale

Kraut *Germany* Sauerkraut (*colloquial*)

Kräuter *Germany* Herbs

Kräuterkäse *Switzerland* Sapsago cheese

Kräuterklösse *Germany* Dumplings coloured green with spinach or herbs

Kräuterleberwurst *Germany, Switzerland* A well-seasoned liver sausage flavoured with herbs and with large pieces of liver embedded in it. Also called **Kräuterwurst**

Kräuterwurst *Germany, Switzerland* Kräuterleberwurst

Kräuterwurst à la Montreux *Switzerland* Liver sausage (**Kräuterwurst**) laid on a bed of baked leeks, napped with a rich brown gravy and heated through

Krautfleckerl *Germany* A dish of boiled cabbage mixed with noodles

Krautkräpfli *Switzerland* A type of ravioli filled with spinach

Kraut mit Eisbein und Erbensuppe *Germany* A national dish of pigs' knuckles with cabbage and pea soup

Krautwürstel *Austria* Cabbage rolls stuffed with minced beef and onions

krawaan *Thailand* Cardamom

krebs *Denmark* Crayfish

Krebs *Germany* Crab

Krebstieren *Germany* Crustaceans

kreeft *Netherlands* Crayfish

Kreivi *Finland* A loaf-shaped cheese resembling **Tilsit**, but not flavoured with caraway seeds

krem *Norway* 1. Whipped cream 2. Custard

Kren *Germany* Horseradish

krendel *Russia* An egg and butter enriched yeasted dough formed after raising into a long cylinder (5 cm diameter) and tied like a pretzel; proved, egg-washed, sprinkled with almond flakes and baked at 200°C, initially covered with foil then uncovered; finally dusted with icing sugar

Krenfleisch 1. *Germany* Sliced hot boiled beef served with horseradish sauce 2. *Austria, Italy* Pork, boiled in vinegar and wine and served with horseradish and potatoes

krenten *Netherlands* Currants, from dried grapes

krentenbrood *Netherlands* Currant bread

krentenbroodjes *Netherlands* Currant buns

kreplach A type of Jewish ravioli with a variety of fillings. Meat or chicken are served in chicken consommé. Fillings based on cheese, soured cream and eggs are served with melted butter and either salt or sugar.

kreps *Norway* Small crayfish

Kreuzkümmel *Germany* Cumin

Krevetten *Germany* Shrimps

kroepoek *Netherlands* A large deep-fried crisp pancake flavoured with dried prawns. See also **krupuk**

Krokette *Germany* Croquette

kromeski, kromesky A small cylindrical croquette of minced meat. See also cromesquis

krona *Mexico* A mild red pepper

kronärtskocka *Sweden* Artichoke

Kronsbeere *Germany* Cranberry

kroppkakor *Sweden* Potato dumplings made with minced raw potatoes mixed with egg, flour and seasoning to give a light mixture. Formed into dumplings around a filling of sweated chopped gammon and onions, boiled in water until they float, plus a further 5 minutes. Served with melted butter and cranberry sauce.

kropsla *Netherlands* Lettuce

kropsua *Finland* A thick pancake

krøsesuppe *Denmark* A soup made from a mixture of dried fruits, apples and chicken giblets

kruiden *Netherlands* Herbs

kruidenagel *Netherlands* Clove, the spice

kruiden azÿn *Netherlands* Herb-flavoured vinegar

kruisbes *Netherlands* Gooseberry

krumpli *Hungary* 1. Potato 2. A stew of mainly vegetables, onions, potatoes, tomatoes, green sweet peppers, etc. with bacon and sausage, seasoned and flavoured with paprika

krung gaeng *Thailand* The general term for curry paste

krung gaeng kao wan *Thailand* A very hot green curry paste made hot by the fresh green chillies which give it its colour

krung gaeng kare leung *Thailand* A mild yellow curry paste coloured using fresh turmeric root

krung gaeng ped daeng *Thailand* A medium to hot commercial and very aromatic curry paste coloured red. A typical formulation contains chopped seeded New Mexico chillies, minced greater galangal root, coriander root and shallots, chopped kaffir lime rind and lemon grass root and shrimp paste.

krung gaeng som An orange-coloured curry paste used in seafood soups and dishes

krupek See krupuk

krupuk *Indonesia* A large deep-fried crisp pancake flavoured with dried prawns, similar to the Indian poppadom or Chinese prawn cracker. Smaller varieties are made with fresh ingredients, e.g. shrimps and tapioca chips, by rolling out and drying. See also singkong, emping melinjo. Also called krupek, kerupuk

krupuk ikan *Indonesia* A rice flour batter flavoured with fish, dried and deep-fried rather like an Indian poppadom or Chinese prawn cracker

krupuk tempeh *Indonesia* A krupuk chip flavoured with tempeh

krupuk udang *Indonesia* 1. A shelled, deveined and flattened shrimp, dried and resembling a crisp 2. A rice-flour batter flavoured with powdered dried shrimp, dried and deep-fried

krusbär *Sweden* Gooseberries

Krustentieren *Germany* Crustaceans

kryddersild *Norway* Spiced herring

kryddor *Sweden* Condiments, spices

Kryddost *Sweden* A cows' milk cheese flavoured with caraway seeds and cloves

kryddpeppar *Sweden* Allspice

Kryddsvecia *Sweden* **Sveciaost** cheese flavoured with various spices

kseksu bidawi *North Africa* Couscous with seven vegetables; the most common seven are cabbage, carrots, pumpkin, peas, artichoke hearts, turnips and sweet potatoes

kskas *North Africa* The upper part of a couscousière in which the couscous is steamed. See also gdra

kuali *Malaysia* Wok

kuba al-aish *Persian Gulf* Stuffed meatballs made from a minced lamb and sticky rice mixture, spiced and processed into a cohering paste. This is formed into small balls around a filling of cooked split peas, fried onions, sultanas, ground cardamom and **baharat**. The balls are flattened into oval cakes and shallow-fried on each side.

kubis bunga *Malaysia* Cauliflower

ku cai *Malaysia* Garlic chive

Kuchen *Germany* Cake

Küchenragout *Germany* A rich stew of chicken, sweetbreads, veal meatballs, clams, asparagus and peas

kudamono *Japan* Fruit. It may be served at the end of a meal in small portions and decorative shapes.

kudzu A pale grey starch rather like arrowroot made from the roots of a vine. See also kuzu

kuei *China* Cassia

kugel A Jewish baked pudding consisting of rice or noodles with dried vine fruits, fresh fruit, chopped nuts, eggs, sugar, spices and margarine or molten chicken fat

Kugelhopf *Germany, Switzerland* Sponge cake or large choux pastry balls filled with whipped cream. Also called Kugelhoph

Kugelhoph *Germany, Switzerland* Kugelhopf

kugelhumf tin A tubular cake tin hinged along the length for cooking long cylindrical cakes

kugelis *Lithuania* A famous dish of grated raw potatoes, salted and drained for 10 minutes, dried, combined with a little flour, baking powder, bacon fat, egg, grated onion, caraway seed and pepper, placed in a baking dish, dotted with butter and baked at 180°C for 35 minutes then at 200°C until browned. Served with fried onions.

ku gua *China* Bitter melon

kuha *Finland* Pike-perch

kühl *Germany* Cool

kui *Korea* **1.** Grilled **2.** Cooked on the griddle

kuiken *Netherlands* **1.** Young chicken **2.** Young pigeon

kukhura ka phul *Nepal* Hen's egg

kukorica *Hungary* Sweetcorn

kuku *Central Asia* An egg dish from Iran either like a Spanish omelette with discrete pieces of vegetables or with the vegetables puréed and mixed with the egg. The dish is usually named after the principal vegetables in it, preceded by *kukuye*, e.g. kukuye sabzi.

kuku choma *East Africa* Roast chicken

kuku paka *East Africa* A Swahili chicken and coconut curry made from onions, sweet peppers and garlic fried in the usual way with spices. Potatoes and water are added and simmered until the potatoes are almost cooked, browned chicken pieces are then added together with tomatoes and coconut milk, the whole being simmered until the chicken is well done and the sauce thick. Served with rice or chapatis.

kukuruza *Russia* Maize

kukuye sabzi *Central Asia* An omelette of herbs and spring greens baked in a 180°C oven for about 45 minutes

kulchas *South Asia* A yeast or other leaven raised white flour dough made into rounds and deep-fried. May be filled with cheese or vegetables before cooking.

kulebiaka *Russia* The original Russian fish pie **coulibiac**. Also called **kulebiak, kulibyaka**

kulfi *South Asia* A type of ice cream made from sweetened full-cream milk thickened with corn flour, mixed with chopped almonds and pistachio nuts and flavoured with rose water

kulfi mould A small conical metal mould used for shaping kulfi

kulich *Russia* A traditional yeast-raised Easter cake made with flour, milk, sugar and butter (11:5:4:2) mixed with eggs and egg yolks to make a firm well-kneaded dough. After allowing a thin batter made with some of the flour, milk and yeast to rise, the dough is mixed after the first proving with sultanas, rum, powdered saffron, crushed cardamom seeds, chopped mixed peel and almond slivers. It is then knocked back, proved and

baked at 200°C for 15 minutes then at 180°C until cooked.

kulikuli *West Africa* A type of biscuit made from freshly ground peanuts from which most of the oil is extracted by kneading and squeezing with a little warm water. The paste is mixed with water, salted, shaped into biscuits and deep-fried.

kulitis *Philippines* Amaranth

kulthi bean Horse gram

kumara *New Zealand* The Maori term for sweet potato

kumin *Japan* Cumin

kumiss A thick slightly alcoholic and sour drink made from fresh mare's milk. See also **koumiss**

kumler *Norway* Potato dumplings

kummel *Sweden* Hake

Kümmel **1.** *Germany* Caraway seed **2.** *Netherlands* A caraway-flavoured liqueur sometimes used for flavouring

Kümmelkase *Germany* A soft surface-ripened caraway-flavoured cows' milk cheese. Contains 58% water, 21% fat and 19% protein.

Kümmelsuppe *Germany* Caraway-flavoured soup

kumquat One of the three principal varieties of citrus, members of the genus *Fortunella*, especially *F. japonica* & *F. margarita* with oval-shaped fruits about 2 to 4 cm in diameter with an edible skin and an unusual bittersweet flavour. Introduced to the UK in 1846, and thence worldwide. Crystallized, made into marmalade, often sliced for decoration and used in sweet and savoury dishes. See also **maru-kinkan, nagami kumquat, meiwa kumquat**. Also called **cumquat**

kumys *Russia* A thick slightly alcoholic and sour drink made from fresh mare's milk. See also **koumiss**

kun choi *China* Chinese celery

kunchor *Malaysia* Lesser galangal

kunde *East Africa* A Kenyan dish of cooked cow peas and ground peanuts (2:1) mixed with chopped onions and tomatoes that have been sautéed in oil and all cooked gently for about ten minutes. Normally served with maize porridge.

kung haeng *Thailand* Dried shrimp

kung yue *China* A small fish similar to an anchovy prepared like **ikan bilis**

kunyit *Indonesia, Malaysia* Turmeric

kunyit basah *Malaysia* Turmeric

kunyit kering *Malaysia* Saffron

kupang *Malaysia* Asian mussel

kura *Russia* Chicken

Kürbis *Germany* 1. Squash 2. Pumpkin 3. Gourd

kure po plzensku *Czech Republic* Chicken cooked in beer with sultanas

kurhai *Nepal, South Asia* A small wok used for one-dish cooking. See also **karahi**

kuri *Japan* Chestnut

kuri ama-ni *Japan* Candied chestnuts similar to marrons glacés

kuritsa *Russia* A boiling fowl, old hen

kurnik 1. *Poland* A double-crust puff pastry pie filled with four thin unsweetened pancakes interspersed with three separate layers: the first, chicken in a cream sauce, then sautéed mushrooms in a sour cream sauce and finally boiled rice mixed with chopped hard-boiled eggs and onions bound in a cream sauce. The pie is egg-washed, baked and served with a suprême sauce. 2. *Russia* A simpler version of the Polish kurnik using a shortcrust pastry and a creamy filling of hard-boiled eggs, cooked rice and chopped roast chicken meat

kuro goma *Japan* Black sesame seeds

k'urt *East Africa* Chopped raw beef mixed with mustard and chilli paste

Kurt *Central Asia* A hard pungent sun-dried ewes' milk cheese from Kazakhstan

kurundu *Sri Lanka* Cinnamon

kurzemes *Latvia* Patties made with a duxelle of onions and mushrooms mixed with minced pork, veal or ham and breadcrumbs, seasoned and flavoured with chopped parsley and dried thyme, bound with egg, fried both sides and served with a sauce made from the reduced deglazed pan juices and sour cream

kushikatsu *Japan* Skewers of pork with a sauce

kushiyaki *Japan* Skewers of pork, chicken, seafood and vegetables, panéed and deep-fried and eaten with a variety of sauces and relishes

Kuttelflech *Austria* Tripe

Kutteln *Germany* Tripe

kutya *Russia* Wheat grains, whole burghul or rice cooked in sweetened milk or almond milk like a rice pudding

kuzu A pale grey starch rather like arrowroot made from the roots of a vine related to jicama. Used in Chinese and Japanese cooking to thicken sauces and make translucent glazes, it is excellent as a coating for fried foods. Also called **kudzu**

kvæder *Denmark* Quince

kvarg *Norway* Quark

kvas *Russia* A slightly alcoholic drink made from stale rye bread and water (1:6), the bread is dried and powdered, steeped for 8 hours, sieved, yeasted and fermented with mint and sugar (1:30 on water) for 8 hours, strained, a few sultanas added and the whole left for about 3 days until the sediment settles and the sultanas float. Decanted and strained before use. Juniper is occasionally used in place of mint.

kveite *Norway* Halibut

kwabaal *Netherlands* Eel pout, the fish

kwah *North Africa* A Moroccan kebab of cubed liver coated with cumin, paprika and salt and wrapped in a sheep's caul before grilling

kwali *Malaysia* A Chinese-style wok used by Malaysian Chinese (Straits Chinese) for cooking **rempah**

kwalima *East Africa* A beef sausage from Ethiopia similar to Spanish chorizo

kwanga *Central Africa* Treated cassava tubers. See also **bâton de manioc**

kwanta *East Africa* The Ethiopian name for preserved beef made by rubbing strips with butter, salt and **berbere** then hanging them out to dry

kwark *Netherlands* 1. Quark 2. Curds

kway tio *Malaysia* Rice ribbon noodles

kyabetsu *Japan* Cabbage

kyainthee *Burma* Candlenut

kyauk kyaw *Burma* Agar agar

kyauk-nga *Burma* Garoupa, the fish

kyckling *Sweden* Baby chicken or **poussin**

kyenam *West Africa* A traditional Ghanaian dish consisting of a whole fish, each side incised with two deep diagonal cuts which are filled with a paste of chillies, root ginger and salt, coated with surplus paste and deep-fried or grilled until crisp. Also called **kenan**

kyet-thun-ni *Burma* Shallots

kyin-kyinga *West Africa* Kebabs of meat and sweet peppers, the meat marinated in a processed mixture of onion, ginger, ground roasted peanuts, tomatoes, garlic and chillies and the kebabs sprinkled with ground peanuts before cooking

kylling *Denmark, Norway* Chicken

kyodo ryori *Japan* Specialities of a region, either single dishes or a complete meal

kypsäksi paiste *Finland* Well done. Used of meat, steaks, etc.

kyringa *Russia* A central Asian fermented milk similar to **koumiss** made in wooden vessels which become impregnated with the starter culture and are not sterilized

kyufte *Bulgaria* Meatballs

kyuri *Japan* Cucumber

la *China* Hot and peppery

laab *Thailand* A mixture of lightly stir-fried meat and onions with herbs and other salad ingredients

la bai cal *China* Peppery pickled cabbage

labelling See **food labelling**, **organic labelling**, **nutritional labelling**

lablab bean Hyacinth bean

lablabi *North Africa* A thick vegetarian purée soup from Tunisia based on chickpeas with garlic and sweated onion, carrots and celery, finished with lemon juice and chopped coriander leaves

Lablab purpureus *Botanical name* Hyacinth bean

labna *Middle East* A cream cheese made from the solids remaining when goats' milk yoghurt is strained through muslin. It is formed into 3 cm balls which are coated with olive oil and chopped herbs or paprika. Eaten with bread and keeps well. Also called **labneh**

labneh See **labna**

labong *Philippines* Bamboo shoot

Labquark *Germany* Quark

Labskaus *Germany* A northern German dish of mashed potatoes, fried chopped onion, chopped corned beef and seasoning, served hot topped with a fried egg and accompanied by pickled beetroot and gherkins. Sometimes well-soaked, filleted and chopped salt herrings are added.

labu air *Malaysia* Bottle gourd

labu merah *Indonesia, Malaysia* Winter squash

labu siam *Indonesia* Choko

la cari *Vietnam* Curry leaves

laccetto *Italy* Mackerel

lace, to To add alcohol, condiments or spices to a dish to make it more tasty or interesting

lacerto *Italy* Mackerel

la chang *China* The standard Chinese pork sausage. See also **lap cheong**

Lachs *Germany* Salmon

Lachsforelle *Germany* Salmon trout

Lachsschinken *Germany* The main muscle of pork loin, lightly smoked and wrapped in a sheet of raw bacon fat and tied into a neat cylinder with string. Eaten raw and thinly sliced as a hors d'oeuvre or sandwich filling. See also **laxschinken**

Läckerli *Switzerland* Sweet biscuits containing chopped nuts and candied peel. Also called **Leckerli**

lacón con grelos *Spain* Boiled cured shoulder of pork with turnip tops

lactalbumin One of the proteins in milk

Lactarius deliciosus *Botanical name* Saffron milk cap

lactase The enzyme that converts lactose into glucose and galactose

lactates Salts of lactic acid used as buffers i.e. to maintain near constant pH in foods and as firming agents. Sodium (E325), potassium (E326) and calcium lactate (E327) are used in the food industry.

lactic acid An important food acid which is the end product of anaerobic fermentation of sugars by *Lactobacillus* spp. Added as a preservative to reduce pH or made naturally in the production of yoghurt, sauerkraut, some cheeses, olives, other varieties of pickles and in continental sausages.

lactic butter Butter made from a cream treated with species of *Lactobacillus* to give it a slightly sour flavour

lactitol A modified lactose used in sugar-free confectionery

Lactobacillus bulgaricus One of the bacteria used in starter cultures for yoghurt and continental cheeses

Lactobacillus caseii A bacterium associated with the ripening of Cheddar cheese

Lactobacillus helveticus One of the bacteria in starter cultures for yoghurt and Swiss cheeses

Lactobacillus plantarum One of the bacteria included in starter cultures for the fermentation of cucumbers and olives

Lactobacillus sanfrancisco Bacteria used for the leavening of sour dough bread

Lactobacillus spp. Bacteria used for the production of lactic acid in cheese and other milk products and in sauerkraut production

Lactococcus lactis A bacteria which can ferment traditional foods made from rice to prevent transmission of infection to weaning children in underdeveloped countries. It has the advantage of producing a safe form of lactic acid, the laevo isomer (L-lactic acid) which cannot harm children. Other lactic fermenters produce both the L and D forms of the acid which are easily tolerated by adults.

lactofil *Sweden* A cultured milk concentrated by removing whey equal to half its volume. It is then enriched with cream to give 5% butterfat and homogenized.

lactoglobulin One of the proteins in milk

lacto-ovo-vegetarian A person who will not eat poultry, animal flesh or fish, but will eat eggs and milk products

lactose The main sugar in milk. It is a disaccharide composed of a glucose and a galactose unit. Less sweet than sucrose. Also called **milk sugar**

lactose intolerance An inability to absorb and metabolize the galactose component of lactose hence the cause of many bowel complaints due to fermentation in the lower gut. Common in persons of Chinese origin.

lacto-vegetarian A person who will not eat animal flesh, fish, poultry or eggs but will eat milk and milk products

Lactuca sativa *Botanical name* Lettuce

låda *Sweden* Casserole

lada cabai *Indonesia* Black pepper

lada hijau *Malaysia* Green chilli

lada hitam *Malaysia* Peppercorn

lada merah *Malaysia* Green chilli

lade *China* Spicy

ladies' cheese A soft rich, cows' milk cheese. See also **Butterkäse**

ladies' fingers Okra

ladies' mustard An old-fashioned name for **tarragon**

ladle A cooking implement for transferring liquids or skimming liquids, consisting of a hemispherical metal scoop attached at an angle to a long handle hooked at the other end. Usually sized in fluid measure.

la dua *Vietnam* Screwpine

Lady Baltimore cake *United States* A white layer cake, layers separated with a meringue-like icing mixed with dried fruits and nuts, the whole covered with white icing (NOTE: This cake is supposed to have originated in the Lady Baltimore Tearoom in Charleston, South Carolina, towards the end of the 19th century. The husband of the original Lady Baltimore was an Irishman who inherited the state of Maryland in 1632.)

lady finger *United States* Sponge finger

lady fingers See **langues de chat**

lady's bedstraw A wild plant, *Galium verum*, of the madder family whose small yellow flowers were once used to curdle milk

lady's fingers A short variety of banana (NOTE: Not to be confused with 'ladies' fingers', which is okra.)

lady's mantle A low growing hardy perennial, *Alchemilla vulgaris*, whose mildly bitter young leaves may be used sparingly in salads. Also called **dewcup**

lady's smock A common wild plant, *Cardamine pratensis*, tasting like cress, which can be eaten young as a salad vegetable. Also called **cuckoo flower**

laevulose See **fructose**

Lafayette gingerbread *United States* A spiced gingerbread with added orange juice and zest

Lageneria siceraria *Botanical name* The **bottle gourd** and **hairy gourd** plant

lagerblad *Sweden* Bayleaf

lagopède *France* Ptarmigan

lagopède d'Écosse *France* Grouse

lagópodo escocés *Spain* Grouse

lagos *Greece* Hare

lagôsta *Portugal* Spiny lobster

lagostim *Portugal* **1.** Prawn **2.** Small lobster **3.** Dublin bay prawn

lagostino *Galicia* **1.** Dublin Bay prawn **2.** A general term for a crayfish or large prawn

Laguiole *France* A semi-hard pressed cows' milk cheese from the mountains of Aquitaine, with a soft dry rind and a supple homogeneous paste whose herby flavour comes from the pasture on which the cows feed, resembling **Cantal**. Protected by an appellation d'origine. Contains 37% water, 28% fat, and 26% protein. Also called **forme de Laguiole**, **Laguiole-Aubrac**

Laguiole-Aubrac See **Laguiole**

laguipierre, sauce *France* Butter sauce with the addition of the juice of one lemon and 60 ml of fish glaze per litre. Used for boiled fish.

laham ajeen *Middle East* Small 12-cm-round tarts from Iraq made with a yeast-raised dough and filled with cooked lamb, onion, garlic, tomato, courgette, parsley, thyme and chilli. Baked for about 10 minutes at 220°C.

lahana dolmasi *Turkey* Blanched cabbage leaves wrapped around a mixture of cooked rice, chopped onions, raisins, pine nuts, seasoning and chopped parsley or dill, baked in the oven and served cold

la han chay *Vietnam* Vietnamese vegetarian stir-fry

la he *Vietnam* Garlic chive

lahm bil bayd *Persian Gulf* A type of Scotch egg. The covering is a well-processed paste of lamb and onion mixed with finely chopped parsley and soft breadcrumbs, panéed and deep-fried as usual.

lait *France* Milk

lait, au *France* Cooked or mixed with milk

lait aigre *France* Sour milk

laitance *France* Soft roe

laitances d'alose *France* Shad roe

lait caillé *France* Milk curds, sour milk

lait d'amande *France* Almond oil

lait de coco *France* Coconut milk

lait écrémé *France* Skimmed milk

lait en poudre *France* Dried or powdered milk

laiterie *France* Dairy

laitue *France* Lettuce

laitue beurrée *France* Round lettuce

laitue romaine *France* **1.** Cos lettuce (UK) **2.** Romaine lettuce (USA)

la jiao fen *China* Chilli pepper

la jiao jiang *China* Chilli sauce

la jiao xiang you *China* Sesame chilli oil

lake bass A freshwater game fish of the genus *Micropterus* caught throughout North America except Alaska, with firm white lean flesh up to 1.5 kg in weight. It is also farmed. Usually eaten baked or fried.

lake herring A freshwater fish of the genus *Leucichthys* from the Great Lakes of North America. Similar in shape and colour to a herring but only medium oily with white flesh. It weighs up to 1 kg and may be poached or fried. Also called **cisco**

Lakeland A variety of **limequat**

lake trout *Canada, United States* A large trout, *Salvelinus namaycush*, light green to near black with oily pink flesh weighing on average 2 kg. Caught all the year round in North American lakes and rivers. Cook as trout. Also called **Great Lakes trout**

lake whitefish *Canada, United States* A fish, *Coregonus clupeaformis*, of the trout and salmon family with a light-brown back and white, medium oily, delicate flesh which cooks in flakes like cod. Found in North American lakes. Cook as trout.

lakka *Finland* Cloudberry

laks *Denmark, Norway* Salmon

laksa 1. *Indonesia, Malaysia* A stew of fish, shrimp or chicken in a well-flavoured and possibly soured curry-type sauce based on coconut milk. Served with rice noodles. **2.** *Philippines* A stew containing a wide variety of vegetables, shrimp and pork, served with fine bean flour vermicelli (**sotánghon**) (NOTE: Literally '10,000', referring to the number of ingredients.)

laksa ikan *Malaysia* A fish soup containing noodles

lala mirich *South Asia* Red chilli

lal mirch *South Asia* Cayenne pepper, chilli powder

lal sarsu *South Asia* Brown mustard seed

lam *Denmark, Netherlands* Lamb

la Mancha saffron Reputed to be the best saffron from Spain. It contains the white styles as well as the red stamens.

lamb A young sheep under 1 year old but preferably 3 to 4 months old and weighing about 10 kg. The meat is tender and suitable for grilling, frying and roasting.

lamballe, crème *France* **Crème Saint Germain** garnished with cooked and washed tapioca

lambascioni *Italy* Bulbs of grape hyacinth served in a sweet-and-sour sauce. See also **copollotto**

lamb backstrap *Australia* The trimmed eye of the middle loin of lamb, free of bone, gristle and fat, usually about 30 cm long

lamb cutlet A transverse slice cut from a skinned and chined best end of lamb containing one rib, the rib sometimes scraped to the bone for 5 to 7 cm

lamb cutlets Reform *England* Lamb cutlets panéed with a mixture of breadcrumbs and finely chopped ham, grilled or fried, garnished **à la Réforme** and served with **Réforme sauce**

lamb flank *Scotland* The Scottish term for breast of lamb

lamb grades *United States* Grades of lamb in the US are prime, choice, good, utility and cull in descending order of quality

lamb herbs The principal herbs used with lamb are basil, chervil, cumin, dill, lemon balm, lovage, marjoram, mint, parsley, rosemary, savory and thyme

lambie *Caribbean* Tenderized conch flesh used as a food

lambie souse *Caribbean* Lambie cut in small pieces and simmered until tender, drained and cooled and served as a salad with chopped shallots, sliced peeled cucumber and sweet pepper, lime juice, chopped parsley and finely chopped chilli pepper

lamb's fry 1. The liver, kidney, sweetbreads, heart and sometimes the brains and some of the internal abdominal fat of a lamb. Generally cut in pieces, panéed and fried. **2.** The testicles of sheep, very rare since most are now castrated by a bloodless method

lamb's kidneys Small kidneys which are skinned and cored in the usual way and cooked whole or halved in kebabs, mixed grills or other dishes

lamb's lettuce A slow-growing hardy annual, *Valerianella locusta*, grown for its leaves which will stand the winter and are used in winter salads. The growing plant may be blanched to reduce the slight bitterness. There are two varieties, a floppy large-leaved version and a smaller, more hardy, upright type. Also called **corn salad**, **mâche**, **field lettuce**

lamb's liver A delicate light-brown liver very popular in the UK. It should not be cooked too long or it becomes tough.

lamb's quarters *Canada* A wild vegetable which is a cross between Swiss chard and spinach and cooked in the same way. Said to have a faint flavour of lamb. Grows profusely in New Brunswick.

lamb's tongues Small pink tongues weighing about 200 g with a good flavour. May be stewed and jellied as other tongues.

lamb's tongue Ste Menehould *France* Lamb's tongues braised, panéed and grilled

lam chiak *Thailand* Screwpine

Lamellibranchiata The scientific name for bivalves, shellfish with two hinged shells, including oysters, clams, scallops, mussels, razor shells, abalone, etc.

Lamington *Australia* A small square cake made from sponge coated with chocolate icing and sprinkled with desiccated coconut

lam keong *China* Greater galangal

lamm *Sweden* Lamb

Lamm *Germany* Lamb

lammasta *Finland* **1.** Mutton **2.** Lamb

lamme *Denmark* **1.** Mutton **2.** Lamb

lamme kotelet *Denmark* Lamb chop

lammesteg *Denmark* Roast lamb

Lammkeule *Germany* Leg of lamb

Lammkotelett *Germany* Lamb chop

lammkotlett *Sweden* Lamb chop

lammstek *Sweden* Roast lamb

Lammzunge *Germany* Scald, the fish

lampaankyljys *Finland* Mutton or lamb chop

lampaanliha *Finland* **1.** Mutton **2.** Lamb

lampaanpaisti *Finland* Roast leg of lamb or mutton

lampada, alla *Italy* Cooked at the table over a portable heat source

lampari *Sri Lanka* Curried rice baked in banana leaves

lampern A fish resembling a small lamprey. Cooked like an eel.

lampone *Italy* Raspberry

lampreda *Italy* Lamprey

lamprey Any of various small round anadromous sea fish rather like eels, with sucking mouthparts and rough tongues. Popular in Spain, Portugal and Southern France. Lampreys require longer cooking than eels.

lampries *Sri Lanka* A mixture of several types of food separately wrapped in banana leaves and baked (NOTE: From the Dutch *lomprijst*. Typical dishes might be frikkadels, buttered rice, various curries and sambals. Very much party food in which the guests make and bake the parcels)

lamproie *France* Lamprey, the fish

lampuga *Italy* Dolphin fish

lamsbout *Netherlands* Leg of lamb

lamsvlees *Netherlands* Lamb

Lanark blue *Scotland* A blue-veined ewes' milk cheese from Strathclyde, similar to **Roquefort**

Lancashire cheese *England* An excellent white melting cheese with a crumbly texture. When new it has a mild flavour but this develops as it matures especially if made with unpasteurized milk.

Lancashire hotpot *England* A casserole of lamb chops from the neck end and kidneys with onions, carrots and potatoes, topped with a layer of sliced potatoes which become brown and crisp in the oven

Lancashire parkin *England* A gingerbread containing oatmeal, chopped candied peel, demerara sugar and caraway seeds

lançon *France* Sand eel

landaise, à la *France* In the style of the Landes in southwest France, i.e. cooked in goose fat with garlic and pine nuts

land cress A slightly peppery leafy plant, *Barbarea verna*, found wild but also cultivated in Europe and North America to provide green leaves for salads in winter. Also called **early flowering yellow rocket**, **American cress**

Landes chicken Chicken from the Landes in southwest France. Usually free-range and maize-fed with dark well-flavoured leg meat, slightly firmer than normal.

Ländjäger *Germany* A small smoked and scalded sausage made from up to 40% pork, beef, garlic, caraway seeds and red wine pressed into a square mould and cold-smoked or air-dried

landlady's loaf Barrel bread

Landmettwurst *Germany* A **Mettwurst** made in the countryside

landrail Corncrake

ländstycke *Sweden* Sirloin steak

Lane cake *United States* A layered cake containing chopped nuts, dried fruit and coconut and covered with a fluffy icing

lange japanische Auster *Germany* Pacific oyster

Langermannia gigantea Giant puffball

langka *Philippines* Jackfruit

lang kail *Scotland* True kale, *Brassica oleraceae* Acephala Group

lángos *Hungary* Fried doughnuts

langosta *Spain* Spiny lobster

langostino *Spain* General term for crayfish or large prawn

langostino moruno *Spain* A large king prawn (**crevette rouge**)

langouste *France* Spiny lobster

langoustine *France* Dublin bay prawn

Langres A soft, surface-ripened and washed curd cows' milk cheese with a tangy flavour and shaped like a squat cylinder (300 g). The salted curd is ripened for 2 to 3 months.

langsam kochen *Germany* To simmer

langsat A round or oval fruit of a tree, *Lansium domesticum*, from Malaysia which is about 4 cm diameter and grows in clusters. The flesh is white, juicy and fragrant, contains one or two large inedible seeds and is enclosed in a tough brown mottled skin. Eaten raw.

Langskaill *Scotland* A cows' milk cheese from Scotland which resembles **Gouda**

Languas galanga *Botanical name* Greater galangal

Languas officinarum *Botanical name* Lesser galangal

langue *France* Tongue

languedocienne, à la *France* In the Languedoc style, i.e. with a garnish of aubergine, mushrooms, tomatoes and parsley

langues de chat *France* Small sweet flat biscuits made by the sugar batter method with butter, icing sugar, egg white, flour and vanilla essence. Can be moulded when hot. Also called **lady fingers** (NOTE: Literally 'cat's tongues'.)

languier *France* Smoked pig's tongue

Languste *Germany* Spiny lobster

Lansium domesticum *Botanical name* Langsat

lansur *Africa* A leaf vegetable from Nigeria rather like a cross between parsley and watercress

lanttu *Finland* Kohlrabi

lanzado *Italy* Mackerel

laos *Indonesia* **1.** Greater galangal **2.** Laos powder

laos ginger Greater galangal

laos powder The dried and ground root of greater galangal, rather like ginger

Laotian caviar Som khay

Laotian coriander Dill weed

Laotian rice A rice grown on the dry hillsides and not in paddy fields. It is soaked before being steamed in a woven cane basket (a **luang prabang**).

lap *Korea* Finely ground raw water buffalo meat or venison, flavoured with chilli and herbs and served wrapped in bite-size rolls using blanched lettuce leaves

lapa *Spain* Limpet

lap cheong *China* The standard pork sausage made from chopped lean pork and pork fat, mixed with sugar, salt, saltpetre and softened grain, flavoured with paprika and soya sauce, moistened with rice wine, filled into casings and air-dried. Usually steamed to soften before use. Also called **la chang**, **lop cheeng**

lapereau *France* Young rabbit

lapin *France* Rabbit

lapin à l'aigre doux *Belgium* Jointed rabbit marinated for 24 hours in white wine and vinegar with sliced onion and herbs, dried off, browned in butter and stewed with **demi-glace** sauce, stock and a little of the marinade until tender, reserved and mixed with pickled cherries and the reduced cooking liquor flavoured with melted dark chocolate

lapin aux pruneaux *Belgium* Jointed rabbit, marinated, dried, browned in butter then simmered in equal parts of water and the strained marinade with destoned prunes plumped in water and white wine until tender. Served with the cooking liquor thickened with redcurrant jelly.

lapjes *Netherlands* Small slices of meat

lap ngup *China* Pressed duck

lapocka *Hungary* A cut of meat from the shoulder

lap of lamb *England* The north of England name for breast of lamb (*colloquial*)

lapskaus *Norway* A thick stew of meat and potatoes

Lapskaus *Germany* Lobscouse. See also **Labskaus**

lapskojs *Sweden* A modern version of lobscouse made with corned beef

lapskous *Netherlands* Lobscouse

lapu lapu *Philippines* Garoupa, the fish

lapwing Plover

lap xuong *Vietnam* Chinese sausage **lap cheong**

lap yoke *China* Dried and smoked belly pork, rather like smoked streaky bacon

laranja *Portugal* Orange, the fruit

laranja cravo *Brazil* A variety of mandarin grown extensively in Brazil. It is medium large and has a rather thick skin. The flavour is appreciated in Brazil, but is too insipid for European and North American tastes.

laranja lima *Brazil* A variety of acidless orange very popular in Brazil where over half a million tonnes are grown annually. Also called **lima orange**

lard 1. *England, France* Rendered-down pig fat, which is white, soft and has a distinctive flavour. The best lard comes from leaf fat, the fat around the kidneys. Often used with equal parts of butter or margarine for pastry-making. **2.** *France* Bacon

lard, to To thread small strips of fat or fat bacon through the lean flesh of game birds, poultry and other meat to keep it succulent during roasting, using a needle with a large eye

larder *France* To lard meat

larding needle A large needle with a wide eye used for larding meat

lard maigre *France* Streaky bacon

lard net Caul

lardo *Italy* Bacon or salt pork

lardo affumicato *Italy* Bacon

lardoire *France* Needle used for larding large cuts of meat

lardon *England, France* Small strips of pork or bacon fat, square in cross section used for larding lean meat, or similar strips of bacon used for flavouring or after cooking as a component of a salad

lardoncini *Italy* Fried cubes or strips of salt pork (**lardons**)

lardy cake *England* A south Midlands cake made from bread dough enriched with lard, sugar and dried vine fruits, baked in small square tins with rounded corners and the tops scored in diamonds. Eaten warm with butter.

large calorie See **kilocalorie**

largemouth black bass A bass-like freshwater game fish, *Micropterus salmoides*, with a silvery skin and a dark tail and mouth parts, found in Europe and North America and weighing up to 10 kg

larger argentine See **argentine**

large round kumquat See **meiwa kumquat**

larger spotted dogfish The most common British dogfish, *Scyliorhinus stellaris*, up to 1.2 m long and with rather coarse tasteless flesh. Also called **nurse hound**

large thread stage See **sugar cooking**

large-toothed flounder *Australia* See **flounder 3**

largo *Mexico* A long thin variety of chilli pepper which is fairly hot

Largo potato soup *Scotland* Neck of mutton, chopped onions and carrots simmered for 90 minutes, sliced potatoes added and cooked a further 30 minutes, bones and fat removed and the meat chopped small and returned, the soup seasoned and garnished with chopped parsley

lark A small wild bird almost hunted to extinction. Eaten as a delicacy in France and Italy, but will soon be protected.

larm yum *China* Chinese olive seeds

Laruns *France* A ewes' milk cheese from the Basque country

lasagna *England, Italy* A wide flat pasta which comes in a strip, rectangle or square about 1 to 2 mm thick. Poached in salted water before incorporation in a made-up dish. Also called **lazagne** (NOTE: The plural is **lasagne**.)

lasagna verde *England, Italy* Lasagna made with a paste coloured green with spinach purée

lasagne alla bolognese *Italy* Poached lasagna layered with a meat sauce and topped with **béchamel sauce** and grated Parmesan cheese

lasagne alla fiorentina *Italy* Poached lasagna with a meat sauce and cheese

lasagne da fornel *Italy* Poached lasagna with a sauce of nuts, raisins, apples and figs

lasagne pasticciate alla napoletana *Italy* Cooked lasagna layered with cooked cheese and Bolognaise sauces, topped with a final layer of cheese sauce and gratinated. Finished in the oven until crisp on top.

lasagnette *Italy* Wide ribbons of flat pasta intermediate in size between lasagna and tagliatelle

lasca *Italy* Roach, the fish

lassan *South Asia* Garlic

lassi *South Asia* Yoghurt diluted with water or mineral water (1 part yoghurt to 1 to 2 parts water), used as a refreshing drink either with sugar or flavoured with e.g. cumin and mint. Sometimes made from salted and sweetened buttermilk.

lasun *South Asia* Garlic

lat chu jeung *China* Chilli bean paste

lath A legume, *Lathyrus sativus*, grown as a fodder plant and, in poor areas, for its seeds which are used like other pulses. Also called **chickling vetch**, **grass pea**

latholemono *Greece* An olive oil and lemon juice (3:1) salad dressing with chopped marjoram and parsley, seasoning and possibly a little sugar

Lathyrus sativus *Botanical name* Lath

latik *Philippines* The brown curds produced by heating coconut milk to separate the oil. Used on desserts and snack foods.

lat jiu jiang *China* A medium to hot, orange red thickish chilli sauce

lat jiu keung yau *China* A ground garlic and chilli paste

latkes The Jewish name for **Rösti**. Also called **potato latka**

lato *Philippines* An edible seaweed with clusters of small bladders rather like a bunch of grapes

latour *France* Porbeagle shark

latte *Italy* Milk

latte acido *Italy* Sour milk

latte di mandorla *Italy* Almond milk. Whole almonds blended with water until creamy, separated from the solid residue, sweetened to taste and possibly flavoured with lemon zest and cinnamon. Served chilled.

latte di pesce *Italy* Soft fish roe

latteria *Italy* 1. Dairy 2. Dairy farm 3. The name generally used for cheeses from the Friule region

latterino *Italy* Smelt, the fish

latte scremato *Italy* Skimmed milk

lattice top A method of covering an open pie in which thin strips of pastry are laid in a crisscross pattern over the top so that the filling is seen in the openings

Lattich *Germany* Lettuce

lattuga *Italy* Lettuce

lattuga a cappuccio *Italy* Round lettuce

lattuga romana *Italy* Cos lettuce

Latviiski *Russia* A cows' milk cheese with a strong smell and pungent taste. Also called **Latviysky**

Latviysky *Russia* Latviiski

lat you *China* Chilli oil

Laubfrösche *Switzerland* A type of cabbage roll made with spinach leaves with a filling of fresh white breadcrumbs, sweated chopped onion, scrambled eggs, seasoning and nutmeg, moistened with water if necessary and cooked in the usual way (NOTE: Literally 'tree frogs'.)

Lauch *Germany* Leek

lauki *South Asia* Wax gourd

laulau *United States* A Hawaiian speciality consisting of taro leaves wrapped around a filling of salt pork and either butterfish, mackerel or salmon, steamed and served hot

Laums *France* A cows' milk cheese from Burgundy made in a brick shape and often soaked in coffee

laung *South Asia* Cloves

laurel The only edible member of the laurel family, *Laurus nobilis*. See also **bay**

laurie *France* Porbeagle shark

laurier *France* Bay, *Laurus nobilis*, but also used of several other toxic members of the laurel family

laurier, feuille de *France* Bayleaf

lauro *Italy* Bay, *Laurus nobilis*, but also used of several other toxic members of the laurel family

Laurus nobilis *Botanical name* Bay

lavagante *Portugal* Large American or European lobster

Lavandula angustifolia *Botanical name* Lavender

Lavarel *Austria, Switzerland* Lake trout

la Varenne The founder of French classical cooking (1618 – 1678)

lavaret de bourget *France* Pollan, the fish

lavender The bitter leaves of lavender, *Lavandula angustifolia*, are used in southern European cooking

laver 1. A red-tinged edible seaweed, *Porphyra umbilicalis* (*P. purpurea*), found round the coasts of South Wales and Ireland, similar to Japanese **nori**. Prepared by cleaning, soaking in sodium bicarbonate solution, then washing and stewing until tender when it resembles spinach purée. Also called **sloke**, **slugane**, **stoke**, **stake**, **slouk**, **slokum** 2. *France* To wash

laver bread *Wales* Cooked laver mixed with porridge oats and fried in bacon fat as a breakfast dish. Popular in south Wales. Also called **bara lawr**

laverello *Italy* Lake trout from the northern lakes

laver sauce *Wales* Laver bread heated and blended with orange juice, butter and lamb stock and/or cream. Served with shellfish and lobster.

lawalu, i'a Fish baked in taro leaves. See also **i'a lawalu**

lawash *Central Asia* A wholemeal flat bread from Afghanistan baked on the side of a tandoori oven and prepared in the same way as the Iranian **nane lavash**

lax *Iceland, Sweden* Salmon

laxforell *Sweden* Brown trout

laxgryta *Sweden* Salmon slices sprinkled with salt and dried dill weed, layered in a pan, covered with equal parts of butter and boiling water and simmered until most of the water has evaporated. Served with new potatoes.

laxpudding *Sweden* Layers of seasoned salmon and raw sliced potatoes alternated in a greased oven-proof dish starting and finishing with potato, covered in an egg custard mix to leave the potatoes showing and baked in a moderate oven for about 1 hour. Also called **salmon pie**

laxschinken A roll of smoked pork loin. See also **Lachsschinken**

layer cake A sponge cake which is baked in several tins then assembled together when cold and the layers sandwiched with various fillings. The top layer is decorated. An example of a layer cake is **Black Forest gateau**. Also called **sandwich cake**

lazagne *Italy* Lasagna

lb Abbreviation for pound weight

L-cysteine hydrochloride See **E920** (NOTE: The l- refers to the naturally occurring laevo form.)

LDL See **low-density lipoprotein**

Lea and Perrins' sauce See **Worcestershire sauce**

leaf beet Swiss chard

leaf fat A sheet of soft fat from the lower part of the abdominal cavity of a pig

leaf gelatine Rectangular shapes of purified gelatine rather like stiff cellophane. Each sheet weighs 2 g and will set 100 ml of water on average, but dependent on temperature and stiffness of gel required. Should be softened in water for 5 minutes prior to using.

leaf lard A very fine quality lard made from **leaf fat**

leaf tube A piping-bag nozzle with a V-shaped opening, used to make leaf shapes

leather *United States* Fruit leather

leathog *Ireland* Plaice

leaven 1. A piece of dough reserved from yeast-based bread making, placed in water possibly with a little sugar and allowed to rise when it can be used in place of yeast for the next batch of dough and is the basis of the sour dough production method. This process may continue indefinitely. **2.** Any yeast or other raising agent used in dough to make leavened bread

leavened bread Any bread using yeast or other raising agent to lighten it and incorporate carbon dioxide or air

leban *Middle East* Yoghurt

Lebanon bologno *United States* A hardwood-smoked Bologna sausage from Lebanon, Pennsylvania made with coarsely ground pre-cured meat

leben *Middle East* Yoghurt

leben raib *Middle East* The Saudi Arabian term for yoghurt

Leber *Germany* Liver

Leberkäse *Germany* A pre-cooked meat loaf from Bavaria made from a mixture of finely minced liver and sausage meat. Usually sliced and grilled or fried.

Leberklösse *Germany* Liver dumplings

leberknodel *Italy* The northern Italian version of liver dumplings, found in the Trentino-Alto Adige region

Leberknödel *Austria, Germany* Liver dumplings made with a processed and seasoned mixture of beef liver, onions, chopped parsley and soaked bread brought together with a little flour and egg, formed into small balls and simmered in beef stock until they rise to the surface

Leberknödelsuppe *Austria, Germany* A clear consommé containing small dumplings made from ground liver, breadcrumbs, herbs and seasonings, garnished with chopped parsley or chives

Lebersalsiz *Switzerland* A **Rohwurst** containing pork meat, pork fat, pigs' liver and beef, air-dried and smoked

Leberspätzle *Germany* Noodles made with flour, eggs, liver and spinach. See also **Spätzle**

Leberspiessli *Switzerland* A kebab of pieces of liver wrapped in sage leaves and bacon and grilled over charcoal

Leberstreichwurst *Austria* A small coarse-textured spreading sausage made with pork and pigs' liver

Leberwurst *Austria, Germany* Liver sausage made from boiled pig meat, pig's liver, salted pork fat, onions fried in lard and seasoning, all pounded to a fine paste and cased, the whole boiled, air-dried and smoked

Lebkuchen *Germany* Highly spiced soft brown ginger cakes with a hard white icing or chocolate covering. Eaten over the Christmas season.

lebonnet rice A type of long-grain rice

lebre *Portugal* Hare

leccia *Italy* Pompano, the fish

lechas *Spain* Soft fish roe

leche *Spain* Milk

lechecillas *Spain* Sweetbreads

leche de manteca *Spain* Buttermilk

leche desnatada *Spain* Skimmed milk

lechón *Spain* Suckling pig

lechoncillo *Spain* Small suckling pig

lechón de leche *Philippines* A whole barbecued sucking pig

lechón sarsa *Philippines* A thick sauce made from ground pig's liver, brown sugar, vinegar, garlic, spices and seasoning, thickened with biscocho. Served with roast pork.

lechuga *Spain* Lettuce

lecithin A natural substance found in egg yolk used as an emulsifier and antioxidant. See also **E322**

Leckerli *Switzerland* Sweet biscuits containing chopped nuts and candied peel. See also **Läckerli**

le colombo *Caribbean* A meat or fish and tropical vegetable curry flavoured with rum, coconut and lime

lecsó *Hungary* A sauce used for flavouring made by sweating green sweet peppers with chopped bacon, onions, paprika, tomatoes and salt in lard until soft, puréeing and straining. Used cold, may be frozen.

lectins A type of protein found mainly in legume seeds, some of which are highly poisonous and believed to act as a protection for the seed against insect and animal attack. They attack different human populations differently depending on their blood type. They are inactivated by boiling at 100°C for at least ten minutes. It has been reported that the lower boiling point of water at high altitude can prevent inactivation. Also called **haemagglutinins**

Lecythis sabucajo *Botanical name* Paradise nut

Lederzucker *Germany* Marshmallow

ledvinková polévka *Czech Republic* Kidney soup made from sliced onions and potatoes sweated in lard, flour added to make a roux and all simmered with white stock, paprika, caraway seeds and garlic, sieved and garnished with sliced and sautéed calves' kidneys

Lee cake *United States* A white sponge cake flavoured with citrus juice and zest

leek A mild-tasting member of the onion family, *Allium porrum*, with a thick multilayered stem which is the part eaten. The stems are white in the centre but may be fully blanched if planted deep in the soil or protected from light with a collar. The edible part is cylindrical up to 30 cm long and 5 cm in diameter.

leek and potato soup Paysanne-cut leek sweated in butter without colour, white stock, a bouquet garni and paysanne-cut potatoes added, seasoned and simmered until all cooked

leek pasty *Wales* A double-crust pie, whose filling consists of a layer of chopped leeks covered with bacon rashers and a little water or beaten egg. The top crust is egg-washed and pierced and all baked at 200°C for between 30 and 45 minutes. Also called **pastai cennin**

leek soup Basic soup with leeks, garnished with a fine cooked **julienne** of leek

leen chee *Thailand* Lychee

leen ngau *China* Lotus

leg chops of lamb *England* A Midlands name for chump chops of lamb and generally used for slices cut from the top end of a leg of lamb

leg of beef *England* The lower part of the hind leg of beef. It is tougher and has more gristle than other cuts and is braised, stewed or casseroled.

leg of lamb A prime roasting joint being the rear leg cut from the carcass at the coccyx and pelvis. Often divided into two, the fillet end nearest the loin and the knuckle or leg end.

leg of mutton As leg of lamb, but from an older sheep

leg of mutton cut A part of the beef carcass which resembles a leg of mutton from just above the shank of the foreleg, below the chuck and in front of the brisket. Used for braising and stewing.

leg of pork A prime roasting joint being the hind leg cut from the carcass at the coccyx and pelvis. Often cut into two joints the fillet and knuckle.

leg of veal A prime roasting joint being the rear leg cut from the carcass at the coccyx and pelvis. Can be roasted whole but is more often divided into knuckle, thick flank, cushion and under cushion.

legumbres *Spain* Vegetables

legumbres secas *Spain* Pulses

legume The general name for plants whose seeds are enclosed in two-sided pods attached along one join. Sometimes the whole pod is eaten, but more often the seeds only, either in the green or dried state, are consumed. When dried, they are known as pulses and are an important source of protein. Well over 10,000 varieties are known, most of which are edible. See also **bean, pea**

legumes *Portugal* Vegetables

légumes *France* Vegetables

légumes, crème de *France* Vegetable soup with added cream, milk or thin **béchamel sauce**

légumes, purée de *France* Vegetable soup

legume soups Soups made from pulses, usually puréed and possibly creamed

légumes secs *France* Pulses

legumi *Italy* Vegetables

leguminous Used to describe plants which are legumes

Leicester cheese *England* A mild-flavoured hard cheese made from pasteurized cows' milk and coloured orange-red with annatto. Also called **Red Leicester**

leichte Kraftsuppe *Germany* Chicken and veal broth

Leiden A highly flavoured yellow cheese with a red wax coating. See also **Leyden cheese**

Leinsamenbrot *Germany* A yeast-raised bread made from wholemeal flour and unground linseed. Said to aid digestion. Also called **linseed bread**

leipä *Finland* Bread

leipäjuustö A Finnish cheese. See also **juustoleipä**

Leipziger Allerlei *Germany* Diced root vegetables, green beans and morels all cooked separately and drained, mixed with cooked green peas and steamed and sliced asparagus tips, buttered and bound with crayfish sauce. Served garnished with crayfish tails, fleurons and small semolina gnocchi.

leitão assado *Portugal* Roast sucking pig

leite *Portugal* Milk

leivokslet *Finland* 1. Pastries 2. Tarts 3. Pies

leivos *Finland* 1. Pastry 2. Tart 3. Pie

lei yu *China* Rock carp

lekach A Jewish New Year cake sweetened with honey and flavoured with spice, raisins and chopped mixed candied peel. Also called **honiglekach**

Le Moine *Canada* A cheese resembling **Port-Salut** made by monks in Quebec

lemon One of the most important fruits of the *Citrus* family from a tree, *Citrus limon*, which grows in Mediterranean climates and is probably a hybrid of Indian lime and pummelo. It originated in the Punjab, was further developed in the Middle East and taken to Spain by the Arabs around 1150 A.D. Although there are many varieties they differ very little more between varieties than a single variety does at different times of the year. The fruit has a tart taste and is shaped like a rugby ball with usually a thick yellow skin. The juice is used extensively for flavouring, for souring and to add bite to sauces. Segments and slices are used as garnishes and for decoration and the zest is an important flavouring ingredient.

lemon aspen *Australia* This fruit of a rain forest tree, *Achronychia acidula*, is the size of a small apple with a thin lemon-coloured skin and grape-like flesh. It has an intense tart lemon eucalypt flavour and is used wherever lemons or lemon grass would be. 15–20 lemon aspens are the equivalent of the zest, juice and flesh of 6 large lemons.

lemon balm A clump-forming perennial plant, *Melissa officinalis*, with lemon-scented oval leaves used as flavouring herb with fish, poultry and ham. Also used in fruit drinks, salads, mayonnaise and sauerkraut. Also called **melissa**

lemon barley water The strained cooking liquor from barley mixed with sugar and lemon juice, used as a high-calorie drink

lemon basil A variety of basil, *Ocimum basilicum* var. *citriodorum*, with lemon-scented green leaves.

lemon butter sauce See **meunière butter sauce**

lemon curd The commonest of the smooth fruit curds made from butter and sugar emulsified and thickened with egg yolks and flavoured with the juice and zest of lemons

lemon dainty *England* A pudding made from milk, sugar, egg, flour and butter (12:12:8:3:2) flavoured with lemon juice and zest. All the ingredients with the exception of the egg whites are mixed, the butter being cut in small pieces. The stiffly beaten egg whites are folded in and all baked at 180°C until the top is firm and browned. It is allowed to stand before serving.

lemon essence An alcoholic extract of lemon zest used for flavouring

lemon fluff *England* A light sugar syrup (250 g per litre) is flavoured by boiling it with lemon peel then thickened with corn flour (50 g per litre) and egg yolks (from 4 eggs per litre). The whites from the eggs are whisked to a soft peak and folded into the cool mixture, which is then decorated with chopped nuts.

lemon grass The fresh or dried stalks and leaves of a perennial grass, *Cymbopogon citratus* and *C. flexuesus*, native to South Asia but widely grown in hot climates. It has a lemony flavour and is common in Southeast Asian dishes particularly in Thai cooking. Also called **citronella**

lemon juice The juice of lemons used for flavouring, souring and to prevent cut fruit and vegetables from browning or to whiten fish and fish bones for stock. The juice of 1 lemon amounts to between 50 and 100 ml, say 60 ml or 4 tablespoons.

lemon meringue pie *United Kingdom* A blind-baked pastry case or base filled with a thick-setting lemon-flavoured sauce, topped with meringue and baked until browned. Served cold. (NOTE: Although of UK origin, it is very popular in the USA.)

lemon mint A type of mint, *Mentha aquatica* var. *citrata*, with smooth lemon-scented green leaves. Used for flavouring.

lemon myrtle *Australia* The leaves of this tropical tree, *Backhousia citriadora*, are used either fresh or dried and ground as a flavouring herb. The taste and aroma are similar to a mixture of lemon, lime, lemon grass and lemon verbena. The essential oil is sold separately.

lemon pudding *United Kingdom* A pudding made from basic steamed pudding mixture flavoured with grated lemon zest

lemon sauce As orange sauce but with lemon zest and juice substituted for orange

lemon-scented verbena See **lemon verbena**

lemon sole A North Atlantic dextral flat-fish, *Microstomus kitt*, similar to plaice with a brownish-yellow upper skin covered with spots and with a faint lemon scent when freshly caught. It has a very small head and can grow to 60 cm long. The flesh is white and lean but not considered as fine as Dover sole. Also called **long flounder**

lemon soufflé A cold soufflé flavoured with finely grated lemon zest. Also called **Milanese soufflé**

lemon squeezer See **juice extractor**

lemon thyme A hardy low-growing thyme, *Thymus x citriodorus*, with lemon-scented leaves used in stuffings, fresh fruit salads and dips

lemon verbena A half hardy shrub, *Aloysia triphylla*, with pointed crinkly leaves which have a sharp lemony fragrance. The chopped young leaves can be used to flavour desserts, cakes, ice cream and the fresh or dried leaves are used in white meat and fish dishes. Can be used as a substitute for lemon grass. Also called **lemon scented verbena**, **verbena**

lemon zester See **zester**

lencse *Hungary* Lentils

Lende *Germany* Loin or sirloin (of meat)

Lendenbraten *Germany* Roast sirloin of beef

Lendenschnitte am Grill *Germany* Grilled fillet of beef

Lendenstück *Germany* Fillet or loin (of meat)

lengkuas *Malaysia* Greater galangal

lengua *Spain* Tongue

lengua asada *Caribbean* A dish from Puerto Rico made from cows' tongue boiled with onions, carrot, thyme, cloves and a bay leaf until almost cooked. The tongue is skinned whilst hot then cooked to completion in a mixture of oil and caramelized sugar. The strained cooking liquor is added together with onion and garlic and all simmered until the sauce thickens. The tongue is then removed and sliced and served with the sauce.

lenguado *Spain* 1. Dover sole 2. Dab

lenguado a la vasca *Spain* Boiled Dover sole with potatoes and mushrooms

lenivyi shchi *Russia* A soup made with water or stock, simmered with a large amount of shredded cabbage and sliced potatoes, tomatoes, carrots, turnips, parsnips and celery. It is flavoured with an onion and bay leaves, which are removed, before being served in large bowls garnished with sour cream and butter. (NOTE: Literally 'lazy soup', referring to the use of cabbage for soup instead of preparing it for sauerkraut.)

lenkuas *Malaysia* Greater galangal

lenrimmad lax *Sweden* Home-salted salmon prepared as gravlax but with twice as much salt as sugar. Cut in very thin slices and served with potatoes mashed with chopped parsley and dill.

Lens culinaris *Botanical name* Lentil

Lens esculenta *Botanical name* Lentil

lentejas *Spain* Lentils

lenticchie *Italy* Lentils

lentil brö *Scotland* A lentil soup from the Shetland Islands made with ham stock and finely chopped onions, carrots and turnips plus pearl barley, the solid ingredients all being first sweated in butter

lentilhas *Portugal* Lentils

lentilles *France* Lentils

lentilles, purée de *France* Lentil soup

lentilles vertes du Puy *France* Very tiny green and expensive lentils regarded as a delicacy

lentils The seeds of the oldest documented leguminous plant, *Lens culinaris* or *L. esculenta*, originating in the Middle East but now common throughout the world. They are about 5 mm in diameter and usually dehusked and split in two. Red, green and brown (orange when dehusked) varieties exist, the latter keeping their shape on cooking. None require soaking prior to cooking. Other seeds are incorrectly called lentils, e.g. black lentil (black gram) and green lentil (mung bean).

lentil soup Washed lentils, chopped carrot and onion, a bouquet garni, knuckle of ham and tomato purée simmered and skimmed with white stock until all cooked, ham removed and the whole liquidized and passed through a chinois, seasoned and served hot with croûtons. Also called **lentilles, purée de**

Lentinus edodes *Botanical name* Shiitake mushroom

lentischio *Italy* Mastic

lentisco *Spain* Mastic

lentisk A straggly bush, *Pistacia lentiscus*, with red berries which grows wild on arid

Mediterranean hillsides. If cut it exudes the aromatic resin, mastic.

León *Spain* A hard cows' milk cheese, dry-salted and ripened for about 20 days. It is made in small cylinders (500 to 800 g) and has a close-textured paste with a hard, yellow and rough rind.

Leoni *Germany* A sausage made from a mixture of coarsely ground beef, pork and pork back fat, with seasoning, sugar, ginger, coriander and nutmeg, packed into beef middles and tied

Lepidium sativum *Botanical name* Cress

Lepiota rhacodes *Botanical name* Shaggy parasol

lepre *Italy* Hare

lepre agrodolce *Italy* Hare cooked in sweet-and-sour sauce and topped with shredded chocolate, almonds and raisins

lepre crostata *Italy* Spit-roasted hare, baked with cream and covered in almond paste

lepre in salmì *Italy* Hare marinated in vinegar and cooked in red wine

lepudrida *Italy* A rich meat and vegetable stew from Sardinia

le rouge royal *United States* A very large, brilliant red and thick-walled sweet pepper

leshch *Russia* Bream

leshch v pergamente *Russia* Fillets of bream, soaked in hot water then cooked **en papillote** with grated carrot, onions and butter with lemon juice and herbs. Served with boiled potatoes and béchamel or fish velouté with pickled cucumbers.

Les Orrys *France* Orrys

Les Riceys *France* A soft cows' milk cheese from Troyes made in discs and covered in wood ash

lessato *Italy* Lesso

lesser argentine See **argentine**

lesser galangal The root of a Chinese plant, *Languas officinarum* or *Alpinia officinarum*, with a reddish-brown skin resembling a smaller version of ginger root. It has a pungent flavour of cardamom and ginger with a hint of eucalyptus. Used extensively in Southeast Asian cooking.

lesser ginger See **kempferia galangal**

lesser spotted dogfish A common British dogfish, *Scyliorhinus caniculus*, up to 75 cm long and slightly better tasting than the larger variety

lesso *Italy* 1. Boiled 2. Boiled meat, especially boiled beef ▶ also called **lessato**

lesso valdostano *Italy* Meat and sausage boiled in a sealed pot

let down, to To dilute or thin with liquid

letsprængt oksebryst *Denmark* Corned beef

letterato *Italy* A small tuna fish

letterbanket *Netherlands* Marzipan

lettuce The most common salad vegetable, which is occasionally braised or stir-fried. It is an annual low-growing plant, *Lactuca sativa*, varying from a 10 to 30 cm spread, usually green-leaved but some varieties are red or brown. They may be loose-leafed, curly or form tight compact heads. The principal types are cos (romaine), semi-cos, butterhead, crisphead and loose leaf. Typical named varieties are Webb, Great Lakes, Little Gem, Sugar Cos, Oak leaf, Lollo rosso and Lollo biondo.

lettuce laver Sea lettuce

lettuce leaf basil A variety of basil with a fruity scent

Leuconostoc The name of the genus of bacteria used for the production of lactic acid in cheese and other milk products and in sauerkraut production

Leuconostoc mesenteroides One of the bacteria included in starter cultures for the fermentation of cabbage, cucumbers and olives and the production of cottage cheeses

leudar *Spain* To leaven or raise with yeast or a chemical raising agent

leuqkuas *Malaysia* Greater galangal

levadura *Spain* Leavening agent such as baking powder, sourdough starter, yeast

levain *France* Leaven, sourdough starter

lever *Denmark, Norway, Sweden* Liver

leveret A young hare up to 1 year old

leverkorv *Sweden* A liver sausage made with pigs' liver, fat bacon and veal, separately minced, combined with seasoning, chopped onion and marjoram, moistened with milk, packed loosely into casings and simmered for 30 minutes

leverpastej *Sweden* Liver pâté

leverpølse *Denmark* A firmer version of the liver sausage **leverpostej**

leverpostej *Denmark* A liver sausage made with pigs' liver, lean pork and flare fat, seasoned, flavoured with anchovies, nutmeg and cinnamon, bound with egg, packed into beef runners and simmered for 2 hours

leves *Hungary* Soup

levistico *Italy* Lovage

Levisticum officinale *Botanical name* Lovage

levraut *France* Young hare

levreteau *France* Young hare

Levroux *France* A soft goats' milk cheese similar to **Valençay**, shaped like a pyramid (300 g)

levulose See **fructose**

levure *France* Yeast, or other leavening agent

levure chimique *France* Baking powder

Lewis kilkenny *Scotland* Equal quantities of cooked potatoes, carrots and well-chopped cabbage mashed together with cream and seasoning. Eaten hot as is or made into cakes and fried.

Leyden cheese *Netherlands* A highly flavoured yellow, semi-hard scalded-curd cheese made from cows' milk with a hard rind and red wax coating. Often flavoured with cumin seed, caraway seed or cloves.

ley nyin bwint *Burma* Cloves

L-glutamic acid See **E620**

liaise, to To thicken with a liaison

liaison *England, France* A combination of ingredients used to thicken and bind soups, sauces, stews, etc. Egg yolks and cream, **beurre manié** and all the starch-based mixtures are typical liaisons

liba *Hungary* Goose

libamáj pástétom *Hungary* A hot puff pastry bouchée or vol-au-vent filled with a mixture of goose liver pâté, butter, **béchamel sauce**, brandy and spices

liboké *Central Africa* A method of preparing fish or meat in the Congo river area by wrapping it in banana leaves two or three layers thick and either steaming or grilling. Marinades and flavourings are used in the usual way. The banana leaves are softened by warming them in water or the oven and the central rib is cut away. Also called **ajomba** (NOTE: The plural is **maboké**.)

lichee Lychee

lichene d'Irlanda *Italy* Carragheen

li chi *China* Lychee

licki kupus *Balkans* A Croatian dish made from three or more different cuts of pork simmered with sauerkraut and served with boiled potatoes

licorice See **liquorice**

Liebig beef extract The original concentrated beef extract named after the German chemist Leibig who developed it for production in South America before refrigerated ships could bring their beef to Europe

liebre *Spain* Hare

Liebstöckel *Germany* Lovage

Liederkranz *United States* A soft golden-yellow cows' milk cheese with an orange rind, somewhat milder than **Limburger**, made in Ohio

liégeoise, à la *France* In the Liège style, i.e. including gin or juniper berries

liemi *Finland* Soup

lien jee *China* Lotus seeds

lien ngow *China* Lotus root

lier *France* **1.** To blend or bring together **2.** To thicken or to bind, hence 'jus lié'

lievero *Italy* Young hare

lievitare *Italy* To leaven or raise with yeast or a chemical raising agent

lievito *Italy* Yeast

lievito chimico *Italy* Baking powder

lievito naturale *Italy* Sourdough starter

lièvre *France* Hare

lièvre en civet *France* Jugged hare. Also called **civet de lièvre**

lifrarpylsa Blood sausage

lift The rising of puff pastry when cooked due to the generation of steam which separates the layers of dough as they are cooked. Also used for the rising of any cooked mixtures such as cakes and soufflés.

light brown sugar *United States* A refined pale brown sugar which looks like damp sand. Also called **soft sugar**, **sand sugar**, **pieces**, **yellows**

light corn syrup *United States* Corn syrup

light cream *United States* Coffee cream

light muscovado A semi-refined soft brown sugar about the same crystal size as granulated or caster sugar

lights Lungs of animals used in manufactured meat preparation but rarely eaten in meals in the UK

light soya sauce A thin, light-coloured and salty soya sauce used where colouring is not required as e.g. with seafood. Also called **thin soya sauce**

light syrup 1. *United States* Corn syrup **2.** See **syrup**

light whipping cream *United States* Cream with 30 to 40% butterfat

Ligueil *France* A strong-flavoured goats' milk cheese from the Loire valley made in a cylindrical shape

ligurienne, à la *France* In the style of Liguria in Italy, i.e. with a garnish of stuffed tomatoes, risotto flavoured with saffron and duchesse potatoes

ligústico *Spain* Lovage

Ligusticum scoticum *Botanical name* Scottish lovage

ligzdinas *Latvia* A type of Scotch egg

liha *Finland* Meat

lihakääryle *Finland* Beef olive

lihaliemi *Finland* Consommé

lihamureke *Finland* Forcemeat

lihamurekepiiras *Finland* Meat pie with a sour cream crust

lihapallero *Finland* **1.** Meat balls **2.** Croquettes

lihapiirakka *Finland* Meat pie or pasty

lihapyörykkä *Finland* **1.** Meat ball **2.** Croquette

liiaksi paiste *Finland* Overdone, overcooked. Used of meat, baked goods, etc.

li jiang *China* Oyster sauce

li ju *China* Carp

likky pie *England* A West Country dish of sliced parboiled leeks and cubed lean pork cooked in milk for about an hour, mixed with cream and eggs, placed in a pie dish, covered with puff pastry and baked at 220°C until brown

Lilium tigrinum *Botanical name* Lily bulb

lily buds The 5 cm long, furry, slim unopened flower buds of a day lily, *Hemerocallis fulva*, with a woody scent, used in Chinese cooking. They are light brown in colour and are soaked in water prior to use. Usually tied up when cooked in simmering dishes to avoid them falling apart. Also called **golden needles**

lily bulb The bulbs of a tiger lily, *Lilium tigrinum*, resembling a head of garlic. Used fresh in Japan and Korea or dried in China. Must be parboiled before use to remove bitterness.

lima *Italy, Spain* Lime, the citrus fruit

lima bean *United States* Butter bean

limanda *Italy* Dab, the fish

limande *France* Dab, the fish

limão *Portugal* Lemon

limão galego *Brazil* West Indian lime

lima orange See **laranja lima**

limau *Indonesia* Pummelo

limau kesturi *Malaysia* A small lime, 1.5 cm diameter, used as a souring agent

limau nipis *Malaysia* Lime, the fruit

Limburger A very strong-smelling, soft, surface-ripened cheese originally from Belgium, then adopted in Germany and now made worldwide. It is made from pasteurized full cream cows' milk started with *Streptococcus lactis* and *S. thermophilus* to develop acidity, coagulated with rennet, the curd formed into small bricks, dry-salted, ripened at high humidity for about 10 days until the surface develops a red colour, then further ripened at lower temperatures until finished. It has a cream-coloured close-textured paste.

lime *England, France* **1.** A small round citrus fruit of which there are four principal species: *Citrus aurantifolia*, the West Indian lime, requires very hot conditions and is not usually exported; *Citrus latifolia*, the Persian or Tahiti lime, is rather larger and is seedless; *Citrus limettiodes*, the Indian or sweet lime, is grown extensively in the Middle East, India, the Caribbean and South America, and *Citrus limetta*, the Tunisian sweet limetta. Limes generally have a thin green skin and few pips; they are sharper and more acid than lemons, but are used in the same way. They are also available dried and as such frequently used in Middle Eastern and East Asian cooking. Often pickled with spices, salted and/or dried or preserved in soya sauce. **2.** Calcium hydroxide, the hydrated form of calcium oxide (E529) used in Southeast Asia to add crispness to batter, to reduce the acidity of fruits in desserts and as a component of **pan**. It is an important source of calcium in the diet. See also **tortilla flour**. Also called **slaked lime**

lime leaves The leaves of the **makrut lime**

limequat A hybrid of the lime and kumquat, *Citrus aurantifolia x Fortunella japonica*. The principal varieties are Eustis and Lakeland which are both small and green with a thin edible skin and very sour flesh. Used as a garnish.

lime sauce As **orange sauce**, but with lime juice and zest substituted for orange

limon *Russia* **1.** Lemon **2.** Lime, the citrus fruit

limón *Spain* Lemon

limoncello *Italy* The zest of Amalfi lemons macerated in alcohol and sugar

limoncillo *Spain* Lemon grass

limone *Italy* Lemon

limone, al *Italy* Sautéed and finished with lemon juice

limone Amalfitano *Italy* Amalfi lemon

limone di mare *Italy* See **violet 2**

limousine, à la *France* In the Limousin style, i.e. with red cabbage, ceps and chestnuts

Limousin tart clafoutis See **tarte limousine clafoutis**

limpa bread *Sweden* A dark yeast-raised bread made with milk, brown sugar and/or treacle and a mixture of wheat and rye flour, flavoured with caraway seed, fennel seed and grated orange zest which has been covered with boiling water then cooled

limpet A single-shelled mollusc, *Paletta vulgaris*, with a shell shaped like a flat cone up to 5 cm diameter and which is commonly seen clinging to rocks. It is found in the Atlantic and the Mediterranean and is prepared and served like cockles. They are not traded and not particularly good to eat on their own but may be used in sauces and stews.

limpet stovies *Scotland* Limpets, soaked in water for 12 hours, are drained then simmered in salted water until they are released from their shells, retaining the cooking liquor. They are then rinsed in cold water and the eyes and sandy trails removed, layered alternately with sliced potatoes ((3:1) on limpet meat) in a pan, covered with the cooking liquor, seasoned, buttered and simmered for 1 hour.

limpin' susan *United States* A dish of rice and red beans

limun helou *Egypt* Sweet lime

limun succari *Egypt* Sweet lime

limu omani *Central Asia* The Iranian name for whole **loomi**

Lincolnshire potato cheesecake *England* A shortcrust pastry flan filled with a mixture of mashed potatoes, butter, caster sugar and well-beaten eggs (2:1:1:1) flavoured with nutmeg, lemon juice and zest. Baked at 200°C for 15 minutes to set the pastry, then for a further 10 minutes without the flan ring. Contains no cheese.

line, to To cover the inside of a cooking utensil e.g. a cake tin, pudding bowl or terrine dish, with edible matter, e.g. bacon, or non-edible matter, e.g. greaseproof paper, for protection, decoration or to prevent the enclosed food sticking to the container

ling A round seawater fish, *Molva molva*, with a brownish-black top, a member of the cod family but longer (up to 2 m) and thinner than cod. Often salted or smoked. Cooked as cod. Also called **sea burbot**, **common ling**

ling fun *China* Tapioca starch

ling gok *China* Water caltrop

lingon *Sweden* Cowberries

lingonberry Cowberry

lingua *Italy, Portugal* Tongue

lingua alla borghese *Italy* Ox tongue, braised with wine, brandy and salt pork

linguado *Portugal* Sole, the fish

linguado com bananas *Portugal* Baked fillets of sole topped with bananas, served with boiled potatoes and salad

linguattola *Italy* General name for small flat seawater fish, dabs

lingue *France* Ling, the fish

lingue di gatto *Italy* Langue de chat

lingue di passero *Italy* Thin strips of noodle-like pasta (NOTE: Literally 'sparrow's tongues'.)

linguica *Portugal* A coarse-textured pungent small sausage, usually grilled or barbecued

linguine *Italy* Small tongue-shaped pieces of flat pasta

link, to A method of dividing long meat-filled casings into short individual sausages by twisting at the division points and plaiting them into a succession of threes. Normally done by butchers who make their own sausages.

Linköping *Sweden* A spreading sausage made from pork and beef and salt-cured

link sausages Frying or grilling sausages made in a long chain with one casing and formed into links by taking them three at a time with a twist between each group of three

linquisa *Portugal* A brine-cured pork-based sausage, flavoured with garlic, cumin and cinnamon. Requires cooking.

linseed bread See **Leinsamenbrot**

linseed oil Cold pressed oil from the seeds of the flax plant which can be used in food and as a nutritional supplement being rich in essential fatty acids (EFAs)

Linsen *Germany* Lentils

Linsensuppe *Germany* Lentil soup often served with chopped sausage

linser 1. *Denmark* Cream tarts **2.** *Norway* Lentils

Linz cake See **Linzertorte**

Linzer Delicatesse A small pleasant-tasting salad potato

Linzertorte *Austria, Germany* A flan made with a base of almond-flavoured pastry filled with raspberry jam and topped with latticework pastry. Eaten warm or cold with whipped cream. Also called **Linz cake**, **Linz tart**

Linz tart See **Linzertorte**

lipase An enzyme that breaks down fats into fatty acids and glycerine for absorption in the gut. It also causes fat to go rancid.

lipeäkala *Finland* Lutefisk

lipid See **fat**

lipoic acid This acid is an essential growth factor for many microorganisms. Whether it has any function in human metabolism is not known.

Liptauer *Germany* A soft strong-tasting ewes' milk cheese with no rind. It is made by ripening the curd for 10 days, removing the rind, blending with salt and ripening for a few more days. Contains 50% water, 22% fat and 21% protein.

Liptauer cheese spread Liptauer cheese mixed at the blending stage with cream and flavourings such as anchovies, onions, capers, caraway seed, chives, paprika, etc.

Liptói *Hungary* A soft creamy ewes' milk cheese, similar to **Liptauer**

liqueur A sweetened alcoholic extract of various herb-, spice- and fruit-based flavourings, used as a drink but also as a flavouring in many dishes, e.g. cointreau, Kümmel, kirsch

liqueur de framboise Raspberry liqueur

liquidize, to To pulverize fruits and vegetables or mixtures of liquids and the same into a soft purée by breaking down the cell walls and releasing their contents

liquidizer See **blender**

liquid measure Volume measure

liquid paraffin See **mineral hydrocarbons**

liquid smoke See **pyroligneous acid**

liquirizia *Italy* Liquorice

liquor See **cooking liquor**

liquorice A Mediterranean plant, *Glycyrrhiza glabra*, which probably originated in China. It is grown for the rhizomes and roots from which, after 3 to 5 years' growth, the flavouring is extracted in water and boiled down to a black tarry substance. The roots used to be chewed by children as a sweet. Also called **licorice**, **Spanish**

liscio *Italy* Smooth

lisette *France* A small mackerel

lissamine green A synthetic green food colouring. See also **E142**

lista *Italy* Menu

Listeria monocytogenes A bacterium causing illness which grows in soft ripened cheeses (unpasteurized milk has been wrongly implicated), pâtés, shop-prepared salads, etc. It will grow in these foods at less than 4°C with a doubling time of 18 hours. Samples cultured at 37°C normally have a doubling time of 7.4 hours but after subjecting them to cold shock at 4°C the doubling time drops to 2.5 hours, at the same time refrigeration appears to select for more virulent strains. The incubation period is up to 4 weeks and the resulting illness can range from a general feeling of malaise to meningitis and septicaemia. It is more likely to cause stillbirths and miscarriages, and for this reason pregnant women are recommended to refrain from the food items mentioned unless home cooked. It does not grow in raw milk farmhouse cheeses due to the low pH (less than 5), and better hygienic practices. Subsequent pasteurization cannot be used as a let-out, and there is more rapid transfer of the milk from cow to cheese making.

listeriosis The disease caused by the bacterium *Listeria monocytogenes*

litchee Lychee

litchi Lychee

Litchi chinensis Botanical name Lychee

litekokt *Norway* Soft-boiled. Used e.g. of eggs.

liter *United States* Litre

Liter *Germany* Litre

lithol rubine BK See **E180**

litre *England, France* The normal measure of volume approximately equal to 1.75 imperial pints or 2.1 US pints, or divided into decilitres (dl) (10 per litre), centilitres (cl) (100 per litre) or millilitres (ml) (1000 per litre). A teaspoon is 5 ml, a dessertspoon 10 ml, a tablespoon 15 ml and an imperial pint 568 ml. Abbreviation **l**, **L**

litro *Italy, Spain* Litre

little cuttlefish A very small cuttlefish, *Sepiola rondeleti*, with a maximum length of 4 cm. Usually cleaned and eaten whole.

Little Gem A semi-cos-type lettuce variety with soft leaves, usually harvested when up to 15 cm high

little neck clam A small (up to 6 cm) and slightly oblong clam, *Venerupis japonica*, found in the Pacific Ocean. May be eaten raw or cooked.

little tuna See **little tunny**

little tunny A tropical seawater fish, *Euthynnus alletteratus*, resembling a small albacore and also related to tuna. It has a firm oily flesh and dark blue to green striped skin on top. Weighs up to 7 kg. Baked or grilled. Also called **bonito**, **little tuna**

liu *China* A method of cooking involving coating with corn flour, frying or steaming then simmering in sauce

lívance *Czech Republic* A mixture of flour, milk, butter, sugar and egg yolks, lightened with stiffly beaten egg whites, shaped into small balls and baked until brown on both sides in the oven. Served coated with plum jam and sprinkled with cinnamon and sugar.

Livarot *France* A soft cows' milk cheese from Normandy cast in small discs (500 g) with a brownish shiny rind and a strong flavour and smell. It is protected by appellation d'origine status and the label should contain the words 'Pays d'Auge'. Contains 51% water, 20% fat and 24% protein.

livèche *France* Lovage

liver A large internal organ in all vertebrates consisting of pink to dark brown soft uniform tissue interspersed with veins, etc. all enclosed in a membrane. It functions as a detoxifying organ for poisons such as alcohol and plant alkaloids, as an energy store (glycogen) and as a source of fat emulsifiers for the bowel. The flavour depends on the age and type of animal. The most commonly used are lamb's, pig's, and calf's livers which are grilled, fried or braised; goose, duck, pig and chicken livers which are made into pâtés; and pig and ox livers which are braised and stewed.

liver herbs The principal herbs used with liver are basil, dill, marjoram, sage and tarragon

liver pudding See **maksalaatikko**

liver sausage A very common sausage made in many countries from a fine paste of cooked liver, sometimes with meat, and with flavourings and seasonings. Can be sliced or spread. See also **Leberwurst**

live yoghurt Yoghurt which still contains live bacteria and hence can be used to inoculate further batches. It is kept at a low temperature to slow down bacterial growth.

livonienne, sauce *France* A fine **julienne** of carrots, celery, mushrooms and onions sweated in butter, added to a fish velouté and finished with julienned truffle and chopped parsley. Served with fish.

livornaise, à la *France* In the style of Livorno in Italy, i.e. accompanied with shallots, tomatoes and truffles. Used especially of poached fish.

livornese, alla *Italy* In the style of Livorno in Italy, i.e. with tomato sauce, especially fish and shellfish

livre *France* Pound of weight; 500 g

li yi *China* Carp

li yu *China* Rock carp

li zhi *China* Lychee

llagosta a la brasa *Catalonia* Lobster cooked over an open flame

llagosta i pollastre *Catalonia* Lobster and chicken in a tomato and hazelnut sauce

llantén *Spain* Plantain

llenguado *Catalonia* Sole, the fish

llesca (*plural* **llesques**) *Catalonia* A slice

llet *Catalonia* Milk

lliseria *Spain* Megrim, the fish

llobarro al forn a rodanxes *Catalonia* Baked sliced sea bass

llom de porc *Catalonia* Pork loin chops

llonganisetta *Catalonia* A fine-textured cured sausage

lluç a la plancha *Catalonia* Hake cooked on a griddle

loach One of three types of small European freshwater fish of the carp family *Cobitidea*. They have a good flavour but lots of small bones and when fried are popular in France. Treat as smelt.

loaf 1. A standard quantity of bread dough usually baked in a rectangular loaf tin to give a characteristic shape **2.** Any type of food baked in a loaf tin, e.g. meat loaf, fruit loaf, etc.

loaf cheese Edamer

loaf pan A rectangular pan with deep, slightly sloping sides, used to bake bread, some cakes and meat loaves

loaf sugar *United States* Cube sugar or sugar cubes (NOTE: Not the same as sugar loaf.)

loaf tin A rectangular tin, of length approximately twice, and width equal to, the depth, with slightly outward sloping sides to allow for easy removal of whatever is cooked in it

lo baak *China* Mooli. Also called **lo bok**

lo baak gor *China* A solid steamed savoury pudding or dumpling made with grated mooli and rice flour, then sliced and fried

lobak *Indonesia, Malaysia* Mooli

lobe leaf seaweed Wakame

lobhia *South Asia* Cow pea

lobia *South Asia* Cow pea

lo bok *China* Mooli. Also called **lo baak**

lobscouse *United Kingdom, United States* A meat and vegetable stew thickened with ship biscuit, once popular on sailing vessels where it could easily be prepared. Variants on the name occur in all north Atlantic seafaring nations. In the UK it is associated with Liverpool, hence the name scouse or scouser for inhabitants of that city. In the USA it is associated with New England. Nowadays it is made without the ship biscuit. Also called **scouse**

lobskovs *Denmark* Lobscouse served with rye bread

lobster *Europe, United States* The largest sea crustaceans, *Homarus gammarus* and *H. americanus*, with eight legs, two forward-facing strong crushing claws, several antennae and a muscular tail. Lobsters are blue-grey when alive and pink when cooked. They are caught on both sides of the Atlantic and in Europe weigh up to 2 kg. The North American variety is larger. Female lobsters, which are more tender, may contain orange eggs called coral. They should feel heavy for their size, generally yield half their weight in edible meat and are normally bought alive. To kill them they can either be suffocated for 30 minutes in de-aerated water (water which has been vigorously boiled and cooled), be dropped in boiling water and held under for 2 minutes or be severed along the centre line of the whole body using a cleaver or heavy knife and starting at the head end. The RSPCA recommend placing them in cold salted water (35 g salt per litre) which is gradually brought to the boil.

lobster bisque Bisque de homard

lobster butter 1. Lobster shell pounded with unsalted butter to a smooth paste, sweated in a pan, a little water added and all boiled for 15 minutes, strained and cooled until the butter fat sets. Used quickly, the water may also be used for its flavour. **2.** A compound butter made with the creamy parts, eggs and coral of lobster pounded together with an equal amount of butter and sieved

lobster mayonnaise Half a cold boiled lobster served in its shell with mayonnaise and salad

lobster Newburg *United States* Cubed cooked lobster meat, sautéed in butter, sherry added, the juices thickened with a liaison of egg yolks and cream and all served on a paprika-flavoured rice

lobster sauce See **homard, sauce**

lobster thermidor Homard thermidor

lobya *South Asia* Cow pea

Loch Fyne kipper *Scotland* An excellent fat and plump kipper from Loch Fyne

Loch Fyne oysters *Scotland* Farmed Pacific oysters from Loch Fyne

lochshen A Jewish term for noodles, traditionally made by cutting thinly rolled pasta dough into strips, now usually commercial vermicelli. Also called **lokshen**

locro *South America* An Ecuadorian potato soup with cheese, garnished with pieces of avocado

locust bean Carob

locust bean gum E410, A plant gum extracted from carob, used as a thickener or gelling agent

lodger's loaf Barrel bread

lodole *Italy* Larks, the birds

lofschotel *Netherlands* Chicory

løg *Denmark* Onion

loganberry A hybrid of a raspberry and blackberry or dewberry looking like a large dark raspberry about 5 cm long, with a sweet-sour taste and fragrant aroma. Use as raspberry.

lohi *Finland* Salmon

lohikeitto *Finland* Salmon soup with potatoes and leeks

lohilaatikko *Finland* As **laxpudding**, but with the addition of chopped onions and breadcrumbs to the layers and gratinated with breadcrumbs

lohipiirakka *Finland* Salmon pie

lohipiiras *Finland* Salmon pie, similar to **koulibiac**

loin The general name for the joint of an animal consisting of the ribless vertebrae up to the pelvis plus up to 4 vertebrae with ribs, cut through the centre of the backbone to include all the longitudinal muscles plus a small portion of the ribs and the abdominal cavity muscles

loin end of lamb The front half of a loin of lamb

loin of lamb *Scotland* A best end of lamb. Also called **single loin of lamb**

loin of veal *United Kingdom* That part of the back between the ribs and leg. May be stuffed, rolled and roasted or cut into chops.

lök *Sweden* Onion

løk *Norway* Onion

lok dow *China* Mung beans

lokhi Bottle gourd

löksås *Sweden* Onion sauce made from finely chopped onions sweated in butter, flour added to make a blond roux and let down to a thin sauce with milk, cooked out and seasoned. Often served with baked potatoes.

lokshen A Jewish term for noodles. See also **lochshen**

lokshyna *Russia* Egg noodles

löksoppa *Sweden* Onion soup

lökströmming *Sweden* Uncleaned sprats marinated in equal parts of white vinegar and water for 12 hours, drained, then layered with sliced onions and a mixture of sugar, black pepper, crushed white peppercorns, cloves and salt in a pot and kept in the refrigerator for 5 days Served with potatoes boiled in their skins

Lollo biondo *Italy* A non-hearting loose leaf lettuce with well-flavoured green frilly leaves. May be harvested over a long period by picking individual leaves or cutting and leaving to resprout. Also called **green lollo lettuce**

Lollo rosso *England, Italy* As **Lollo biondo**, but with frilly leaves tinged with red/bronze and of excellent flavour. Also called **red Lollo**

lombarda *Spain* Red cabbage

lombata *Italy* Loin (of meat)

lombatina *Italy* 1. Entrecôte steak of beef 2. Loin chop

lombo *Italy, Portugal* Loin (of meat)

lombo di maiale al latte *Italy* A pork loin, piquéed with cloves and cinnamon bark and braised in milk

lombok chilli A deep-red pointed chilli from Indonesia and used in its cuisine

lo mein *China* Fresh egg noodles

lomi-lomi salmon *United States* A Hawaiian dish of salted salmon cooked with chopped tomatoes, sweet mild onions and spring onions

lomo *Spain* 1. Saddle, loin or back (of meat) 2. The eye of a loin of pork, cured and packed without further treatment into a close fitting casing. Usually eaten raw.

lon 1. *Thailand* Various cooked sauces made with ingredients such as shellfish, fish and meat with flavouring agents and seasoning and simmered in coconut milk until thick 2. *Vietnam* Pork

lonac *Balkans* A deep earthenware casserole dish

London broil *United States* Boneless flank of beef, marinated and grilled then cut on the slant

London particular *England* A bacon and green split pea soup made with a chicken or ham stock with aromatic vegetables, puréed, strained, seasoned and finished with cream or yoghurt and garnished with chopped grilled bacon and croûtons (NOTE: Named after a particularly nasty London fog whose colour it resembled.)

longa *Ireland* Ling, the fish

longan A small round tropical fruit, *Nephelium longana*, from Southeast Asia and China resembling a lychee. It has a brown and brittle skin, a central inedible stone and a sweet aromatic white flesh. Also called **dragon's eye**, **lungan**

longaniza *Portugal* A large sausage similar to chorizo

long back bacon Long rashers of bacon from that part of a side of bacon without ribs

long bean *Vigna sesquipedalis*, a relative of the cow pea grown extensively in India, China and Southeast Asia both for the mature yellow beans which are harvested from pods (up to 1 m long) or for the young pods (up to 35 cm) which are cooked whole. The plants need high supports. Also called **yard long bean**, **long-podded cow pea**, **snake bean**

Longchamp, crème *France* **Crème Saint Germain** garnished with cooked and washed vermicelli and a **julienne** of sorrel cooked in butter

long cucumber Indoor-grown cucumbers, 25 to 65 cm in length with usually smooth skins. They do not require fertilization. If fertilized they produce bitter fruits and it is for this reason that they must be grown in the absence of insects.

longe *France* Loin (of veal or pork)

longeole *Switzerland* A sausage from Geneva made with chopped pork filled into a casing, air-dried for 2 days and cooked for 2 hours. Served hot.

long fin tuna Albacore

long flounder Lemon sole

long-grain rice Rice which releases little starch when boiled thus remaining in separated grains. See also **brown long-grain rice**, **white long-grain rice**

Long Island duck *United States* An intensively raised duck killed at 1.5 to 2.5 kg, 7 to 8 weeks old

long-life Used to describe foods, usually milk, cream, other liquid dairy products and fruit juices, which have been heated to 132°C for 1 to 2 seconds (occasionally up to 6 minutes depending on the foodstuff) rapidly cooled and aseptically packaged. Also called **UHT**, **ultra heat-treated**

long-neck clam Soft-shell clam

longnose Garfish

long pepper A plant *Piper longum* (India), *P. retrofractum* (Indonesia), related to the pepper vine whose berries are harvested green and sun dried. Its flavour resembles a milder black pepper. It is grown only in India and Indonesia and is used in East Asian cooking. Also called **pippali**

long-podded cow pea See **long bean**

longsong *Laos* A type of **fondue chinoise** in which thin strips of buffalo meat or venison are cooked at the table in a pot of simmering flavoured stock and dipped in a peanut sauce

long xia *China* Lobster

long xu niu rou *China* Thin-sliced beef and asparagus shallow-fried

lontong *Indonesia* Boiled short-grain white rice pressed into a greased square dish, covered with banana leaf, cooled and cut into cubes. Served with satay.

lonza *Italy* The eye of a loin of pork, salted and air-dried. Eaten raw in very thin slices.

loofah The slightly bitter gourd from a plant, *Luffa cylindrica*, which looks like a cucumber when young and can be used as a vegetable after soaking in salted water to remove the bitter flavour. When old it is made into a rough bath sponge. Grown in China and the Caribbean. See also **angled loofah**. Also called **sponge gourd**, **luffa**

loomi *Middle East, Persian Gulf* Dried limes which have first been boiled in salted water for five minutes then halved and dried in the sun or a very cool oven until dark and brittle with the flesh completely dehydrated. May be powdered for use as a spice. Lime or lemon zest is used as a substitute if not available.

loose-leaf lettuce A type of lettuce with leaves often indented and very decorative but not forming a heart. The most nutritious type of lettuce.

lop cheeng *China* The standard Chinese pork sausage. See also **lap cheong**

loquat The fruit of a tree, *Eriobotrya japonica*, once from Japan but now grown in Mediterranean and similar climates. It looks like a small golden yellow plum and has a sweet slightly tart flesh with a fruity aroma and a large central stone. Use as plums. Also called **Japanese medlar**

Lorbeer *Germany* Bay, *Laurus nobilis*, but also used of several other toxic members of the laurel family

lorgnettes *France* **1.** Fried onion rings **2.** Small dessert biscuits **3.** Candied fruit

Lormes *France* A goats' milk cheese shaped like a cone from Nivernais

lorraine, à la *France* In the Lorraine style, i.e. garnished with small potatoes sautéed in butter and balls of red cabbage

Lorraine *France* A whitish cows' milk cheese with a distinct lactic flavour formed into stubby cylinders. Similar to **Münster** and **Géromé** cheeses. Also called **Gérardmer**, **Gros Lorraine**

Lorraine soup *Scotland* A soup made from a processed paste of cooked chicken meat, cooked veal, almonds, hard-boiled egg yolks and breadcrumbs soaked in milk. This paste is thinned to the desired consistency with chicken and veal stock, seasoned and flavoured with lemon juice and zest and a little ground mace and finished with cream and chopped parsley. (NOTE: Said to be named after Mary of Lorraine, wife of James V of Scotland.)

losh kibbehskiye kebaby *Central Asia* Azerbaijani kebabs made from a processed mixture of soaked bulgar, minced lamb, chopped onion, tomato purée, parsley, allspice, cayenne pepper, lemon zest and seasoning, formed into cylinders around skewers, brushed with oil and grilled for 10 to 15 minutes. Served with chopped sweet red peppers and parsley.

löskokt *Sweden* Soft-boiled. Used of eggs.

losos *Russia* Salmon

lota *Spain* Eel pout

lote Eel pout

loto *Italy, Spain* Lotus

Lotos *Germany* Lotus

Lotosblume *Germany* Lotus flower

lotte *France* Burbot, the freshwater fish

lotte de mer *France* Monkfish

lotte de rivière *France* Eel pout

loture *Italy* A type of bread from Sardinia

lotus *England, France* A water plant, *Nelubium nuciferum*, related to the water lily and used in Chinese and Indian cooking. The leaves are used for wrapping food, the tuberous roots which have internal holes are used as a vegetable and the black seeds are used like a nut when ripe and after removing the bitter germ. The young stems are eaten as a vegetable in Southeast Asia. See also **lotus root**, **lotus flowers**. Also called **Chinese water lily**, **Indian lotus**

lotus flowers The petals of the lotus flower are used as a garnish in Chinese and Thai cuisines and the open flower is used to contain food

lotus jujube A species of jujube, *Zizyphus lotus*, from North Africa, only noted because its fruits were mentioned by Homer as the food of the lotus eaters

lotus root The tuberous roots of the lotus with many longitudinal internal holes are eaten young and taste rather like artichokes. The Japanese value them for their appearance. They are often stuffed and deep-fried or braised before slicing.

lotus root starch A grey-coloured and slightly granular starch made from lotus' roots and used for soft cakes and sweet dishes

lotus seeds Seeds of the lotus used in desserts and stews or roasted as a snack

Lotus tetragonolobus *Botanical name* Asparagus pea

Louisiana yam Sweet potato

Louis sauce *United States* Mayonnaise incorporating whipped cream, flavoured with chilli sauce, finely chopped green sweet peppers and spring onions, and lemon juice. Served with seafood.

loukanika *Greece* A sausage made with seasoned pork belly marinated with red wine, salt and some or all of cinnamon, coriander, allspice, herbs and orange for a week, packed into hog casings and air-dried for a week

lou-kenkas *France* A small spicy garlic-flavoured sausage from the Basque country. Sometimes eaten hot with cold oysters. Also called **loukinka**

loukinka *France* Lou-kenkas

loukoum *North Africa* Turkish delight

Lou Palou *France* A hard scalded-curd ewes' and/or cows' milk cheese with a thick black, dry rind and a dense paste whose flavour depends on the milks used varying from strong and aromatic to mild and nutty

loup de mer *France* Sea bass

loup marin *France* Catfish

lovage 1. A perennial herb, *Levisticum officinale*, with a sharp peppery flavour rather like celery. Used in strong-tasting dishes and soups. The seeds can also be used in bread and pastries and sprinkled on salads, rice and mashed potatoes. The stems are occasionally candied like angelica. **2.** An Indian name for **ajowan**

lövbiff *Sweden* Sliced beef with **béarnaise sauce**

love and tangle *United States* Deep-fried twisted and tangled doughnuts

love apple *England* The original name given to the tomato when it was introduced, probably as a marketing ploy

love in disguise *England* Calf's heart stuffed and baked in the oven, served with gravy and bacon

low-calorie With a low energy value. The guidelines (not law) used in the EU require such foods to have less than 40 Kcal per 100 g of food.

low-density lipoprotein A specific complex of a lipid (fat) and a protein that transports cholesterol in the blood. High levels appear to increase the risk of heart and vascular disease. See also **cholesterol**, **high-density lipoprotein**

low-fat A term used for any food which contains less fat than normally expected or a low-fat substitute for a fatty food. Examples are milk, cheese, yoghurt, substitute butter spreads, etc. Guidelines (not law) in the EU require foods so labelled to have less than 5 g of fat per 100 g of food.

low-fat milk *United States* Milk with no more than 2% butterfat

low-methoxyl pectin Pectin treated to remove methoxyl groups. It can form a gel without sugar.

low mull *United States* A vegetable and meat stew related to the Irish Mulligan stew

low-starch flour Flour from which most of the starch has been removed. Used for diabetics and makes a bread rather like an open foam or sponge.

lox *United States* Smoked salmon

loza de barro *Spain* Earthenware

lsanat matabbli *Middle East* A salad from Syria and the Lebanon of lambs' tongues boiled in water with aromatic vegetables and a bouquet garni until tender, cooled, skinned, sliced and arranged decoratively, chilled, dressed with olive oil and lemon juice and garnished with paprika, chopped parsley and lemon wedges

lua *Thailand* Blanched

luang prabang *Laos* A round handwoven basket in which rice is steamed and served. The rice is normally formed into small balls with the fingers and eaten by hand.

luau soup *United States* A cream soup from Hawaii made with puréed taro leaves, stock and seasonings

lubia *Middle East* Hyacinth bean

lubina *Spain* Bass, the fish

lucanica *Italy* Luganega

luccio *Italy* Pike, the fish

luccio del trasimeno arrostito *Italy* Pike, larded with bacon and anchovies, roasted and served with a sharp mayonnaise

luccio marino *Italy* Barracuda, the fish

luccioperca *Italy* Pike-perch

lucines *France* Clams or mussels

lucio *Spain* Pike, the fish

luciperca *Spain* Pike-perch

luffa See **angled loofah**, **loofah**

Luffa acutangula *Botanical name* Angled loofah

Luffa cylindrica *Botanical name* The loofah plant

lufttrockene Mettwurst *Germany* An air-dried Mettwurst from Westphalia

luganeaga *Italy* Luganega

luganega *Italy* A small pure pork-based sausage flavoured with Parmesan cheese from northern Italy that looks rather like a Cumberland sausage. Also called **lucanica**, **luganeghe**, **luganiga**

luganeghe *Italy* Luganega

luganiga *Italy* Luganega

luk (*plural* **luki**) *Russia* Onion

lukanka *Bulgaria* A slightly salted and spiced pork sausage eaten raw or cooked

luk chand *Thailand* Nutmeg

lukewarm Around 37°C. Also called **blood heat**

luk jun *Thailand* Nutmeg

luk kra waan *Thailand* Cardamom

luk mangkak *Thailand* Hairy basil

luk taan *Thailand* Palm nut

lumache *Italy* Snail-shaped pasta

lumachi 1. *Italy* Snails **2.** *Switzerland* Snails served with walnut paste

lumberjack pie *United States* Venison and vegetable pie

lumi *Malaysia* Bummaloe, the fish

lumpfish A grey or green seawater fish, *Cyclopterus lumpus*, with a humped back and knobbly skin, found in the North Atlantic and Baltic and growing to about 60 cm. The male is oily but can be poached. The female is not eaten but caught for the lumpfish roe. Also called **lump sucker**, **sea owl**, **cock paddle**

lumpfish roe The eggs of the lumpfish used as a substitute for caviar especially as a garnish. Coloured white, black, orange or red. See also **imitation caviar**

lumpia *Southeast Asia* A type of spring roll in which the wrapping is a thin sheet of cooked beaten egg

lump sucker Lumpfish

lump sugar 1. See **cube sugar 2.** Irregularly shaped pieces of sugar made by crushing a sugar loaf **3.** A semi-refined sugar from

Southeast Asia and China compressed into flat slabs and cut into 15 x 3 x 3 cm fingers. Also called **brown slab sugar**, **rock sugar**, **yellow rock**

lunch *England, Sweden* A meal taken between around 12 noon to 1.30 p.m.

luncheon A more formal lunch

luncheon meat A mixture of pork, ham, cereal, fat, colouring and seasoning usually cooked in deep rectangular cans to form a solid pink mass which can be sliced and eaten cold or hot. A superior version known as **spam** (spiced ham) was shipped in great quantities during World War II from the USA to the UK.

luncheon sausage A slicing sausage made with ground beef and salt pork mixed with saltpetre, sugar and flour or starch, seasoned, spiced and coloured pink, filled into ox bungs, simmered at 75 to 80°C for 3 hours, smoked and oiled

lungan Longan

lungfish Barramunda

lungs The soft spongy tissue used in vertebrates to transfer oxygen from air to blood and carbon dioxide from blood to air. Known normally as lights when in manufactured meat products, but not normally eaten in the UK except by pets. Sometimes eaten as a part of a cooked dish in other cuisines.

lunsj *Norway* Lunch

luo bo gao *China* A **dim sum** made from a type of turnip cake

luoc *Vietnam* To boil, boiled

luo han zhai *China* Bamboo shoots, nuts and mushrooms, stir-fried with soya sauce and rice wine or sherry (NOTE: Literally 'Buddha's vegetables'.)

Luostari *Finland* A cows' milk cheese resembling **Port-Salut**

luppoli *Italy* Hops

lúpulos *Spain* Hops

lu rou *China* Deer

lu shui *China* Lu soy

Lusignan *France* A fresh goats' milk cheese from Poitou

lu soy *China* A mixture of soya sauce with sugar, ginger and five spices used as a basic flavouring for cooking liquors used for simmering meat and poultry

lustrer *France* To glaze with aspic

lustro *Italy* A Calabrian name for grey mullet

lute A flour and water paste used to seal the lids of casseroles, terrines and other cooking pots for baking in the oven

lute, to 1. To seal the gap between the lid and body of a cooking dish with a flour and water paste which bakes hard in the oven. Used for slow cooking casseroles, etc. **2.** To place a strip of pastry around the rim of a pie dish to seal on the pastry cover

lutefisk *Norway* Air-dried cod, cut into pieces, soaked in water for 12 to 14 days, then in dilute caustic soda solution for 2 days, resoaked in water for 3 to 4 days, boiled and served with fried bacon and its fat. An acquired taste.

lutein See **E161(b)**

lutfisk *Sweden* Lutefisk

lut tzee *China* Chestnut

luumu *Finland* Plum

luumut *Finland* Plums

luvasu *Italy* A Sicilian name for either pandora or sea bream

luwombo *East Africa* A celebratory dish from Uganda of boneless meat or fish wrapped in banana leaves. See also **oluwombo**

luxerna *Italy* The name used on the Italian Riviera for grouper, the fish

luya *Philippines* Ginger

Luzener Allebei *Switzerland* A vegetable and mushroom salad

lychee The fruit of a Chinese subtropical evergreen tree, *Litchi chinensis*, now grown worldwide. The small fruits grow in bunches and are about 4 cm long with a central stone, sweet juicy white grape-like flesh and a hard rough pink to brown skin. May be eaten raw or cooked after peeling and destoning. Available canned. Also called **Chinese cherry**, **lichee**, **litchee**, **litchi**, **lizhi**

lycopene An extract of ripe fruit, especially tomatoes, used as a natural red food colour. See also **E160(d)**

Lycoperdon perlatum Common puffball

Lycopersicon esculentum Botanical name Tomato

lye A dilute solution of sodium hydroxide

Lymeswold *England* A so-called designer cheese deliberately developed and marketed commercially in 1982 as the UK answer to soft blue cheeses. It did not survive.

Lyoner *Germany* The German version of the French **saucisson de Lyon**, made with beef, pork and veal and containing pistachio nuts

lyonnaise, à la *France* Containing fried chopped onion

lyonnaise, sauce *England, France* Onion sweated to a light colour in butter, vinegar added and reduced completely, **demi-glace** added, simmered, skimmed and seasoned. Served with Vienna steak or fried liver. Also called **brown onion sauce**

lyre of beef *Scotland* The term used in the east of Scotland for **clod** of beef

lysozyme An enzyme found in egg white which protects the egg from bacterial contamination by destroying the cells of any invading bacteria

lys saus *Norway* Light sauce, e.g. thin béchamel, etc.

MNOPQRS

maafe *West Africa* **1.** Sautéed chicken pieces simmered with onions, chopped chillies, tomato paste, peanut paste and vegetables including okra and flavoured with cinnamon and paprika **2.** A groundnut stew from Senegal. See also **mafé**

maanz *South Asia* Meat

maas *South Africa* A thick naturally curdled milk

maasa *West Africa* Millet flour and possibly other flours sweetened and allowed to ferment with yeast and water, possibly with a chemical raising agent, then brought to the consistency of a pancake batter, shallow-fried and sprinkled with sugar before service. From Mali.

Maasdam *Netherlands* A yellow wax-coated cows' milk cheese resembling **Emmental**

maatjes haring *Netherlands* Lightly cured young herrings which have not yet developed roe. Eaten as a snack or as a main course with boiled potatoes and salad. (NOTE: Not to be confused with **matjes herring**.)

maayi *Middle East* A popular Iraqi **mezze** dish of turnips peeled, diced and simmered in salted water for 30 to 45 minutes with beetroot cut in quarters. The beetroot is discarded and the turnips drained and served hot, sprinkled with salt.

mabalo A species of persimmon, *Diospyros discolor*, grown in the Philippines, Malaysia and Sri Lanka. Also called **velvet apple**

mabela *South Africa* A type of sorghum which when ground is made into mabela porridge

maboké *Central Africa* The plural of **liboké**

maçã *Portugal* Apple

Macadamia integrifolia *Botanical name* Macadamia nut

macadamia nut The fruit of a tree, *Macadamia ternifolia* (with hard-shelled nuts) and *M. integrifolia* (with softer-shelled nuts), originally from Australia, developed in Hawaii and now grown worldwide. Rather like a large hazelnut with a very hard shell.

Usually sold shelled. Use as hazelnuts. Also called **Queensland nut**

Macadamia ternifolia *Botanical name* Macadamia nut

maçã do pieto *Portugal* Brisket of beef

maçapão *Portugal* Marzipan

macaron *France* Macaroon

macaroni *England, France* Thick hollow tubes of pasta, often cut into short lengths

macaroni alla veronese *Italy* Potato gnocchi served with butter and grated Parmesan cheese

macaroni cheese *United Kingdom* Cooked macaroni mixed with cheese sauce, gratinated with cheese and browned under the grill

macaroon A small light crisp cake or biscuit made from ground almonds, sugar and egg white (6:5:1), the egg white being whisked to a stiff peak with the sugar and baked at 150°C after resting on rice paper. Used as petit fours or crushed for use in desserts. The mixture may be cooked in a pastry tartlet.

macarrão *Portugal* Macaroni

macarrones *Spain* Macaroni

macassar gum Agar-agar

maccarello *Italy* Mackerel

maccheroncini *Italy* A thinner version of macaroni

maccheroni *Italy* Macaroni, sometimes used as a general description of all types of dried pasta

macco *Italy* Mashed boiled beans mixed with oil and fennel, from Sicily. Also called **maccu**

maccu *Italy* Macco

mace The lacy covering (**aril**) that surrounds the stone (nutmeg) in the apricot-like fruit of an evergreen tree, *Myristica fragrans*, originally from the Moluccas but now grown extensively in maritime tropical areas. It has a slightly bitter aromatic flavour and is widely used in both sweet and savoury dishes. Sold as blades (whole mace), chips or powder.

macédoine *England, France* **1.** A cut for vegetables and fruit consisting of small cubic dice **2.** A mixture of diced fruit or vegetables

macédoine de fruits *France* Fruit salad

macedone *Italy* Macédoine

macedònia *Catalonia* Fresh fruit salad

macedonia di frutta *Italy* Fruit salad, usually with a liqueur

macelleria *Italy* Butcher's shop

macerate, to To leave a solid in contact with a liquid either to soften the solid, to reconstitute it, to extract flavour from it or to add flavour to it. Also called **steep, to**

macérer *France* To macerate, steep or soak

mach *Italy* A northern soup of milk with chestnuts and rice. See also **al macc**

machado *Spain* Bread fried in olive oil until crisp, pounded or blended with white wine and used as a thickening agent for stews and soups, etc.

machbous *Persian Gulf* A type of spicy prawn paella

mâche *France* Lamb's lettuce

machi *South Asia* Fish

ma chin *China* Cumin

macia *Spain* Mace

macinare *Italy* To grind

macinato *Italy* Ground, pounded or minced

macis *France, Italy, Spain* Mace

mackerel A round seawater fish, *Scomber scombrus*, up to 55 cm long with blue-black stripes on its back and off-white, firm, well-flavoured oily flesh. Available fresh or smoked. Cooked whole in fillets or in steaks and often served with gooseberry sauce. Also called **Atlantic mackerel**

mackerel shark Porbeagle shark

mâconnaise, à la *France* In the Mâcon style, i.e. garnished with croûtons, braised button onions or shallots and button mushrooms. Used especially of poached freshwater fish.

macque choix *United States* A Cajun Christmas dish of tomatoes stewed with sweetcorn, hominy, green sweet peppers, celery, lemon juice, and seasoning. Served as an accompaniment to duck.

macquée *Belgium* A soft, mild, brick-shaped cheese made from skimmed cows' milk

macreuse *France* Scoter duck

macrobiotic A philosophy of eating or diet developed by Japanese Zen Buddhists. Each person's diet seeks to complement their Yin and Yang components or tendencies. The diet is very restrictive but adherents claim it promotes health and spiritual harmony.

Madagascar bean Butter bean

Madagascar green peppercorns Green peppercorns

maddalene *Italy* Madeleine, a sponge cake baked in a madeleine mould

made *Finland* Burbot, the fish

Madeira A fortified and heat-treated wine from Madeira used to flavour foods especially sauces and once popular as the drink to be taken with the Victorian madeira cake

Madeira cake A rich yellow sponge cake flavoured with lemon juice and zest and decorated with candied citron peel during the baking process

Madeira sauce 1 part Madeira to 10 parts **demi-glace**, seasoned, passed through a chinois and butter added. Served with braised ox tongue.

madeirense, à *Portugal* In the style of Madeira, i.e. with tomatoes, onions and garlic

madeleine 1. *United Kingdom* A small cake made from Victoria or Genoese sponge, baked in a dariole mould, coated with jam, dredged with desiccated coconut and decorated with a glacé cherry and angelica. Also called **madeline 2.** *France* A small sponge cake baked in a madeleine mould

madeleine mould A hinged scallop-shaped mould which completely encloses the cake baked in it

madeline *United Kingdom* Madeleine

madère, sauce *France* Madeira sauce

Madras curry powder A fragrant, fairly hot, ground spice mixture made from deseeded and dried red chillies, coriander seeds, cumin seeds, mustard seeds, black peppercorns, curry leaves, all dry-roasted, plus dry ginger and turmeric

Madras gram Horse gram

madrilène, à la *France* In the Madrid style, i.e. garnished with or incorporating tomatoes

maduixa (*plural* **maduixes**) *Catalonia* Strawberry

madun *Thailand* **1.** Belimbing, the fruit **2.** A small juicy sour fruit from the tree *Gardinia schomburgiana*, similar to a small star fruit. Used as a souring agent.

maduru *Sri Lanka* Fennel

mafalde *Italy* Long flat ribbons of pasta with crinkly edges

mafé *West Africa* The standard groundnut stew from Senegal made with any meat or even in a vegetarian version. Meat and onions are sautéed in oil then cooked very slowly with as little water as possible with chopped vegetables, chilli pepper, tomatoes and tomato paste. When all is cooked peanut butter and a little stock are added to make a smooth sauce. Served with rice. Also called **maafe**

magdalena *Spain* A popular breakfast food often dunked in coffee. The traditional recipe uses equal weights of eggs in the shell, sugar, flour and aniseed-flavoured olive oil. The ingredients are vigorously beaten into the oil to incorporate as much air as possible. They are then spooned into paper cases with flavourings and baked at 180°C for about 20 minutes. Nowadays egg whites may be whisked separately before folding them in and baking powder is usually added.

Magenbrot *Switzerland* A bitter-sweet cake flavoured with cinnamon (NOTE: Literally 'stomach bread'.)

Magerquark *Germany* Fat-free quark, i.e. containing less than 1% butterfat. Also called **skimmed milk quark**

maggengo *Italy* Parmesan chesse made between April and November. See also **Parmigiano Reggiano**

maggiorana *Italy* Marjoram

magnesium An essential element required for health and a constituent of many enzymes, necessary for bone and teeth growth and repair. Available from all seeds but often taken as a supplement in the form of Epsom salts.

magnesium carbonate See **E504**

magnesium hydroxide See **E528**

magnesium oxide See **E530**

magnesium silicate See **E553(a)**

magnesium stearate See **E572**

magnesium sulphate See **E518**

magnesium trisilicate See **E553(a)**

Magnifera indica Botanical name Mango

magnonese *Italy* Warm mayonnaise served with fish or boiled meat

magnosa *Italy* A flat Mediterranean lobster-like crustacean. See also **cigarra**

magnum *France* A large bottle of about 1.5 litre capacity

Magnum *France* A rich creamy cows' milk cheese from Normandy made in the shape of a disc and similar to **Brillat-Savarin**

magoro *Italy* Tuna

magret *France* Grilled and sliced underdone breast of duck or goose taken from a force-fed bird. Also called **maigret**, **maigret de canard**

magro *Italy* Not containing meat

magrut *Thailand* Makrut lime

maguro *Japan* Bluefin tuna, excellent for sushi and sashimi and when cooked for shioyaki and teriyaki

magyar gulyás leves *Hungary* Soup made like a thin goulash from sweated onions and diced beef simmered in water with seasoning, paprika, marjoram and crushed caraway seeds. Strips of sweet red pepper, diced tomatoes and **csipetkes** are added at intervals so that all are cooked at the same time.

magyar halleves *Hungary* A fish soup made from sweated onions sprinkled with flour and simmered with fish stock, seasoned and flavoured with paprika. Towards the end blended with sour cream and garnished with small pieces of fish roe and **csipetkes** and all cooked out.

ma-gyi-thi *Burma* Tamarind

mahallebi *Turkey* A dessert of sweetened milk thickened with rice starch, flavoured with rose water, poured into a mould and chilled

mahamri *East Africa* Deep-fried dough cakes from Kenya and Tanzania. See also **mandaazi**

maharagwe *East Africa* Red kidney beans from Kenya often cooked in coconut milk, flavoured with cardamon or cinnamon. Sometimes chopped vegetables are added towards the end of the cooking period.

mahlab Small beige oval kernels of the black cherry tree, *Prunus mahaleb*, with a bitter, rather sour taste used when dried and ground to flavour breads and pastries in Turkey and the Middle East

mahlen *Germany* To grind

mah mee *Southeast Asia* A soup from Singapore consisting of a clear stock with noodles, shellfish, pork, vegetables and seasoning

Mahón *Spain* A semi-hard cows' and ewes' milk cheese from the Balearic islands, white, soft and creamy when young but becomes harder, darker and more tasty as it matures. It is cast in a rounded brick shape and normally brined, matured for 3 weeks, then coated with olive oil.

mahonesa *Spain* Mayonnaise

Mährische *Austria* A sausage made from lean pork, beef and bacon fat (2:1:1) plus seasoning

mah tai *China* Water chestnut

maiale *Italy* Pig or pork

maiale ubriaco *Italy* Pork chops cooked in red wine (NOTE: Literally 'tipsy pork'.)

maialino *Italy* Sucking pig

maida flour A soft white flour for making naan, from the north of India

maidenhair fern A feathery fern, *Adiantum capillus-veneris*, which can be used for decoration or when extracted with water is used to make capillaire syrup

maidenhair tree The tree, *Ginkgo biloba*, from which ginkgo nuts are obtained

maid of honour *England* A small puff pastry tartlet with a filling made from milk curds or curd cheese, egg yolks and butter or clotted cream (5:3:5), with sugar to taste and flavoured with lemon zest and possibly cinnamon and nutmeg. Other additions to the filling include coconut, flour or ground almonds and some recipes give orange flower water as a flavouring. (NOTE: It is said to have been invented by Anne Boleyn when she was a maid of honour to King Henry VIII's first wife, Catherine of Aragon)

Maidstone biscuit *England* A light crisp biscuit made with plain flour, caster sugar and butter (5:4:4), using the creaming method and flavoured with rose water and chopped blanched almonds. Baked at 180°C.

Maifisch *Germany* Shad

maigre *France* Lean, low-fat, clear (of soup)

maigre, au *France* Not containing meat

Maigrelet *Canada* A medium soft cheese made from skimmed cows' milk in Quebec

maigret, maigret de canard *France* Grilled and sliced underdone breast of duck or goose. See also **magret**

maik yu *China* Cuttlefish

maillard reaction A reaction between a sugar and an amino acid, both of which are usually part of a carbohydrate and a protein respectively. It is responsible for the browning of meat, bread, chocolate, coffee and other roasted food.

maillot, à la *France* Garnished with turnips, carrots, French beans, braised lettuce and peas

Mainauerkäse *Germany, Switzerland* A semi-hard, surface-ripened, scalded-curd cows' milk cheese with a smooth texture and slightly acid pleasantly aromatic taste. Contains 43% water, 25% fat and 24% protein.

main course The central and most substantial dish of a meal, usually containing a fair amount of meat, fish or pulse protein

maintenon, à la *France* Garnished with an onion sauce containing puréed onions and chopped mushrooms

Mainz *Germany* A hand-moulded cheese similar to **Harzerkäse** and often flavoured with cumin

Mainzer Rippchen *Germany* Pork rib chops

maionese *Italy* Mayonnaise

maioran *Russia* Marjoram

maïs *France* 1. Maize 2. Sweetcorn

Mais *Germany* 1. Maize 2. Sweetcorn

maïs en épi *France* Corn on the cob

Maismehl *Germany* Corn flour

maison *France* Used to indicate that the food was made on the premises, e.g. pâté maison

maison, de la *France* Made on the premises (NOTE: Literally 'of the house'.)

Maistorte *Germany* A type of pudding made with cornmeal

maito *Finland* Milk

maitoporsas *Finland* Sucking pig

maître d' *United States* Maître d'hôtel. Pronounced 'maître dee'. (*colloquial*)

maître d'hôtel *France* The person in charge of a dining room in a restaurant or hotel; the head waiter or waitress. See also **beurre (à la) maître d'hôtel**

maíz *Spain* 1. Maize 2. Corn on the cob

maize A Central American cereal, *Zea mays*, now grown worldwide, which is a tall large-leaved grass with an ear consisting of a large number of individual white, yellow, red or blue seeds packed in a single layer around a cob, a central wide stalk tapering to a point, the whole enclosed in several papery leaves with a tassel emerging from the point. Several of these cobs, which are about 6 to 8 cm diameter and up to 30 cm long, sprout from the leaf bases. The individual seeds (kernels) are stripped from the cob for further processing, the white and yellow being used for human consumption. Maize is an important source of carbohydrate for both humans and animals. There are various types: Dent (var. *indentata*) is soft, has a depression in the seeds, and is used for flour. A hard type, flint (var. *indurata*) is used for popcorn and a sweet sugary type, (var. *saccharata*) is used as a vegetable. See also entries for sweet corn, miniature corn, popcorn, hominy, corn syrup, etc. Also called **corn**, **Indian corn**, **mealies**

maize meal *United States* Coarsely ground dehusked maize kernels

maize oil See **corn oil**

majonnäs *Sweden* Mayonnaise

Majoran *Germany* Marjoram

majorana *Spain* Sweet marjoram

makapuno *Philippines* A mutant coconut which cannot mature and in which the fruits are full of a soft gelatinous meat instead of separate liquid and flesh. Used as a dessert and for making ice cream.

makaronilaatikko *Finland* Macaroni baked in milk and cream thickened with egg yolks

ma kham *Thailand* Tamarind

makhan *South Asia* Butter

makhanas *South Asia* Roasted seeds of the lotus plant which puff up when fried. Generally served salted as a snack or sometimes made into a kind of sweet by boiling them in milk with flavourings. See also **makhane ki kheer**

makhane ki kheer *South Asia* A thinnish dessert of makhanas simmered in milk for about 30 minutes, sweetened with sugar and combined with almond pieces and grated coconut

makhani chawal *South Asia* Buttered rice made from cooked rice and molten butter (5:1) heated gently with various flavourings, diced or raw vegetables and sometimes chopped or flaked cooked fish and shellfish. Served when the rice is steaming.

makhani khumbi *South Asia* Grilled mushrooms sweated with butter (10:1), minced chives, paprika, and cardamon seeds previously fried in the butter for 10 minutes

makisu *Japan* A flexible mat made of strips of bamboo, used for rolling up sushi

maki-sushi *Japan* A type of sushi made without being wrapped in nori. See also **nori-maki**

maki-yakinabe *Japan* A rectangular omelette pan the same shape as a Swiss roll tin. See also **tamago-yakiki**

makkara *Finland* Sausage

Makkaroni *Germany* Macaroni

makki ki roti *South Asia* A thin bread from the Punjab made from fine cornmeal. It is soft on the inside and crisp on the outside.

mak mo *China* Cuttlefish

mako shark *Isurus oxyrhynchus*, a member of the shark family which makes good eating

makreel *Netherlands* Mackerel

makrel *Denmark* Mackerel

Makrele *Germany* Mackerel

makrell *Norway* Mackerel

makrill *Sweden* Mackerel

makrillgryta *Sweden* Pieces of seasoned mackerel fillet, layered with thin slices of lemon and peeled tomatoes in a pot, a little stock and butter added and simmered with a tight fitting lid for 20 minutes. Finished with chopped parsley or dill.

makrilli *Finland* Mackerel

Makrone *Germany* Macaroon

makroner *Denmark* Macaroons

makrut lime This citrus fruit from Southeast Asia, *Citrus hystrix*, is not a true lime but is picked in the immature state and used as such. The rind is irregular and very bumpy with a pronounced smaller stem end. There is very little juice. The rind and leaves are used to flavour curries, soup, salads and vinegar. Known in Paris as combava. Also called **kaffir lime**

maksa *Finland* Liver

maksalaatikko *Finland* A liver pudding made with liver, rice, onions, milk, water, golden syrup, raisins, eggs, marjoram and seasoning. Served with melted butter, boiled potatoes and cranberry sauce.

makua *Thailand* Aubergine

makua phuong *Thailand* Pea aubergine

malacz kövesonya *Hungary* Brawn made from pig's head boiled with a minimum of water with garlic, carrots, onion, Hamburg parsley, seasoning and spices

maladi *Middle East* Common orange

Málaga *Spain* A soft cream-coloured cheese made from goats' milk, covered with a yellow rind, with a mild goaty flavour and many fine holes. Eaten fresh within a few days of manufacture.

malagliata *Italy* Roughly cut elongated diamonds of pasta (NOTE: Literally 'badly cut'.)

malai *South Asia* Cream used in Indian cooking, similar to **clotted cream** but made by repeatedly boiling the milk and removing the skin from the top until it is all reduced to a crumbly texture

Malakoff, tarte *France* A cake made from layers of rum-soaked sponge fingers in a rich cream mixture made from butter, sugar, ground almonds and cream, flavoured with coffee or vanilla essence (NOTE: Named after the suburb of Paris.)

malanga, malanga isleña 1. The Columbian name for **taro 2.** A Latin American name for yautia and other tuberous starch plants of different species and genera

malasado *Portugal* An egg-enriched puff pastry deep-fried and dredged with sugar (NOTE: Literally 'unlucky'.)

Malay apple *United States* A crisp red bland-flavoured and pear-shaped fruit

Maldive fish *Sri Lanka* Various fish species local to Sri Lanka, dried and crumbled or powdered for use in cooking. See also **bummaloe**

malet kött *Sweden* Minced beef

malfatta *Italy* Home-made balls of pasta dough (NOTE: Literally 'badly made'.)

malfatti *Italy* Gnocchi coloured with spinach and flavoured with ricotta cheese

malfattina *Italy* Finely chopped sheets of pasta dough

mali *Thailand* Jasmine flowers and jasmine essence used as flavouring

malic acid A fruit acid, E296, found in underripe apples, rhubarb and some berries. It is not suitable for setting jams. Used as a flavouring in soft drinks, dessert mixes and pie fillings.

malinovyi sup *Russia* A cold soup from the Baltic region made from the strained juice of summer fruits sweetened with brown sugar and flavoured with cinnamon, lemon juice and lemon zest and slightly thickened with corn flour

malka sabat *South Asia* Dehusked and split red lentils

mallard A wild duck, suitable for one or two servings depending on size. Brushed with oil and roasted at 200°C for approximately 50 minutes and then treated as duck. Shooting season 1st September until the 31st of January, or until the 21st of February if shot below the high water mark of spring tides. Hanging time 2 to 3 days.

mallow A family of plants many of which are edible, e.g. abelmusk, Jamaica flower, abutilon, marshmallow, okra, and meloukhia

malong *Malaysia* Eel

malosol *Russia* Fresh caviar prepared with only a little salt

malosolnyi *Russia* Lightly salted. Used e.g. some Russian caviar.

mal passado *Spain* Rare. Used of meat, steaks, etc.

Malpighia glabra *Botanical name* Acerola

malpuri *South Asia* Puri bread flavoured with crushed fennel seed

malt *England, France* Barley which has been germinated and allowed to sprout under warm humid conditions. The sprouting liberates enzymes which convert the starch into a variety of sugars and polysaccharides of which maltose is the most important. Heat is used to denature the enzymes and the malt is then dried and crushed. The soluble sugars are extracted with water either for brewing or for concentration into malt extract, a thick brown sweetish syrup.

malta *Spain* Malt

maltaise, à la *France* In the Maltese style, i.e. with the addition of orange zest and juice

maltaise, sauce *England, France* Hollandaise sauce flavoured with the strained juice of blood oranges and orange zest. Also called **Maltese sauce**

maltase The enzyme which splits maltose into its constituent glucose units

malt bread A yeasted bread dough enriched with malt extract, black treacle and dried vine fruits prior to baking to a soft moist loaf

malted milk A mixture of dried milk powder and ground malted barley reconstituted with milk. Served hot or cold.

Maltese sauce See **maltaise, sauce**

malt extract A concentrated solution of the soluble sugars extracted from malt. Used in cakes, bread and puddings in the West and as a constituent of sauces and meat glazes in China.

malto *Italy* Malt

maltose A disaccharide consisting of two glucose units. The principal sugar in malt. Also called **malt sugar**

malt sugar See **maltose**

malt vinegar A brown vinegar made by partial oxidation of the alcoholic liquor (ale) made from the water extract of malt. Contains about 5% acetic acid.

Malus pumila *Botanical name* Crab apple

Malus sylvestris var domestica *Botanical name* Apple

Malva moschata *Botanical name* Muskmallow

malvavisco *Spain* Marshmallow

Malvern apple pudding *England* Equal quantities of butter, sugar, eggs and flour made up using the creaming method and combined with half the mixture's weight of cored, peeled and chopped russet apples and one eighth its weight of currants. The mixture is flavoured with lemon juice and zest and brandy, put in a lined pudding basin, covered and steamed for 2 hours.

Malz *Germany* Malt

mămăligă *Romania* Cornmeal cooked slowly in salted water with butter until thick and served with melted butter. A national dish of Romania.

mămăligă cu ochiuri românesti *Romania* Mămăligă topped with poached eggs and melted butter with sour cream served separately

mamalyga *Russia* The Russian Moldavian version of **mămăligă** made from polenta, butter and melting cheese (3:1:4 based on cornmeal), flavoured with marjoram and pepper, put in a buttered dish and baked at 190°C until skinned over, cooled, divided in squares and served gratinated with cheese and grilled

mamelle *France* Udder

mamey The spherical fruit of a tree, *Mammea americana*, from the Carribean and South America, up to 15 cm in diameter with a brown to grey rough outer skin, a thin bitter, yellow, inner skin and yellowish flesh tasting of raspberries and apricots, surrounding up to 4 inedible seeds. May be eaten raw. Also called **mammee**

Mamirolle *France* A semi-hard washed-rind cows' milk cheese made in the same way as **Limburger** but not as pungent. Usually brick-shaped (600 g).

Mammea americana *Botanical name* Mamey

mammee See **mamey**

mammella *Italy* Udder

mämmi *Finland* A pudding made from rye meal sweetened with molasses and flavoured with Seville oranges. Usually baked in the oven in birch bark baskets for Easter and served with cream.

Mamsell Babette *Germany* A firm, loaf-shaped mild-flavoured cows' milk cheese from Bavaria which contains small pieces of smoked ham

mam tom *Vietnam* Shrimp paste

manaita *Japan* A chopping board

manalsama *Middle East* As **klaicha** but filled with a mixture of coarsely ground walnuts and caster sugar (8:1)

ma-nao *Thailand* Lime, the fruit

manapua *United States* A dough bun from Hawaii filled with various savoury fillings and steamed

manbollen *Netherlands* Edam

mancare cu bame *Romania* Diced pork and fried onions stewed in tomato juice with herbs and seasonings. Served with bread.

manchant *England* Manchet

manche *France* The scraped bone end of a cutlet or the knuckle of a leg of lamb (NOTE: Literally 'handle'.)

Manchego *Spain* A strong-tasting, pale-coloured, hard scalded-curd cheese with a sprinkling of small holes, made from ewes' milk. It uses a lactic starter and the yellow paste is covered with a greenish black mould. Very popular and eaten both fresh and matured to varying degrees of hardness and dryness. The mature varieties are washed and oiled.

Manchester pudding *England* Soft white breadcrumbs mixed with egg yolks, sugar and milk infused with lemon peel, cooked until set in a bain-marie in individual dishes. Cooled, covered with raspberry jam, piped with meringue, coloured under the grill and dredged with icing sugar.

manchet *England* The Old English term for the finest wheaten bread eaten only by the well off, now applied in Cornwall to any loaf of bread shaped by hand. Also called **manchant** (NOTE: Possibly from Anglo-Norman *pain demaine*, from medieval Latin *panus dominicus*, 'lord's bread', and *cheat*, 'poor quality wheat bread'.)

manchette *France* Cutlet frill

manchon, en *France* A method of presenting panéed and deep-fried small fish by cutting off the head and tail after cooking so that they appear to be served in sleeves

mancu A black colouring used in black puddings

mandaazi *East Africa* Sweet, puffy, deep-fried dough cakes from Kenya and Tanzania, served hot at breakfast and cold and rather solid at dinner. Similar to doughnuts but not as sweet and not sugar glazed. Sometimes they are spiced. Also called **mahamri**, **mandazi**

mandaliya *South Asia* An almost vegetarian sausage consisting of marrow and spices stuffed into a casing

mandarin The general name of a group of citrus fruits, *Citrus reticulata*, which are all generally sweet and have very easily separable thin orange skins and segments. Generally classified as: satsuma or unshui mandarin, *Citrus unshui*; Mediterranean mandarin, *C. deliciosa*; king mandarin, *C. nobilis*; and common mandarin, *C. reticulata*. The zest is not usually used except dried and ground as a spice. Also called **tangerine**

mandarina *Spain* Mandarin orange

mandarin cooking The haute cuisine of Chinese cooking originating in the royal court and combining Peking (Beijing) and Shanghai styles

mandarine *France* Mandarin, the fruit

Mandarine *Germany* Mandarin, the fruit

mandarino *Italy* Mandarin, the fruit

mandarin pancake The pancake in which Peking duck is wrapped, made from a flour and boiling water dough (5:3) which is kneaded until silky with a further part of cold water. It is rolled out, cut in squares, one side of each coated in sesame seed oil and sandwiched in pairs with the oiled sides together. These are rolled out again, fried in an oiled pan until browned on each side, separated and folded in triangles.

mandarin peel See **tangerine peel**

mandazi *East Africa* Deep-fried dough cakes from Kenya and Tanzania. See also **mandaazi**

Mandel *Germany* Almond

mandelbiskvier *Sweden* Almond biscuit

Mandel Halbmonde *Germany* Almond crescent biscuits made by the creaming method from flour, butter, sugar and egg yolks (6:4:3:1) in which two thirds of the egg yolks are hard-boiled and sieved before incorporation. Formed into crescents from bent and flattened cylinders of paste, dipped in egg white and coated with a mixture of almond nibs, sugar and cinnamon, then baked at 160°C until firm.

Mandeltorte *Germany* An almond layer cake with a filling of jam or crème pâtissière and covered with a royal icing flavoured with rum or butter icing or the like. The cake mixture is a type of fatless cake mixture with mainly ground skinned and dry-roasted almonds mixed into an egg yolk, egg and sugar batter with a little flour and stiffly whisked egg whites folded in at the end. The baking tins are coated with melted butter and dredged with fine dried breadcrumbs before filling.

mandioca *Spain* Cassava

mandlar *Sweden* Almonds

mandler *Denmark, Norway* Almonds

mandolin An implement for slicing any firm vegetable or fruit or making it into batons or julienne strips. It consists of a strong rectangular metal frame supported at an angle to the bench top with various transverse cutting blades and attachments. The food to be sliced is moved by hand downwards across the blade and the cut pieces fall beneath.

mandonguilles *Catalonia* Meatballs

mandora *Cyprus* Ortanique

mandorla *Italy* Almond

mandorlato *Italy* 1. Almond cake 2. Nougat

mandur *Balkans* A hard grating cheese made from a mixture of cows' and ewes' milk and the whey from cheese making

maneira de, à *Portugal* In the style of

mangetout *England, France* A variety of pea, *Pisum sativum* var. *macrocarpum*, which has a delicate pod and is eaten whole when young. Also called **snow pea**, **sugar pea**, **sugar-snap pea**, **Chinese pea** (NOTE: Literally 'eat all'.)

manggis *Indonesia, Malaysia* Mangosteen

mang guo *China* Mango

mangkut *Thailand* Mangosteen

mango *England, Italy, Spain* A large round to pear- or kidney-shaped tropical fruit weighing between 0.25 and 1 kg, from a tree, *Magnifera indica*, which is widely grown. The fruit when ripe has a juicy, slightly fibrous orange flesh with a distinctive flavour, a large central stone and a thickish green through yellow to red inedible skin. Sold whole or skinned and destoned in canned or dried form.

Mango *Germany* Mango

Mangold *Germany* Spinach beet

mango pickle An Indian pickle made from chopped very underripe raw mango, destoned but not peeled mixed with turmeric, ground cinnamon, nigella, fennel seed, soaked fenugreek seed, salt and chilli powder, left for two days then covered with warm oil flavoured with dried chillies and allowed to mature

mango powder See **amchoor**

mango squash Choko

mangostan Mangosteen

mangosteen The fruit of a Malaysian evergreen tree, *Garcinia mangostana*, which grows in wet tropical regions. It has a deep purple fibrous outer casing enclosing segments of juicy, creamy white flesh containing an inedible seed. The flesh has a sweet-sour flavour reminiscent of molasses. The skin contains an indelible dye. See also **kokum**. Also called **mangostan**

mang tre *Vietnam* Bamboo shoot

mangue *France* Mango

maniche *Italy* Wide tubes of pasta resembling short cannelloni

manicotti *Italy* Large cannelloni often stuffed with a Ricotta cheese mixture and baked in a sauce (NOTE: Literally 'muffs'.)

manicou *Caribbean* The opossum, *Didelphys marsupialis insularis*, from Central and Northern America now widely distributed, and appreciated for its fine-tasting meat. In the Caribbean it is generally smoked then stewed in red wine or curried. See also **opossum**

maniera di, alla *Italy* In the style of

manina ferrarese *Italy* A crisp bread roll in the shape of a double horseshoe

manioc *England, France* Cassava

manioca *Italy* Cassava

manjar blanco *Mexico, Spain* A dessert made from caramelized milk and sugar. See also **arequipe**

manju *Japan* A cake eaten with tea

mannagrynspudding *Sweden* Semolina pudding

mannaia kasha, mannaya kasha *Russia* A type of slightly sweetened gruel made from semolina with milk and salt

mannish water *Caribbean* A soup made from goat meat, including the testicles, served to a Jamaican groom on his wedding night

mannitol A compound similar to sorbitol found in many plants, now synthesized from sucrose for use as a humectant. See also **E421**

mano *Mexico* A stone ball-like roller used on a **metate** to grind grains and spices

manoa *United States* A variety of butterhead lettuce from Hawaii

Manoori, Manouri *Greece* A ewes' milk cheese from Crete eaten with honey as a dessert

mansikkasoppa *Finland* Strawberries with cream and sugar

mansikkat *Finland* Strawberries

mansikkatorttu *Finland* Strawberry tart

mantar *Turkey* Grilled mushroom caps with a garlic filling

man tau *China* Steamed buns

manteca 1. *Italy* A small, mild, pear-shaped cheese with a butter centre. See also **burrino** 2. *Mexico* Lard

manteca de cerdo *Spain* Pig's lard

mantecado *Spain* Ice cream with added whipped cream

mantecare *Italy* To whip or whisk

mantecato *Italy* **1.** Softened **2.** Pounded **3.** Soft ice cream made by adding whipped cream to ice cream

manteenmäti *Finland* The roe of the burbot processed like caviar and very expensive

mantega *Catalonia* Butter

mantega bean A bean from Chile which does not cause flatulence and which is being used to breed more popular varieties with the same properties

manteiga *Portugal* Butter

manteli *Finland* Almond

mantelimassa *Finland* Marzipan

mantequilla *Spain* Butter

manti *Turkey* Fresh ravioli, poached, drained and coated with a sauce made from yoghurt, melted butter, chopped garlic and paprika

mantis shrimp A large crustacean, *Squilla empusa* from the eastern coast of the USA and *S. mantis* from the Mediterranean, somewhat larger than a prawn and when eating resembles a praying mantis. It is related to the crab but looks more like a prawn. Usually only found where landed. Cooked like prawns.

manty *Central Asia* Steamed filled dumplings from Uzbekistan made with a flour and water dough, rolled out, cut in 10 cm circles each of which is wrapped around a teaspoonful of filling and some butter. Usually served with yoghurt or vinegar as a dipping sauce.

man yu *China* Eel

manzana *Spain* Apple

manzo *Italy* Beef from cattle under 4 years old

manzo alla certosina *Italy* Beef stewed with bacon, anchovies and herbs

manzo arrosto *Italy* Roast beef

manzo brasato *Italy* Braised beef

manzo lesso *Italy* Boiled beef

manzo salato *Italy* Corned beef

manzo stufato *Italy* Stewed beef

manzo uso *Italy* Pot-roasted beef

maple sugar *Canada, United States* A solid sugar (saccharose) with a characteristic flavour crystallized from the sap of the sugar maple tree, *Acer saccharum*

maple syrup *Canada, United States* A sweet sugar syrup prepared from the sap of the sugar maple tree, *Acer saccharum*, which is collected by boring a hole into the trunk during March. Used as a sweetening agent especially to produce a sauce for waffles and hot cakes.

maple syrup pie *Canada* A double-crust pie filled with a mixture made from maple syrup, corn flour, butter and chopped nuts

maprao *Thailand* A young coconut

maque choux *United States* A sweet, highly seasoned Cajun dish of maize

maquereau *France* Mackerel

maquereaux au vin blanc *France* Mackerel fillets poached in white wine and served cold as a starter

maracuya *South America* Purple passion fruit grown in Columbia

maraîchère, (à la) *France* In the market gardener's style, i.e. garnished with salsify, Brussels sprouts, potatoes, onions and carrots. Used of meat.

maräng *Sweden* Meringue

maranta *Italy* Arrowroot

Maranta arundinacea Botanical name Arrowroot

maraq al-bamiya *Persian Gulf* A stew of beef or lamb with okra, flavoured with onions, garlic, tomatoes, sugar and **baharat**

marasche *Italy* Morello cherries

maraschino A colourless liqueur flavoured with maraschino cherries and their crushed kernels. Used for flavouring.

maraschino cherries Cherries preserved in a red coloured sugar syrup flavoured with almond oil, or in maraschino liqueur

Marasmius oreades Fairy ring mushroom

maratello rice *Italy* A moderately priced semi-fino, oval, slightly sticky rice suitable for minestrone

marbled **1.** Interspersed with long visible flecks of fat, usually a sign of high quality in lean beef. The fat helps to prevent the meat drying out. **2.** In pastry or cake-making, made from two contrasting coloured pastes mixed together to resemble marble when cooked

marbrade *France* A dish from the southwest consisting of a cooked pig's head in aspic

marbré *France* Striped bream

marc An alcoholic spirit distilled from the fermented skins and pips of pressed grapes. Used as a cheap substitute for brandy.

marcassin *France* A young wild boar

marchand de vin *France* Cooked with red wine and shallots, especially steak

marchand de vin, sauce *England, France* A chasseur sauce based on red wine as well as stock

marche Lamb's lettuce

marchepain Marzipan

maréchal, à la *France* In the marshal's style, i.e. garnished with asparagus tips, truffles, cockscombs and peas

Maredsous *Belgium* A rectangular cows' milk cheese similar to **Saint-Paulin**

marée *France* Fresh seawater fish and shellfish

marees *Middle East* A mixture of date syrup and butter, used in Iraq in the same way as jam

Marengo See **poulet sauté Marengo**

marennes *France* A variety of small oysters

margarine *England, France* A butter substitute made by hydrogenating liquid vegetable and deodorized fish oils to give a fat solid at room temperature. Once thought to be healthier than butter due to its lower proportion of saturated fat. Unfortunately the chemical processes produce fats which do not occur in nature (trans- as opposed to cis-forms) which, although they do appear in butter at a lower concentration, may be deleterious to health in some as yet unknown way. One of the more successful examples of persuading the public to substitute a factory product for a farm-produced equivalent.

margarita *Spain* Golden carpet shell clam

marge *United Kingdom* Margarine (*colloquial*)

Margotin *France* A soft buttery cows' milk cheese from Périgord, flavoured with pepper or herbs

Marguery, fish As for **fish Bercy**, but garnishing the fish with cooked prawns and mussels before coating it with sauce and glazing

marha gulyás *Hungary* A goulash of diced beef heart, ox liver and cows' udder with chopped onions and garlic sweated in lard, flavoured with paprika, crushed caraway seeds and marjoram, seasoned and stewed with tomato purée and water with diced potatoes and **csipetkes**

marhahús *Hungary* Beef

Maribo *Denmark* A semi-hard, scalded-curd open-textured cows' milk cheese, cream coloured with a slightly lactic flavour and many small holes. The curd which is cast in large rounds (up to 14 kg) is salted and ripened for 3 to 5 weeks and covered in yellow wax. The white paste has a mild to strong aromatic flavour depending on age.

Marie-Louise, à la *France* In the Marie-Louise style, i.e. garnished with onion purée, artichoke hearts, mushrooms and potatoes

Marienhofer *Austria* A cheese from the Austrian Tyrol resembling **Limburger**

Marienkraut *Germany* Sweet marjoram

marignan *France* A type of rum baba with an apricot glaze and filled with crème chantilly

marigold A hardy annual, *Calendula officinalis*, grown as a garden plant. The petals can be used to colour and flavour a variety of dishes and as a garnish. The leaves can be used sparingly in salads. Also called **calendula**, **pot marigold**

Marille *Austria* Apricot

mar i muntanya *Catalonia* A dish containing both seafood and meat (NOTE: Literally 'sea and mountain')

marinade *England, France* A mixture of various tenderizing and flavouring agents, usually including an oil, an acid such as vinegar or lemon juice and a selection from wine, sherry, yoghurt, coconut milk, fruit juices and similar liquids, herbs, spices, seasonings and flavour enhancers such as soya sauce. Used to treat raw meat and fish for periods from an hour upwards to tenderize, flavour and add moisture. Sometimes the strained marinade is used in the resulting dish. The classic marinade contains 1 litre of wine, 0.5 litres of vinegar and 0.2 litres of oil to 200 g of chopped aromatic vegetables plus garlic, parsley stalks, bay leaf, peppercorns and cloves and may be cooked or uncooked.

marinades *Canada* Pickles

marinar *Spain* To marinate

marinara *Italy* A rich tomato sauce prepared very quickly from ripe tomatoes

marinara, alla *Italy* In the sailor's style, e.g. with seafood, or, of shellfish, simmered with oil, wine, parsley and garlic

marinare *Italy* To marinate

marinate, to To treat raw meat, poultry, game or fish with a marinade

marinato *Italy* 1. Marinated 2. Pickled

mariné(e) *France* 1. Marinated 2. Pickled or soused

mariner *France* To marinate

marinerad böckling *Sweden* Cleaned, filleted and deboned (as far as possible) buckling, marinated for 2 hours in oil, vinegar and seasoning, drained and garnished with chopped dill or chives

marinière, à la *France* In the boatman's style, i.e. garnished with mussels. See also **moules marinière**

marinière, sauce *France* **Sauce Bercy** with 100 ml of reduced mussel cooking liquor per litre and finished with 6 egg yolks per litre

marinieren *Germany* To marinate

mariniert *Germany* 1. Marinated 2. Pickled

Marinierter Hering *Germany* Soused herring

marinovannaia arbuznaia korka *Russia* Pickled watermelon rind from which all the pink flesh and the green skin has been removed. It is brined (50 g per litre) overnight, drained and rinsed, boiled until soft in vinegar and water (2:1), sugar equal in weight to the rind added plus cinnamon, cloves, root ginger and allspice in a muslin bag and all boiled until the rind is transparent. The rind is then bottled with the reduced syrup and served on the hors d'oeuvre (**zakuski**) table.

marinovannie griby *Russia* A type of mushroom **à la grecque** made with a variety of edible fungi cooked in wine vinegar and water (3:2) with garlic, cloves, bay, salt, sugar and peppercorns, bottled in the cooking liquor, covered with oil and refrigerated for at least 10 days before use

marisc *Catalonia* Seafood

mariscos *Spain* Shellfish

maritozzo *Italy* A currant bun

marjolaine *France* 1. Marjoram 2. A pie case made of meringue mixed with almonds and filberts, layered with chocolate, praline and butter cream

marjoram The name given to species of *Origanum*, in particular *Origanum majorana*, sweet or knotted marjoram; *Origanum onites*, pot or French marjoram; and *Origanum heracleoticum*, winter marjoram. See also **oregano**

Mark *Germany* Bone marrow

market crab Dungeness crab

market measure The system of volume measures used for large quantities of goods, now in hectolitres (100 litres). In the pre-metric system the most common were the bushel (equal to 8 gallons, either imperial or US), the quarter (equal to 8 bushels), the bag, sack, chest, hogshead and barrel. Because many dry goods were originally sold by volume, the weights of a bushel and other volume measures were standardized, e.g. a bushel of wheat equals 60 lb, of maize, 56 lb, of oats, 39 lb in the UK and 32 lb in the USA and so on. See also **liquid measure, dry measure, cup measure, can measure, volume measure**

Markklössen *Germany* Bread dumplings mixed with beef marrow. Served with consommé.

Markknochen *Germany* Marrow bone

mark yang tong *China* Malt extract or maltose

Marlborough pie *United States* A blind-cooked pie case filled with a mixture of sweetened apple purée and cream flavoured with nutmeg and sherry and thickened with eggs. The whole baked until the filling sets.

marlin A seawater game fish, *Makaira nigricans* (blue) and *M. albida* (white), with a long pointed upper jaw. It is similar to the swordfish but with not so good a flavour.

marmalade A jam made from citrus fruit, especially Seville oranges, by boiling the juice with water, shredded peel and a muslin bag containing all the pips, pith and excess peel for several hours to extract pectin. The muslin bag is removed, sugar added and the whole boiled for a short time until it reaches setting point.

marmalade pudding *United Kingdom* A pudding made from the basic steamed pudding mixture poured into a greased basin whose base is covered with marmalade

marmalade sauce As apricot sauce but using marmalade in place of apricot jam. Served with steamed and baked sponge puddings.

Marmande A variety of large ribbed tomato up to 10 cm in diameter

Marmande farcie *France* A Marmande tomato stuffed with e.g. tuna, onion and olive oil or minced lamb and onion. Served as a starter.

marmelad *Sweden* Marmalade

marmelada *Spain* Jam

marmelade *France* A thick purée of fruit made by stewing until well reduced

Marmelade *Germany* 1. Jam 2. Marmalade

marmellata *Italy* 1. Jam 2. Marmalade

marmelo *Portugal* Quince

marmite 1. *France* A special metal or earthenware pot with a lid and handles used for long slow cooking 2. *United Kingdom* Marmite, the trade name for a thick dark brown extract of hydrolysed yeast protein used for spreading on bread or to flavour soups, sauces and vegetarian dishes

marmite dieppoise A fish soup made of sole, turbot and red mullet cooked in mussel liquor, white wine or cider and vegetables, garnished with mussels, shrimps and finished with cream

marmitta *Italy* A cooking pot similar to a marmite

marmora *Italy* Striped sea bream

Marmorgugelhopf *Austria* A chocolate and vanilla-flavoured cake

Marmorkuchen *Germany* Marbled cake

maro *Italy* Pounded and sieved cooked beans mixed with chopped mint, garlic, cheese and oil. Also called **pestun de fave**

marocaine, à la *France* In the Moroccan style, i.e. garnished with courgettes, sweet peppers, saffron-flavoured rice and tomatoes

Maroilles, Marolles *Belgium, France* A soft, thick, square cheese from the French/Belgian border region (Aisne and Nord), pale yellow and slightly elastic with a strong taste and smell. It is started with a mixed culture of *Streptococcus cremoris, S. lactis, S. diacetilactis* and *Leuconostoc citrovorum*. The curd is drained, moulded and brined and kept so as to allow surface moulds and yeasts to develop when the rind becomes rough and red. It is ripened for 6 months and brine-washed regularly. Contains 50% water, 25% fat and 23% protein and has appellation d'origine status in France. Sold as a quart (180 g), mignon (360 g), sorbais (540 g) and the full Maroilles (720 g).

Marone *Germany* Chestnut

marquise *France* A frozen dessert made from a fruit sorbet mixed with a liqueur and whipped cream

Marrajo *Germany* Porbeagle shark

marron 1. *France* Chestnut **2.** *Australia* A fine-tasting crayfish, *Cherax tenuimanus*, from Western Australia which weighs up to 2 kg

marrona *Spain* Chestnut

marroni *Italy* Chestnuts

marrons, purée de *France* Chestnut purée with or without vanilla and sugar

marrons glacés *England, France* Shelled chestnuts boiled in sugar syrup and drained for use as a dessert, as a decoration, or, when puréed and sieved, as a flavouring and bulking agent for meringue and whipped cream

marrons Mont Blanc *France* Chestnut purée heaped into a cone and topped with whipped cream to resemble the mountain

marrons plombières *France* Iced custard with chestnuts, rum, vanilla and kirsch

marrow 1. See **vegetable marrow 2.** The blood-forming tissue of the body which takes the form of pink pulpy material in the hollow centres of some of the larger skeletal bones especially thigh and leg bones. Beef marrow is often poached in the bone wrapped in a cloth for an hour, for use as a garnish and sometimes served in the bone with a special metal scoop to extract it.

marrow bone The large hollow bones of the skeleton which contain marrow, especially the thigh bone of beef

marrowfat pea The original European pea now grown mainly for canning, drying or to make mushy peas

Marsala *Italy* A sweet fortified wine from Sicily used to make **zabaglione** and for general flavouring

marseillaise, à la *France* In the Marseilles style, i.e. garnished with tomatoes, anchovies and olives. Used especially of steaks.

marsepein *Netherlands* Marzipan

marshmallow 1. A tall hardy perennial, *Althaea officinalis*, from whose roots and leaves a thickening agent used to be extracted which, with sugar, made the original marshmallow confection. The seeds and flowers are edible and the young leaves can be used in salads or steamed and served as a vegetable and were used as such by the ancient Romans. **2.** A soft, sweet, opaque jelly-like confection cut in 2 to 3 cm cubes and rolled in icing sugar. Sometimes used in desserts.

marsh samphire Samphire, *Salicornia europaea*

Marsh Seedless The commonest variety of grapefruit grown worldwide since it keeps well and is easily processed for juice and segments

maru-kinkan *Japan* A round kumquat, *Fortunella japonica*, weighing about 12 g and grown mainly in East Asia. The rind is thinner and sweeter than the **nagami kumquat** and has slightly more segments and seeds but is otherwise similar. Also called **oval kumquat**

marula The light yellow, 3.5 cm-diameter fruit of a South African tree, *Scelerocarya birrea*, with an intense fragrance and a white fibrous flesh enclosed in a leathery skin with one central stone. The stone contains 2 or 3 kernels (marula nuts) slightly bigger than a peanut and similar in shape to a pine nut. The flesh is a good source of vitamin C and the nut of protein. Not yet marketed commercially.

Maryland *United States* Served in a butter and cream sauce. See also **chicken Maryland**

Maryland cookies Chocolate chip cookies

marzapane *Italy* Marzipan

marzipan A kneaded paste of ground almonds and sugar bound with sugar syrup (at the **hard crack stage**) or white of egg or whole egg, used for covering cakes or producing various sweetmeats. Also called **marchpane, almond paste**

Marzipan *Germany* Marzipan

masa 1. *Spain* Dough **2.** *Mexico* A cornmeal dough used for making tortillas, tamales and enchiladas

masa harina *Mexico* A heavy type of white flour made from maize with a much larger particle size than corn flour, treated with lime water and used for making masa. See also **nixtamal**. Also called **tamale flour**

masala *South Asia* A general term for a blended mixture of ground spices, either produced commercially or in the home. Varieties include garam masala, chaat masala and dhansak masala.

masala dosa *South Asia* A South Indian pancake made from a lentil flour and water batter which is allowed to ferment overnight. After frying, it is stuffed with mashed potato and spices.

masar dal *South Asia* Split dehusked lentils which are pink and easy to cook. See also **masoor dal**

mascarpone *Italy* A rich unsalted cream-cheese-like confection made from cows' cream heated to 90°C, curdled with citric or tartaric acid, drained then beaten or whipped and eaten freshly made. Sometimes flavoured with chocolate, coffee, liqueur, brandy, etc. for use as a dessert. Contains around 45% water, 45% fat, 7% protein and 2 to 3% lactose. Also called **Maschepone**, **Mascherpone**

Maschepone, **Mascherpone** Mascarpone

mascotte, à la *France (of a roast joint)* Garnished with artichoke hearts, truffles and potatoes

masculini *Italy* Tiny anchovies from Sicily, served with spaghetti

masgoof *Middle East* Fish from the River Tigris in Iraq, gutted and opened out, impaled on skewers, seasoned and barbecued slowly with the skin side away from the heat. When the flesh is cooked through the skin side is placed on the glowing charcoal to crisp it. Served as is with sliced onions, tomatoes and bread.

mash 1. *United Kingdom* Seasoned boiled potatoes formed into a stiff purée with margarine or butter and milk. See also **bangers and mash 2.** *South Asia* Black gram

mash, to To pound or process a soft fruit or vegetable to a smooth paste

mashamba *East Africa, South Africa* A type of pumpkin from Zimbabwe which resembles a melon and has green flesh

mashed potatoes Floury potatoes cooked in their jackets, skinned, dried over heat and mashed with milk, butter (5:2:1) and seasoning until smooth and creamy □ See **mash**

mashkoul *Persian Gulf* Long-grain rice cooked then mixed with finely chopped onion that has been fried until crisp in oil. It is served topped with more of the crisped onion.

mashwi *North Africa* A Berber festive dish consisting of a whole lamb barbecued on a spit over a pit in the ground which is coated inside and out and basted at 15 minute intervals with a mixture of butter, cumin, salt, pepper and paprika. This gives it a rich crust.

mask, to To cover or coat a piece of cooked meat, fish or similar item with a savoury sauce, glaze or jelly or to coat the inside of a mould with the same

maslina *Russia* Olive

maslo *Russia* Butter or oil

Masnor *Balkans* A semi-hard cooked-curd pear-shaped goats' milk cheese made in the same way as Ricotta, dry-salted and ripened for 1 to 2 months

masoor *South Asia* Lentils either whole or dehusked and split. See also **saabat masoor**, **masoor dal**. Also called **Egyptian lentils**

masoor dal *South Asia* Split dehusked lentils which are pink and easy to cook

masquer *France* To mask or nap

massa 1. *Portugal* Noodles and other similar pasta products **2.** Dough **3.** Paste

massa de pimentão *Portugal* A chilli pepper paste

massa folhada *Portugal* Puff pastry

Masséna, à la *France (of steak)* Garnished with artichoke hearts, **béarnaise sauce** and bone marrow

massepain *France* **1.** Marzipan **2.** A cake made with marzipan

mast *Iran* Yoghurt

Mastgeflügel *Germany* Corn-fed poultry of high quality

mastic The resin exuded by the Mediterranean plant lentesk and other similar plants used as a flavouring in some Greek dishes and in Turkish delight

mastice *Italy* Mastic

mastique *Spain* Mastic

Mastix *Germany* Mastic

mastokhiar *Iran* A light Iranian version of tsatsiki containing sultanas and chopped cucumber combined with yoghurt and garnished with dry mint

mastuerzo de jardín *Spain* Cress

mast va khiar *Central Asia* A cold yoghurt soup from Iran rather like a thin *tsatsiki*, with chopped green herbs, sultanas, spring onions and hard-boiled eggs all let down with iced water. It is also served as a salad (**borani**) by not adding water.

masuka nani *Japan* A decorative carrot garnish made from a flat rectangle of carrot part cut through from each of the two short ends and twisted so that one length is trapped between the two remaining

ma taai *China* Water chestnut

matafan aux pommes *France* Sliced, peeled and cored dessert apples mixed into a baking powder raised batter flavoured with brandy, cooked in a frying pan over a low heat for 30 minutes, turned, cooked a further 15 minutes and served dredged with icing sugar. Other fruit can be used. Also called **matefaim**

matambre *Argentina* A long thin slice of meat rolled round a filling of spinach, onion rings, sliced carrots and quarters of hard-boiled eggs, simmered in stock until tender, drained, cooled and sliced for use as an appetizer

matapa *South Africa* A dish from Mozambique consisting of cassava leaves cooked in a peanut sauce, often with prawns or other additions

matar dal *South Asia* Yellow dal

matbucha *North Africa* A sweet tomato chutney from Morocco

matefaim *France* Matafan aux pommes

matelote *France* A rich freshwater fish stew made with wine, onions and mushrooms

matelote blanche, sauce *France* **Sauce canotière** with the addition of button onions glazed in butter and blanched button mushrooms

matelote d'anguilles *France* Eels stewed in a wine sauce

matha *South Asia* Buttermilk

matière grasse *France* Fat (indicating the fat content on a product)

matignon *France* Minced or finely chopped aromatic vegetables used in the same way as a **mirepoix**

matisha mesla *North Africa* A Moroccan dish of chicken cooked in a sauce of tomatoes, honey, ginger and cinnamon

Matjeshering *Germany* Lightly cured young virgin herrings which have not yet developed roe

matjes herrings Gutted herrings if small or gutted and filleted if large, lightly cured in salt, sugar and saltpetre used in made-up dishes or served with raw onion and boiled potatoes (NOTE: Not to be confused with **maatjes haring**.)

matjessill *Sweden* Rinsed and wiped but not cleaned salt herring, layered in a pot with brown or granulated sugar and saltpetre (140:1) and covered with milk for 3 weeks in a cool place, then filleted as required. Traditionally served on Midsummer's day.

matjessill à la russe *Sweden* Fillets of matjessill covered with a sauce of mayonnaise mixed with French mustard, wine vinegar, sugar and cream and decorated with diced hard-boiled eggs, chives, beetroot and capers

mató *Catalonia* Fresh goats' cheese usually eaten with honey, sugar or jam

matoke *East Africa* Previously fried onions, tomatoes, sweet peppers, chilli pepper and spices are simmered in beef stock with seasoning and coriander leaves and, in Kenya, Tanzania and Zanzibar, diced or minced beef. Plantains which have been chopped and marinated in lemon juice are

added towards the end of the cooking process.

matrimony vine Various shrubs of the genus *Lycium*, related to the boxthorn, whose minty-flavoured leaves are used for tea and to flavour soup. All parts of the plant are used in Chinese medicine.

matsedeln *Sweden* Menu

matsoon *Southwest Asia* The Armenian term for yoghurt

matsuba *Japan* The pine needle garnish made from an 8 cm long halved piece of thin cucumber with many 0.5 cm deep longitudinal cuts made on the skin side followed by a series of oblique 2 cm slashes across the length, the slashes being pushed to alternate sides to give what looks like a series of rows of pine needles

matsutake *Japan* A dark-brown thick capped mushroom, *Armillaria edodes*, which grows under red pine. They are very expensive and are eaten fresh and cooked very simply as a single dish. Also called **pine mushroom**

matsutake fu *Japan* Baked gluten dough cut to resemble mushroom slices and flavoured and aromatized with an extract of matsutake or shiitake mushrooms. Sometimes used in sukiyaki.

Matteuccia struthiopteris *Botanical name* The fiddlehead fern

mattha *South Asia* Seasoned yoghurt flavoured with dry-roasted cumin and chopped fresh mint. May be let down as a drink.

mature Kept for a considerable time to develop flavour especially of fermented and cured products such as cheese, salami, etc.

matzo A large thin piece of very dry unleavened Jewish bread eaten during Passover. The bread is rather like a water biscuit or cream cracker. Crushed matzos are used in Jewish cooking. Also called **passover bread**

matzo meal, matzo mel Finely powdered matzos often used as a flour substitute in Jewish cooking and as the equivalent of dried breadcrumbs

maui onion *United States* A very mild sweet onion from Hawaii which may be eaten raw without treatment

ma uk *Thailand* Hairy aubergine

mau lai *China* Oyster

Maultasche *Germany* A filling of minced pork, veal, brains, spinach, spices, etc. wrapped in a thin sheet of noodle dough and braised in gravy

maund *South Asia* A unit of weight equal to 40 seers, approximately 36 kg, 80 lb

Mauritian jujube A species of jujube, *Zizyphus mauritiana*. Also called **Chinese date**

maush *Central Asia* Mung beans

maushawa *Central Asia* A kind of thin stew or thick soup from Afghanistan made by mixing various kinds of cooked pulses and rice with small spiced meatballs and chopped onion fried in oil This is then simmered with chopped tomatoes, water and dill and finished with yoghurt

maust *Central Asia* Yoghurt

Maximillian sauce Mayonnaise flavoured with tomato purée and chopped gherkins, capers and parsley, served with fish

ma yau *China* Sesame seed oil

Mayence red sausage A type of fat sausage or pudding from Germany consisting of the chopped neck meat, rind and tongue of pig moistened with pigs blood, flavoured with white pepper, peppermint, cloves, marjoram and mace, stuffed into a pig's stomach and boiled until cooked

mayonesa *Spain* Mayonnaise

mayonnaise See **mayonnaise, sauce**

mayonnaise, sauce *England, France* Egg yolks, vinegar, French mustard and seasoning combined, oil poured in slowly with vigorous whisking until the consistency of the resulting emulsion is as desired. More oil makes it thicker and stiffer, more vinegar less so. Generally nowadays made with a blender. Served cold and used as a base for many other cold sauces.

mayonnaise à la russe *France* Mayonnaise whisked over ice with a little melted aspic jelly, tarragon vinegar and grated horseradish until frothy. Used for binding Russian salad, etc.

mayonnaise chantilly *France* Sauce chantilly

mayonnaise collée *England, France* Mayonnaise mixed with melted aspic jelly (7:3), used to bind vegetable salads or to coat à la russe, chaud-froid dishes. Also called **jellied mayonnaise**

mayonnaise verte *France* Mayonnaise coloured with a raw green purée of spinach, watercress, parsley or tarragon or any combination

mayorana *Spain* Sweet marjoram

Maytag Blue *United States* A local speciality blue cows' milk cheese from Newton, Iowa

mazamorra *South America* A sweet dessert made from **chuño blanco**, fruit and molasses

mazapán *Spain* Marzipan

maziwa *East Africa* Milk

maziwalala *East Africa* Fermented milk from Kenya (NOTE: Literally 'sleeping milk'.)

maziwa mabichi *East Africa* Curdled milk, similar to cottage cheese. Also called **gururu**, **maziwa ya robu**

maziwa ya robu *East Africa* Maziwa mabichi

mazoon *Southwest Asia* See **matsoon**

mazurek *Poland* A Polish cake made from a flat pastry base spread with jam or vanilla cream and sprinkled with dried fruit and nuts

mazza bishurba *Persian Gulf* Lamb knuckles, blanched then simmered with whole **loomi**, cinnamon quills, fried onions and **baharat**

mazzacuogni *Italy* A Mediterranean king prawn. See also **caramote**

mazzafegati *Italy* A pork liver and pine kernel sausage from Umbria flavoured with fennel and garlic

mazzancolla *Italy* A Mediterranean king prawn. See also **caramote**

mbaazi wa nazi *East Africa* Soaked and cooked pigeon peas, cow peas, black eyed peas or similar simmered in coconut milk until almost dry. A fried chopped onion, chilli and curry powder mixture is added and all finished by simmering with thick coconut milk for ten minutes.

mbanga soup *Central Africa* Pieces of fresh fish skinned and deboned, simmered in stock with onion, chilli pepper and seasoning for 10 minutes, **moambé sauce** added and simmered for a further 10 minutes, finally smoked or dried fish and dried shrimp added and simmered for another 10 minutes or until the soup is thick enough. Served with rice, yams, plantain or fufu. Greens can also be added.

mbaqanga *East Africa* A yellow-fleshed pumpkin from Tanzania

mbatata *East Africa* A type of soufflé dessert from Malawi made from cooked sweet potatoes mixed with honey, brandy or sherry, butter, the zest and juice of an orange and egg yolk, the stiffly beaten egg white folded into the mixture and all baked at 200°C for about an hour

mbika *Central Africa* Seeds of pumpkins etc. See also **egusi**

mboga *East Africa* Vegetables, usually potatoes, carrots and onions in a meat gravy. Served in Kenya.

mbuta *Central Africa* Capitaine

mchele *East Africa* Kenyan for plain white rice

mchicha *East Africa* A type of spinach grown in most gardens and much used in Tanzanian cooking

m'choui *North Africa* Mechoui

mchuzi *East Africa* A beef and vegetable stew lightly flavoured with curry powder

mchuzi wa biringani *East Africa* A coastal Swahili standard curry made with aubergines and the usual sautéed onions, garlic, potatoes, tomatoes and tomato paste with curry spices, chopped ginger and chilli peppers, cumin, coriander, turmeric, cardamom etc. all brought together and simmered with coconut milk or yoghurt

mchuzi wa kamba *East Africa* As mchuzi wa samaki, but with peeled shrimps instead of fish. The shrimps are not precooked.

mchuzi wa samaki *East Africa* A fish curry from Zanzibar made from whole or filleted firm fish, seared on the outside and steeped in coconut milk and tamarind. Chopped onions, tomatoes, sweet peppers, garlic and spices are fried in the usual way then added to the fish mixture and all simmered until the fish is cooked through. Served with rice or chapatis.

me *Vietnam* Tamarind

meadowsweet A hardy perennial herb, *Filipendula ulmaria*, up to 1 m high, whose flowers give a slight almond flavour to jams and fruit. Leaves may be added to soups. (NOTE: Once used for flavouring mead and called meadsweet, hence the current name.)

meal 1. Any combination of foods eaten at a single sitting 2. The ground edible parts of any grain, seed, nut, etc. usually coarser than flour. The word is often added to the end of the seed's name, e.g. wheatmeal, oatmeal, cornmeal.

mealie meal *South Africa* Ground maize used to make a porridge, which is used as a staple carbohydrate source

mealie pudding *Scotland* White pudding

mealie rice *South Africa* Crushed or cut maize made to resemble rice and used in the same way

mealies *Caribbean, South Africa* Maize

mealy endosperm An endosperm with an open structure containing voids and which is not very tough

mean see jiang *China* Soya bean paste

measuring cup The standard volume measure used in North America and Australasia, equal to 236 ml and used in recipes for both free-flowing solids and liquids. Referred to as a 'cup', as in '2 cups of flour'.

measuring jug A toughened glass, metal or plastic jug inscribed on the side with volume measure usually in millilitres, litres, fluid ounces and pints. The ideal shape tapers towards the base so that small quantities can be measured accurately.

measuring spoon Plastic or metal, usually hemispherical spoons used for measuring small quantities of liquid or powder, graded one quarter, one half or one teaspoon (1.25, 2.5 or 5 ml), dessertspoon (10 ml) and tablespoon (15 ml)

meat 1. The edible muscle of any animal including vertebrates, invertebrates, molluscs, crustaceans, etc. Sometimes used of soft tissues not necessarily muscular as in molluscs 2. The central edible part of a fruit or nut

meat birds Any paupiette of meat with a savoury stuffing, usually browned then braised. Also called olive

meat cleaver A heavy chopping implement which can cut through bone

meat extract The soluble components of meat extracted by heating with water sometimes under pressure above its normal boiling point, filtering off the debris and reducing the solution to a thick dark syrupy paste. Used for spreading, making drinks and as a flavouring.

meat glaze White or brown beef stock, reduced by boiling until a sticky consistency. Used as a base for sauces or to improve their flavour. Also called glace de viande

meat grading *United States* Beef is graded in the USA as prime, choice, good, standard and commercial or utility. See under each name. There are no official gradings in the UK.

meat loaf Minced raw meat mixed with flavourings, seasoning and extenders, bound with egg or flour, baked in a tin, demoulded and sliced. Served hot or cold.

meat pie A pie filled with precooked meat, gravy, flavouring and seasoning prior to baking

meat press *United States* A heavy piece of metal with a heat-proof handle which is placed on food being cooked on a griddle in order to maintain good contact between the food and the hot surface and to prevent curling

meat safe A well-ventilated cupboard in a cool place with wire mesh or perforated metal over all ventilation holes. Used to keep meat or other food in a relatively uncontaminated state before refrigerators were in common use. Also called food safe

meat tenderizer Some form of proteinase, often from papaya or pineapple, which in a water solution is used to break down the muscle fibres in meat. Care must be taken not to use for too long as the enzymes are not used up and the meat may be reduced to soft slush. The enzymes can be deactivated by heat or alcohol.

meat thermometer A metal thermometer with the measuring element in a sharp point and a circular indicating dial, placed with its point in the thick part of a joint so as to indicate its internal temperature. Beef and lamb temperatures are 51°C, 60°C and 70°C for rare, medium and well done, pork and veal are 75°C, chicken, ducks and turkey 80°and goose 85°C.

mebos *South Africa* Pickled, sugared and dried apricots

mechanically recovered meat The waste meat, etc. left on animal carcasses and bones after trimming, removed as a soft pink slurry by subjecting the bones to very high pressure under a piston. All the soft tissues and marrow are squeezed out leaving bone fragments behind. Abbreviation **MRM**

mechoui *North Africa* A lamb, or occasionally a young camel, roasted on a spit or baked in a special oven and served whole to be carved at the table. Accompanied by ground cumin seed and bread.

mechouia *North Africa* A Tunisian salad of assorted vegetables

Mecklenberg *Germany* A hard cheese made from skimmed cows' milk

Mecklenburger Bratwurst *Germany* A **Bratwurst** made of equal parts of lean and fat pork, seasoned, spiced and moistened with brandy

Mecklenburger Leberwurst *Germany* A liver sausage of coarsely minced pig's liver mixed with chopped boiled breast of pork, pork kidney, tongue and back fat, pepper, allspice and powdered sage, filled into casings, boiled in the cooking liquor, refreshed then dried and smoked

medaglioni *Italy* 1. Small slices of fillet steak or slices of veal 2. Medallions

médaillon *France* Medallion

medallion A small round piece of tender meat easily cooked by frying or grilling, especially of beef or veal. Also called **médaillon**

Médici, à la *France* Garnished with artichoke hearts, peas, carrots, turnips and sometimes tomatoes. Used of steak. (NOTE: Named after Catherine de Médici.)

medio *Portugal* Medium cooked. Used of steaks, meat, etc.

medister pølse *Denmark* A sausage made with pork and pork fat with the possible addition of beef, seasoned, packed into 4 cm diameter casings and hot smoked. May be fried, grilled or boiled.

Mediterranean grouper A grouper, *Epinephelus caninus*, with a grey-green to reddish-brown skin, weighing normally around 2 kg. Often baked whole at 200°C from 30 minutes to 1 hour if stuffed. Also called **rock bass**

Mediterranean hare A strong-coloured small hare, *Lepus capensis*, found in Spain and Mediterranean islands

Mediterranean mandarin The first mandarin, *Citrus deliciosa*, introduced to England from China in 1805, from where it spread to the Mediterranean and throughout the Western world. The fruit is small to medium with a small, heavily furrowed neck and sometimes a navel. It peels very easily, the segment walls are fairly tough but the flesh is very juicy with an aromatic and sweet taste. It does not ship or store very well. Essential oils are produced from the rind and the leaves and twigs. Also called **willowleaf mandarin**, **thorny mandarin**

Mediterranean medlar Azarole

Mediterranean mussel A mussel, *Mytilus gallaprovincialis*, very similar to the common variety with an overlapping range

Mediterranean rocket See **rocket**

Mediterranean squid The common squid, *Loligo vulgaris*, traded in Europe and up to 50 cm in length

Mediterranean sturgeon Common sturgeon

Mediterranean sweet lime, Mediterranean sweet limetta Tunisian sweet limetta

medium-fat Containing between 10% and 20% butterfat according to type. Used e.g. of cheese, yoghurt.

medium oily Containing between 2% and 6% fat or oil. Used of fish flesh.

medium rare Cooked so that the centre of the meat is just pink but set. Used of steaks.

medium syrup See **syrup**

medium white sauce *United States* A sauce made with a blond roux and with a liquid to flour ratio of 14:1

medivnyk *Russia* A rich, heavily spiced and fruited, chemically raised honey cake for Christmas made with creamed butter, brown sugar and egg yolks mixed with a molten honey, spice and baking soda mixture then flour, yoghurt and cottage cheese with orange zest are alternately folded in followed by the fruit and stiffly beaten egg whites. All baked in a tube tin, cooled, brushed with honey and matured for several days.

medjool *North Africa* A particularly fine date from the Mahgreb

med-kha-noon *Thailand* A kind of dessert which looks like jackfruit seeds

medlar A small brown fruit about the size of an apple from a deciduous tree, *Mespilus germanica*, which grows in temperate climates. The sharp-flavoured flesh can be eaten raw if very overripe (**bletted**), i.e. after the first frost; otherwise they are used to make jam.

medvurst *Sweden* A Rohwurst similar to **Mettwurst** usually moistened with stock and brandy.and either hot or cool-smoked. May be eaten raw or cooked in any way.

mee krob *Thailand* Deep-fried puffed-up rice noodles mixed with stir-fried fish, pork and vegetables flavoured with lemon juice, vinegar and sugar and garnished with strips of egg omelette, chopped spring onions and coriander leaves. Also called **mi krob**

meenchi *Sri Lanka* Mint

mee noodles Chinese egg noodles

Meer *Germany* Bass, the fish

Meeraal *Germany* Conger eel

Meerbarbe *Germany* Red mullet

Meerengel *Germany* Angel fish

Meerfenchel *Germany* Samphire, *Crithmum maritimum*

Meerpolyp *Germany* Octopus

Meerrettich *Germany* Horseradish

Meersalz *Germany* Sea salt

Meerschildkröte *Germany* Turtle

mee siam *Malaysia* A noodle dish made by frying a pounded mixture of spring onions, red chillies and shrimp paste in oil, adding mashed soya beans, sugar, fried onions and coconut milk, simmering, then adding rice vermicelli, dried shrimp powder, fried bean curd and peeled and fried shrimps. The whole is heated through, seasoning corrected, finished with lime juice and garnished with sliced hard-boiled eggs and shredded spring onions.

meggyleves *Hungary* A cold summer soup based on cherries

megrim A rather dry sinistral flat-fish, *Lepidorhombus whiffiagonis*, lacking in any distinctive flavour of its own. Requires a strong-tasting sauce. Also called **whiff**

mehemalou *Iran* Cubed lamb or mutton, marinated in lemon juice with chopped onions, bay leaf, garlic, cloves and peppercorns; meat drained, floured and browned then simmered in stock with salt, sugar and saffron; stoned prunes and raisins added at the half-cooked stage; and the sauce finished with grape juice syrup. Served with a topping of dry-roasted almond slivers.

Mehl *Germany* Flour

Mehlpüt *Austria* Stewed pears with sweet dumplings

Mehlspeise *Austria* A sweet pastry dish or pudding

mehraz *North Africa* A heavy brass mortar and pestle for pounding spices and herbs

mei fun *China* Rice vermicelli

mei gee *China* Rice paper

mei jing *China* Monosodium glutamate

mein jin pau *China* Small balls of cooked gluten dough which are deep-fried and may be added to soups and stews

mein noodles Chinese egg noodles

meiwa kumquat A hybrid kumquat, *Fortunella margarita x F. japonica*, grown in China and Japan. It is larger than either of the parent species, has a thicker peel and fewer seeds, is the sweetest of the three and is considered to be the best eating variety. Also called **large round kumquat**

mei zi *China* Prunes

mejillón (*plural* **mejillones**) *Spain* Mussel

mejillones rellenos *Spain* Stuffed and baked mussels

mejiso *Japan* Shiso seed sprouts used as a garnish

mejorana *Spain* Marjoram

mekabu *Japan* The root or thickened base of **wakame** used whole or shredded in stews or as a separate vegetable

mel *Catalonia, Portugal* Honey

mela *Italy* Apple

melaço *Portugal* Molasses

melacotogna *Italy* Quince

melagrana *Italy* Pomegranate

melancia *Portugal* Watermelon

mélange *France* Blend or mixture

melanger *France* To mix or blend

melanzana *Italy* Aubergine

melanzane alla finitese *Italy* A Calabrian dish of aubergines stuffed with cheese, basil and peppers and deep-fried

melão *Portugal* 1. Melon 2. Bread roll

melassa *Italy* 1. Treacle 2. Molasses

mélasse *France* 1. Treacle 2. Molasses

Melasse *Germany* 1. Treacle 2. Molasses

melaza *Spain* 1. Treacle 2. Molasses

Melba sauce A sweet sauce made from puréed and sieved fresh raspberries. Used on fruit sundaes and similar desserts.

Melba toast Very thin (3 mm) slices of bread, dried and browned in the oven or under the grill. Served with soup or as a base for hors d'oeuvre and appetizers.

melboller *Denmark* Dumplings

Melbury *England* A soft mild white mould-ripened cheese with a mellow taste and formed in the shape of a loaf

mele alla certosa *Italy* Baked stuffed apples

melegueta pepper Grains of paradise

mele in gabbia *Italy* Apple dumplings (NOTE: Literally 'apples in a cage'.)

meli *Greece* Honey

melilot A hardy biennial, *Melilotus officinalis*, whose faintly aromatic leaves are used to flavour the Swiss cheeses Gruyère and Sapsago. It may also be used in small amounts in sausages, stuffings and marinades. Also called **sweet clover**

Melilotus coeruleus *Botanical name* Blue melilot

Melilotus officinalis *Botanical name* Melilot

melindres de Yepes *Spain* Dessert fritters

melinjo *Indonesia* The small red fruit of a tree, *Gnetum gnemon*. The kernel and its covering are used to make **emping melinjo** and the young flowers and leaves are used as a vegetable, raw or cooked. The ripe peel is fried in oil and served with rice as a side dish. The immature nuts can be added to soup. Also called **belinjo, blindjo**

melissa Lemon balm

Melissa officinalis *Botanical name* Lemon balm

melitzanes *Greece* Aubergine

melitzanes me domata *Greece* A type of ratatouille made from chopped onions softened in olive oil mixed with chopped tomatoes and peeled garlic cloves, simmered 15 minutes, diced grilled aubergine which has previously been salted and drained added and the whole simmered over a low heat until all tender

melitzano salata *Greece* **1.** A salad made from chopped cooked aubergine, onions, garlic and tomatoes, garnished with black olives, parsley and rings of sweet green pepper and dressed with oil, vinegar, lemon juice and seasoning **2.** Roasted aubergine flesh puréed to a fine paste with chopped onions, garlic, skinned tomatoes, oil, lemon juice and fresh herbs, spread over a flat dish, covered with olive oil and garnished with olives. Served as a starter with pitta bread.

melk *Netherlands, Norway* Milk

melkbrood *Netherlands* Milk bread, i.e. made with milk instead of water

melkchocolade *Netherlands* Milk chocolate

melktert *South Africa* A corn flour thickened and sweetened egg custard made with egg yolks, flavoured with cinnamon. The egg whites are whisked to a peak and folded into the cooled custard which is then put into a pastry case and cooked in the oven with a topping of cinnamon and sugar.

melò *Catalonia* Melon

melocotón *Spain* Peach

melocotón en almíbar *Spain* Peach in syrup

meloen *Netherlands* Melon

melokhia A plant related to okra. See also **meloukhia**

melon *Denmark, England, France, Norway, Spain, Sweden* The fruit of a climbing annual vine, *Cucumis melo*, related to cucumber. It is round or oval with a hard thick skin enclosing a thick layer of sweet (when ripe) juicy flesh with a mass of inedible seeds at the centre. The three principal types are **cantaloupe, winter** and **musk**. See also **water melon**. Also called **sweet melon**

melon baller A **parisienne cutter** used to make melon balls

melón de agua *Spain* Watermelon

melón de verano *Spain* Cantaloupe melon

melone *Italy* Melon

Melone *Germany* Melon

melon pear Pepino

meloukhia *Egypt, Middle East* A plant, *Corchorus olitorius*, related to okra and hibiscus. The leaves, which are used in cooking and soup-making, release a gelatinous thickening agent similar to that from okra. See also **molohia**. Also called **melokhia, molokhia, jew's mallow, naita jute, tussa jute**

Melrose pudding *Scotland* A pudding made with self-raising flour, eggs, butter, sugar and ground almonds (8:4:4:3:2) made by the creaming method and with sufficient milk added to make it of dropping consistency. Put in a buttered pudding basin lined with halved glacé cherries and steamed for 2 hours.

melt The spleen of an animal, sometimes classed as offal. Also called **milt**

melt, to To convert a solid to a liquid by heating

melted butter sauce See **beurre fondu**

melting cake method A method of making cakes such as parking by melting and mixing together all liquid, liquefiable and soluble ingredients such as fat, sugar, milk, etc., but not eggs, then folding in the sieved dry ingredients and beaten eggs if any

melting moments Small crisp round biscuits covered with oats which melt in the mouth

Melton Mowbray pie *England* A raised pork pie from Leicestershire, with a flavoured chopped (not minced) pork filling flavoured with ground mace and ground ginger

melu *Italy* Blue whiting, the fish

membrillo *Spain* Quince

men *China* Red cooking

mendoan *Indonesia* A fermented paste similar to tempe made from the residual solids after making bean curd and from peanuts. It has a finer texture than tempeh and is usually fried.

mendo limón *Spain* Lemon sole

menegi *Japan* The very young shoots from a spring onion that is grown to a maximum height of 8 cm. Used as a decoration and garnish for sashimi and sushi. Chives can be substituted.

menestra *Spain* Stew

menestra a la castellana *Spain* Meat and vegetable stew in a wine and tomato sauce

menestra de legumbres frescas *Spain* Mixed cooked vegetables with a poached egg

menjar blanc *Catalonia* Almond blancmange

mennola *Italy* Picarel, a type of sea bream

menrui *Japan* Noodles

men-ryori *Japan* Noodles

menta *Italy, Spain* Mint, the herb

menta piperita *Italy* Peppermint

Mentha Botanical name Mint

Mentha aquatica var. *citrata* *Botanical name* Lemon mint

Mentha pulegium *Botanical name* Pennyroyal

Mentha raripila rubra Botanical name Red raripila spearmint

Mentha requiena Botanical name Corsican mint

Mentha spicata Botanical name Spearmint

Mentha suaveolens *Botanical name* Applemint

Mentha x gentilis 'variegata' Botanical name Ginger mint

Mentha x piperita *Botanical name* Peppermint

menthe poivrée *France* Peppermint

menthe verte *France* Spearmint, garden mint

mentonnaise, à la *France* In the Menton style, i.e. garnished with vegetable marrow or courgette, potatoes and artichokes. Used especially joints of meat.

menu 1. *France* Meal or diet 2. *England, France* A list of foods available at a restaurant or eating establishment with the prices of individual dishes or of whole meals and the conditions of sale, or the list of items at a meal without prices if a formal meal where the participants do not pay at the time

Menü *Germany* Fixed-price menu

menudillos *Spain* 1. Giblets 2. Offal

menudo *Spain* A maize and tripe stew

menukort *Denmark* Menu

merca *Italy* Grey mullet boiled in a court bouillon then rolled into a cylindrical shape with a coating of herbs

merenda *Italy* Snack, light meal

merendeiras *Portugal* Small fresh 50 g ewes' milk cheeses kept in olive oil prior to sale (NOTE: Literally 'intended for lunch'.)

merguez *France, North Africa* A highly spiced short stumpy beef or lamb sausage from Algeria, now popular in France and generally in North America. Usually grilled.

merica cabai *Indonesia* White pepper

merica hitam *Indonesia* Peppercorn

merienda *Spain* Snack

meriendas *Philippines* Tapas-like dishes

meringato *Italy* With meringue

meringue *England, France* A whisked mixture of egg white and caster sugar in which a large amount of air is incorporated. The mixture is dried in a slow oven. The principal types are meringue suisse (often known simply as meringue), meringue cuite, Italian meringue and American meringue. All are shaped before drying and all use about 50 g of sugar per egg white.

meringue cuite *France* Professional meringue made by whisking the egg whites over a boiling bain-marie whilst incorporating the sugar. It is harder, whiter and more powdery than meringue suisse and requires more care and intenser mixing, but keeps better.

meringue suisse *France* Meringue in which half the sugar is incorporated during whisking, the remainder being folded in. The mixture is firm and glossy. Also called **Swiss meringue, meringue**

merinhe *Italy* Meringues

merise *France* Wild cherry

merlan *France, Spain* Whiting

merlano *Italy* Whiting

merlo marino *Italy* Wrasse, the fish

merlu *France* Hake

merluche *France* 1. Dried cod or stockfish 2. Hake

merluza *Spain* 1. Haddock 2. Cod 3. Hake

merluza a la plancha *Spain* Hake cooked on a griddle

merluzzo *Italy* Hake

merluzzo comune *Italy* Cod

mermez *North Africa* A mutton stew from Tunisia

mero *Spain* Mediterranean grouper

mérou *France* Mediterranean grouper

mersin *Turkey* Smoked swordfish

Mesambryanthemum crystallinum Botanical name Iceplant

mescal *Mexico* The generic name for all spirits distilled from the fermented sap of the agave plant of which there are over 300 varieties. Generally produced in the southern states of Mexico and may be bottled there or shipped in bulk for bottling elsewhere. Also called **mezcal**. See also **tequila** (NOTE: The practice of putting into the bottle the butterfly larva, *Hipopta agavis*, which feeds on the agave plant was started in the USA in the 1940s as a marketing ploy. It is known as *gusano de maguey*, 'worm of the agave', and may be gold or the more prized red.)

mesclun *France* A mixed green salad from Provence

mesentery A deep frilly fold in the interior lining of the abdominal cavity (the peritoneum) which is used to keep the intestines in position and attach a part of them to the back wall. Also called **mudgeon**, **frill**, **crow**

Meshanger *Netherlands* A soft cows' milk cheese with a delicate tasting and smooth paste covered with a thin natural rind. Contains 53% water, 23% fat and 21% protein.

mesi *Finland* Honey

mesimarja *Finland* The honey berry or arctic bramble, found in the Arctic and used for flavouring

mesocarp Albedo

Mesost *Sweden* A cows' milk whey cheese made in the same way as **Gjetöst**

Mespilus germanica *Botanical name* Medlar

mesquite *United States* A tree whose wood is used as part of barbecue fuel to add a strong flavour to the food cooked over it

mesquite bean The seeds of various spiny shrubs, *Prosopis glandulosa, P. juliflora* and other species, mainly used as cattle fodder but also ground for pinole.

mess A portion of food for 2 to 4 persons served on a trencher in medieval times

messicani *Italy* Stuffed paupiettes of veal

messina cob Turkish hazelnut

mesticanza *Italy* A dressed mixture of tender salad leaves

metabisulphites Salts similar to the sulphites and hydrogen sulphites used both as sterilants and food preservatives. Sodium-metasulphites, E223, and potassium-metasulphites, E224, are used in the food industry.

metabolism The process of converting circulating blood components derived from food or the breakdown of body tissues, principally fats, sugars and amino acids, into new or repaired body tissues and into energy by chemical reaction and conversion in the body's cells. The end products of these reactions are transported by the blood and excreted via the lungs, skin or kidneys.

metabolize, to To convert food, which has been broken down in the gut and transported in the blood to the cells of the body, into new or repaired cell material and tissues and energy

metagee *Caribbean* A traditional stew from St Lucia made from cubed salt beef sautéed with garlic and onions in coconut oil, saltfish, green bananas and seasonings added, then in order according to cooking time, potatoes, pumpkin, plantain, okra and tomato followed by coconut milk and chilli peppers. It is then cooked a further 20 minutes or so.

metatartaric acid See **E353**

metate *Mexico* A large stone with a dished upper surface used for grinding grains and spices using a mano

metchnikoff *Russia* A soured milk product named after the Russian bacteriologist who isolated the important bacterium *Lactobacillus bulgaricus* used for yoghurt and similar products

metété *Caribbean* A type of risotto from Martinique using fried meat, fish or shellfish, often crab meat, with onions, garlic, chillies and rice, flavoured with herbs and using vegetable or other stock. A more French version of the West African jollof.

methai *South Asia* Indian sweetmeats often based on evaporated or condensed milk. See also **mithai**

methe *South Asia* Fenugreek

methi ka beej *South Asia* Fenugreek seeds

methi ka saag *South Asia* The leaves of **fenugreek** with a bitter taste and strong aroma. Often cooked with starchy root vegetables. The bitter taste disappears on cooking.

methis *Indonesia* Fenugreek

methods of cookery See under particular class of items to be cooked such as biscuit, cake, fish, meat, etc.

metre The normal measure of length approximately 3 feet 3 inches, abbreviated m, divided into centimetres (cm) (100 per metre) and millimetres (mm) (1000 per metre). One inch is approximately 2.5 cm, one foot 30 cm and one yard 91 cm.

Metroxylon sagu *Botanical name* Sago palm

metso *Finland* Capercaillie, the game bird

metton *France* A spread made from evaporated whey similar to a soft **Gjetöst**. Made in the Jura.

mettre en boîte *France* To can

Mettwurst *Germany* A **Rohwurst** of equal parts of lean pork, lean beef, and fine diced fat bacon, seasoning, spices such as cloves, paprika and nutmeg and a little sugar and saltpetre, filled into casings, cooled and dried then dry-cured with salt, sugar and saltpetre for 2 days, retied and cool smoked. It may be coarse-textured (grosse Mettwurst) or smooth and fine textured (feine Mettwurst). Cooked in any way. Also called **Metwurst**

Metwurst *Germany* Mettwurst

Metzithra *Greece* A Cretan cheese

meunière, à la *France* Cooked in butter and finished with **beurre noisette** or lemon juice and chopped parsley. Applied especially to shallow-fried fish.

meunière, fish Shallow-fried fish cooked à la meunière. See also **amandes, fish aux**, **belle meunière, fish**, **doria, fish**, **grenobloise, fish**, **bretonne, fish**

meunière butter sauce Clarified butter heated until it just starts to brown then cooled with lemon juice and finished with parsley and ground white pepper. Used with fish. Also called **meunière butter**, **beurre noisette**

meurette *France* A mixture of fish stewed in red wine from Burgundy

Mexi-bell pepper *United States* A mildly hot sweet pepper-sized capsicum

Mexicaine, à la *France* In the Mexican style, i.e. garnished with tomatoes, mushrooms, sweet peppers, rice and sometimes aubergine

Mexican bean Red kidney bean

Mexican black bean See **black bean**

Mexican lime West Indian lime

Mexican saffron Safflower

Mexican tea Epazote

Mexican yam bean Jicama

mexikansk vårkyckling *Sweden* Mexican spring chicken made from pot-roasted and boned poussins laid on a sort of risotto made with half and half wild rice and short-grain rice, separately cooked with chopped fried onion, mushrooms and green and red sweet peppers plus petit pois and chopped parsley. Served with a red wine sauce.

mexilhão *Portugal* Mussel

meyve *Turkey* Fruit

mezcal See **mescal**

mezclar *Spain* To mix or blend

meze, mezes A selection of small dishes of food similar to hors d'oeuvres. See also **mezze**

mézeskalács *Hungary* Honey cake

mezethes *Greece* Appetizers

mezzaluna *Italy* A two-handled crescent-shaped chopping knife which is rocked back and forth over the food to be chopped. Versions with two and more blades are available. Also called **hachoir**

mezzani *Italy* Pasta tubes

mezze *Greece, Turkey* A selection of small dishes of food similar to hors d'oeuvres, appetizers or tapas served as starters or as a main meal. Both hot and cold dishes are served with pitta bread. Also called **mezes**, **meze**

mezzefegati *Italy* Mazzafegati

mezze penne *Italy* Short pasta quills

mezze ziti *Italy* Long lengths of macaroni slightly thinner than **ziti mezze**. See also **ziti**

mezzi rigatoni *Italy* Ridged pasta tubes

mezzo *Italy* Half, semi-

mfumbwa *Central Africa* The leaves of a forest plant eaten as a vegetable. See also **afang**

mhaans turcarri khasta *South Asia* A piquant mutton curry made by cubing and piquéing mutton, rubbing in a pounded paste of minced onion, black pepper, paprika, dry-roasted mustard seeds and ground cinnamon with oil, leaving 2 hours then layering the meat in a buttered pan with onion rings, ground fenugreek, chopped ginger and garlic, finishing with onion rings and chopped mint. This is covered with mutton stock and simmered until the meat is tender, skimming and adding stock to keep the level high. Finally it is mixed, a little asafoetida added, and the whole kept warm for 15 minutes before serving. See also **turcarri**

mhaans turcarri sadah *South Asia* A simple mutton curry made by browning chopped onion in ghee and reserving, browning the trimmed and cubed shoulder of mutton in the same ghee for 10 minutes, adding turmeric and ground coriander, and cooking briefly. The reserved onion and cayenne pepper are added and cooked briefly, then seasoned, and a little water added to deglaze the pan. The whole is then covered with water and simmered until the meat is tender, and finished with chopped parsley or coriander leaf and kept warm for 15 minutes before serving. Potatoes may be added towards the end. See also **turcarri**

mhannsha *North Africa* A large coil of pastry dusted with icing sugar. From Morocco. (NOTE: Literally 'the snake'.)

mhon-la-u *Burma* Mooli

mi *Vietnam* Wheat flour noodles

miascia *Italy* A baked bread pudding from Lombardy containing apples, pears, raisins and herbs

miaso *Russia* Meat

miata *Russia* Mint

Michaelmas *United Kingdom* The feast of St Michael on the 29th of September regarded as being the end of the harvest, used as an adjective to describe particular food served to celebrate the occasion such as Michaelmas goose

Michaelmas goose *England* A traditional Devonshire method of roasting a stuffed goose by basting it with its own fat and dredging it with seasoned flour at half-hourly intervals to form a thick crust. This crust would be eaten with the goose and its gravy or, if the person were rich, fed to the dogs.

miche *France* A cob or round loaf

Michelin guide *United Kingdom* One of the restaurant guides to whom complaints and experiences may be sent. Address: Michelin Tyre plc, Tourism dept., 38 Clarendon Rd., Watford, Herts WD1 1SX. (NOTE: The other guides with the same status are the Egon Ronay and Good Food Guides.)

mi-chèvre *France* Cheese made from a mixture of goats' and cows' milk containing at least 25% goats' milk

Michigan banana Papaw

microcrystalline cellulose E460(i), a very finely divided form of cellulose used to add bulk and fibre to slimming food, convenience foods, desserts and the like

microcrystalline wax See **E907**

microorganism A microscopic form of life such as a bacterium, virus, yeast etc.

microwave cooker A small oven fitted fitted with a timer, power variation and sometimes elaborate programmers, which cooks by subjecting the food to very high frequency electromagnetic radiation (microwaves) similar to radio waves, generated in a magnetron and piped to the oven through a wave guide. The microwaves are contained within the cooking chamber by the reflective walls but are absorbed by the food, which should be contained in materials such as ceramics, glass and plastics which do not absorb microwaves and so do not themselves get hot. See also **microwaves**

microwaves Very-high-frequency electromagnetic radiation used to heat up and cook foods. Microwaves transfer their energy to food by causing certain types of molecules to vibrate at their frequency. They are generally absorbed in the first cm of the surface and hence solid food to be cooked should be less than 2 cm thick or well stirred from time to time if contained in a deep container. Microwaves are reflected off metal surfaces but isolated metal within an enclosure will heat up and sometimes cause sparking.

microwave thermometer A thermometer without any metal parts which can be used inside a microwave cooker

middag *Denmark, Norway, Sweden* Dinner

middellandse-zeetapijtschelp *Netherlands* Carpet shell clam

middle See **ox casings**

middle bacon Bacon from the centre of the pig combining streaky and back bacon. May be sliced for rashers or stuffed, boiled or baked.

middle gammon A lean cut of bacon from between the corner gammon and the hock

middle neck of lamb *United Kingdom* The cutlets, rib bones, vertebrae and longitudinal muscles which lie between the best end and the scrag end (neck) behind the shoulder. Used for stewing or sometimes passed off as cutlets.

middle rib of beef *United Kingdom* The 3rd to the 6th ribs of beef counting from the head end. Used as a second class roasting joint or for braising, e.g. beef olives.

midolla *Italy* Crumb of a loaf, flesh of a fruit

midollo *Italy* Bone marrow

mie *France* The soft crustless interior of white bread

miel *France, Spain* Honey

miele *Italy* Honey

mien bao *China* Bread

mien see *China* Yellow bean sauce

mien tiao *China* Noodles

Miesmuschel *Germany* Mussel

miette *France* Crumb

mi fan *China* Rice

miga *Spain* Crumb

migas 1. *Spain* A Spanish breakfast dish consisting of fried breadcrumbs, flavoured with garlic, bacon and peppers **2.** *Portugal* Tender cubed lean pork and beef, coated with massa de pimentão overnight and each sautéed separately in olive oil and bacon fat until brown. The pan juices deglazed with water, mixed with fried diced bacon, sweated garlic and chunks of moistened stale bread, seasoned as required, beaten until fluffy and served with the beef and pork. **3.** *Portugal* Panada

migiod *Wales* Yeast buns

migliaccio *Italy* Pig's blood mixed with a variety of nuts, spices, dried vine fruits, honey, etc. and baked in a tart or fried as a flat cake. Also called **sanguinaccio alla fiorentina** (NOTE: From central Italy)

miglio *Italy* Millet

mignardise *France* Small and dainty made-up dishes

mignon *France* **1.** Small and dainty especially when applied to cuts of meat, e.g. the small muscle in a chicken breast or the small end of a fillet of beef (NOTE: Literally 'dainty'.) **2.** A smaller size of **Maroilles** cheese

mignonette *France* Small round fillets of lamb

mignonette pepper Coarsely crushed white peppercorns. Also called **shot pepper**

Mignot *France* A cheese from Normandy similar to **Livarot**

mignuic, mignule *Italy* Pasta curls served with sauces or cheese. See also **cavatieddi**

mihun *Indonesia, Malaysia* Rice vermicelli

mi-iro gohan *Japan* Boiled rice dressed with the cooking liquor from the meat served in individual dishes with petit pois, seasoned egg scrambled with a little sugar and minced topside of beef, lightly cooked with soya sauce, salt, sugar and **dashi**, all arranged decoratively on top of the rice

mijin-giri *Japan* Finely shredded or brunoise vegetable

mi jiu *China* Yellow rice wine

mijo *Spain* Millet

mijoter *France* To simmer or cook very slowly

mikan *Japan* Mandarin orange, often hollowed out and used as a dish e.g. for orange-flavoured jelly or seafood

mike cho *China* Rice vinegar

mi krob Deep-fried puffed-up rice noodles mixed with stir-fried fish, pork and vegetables. See also **mee krob**

milagia podi *South Asia* A condiment from the south made from dry-roasted sesame and coriander seeds, red chillies and black gram, dehusked chick peas or similar and all coarsely ground. Used on bread or vegetarian snacks.

milanaise, à la *France* In the Milan style, i.e. garnished with spaghetti or macaroni, tomato sauce and ham or tongue or panéed with breadcrumbs and grated cheese prior to frying

milanese, alla *Italy* In the style of Milan, i.e. panéed, fried in butter and finished with lemon. Used especially of escalopes and liver.

Milanese soufflé Lemon soufflé

Milch *Germany* Milk

milchig A Jewish term describing food containing or derived from dairy products, or equipment used in preparing such food. See also **fleishig**

Milchrahmstrudel *Austria* Strudel pastry wrapped round a light curd cheese and baked in a cream sauce

mild-cure Cured by the quick method using a solution of salt, saltpetre, flavourings and sometimes polyphosphates, which is either injected into the food or in which the food is immersed

mildew A fungus which grows on the surface of food exposed to a warm humid atmosphere, usually in the form of green furry blotches, each of which has grown from a single organism

mil folhas *Portugal* Flaky pastry, millefeuille

milho *Portugal* Maize

milk The liquid food provided by all mammals for new-born young, consisting of a water solution of sugars and proteins with emulsified fats, various minerals, vitamins and health protective substances. The most important milk in cooking is from the cow, but milk from sheep, goats, buffalo, camels and horses, etc. is used in various cultures, especially for cheese and yoghurt manufacture. Cows' milk is available with various fat contents and in various forms. The first milk drawn at a particular time from a mammal is usually high in sugar and low in fat and becomes progressively less sugary and more fatty as the glands are emptied, thus allowing some control over quality.

milk bread A white yeast-raised bread containing about 6% of dried milk by weight of the dry ingredients

milk chocolate A high sugar content (greater than 48%) chocolate confectionery with added milk solids

milk-fed lamb 3 to 4 week old, unweaned lamb weighing 4 to 5 kg. Usually born in winter and raised indoors on milk only. Should be eaten fresh not more than 3 days after slaughter. Also called **house lamb**

milkfish Bangus

milk pudding Grain, either whole or ground, and other starch products cooked in sweetened milk, e.g. rice pudding, semolina, sago, tapioca

milk substitute Creamer

milk sugar See **lactose**

mill An implement used to reduce a solid to a fine powder, as with pepper, salt crystals, coffee, spices, etc.

mill, to To reduce foods to a powder or paste, generally by grinding or squeezing the material through close, counter-rotating or moving metal, stone or other hard solid plates, rollers or discs

millassata *Italy* A cheese omelette from Sicily filled with artichokes and asparagus

millefeuille *France* Cream slice. Also called **Napoléon** (NOTE: Literally 'a thousand leaves or sheets'.)

mille foglie *Italy* Puff pastry

millet *England, France* The general name for a variety of small seeds produced by grasses used as food sources for both humans and animals. Millets tend to be drought and waterlogging resistant and hence important food sources in drought prone or marshy areas. Millet has a delicate bland flavour and is cooked as any other grain. See common millet, sorghum, finger millet, kaffir corn, bulrush millet, hungry rice, etc.

milo maize *United States* A variety of sorghum, *Sorghum vulgare* subspecies *glabrescens*, used to make sorghum flour

milt 1. Soft roe **2.** See **melt**

milza *Italy* Spleen, occasionally fried with herbs and anchovies

milzschnittensuppe *Italy* Beef broth served with fried bread spread with a mixture of minced spleen with eggs and garlic

Milzwurst *Germany* A Bavarian veal sausage usually fried in butter, probably contains spleen

Mimolette *France* An Edam-type cows' milk cheese coloured a dark orange

mimosa A garnish or decoration made by forcing hard-boiled egg yolk through a sieve to resemble the petals of the mimosa flower

mince The name given to any foodstuff processed by a combination of chopping and crushing as in a mincer, especially for meat and dried vine fruits. See also **minced meat**, **mincemeat**

mince, to To reduce the size of solid or semi-solid foodstuffs by a combination of chopping and crushing usually in a mincer or food processor

minced meat Meat which has been finely divided by being chopped or passed through a mincer. Used in stews, hamburger, pies, etc. Mincing converts tough meat into a more palatable and tender form. Also called **ground meat**

mincemeat A mixture of dried vine fruits, chopped mixed peel, apples and suet, with sugar, nutmeg, cinnamon, grated lemon zest, lemon juice and sometimes spirits all passed through a mincer, allowed to mature and used as a filling for mince tarts and other sweets, cakes and puddings

mince pie A small round pastry tartlet with a pastry top, filled with mincemeat, baked and sprinkled with icing sugar. Also called **mynce pie**, **shred pie**

mincer A culinary implement used for mincing, consisting of a barrel with a hopper above possibly tapering towards one end, into which fits a well-fitting scroll feeder with a pitch which reduces towards the output end. When the scroll is turned either manually or mechanically it forces food towards the output end slightly crushing it. A knife with three or four blades rotates with the scroll and cuts the crushed food as it is forced through a stationary circular disc containing a number of holes. The holes in

the stationary disc may be of various sizes to give varying degrees of size reduction.

minchet abesh *East Africa* Minced beef or lamb in a hot berbere sauce from Ethiopia

Mineiro Frescal *Brazil* Queijo Minas frescal

mineola A variety of **tangelo**

mineral hydrocarbons Highly purified oils derived from crude oils with high boiling points and usually colourless and transparent. Technical white oils come in a range of viscosities. The highest-viscosity oil is called liquid paraffin. Once used as fat or oil substitutes in slimming foods since they are not metabolized. Used as release agents to prevent dried vine fruits sticking together. See also **E905**

minerals The name given to various metals and other elements usually in the form of salts, oxides or organic compounds which are necessary for health. See under individual names e.g. calcium, chromium, copper, iodine, iron, magnesium, potassium, selenium. Those required in very small amounts are called **trace elements**.

mineral water See **carbonated water**

miner's lettuce Winter purslane

minestra 1. *Italy* The first course of a meal after the antipasto either soup, pasta, rice, gnocchi or similar **2.** *Catalonia* Vegetable stew

minestra asciutta *Italy* Dry minestra, i.e. pasta, rice, etc. eaten with a fork, not a spoon

minestra col battuto alla romana *Italy* Soup with pasta containing ham fat, onions and garlic

minestra di riso alla cappuccina *Italy* Thick rice soup with pounded anchovies

minestra in brodo *Italy* Pasta or rice cooked in broth

minestrina *Italy* A light broth

minestrina tricolore *Italy* Potato soup garnished with diced cooked carrots and chopped parsley

minestrone 1. *Italy* A substantial thick, mixed vegetable soup with the addition of some of pasta, rice, beans and potatoes in many local variations. The UK version is given in the next entry. **2.** *United Kingdom* A soup made from paysanne-cut mixed vegetables sweated in oil without colour, white stock, a bouquet garni and seasoning added and simmered 20 minutes, peas and diamond-cut green beans added and simmered 10 minutes, paysanne-cut potatoes, short lengths of spaghetti, tomato purée and diced, skinned and deseeded tomatoes added and simmered until all cooked. A processed mixture of fat bacon, garlic and parsley formed into pea-sized balls dropped into the boiling soup, the bouquet garni removed and all served with grated Parmesan cheese and toasted slices of French bread.

minestrone alla milanese *Italy* The classic minestrone with tomatoes, peas, beans, courgettes, potatoes, cabbage, bacon and rice, often served at room temperature or chilled

minestrone alla sarda *Italy* A minestrone with beans, chick peas, potatoes, cabbage, fennel, pasta and pork

Ming dynasty egg Chinese preserved eggs

minhota, à *Portugal* In the style of Minho, i.e. with chopped ham and vinho verde

miniature corn Small (up to 10 cm long) cobs of sweet corn used as a vegetable and eaten whole. Also called **baby corn**

Minneola A variety of **tangelo**

Minnesota blue *United States* An American copy of **Roquefort** cheese, but made from cows' milk instead of ewes' milk

Minnesota slim *United States* A moist, open-textured cows' milk cheese coloured orange, which easily melts

mint A large group of hardy herbaceous perennials of the genus *Mentha*, which interbreed readily to form hybrids. Generally up to 1 m high with oval pointed aromatic leaves, deep veined and set in pairs up a square green to purple stalk. Some varieties are variegated (two colours). All are edible save that penny royal should only be used in small quantities. See also *Mentha*

mint sauce *United Kingdom* Chopped mint leaves, macerated with boiling water and sugar and combined with an equal amount of vinegar. Served with roast lamb.

mintuba *Central Africa* Treated cassava tubers. See also **bâton de manioc**

minute *France* Cooked quickly

minute steak Lean pieces of beef which have been passed through rollers covered with sharp projections. These have the effect of breaking down the fibres in the steak so that it cooks quickly when grilled or fried. Also called **flash-fry steak**

minyak kelapa *Indonesia, Malaysia* Coconut oil

Minze *Germany* Mint, the herb

miolos *Portugal* 1. Brains 2. The soft crumb inside a loaf of bread

Mirabeau, à la *France* Garnished, especially of grilled meats, with anchovies, olives and pats of anchovy butter

mirabelle *France* A small, golden, cherry-sized variety of plum, *Prunus insititia*, very popular as a dessert fruit in Europe, also the alcoholic liqueur made from the same. Also called **golden gage**

mirasol *Spain* Sunflower

mirchi *South Asia* Chilli peppers

mirepoix *England, France* A mixture of rough cut aromatic vegetables used as a bed on which to braise meats and to flavour sauces. Often browned in fat in the oven before use.

mirin *Japan* A sweet rice wine used almost exclusively for cooking and not classed as an alcoholic drink. Used in basting sauces to give food a translucent glaze. A well-flavoured sweet sherry with a little extra sugar may be substituted. Also called **honmirin, Japanese sherry, sweet sake**

mirliton 1. Choko **2.** *France* A small almond-flavoured pastry cake from Normandy

miroton *France* A dish of boiled beef warmed up with an onion and mustard sauce. Also called **boeuf miroton**

mirride odoroso *Italy* Sweet cicely

mirtilli *Italy* Bilberries

mirto *Italy, Spain* Myrtle

mirto holandés *Spain* Bog myrtle

mirugai *Japan* A gaper clam, *Tressus keenae*, around 14 cm across and 9 cm thick with a large projecting syphon, The syphon is skinned and used for sushi, sashimi and sunomono but is very chewy. The rest is also eaten but is has a poor flavour. Also called **mirukui**

mirukui *Japan* Mirugai

mischen *Germany* To mix or blend

mischiare *Italy* To mix or blend

Mischling *Austria* A hard scalded-curd strong-flavoured mountain cheese made from cows' milk coagulated with a natural lactic starter. The paste contains a few irregular shaped holes and cracks but the rind is dry, hard and unbroken.

mise en place *England, France* The collection, weighing and preparation of all ingredients for a recipe before it is assembled and cooked (NOTE: Literally 'putting into place'. It is an essential in a commercial kitchen and will save time in a domestic situation.)

miser's feast *Wales* A very simple traditional dish from 19th-century Carmarthenshire consisting of peeled potatoes and sliced onions seasoned, covered with a piece or slices of bacon, a small amount of water added and all covered with a lid and simmered until the potatoes are cooked and most of the water absorbed. The potatoes and onions were mashed with a little of the liquid for one meal and the bacon eaten with boiled potatoes the next day.

Mish *Egypt* A soft buffalo milk cheese which is kept for up to a year in salted buttermilk

mishkaki *East Africa* Beef kebabs in which the beef has been marinated for several hours in a mixture of ginger, tomato, garlic, tamarind paste, curry powder and seasoning processed in a mixture of oil and water. Popular all along the coast.

miso *Japan* A dark brown salty paste tasting rather like soya sauce. It is made by a two step fermentation first producing koji from grains or beans then fermenting the koji mixed with mashed, well cooked soya beans and salt, stirring at intervals. It is aged for up to 3 years. Used as a flavouring and condiment. A good source of B vitamins. See also **hatcho-miso, inaka-miso, shinshu-miso, shiro-miso**. Also called **bean paste, bean sauce**

miso-dengaku *Japan* Grilled, skewered and coated with a sweetened **miso**

misoltini *Italy* Salted and dried agoni. Also called **missoltitti**

miso-ni *Japan* Cooked in miso

miso-ramen *Japan* A white curly noodle containing the cream coloured miso

miso-shiru *Japan* A traditional soup made from kombu and shiitake mushrooms simmered in **dashi** and finished with shredded spring onions, diced bean curd and red miso. It must not be boiled at the finishing stage.

Mispel *Germany* Medlar

missoltitti *Italy* Misoltini

misticanza *Italy* Mixed salad

misto *Italy* Mixed

mistol jujube Argentinian jujube

misto mare *Italy* Mixed fried seafood

miswa *Philippines* Fine white wheat flour noodles similar to **hiyamugi** noodles. Sold in bundles and should be cooked carefully to avoid breaking up.

mithai *South Asia* Indian sweetmeats made in various ways but often based on evaporated or condensed milk (**khoya**) and nuts. Also called **methai**

mitha nimboo *South Asia* Sweet lime

mithia tiganita *Greece* Cooked mussels, battered and deep-fried at 180°C. Served with lemon wedges.

mitili *Italy* Mussels

mititei *Romania* Skinless sausages flavoured with garlic and ground caraway seed and containing bicarbonate of soda which gives them an unusual texture and flavour

mitmita *East Africa* A hot yellow chilli pepper from Ethiopia

mitsuba *Japan* A herb resembling Italian parsley whose leaves are used as a garnish either chopped or whole. Also called **Japanese parsley, trefoil**

Mittagessen *Germany* Lunch

miúdos *Portugal* Giblets

miveh dami *Central Asia* An Iranian rice, meat and fruit dish, made like a risotto by frying onion and diced lamb or veal in clarified butter and adding cinnamon, sour cherries, chopped walnuts, currants, chopped dried apricots and washed basmati rice with enough water to cook on a low heat in a tightly closed pan

mix A mixture of dry ingredients to which water, milk, eggs or a combination of these is added and the result may be eaten as is, left to set, or further cooked, e.g. bread mix, soup mix, cake mix

mix, to To combine two or more ingredients so that they are intimately and irrevocably mingled

mixed grill A mixture of small portions of various grilled meats, offal, bacon, ham, sausage together with grilled mushrooms and tomatoes, served as a main meal or breakfast dish

mixed herbs Mixtures of dried herbs supplied for flavouring, often proprietary brands formulated for different applications such as sausages and the like

mixed salad An assortment of raw or cooked vegetables, leaves, fruit, cheese, sometimes with cooked fish, shellfish, meat, offal or egg assembled together as a single dish of attractive appearance and treated or served with a suitable dressing. Served warm or cool.

mixed spice Mixtures of ground spices supplied for flavouring, often proprietary brands formulated for various cakes, biscuits, desserts, etc.

mixed vegetable soup See **potage paysanne**

mixer Any hand-operated or machine operated implement used for mixing ingredients ranging from a simple spoon to a complex food processor. See also **whisk, food processor, blender**

Mizithra *Greece* A Ricotta-like cheese made from the whey remaining after conventional cheese making with ewes' milk

mizu *Japan* Water

mizuna *Japan* A bitter leaf used as a herb

mizuna greens An annual or biennial oriental brassica, *Brassica rapa* var. *nipposinica*, with dark green, glossy, almost feathery leaves with white stems which form large rosettes rather like endive but not bitter. They may be eaten at any stage of growth up to 10 weeks and are cooked as a vegetable or the young tender leaves used in salads.

m'jadarah *Middle East* Sliced onions fried until crisp in olive oil, most removed and drained and reserved, cooked lentils and rice added to the leftover oil and onions with cinnamon, allspice and pepper and cooked until dry. Served covered with the reserved crisp fried onions.

mjölk *Sweden* Milk

mjuka småfranska *Sweden* Soft bread rolls

mkate mayai *East Africa* A light wheat flour pancake wrapped around fried eggs and fried minced meat, from Kenya. Also called **egg-bread**

mkate wa ufute *East Africa* A type of flat bread from Zanzibar made with a yeast raised flour batter (equal parts of milk and water), fried in oil like a pancake and sprinkled with sesame seeds

moa luau *United States* A Hawaiian dish of diced boiled chicken mixed with cooked taro leaves, butter and seasoning

moambé sauce *Central Africa* A sauce made from palm nuts boiled in water until the skin comes off, drained, mashed into a pulp, mixed with water and strained through a sieve to remove skin and kernels. The pulp and oil are then cooked until thick to make the sauce. Used as a base for many soups and stews. Also called **nyembwe sauce**, **palm butter**

moa niu *United States* A Hawaiian dish of boiled chicken in a white sauce placed in a halved coconut shell still containing coconut flesh, covered in cooking foil and baked in a bain-marie in the oven

mocetta, la *Italy* 1. A large salami 2. Dried salted chamois or goat flesh served in very thin slices as an antipasto

Mocha A strongly flavoured coffee. The word is also used for a mixture of coffee and chocolate flavours used for cakes and puddings and sometimes the cake itself.

mochi *Japan* Steamed glutinous rice pounded to a smooth paste and made into small sweet or savoury cakes or dumplings. May be grilled and served with soya sauce.

mochi-gome *Japan* A very small grain glutinous rice. Used to make mochi cakes.

mochiko *Japan* Ground mochi-gome used as a thickening agent

mochomos *Mexico* Cooked, shredded and crisply fried meat

mock crab *England* Chopped hard-boiled egg and egg yolk mixed with grated red Leicester cheese and shredded cooked chicken breast bound with a mixture of cooked egg yolk, mustard, anchovy essence, butter and pepper. Rested, then presented on crab shell and garnished as for dressed crab.

mock cream A creamed mixture of fat and sugar, mixed with a corn flour thickened milk-based white sauce. Used as a cake filling especially in the UK during World War II.

mock hollandaise See **Dutch sauce**

mock turtle soup *England* Soup made from stock derived from calf's head, aromatic vegetables and turtle herbs, strained, thickened and coloured brown, garnished with diced lean meat from the calf's head

moda, à *Portugal* In the style of

moda di, alla *Italy* In the style of

mode, à la 1. *France* In the fashion **2.** *United States* Served with a scoop of ice cream **3.** *France* With carrots, onions and a calf's foot braised in wine. Used of beef dishes.

mode de, à la *France* In the style of

moderne, à la *France* In the modern style, i.e. garnished with cauliflower sprigs coated with cheese sauce, tomatoes and duchesse potatoes

moelle *France* Bone marrow

moelle, sauce *France* Bordelaise sauce finished with poached and diced bone marrow and chopped parsley

moeum spey sar *Cambodia* Mooli

mofo *South Africa* The traditional bread of Madagascar, usually baguette-shaped

Moghul masala A mild Indian spice blend containing green cardamoms, cinnamon, black peppercorns, mace and cloves

mo gwa *China* Bitter gourd

mohali mandarin *Ponkan* mandarin

mohingha *Burma* A spicy fish soup based on coconut milk with local vegetables, served with noodles, hard-boiled eggs, raw onions, chillies and lemon. The national dish of Burma.

mohi shekumpour *Central Asia* A large fish, slashed and marinated in lemon juice and oil, the cavity stuffed with chopped spring onions and herbs mixed with some of the marinade, and baked at 190°C for about 45 minutes. From Iran.

moh lung ye baw *Burma* Small flour and grated coconut dumplings filled with **jaggery** and cooked in a sauce based on coconut milk. Eaten to celebrate the cutting of a baby's first tooth, which meant it had survived the first hazardous months of life. Also called **teething cake**

Mohnbrötchen *Germany* Poppy seed rolls

Mohnkipfel *Germany* Poppy seed crescent rolls

Mohnkuchen *Austria, Germany* A cake made from a base of white yeast-raised dough topped with a sweet rich mixture containing poppy seeds. Served in pieces dredged with icing sugar.

Mohnsamen *Germany* Poppy seed

Mohnspielen *Germany* Christmas bread soaked in milk and sprinkled with poppy seeds, currants and sugar

Mohnstriezel *Germany* Poppy seed cake made from a yeasted egg and butter enriched stiff dough, rolled in a ball, submerged 5 to 8 cm below cold water and left until it rises above the surface; dried, punched down and kneaded and allowed to prove; rolled into a 6 mm thick rectangle about 25 by 40 cm and covered with a filling of ground poppy seeds, raisins and almond nibs (5:3:1), mixed with an egg yolk-enriched and sweetened béchamel with stiffly beaten egg whites folded in at the end; then brushed with melted butter. The rectangle is rolled from either short side like palmiers and baked seam side down at 190°C until golden brown and crusty.

Möhre *Germany* Carrot

Mohrenkopf *Germany* A Genoese sponge cooked in hemispherical moulds. Two placed together with a chocolate filling and covered with whipped cream. (NOTE: Literally 'Moor's head'.)

Mohr im Hemd *Austria* A chocolate pudding topped with ice cold whipped cream and covered with hot chocolate sauce (NOTE: Literally 'Moor in a shirt'.)

Mohrrüben *Germany* Carrots

moilee *South Asia* A dish of fish or meat containing thick coconut milk in the sauce. See also **molee**

moi-moi *West Africa* A dish based on black-eyed peas, soaked, skinned and ground. See also **moyin-moyin**

moisten, to To add a little liquid to a dry mixture of foods so as to soften or flavour it, but not so as to be able to see free liquid

moist sugar *United States* Muscovado sugar

moixama *Catalonia* Thinly sliced, dried and cured, e.g. of fish or meat

mojama *Catalonia* Thinly sliced, dried and cured. Used e.g. of fish or meat.

mojettes *France* White cooked haricot beans, eaten warm or cold as a salad

moka *France* Mocha

moke-kaung *Burma* Ridged sand clam

Mokka *Germany* Mocha

molahu kozhambhu *South Asia* A well-seasoned and spiced soup made with yoghurt, coconut, lentils and tamarind thickened with a little rice flour

molasses The thick brown drainings from raw and recrystallized sugars which is a complex mixture of sugar, invert sugar and other plant derived components and minerals. Cane sugar molasses are used to produce treacle. Beet sugar molasses contains too many bitter and astringent beet compounds to be palatable.

molasses sugar A fine grained unrefined sugar containing a large admixture of molasses so that it is very soft. Used in cakes and puddings.

Molbo *Denmark* An Edam-type cows' milk cheese covered in red wax

mold *United States* Mould

Moldavia *Russia* A hard smoked scalded-curd ewes' milk cheese made in the form of a cylinder (up to 25 kg). Contains 42% water, 31% fat and 25% protein.

mole *Mexico* As **mole poblano**, but with added tomatoes, thickened with tortillas and sweetened with raisins. Also called **molli**

moleas de vitela *Portugal* Veal sweetbreads

moleche *Italy* Small shore crabs cultivated in the Venice lagoon and eaten just after they have shed their shells and before the new shells have hardened

moleche alla muranese *Italy* Moleche floured, egged and fried

moleche ripiene *Italy* Moleche, killed by being left in beaten egg for 2 hours, then floured and fried

molee *South Asia* A dish of fish or meat containing thick coconut milk in the sauce which is usually made from sweated onions, garlic, chillies and fresh ginger with spices to which the coconut milk is added. The fish or meat are then cooked in this sauce without boiling. Also called **moilee**

mole poblana con guajalote *Mexico* Boiled turkey served with mole or mole poblano sauce

mole poblano *Mexico* A sauce made from deseeded chile poblano puréed and fried with onion, coriander and garlic and combined with a small amount of unsweetened chocolate. Individual cooks may add other chillies for their own special flavour.

moler *Spain* To grind

molho *Portugal* A bunch

môlho *Portugal* **1.** Gravy **2.** Sauce

môlho branco *Portugal* White sauce

môlho de maças *Portugal* Apple sauce

mølja *Norway* Cod steaks boiled in water and served with sliced, cold, boiled cod's roe and a sauce made from boiled cod's liver heated with onion and water and the oil which floats on the top of the water in which the liver is boiled

moll de roca *Spain* Red mullet, *Mullus surmuletus*

molle, molletto *Italy* 1. Soft 2. Soft-boiled

mollejas *Spain* Sweetbreads

mollet *France* Soft or soft-boiled, especially of eggs

molletto *Italy* Molle

molli A sauce made from deseeded chile poblano. See also **mole**, **mole poblano**

mollica *Italy* Crumb

molls a la brasa *Catalonia* Red mullet cooked over an open flame

mollusc The general term for a creature with a soft body and a hard either external or internal shell, but which is not segmented. Many molluscs live in the sea. Molluscs are divided into univalves (gastropods) with a single solid external shell, bivalves which have a hinged two part external shell and the cephalopods, some of which have an internal shell.

molluschi *Italy* Molluscs

mollusk *United States* Mollusc

molohia *Egypt* A thick green soup made by boiling finely chopped meloukhia leaves (or spinach beet if not available) in stock and adding chopped garlic and ground coriander seeds fried in butter. Sometimes named after the vegetable.

molokhia A plant related to okra. See also **meloukhia**

moloko *Russia* Milk

molt fet *Catalonia* Well done. Used of meat.

molto cotto *Italy* Well done, cooked through

molva occhiona *Italy* Ling, the fish

momendofu, momentofu *Japan* Bean curd which has been strained through cloth, slightly pressed and presented in cubes or similar

momiji-oroshi *Japan* A mixture of finely grated mooli and red chillies served wet as a condiment or dry after expelling the juice through a cloth. The juice may be used for flavouring other dishes. The grating of the chillies is achieved by inserting the long red variety into holes pierced in the mooli then grating the combination.

Momordica charantia *Botanical name* The bitter gourd

Momordica cochiniensis *Botanical name* The spiny bitter gourd

Momordica muricata *Botanical name* Kantola

Monarda didyma *Botanical name* The herb bergamot

Monascus purpureus A fungus used in addition to the alcohol producing microorganism to impart a purplish red colour to the rice which is used to make ang-kak or rice wine. See also **red rice**

mondé(e) *France* 1. Hulled. from *monder*, 'to hull'. 2. Formed into a round ball shape e.g. when a tomato is cored and skinned

mondeghili *Italy* Meatballs from Lombardy made with minced beef and cheese then panéed and fried

Mondseer *Austria* A semi-hard, cooked-curd cows' milk cheese made with a lactic starter. The cheeses are brined then ripened for up to 8 weeks. The supple yellow paste contains small irregular holes and is enclosed in a thin dry rind. The taste varies from mild to piquant depending on age.

mongete *Spain* Dried kidney bean. Also called **monguete**

mongetes tendres i patates *Catalonia* French beans and potatoes

mongo-ika *Japan* Cuttlefish strips used for flavouring stocks and soups

Mongolian barbecue An upwardly convex domed steel plate set over a fierce heat source and usually with a gutter round the edge. Finely chopped foods (often self selected by the guest) are cooked rapidly on the plate in small quantities. Said to be derived from the upturned shield on which Mongolian horsemen cooked their food. Also called **Genghis Khan griddle**

Mongolian fire-pot See **Mongolian hot pot**

Mongolian hot pot A large pot with a funnel through the middle somewhat like a ring mould, and with a burner below which uses the funnel as a flue. Food is cooked at the table, possibly a stew or a stock into which finely sliced raw meat is briefly dipped as in **flying lamb slices**. Also called **Mongolian fire pot**

monguete *Spain* Dried kidney bean

mong yau *China* Caul

monkey bread 1. Baobab 2. *United States* A sweet bread made by placing separate pieces of dough at random into a bread tin and baking. The bread may be enriched and flavoured.

monkey nut Peanut

monkfish 1. A round seawater fish, *Lophius piscatorius*, with a large ugly head and very fine-tasting white tail flesh often used as a substitute for scampi. The whole tail can be roasted like a leg of lamb. The fish can grow up to 2 m in length and 30 kg, but is usually sold smaller. It is found in the Mediterranean and the Atlantic. Also called **anglerfish**, **goosefish** 2. A name sometimes given to the **angel fish**, a type of shark

monk's hotchpotch See **ghiveci călugăresc**

Monmouth pudding *Wales* A pudding made with soft white breadcrumbs, sugar, butter and strawberry jam into which beaten egg whites are folded and all baked together

món ngôi *Vietnam* A cold dish of food

monoacetin See **glycerol monoacetate**

Monoatriumglutamat *Germany* Monosodium glutamate

monopotassium glutamate See **E622**

monosaccharide A simple sugar consisting of a 6-membered ring structure. The important monosaccharides in food are glucose, fructose and galactose which in various combinations form most of the sugars, starches and carbohydrates found in food.

monosodium glutamate The white crystalline sodium salt of the amino acid, glutamic acid, a constituent of proteins now produced by fermentation. It has a distinctive meaty taste in itself but is used to enhance the flavour of other foods especially in Chinese cooking and in convenience foods. See also **E621**. Also called **MSG**, **aji-no-moto**, **taste powder**, **gourmet powder**, **ve tsin**

monounsaturated As polyunsaturated but only one carbon atom has less than two hydrogen atoms or other groups attached

monounsaturated fat A fat or oil which contains a single unsaturated (i.e. double) bond in the chain of carbon atoms which make up the fatty acid part. Olive oil is the commonest example.

monsieur *France* Monsieur fromage

monsieur fromage *France* A small double cream cows' milk cheese from Normandy with a strong flavour and in the shape of a tall cylinder. Also called **monsieur**

monstera deliciosa The fruit of a tropical tree, *Monstera deliciosa*, with a green scaly skin about the size of a large maize cob. The ripe pulpy flesh is white and has a strong flavour similar to that of pineapples and bananas. Also called **ceriman**

Montasio *Italy* A hard, cooked-curd wheel-shaped (up to 15 kg) cows' milk cheese made with a whey starter, pressed, salted 10 days, brined for 7 days and ripened for 6 to 12 months and varies from a dessert cheese to a grating cheese as it ages. Resembles Asiago.

montata *Italy* Whipped

Mont Blanc *France* A dessert of sweetened chestnut purée topped with whipped cream

monté, to The shortened anglicization of **monter au beurre**, meaning to add butter to a sauce before service to enrich, thicken and gloss it

Monte Bianco *Italy* As **Mont Blanc**, with chocolate and rum

Montecenisio *France, Italy* A soft blue cheese made with cows' milk possibly mixed with goats' milk from the region west of Turin

monter *France* To increase the volume of an ingredient by whipping to incorporate air

monter au beurre *England, France* To add butter to a sauce at the last moment to give it a sheen

Monterey Jack *United States* A scalded-curd bland Cheddar-like cows' milk cheese made in dessert, semi-hard or grating textures depending on the ripening time. The grating version is known as Dry Jack. Originally from Monterey, California.

Montia perfoliata *Botanical name* Winter purslane

Montmorency, à la *France* **1.** Dishes dedicated to the Montmorency family especially various cakes and sweet and savoury dishes containing Montmorency cherries **2.** Garnished, especially steaks, with artichokes, carrots, potatoes and sometimes with Madeira sauce

Montmorency cherry A particularly prized variety of cherry used in many sweet and savoury dishes

Montoire *France* A mild, pleasant-tasting goats' milk cheese from the Loire

montone *Italy* Mutton

Montpellier butter This butter without the oil and egg yolks is sometimes chilled and cut into decorative shapes for cold buffets. See also **beurre de Montpellier**

Montpensier, garnish *France* A steak garnish of artichokes, asparagus, truffles and potatoes

Montrachet *France* A small, delicate and creamy goats' milk cheese made in the shape of a small cylinder and wrapped in grape or chestnut leaves

montreuil *France* With peaches

Montreuil *Germany* Fish poached in white wine and served with potatoes and shrimp sauce

Montrose cakes *Scotland* Self-raising flour, caster sugar, butter, eggs and currants (4:4:4:4:3) made up by the creaming method, flavoured with brandy, rose water and nutmeg and baked in buttered bun tins at 190°C for 10 to 15 minutes

Montségur *France* A bland cows' milk cheese from Languedoc-Roussillon

monzittas *Italy* Snails (*Sardinia*)

moo *Thailand* Pork

moolee *South Asia* Cooked in a coconut sauce

mooli *South Asia* The long white tubers of a species of radish, *Raphanus sativus*, with a similar and sometimes hotter taste. Up to 40 cm long and eaten raw, pickled or cooked. Also called **Japanese radish**, **white radish**, **giant white radish**, **mouli**, **muli**, **daikon**

moong dal Mung bean

moong ke dal *South Asia* Dehusked and split mung beans

moongphali *South Asia* Peanut

moon sin *China* Eel

moorcock See **grouse**, **black grouse**

moorfowl See **grouse**, **black grouse**

moorkoppen *Netherlands* Filled tarts piled high with whipped cream (NOTE: Literally 'Moors' heads'.)

Moor's head Edam

Moors' heads *United States* As **Mohrenkopf**, but with various fillings and coverings

Moosbeere *Germany* Cranberry

moose A large wild herbivore, *Alces americana*, from the north of Canada. The membrane around the muscles gives the flesh a gamey flavour and should be removed before cooking. Marinating is recommended.

moo shu zoh *China* A pancake rolled around a filling of chopped pork stir-fried with spring onions, cloud ear fungus and eggs

mo qua *China* Fuzzy melon

mora *Italy, Spain* Blackberry

mora di gelso *Italy* Mulberry

morango *Portugal* See **strawberry**

Moravsky bochník syr *Czech Republic* A cows' milk cheese similar to Emmental

Moray eel A warm seawater fish, *Muraena helena*, with a brown and fawn mottled skin. It is up to 1.5 m in length, has excellent flesh although with many bones and is suitable for poaching or boiling.

morbidelle *Italy* Tiny dumplings used to garnish soup

Morbier A hard cows' milk cheese from Franche-Comté with a delicate flavour. The milk is treated with a lactic starter, coagulated with rennet and the curd, drained, pressed, brined and ripened for 2 to 3 months. Before brining, the cylinder of immature cheese is cut in half horizontally with a knife dipped in soot to give a characteristic black line when it is finally cut in wedges.

mørbrad *Denmark* Tenderloin of pork, i.e. that muscle corresponding to the fillet of beef

morceau *France* A small portion

morcela *Portugal* The Portuguese version of **boudin noir**

Morchel *Germany* Morel

morchella *Italy* Morel

Morchella esculenta *Botanical name* Morel

morcilla *Spain* The Spanish version of **boudin noir** from Asturia. Also called **boudin Asturien**

morcilla blanca *Spain* A **boudin blanc** made with chicken meat and hard-boiled eggs

morcilla negra *Spain* A **boudin noir** from Andalusia made from pig's blood, minced almonds, sweet peppers and parsley

more *Italy* Blackberries

morel The fruiting body of a highly prized wild fungus, *Morchella esculenta*, the commonest of the *Morchellaceae*, all of which are edible. It has an erect brownish fruit body with deep pits surrounded by irregular ridges 3 to 10 cm high and 3 to 7 cm in diameter, attached to a whitish stem which thickens towards the base. It must be washed carefully to remove grit and dirt from the pits. Available dried, fresh or canned. Also called **common morel**

morello cherry The best cooking variety of cherry, almost black in colour and slightly tart when ripe

morena *Spain* Moray eel

Moreton Bay bug *Australia* Sand lobster

morgen complet *Denmark* Full breakfast

morgenmad *Denmark* Breakfast

Morgenrot *Germany* A chicken broth with tomato purée and pieces of chicken meat (NOTE: Literally 'dawn'.)

morgh shekumpour *Central Asia* Iranian roast chicken stuffed with a mixture of chopped prunes, sultanas, dried apricots and chopped apple, flavoured with cinnamon and brown sugar. Served with **chelou**.

moriawase *Japan* A celebratory display of sashimi, yakitori, or other food arranged artistically on a wooden platter and garnished

moriglione *Italy* Pochard, a red headed diving duck

morille *France* Morel, the fungus

Moringa oleifera *Botanical name* The drumstick bean

Moringa pterygosperma *Botanical name* Drumstick vegetable

morkovka (*plural* **morkov**) *Russia* Carrot

mörkt rågbröd *Sweden* Toast

Morlacco *Italy* A semi-hard, scalded-curd cows' milk cheese similar to Montasio with a smooth rind and a firm paste with a few holes

mormora *Italy* Striped bream

Mornay, à la *France* With Mornay sauce

Mornay, fish White fish poached in fish stock, drained and kept warm, reduced cooking liquor added to boiling **béchamel sauce**, egg yolk whisked in, removed from heat, grated cheese added, seasoned, strained, butter and cream added, fish coated with sauce and gratinated with grated cheese

Mornay, sauce *England, France* Cheese sauce

Moroccan spearmint See **spearmint**

moroko *South Africa* Equal weights of greens (Swiss chard, spinach or similar, cleaned and chopped) and potatoes. The greens are placed in the bottom of the pan with chicken stock and the potatoes on top so that they are steamed. More stock or water is added as required until the potatoes are tender then all are mashed together. From the highland regions where potatoes can be grown.

Morón *Spain* A mild and delicate white cheese made from a variety of milks in the Seville region and often consumed within 24 hours of production. If kept longer it is steeped in olive oil and rubbed with paprika.

moros y cristianos *Caribbean* A Cuban dish of black eyed beans and long-grain rice cooked and mixed together with fried finely diced onion and garlic (NOTE: Literally 'Moors and Christians'.)

morötter *Sweden* Carrots

morozhenoe *Russia* Ice cream

mortadella *Italy* The original Bologna sausage, noted for its size and dating from the 12th century if not before. The composition is variable but the best contain only pork, garlic and seasoning. Cheaper ones may contain in addition, veal, tripe, donkey and spices, etc. All are ground to a fine paste and stuffed into pig's or beef bladders, boiled and hung up to dry for a few days.

mortadella di campotosta *Italy* A type of mortadella with a cylinder of bacon through the centre

mortadelle *France* A version of mortadella made from pork, salt pork fat and fresh pork fat, soaked in wine and smoked

mortar The round ceramic, stone or steel bowl in which food is placed to be broken down by the **pestle**. See also **pestle and mortar**

mortella *Italy* Myrtle

mortella di palude *Italy* Cranberry

mortifier *France* To hang meat or game

mortpølse *Norway* A sausage made from a mixture of beef, mutton and reindeer meat

morue *France* Cod, also used for salt cod

morue salée *France* Salt cod

Morus nigra *Botanical name* Mulberry

Morven *Scotland* A soft cows' milk cheese with a yellow rind from Scotland made into square blocks. It is similar to **Butterkäse** and like that cheese is flavoured with caraway seeds.

morwong *Australia* A perch-like fish, *Nemadactylus* family, sometimes called and sold as sea bream because of a superficial resemblance. It is found from New South Wales along the south coast to Western Australia and Tasmania. It has a grey back and a silver underside and grows to 4 kg. They are reasonably cheap, have a moist flesh with medium-sized flakes and can be cooked in any fashion. Also called **queen snapper**, **sea bream**

mosbolletjie *South Africa* A sweetish bun, eaten fresh or dried like a rusk, often flavoured with aniseed

moscardino bianco *Italy* Curled octopus

moscovita *Italy* A rich dessert mousse

moscovite, sauce *England, France* **Poivrade sauce** made with venison stock and finished at the last minute with a sweet fortified wine infused with juniper berries, soaked and plump currants and toasted pine nuts or chopped almonds

mosede kartofler *Denmark* Mashed potatoes

moskovitaeg *Denmark* Egg mayonnaise

Moskovski *Russia* A hard cows' milk cheese with a good flavour matured for 3 to 4 months

moss curled endive See **endive**

moss curled parsley Parsley

mossel *Netherlands* Mussel (blue)

Mosslands saddle of lamb *England* A boned and skinned saddle of lamb with the bone replaced by a pork fillet, the whole seasoned, rolled, tied and roasted in the oven at 180°C for about 70 minutes per kg or until cooked

mostacciolo *Italy* A rich fruit cake with almonds, chocolate and candied fruit

mostarda *Italy, Portugal* Mustard

mostarda di Cremona *Italy* A mixture of fruits preserved in a mustard-flavoured sugar syrup served with boiled meats. Also called **mostarda di frutta**

mostarda di frutta *Italy* Mostarda di Cremona

mostaza *Spain* Mustard

mostelle *France* Three-bearded rockling, the fish

mosterd *Netherlands* Mustard

mosto *Italy* Unfermented grape juice, must

Motal *Russia* A salty ewes' or cows' milk cheese from the Caucasus matured in brine for 3 to 4 months

motella *Italy* Three-bearded rockling, the fish

moth bean One of the most recently domesticated legumes, *Phaseolus aconitifolius*, which is very drought-resistant and is grown in India for its green or black seeds

mother The name often given to a undefined mass of microorganisms, yeasts, bacteria, etc. which are used to start a fermentation

mother of vinegar The whitish flora which grows on the surface of naturally brewed vinegar used as a starter for vinegar

moti sonf *South Asia* Fennel

mouclade *France* A mussel stew with a white wine and cream sauce thickened with egg yolks

moudre *France* To grind

moufflon See **mouflon**

mouflon *England, France* A wild sheep originally from Corsica but now the name applies to all large horned wild sheep. Also called **moufflon, muflon**

mouhalabiah *North Africa* Sweetened milk thickened with rice flour or puréed soft rice and flavoured with orange flower water. Served as a cold sweet.

mould 1. A hollow container of metal, ceramic, glass or plastic in which liquids are placed so as to set and take up the shape of the mould. Used for jellies, blanc-mange and a variety of solid foods set in aspic. 2. The fungi which grow on the surface of food left exposed to ambient conditions. Often moulds are not noticed until the fruiting bodies appear. These are usually either a white coating or a furry white, grey or green growth, both of which grow outwards from the original inoculating spore. Some moulds are deliberately encouraged as on the surface of Camembert and in blue cheeses where they are deliberately introduced into the centre by needling. Mould growth is also important in many fermented foods such as soya sauce and tempeh. Very few moulds are toxic and many have antibiotic (anti-bacterial) properties.

mould, to To form into a desired shape either by hand or in a mould

moule *France* 1. Mould for jellies, etc. 2. Mussel

moule à gateaux *France* Cake tin

moule à manqué *France* A deep cake tin with outward sloping sides. This facilitates icing or coating the sides of cakes baked in it.

moule à tarte *France* 1. Pie plate 2. Flan dish

moules à la marinière *France* Moules marinière

moules à l'escargot *Belgium* Mussels, stuffed and prepared to look like snails

moules marinière *England, France* Cleaned and debearded mussels cooked in a deep closed pan with dry white wine, chopped onion, chopped parsley and seasoning. When the mussels open they are served with the cooking liquor. Any which do not open must be discarded. Also called **moules à la marinière**

moules poulettes *France* Mussels presented in timbales with creamed mushrooms, parsley and lemon sauce

mouli 1. *France* A hand-operated food mill for puréeing soft food or slicing raw vegetables consisting of various perforated discs over and through which food is forced by rotating blades operated via a cranked handle 2. See **mooli**

mountain ash 1. Rowanberry 2. *United States* Various trees, *Sorbus americana* and *S. scopulina*, with larger fruit similar to the rowan, with berries used in the same way.

mountain cheese Bergkäse

mountain chicken *Caribbean* 1. Crapaud 2. Frog's legs

mountain cranberry Cowberry

mountain grouse Ptarmigan

mountain ham See **jamón serrano**

mountain hollyhock Wasabi

mountain oysters Prairie oysters

mountain pepper *Australia* The commonest Australian pepper grows on a small bush, *Tasmania lanceolata*, in Tasmania and Victoria. The leaves and the berry have an aromatic taste followed a few seconds later by the heat of the pepper. The leaves are usually dried and ground and used in the same way as pepper.

mountain pepper bread *Australia* Bread flavoured with mountain pepper added to the flour at the rate of 1 teaspoon (6 ml) per kg of flour. Also called **high country bread**

mountain spinach Orach

mountain yam A temperate climate variety of yam, *Dioscorea japonica*, which grows in Japan. It has a gluey texture and is often grated and used as a binder.

mousaka *Greece* Moussaka

mousetrap cheese *United Kingdom* Various types of bland tasteless Cheddar-type cheese imported from different countries and occasionally from British commercial cheese makers. Only suitable for baiting mousetraps. (*colloquial*)

mousquetaire, sauce *France* Mayonnaise flavoured with chopped onion or shallot which has been simmered in dry white wine. Served cold. (NOTE: Literally 'musketeer's sauce')

moussaka *England, Greece* Alternating layers of partially cooked and flavoured minced lamb and fried aubergine slices in a deep dish, topped with a **béchamel sauce** or a yoghurt, eggs and cheese mixture, flavoured with nutmeg, gratinated with breadcrumbs and cheese and baked in the oven. Served with salad and pitta bread. Also called **mousaka**

mousse *England, France* A flavoured egg mixture or purée of fruit, vegetables, fish or shellfish into which whisked egg whites and whipped cream are folded to make a stiff foam, this poured into a mould, set and demoulded. Gelatine may be used in the base mix as a setting agent or the mousse may be frozen. Served as a cold dessert, as a starter or sometimes used as a filling for fish paupiettes, etc.

mousse de foie gras *France* As pâté de foie gras but need contain only 55% or more of goose liver, almost as good as the pâté but will melt if heated

mousseline *France* A small individually served sweet or savoury mousse

mousseline, sauce *England, France* Hollandaise sauce mixed with whipped double cream prior to serving. Used with asparagus, broccoli and poached fish, chicken and egg dishes. Sometimes called sauce chantilly.

mousse perlée d'Irlande *France* Carragheen

mousseron *France* St George's mushroom, meadow mushroom

mousseuse, sauce *France* A type of compound butter made by whisking the juice of half a lemon, 16 g of salt and 800 ml of cream into a litre of softened butter which is then chilled and sliced for use with boiled fish

moutabel A purée dip similar to **hummus-bi-tahina**, made with aubergine. See also **mutabbal**

moutarde *France* Mustard

moutarde, sauce *France* Mustard sauce

moutarde de Meaux *France* A whole grain mustard made from a mixture of mustard seeds with their husks

moutarde extra-forte *France* English mustard

moutarde forte *France* English mustard

mouton *France* Sheep, mutton

mowra butter *South Asia* A soft yellow oil extracted from the seeds of the Indian butter tree. Used locally for cooking and exported for margarine manufacture. Also called **bassia fat, illipe butter**

moyashi *Japan* Bean sprouts

moyin-moyin *West Africa* Soaked and skinned black-eyed peas, partially cooked, are ground to a thick paste and oil added if preferred. Dried shrimp powder, tomatoes, onion, chilli pepper and seasoning are processed and mixed with the bean paste, which can then be steamed in banana-leaf parcels or baked in muffin tins at 200°C. All sorts of additional ingredients are added to the mixture according to the cook's fancy. Also called **moi-moi**

Mozzarella *Italy* A soft pale spun-curd cheese made from buffalo or cows' milk eaten very fresh. Formed into a round or pear shape and often stored in brine. Used for pizzas, lasagne and in salads. It becomes characteristically stringy when cooked. Contains 55 to 65% water, 18 to 20% fat and 16 to 21% protein.

Mozzarella affumicata *Italy* A smoked Mozzarella cheese

Mozzarella di bufala *Italy* A Mozzarella cheese made with pure buffalo milk and given legal protection. Also called **Trecce di bufala**

mozzarella in carrozza *Italy* A fried sandwich filled with Mozzarella cheese

MRM See **mechanically recovered meat**

mrouziya *North Africa* A Moroccan **tagine** made from middle neck of lamb rubbed with **ras el hanout**, powdered saffron, cinnamon and seasoning, simmered with blanched almonds, onions, butter and a little water and finished with raisins and honey about 30 minutes before serving

mruziyya *North Africa* A sweet-and-sour **tagine** from Morocco made with mutton, raisins, lemon, almonds and spices in a thick brown sauce. Reputed to last for up to a month without refrigeration.

MSG See **monosodium glutamate**

mtindi *East Africa* Buttermilk or cream

mtori 1. *East Africa* A thick Tanzanian soup from the Kilimanjaro region made from plantains, onions and tomatoes simmered in a strong beef stock until tender. This is then all mashed together and finished with butter. Sometimes meat that has been cooked to make the broth is removed from the bones, chopped into small pieces and added to the soup. **2.** *West Africa* A sort of mash made from boneless meat browned and boiled to which are added plantains, potatoes, onions, tomatoes, chilli pepper and seasoning. When all is soft the mixture, less the meat, is mashed or processed, the chopped meat is returned and finally coconut milk or butter is added before service.

muaba nsusu *Central Africa* A chicken and peanut butter soup from Angola and the two Congos. The chicken meat is removed from the bones after cooking and mixed with the soup made from the chicken broth thickened with tomato purée and peanut butter. Usually, chopped onions sautéed in palm oil are added.

muaddas *Persian Gulf* A type of risotto made with well-washed brown or green lentils, chopped onion and oil or clarified butter but with water in place of stock and wine

muamba de galinha *Central Africa* Chicken, marinated in lemon juice, browned in oil, cooked with onions, chilli pepper and tomatoes and towards the end with aubergine or squash. Finally moambé sauce and okra are added and all cooked until tender. From Angola.

mucca *Italy* Cow

Mucor A class of white moulds which grow on foods

Mucor pusillus A microorganism used for the production of a protease used in curdling milk for cheese production. Acceptable to vegetarians.

mud crab A dull green crab, *Scylla serrata*, growing up to 2 kg in weight and found throughout Southeast Asia in shallow muddy water. The claw meat is especially prized.

mudgeon Mesentery

mudjemeri *Turkey* Very similar to **kadin budu köfte**, but mutton finely minced and made into small balls fried in mutton fat

mu er *China* Cloud ear fungus

muesli A mixture of raw or semi-processed and dry cereals with dried vine fruits, chopped nuts, bran, sugar and chopped dried fruit, used as a breakfast cereal and eaten uncooked. Typical cereals used are wheat, rye, barley and oat flakes as well as others less common.

muffin 1. *England* A yeast-raised dough made with strong flour, milk, a little semolina and salt, rolled out and cut in 8 cm rounds, proven and cooked on a griddle or hot plate for about 7 minutes each side until golden brown **2.** *United States* A baking powder raised sweet sponge mix baked in deep patty tins to a soft doughy consistency. Sometimes flavoured with fresh or dried fruit, glacé cherries, honey or maple syrup.

muflon *England* Mouflon

mugicha *Japan* Roasted barley made into a tea which is very popular as an iced drink in summer

mugwort A wild perennial herb, *Artemesia vulgaris*, originally used in place of hops. The crushed dried leaves may be sprinkled on fatty meats and poultry prior to roasting. See also **white mugwort**

muhamara *Middle East* Red chilli pepper blended with a little water, olive oil, ground walnuts and a few stale breadcrumbs, allspice, ground cumin, salt and pomegranate (or lemon) juice until a smooth paste. Chilled and garnished with chopped parsley and served as a **mezze** dish. Also called **garmerong**

muhammar *Persian Gulf* Parboiled long-grain rice drained and mixed with sugar or honey (1:6 on uncooked rice) and poured over molten butter in a pot with a tight-fitting lid. A mixture of rose water infused with saffron and cardamom seeds is poured over and the pot sealed and cooked over a low heat for 20 to 25 minutes until the rice is cooked and has absorbed all the liquid. Served with meat or fish.

muhennettu *Finland* Stewed

muhennos *Finland* Stew

muik *Korea* Kombu

muikku *Finland* A tiny white fish similar to whitebait

mui kwai cheung *China* A sausage from Hong Kong made from a mixture of lean and fat pork, soya sauce, rosé wine, salt and sugar

mújol *Spain* Grey mullet

muk bampound *Cambodia* Squid

muki goma *Japan* Hulled sesame seeds

muktuk *Canada* The tough outer flesh of whales used by the Inuit people of Canada as food

mulard *France* A modern crossbred duck bred for the table and its liver. It is fleshier and leaner than the standard French breeds.

mulato *Mexico* A large brown chilli pepper, usually dried

mulberry The soft very perishable blackberry-like fruit of a tree, *Morus nigra*, which grows to about 10 m. Treat as blackberries.

mulet doré *France* Golden grey mullet

mulet farci *West Africa* Mulet farci à la Saint-Louisienne

mulet farci à la Saint-Louisienne *West Africa* A Senegalese dish of stuffed fish in the French style. A large 2 kg mullet is cleaned and skinned from the dorsal ridge without tearing the skin. The fish flesh is removed from the bones and mixed with soft breadcrumbs and a processed paste made from coriander, parsley, garlic, green onions and salt plus chopped tomatoes and tomato purée. This mixture is sewn back into the fish skin which is baked in the oven on a **mirepoix** of onions, tomatoes and chilli peppers sprinkled with thyme and oil. After baking for 25 minutes the covering is removed and fish stock poured over the vegetables and all cooked until the vegetables are soft and the fish browned. Also called **dem à la Saint Louisienne, dem farci, mulet farci**

mulet gris *France* Grey mullet

muli Mooli

mülk *Denmark* Milk

mull, to To heat wine or beer with or without spices and sugar

mulled wine Red wine heated with a sugar syrup flavoured with cinnamon stick, bruised dried ginger, cloves and orange zest. Traditionally heated by immersing a red hot poker in the mixture.

mullet See **grey mullet**, **red mullet**, **yellow eye mullet**, **sea mullet**

mulligan stew *United States* Burgoo

mulligatawny soup *England* A Victorian soup made from pre-browned chopped onions fried in oil with curry powder and flour, stock; tomato purée, chopped apple, chutney and desiccated coconut added; simmered and skimmed for 1 hour; liquidized, strained, seasoned and consistency corrected and served with a garnish of boiled rice. An alternative uses only chicken stock, fried curry powder (mixed Indian spices) and yoghurt. (NOTE: Adapted from the Tamil **milakutanni** ('pepper water') during the British occupation of India.)

mulloway *Australia* A fish, *Argyrosomus hololopidotus*, generally from the northern waters of Australia, although it is found in all states with the exception of Tasmania. They can grow to 50 kg but average 2 to 8 kg. The flesh is white and the smaller fish make excellent eating. They are normally grey-blue above shading to a silver belly. Also called **jewfish**, **butterfish**,

multer *Norway* Cloudberry

mum bar *Middle East* A highly spiced sausage from Iraq containing lamb and rice

muna *Finland* Egg

muna ja pekoni *Finland* Eggs and bacon

munakas *Finland* Omelette

munakokkeli *Finland* Scrambled eggs

muna kova *Finland* Hard-boiled eggs

muna pehmeä *Finland* Soft-boiled eggs

Münchener Weisswurst *Germany* A Brühwurst made from veal and possibly beef with parsley, filled into a light coloured casing. Served steamed or grilled with sauerkraut, puréed potatoes and sweet Bavarian mustard.

munchies *United Kingdom, United States* **1.** Snack foods **2.** The state of being peckish, hungry, e.g. to have the munchies

mung bean A small spherical green bean, *Phaseolus aureus*, with a white hilum, used as a source of **bean sprouts**, but may be eaten as a vegetable when the pod is young. Its principal use is as a pulse which is also made into a flour used in Indian cooking. If used as a pulse, it requires 8 hours soaking and long cooking. It may also be candied as a snack food or used to make a type of bean curd. Also called **golden gram**, **moong dal**, **green gram**, **green lentil**

mung bean flour Flour made from mung beans, sold natural colour or pink or green for use in making Southeast Asian sweetmeats

mung dal *South Asia* Dehusked and split mung beans

mungerela *South Asia* Nigella

munk *Sweden* Doughnut

munkar *Sweden* Dumplings

munna juusto *Finland* A delicately flavoured golden-coloured cheese made from cows' milk mixed with eggs

Münster *France, Germany* A soft yellow, surface-ripened cows' milk cheese with an orange-red rind from Alsace. It uses a lactic starter and has an open textured delicately flavoured paste with some cracks. It has a recorded history going back to the 7th century. The German variety is milder than the French. Traditionally served with Gewürztraminer and a bowl of cumin seeds. The French version has appellation d'origine status.

mun sum palung *Thailand* Cassava

munthari berry *Australia* Muntries

muntries *Australia* A pea-sized fruit from a low growing plant, *Kunzia pomifera*, that tastes like a cross between Granny Smith apples and sultanas. Their reddish green colour changes to a dull brown on cooking. They are used like dried vine fruits in pies, cakes and biscuits. Also called **munthari berry**

muòi *Vietnam* Salt

murag *Middle East* A meat and vegetable sauce from Iraq (NOTE: Literally 'sauce'.)

Murazzano *Italy* A soft cheese made from a mixture of 60% ewes' milk and 40% cows' milk. It is formed into small cylinders (up to 400 g), dry-salted, and then washed daily for 7 days. It has no rind and a dense texture.

Mürbeteig *Germany* Short pastry

Murbodner *Austria* A large (up to 15 kg) hard, cooked-curd cows' milk cheese resembling Emmental which is ripened for 2 months. It contains 39% water, 28% fat and 26% protein.

Murcott tangerine Honey tangerine

mûre *France* Mulberry

mûre de ronce *France* Blackberry

murena *Italy* Moray eel

murène *France* Moray eel

mûre sauvage *France* Blackberry

murex A small gastropod mollusc from the Mediterranean, the original source of the Roman imperial purple dye

murgh *South Asia* Chicken

murgh musallam *South Asia* A Pakistani dish of chicken roasted with spices

muriche *Italy* Murex, the shellfish

murlins Alaria

Murol *France* A semi-hard washed-rind pressed cows' milk cheese from the Auvergne made in 500 g discs with a hole in the centre. It has a red rind and the flavour of the paste starts off mild but gradually becomes strongly aromatic over the 7 week ripening period.

murraba tamar *Middle East* An Iraqi method of preparing dates. They are pitted, stuffed with halved walnuts, boiled and then left to soak in a heavy sugar syrup flavoured with lemon rind, cloves and cinnamon.

murraba tringe *Middle East* An Iraqi sweetmeat made from small triangles of citrus peel which are boiled in water repeatedly to remove bitterness then boiled in a heavy sugar syrup, left overnight, reboiled to 110°C, cooled and served with the syrup as a sweet

Murraya koenigii *Botanical name* Curry leaf

Murray river crayfish *Australia* A crayfish, *Euastacus armatus*, with a spiny blue shell and weighing up to 2 kg

murseddu *Italy* A flat bread from Calabria filled with a mixture of tripe, offal, tomatoes and spices

mursiellu alla cantanzarese *Italy* Pork stewed in wine

murtabah *South Asia* A southern dish consisting of a very large pancake filled with curried meat and onions

murtabak *Southeast Asia* Pasties with a savoury meat and vegetable filling, fried and eaten as a snack

mus *Italy* Polenta, wheat flour and milk boiled to a gruel with poppy seeds and sweetened. See also **farinata alla contadina**

musaca *Romania* Moussaka topped with soured cream instead of the customary cheese sauce

musakka *Turkey* A type of moussaka made with layers of fried sliced aubergine, fried onions, minced lamb or beef, sliced tomatoes and halved green peppers, baked or simmered very slowly

musaman curry A heavily spiced beef curry with coconut and peanuts. See also **gaeng mussaman**

Musa paradisica *Botanical name* The plantain

musaria *South Asia* A brass or cast iron pestle used with a matching mortar (**khalia**). Used for hard grains and spices.

Musa sapientum *Botanical name* The banana

muscade *France* Nutmeg

muscadine *United States* A white grape used for the table and for making raisins

muscatel raisins Dried muscat grapes, sometimes still in the original bunch

muscat grape Dessert grape

Muscheln *Germany* Shellfish

muscle *Spain* Mussels

musclos *Catalonia* Mussels

muscoletti *Italy* Muscolo

muscoli *Italy* Mussels

muscolo *Italy* Beef or veal shank. Also called **muscoletti**

muscovado sugar A soft and sticky partially refined cane sugar with fine crystals. Both light and dark varieties are available. Also called **Barbados sugar**, **moist sugar**

muscovy duck Barbary duck

musgo de Irlanda *Spain* Carragheen

mush *United States* A cooked porridge made from maize meal similar to polenta

mushi See **mushimono**

mushi-ki *Japan* A steamer, usually 2 or 3 tiered dishes with a topmost lid which fit over a pan of boiling water. The steamer dishes may be in metal or bamboo. Also called **seiro**

mushimono *Japan* Steamed or steaming as applied to cooking methods (NOTE: Abbreviated in recipes to 'mushi'.)

mushizakana to daikon to tamago tsuke awase *Japan* Pieces of white fish placed in individual bowls, moistened with sake, covered with a mixture of egg, sake, sugar and grated mooli, garnished with a spinach leaf, steamed until set, sprinkled with grated ginger and served immediately

mushkaki *East Africa* A Kenyan kebab of marinated meat

mushroom A general name given to various edible fungi but in the UK the name is generally applied to the common mushroom, *Agaricus bisporus*, which is widely cultivated and the field mushroom, *Agaricus campestris*. Common mushrooms are sold as buttons (completely closed caps to 2 cm diameter), closed cup (skin still closed below cup to 4 cm diameter), open cup (pink gills visible) and flat (fully open with dark brown gills). Other common types of cultivated mushroom in the UK are oyster, chestnut and shiitake. See also **fungi**

mushroom essence The juices extracted from mushrooms. This is best done by freezing them, thawing them and squeezing out the liquid. The tissue remaining may be chopped and added to duxelles before preparation.

mushroom ketchup A dark brown salty cold condiment sauce made with mushrooms

mushroom sauce 1. A suprême sauce but with sliced and sweated button mushrooms added after the velouté sauce has been strained. Used for boiled chicken, sweetbreads, etc. **2.** Fish velouté, consistency adjusted with fish stock or cream, seasoned, strained and finished with sliced button mushrooms sweated in butter and lemon juice. Served with boiled or poached fish. Also called **champignons, sauce aux**

mushroom sausage *England* A link sausage containing about 5% chopped fresh mushrooms in the usual rusk/meat mixture

mushroom soup A **mirepoix** of onions, leek and celery sweated in butter, flour added and cooked out without colour, white stock, a bouquet garni and chopped mushrooms added, simmered and skimmed for 1 hour, bouquet garni removed, liquidized, strained, seasoned and consistency adjusted. Finished with cream. Also called **crème de champignons**

mushroom soya sauce Soya sauce flavoured with an extract of straw mushrooms

mushy peas Marrowfat peas, cooked until soft and mashed. May be forced through a sieve to remove the skins. Served as an accompaniment.

musillo *Italy* The thick central cut of salt cod

muska börek *Turkey* A deep-fried puff pastry pasty (**börek**) filled with feta cheese and chopped parsley

Muskatblüte *Germany* Mace

Muskatnuss *Germany* Nutmeg

muskatnyi orekh *Russia* Nutmeg

musk mallow A bushy perennial, *Malva moschata*, growing to 60 cm. The leaves can be boiled and eaten as a vegetable.

musk melon A variety of sweet melon, *Cucumis melo*, smaller than the cantaloupe or winter melon but variable in size and with fine reticulate markings (a raised network) on smooth or ribbed yellowish or green skins. The aromatic flesh is green to salmon orange. It was the common variety grown in UK hothouses. When ripe the skin at the stalk end will give slightly when pressed. Also called **netted melon, nutmeg melon, cantaloupe**

Muslim curry A heavily spiced beef curry with coconut and peanuts. See also **gaeng mussaman**

muslin A relatively open simple woven cotton used for straining liquids or to wrap up a bouquet garni, dried herbs, spices, etc. from which the flavour is to be extracted in a simmering liquid

muslinger *Denmark* Mussels

muslo *Spain* Leg (of meat)

muso *Italy* Beef muzzle and nose

musola *Spain* Smooth hound, the fish

mussel A very common bivalve mollusc (various species) found worldwide usually attached to rocks near the water line, but some bury themselves in the sand. Most have dark blue to black shells up to 8 cm long, but some from New Zealand have blue and green shells. Generally sold live in their shells or removed, cooked and preserved in brine, sauce or by canning. Sometimes sold smoked. Cooked as any other mollusc. The mussel is a highly productive shellfish producing up to 10000 kg of meat per hectare per year. Varieties include the common mussel, green-lipped mussel, horse mussel and fan mussel.

mussel brose *Scotland* A soup made with cleaned and selected mussels covered with water and heated until they open, the liquor strained off and an equal amount of milk added. Lightly toasted oatmeal added, seasoning adjusted, all warmed and the reserved mussels added just before service.

Musselburgh pie *Scotland* Beef olives made with rump steak beaten out thin, each piece stuffed with a few mussels and some suet. After tying, the olives are dipped in seasoned flour and packed upright in a pie dish with chopped onions and water, then covered with foil and braised until cooked (1 to 2 hours). The dish is then allowed to cool, the strings removed and the olives covered with pastry, which is glazed with egg and baked at 220°C for 30 minutes until golden brown. Originally oysters were used.

mussel pâté *Wales* A pâté from the north of Wales made with mussels, egg yolk, soft herring roe, chopped celery, chopped carrots and breadcrumbs (5:4:3:2:2:2) processed with garlic and fresh herbs, consistency adjusted with double cream and brandy and cooked in a bain-marie in the oven at 180°C for 30 to 40 minutes

mustard 1. The name of a range of seeds with a generally hot taste native to Europe and India. None have any smell. Varieties include black mustard, brown mustard, white mustard and oriental mustard. **2.** A mixture of various ground or whole mustard seeds and other spices, etc. often moistened with vinegar, wine, verjuice or water, used as a condiment or for flavouring other dishes **3.** A fast growing brassica, *Brassica hirta*, usually grown as sprouted seed for the sharply flavoured seedling leaves and stems which are used in salads or as a garnish. If allowed to grow on, the young leaves may also be used in salads. See also **mustard and cress**

mustard and cream sauce Double cream whipped into English mustard let down with lemon juice as when making mayonnaise. Used on hors d'oeuvres and canapés.

mustard and cress Seeds of mustard and cress laid thickly on a water saturated substrate and root support, allowed to grow to the two-leaf stage and a height of 5 to 7 cm and sold in this form for cutting to use as a garnish. The mustard is sown 2 days after the cress so that both are of equal height.

mustard butter A compound butter made with 120 g of French mustard per kg of softened butter. It is shaped into a 2.5 cm roll, refrigerated and cut in 6 mm slices for use as a garnish on grilled meats, mackerel and herrings.

mustard greens Oriental mustard

mustard oil A deep yellow highly flavoured oil extracted from mustard seeds. Used in Indian cooking and in pickles and chutneys. Usually diluted with a blander oil.

mustard pickle See piccalilli

mustard sauce Béchamel sauce with the addition of English or French mustard and possibly vinegar. Used with pork, ham or cheese dishes, with fried or grilled herring or mackerel and with hot boiled tongue. Also called **moutarde, sauce**

mustard seeds Small (up to 1.5 mm diameter) seeds used extensively in Indian cooking. Usually fried before use to bring out the pungent flavour. See also **mustard**

mustella Italy Forkbeard, a fish similar to whiting

Musteweck Germany A bread roll with chopped pork

mustikka Finland 1. Blueberry 2. Bilberry

mustikkakeito Finland A dessert made from corn flour-thickened blueberry juice

mustikkapiiras Finland Blueberry tart

mutabbal Middle East A purée dip or **mezze** similar to **hummus-bi-tahina**, but substituting the flesh of grilled aubergines for the chick peas. Also called **moutabel**

mutton The meat of sheep older than one year but nowadays over two years. The meat is darker and stronger-flavoured than lamb and was preferred in Victorian times. Most mutton sold today is from old breeding ewes killed at 3 to 5 years and is generally tough and only suitable for boiling. The best mutton, now difficult to find, is killed at 18 months and is more expensive than lamb.

mutton broth Blanched neck or scrag end of mutton simmered with water or stock and washed barley, skimmed, brunoise carrot, leek, turnip, celery and onion and a bouquet garni added, simmered and skimmed, meat removed, diced lean meat returned, bouquet garni removed, seasoned and served with chopped parsley

mutton fat A hard highly saturated fat from lamb and mutton used for cooking in the Middle East. Contains 50% saturated, 45% monounsaturated and 5% saturated fat.

mutton fish 1. A type of abalone, Haliotis naevosa, from Australian waters **2.** Ocean pout **3.** See **mutton snapper**

mutton ham Cured leg of mutton. Used in Muslim cooking.

mutton sausage England An English-type sausage made with lean mutton, mutton suet, breadcrumbs, chopped boiled bacon and seasoning, moistened with mutton stock

mutton snapper An olive-green snapper, Lutjanus analis, fished for sport in the warm western waters of the Atlantic

muy hecho Spain Well done. Used of meat, steak, etc.

myaso Russia Miaso

myaso po-tatarsky Russia Steak tartare made with triple minced seasoned fillet steak mixed with egg yolks, chopped spring onions and capers, horseradish sauce, Worcestershire sauce, oil and pepper vodka

myata Russia Miata

mycella Denmark A semi-hard full-fat cows' milk cheese shaped in cylinders and with a creamy yellow blue-veined paste. Milder than Danish blue.

mylta med grädde Sweden A compote of cloudberries with cream

mynce pie United Kingdom Mince pie

myoban Japan Alum

myoga Japan Ginger buds

Myristica fragrans Botanical name Mace and nutmeg

myrobalans Cherry plum

myrrh Sweet cicely

Myrrhis odorata Botanical name Sweet cicely

myrte France Myrtle

Myrte Germany Myrtle

myrte des marais France Bog myrtle

myrtille France Bilberry, blueberry

myrtle A half-hardy evergreen shrub, Myrtus communis, growing to 3 m with small shiny leathery leaves which have a spicy orange fragrance used for stuffings and with pork or lamb. The small white flowers excluding the green calyx may be used in fruit salads and the dried black berries have a mild juniper flavour and may be used as juniper berries. Grows in Mediterranean climates and is common in Corsican and Sardinian cooking. An oil is extracted from the ripe berries.

myrtle pepper Allspice

Myrtus communis *Botanical name* Myrtle

myśliwska *Poland* An expensive smoked and linked pork sausage in a natural casing

Mysore coffee A rich full-flavoured coffee from Mysore in Southern India

Mysost *Norway* A fawn, slightly sweet caramel-flavoured cheese made from the whey from a mixture of cows' and goats' milk in a similar manner to Ricotta. The whey is boiled and reduced to a brown sticky mass containing whey proteins, lactose and caramelized sugars. It is stirred whilst cooling to a solid to prevent crystallization of the sugars. Usually cut or shaved in very thin slices and served on crispbread, but also used in cooking. Also called **Gjetöst**, **Norwegian whey cheese**

Mysuostur *Iceland* A cheese very similar to Mysost made from the whey of cows' milk

naam gwa *China* Winter squash

naan *South Asia* Nan bread

naartjie *South Africa* A variety of tangerine

naawr mai *China* Glutinous rice

naba *Spain* Kohlrabi

nabemono *Japan* A single-pot meal cooked at the table using sliced raw prepared ingredients and usually a central casserole of simmering stock. **Sukiyaki** and **shabu shabu** are the two most famous.

nabo *Portugal, Spain* Turnip

nabo sueco *Spain* Swede

nachos *Mexico* Pieces of fried tortilla topped with grated cheese, browned under the grill and garnished with green chillies. Served as a snack.

Nachspeise *Germany* Dessert, sweet

Nachtisch *Germany* Dessert, sweet

nadru *South Asia* Lotus

nagaimo *Japan* Yam

nagami kumquat The commonest kumquat in Europe and the USA, Fortunella margarita, grown mainly in Morocco, Palestine, Brazil and the USA. It is an oval fruit with a smooth rind and a pronounced spicy citrus flavour. The flesh is acidic with a few seeds. Also called **oval kumquat**

naganegi *Japan* Asian leek

nagashi-bako *Japan* A small square mould used for making jellies and jellied (e.g. aspic coated) food

nage, à la *France* Shellfish cooked in white wine with aromatic vegetables and herbs

nagelkaas *Netherlands* A pale strong-flavoured and very hard and dense cows' milk cheese made with a lactic starter, flavoured with cumin and cloves and matured for six months. The hard yellow rind is usually oiled. The unspiced version is Kanterkaas. Also called **Friese nagelkaas**, **Friese**

Nagelrochen *Germany* Thornback ray

nagerecht *Netherlands* Dessert

nagkesar *South Asia* Cassia buds

naita jute *Middle East* A plant related to okra. See also **meloukhia**

nai tsom *East Africa* The Eritrean name for **ye som megeb**

näkinkenka *Finland* Mussel

nakiri bocho *Japan* A vegetable knife rather like a very sharp diminutive chopper. Used for peeling and the production of the characteristic vegetable cuts of Japan.

näkkileipä *Finland* Crispbread, hard rye bread, hardtack

naky pliak *Eastern Europe* A cabbage soufflé considered to be a good test of a Ukrainian cook. It is made from shredded cabbage which has been lightly salted and pressed, then covered in boiling water and left for 3 to 4 days to partially ferment. The drained, rinsed and dried cabbage is mixed into an onion-, garlic- and milk-based roux sauce, flavoured with cheese, thickened with egg yolks and lightened by folding in stiffly beaten egg whites (cabbage to eggs 2:1), placed in a buttered soufflé dish, dotted with butter sprinkled with breadcrumbs and baked at 190°C.

naleśniki *Poland* Fritters made from cottage cheese mixed with egg yolks and butter sandwiched between thin pancakes, cut into squares, dipped in batter and deep-fried

nama-age *Japan* Lightly fried bean curd

nama fu *Japan* Fresh gluten cake

namagashi *Japan* Soft cakes usually including adzuki bean paste (**anko**)

namasu *Japan* Julienned mooli and carrot salted in a bowl for 30 minutes, wrung out and dressed with a rice vinegar flavoured with soya sauce, chopped ginger root and sugar. Best left to mature for 8 hours.

nama-uni *Japan* Raw sea urchins

nambanzuke *Japan* Soused fish made as for **escabeche** from fried fish using **mirin**, soya sauce, chillies and **dashi** in the marinade (NOTE: Namban means 'southern savages', referring to the Spanish and Portuguese who brought this dish with them)

nam dong ca *Vietnam* Shiitake mushroom

ñame *Spain* Yam

nameko *Japan* A small gelatinous mushroom native to Japan, used in soups and sunomono. Usually sold preserved in a light brine.

nameshi *Japan* Green rice made by mixing salted plain boiled rice with shredded spinach that has been cooked 5 minutes and wrung out

namida *Japan* See **wasabi** (NOTE: Literally 'tears'.)

nam jim kratiem *Thailand* A sweet-and-sour garlic sauce with chillies, made by slowly cooking the ingredients with a little water until soft and reduced to a sauce, then salting to taste

na mool *Korea* Accompaniments and side dishes at Korean meals, often marinated or cold cooked vegetables

nam pa *Laos* A thin straw coloured fish sauce similar to **nuoc mam**

nam pla *Thailand* The salty brown liquid which drains from salted and fermented fish used as a flavouring in the same way as soya sauce. Also called **fish sauce**

nam pla ra *Thailand* A thin sauce made by boiling nam pla with lemon grass and makrut lime leaves and straining

nam prik *Thailand* The general name for Thai relishes made from a mixture of spices, herbs and other flavouring agents such as red chillies, dried shrimps, garlic, trassi, fish sauce, brown sugar, shallots, tamarind, lime juice, peanuts, sour fruits, etc. all processed together

nam prik pao *Thailand* A hot chilli sauce made from roasted red deseeded chillies fried in oil with garlic, onions and shrimp paste, then all processed with brown sugar and tamarind to a thin paste. Also called **roasted chilli paste**, **roasted curry paste**

nam som *Thailand* Rice vinegar

nan (bread) 1. *South Asia* A yeast-raised bread made from white flour and yoghurt, cooked very quickly as a large flat pear shaped bread on the side of a tandoori oven. The shaped dough is moistened so that it sticks to the side of the oven and is hooked off when cooked. Served with Indian meals. **2.** *Iran* Bread

nane lavash *Central Asia* The Iranian yeast-raised flat bread made with a mixture of wholemeal and plain flour beaten or kneaded for at least 20 minutes with as much water as it will take added. The dough is then rolled out very thin, stretched and pressed onto an oiled preheated smooth griddle plate with a cloth-covered cushion, baked at 290°C until the surface bubbles then turned over to complete the cooking (about 5 minutes in all). The dough is not proved or rested.

nangka *Indonesia, Malaysia* Jackfruit

nangpur suntara *South Asia* Ponkan mandarin

nan nan bin *Burma* Coriander leaves

nan nan zee *Burma* Coriander seeds

nannee *Caribbean* Anise seeds

nannygai *Australia* Redfish

nano dok *Central Asia* A flavouring mix from Iran made of turmeric browned in clarified butter, with powdered dried mint added off the heat. It is used for flavouring soups, salads etc.

Nantais *France* **1.** A semi-hard smooth-textured, washed-rind cheese made from cows' milk. The rind is light brown and the smooth paste has a strong flavour and smell. Also called **Véritable Nantais 2.** A small almond cake

Nantais duck See **Nantes duck**

nantaise, à la *France* In the Nantes style, i.e. garnished with peas, potatoes and turnips. Used especially of roasts.

Nantes duck One of the two main breeds of French domesticated duck, similar to the Aylesbury and less plump than the Rouen duck. It is usually killed at about 2 kg and provides 4 portions It may be braised or poêléed as well as being roasted.

Nantua, à la *France* In the Nantua style, i.e. garnished with crayfish tails and truffles. Used especially of fish.

Nantua, sauce *England, France* 200 ml of cream per litre of **béchamel sauce**, reduced by one third, consistency adjusted with more cream and finished with crayfish butter and a few small cooked and shelled crayfish tails

nap, to To cover a food item, usually a piece of meat or fish on a plate or dish, with sauce

Napfkuchen *Germany* A yeast-raised sweet bun with raisins

Napfschnecke *Germany* Limpet

Naples biscuit *United States* A light dessert or tea biscuit similar to a sponge finger

Naples medlar Azarole

Napoléon *France* Cream slice made with layers of puff pastry

Napoléon biscuits Two biscuits sandwiched together with a filling of jam and dusted with icing sugar

napolitaine, à la *France* In the Neapolitan style, i.e. garnished with spaghetti in tomato sauce, grated cheese and chopped tomatoes. Alternatively a description of spaghetti served with a tomato sauce and grated cheese.

nappa cabbage *United States* Chinese leaves

napper *France* To nap

naranja *Spain* Orange, the fruit

naranja amargo *Spain* Seville orange

nara nut The seed of a gourd from a spiny shrub, *Acanthosicyos horrida*, that grows in South West Africa and is about the size of a large melon seed. Also called **butternut**, **butter pit**

narbonnaise, à la *France* In the Narbonne style, i.e. garnished with haricot beans, aubergine and tomatoes

nargisi *South Asia* A forcemeat of finely ground meat blended with aromatics and herbs, moulded around a hard-boiled egg rather like a Scotch egg and baked or fried (NOTE: Literally 'narcissus'.)

narial *South Asia* Coconut

narijal *South Asia* A young coconut

narm yu *China* Bean curd cheese

narrow-headed softshell turtle A species of turtle from Thailand now endangered due to over exploitation

narrow-leaf sage See **Spanish sage**

naruto *Japan* A Japanese fish cake formed into a cylinder and the surface decorated with red colouring after steaming to give an attractive garnish when sliced. See also **kamaboko**

naseberry Sapodilla

nasello *Italy* Hake, the fish

nashab *Persian Gulf* Deep-fried filo pastry rolls about 12 cm by 10 to 15 mm in diameter, filled with a mixture of ground cashew nuts and walnuts, caster sugar and ground cardamom seeds then deep-fried at 190°C

nashi Asian pear

nasi *Indonesia, Malaysia* Rice

nasi goreng *Indonesia* Fried rice with chopped pork, ham, onion, garlic, seafood and vegetables. Served with acar, krupek and strips of cooked egg omelette.

nasi padang *Indonesia* A very hot-flavoured and spicy rice dishes from Padang, Sumatra

nässelkål *Sweden* Nettle soup made from fresh young nettles cooked like spinach, chopped and added to a seasoned beef stock thickened with a blond roux, the whole finished with chopped chives and served with one poached egg per portion

nasturtium A trailing plant, *Tropaeolum majus*, with bright red to yellow trumpet-shaped flowers and round green leaves. The leaves and flower buds may be used in salads, the flowers as decoration and the young green seeds may be pickled in vinegar and resemble capers. Also called **Indian cress**, **Jesuits' cress**

Nasturtium officinale *Botanical name* Watercress

nasturzio *Italy* Nasturtium

nasu *Japan* Aubergine

nata 1. *Spain* Cream 2. *Philippines* A translucent degraded starch, probably a dextran, which appears on the surface of fruits after they are inoculated with a dextranase producing bacteria. It is scraped off, washed and boiled and used as a flavouring for desserts.

nata batida *Spain* Whipped cream

nata de coco *Philippines* A **nata** produced on coconut flesh

nata de pina *Philippines* A **nata** produced on pineapple flesh

natillas *Spain* A soft custard dessert made with ewes' milk and flavoured with cinnamon and lemon

natillas piuranas *Spain* A dessert made from a caramelized milk and sugar. See also **arequipe**

native mint *Australia* A common ornamental garden bush in the southeastern states with edible flowers and strong mint flavoured leaves which are used fresh or dried and ground. The flavour intensifies over time and it should be used sparingly. There are a number of indigenous plants which are called native mints. Used in dressings, sauces, curries and in baking and desserts.

native oyster A smaller variety of oyster, *Ostrea edulis*, with a smooth flat shell famous for its flavour. Can grow to 12 cm, but normally sold somewhat smaller.

native peach *Australia* Quandong fruit

native pepperberry *Australia* Small fruits intermediate in size between a peppercorn and a pea which can be used whole or dried and ground as a substitute for pepper

native peppermint *Australia* A widespread eucalyptus, *Eucalyptus dives*, whose grey-green leaves have a strong peppermint flavour with a hint of eucalyptus. They are best used dried and ground in desserts and cakes, or the whole leaves may be used to make a tea. The essential oil is sold separately.

native spinach *Australia* Warrigal greens

native tamarind *Australia* A relative of the lychee, *Diploglottis cunninghamii* and *D. campbellii*, with a hard woody orange-coloured shell and segmented fleshy pulp around a central stone. The brilliant orange flesh has a sharp, sour, mandarin type flavour and is excellent in sauces, jams, ice cream and the like.

native thyme *Australia* Wild thyme

natsudaidai *Japan* A naturally occurring hybrid of *Citrus* relatively unknown outside Japan

natsumegu *Japan* Nutmeg

Natterkopf *Germany* Viper's bugloss

nattmat *Sweden* Solitary midnight snacks, or **vickning** (NOTE: Literally 'night food'.)

natto *Japan* Soaked and steamed soya beans inoculated with *Bacillus natto*, made up into small parcels with rice straw and allowed to ferment for a day in a hot humid conditions when they develop a strong flavour and stickiness. Usually served with hot rice, but sometimes in soup and salads.

natur *Germany* Plain, not garnished or decorated

naturale *Italy* Plain, not garnished or decorated

nature *France* Plain as in omelette nature, or a description of tea or coffee without the addition of milk

naturel, au *France* Plainly cooked without sauces or garnish or served in its plain uncooked state as e.g. huîtres au naturel

Naturschnitzel *Germany* Plain veal cutlet or escalope, not panéed

nau *Vietnam* To cook

naudanliha *Finland* Beef

naudanpaisti *Finland* Beefsteak

naun *Central Asia* A yeast-raised bread from Afghanistan made with a mixture of equal parts of wholemeal and white flour. After rising it is formed into tear shapes about 1 cm thick which, when proved, are marked with the fingers in three long grooves before being baked at 220°C on a flat sheet for about 15 minutes.

nauris *Finland* Turnip

navaja *Spain* Razor shell

navarin *France* A lamb or mutton stew with onions and potatoes

navarin à la printanière *France* A lamb or mutton stew with onions, garlic, root vegetables, peas, green beans, herbs and seasoning

navel orange A type of sweet orange which has a small secondary fruit embedded in the apex of the primary fruit. They are seedless, with deep orange, easily peeled rinds and with a rich sweet flavour. One of the best dessert fruits. They are unsuitable for processing as the juice develops bitterness on standing. The two common varieties are the Washington and the Bahia.

navet 1. *France* Any type of turnip **2.** *England* Small immature and tender white turnips tinged with red, generally require no peeling

navets, purée de Turnip soup

navone *Italy* Swede

navy bean *United States* A variety of haricot bean used for making the ubiquitous canned baked beans. Also called **American navy bean**, **Boston bean**, **great northern bean**, **pea bean**, **yankee bean**

nazi *East Africa* The Tanzanian word for coconut

nazuna *Japan* Salt pickle made with a variety of green leaves

'ncapriata *Italy* A bean purée flavoured with chillies and other spices (NOTE: From Puglia)

ndayu *East Africa* Roasted young goat served as a celebratory meal in Tanzania

n'dizi *East Africa* Plantain

n'dizi na nyama *East Africa* Cubed boneless beef simmered with seasoning, curry powder and cayenne pepper until almost cooked, then sliced plantains added for a further 10 minutes cooking. Finally, onions, tomatoes and tomato paste which have been fried in oil then simmered with a bay leaf in coconut milk are added to the meat plantain mixture. Served with rice or **ugali**.

neapolitan Made in multicoloured layers

Neapolitan ice cream See **cassata**

Neapolitan parsley A type of parsley grown for its leaf stalks used in the same way as celery

Neapolitan sauce A tomato sauce from Naples flavoured with onion, basil and parsley

nebu *South Asia* Lemon

necares *Spain* The blue velvet swimming crab most favoured by Spanish gourmets

neck end of pork A joint of meat from the shoulder of the pig near the neck. Usually boned and rolled.

neck end of veal The ribs and muscles behind the shoulder and in front of the best end. Used for stewing and sautéing after boning out.

neck fillet *United Kingdom* Scrag end of lamb

neck of beef *United Kingdom* Clod

nectar 1. The sugary liquid extracted from flowers by bees which after ingestion is chemically transformed and regurgitated as honey **2.** Any thick sweetened fruit juice

nectarine The fruit of a deciduous tree, *Prunus persica* var. *nectarina*, with a worldwide distribution. The fruit is a variant of the peach with a smooth shiny orange red skin and white to red firm flesh surrounding a rough central stone. Use as peach.

needle A thin steel rod, sharpened at one end and pierced with a flattened hole at the other, used for trussing or larding a bird or piece of meat

needle, to To pierce food singly or repeatedly with single or multiple needles either to make it more absorptive, to introduce microorganisms as e.g. in making blue cheeses, or to inject fluids through hypodermic needles (hollow needles) as in quick curing or tenderizing of meats

needle cut A very fine **julienne** vegetable cut. See also **sen-giri**

needlefish A fish similar to the garfish found in the Atlantic and Pacific oceans

neep *Scotland* Scottish for swede although sometimes thought to be a turnip. The English white turnips are called new turnips in Scotland, e.g. bashit neeps, mashed swede. (*colloquial*)

neep bree *Scotland* A soup made from chopped swedes blanched then sautéed in butter with onion and a pinch of ginger for 10 minutes and simmered with stock and milk until soft prior to puréeing. Equal weights of liquid and vegetables are used.

neep purry *Scotland* A purée of swede or turnip, mashed with butter and a little ground ginger

neeseberry Sapodilla

nèfle *France* Medlar

nèfle d'Amérique *France* Sapodilla

negi *Japan* Asian leek

negi shigi-yaki *Japan* Broiled leeks. See also **Japanese broiled vegetables**

négresse en chemise *France* A dessert made of a chocolate ice cream or mousse, heaped up in the centre of a plate with cream over and surrounding it

negretti *Italy* Individual square chocolate coated almond cakes

negritas *Spain* Chocolate mousse topped with whipped cream

neguilla *Spain* Nigella

neige *France* White of egg beaten to a froth (NOTE: Literally 'snow', as in *oeufs à la neige* 'floating islands'.)

neige, monter en *France* To whisk egg whites to a stiff peak

neige de Florence *France* Very small thin flakes of pasta

neiha kinkan *Japan* Meiwa kumquat

Nelke *Germany* Clove, the spice. Also called **Gewürznelke**

Nelubium nucifera *Botanical name* The lotus plant

nenna *South Asia* Loofah

neohesperidin The compound responsible for the bitterness of the Seville orange

nep *Vietnam* Uncooked glutinous rice. See also **xoi nep**

Nepal cardamom A cheap cardamom substitute from a perennial plant, *Amomum subulatum*, which has ribbed and deep red pods becoming black or brown when dried and resembling a small coconut (up to 2.5 cm long). The seeds have a distinctly camphorous flavour.

nepaul pepper *United States* A chilli pepper similar to cayenne with a sweet pungent flavour

Nepeta cataria *Botanical name* Catmint

Nephelium lappaceum *Botanical name* Rambutan

Nephelium longana *Botanical name* Longan

Nephelium mutabile *Botanical name* Pulasan

nero *Italy* Black

neslesuppe *Norway* Nettle soup

nespola *Italy* Medlar

nespola del Giappone *Italy* Loquat, Japanese medlar

Nessel *Germany* Nettle

Nesselrode *France* Containing chestnut purée

Nesselrode pudding A dessert made from chestnut purée, egg yolks, cream and possibly candied fruits, cooked without curdling then frozen in a mould. See also **pouding Nesselrode**

nesting frying baskets Two wire mesh baskets one slightly smaller than the other, used to make edible bowls by trapping finely shredded or precooked ingredients between the two baskets before deep-frying them

netted melon Musk melon

nettle A wild plant, *Urtica dioica,* which grows in clusters on well-manured ground with leaves that sting the exposed skin. The young leaves may be used as spinach or to make soup and lose their stinging capacity on boiling. Also called **stinging nettle**

nettle kail *Scotland* A boiling fowl stuffed with a mixture of sweated onions cooked in suet, thickened with oatmeal and flavoured with ransons or mint is simmered in seasoned water for 60 to 80 minutes and young nettles or spinach added for the last 10 minutes of cooking together with a little fine oatmeal or barley flour to thicken. Served with the buttered nettles.

nettoyer *France* To clean

Neufchâtel *France* A soft white creamy cows' milk cheese from Normandy with a rind like Camembert and a salty lactic taste. It is produced in various small shapes and eaten young. See also **Bondon**, **carré de Bray**. Also called **Coeur**, **Briquette**

neutral fat Fat with no excess fatty acid

New Bedford pudding *United States* A molasses-sweetened pudding made with cornmeal, flour, milk and eggs

Newburg, sauce *England, France* Diced lobster meat cooked in court bouillon or oil and butter, drained, covered with Madeira wine and reduced, seasoned with cayenne pepper, cream and fish stock added, simmered then thickened with egg yolks. The lobster may be flamed with brandy and the pounded coral and creamy parts may be added towards the end.

new cheese Caerphilly

new cocoyam A plant with yam-like fruit. See also **tannia**

New England boiled dinner *United States* A one-pot dinner of corned beef or chicken cooked with cabbage, potatoes, carrots, etc. and served with horseradish sauce or mustard

New Mexico chilli A variety of red and hot chilli pepper about 8 cm by 0.5 cm from Mexico and the southern USA. They are used in curries and sauces and are often dried and ground. In New Mexico green chillies are included in this category.

newrex rice A type of long-grain rice

newspaper cooking *United Kingdom* A method of cooking cleaned whole fish by wrapping in 8 or 9 layers of newspaper, thoroughly soaking in water then cooking in a moderate oven until the paper is completely dry (approximately 1 hour for a 1.5 kg fish)

new turnips *Scotland* The English turnip 1

New Zealand grapefruit A citrus hybrid with characteristics similar to grapefruit but not directly related. Taken from Shanghai to Australia in 1820. It has a straw-coloured coarse flesh which is tender and far more juicy than most grapefruit. The flavour combines that of grapefruit with a trace of lime and lemon. Usually used as a breakfast fruit. Also called **poorman orange**

New Zealand spinach A half-hardy creeping perennial, *Tetragonia tetragonioides* or *T. expansa*, grown as an annual. The thick triangular leaves are used in the same way as spinach. It is at its best eaten young and the water should be changed during the cooking. See also **Warrigal greens**

nfissat *North Africa* A thin mutton broth from Morocco

nga *Thailand* Sesame seed

nga choy *China* Mung bean sprouts

nga hnap *Burma* Bummaloe, the fish

ngalakh *West Africa* A sweetened porridge from Senegal made from couscous or **karaw** cooked as normal with some butter then mixed just before service with a sauce made from equal parts of baobab fruit juice or tamarind juice and peanut butter with sugar, vanilla essence, nutmeg, orange flower water and raisins. Also called **ngallax**

ngallax *West Africa* Ngalakh

nga-man-gyaung *Burma* Small fish similar to anchovy, prepared like **ikan bilis**

nga-mote-phyu *Burma* Pomfret, the fish

ngan pye ye *Burma* Fish sauce similar to **nuoc mam**

ngan pye ye chet *Burma* A strong-flavoured sauce made from fish sauce (**ngan pye ye**), lemon grass, garlic and chilli powder

ngapi *Burma* A dark grey paste made from fermented fish commonly used as a flavouring in Burmese cooking (NOTE: Literally 'rotten fish'.)

ngapi htaung *Burma* A pungent dipping paste made from a finely ground mixture of ngapi, onions, garlic and dried shrimps

ngapi nut The seed of a Burmese jungle tree, *Pithecolobium lobatum*, with a smell similar to ngapi. Used raw or cooked.

nga-youk-kuan *Burma* Peppercorn

nga yut thee *Burma* Chilli pepper

ngege *East Africa* A type of tilapia, *Oreochromis esculentus*, from the Great Lakes region of East Africa

ng he *Vietnam* Turmeric

ng heung fun *China* Five-spice powder

ngun jump fun *China* Wheat starch

ngun nga choy *China* Silver sprouts

ngup jern *China* Duck feet

ngup yu *China* Cuttlefish

ngu vi huong *Vietnam* Five-spice powder

nho *Vietnam* Raisin or grape

nhopi *South Africa* **Sadza** dumplings mashed and mixed with cooked and mashed pumpkin (3:1), flavoured with sugar and peanut butter, cooked for a few minutes and thinned with the pumpkin cooking water to the desired consistency. Served with green vegetables.

niacin See **vitamin B3**

niacinamide See **vitamin B3**

niban dashi *Japan* The second infusion in making dashi. See also **dashi**

niboshi *Japan* Dried and salted fish similar to Bombay duck. Used for flavouring or fried as a snack food or side dish.

nibuta *Japan* Boiled and seasoned pork

niçoise, à la *France* In the Nice style, i.e. garnished with olives, tomatoes, garlic, French beans, etc.

niçoise, salade *France* Salade niçoise

niçoise, sauce *England, France* Vinaigrette with French mustard, diced anchovies and chopped capers, olives and parsley. Served with meat salads and hard-boiled eggs.

nicotinic acid See **vitamin B3**, **E375**

nidi *Italy* Tangles of thin pasta (NOTE: Literally 'nests'.)

nido, al *Italy* In a nest, i.e. one ingredient in another

niébé et maïs *West Africa* A dish based on soaked dried cow peas, boiled. See also **adalu**

Nieheimer *Germany* A soft cheese made with skimmed cows' milk coagulated with lactic acid. The curd is salted and flavoured with caraway seeds, formed into 40 g cheeses, ripened for a short time and wrapped in hop leaves. Also called **Hopfenkäse**

Nieren *Germany* Kidneys

Nierenfett *Germany* Suet

nigella *England, Italy* The small black seeds of an annual plant, *Nigella sativa*, related to love-in-a-mist and resembling onion seeds. They have a delicate, slightly peppery flavour and are used in Indian spice mixtures and to flavour bread in India and the Middle East. (NOTE: Not to be confused with **black cumin**.)

Nigella sativa *Botanical name* Nigella

nigelle *France* Nigella

niger oil A highly flavoured oil extracted from the seeds of a plant, *Guizotia abyssinica*, which grows in Africa and India. It has a pleasant nutty flavour.

nigiri-zushi *Japan* A hand-moulded sushi made in an oval shape with the fillings placed on top after smearing the ball with a little **wasabi**

nihai-zu *Japan* A vinegar-based dressing for **sunomono** consisting of a mixture of rice vinegar, soya sauce and **dashi**

nihura *Nepal* Drumstick vegetable

nijuseki, nijusseki *Japan* Asian pear

nikiri sake *Japan* Sake boiled to remove alcohol before incorporating in cold uncooked dips and sauces

niku-ryori *Japan* Meat

nikuzuku *Japan* Nutmeg

Nile perch *Central Africa* Capitaine

nimboo acar *South Asia* A lemon pickle made from quartered lemons with the pips removed. These are layered in a jar with a little salt, chopped ginger, bay leaf and chilli between each layer then covered with lime juice and finally a thin layer of salt. The pickle is left covered for at least 2 weeks to mature.

nimono *Japan* Simmered, e.g. of meats or vegetables in a well-flavoured stock using an

otoshibuta. The solids are usually served with a little of the stock.

ninfea *Italy* Lotus

Niolo *France* A soft, washed-rind cheese from Corsica made in a brick shape (600 g) from a mixture of ewes' and goats' milk. It is dry-salted and ripened for 15 days.

nishin *Japan* Herring

nisin See **E234**

níspola *Spain* Medlar

nitrate of potash See **saltpetre**

nitrites Salts of nitrous acid which are involved in producing the pleasant pink colour of cured meat. They are formed by reduction of nitrates (saltpetre) by bacterial action in the meat or can be included in the curing liquor. Because of the method of production sal prunella contains a little nitrite as impurity.

nitrogen The inert gas which forms 79% of air, used to fill sealed packaging so as to displace air and prevent oxidation

nitrogen trichloride A compound used for bleaching flour

nitrous oxide Laughing gas, once used as an anaesthetic, now used as a propellant in aerosol packs of whipped cream

nitsuke *Japan* Simmered, in clear liquid or thin sauce

niu *Catalonia* A fish and meat stew from the Costa Brava containing, amongst other things, pigeon, cuttlefish, cod, tripe, pigs' trotters, egg and garlic mayonnaise

Niva *Czech Republic, Russia* A soft blue-veined cheese similar to **Roquefort**, made from a mixture of ewes' and cows' milk and surface-ripened. Contains 47% water, 23% fat and 22 % protein.

nixtamal *Mexico* Maize kernels treated with water and lime (15:30:1) until the skins can be rubbed off, washed until white in clean water then used for making **masa** or **masa harina**

nizakana *Japan* Oily fish such as herring, mackerel, sardine, etc. cleaned and gutted, slashed and placed in a boiling mixture of equal parts of **dashi**, soya sauce and sake with a little sugar, and simmered until cooked on a very low heat. Served immediately with some of the cooking liquor.

njamma-jamma *Central Africa* Shredded greens cooked with a little sweated onion and garlic, then all simmered in stock with seasoning to taste until tender. The name also refers to the leaves of a plant used as a vegetable in Central Africa.

Njeguski *Balkans* A hard, scalded-curd, pressed ewes' milk cheese made in a drum shape (up to 3 kg). It is dry-salted and ripened for up to 4 months. Contains 33% water, 33% fat and 31% protein.

njure *Sweden* Kidney

njursauté *Sweden* Cleaned and blanched calves' or lambs' kidneys diced or sliced and sautéed with mushrooms in butter. Flour, stock, mushroom juices and cream added, seasoned and simmered 10 minutes and finished with Madeira wine.

njursoppa *Sweden* Kidney soup made from diced kidney flesh sweated with chopped onion and parsley, flour added to make a roux and let down with beef stock, boiled 10 minutes and finished with a whisked mixture of eggs and sour cream. Served over toast.

nocciola *Italy* 1. Hazelnut 2. Noisette of meat

nocciola di burro *Italy* Beurre noisette

nocciolina *Italy* Peanut

noce *Italy* 1. Nut, walnut 2. Rump (of meat) 3. Knob (of butter)

noce del Brazile *Italy* Brazil nut

noce del para *Italy* Brazil nut

noce di acagiu *Italy* Cashew nut

noce di areca *Italy* Betel nut

noce di cocco *Italy* Coconut

noce moscata *Italy* Nutmeg

nocepesca *Italy* A nectarine

nødder *Denmark* Nuts

nodino *Italy* Meat chop

noisette *France* 1. Hazelnut 2. A neatly trimmed and tied boneless piece of meat at least 1.5 cm thick, cut from the eye of the loin of lamb, the filet mignon of beef or a small grenadin of veal, usually surrounded on its edge with a thin layer of fat 3. Knob (of butter)

noisette, beurre *France* Beurre noisette

noisette, beurre de *France* Beurre de noisette

noisette, sauce *France* **Hollandaise sauce** finished at the last moment with 150 g of **beurre noisette** per kg of butter used in making the hollandaise. Used with poached salmon and trout.

noisette cutter A larger version of the Parisienne or Paris cutter used for scooping balls out of raw vegetables and fruit, etc.

noix *France* 1. Walnut 2. Eye of a chop or cutlet, i.e. a round piece of lean meat cut from across a long circular muscle 3. Knob (of butter) 4. Cushion of veal

noix d'arec *France* Betel nut

noix de cajou *France* Cashew nut

noix de coco *France* Coconut

noix de muscade *France* Nutmeg

noix de pecan *France* Pecan nut

noix de veau *France* Cushion of veal

noix du Brésil *France* Brazil nut

noix pâtissière *France* A cut of veal or beef. See also **gîte à la noix**

Nøkke *Norway* Nøkkelost

Nøkkelost *Norway* A hard scalded-curd cheese made in wheels (up to 15 kg) from semi-skimmed cows' milk and flavoured with cumin and caraway. It contains 43% water, 20% fat and 33% protein. Also called **Nøkke**

non *Russia* A flat onion-flavoured bread from Asiatic Russia, similar to the Indian paratha

nonats *France* Gobies, Mediterranean fish similar to whitebait

non-dairy creamer Creamer

nonna, alla *Italy* In the style of grandmother, i.e. home cooked

nonnati *Italy* Goby, the fish

nonnette *France* Spiced bun

nonnette de Dijon *France* Iced gingerbread cake

nonpareille *France* Hundreds and thousands

nonya cuisine The distinctive cuisine of the Chinese Malaysians and Singaporeans (Straits Chinese), which marries Chinese and Malaysian ingredients

noodle basket A container made by lining a wire mesh frying basket with softened and drained noodles, placing a slightly smaller basket inside to hold the noodles in place and deep-frying until the noodles are crisp and adhering together. The noodle basket is used to serve some stir-fried Chinese dishes. Also called **noodle nest**

noodle nest See **noodle basket**

noodles A mixture of grain or pulse flour or other starch product with egg and/or water and salt formed into a long flat ribbons of various thicknesses and cross sections. Available in most cuisines. Cooked by boiling, stir-frying or deep-frying and may be soft or dried. Typical names are listed under egg, rice, cellophane, soba, cha-soba, udon, somen, shirataki, bean thread, e-fu, miswa, Shanghai and all the Italian pasta types.

noomi *Middle East* The whole, not powdered, version of **loomi**

Noorse kreeft *Netherlands* Dublin bay prawn

nopal *Spain* Young leaf of the prickly pear cactus, *Opuntia vulgaris*, sold skinned, trimmed and chopped and used after cooking in stews and salads. Common in Mexico and southern USA. Also called **nopalito** (NOTE: Plural is **nopales**.)

nopalito Nopal

noques *France* Gnocchi

ñora A round red chilli from Spain, not particularly hot, almost a sweet pepper. Usually dried.

norbixin A golden yellow food colouring obtained from the seeds of achiote. See also **annatto**

nordische Meerbrassen *Germany* See **bream 1**

Norfolk apple cake *England* A shortcrust pastry case with a pastry top filled with a mixture of stewed apples, orange marmalade and currants. Also called **apple cake**

Norfolk black *England* A breed of turkey similar to the bronze but with a slightly less plump breast

Norfolk dumpling *England* A dumpling made of flour, eggs and milk sometimes with added yeast to cause it to rise before boiling

Norfolk knobs *England* Hollow biscuits made with a sweetened and butter enriched yeast-raised soft dough, kneaded, rolled, docked to remove all air, cut in 3 cm discs, proved until doubled in size and baked at 220°C then completely dried in the oven at 90°C. Eaten with cheese or jam, or the like. Introduced by the Flemish weavers.

Norfolk plough pudding *England* A pudding basin lined first with suet pastry, then with sausagemeat, the centre filled with a mixture of chopped onion, bacon flavoured with a little sage and brown sugar plus stock, this layered with more sausagemeat and everything topped with suet pastry well sealed to the sides. The basin is covered, then steamed for 3 to 4 hours. (NOTE: This dish was traditionally served on Plough Monday, the first Monday after Twelfth Night when spring ploughing started.)

Norfolk rusks *England* A hard biscuit made with self-raising flour, butter and egg (12:5:4) mixed by the rubbing-in method, rolled out to 7 mm thick and cut in rounds. These are baked at 200°C for 20 minutes or until golden, cooled, split in half and baked cut side uppermost for a further 5 minutes.

nori *Japan* A marine alga, *Porphyra tenera* or *P. umbilicalis*, found on the surface of the sea off Japan, China and Korea. It is formed into paper-like sheets, compressed and dried and has a colour ranging from green through purple. It is used in Japan to wrap around rice and various fillings to make sushi. It may also be shredded for use as a condiment or flavouring or may be formed into baskets by deep frying. Also called **green laver, purple laver, sea laver**

noriega *Spain* Common skate

nori-maki *Japan* A sushi wrapped in **nori** with the filling in the centre of the sushi-meshi rice. Rolled up using a bamboo mat (**makisu**). The roll is cut in 3 cm pieces to show the decoratively arranged filling. See also **maki-sushi**

normande, à la *France* In the Normandy style, i.e. containing cream, apples, cider, calvados or seafood. Also used of fish served with sauce normande and garnished with truffles, shrimps and crayfish or mussels.

normande, sauce *France* A fish velouté sauce enriched with cream, egg yolks and butter and served with fish and shellfish. Also called **Normandy sauce**

Normandy sauce See **normande, sauce**

Normanna *Norway* A semi-hard cows' milk cheese made with a lactic starter. The cylindrical cheeses (up to 3kg) are ripened for 2 months and develop a sharp flavour and patches of greenish blue colouration in the white paste.

North American lobster A larger variety of lobster, *Homarus americanus*, than the European, *Homarus vulgaris*

northern fluke Summer flounder

northern prawn Deepwater prawn

North Staffordshire black pudding *England* Black pudding flavoured with thyme, allspice, marjoram, pennyroyal and coriander

Norvegia *Norway* A semi-hard cows' milk cheese resembling Gouda. The paste contains small holes.

norvégienne, sauce A type of mayonnaise made from pounded hard-boiled egg yolk with vinegar and mustard into which oil is beaten to give a thick sauce

Norway haddock Redfish

Norway lobster Dublin bay prawn

Norwegian omelette Baked Alaska

Norwegian whey cheese Mysost

nosh *England* Food, from the Yiddish for titbits or appetizers (*colloquial*)

nostrano *Italy* Home-grown

noten *Netherlands* Nuts

nötkött *Sweden* Beef

nötter *Sweden* Nuts

nøtter *Norway* Nuts

nøtteterte *Norway* Nut cake

Nottingham pudding *England* The centres of peeled and cored Bramley cooking apples are filled with a creamed mixture of equal parts of butter and sugar flavoured with cinnamon and nutmeg, then placed in a greased baking dish, covered with an egg and milk batter stabilized with flour at the rate of 2 tbsp per egg and baked at 200°C for 50 minutes

nougat *England, France* Any sweetmeat made with a mixture of nuts and sugar, syrup or honey with possibly white of egg and glacé fruits. The white French version is common in the UK. In Germany it is light brown and smooth.

nougatine *England, France* A confection similar to **praline** made from a light caramel mixed with crushed almonds or hazelnuts, poured onto a flat sheet and cut into small decorative shapes, or moulded when warm into baskets and the like to contain other foods, or cut in a large circle to be used as a base for a gateau or dessert

nouilles *France* 1. Pasta 2. Noodles

nouvelle cuisine *England, France* A fashionable 1980s style of cooking using small amounts of very fresh food artistically arranged on the plate together with purées and reduced cooking liquors without cream, flour, egg or butter thickening, as sauces. Portions and sauces have now reverted to normal although much of the artistic merit has persisted. This type of cuisine tends to arise in history at favourable economic times.

nova *United States* Cold-smoked salmon. Eaten with cream cheese and bagels.

noyau *France* Kernel, stone or pit of a fruit

noyau, liqueur de 1 *France* A liqueur flavoured with kernels of cherry and apricot stones used as a flavouring

noz *Portugal* Walnut

nozzle An open-ended hollow metal or plastic cone in varying sizes used in the end of a piping bag. The smaller end may be a plain circle, star-shaped or other shapes to give different decorative effects.

nsusu na buha *Central Africa* A similar Congolese dish to **muaba nsusu** made with smoked chicken

Nudeln *Austria, Germany* Egg noodles not made with durum wheat flour

Nudelschöberl *Austria* Noodle pie, served as an accompaniment to meat

nudlar *Sweden* Dumplings

nuea *Thailand* Beef

nueces *Spain* 1. Nuts 2. Walnuts

nueng *Thailand* Steamed

nuez *Spain* 1. Nut 2. Walnut (NOTE: Plural is **nueces**.)

nuez americana *Spain* Hickory nut

nuez de anacardo *Spain* Cashew nut

nuez de areca *Spain* Betel nut

nuez de Brasil *Spain* Brazil nut

nuez moscada *Spain* Nutmeg

nuez nogal *Spain* Walnut

nuka *Japan* Rice bran. See also **nuka-zuke**, **nukamiso-zuke**

nukamiso-zuke *Japan* A mixture of rice bran, salt, beer and mustard made into a paste with water. Salted vegetables are immersed

in the mixture and left for from 1 to 30 days to mature and become preserved.

nuka-zuke *Japan* 1. Nukamiso-zuke 2. A method of preserving in which salted vegetables are immersed in rice bran

num krathi *Thailand* Coconut

num taan *Thailand* Sugar

num taan peep *Thailand* Palm sugar

num taan sai *Thailand* Sugar

nun's beads *Scotland* Grated Dunlop cheese, egg yolks and breadcrumbs (4:1:1), made into a paste, formed into walnut-sized balls, each ball covered in thin puff pastry and deep-fried until golden brown

nun's toast *United States* Hard-boiled eggs in thickened milk, served over toast

nuoc cham *Vietnam* A condiment and dipping sauce made from dried red chillies, garlic and sugar, processed with water, fish sauce and lime juice. Will keep fresh for 3 days in the refrigerator.

nuoc cham tuong gung *Vietnam* Tuong sweetened with sugar and processed with ginger and chillies. Served with roast meats.

nuoc cot dua *Vietnam* Coconut milk

nuoc dua tuoi *Vietnam* Coconut water

nuoc mam *Thailand, Vietnam* A thin fish sauce made from the liquid which drains from salted and fermented anchovies or other small fish. Also called **nuoc-nam**

nuoc mau *Vietnam* Caramelized sugar used as a colouring and for glazing grilled food. Sometimes used of brown sugar.

nuoc-nam See **nuoc mam**

nuoc tuong *Vietnam* Soya sauce

nuoc tuong hot *Vietnam* Bean paste

nuo mi zong zi *China* Lotus leaves stuffed with sweet rice and meat

nuong *Vietnam* Grilled

Nur Hier *Germany* A solid black bread only available in Hamburg (NOTE: Literally 'only here'.)

Nürnberger *Germany* Nürnbergerwurst

Nürnbergerwurst *Germany* A sausage made from minced lean pork mixed with diced bacon fat, seasoned, flavoured with kirsch, thyme and marjoram, packed into casings and linked. Fried in butter and served with horseradish sauce and sauerkraut. Also called **Nürnberger**

nurse hound Larger spotted dogfish

Nuss *Germany* Nut

Nusstorte *Central Europe* A speciality cake containing ground almonds or walnuts filled and coated with whipped or butter cream

Nuss und Mohnstrudel *Austria* A walnut and poppy seed strudel with a filling made from ground walnuts, sugar, butter, raisins, cinnamon, lemon zest, rum and biscuit crumbs. Sprinkled with poppy seeds.

nusu *East Africa* The name given to a half portion of food in Kenya

nut The seed of a plant usually enclosed in a fruit and edible when ripe without further cooking or processing. The term is also applied to or some underground seed-like tubers. Most, apart from chestnuts, contain large amounts of protein and oil or fat. The most important in commerce are almonds, brazil nuts, cashews, chestnuts, cobnuts, filberts, macadamia nuts, peanuts, pecans, pine nuts, pistachios and walnuts. The coconut is an unusual hollow nut and there are many others of regional interest.

nut brittle See **praline**

nut cracker An implement used to crack the hard outer shell of nuts using a lever or screw thread action

nu tieu *Vietnam* White rice noodles about 3 mm wide. See also **banh pho**

nut meal Ground nuts used to substitute for some of the flour in biscuit and cake mixes and in fillings

nutmeg The hard, dried, oval, shelled seed (up to 2 cm long) of which the outer covering is mace, from the fruit of an evergreen tree, *Myristica fragrans*. It has a warm sweetish aromatic flavour and is used when grated to a fine powder to flavour both sweet and savoury dishes, vegetables and cakes, etc. especially by the Dutch. Also used as a condiment. It is hallucinogenic if taken in large quantities (1 – 3 whole nutmegs) and can be poisonous. See also **mace**

nutmeg melon Musk melon

nut of veal *United Kingdom* Cushion of veal

nut oil Any oil expressed or extracted from a nut, usually carrying the particular flavour of the nut

nutraceuticals See **functional foods**

nutria, nutria rat A small rat-like herbivore from Louisiana, USA, considered to be a luxury. Generally stewed in a tomato sauce.

nutrient Any substance in food which is utilized in the body for energy production, for the growth, reproduction and repair of tissues or for other physiological functions such as providing bulk or a substrate for micro-organism growth in the bowel

nutrition The study of the food requirements of humans and animals in terms of quantity, quality and the content of protein, fat, carbohydrate, fibre, vitamins, mineral, and trace elements, etc.

nutritional labelling In the EU, nutritional labelling is optional, but if given, must contain the energy value and the amounts of protein, carbohydrate and fat. It may also show, sugar, saturated fats, fibre and sodium.

nutritional needs The amounts of the various components of food required to be eaten for health and well being

nutritionist A person who makes a study of and is an expert in nutrition and nutritional needs. Often works with the kitchens and chefs of hospitals, schools and other institutional food providers.

NVQ National vocational qualification. The UK craft training qualification which consists, for cooking, of on-the-job training with agreed competencies but no formal externally marked examinations or time limits for completion. Exact details of certificated competencies should always be examined if this qualification is offered and the reputation of the training school or workplace is important. The question of formal examinations is under consideration.

nyama *East Africa* The Tanzanian name for beef

nyama choma *East Africa* Roast meat brought to the table on a wooden platter where it is chopped for service. The meat has often been marinated in lemon juice with spices and garlic before roasting. A Kenyan dish usually accompanied with ugali and spinach.

nyana creole *West Africa* A stew from Ghana made from oysters, onions, green sweet peppers, tomatoes, garlic, chilli pepper, oil and seasoning. Served with rice or bread.

nyavhi *South Africa* A wild native plant of Zimbabwe with small narrow green leaves harvested just before the rainy season. It is cooked and used as a vegetable.

nyembwe sauce *Central Africa* Moambé sauce

Nymphaea lotus *Botanical name* The Egyptian lotus

nymphes à l'aurore *France* Frogs' legs poached in white wine and covered with pink chaud-froid sauce and garnished with chopped aspic

nyoyo *East Africa* A Kenyan dish of equal quantities of cooked cow peas or black-eyed beans and maize kernels mixed with a kind of ratatouille of onions, sweet peppers and tomatoes, seasoned and flavoured with paprika and cooked in a covered pot for 15 minutes, adding a little water if necessary. Served with rice and salad, or fried as a snack. Also called **githeri**

nypon *Sweden* Rose hips

nyponsoppa *Sweden* Rose hip soup

nyre *Denmark, Norway* Kidney

nyrøket laks *Norway* Smoked salmon

OPQRSTU

oak leaf lettuce A loose-leaf lettuce with deep bronze serrated leaves and a mild flavour. Also called **red oak leaf lettuce**, **red salad bowl lettuce**

oak mushroom Shiitake mushroom

oast cake *England* A type of thin chemically raised scone containing currants, not baked but fried in oil and butter until golden brown

oat bran The fibrous outer layer of the whole oat grain separated during the process of making oat flour. Usually mixed with **oat germ**.

oatcake *Scotland, England* An unsweetened Scottish and Northern English unleavened bread or biscuit made with oatmeal, water, fat and salt. Some are relatively thick and baked in the oven or on a griddle, others are made like a pancake batter, cooked and sometimes dried.

oat flakes See **porridge oats**

oat flour Flour ground from oats. Does not contain much gluten and must be combined with wheat flour to make a bread which rises.

oat germ The germ of the oat grain separated during the process of making oat flour. Usually mixed with oat bran to a brown powder which can be used to make a thin porridge or added to other flours for use in bread making.

oatmeal Coarsely ground or cracked dehusked oats separated by sieving into various particle sizes, usually fine, medium and coarse, but superfine and pinhead can be found

oats The seeds of a cereal grass, *Avena sativa*, extensively grown in cool wet climates on poor soils. Once considered a herbal medicine now known to be an excellent source of dietary and soluble fibre. Used extensively in cooking especially as a breakfast cereal and for cakes, biscuits and scones and for coating herring.

Oaxaca *Mexico* A fresh spun-curd cows' milk cheese similar to **Provolone**

ob cheuy *Thailand* Cinnamon

obed *Russia* The main meal of the day taken any time between 13.00 and 17.00 hours

obeni-mikan *Japan* Dancy tangerine

obento *Japan* Different cold foods served in a lunch box (**bento bako**). See also **bento**

Oberland Leberwurst *Germany* A liver sausage made from a boiled skinned and boned shoulder of pork, drained and the pork flesh minced with half its weight of pigs' liver, mixed with diced, boiled and drained pork fat, chopped onion, seasoning and nutmeg, packed into casings, boiled 45 minutes, refreshed and air dried

Obers *Austria* Whipped cream (*colloquial*)

oblada *Spain* Saddled bream

oblade *France* Saddled bream

oboro ebi *Japan* Shrimp paste

oboru kombu *Japan* Shavings from soaked **kombu** cut across the grain leaving the tough membrane

O'Brien *United States* A garnish of crisp fried bacon pieces with fried chopped onions and red and green sweet peppers. Often served with potatoes.

Obst *Germany* Fruit

Obstkuchen *Germany* Fruit cake

Obstsosse *Germany* A sweet-and-sour fruit sauce such as apple or redcurrant, served with roast meat

Obstsuppe *Germany* A puréed fruit soup

Obsttorte *Germany* A glazed open mixed fruit tart. The pastry is made with flour, sugar, raw egg yolks, sieved hard-boiled egg yolk and melted butter (25:4:2:1:25) kneaded and rested before baking blind at 165°C until slightly brown. The filling is mixed fresh or tinned fruit set in jelly.

Obst Traubensaft *Germany* Verjuice

oca 1. *Italy* Goose 2. See **occa**

oca amb peres *Catalonia* A festive dish of goose with pears

oca di guerra *Italy* Goose poached in water and the flesh cooled in molten goose fat like confit

oca farcita alla borghese *Italy* Roast goose stuffed with chopped pork, apples, chestnuts and the goose liver

occa An important white to brown tuber, *Oxalis tuberosa*, from the South American Andes region. It is said to have gone wild in parts of France. Requires careful cooking to rid it of oxalates. Also called **oca**, **oka**

occhialone *Italy* See **bream 1**

occhiata *Italy* Saddled bream

occhi di lupo *Italy* Short pasta tubes

oceanic bonito Skipjack tuna

ocean perch Redfish

ocean pout A seawater fish, *Macrozoarces americanus*, found in coastal waters off the northeast coast of North America. It has a sweet white flesh with few bones. Also called **mutton fish**

ocean quahog A bivalve mollusc, *Arctica islandica*, similar in appearance to the quahog clam but with a dark shell and flesh which sometimes has a strong taste. Found in the North Atlantic but only fished in the USA where it is used in manufactured clam products.

ochazuke *Japan* Boiled rice served with crumbled crisp **nori** and hot green tea poured over it. Eaten as a snack.

ochro Okra

Ochse *Germany* Ox, beef

Ochsenauge *Germany* Fried egg (*colloquial*) (NOTE: Literally 'ox eye'.)

Ochsenbraten *Germany* Roast beef

Ochsenfleisch *Germany* Beef

Ochsenlende *Germany* Fillet of beef

Ochsenmausalat *Germany* A salad of sliced cold beef with onions and vinegar

Ochsenniere *Germany* Beef kidney

Ochsenschwanz *Germany* Oxtail

Ochsenschwanzsuppe *Germany* Oxtail soup

Ochsenzunge *Germany* Ox tongue

Ocimum basilicum *Botanical name* Basil

octadecyl ammonium acetate An anti-caking agent for yeast foods used in bread making. Aids dispersion throughout the mix.

octopus An eight-armed cephalopod, *Octopus vulgaris*, found worldwide in warm seawater and usually in the range 30 cm to 1 m long (head and tentacles), although they can reach 3 m. They vary in colour from transparent to blue-black. The tentacles and head flesh of larger animals are usually cooked after pounding to soften the tissues. To cook, put a cork in the head and place in boiling unsalted water and boil for 10 to 20 minutes depending on size, alternatively smaller ones are tender if cooked very quickly e.g. by deep-frying or stir-frying. See also **warm-water octopus**, **red octopus**, **curled octopus**

Odelsostur *Iceland* A cows' milk cheese which resembles **Emmental**

oden *Japan* A stew of squid, turnips, carrots, potatoes, **konnyaku**, **abura-age**, hard-boiled eggs and deep-fried Japanese meatballs all simmered in **dashi** with soya sauce and sugar for 2 to 3 hours. Bean curd is added towards the end and the stew is served with mustard. The ingredients are normally cut in decorative shapes. Also called **Tokyo hotchpot**

Oderberger *Austria* A sausage similar to the German Brunswick sausage

odika *West Africa* The seeds of the wild mango tree

odour The property of a substance which causes the sensation of smell. It is caused by molecules from the substance binding to receptors in the nasal cavity which send specific signals to the brain. The six main odour qualities are fruity, flowery, resinous, spicy, foul and burnt. See also **flavour**. Also called **smell**

oeil d'anchois *France* A raw egg yolk surrounded by chopped onion and anchovies served as a hors d'oeuvre

Oelenberg *France* A mild-flavoured, cows' milk cheese from Oelenberg monastery, suitable for cooking as well as dessert uses. Also called **Trappiste d'Oelenberg**

Oenothera biennis *Botanical name* Evening primrose

oester *Netherlands* Oyster, originally the European flat oyster

oeuf *France* Egg

oeuf à la poêle *France* Fried egg

oeuf dur *France* Hard-boiled egg

oeuf frit *France* Fried egg

oeuf mollet *France* A shelled soft-boiled egg

oeuf poché *France* Poached egg

oeufs, sauce aux *France* Egg sauce

oeufs à la bénédictine *France* Poached eggs served on a base of creamed salt cod

oeufs à la causalade *France* Fried eggs and bacon

oeufs à la coque *France* Eggs in their shell, generally soft-boiled

oeufs à l'agenaise *France* Eggs fried in goose fat with aubergines and onions

oeufs à la neige *France* Îles flottantes

oeufs à la tripe *France* A Normandy dish of chopped hard-boiled eggs with onions

oeufs au chasseur *France* Scrambled eggs with chicken livers

oeufs au lait *France* Egg custard

oeufs brouillés *France* Scrambled eggs

oeufs bûcheronés *France* Beaten eggs poured over slices of ham on toast and baked in the oven

oeufs de lump *France* Lumpfish roe

oeufs de poisson *France* Hard fish roe

oeufs en cocotte See **cocotte, en**

oeufs en gelée *France* Poached eggs in aspic

oeufs en gelée Stendhal *France* Poached eggs in aspic flecked with ham

oeufs en meurettes *France* Eggs poached in red wine with lardons

oeufs farcis *France* Stuffed eggs

oeufs florentine Freshly poached eggs laid on a bed of spinach, topped with cheese sauce, gratinated with cheese and breadcrumbs and browned under the grill

oeufs Justine *France* Hard-boiled eggs stuffed with mushrooms in a thick cream sauce, reassembled, panéed and fried in butter

oeufs montés (en neige) *France* Egg whites beaten to a peak

oeufs Rossini *France* An elaborate shirred egg dish in which the egg yolks are baked in depressions in a stiffly beaten egg white base

oeufs sur le plat *France* Eggs baked in a shallow, greased, oven-proof dish. Also called **shirred eggs**

Ofentori *Switzerland* Mashed potatoes mixed with fried finely diced bacon

offal The edible internal parts of an animal including brains, chitterlings, heart, kidneys, liver, lungs, spleen, sweetbreads (pancreas and thymus gland) and tripe. Tongues, heads, tails, trotters and testicles are sometimes included in this classification.

Öffelkes *Germany* Small cakes

office knife A small knife with a 10 cm blade shaped like a cook's knife. Used for fine cutting and paring and for testing food to see if it is cooked.

ogbono *West Africa* The Nigerian name for the kernels of the wild mango tree, *Irvingia gabonensis* and *I. wombolu*, which when crushed are a very powerful thickener and are therefore used sparingly in soups and stews. Also called **apon**, **agbono**

ogbono soup *West Africa* A typical West African soup/stew made with meat, palm oil, dried fish or shrimps, onions and tomato, thickened with crushed ogbono and seasoned with salt and cayenne pepper. Often chopped greens are added. Okra in

sufficient quantity will give the same mucilaginous effect as ogbono.

ogen melon A variety of cantaloupe melon bred on an Israeli kibbutz. The fruit is about 15 cm across with a bright orange/yellow green ribbed skin and a pale green, sweet, juicy and fragrant flesh.

oggy *England* Cornish pasty (*colloquial*)

ogi-giri *Japan* A fan cut of circular soft vegetables such as cucumber or thin aubergine made from a quarter of the cylinder cut lengthwise with close evenly spaced cuts to within 1 cm of the end and then pressed flat to make the fan

ögle yemegi *Turkey* Lunch

ogonowa *Poland* A skinless spicy smoked pork sausage common throughout the country

ogopogo apple dumpling *Canada* A rectangular baked apple turnover made from a square of pastry folded over the apple filling, sealed, coated with syrup and baked in the oven (NOTE: From British Columbia)

ogurtsi *Russia* Gherkins

Ohio pudding *United States* Sweet potatoes, carrots and squash, all cooked, mashed and mixed with brown sugar, breadcrumbs and single (light) cream, then baked until firm. Served with an uncooked sweet sauce made from butter, cream, icing sugar and lemon juice.

Ohrmuschel *Germany* Abalone

ohukas *Finland* A small thin crêpe

oie *France* Goose

oie à l'instar de Visé *Belgium* Roast goose in a rich cream and garlic sauce

oie cendrée *France* Greylag goose

oie sauvage *France* Wild goose

oi gimchi *Korea* Cucumbers stuffed with radish and pickled with ginger, garlic, chillies and salt

oignon *France* Onion

oignon clouté *France* Onion clouté

oignons, purée d' *France* White onion soup

oignons, sauce aux *France* Onion sauce

oil Fat, which is liquid at ambient temperatures, comprising glycerol esters of a variety of mainly unsaturated, fatty acids. They are extracted from seeds, nuts, fruit, fish and other cold blooded animals. Most natural oils contain complex flavouring compounds some of which are **essential oils**. The common seed, nut and fruit oils are almond, coconut, corn, cottonseed, grapeseed, hazelnut, mustard, olive, palm, peanut, poppy seed, rape seed, safflower, sesame, soya, sunflower and walnut. The animal oils are cod liver, halibut liver, whale and snake. See also **essential oil, essential fatty acids, cold-pressed, virgin oil, hydrogenation**

oil-down *Caribbean* A Trinidadian dish of vegetables, particularly cassava tubers or breadfruit, stewed in coconut milk

oil pastry A short crust pastry made with oil instead of hard fat. Because of its fragility it is rolled out between sheets of non-stick paper.

oil sardine A small fish, *Sardinella longiceps*, similar to the sardine

oily fish Fish whose flesh contains more than 6% of fat by weight

oiseau *France* Bird

oiseaux sans têtes *Belgium, France, Netherlands* Beef olives (NOTE: Literally 'birds without heads'.)

oison *France* Gosling, young goose

oka 1. *Canada* A semi-hard cows' milk cheese resembling **Port-Salut** from the village of Oka near Montreal **2.** See **occa**

Okanagan savoury tomato *Canada* Tomato stuffed with a filling made from fried chopped onions, flour, milk, breadcrumbs, herbs, spices and grated Cheddar cheese (NOTE: From British Columbia)

okashi *Japan* Sweets and desserts, usually served with tea to visitors but not at formal meals

okasi *West Africa* The leaves of a forest plant eaten as a vegetable. See also **afang**

okayu *Japan* A rice gruel

okorok v rzhanom teste *Russia* Canned or cooked ham with the jelly removed, coated with a mixture of dark brown sugar, dry English mustard, ground cloves and cinnamon then wrapped in a yeast-raised rye flour pastry flavoured with caraway seeds and black treacle and completely sealed. This is then glazed with milk and baked in the oven at 180°C for 2 hours or more and allowed to rest for 15 minutes. The pastry case is usually discarded.

okra The seed pod of a plant, *Abelmoschus esculentus*, used when young as a vegetable or when mature, dried and powdered as a flavouring. Generally about 5 to 10 cm long, green, deeply ridged and full of seeds. They liberate a gelatinous material when cooked unless treated with lemon juice and salt prior to frying. In the Middle East great care is taken not to cut the pod if the release of gelatinous material is not wanted. Grown in most hot areas of the world. Also called **gumbo, gombo, lady's fingers, ochro, bhindi, bindi, bamiya.** See also **Chinese okra**

ok-rong *Thailand* A pale yellow mango considered to be the best dessert variety

okroshka *Russia* A cold uncooked soup made from cooked egg yolks mashed with dry English mustard and sour cream and let down with **kvas** (or flat beer or semi-sweet cider) and mixed with chopped white of egg, cooked potatoes, spring onions and cold roast meat all diced, flavoured with cayenne pepper and garnished with chopped dill

oksebryst *Denmark* Brisket of beef

oksefilet *Denmark* Fillet steak

oksekjøtt *Norway* Beef

oksekød *Denmark* Beef

oksekødsuppe *Denmark* Beef broth

oksesteg *Denmark* Roast beef

oksestek *Norway* Roast beef

oksetunge *Denmark* Ox tongue

Öl *Germany* Oil

olallieberry *United States* A hybrid of the loganberry and the youngberry, grown in the southwestern states of the USA

olandese, all' *Italy* With hollandaise sauce

olandese, salsa *Italy* Hollandaise sauce

Oldbury tart *England* A raised fruit pie from Gloucestershire filled with gooseberries and eaten hot

Old Heidelberg A small cows' milk cheese from Illinois, USA, resembling Liederkranz

old wife Black bream

Olea europa *Botanical name* Olive

olean The commercial name for **olestra**

oleic acid A monounsaturated fatty acid which when esterified with glycerol produces a low melting point fat which is a constituent of lard making it soft and of many vegetable oils including olive oil

Olenda *Italy* A cheese similar to Edam

óleo *Portugal* **1.** Oil **2.** Fat

Oléron *France* A mild creamy ewes' milk cheese from the Ile d'Oléron on the Atlantic coast

olestra An ester of fatty acids and sugar, which behaves in cooking like oil or fat but which is not absorbed by the human body. Thus it can be used as a non-fattening fat. It has been licensed in the USA for cooked snack foods such as crisps. Because of its ability to sequester vitamins A, D, E and K plus carotenes and possibly other nutrients, foods cooked with it carry a health warning. Extra vitamins are required to be added back to the food which uses olestra.

olie *Denmark, Netherlands* Oil

oliebollen *Netherlands* Deep-fried doughnuts

olijfolie *Netherlands* Olive oil

olijven *Netherlands* Olives

olio *Italy* Oil

olio, all' *Italy* Cooked in oil

olio, sott' *Italy* Preserved in oil

oliva *Italy, Spain* Olive

olive *England, France* The oval fruit of a long-living evergreen tree, *Olea europa*, which grows in areas with hot summers and cool winters. The fruits, up to 4 cm long, are green when unripe and turn black when fully ripe. Both green and black olives are eaten raw, the green after treatment. Both kinds may be fermented (lactic fermentation) in a 10% brine. The black are often partially dried and stored in oil. The fully ripe black olives are the source of olive oil. See also **green olive**

Olive *Germany* Olive

olive all' anconetana *Italy* Large green olives, pitted, stuffed with meat, ham or chicken and deep-fried

oliven *Denmark, Norway* Olives

olive oil The monounsaturated oil obtained from the ripe fruit of the olive tree. The first cold pressing of the hand-picked, destoned and skinned ripe fruit from a single producer is usually the finest flavoured and most expensive, and is treated with the respect accorded to fine wines. Most olive oil is hot-pressed or solvent-extracted from the whole fruit. Olive oils are classified according to the method of production and the acidity (free oleic acid) of the oil. The Italian grades are *afiorato*, extra virgin *(extra vergine)*, superfine *(sopraffino)*, fine *(fino)*, virgin *(vergine)*, and finally the pure or 100% pure commercially blended oils. See under each heading for details.

oliver *Sweden* Olives

Olivet *France* A soft cows' milk cheese made in the same way as Camembert in Loiret. It is eaten after 2 days ripening or left to ripen for a month in damp cellars when it develops a stronger flavour due to the growth of mould on its surface. It is then known as Olivet bleu.

Olivet bleu *France* Olivet

Olivet cendré *France* As Olivet bleu but the rind dried off in wood ashes

olivette 1. *France* Plum tomato **2.** *Italy* Beef or veal olive, paupiette

olivette cutter A sharp-edged scoop-shaped implement for cutting out oval shapes (olive-shaped) of potato or other vegetables or fruit

olivette de vitello *Italy* Stuffed paupiettes of veal, veal olives

olivkovoe maslo *Russia* Olive oil

olja *Sweden* Oil

olje *Norway* Oil

olla *Spain* Cooking pot or stew

olla de San Antón *Spain* Pork with rice, beans and fennel. A traditional Andalusian dish for the feast of San Anton on the 19th of January.

olla gitana *Spain* A vegetable stew

olla podrida *Spain* Beef brisket, rolled rib of beef, soaked chick peas or other beans, hard sausage and salt pork or bacon (roughly 8:6:3:2:1) simmered in seasoned water with a bouquet garni until tender, aromatic vegetables and any other solid vegetables to hand added and cooked until tender and finished with chopped parsley. A traditional Spanish dish named after the pot in which it is cooked. Also called **cocido**, **puchero**

øllebrød *Denmark* A soup made from black bread and a non-alcoholic malt liquor

Olmützer *Austria* A strong-flavoured cows' milk cheese similar to **Handkäse**, sometimes flavoured with caraway seeds

Olmützer Quargel *Germany* Very small (up to 20 g) soft low-fat cows' milk cheeses with a strong flavour made by coagulating the milk with acid. The paste has no holes and there is no rind save for the soft skin.

Olomoucké syrecky *Czech Republic* A strong cows' milk cheese similar to Handkäse. Also called **Syrecky**, **Tvarvzky**

oluwombo *East Africa* A classic dish from Uganda, once served to royalty and now on celebratory occasions. Single servings of boneless meat and/or smoked fish or meat are browned and steamed for an hour or so **en papillote**, using banana leaves presoftened by heating, together with a smooth peanut, onion, and tomato sauce as flavouring. Plantains are also steamed in the same way and the dish is assembled by mashing the plantain on the plate, then topping it with the meat and sauce. This may be done in the kitchen or individually at the table. Also called **luwombo**

Olympia oyster A small delicate oyster, *Ostrea lurida*, found off the Pacific coast of the USA

omble chevalier *France* Arctic char

ombrina *Italy* Arctic char

omelet *Denmark, Netherlands, United States* Omelette

omeleta *Greece* Omelette

omelett *Norway, Sweden* Omelette

omeletta *Italy* Omelette

omelette *England, France* Whole shelled eggs, lightly stirred to mix the white and the yolk, seasoned, then poured into a hot frying or omelette pan greased with butter. As the egg sets, the unset egg is run underneath so that the whole of the egg mixture cooks rapidly with a slightly brown lower surface. The omelette my be turned over to harden the upper surface or folded in half or thirds with or without a precooked filling or topping and served immediately. Generally served slightly runny (**baveuse**) in the centre. See also **soufflé omelette**

omelette landaise *France* Pine nuts fried gently in the butter before adding the eggs in the usual way

omelette (à la) norvégienne *France* Baked Alaska

omelette pan A heavy-based frying pan with rounded sloping sides, usually kept exclusively for omelettes and never washed after use but cleaned with absorbent paper. Omelette pans are proved before first use by heating salt in them.

omelette soufflée en surprise *France* Baked Alaska

omelette Stéphanie *Austria* A light and fluffy soufflé omelette from Vienna

omena *Finland* Apple

omenahilloke *Finland* Compote of apples

omenalumi *Finland* Apple snow, the dessert

omenasose *Finland* Apple sauce

omnivore A person or animal who will eat anything edible, either of animal or vegetable origin

omul *Russia* A relative of the salmon found in Lake Baikal, Siberia

omum *South Asia* Ajowan

omuretsu *Japan* Omelette

oncom *Indonesia* A fermented paste made from peanuts and subsequently fried. Similar to tempe.

ong choi *China* Swamp cabbage

onglet *France* Thin flank of beef. Also called **hampe**

onigiri *Japan* Cooked rice moulded around a sweet or savoury filling and possibly wrapped in sheets of seaweed. The Japanese equivalent of the sandwich.

onion A white pungent bulb from a plant, *Allium cepa,* originating in Asia but now grown all over the world. It is the most important culinary vegetable and comes in many varieties. Scallions and spring onions are immature forms of onion harvested before the bulb has swollen. Varieties include globe, Spanish, Italian red, white, button, silverskin and spring onion.

onion and liver sausage *England* A sausage made with minced pigs' liver and lean pork mixed with chopped onions and sliced lights, all fried in lard, mixed with seasoning, nutmeg and marjoram, packed into hog fat ends or bungs, simmered for 30 minutes, refreshed and air dried

onion cake *Wales* As **pommes Anna**, but with finely chopped onion between the potato

layers. Sometimes beef stock is added. Also called **teisen nioned**

onion clouté *England* A peeled onion studded with cloves some of which may hold a piece of bay leaf, most commonly used to flavour the milk used for **béchamel sauce** (NOTE: Literally 'nailed onion'.)

onion kachumber *South Asia* Sliced onions salted and drained for an hour, mixed with a mixture of equal proportions of water, brown sugar and tamarind then combined with chopped tomato, minced ginger, chopped coriander leaves and chopped and deseeded green chillies

onion rings Onions sliced across the root stem axis and the large outer rings battered and deep-fried

onion sauce Finely diced onions, boiled or sweated in butter added to **béchamel sauce**. Used for roast mutton. Also called **oignons, sauce aux**

onion seeds Used in India as a spice, often fried with vegetables

Onopordum acanthum *Botanical name* Cotton thistle

ontbijt *Netherlands* Breakfast

ontbijtkoek *Netherlands* **1.** A spiced breakfast bun **2.** Honey cake

oodovolstvie testya *Russia* See **udovolstvie testia** (NOTE: Literally 'father-in-law's delight'.)

ookha *Russia* See **ukha**

opal basil A variety of basil with a heavy perfumed scent

open sandwich A Scandinavian speciality consisting of a single slice of buttered bread on which food and garnishes are arranged in a decorative and artistic manner. Eaten with a knife and fork.

opéra, à l' *France* In the opera style, i.e. garnished with chicken livers, duchesse potatoes and asparagus tips

Opera dell'arte del cucinare *Italy* One of the most influential early Italian cookery books by Bartalomeo Scappi, cook to Pope Pius V, 1566 to 1572 A.D. See also **Scappi's spice mix**

operatårta *Sweden* A cream-filled layer cake

opgerolde koek *Netherlands* A Swiss roll

opisthorchis A species of fluke common in Russia and parts of Southeast Asia which is transmitted by carp and other fresh water fish. Causes liver damage.

oplet A **sea anemone**, *Anemonia sulcata*, eaten in France. Also called **snakelocks**

opossum Small marsupials from the USA, principally the Virginian opossum, *Didelphis virginiana*, and from Australia, the brush-tailed opossum, *Trichosurus vulpecula*. They are eaten as food.especially in southeastern USA. The American variety can weigh up to 5 kg. There are many other species of opossum which are generally smaller and of no value as food. See also **manicou**. Also called **possum**

Opuntia ficus-indica *Botanical name* Prickly pear cactus

orach A hardy annual, *Atriplex hortensis*, growing to 1.5 m with large indented leaves also available in gold and purple varieties. The young leaves may be used in salads, older leaves are cooked as spinach. Used in France for soups. Also called **garden orach**, **mountain spinach**

orada a la sal *Catalonia* Gilthead bream cooked in a salt crust which is removed before service

orange See **sweet orange**

Orange *Germany* Orange, the fruit

orange amère *France* Seville orange

orangeboom *Netherlands* Orange, the fruit

orange essence A strong extract of orange zest used as a flavouring

orange flower water An alcoholic extract from Seville orange flowers used as a flavouring

orange marmalade *Denmark, England* Marmalade made with oranges

orange passion fruit Sweet granadilla

orange pudding *United Kingdom* A pudding made from basic steamed pudding mixture flavoured with grated orange zest

orange roughy *New Zealand* A seawater fish from the South Pacific with firm white, tasteless flesh, exported as boneless fillets

orange sauce 1. A 20% sugar syrup thickened with corn flour or arrowroot, cooked out, strained then strained orange juice and blanched **julienne** of orange zest added **2.** See **bigarade, sauce**

orata *Italy* Gilt head bream

Orbignija martinana *Botanical name* Babassu

Orbignija speciosa *Botanical name* Babassu

ördek *Turkey* Duck

ordinaire *France* Ordinary, not distinguished in any way

Orduña *Spain* A hard cylindrical (up to 1.5 kg) ewes' milk cheese with no holes, ripened for 30 to 40 days

orecchia di San Pietro *Italy* Abalone

orecchia marina *Italy* Abalone

orecchiette *Italy* Small ear-shaped or shell-like pasta shapes

orecchio *Italy* Ear, e.g. of a pig

oregano A more aromatic and strongly flavoured herb, *Oregano vulgare*, than the

marjorams. It has a slightly sprawling habit and white or pink flowers. Available dried or fresh and used with meat, sausages, in salads and in many Italian dishes. Also called **common marjoram**, **wild marjoram**

orégano *Spain* Oregano

Oregano *Germany* Oregano

Oregon grape *United States* Barberry

oreille *France* Ear, especially of a pig

oreille de mer *France* Abalone

oreja de mar *Spain* Abalone

orekh *Russia* Nut

organic food Food which has been grown or reared without synthetic or chemically produced fertilizers, pesticides and herbicides on land which itself has been organic for 2 years

organic labelling In the EU, any food product with organic claims on the label must have been produced according to the rules on organic agricultural production. No irradiated or genetically engineered ingredients can be included.

organ meat *United States* Offal

orge *France* Barley

orge perlé *France* Pearl barley

oriental brassicas Brassicas cultivated mainly for their leaves, stems and young flowering shoots. They tend to grow faster and have a wider range of uses than the western varieties.

oriental bunching onion A bunching onion developed from the Welsh onion with thickened white leaf bases up to 15 cm long. Usually grown as an annual or biennial plant. All parts are edible and are used at all stages of growth. Often used as a substitute for spring onions.

orientale, à l' *France* In the eastern Mediterranean style and the Balkan style, i.e. with tomatoes, garlic and saffron

orientale, sauce *France* **Sauce américaine** flavoured with curry powder, reduced and let down with cream

oriental mustard The name of a variety of annual and biennial, often coarse-leaved plants, *Brassica juncea*, with seeds the same colour as white mustard, grown in Japan for use in cooking and as a condiment. The leaves which come in various colours and textures are cooked as a vegetable or eaten raw in salads when young and are becoming popular in the west. The flavour of the leaves becomes stronger as they age. Also called **mustard greens**

oriental sesame oil Sesame seed oil

origan *France* Oregano

origano *Italy* Oregano

Origanum heracleoticum Botanical name Winter marjoram

Origanum majorana Botanical name Sweet marjoram, knotted marjoram

Origanum onites Botanical name Pot marjoram, French marjoram

Origanum vulgare Botanical name Oregano

Orkney Scotland A firm cows' milk cheese from Orkney, resembling Dunlop

Orkney broonies Scotland Similar to parkin but made with buttermilk instead of milk

Orlando A variety of **tangelo**

orléanaise. à l' France In the Orleans style, i.e. garnished with braised chicory and potatoes

Orly, fish à l' Fish, usually fillets of white fish marinated in oil and lemon juice, passed through seasoned flour, coated in a frying batter, deep-fried at 175°C, drained, garnished with lemon and picked or deep-fried parsley and served with separate tomato sauce

ormer The European version of the Pacific **abalone**, found in the Mediterranean and around the Channel Islands. Up to 10 cm long.

ornato Spain A decorative bread from Estremadura with chorizo sausage inside

oronge France Orange agaric, an edible fungus

Oropesa Spain A hard ewes' milk cheese from Toledo cast in cylinders (up to 2 kg). It has a dark paste containing small holes and a hard thick rind after ripening for 2 to 3 months. Similar to **Manchego**.

oroshigane Japan A long thin grater resembling a wood rasp or surform with one sharpened edge used for peeling and grating ginger root

orozuz Spain Liquorice

orphie France Needlefish or garfish from the Mediterranean. See also **aiguille**

orre Sweden Black grouse

ørred Denmark Trout

ørret Norway Trout

Orrys France A hard strong-tasting cows' milk cheese from Languedoc-Roussillon made in the shape of a large flat disc. May be used for grating.

ort See **orts**

ortaggi Italy Vegetables, greens

ortanique Caribbean A naturally occurring hybrid of the genus *Citrus* from Jamaica, which is grown in many semi-tropical climates under other names e.g. australique (Australia), mandora (Cyprus), topaz and tangor (Middle East) and tambor (South Africa), because the original name is a

trademark (from orange, tangerine un*ique*). The flesh is extremely tender with a very sweet aromatic juice, few if any pips and a thin easily peelable skin. It does not develop off flavours.

ortega Spain Grouse

orthophenyl phenol See **E231**

orthophosphates, ammonium Ammonium dihydrogen and diammonium hydrogen orthophosphate, used as buffers and as yeast food

orthophosphates, calcium Calcium salts of orthophosphoric acid used as firming agents, anti-caking agents and raising agents in cake mixes, baking powder and dessert mixes. E341 covers calcium tetrahydrogen diorthophosphate, calcium hydrogen orthophosphate and tricalcium diorthophosphate.

orthophosphates, sodium and potassium Sodium and potassium salts of orthophosphoric acid used as buffers, sequestrants and emulsifiers in dessert mixes, non-dairy creamers, processed cheese and the like. E339 covers sodium dihydrogen-, disodium hydrogen- and trisodium orthophosphate, E340 covers the equivalent potassium salts.

orthophosphoric acid An inorganic acid used as a buffering agent, and in the form of its salts (orthophosphates) as buffers, sequestrants, anti-caking agents, emulsifiers and firming agents in cake and dessert mixes, creamers and processed cheese. See also **E338**

ortiche Italy Nettles

ortie France Nettle

ortie de mer France Sea anemone

ortiga Spain Nettles

ortolan A small wild bird, *Emberiza hortulana*, up to 15 cm long, once popular in France, now a protected species due to over-hunting

orts England Remains of food left over from a meal often eaten as a snack or at a subsequent meal (*colloquial*)

oruga Spain Rocket, the plant

Oryza glaberrima Botanical name Red rice (2)

Oryza sativa Botanical name Rice

orzo Italy 1. Barley 2. Rice-shaped pasta used in soups

orzo perlato Italy Pearl barley

os France Bone

os, à l' France Garnished or flavoured with bone marrow

os à moelle France Marrow bone

Osborne pudding England A bread and butter pudding made with brown bread and butter spread with marmalade but without dried fruit

oscetrova Caviar from the **osetrina sturgeon**

oseille France Sorrel

osetrina sturgeon A somewhat larger sturgeon, *Acipenser guldenstädti*, than the sevruga. It weighs up to 18 kg and yields about 4 to 7 kg of caviar. The caviar, known variously as osciotre, ossetra, osetrova in the West, is considered to be one of the finest. Also called **white sturgeon**

oshifima South Africa The Namibian name for the standard corn or maize meal porridge

oshinko maki Japan A sushi roll containing pickle and salted mooli

oshi-zushi Japan Sushi-meshi rice packed into a square wooden mould, covered with filling which is pressed into place. The mould sides are removed and the rice cake cut into squares.

Osmanli kebabi Turkey A kebab of cubed fatty mutton or lamb marinated in vinegar with chopped onions and seasoning and grilled

osmanthus flower A tiny scented white flower from China used as a garnish. They may be fresh, candied or preserved in sweetened alcohol.

oss buss Italy Ossobuco

ossehaas Netherlands Fillet of beef

ossestaartsoep Netherlands Oxtail soup

ossetra Caviar from the **osetrina sturgeon**

ossibuchi Italy Ossobuco

osso Italy Bone

osso bucco See **ossobuco 2**

ossobuchi Italy Ossobuco

ossobuco Italy 1. Marrow bone 2. Knuckle or shin of veal cut in steaks across the bone, sautéed on the bone and then simmered with garlic, onions and tomatoes, sprinkled with a mixture of chopped parsley, garlic and grated lemon zest and served with spaghetti or rice, especially **risotto alla milanese**. Also called **osso bucco, ossibuchi, ossobuchi, oss buss**

ost Denmark, Norway, Sweden Cheese

østers Denmark, Norway Oysters

ostia Italy Wafer

ostkaka Sweden A type of cheesecake baked in a mould

ostra Portugal, Spain Oyster, originally the European flat oyster

ostra de Portugal Spain Portuguese oyster

ostrica giapponese Italy Pacific oyster

ostrica piatta Italy European flat oyster

ostrica portoghese Italy Portuguese oyster

ostrich A very large flightless bird, *Struthio camelus*, with a long bare neck, small head and two toed feet. It is now being farmed for its flesh which is very lean, its feathers and its skin which makes good leather. The meat is best with little cooking.

ostriche Italy Oysters

ostrich fern Fiddlehead fern

ostron Sweden Oyster

ostsås Sweden A type of cheese or rarebit sauce made from diced cheddar cheese melted with butter and cream over a low heat, seasoned with salt and cayenne pepper, flavoured with a little dry mustard and diced gherkin and finished with beaten egg. Used with fish.

ostsoppa med åggkulor Sweden Veal or chicken stock, thickened with a blond roux, flavoured with salt, paprika and white wine, boiled and whisked into a frothy but not too thick mixture of double cream, egg yolks and grated cheese. Served hot, garnished with chopped parsley, chervil and egg balls (**äggkulor**).

osuimono Japan Suimono

osyotrina sturgeon Russia See **osetrina sturgeon**

ot Vietnam Chilli pepper

otaheite apple A very sweet variety of **hog plum** from the tree *Spondias dulcis*

otak-otak Malaysia A mixture of chopped raw fish, chopped onions, grated coconut, herbs and spices, bound with egg and wrapped in banana leaf or aluminium foil prior to steaming

o'teano Italy A Neapolitan vegetable pie made with steamed potatoes, zucchini and aubergines, flavoured with oregano (NOTE: Literally 'saucepan', in local dialect.)

otkrytyi buterbrod Russia Open sandwich

otoro Japan A very expensive cut from the middle of the middle section of tuna belly (**toro**). See also **chutoro**

otoshibuta Japan A circular piece of wood with a central handle placed directly on simmering food to prevent too much turbulence and the food breaking up

ottarde Italy Bustard, the bird

ou China Lotus root

ouaouaron Canada, United States Bullfrog in the Cajun patois

ouillade France A bean and vegetable soup from Languedoc, well flavoured with garlic

oukha Russia See **ukha**

oukrop Russia Ukrop

ounce A unit of weight equal to one sixteenth of a pound. Still in use in the USA. Abbreviation **oz**

oursin France Sea urchin

ous remenats amb camasecs *Catalonia* Scrambled eggs with wild mushrooms

outlaw soup See **bakonyi betyárleves**

ouvrir *France* To open

ouzhin *Russia* See **uzhin**

ouzo *Greece* An aniseed-flavoured liqueur also useful as a culinary flavouring

ovalbumin The main protein comprising about 70% of egg white protein. It is partially coagulated by fast beating especially at higher temperatures and is responsible for the stability of whipped egg white. It starts to coagulate with heat at around 60°C.

oval kumquat Nagami kumquat

Ovár *Hungary* A supple-textured, yellow cows' milk cheese with a reddish-brown rind resembling **Tilsit**

Ovcí Hrudkovy syr *Czech Republic* A semi-hard unpressed ewes' milk cheese made in spheres or brick shapes (up to 10 kg) and ripened in brine for a week

oven An insulated enclosed space, usually rectangular but may be other shapes, heated by any type of fuel including solar radiation, either directly or indirectly, with a door or opening and in which food is baked, roasted or cooked

oven-fry, to *United States* To pass meat through seasoned flour, brush with molten fat or oil and bake in the oven on a flat sheet or dish until brown and cooked through

oven-ready Sold in a state ready to be put in the oven for heating or cooking after removing any unwanted packaging, usually descriptive of chickens, potato chips or prepared meals

oven temperature Oven temperature is set according to four different scales, three quantitative, i.e. Fahrenheit °F, Centigrade °C, or gas mark GM, and one qualitative, i.e. cool <120°C, slow 120°C, moderate 180°C, hot 220°C and very hot 250°C. As a rule of thumb °F are twice °C. This is exactly so at 144 °C; above this °F are slightly less than double and below slightly more than double. See also **gas mark**

oven toast Bread lightly buttered on each side and baked in the oven until golden brown

ovini *Italy* Sheep

ovo *Portugal* Egg

ovoli *Italy* 1. A small ball-shaped Mozzarella cheese sometimes eaten with Parma ham 2. An egg-shaped mushroom with a bright orange cap which is highly prized and eaten raw/NX/. Also called **Caesar's mushroom**, **imperial agaric**

ovos duros *Portugal* Hard-boiled eggs

ovos escalados *Portugal* Poached eggs

ovos estrelados *Portugal* Fried eggs

ovos mexidos *Portugal* Scrambled eggs

ovos moles *Portugal* Egg yolks mixed with sugar and used as a sauce or filling or poached in spoonfuls and dusted with cinnamon

ovos quentes *Portugal* Soft-boiled eggs

ovotarica *Italy* Botargo

ox 1. A general name for the male or female of common domestic cattle (bulls and cows), especially a castrated male. The name is still used as a prefix for some items of offal e.g. liver, kidney, heart, etc. **2.** *Sweden* Indicating beef

oxalic acid The acid found in spinach, rhubarb and some other leaves, stems and tubers which serves to prevent insect attack. It has no known benefit to humans and may be deleterious especially for certain health conditions.

Oxalis tuberosa Botanical name Occa

ox brains The brains of older cattle, not now used in the UK because of BSE

oxbringa *Sweden* Brisket of beef

ox casings The trade term for casings (cleaned intestines) of cattle, known as runners to 48 mm diameter, middles 45 to 55 mm diameter and bungs 75 to 150 mm diameter

ox cheek Very gelatinous and tasty meat from the cheek of cattle generally classed as offal. Requires long slow cooking and is used in soups, stews and casseroles.

oxfilé *Sweden* Fillet of beef

Oxford cheese *England* A cheese intermediate in flavour and texture between Cheddar and Cheshire. May be smoked.

Oxford John steak *England* A speciality of Oxfordshire, consisting of leg steaks of lamb including the bone, fried with onion, thyme and parsley and served with a brown gravy flavoured with port and lemon juice

Oxford pudding *England* A pastry tart lined with apricot jam and filled with meringue

Oxford sauce As **Cumberland sauce**, but finished with chopped blanched orange and lemon zest instead of **julienne** of orange

Oxford sausages *England* Sausages made from minced pork, minced pork fat and fresh white breadcrumbs (2:1:1), mixed, seasoned and flavoured with sage, winter savory and marjoram and grated lemon zest, moistened with water and may be packed into casings and linked or left skinless. Fried and served hot. A 19th century version substituted veal for half the pork, suet for pork fat and reduced the breadcrumbs by half.

oxidation In cooking, the reaction of a food with the oxygen of the air which usually produces off flavours. Oxidation reactions are often promoted by light and high temperature increases the rate of reaction (approximate doubling for every 10°C rise). Anti-oxidants are used to inhibit the reaction.

ox kidney The large dark red kidney from mature cattle. It has a core of fat and requires long slow cooking. Often soaked in warm salted water with a little vinegar prior to cooking to reduce the strong flavour. Used in steak and kidney puddings and pies.

oxkött *Sweden* Beef

ox liver The deep brown-coloured and strong-flavoured liver from mature cattle. It requires long cooking and is suitable for stewing, braising and for casseroles and coarse pâtés. The flavour may be reduced by soaking in milk.

oxstek *Sweden* Roast beef

oxsvans *Sweden* Oxtail

oxsvanssoppa *Sweden* Oxtail soup

oxtail The tails of beef cattle usually weighing about 1.4 kg when skinned. There is a fair amount of lean meat with a good meaty flavour and a thin layer of firm white fat. Usually braised or made into soup.

oxtail soup 1. Disjointed oxtail and a **mirepoix** of onion, garlic, carrot and turnip browned in fat; flour added to make a brown roux; tomato purée, a bouquet garni and brown stock added, simmered and skimmed for 4 hours; oxtail and bouquet garni removed; oxtail deboned and flesh returned; the whole liquidized, strained, seasoned and consistency corrected; finished with sherry and garnished with diced or balled carrots and turnips and the tip of the oxtail cut in rounds. See also **thick oxtail soup 2.** As thick oxtail soup, but omitting the flour and slightly thickening before garnishing using arrowroot and cooking until clear. See also **clear oxtail soup**

ox tongue The large tongue of mature cattle weighing about 3 kg. Sold fresh or brined and often cooked, jellied and pressed as a slicing meat and sandwich filling. When cooked it has a rich flavour and may be served hot with mustard sauce or Madeira sauce.

oxtunga *Sweden* Ox tongue

oxygen The gas which is necessary for most animal life and which forms about 20% of the air. At high temperatures it causes oxidation and deterioration of food. The rate of oxidation doubles for every 10°C increase in temperature. Occasionally used as a packaging gas.

oxymel A mixture of 4 parts honey to 1 part vinegar which may be used as a marinade or, after diluting with water, as a drink

oxystearin A sequestering agent and inhibitor of fat crystallization used in salad creams and similar foodstuffs

oyakonabe *Japan* A small round frying pan

oyster 1. A seawater bivalve of the genera *Ostrea* and *Crassostrea* and the species *Saccostrea commercialis*, once the food of the poor but now a gourmet delicacy. May be wild or farmed, sold alive or in dried or other preserved form. Since they are static feeders, they are influenced by sea conditions and hence known by the name of a district, e.g. Whitstable and Colchester in the UK, Galway in Ireland, Belon and Armoricaine in France. Not at their best when spawning, hence traditionally eaten in the Northern Hemisphere in months with an 'R' in them, i.e. September to April. See also **native oyster**, **Pacific oyster**, **Portuguese oyster**, **American oyster**, **Indian oyster**, **Australian oyster**, **South American oyster**, **Olympia oyster 2.** A prized small muscle in poultry which sits in an indentation in the carcass just in front of where the thigh bone is attached

oyster bacon A round cut of bacon from the end of the back containing a fair amount of fat

oyster crab A very small (1 cm) crab which lives in the shells of live oysters. May be eaten raw or fried. Also called **pea crab**

oyster fungus See **oyster mushroom**

oyster knife A knife with a thin, strong, sharp-pointed blade, used to open oysters

oyster meat See **oyster 2**

oyster mushroom An edible wild mushroom, *Pleurotus ostreatus*, with a short stalk on one side of the smooth bare oyster-like cap which is up to 15 cm in diameter and blue-grey when young. It grows on the trunks of deciduous trees and has a rather tough, juicy flesh with no smell but a slightly fishy flavour. Now cultivated. Also called **oyster fungus**, **abalone mushroom**, **tree oyster mushroom**

oyster of veal A prime roasting cut of veal from the forequarter, generally boned and rolled

oyster plant Salsify

oyster sauce 1. *China* A condiment and flavouring sauce consisting of soya sauce combined with dried oysters. It has a strong shellfish flavour. **2.** See **huîtres, sauce aux 3.** *United Kingdom* A **béchamel sauce** with cream, a little cayenne pepper, oyster juice and poached and bearded oysters

oyster sausage *England* A traditional sausage made when oysters were the food of the poor. Made from pounded veal, chopped or minced oysters and breadcrumbs soaked in oyster liquor, seasoned and bound with egg before being packed in casings. Not made commercially nowadays but almost certain to be taken up by expensive restaurants specializing in traditional English cooking.

oysters Bienville *United States* Oysters on the half shell covered with a **béchamel sauce** containing chopped and sweated green sweet peppers and onion, gratinated with breadcrumbs and cheese and grilled

oysters Mombasa *East Africa* Shucked oysters baked in the oven for 6 to 8 minutes. Each oyster is topped with a little sauce made by sautéeing garlic and coriander or parsley in butter, adding piri-piri or similar hot sauce, white wine and seasoning and processing in a blender.

oysters outback *Australia* Shucked oysters topped with a mixture of grated cheddar cheese and akudjura, salted and grilled until the cheese melts

oysters Rockefeller *United States* A New Orleans speciality of oysters topped with a Pernod-flavoured savoury breadcrumb mixture and baked quickly on the half shell

oysters Van Diemen *Australia* Shucked oysters each covered with a slice of Tasmanian Brie, seasoned with mountain pepper and garnished with a native pepperberry

oz Ounce

PQRSTUV

pa *Catalonia* Bread
paahdeleipää *Finland* Toast
paahdepaisti *Finland* Roast beef
paak cheong *China* White pomfret, the fish
pa amb oli *Catalonia* A snack made from a thick slice of crusty bread rubbed with a vine-ripened cut tomato, sprinkled with good oil and salted
pa amb tomàquet *Catalonia* Bread rubbed with tomato and garlic and drizzled with olive oil. Served as tapas.
paan *South Asia* A breath freshener taken after a meal usually consisting of a mixture of aromatic seeds, often garishly coloured. See also **pan 2**
paarl lemoen *South Africa* A classic Cape recipe for abalone (**perlemoen**) which is simmered in white wine and water (1:3) with butter, lemon juice and seasoning for 2 hours then served with cooking liquor thickened with soft white breadcrumbs and flavoured with a little nutmeg
paayap *Philippines* Long bean
PABA This constituent of sunscreen agents appears to maintain hair colour and skin conditions in rodents, but its function in humans is obscure. It is found in whole grains and wheat germ and is an essential growth factor for many microorganisms. Also called **para-amino-benzoic acid**
pabellon caroqueno *Venezuela* A national dish consisting of a mixture of steak, rice, black beans and plantains or bananas topped with a fried egg
pa boeuk *Laos* A very large fish (up to 2 m) caught in the Mekong river. Its roe alone can weigh up to 10 kg. The flesh may be eaten fresh, but because of the amount is usually preserved by fermentation.
pabulum An archaic term for food of any kind especially of animals and plants
paca *South America* An edible rodent from the north of South America with a white spotted brown coat

pachadi *South Asia* Chopped vegetables bound with yoghurt and flavoured with mustard seeds
Pachyrrhizus erosus *Botanical name* The jacama plant
Pacific bonito Skipjack tuna
Pacific cod A relative, *Gadus macrocephalus* of the Atlantic cod with a brown to grey back weighing 2 to 4 kg and up to 60 cm long. Treat as cod.
Pacific dogfish Rock salmon
Pacific hake A variety of hake caught in the Pacific Ocean, used mainly for processed fish products
Pacific halibut The halibut, *Hippoglossus stenolepsis*, found in the northern Pacific Ocean
Pacific mackerel The mackerel, *Scomber japonicus*, found off Japan and California
Pacific oyster A variety of disease-resistant oyster, *Crassostrea gigas*, used to restock many European farmed oyster beds wiped out by disease in the 1970s. Has a craggier and deeper shell than the Portuguese oyster and can grow to 30 cm but normally sold at 6 to 12 cm. Also called **Japanese oyster**
Pacific thread herring A relative of the thread herring found off the west coast of North America
packet *Ireland* A black pudding from Limerick similar to **drisheen**. Eaten with tripe.
Pacrasma excelsa *Botanical name* Bitter ash from which quassia is extracted
pad *Thailand* Stir-fried
paddestoel *Netherlands* Mushroom
paddy rice Freshly harvested rice still with its husk
paddy straw mushroom See **straw mushroom**
pa de fetge *Catalonia* Liver pâté
pa-de-gaw-gyi *Burma* Greater galangal
padeira, à *Portugal* Baked in an ovenproof dish in a hot oven (NOTE: From *padeiro*, 'baker'.)

padek *Laos* A fish paste made by salting fish or fermenting it with rice bran

padella *Italy* Frying pan

padrushka *Poland* Hamburg parsley

paella 1. A savoury mixture of rice, vegetables, chicken and shellfish cooked in a large pan called a paellera in the same way as risotto, but with a less starch-releasing rice such as Valencia. Shellfish are normally added about 5 to 10 minutes after adding stock, so that they are not overcooked, and paella is finished with liquidized garlic and decorated before service from the pan. **2.** *Catalonia* The same as Spanish paella but using seafood on the coast and game inland

paella de campiña *Spain* Paella with ham, bacon, chicken and sausage

paella powder A colouring agent, usually synthetic tartrazine, used to colour paellas instead of saffron. Not recommended.

paella valenciana *Catalonia* Paella with chicken, shellfish, peas, beans and artichokes

paellera *Spain* A wide, round, shallow, 3 to 5 cm deep pan with 2 handles. The diameter, which can be up to a metre, depends upon the number of servings required. Used for cooking paella which is served direct from the pan.

pære *Denmark, Norway* Pear

paesana, alla *Italy* In country style, i.e with bacon, mushrooms and tomatoes, especially of pasta.

paeta *Italy* Turkey

pagello *Italy* Sea bream, the fish. Also called **fragolino**

pageot rouge *France* Pandora, the fish

Paglia *Switzerland* A soft cheese similar to **Gorgonzola** from Ticino

paglia e fieno *Italy* Thin green and yellow dried noodles sold mixed in the packet (NOTE: Literally 'straw and hay'.)

pagnotta *Italy* A round loaf of bread

pagnotta Santa Chiara *Italy* A potato bread from Naples filled with tomatoes, anchovies and herbs

Pago *Austria* A ewes' milk cheese

pagre *France* Sea bream

pagro comune *Italy* Sea bream

paguro *Italy* Hermit crab

pahari mirich *South Asia* Sweet peppers

pähkinäkakku *Finland* A rich cake containing ground walnuts and smothered in whipped cream

pähkinäpaisti *Finland* A vegetarian patty made from ground nuts and cream

pai chi *China* The dried root of a relative of **angelica**, *Angelica sinensis*. See also **dang gui**

paillard 1. *France* A thin escalope or slice of meat or fish **2.** *Italy* Grilled sirloin steak

paillard di vitelle A grilled veal cutlet served with lemon juice

paillettes *France* Thin slivers or rings, e.g. of potatoes, pastry, onions, etc (NOTE: Literally 'spangles, flakes'.)

paillettes d'oignons frits *France* Fried onion rings

paillettes dorées *France* Cheese straws

paimi Conkies

pain *France* Bread, also used for the long 400 g baguette type of loaf

pain à cacheter *France* Wafer

pain à la grecque *Belgium* Small cakes made from a rich cake mixture

pain au chocolat *France* A rectangular-shaped croissant-type pastry with chocolate in the centre. Eaten warm.

pain au sucre *Canada* A French Canadian speciality of bread toasted on one side, the untoasted side covered with maple sugar, grilled until the sugar melts then served with cream

pain bis *France* Wholemeal or brown bread

pain blanc *France* White bread

pain complet *France* Wholemeal, wholewheat or granary bread

pain de Gênes *France* Genoa cake

pain de la Mecque *France* A cream-filled puff pastry

pain de ménage *France* Home-made bread

pain de mie *France* Soft crusted English-style white bread for sandwiches

pain d'épices *France* Well-spiced gingerbread

pain de seigle *France* Rye bread

pain de son *France* Wholemeal bread

pain des paysans *France* Chestnut flour

pain de veau *Belgium* A meat loaf made with veal

pain de volaille *France* A finely processed chicken meat loaf or mould

pain doré *France* Pain perdu

pain entier *France* Wholemeal bread

pain épi *France* A large French bread stick, shaped like an ear of corn, weighing about 250 g

pain fig banane *Caribbean* A speciality of St Lucia consisting of banana bread flavoured with cinnamon, nutmeg, ginger and cloves eaten like cake. Also called **Caribbean banana cake**

pain grillé *France* Toast

pain intégral *France* Wholemeal bread

pain noir *France* Wholemeal bread or brown bread

pain parisien A long loaf of bread rather like a large baguette

pain perdu *France* Stale bread slices dipped in an egg and milk mixture, sweetened and flavoured with vanilla for the dessert version, then fried in (clarified) butter until crisp and golden. Also called **pain doré**, **French toast**

pain pistolet *France* Pistolet

pain rôti *France* Toast

Painswick chop *England* A bacon chop from the West country often baked in the oven with cider, brown sugar and mustard

pain trouvé *Belgium* **Pain perdu** topped with a mixture of **béchamel sauce** and chopped ham and sprinkled with grated Parmesan cheese

paio *Portugal* A thick garlic-flavoured pork sausage

Paisley almond cakes *Scotland* Well beaten eggs, butter, caster sugar, rice flour, corn flour and ground almonds (8:6:6:4:4:3) with 3 tbsp of baking powder per kg of flours made up by the creaming method and baked in bun tins at 180°C for 10 to 15 minutes

paistettu *Finland* **1.** Roasted **2.** Fried

paistettu kana *Finland* Fried chicken

paistettut sienet *Finland* Fried mushrooms

paisti *Finland* Steak, roast (as of meat)

paistinperunat *Finland* Fried potatoes

paj *Sweden* Pie

pak *Thailand* Vegetables

pak bung *Thailand* Swamp cabbage

pak chai *China* Pak choy

pak chee *Thailand* Coriander seed and leaves

pak chee lao *Thailand* Dill seed

pak chi met *Thailand* Coriander

pak choi Pak choy

pak choy A loose-leaved Chinese brassica, *Brassica rapa* var. *chinensis*, with white leaf stems and dark, succulent mild leaves, very fast growing and cooked when young with at most 12 opened leaves. Also called **pak choi**, **pak soi**, **bok choy**, **bok choi**, **celery cabbage**

pak hom ho *Vietnam* Mint

pak kard hom *Thailand* Lettuce

pak kok *China* Star anise

pakode *South Asia* Fritters

pakora *South Asia* Bite-sized fritter made with a batter containing **besan** or chickpea flour. Deep-fried and served hot with chutney. The fritters usually contain vegetables, but can be made with shellfish, fish, cooked rice,

cheese or meat. (NOTE: They are the north Indian equivalent of **bhajias**.)

paksiw *Philippines* Large pieces of fish simmered until cooked in a clay pot with vinegar, salt and possibly ginger and sugar. Allowed to cool in the liquid and served cold with some of the pickling liquid.

pak soi See **pak choy**

pala *Indonesia* Nutmeg

palabok *Philippines* Garnishes, usually to give added flavour, such as dried fish flakes, pork crackling, chopped scallions, dried shrimps, chopped hard-boiled eggs, etc.

palacinky *Czech Republic* Light batter pancakes filled with grated chocolate, apricot jam or a sweetened mixture of cream cheese and sultanas

palacsinta *Hungary* Small pancake, crêpe

pålæg *Denmark* The filling on open-topped Danish sandwiches

palak *South Asia* Spinach

palamita *Italy* Bonito, the fish

Palatschinken *Austria* Thin pancakes filled with marmalade, chocolate, chopped nuts and/or sweetened cheese

palayok *Philippines* A terracotta cooking pot similar to the Indian chatty

paleron *France* A cut of beef including part of the chuck and clod used for stewing or braising; parts are sometimes marinated in the piece and roasted

Palestine, crème *France* Artichoke soup finished with cream, milk or thin **béchamel sauce**. Also called **cream of artichoke soup**

Palestine sweet lime See **sweet lime**

palette *France* Blade of pork or lamb from the shoulder

palette knife A 2 to 3 cm wide, flexible handled blade with a round blunt end and not sharpened. Used for manipulating food, e.g. fish fillets, and for smoothing icings and toppings.

palm Any member of an important family of plants, *Palmae*, of which there are over 4,000 species, generally tropical or subtropical and mostly trees with the characteristic tuft of fan-like leaves, although a few are climbers, e.g. the rattan palm. They supply edible vegetable matter, fruit, nuts, oil and sap as well as building materials.

palma *Italy, Spain* Palm

palm butter 1. *Central Africa* Moambé sauce **2.** *West Africa* A pulp made from palm nuts similar in consistency to peanut butter **3.** *West Africa* Palm kernel oil

palm cabbage The growing tip of the coconut palm considered to be a delicacy and eaten as a vegetable in tropical Asia

palme *France* Palm

Palme *Germany* Palm

palmetto A palm tree, *Sabal palmetto*, which grows in the southeast of the USA and in Mexico. Its main use is for brushes but the growing tips are boiled as heart of palm and eaten hot as a vegetable or cold as a salad. Also called **cabbage palm**

palm heart Heart of palm

palmiers *England, France* A square of sugared puff pastry rolled like a scroll from opposite sides to meet in the middle, egg-washed, cut into 2 cm slices, one side sugared and baked sugar side down for about 10 min. in a hot oven, turned and sugar caramelized.

palmitic acid A saturated fatty acid found in its glycerol ester form in beef and lamb fat and other hard fats

palmito *Portugal, Spain* Heart of palm

palm kernel oil A white oil extracted from the kernels of the fruits of the oil palm, *Elaeis guineensis*, mainly used for margarine manufacture. See also **palm oil**. Also called **palm butter**

palm nut The fruit of the **palmyra palm** about 9 cm long and containing 3 kernels in each. The immature kernels are used in desserts and have a taste of coconut. The mature kernels are a source of palm kernel oil but may be germinated to give an enlarged fleshy embryo used as a vegetable. Also called **palmyra fruit**

palm oil The oil extracted from the fruits of the oil palm, *Elaeis guineensis*, which originated in Africa but is now grown in Malaysia, Indonesia and other high rainfall tropical areas. About half the African production is used as cooking oil, the remainder is used for soap and industrial purposes and after treatment for margarine. The oil sets to a soft solid after extraction. It contains 40% saturated, 40% monounsaturated and 10% polyunsaturated fat. See also **palm kernel oil**

palm-oil chop *West Africa* A celebratory dish made by browning beef or chicken pieces in palm oil with ground ginger or cinnamon, The meat is removed and vegetables are sweated in the same oil and simmered for 20 minutes and partially mashed. Prawns, tomato purée, palm fruit pulp, thyme and spices are added together with water to make a smooth sauce. The reserved meat is added and simmered until cooked. Served over rice with a selection of garnishes for the guests to choose at will.

palm sugar A sugary substance obtained by boiling down the sap from the palmyra palm or sugar palm. Also called **jaggery**, **java sugar**, **coconut sugar**

palm tree See **palm**

palmyra fruit Palm nut

palmyra palm A palm tree, *Borassus flabellifer*, from India, Africa and Asia. Sap is extracted by tapping the unopened male or female flower stalks and immediately boiled down to produce palm sugar or fermented to toddy. Alternatively the fruits (palm nuts) are allowed to grow. Their sap is used as a drink, the soft kernel is also eaten and the germinated nuts produce an enlarged fleshy embryo which is used as a vegetable. Also called **borassus palm**

paloise, sauce *England, France* As **hollandaise sauce**, but with chopped mint in the initial reduction and finished after straining with chopped fresh mint

paloma *Spain* Pigeon

palomba *Italy* Wood pigeon

palombacce *Italy* Wood pigeon

palombe *France* Wood pigeon

palombo *Italy* **1.** Smooth hound, the fish **2.** Ring dove

palometa *Spain* Pomfret, the fish

palourde *France* Cockle, clam, carpet shell or similar bivalve mollusc

palwal *South Asia* A small elongated green squash. See also **tindoori**

pámpano *Spain* Vine leaf

Pampelmuse *Germany* Grapefruit

pamplemoes *South Africa* **1.** Grapefruit **2.** Pummelo

pamplemousse *France* **1.** Grapefruit **2.** Pummelo

pan 1. A metal, glass or ceramic vessel usually deep and round but may be other shapes, fitted with one long handle or two small handles **2.** *Italy, Spain* Bread, cake **3.** *South Asia* A betel leaf folded into a parcel containing a betel nut, spices and a little lime paste. Chewed to extract the flavours and considered by some to be an aid to digestion to be taken after a meal. The lime provides much needed calcium. The fibrous mass left after all the flavour has been extracted is not swallowed. Sometimes spelled paan but this refers to another mix.

pan, to *United States* To cook vegetables without water in a tightly closed pan with a little fat

panaché(e) *France* **1.** Multicoloured or layered, e.g. desserts, salads, ice creams, etc. **2.** Garnished with a mixture of flageolet and French beans

panada 1. *England, Spain* A stiff pounded and boiled mixture of stale bread and water with possibly oil, used for thickening and binding **2.** *England, France* A double-thickness **béchamel sauce** used as a binding agent **3.** *Italy* A broth thickened with breadcrumbs and egg and finished with grated Parmesan cheese

panade *France* **1.** See **panada 2.** A peasant soup based on water, stock or milk and thickened with bread

panadó, panadons d'espinacs *Catalonia* A small spinach, pine nuts and raisin pasty, often served as tapas

panafracchi *Italy* Ring-shaped cakes or pastries with nuts and candied fruit. See also **ciambelle**

panais *France* Parsnip

Panama orange Calamondin

panarda *Italy* A celebratory feast of 20 or more dishes traditional in the Abruzzo region

panato *Italy* Panéed, breaded

pan bagnat *France* A sandwich from Provence containing salade niçoise ingredients. A hollowed out loaf or roll is often used as the bread base.

pan blanco *Spain* White bread

pan-broil, to *United States* To cook meat in a very hot iron (non-stick) frying pan with no fat by rapidly browning all sides to seal in the juices

pancake A thin flat cake cooked on both sides with oil or fat in a pancake or frying pan, made from a thin pouring batter of milk, egg, flour and possibly sugar, normally served with a sweet or savoury filling or sauce. In the UK served with lemon juice and sugar on Shrove Tuesday.

pancake omelette *Wales* Plain flour and beaten egg (2:1) mixed and brought together with a little milk to form a thick batter, seasoned and flavoured with chopped parsley and shallots and fried until golden brown on both sides. Also called **crempog las**

pancake pan A pan similar to an omelette pan reserved for pancakes and crêpes

pancake roll See **spring roll**

pancetta *Italy* Belly of pork cured with salt and spices, rolled up and eaten either raw in thin slices or cooked in thicker slices. Also called **panchetta**

panchetta *Italy* Pancetta

panch foran *South Asia* A Bengali spice mix consisting of cumin, nigella, aniseed, fenugreek and brown mustard seeds ground to a well mixed powder. Used to flavour oils as well as in made up dishes. Also called **panchphoran, panch poran**

panchphoran, panchporan *South Asia* Panch foran

panchporan *South Asia* Panch foran

pancit canton *Philippines* E-fu noodles made with duck eggs

pancotto *Italy* A soup thickened with stale bread, containing seasonal vegetables and finished with oil and cheese. Also called **pappa**

pancreas An abdominal gland which supplies insulin to the blood and digestive juices to the small intestine. Together with the thymus it comprises the sweetbreads.

pancreatin A protease produced by various microorganisms and used to convert proteins into emulsifying agents

Pandanus amaryllifolius *Botanical name* The more aromatically flavoured variety of screwpine

pandanus leaf The leaf of the screwpine used both for its colouring and flavour

Pandanus odoratissimus *Botanical name* Screwpine

pandekager *Denmark* Pancakes

pan di frizze *Italy* A bread containing pork scratchings

pan di Genova *Italy* Genoa cake

pan di natale *Italy* A soft yeast-raised enriched dough mixed with a variety of candied fuits, nuts, raisins, pine nuts, etc. and formed into various shapes (NOTE: Literally 'Christmas bread'.)

pan di Spagna *Italy* A liqueur soaked sponge cake filled with cream or jam

pan dolce *Italy* A tall octagonal sweet yeast-raised and enriched bread from Verona, Served at Christmas. Also called **pandoro**

pandora A pink seawater fish, *Pagellus erythrinus*, similar in size and appearance to the sea bream

pandorato *Italy* Pain perdu, French toast, often with Mozzarella cheese and anchovies spread on the bread before egging

pan d'oro *Italy* A round sweet yeasted bun

pandoro *Italy* Pan dolce

pandowdy *United States* A type of apple pie made from stewed sliced apples layered in an ovenproof dish with butter, brown sugar and spice, moistened with cider, covered with biscuit dough then baked until golden brown

pan-dressed *United States* (Fish) gutted and scaled with the head and fins removed ready for baking, grilling or frying

pan drippings *United States* Residues in the pan left after roasting or frying meat or vegetables used as a basis for gravy

pane *Italy* Bread

pané, to An anglicization of the French *paner*, meaning to coat foods with seasoned flour, beaten egg and breadcrumbs in that order, prior to frying them

pane bianco *Italy* White bread

pane bigio *Italy* Brown bread

pane bolognese *Italy* A sweet bread made from cornmeal and containing candied fruit and nuts

pane carasau *Italy* A very thin bread from Sardinia

pane di frumento *Italy* Whole wheat bread

pane di segale *Italy* Rye bread

panée à l'anglaise *France* Panéed

paneer *South Asia* Curds made from boiling milk acidified with lemon juice. Used for making desserts and as an accompaniment to vegetarian meals. May be fried. Also called **panir, chenna, chhena, channa**

paneermeel *Netherlands* Breadcrumbs

paneer tikki *South Asia* Fresh curds (**paneer**) pressed overnight in a cheese cloth to make a fairly solid curd cheese

pane grattugiato *Italy* Pangrattato

panela *South America* A hard dark sugar from Colombia formed into loaves

panelle *Italy* Fritters made in Sardinia from chick pea flour

paner *France* To pané

pane scuro *Italy* Dark bread

panetière *France* A baked pastry case filled with precooked food or a small precooked bird and served hot

pane tostato *Italy* Toast

panettone See **pannetone**

Panfisch *Germany* A mixture of cooked minced fish and onions served on mashed potatoes

panforte *Italy* A rich cake from Sienna containing glacé fruits and nuts

pan-fry, to To cook in a frying pan with a small quantity of fat or oil

panggang *Indonesia* Spit-roasted. The food is usually marinated.

pang kao niew *Thailand* Glutinous rice flour

pang khao chao *Thailand* Rice flour

pang khao phod *Thailand* Corn flour

pang mun *Thailand* Tapioca starch

pangrattato *Italy* Dried stale bread reduced to fine breadcrumbs

pang tao yai mom *Thailand* Arrowroot

pang xie *China* Crab

pan haggerty *England* A Northern dish made in a wide shallow pan with heated butter and oil, layered with sliced raw waxy potatoes, onions and grated Cheddar or Lancashire cheese and seasoning, topped with cheese and cooked in the oven on a low heat for 30 minutes uncovered, then grilled to brown the top. Served from the pan.

paniccia *Italy* Panissa

panicia *Italy* A barley soup from the Dolomite region

Panicum miliaceum *Botanical name* Common millet

paniert *Germany* Panéed

panini imbottini *Italy* Sandwiches

panino *Italy* Bread roll

panir *South Asia* Curds made from boiling milk acidified with lemon juice. See also **paneer**

paniscia *Italy* Rice, beans and sausage cooked in broth

panissa *Italy* A dough made from boiled chick pea flour and finely chopped and sweated onions, sliced and fried

panitsa *Philippines* Palm sugar

panko *Japan* Large-sized toasted dry breadcrumbs used for coating fried foods

pan loaf *Scotland* A loaf of bread baked in a tin

pan moreno *Spain* Brown bread

panna *Italy* Cream

panna cotta *Italy* **1.** A rich dessert made from cream and milk flavoured with vanilla and set with gelatine. Often served with a fruit sauce. **2.** Coffee-flavoured cream custard (NOTE: Literally 'cooked cream'.)

panna fermentata *Italy* Sour cream

panna montata *Italy* Whipped cream, usually sweetened

Pannarone *Italy* A rich, soft, quick ripening cheese from south Lombardy, made from whole milk, the curds not salted but gathered in cheese cloths, drained, kept at 28°C for 7 days and ripened for a further 8 to 19 days at a lower temperature. It has a thin yellow rind and a white to fawn, mild and slightly bitter paste with lots of small holes. Also called **Pannerone**

pannbiff med lök *Sweden* Chopped beef steak and onions

pannekoeken *Netherlands* Pancakes

pannequet *France* A small crêpe filled with a sweet or savoury mixture and folded into quarters

Pannerone *Italy* Pannarone

pannetone *Italy* A tall yeast-raised cake from Milan containing nuts, spices, sultanas and candied peel often associated with Christmas and New Year's eve. Also called **panettone**

pannkakor *Sweden* Pancakes

pannkoogid A large soufflé type of pancake from Estonia made from a flour, egg, milk and sugar batter (4:4:8:1) flavoured with vanilla essence. The egg whites are reserved whilst the batter matures for 12 hours, beaten to a stiff peak and folded into the batter just before it is fried in 100 ml lots. Filled with a thickened soft fruit compote.

pannocchia *Italy* Mantis shrimp

Pannonia *Hungary* A hard cows' milk cheese similar to Gruyère and made in cylinders (up to 40 kg). The paste has a few holes and a pleasant flavour. Contains 38% water, 31% fat and 30% protein.

pannukakku *Finland* An oven-baked sweet pancake

panocha, panoche *Mexico* A dark unrefined sugar similar to muscovado. See also **piloncillo**

panoche *Mexico* Piloncillo

pan pepato *Italy* A nutmeg and pepper-flavoured cake containing raisins, almonds, hazelnuts and chocolate

pansit *Philippines* Noodles fried with various ingredients such as garlic, onions, vegetables, shrimps, meat, etc.

pansoti *Italy* Pansotti

pansotti *Italy* Triangular-shaped ravioli filled with meat, offal or cheese. Also called **pansoti, panzerotti**

pansy A plant, *Viola tricolor* with edible flowers used for decoration and to add a subtle flavour to salads

panthe kaukswe *Bulgaria* A mild chicken curry flavoured with onions, garlic, chillies, coconut milk and turmeric, served with noodles, hard-boiled eggs, raw onion slices, lemon quarters and prawn crackers

pantosta *Italy* Toast

pantothenic acid See **vitamin B5**

pantserkreeft *Netherlands* Spiny lobster

panucha *Philippines* Palm sugar

panucho *Mexico* A small tortilla from the southwest, part fried to make it puff up, partially split, filled with a savoury filling then fried until crisp

panunto *Italy* Bruschetta (*Tuscany*)

panure 1. *France* Breadcrumbs **2.** A coating of flour, beaten egg and breadcrumbs. See also **pané, to**

panurette *France* Finely grated rusks used as a lining in moulds

panvis *Netherlands* Fried fish, also a casserole made with dried codfish, onions and potatoes

pan white pudding *Scotland* A type of **skirlie** from Mull made with dripping from the roast meat rather than butter. The medium oatmeal is generally twice the weight of the dripping.

panzanella *Italy* A bread salad from Tuscany made from coarse bread soaked in water and squeezed dry, mixed with chopped tomatoes, basil and other salad vegetables, dressed with oil and vinegar and left to develop the flavours for a few hours before serving

panzarotti *Italy* Deep-fried pastry turnovers filled with a chopped ham, cheese, parsley and egg filling or as an alternative, anchovies, basil and egg

panzerotti *Italy* Triangular-shaped ravioli. See also **pansotti**

pão *Portugal* Bread

pao yu *China* Dried abalone. It requires soaking for 4 days.

pap 1. Soft mushy foods served to weaning infants and persons with eating or swallowing difficulties **2.** *Netherlands* Porridge

papa *Mexico* Potato

papadam *South Asia* Poppadom

papads *South Asia* Poppadom

papadum *South Asia* Poppadom

papaia *Italy* Papaya

papain A protease derived from papaya latex, used to remove protein hazes from beer, in bread dough modification, for yeast autolysis and for tenderizing meat for manufacturing purposes. It is also present in pineapples and figs.

Papaja *Germany* Papaya

papalina *Italy* Sprat. Also called **spratto**

papalina, alla *Italy* In the style of the pope (strictly 'of the pope's skullcap'), i.e. with ham, cream, eggs and Parmesan cheese

papanasi cu smantană *Romania* Sieved cottage cheese mixed with butter, eggs, egg yolks, double cream and a little sugar, seasoned and flavoured with grated lemon zest, made into small patties, fried and served with sour cream

papanasi fierti *Romania* Curd cheese dumplings, poached in water, drained and coated with melted butter, breadcrumbs and caster sugar

papa seca *South America* Boiled and peeled non-bitter potatoes from Peru, dried in the sun and then ground. Used for the preparation of carapulca.

papas rellenos *South America* A type of cottage pie with a base of meat, vegetables, hard-boiled eggs, olives, raisins and spices topped with mashed potatoes

papatzul *Mexico* Tortilla filled with egg and pumpkin seeds

papavero, al *Italy* With poppy seeds

Papaver rhoeas *Botanical name* Field poppy, corn poppy, a source of poppy seed

Papaver somniferum *Botanical name* Opium poppy, a source of poppy seed

papaw 1. A variety of green custard apple, *Asimina triloba*, which grows in temperate regions of the USA. It is kidney-shaped with smooth yellow skin and large brown seeds surrounded by a sweet yellow pulp tasting of bananas and pears. **2.** Papaya

papaya *England, Spain* A large pear- or melon-shaped fruit to 20 cm long, from the tree *Carica papaya* which grows in most tropical and sub-tropical regions and is second only in importance to the banana amongst tropical fruit. When ripe it has a yellow/orange skin and a juicy pink/orange flesh tasting like a mixture of roses, peaches and strawberries with many black seeds in a central cavity. The unripe fruit can be boiled and used as a vegetable in the same way as a marrow. The juice contains the protease papain and the seeds may be used as a condiment. Also called **pawpaw**

papaye *France* Papaya

papaz yahnisi *Turkey* Thick slices of mutton or lamb stewed in mutton fat with sliced onions, garlic, seasoning, cinnamon and a little vinegar

papel de paja de arroz *Spain* Rice paper

paper bark *Australia* The bark of large trees which is used as a food wrapping and imparts a woody smoky flavour to the meat or fish cooked in it

paper frill See **cutlet frill**

paperino *Italy* Gosling

Paphos sausage *Cyprus* Seasoned minced lean leg of pork mixed with chopped pork fat, flavoured with ground coriander and herbs, marinated with red wine for 2 days, filled into pricked casings and air-dried for 5 to 10 days, fried or grilled. May be preserved after drying in rendered pork fat.

papier de riz *France* Rice paper

papillon *France* A butterfly-shaped small cake of flaky pastry dredged and possibly glazed with sugar

papillote *France* Cutlet frill or the paper frill on the bone of a leg of lamb

papillote, en *England, France* Baked in a buttered greaseproof paper or aluminium foil packet. Usually used of a piece of meat or fish with flavourings which is served from the packet.

papo de anjo *Portugal* Small spherical cakes made with mostly egg yolks and served with syrup, alternatively a frothy dessert made with egg white

papo seco *Portugal* Bread roll or ordinary bread without butter

pappa *Italy* A soup thickened with stale bread. See also **pancotto**

pappa al pomodoro *Italy* A Tuscan bread soup with tomatoes cooked in oil, garlic and basil

pappadam *South Asia* Poppadom

pappadum *South Asia* Poppadom

pappardelle *Italy* Wide egg noodles with crinkly edges

paprica dolce *Italy* Paprika

paprika *England, France* A variety of sweet red pepper, *Capsicum annuum*, from Hungary, used fresh or more commonly dried and ground as the flavouring of the same name

paprika butter See **beurre de paprika**

Paprikapfeffer *Germany* Powdered paprika

paprikas *Netherlands* Sweet peppers, capsicums

paprikás borjúszelet *Hungary* Veal escalopes seasoned and sprinkled with paprika, floured and fried in lard with chopped onions, simmered in white stock with sliced sweet green peppers and served with the reduced cooking liquor and sour cream as a sauce

paprikás csirke *Hungary* A chicken stew flavoured with onions, sweet peppers, tomatoes, paprika, soured cream and seasonings. Served with pasta or **tarhonya**

Paprikáskrumpli *Austria* A type of goulash. Sliced onions and garlic are sweated in oil; sliced potatoes and sausages (**debrecen** or **chorizo**), paprika and chilli powder are added and cooked. Then peeled and diced tomatoes, stock, sliced green sweet peppers and dried Hungarian peppers and seasoning are added, and the whole is simmered until cooked.

paprika spice mix A pungent blend of flavouring agents used to coat chicken prior to barbecueing, consisting of fresh ginger, fresh garlic, paprika and ground cumin pounded into a paste

papu *Finland* Bean

păpusi de cas *Romania* A hard spun-curd and smoked ewes' milk cheese with a sharp salty taste made in 500 g cylinders or bricks

paquette *France* The dark green mature lobster roe about to be laid or the lobster carrying such roe

para-amino-benzoic acid See **PABA**

paradicsommártás *Hungary* Ketchup

Paradiesapfel *Germany* Tomato

Paradieser *Austria, Germany* Tomato

paradise cake Carrot cake

paradise nut *South America* A nut from a tree, *Lecythis sabucajo*, which resembles the

Brazil nut but has a more delicate flavour and a thinner shell. Also called **sapucaya nut**

paragonimus A species of fluke endemic in Asia and parts of Africa, transmitted mainly in freshwater crabs and crayfish, causes tuberculosis-like symptoms since it lives in the lungs. It can also affect the brain. Easily cured with 1 dose of praziquantel.

Paranuss *Germany* Brazil nut

parasol mushroom An edible fungus, *Lepiota procera*, found in grassy areas and resembling a light brown umbrella. The cap, which has a scaly surface which should be removed, can be up to 15 cm in diameter. Best eaten when young. Also called **umbrella mushroom**

paratha *South Asia* Flaky unleavened bread made from a mixture of white and brown flour, water and salt, the dough formed into rounds coated with ghee and fried until crisp on the outside

parboil, to To boil foods until they are about half cooked

parboiled rice See **converted rice**

parch, to To dry-roast until slightly brown

parcha *South Asia* Parcha-style, i.e. cooked **en papillote** in a banana leaf or completely encased in pastry and steamed, grilled, barbecued or cooked in the oven. It also refers to the process of dry-roasting with a crust formed by basting at intervals with a marinade of yoghurt and spices.

parched corn Maize kernels which have been cooked or dry-roasted slightly

pare *Indonesia* Bitter gourd

pare, to To peel thinly, e.g. skins from potatoes, apples, etc.

párek v rohlíku *Czech Republic* Hot dog, boiled or steamed sausage in a roll

parenica *Czech Republic, Hungary, Russia* A soft spun-curd ewes' milk cheese cut into long strips, rolled up and smoked. Also called **ribbon cheese**

pareve A Jewish term describing food made without milk or meat or derivatives of them, so that it may be eaten with either type

parfait *France* A frozen, flavoured, cooked egg custard mixture in which the eggs have been well beaten to incorporate air, served as a dessert. Flavourings included coffee (traditional), chocolate, fruit, vanilla, liqueurs and praline.

parfum *France* 1. Flavour 2. Aroma

pargo 1. *Portugal* Barbel, the fish 2. *Spain* Sea bream

paria *Indonesia* Bitter gourd

paring knife A smaller version of an office knife, used to peel fruit and vegetables

parique *South Africa* A mixture of peanuts, cooked rice and sugar wrapped in banana leaves, baked and then sliced. From Madagascar.

Paris-Brest A cake consisting of three concentric baked rings of choux pastry, split in half and filled with whipped cream or crème pâtissière mixed with a fine praline and decorated with icing sugar and flaked almonds (NOTE: It is named after a famous 19th-century bicycle race.)

Pariser Schnitzel *Austria* Veal escalope, dipped in flour and lightly beaten egg and fried in butter

parisersmörgås *Sweden* An open sandwich consisting of a thick slice of bread and butter topped with a forcemeat of minced beef, egg yolk, breadcrumbs, grated onions, finely chopped pickled beetroot and seasoning. The whole fried both sides, meat side first.

Parisian spice *United States* A mixture of dried thyme, bay, basil and sage ground with coriander seed, mace and black peppercorns used for flavouring

parisien *France* Gros pain

parisienne, à la *France* Garnished with parisienne potatoes and artichoke hearts, and sometimes other vegetables

parisienne, sauce *England, France* Allemande, sauce

parisienne cutter A sharp edged scoop-shaped implement for cutting out balls of potato or other vegetables or fruit

parisienne potatoes Potatoes scooped out with a parisienne cutter, browned in a frying pan, finished in the oven at 240°C and coated with meat glaze just before serving

Parker House Roll *United States* A yeast-raised dough formed into a roll and folded in two before proving and baking

parkia A medium-sized leguminous tree, *Parkia speciosa*, from Thailand and Indonesia which produces flat seed pods about the size of broad beans with a peculiar smell. The pods are eaten as a vegetable and the sun-dried and peeled beans are fried in oil or softened in water and eaten as a snack. Also called **stink bean**, **twisted cluster bean**

Parkia speciosa Botanical name Parkia

parkin *England* A moist and dense dark brown ginger cake from Yorkshire made with oatmeal and sweetened with black treacle. Usually served in squares after maturing for a week.

párky *Czech Republic* Frankfurter type sausages often boiled or steamed in pairs. Popular as a street snack in Prague.

Parma ham A dry-cured ham eaten raw as **prosciutto**. It must come from around the town of Parma in Italy, have been air-dried for at least 8 months and be branded on the skin.

Parmentier *France* Containing potatoes

Parmentier, purée *England, France* Sliced onion and leek sweated in butter, bouquet garni, stock and sliced peeled potatoes added, simmered, skimmed, bouquet garni removed, passed through a sieve or liquidized, seasoned, consistency adjusted and served hot with croûtons

Parmesan A very hard Italian grating cheese with a strong and distinctive flavour made from unpasteurized skimmed cows' milk. The curds are heated and packed into very large circular moulds and matured for well over 2 years, ending up with a pale straw colour and a black rind. When grated it is used on a wide variety of Italian dishes. The composition depends on age, at 18 months it is 27% water, 37% fat and 31% protein. See also **Parmigiano Reggiano**

parmesane, à la *France* Containing or sprinkled with Parmesan cheese

parmigiana, alla *Italy* Finished with butter and grated Parmesan or an escalope panéed with a mixture of grated Parmesan cheese and breadcrumbs

Parmigiano Reggiano *Italy* The finest and most authentic Parmesan cheese, made in squat barrel shapes (up to 35 kg) which are salted in brine and turned and brushed regularly. It is unique to its particular region and although it may be made at any time it has special names according to the date of manufacture, 'maggengo' April to November and 'invernengo' December to March. The non-winter period can also be split, 'ditesta' April to June, 'agostano' or 'di centro' July and August and 'tardno' September to November. One year old cheeses are called 'vecchio' and two year old 'stravecchio'. Always stamped with the name. It may be eaten young as a dessert.

päron *Sweden* Pear

parr A young river salmon in its second or third year before it leaves for the sea. Protected from fishing. Also called **samlet**

parrilla *Spain* Grill

parrillada *Argentina* Barbecue

parrillada de pescado *Spain* A mixed seafood grill

parsa *Finland* Parsley

parsi dhansak masala *South Asia* A hot spice mix containing in addition to those listed under garam masala, fenugreek seeds, mustard seeds, chillies and turmeric

parsley A hardy biennial plant with either bright green very curly leaves, *Petroselinum*

crispum, or flat duller leaves, *P. crispum* 'Neapolitanum'. The flat-leaved variety which is common outside the UK has a stronger flavour. It is very widely used as a culinary herb, as a decoration or garnish either in sprigs or chopped, and as an essential part (esp. the stalks) of a bouquet garni. See also **French parsley, Italian parsley**

parsley butter See **beurre (à la) maître d'hôtel**

parsley ham See **jambon persillé**

parsley root Hamburg parsley

parsley sauce 1. Béchamel sauce with finely chopped parsley. Used for poached and boiled fish and vegetables. **2.** A fish velouté mixed with a strong infusion of parsley, chopped parsley and a little lemon juice

parsnip A biennial plant, *Pastinaca sativa*, whose long (up to 25 cm) conical tap root is harvested as a winter root vegetable in the first year. The roots have a cream sweetish flesh with a distinctive flavour and are best after being frosted. Served boiled, roasted, fried or puréed, etc.

parson's nose The small projecting fatty tissue growth at the rear of a chicken which carries the tail feathers and, in the case of the male, the sexual organs and glands. It has a strong flavour and is not usually eaten except by those who wish to draw attention to themselves.

parson's venison *England* A skinned and boned leg of lamb, stuffed with a duxelle mixed with chopped ham and chives, marinated for 24 hours in port, red wine, red wine vinegar, juniper, allspice, bay leaf and grated nutmeg, drained, dried, seared then braised in the marinade in a covered dish at 180°C for up to 2 hours until cooked and served with the reduced strained cooking liquor

partan bree *Scotland* Puréed soup from Scotland containing crab meat and rice

partridge 1. *United Kingdom* A greyish-brown game bird widespread in Europe and the Middle East weighing about 450 g at 2 to 4 months and serving 1 person. Barded and roasted at 200°C for 1 to 2 hours. They come in two varieties:grey-legged, *Perdrix perdrix*, and red-legged, *Alectoris rufa*. The shooting season is the 1st September to 1st February, and the hanging time 3 to 5 days. **2.** *United States* The general name for various game birds including the American ruffed grouse, quail, pheasant and bobwhite

parut *Indonesia, Malaysia* Coconut grater

parwal *South Asia* A small elongated oval green squash. See also **tindoori**

pasa *Mexico, Spain* Raisin

pasa de Corinto *Spain* Currant, from grapes

pasha *Finland* A type of cheesecake introduced from Russia

pashka See **paskha**

pashtet iz tieliatiny *Eastern Europe* A veal and liver pâté from the Ukraine made with fried calves' liver, veal, bacon and vegetables simmered with chicken stock and dried mushrooms, strained, processed with softened bread, bound with egg, seasoned and flavoured with allspice then baked in the oven at 180°C

Pasiego prensado *Spain* A soft mild white smooth cream cheese from Santander made from ewes' and semi-skimmed cows' milk. Eaten after 2 weeks maturation. The white paste contains small holes and has a decided flavour.

Pasiego sin prensar *Spain* A cheese similar to Pasiego prensado but hand-moulded into various shapes

pasilla chile *Mexico* A variety of long, hot and dark brown chilli, commonly dried

pasionara *Spain* Nigella

paskha *Russia* A rich dessert made from a mixture of curd cheese, cream, almonds and dried fruits placed in a muslin-lined sieve or unglazed earthenware (flower)pot, weighted and left to drain for 24 hours, then turned out, muslin removed, and decorated. Traditionally served at Easter. Also called **pashka**

pass, to 1. To pass a food item through an excess of flour, beaten egg, oil or similar so as to completely coat it with the material **2.** To make something pass through a sieve or strainer as in making a purée or coulis

passa *Portugal* Raisin

passa de Corinto *Portugal* Currant, from grapes

passata *Italy* Purée, in the UK usually of raw tomatoes

passato *Italy* **1.** Purée soup **2.** Well done, overcooked **3.** Skinned and deseeded tomatoes simmered with chopped onions (10:1) with garlic, basil, bay and celery until reduced by half, then seasoned and passed through a sieve. May be frozen.

passé l'an *France* **1.** A hard cooked-curd cows' milk cheese from Languedoc weighing to 40 kg. Similar to Parmesan but with a more mellow flavour. (NOTE: Literally 'passed the year', i.e. more than 1 year old.) **2.** Ripened, of cheese

Passendale *Belgium* A semi-hard loaf-shaped cows' milk cheese weighing up to 7 kg. The moist and supple paste has many small holes.

passer *France* **1.** To pass (food through flour, beaten egg, etc.) **2.** To quickly seal the surface of food in a hot frying pan prior to cooking by another method

passera *Italy* Plaice

passera pianuzza *Italy* Flounder

passerino *Italy* Plaice

Passiflora edulis *Botanical name* Purple passion fruit

Passiflora edulis var. **flavicarpa** *Botanical name* Yellow passion fruit

Passiflora laurifolia *Botanical name* Yellow granadilla

Passiflora ligularis *Botanical name* Sweet granadilla

Passiflora maliformis *Botanical name* Curuba

Passiflora quadrangularis *Botanical name* Giant granadilla

passion cake Carrot cake

passion fruit The globular fruit of climbing plants, *Passiflora edulis*, *P. edulis* v. *flavicarpa* and *P. ligularis*, which grow in warm, humid, frost-free climates. See purple passion fruit, yellow passion fruit and sweet granadilla. Passion fruit on its own generally refers to the purple variety.

passoire *France* Colander, strainer, sieve

passover bread See **matzo**

pasta 1. *Italy* Dough, paste **2.** *England, Italy* A variety of extruded, cut or pressed shapes and sheets of pasta dough made either fresh and soft, or dried, from a basic dough of water and/or eggs, salt and hard durum wheat flour and sometimes oil. The simplest pasta is made from strong flour and eggs only (9:5), kneading up to 10 minutes until small blisters appear. There are innumerable names and shapes but the main types are spaghetti, macaroni, noodles, vermicelli, lasagne, canneloni and ravioli. Most pastas are cooked and served with a sauce. **3.** *Spain* Pasta or pastry **4.** *Italy, Spain* Noodle

pasta alla sarde *Italy* Alternate layers of macaroni, fennel and fresh sardines, cooked in a pie dish and served cold

pasta alle acciughe *Italy* Pasta with tomato sauce, anchovies and clams

pasta all'uovo *Italy* Pasta made from flour and eggs only without water or oil. Available in various shapes and usually made on the premises where cooked or sold. By law it must contain at least 4 eggs per kg of flour.

pasta cresciuta *Italy* Vegetable, etc. fritters made with a yeast-raised flour, water and salt batter

pasta d'acciughe *Italy* Anchovy paste

pasta de hojaldre *Spain* A patty made from puff pastry

pasta e fagioli *Italy* A traditional soup made with pasta, white beans and salt pork

pasta fatta in casa *Italy* Fresh pasta usually made in the place where it is cooked

pasta filata *Italy* The term for scalded milk curds that are kneaded until they become an elastic dough and easy to shape

pasta frolla *Italy* Shortcrust pastry

pastai cennin *Wales* Leek pasty

pastai cocos *Wales* Cockle pie

pasta in brodo *Italy* Pasta cooked and served in broth

pastai persli *Wales* Welsh parsley pie

pasta italiana *Spain* Spaghetti

pasta liscia *Italy* Smooth pasta

pastanaga *Catalonia* Carrots (NOTE: The plural is **pastanagues**.)

pasta reale *Italy* Small pasta grains for soup

pasta rigata *Italy* Ridged pasta which traps more sauce than smooth

pasta rossa *Italy* A red or pink pasta coloured with tomatoes

pastasciutta *Italy* Pasta in a sauce

pasta secca *Italy* Dried pasta usually manufactured and sold through retail outlets

pasta sfoglia *Italy* Puff pastry

pasta trinata *Italy* Flat pieces of pasta with frilly or lacy edges wedges

pasta verde *Italy* A green pasta coloured with spinach

paste The name given to any thick relatively smooth semi-solid which is spreadable, such as a flour water paste or pastry but more specifically to cooked and pounded meat and fish mixed with flavourings and extenders

pastei *Netherlands* A pie or pasty usually containing meat in a thick sauce

pasteijes *Netherlands* Blind-cooked pastry shells

pastéis *Portugal* A round patty-shaped food item, may be a sweet cake or a savoury item such as a fish cake or rissole

pastéis de bacalhau *Portugal* Dried salt cod, cooked and then recooked en croûte

pastej *Sweden* Pie

pastel *Spain* Pastry, cake, pie or pâté

pastel, en *Spain* In batter

pastél *Portugal* Pie, tart or pastry

pastela *Spain* An Andalusian speciality consisting of shredded beef cooked with cumin, nutmeg and honey in a pastry case

pastelería 1. *Portugal, Spain* Pastries **2.** *Spain* Cake shop

pastelillos *Caribbean* Small deep-fried pasties containing meat or cheese served as a hors d'oeuvre or appetizer

pastélinho *Portugal* Small pie

pastelito de almendra *Spain* Almond cake

pastelitos *Mexico* Biscuits or small cakes

pastella *Italy* Batter

pastels *West Africa* The West African version of the **Cornish pasty**, the Hispanic **empanadas** and the Indian **samosa**, usually filled with a savoury fish stuffing and served with a hot chilli sauce based on tomatoes, sweet peppers and onions

pastèque *France* Watermelon

Pastete *Germany* Pie

pastetice od sira-skute *Balkans* Turnovers from Serbia filled with ham and using a pastry made from flour, butter and cottage cheese

pasteurize, to To heat a substance, usually a liquid, to a temperature between 60 and 100°C to kill particular pathogenic organisms, e.g. milk may be pasteurized at 62.8°C for 30 minutes or at 72°C for 15 seconds, shelled eggs at 64.4°C for 2 to 5 minutes, etc. This process does not completely sterilize the substance

pasteurized milk Milk pasteurized at 72°C for 15 seconds and then rapidly cooled. This does not affect the flavour of the milk but causes the cream to rise unless it is homogenized.

pasticceria *Italy* **1.** Pastry **2.** Pastry-making **3.** Cake **4.** Cake shop

pasticciata *Italy* Baked pasta with a savoury sauce, cheese and cream

pasticcino *Italy* Fancy cake or pastry

pasticcio *Italy* **1.** A savoury pie of meat, pasta, vegetables or cheese or a combination of these **2.** Pâté, meat loaf, any mould of processed fish, meat, etc.

pasticcio di maccheroni *Italy* A large double-crust deep pie made in a cake tin with a removable base, lined with a sweet egg and butter enriched pastry filled with a mixture of cooked pasta, meatballs, peas, rich tomato sauce and diced Mozzarella cheese heaped up in the centre and filled with a sweetened egg custard (5 eggs per litre of milk), covered with a pastry lid, decorated and glazed, then baked at 190°C for 45 minutes. Rested 10 minutes in the tin.

pastiera *Italy* A tart filled with ricotta cheese

pastiera Napoletana *Italy* A puff pastry case filled with fruit

pasties See **pasty**

pastilla A type of filled pastry. See also **bastilla**

pastillage A dough-like mixture of icing sugar, water and gum tragacanth which can be coloured and moulded or shaped to make cake coverings and decorations

Pastinaca sativa Botanical name Parsnip

Pastinake *Germany* Parsnip

pastine *Italy* Tiny pasta shapes for soup

pastís *Catalonia* Pie or cake. See also **tarta**

pastitsio *Greece* Cooked pasta layered with a cooked meat sauce, usually lamb, an egg-enriched and cinnamon-flavoured béchamel and grated cheese, finishing with a final layer of grated cheese and fresh breadcrumbs then baked at 190°C until the top is golden brown (40 minutes)

Pastorella *Italy* A small version of **Bel Paese** cheese

pastrami *United States* Dry cured and smoked brisket or other similar cut of meat usually boiled then thinly sliced for use as a sandwich filling

pastries Various types of small cakes, often iced, filled or decorated and made of pastry or various sponge or cake mixtures

pastry A mixture of flour, fat, possibly egg and sugar, the fat usually dispersed as small solid globules coated with flour and the whole brought together with liquid prior to shaping and baking. There are many types of pastry, including shortcrust, flan, sweet, flaky, puff, rough puff, hot water crust, suet crust, choux and filo.

pastry board A square or oblong board preferably marble but usually wood on which pastry is rolled out

pastry brake Opposed and contra-rotating rollers with a variable gap through which pastry can be worked and reduced in thickness for commercial production. A very small version is used domestically for pasta production.

pastry case An uncooked or blind baked pastry container used to hold savoury or sweet mixtures

pastry cream See **crème pâtissière**

pastry crimper A tool used to scallop or crimp the edges of pies, tarts etc.

pastry cutters Various metal or plastic outlines of shapes, e.g. circles, fluted circles, diamonds, gingerbread men, etc. sharpened on one edge and used to cut out corresponding shapes from biscuit, scone, pastry or cake mixtures, etc.

pastry wheel A small wooden wheel with a serrated edge attached to a handle, used to crimp edges of pastry etc.

pasty A doubled over sheet of pastry containing a savoury filling, sealed around the edges and baked flat on a baking tray without support. Usually a half circle.

pasztetowa *Poland* Seasoned pigs' liver and veal processed and packed into casings

pat A small shaped amount of solid or semi-solid such as a butter pat

pat, to To shape a solid or semi-solid into a pat by using two flat wooden paddles, by forming into a roll, refrigerating and slicing, or by use of a mould

pataca *Spain* Jerusalem artichoke

pata de mulo *Spain* **Villalón** cheese made in the shape of a hoof (NOTE: Literally 'mule's foot or shoe'.)

Patagonian black cake *Wales* A rich fruit cake similar to the Scottish black bun but containing rum and encased in glacé icing instead of pastry. The icing is put on while the cake is still warm from the oven.

Patagonian cream tart *Wales* Flour, butter and egg yolks (8:4:1) made into a paste, rested for several hours then used to line a pie dish. This is filled with a vanilla-flavoured mixture of double cream and egg whites (5:1), the egg whites being whisked to a stiff peak and folded into the cream. All baked at 179°C for 35 to 40 minutes.

patagras *South America* A semi-hard cows' milk cheese resembling Edam and Gouda

patakukko *Finland* A double-crust pie from Karelia made with rye flour and filled with muikko fish, fat pork and seasoning, cooked very slowly to completely soften the filling

patata *Italy, Spain* Potato

patata, purea di *Italy* Mashed potato

patata arrostita *Italy* Roast potato

patata asada *Italy* Baked potato

patata bollita *Italy* Boiled potato

patata dolce *Italy* Sweet potato

patatas bravas *Catalonia* Cubed and fried potatoes in a spicy tomato sauce, often served as tapas

patata sfogliata *Italy* Deep-fat-fried potato, chips, French fries

patatas fritas *Spain* Chips, fried potatoes

patata stacciato *Italy* Mashed potato

patate (douce) *France* Sweet potato

patate alla borghese *Italy* Potatoes with butter and lemon

patate alla veneziana *Italy* Diced potatoes fried with onions and herbs

patate fritte *Italy* Potato crisps, game chips

patate lesse *Italy* Boiled potatoes

patates *Turkey* Potato

patate sabbiose *Italy* Sauté potatoes

patate tenere *Italy* New potatoes

pâte *France* **1.** Pastry (NOTE: The 'e' is unaccented.) **2.** A softish mixture such as batter, etc. **3.** Paste, e.g. of cheese

pâté 1. *France* A raised pie with a meat filling completely enclosed in pastry. Eaten hot. **2.** *England, France* A cooked, smooth or coarse meat paste made from a variety of meats, often liver and belly pork or bacon plus flavourings and seasoning. Allowed to cool in the mould then turned out and eaten cold, usually as a hors d'oeuvres. As a rule of thumb there should be equal amounts of lean meat and fat to which are added binders such as eggs, flour, choux pastry or white sauces. Sometimes vegetarian pastes with a similar texture are so called.

pâte à choux *France* Choux pastry

pâte à crêpes *France* Pancake batter

pâte à foncé *France* Shortcrust pastry

pâte à frire *France* Batter

pâte à sucre *France* Sugar pastry

pâte brisée *France* Shortcrust pastry

pâte croquante *France* A crisp ground almond and sugar pastry

pâte d'amandes *France* Marzipan

pâte d'anchois *France* Anchovy paste

pâté de campagne *France* Farmhouse pâté, usually made from coarsely chopped pork with garlic and herbs

pâté de foie gras *England, France* An expensive gourmet pâté made with the enlarged livers (foie gras) of force-fed geese, seasoned and flavoured with truffles. The best pâté is made from livers trimmed of any yellow gall stains, rested or soaked overnight, trimmed of connective tissue, seasoned, possibly marinated, piquéed with truffle slivers, squashed into a terrine, sealed with a flour and water paste and cooked in the oven in a bain-marie. By law, pâté de foie gras must contain 80% goose liver.

pâte de fruit, en *France* Fruit jelly as in framboise en pâte de fruit (raspberry jelly)

pâté de Pâques *France* Veal and pork pie

pâté de Pâques au biquion *France* An elaborate Easter pie made with puff pastry which uses a mixture of butter and goats' cheese (3:2) instead of all butter. The filling is a mixture of diced pork, veal and kid, fried in butter and mixed with finely chopped onion, parsley and egg yolk, seasoning and nutmeg. The pie is assembled on a baking sheet from a circle of puff pastry with the filling heaped in the centre, halved hard-boiled eggs on the top and all covered with another circle of puff pastry sealed around the edges and crimped. Baked at 200°C for 20 minutes, then at 170°C until cooked.

pâtée *France* The mash that is force fed to geese and chickens

pâté en croûte *France* Meat pie

pâte feuilletée *France* Flaky or puff pastry

pâte frollée *France* Almond-flavoured pastry

patella *Italy* Limpet

patelle 1. *France* Limpet 2. *Italy* Limpets, the shellfish

pâté maison *France* A cold pâté produced on the premises usually cut in slices as a hors d'oeuvre and served with a garnish and fingers of hot toast

patent blue V A synthetic blue food colouring. See also **E131**

paternostri *Italy* Small squares of flat pasta

pâtes *France* 1. Pasta 2. Noodles

pâte sablée *France* Sugar pastry (UK), sugar crust pastry (USA)

pâtes alimentaires *France* 1. Pasta 2. Noodles

pâtes de fruits *France* Pieces of crystallized fruits

pâte sucrée *France* A sweetened shortcrust pastry (**pâte brisée**) used extensively for patisserie. Quite fragile and requires careful handling.

patience A sorrel-like herb, *Rumex patientia*, with a slightly acidic taste. Used like sorrel or spinach.

patila *South Asia* A tinned brass cooking pot. See also **degchi**

patinho *Portugal* Duckling

patis *Philippines* A fermented fish sauce

pâtisserie *France* 1. Cake shop 2. Sweet items generally made of pastry, filled and decorated. The filling is often **crème pâtissière** overlaid with glazed fruit or cream, chocolate, jam and the like. 3. The art of cake and pastry making and baking

pâtissier,-ière *France* Confectioner or pastry cook

patlican dolmasi *Turkey* Aubergine halves, filled with a mixture of minced beef, chopped onions, tomatoes, rice and seasonings, baked in the oven and served hot

patlican salatasi *Turkey* Cooked aubergine flesh puréed with lemon juice and olive oil, served cold garnished with tomato wedges, strips of green sweet pepper and black olives

Patna rice A north Indian long-grain rice which stays separate during cooking. Similar to basmati rice but not so fragrant. Excellent for rice salads.

pato *Portugal, Spain* Duck

pato bravo *Portugal* Wild duck

patola *Philippines* Angled loofah

patra Dasheen leaves used as a vegetable

patrijs *Netherlands* Partridge

pattegris *Sweden* Sucking pig

pattie *Caribbean* A snack food from Jamaica consisting of a flaky pastry case filled with a highly spiced beef or other filling

patty A small pie or pasty

patty pan squash A summer squash, *Curcubita pepo*, common in the USA. The creamy white skin and flesh and the seeds are eaten as a vegetable when it is very young. Also called **scallop squash**, **custard marrow**, **cymling** (NOTE: So called because of its dish shape with scalloped edges.)

patty shell *United States* A puff or short pastry shell for serving hors d'oeuvres, bouchées, vol-au-vents, barquettes, etc.

patty tin See **bun tin**

pau *South Asia* An old unit of weight. See also **powa**

paua *New Zealand* A type of abalone, *Haliotis iris*, with a rainbow-coloured shell which is often used as an ornament

Pauillac lamb Milk-fed lamb from Pauillac, France

paunce bourré *United States* A Cajun dish of stuffed pork stomach

paunch, to To remove the entrails, heart and lungs of an animal, especially a hare

paupiette 1. *England, France* A stuffed and rolled thin fillet of fish **2.** *France* Beef or veal olive

paupiettes d'anchois *France* Anchovy paupiettes

pau ts'ai *China* Pak choy

pav *South Asia* An old unit of weight. See also **powa**

pava *Spain* Hen turkey

pavé *France* A thickish square or rectangle e.g. of steak, cheese, cake or mousse (NOTE: Literally 'cobblestone or paving stone'.)

pavé d'Auge *France* Pont l'Evêque

pavé de Moyaux *France* Pont l'Evêque

Pavlova *Australia* Meringue piped into a shallow basket, dried, filled with whipped cream and decorated with fresh fruit. Named in honour of the famous Russian ballet dancer.

pavo *Spain* Turkey

pavo relleno a la catalana *Spain* Stuffed and roasted turkey

pavot *France* Poppy seed

pawpaw See **papaya**

payasam *South Asia* A paste made from various ingredients but always containing coconut milk, eaten as a sweet snack or accompaniment to a meal. Typical ingredients are cooked and mashed pulses, cooked rice, cooked sago, cashew nuts, jaggery or sugar.

pay darn *China* Chinese preserved eggs

paymi *Caribbean* A dessert from Antigua. See also **dukuna**

payousnaya *Russia* Payusnaia

pays *France* Country or region, as in vin de pays, locally produced wine

paysanne A vegetable cut in thin slices and small (1 cm) triangular, square or round shapes

paysanne, à la *France* In the peasant style, i.e. a simple dish containing onions, carrots and bacon

payusnaia *Russia* The less mature eggs of sturgeon treated with hot brine to coagulate them and packed into small wooden tubs. Also called **pressed caviar**

pazlache *Italy* A type of lamb-stuffed ravioli. See also **agnolotti**

pazon ng api *Burma* Shrimp paste

pazun nga-pi *Burma* A pungent fermented fish sauce made from shrimps

pea The fruit of a climbing legume, *Pisum sativum*, grown extensively in temperate climates, consisting of a green pod to 10 cm long containing a row of soft, round green seeds which become brown and hard when ripe. Some varieties (e.g. mangetout) have edible pods which are eaten whole before the seeds begin to swell, but most have inedible pods and the green underripe seeds are eaten either raw if very young or cooked. Most peas are frozen in the developed world. Some are dried, possibly dehusked and split or further processed. The fully ripe seed is brown and used as animal and bird food in developed countries but may also be used as a pulse. See also **pea leaf**. Also called **garden pea**

pea aubergine Tiny pale green, white/yellow or purple/brown relatives of the aubergine, *Solanum torvum*, grown in the Seychelles, Thailand and the Caribbean, which look like a rather straggly bunch of grapes. They are picked while unripe and used raw in hot sauces and chutney. Used in nam prik. Also called **susumber**, **gully bean**

pea bean Navy bean

peaberry A mutant arabica coffee which is a single round bean instead of the two matching hemispheres as is normal

peach The fruit of a deciduous tree, *Prunus persica*, originally from China but now cultivated worldwide in temperate climates. Most fruits are spherical up to 7.5 cm diameter with a single longitudinal indentation from the stalk to the calyx end. The sweet juicy flesh may be white, yellow or orange, surrounds a large rough central stone and is enclosed in a downy skin ranging in colour from cream to orange/pink. Used both raw and poached as a dessert and for jam.

peach Melba An individual dessert made with vanilla ice cream plus poached, skinned and destoned peaches with a topping of fresh raspberry sauce. Served in a coupe dish.

pea crab A very small crab from New England, USA which lives in empty oyster shells and is eaten whole after stewing in cream. Also called **oyster crab**

pea flour Flour produced from fully mature dried peas used for soups and thickening sauces. Also called **pea starch**

pea leaf The young leaves and shoots of the garden pea which have been prevented from flowering. Used as a gourmet vegetable in stir fries and soups. Also called **pea sprout**

pea man *Japan* another spelling of **piman**

peanut A plant, *Arachis hypogaea*, from South America whose fertilized flowers send shoot-like structures into the soil where the immature fruits develop as two to four nuts in a light brown, dry and soft shell or pod, each nut being covered by a thin papery skin. The Spanish type has 2 light brown seeds per pod, the Valencia type up to 4 dark red seeds per pod and the Virginia type 2 dark brown seeds per pod. They are eaten raw or roasted as a snack food and are a major source of oil and protein. Peanuts are made into peanut butter and are used to thicken and flavour many sauces and stews. Also called **groundnut, monkeynut**

peanut butter Ground peanuts sometimes with added peanut oil, salt or sugar with a buttery consistency. Sold as smooth or crunchy, the latter containing chopped peanuts. Used as a sandwich spread or to flavour some dishes.

peanut flour *United States* Ground peanuts sometimes used to enrich baking flours

peanut oil Oil extracted from peanuts containing 20% saturated, 50% monounsaturated and 30% polyunsaturated fat. It has a rather high melting point (freezing point) and a high smoke point. Used for deep-frying. Also called **groundnut oil, arachis oil**

pear The fruit of a deciduous tree, *Pyrus communis* var. *sativa*, native to Europe and western Asia which requires cool winters to fruit. The thin, usually smooth, green through yellow to brown and often mottled skin encloses a firm, juicy, delicately flavoured flesh surrounding a core of seed somewhat smaller than an apple. The fruit is narrow at the stalk end widening towards the calyx. There are both cooking and dessert varieties and they may be eaten raw, poached, baked, etc.

pear apple Asian pear

pear Condé A Condé dessert, possibly made with a short-grain rice, topped with a fanned poached pear. Also called **poire condé**

pearks sakhoo *Thailand* Tapioca

pearl barley Pot barley which has been steamed and tumbled in a revolving cylinder to remove the outer coating. Softens more quickly than pot barley.

pearl millet A white-seeded variety of bulrush millet

pearl moss Carragheen

pearl onion Button onion

pearl rice *United States* A short-grain soft sticky rice

pearl sago See **sago**

peasant's cabbage Kale

pea sausage *England* A vegetarian sausage made from mashed cooked yellow peas with a little grated carrot, onion, nutmeg and seasoning, possibly bound with a little fat and flour, packed in non-animal casings

pease pudding Split dehusked dried green peas, soaked, boiled, drained and mashed with butter, egg yolks and seasoning. Reheated in the oven before serving.

pea sprout Pea leaf

pea starch Pea flour

peau blanche *France* Ziste

peber *Denmark* Pepper

pebernødder *Denmark* A spiced Christmas biscuit

pebre *Catalonia* Pepper, the condiment

pebrots *Catalonia* Red sweet peppers

pecan nut The central stone of the fruit of a large hickory (pecan) tree, *Carya illinoensis*, from central and southern USA. It has walnut-like wrinkled flesh enclosed in a smooth oval brown outer shell (up to 2.5 cm long). Eaten raw or cooked.

pecan pie *United States* A sweet open-topped pie filled with pecan nuts often served at Thanksgiving

pechay *Philippines* Chinese leaves

pêche *France* Peach (NOTE: Also means 'fishing')

pechena tikva *Bulgaria* Pumpkin slices baked with honey, walnuts, cinnamon and lemon zest

pechenye, pyechenye *Russia* Tart

pêches Melba *France* Peach Melba

pecho de ternera *Spain* Breast of veal

pechuga *Spain* Chicken breast

pechuga de ave a la Sarasate *Spain* Chicken breast filled with chopped veal

pechyen-grill, pyechen-grill *Russia* Liver and onion kebabs basted with mutton fat from Asiatic Russia. The liver can be wrapped in bacon for non-Muslims.

pechyenka, pyechyenka *Russia* Liver

pechyen kur v madere, pyechyen kur v madere *Russia* Floured chicken liver pieces sautéed with sweated onions, stewed in chicken stock and Madeira until cooked and served with the reduced cooking liquor blended with sour cream and garnished with chopped parsley

pecora *Italy* Sheep, ewe, mutton

Pecorino, Pecorino canestrato A semi-hard scalded-curd Sicilian cheese. See also **Canestrato**

Pecorino canestrato See **Canestrato**

Pecorino foggiano *Italy* A hard ewes' milk cheese made in cylinders (up to 7 kg), dry-salted and cured for 6 months. It has a sharp flavour and a hard rind. Contains 40% water, 29% fat and 25% protein.

Pecorino Romano *Italy* A hard cooked-curd ewes' milk cheese made around Rome and in Sardinia and shaped into cylinders (up to 20 kg). The curds are tapped and pierced in their moulds to promote drainage of whey, and the cheeses are dry-salted and needled to allow salt to penetrate over a period of 3 months. They are then ripened for a further 5 months. It has a dense white to yellow paste with a sharp ewes' milk cheese flavour and a brown oiled rind. Used as a dessert cheese since Roman times. Contains 31% water, 33% fat, 28% protein and 4 to 5 % salt.

Pecorino Siciliano *Italy* A hard ewes' milk cheese made between October and June and formed in a basket mould. The cheeses are dry-salted and ripened for 8 months. They have a pale yellow oiled rind and the pale paste which contains a few peppercorns has a sharp flavour and a few holes.

Pecorino Siciliano bianco *Italy* Pecorino Siciliano without peppercorns. Also called **Pecorino Siciliano calcagno**

Pecorino Siciliano calcagno *Italy* Pecorino Siciliano bianco

pectin A natural hemicellulosic carbohydrate gelling agent which in acid conditions (less than 3.46 pH) causes jam and marmalades to set. If the acidity is too low, less than 3.2 pH, then the jelly will weep, boiling also reduces the gelling power. Citrus fruits, apples, currants and some plums are rich in pectin and acids. Other fruits require added pectin and acid to make a satisfactory jam. See also **E440(i)**

pectinase An enzyme obtained from *Aspergillus niger*, used for the clarification of wines and beers and for the extraction of fruit juices by breaking down pectin

peda *South Asia* Milk fudge formed into small rounded blocks and garnished with pistachio nuts

pedas *South Asia* Hot-flavoured as from chillies

Pediococcus cerevisiae Bacterium used as a starter culture for lactic fermentation in meat products, e.g. salami, and in vegetables, e.g. cucumbers

Pediococcus halophilus Bacterium uses for the second-phase acidification of soya sauce

pedra, a la *Catalonia* Cooked on a hot stone or hot-plate

Pedroches *Spain* A hard ewes' milk cheese with holes in the paste, ripened for 1 to 2 months. Contains 40% water, 30% fat and 24% protein.

peel 1. The outer skin or rind of fruits and some, principally root, vegetables **2.** The long handled paddle used to move bread, baked goods, pizzas, etc. in and out of ovens

peel, to To remove the skin or rind from fruit or vegetables or to remove any outer covering, e.g. paper from a cake or rind from a cheese

peeler An implement used for peeling, consisting of a handled steel blade in which a longish slot with a raised sharp edge has been formed. This is used to remove a uniformly thick continuous slice from the surface of the object being peeled. Also called **potato peeler, vegetable peeler**

peelings The lengths of peel produced by a peeler

peertjes *Netherlands* Cooking pears

pee tee *Thailand* A deep saucer-shaped mould on the end of a long handle which is dipped in oil, then in batter, and deep-fried to produce a thin crisp case for filling with appetizers and the like

pei sooli *China* Asian pear

peix *Catalonia* Fish

peixe *Portugal* Fish

peixelua *Portugal* Sunfish, a type of basking shark

peix espasa *Catalonia* Swordfish

pejerrey *Spain* Smelt

pekin duck *England* One of the two standard duck breeds, Aylesbury is the other. It matures in about 7 weeks from hatching and contains a lot of fat.

Peking cooking The style of cooking practised in the northeast of China around Beijing. It is suited to a colder climate and includes carp, crab and giant prawns, roasts, hotpots, wheaten bread and noodles. Typical flavourings included garlic, ginger, onions, chives and leeks.

Peking duck A renowned Chinese speciality of crisp, marinated and roasted duck, pieces of which are wrapped up in a small pancake with spring onions, strips of cucumber, and a soya-based sauce prior to eating with the fingers. The ducks are specially bred with a meaty breast and an even layer of fat between the skin and the carcass so that the skin separates when roasted and becomes crisp. Also called **Beijing duck**

Peking pear Asian pear

pekoni *Finland* Bacon

pelagic Fish which move about in large shoals in the open sea

Pelardon *France* A mild, smooth, close-textured, white goats' milk cheese from Languedoc, formed into small rounds and often cured in the local brandy

pelargonium Scented geranium

Pelargonium capitatum *Botanical name* A rose-scented geranium used as an infusion to flavour sauces, custards, jellies, etc.

Pelargonium crispum **'Prince of Orange'** *Botanical name* An orange-scented geranium used as an infusion for general flavouring

Pelargonium graveolens x tomentosum *Botanical name* A rose-peppermint-scented geranium used to flavour liver pâté

Pelargonium odoratissimum *Botanical name* An apple-scented geranium used with fish baked in cider

Pelargonium quercifolium *Botanical name* An oak-leaved incense-scented geranium

Pelargonium radens *Botanical name* A rose-lemon scented geranium. An infusion of the leaves is used for general flavouring.

Pelargonium x fragrans *Botanical name* A pine-scented geranium used in soup and Welsh rarebit

pelato *Italy* Peeled, skinned

pelau *Caribbean* 1. A version of rice pilaff including boiling fowl meat, salt beef, almonds, sugar, butter, chopped onions, tomatoes, herbs, spices and seasoning 2. A Trinidadian dish of chicken or other boneless meat, long-grain rice and pigeon peas (4:2:1), flavoured with caramelized brown sugar and simmered with coconut milk so as to produce a moist mixture

pelle di porco *Italy* Pork crackling

pelli-pelli A simple sauce made from hot chillies. See also **piri-piri sauce**

Pellkartoffeln *Germany* Potatoes boiled in their skins

pelmeni *Russia* A type of ravioli made in the same fashion and filled with three different

freshly minced meats mixed with just enough water to keep them juicy, and carefully sealed in an envelope of extra-thick dough. Traditionally made at the beginning of winter, left frozen outside in the snow and used as required.

pelota *Spain* Meatball

peltopyy *Finland* Grey-legged partridge

Pembrokeshire broth *Wales* Equal weights of salted beef and bacon in a piece simmered in water for 2 to 3 hours, finely shredded or chopped carrots, turnips, onions and cabbage added and simmered a further 30 minutes, meat removed and kept warm and the broth thickened with oatmeal. The broth is served in bowls with finely chopped and cooked leeks and the meat is served as a second course with boiled potatoes. Also called **cawl sir benfro**

pemican See **pemmican**

pemmican *United States* Lean dried meat pounded to a paste with molten fat and used by the native Indians as an easily transportable energy source. It will keep for some time. Occasionally used with an admixture of dried vine fruits as iron rations. Also called **pemican**

Penang sugar A crude unrefined sugar containing a high proportion of molasses

Peña Santa *Spain* 1. A dessert similar to **baked Alaska 2.** An Asturian cheese

Pencarreg *Wales* A Welsh cheese made from pasteurized cows' milk resembling Brie in appearance but softer and with a stronger flavour

peng *China* A method of cooking in which ingredients are first deep-fried to seal the surface quickly and then stir-fried

Penicillium camembertii One of the penicillium moulds associated with the ripening of soft Camembert type cheeses

Penicillium candidum A strain of the penicillium mould used to give the characteristic skin and flavour to Camembert cheese

Penicillium glaucum A strain of the penicillium mould used for the production of bleu d'Auvergne cheese

Penicillium roquefortii A strain of the penicillium mould used to produce the veining in Roquefort and Stilton cheese

penne *Italy* Short tubes of pasta about 4 cm long and cut on the diagonal to resemble quill pens

penne rigate *Italy* Finely ribbed penne

pennette *Italy* Thin penne

Pennisetum typhoideum *Botanical name* Bulrush millet

pennone *Italy* Large penne

penny bun Cep

pennyroyal A type of mint, *Mentha pulegium*, with bright green peppermint scented leaves. There are two main varieties 'creeping' which grows to a height of 15 cm and 'upright' with upright stems to 30 cm. It should only be used in small quantities and not when pregnant or suffering from kidney problems. Also called **pudding grass**

pensées brouillées *France* Crisply fried pastries

pen shell Fan mussel

Penteleu *Romania* A ewes' milk cheese very similar to **Kashkaval**. Also called **dobrogea**

penyu *Indonesia, Malaysia* Turtle

peoci *Italy* Oven-browned mussels

pepato *Italy* A Pecorino type of cheese containing crushed peppercorns

pepe *Italy* Pepper

pepe di caienna *Italy* Cayenne pepper

pepe forte *Italy* Chilli pepper

pepe nero *Italy* Black pepper

peper *Netherlands* Pepper

peperata *Italy* A peppery sauce served with roasts. Also called **peverada**

peperkoek *Netherlands* Gingerbread

pepermunt *Netherlands* Peppermint

pepernoten *Netherlands* Tiny cubes of spiced ginger cake served on the 5th of December, the eve of St Nicholas' day when the Dutch give presents

peperonata *Italy* A type of **ratatouille**, made with sweet onions, red and yellow sweet peppers, tomatoes and a little garlic finished with chopped fresh parsley. Often served cold as an antipasto.

peperoncino *Italy* **1.** Hot chilli pepper **2.** Paprika

peperone *Italy* Sweet pepper, capsicum, occasionally used for chilli peppers and grains of paradise

peperoni gialli *Italy* Sweet yellow peppers

pepinillo 1. *Spain* Gherkin **2.** Choko

pepino 1. A large round or oval fruit of a plant related to the tomato. It has a yellow to green, smooth, shiny and bitter skin streaked with purple, a sweet, slightly acid, yellow flesh and a central mass of white seeds. Eaten fresh or in cooked sweet or savoury dishes. Also called **melon pear 2.** *Portugal, Spain* Cucumber

pepino de mar *Spain* Sea cucumber

pepita *Spain* Pumpkin seed

pepitoria *Spain* Meat hash or stew

pepitoria de gallina a la española *Spain* A chicken fricassée with peas, flavoured with nutmeg and saffron

pepo A type of marrow with a hard rind and many seeds. Also called **pepos**

pepos See **pepo**

peppar *Sweden* Pepper

pepparkakor *Sweden* A traditional crisp biscuit, variously flavoured with powdered cinnamon, cloves and cardamom seeds, served especially at Christmas

pepparrot *Sweden* Horseradish

pepparrotskött *Sweden* Brisket of beef boiled with vegetables and herbs and served with a velouté sauce made from the skimmed and strained cooking liquor flavoured with grated horseradish and finished with cream

pepparrotskött Sacher *Sweden* Boiled beef with Sacher sauce

pepper 1. Either the capsicum, sweet or hot, or the spice, *Piper nigrum* **2.** *Norway* Pepper, the spice

pepper, to To sprinkle or season with ground pepper

peppercorn The berries from a perennial vine, *Piper nigrum*, harvested at different stages of maturity with a pungent taste. Unripe green peppercorns can be preserved in brine or vinegar and are used whole or crushed. If the green berries are allowed to ferment and then dried they become black peppercorns. White peppercorns are the dried, dehusked ripe berries. All forms are used whole for flavouring. Black and white are also ground for use as a flavouring agent or as a condiment. See also **long pepper**

peppercress See **cress**

pepper dulse A seaweed, *Laurencia pinnatifida*, with a strong flavour once used as a condiment and chewed like tobacco in Iceland

peppergrass See **cress**

pepper jelly *United States* A Cajun condiment from Louisiana made with chillies, sweet peppers, sugar, vinegar and pectin and coloured red or green. It has a very hot taste.

pepper mill A hand-operated implement for grinding dried peppercorns to a powder as required

peppermint A strongly scented plant of the mint family, *Mentha x piperita*, with dark green pointed leaves and small pink or purple flowers. Mainly cultivated for its oil which is used as a flavouring, but may be used as a culinary herb.

peppermint cream A peppermint-flavoured fondant very popular in chocolates served with coffee at the end of a meal

peppermint oil The essential oil extracted from peppermint used as a flavouring

pepperoncini *United States* A small, mild, green chilli pepper used sparingly in salads

pepperone *Italy* A sausage made from beef and pork with chopped sweet red peppers and fennel. Cannot be kept.

pepperpot *United States* A highly seasoned thick soup or thin stew made with tripe

pepperpot soup *Caribbean* A rich soup made from beef, oxtail, pigs' trotters, chicken and mixed vegetables including okra, pumpkins and yams, flavoured with chillies and often containing cassava juice

pepperrotsaus *Netherlands, Norway* Horseradish sauce

pepper salami A salami covered in crushed peppercorns instead of a casing

pepper sauce See **poivrade, sauce**

pepper steak A beef steak coated with crushed peppercorns before frying and served with a sauce made from the deglazed pan juices and cream. Also called **steak au poivre**

pepper tree Various evergreen trees of the genus *Schinus* especially *S. molle*, found in South America and from which a commercial food-flavouring oil is obtained.

pepsin One of the proteases found in the human digestive system and also extracted from pigs' stomachs for use in cheese making

pera *Catalonia, Italy, Spain* Pear

pêra *Portugal* Pear

perca *Spain* Perch

percebes *Spain* Goose barnacles which grow along the northern Galician coast of northwest Spain. Cannot be frozen or canned and are eaten after boiling for 10 minutes. Very expensive.

perch A round freshwater fish of the genus *Perca*, especially *P. fluviatilis*, with a fine delicate flesh but many bones; found in the northern hemisphere. It has a greenish yellow back and is usually up to 30 cm long (500 g). Cooked in any way.

perche *France* Perch, the freshwater fish (NOTE: Also means **pole, stick**)

perche-soleil *France* Butterfish (3)

perche-truite *France* Largemouth black bass

perchia *Italy* Comber, the fish

perciatelli, perciatelloni *Italy* A type of macaroni. See also **bucatini**

perciatelloni *Italy* Bucatini

percolator A coffee maker in which liquid heated to boiling point at the base rises through a central tube and sprays over a container of ground coffee. As it percolates through it extracts the solubles from the coffee and returns to the base to rise up through the tube again until all the solubles are extracted.

perdigón *Spain* Partridge

perdikes *Greece* Partridge

perdiu *Catalonia* Partridge

perdiz *Portugal, Spain* Partridge

perdiz a la moda de Alcántara *Spain* Stuffed and roasted partridge

perdiz blanca *Spain* Ptarmigan

perdiz en chocolate *Spain* Partridge baked in a casserole with onions, garlic, parsley and vinegar and topped with chocolate

perdiz estofada a la catalana *Spain* Partridge stuffed with sausage and served with a wine and vinegar sauce with chocolate

perdreau *France* Young partridge

perdrix *France* Partridge

pere *Italy* Pears

perejil *Mexico, Spain* Parsley

peren *Netherlands* Pears

peres amb vi negre *Catalonia* Pears poached in red wine

perets *Russia* Pepper

perets farshirovannyi *Russia* Stuffed sweet peppers. See also **farshirovannyi perets**

pericarp The bran layer on cereal grains inside the outer husk

perifollo *Spain* Chervil

perifollo oloroso *Spain* Sweet cicely

périgord, à la See **périgourdine, à la**

Périgord black truffle An edible truffle, *Tuber melanosporum*, from Périgord, France, which has a wrinkled warty appearance and a strong distinctive fragrance but with a somewhat mild flavour. Very rare and expensive. See also **truffle**

périgourdine, à la *France* In the Périgord style, i.e. sometimes including truffles and/or foie gras

périgourdine, sauce *France* As sauce Périgueux but with parisienne-cut balls or thick slices of truffle instead of chopped truffle

Périgueux, à la See **périgourdine, à la**

Périgueux, sauce *England, France* An **espagnole sauce** to which port and finely chopped truffles are added. Served with meat and omelettes.

perilla 1. A member of the mint family. See also **shiso 2.** A soft white cheese. See also **Tetilla**

Perilla arguts Botanical name Shiso

perilla oil Oil from the roasted seeds of a variety of perilla, *Perilla frutescens*, grown in north India, China and Japan and used in Asian cooking

peri-peri A simple sauce made from hot chillies. See also **piri-piri sauce**

perisoare cu verdeaţă *Romania* Meatballs made of a mixture of minced beef and fat pork (1:3) with plenty of chopped and fried onions and seasoning, shaped into small balls, rolled in a mixture of chopped green herbs and fried very slowly in butter. Served with **demi-glace** sauce.

periwinkle See **winkle**

perlé(e) *France* Polished or pearl-shaped

perleløge *Denmark* Silverskin onions

perlemoen *South Africa* Afrikaans for **abalone**. Also called **klipkous**

perles du Japon *France* Tapioca pearls

Perlhuhn *Germany* Guinea fowl

perline *Italy* Tiny balls of pasta used in soup

Perlmoos *Germany* Carragheen

perna de carne *Portugal* Leg of meat

pernice *Italy* Grey-legged partridge

pernice di montagna *Italy* Ptarmigan

pernice rosa *Italy* Red-legged partridge

pernil *Catalonia* Cured and air-dried ham often used for tapas

pernil dolç *Catalonia* Cooked ham

pernil serrà *Catalonia* Cured ham

perpetual spinach See **spinach beet**

Persea americana *Botanical name* Avocado

Pershore egg plum *England* A yellow, almost pear-shaped plum used in cooking and jam making

Persian leek A small variety of leek about the size of a spring onion used as a flavouring

Persian lime A lime, *Citrus latifolia*, with a very thin skin and a distinctive aroma, usually picked when dark green. It has a very juicy and acid flesh with no seeds and is unsuitable for manufacturing purposes. It is produced in the USA, Israel and Australia. Also called **Tahiti lime, bearss lime**

Persian melon *United States* A large spherical dark green netted melon with a bright pink-orange flesh. It has finer netting than the musk melon.

Persian-style rice *United States* Plain boiled rice with a crust similar to **kateh**

persicata *Italy* A paste made from peaches which is dried and cut into squares

persico comune *Italy* Perch

persico sole *Italy* Butterfish (3)

persico trota *Italy* Largemouth black bass

persika *Sweden* Peach

persil *France* Parsley

persil, sauce *France* Parsley sauce

persilja *Sweden* Parsley

persiljespäckad kalv *Sweden* Fillet or cushion of veal stuffed with chopped parsley and chervil, browned in butter then pot-roasted with **tomato concassée** and stuffed

olives. The meat is cut in thick slices and served over the reduced cooking liquor.

persillade *France* A mixture of chopped garlic or shallots and chopped parsley used as a flavouring

persillade, sauce *France* A vinaigrette dressing flavoured with persillade

persille *Denmark* Parsley

persillé(e) *France* **1.** Sprinkled with parsley **2.** The name of many local goats' milk cheeses from the Savoie, each named after a village as e.g. Persillé de Thônes, meaning veined **3.** (*of beef*) Marbled

persimmon A large tomato-like fruit from a large group of tropical trees of the genus *Diospyros* but normally *D. kaki*. The fruit has a central core of seeds like an apple and a large calyx, and its green inedible skin turns a glossy yellow-orange as the fruit matures. Found in three principal varieties, i.e. kaki (Japan and China), Sharon fruit (Israel) and **mabalo**. Eaten as a dessert in fruit salads or other dishes. May be used as a decoration, in jam-making or may be dried. Also called **kaki** (NOTE: The persimmon is traditionally known as 'the apple of the Orient' because it originated in Japan and China)

peru *Portugal* Turkey

peruna *Finland* Potato

peru paulistano *Brazil* Turkey stuffed with a mixture of bread, tapioca and chopped ham, braised and served with thickened cooking liquor

perzik *Netherlands, Russia* Peach

pesca *Italy* Peach (NOTE: Also means 'fishing'.)

pescada *Portugal* Haddock, cod and similar fish

pescadilla *Spain* Whiting

pescaditos *Spain* Small fried fish, similar to whitebait, served as tapas

pescado 1. *Portugal* Any food fish **2.** *Spain* Fish

pescado a la asturiana *Spain* Fish cooked in wine with onions and chocolate and served with mushrooms

pescado a la sal *Spain* Whole unskinned fish baked in hot rock salt

pescado blanco a la malagueña *Spain* Cold skinned and deboned whitefish served with a covering of mayonnaise

pescado frito a la andaluza *Spain* Fish coated in an egg and flour batter and fried in olive oil

pesca nettarina *Italy* Nectarine

pesce *Italy* Fish

pesce al cartoccio *Italy* Fish baked **en papillote**

pesce cane *Italy* Dogfish

pesce cappone *Italy* Scorpion fish

pesce castagna *Italy* Pomfret, the fish

pesce da taglio *Italy* Halibut

pesce di castagna *Italy* Fish baked with chestnuts and served with mint sauce

pesce forca *Italy* Gurnard, the fish

pesce gatto *Italy* Channel catfish

pesce martello *Italy* Hammerhead shark

pesce persico *Italy* Perch

pesce San Pietro *Italy* John Dory

pesce sciabola *Italy* Scabbard fish

pesce spada *Italy* Swordfish

pesce stocco *Italy* Stockfish, dried cod

pesce turcino *Italy* Mackerel

pesce violino *Italy* Guitar fish

pesce volante *Italy* Flying fish

pesche *Italy* Peaches

pesciolini *Italy* Young fish similar to whitebait but of the local fish varieties, mainly sardines. Cooked as whitebait.

pêssego *Portugal* Peach

pesticide Any natural or synthetic chemical which kills insects such as flies

pestiño *Spain* A sweet honey fritter

pestle A heavy and short stumpy stick-like implement with a rounded end of ceramic, glass, metal or other hard material for use with a **mortar**. See also **pestle and mortar**

pestle and mortar The pestle and mortar are used in combination to crush and/or to grind by hand foods, spices and the like to a fine powder or paste

pesto *England, Italy* A mixture of basil, parsley, pine kernels and olive oil pounded together or processed. Used to flavour pasta and as a general flavouring. Sometimes contains grated Parmesan cheese. (NOTE: So called because once prepared in a pestle (*pesto* in Italian) and mortar.)

pestun de fave *Italy* Pounded and sieved cooked beans mixed with chopped mint, garlic, cheese and oil. See also **maro**

petacciuola *Italy* Plantain

petai *Indonesia* Parkia

petcha A Jewish appetizer made from calf's foot jelly flavoured with garlic and vinegar, seasoned and studded with wedges of hard-boiled egg. Also called **cholodyetz**, **fisnoga**, **pilsa**, **putcha**

pet de nonne *France* A light deep-fried sweet fritter similar to a beignet. From Burgundy. (NOTE: Literally 'nun's fart'.)

pétéram *France* A rich offal stew containing sheep's trotters and tripe from Languedoc

Petersilie *Germany* Parsley

petha *South Asia* Strips of wax gourd softened with lime water (Calcium hydroxide), then boiled in sugar syrup to form a candied confection

petis *Indonesia* A fermented fish sauce

petit beurre *France* A small biscuit made with butter. Butter cookie (USA).

petit déjeuner *France* Breakfast (NOTE: Literally 'small lunch'.)

petit-duc, au *France* In the style of the minor duke, i.e. garnished with asparagus tips, truffles, creamed chicken in small pastry cases and possibly mushrooms

petite marmite 1. *England, France* Double-strength consommé in which are simmered progressively diced lean beef, blanched pieces of chicken winglets, turned carrots, pieces of celery, leek and cabbage and turned turnip so that all are cooked at the same time, the whole seasoned, degreased and served in a marmite dish garnished with slices of beef bone marrow and accompanied by a slice of toasted French bread and grated cheese **2.** *France* A small earthenware bulbous dish with two moulded handles used to serve consommé

petite roussette *France* Lesser spotted dogfish

petites *France* Sheep's or calves' tripe

petit four See **petits fours**

petit gris *France* A small dark brown snail from the north of France

petit lait *France* Milk whey

petit pain *France* A quarter-sized baguette weighing about 50 g

petit pain fourré *France* A filled roll or bridge roll

petit pâté *France* A small pork pie or meat patty

petit salé *France* Small pieces of salt pork

petits fours *England, France* Small sweetmeats, chocolates and tiny decorated cakes served with the coffee at the end of a meal

petits pois *England, France* A small variety of a very tender pea with a delicate flavour

petits secs *France* Small cream biscuits

petit-suisse *France, Switzerland* A 30 g Suisse cheese. Also called **demi-suisse**

petonchio *Italy* Variegated scallop

pétoncle *France* Variegated scallop

pétrir *France* To knead

Petroselinum crispum *Botanical name* Curly parsley

Petroselinum crispum 'Neapolitanum' *Botanical name* Flat leaved (Italian or French) parsley

Petroselinum crispum 'tuberosam' *Botanical name* Hamburg parsley

Petrus *Belgium* A pale yellow, supple textured, strong smelling but mild-flavoured cows' milk cheese from Loo with an orange rind. The cheese contains many small holes.

petruska kudryavana *Russia* Flat leaved parsley

pe tsai *China* Chinese leaves

petticoat tails *Scotland* Skirt-shaped shortbread biscuits from Scotland

petti di pollo *Italy* Chicken breasts

pettine *Italy* Small scallops

pettitoes Young sucking pigs' trotters which may be braised or grilled or used for their gelatine content

petto *Italy* Breast of an animal, brisket, etc.

petto di tacchino alla milanese *Italy* Panéed and fried breast of turkey

peultjes *Netherlands* 1. Small young peas 2. Mangetout

peus de porc a la llauna *Catalonia* Pigs' trotters in a spicy sauce

peverada *Italy* Peperata

peynir *Turkey* Cheese

pez *Spain* Fish

pez cinto *Spain* Scabbard fish

pez de limón *Spain* Amberjack

pez de San Pedro *Spain* John Dory

pez espada *Spain* Swordfish

pez martillo *Spain* Hammerhead shark

pezzo *Italy* A piece (of cake, etc.)

Pfahlmuschel *Germany* Farmed mussel

Pfälzer Leberwurst *Germany* Smooth liver sausage containing coarse pieces of offal

Pfannkuchen *Germany* Pancake. The German variety tend to be thicker than in the UK or France.

Pfeffer *Germany* Pepper

Pfeffergurke *Germany* Gherkin

Pfefferkuchen *Germany* A spice cake similar to gingerbread eaten at Christmas

Pfefferminz *Germany* Peppermint

Pfeffernüsse *Germany* Spiced ginger biscuits made by the blending method e.g. from self-raising flour, golden syrup, honey, sugar and butter (12:8:6:4:1) well-flavoured with spices and baked at 205°C

Pfefferpotthast *Germany* Boned and trimmed stewing steak cut in large pieces, simmered with sliced onions, a bouquet garni and seasoning until cooked, bouquet garni removed and all thickened with breadcrumbs and flavoured with plenty of pepper and lemon

Pfeilwurz *Germany* Arrowroot

Pfifferling *Germany* Chanterelle

Pfirsich *Germany* Peach

Pflaume *Germany* Plum

Pflaumenschlehe *Germany* Bullace, the fruit

Pfnutli *Switzerland* Apple fritters

pH A measure of acidity or alkalinity related to the concentration of hydrogen ions (positively charged hydrogen atoms) in solution. Values range from 1 the most acid through 7, neutral, to 14 the most alkaline. Some typical pH values are: gastric juice 1.3 to 3.0, lemon juice 2.1, cranberry sauce 2.6, orange juice 3.0, apples 3.4, tomatoes 4.4, black coffee 5.0, egg yolk 6.0 to 6.6, milk 6.9, baking soda solution 8.4, egg white 9.6 to 10.0, household ammonia 11.9.

phai tong *Thailand* Bamboo shoot

phak hom pom *Laos* Coriander leaves

phak si *Laos* Dill seed

phalazee *Burma* Cardamom

pharma foods See **functional foods**

phase A physical state of matter such as gas, vapour, liquid or solid. Two or more phases are common in many foods, e.g. milk and cream contain two liquid phases, water and butterfat, whipped eggs contain liquid and gas phases, cooked meringue contains a solid and gas phase and some cake mixtures are very complex mixtures of phases. See also **dispersed phase**, **continuous phase**

Phaseolus aconitifolius *Botanical name* Moth bean

Phaseolus acutifolius *Botanical name* Tepary bean

Phaseolus aureus *Botanical name* Mung bean

Phaseolus canceratus *Botanical name* Rice bean

Phaseolus coccineus *Botanical name* Runner bean

Phaseolus limensis *Botanical name* Butter bean

Phaseolus lunatus *Botanical name* Butter bean

Phaseolus mungo *Botanical name* Black gram

Phaseolus vulgaris *Botanical name* French bean, kidney bean, etc.

pheasant The most widespread of all game birds, *Phasianus colchicus*, weighing about 1 to 1.5 kg and suitable for two persons. Hen birds are less tough than the cock, but the cock has a better flavour. The feathered birds should be hung by the feet for 3 to 10 days until blood begins to drip from the beak. The young birds are barded, not larded, with fatty bacon and roasted at 190°C for 45 to 60 minutes. Shooting season in the UK 1st October to the 1st of February. Hanging time 3 to 10 days, some say 12 to 15 days, at 6°C.

phen *Vietnam* Alum

phenol oxidase The enzyme which causes the cut surfaces of apples, potatoes etc. to brown in air

phenyl benzene See **E230, diphenyl**

Philadelphia cheese steak *United States* A crisp roll covered with thin slices of beef and/or cheese, with relishes, etc.

Philadelphia cream cheese A heavily promoted and well-known brand of processed **cream cheese**

Philadelphia eggs *United States* A split muffin covered with cooked sliced breast of chicken, a poached egg and **hollandaise sauce**

phil noi *Laos* Peppercorn

philpy *United States* A rice bread from South Carolina

pho *Vietnam* A traditional rice noodle soup made with beef stock, and served with limes and chillies. It is eaten for breakfast, lunch or dinner.

phong jau *China* Chicken feet

phool gobi *South Asia* Cauliflower

phooti *South Asia* A variety of melon which bursts open when ripe. Used in the unripe state as a vegetable.

phosphated flour *United States* Flour with added salt, yeast and yeast nutrients which only needs mixing with water to make dough. Does not keep well.

phosphates Salts of phosphoric acid used for flavouring and as stabilizers. The important ones used in the food industry are disodium dihydrogen, tetrasodium, tetrapotassium and trisodium diphosphate all classified as E450(a) and pentasodium triphosphate and pentapotassium triphosphate classified as E450(b). See also **polyphosphates**

phosphoric acid See **orthophosphoric acid, E338**

phosphorus An essential inorganic element necessary for health. Usually in the form of phosphates which are essential for cellular processes as well as for the construction of bones and teeth.

phul *Nepal* Egg

phul gobhi *South Asia* Cauliflower florets briefly fried in butter which has already been aromatized with mustard seeds, chopped ginger and turmeric, all the florets to be well-coloured with the turmeric. Cumin, paprika, pepper and salt are added with a little water, then the pan covered and left on a low heat until the cauliflower is al dente. It is then dried off over a high heat before serving.

phulka *South Asia* A small chapati

phyllo pastry Filo pastry

Phyllostachys pubescens *Botanical name* One of the cultivated bamboo shoots

physalis Cape gooseberry

Physalis alkekengi *Botanical name* Chinese lantern

Physalis ixocarpa *Botanical name* Tomatillo

Physalis peruviana *Botanical name* Cape gooseberry

Physalis pruinosa *Botanical name* Dwarf cape gooseberry

phytic acid A plant acid which tends to bind iron and zinc in the plants and to carry these trace elements through the human gut without absorption. The amino acids methionine and cysteine present in animal products but not in plant-derived protein promote the release of these trace elements and hence their absorption.

Phytolacca americana *Botanical name* Pokeweed

phytomenadion See **vitamin K**

piacere, a *Italy* At choice, free choice of menu items

piada *Italy* Piadina

piadina *Italy* A soft flat bread usually served warm filled with sausage, ham or spinach and/or Ricotta cheese. Also called **piada, pie**

piantaggine *Italy* Plantain

pianuzza *Italy* Dab, the fish

piatti *Italy* Dishes, plates (of food)

piatto, al *Italy* Shirred or gently cooked in a dish, usually eggs

piatto del giorno *Italy* Dish of the day

piaz *South Asia* Onion

pibil pork *Mexico* Cochinita pibil

picada 1. *Mexico* A filled turnover made with tortilla dough. See also **garnacha 2.** *Catalonia* A sauce whose principal ingredients are garlic, ground nuts, toasted bread, spices and parsley, with ground almonds used instead of flour for thickening

picadillo 1. *Spain* Minced meat **2.** *Mexico* A cooked savoury mixture of minced pork and beef with onions, oil, tomatoes, garlic, vinegar, raisins, chopped almonds, spices, herbs and seasonings, used as a filling or served with rice **3.** A salad of orange, onion, sweet peppers and cooked shredded salt codfish

picadinho *Brazil* Minced beef simmered in stock with chopped onions and tomatoes. Served with the addition of chopped hard-boiled eggs and olives, accompanied by rice or mashed potatoes.

picado *Portugal* A type of meat hash

Picadon *France* A soft goats' milk cheese from the Rhône valley cast in 100 g discs. The white paste has a sharp nutty-flavoured taste after maturing for 1 to 4 weeks. It has AOC status. Contains 45% fat.

picante *Spain* Piquant, hot and spicy

pica-pica *Catalonia* A selection of different dishes for sharing

picatostes *Spain* Deep-fried bread slices

piccalilli A bright yellow mustard-flavoured pickle made from brined pieces of cauliflower, marrow, green beans, pickling onions and cucumber in a sauce made from white vinegar, flour, sugar, mustard, ginger and turmeric. Also called **mustard pickle**

piccante *Italy* Piquant, hot and spicy

piccata *Italy* A small medallion or escalope of meat, usually a thin fried escalope of veal served in a sour lemon sauce and garnished with lemon wedges

piccioncello *Italy* Pigeon

piccioncino *Italy* Pigeon

piccione *Italy* Pigeon

piccolo *Italy* Small

Pichelsteiner *Germany* Pichelsteinerfleisch

Pichelsteinerfleisch *Germany* A flame-proof earthenware dish filled with alternate layers of meat (sliced marrow, beef, pork, veal and mutton mixed together) and vegetables (sliced onions, carrots, celeriac, potatoes and savoy cabbage), seasoned, moistened with water, covered and baked in the oven. Served from the pot. Also called **Pichelsteiner**

pichón *Spain* 1. Pigeon 2. Squab

pickerel 1. A young pike 2. A small relative of the pike found in North America

Pickert *Germany* A type of peasant bread made from potato flour or grated potatoes and wheat flour or buckwheat meal, fried or baked

pickle Food, usually chopped vegetables and fruits, preserved in a flavoured sauce or solution which prevents the growth of microorganisms. Usually used as a condiment or accompaniment and appreciated for its salty or sharp acidic flavour.

pickle, to To preserve food by placing it in brine, vinegar or other acid solutions together with flavourings. The low pH or high salt concentration prevents the growth of microorganisms.

pickled bean curd See **bean curd cheese**

pickled cucumber Cucumbers or cucumber pieces or slices pickled in spiced brine or vinegar

pickled eggs Shelled hard-boiled eggs pickled in spiced and seasoned vinegar. Usually eaten between 1 and 4 months after pickling.

pickled fish Caveach

pickled garlic Peeled garlic cloves pickled in vinegar, possibly with the addition of sugar. Eaten as a snack or side dish.

pickled limes Limes are preserved by immersing in soya sauce with sugar, salt and vinegar (across Southeast Asia), by salting and drying (in China), or by slitting, filling with spices and immersing in oil (in Indonesia)

pickled shallots Shallots pickled in a vinegar and sugar mixture, used as a snack or side dish in China and Japan

pickled testicles *Iceland* Testicles pickled in whey

pickling brine A mixture of 500 g salt, 40g of saltpetre and 20 g of brown sugar per litre of water. This mixture is oversaturated and will contain solid salt but this will disappear as pickling progresses. Various spices and herbs may be added. Joints of meat are normally pickled for about 8 days and if weighing over 4 kg should be injected with the brine.

pickling onion Button onion

pickling salt *United States* Pure salt without additives such as anti-caking agents which are often insoluble and would cloud the pickle

pickling spice *United Kingdom* A mixture of whole spices used to flavour vinegar for preparation of pickles and chutney, consisting of a selection from dried ginger, mustard seed, cloves, black peppercorns, small chilli peppers, mace, coriander seed and allspice berries

picnic A meal taken in the open air usually from food laid out on a cloth on the ground or on collapsible tables

picnic ham *United States* A cured and smoked front leg of pork, similar in taste to ham

Picodon *France* The name of various goats' milk cheeses from the Drôme-Rhône valley

Picón *Spain* An Austurain semi-hard cheese. See also **Cabrales**

pi dan *China* Salted duck eggs

pie 1. A sweet or savoury mixture enclosed totally in pastry and cooked in a container or placed in a pie dish and covered with pastry prior to cooking 2. *Italy* Foot 3. *Italy* Piadina

pie, à la *France* Black and white like a magpie

pièce de boeuf *France* A prime cut of beef

pièce montée *France* The centrepiece of a cold or hot buffet or other display of food; alternatively a French wedding cake of profiteroles built up into a cone and held together with caramel

pieces Light brown sugar

pie cherry Acid cherry

piecrust pastry *United States* Shortcrust pastry

pied *France* Foot or trotter

pie d'asino *Italy* Dog cockle

pied de cochon *France* Pig's trotter

pied de porc *France* Pig's trotter

piedini *Italy* Feet, trotters, e.g. of a pig

piedini di maiale alla piemontese *Italy* Pigs' trotters, panéed and deep-fried

pie dish A round or oval dish with a rim on which the pastry crust is supported, sometimes with a projection rising from the centre to also support the pie crust

Piedmontese truffle The **Italian white truffle**, *Tuber magnatum*

'*(Tuber magnatum)*'

Piedrafita *Spain* A hard, mushroom-shaped, mountain cheese. See also **Cebrero**

pieds cendrillons *France* A mixture of seasoned meat from pigs' trotters minced with mushrooms and truffles either made as a crépinette, wrapped in pastry and baked in the oven or wrapped in greased paper and cooked in hot ashes

pieds et paquets *France* A Provençal dish of sheep's tripe folded into packets filled with a savoury mixture and cooked slowly with trotters, skinned tomatoes, herbs and seasoning. Also called **pieds-paquets, pieds-en-paquets**

pie floater *Australia* A meat pie floating on mushy peas with tomato sauce on top. From South Australia.

pie marker A round metal frame supporting radial cutters, used for accurately portioning pies and cakes, usually into quarters, sixths, eighths or smaller

piémontaise, à la *France* In the style of Piedmont in Italy, i.e. garnished with polenta or risotto, white truffles and sometimes tomato sauce

pie plant *United States* Rhubarb

pierna *Spain* Leg of meat

pierna de cordero *Spain* Leg of lamb

piernik *Poland* A Christmas gingerbread cake made by the melting method sweetened with sugar and honey, raised with baking powder and flavoured with ground ginger, cinnamon and nutmeg

pierogi *Poland* A type of ravioli usually filled with either curd cheese, sauerkraut or mushrooms. Larger than Italian ravioli.

pierozki *Poland* Small savoury semi-circular pasties made from 10 cm rounds of choux, sour or puff pastry with a variety of fillings, baked at 200°C or deep-fried. Often served as an accompaniment to soup or as a snack.

pierrade *France* Meat, fish or vegetables cooked without oil or fat on an electric hot-plate (a 'pierrade électrique') brought to the table

pieterman *Netherlands* Weever fish

pie tin A round shallow baking dish with sloping walls

pieuvre *France* Octopus

pie veal *United Kingdom* Diced meat from cheap secondary cuts of veal e.g. neck, scrag and breast

pig 1. *United Kingdom* Any member of the *Suidae* family, intelligent animals with a bristly skin and long snouts with which they can root about in earth and leaf litter looking for food; especially *Sus scrofa*, the domesticated pig, and European wild boar. Also called **porker 2.** *United States* A sucking pig or young immature pig

pigeon *England, France* A rather tough wild bird or more tender domesticated bird weighing about 450 to 700 g. Part roast at 200°C for 15 minutes, remove breasts and poach in stock made from the remainder of the carcass, using reduced cooking liquor as sauce. The domesticated bird is treated like chicken. There are no restrictions on shooting. See also **wood pigeon**. Also called **wood dove**

pigeonneau *France* Squab or young pigeon

pigeon pea The peas from a short lived perennial shrub, *Cajanus cajan,* which are a staple food and grown in Africa, India and the Caribbean. The peas may be red to white, brown, mottled or black and the green pods can be used as a vegetable. Also called **cajan pea, red gram, gunga pea, toor dal, red chick pea, tuware, tur, tuvaran, rarhar, arhar**

piggvar *Norway, Sweden* Turbot

pig-in-a-blanket *United States* Sausage roll

pigmented grapefruit A comparatively recent development of grapefruit, some varieties having occurred naturally and other having been produced by irradiating seed (e.g. rio red). All are characterized by a red pigmentation of the flesh and in some varieties, of the rind. The pigment is lycopene (as in tomatoes) and is produced by prolonged high temperature. The common variety is ruby but many new varieties are in the process of development.

pigmented orange A type of sweet orange which develops red pigmentation (**anthocyanins**) in the flesh adjacent to segment walls and near the flower end. The flavour is distinctive and is sometimes said to resemble that of a raspberry or cherry. As they require low night temperatures to develop the red colour they tend only to be grown in the Mediterranean and similar climates. Also called **blood orange**

pigment rubine See **E180**

pignatta *Italy* Earthenware cooking pot

pignola *United States* Pine nut

pignoli *Italy* Pine nuts

pignolia Pine nut

pignons *France* Pine nuts

pignut Tiger nut

Pigouille *France* A creamy cheese from Charente made from any milk and usually sold wrapped in straw

pig's cheek Half the lower part of the pig's cheek including the jaw bone, and half the tongue and snout, pickled, boiled, boned and coated with breadcrumbs, sliced and served cold or for frying. Alternatively dried and cured. Also called **Bath chap**

pig's ear Pig's ears may be cooked together with pigs' trotters but are generally used for manufactured meat products

pig's fry 1. Haslet **2.** Heart, liver and sweetbreads of a pig, cut in pieces, boiled until tender, drained, coated with a mixture of seasoned flour and rubbed sage and fried. Served with fried potatoes, greens and gravy.

pig's head The major source of meat for **brawn**, occasionally used as a source of meat for pie fillings and sometimes roasted whole, glazed and an apple placed in its mouth for use as a table decoration especially at theme banquets

pigs in blankets *United Kingdom* Cabbage rolls

pig's kidney Small but elongated kidneys with a good flavour which may be cooked in any way. Allow one per person.

pig's liver A strong-flavoured liver which should be soaked in milk for at least 1 hour. Generally stewed or casseroled, made into pâté or used in stuffings.

pig's trotters Pigs' feet used like calves' feet as a source of gelatine or may be boned, stuffed and roasted or the meat used in brawn. Boiled pigs' trotters used to be eaten dressed with vinegar as a northern UK delicacy.

pig weed Summer purslane

pihvi *Finland* Beef steak

piimä *Finland* **1.** Curdled milk **2.** Junket **3.** Clabber **4.** Buttermilk

piirakka *Finland* Meat or fish and rice cooked in a pasty

pijlinktvis *Netherlands* Squid

pikant *Germany* Piquant, spiced; often denotes coated with a hot prepared mustard

Pikantensosse *Germany* Piquant sauce

Pikantwurst *Austria* A spicy sausage similar to **Csabai**

Pikatinij *Russia* A semi-hard surface-ripened cows' milk cheese with scattered holes. Contains 45% water, 25% fat and 23% protein.

pike A large (up to 4 kg commercially but can be 20 kg) freshwater fish of the genus *Esox*, with a long pointed nose, greenish yellow back and lighter underside found in temperate waters of the northern hemisphere. The flesh is lean, white and dry with an excellent flavour but very bony. Usually soaked before cooking in any way. Also called **jackfish**, **freshwater shark**, **waterwolf**

pikefleisch *France, Germany* Boeuf salé

pikelet *Scotland, England* A name used for a variety of teacakes, in particular the crumpet (in Yorkshire) and the Scottish pancake, either the yeasted or non-yeasted types. Usually eaten warm.

pike-perch A temperate freshwater fish from the northern hemisphere of the genera *Stizostedion* or *Lucioperca* which has the body of a perch but a pike's nose and a brown striped back. Cooked like pike or perch.

pilaf *Turkey* Pilav

pilaff *Greece* A rice dish made from finely chopped onions sweated in butter, rice added and sweated 2 minutes, twice the volume of boiling seasoned white or fish stock added with a bouquet garni and all cooked under a cartouche in a 240°C oven for 15 to 20 minutes until cooked. The bouquet garni is removed, the dish seasoned and butter stirred in. Often served with cooked meat, fish or vegetables. See also **pilaw, pilau**

pilafi 1. Grains of pasta resembling rice **2.** Rice fried to a cream colour in butter then simmered in stock until tender

pilaki *Turkey* Fish cutlets or steaks braised with vegetables and garlic then served cold, dressed with lemon juice and garnished with chopped parsley

pilao *South Asia* Pilau

pilau *South Asia* A savoury rice dish made from spices, garlic and chilli fried in butter or ghee, meat added and fried 5 minutes; yoghurt progressively added until no more is absorbed; soaked and drained Basmati rice added with saffron and salt and fried. The whole is then covered with stock, brought to the boil and cooked on a very low heat until the rice is tender adding more stock if too dry. Garnished with crisply fried onions before service. Fruits and vegetables may be added with the rice. Also called **pilao**, **pulao**, **pullao**

pilav *Turkey* Round grain rice or bulgar wheat cooked until tender then mixed with butter or oil. Also called **pilaf**

pilaw *Poland* A type of pilaff with lamb and tomato purée

pilchard A small round oily sea fish, *Sardina pilchardus* and *Clupea pilchardus*, which when immature is called a sardine. Often canned in brine or tomato sauce, but can be cooked whole. Found off the south-west coast of the UK. Fresh pilchards can be distinguished from small herring by raised lines that run back from the eyes and from sprats by their lack of the line of spiny scales along the centre line of the belly.

Pilgermuschel *Germany* Pilgrim scallop

pilgrim scallop The Mediterranean scallop, *Pecten jacobaeus*, slightly smaller than the great scallop. Also called **coquille Saint Jacques**

piliç *Turkey* Chicken

pili pili *Central Africa* Chilli pepper

pili pili sauce *Central Africa* A very hot sauce made from finely chopped chilli peppers, lemon juice, garlic, parsley, salt and oil, all processed and heated in a hot frying pan for a few minutes then bottled

pillau Pilau

piloncillo *Mexico* A dark unrefined sugar similar to muscovado, formed into small cylinders and sometimes wrapped in raffia. Also called **panoche**, **panocha**

pilon de cuisse *France* Chicken drumstick

pilot biscuit Hardtack

pilsa A Jewish appetizer made from calf's foot jelly. See also **petcha**

Pilz *Germany* 1. Mushroom 2. A crumbly, yellowish, blue-veined semi-soft cows' milk cheese (up to 5 kg) with a strong distinctive flavour and a soft or dry rind. Usually served as a dessert cheese. Contains 49% water, 27% fat and 18% protein. Also called **Edelpilzkäse**

Pilzschnitzel *Austria* A vegetarian cutlet made from mushrooms, carrots and peas

piman, **pimen** *Japan* Sweet pepper

piment *France* Capsicum

pimenta-da-caiena *Portugal* Cayenne pepper

Pimenta dioica *Botanical name* Allspice

pimentão-doce *Portugal* Sweet red or green pepper

Pimenta officinalis *Botanical name* Allspice

piment doux *France* Sweet pepper

piment fort *France* Chilli or cayenne pepper

pimento 1. *Italy* Allspice 2. See **pimiento** 3. A very mild chilli pepper

pimento butter Red peppers pounded with butter and sieved

pimento-do-reino *Portugal* Black pepper

pimentón *Spain* Dried and ground red pepper, generally bright red and with a strong aroma, similar to paprika

piment rouge *France* Chilli pepper

pimient *Russia* Allspice

pimienta 1. *Portugal*, *Spain* Pepper, capsicum 2. *Spain* Pepper *P. nigrum*.

pimienta inglesa *Spain* Allspice

pimienta negra *Spain* Black pepper

pimiento 1. *Spain* A variety of red, yellow or green sweet pepper with a good flavour often sold canned or bottled. Also called **pimento** 2. *United States* Sweet pepper

pimiento de Jamaica *Spain* Allspice

pimpinela *Spain* Salad burnet

pimpinella *Italy* Salad burnet

Pimpinella anisum *Botanical name* Anise

Pimpinelle *Germany* Salad burnet

pimprenelle *France* Salad burnet

piña *Spain* Pineapple

pinaattiohukaiset *Finland* Spinach-flavoured pancakes

pinaksiw *Philippines* Sardines or similar fish layered in a pot with banana leaves, salt and coconut vinegar and simmered for 20 minutes

pinaroli *Italy* A small fungus found in pine woods

pin bone of beef *Wales* Welsh and west country term for rump of beef

pinbone steak *United States* A steak cut from the **sirloin**

pinch A dry measure often used in recipes for a small quantity of powder. The amount of powder held between the thumb and forefinger, roughly equal to one quarter of a gram. 15 pinches per teaspoon.

pin cherry *United States* Bird cherry

pincisgrassi *Italy* Lasagne layered with ceps, cream and parma ham, topped with Parmesan cheese and white truffle shavings. See also **vincisgrassi maceratese**

pinda *Netherlands* Peanuts

pindakaas *Netherlands* Peanut butter

pindangga *Philippines* Eel

Pindos *Greece* A cheese similar to **Kefalotiri**

pineapple The fruit (up to 30 cm long and 15 cm diameter) of a tropical plant, *Ananas comosus*, which is the result of the coalescence of the fruits of a hundred or more flowers. It grows at the top of a thick stalk which springs from the centre of a rosette of long spiky leaves. The golden-yellow flesh is firm, juicy and fibrous with a central inedible core. The skin varies from green to yellow or red as it matures. Sold whole or tinned with the skin and central core removed. Used as a dessert fruit or in savoury dishes, e.g. with pork. The uncooked juice, which contains active proteases, may be used to tenderize meat and will prevent gelatine-based jellies from setting.

pineapple cheese *United States* A pink-coloured soft textured Cheddar-like cheese from Connecticut

pineapple fritter A slice of pineapple, skinned, cored, floured, coated with a batter and deep-fried

pineapple guava Feijoa

pineapple melon A Japanese melon rather like a water melon with a green striped skin and a crisp, sweet, golden flesh tasting slightly of pineapple. now grown in Israel.

pine kernel See **pine nut**

pine mushroom Matsutake

pine nut The seed of the Mediterranean stone pine tree, *Pinus pinea*, from the Mediterranean and North Africa. They are sold shelled, are cream coloured with a slightly resinous flavour and oily texture and about the size of a lemon pip. Popular in Middle Eastern and Italian cooking and used to make **pesto**. The seeds of various other pine trees are eaten worldwide e.g. *P. koraiensis* (Korea), *P. gerardiana* (Himalayas), *P. cembroides* (Mexico and southwest USA). In fact most pine tree seeds if sufficiently large are eaten somewhere. Also called **Indian nut, pignola, pine kernel**

pine nut oil An expensive fine oil extracted from pine nuts. Used for salad dressings.

ping *Thailand* Dry cooking of food in the oven or over a source of heat such as charcoal. Also called **bing**

ping guo *China* Apple

pinhead oatmeal Dehusked whole oats cut into 3 or 4 pieces per individual grain. Also called **steel-cut oatmeal**

Pinienkern *Switzerland* Pine nut

Piniennuss *Germany* Pine nut

pinion The wingtip or winglet of a bird (poultry or game)

pinipig *Philippines* Toasted and flattened glutinous rice used in cakes and desserts and after deep-frying used as a crisp topping for sweets and ice cream

pink bean *United States* Pinto bean

Pinkel *Germany* A type of sausage from Bremen made from beef and/or pork,

onions, oats and seasonings and sometimes lightly smoked. Boiled or cooked with other foods. Also called **Pinkelwurst**

Pinkelwurst *Germany* Pinkel

pink fir apple An irregularly shaped potato with a pink skin, a smooth waxy flesh and a fine nutty flavour. Used for potato salad.

pink gingerbuds Ginger buds

pink peppercorn See **schinus molle**

pink salmon The smallest of the Pacific salmon, *Oncorhynchus gorbuscha*, with a dark blue spotted back and silvery underside weighing to 2.5 kg. The flesh is pink, oily and firm textured and it may be cooked in any way. Also called **humpback salmon**

pink sauce *United States* Marie-rose sauce

pink shrimp One of the common British varieties, *Pandalus montagui*, of shallow water shrimps. Not as good tasting as the brown shrimp.

pink trout See **salmon trout**

pinne *Italy* Fan mussels

pinnekjøtt *Norway* Salt-cured mutton chops steamed over peeled birch twigs

pinocchio *Italy* Pine nut

pinole A mixture of finely ground maize or wheat flour made from the parched grain and mesquite beans sometimes used to make a sweet drink. Used in Mexico and southwestern USA.

pinoli *Italy* Pine nuts

pinolli *South America* A mixture of powdered vanilla, spices and ground and toasted chocolate beans

pinolo *Italy* Pine nut

piñón *Mexico, Spain* Pine nut

pint A non-metric fluid measure still in use in the USA and still seen in English recipes. The UK measure is divided into 20 fluid ounces and is 567.5 ml (0.57 litres). The USA measure is divided into 16 fluid ounces and is 0.8 times the UK measure i.e. 473 millilitres. Both are abbreviated pt. See also **gallon, cup measure, liquid measure, volume measure, dry measure**

pintada *Spain* Guinea hen

pintade *France* Guinea fowl

pintadeau *France* Young guinea fowl

pintail duck A wild duck, *Anas acuta*, shot for the table

pintarroja *Spain* Dogfish

pinto bean A variety of pale kidney bean, *Phaseolus vulgaris*, with bright red markings, popular in Spain, Mexico and North America

pin tong *China* Lump sugar (3)

Pinus *Botanical name* The genus of pine trees, the source of **pine nuts**

Pinzgauer Bier *Austria* A distinctive, full-flavoured cows' milk cheese from the district around Salzburg

pinzimonio *Italy* A mixture of olive oil, salt and pepper used as a dressing for raw vegetables

Piora *Switzerland* A hard scalded-curd cows' milk cheese shaped like a cylinder (up to 12 kg). The cheeses are salted and ripened for up to 6 months.

pip The small seed of which several are usually found in fruits such as apples, citrus, grapes and melons

pip, to To remove seeds or pips from fruit or vegetables

pipe, to To force a semi-solid mixture through the nozzle of a piping bag and lay it down on some surface. See also **piping bag**

piperade *France* Tomatoes, sweet peppers, onions and garlic cooked in olive oil or goose fat until soft, then chopped herbs and beaten eggs added to the mixture and lightly scrambled. Served with fried or grilled ham and garnished with triangular pieces of fried bread.

Piper betle *Botanical name* The betel pepper vine from which **betel leaf** is obtained

Piper cubeba *Botanical name* Cubeb

Piper longum *Botanical name* Long pepper (In)

Piper nigrum *Botanical name* Pepper

Piper retrofractum *Botanical name* Long pepper

pipi Smooth-shelled seawater bivalves found in New Zealand, *Mesodesma nova-zelandiae*, and Australia, *Plebidonax deltoides*

pipián *Mexico* A sauce served with chicken made from ground sesame and pumpkin seeds, spices and ground peanuts or almonds and coloured red

pipikaula *United States* A Hawaiian dish of dried beef cooked with soya sauce

piping The decorative lines of icing piped onto a cake

piping bag A triangular-shaped bag made of a flexible impervious material with a hole at the pointed end into which a metal or plastic cone with a plain circular or star shaped hole may be fitted. Used for piping any soft but self supporting mixture such as whipped cream, icing, mashed potatoes, meringue mix, etc. into various patterns prior to cooking or for decoration. Also called **forcing bag, icing bag**

Pipo crem' *France* A log-shaped blue-veined cows' milk cheese from Grièges with a similar flavour to Bleu de Bresse. Also called **Grièges**

pippali *South Asia* Long pepper

pippuri *Finland* Pepper

piquant *France* Highly seasoned, sharp

piquante, sauce *France* Piquant sauce

piquant sauce Chopped shallots and vinegar, reduced by half, **demi-glace** added, simmered and seasoned. Finished with chopped gherkins, capers, chervil, tarragon and parsley. Served with made up dishes and grilled meats. Also called **piquante, sauce**

piquant Welsh sauce *Wales* 6 lemons cut in eighths mixed with 1 litre of malt vinegar, 450 g of salt, 50 g each of grated horseradish and English mustard, 6 cloves of garlic and 1 tbsp each of ground mace, cloves, nutmeg and cayenne pepper, all brought to the boil in an enamel or glass pan, left to steep for 6 weeks in a jar, stirring daily, then strained and bottled

piquer *France* To pierce a joint of meat at various points on its surface with the point of an office knife so as to be able to insert slivers or cloves of garlic or sprigs of herbs

piquín *Mexico* A very small, hot and dark green chilli pepper

pirinç *Turkey* Rice

piri piri *Africa, Portugal* **1.** A hot chilli pepper **2.** Meat or fish dishes served with a sauce made from piri piri chillies, originally from Portuguese Africa. Also called **peri-peri, pilli-pilli**

piri-piri sauce A simple sauce made from hot chillies in various ways, e.g. by simmering red sweet peppers and red chilli peppers in lemon juice for 5 minutes, passing through a sieve, salting and simmering further or by infusing small red chillies in warm oil

pirog c limonem *Russia* Lemon tart

pirogen Semicircular Jewish turnovers similar to piroshki, made with a kneaded dough and a variety of fillings, some specific to particular festivals. Also called **knishes**

pirogi *Hungary, Russia* Potato dough balls stuffed with potato and onion, served fried with sour cream

pirozhki *Russia* Small semicircular pasties made from 10 cm rounds of choux, sour or puff pastry with a variety of fillings, baked at 200°C or deep-fried. Often served as an accompaniment to soup or as a snack.

pirurutung *Philippines* A dark purple-coloured rice grown around Luzon

pisang *Indonesia, Malaysia* Banana

pisang goreng *Netherlands* Indonesian-style fried or baked bananas

pisang-pisang *Malaysia* Bangus, the fish

pisang starch Banana flour

piselli *Italy* Peas

piselli all'antica *Italy* Peas cooked with lettuce and finished with cream

piselli alla romana *Italy* Peas cooked in butter with chopped onions and ham

piselli secchi *Italy* Split peas

Pishingertorte *Austria* A cake made from circular wafers sandwiched with chocolate hazelnut cream and covered with chocolate

pisi hui lal mirich *South Asia* Chilli powder

pismo clam A very large hard-shell clam, *Tivela stultorum*, up to 500 g in weight from the coasts of southern California, USA. It makes excellent chowder.

pissaladière *France* A savoury open tart filled with cooked tomatoes and onions, black olives and anchovy fillets from Provence. Eaten hot or cold.

pissaldeira *Italy* A flat bread covered with onions, black olives, tomatoes, cheese and anchovies similar to pissaladière

pissenlit *France* Dandelion

pista *South Asia* Pistachio nut

pistacchio *Italy* Pistachio nut

pistache *France* Pistachio nut

pistachio nut The fruit of a small tree, *Pistacia vera*, from the Middle East and Central Asia, with bright green kernels in a beige shell which splits but does not detach itself when ripe. Often soaked in brine and dried. Used as a snack, flavouring, garnish or in nougat, halva, ice cream and mortadella. Also called **green almond**

pistacho *Spain* Pistachio nut

Pistacia lentiscus *Botanical name* Lentisk

Pistacia vera *Botanical name* Pistachio nut tree

Pistazie *Germany* Pistachio nut

pisto *Spain* Chopped tomatoes, courgettes, onions and sweet peppers, fried and stewed together. Also called **samfaina**, **frito de verduras**

pistocco *Italy* Carta di musica

pistol Barrel bread

pistoles *France* Peeled, stoned and flattened prunes

pistolet *France* A third-sized baguette used for sandwiches. Also called **pain pistolet**

piston Barrel bread

pistou *France* 1. A dip or accompaniment similar to pesto made from basil, garlic and Gruyère cheese processed to a soft paste with olive oil 2. A rich soup containing green beans, potatoes, tomatoes, garlic and vermicelli

Pisum sativum *Botanical name* Pea

Pisum sativum var. microcarpum *Botanical name* The mangetout pea

pit *United States* The stone of a fruit

pit, to To stone

pita bread See **pitta bread**

pitahaya The fruit of a cactus from Central and South America with a scaly reddish purple skin and sweet pink but bland flesh containing embedded tiny black edible seeds

Pitcaithly bannock *Scotland* Scottish shortbread containing chopped mixed peel and caraway seeds and topped with flaked almonds before baking

pitepalt *Sweden* Potato dumplings stuffed with pork

pith The soft white tissue found beneath the zest of citrus fruits and in the centre of some stalks. Citrus pith is usually bitter and is removed in all dishes except marmalade where its pectin content is required.

Pithecolobium lobatum *Botanical name* Ngapi nut

Pithiviers *France* A puff or flaky pastry tart or cake filled with almond paste or Pithiviers cream (NOTE: From the town of the same name)

Pithiviers au foin *France* A soft cheese shaped like a disc and covered with dried grass

Pithiviers cream A French cake filling made from butter, sugar, eggs, ground almonds and flavourings

pito-ja-joulupuuro *Finland* A pudding made from pearl barley cooked in milk and served with rosehip or raisin purée

pi-tsi *China* Water chestnut

pitta *Italy* A flat bread or pizza from Calabria with various toppings

pitta bread *Middle East* Yeast-raised dough formed into thin flat ovals and baked in the oven. Allowed to cool in a humid atmosphere or wrapped in a damp cloth to make the surface leathery. Often opened along one side to make a pocket which can be filled with cooked meat, salad, etc. Known as khubz in Arabic. Also called **pita bread**

pitta maniata *Italy* A sandwich of pitta filled with eggs, cheese, sausages and peppers

pitta 'nchiusa *Italy* A sandwich of pitta filled with nuts and raisins moistened with grape juice

pitulle *Italy* A yeasted plain-flour dough with a little olive oil and coarse sea salt, proved until doubled, mixed with a selection of chopped onions, sun-dried tomatoes, olive, capers, anchovies, mushrooms, etc. proved again, then fried in small teaspoonfuls until golden and puffed up

piviere *Italy* Plover

pizza *Italy* A popular and cheap meal, which was once used for leftover dough from bread baking. The yeast-raised dough is rolled out into a thin circle, covered with sieved tomatoes, oregano and pieces of Mozzarella cheese together with various toppings such as ham, salami, hard-boiled eggs, tuna, anchovies, olives, etc. all in small pieces. This is cooked quickly in the oven on a flat sheet or in a shallow dish until the cheese melts and bubbles.

pizza cheese *United States* A soft spun-curd cheese similar to Mozzarella made from cows' milk using either a starter of *Lactobacillus bulgaricus* and *Streptococcus thermophilus* or citric acid to curdle the milk. Used particularly for pizzas and contains somewhat less water than real Mozzarella, roughly 47% water, 24% fat and 25% protein.

pizza di ricotta *Italy* Cheesecake

pizza dough A typical yeasted dough made of strong flour and tepid water with 30 to 60 ml of olive oil, 10 to 30 ml of active dried yeast and 10 ml of salt per kg of flour. Proved, knocked back and proved again. Exact proportions of flour and water depend on the flour. This dough will keep for 7 days in the refrigerator if oiled and covered with film.

pizzaiola *Italy* A sauce made from skinned and deseeded tomatoes, garlic, parsley, oregano and seasoning. The word is also used for dishes served with this sauce.

pizza oven The traditional pizza oven was brick with a stone floor and a wood fire to one side radiating heat from the brick roof onto the pizza. Modern ovens mimic these characteristics by having a large hot mass of metal.

pizzelle *Italy* **1.** Deep-fried pizza dough served with tomato sauce and a variety of fillings **2.** A thin circular biscuit baked on a patterned griddle and bent when hot to form a cone or similar for filling with various creams

pizzetta *Australia* Cooked pasta baked into a pizza base

pizzette *Italy* A dough made from flour, eggs, Gorgonzola or similar cheese and butter (4:2:2:1) plus seasoning, rested, rolled out, cut in shapes, glazed with egg white and baked at 200°C. Eaten as a snack.

pizzoccheri *Italy* Short stubbly noodles made from buckwheat flour

pkhala *Southwest Asia* A Georgian dish made from a purée of cooked and wrung out spinach with sweated chopped onion and garlic and chopped parsley and coriander leaves mixed with soaked saffron, vinegar and lemon juice, finely chopped walnuts and sufficient chicken stock to make a stiff paste. Served after standing 3 hours as a hors d'oeuvre scattered with chopped walnuts and/or toasted pine nuts.

pla *Thailand* Fish

placali *Central Africa* Treated cassava tubers. See also **bâton de manioc**

pla chalard *Thailand* Dried fish used for flavouring

pla chalarm *Thailand* Shark

plăcinte moldovenesti *Romania* Puff pastry turnovers filled with a mixture of sieved cottage cheese, egg yolks, butter, sugar and salt, egg-washed and baked at 210°C

pla duk *Thailand* Catfish

pla haeng *Thailand* Dried fish

pla hai ling *Thailand* Bangus, the fish

plaice A flat seawater fish, *Pleuronectes platessa*, with orange or red spots on a brown upper skin weighing up to 1.5 kg. Found throughout the Atlantic and North Sea. Cooked as any white fish.

plain bacon Green bacon

plain cakes Cakes made by the rubbing in method with a low ratio of fat to flour (1 or less to 2)

plain chocolate Chocolate confectionery with a low percentage of sugar (less than 30%) and no milk solids

plain court bouillon A cooking liquor for deep poached or boiled fish consisting of water, milk, salt and lemon juice, used for large cuts of turbot and brill

plain flour Wheat flour made from any type of soft wheat with between 9 and 10% protein with no added raising agents. Used mainly for cakes and pastries where less rise and a finer texture than bread is required. Not used for puff pastry. Also called **household flour**

plain-leaved escarole Batavian endive

plain omelette An omelette made with no filling or addition to the eggs except seasoning and possibly water

pla in-see *Thailand* Mackerel

plain tripe Blanket tripe

pla jalamed *Thailand* Pomfret, the fish

pla jara met khao *Thailand* Pomfret, the fish

pla jien *Thailand* Steamed filleted fish in a light soya sauce

pla kapong *Thailand* Sea bass

pla karang *Philippines, Thailand* Garoupa, the fish

pla karang daeng jutfa *Thailand* Garoupa, the fish

pla lai *Thailand* Eel

pla mangkor *Thailand* Eel

pla muk *Thailand* Squid

planche de charcuterie *France* A platter of cold meats

plank A well-seasoned hardwood board usually with a groove or gutter to catch juices cut into the surface around the outer edge. The plank is warmed, oiled and used to serve and sometimes to grill and serve meat or fish dishes.

plank, to *United States* To bake or grill meat or fish on a plank

plantain *England, France* A type of banana, genus *Musa*, sometimes named *M. paradisica*, with firm and starchy flesh cooked either in the green (if dessert types) or ripe (if non-sweet types) state; used as a staple food in Africa, the Caribbean and South America. Also called **adam's fig**, **green banana**

plantain flour Banana flour

plantation shortcake *United States* Hot corn bread topped with chopped chicken or ham in a cream sauce

planxa, a la *Catalonia* Cooked on a flat metal sheet

pla o *Thailand* Tuna

pla pak khom *Thailand* Bummaloe, the fish

pla ra *Thailand* A freshwater mud fish, gourami, from the north of Thailand which is fermented with roasted rice for several months and has a very pungent smell and flavour. It is sometimes deep-fried and dressed with finely sliced shallots, chillies and lemon grass but is more usually made into a seasoning by boiling in water with shallots, lemon grass and kaffir limes and then straining. It is sold in the West as pickled gourami.

plasas *West Africa* A sauce from Gambia and Sierra Leone made from any greens sweated in oil with chilli peppers and onions then simmered in stock until cooked. This is then thickened with **egusi** or peanut butter let down with a little water and all simmered until smooth. Meat, dried shrimps and pieces of salted or smoked fish, previously cooked are often added at the end. Served with **fufu** or rice.

plastic icing *Australia* A thick icing resembling fondant icing made from a mixture of granulated and icing sugar with water, gelatine, lemon juice and butter which after resting can be rolled out or moulded. Also called **Australian fondant icing**

plat *Balkans* Turbot

plàtan *Catalonia* Banana

plátano *Spain* Banana

plátano manzano *Mexico* A stubby banana with a hint of strawberry and apple in its flavour

plat à sauter *France* A large diameter shallow copper pan with straight vertical sides, tinned on the inside and used professionally for sautéing and shallow frying. The sides are almost as hot as the base and are used to cook the sides of steaks chops, etc.

plat-de-côte *France* A cut of beef from the lower centre of the animal including the plate and parts of the rib bones which would be included with the ribs in English butchery. It is either boned or left on the bone and used for braising, pot roasts or boiled beef.

plat-de-côtes *France* The front of the pork belly containing the ribs. Used for braising, pot-roasting or casseroles.

plat du jour *France* The special dish for the day in a restaurant. Normally changed daily and cheaper or better value than other menu dishes.

plate 1. A flat oval or round piece of crockery on which food is served **2.** *United Kingdom* The rear part of the lower half of the ribs of beef behind the brisket, usually used for stewing and manufacturing

plate, to To place food and garnishes on a plate preparatory to serving it to a customer

Plateau *Belgium* A soft cows' milk cheese similar to Saint-Paulin and Herve. It has a smooth pungent taste and a yellow crusty rind.

plateau de fromages *France* Cheeseboard

plateau de fruits de mer *France* A speciality of Brittany and northern France consisting of a mixture of shellfish and crustaceans served cold on a plate

plate of beef *Scotland* The Scottish name of a tough lean cut from the shoulder

plate ring A metal ring used for stacking plates with food on them so as to prevent the food on one plate touching the base of the one above. Commonly used in restaurants and at banquets.

plate waste Food left on the plate in a restaurant, indicating either low quality or excessively large portion sizes. Usually carefully monitored.

platija *Spain* Flatfish: plaice, flounder or dab

pla too *Thailand* Fried fish such as salted mackerel, trout and herring. Served with **nam prik**.

plat siew *Thailand* Dried fish, fried with dried noodles and a black bean sauce

plättar *Sweden* Small pancakes made with a butter and egg-enriched sweet batter, flavoured with brandy and served with a jam or fresh fruit and cream stuffing

Plättchen *Germany* Pretzels

plattekaas *Belgium* A curd cheese usually made from cows' milk

platter A large plate generally used for serving food to several people or for serving several foods on the same plate, e.g. seafood platter

Plattfisch *Germany* Plaice

plava A fatless sponge cake made with matzo meal and flavoured with almonds for use at the Jewish Passover meal

plegonero *Spain* Whiting, the fish

pletzlach Squares of pastry with an apricot or plum filling served at the Jewish Passover feast

pleurote *France* Oyster mushroom

pleurotis mushroom *United States* Oyster mushroom

Pleurotus ostreatus *Botanical name* Oyster mushroom

plie *France* Plaice

Plinz *Germany* Fritter or pancake

ploat, to To pluck

Plockwurst *Germany* An air-dried, smoked slicing sausage with a deep red colour, made from a variety of meats e.g. beef, pork, ham, pickled pork, etc.

Ploderkäse *Switzerland* A soft scalded-curd surface-ripened cows' milk cheese coagulated with a lactic starter, formed into blocks (up to 10 kg), dry-salted and ripened. The paste is smooth with a slightly bitter taste.

plombières *France* Tutti frutti ice cream

plomme *Norway* Plum

plommegrøt med fløtemelk *Norway* A milk and cream pudding thickened with groats and mixed with plums

plommon *Sweden* Plum

plommonspäckard fläskkarré *Sweden* Loin of pork with a prune stuffing

plot toffee *United Kingdom* A treacle toffee served on Guy Fawkes night (5th of November)

ploughman's lunch *United Kingdom* A typical public house lunch of cheese, crusty bread, butter and pickles

plov *Russia* Rice pilaf

plover A small wild wading bird common in Norfolk but now rarely hunted for the table. There are several varieties of which the lapwing, *Vanellus vanellus,* the golden plover, *Pluvialis apricaria* and the grey plover, *Pluvialis squatarola,* are the most well known. The golden plover is the most sought after. Usually roasted with or without the innards at 220°C and served on buttered toast with lemon and watercress garnish. Also called **bustard plover, green plover**

plover's eggs The eggs of plovers considered to be a delicacy, generally cream or buff-coloured with dark brown spots or blotches, generally replaced by eggs of various species of gull (black- headed, lesser black-backed, great black-backed, etc.), which are similar in colour. In the UK they can only be gathered up to April the 14th and for home consumption only. Their sale is prohibited.

plov iz rybi *Russia* A risotto made from rice, fish, tomatoes, onions and butter

pluches *France* A spray of chervil or other fresh herb used as a garnish

pluck The liver, lungs and heart of an animal

pluck, to To remove the feathers from poultry and birds. Also called **ploat, to**

plum The fruit of deciduous trees, *Prunus domestica* and other species of *Prunus,* with yellow through purple skin usually with a fine bloom of wild yeast, a central stone and a generally sweet flesh. All need cool winters to fruit. There are many varieties, e.g. greengage, damson, cherry plum, mirabelle, quetsch plum, bullace, Japanese or salicine and Victoria. Dried plums are known as prunes.

plumb An old English name for a raisin

plumcot A rediscovered eighteenth-century fruit. The taste is intermediate between plum and apricot. Also called **violet apricot, pope's apricot**

plum duff Suet pudding containing currants, raisins, spices and brown sugar. Boiled in a cloth and served hot with English custard or cream.

plum pudding 1. See **Christmas pudding 2.** A porridge-like mixture of raisins (otherwise called plumbs), dried fruits, spices, oranges, lemons, sugar, minced veal or beef and sherry, thickened with bread. Once popular in the UK but since evolved into Christmas pudding.

plum sauce A Chinese condiment made from dark red plums, sugar and water. Also called **Chinese plum sauce**

plum tomato A bright red elongated Italian tomato with a good flavour. The principal variety used for canning.

pluvier *France* Plover

Plymouth onions *England* Large Spanish onions wrapped in foil and baked in the oven for about 40 minutes until soft, then cut in half and eaten with butter and cheese

plyskavice *Balkans* Grilled hamburgers from Serbia

poach, to To cook food, usually eggs or fish, in a cooking liquor at the simmer, i.e. at around 96/7°C in an open or closed pan on the stove or in the oven. Coddling is a kind of poaching and is as equally successful with fish and small pieces of tender meat as with eggs.

poached eggs Shelled eggs, yolk intact, placed in acidulated water just below simmering point for about 3 minutes until set then carefully removed. May be poached in other cooking liquors.

poached white fish Fillets of white fish or whole, skinned and trimmed sole, shallow-poached and served with a sauce usually derived from the cooking liquor. See also **Bercy, fish, bonne femme, fish, bréval, fish, Dugléré, fish, florentine, fish, Marguery, fish, Mornay, fish, Véronique, fish, vin blanc, fish, Walewska, fish**

poacher's pie *England* A pie made from alternate layers of boned rabbit, bacon, potatoes and leeks in a pie dish, seasoned, flavoured with herbs, half filled with stock and topped with shortcrust pastry. Baked covered at 190°C for 30 minutes and finished uncovered at 180°C until brown and cooked.

po boy *United States* Poor boy

pocha bruide *Scotland* Deer tripe cleaned immediately after slaughter, soaked in water for 24 hours and boiled for 8 hours then cooked in the normal way in thickened milk with onions. See also **tripe and onions**

pochade *France* A freshwater fish stew from Savoie containing raisins and carrots

pochard A wild duck, *Aythya fernia*, shot for the table in the UK

poche *France* Caecum

poché(e) *France* Poached

pocher *France* To poach

pocheret *Denmark* Poached

pocheteau *France* Common skate

po chio *China* Aniseed

pochouse *France* A mixture of various freshwater fishes, especially eel, stewed in white wine from Burgundy

pochti nichevo, pochty nichevo *Russia* Soup made from equal quantities of mixed bones and water (1.5 kg of each) simmered with a cleaned but unpeeled onion until the liquid has reduced by half. The liquid is strained. Chopped onion and clean potato peelings, sautéed in bacon fat, are simmered with the strained stock, then puréed. The seasoning and consistency are adjusted, and the whole finished with cream and chopped chives. (NOTE: Literally 'almost nothing (soup)'.)

poco hecho *Spain* Rare, underdone. Used of meat, steak, etc.

poco pasado *Spain* Rare. Used of meat, steak, etc.

pod The elongated seed capsule of leguminous plants which contains a row of seeds and splits lengthways into two halves to release the seeds when ripe. Usually

picked before maturing, unless ripe seeds are to be harvested as pulses. Sometimes eaten whole; otherwise, immature seeds are removed.

pod, to To remove seeds from a pod

poddy mullet *Australia* Sea mullet

podina *South Asia* Mint

podlivka *Russia* Sauce, usually a thickened gravy made with the meat juices from frying or roasting. It is often enriched with chopped ingredients such as fried onions or mushrooms, bacon bits, chopped hard-boiled eggs, capers etc. and whatever other flavourings are available such as sour cream, tomato purée, chilli sauce or mustard.

podsolnechnoe maslo *Russia* Sunflower oil

poêle *France* 1. Frying pan 2. Stove

poêlé(e) 1. *England* Braised or pot-roasted 2. *France* Fried

poêlon *France* A casserole, a small tight lidded heavy pan with a long handle used for slow cooking

poem card cut Tanzako giri

poffertjes *Netherlands* Puffed up fritters made with a chemically raised batter

poffertjies *South Africa* Apple fritters made from sieved apple purée, milk, flour, sugar, egg and raisins (12:3:2:2:1:1), beaten together into a stiff batter then deep-fried in small quantities, drained and served with cinnamon and sugar

po gwa *China* Hairy gourd

poha The wild dwarf cape gooseberry found in Hawaii

poh pia *China* Spring roll

poi A staple food of the Pacific islands made from the boiled and mashed tubers of taro or sweet potato with possibly banana and breadfruit

point, à See **à point**

pointe *France* 1. Tip, as in pointes d'asperge, asparagus tips 2. A small amount as in pointe d'ail; a small amount of any ingredient that can be held on the tip of a knife

pointe de filet *France* Pork fillet (tenderloin)

point steak *United Kingdom* The thin end of a slice of beef rump steak

poire *France* Pear

poireau *France* Leek

poireaux, purée de *France* Leek soup

poire condé *France* Pear Condé

poirée *France* Chinese leaves

poires Alma *France* Pears poached in port

poires Belle Hélène *France* Pear halves, poached in sugar syrup and served with vanilla ice cream and chocolate sauce

pois *France* Peas

pois à la française *France* Peas braised with lettuce, a little sugar, chopped spring onions and parsley and a small amount of water

pois cassés *France* Split peas

pois chiches *France* Chickpeas

pois rouges maconne *Caribbean* A dish of rice and beans (not peas) from Martinique, made by gently frying chopped onion, garlic, chillies and bacon in peanut oil, adding red beans and water, simmering until the beans are almost cooked then adding the rice to finish cooking, finally thickening with cassava

poisson *France* Fish

poisson brun *Belgium* Browned fish with a wine and herb sauce

poisson-chat *France* Channel catfish

poisson fumé *France* Smoked fish

poisson meunière aux amandes *France* Amandes, fish aux

poissonnière *France* Fish kettle

poisson volant *France* Flying fish

poisson yassa *West Africa* As **poulet yassa**, but with any firm-fleshed fish in place of the chicken

poitrine *France* **1.** Breast (of lamb or veal), stewed or boned out and stuffed rolled and roasted **2.** The abdominal part of pork belly **3.** A cut of lean beef from the shoulder immediately in front of the jumeau, used for braising, pot-roasting and boiled beef

poitrine de porc *France* Pork belly

poitrine fumée *France* Smoked streaky bacon

poivrade *France* Vinaigrette sauce with pepper

poivrade, à la *France* Containing freshly ground pepper or dried green peppercorns

poivrade, sauce *England, France* A **mirepoix** of onion, carrot, celery, bay leaves and thyme, sweated in butter, fat removed, reduced with wine, vinegar and mignonette pepper, simmered with **demi-glace** for 30 minutes, strained and seasoned. Served with venison. Also called **pepper sauce**

poivre *France* Pepper

poivre, au *France* With pepper, usually coarsely crushed peppercorns

poivre d'âne *France* **1.** A goats' milk cheese from the Alpes Maritime with a distinctive flavour of herbs, probably savory **2.** The Provençal name for savory, the herb (*colloquial*)

poivre de la Jamaïque *France* Allspice

poivron *France* Sweet pepper, capsicum

poke *United States* A Hawaiian dish of fish marinated in a highly spiced sauce

Pokel *Germany* Pickle

pokeweed A shrub, *Phytolacca americana*, from North America with poisonous roots but whose young leaves (up to 15 cm) may be boiled and treated like asparagus. The red berry may be used as a food colouring. The whole plant is classified as poisonous in the UK.

pok fet *Catalonia* Rare. Used of meat.

pok kak bua *Thailand* Star anise

pole dab *United States* Witch sole

Polędwica sopocka *Poland* As **Polędwica tososiowa**, but not packed in casings

Polędwica tososiowa *Poland* A hard smoked sausage from Gdansk made of pork and pork back fat, packed in casings and knotted

Polei *Germany* Pennyroyal

polenta *England, Italy* Fine yellow cornmeal, dry-fried until it loses its colour It is used as a thick porridge, and to make some types of bread and gnocchi. This porridge, also known as polenta, is made by mixing the cornmeal with salted water (150 g per litre). This is brought to the boil then simmered with stirring until thick and the paste leaves the side of the pan. It is a major source of carbohydrate in Italy and is often left to cool then sliced and fried as an accompaniment to meat dishes.

polenta al forno *Italy* Polenta casseroled with sausages in a meat sauce covered with cheese

polenta alla bergamasca *Italy* Polenta baked with tomatoes, sausage and cheese

polenta d'ivrea *Italy* A cake resembling polenta made with buckwheat flour flavoured with vanilla

polentagrøt *Norway* Cornmeal pudding

polenta taragna *Italy* Polenta liberally sprinkled with grated Bitto cheese and covered with melted butter

poleo *Spain* Pennyroyal

polewka *Poland* A very simple soup of seasoned water thickened with rye flour and blended with cream

pólipo *Spain* Octopus

poliporo *Italy* An edible fungus which grows on trees

polished rice Rice from which the vitamin B-rich outer coating has been removed during processing. Prized because of its whiteness.

Polish sausage A generic term for a variety of sausages using the usual pork, beef and pork fat with flavourings, saltpetre and sometimes dextrose to facilitate lactic fermentation, normally cased, air-dried and smoked until hard

polla *Spain* Young chicken

pollack A coastal seawater fish, *Pollachius pollachius*, of the cod family with a protruding lower jaw and a dark green upper skin, found throughout the North Atlantic. It does not have as fine a flavour as cod but is otherwise similar and cooked in the same way. Generally sold at 50 cm in length. Also called **green cod**, **pollock**

pollame *Italy* Poultry

pollan See **pullan**

pollanca *Italy* Young chicken

pollastre *Spain* Young chicken

pollastre rostit amb samfaina *Catalonia* Roast chicken with samfaina sauce

pollastro *Italy* Young chicken

pollito *Spain* **1.** Pigeon **2.** Squab

pollo *Italy, Spain* Chicken

pollo a la chilindrón *Spain* Sautéed chicken

pollo a la extremeña *Spain* Chicken with sausages and baked tomato

pollo a la navarra *Spain* Chicken casseroled in wine with carrots, onions and strips of ham

pollo alla cacciatora *Italy* Chicken stewed in stock with mushrooms and seasoning and flavoured with Marsala. Served with fresh pasta.

pollo alla contadina *Italy* Portioned chicken fried in oil for 20 minutes, mixed with potatoes cut in 2 cm slices and fried separately, then, both stewed in chopped deseeded tomatoes with seasoning and a little wine until all tender (NOTE: Literally 'peasant woman's chicken'.)

pollo alla marengo *Italy* Chicken stewed in stock and white wine with tomatoes, mushrooms, parsley, black olives and seasoning. See also **poulet sauté Marengo**

pollo alla padovana *Italy* Chicken browned, then braised in the oven with onions and finished with egg and lemon

pollo all'arentina *Italy* Chicken stewed in wine

pollo alla romano *Italy* Chicken simmered with white wine, tomato, ham, sweet pepper and herbs

pollock 1. See **pollack 2.** Coley

pollo de naranja *Spain* Chicken pieces marinated in sherry and orange juice and shallow-fried in butter

pollo en chanfaina a la catalana *Spain* Chicken sautéed with sweet peppers, aubergine and tomato sauce

pollo fandango *Spain* Chicken cooked in a creamed sauce and served with braised celery

pollo rebozado *South America* A Bolivian speciality of chicken joints coated in an egg, milk and polenta batter, fried, then

simmered in a sauce made from wine, tomatoes, spices and seasoning

pollo ripieno alla trentina *Italy* Chicken stuffed with a mixture of chopped nuts, breadcrumbs, beef marrow and chopped liver, then boiled

pollo salteado *Spain* Chicken sautéed with onion and served with artichoke hearts and tomato sauce

polmone *Italy* Calves' lungs

polo *Iran* Cooked rice

polonaise, à la *France* In the Polish style, i.e. containing soured cream, red cabbage or beetroot, or vegetables topped with a mixture of chopped hard-boiled eggs and parsley with fried breadcrumbs

poloney The name of a sausage common in English-speaking countries, probably a corruption of Bologna or Polonia since it has the characteristics of both Italian and Polish sausages. All are coloured red.

polony See **poloney**

polou *Central Asia* An Iranian-style dish combining rice with another ingredient such as chicken, lamb or veal together with pumpkin, potatoes, beans etc. The meat and vegetables are generally precooked and usually fried in clarified butter and reserved. Partly cooked rice as in **chelou** is put in the bottom of the pan and pressed down, followed by the meat and vegetables. The other half of the rice is put on top, excess frying butter is poured over and the whole cooked slowly, either on the stove or in the oven with a tight-fitting lid. Sometimes vegetables may be mixed with the top layer of rice. The contents may be removed in one piece, in which case high heat is used to form a crust in the initial stage.

polpa *Italy* Lean meat, flesh of fruits

polpessa *Italy* Warm water octopus

polpetiello *Italy* Polpo

polpetta *Italy* Croquette, meatball, rissole

polpettine *Italy* Meatballs

polpettine di spinaci *Italy* Spinach-flavoured and coloured dumplings

polpettone *Italy* **1.** Meat or fish loaf **2.** A baked mixture of vegetables bound with egg

polpettone alla genovese *Italy* A mixture of chopped cooked potatoes and French beans bound with grated cheese and eggs and baked in a loaf tin

polpettone alla toscana *Italy* A minced meat and cheese loaf bound with egg and braised, fried or poached

polpo *Italy* Octopus

pølser *Denmark, Norway* Sausages

Polsterzipfel *Austria* A jam filled turnover

451

polvere di curry *Italy* Curry powder

polydextrose A bulking agent used in reduced and low calorie foods

polygonum Vietnamese mint

polyoxyethylene (20) sorbitan esters See **E432 – 436**

polyphenol oxidase The enzyme in plants which causes browning of fruits and vegetables on exposure to air by oxidation of phenolic compounds to melanin pigments. Its effects are being eliminated by genetic engineering of plant varieties.

polyphosphates Complex phosphates of sodium and potassium used mainly to retain added water without exudation in frozen chickens, ham, bacon and other similar meat products, and also as stabilizers and emulsifiers. See also **E450(c)**

polysaccharide Long chains or branched chains of simple sugars which make up starch, dextrins, cellulose and other carbohydrates of natural origin

Polyscias scutellarium *Botanical name* Daun mangkok

polysorbate ( ) The alternative names for polyoxyethylene (20) sorbitan esters. See also **E432 – 436**

polyunsaturated A description of long chains of carbon atoms that occur in fats, oils and fatty acids in which several of the carbon atoms do not have as many hydrogen atoms attached as they could and are therefore connected to neighbouring carbon atoms by double or triple bonds. Hence polyunsaturated fats.

poma *Catalonia* Apple

pomace The residue after juice or oil has been physically crushed out of fruit. The pomace from oil bearing fruits is often treated by solvent extraction to produce inferior oils.

pombé *South Africa* Beer produced from sprouted millet seed, an important source of vitamins. Also called **Kaffir beer**

pomegranate The beige to red fruit of the pomegranate tree, *Punica granatum*, up to 8 cm in diameter with a hard skin filled with numerous seeds each in a red, juicy, fleshy sac. Sweet varieties are eaten (rather messily) as a dessert. Seeds of the sour pomegranate have a sweet-sour taste and are used as a garnish in the Middle East. The dried, ground seeds, known as anardana, are used as a souring agent and with bread, vegetables and pulses in North India. Also called **Chinese apple**

pomelo 1. See **pummelo 2.** *Spain* Grapefruit

pomfret A tropical seawater fish, *Pampus argenteus*, with a silvery skin and tiny black spots, found around and used in India, China and Southeast Asia. It has white flesh similar to, but not as tasty as, that of turbot or sole and is cooked in the same ways. There is also a darker variety with a brownish-grey skin found in Indonesia and the Phillipines with an inferior flavour. The Chinese smoke pomfret over tea leaves. Also called **Ray's bream, white butter fish**

pomfret cake Pontefract cake

pomme *France* **1.** Apple **2.** Potato (NOTE: Abbreviated from *pomme de terre*.)

pomme de terre *France* Potato, often abbreviated to pomme, especially with potato dishes

Pommel *France* An unsalted double-cream cows' milk cheese similar to Petit-Suisse

pommes à l'anglaise *France* Plain boiled potatoes

pommes allumettes *France* Very thin potato chips

pommes amandine *France* Potatoes made in the same way as croquette potatoes but panéed with flour, egg and nibbed almonds instead of breadcrumbs

pommes Anna *France* Layers of thinly sliced potatoes, melted butter and seasoning, baked in a straight sided metal dish in the oven in a dish until browned, inverted on a plate and served in slices or wedges (NOTE: The dish for pommes Anna should not be washed.)

pommes boulangère *France* Roast potatoes

pommes dauphine *France* A mixture of potato croquette mixture and choux pastry (3:1) formed into small cylinders, panéed and deep-fried

pommes dauphinoises *France* Sliced potatoes layered in a dish with milk, grated cheese, garlic and butter and cooked in the oven. Egg and cream may be added but the egg tends to scramble. Also called **gratin dauphinois**

pommes de terre en robe des champs See **pommes en robe de chambre**

pommes duchesses *France* Duchesse potatoes

pommes en copeaux *France* Grated potatoes or potato shavings

pommes en robe de chambre *France* Potatoes boiled or steamed in their skins

pommes frites *France* Potato chips, thinner and crisper than the UK variety

pommes mousselines *France* Mashed potatoes

pommes pailles *France* Straw potatoes

pommes sauvages *France* Crab apples

pommes savoyarde *France* As **gratin dauphinois**, but substituting stock for cream. Also called **gratin savoyard**

pommes vapeur *France* Boiled or steamed potatoes

pomodori di magro alla sarda *Italy* Tomatoes stuffed with anchovies, tuna and aubergine flesh and baked

pomodorini *Italy* Small tomatoes

pomodori ripieni alla novarese *Italy* Tomatoes stuffed with rice, onions and cheese, panéed and deep-fried

pomodoro *Italy* Tomato

pompano A small, oily, round seawater fish of the genus *Trachinotus*, with a high yellow to green-blue back, a deep belly and deeply forked tail fin from the Mediterranean, Caribbean and southeast USA. It can weigh up to 3 kg but is better at 1 kg and has a sweet-flavoured, rather dry, white flesh. Often cooked **en papillote**. Prepared like perch.

pompano rellena *Mexico* Pompano stuffed with a mixture of chopped onions and tomatoes sweated in oil, chopped hard-boiled eggs, parsley and spices then poached and served with a fish velouté

pompelmo *Italy* Grapefruit or pummelo

pompelmoes *Netherlands* Grapefruit

pompoen *Netherlands* Pumpkin

pomtannia A plant with yam-like fruit. See also **tannia**

ponceau 4R A synthetic red food colouring banned in the USA. Also called **cochineal red**. See also **E124**

poncirus One of the three important genera of Citrus. Also called **trifoliate orange**

pondah *Indonesia* Ubod, palm pith

pone *Caribbean, United States* A general name for a baked carbohydrate mixture in the Caribbean and southern USA. It is usually unleavened and may be made from cornmeal, sweet potatoes, pumpkin etc. and flavoured or merely salted.

ponkan mandarin The most widely grown mandarin in the world, found in Japan, the Phillipines, India, south China and Brazil. The rind is moderately thick and very loose, the juice content whilst sweet and pleasant-tasting is rather low in quantity and the segment walls are somewhat tough. Also called **Chinese honey orange, mohali mandari**

Pontac ketchup *England* Ripe elderberries covered with warm boiling vinegar and kept hot in the oven for 3 hours. Juice strained off without pressure and boiled with mace, peppercorns, shallots and salted anchovies (250 g per litre of juice) until the anchovies have disintegrated, strained and bottled. Also called **Pontac sauce**

Pontac sauce *England* A sharp condiment sauce based on elderberries (NOTE: Invented by a Monsieur Pontac of Lombard St. London.)

Pontefract cake A small flat round (up to 2 cm in diameter) liquorice-based sweet usually embossed as though by a seal. Also called **pomfret cake**

Pont l'Evêque *France* A soft orange-coloured cows' milk cheese from Normandy, made in a square about 10 cm on the side and 4 cm deep with a thick brown rind mottled with thin smears of mould. The paste contains a few round holes and has a strong smell and a less strong taste. It has AOC status. Contains 47% water, 27% fat and 20% protein.

Pont Moutier *France* A soft square-shaped cows' milk cheese weighing to 2.5 kg. The brown rind had a white bloom and the smooth fragrant and aromatic tasting paste has a few cracks and holes.

ponzu, ponzu-shoyu *Japan* A dipping sauce, especially for **oden** or **yosenabe** and condiment use, made from **yuzu** juice, soya sauce, **mirin**, sake and dried bonito flakes (20:20:3:3:1 by volume) with a piece of **kombu**, all macerated for 24 hours then strained

poong dang *Thailand* 1. Alum 2. A paste of lime (Calcium hydroxide)

poor boy *United States* A Cajun sandwich from Louisiana consisting of a French bread stick split lengthwise and filled with a savoury mixture of foods, salads, etc. similar to **casse-croûte**. It originated in New Orleans in the 19th century when oyster sandwiches were given as charity to the poor. See also **hoagie**. Also called **po boy**

poori *South Asia* A deep-fried chapati. See also **puri**

poor knights of Windsor *England* Fingers of bread dipped in egg and milk mixture sometimes flavoured with liqueur or spirits, deep-fried and eaten hot sprinkled with cinnamon and caster sugar. See also **pain perdu**

poorman orange New Zealand grapefruit

poor man's beefsteak Beefsteak fungus

poor man's caviar A dip made from the flesh of roasted aubergines processed with garlic and olive oil to a thick purée, seasoned, let down with a little lemon juice and garnished with chopped parsley

poor man's goose *Wales, England* Faggot

pop *Catalonia* Octopus

popara *Bulgaria* A porridge made from bread, butter, cheese and milk, eaten at breakfast

popcorn A variety of maize kernels, *indurata*, which when heated in a closed container are blown up into a soft foamed starch as the bound water turns to steam. Eaten as a snack with salt, sugar or butter.

pope A freshwater fish similar to the perch. Also called **ruffe**

pope's apricot Plumcot

pope's eye 1. *England* The small circle of fat in the centre of a leg of lamb or pork **2.** *Scotland* Prime rump steak

pope's nose The equivalent of the **parson's nose** on a duck or goose

popets *Catalonia* Baby octopi used for tapas

popone *Italy* Melon

popover 1. *England* A small individual Yorkshire pudding, often flavoured with grated cheese, chopped onions, bacon and herbs or in a sweet version with chopped fruit and sugar **2.** *United States* A quickly made type of muffin using a Yorkshire pudding batter baked in the oven

poppa *Italy* Udder

poppadom *South Asia* A thin round pancake made from a lentil flour batter which is occasionally spiced, deep-fried until crisp and served as an appetizer or accompaniment to Indian food. Sometimes the lentil flour is mixed with or substituted by rice or potato flour. Also called **papadum**, **papadam**, **pappadam**, **pappadum**, **puppodom**, **papads**

popper *United States* A type of pan used to prepare popcorn

poppy seed The ripe seeds of an annual poppy, *Papaver somniferum* and *P. rhoeas*, which vary in colour from cream through to almost black according to origin. They have a slightly nutty aroma and flavour and are often sprinkled on bread and cakes or crushed with honey or sugar to make pastry fillings. Used with other spices in Indian cooking.

poppy seed oil A light odourless oil with a faint almond taste from the first cold pressing of poppy seeds. Used for salads.

poppy seed paste Roasted and ground poppy seeds formed into a paste much used in Turkish cooking

pop tart *United States* A thin pastry turnover with various fillings which can be heated in a pop-up toaster or in the oven

porbeagle shark A member, *Lamna nasus*, of the shark family which grows to 4 m and is common in the Atlantic. It makes good eating and is often larded and grilled as steaks.

porc *France* Pig or pork

porcella *Catalonia* Suckling pig

porché *France* A Breton dish of stewed pigs' ears and trotters

porchetta *Italy* Sucking pig

porcini *Italy* Ceps, usually sliced and dried

porco *Portugal* Pork

porc salé *France* Salt pork

porgy Various deep-bodied seawater fishes of the genus *Calamus*, especially *Pagrus pagrus* with long spiny dorsal fins chiefly found in the Mediterranean and the Atlantic Ocean and similar to bream. They have delicate, moist, sweet flesh but many bones.

pork The flesh of the pig

pork belly Meat from the underside of the abdominal and chest cavity of the pig equivalent to breast of lamb and consisting of alternating layers of fat and lean muscle. Used in sausages, pâtés and terrines or may be cooked as a dish in its own right. Also called **belly pork**

pork chop A transverse slice from a loin of pork

pork crackling Crackling

porker See **pig**

pork fat Fat from the pig is graded according to hardness and has many uses in sausages, terrines, pâtés and other items. Back fat tends to be the hardest and belly fat the softest. Lard is rendered pork fat and is traditionally used in pastry and in the cooking of eastern France. It contains about 49% saturated, 42% monounsaturated and 9% polyunsaturated fat.

pork fillet Tenderloin of pork

pork grades *United States* Grades of pork in the US are 1, 2, 3 and cull, in descending order of quality

pork herbs The principal herbs used with pork are chervil, coriander, fennel, lovage, marjoram, rosemary, sage, savory and thyme

porkkana *Finland* Carrot

pork oaties *England* Cold cooked pork, onion, apple and breadcrumbs (2:1:1:1) are minced together, seasoned and flavoured with dried sage then brought together with beaten egg and formed into small flat cakes which are panéed with oatmeal and fried in pork dripping for 6 minutes a side

pörkölt *Hungary* **1.** Roasted **2.** A thick braised stew with very little added water made with fried meat, poultry or game pieces, tomatoes, green sweet peppers, onions, paprika and seasoning, served with boiled potatoes or rice, green salad and/or pickled cucumbers

pork pie *United Kingdom* A raised pork pie similar to a Melton Mowbray pie but the cooked pork is in cubes and/or minced and whole hard-boiled eggs are sometimes included in the filling of the larger ones

pork sausage The most common sausage of English-speaking countries, made from ground pork, flavourings, extenders and binders filled into casings and linked. Quantities of extenders depend on the price and local laws. In the UK many suspect extenders which legally count as meat such as drinde, MRM, etc. are incorporated in the cheaper versions, together with a high proportion of rusk and cereal fillers. UK sausages are usually flavoured with sage, cayenne pepper and possibly cloves, ginger, nutmeg or mace. USA sausages are normally flavoured with cardamom, coriander and nutmeg.

pork scratchings See **scratchings**

pork vindaloo A dish of lean pork, cubed, piquéed, rubbed with a paste of dry-roasted coriander and cumin seeds plus cardamom seeds, cinnamon, cloves, black peppercorns, turmeric, onion salt, ground ginger and cayenne pepper to taste, all well pounded, then marinated in vinegar or vinegar and water (1:1) with bay leaves for 24 hours. The meat and its marinade are then simmered slowly with mustard seeds fried in ghee until tender, adding water as required.

poron *Finland* Reindeer

poronkäristys *Finland* Very thin slices of braised reindeer

poronkieli *Finland* Reindeer tongue

poronliha *Finland* Reindeer meat

poronpaisti *Finland* Reindeer steak

Porphyra tenera *Botanical name* Nori

Porphyra umbilicalis *Botanical name* Nori

porpore *Italy* Murex, the shellfish

porridge A kind of gruel made by boiling porridge oats with water or milk or mixtures of both and salt until the desired consistency is reached. Eaten as a breakfast dish with sweetening and milk or cream. The name is also used for oatmeal, maize, etc. boiled to the same consistency with water.

porridge oats The breakfast cereal produced by heating either pinhead oatmeal or whole oats with steam as they are passed through rollers to flatten them. The pinhead oatmeal produces the normal porridge oats, whilst the whole oats produce oat flakes which can be used in muesli. Also called **rolled oats**

porro *Italy* Leek

porsaankyljys *Finland* Pork chops

port A fortified wine from Portugal made by stopping the fermentation of full-bodied grape juice with brandy before all the sugar has been fermented to alcohol. Used as a flavouring in sauces and served with melon.

Port-du-Salut *France* The original **Port-Salut** cheese made by the Trappist monks of Port du Salut monastery at Entrammes. The name was sold to commercial cheese makers in the late 1940's.

porter cake *Ireland* A chemically raised basic cake mixture flavoured with mixed spice and grated lemon zest with 3 parts dried vine fruits to 2 parts flour, brought together with a dark stout and all ingredients whisked together for a few minutes and baked at 170°C until cooked (NOTE: From Northern Ireland)

porterhouse steak A steak without bone cut from the large end of the short loin of beef possibly including some of the sirloin and including the fillet. It is usually about 5 cm thick and will easily feed 2 people. Grilled or fried.

portion control The establishment of standards in a catering establishment for the size, weight or number of each item served

portion size The weight or number of each item in one serving

Portland-style mackerel *England* Seasoned and floured mackerel, grilled until golden brown and served with a sweetened coulis of gooseberries flavoured with a little nutmeg

portmanteau lamb chops *England* Lamb loin chops pocketed from the skin side to the bone and filled with a cooled and seasoned cooked mixture of finely chopped chicken liver and mushrooms, sealed with a stick, panéed and baked in melted butter at 200°C until brown on both sides

Portnockle shortbread *Scotland* A less buttery shortbread made from flour, margarine, sugar, rice flour, and butter (12:8:5:5:4) rolled out to 5 mm, cut into rounds and baked at 180°C for 15 to 20 minutes

porto, sauce *France* Port-wine sauce

Port-Salut *France* A semi-hard mild-flavoured cows' milk cheese from the west of France. Made in large rounds (up to 2 kg) with an orange rind. Used as a dessert cheese.

portugaise, à la *France* 1. A method of cooking vegetables similar to **à la grecque**, using a cooking medium consisting of water, olive oil, skinned and deseeded tomatoes, chopped onion, tomato purée, garlic, parsley, bay leaf, thyme and seasoning, served hot or cold 2. In the Portuguese style, i.e. including onions, tomatoes and garlic

portugaise, crème *France* Crème de tomate, cream of tomato soup, garnished with plain boiled rice

portugaise, sauce *France* A type of **espagnole sauce** made with fresh tomatoes instead of tomato purée

Portugiesische Auster *Germany* Portuguese oyster

Portuguese boiled dinner See **cozido à portuguesa**

Portuguese cabbage A smooth-leaved, blue-green cabbage, *Brassica oleracea* var. *tronchuda*, from Portugal used in their national dish **caldo verde**. Kale or Savoy cabbage may be substituted. Also called **Braganza cabbage**, **Galician cabbage**, **couve gallego**, **couve tronchuda**

Portuguese oyster A variety of oyster, *Crassostrea angulata*, once popular as the farmed European oyster now displaced by the Pacific or Japanese variety. It is elongated in shape and up to 17 cm long. It is best used in cooked dishes.

portulaca Summer purslane

Portulaca oleracea *Botanical name* Summer purslane

port-wine jelly *United Kingdom* A gelatine-based sweetened jelly flavoured with port and spices, moulded, cooled, demoulded and served with whipped cream

port-wine sauce As **Madeira sauce**, but substituting port

poshekhonski, poshekhonskij *Russia* A hard scalded-curd cows' milk cheese with a hard dry rind and containing small irregular holes. Contains 41% water, 26% fat and 26% protein.

posset 1. *England* An old English dessert made from a rich egg custard flavoured with sherry, lemon and sometimes almonds **2.** *United Kingdom* A hot, spiced and sweetened milk drink mixed with ale or wine

possum See **opossum**

posta de carne *Portugal* A slice, not a steak, of beef

postej *Denmark* Pâté or paste

postnyi farshirovonnyi baklazhana *Russia* Pulped aubergine flesh mixed with fried onions and tomatoes, chopped hard-boiled eggs, parsley and seasoning, stuffed into aubergine skins, two sandwiched together and baked in a little water and lard

postre *Spain* Dessert course

postres *Catalonia* Dessert

postres de músic *Catalonia* A bowl of mixed nuts and dried fruit

pot 1. A deep ceramic or metal cylindrical container with a lid and two handles used on the stove for slow cooking of stews, etc. **2.** A cylindrical container usually of ceramic or glass in which food is placed for serving or storage as in potted meat or jams, etc. **3.** General term for crockery (**pots**)

pot, to To put food into jars or ramekins and seal with molten butter, fat, greased paper, etc. for presentation at the table or so as to preserve it for a long or short time

potable Safe to drink

potage 1. *France* A light soup or broth **2.** *England* A meat or vegetable stock with added paysanne-cut vegetables, e.g. minestrone

potage à la bressane *France* Pumpkin soup

potage à l'albigeoise *France* A soup from Albi based on beef stock with a selection from preserved goose, calves' feet, ham, sausage and various vegetables

potage bonne femme *France* Leek and potato soup finished with cream and butter. Some recipes add carrot but this spoils the colour.

potage de tomates *France* Tomato soup

potage paysanne *France* Paysanne-cut mixed vegetables sweated in butter without colour until tender, white stock and a bouquet garni added, seasoned, simmered and skimmed for 20 minutes, peas and diamond cut green beans added and the whole simmered until all cooked. Also called **mixed vegetable soup**

pota i tripa *Catalonia* Lambs' trotters cooked with tripe

potaje *Spain* A thick soup or stew

potassium An important mineral essential for health, especially to maintain the fluid balance in the body and the correct working of muscles and nerves. Found in all plant and animal cells.

potassium acetate E261, the potassium salt of acetic acid used as a preservative and firming agent

potassium bisulphite See **E228**

potassium bromate A flour improver and bleaching agent

potassium carbonate See **E501**

potassium chloride See **E508**

potassium gluconate See **E577**

potassium hydrogen carbonate See **E501**

potassium hydrogen L-glutamate See **E622**

potassium hydrogen tartrate See **cream of tartar**

potassium hydroxide See **E525**

potassium lactate See **E326**

potassium nitrate See **saltpetre**

potassium nitrite E249, the potassium salt of nitrous acid used in curing mixtures to preserve meat and maintain the pink colour

potassium sorbate See **E202**

potassium sulphate See **E515**

potassium tartrate See **cream of tartar**

potatis *Sweden* Potatoes

potatiskaka med ost *Sweden* Cheese potato cakes made from a mixture of grated potatoes and onions, half fried in butter, mixed with grated Gruyère cheese, brought together in the frying pan and fried until browned, turned over, refried and topped with slices of Gruyère cheese which should just melt. Also called **Käserösti**

potatismos *Sweden* Mashed potatoes

potatis och purjolöksoppa *Sweden* Potato and leek soup, the same as potage bonne femme

potato One of the commonest and most versatile of vegetables which is the swollen tip of an underground stem of the plant *Solanum tuberosum*, used as a store of starch to support the growth of new stems from the eyes. The two main types are floury and waxy, distinguished by the cohesiveness of the tissues. Waxy potatoes are less dense than floury and will float in a brine of 1 part salt to 11 parts water. Stem end blackening due to the reaction of compounds in the potato with iron during cooking can be minimized by boiling with acidulated water (0.5 tsp of cream of tartar per pint). Common varieties of waxy potatoes in the UK are Arran Comet, Ulster Sceptre, Maris Bard, Pentland Javelin, Alcmaria and Romano and of floury potatoes, Desirée, Estima, Home Guard, Kerrs Pink, King Edward, Maris Peer, Maris Piper, Pentland Dell, and Pentland Squire.

potato and turnip soup See **Freneuse, purée**

potato cakes *England* A northern speciality of floury potatoes, mashed with salt and butter and enough plain flour worked in to make a stiff dough, rolled, cut in shapes, floured, fried on a griddle and served hot with butter. Also called **potato scones**

potato chips See **chips**

potato crisps See **crisps**

potato croquettes Mashed potato with butter, milk, seasoning and possibly eggs, formed into small cylinders and deep-fried

potato dumplings Dumplings made from potatoes, e.g. Kartoffelklösse

potato flour Fécule

potato latkes Jewish potato pancakes made with grated raw potatoes, chopped onions, eggs, flour and seasoning, fried until crisp

potato masher A flat perforated metal or plastic circle or oval with an upright handle used to mash cooked potatoes by forcing them through the perforations with an up and down movement

potato peeler See **peeler**

potato ricer A two part potato masher consisting of a receptacle for the boiled potatoes with a fine perforated plate at the base and a solid plate on a lever which forces the potatoes through the perforations. Rather like an oversize garlic press.

potato salad Cooked waxy potatoes, diced and bound together with mayonnaise and sometimes with a little chopped onion and parsley or other herb

potato sausage *Sweden* Beef, fat pork, cold cooked potatoes and onions, all minced, seasoned, and flavoured with mace, ginger and sage, packed into thin hog casings and cooked by boiling

potato scones *England* Potato cakes

potato skins The skins of baked potatoes after the cooked potato has been removed for e.g. duchesse potatoes. They are often served with a filling or deep-fried until crisp.

potato snow *United States* Riced cooked potato, not mixed or treated in any way

potato soup See **Parmentier, purée**

potato starch Fécule

potato yam Aerial yam

pot au feu *France* A traditional French stew of meat or poultry sealed in fat and braised or simmered in stock with a variety of vegetables. The broth and the meat are often served separately.

pot barley Dehusked whole-grain barley with no other treatment. Requires long soaking and cooking to soften. Used for soups and stews. Also called **Scotch barley**

pot cheese *United States* Cottage cheese

potée *France* A thick soup containing sausage, salt pork or streaky bacon, cabbage, potatoes, onions and possibly beans, lentils and other vegetables, seasoned and flavoured with nutmeg and bay. Sometimes reduced to a stew or hotpot.

potée champenoise *France* A thick soup or stew made with salt belly of pork, ham, haricot beans and vegetables. The liquid is served as soup and the meat and vegetables as a main course dish.

pote gallego *Spain* A thick stew of pork, bacon, beans and cabbage, from Galicia

poten dato *Wales* Floury potatoes boiled until soft then mixed with a little flour, sugar, spice, currants, butter, an egg and enough milk to give a soft consistency. Baked in the oven at around 180°C.

Poterium sanguisorba *Botanical name* Salad burnet

poteter *Norway* Potatoes

poteter stappe *Norway* Mashed potatoes

potetkaker *Norway* Potato cakes made from fried mashed potatoes

potetstappe *Norway* Mashed potatoes

pot herbs Leaves or stems of green plants used as vegetables or culinary herbs

potica *Balkans* A walnut strudel from Slovenia known as **povitica** in Croatia

potiron *France* Pumpkin

potje *Belgium, France* Pâté

potjiekos *South Africa* A mixture of meat, vegetables and spices cooked very slowly in a large cast iron pot. The original dish dates from the 16th century and is probably Dutch.

potlikker *United States* Pot liquor

pot liquor *United States* The liquid in which vegetables have been cooked or blanched. May be used as a basis for vegetarian soups especially if not salted and the same water used for several batches. Also called **potlikker**

potli samosa *South Asia* An Indian pasty filled with shrimps in a cumin and cardamom-flavoured yoghurt sauce

pot luck Whatever food is available for eating when arriving somewhere unannounced, thus to take pot luck

pot marigold See **marigold**

pot marjoram A type of marjoram, *Origanum onites*, which originated in Sicily and has a much stronger flavour than sweet marjoram. Also called **French marjoram**

potpie *United States* A dish of meat and vegetables in a rich gravy baked in a deep dish and covered with pie crust to finish

pot-roast, to To cook meat which has been sealed in hot fat in a covered pan or casserole with a little fat and a small amount of liquid or vegetables over a low heat for a considerable time

pottage Broth containing mashed vegetables and chopped up pieces of meat to make a thick substantial meal in itself. Originally any food served in a pottager, a kind of medieval dish.

pottager The dish in which pottage was served made of metal, earthenware or wood

potted char An old English delicacy made from char, a freshwater fish still available in the Lake District. Popular as a breakfast dish in the 19th century. It is made from unwashed skinned and bone fillets of char, rubbed with a mixture of ground pepper, allspice, mace, cloves and nutmeg (2:1:4:1:2), baked with butter for 5 hours at 120°C, drained, pressed into pots and covered with some of the melted butter.

potted fish As potted meat with fish substituted for meat

potted hough *Scotland* A Scottish brawn made from shin and knuckle of beef, peppercorns and seasoning, simmered until tender, bones removed and the liquid reduced until setting consistency

potted meat 1. Cooked meat either reduced to a paste or chopped into pieces, placed in a container and sealed with molten fat or clarified butter. Commercial varieties contain preservatives. **2.** Shin beef, cooked until tender with calves foot, herbs and seasonings, bones removed, meat coarsely chopped, mixed with reduced cooking liquor and allowed to set in a pot

potted shrimps *England* Cooked and peeled whole shrimps placed in a container and covered with molten clarified butter. Popular in the north of England.

potwarak *Balkans* Duck, browned then braised on a bed of sweated sliced onions, mixed with chopped sauerkraut, peppercorns and a little of the liquid from the sauerkraut. When cooked, sliced and served on the sauerkraut.

pouce pied *France* Barnacle

pouding *France* Pudding

pouding au pain *France* Bread pudding

pouding de cabinet *France* Cabinet pudding

pouding de Noël *France* Christmas pudding (UK)

pouding diplomate *France* Diplomat pudding

pouding Nesselrode *France* Sweetened chestnut purée, combined with egg custard, raisins and currants, flavoured with maraschino liqueur, half frozen, cream folded in then placed in a mould, cooled, demoulded and served with maraschino-flavoured custard

poudre de colombo *Central America, France* A mixture of garlic, deseeded red chillies, turmeric, coriander seeds and mustard pounded together to make a paste. It originated in the French Caribbean and is used to make colombo, a type of curry.

poudre de curry *France* Curry powder

pouile dudon *Caribbean* Chicken stew with garlic, onions, sweet peppers, caramelized sugar, coconut oil, spices and seasoning. Served with rice and pigeon peas.

poularde *France* A large fattened chicken between 1.5 and 2 kg

poularde demi-deuil *France* Poached chicken masked with suprême sauce and surrounded with tartlets containing a salpicon of braised calves' or lambs' sweetbreads bound with suprême sauce each topped with a slice of truffle

poule *France* A boiling fowl suitable for stewing, slow braising or stock

poule-au-pot *France* Stewed chicken and vegetables served with the reduced cooking liquor

poulet *France* Chicken usually between 3 and 8 months old. Suitable for 2 to 4 portions depending on size. Roasted, grilled or sautéed.

poulet à la crapaudine *France* Spatchcock

poulet au vinaigre *France* A Lyonnaise dish of chicken and shallots cooked in wine vinegar and finished with cream

poulet de grain *France* Corn-fed and free-range chicken

poulet moambé *Central Africa* This very popular chicken dish from the Congo river area is similar to **muamba de galinha**. Under its alternative name of 'poulet nyembwe' it is considered to be the national dish of Gabon in West Africa.

poulet noir *France* A superior variety of chicken with black feathers and a delicious slightly gamey flavour

poulet nyembwe *West Africa* Poulet moambé

poulet sauté Marengo *France* A classic dish reputed to have been cooked by Napoleon's chef after the battle of Marengo from what could be found quickly, i.e. a cock, wild mushrooms, crayfish, eggs, garlic and brandy. Also called **chicken Marengo**

poulette *France* Pullet, immature chicken

poulette, à la *France* Served with sauce poulette or garnished with onions and garlic

poulette, sauce *France* A sauce made from white stock combined with lemon juice, butter and chopped parsley thickened with egg yolks

poulet yassa *West Africa* A Senegalese dish of chicken pieces marinated overnight in 250 ml of equal parts of lemon juice and vinegar per chicken together with minced garlic, bay leaf, French mustard, chopped chilli pepper, soya sauce, seasoning and a large quantity of chopped onions. The chicken is then browned in a frying pan or on a grill and slowly cooked in a sauce made from the marinade together with a few vegetables. Served with rice, **fufu** or couscous. Also called **chicken yassa**

Pouligny-Saint-Pierre *France* A soft goats' milk cheese shaped like a pyramid (250 g), which is dry-cured for a month. It is protected by an appellation d'origine.

pouliot *France* Pennyroyal

poulpe *France* Octopus

poultry The name given to all domesticated birds bred for the table or for their eggs, as opposed to game birds which are wild. Includes chickens, hens, turkeys, ducks, ducklings, geese, and guinea fowl.

poultry grades *United States* Grades of poultry in the US are AA, A, B and C, in descending order of quality

poultry herbs The principal herbs used with domesticated poultry are bay, chervil, chives, fennel, lemon balm, marjoram, mint, parsley, sage, savory, tarragon and thyme

poultry needle A large curved bodkin-type needle used for sewing up the abdominal cavity of poultry and game birds

poultry shears Heavy scissors or secateurs with a serrated edge and a good hand grip used for cutting through the bones of poultry

pound The original unit of weight in the British system still in use in the USA and equal to 453.6 g. Divided into 16 ounces. Abbreviated lb. It still lingers on in mainland Europe, e.g. the French livre, but is taken as being 500 g.

pound, to 1. To bruise, break up and crush any hard food item to reduce it to a smooth consistency or a fine powder. Once done in a pestle and mortar but now usually done by mechanical means, e.g. food processor, grinder or powder mill. **2.** To beat meat with a bat or specially-shaped hammer in order to tenderize it or flatten it into e.g. an escalope

pound cake A fruit cake originally made from pound (454 g) quantities of the main ingredients, fat, flour, sugar and eggs, using the creaming method to make two 20 cm. diameter round cakes.

poupeton *France* Veal slices with minced meat

pour batter *United States* Thin batter

pourgouri Powdered wheat. See also **burghul**

pouring batter *United Kingdom* A thin batter made from flour, egg, milk, salt and sometimes sugar, used for pancakes, Yorkshire puddings, etc.

pouring sauce Any flowing sauce used to cover foods usually on the plate, thickened with approximately 50 g of flour or starch per litre

Pourly *France* A white creamy and mild goats' milk cheese from Burgundy with a greyish blue rind

pour-on cheese *United States* A bottled processed coating consistency cheese topping

pousse de bambou *France* Bamboo shoot

pousser *France* To rise, as of dough

poussin *England, France* A single portion, small and tender chicken 4 to 6 weeks old. Usually grilled or roasted. Also called **broiler chicken**

poussin double *France* A double portion 10 to 12 week old chicken, usually grilled or roasted

poutargue *France* A relish made from botargo. Also called **boutargue**

Pouteria caimito *Botanical name* Abiu

povitica *Balkans* The Croatian name for **potica**

powa *South Asia* A unit of weight in the old system equal to 4 chattaks, approximately 225 g or 8 oz. Also called **pau, pav**

powdered cellulose Finely divided cellulose used to add bulk and fibre to slimming foods, convenience foods, etc. See also **E460(ii)**

powdered eggs Spray-dried mixed eggs used for manufacturing purposes. During World War 2 large quantities of eggs dried on heated revolving cylinders were imported into the UK from the USA for domestic consumption.

powdered sugar *United States* Icing sugar

pozole *Mexico* A thick soup made with sweet corn and chicken or pork, flavoured with chilli powder, oregano and pepper and served with chiffonade of lettuce and fried tortilla strips

ppb Parts per billion. Similar to ppm: 1000 ppb equals 1ppm. See also **ppm**

ppm Parts per million: normally used to indicate the levels of contaminants, trace elements or vitamins in food. 10,000 parts per million equals 1%.

praakes A Jewish speciality consisting of blanched cabbage leaves wrapped around a filling of meat and rice. See also **holishkes**

Pragerschinken A small ham on the bone. See also **prazská sunka**

Prague ham See **prazská sunka**

Prague powder See **saltpetre**

prahok *Cambodia* A fish paste prepared using the residue from preserved cleaned fish which have been used to make a fish sauce

praio *Italy* Sea bream

praire *France* Warty venus clam

prairie chicken *United States* A type of wild grouse with mottled brown plumage, *Tympanuchus cupido* or *T. pallidicinctus*, found on the great plains of western North America.

prairie oyster 1. *United States* Ox, pig or lamb testicles usually panéed and fried. Also called **mountain oyster, rocky mountain oyster 2.** A hangover cure consisting of a shelled egg with an intact yolk, flavoured with Worcestershire sauce, lemon juice and salt

praline *England, France* Nut brittle made from toasted (dry-fried, roasted or grilled) or boiled nuts, skins removed, retoasted, mixed with an equal weight of sugar and some water, caramelized to a rich golden brown, allowed to cool and broken down to a coarse powder

praliné(e) *France* Caramelized or covered with praline

praline cream *United Kingdom* Praline folded into softly whipped cream, used to accompany apple tart

pranzo *Italy* 1. Lunch 2. Dinner (*rare*)

Prästost *Sweden* A semi-hard, creamy cows' milk cheese with an open texture and some scattered holes. Sometimes covered in wax. Contains 40% water, 30% fat and 25% protein. (NOTE: Literally 'priest's cheese'.)

prataiolo *Italy* Of the field, e.g. mushrooms

pratie *Ireland* Potato from the Irish práta, potato (*colloquial*)

pratos de carne *Portugal* Meat dishes

prawn The name given to various species of small clawless crustaceans with long curved tails and large heads varying in colour from white translucent to red and brown and from 7 to 20 cm long found all over the world's oceans. Available raw or cooked, shelled or unshelled and fresh, frozen or dried. The tails only are eaten. Varieties include common prawn, spot prawn, northern prawn, deepwater prawn and king prawn.

prawn cocktail A stemmed glass containing a base of chiffonade of lettuce topped with prawns bound in a cocktail or marie-rose sauce. It should be assembled just before serving.

prawn crackers A Chinese snack food made from a dried, prawn-flavoured rice flour batter which when deep-fried, puffs up to a light crunchy hard white foam-like biscuit or crisp

prawn ondines *Australia* Ramekins lined with mashed cooked white fish mixed with creamed butter and whipped cream, centre filled with prawns in mayonnaise, chilled, then covered with a white wine aspic

prawn pudding See **shrimp pudding**

prazheni filii *Bulgaria* French toast (**pain perdu**) flavoured with cinnamon and served with honey

prazská sunka *Czech Republic* A small ham on the bone cured for several months in mild brine, smoked over beech wood, then baked or boiled whole. Considered to be the best ham for serving hot. Also called **jambon cuit de Prague, Pragerschinken, Prague ham**

prebiotics Polysaccharides, principally fructo-oligosaccharide made up of fructose units and galacto-oligosaccharide made from galactose units, which resist digestion in the stomach and small intestine and reach the colon intact. They are then selectively metabolized by the so-called beneficial bacteria, bifido bacteria and lacto bacilli. Now being added to foods as a selling point although they are of no use without the presence of these bacteria and increase flatulence.

precio fijo, a *Spain* Fixed-price

precipitated chalk See **calcium carbonate**

preço fixo, a *Portugal* Fixed-price

pre-cook, to To cook one or more ingredients in advance of their use in another dish, e.g. a duxelle, or of their assembly into a finished dish, e.g. for a salad

precooked rice Rice that had been completely cooked then dehydrated. Also called **quick-cooking rice**, **instant rice**

Preiselbeere *Germany* Cranberry

prepared mustard Various mustard seeds finely or coarsely ground and mixed with a selection of vinegars, spices, herbs and seasoning for use as a condiment or as a flavouring for other dishes

pré-salé *France* Lamb or sheep raised on salt marshes

presame *Italy* Rennet

preservation See **food preservation science**

preservative Any substance added to food capable of inhibiting, retarding or arresting the growth of microorganisms or of any deterioration of food caused by microorganisms or capable of masking the evidence of any such deterioration. Traditional preservatives included salt, sugar, saltpetre, acids or alcohol. Numbers of synthetic substances and derivatives of natural substances are also used. These are identified by E numbers between 200 and 299.

preserve A jam or marmalade preserved by cooking or boiling the fruit with a high concentration of sugar

preserve, to To make food suitable for long term storage by preventing growth of microorganisms or enzyme attack using a variety of techniques such as freezing, canning, bottling, drying, curing, salting, pickling, fermenting or preserving with sugar, chemical preservatives or alcohol

preserved fruit See **candied fruit**

preserved ginger Ginger rhizomes from young plants, skinned, soaked in brine for several days, refreshed in water, boiled in water then in sugar syrup. Used for decoration of cakes, in jam and as a sweetmeat.

preserves *United States* Large pieces of fruit or whole fruit preserved in a heavy sugar syrup which may be slightly jellied with pectin

preserving pan A large deep, wide pan with outwardly sloping sides, a thick base and a large handle, once made of brass or untinned copper, now usually aluminium or stainless steel. Used for making jam and marmalade.

preserving sugar A refined white sugar in large crystals used for jam-making, supposed to minimize scum formation and reduce caramelization when being dissolved

press, to 1. To shape food, usually meat but sometimes fruit, by compacting it in a bowl or basin with a weight so that when turned out it forms a solid mass which can be easily sliced **2.** To squeeze juice out of fruit **3.** To squeeze milk curds so as to remove excess whey thus making a harder cheese

Pressburger Beugel *Austria* A rich pastry with a ground walnut filling

pressé(e) *France* Pressed

préssec *Catalonia* Peach

pressed bean curd Bean curd wrapped in cheese cloth and pressed to reduce the water and increase the solids content. Used as a cheese substitute.

pressed caviar See **payousnaya**

pressed duck Deboned duck with wing and drumstick bones left in, seasoned with salt and spices, pressed flat and dried. Used as a flavouring agent in Chinese cooking. Also called **dried duck**

pressgurka *Sweden* Cucumber salad or relish

Presskopf *Austria, Germany* A sausage similar to the German **Presswurst** but with larger pieces of meat

press-sylta *Sweden* Brawn

pressure-cook, to To cook food in the presence of water or steam in a pressure cooker at a temperature above the normal boiling point of water by allowing the pressure to rise to some predetermined value. Food cooks much quicker than normal under these conditions.

pressure cooker A vessel which can be completely sealed with a tight fitting lid, fitted with a pressure regulator and a pressure relief valve so that when heated with water inside, the internal pressure rises to some predetermined value above atmospheric pressure with a consequent increase in temperature above the normal boiling point. See also **pressure-temperature relationship**

pressure fryer A deep-fryer with a sealed lid which holds steam under pressure over the surface of the hot fat, thereby reducing the cooking time. Similar in action to a pressure cooker.

pressure-temperature relationship The boiling point of water depends on the pressure exerted on its surface and is 100°C at sea level in an open vessel. This rises to 120.5°C at a pressure of 15 psi (pounds per square inch, equivalent to 1 bar) above atmospheric pressure and decreases by approximately 2.7°C for every 1000 m above sea level.

presswurst *Hungary* The Hungarian version of the German Presswurst made from pigs' trotters, neck and head boiled with onions, garlic, seasoning, bay, marjoram and paprika, bones removed and when cool pigs' blood added, filled into casings simmered for 2 hours and pressed under a weight

Presswurst *Germany* A pig's stomach loosely filled with a mixture of diced pickled pork shoulder, pigs' head meat and salted pigs' tongue, salted pork rind, calves' feet and chopped shallots, all chopped until individual pieces are no bigger than a pea, bound with meat glaze, seasoned and flavoured with nutmeg and coriander, simmered for up to 2 hours and pressed in a mould until cool

presunto *Portugal* Smoked ham

presunto de lamego *Portugal* Salted, smoked and air-dried ham made from pigs fed on acorns from the cork oak forests

présure *France* Rennet

prêtre *France* Smelt

pretzel A glossy brittle non-sweet snack biscuit sprinkled with coarse salt resembling a capital B, figure of 8 or lover's knot. Made by poaching the shaped dough then baking it hard in the oven. Also called **bretzel**, **salt stick**

preziosini al pomodoro *Italy* Fried bread dumplings with cheese and tomato sauce

prezzemolo *Italy* Parsley

prezzo fisso *Italy* Fixed price

prickly cockle A variety of cockle, *Acanthocardia echinata*, with raised projections on the shell

prickly custard apple Sour sop

prickly pear A small greenish-orange fruit from a large cactus, *Opuntia ficus-indica*, shaped like a 4 to 7 cm long flattened pear. The sweet juicy flesh contains edible seeds which become hard on cooking. It should be handled with leather gloves when skinning although they can be bought with the spines removed. Also called **barbary pear**, **cactus pear**, **Indian pear**, **Indian fig**, **tuna fig**

prik *Thailand* Chilli pepper

prik bod Chilli paste

prik chee far *Thailand* Cayenne pepper

prik khee noo *Thailand* Bird's eye chilli

prik khee noo kaset *Thailand* Serrano chilli

prik khee noo luang *Thailand* A small very hot chilli

prik khee noo suan *Thailand* Bird's eye chilli

prik leung A mild yellow chilli

prik pon *Thailand* Red chilli powder

prik thai *Thailand* Peppercorn

prik yuah *Thailand* Sweet pepper

prik yuak *Thailand* Medium to large, green to red mild chillies, usually stuffed and fried

prima colazione *Italy* Breakfast

primavera *Italy* A garnish of raw or blanched spring vegetables

prime beef *United States* The best quality beef from young specially fed cattle. It is tender, with an excellent flavour and texture and is well marbled and usually well hung.

prime cut A top-quality cut of meat or fish

primer plat *Catalonia* Main course of a meal

primeurs *France* Early forced fruit and vegetables. Also used as an adjective especially of wines.

primizie *Italy* First early vegetables

Primost *Scandinavia* A soft form of **Gjetöst**

Primula veris Botanical name Cowslip

Prince Albert pudding *England* A Victoria sponge sandwich mixture in which half the flour may be replaced by breadcrumbs, steamed in a basin lined with precooked prunes

Prince Jean *Belgium* A soft surface-ripened cows' milk cheese made in the shape of a cylinder (up to 450 g) with an even-textured aromatic paste

princesse, à la *France* In the princess's style, i.e. garnished with asparagus tips and truffles or noisette potatoes, and sometimes with **béchamel sauce**

pringar *Spain* To baste or sprinkle with liquid

pringue *Spain* Dripping

prinskorv *Sweden* Small sausages

printanière, à la *France* In a spring-like fashion, i.e. garnished with a mixture of spring vegetables coated with melted butter

Printen *Germany* Honey biscuits with nuts

prix fixe *France* A fixed-price menu

probecho *Spain* See **violet 2**

probiotics A rather vague name sometimes used for **functional foods** but more often for the various beneficial bacteria which hopefully grow in the colon and crowd out the more hostile ones. Typical are *Lactobacillus acidophilus* and *Bifidum longum*, which can be obtained in capsule form or in various yoghurt-type foods.

process, to To grind to a fine or coarse consistency in a food processor

processed cheese Fairly bland cheese compounded with flavourings, emulsifiers, preservatives, extenders and stabilizers, then formed into blocks, portions, wedges, slices, etc. or filled into squeezy tubes or sausage casings

processed peas Marrowfat peas, cooked in their cans and coloured a particularly bright green

profiterole *England, France* A light cake filled with cream or custard usually served with chocolate sauce, now restricted to choux pastry balls about 3 to 5 cm diameter with the centre hollow filled with whipped cream, Chantilly cream, ice cream or crème pâtissière

profumata, alla *Italy* Flavoured with

prolamin One of the proteins in seeds and grains. It is soluble in the water-ethanol mixtures formed during dough proving and affects the texture of wheat dough during proving and baking.

proof cabinet A controlled temperature and humidity enclosure, used for proving baked goods

propan-1,2-diol A solvent used for food colours and flavourings. Also called **propylene glycol**

propan-1,2-diol alginate E405, an ester of alginic acid which is partially soluble in fats

propan-2-ol See **isopropyl alcohol**

proprionates Salts of proprionic acid used as flour improvers and food preservatives. The sodium- E281, calcium- E282 and potassium proprionates E283 are used.

Proprionibacterium A genus of microorganisms associated with the ripening of Swiss cheese and the development of the holes

proprionic acid E280, a simple fatty acid which occurs naturally in dairy products, now synthesized for use as a flour improver and preservative

propylene glycol See **propan-1,2-diol**

prosciutto *Italy* Fresh uncooked ham preserved by curing and/or air-drying. Usually served in very thin slices as antipasto.

prosciutto cotto *Italy* Cooked ham often boned and pressed into shape

prosciutto crudo *Italy* Raw smoked ham

prosciutto di montagna *Italy* A type of Parma ham but with a more powerful flavour and darker colour

prosciutto di Parma *Italy* Parma ham

proso Common millet

Prosopis glandulosa *Botanical name* Mesquite bean

Prosopis juliflora *Botanical name* Mesquite bean

prostokvash *Russia* Milk soured at around 30°C

protease A specialized group of enzymes which attack the peptide links (i.e. between the amino acids) in proteins causing a variety of changes including complete digestion of proteins to amino acids. Used in brewing, baking, cheese making and for flavour enhancement and meat tenderization.

protein Long chains of amino acids which arrange themselves in many different shapes, some for use as muscle fibres, others to act as structural building blocks of body tissue and others as the enzymes which mediate most body processes. Of the 20 amino acids required 8 (9 in the case of infants) cannot be synthesized by the body and must be supplied in the diet. These are known as **essential amino acids**. Proteins in food are broken down into amino acids in the gut, these are absorbed into the blood and reassembled as required or burnt to provide energy.

protein bodies These are roughly spherical structures consisting of protein encapsulated in a membrane which occur in all seeds including cereals. They cannot be broken mechanically but water causes them to swell and break open, this being the process occurring in germination and also in dough production. See also **gluten, glutenin, gliadin, prolamin, lectins**

proteolytic enzyme See **protease**

protose steak *United States* A type of textured vegetable protein made to resemble steak

prove, to 1. To allow a yeast dough to rise both before and after shaping. Even rising depends on the incorporation and dispersion of the correct amount of air in the dough by the mixing and kneading processes. **2.** To heat a new frying pan to a high temperature with oil or salt prior to using it so as to fill in minute imperfections in the surface. This prevents certain mixtures containing eggs or other proteins from sticking to it. Such pans should not be washed in detergents.

provençale, (à la) *France* In the Provence style, i.e. with olive oil, garlic, olives and tomatoes, and sometimes mushrooms or anchovies

provençale, sauce *France* A fondue of concassée tomatoes fried briefly in hot oil then cooked very slowly in a covered pan with crushed garlic, chopped parsley, seasoning and a little sugar

provision, to To purchase or acquire all the foods necessary for a particular task, usually for a voyage or expedition

provisions 1. Foodstuffs acquired for use or storage **2.** *Caribbean* A general name for edible tubers such as eddoes, dasheen and cassava or starchy fruit and vegetables, i.e. main carbohydrate sources

provitamin A See **carotenes**

Provola *Italy* A soft spun-curd cheese made with buffalo or cows' milk in the same way as Mozzarella but ending up rather more firm. It is formed into 500 g pear shapes and a string tied around the top leaves a small sphere where the stalk of the pear would be.

Provolone *Italy* A hard, scalded and spun-curd smooth-textured, pale yellow cheese made from unpasteurized cows' milk. It is started with fermented whey and rennet and the curd is warmed and washed to reduce calcium which makes it more pliable. It is then cheddared and drained, moulded by hand into a variety of shapes, cooled, brined and ripened at high humidity and strung in pairs when moulds develop on the surface. It is brushed and washed before sale. Used for dessert and cooking, as it matures the flavour increases in intensity. The mature form contains 33% water, 35% fat, 28% protein and 4% salt.

Provolone affumicato *Italy* A smoked Provolone cheese

Provolone piccante *Italy* A type of grating provolone in which the milk is coagulated with kid's rennet and the cheese is left to mature for up to 2 years when it becomes dark, hard and strong

prugna *Italy* Plum

prugna secca *Italy* Prune

prugna selvatica *Italy* Sloe

prugnolo *Italy* Sloe

prugnuoli *Italy* Saint George's mushrooms

pruim *Netherlands* Plum

prune 1. A whole plum with or without the stone dried to a black colour **2.** *France* Plum

pruneau *France* Prune

prune d'Agen *France* One of the best French plums, used for making prunes

prune de Damas *France* Damson

prunelle *France* Sloe

Prunus armeniaca *Botanical name* Apricot

Prunus avium *Botanical name* Sweet cherry

Prunus cerasifera *Botanical name* Cherry plum

Prunus cerasus *Botanical name* Acid or sour cherry

Prunus communis var. sativa *Botanical name* Pear

Prunus domestica *Botanical name* Plum and gage

Prunus dulcis var. amara *Botanical name* Bitter almond

Prunus dulcis var. dulcis *Botanical name* Sweet almond

Prunus insititia *Botanical name* Damson, gage, mirabelle and bullace

Prunus mahaleb *Botanical name* Mahlab

Prunus pennsylvanica *Botanical name* Bird cherry

Prunus persica *Botanical name* Peach

Prunus persica var. nectarina *Botanical name* Nectarine

Prunus salicina *Botanical name* Japanese or salicine plum

Prunus spinosa *Botanical name* Sloe

Prunus triflora *Botanical name* Japanese or salicine plum

Prunus virginiana *Botanical name* Chokecherry

psarassoupa *Greece* A thick fish soup made from fish stock simmered for 30 minutes with sliced onions, celery, carrots, potato and garlic all sweated in olive oil, plus **tomato concassée** and bay leaf. Skinned boned and portioned white fish (about 1:2 on the original stock) and white wine added, simmered 10 minutes then seasoned and finished with lemon juice and simmered a further 2 minutes. Served with chopped parsley. Also called **kakavia**

psari *Greece* Fish

pshennaya kasha *Russia* A porridge made from millet and milk with salt and sugar

Psidium guajava *Botanical name* Guava

psiti crema *Greece* A baked custard made from plain yoghurt, sugar and egg yolks (15:3:2) flavoured with cinnamon. The yoghurt is whisked into the creamed egg and sugar and all cooked in a bain-marie.

psito arni *Greece* Roast lamb

Psophocarpus tetragonolobus *Botanical name* Goa bean

ptaquiloside The compound in bracken, *Pteridium aquilinum*, which is broken down in the body into dienone, a potent carcinogen. This may explain the high incidence of throat cancer amongst the Japanese who eat bracken shoots.

ptarmigan A small rarely seen wild bird, *Lagopus mutus*, of the grouse family from northern Europe and North America, which goes white in winter. It is generally cooked in the same way as grouse. Shooting season 12th of August to the 10th of December. Hanging time 2 to 4 days. Also called **willow partridge**, **rock partridge**, **mountain grouse**

puak *Thailand* Taro

Pucheria campechiana *Botanical name* Canistel

puchero 1. *Spain* Olla podrida **2.** *Argentina* An **olla podrida** containing diced pumpkin and quarters of corn on the cob

puchero argentina *Argentina* A complex stew of cubed brisket of beef, lamb's and pig's heads, portioned chicken and chick peas, simmered slowly with diced bacon, chorizo sausage, cabbage, potatoes, rice and tomatoes added towards the end

puchero mexicana *Mexico* A one-pot meal of beef, veal, pickled pork and goose giblets cooked in plenty of water with carrots, turnips, onions, Hamburg parsley and chick peas in a special earthenware pot and served as both soup and main course

puddenskins *England* A Cornish sausage of slightly salted pork, potatoes, turnips and onions, seasoned and baked in the oven in a covered dish, chopped and mixed with flour, suet, oatmeal and raisins, bound with egg and filled into large casings, tied and baked or fried until coloured

pudding 1. The general term for sweet or savoury dishes cooked or assembled and set in a pudding basin or other type of mould **2.** The general term for hot sweet dishes served at the end of a meal **3.** The Old English term for minced meat or offal and cereal packed into a casing and boiled. Haggis and black pudding are the two common survivors of this once common practice.

pudding grass Pennyroyal

pudding iz kartofelia i iablok *Russia* A Baltic dish of equal parts of mashed potatoes mixed with mashed cooking apples sautéed in butter, flavoured with sugar and nutmeg and mixed with a little cream, placed in a baking dish covered with breadcrumbs and butter and baked at 200°C until golden

pudding rice A short-grain rice, chalky when raw and sticky when cooked. Requires 40 minutes to cook.

pudding spice *England* An English blend of ground spices used in cakes, biscuits and puddings selected from cinnamon, cloves, mace, nutmeg, coriander seeds and allspice

pudeena *South Asia* Mint

pudim *Portugal* Pudding

pudim de nozes *Portugal* Custard with cinnamon and walnuts

pudim de ovos *Portugal* Caramel custard flavoured with lemon and cinnamon

pudim flan *Portugal* Crème caramel

pudim português *Portugal* Orange custard

pudín *Spain* Pudding

pudina ki patti *South Asia* Mint

puerco *Spain* Pig or pork

puerro *Spain* Leek

puffball An edible pear-shaped or spherical fungus of two distinct types called the **common puffball** and the **giant puffball**

Puffer *Germany* **1.** Fritter **2.** Potato pancake

puffer fish A yellow and black fish, *Fugu rubripes*, with a white underside whose raw flesh is prized by Japanese gourmands for use in sashimi. It contains a powerful toxin which kills several consumers each year. See also **fugu**

puff pastry Pastry made from 700 to 1500 interleaved layers of a very short flour dough and fat formed by rolling out a rectangular layer of the short flour dough, coating or sandwiching with fat, folding in 3 (3-fold turn) or folding the ends to the centre and then together like a book (book turn), rotating a quarter turn and repeating this, resting for 20 minutes in the refrigerator between turns. 5 book folds and 6 3-fold turns are required. The fat used must be of the same consistency as the dough. Margarine or pastry fat requires a strong flour, butter a softer flour. The ratio of fat to flour in the dough is roughly 1:8 whilst overall, the fat flour ratio is 1:1. See also **French puff pastry method, puff pastry, rough puff pastry, virgin pastry**

puff pastry fat A high-melting-point fat which can be used to make puff pastry in warm conditions and which will withstand rough handling. Usually free of water. If it contains water the amount of fat in the puff pastry must be increased to give the correct ratio of pure fat to flour.

puffs Small cakes or tarts made with a casing of puff pastry filled with jam, custard, whipped cream, etc.

puila A sweet bread from Finland flavoured with cardamom

pui la ceaun cu mujdei *Romania* Roast chicken served with a sauce made from chicken stock and garlic

puits d'amour *France* A small round pastry filled with cream, jelly or fruit (NOTE: Literally 'well of love'.)

pulao *South Asia* Pilau

pulasan The fruit of a small tree, *Nephelium mutabile*, covered with red to yellow warts, similar to the lychee and used in the same way

puleggio *Italy* Penny royal

puli *Indonesia* Blade mace

pulla *Finland* A roll or bun especially an enriched and sweetened yeast-raised dough formed into a braid or plats before proving

pullan *Ireland* A white-fleshed fish, *Coregonus lavaretus*, similar to vendace found in freshwater lakes especially in Ireland. Also called **white fish**

pullao *South Asia* Pilau

pulled bread *United States* Freshly baked bread with its crust removed

pullet A young hen or laying fowl

pullet eggs The small eggs laid by pullets when they first start to lay. Not normally sold through other than producer outlets.

pulp 1. The soft, somewhat formless, interior of a fruit or vegetable **2.** A thick or coarse purée of fruit or vegetables **3.** The residue of cooked or uncooked fruit or vegetables after sieving or pressing out the juice. Citrus pulp is sometimes used in manufactured orange drinks.

pulpeta *Spain* Slice of meat

pulpo *Spain* Octopus or squid

pulp wash The liquid containing sugars, acids and minerals obtained by washing the pith and cell walls left when orange juice is separated from whole oranges. It is illegal to add it to pure orange juice in the UK but not in the USA.

pulse The general name for most dried leguminous seeds used for their protein content, such as beans, peas, lentils, etc.

Pultost *Norway* A soft cooked-curd naturally curdled cheese made from very low-fat cows' milk. The curds are salted and often flavoured with caraway seeds to give a very tasty paste. Contains 60% water, 3% fat and 30% protein. Also called **knaost**, **ramost**

pummelo The fruit of a tree, *Citrus grandis*, which looks like a large pale green grapefruit and has a firm sharp-tasting white or pink flesh and a very thick skin. It probably originated in southern China but is now grown throughout Southeast Asia. There are 3 main groups: the Thai which is relatively small and of high quality, the Chinese which is medium-sized with a coarse juicy flesh and the Indonesian which is the largest and is perfectly spherical. They are usually eaten by removing a segment and peeling away the walls on two sides. Also called **pomelo**, **shaddock**

pumpa *Sweden* Pumpkin

pumpernickel A dark brown slightly sticky dense German-style bread made from coarse rye flour and steamed for up to 20 hours. Usually eaten in very thin slices. Also called **black bread**

pumpkin The various yellow to orange fruits of a vine, *Cucurbita pepo,* a member of the *Cucurbitaceae* family native to America. Pumpkins are usually used for decoration e.g. jack o' lantern and Connecticut field cultivars. Pumpkin pie is usually made from squash which have better cooking qualities; New England sugar however is a small pie pumpkin.

pumpkin pie *United States* A dessert served with whipped cream consisting of a cooked pumpkin or squash purée mixed with eggs, sugar, cream, black treacle or molasses and spices, baked in a precooked open pastry case until set

pumpkin seeds Large flat green seeds from pumpkins and squashes eaten raw or cooked, in sweet or savoury dishes or as a snack food. Can be sprouted.

punajuuri *Finland* Beetroot

punajuurikeitto *Finland* Borscht

punch, to To fold dough in triple or bookfold and literally punch it to expel air

punchero *Mexico* A one-pot meat, bean and vegetable stew. The broth is served first, then the meat and vegetables.

Punica granatum *Botanical name* Pomegranate

Punkersdorker *Germany* A strong juicy salami-style sausage

punnet A small square, rectangular or oval basket originally of woven wood or leaves but now plastic or card, used to hold soft fruit, mushrooms and the like for sale

Punschtorte *Germany* A rum-flavoured cake

punt, al *Catalonia* Medium cooked (of meat)

punta di vitello *Italy* Breast of veal

puntarelle *Italy* A winter salad green with thin serrated leaves on long stalks

puntina *Italy* Pinch, e.g. of salt

puntine *Italy* Tiny pasta seeds, smaller than semini

puntino, a *Italy* Medium well done as applied to meat

puntitas Paco Alcade *Spain* An Andalusian speciality of beef sautéed with fresh tomatoes, black olives and garlic

punto, en su *Spain* Medium-cooked. Used of meat steaks, etc. See also **à point**

puppadom *South Asia* Poppadom

pur chèvre *France* Cheese made only from goats' milk

purea *Italy* Purée

puré de patata *Spain* Mashed potato

purée *England, France* **1.** A type of soup in which fresh vegetables and pulses are simmered in stock with flavouring then forced through a sieve or liquidized to give a smooth consistency. Usually served accompanied with croûtons in a separate dish. **2.** Any food processed or pounded to a smooth consistency, somewhere between coating and pouring

Püree *Germany* Purée

pure olive oil Blended olive oil made by larger companies from a mixture of refined oils from various sources. Also called **100% pure olive oil**

puri *South Asia* A deep-fried chapati which puffs and swells as it is cooked. Served hot, often with a hot spicy filling for use as a snack. Also called **poori, bhatura, bhatoora**

purjo *Sweden* Leeks

purple basil A type of basil from Southeast Asia with red to purple tinged leaves and red stalks. The flavour and aroma become intense when it is cooked.

purple granadilla See **purple passion fruit**

purple guava See **strawberry guava**

purple laver Nori

purple passion fruit A large (up to 7.5 cm diameter) globular fruit, *Passiflora edulis*, with a hard wrinkled purple to black skin containing a deliciously flavoured mucilaginous yellow pulp full of small edible seeds. The pulp is scooped out for eating or use in desserts, or it may be sieved to use as a flavouring. Also called **maracuya, purple granadilla**

purple sage A variety of sage, *Salvia officinale* 'Purpurascens', with very strong-flavoured purple leaves, good for tea

purple sprouting broccoli See **sprouting broccoli**

pursindah seekhi *South Asia* An elaborate way of skewering lamb fillet by first trimming it to a block 75 mm long by 60 mm wide by 20 mm deep. The block is then cut once from either end into a 6 to 7 mm thickness without completely finishing the cut so as to form a long strip roughly 210 by 60 by 7mm. This strip is pierced along its length in a series of S curves with a greased skewer then grilled, with flavourings added either before or after cooking.

purslane A plant of two distinct types, **summer purslane** which is a half-hardy annual and **winter purslane** which is fully hardy

pusit calmar *Philippines* Squid

puso no saging *Philippines* Banana flower

pu tao *China* Grapes

pu tao gan *China* Raisins

pu tao jiu *China* Wine made from grapes

putcha A Jewish appetizer made from calf's foot jelly. See also **petcha**

Pute *Germany* Hen turkey

Puter *Germany* Cock turkey

puttanesca, alla *Italy* In the style of the harlot, i.e. with tomatoes, garlic, capers, olives and anchovies

puuro *Finland* Porridge

Puzol *Spain* A soft ewes' milk cheese eaten very fresh. Contains 61% water, 21% fat and 18% protein.

pwdin cymreig *Wales* Welsh pudding

pwdin eryri *Wales* Snowdon pudding

pwdin gwaed *Wales* A Welsh black pudding made of salted fresh pig's blood mixed with a little water, allowed to stand overnight, chopped onions and a little fat coated with oatmeal, herbs and seasoning added, this then mixed with the blood, all packed into hog casings, boiled 30 minutes then dried. Served sliced and fried.

pwdin gwaed gwyddau *Wales* As **pwdin gwaed** but using goose blood instead of pig's blood

pyaaj *Nepal, South Asia* Onion

pyechenka *Russia* Pechyenka

pyechenye *Russia* Pechenye

pyechyen-grill See **pechyen-grill**

pyechyen kur v madere See **pechyen kur v madere**

pyin daw thein *Burma* Curry leaf

pyin tha-leik *Burma* Turtle

p'yogo *Korea* Shiitake mushroom

pyramide *France* A soft surface-ripened goats milk cheese with a sweet flavour which becomes stronger as it ripens. It is formed in the shape of a truncated pyramid and sometimes coated with ashes to dry it out.

pyrethrum A nontoxic pesticide made from dried pyrethrum flowers that can be used near food

pyridoxal See **vitamin B6**

pyridoxamine See **vitamin B6**

pyridoxine See **vitamin B6**

pyridoxol See **vitamin B6**

pyroligneous acid A yellow liquid obtained by condensing the vapours obtained by heating sawdust in a closed metal retort. Used to impart a smoky flavour to some foods.

Pyrus communis Botanical name Pear tree

Pyrus pyrofolia Botanical name Asian pear

Pyrus ussuriensis Botanical name Asian pear

pytt i panna *Sweden* Fried cubes of potato, ham and beef, mixed with fried onions and chopped parsley, the whole topped with a raw egg yolk which is stirred into the mixture at the table. Also called **Swedish hash**

pyy *Finland* Hazel hen

QRSTUVW

qâlat daqqa *Middle East, North Africa* An Arabian spice blend of ground black peppercorns, cloves, grains of paradise, nutmeg and cinnamon used in vegetable dishes and with lamb

qa tagine *North Africa* A deep copper dish in which a **tagine** is served at the table so as to protect the table's surface

qataif *Middle East* A pancake made from flour, water and yeast, dipped after cooking in lemon-flavoured syrup scented with orange flower water. Can be stuffed, folded and deep-fried.

qawwrama *Middle East* Lebanese preserved meat made from the rendered fat of specially fattened sheep in which cubes of lean mutton which have been pressed to remove moisture are fried and the fried meat and fat to cover, packed in earthenware pots. Will keep for several months.

quadrello *Italy* Rack of lamb or loin of pork

quadretti di riso alla piemontese *Italy* Rice fritters with meat sauce and cheese

quadrucci *Italy* Small squares of egg pasta used in soups

quaggiaridda *Italy* A mixture of sheep's offal, sausage and cheese wrapped in a pig's caul and baked

quaglia *Italy* Quail

quaglie alla borghese *Italy* Quails wrapped in vine leaves and roasted on a bed of puréed peas and lettuce

quaglie rincartate *Italy* An Umbrian dish of quails wrapped in bread dough and baked

quagliette *Italy* Cabbage rolls and similar

quagliette di vitello *Italy* Paupiettes of veal stuffed with ham and grilled on a skewer

quahog clam An Atlantic Ocean clam, *Mercenaria mercenaria*, up to about 13 cm in diameter with a dull grey to brown exterior and purple interior shell. Eaten raw or cooked. Also called **hard clam**, **hard shell clam**, **hard-neck clam**, **cherrystone**

quaietta *Italy* A dish from Turin of veal cutlets stuffed with meat, cheese and truffles

quail A small game bird, *Coturnix coturnix*, now protected in the wild but farmed for table use. The English version is usually more tasteless than the French which has a yellow flesh from being corn-fed. Usually barded and roasted at 220°C for 25 minutes and served one per person on buttered toast garnished with watercress.

quails' eggs Small eggs regarded as a delicacy, boiled for 1 minute or hard-boiled and served with a dip as an appetizer or used as a garnish for cold buffets

quaking custard *United States* A New England demoulded egg custard garnished with egg white which tends to shake easily on the plate

qualheim cutter *United States* A type of **mandolin** that also dices food

quandong fruit *Australia* One of the best known wild fruits of the continent, *Santalum acuminatum*, now grown in considerable commercial quantities. It is bright red, mildly tart and the flavour is a mixture of apricot and peach with a touch of cinnamon. It is used in sauces, desserts etc. The seed kernels are toxic unless roasted to a light chocolate colour. Also called **native peach**

quarg See **quark**

quark, Quark *Central Europe, England, Germany* A soft, slightly sour, curd cheese sometimes flavoured with fruit or herbs, made from skimmed, whole or buttermilk possibly with added cream. Eaten as a dessert. Contains 70 to 80% water, and less than 3 % fat. Also called **kvarg**, **quarg**, **Buttermilchquark**, **Labquark**, **Speisequark**

Quarkklösse *Germany* Dumplings made with quark

Quarktorte *Germany* A type of cheesecake with a short pastry base. The filling is strained quark creamed with butter, sugar and egg yolk flavoured with lemon zest and cinnamon and with currants and stiffly beaten egg whites folded in. The base and fillings are baked in a very slow oven and served cold dusted with icing sugar.

quart 1. 2 pints in either imperial or USA volume measure **2.** *France* A quarter, one fourth part

quarter A volume measure equal to 8 bushels or 64 gallons in either imperial or USA measure

quarter of meat See **forequarter**

quartier *France* Fore or hindquarter of an animal carcass

Quartirolo *Italy* A soft, cows' milk cheese similar to Taleggio made with a lactic starter and having a distinctive mushroom flavour

quarto *Italy* **1.** A quarter, one fourth part **2.** Leg, haunch or hindquarter of meat

quasi *France* The top of the leg of veal cut from the English cushion and undercushion and the rear of the loin

quasi de veau bourgeoise *France* Boneless quasi of veal casseroled with pork, calf's foot and vegetables

quassia A bitter flavouring extracted from the wood and bark of a South American tree, *Quassia amara*, or West-Indian tree, *Pacrasma excelsa*, mainly used for drinks and tonics

Quassia amara *Botanical name* Quassia

quatre-épices *France* The classic French spice blend used in charcuterie and stews, consisting of 5 parts black peppercorns, 2 parts nutmeg, 1 part cloves and 1 part dried ginger ground to a fine powder. Cinnamon is substituted for black pepper if used in sweet dishes and the proportions vary from place to place.

quatre-quarts *France* The French version of **pound cake**

quattro spezie *Italy* A spice mix of pepper, nutmeg, juniper and cloves (NOTE: Literally 'four spices'.)

quattro stagioni *Italy* **1.** A butterhead lettuce with dimpled soft and glossy leaves tipped with red **2.** A type of pizza in which the four quarters have different additions to the tomato and cheese base to represent the four seasons

quay *Vietnam* Roast

que *Vietnam* A type of mint

queen cake A small individual cake made from the basic cake mixture using the creaming method with a final addition of washed and dried mixed dried vine fruits

queen crab See **snow crab**

queenie Queen scallop

queen of puddings *England* Bread or cake crumbs covered with a sweetened and flavoured egg custard mixture baked in the oven in a bain-marie until set, cooled, spread with warmed jam or fruit, topped with a meringue mixture and browned in the oven

queen scallop A small variety of scallop, *Pecten opercularis* or *Chlamys opercularis*, with an almost circular shell up to 10 cm diameter and a vivid red roe. Found in deeper waters than the great scallop. The flesh weighs about 12 g. Also called **queenie**, **quin scallop**

Queensland nut Macadamia nut

Queensland school mackerel *Australia* An important commercial fish, the school mackerel, *Cybium queenslandicus*, makes excellent eating. It can grow to 8 kg but is generally available at between 1 and 3 kg. It is green on top and silver below and its alternative name, **blotched mackerel**, refers to the several rows of light grey blotches along the sides. Also called **blotched mackerel** (NOTE: Not to be confused with the common mackerel, *Scomber australasicus*, which rarely weighs more than 800 g in Australia.)

queen snapper *Australia* Morwong

queijadas de sintra *Portugal* Unsweetened patties made with eggs, almonds and cheese served with French beans

queijo *Portugal* Cheese

queijo arreganhado *Portugal* A mild and mellow cheese made from the first milk drawn from the ewe which doesn't contain much fat

queijo da Ilha *Portugal* A hard cows' milk cheese from the Azores resembling a mature Cheddar, used mainly for cooking. Also called **queijo da Terra**

queijo da Serra *Portugal* The famous semi-hard high-fat cheese made from the milk of ewes pastured on the high meadows of the north East. It resembles a well-flavoured Brie and is eaten either runny or ripened until firm and pungent. Its origin and method of production are controlled by the government. Also called **Serra**

queijo da Terra *Portugal* Queijo da Ilha

queijo do ceu *Portugal* A cheese dessert

queijo Minas *Brazil* A white scalded-curd cheese made from cows' milk eaten fresh as a dessert or allowed to mature and become yellow

queijo Minas curado *Brazil* The mature, semi-hard version of Minas with a thin rind and paste containing scattered holes. Contains 45% water, 20% fat and 28% protein.

queijo Minas frescal *Brazil* A soft fresh cows' milk cheese with a pleasant acid taste. Contains 60% water, 16% fat and 17% protein. Also called **Mineiro Frescal**

queijos frescos *Portugal* Fresh cheeses made from ewes' or goats' milk sometimes allowed to ripen

quemada *Mexico* Milk which has been boiled until it turns a caramel colour

quenelle *England, France* Fish, meat or poultry meat processed to a very fine forcemeat, bound with eggs or fat, shaped with two spoons into small round or oval dumplings and poached in a cooking liquor. Served as a garnish or as a main course with a sauce.

quenelles de brochet *France* Quenelles or dumplings made with the flesh of pike

quente *Portugal* Warm, hot

quesillo *Caribbean* Crème caramel from Dominica

queso *Spain* Cheese

queso blanco *South America* A soft cheese made from cows' milk curdled with acetic acid, the curds kneaded, pressed and salted. Eaten fresh or after ripening for up to 3 months. Contains 50% water, 19% fat and 25% protein.

queso Ciudad Real *Spain* A smoked goats' milk cheese

queso de bola *Spain* A round ball-shaped Dutch-style cheese

queso de cabra *South America* A soft cylindrical (up to 1 kg) goats' milk cheese from Chile with a sharp flavour

queso de cerdo *Spain* Brawn made from pig's head

queso de los Bellos *Spain* A hard cheese. See also **Bellos**

queso de nata *Spain* Cream cheese

queso helado *Spain* An ice cream brick

queso manchego *Spain* A hard sheeps' milk cheese

quesong puti *Philippines* Kesong puti

quetsche *France* A variety of dark purple plum

queue *France* 1. Tail, of an animal 2. Handle of a pan

queue de boeuf *France* Oxtail

queue de boeuf claire *France* Clear oxtail soup

queue de boeuf liée *France* Thick oxtail soup

queues d'écrevisses *France* Crayfish tails

quiche A savoury custard tart made from a shortcrust or puff pastry-lined quiche dish or flan ring, possibly precooked, filled with various solid savoury and raw salad or vegetable items which are then covered with a seasoned mixture of eggs and milk and/or cream, possibly gratinated and/or decorated, then baked in the oven at 200 to 230°C until cooked and browned

quiche dish A shallow (about 3 cm deep), round, glazed ceramic dish used for cooking quiches

quiche lorraine *England, France* A quiche made with a filling of chopped ham or bacon and grated cheese or slices of Gruyère

quick bread *United States* Bread made with chemical raising agents

quick cooking rice See **precooked rice**

quick freeze, to To freeze food so that it spends a minimum of time between 0°C and –4°C, the region where ice crystals would, if given the time, grow to such a size as to rupture cell walls releasing their contents on thawing. Usually done by blasting with liquefied gases. Quick frozen food is usually stored at around – 30°C.

quiejo do Reino *Brazil* A cows' or goats' milk cheese similar to the Portuguese Serra cheese

quiejo Prato *Brazil* A flat semi-hard Edam-like cows' milk cheese with a few small holes and a tender rind

quignon *France* Crust or hunk (of bread)

quill Cinnamon bark rolled up into a cigar-like tube

quillaia The compound extracted from the bark of the soap bark tree from SA used as a foaming agent in soft drinks. Permitted for use in the UK.

quillings Small broken pieces of cinnamon bark often rolled up within larger quills

quince The apple or pear-shaped fruit of a temperate climate bush, *Cydonia oblonga*, with a green skin which turns to gold when ripe and is covered by a greyish-white down. The ripe flesh is sweet, juicy and yellow with a pronounced scent and is always cooked. Used as apples or made into jam without the need of added pectin. They originated in western Asia but are now grown worldwide especially in Uruguay.

quin choy *China* Winter rape

quing dou *China* Fresh soya beans

quing suan *China* Asian leek

quinoa A tiny golden seed from South America cultivated since 3000 BC. It is rather like rice but has a higher protein content. Requires 10 to 15 minutes boiling. Can be grown in temperate climates.

quinoline yellow E104, a synthetic yellow food colouring

quin scallop Queen scallop

quire of paper *England* An old English cake made from very thin pancakes cooked on one side only, sprinkled with sugar and built up into a cake. The pancake mixture is rich in eggs, cream and melted butter and flavoured with sherry, rose water and nutmeg.

quisquilla *Spain* Shrimp

quisquilla gris *Spain* Brown shrimp

Quitte *Germany* Quince

Quittengelee *Germany* Quince jam

quorn The thread-like mycelium of a fungus grown industrially in a medium made principally from the starch content of field beans. It contains about 45% protein and 13% fat together with dietary fibre, and after drying and compounding is used as a high-class protein in vegetarian meals, both made up and home cooked.

quroot *Central Asia* Yoghurt or sour milk drained and dried to form a cheese-like substance which can be stored. It is usually reconstituted with water and used as a base for sauces.

quwarmah ala dajaj *Persian Gulf* A lightly curried chicken flavoured with garlic, fresh ginger root, a little chilli powder, turmeric and **loomi** powder

rã *Portugal* Frog finished with cream and chopped dill

rabaçal *Portugal* A mild, white and soft curd cheese made from a mixture of ewes' and goats' milk. Eaten young but the taste intensifies as it ripens. Often cured in the sun.

rabadi *South Asia* Condensed milk

rabanadas *Portugal* A dessert made from sweetened fried bread

rabanete *Portugal* See **radish**

rábano *Spain* Radish

rábano picante *Spain* Horseradish

rabarbaro *Italy* Rhubarb

rabarber *Denmark, Sweden* Rhubarb

rabarbra *Norway* Rhubarb

rabbit A small furry burrowing game animal, *Oryctolagus caniculus*, of the hare family sometimes farmed and weighing when dressed around 1.2 kg to 4 kg for some of the farmed animals. The farmed animal's flesh resembles chicken, the wild animals are more gamey but this may be reduced by soaking in salted water and briefly blanching. They are not hung. Cooked in any way, traditionally served with onion sauce.

rabbit-eye blueberry See **blueberry**

rabbit Latrobe *Australia* Marinated pieces of rabbit stewed in a sour cream sauce

rabbit sausage *England* Meat from cooked rabbit, shredded and mixed with one third its weight of coarsely chopped bacon, seasoned, flavoured with ground cloves and mace, packed into casings and boiled or fried. Eaten hot or cold.

råbiff *Sweden* Raw beef, steak tartare

râble *France* Saddle of hare or rabbit

rabo de buey *Spain* Oxtail

rabotte *France* An apple cooked in pastry as a dessert (NOTE: From Champagne)

raccoon *United States* A small furry carnivorous animal sometimes used in Cajun cuisine

rachel, à la *France* In Rachel's style, i.e. steaks garnished with artichokes, bone marrow and parsley

racine *France* Root vegetable

ració *Catalonia* A large tapas, almost sufficient for a meal

rack of lamb One half of the vertebrae and first six rib bones counting from the rear end of the lamb equivalent to the best end. Usually chined, skinned and roasted.

raclette *Switzerland* **1.** An unpasteurized cows' milk cheese similar to **Gruyère** and made in small rounds. See also **Valais raclette 2.** A dish made by halving a raclette cheese, toasting it in front of the fire or grilling it and serving the molten centre with boiled potatoes and pickles

radappertization The production of food free from spoilage microorganisms using ionizing radiation

radicchio Red chicory

radici *Italy* Radishes

radicidation The elimination of pathogens in food using ionizing radiation

Radieschen *Germany* Radishes

radijs *Netherlands* Radish

radis *France* Radish, radishes

radish The root of a plant, *Raphanus sativus* and *R. sativus* Longipinnus Group, of the mustard family grown in many forms and colours from 1 cm diameter spheres to 30 cm long carrot-like roots and with colours from white through red to black. The crisp white flesh has a slightly peppery flavour of varying degrees of strength. Generally used raw in salads and for decoration in many sculpted shapes. The larger varieties, e.g. mooli, may be eaten raw, cooked or pickled. The young leaves are also edible.

radis noir *France* Horseradish

radisor *Sweden* Radish

radisser *Italy* Radishes

rådjurssadel *Sweden* Roasted saddle of venison

rådjursstek *Sweden* Venison steak

radurization The reduction of the content of spoilage organisms in perishable food using ionizing radiation

rådyr *Norway* Venison

rafano *Italy* Radish

rafano tedesco *Italy* Horseradish

raffreddato *Italy* Chilled

rafinat *France* A refined product

rafraîchi(e) *France* Refreshed or chilled, the past participle of *rafraîchir*, 'to refresh or cool down'

ragee See **ragi**

raggee See **ragi**

raggmunkar *Sweden* Potato (pan)cakes

raggy See **ragi**

ragi 1. The seeds of an East Indian grass, *Eleusine caracana*, used as a cereal grain in Africa and India and used for bread and beer. Also called **ragee, raggee, raggy, finger millet 2.** *Southeast Asia* A rice cake, widely sold as street food

ragno di mare *Italy* Spider crab

ragoo *England* An English spelling of ragoût, used of a rich meat and vegetable casserole

ragoût *France* A thick stew with a high proportion of meat or poultry sometimes including offal and sausages

Ragoût fin *Germany* Sweetbreads, brains and other fine offal cooked with mushrooms in a cream and wine sauce

ragú 1. *Italy* Ragoût **2.** *Italy* A sauce made from olive oil, butter, cooked meat and garlic **3.** *Denmark, Norway, Sweden* Stew

Ragusano *Italy* A hard, scalded and spun curd cheese from Sicily made in rectangular blocks (up to 12 kg). It is matured for 3 months for dessert use or up to 12 months for grating. The dessert cheese has a mild delicate flavour, the grating cheese which had an oiled dark brown rind is sharp and savoury.

rahat lokum *Turkey* A type of Turkish delight mixed with almond slivers, pistachios and hazelnuts after it is cooked but before setting

Rahm *Germany* Cream

Rahmfrischkäse *Germany* A soft fresh cheese made with acid curdled cows' milk. Contains 70% water, 18% fat and 9% protein.

Rahmkäse *Germany* Cream cheese

Rahmschnitzel *Switzerland* Veal escalopes in a cream sauce

Rahmsosse *Germany* Cream sauce

rai *South Asia* Black mustard seeds

raia blanca *Portugal* White skate

raie *France* Ray or skate, the fish

raie blanche *France* White skate

raie bouclée *France* Thornback ray

raifort *France* Horseradish

raifort, sauce *France* Horseradish sauce

raïm *Catalonia* Grape

rainbow sardine A small fish, *Dussumiera acuta*, similar to the sardine. It is fished off the southwest coast of India and canned in the same way.

rainbow smelt See **smelt**

rainbow trout A generally freshwater trout, *Salmo gairdneri*, occasionally found in the sea, with a silvery green back, banded with pink and weighing about 500 g, now usually farmed. The flesh may be white or pink depending upon the diet. Grilled, poached, shallow-fried or baked **en papillote**.

Rainfarn *Germany* Tansy

rainforest oysters *Australia* Avocado flesh, lemon aspen juice, and salt processed to a fine purée, piped onto shucked oysters and garnished with an edible flower

Rainha Claudia *Portugal* A type of greengage. See also **reine-claude**

raise, to To lighten baked doughs and cake mixtures by the addition of raising agents or by fermentation with yeast prior to cooking

raised pie A pie made with a very stiff pastry (hot-water pastry) which is self-supporting, will hold the filling without support and can be moulded by hand sometimes around a tin or more commonly in a fluted oval mould which separates into pieces. **Melton Mowbray pie** and **pork pie** are types of raised pie.

raisin 1. Dried white grapes made from either the naturally seedless Thompson type or the muscatel grape **2.** *France* Grape

raising agent Any chemical mixture which liberates carbon dioxide on heating so as to form small bubbles and hence lighten the mixture it is in. Bicarbonate of soda and baking powder are typical examples.

raisin oil Oil pressed from the seeds of Muscat grapes, used to keep raisins soft

raisins de Corinthe *France* Currants (the dried vine fruits)

raisins de Smyrne *France* Sultanas

raisins secs *France* Raisins

raisu *Japan* Cooked rice served on a plate, Western-style. See also **gohan**

raita *South Asia* A combination of chopped vegetables and fruit, usually cucumber, onion and bananas mixed with thick yoghurt and flavoured with cumin, coriander and seasoning, served as an accompaniment to other foods

rajas *Mexico* Strips of **chilli poblano** fried with onion, potatoes and/or tomatoes and garnished with melted cheese

rajma *South Asia* Red kidney beans

rakkyo *Japan* Pickled shallots

räkor *Sweden* 1. Prawns 2. Shrimps

rakørret *Norway* Salted and cured trout

rakott káposzt *Hungary* Sauerkraut layered in a dish with slices of smoked bacon covered with chopped lean pork which has been browned in lard with garlic and paprika, slices of debreszin sausage and with a final layer of sauerkraut, then covered with sour cream and baked in the oven

räksås *Sweden* Shrimp sauce. Chopped and cooked shrimps, sweated with butter and flour, combined with fish stock.

rambutan *England, Indonesia* The oval fruit of a tropical tree, *Nephelium lappaceum*, about 5 cm long with a central inedible stone, a delicate sweet white flesh tasting of raisins and a green skin turning to red when ripe, covered with soft spines. Eaten raw. Also called **hairy lychee**

ramekin 1. A small individual circular, usually white, porcelain, glass or earthenware oven-proof dish from 4 to 15 cm in diameter used for pâtés, mousses, egg custards, baked eggs and soufflés, etc. 2. A mixture of cheese, eggs and bread crumbs or unsweetened puff pastry baked in an individual dish

ramen *Japan* The common noodle of Japan, thin, yellow and made from wheat flour and egg

ramequin *France* 1. Ramekin 2. A type of cheese fritter

ramequin au fromage *France, Switzerland* A cheese tart or fritter served hot or cold

ramereau *France* Young wood pigeon

ramier *France* Wood pigeon

ramo de cheiras *Portugal* Flavourings wrapped in muslin like a bouquet garni always containing garlic, parsley and bay leaf plus other herbs according to the dish

ramolaccio *Italy* Horseradish

ramost A soft cooked-curd cheese. See also **Pultost**

ramp *United States* A wild leek with a strong flavour

rampe *South Asia, Sri Lanka* Screwpine

ramphal Bullock's heart

rampion A European flowering plant, *Campanula rapunculus*, of the harebell family. The leaves and roots are eaten.

ram's head pea Chick pea

ramsons *United Kingdom* A wild plant of river banks and damp woodlands, *Allium*

ursinum, with clusters of white flowers and dark-green strap-shaped leaves. The leaves impart a mild garlic flavour to a mixed-leaf salad and all parts of the plant can be used for flavouring. It is easily grown in the herb garden. (NOTE: From the Old English *hramsan*, 'wild garlic')

ram tulsi *South Asia* White basil

rana comune *Italy* Edible frog

rana pescatrice *Italy* Monkfish

ranchero, ranchera *Spain* In a country style

rancid The unpleasant smell of oxidized stale fats which is due to liberated free fatty acids and other oxidation compounds

rane fritte *Italy* Fried frogs' legs

range A large cooking stove with several burners and one or more ovens which are usually kept hot and ready for use

ranghi Abutilon

rango ko maasu *Nepal* Water buffalo meat

rankins *United States* A type of light cheese pudding or soufflé containing stiffly beaten egg whites

ranocchio *Italy* Edible frog

rapa *Italy* Turnip

rap a l'all cremat *Catalonia* Monkfish served with crisped garlic

raparperi *Finland* Rhubarb

rapa svedese *Italy* Swede

rapata *Italy* A rice and turnip soup from Lombardy

rape 1. The plant, *Brassica napus*, from which rapeseed is obtained. Some varieties known as salad rape are used in the west as a source of salad leaves. It is used as a vegetable in northern China where 3 types, broccoli rape (probably the same as broccoli raab), heart of rape and winter rape are used. Also called **cole, coleweed, coleseed** 2. *Spain* Monkfish

râpe *France* Grater

râpé(e) 1. *France* Grated, past participle of *râper*, 'to grate' 2. Grated cheese (from fromage râpé)

rape rosse *Italy* Beetroot

rapeseed The seed of a yellow flowered plant, *Brassica napus*, closely related to the swede, now commonly grown for its oil, but can also be sprouted as a substitute for mustard in mustard and cress. Also called **canola**

rapeseed oil The oil from the rapeseed, grown in great quantities in the EU. Used as a cooking oil and for margarine manufacture. Low erucic acid strains of rape are now normal. Also called **colza oil**

Raphanus sativus *Botanical name* Mooli

***Raphanus sativus* Longipinnatus Group** *Botanical name* Radish

raphøne *Denmark* Pheasant

rapini *Italy* Broccoli raab

rapphöna *Sweden* Partridge

rapphøne *Norway* Partridge

Raps *Germany* Rape, *Brassica napus*

Rapsöl *Germany* Rapeseed oil

rårakor *Sweden* A type of crêpe made from grated or processed raw potato and onion, seasoned, bound with egg and fried as very thin pancakes in hot butter

rare Cooked so that the inside of the meat is still red or pink

rarebit See **Welsh rarebit**, **buck rarebit**

rarhar *South Asia* Pigeon pea

rarrah *South Asia* Saddle, usually of lamb

rasadarh chawal *South Asia* Flavoured rice made by steaming or boiling the rice in the usual way with paprika and seasoning but mixing in flavourings according to use, e.g. tomato purée, beetroot purée, stock, ground herb pastes, sieved vegetables and the like

rasam *South Asia* A lentil broth soured with tamarind

rascasse *France* Scorpion fish, used in bouillabaisse. Also called **rascasse rouge**

rascasse de fond *France* Bluemouth, the fish

rascasse rouge *France* Rascasse

Raschera *Italy* A semi-hard cows' milk cheese sometimes with ewes' or goats' milk added. It is made in squares (up to 8 kg) and has a yellow, supple paste with a delicate taste and containing a few holes. Also called **Raschiera**

Raschiera *Italy* Raschera

rasedar *South Asia* Vegetables in a thin sauce

ras el hanout *North Africa* A mixture of many spices, herbs and other items, up to 20 or more in number including so-called aphrodisiacs such as Spanish fly (**cantharides**), ash berries and monk's pepper. Sold whole by the merchants who each have their own recipe and grind as required. Used in sweet and savoury dishes. (NOTE: Literally 'head of the shop'.)

rasgullas *South Asia* Cheese quenelles eaten as a dessert. They are made from a **paneer tikki** mixed with semolina to a smooth paste, then formed into walnut-sized balls. A little sugar and some chopped almonds are pressed into the centre of each then they are poached in a medium sugar syrup for 90 minutes. Served hot or cold, sprinkled with rose water.

rashad *Middle East* A herb from Iraq resembling a coarse dill weed with a peppery flavour

rasher See **bacon rasher**

rasolnik *Russia* A soup based on beef stock simmered with presweated aromatic vegetables, wilted sorrel or spinach, bay leaf and seasoning until cooked, bay leaf removed, all puréed, finely chopped gherkins, pickling juice and prefried, floured pieces of lambs' kidney added and simmered 5 minutes then thickened with egg yolk and served hot or chilled with sour cream

rasp Barrel bread

rasp, to To grate or break up into raspings

raspberry A fruit similar to the **blackberry** but softer, light red, occasionally white or black, with a covering of fine down and a sweet, slightly acid, fruity, perfumed flavour. The wild variety are small to 5 mm but domesticated varieties can grow to 2.5 cm long. It is grown on a cool-climate rambling plant, *Rubus idaeus*, which is cultivated so as to produce new, relatively short canes each year. The fruit tend to soften and go mouldy quickly and must be used when fresh, canned or deep-frozen. Used raw or cooked and often puréed to form a coulis or sauce. One of the fruits in summer pudding.

raspberry sauce As apricot sauce but made with raspberries

raspings Breadcrumbs

Rässkäse *Switzerland* A hard cooked-curd cows' milk cheese similar to but stronger tasting and less supple than Appenzell and with more holes. It is slightly bitter.

råstekt potatiskaka *Sweden* A type of Rösti made from grated potatoes, seasoned and fried in butter in a closed pan as a solid cake. Butter is put on top and the pan is left on a very low heat until the base of the cake is browned. Served browned side up.

rat Grenadier

ratafia 1. A liqueur flavoured with the kernels of cherries, almonds, peaches and other stone fruits **2.** A small sweet macaroon-like biscuit flavoured with ratafia essence. Once eaten with the liqueur but now used for decoration, as a base for cold desserts or, when crushed, as a constituent of various dessert creams. See also **macaroon**

ratafia essence An alcoholic extract of the kernels of cherries, peaches, almonds and other stone fruits used as a flavouring

ratalu *South Asia* White yam

rață pe varză *Romania* Duck browned in fat then braised in the oven on a deep bed of sauerkraut mixed with chopped onions browned in lard and moistened with sauerkraut juice, defatted and the duck carved and served on the sauerkraut and onion mixture

ratatouille 1. *England, France* A Provençal dish made from a mixture of tomatoes, aubergines, green and red sweet peppers, onions, garlic and olive oil seasoned and flavoured with marjoram or oregano. Courgettes and stoned olives are sometimes included. Traditionally each vegetable is fried or grilled separately and then combined. In the UK and commercially all tend to be stewed together. **2.** *France* Bad stew, lousy food

rathu miris *Sri Lanka* Chilli pepper

raton *France* A type of cheesecake

rat's ear Cloud ear fungus

rattan palm A climbing palm, *Calamus rotang*, whose shoots and seeds are edible but whose main use is as a source of cane for weaving furniture and baskets

rattatuia di frutti di mare alla marchigiana *Italy* A stew of seafood and tomatoes in wine, served with rice

rattle A variety of salad potato

rau *Vietnam* A generic term for leaves of all kinds, the following word indicates the type

Raubreif *Germany* A dessert of chilled Chantilly cream blended at the last moment with peeled and cored dessert apples which have been coarsely grated into a mixture of orange juice, lemon juice and sugar (6:3:4) previously prepared and chilled

rau cai tau *Vietnam* Chinese cabbage

rau can *Vietnam* Celery leaves

Räucheraal *Germany* Smoked eel

Räucherkäse *Germany* Naturally smoked cheese, often of the processed kind and with various flavourings and additives

Räucherlachs *Germany* Smoked salmon

räuchern *Germany* To smoke

Rauchfleisch *Germany* Smoked meat

rau hun cay *Vietnam* Mint

Rauke *Germany* Rocket, the plant

Raukenkohl *Germany* Rocket, the plant

rau la tia to *Vietnam* Caraway mint

rau muong *Vietnam* Swamp cabbage

rau ngo *Vietnam* Coriander leaves

rau que *Vietnam* Basil

rau ram *Vietnam* Vietnamese mint

Raute *Germany* Rue, the herb

rau thom *Vietnam* Mint

rau trôn *Vietnam* Salad (NOTE: Literally 'mixed leaves'.)

rava *South Asia* Semolina

ravanelli *Italy* Radishes

ravier *England, France* A dish in which compound hors d'oeuvres are presented, usually rectangular (10 by 20 cm) in shape

ravigote, sauce *England, France* **1.** A reduction of white wine and vinegar mixed with a velouté sauce and finished off the heat with shallot butter and chopped chervil, tarragon and chives. Served hot. **2.** A vinaigrette made with oil and vinegar, small dried capers, chopped parsley, tarragon, chervil, chives, onion and seasoning

ravigote butter A compound butter made by mixing butter with blanched, refreshed and dried chopped shallots, parsley, chervil, tarragon, chives and salad burnet which have been pounded to a paste, the whole passed through a sieve. Also called **beurre Chivry**, **beurre ravigote**, **beurre vert**, **green butter**

ravioli *England, Italy* A filling made from cheese, spinach, ground meat or similar items piped gridwise on to a sheet of pasta, egg-washed, a similar-sized sheet laid over and small squares or circles cut out with a filling in the centre of each. Poached and served with a sauce.

ravioli alla calabrese *Italy* Ravioli with a filling of sausage, cheese and egg and served with a sauce sprinkled with cheese

ravioli alla napoletana *Italy* Ravioli filled with a mixture of ham, ricotta, Mozzarella and Parmesan cheese

ravioli caprese *Italy* Ravioli stuffed with cheese, eggs and herbs

ravioli della val pusteria *Italy* Ravioli made with rye flour, filled with spinach, cheese or sauerkraut and poached or fried

ravioli dolci *Italy* Ravioli from Liguria stuffed with beef marrow and candied fruit, fried and dredged with sugar

raviolini *Italy* Very small ravioli

ravioli trentini *Italy* Ravioli stuffed with a mixture of meat and chicken

ravo *South Asia* Semolina

raw Not cooked

raya de clavos *Spain* Thornback ray

rayed-trough shell clam A cream-coloured clam with purple markings about 13 cm in diameter

ray's bream Pomfret

raznjici *Balkans* Grilled meat kebabs from Serbia

razor shell A cut-throat razor-shaped mollusc, *Solen vagina*, about 6 cm long. Treat as mussels.

razor shell clam A long thin bivalve mollusc, *Ensis ensis*, resembling a cut-throat razor up to 13 cm long and found on sandy beaches. Not traded commercially but may be eaten raw or cooked like mussels if gathered in unpolluted water. Toughens with overcooking.

razza *Italy* Common skate, the fish

razza chiodata *Italy* Thornback ray

rBST Recombinant BST made by genetic engineering not involving the cow

RDI See **recommended daily intake**

ready basted poultry Poultry, usually turkeys, which have fat, emulsifiers, flavourings, etc. injected and massaged into the flesh to improve the apparent quality of intensively reared birds

Rebenblatt *Germany* Vine leaf

Rebhuhn *Germany* Partridge

Reblochon *France* One of the oldest mild French cheeses from Haute Savoie made with the later part of the cows' milking which has the higher fat content. It is shaped like a wider and thinner Camembert with a soft supple centre and a deep orange to red-coloured washed rind. It is packed between very thin wooden discs and does not go runny like Camembert. It has a pleasant buttery flavour with a fruit finish when young but becomes bitter when old. Protected by an appellation d'origine.

rebong *Indonesia, Malaysia* Bamboo shoot

receipt An old English word for recipe

reçel *Turkey* Jam

recette *France* Recipe

réchaud *France* Hot plate or small stove used at the table

rechauffé(e) *France* Made of food already cooked and then reheated, such as rissoles, croquettes, hash, cottage pie, etc.

rechauffer *France* To reheat, to warm up

recheado *Portugal* **1.** Stuffed **2.** Stuffing

recheio *Portugal* Stuffing, filling

recipe The list of ingredients with quantities and the instructions for making a dish

recommended daily intake The amounts of vitamins, minerals and other micro-nutrients (sometimes fat, fibre, carbohydrate and protein) that the government recommends people take in their food or otherwise every day. They tend to be set so as to avoid ill health rather than to promote optimum health and are not related to body weight, age, physical activity, type of work, state of health, etc. Most can be exceeded with safety. The amount of vitamins and some micro-nutrients that remain in food depends on its age, storage conditions and cooking methods. Abbreviation **RDI**

reconstitute, to To add back liquid, usually water, to dried foods so as to restore them to some semblance of their original state

recovery time The time it takes for a cooking appliance (deep fat fryer, oven, blanching liquor, etc.) to return to the required temperature for another batch of food after a batch of cooked food has been removed from it

rectifier (l'assaisonnement) *France* To adjust the seasoning according to taste

recuit *Catalonia* Curdled sheep's or cows' milk served in a small pot

red 2G A synthetic red food dye, E128, used for sausages. Licensed for use in the UK but not generally in the EU.

red banana *United States* A short stumpy banana with a purplish red skin and a very sweet tasting flesh

red bean curd See **bean curd cheese**

red beans and rice *United States* A Louisiana dish of red kidney beans cooked with a ham hock and served over rice

red bean sauce A Chinese paste made from fermented soya beans used as a condiment or flavouring

red braising See **red cooking**

red bream See **bream**

red cabbage A cabbage, *Brassica oleracea* var. *capitata*, with red to purple leaves and a round firm head, generally available in autumn and winter, often casseroled with sugar, sultanas and vinegar, or pickled.

red caviar Ketovaia

Red Cheshire A deep orange-coloured Cheshire cheese dyed with annatto

red chick pea Pigeon pea

red chicory A low growing perennial chicory, *Cichorium intybus* var. *foliosum*, grown as an annual. It has slightly bitter red leaves with white veins and a compact heart rather like a loose red cabbage. Used in salads and as a garnish. Also called **radicchio**, **red-leaved chicory**

red cooking A Chinese technique of cooking meat by first browning it then slow cooking it in a tightly sealed casserole with dark soy sauce, sherry, sugar and spices which turns the meat a dark reddish brown colour. Also called **red braising**, **red stewing**

red crab *United States* A bright red crab, *Geryon quinquedens*, up to 15 cm across found in deep water along the eastern coast of North America. It has thin legs and a good flavour.

redcurrant A small red fruit similar to the black currant but more acid and from a more hardy bush *Ribes sativum*. Usually cooked for jams, jellies and sauces.

redcurrant and horseradish sauce *United Kingdom* Port wine reduced with seasoning, ground nutmeg and cinnamon, mixed with redcurrant jelly and finely grated horseradish. Served cold.

redcurrant jelly This jelly used in many sauces is made from redcurrants, boiled with a little water until the skins break, strained, sugar equal in weight to the juice added and all boiled for 3 to 4 minutes to produce a setting jelly

redcurrant sauce As **apricot sauce**, but made with redcurrants

red curry *Sri Lanka* An intensely hot curry coloured a deep red from the number of red chillies used

red curry paste *Thailand* A paste used for beef and similar curries made from dry-fried shallots and garlic, lemon grass, coriander seeds and cumin seeds, blended with black peppercorns, dried red chillies, coriander root, galangal, lime peel, trassi and salt

red date Jujube

red deer A species of deer, *Cervus elaphus*, found in Scotland. The meat is inferior to that from roe deer.

reddiker *Norway* Radishes

redeye gravy *United States* The gravy made by deglazing the dish in which ham is baked or roasted with water or coffee plus a little brown sugar

redfish 1. A short thick-bodied orange-red deep-sea fish of the genus *Sebastes*, especially *S marinus* and *S. viviparus*, up to 25 cm long and found in the North Atlantic. The delicately flavoured flesh is white and flaky and the fish may be cooked in any way. Also called **ocean perch**, **Norway haddock**, **red perch 2.** *Australia* A relatively small fish, *Centroberyx affinis*, with a deep, short body and large eyes which is fished both commercially and recreationally. They are predominantly red, deepest on top and fading towards the belly. They have a moist, finely flaked flesh with a good flavour and are cooked only as skinned fillets. They can be fried, grilled or baked, the latter requiring constant basting. Also called **nannygai**, **goatfish**

red flannel hash *United States* Chopped onions, bacon, corned beef and cooked beetroot, often the leftovers from New England boiled dinner seasoned and mixed with mashed potatoes, shallow-fried on both sides and served in wedges with fried or poached eggs

red garoupa See **garoupa**

red girl wine *China* The classic Chinese rice wine made from a cooked glutinous rice and millet mash fermented with yeast, often aged for up to 10 years and possibly to 100 years. The younger wines are used in Chinese cooking in the same way that wines, fortified wines and brandy are used in the west. (NOTE: So called because a bottle would be laid down on the birth of a girl in anticipation of her marriage.)

red gram Pigeon pea

red grouse The finest flavoured of the grouse family, *Lagopus lagopus scoticus*, is found only in the UK and Ireland. It is a sub species of the willow grouse, which is ruddy brown and does not go white in winter. Also called **Scottish grouse**

red gurnard A variety of gurnard, *Trigla pini*, sometimes confused with red mullet. Red gurnard does not have long feelers (barbels) hanging from the underside of the mouth as does red mullet. See also **gurnard**

redhead duck *United States* A highly prized wild duck, *Nyroca americana*, shot for the table

red herring Whole herring cured in brine for several weeks then smoked until a mahogany colour. Must be desalted by soaking before eating. Usually used as part of a mixed hors d'oeuvres or as decoration for egg-based canapés. Also called **hard smoked herring**

red kidney bean The reddish brown French bean shaped like a kidney used in chilli con carne and other dishes. Must be boiled vigorously to destroy toxins. Often sold precooked in cans. Also called **Mexican bean**, **chilli bean**

red-leaved chicory See **red chicory**

red-legged partridge The French native partridge, *Alectoris rufa,* distributed from central UK to Spain. It is plumper but less tasty than the grey-legged. Roast as grey-legged.

Red Leicester See **Leicester cheese**

red lollo lettuce Lollo rosso

red mash Fermented red rice

red meat Meat which is red in appearance in its raw state as opposed to the paler types such as chicken, veal, rabbit, etc.

red miso Inaka-miso

red mullet A small crimson to dull pink seawater fish of the genus *Mullidae*, especially *Mullus surmuletus* (red) and *M. barbatus* (pink), not related to the grey mullet. It has a delicate flavour and is generally cooked whole with its liver which is considered a prized delicacy. It can be hung for 24 hours to give it a gamey flavour. It can weigh up to 1 kg but is usually caught much smaller. Also called **goatfish**, **golden mullet**

red mustard A prepared mustard made with a mixture of whole mustard seeds and crushed dried red chillies

red octopus A small octopus, *Eledone moschata*, more tender than the curled octopus but with a musky flavour

red onion 1. Italian red onion **2.** A small red skinned onion similar to a shallot used in Asian cooking and pickled in China

red palm oil *Central Africa* Unrefined palm oil which has a red colour due to naturally occurring carotenoids. It is said to have more than 15 times the carotenoids in carrots on a weight for weight basis. See also **palm oil**

red pepper 1. A general term for dried and ground red capsicums such as cayenne and chilli peppers or paprika **2.** Red sweet peppers

red perch Redfish

red porgy See **porgy**

red pork Char siu

red pottage *Scotland* A purée soup made with soaked haricot beans, onions, tomatoes and celery sweated in butter then simmered in stock for 3 hours. A beetroot is added to colour the soup. The soup is then liquidized, sieved, reheated and garnished with chopped parsley.

red prawn See **crevette rose du large**

red raripila spearmint A type of spearmint, *Mentha raripila rubra*, with pointed dark green leaves, a sweet spearmint flavour and purple stems

red-red *West Africa* A Ghanaian dish of dried cow peas or black-eyed beans soaked in water, skins and all debris removed, then boiled with just sufficient water to cook them. They are then mixed with onions and tomatoes fried in red palm oil together with red pepper. Reconstituted dried shrimps or fish or smoked fish may be added and simmered with a little extra water. Often served with **kelewele**.

red rice 1. Fermented red rice **2.** An inferior dull reddish strain of rice, *Oryza glaberrima*, grown in many parts of Asia for processing. Not generally used in cooking.

red salad bowl lettuce Oak leaf lettuce

red salmon The flesh of the sockeye salmon, usually canned

red sauce *United States* Any Italian type of tomato sauce

red sea bream A type of **sea bream** eaten raw in Japan as sushi. Also called **tai**, **dai**

red seedless watermelon *United States* A spherical (diameter 30 cm) water melon with no seeds

red shiso The leaves of the red variety of **shiso** used to colour and flavour umeboshi as well as being used as a vegetable

red snapper A seawater fish, *Lutjanus campechanis*, of the snapper family with a distinctive red skin and fine white flesh, weighing between 0.5 and 2 kg. Baked, grilled, deep-fried or stir-fried. Often used in Eastern dishes.

red sorrel Jamaica flower

red stewing See **red cooking**

red top milk *United Kingdom* Homogenized whole milk containing 3.8% butterfat on average. The cream does not separate out.

reduce, to To boil a liquid so as to remove water and thus thicken the liquid and intensify the flavour. Often done during sauce making with wine and stock.

reduced-fat EU guidelines (which do not have the force of law) state that this means the foodstuff contains less than 25% of the fat normally found in the product

reduction milling The stage in the conversion of grain to flour where the endosperm is ground from semolina size particles to flour after the preceding bran separation

reduction sauce Any sauce based on vinegar, wine or stock concentrated by boiling to give an intense flavour and sometimes a pouring consistency

réduire *France* To reduce a liquid by boiling

red vinegar A slightly salty clear pale red vinegar made in China. Used as a condiment and added to soups to give them a lift.

red wine court bouillon Equal quantities of red wine and water with 120g each of onion and carrot and 12 g of salt per litre together with parsley stalks, a little thyme and bay leaf and peppercorns added. Used for trout and carp.

red wine sauce See **vin rouge, sauce**

ree *Netherlands* Roe deer

reebout *Netherlands* Haunch of venison

reedmace Bulrush millet

refined microcrystalline wax See **E907**

refined oil Culinary oil which has been treated to remove flavouring and other compounds which oxidize easily, which would reduce its shelf life and would depress the maximum temperature at which it could be used

refogado *Portugal* An onion and tomato sauce

Réforme, à la *France* In the Reform Club's style, i.e. garnished with strips of carrot, ham and gherkin and white of egg, and slices of mushrooms and truffles

Réforme, sauce *England, France* A **mirepoix** of carrot, onion, celery, bay leaf and thyme, fried in butter, fat drained off, vinegar and crushed peppercorns added and reduced, **demi-glace** added, simmered and skimmed, redcurrant jelly added, strained through a chinois and garnished with a **julienne** of cooked beetroot, hard-boiled egg white, gherkin, mushroom, truffle and tongue. Served with lamb cutlets.

refresh, to 1. To immerse blanched vegetables in fast running cold water so as to cool them quickly and prevent further cooking **2.** To freshen up herbs, leaves and vegetables by immersing them in cold water.

Any plant cells which have lost water and crispness will replace some of it.

refreshments Light food and drink taken between meals or on some informal occasions

refried beans *United States* Frijoles refritos

refrigerator A cooled sealed storage box, usually with shelves and a front opening door which maintains food at a preset temperature between 1 and 6°C

refrigerator cookies *United States* Biscuits prepared and baked as needed by slicing them from an uncooked roll of thick biscuit dough usually wrapped or cased in plastic and kept in the refrigerator

refroidir *France* To refresh, cool, chill

regaliz *Spain* Liquorice

regattakotlett *Sweden* Pork chops rubbed with seasoning and paprika, browned in butter, reserved, chopped onion fried in the same pan until golden, **tomato concassée**, a bayleaf and thyme added, all reduced, chops added back and simmered until cooked (NOTE: Literally 'yachtsman's chop'.)

Regenbogenforelle *Germany* Rainbow trout

regenboog forel *Netherlands* Rainbow trout

régence, sauce *France* For meat, a **mirepoix** sweated in butter with a reduction of white wine mixed with **demi-glace** sauce and truffle essence, simmered and strained. For fish and poultry, sauce normande with a reduction of white wine, mushroom and truffle trimmings, strained and finished with truffle essence.

Regenpfeifer *Germany* Plover

Regensburger *Germany* Short sausages from Bavaria rather like Frankfurters, made from ground pork and beef with embedded small pieces of bacon. Boiled before consumption. May be eaten hot or cold.

regina in porchetta *Italy* Carp from Umbria, stuffed and baked in a wood burning stove

réglisse *France* Liquorice

regular milled white rice *United States* American long-grain rice

regulo See **gas mark**

Reh *Germany* Deer

Rehbraten *Germany* Roast venison

Rehrücken *Germany* 1. Saddle of venison 2. A long thin chocolate cake made with egg yolks, sugar, ground hazelnuts and breadcrumbs by the creaming method, flavoured with vanilla and grated chocolate and into which the stiffly beaten egg whites are folded and all baked at 175°C (NOTE: So called because of its resemblance to a loin of venison.)

Rehrücken mit Rahmsauce *Germany* Saddle of venison, larded, marinated in wine, cloves, juniper berries, bay leaves, peppercorns and grated nutmeg for a day, browned in lard with aromatic vegetables, covered with reduced marinade and baked in the oven. Served with noodles, cranberry sauce and poached pears with a sauce of reduced cooking liquor and cream.

Rehrücken mit Schlag *Germany* A pastry (resembling a saddle of venison) with almonds, chocolate and whipped cream

Rehschnitzel *Germany* Venison cutlets

rehydrate, to To add back the water lost by dehydration either by soaking or cooking in water

Reibeküchen *Germany* Grated potato pancakes

reindeer meat *Scandinavia* The meat of reindeer, usually smoked and salted

reine, à la *France* Made from chicken, especially coated with an allemande or chicken velouté sauce and garnished with mushrooms and sliced truffles

reine, crème *France* Chicken soup

reine-claude *France* A variety of greengage very popular in France

reinette grise *France* Russet apple

reinsdyr *Norway* Reindeer

reinsdyrpølse *Norway* A spiced reindeer meat sausage

reinsdyrstek *Norway* Reindeer steak

Reis *Germany* Rice

Reisauflauf *Germany* Rice pudding

Reispapier *Germany* Rice paper

Reiswurstchen *Austria* A forcemeat of minced and cooked veal mixed with cold boiled rice, bound with egg, wrapped in rice paper, panéed and fried. Used in soups.

rejemad *Denmark* The piles of tiny shrimps put on Danish open sandwiches

rejer *Denmark* Shrimps

rekening *Netherlands* The bill

reker *Norway* Shrimps

relative density See **specific gravity**

relative humidity The amount of water vapour in air as a percentage of the total amount the air could hold at the same temperature and pressure. If liquid water is present as fog or steam then the relative humidity will be 100%. At 100% relative humidity no evaporation of sweat or water can take place. Abbreviation **RH**

relevé *France* Originally the second meat course of a formal dinner in the days when there were many courses, usually a large joint or bird. Nowadays the course between the fish and entrée or the soup and entrée if no fish course, in a formal meal.

relevée, sauce *France* Ketchup

religieuse *France* A cooked choux pastry sphere filled with whipped cream, topped with a smaller choux pastry sphere and coated with coffee or chocolate icing so as to resemble the rear view of a nun

religious food laws Some religions have particular food prohibitions in particular; Buddhism, usually vegetarian; Hinduism, complex laws depending on caste, but generally no beef; Jainism, strict vegetarian with no eggs but dairy products allowed; Judaism, no horse or pig, seafood must have fins and scales, unfertilized eggs only, dairy products and meat must not be mixed and animals are examined for blemishes, slaughtered and prepared by licensed persons; Islam, no pork or alcohol, special slaughter of animal and no gold or silver plate; Sikh, Muslim or Jewish slaughter not allowed

relish *United States* Pickles and highly seasoned sauce-like condiments

rellenos *Spain* 1. Stuffed 2. Stuffing

remis *Malaysia* Surf clam

remolacha *Spain* Beetroot

Remoudou *Belgium* A strong-flavoured, soft, cows' milk cheese matured for 3 months and made in 200 g loaves. The brownish orange rind has a stronger smell than the centre.

remoulade, sauce *England, France* Tartare sauce plus anchovy essence. Served with fried fish.

remouladsås *Sweden* Remoulade sauce usually served with panéed and fried plaice

rempah *Indonesia, Malaysia* A spicy paste made by grinding, pounding or processing shallots, garlic and some or all of lemon grass, coriander, cumin, turmeric, candlenut, cinnamon, ginger, galangal, chillies, peppercorns, sugar and salt. Sometimes fried in oil. Used for flavouring curries or to season meat for satays.

rendang *Indonesia* A coconut-based highly flavoured curry cooked until all the liquid is absorbed

rendang chicken Seasoned and browned chicken pieces mixed with a cooking liquor made from thick coconut milk simmered with a fried paste of spring onions, garlic and chillies together with lemon grass, lime leaves, tamarind, turmeric and seasoning and simmered until tender

render, to To heat animal fat tissues so that the fat content is released and can be separated from the remaining tissue. Usually done in a heavy pan over a low heat or in the oven at 150°C.

rene *Italy* Kidney

Reneklode *Germany* A type of greengage. See also **reine-claude**

Renette *Germany* Rennet

renkon *Japan* Lotus

renne *France* Reindeer

rennet A mixture of enzymes extracted from the stomachs of suckling animals such as calves, kids and lambs, but usually from the fourth stomach of the unweaned calf. Is is used to curdle milk as the first stage in cheese making. Vegetarian rennets are now made using microorganisms. Some extracts of plants, especially cardoon, are used for the same purpose.

rennin The main protease enzyme in rennet

renstek *Sweden* Roast reindeer

renversé(e) *France* Past participle of *renverser*, 'to turn out or demould'

repápalos *Spain* Sweet bread fritters. Eggs mixed with soft breadcrumbs fried in spoonfuls in olive oil, then placed in a pan with orange peel, cinnamon, sugar and milk, simmered for 15 minutes and allowed to rest for 15 hours. Served chilled.

repas *France* Meal

repasser *France* To strain or pass through a sieve a second time

repast The Old English term for meal

repollo *Spain* Cabbage

repollo relleno *South America* A speciality of Bolivia consisting of a hollowed out cabbage stuffed with a meat mixture and simmered in stock. Served with rice.

requeijão 1. *Portugal* A cheese similar to Ricotta made from the whey of ewes' milk, often enriched with butter and cream. It is white, smooth and has a fresh taste. Sold in straw baskets and served on fig or cabbage leaves. 2. *Brazil* A soft cooked-curd cows' milk cheese made with a lactic starter. The hot, washed and salted curd is placed in oblong or cylindrical moulds to make 500 g cheeses.

requin marteau *France* Hammerhead shark

réserver *France* To put aside to be used later in the same recipe

resin Solid exudate from plants and trees used to seal wounds in the bark or skin and prevent infection. Some such as asafoetida, mastic and pine resin are used as flavourings.

restaurant A place where complete meals are sold for consumption on the premises

resurrection pie *England* Cooked vegetables layered alternately with a cheese sauce flavoured with mustard, each vegetable layer being of a different kind. After all vegetable types are used up the pie is finally covered with more sauce, gratinated with cheese and browned in the oven at 200°C.

rete *Italy* Pig's caul

reticella *Italy* Pig's caul

retinol See **vitamin A**

retort, to To treat food by heating to 121°C in order to kill all microorganisms. Usually used for canned foods.

Rettich *Germany* Radish

reuben *United States* A corned beef and Swiss cheese sandwich dressed with mayonnaise topped with sauerkraut and grilled

revbensspjäll *Sweden* Spare ribs

Réveillon *France* The festive meal held in France after midnight mass on Christmas Eve and on New Year's Eve. Usually includes traditional foods according to region, often **boudin noir**.

reven *Southwest Asia* Rhubarb, often made into a sweet drink flavoured with lemon and mint in Uzbekistan and Kazakhstan

revenir, faire *France* Faire revenir

revuelto de triguero *Spain* An Estremaduran dish consisting of wild asparagus tips mixed with ham, garlic, cumin and bay, fried in olive oil then beaten eggs added and gently scrambled

revythia soupa *Greece* A meatless chick pea soup made from chick peas parboiled for 15 minutes and drained, boiled in water until tender and a few reserved, a sauté of onions, carrots, garlic, tomato purée and **tomato concassée** added to the chick peas and water, all puréed, seasoned and finished with lemon juice, chopped parsley and the reserved chick peas

rghayif *North Africa* Various types of dough folded and interleaved with butter or oil to give a flaky texture when cooked, sometimes filled with **khli'** and onions or served plain with sugar or honey

rghayif el mila *North Africa* An egg-enriched rghayif dough used on celebratory occasions in Morocco

Rhabarber *Germany* Rhubarb

Rheinlachs *Germany* Rhine salmon

Rheinsalm *Germany* Rhine salmon

Rheum x cultorum *Botanical name* Rhubarb

Rhizopus oligosporus The fungal organism used in the manufacture of tempeh. It also has the beneficial effect of removing the bean flavour.

Rhode Island johnny cake *United States* Johnny cake

rhodoxanthin See **E161(f)**

rhubarb A deep-rooted perennial plant, *Rheum x cultorum*, which produces thick pink to red stems at ground level each topped with a large green leaf. The stems are stewed with sugar and used as a dessert, in pies, crumbles, fools, etc. and for jam making. Early rhubarb is forced by excluding light and is the most tender. The leaves are poisonous.

rhubarbe *France* Rhubarb

rhum *France* Rum

Rhus coriaria *Botanical name* Sumac

riatto *Italy* Reheated

rib That part of the carcass of an animal comprising the vertebrae and associated muscles plus a length of attached rib bone equal in length to twice the diameter of the main muscle or less in the case of large animals. It is usually divided along the spinal column and may be cut into single rib portions (cutlets, etc.) or 3 or more ribs (rib roasts).

ribbe *Norway* Pork chops from the rib

ribbon cheese Parenica

ribbon stage The stage at which whipped eggs or cream become just stiff enough to form ribbons when dropped from a spoon

riberry *Australia* The small pink to purple, pear-shaped fruit of various trees of the genus *Sysygium*, known by the indigenous population as lilly pilly trees. They have an aromatic flavour with cinnamon and clove notes and can be eaten fresh or cooked as a dessert, in fruit salads, in baking or to make sauces for use with meat. They become pale pink when cooked.

ribes *Italy* Redcurrants

ribes comune *Italy* Redcurrant

ribes nero *Italy* Black currant

Ribes nigrum *Botanical name* Blackcurrant

Ribes sativum *Botanical name* Redcurrants and whitecurrants

Ribes uva-crispa *Botanical name* Gooseberry

rib of beef *United States* The wing, fore and middle ribs of beef extending about half way down the animal to the short plate. Often cut into steaks, each including one rib bone. See also **ribs of beef**

riboflavin Vitamin B2, essential for health, also used as an orange food colouring E101

riboflavin-5' phosphate See **E101**

ribollita *Italy* A cabbage and bean soup from Tuscany which is reboiled *(ribollita)* each day and thickened with bread

ribs of beef Half of the ribs and the vertebrae together with associated muscle from a side of beef. In total there are 13 which are numbered from the head end. The English cuts are 1 and 2 **chuck ribs**, 3 to 6 **middle ribs**, 7 to 10 **fore ribs** and 11 to 13 **wing ribs**.

rib steak *United States* A steak cut from the rib one rib thick and including the outer layer of fat. May be on or off the bone.

ricciarelli *Italy* Almond biscuits

riccio di mare *Italy* Sea urchin

ricciola *Italy* Amberjack, the fish

ricciolina *Italy* Curly endive

ricciolini *Italy* Pasta curls

ricco *Italy* (of food) Rich

rice A cereal grain, *Oryza sativa*, cultivated in China since 6000 BC, grown extensively in warm moist climates and forming the principal energy source for a major part of the world's population. There are thousands of different varieties but all have a high starch content and are between 3 and 6 mm long and about 2 mm in diameter. Varieties include long-grain, short-grain, brown, white, glutinous, pudding, polished, prefluffed, Arborio, basmati, Carolina, fragrant, jasmine, Patna and Thai.

rice, to To force a semi-solid such as puréed potato through a perforated plate or mesh so as to form thin fragile strands

rice bean A small yellow to deep red dried bean, *Phaseolus canceratus*, from Southeast Asia, grown in the Nepal and Assam and similar in size to the adzuki bean but less rounded, with a larger hilum running the length of the bean and crinkly edges. Said to taste like rice when cooked and reputed to have the highest calcium content of all beans.

rice bubbles *Australia* Rice crispies

rice cakes *Wales* Cooked rice, flour, milk and egg (5:5:3:1) mixed with 4 tbsp of melted butter and 8 tsp of baking powder per kg of flour to form a thick batter. Large tablespoonfuls of the mixture are dropped onto a well greased griddle or thick frying pan and cooked for 4 minutes a side until golden brown. Served hot with a sweet sauce or syrup. Also called **teisen reis**

rice crispies *United Kingdom* Steamed cooked rice, put under reduced pressure, so that the internal water expands puffing up the rice grain to about three times its size, then dried and browned slightly

rice dough Rice flour mixed with boiling or cold water to make a dough which is used for wrappers, cakes or dumplings. Boiling water makes a translucent wrapper for won ton.

rice flakes Rice grain steamed or softened by partial cooking and flattened through rollers, may be cooked or eaten uncooked in e.g. muesli. Also called **flaked rice**

rice flour Ground polished rice which is mainly starch with very little gluten. Used in the same way as corn flour and for noodles, sweets and short pastry.

rice gruel Congee

rice noodles Noodles made with rice flour in very long strands and of varying thicknesses and widths. Very common in Vietnam. Usually folded into a compact bundle. When deep-fried they puff up. Also called **rice stick noodles**

rice paper A very thin edible white paper made from the pith of a small tree, *Tetrapanax papyriferum*, grown in Taiwan. It is used to line baking trays used for sticky baked goods such as macaroons and similar, and does not need greasing. Usually sticks to the base of the biscuit or cake.

rice pudding *United Kingdom* Short-grain rice covered with sweetened milk and baked slowly in the oven in a covered dish. Sultanas or other dried fruit may be added and the top is usually sprinkled with grated nutmeg. Proportions may be adjusted to give thin or stiff finished results and the lid left off towards the end to give a crisp top.

ricer An implement rather like a large garlic press in which boiled potatoes are forced through fine holes. Used to produce superfine mashed potatoes.

rice ribbon noodles Flat noodles about 1 cm wide made from a thin rice flour and water dough which is cooked in thin sheets to a firm jelly-like texture, brushed with oil and cut into strips to be sold as fresh noodles in most Chinese communities in Southeast Asia. The same dough cut in 20 cm squares is used when filled with meat or shrimps as **dim sum**.

rice soup Congee

rice stick noodles See **rice noodles**

rice vermicelli Very thin rice noodles which only require softening in hot water, or they may be deep-fried in the dried state

rice vinegar Vinegar made by oxidizing the alcoholic beer or wine made from fermented rice starch. There are several varieties in use in Asia. See also **black vinegar**, **red vinegar**, **sweet vinegar**

rice wine An alcoholic liquid made by fermenting a cooked ground rice mash. It has a sherry-like taste and is both used as a drink and as a cooking liquid. Clear and amber-coloured varieties are available. See also **red girl wine**, **sake**

rich Very sweet, high in fat, oil or cream content or highly seasoned

rich cakes See **creamed cakes**

riche, sauce *France* Sauce diplomate finished with truffle essence and finely diced black truffles

richelieu *France* A layer cake with apricot glaze and frangipane cream between the layers, the whole iced with a maraschino-flavoured fondant and decorated with angelica strips

richelieu, à la *France* In the Duc de Richelieu's style, i.e. garnished with stuffed tomatoes, mushrooms, potatoes and braised lettuce. Used especially of roasts.

Ricotta *Italy* A soft cows' or ewes' milk cheese made from whey which may be enriched with milk or cream. The whey is heated with citric or tartaric acid to cause the proteins to coagulate. These are separated off, drained, usually in basin-shaped baskets and demoulded. Used widely in Italian cooking or may be eaten as a dessert with fruit, chopped nuts, chocolate or instant coffee. May be matured and hardened for grating. Contains 50 to 60% water, 15% fat, 23 to 26% protein, mainly albumen, and 3% lactose. Not usually salted.

Ricotta Piemontese *Italy* Ricotta made from cows milk whey enriched with 10 to 20% milk

Ricotta Romana *Italy* Ricotta made with the whey left over from making **Pecorino Romano**

Ricotta salata moliterna *Italy* A semi-hard cooked curd cheese made from the whey of ewes' milk heated to 90°C to precipitate soluble proteins. The filtered curd is salted and formed into cylinders. It may be eaten young as a dessert cheese or ripened for grating.

Ridderost *Norway, Sweden* A semi-hard, deep yellow, cows' milk cheese similar to Saint-Paulin with an orange rind and slightly nutty flavour, surface-ripened for 5 to 6 weeks. Suitable for dessert and as a melting cheese.

ridge cucumber An outdoor cucumber often with a grooved, indented or knobbly skin, usually smaller than long cucumbers. They require fertilization. (NOTE: So called because they used to be planted on ridges in the open field)

ridged sand clam A clam which is found in Southeast Asia on beaches with surf and strong tidal currents

Riebisel *Germany* Redcurrant

riekko *Finland* Ptarmigan (white or willow)

rigaglie *Italy* Giblets

Rigatello *Italy* A hard scalded-curd cows' milk cheese made in cylinders (up to 3 kg). The paste is hard, dense with a few cracks and strong-tasting. Eaten for dessert or used for cooking. See also **Canestrato**

rigato *Italy* **1.** A semi-hard scalded-curd Sicilian cheese. See also **Canestrato 2.** Ridged as applied to pasta shapes

rigatoni A large ridged macaroni cut in pieces about 5 cm long and 1 cm in diameter

rigg Dogfish

Rigottes *France* A soft surface-ripened goats' milk cheese from the Ardèche with a delicately flavoured velvety paste made in 60 g cylinders. Contains 45% water, 22% fat ad 24% protein.

riisi *Finland* Rice

riisivanukas *Finland* Rice pudding

rijst *Netherlands* Rice

rijsttafel *Netherlands* An Indonesian inspired meal of many contrasting savoury dishes each accompanied by rice or noodles

riklingur *Iceland* An air-dried fish (**hardfiskur**) made from halibut or catfish

rillettes *France* A rich meat paste made by simmering herbs and pork or goose meat in its own fat until tender then pounding it to a smooth texture

rillons Crisply fried or grilled pieces of cooked pork or goose preserved in fat

rim *Portugal* See **kidney**

rimestato *Italy* Stirred or scrambled

rimmad skinka *Sweden* Salted ham

rimmat kött *Sweden* Salt meat

rind The outer skin of bacon, ham, pork, cheese, and some fruits and vegetables

Rind *Germany* Beef

Rinderbraten *Germany* Roast beef

Rinderbrust *Germany* Brisket of beef

Rinderleber *Germany* Ox liver

Rindermark *Germany* Beef marrow

Rindfleisch *Germany* Beef

Rindfleischkochwurst *Germany* A sausage made from a mixture of 75% lean beef and 25% pork fat with saltpetre and seasoning, packed into casings, linked in pairs and air-dried for 2 days. Boiled before serving.

Rindfleischwurst *Germany* A sausage filled with a mixture of minced lean beef, lean pork, bacon fat, saltpetre and seasoning, flavoured with garlic and ground cloves. Simmered for an hour before serving.

Rindkraftfleisch *Germany* Corned beef

Rindsrouladen *Germany* Beef olives

ring doughnut The ring form of the **doughnut**

Ringelblume *Germany* Marigold

ring mould A round mould in the shape of a half torus so that when the food is demoulded it forms a round ring on the plate.

Used for cakes, desserts, jellies, savoury custards, etc. Also called **border mould**

ring-neck dove *United States* A highly prized wild duck, *Aythya collaris*, shot for the table

riñones *Spain* Kidneys

riñones a la española *Spain* Kidneys sautéed with onions, tomatoes and sweet peppers

Rio red A highly pigmented grapefruit variety which was produced by inducing mutations using ionizing radiation

ripa *Sweden* Grouse

ripe Fully developed or matured and ready for eating, usually used of fruits, vegetables and cheese

ripen, to To allow time for fruit, vegetables and cheese to become ripe. Fruit may be ripened more quickly by putting it in a plastic bag with a ripe tomato.

ripening lamp An ultraviolet lamp used to ripen fruit and vegetables quickly

Ripennstück *Germany* Beef ribs

ripe tart *England* A butter-based shortcrust pastry brought together with egg yolk and water, baked blind in a flan tin, lined with stoned cherries, filled with an egg, icing sugar and ground almond mixture and baked at 170°C until golden brown

ripiddu nivicatu *Italy* A Sicilian dish of rice cooked with cuttlefish and their ink, put in a heap and topped with Ricotta cheese and tomato sauce so as to resemble Mount Etna

ripieno *Italy* Stuffed with or stuffing

Rippchen *Germany* Rib chops, cutlets usually of smoked pork

Rippe *Germany* Rib of meat

Rippenbraten *Germany* Roast loin

Rippenspeer *Germany* Spareribs of pork

ripple ribbon tube A nozzle for a piping bag that produces a ribbed ribbon shape

ris 1. *France* Sweetbreads, esp of veal, ris de veau or lamb, ris d'agneau **2.** *Denmark, Norway, Sweden* Rice

ris à l'amande *Denmark* Rice pudding mixed with whipped cream and chopped almonds served with cherry sauce

ris d'agneau *France* Lamb sweetbreads

ris de veau *France* Veal sweetbreads

rise, to To allow a yeast dough to increase in size by the production of bubbles of carbon dioxide within it or a baked dish or cake to similarly increase in size by the action of heat on air bubbles entrapped in the mix, e.g. soufflés, or the production of carbon dioxide by reactions of chemical raising agents. See also **prove, to**, **lift**

risengrød *Denmark* A sweetened rice soup or porridge sprinkled with cinnamon and topped with butter served at Christmas before the main course of the meal. The person who receives the one almond in the mixture receives a present.

risengrynsklatter *Denmark* Rice fritters

risengrynslapper *Norway* Rice flour pancakes

risetto *Italy* Croquettes made with tiny anchovies and sardines

risgrøt *Norway* Rice pudding

risgryn *Sweden* Rice

risgrynsgröt *Sweden* Rice pudding

risi e bisi *Italy* A mixture of cooked rice and peas in a small amount of thick stock sprinkled with grated Parmesan cheese

riso *Italy* Rice

riso al forno *Italy* A meat sauce with rice baked in the oven

riso al forno in peverada alla rovigina *Italy* Rice baked with chicken livers, mushrooms and anchovies

riso alla canavesana *Italy* Rice boiled in meat broth and finished with Fontina, Grana and Emmental cheeses

riso alla milanese *Italy* Rice boiled in meat broth with saffron and served with butter and cheese

riso alla piemontese *Italy* Rice with a chicken or meat sauce

riso alla ristori *Italy* Rice with cabbage, bacon and sausage

riso alla siciliana *Italy* Rice with aubergines, tomato, parsley and basil, gratinated with cheese and baked

riso commune *Italy* The cheapest rice

risoles *Mexico* Fritters

riso ricco *Italy* Boiled rice with a cream and cheese sauce

risotto *Italy* A classic Italian dish best made with arborio or carnaroli rice fried in butter and/or olive oil with chopped onion and any other flavouring elements (cooked chicken, shellfish, vegetables, etc.), a splash of white wine added over the heat until absorbed, then hot stock added progressively with stirring until no more can be absorbed and the dish is moist and creamy. May be finished with grated Parmesan cheese and butter.

risotto alla certosina *Italy* Risotto with prawns, mushrooms, peas and frogs' legs

risotto alla chioggiotta *Italy* A risotto from Chioggia with gobies (fish), white wine and Parmesan cheese

risotto alla milanese *Italy* A risotto made with chopped onions, flavoured with saffron and grated Parmesan cheese only. Served by itself or as an accompaniment to osso bucco.

risotto alla monzese *Italy* Risotto with sausages and tomato sauce

risotto alla toscana *Italy* Risotto with beef, calves' kidney and liver and tomatoes

risotto al salto *Italy* Cooked risotto formed into a thick round and fried

risotto kalamara *Balkans* A risotto flavoured with chopped squid, coloured with the ink from the squid and sprinkled with grated Parmesan cheese

risotto polesano *Italy* Risotto with eel, mullet and bass

rissole 1. *United Kingdom* A small shaped patty or roll of minced meat bound with mashed potatoes or similar vegetarian mixtures, panéed and fried **2.** *France* A small sweet or savoury filled (puff) pastry turnover usually deep-fried and served with a sauce

rissolé(e) *France* **1.** Baked or fried until brown; past participle of *rissoler*, 'to brown' **2.** Pork crackling

ristet *Norway* Grilled, fried or roasted

ristet brød *Denmark, Norway* Toast

ristet loff *Norway* Toast

ristretto *Italy* Reduced, concentrated, of stock, sauce and soup

river trout Brown trout

rivierkreeft *Netherlands* Freshwater crayfish

riz *France* Rice

riz, au *France* Served with rice

riz à l'imperatrice *France* A cold dessert made from a layer of set red jelly in the base of a charlotte mould. Short-grain rice cooked in milk until tender is mixed with sugar, vanilla essence, gelatine, diced angelica and glacé cherries and when near the setting point has stiffly beaten egg whites and whipped cream folded in. This is poured over the jelly and when all set, the dessert is demoulded and turned out on a plate. (NOTE: Created for Empress Eugénie)

riz au blanc *France* Plain boiled rice

riz au gras *France* Fried rice

riz complet *France* Brown rice

rízek *Czech Republic* Schnitzel, pork cutlet

riz et pois colles *Caribbean* Red kidney beans cooked in four times their weight of water and the liquor reserved, a little salt pork and onion finely chopped and fried in hot oil with chives and chilli pepper, this put in the bean water with rice equal to twice the dried weight (or equal to the cooked weight) of the beans, a little butter and simmered for about 20 minutes until the water is absorbed, then mixed with the cooked beans before service

rizi pilafi me garithes *Greece* A pilaff of rice fried with chopped onions and garlic previously sweated in olive oil, simmered with water, **tomato concassée**, sugar, chopped herbs and lemon juice until 5 minutes before the rice is cooked and all liquid absorbed, cooked and peeled prawns added and then all cooked 5 minutes. Feta cheese is added off the heat until melted, and the dish is finished with chopped parsley.

rizi pilafi me mithia As **moules marinière**, but with the chopped onions sweated in olive oil and the shelled mussels mixed with long-grain rice boiled in the mussel cooking liquor for about 12 minutes

riz sauvage *France* Wild rice

rizzared haddock *Scotland* Cleaned unskinned haddock rubbed inside and out with salt and left in a cool place for 3 hours, then floured and grilled for about 8 minutes a side until browned

roach A small red freshwater fish, *Rutilis rutilis*, similar to carp. Rarely eaten because of the numerous bones but if to be eaten then best fried after soaking in salted water.

roast A joint of piece of meat cooked in the oven on a trivet without any cover at around 230 to 250°C

roast, to To cook food in the oven by a combination of convected and radiated heat with good air circulation around it and usually with fat. The object is to brown the surface of the food, to make it crisp and tasty and to just cook the interior to the right degree. Generally used for meats and root vegetables. See also **spit-roast, to**

roast beef *United Kingdom* A classic dish ideally of sirloin, wing rib, fore rib or fillet, but often nowadays of topside or middle rib. Traditionally cooked slightly underdone and served with Yorkshire pudding, horseradish sauce and roast gravy and garnished with watercress.

roasted cheese *Wales* The original Welsh rarebit made by toasting one side of a slab of hard cheese supported on wholemeal bread either in front of the fire or nowadays in the microwave oven. Also called **caws pobi**

roasted cheese canapés *Caribbean* A seasoned cheese and breadcrumb mixture spread over slices of toast, grilled and cut into fancy shapes and served hot

roasted chilli paste See **nam prik pao**

roasted curry paste See **nam prik pao**

roast gravy All fat poured off the roasting pan, deglazed with the appropriate brown stock, simmered, skimmed, strained and seasoned. Served with roast meat. Also called **jus de rôti**

roasting pan A large rectangular metal pan about 8 cm deep

roastit *Scotland* Roast (adj.)

roast pork spice A spice mix containing five-spice powder, sugar, salt, dried soya sauce and ground annatto seed. Rubbed over pork before roasting to give the characteristic Chinese colour and flavour. Also called **char siu powder**

roast potatoes Parboiled potatoes roasted in the oven at a temperature of 230 to 250°C in a tray containing hot fat which is used to baste the potatoes until the surface is crisp and brown

robalo 1. The general name for various pike-like fish, especially *Centropomus undecimalis*, which has a particularly fine-flavoured flesh, caught in tropical seas. Also called **snook 2.** *Spain* Bass, the fish

Robbiola *Italy* Robiola

Robert, sauce *England, France* Chopped onion sweated in butter, vinegar added and reduced completely, **demi-glace** added, simmered, mustard diluted with water and caster sugar added, skimmed and seasoned. Served with fried pork chop.

Robiola *Italy* A soft surface-ripened cows' milk cheese from Lombardy and Piedmont made using a natural or cultured lactic starter and rennet coagulation. The curd is cast in square moulds (20 by 20 cm) to drain, demoulded, cut in 4 pieces, dry-salted or brined and ripened at high humidity. Also called **Robbiola**

Robiolini *Italy* Very small (up to 70 g) soft raw cows' milk cheeses curdled with acid whey and rennet and ripened for 10 to 15 days at high humidity. Also called **formaggini**

robusta coffee A high yielding variety of coffee but with a flavour inferior to that of the arabica variety

rocambole Giant garlic

rocciata di Assisi *Italy* Pastry filled with a mixture of nuts, raisins, chopped dried figs and prunes

rochambeau *France* A garnish for large cuts of meat of carrots in duchesse potato baskets, stuffed lettuce, cauliflower florets à la polonaise and pommes Anna

Rochen *Germany* Skate, the fish

rock bass Mediterranean grouper

rock cakes Small individual cakes made from the basic cake mixture with dried fruit using the rubbing in method. Baked in rough irregularly-shaped mounds.

rock carp A variety of carp with a large head, a thick body, small bones and a delicious rich meat. Popular with the Chinese.

rock cornish A breed of table chicken with a finer flavour than standard breeds. It thrives in free-range and is popular in the USA.

rock crab A crab, *Cancer irroratus,* (Atlantic) or *C. autannarius,* (Pacific) with a yellowish shell marked with purple or brown spots and up to 10 cm wide. They are not particularly well-flavoured and are often eaten after they have shed their shell.

rock dove A wild pigeon, *Columba livia,* treated as wood pigeon

rock eel Dogfish

rocket A slightly bitter, peppery-flavoured plant, *Eruca vesicaria*, which grows wild in cold climates and is cultivated in Italy and Cyprus. The dandelion-shaped leaves are used in salads. Also called **arugula, rokko, salad rocket, Mediterranean rocket, erugala, roquette)**

rockfish A large group of seawater fish of the genus *Sebastodes* found off rocky coasts in most parts of the world. Generally 30 to 90 cm long weighing 1 to 2.5 kg. The flesh is white to pink turning to white when cooked, and is firm, flaky and mid-oily. May be poached, baked or grilled. One of the more common in the USA is the **striped bass**.

rock herring Shad

rock lobster *United States* The name given for legal reasons to the spiny lobsters which are caught in Australia and shipped in large quantities to the USA. See also **eastern rock lobster, southern rock lobster, western rock lobster**

rock melon Cantaloupe melon

rock partridge Ptarmigan

rock salmon A small shark, *Squalus acanthias*, 2 to 3 kg in weight and up to 60 cm long with a medium oily delicate white flesh. Very widely distributed and commonly served as deep-fried battered fish where the type is not otherwise named. Cooked in any way. Also called **spurdog, Pacific dogfish, spiny dogfish**

rock salt Unrefined salt as mined, used as a heat transfer medium e.g. in baking potatoes and heating oysters, or as a freezing mixture with ice

rock samphire Samphire, *Crithmum maritimum*

rock sole A flat seawater fish, *Lepidopsetta bilineat,a* about 20 cm with a brown to grey skin and a non-oily white flesh. Caught off the west coast of Canada. Also called **roughback**

rock sugar Large brown transparent irregularly-shaped crystals of sugar. See also **lump sugar 3**

Rocky Mountain oyster *United States* Prairie oyster

röd *Sweden* Red

rød *Denmark, Norway* Red

rodaballo *Spain* Turbot

rodaballo menor *Spain* Brill, the fish

rødbeter *Norway* Beetroot

rödbetor *Sweden* Beetroot

rode kool *Netherlands* Red cabbage

rødgrød med fløde *Denmark* Stewed and sweetened summer fruits (berries and currants) thickened with arrowroot. Served cold when set in individual dishes topped with Chantilly cream.

rødgrot *Norway* A dessert made from thickened and sweetened purée of redcurrants and raspberries

rödkål *Sweden* Red cabbage

rødkål 1. *Denmark* Red cabbage cooked with chopped apple and flavoured with caraway seeds. Served with poultry, pork and meatballs. **2.** *Norway* Red cabbage

rodovalho *Portugal* Turbot

rødspætte *Denmark* Plaice

rödspätta *Sweden* Plaice

rödspätta i sardellsås *Sweden* Skinned and gutted whole plaice simmered in a little water with salt and lemon juice until cooked (up to 20 minutes), fish removed and flesh reserved, the cooking liquor made into a velouté sauce and finished with cream and diced fillets of anchovy. The sauce is poured over the fish, gratinated with breadcrumbs and all put into a medium oven and browned.

rödtunga *Sweden* Lemon sole

rödvinssås *Sweden* Red wine sauce made by simmering a well cleaned cod's head in red wine with a bouquet garni for 30 minutes, then straining, seasoning and thickening it with **beurre manié**

roe The egg or sperm of fish or the eggs of shellfish. It can be hard or soft.

roebuck The male roe deer

roebuck sauce A reduction of vinegar with a bouquet garni and a brunoise of onion and raw ham browned in butter, **espagnole sauce** added and simmered 15 minutes, bouquet garni removed and the sauce finished with port and redcurrant jelly. Used for venison.

roe cakes *Scotland* Skinned cooked roe, cooked potatoes and finely chopped onion sweated in butter (4:2:1) mashed together, formed into round cakes 1 cm thick, floured, rested then shallow-fried in oil with a little butter. Served with fried bacon etc.

roe deer A species of deer, *Capreolus capreolus*, which is very common in the UK

and Northern Europe. The meat is known as venison and is considered to be the best of its type.

roereieren *Netherlands* Scrambled egg

roff *West Africa* Roof

rogan josh *South Asia* Lamb or beef cooked in a yoghurt-based sauce with sweet peppers, tomatoes and aromatic spices including chilli powder and paprika to give a red colour

Rogen *Germany* Fish roe

roger *Catalonia* Red mullet

Rogeret de Cévennes *France* A goats' milk cheese similar to Pélardon

røget *Denmark* Smoked

røget sild *Denmark* Smoked herring

roggebrood *Netherlands* Rye bread

Roggen *Germany* Rye

Roggenbrot *Germany* Rye bread

roghan *Central Asia* The Afghanistan word for **ghee**

rognon *France* Kidney

rognone *Italy* Kidney

rognons blancs *France* Veal testicles, usually floured and shallow-fried

rognons en chemise *France* Veal kidneys still surrounded with suet, seasoned, laid on rosemary or thyme sprigs on a rack and roasted at 180°C for about 25 to 30 minutes until all the suet has melted, rested 10 minutes and served with the pan residues, defatted and deglazed with wine

rognons turbigo *France* Skinned split kidneys, sautéed in butter, presented around a centre garnish of grilled mushrooms and chipolata sausages and napped with a sauce made from the white wine deglazed pan juices mixed with a tomato flavoured and seasoned **demi-glace** sauce

rognures *France* Trimmings

roh *Germany* Raw

roher Schinken *Germany* Raw ham

Rohkost *Germany* Crudités, raw vegetables mainly used as a hors d'oeuvre

Rohkostplatte *Germany* A salad of raw vegetables

Rohwurst *Austria, Germany* A group of German/Austrian slicing or spreading sausages such as salami, Mettwurst, Ländjäger, Plockwurst and Teewurst, which are made of raw meat then cured, air-dried and/or smoked. All can be kept.

rokko Rocket

rökt *Sweden* Smoked

røkt *Norway* Smoked

rökt ål *Sweden* Smoked eel

rökt lax *Sweden* Smoked salmon

roll 1. A small bread separately cooked from about 50 to 60 g of raw dough **2.** Any food item shaped like a cylinder e.g. Swiss roll, meat roll, etc.

roll, to 1. To thin out, e.g. pastry or dough, with a rolling pin by compressing it between the rolling pin and a flat surface with a to and fro rolling motion. More accurately, to roll out. **2.** To form in to a cylinder. More accurately, to roll up.

rolle *Italy* Roll of veal or beef

rolled bean curd See **bean curd sticks**

rolled cutlets *United States* Beef and veal olives (**paupiettes**)

rolled oats See **porridge oats**

rolled rump *United States* The top of the round of beef without bone used for roasting

roller milled flour Flour produced from cereal grains by passing the larger pieces or whole grains though rollers set close together and rotating at slightly different speeds so as to shear the grain

rolling pin A wooden or ceramic cylinder about 5 cm in diameter and 25 to 50 cm long used for rolling out pastes and doughs or crushing brittle foods such as nuts, praline, etc. Some rolling pins, e.g. for making pasta, are longer and thinner

roll mac *United Kingdom* Mackerel fillets filled with fruit chutney and rolled up, laid on a bed of chopped onions and mushrooms, moistened with white wine, topped with more chutney and cooked in a 200°C oven until a crust forms on top. Served with soured cream.

rollmop herring Fillets of herring rolled with chopped onions, gherkins and peppercorns, secured with a sliver of wood and marinated in spiced vinegar for 7 to 10 days

Rollmops *Germany* Rollmop herring

roly-poly pudding *United Kingdom* Suet pastry rolled out into an oblong, spread with jam, mincemeat or any sweet filling, rolled up, wrapped in a cloth or foil and steamed or baked for 1.5 to 2 hours. Served with English custard.

Romadur A soft, smooth-textured and surface-ripened block-shaped cows' milk cheese with a yellowish brown washed rind. It tastes like a milder and sweeter version of **Limburger** cheese. Made in central Europe.

romaine, à la In the Roman style, i.e. roasts garnished with tomatoes, or tomato sauce, spinach and occasionally, potatoes

romaine, sauce *France* Caramel dissolved in vinegar as soon as it is made, **espagnole sauce** and game or brown stock added, reduced by one quarter, strained and

finished with pine nuts and a few currants and raisins soaked in water until plump

romaine lettuce See **cos lettuce**

romana, a la *Catalonia* Deep-fried in batter

romanesco A pale green, very decorative variety of cauliflower in which each floret rises to a peak and can be seen individually although they are all bunched together like a true cauliflower

Romano *United States* A hard, drum-shaped cooked-curd cows' milk cheese made in the Pecorino Romano manner. It is close-textured with a strong taste and thin rind. Contains 32% water, 26% fat and 33% protein.

roman pot Chicken brick

roman snail An edible European snail, *Helix pomatia*

romarin *France* Rosemary

romazava *South Africa* A beef and vegetable stew from Madagascar

rombo *Italy* Turbot

rombo chiodato *Italy* Turbot

rombo giallo *Italy* Megrim, the fish

rombo liscio *Italy* Brill, the fish

romdeng *Cambodia* Greater galangal

romero *Spain* Rosemary

Römertopf *Germany* Chicken brick

romesco *Catalonia* A famous spicy sauce made with toasted nuts, garlic, tomatoes, nyora peppers and bread

romesco chilli A mildly piquant smoky-flavoured dried chilli from Spain used to make romesco sauce. No other should be substituted.

romesco de peix *Catalonia* Seafood with romesco sauce

romesco sauce *Spain* Romesco chilli, blistered in the oven and peeled, blended with oven softened garlic and skinned tomatoes, roasted hazelnuts and almonds, chopped parsley, wine vinegar, olive oil and seasoning to form a smooth paste. Sweet red pepper and cayenne pepper may be substituted for the romesco chilli.

romiet *Cambodia* Turmeric

Romorantin *France* Selles-sur-Cher

ron *Spain* Rum

Roncal *Spain* A hard ewes' milk cheese made in 2 kg rounds and matured for 4 months. It has a yellowish white, hard but open textured paste with a pungent taste. The rind is light brown and slightly greasy. Used as a dessert cheese or for cooking.

rond de gigot *France* A thick leg steak of lamb or mutton

rondelle *France* A round thin slice of carrot, lemon. salami, etc.

rondinella *Italy* Flying fish

rondino *Italy* Pomfret, the fish

ronnach *Ireland* Mackerel

roof *West Africa* A mixture for stuffing fish from Senegal consisting of sweet peppers, onions or leeks or similar, garlic, parsley or other fresh herb, salt and a chopped chilli pepper, all processed to a fine smooth paste with a little oil or water. Also called **roff**

rookworst *Netherlands* A spiced and smoked sausage

roomali roti *South Asia* A very thin bread somewhat like a pancake

root celery Celeriac

root ginger The solid root form of **ginger**, either fresh or dried

roots A general name for the common root vegetables, as in *bed of roots* which is a **mirepoix** of carrots, turnips and swedes

root vegetables The general name for vegetables consisting of the swollen roots of plants from which the leaves and flowers spring. Common examples are carrots, turnips, swedes, beetroot, parsnips, salsify and radish. Also called **roots**

roppo muki *Japan* A cut for small vegetables such as baby turnips in which the top and base are trimmed flat and they are cut into hexagons

Roquefort *France* A soft, virtually rindless blue cheese made from unpasteurized ewes' milk, the curds of which are sprinkled with *Penicillium roquefortii* mould spores as they are being formed into 2.5 kg rounds. The cheeses are matured for 3 months in underground caves in currents of air at a constant temperature and humidity. The cheeses are needled to assist mould growth. It has a delicate and subtle tangy flavour and production is strictly controlled. It has AOC status.

roquette Rocket

röra *Sweden* Scrambled as in ägg röra, scrambled egg

rØræg *Denmark* Scrambled egg

rörd smörsås *Sweden* A stirred butter sauce made by creaming butter and egg yolk (3:1), seasoning and whisking in lemon juice

Rorippa nasturtium-aquaticum *Botanical name* Watercress

Rosa *Botanical name* See **rose**

Rosa canina *Botanical name* Wild rose, dog rose

Rosa eglanteria *Botanical name* Eglantine, sweet brier

rosa Krebse *Germany* Prawn

rosbif *France, Italy, Spain* Roast beef, usually very rare

rose A hardy shrub with pink to red fragrant flowers of the genus *Rosa*. The wild rose or dog rose, *R. canina*, and the eglantine or sweet brier, *R. eglanteria*, have large red seed capsules known as hips or rose hips. The flower petals with the bitter white heel removed may be crystallized or used for decoration, in salads, in fruit pies or as a general flavouring. The bright red rose hips, after dehairing, may be used in jams or puréed for use in sauces or to make a sweet syrup high in vitamin C. See also **rose water**

rose apple A fruit which grows in clusters on a tree, *Syzygium malaccensis*, from East Asia. They are small, pink and white, pear-shaped and have an apple flavour, but are rather soft and full of seeds.

rose cocoa bean, rose coco bean Borlotto bean

rose hip The orange to dark red fruit of the rose, especially *R. canina* and *R. eglantina*, with an edible fleshy casing up to 2.5 cm long containing a mass of inedible seeds. Usually used to make syrups and jams and valued for their high vitamin C content.

rose hip catsup *Canada* A cold sauce or ketchup made in Alberta from rose hips, onions, garlic, sugar, spices, vinegar and water

rosehip syrup A sweetened extract of rosehips used for flavouring and colouring (pink) drinks and desserts and as a source of vitamin C

rosella Jamaica flower

rosemary An evergreen perennial shrub, *Rosmarinus officinalis*, with woody upright stems and thin pointed aromatic leaves which grows in temperate and Mediterranean climates. Used to flavour meat dishes especially lamb and strong-flavoured soups. A twig of rosemary is often laid on fish or meat as it is being cooked.

Rosenkohl *Germany* Brussels sprouts

rose oil The essential oil extracted from rose petals used as a flavouring and perfume

roseroot A perennial rock plant, *Sedum rosea*, whose thick succulent leaves are eaten in salads in Greenland

rosette de Lyon *France* A large coarse-textured salami-like dried pork sausage made with chopped pork shoulder and matured very slowly. Eaten raw.

rose tube A nozzle for a piping bag with an elongated teardrop-shaped opening to produce petals and other decorative shapes

rose water Diluted essence of rose petals used as a flavouring in confectionery and desserts especially in Middle Eastern, Indian and Southeast Asian cooking

Rosinen *Germany* Raisins

Rosmarin *Germany* Rosemary

rosmarino *Italy* Rosemary

Rosmarinus officinalis *Botanical name* Rosemary

rosmerino *Italy* Rosemary

rosół *Poland* A mixed beef and chicken broth thickened with buckwheat groats and garnished with diced chicken, diced bacon and chopped parsley and fennel

rospa *Italy* Monkfish

rossetti *Italy* Goby, the fish

rosso *Italy* Red

rossolye *Russia* A traditional Baltic salad of diced cooked beetroot, cooking apples, boiled potatoes, gherkins, pickled herring and cold cooked meat dressed with cream lightly whipped with dry English mustard and caster sugar, all chilled and served on lettuce decorated with chopped hard-boiled egg and some of the dressing

rosta *Italy* Roasted

rostat bröd *Sweden* Toast

Rostbratwurst *Germany* A sausage made from a seasoned mixture of mainly lean pork with one half its weight of fat pork and veal all finely chopped, packed into narrow hog casings and linked

rösten To grill, roast or fry

Rösti *Switzerland* A mixture of grated parboiled potatoes, chopped onion and seasoning, formed into pancakes or patties and shallow-fried

rosticceria *Italy* Rotisserie, delicatessen

rostit *Catalonia* Roasted

Röstkartoffeln *Germany* Fried potatoes

rotary beater A hand-held and hand-operated mechanical whisk or beater consisting of two counter rotating intermeshed metal loops, now generally superseded by electrically powered mixers, beaters or whisks. Also called **rotary whisk**, **egg beater**

rotary whisk See **rotary beater**

Rotbarbe *Germany* Red mullet, *Mullus barbatus*

Rotbart *Germany* Red mullet, *Mullus barbatus*

Rotegrütze *Germany* Strained and sweetened fruit juice thickened with corn flour or potato flour, cooled and set in individual dishes and served with cold milk or cream

rote Johannisbeere *Germany* Redcurrant

rotelli Fusilli

Roterübe *Germany* Beetroot

Rotforelle *Germany* Arctic char, the fish

roti 1. *South Asia* Bread, of any kind **2.** *Sri Lanka* An unleavened flat bread made from wheat flour and grated coconut

rôti *France* **1.** Roasted; past participle of *rôtir*, 'to roast' **2.** Roast of beef, pork, etc.

roti jala *South Asia* A thick pouring batter made with flour, eggs, salt and thin coconut milk dripped in a continuous stream through a perforated cup into a hot greased frying pan to form a lacy pattern. Cooked both sides and then rolled up.

roti jala cup A metal vessel with four spouts issuing from the base each with a fine hole. Used for making roti jala and **string hoppers**.

rotini *Italy* Ruoti

rôtir *France* To roast

rôtisserie 1. *France* The section of the kitchen equipped for roasting meat **2.** *France* A steakhouse type of restaurant or shop selling roast meat **3.** *England* A rotating spit within a conventional oven on which joints of meat or poultry may be turned as they are roasting. Used to give more even cooking and browning.

Rotkohl *Germany* Red cabbage

Rotkraut *Germany* Red cabbage cooked with apples and vinegar

rotmos *Sweden* Mashed boiled turnips

rotolo *Italy* Roll

rotolo alla marmellata *Italy* Swiss roll

rött *Sweden* Red

Rotwurst *Germany* A well-seasoned blood sausage containing large chunks of meat

Rotzunge *Germany* Witch sole

rou *China* Meat

rouelle *France* Leg of veal excluding the jarret and the very top of the cushions or a thick slice cut across same

Rouen duck One of the two main types of French domesticated duck. It is usually killed by suffocation or strangulation and eviscerated carefully so that no blood escapes. Usually roasted slightly underdone and used e.g. for **canard à la presse**.

rouennaise, sauce *France* Hot bordelaise sauce mixed with processed raw duck liver, heated very gently so as not to harden the liver then strained and seasoned

rougail *United States* A highly spiced Creole condiment served with rice dishes

rougaille *South Africa* A savoury sauce from Madagascar made from peeled tomatoes, ginger, onions, lemon juice and zest and chillies

rouget *France* Mullet, the fish

rouget barbet *France* Red mullet, *Mullus barbatus*

rouget de roche *France* Red mullet, *Mullus surmuletus*

rouget grondin *France* Gurnard

roughage See **dietary fibre**

roughback Rock sole

rough puff pastry A puff pastry made with the conventional turns to build up layers but the fat is mixed with the flour in the form of solid cubes 1 to 2 cm on the side and water added to make the dough, keeping the cubes as intact as possible. The flour fat ratio is 4:3. Used only where scrap puff pastry would be used e.g. pies, palmiers.

rouille *France* A processed sauce of water softened and squeezed bread, garlic, salt, deskinned red peppers, and olive oil with possibly cayenne pepper or paprika. It is not cooked. Spread on bread and served with bouillabaisse and other fish soups in Provence.

roulade A type of presentation of sweet cakes, savoury mixtures, cheeses, layered meats or fish, cooked egg mixtures, etc. by taking a rectangle of one item, covering it with a filling or layer in contrasting colour or texture, then rolling up into a spiral which may be served as is, sliced or further cooked. Examples are Swiss rolls, salmon and turbot roulades, nut and vegetable roulades and similar.

Rouladen *Germany* Beef olives

roulé *France* 1. Swiss roll, rolled meat or similar 2. A fresh soft cows' milk cheese made into a roulade with layers of flavourings such as garlic, herbs and peppercorns. Also called **roulette**

rouler *France* To roll

roulette *France* 1. Roulé 2. A pastry or pasta cutting wheel

round fish Fish which may be round or elliptical in cross section and have an eye on each side of the head

round gourd Tinda

round kumquat See **maru-kinkan**

round lettuce Butterhead lettuce

round of beef *United States* The whole of the rear leg of beef excluding the shin but including the rump, topside, silverside and part of the thick flank. It is cut into a number of joints and steaks ranging from rump at the top to round steak at the bottom.

round of bread A single slice of bread

round steak *United States* Steak cut form the lower part of round of beef. It may be fried but is not very tender. When tenderized it is called Swiss steak.

round yam *Australia* A ball-shaped yam from the native Burdekin vine, *Dioscorea bublifera*, which also has edible black berries

roux *England, France* A combination of fat and flour cooked together to varying degrees of colour, i.e. **white roux**, **blond roux** or **brown roux**. Used to thicken liquids to make sauces of various kinds. See also **block roux**

roux blond *France* Blond roux

Rouy *France* A soft strong-smelling cows' milk cheese from Dijon, packed in square boxes

rova *Sweden* Turnip

rovello *Italy* Blue-spotted sea bream

rovellons *Catalonia* Wild mushrooms

roventini alla toscana *Italy* Fried pigs' blood and Parmesan cheese

rowanberry The small red berries of the mountain ash or rowan tree, *Sorbus aucuparia*, which grows in temperate climates. The soft, orange to red berries grow in clusters and although too bitter to eat on their own, their high pectin content is useful when combined with other fruits to make jams. Also called **sorb**

rowanberry jelly *Scotland* A condiment jelly made in Scotland from rowanberries, apples, sugar and water

royal See **royale**

royal chinook See **chinook salmon**

royal custard See **royale**

royale *France* A savoury egg custard made from equal parts of egg and stock or milk, seasoned, strained and poached in a buttered mould in a bain-marie. Cut into neat shapes and used as a garnish especially for consommé. Also called **royal**, **royal custard**

royale, à la In the royal style, i.e. coated with a rich white sauce and garnished with truffles and button mushrooms. Also used of a consommé garnished with a royale.

royale cherry Duke cherry

royal glaze *United States* Royal icing

royal icing A hard white icing made from lightly beaten egg whites into which is beaten icing sugar, lemon juice and at the end a little glycerine. Also called **royal glaze**

royal icing praline Egg whites and icing sugar whipped to the ribbon stage and mixed with finely chopped almonds to the required consistency

Royalp *Switzerland* A mild, semi-hard cheese made from unpasteurized cows' milk cast in large rounds (up to 5 kg), similar to **Tilsit** with a buttery paste and moist reddish brown rind. Contains 39% water, 28% fat and 27% protein.

Royal Wazwaam *South Asia* A Kashmiri meal of 36 courses of which between 15 and 30 will be meat dishes cooked by the master chef, the *Vasta Waza*. Guests are seated in groups of four and share the meal out of a large metal dish.

royan *France* Pilchard

roz bil habib *North Africa* A sweetened rice dessert cooked in milk, flavoured with almonds, vanilla and orange-flower water

roz bil tamar *Middle East* Cooked rice, almonds, dates and sultanas (2:1:1:1), the last three all fried, are assembled with the rice heaped on top of the fruit and nut mixture, then all baked in the oven at 120°C. Served with a sprinkling of rose water.

rozijnen *Netherlands* Raisins

rubanné(e) *France* Made up of well defined layers of different colours and flavours

rubbing in biscuit method A method of making biscuits by rubbing the fat into the flour as in short pastry making, then adding the liquid ingredients and sugar and mixing as little as possible e.g. shortbread and ginger biscuits

rubbing in cake method A method of making cakes by combining fat and sieved flour and raising agent to a sandy (breadcrumb) texture, mixing in other dry ingredients then adding liquid to make a dough, e.g. rock cakes, raspberry buns

Rübe *Germany* Turnip

Rubens, sauce *France* A slow reduction (25 minutes) of white wine, fish stock and a fine brunoise of aromatic vegetables, thickened with yolk of egg and finished with Madeira wine, crayfish butter and anchovy essence

rub in, to To combine hard fat with flour and other dry ingredients using the tips of the fingers or a food processor so as to end up with a dry flowable mixture resembling breadcrumbs in which small particles of solid fat are coated with the dry ingredients

rubixanthin See **E161(d)**

Rubus The genus containing hybrids of the wild blackberry, raspberry and other similar soft fruits

Rubus idaeus *Botanical name* Raspberry

Rubus phoenicolasius *Botanical name* Wineberry

ruby Pigmented grapefruit

ruchetta *Italy* Rocket

rucola *Italy* Rocket

ruda *Spain* Rue, the herb

rudder-nosed lobster Sand lobster

rue A hardy evergreen shrub, *Ruta graveolens*, with small lobed bluish green leaves which have a strong bitter flavour and pungent aroma. Used in small quantities as a garnish and in egg, cheese and fish dishes. The seeds are infused together with lovage and mint in marinades for partridge. It is said to be poisonous in large quantities. Also called **garden rue**

Ruegenwalder Teewurst *Germany* A smooth spreading sausage made with pork and collar bacon, smoked over beechwood

rue kewra *South Asia* Screwpine

rue odorante *France* Rue, the herb

ruffe Pope

Ruffec *France* A strong-tasting goats' milk cheese from Charentais

rugbrød *Denmark* Dark rye bread

rugde *Norway* Woodcock

rughetta *Italy* Rocket

rugola *Italy* Rocket

Rühreier *Germany* Scrambled eggs

ruibarbo *Spain* Rhubarb

ruladă de nuci *Romania* A Swiss roll filled with a mixture of ground walnuts, sugar, milk, rum and grated lemon zest

rulader *Sweden* Beef roll, beef olive

rullepølse *Denmark* A type of roulade made with the belly meat of any animal spread with a mixture of minced onion, spices and herbs, tightly rolled, tied then either dry-salted with salt and saltpetre for a week and simmered in water or braised as is

rullesild *Norway* Rollmop herring

rum *England, Italy* An alcoholic spirit distilled from a fermented molasses solution, used as a flavouring

Rum *Germany* Rum

rumaki *United States* A cocktail snack consisting of chicken liver and water chestnuts, wrapped in bacon, grilled and dipped in a savoury sauce

rum baba A baba cake soaked in rum-flavoured sugar syrup and decorated with whipped cream, glacé cherries and angelica strips. It was created for the King of Poland when living in Alsace Lorraine and is based on the recipe for Kugelhopf. See also **baba**

rumble-de-thumps *Scotland* Cooked potatoes and chopped cooked cabbage, mixed together and browned in the oven

rum butter A mixture of softened butter, brown sugar and rum and sometimes cinnamon. When cool used as an accompaniment to hot puddings.

Rumex acetosa *Botanical name* Sorrel

Rumex patientia *Botanical name* Patience

Rumex scutatus *Botanical name* Buckler leaf sorrel

rump *United Kingdom* A cut of beef from the hindquarter, being a vertical slice from the coccyx (fused vertebrae near the tail) behind the sirloin and extending down to the thick flank. It is a prime joint which can be roasted, fried or grilled. A rump and sirloin of beef joined together is called a choice.

rump steak *United Kingdom* A slice of beef cut from the rump

rum sauce *United Kingdom* A sweet white sauce flavoured with rum, usually served with Christmas pudding or mince pies

rundergehakt *Netherlands* Minced beef

runderlapje *Netherlands* Beefsteak

rundown *Caribbean* A Jamaican dish of flaked smoked fish simmered with coconut milk, onions and seasonings

rundstycke *Sweden* Bread roll. Also called **franksbröd**

rundstykke *Denmark, Norway* Bread roll

rundvlees *Netherlands* Beef

runner Used for black and white puddings, Bologna sausage, etc. See also **ox casings**

runner bean The pods and beans from a climbing legume, *Phaseolus coccineus*, which was introduced into Europe from South America as a flowering plant in the 18th century. The long narrow green pods are generally cooked and eaten whole when young since the pods tend to become stringy with age. The unripe beans may also be used at a later stage and the ripe beans may be dried. Also called **scarlet runner**, **string bean**, **stick bean**

runny Baveuse

ruoka *Finland* Food, meat, dish or course

ruokalista *Finland* Menu

ruoti *Italy* Small cartwheel-shaped pieces of pasta. Also called **rotini**

ruotini *Italy* Small ruoti

ruou *Vietnam* Wine

rushnut Tiger nut

rusinakakku *Finland* Fruit cake

rusinat *Finland* Raisins and sultanas

rusk Ground rusks made from unleavened bread used as an extender in sausages and sausage meat. Yeast-raised bread rusk can cause off flavours in the sausage.

rusks Small pieces of bread, dried and baked until golden brown

russe, à la *France* In the Russian style, i.e. garnished with beetroot, soured cream, hard-boiled egg and sometimes salt herring

russet apple A reddish brown apple with a dull non-shiny skin and crisp sweet/sour flesh

Russian dressing 1. *Russia* Mayonnaise combined with a little dry white wine, horseradish and Worcestershire sauces and tomato ketchup **2.** *United States* Mayonnaise combined with tarragon vinegar or lemon juice, parsley and chopped hard-boiled egg

Russian fish pie *United Kingdom* As **coulibiac**, but with any suitable cooked fish and using puff pastry only

Russian salad A mixture of cooked diced potatoes and carrots with peas and sliced green beans bound together with mayonnaise. Usually served on lettuce garnished with sliced hard-boiled egg, sliced gherkins and diced beetroot.

Russian service The method of serving food from platters to individual diners at the table

Russian tarragon A milder tarragon, *Artemesia dracunculoides*, than the French variety. It may be distinguished from the French by its ability to set seed.

russin *Sweden* Raisin

russische Eier *Germany* Sliced hard-boiled egg dressed with mayonnaise, served with salad (NOTE: Literally 'Russian eggs'.)

russole *Italy* A type of fungus

rustica, alla *Italy* In the rustic style, e.g. used of spaghetti served with an anchovy and cheese sauce flavoured with garlic and oregano

ruta *Italy* Rue, the herb

rutabaga 1. A variety of swede, *Brassica campestris* var. *rutabaga*, with yellow flesh. **2.** *United States* Swede, kohlrabi **3.** *France* Swede

Ruta graveolens *Botanical name* Rue

rutin One of the **bioflavonoids** found in high concentration in buckwheat

Rutland *England* Cheddar cheese flavoured with beer, chopped parsley and garlic

ryba *Russia* Fish

rybia polewka *Poland* A fish soup made from fish stock simmered with carrots, celeriac, onions, cabbage, parsley and cauliflower until all tender, sieved, finished with egg yolks and milk and garnished with sliced hard carps' roes poached in fish stock

rye A cereal grain, *Secale cereale*, which grows mainly in Baltic areas. Used for dense breads and crispbreads. A fungus, *Claviceps purpurea*, which grows on the seed heads, especially during wet harvesting weather, is responsible for a sickness 'St Anthony's fire', characterized by hallucinations and mental derangement. An extract of the fungus is used to induce labour and as an illegal abortifacient.

rye bread A bread usually shaped like a baton and flavoured with caraway seeds, made from a mixture of rye and wheat flour

rye flakes Flakes made by rolling steamed or softened rye grains. Used in muesli and for a cooked breakfast cereal.

rye flour Flour made from rye which has a more sticky and less elastic gluten than wheat and is thus usually mixed with wheat flour to make bread. Used on its own for unleavened bread and crispbreads.

rye meal Coarsely ground rye

rygeost *Denmark* Smoked cream cheese

ryotei *Japan* The extremely expensive restaurants that serve the traditional haute cuisine of Japan in private Japanese-style rooms. The menu is decided by the chef.

rype *Denmark, Norway* Grouse or ptarmigan

rype i fløtesaus *Norway* A famous dish of ptarmigan in a cream sauce

rysk kolja *Sweden* Haddock à la russe

STUVWXY

saabat masoor *South Asia* Lentils with a dark brown or pale green skin which when dehusked are a pale pink-orange. They take a considerable time to cook.

saabat moong *South Asia* Whole mung beans

saabat urad *South Asia* Whole seeds of black gram

saag *South Asia* A general term for green vegetables

saa got *China* Yam bean

Saanenkäse *Switzerland* A hard, cooked-curd cows' milk cheese similar to **Sbrinz**, suitable for slicing or grating. The cheeses are dry-salted and matured in cool damp conditions for up to 5 years. Also called **Walliskäse**

saang choy *China* Cos lettuce

saba 1. *Japan* Mackerel **2.** *Philippines* Banana

sábalo *Spain* Shad

Sabal palmetto *Botanical name* Palmetto

saba no miso-ni *Japan* Mackerel simmered in miso

sabayon A mixture of egg yolk and a little water whisked to the ribbon stage over gentle heat. Added to sauces to assist glazing under the grill.

sabayon sauce A French, thinner, lighter and frothier version of **zabaglione** made from egg yolks, sherry or rum and sugar, sometimes with whipped cream folded into the mixture. Served with fruit desserts and rich sponge puddings.

sabb al-gafsha *Persian Gulf* An enriched yeast-raised thick batter made with a mixture of **besan**, wheat flour, eggs and clarified butter (2:1:4:1) with a little ground rice to give the right consistency, then flavoured with ground cardamom seeds and saffron powder. Spoonfuls are deep-fried at 190°C for about 4 minutes, drained and soaked in a cardamom-flavoured heavy sugar syrup. Served warm.

sablé biscuits A rich sandy-textured biscuit made from a buttery paste containing granulated sugar, formed into a roll, chilled, sliced and the round slices baked in the oven. Also called **sand biscuits**

saboga *Spain* Twaite shad

sabor *Spain* Flavour

sabre *France* Scabbard fish

sabre bean Sword bean

sabroso *Spain* Savoury, tasty

sabzee *Central Asia* The Afghan name for spinach

sabzi *South Asia* Vegetables

sabzi khordan *Central Asia* A platter of washed, drained and chilled herb sprigs arranged in an attractive fashion and served with cubes of cheese and bread. Eaten as an appetizer in Iran.

sac *France* Caecum

saccharin A synthetic chemical which weight for weight is 400 times sweeter than sugar. It is approved for use in the UK for soft drinks, cider and diet products. It does not have an E number and is therefore not universally approved in the EU.

saccharometer A **hydrometer** which is directly calibrated with the percentage of sugar in the sugar/water solution

Saccharomyces cerevisiae The most common yeast used for converting sugars into alcohol or water and carbon dioxide, for making bread and as a source of some enzymes, e.g. invertase

Saccharomyces exiguus A yeast used for the leavening of sour dough bread

Saccharomyces inusitatus A yeast used for the leavening of sour dough bread

Saccharomyces rouxii A yeast used in the third phase of the production of soya sauce

saccharose See **sucrose**

sacchetto *Italy* Sea perch

sacher sauce A blond roux made into a thin sauce with equal parts of consommé and cream, flavoured with Worcestershire sauce, thickened with egg yolks and finished with chopped chives

Sachertorte *Austria* Vienna's most famous torte, created by Franz Sacher in 1832, made from a butter, sugar and egg yolk creamed batter into which rum or Madeira-flavoured molten chocolate is beaten, this followed by folding in flour and stiffly beaten egg whites and baking at 180°C. The cake is rested and covered with chocolate icing to make a rather dry torte which is best served with whipped cream.

Sacherwürstel *Austria* A **Bratwurst** containing mainly beef and bacon fat

sacristain *France* A spiral-shaped puff pastry with almonds and sugar or cheese

sad (A cake or loaf) which is heavy, sunken or has not risen as required

saddle A large joint of meat from smaller animals, consisting of two joined loins and sometimes including ribs

saddled bream A small seawater bream, *Oblada melanura*. The grey-blue skin has longitudinal stripes.

saddle of lamb The two joined loins of a lamb before cutting through the backbone. Normally skinned and roasted, garnished with water cress, carved longitudinally in thick slices and served with gravy, mint sauce, and redcurrant jelly.

sadikka *Sri Lanka* Nutmeg

sadza *South Africa* A type of steamed dumpling made from red millet flour or cornmeal, popular in Zimbabwe and usually served with some kind of sauce or stew

safardjaliyya *North Africa* Lamb or beef chunks browned in oil and simmered with sweated onions, skinned tomatoes, cinnamon and ginger until tender, then cooked with cored, unpeeled and quartered quinces or, if unavailable, hard pears or apricots until the fruit is soft

safflower A thistle-like plant, *Carthamus tinctorius*, with large orange-red flowers, cultivated in India, China and the Middle East. The flowers are used as a yellow colouring and oil is extracted from the seeds. The styles are sometimes sold as true saffron to unsuspecting customers. Also called **saffron thistle**, **Mexican saffron**

safflower oil A mild-flavoured, high polyunsaturated oil from the seeds of the safflower, which is a good source of vitamin E. Not suitable for deep-frying. Used for margarine manufacture and in salad dressings. Contains about 10% saturated, 15% monounsaturated and 75% polyunsaturated fat.

safflower styles The style of the safflower is often used to replace or adulterate saffron by unscrupulous traders, but it is yellow as opposed to the red of real saffron. Will colour dishes orange but has no flavour. Also called **bastard saffron**

saffransbröd *Sweden* A yeast-raised fruit bread flavoured and coloured with saffron. Served on St Lucia's feast day, the 13th of December.

saffron The red/orange thread-like 3 branched styles of the perennial crocus, *Crocus sativus*, about 2.5 cm long with a penetrating aromatic flavour that is medicinal in high concentration. Cultivated from the Mediterranean to Kashmir. It is the most expensive spice known but a small amount (0.1 g) will both flavour a dish and colour it a brilliant gold. Sold either as strands which should be infused in hot water for at least 8 hours or as a red powder which gives a fast release of aroma. Used with fish and rice dishes and in buns. Often adulterated, and should only be purchased from reputable merchants. See also **safflower styles**

saffron cake Cornish saffron cake

saffron milk cap An edible mushroom, *Lactarius deliciosus*, with an irregular orange circular cap containing a central depression. The yellow sap turns green on drying and is a positive identification of the species. Pickled and used in cooking.

saffron sauce Finely chopped shallots or onions cooked in white wine, the volume reduced to about one sixth of the original, double cream, equal in amount to the original wine, whisked in off the heat and saffron powder added to colour and flavour

saffron thistle Safflower

Saflor *Germany* Safflower

safran *France* Saffron

safran d'Inde *France* Turmeric

Safrangewürz *Germany* Saffron

saft *Denmark, Norway* Juice

Saft *Germany* **1.** Juice **2.** Gravy

Saftbraten *Germany* A thin beef stew or braised beef

Saftig *Germany* Juicy, spicy

safuran *Japan* Saffron

sag See **amaranth 1** (NOTE: In Europe, this is usually spinach.)

sagaloo See **amaranth 1** (NOTE: In Europe, this is usually spinach.)

saganaki *Greece* Thick slices of Kessari or Kefalotiri cheese, floured, deep-fried and served with lemon wedges as an appetizer

sage A perennial bush herb, *Salvia officinalis*, of the mint family which grows worldwide. It has silvery leaves, a highly aromatic flavour and aroma and is used as a flavouring especially in Italian cooking. It goes well with fatty meats and liver and is used to flavour sausages, vinegar, and compound butters. It is also available in a prostrate form, *S. officianils 'Prostratus'*, which has a very balsamic flavour. Also called **broad leaved sage]**

sage and onion stuffing *United Kingdom* Onions baked in the oven, the inner soft flesh mixed with white bread which has been soaked in milk and squeezed out, seasoning and chopped sage. Chopped beef suet may be added. Used as a stuffing for poultry or may be diluted with gravy for use as a sauce.

Sage Derby *England* A hard, mild cheese with a slightly flaky texture and marbled appearance made by adding the juice of sage leaves mixed with chlorophyll to the curds

Sägegarnele *Germany* Common prawn

sage grouse *United States* A species of grouse, *Centrocerus urophasianus*, which feeds on sagebrush buds. The crop must be removed as soon as it is shot, otherwise it would give the bird an objectionable flavour.

Sage Lancashire *England* Lancashire cheese flavoured with chopped sage

saging *Philippines* Plantain

Sagittaria sagittifolia *Botanical name* Arrowhead

sago A starch extracted mainly from the pith of the sago palm, *Metroxylon sagu*, using water. The starch is then dried and granulated into small balls known as pearl sago. Used for milk puddings. Many palm trees which grow in India and Southeast Asia, the cabbage palm from the American tropics and cyclads which grow in Sri Lanka, India and Japan all have a starchy pith at a certain phase in their life cycle and are used as a source of starch.

Sago *Germany* Sago

sago palm A palm tree, *Metroxylon sagu*, which grows wild in fresh water swamps in Southeast Asia. Just before flowering at about 15 years, starch reserves build up in the pith and the palm is felled to extract the starch from which sago is produced.

sagú *Italy, Spain* Sago

Sahne *Germany* Cream

Sahnequark *Germany* Cream cheese

Sahnetorte *Germany* Cream cake

saiblinge *France* A fish of the salmon family

sai dau naga choy *China* Mung bean sprouts

saignant(e) *France* Rare or underdone especially of meat (NOTE: Literally 'bleeding'.)

saigneux, bout *France* Neck of lamb or veal

sai gwa *China* Water melon

sai jar *Indonesia* Drumstick vegetable

sailor's beef Sjömansbiff

saín *Spain* Suet

saindoux *France* Pig's lard

saingorlon *France* A soft blue-veined cows' milk cheese similar to Gorgonzola and cast in 5 to 10 kg cylinders. Contains 55% water, 21% fat and 20% protein.

sainome-giri *Japan* Dice cut food (1 cm)

Saint Albray A semi-soft, mellow and delicate cows' milk cheese from Béarn produced in a 2 kg flower shape. It has a pale orange bloomed rind with a pale yellow paste containing small holes. Suitable for dessert and sandwiches.

Saint-Benoît *France* A round cows' milk cheese from the Loire with a fruity flavour

Saint Chevrier A mild and creamy goats' milk cheese covered with ash

Sainte-Maure *France* A soft creamy goats' milk cheese from the Loire made in long cylinders often moulded around a straw

Sainte-Menehould *France* Cooked and then coated with mustard, dipped in melted butter, covered with breadcrumbs and grilled, a method originating in the Champagne region of France. Pigs trotters are traditionally treated in this way.

Saint-Florentin *France* A washed rind, full-flavoured cows' milk cheese from Burgundy

Saint George's mushroom An edible mushroom, *Tricholoma gambosum*, with a cream-coloured irregular cap on a thick stem found in grassland in spring and early summer. Used as a flavouring for soups and stews.

Saint Germain, à la *France* In the Saint Germain style, i.e. including peas

Saint Germain, crème *France* Onion, leek and celery sweated in butter, white stock, mint, a bouquet garni and shelled green peas added, boiled 5 minutes, bouquet garni removed, an equal quantity of béchamel added, boiled, consistency adjusted, liquidized, seasoned and passed through a chinois and finished with cream. Also called **cream of green pea soup**

Saint Germain, fish Fillets of fish passed through seasoned flour, melted butter containing English mustard, and breadcrumbs. Breadcrumbs neatened on the presentation side with a palette knife and marked with a diamond pattern, grilled and served with **béarnaise sauce**.

Saint Germain, purée *France* Soaked dried or washed fresh peas, whole carrot, chopped green leek and onion, a bouquet garni and a knuckle of ham added to white stock, simmered and skimmed until all tender, carrot and ham removed, the remainder liquidized or passed through a sieve, strained, seasoned, consistency adjusted and served hot accompanied with croûtons. Also called **green pea soup**

Saint-Gildas-des-bois *France* A triple cream cows' milk cheese from Brittany with a rather mouldy smell

Saint Honoré The patron saint of pastry cooks. See also **gâteau Saint Honoré**

Saint-Jacques *France* Coquilles saint-jacques

Saint John's bread See **carob powder**

Saint Laurence The patron saint of cooks

Saint-Malo, sauce *France* Sauce vin blanc with mustard, chopped shallots cooked in white wine and a little anchovy essence

Saint-Marcellin *France* Tomme de Saint Marcellin

Saint-Nectaire *France* A semi-hard cows' milk cheese from the Dordogne cast in large discs (up to 2 kg). It is salted and ripened in caves for 60 days. The smooth paste has an aromatic flavour and a slight smell of mildew. It has appellation d'origine status. Contains 45% water, 25% fat and 23% protein.

Saint-Paulin *France* A semi-hard creamy yellow round cheese with a mild delicate flavour made from cows' milk and cast in discs (up to 2 kg). It is made with a lactic starter, is washed in weak brine, salted in brine and cured at high humidity. Sometimes sold as Port Salut.

Saint Peter's fish Tilapia

Saint-Pierre *France* John Dory

Saint-Rémy *France* A soft, washed rind cows' milk cheese from Lorraine with a strong-smelling paste and a reddish brown rind. Made in squares.

saisir *France* To sear

Saiten *Germany* A juicy sausage often served with lentils

saithe Coley

saka madesu *Central Africa* A mixture of white beans, soaked and cooked until tender, and cassava leaves, which have been crushed in a pestle and mortar and simmered in water with sautéed onions for 1 to 2 hours. The mixture is simmered with salt in a large pot for a further 15 minutes and is eaten with any staple carbohydrate source.

saka-mushi *Japan* A method of steaming food over sake and water or steaming food which has been marinated in sake

sakana, sakana-ryori *Japan* Seafood, or a seafood dish

sakana shioyaki *Japan* Cleaned and gutted herring, dried, sprinkled with salt and allowed to rest for 30 minutes, sprinkled with more salt especially on the tail and grilled or barbecued for 15 to 20 minutes, turning as required

saka-saka *Central Africa* Congolese for cassava leaves which normally are only eaten in this region. They can be very tough and require long cooking.

sake *Japan* **1.** A rice wine used principally for drinking but can be used as a substitute for **mirin** in cooking. It is brewed from steamed rice using the mould, *Aspergillus oryzae*, as the fermentation agent. Lactic acid is added to reduce the pH and prevent contamination with a yeast. It is filtered and used immediately. See also **Japanese rice wine 2.** Salmon

saki *Japan* another spelling of **sake**

sakizuke *Japan* A seasonal appetizer served especially in expensive restaurants, e.g. aemono

saku *Thailand* Sago

sakura denbu *Japan* A mixture of dried and ground codfish and sugar-coloured pink and used as a garnish

sal *Portugal, Spain* Salt

salaatti *Finland* Salad

salaattikastike *Finland* Salad dressing

Salacca edulis *Botanical name* Snake fruit

salad A mixture of raw leaves, vegetables, fruit, warm or cold cooked vegetables, sausages, ham, cheese, fish, shellfish, cereal grains, pasta, etc. Virtually any edible foodstuff may be incorporated in a salad but, save for pure fruit salads, all are dressed with some kind of acid-based sauce or dressing and seasoned. Served as a course or meal in its own right or as an accompaniment to other food. well-known varieties include Russian salad, green salad, fruit salad and salade niçoise.

salada *Portugal* Salad

salad bar A range of salad ingredients in separate containers displayed on a refrigerated counter for self-service by the customer

salad burnet A perennial hardy evergreen herb, *Sanguisorba minor*, with tiny green/red spherical flowers. The lacy leaves have a slightly nutty flavour with a hint of cucumber. Used in salads, sauces, soups and stews.

salad cream A commercial emulsion sauce made to resemble mayonnaise but deriving its texture more from thickeners than from emulsified oil

salad dressing A sauce usually based on oil and an acid such as vinegar, lemon juice or possibly yoghurt, either a stable or unstable emulsion, seasoned and flavoured with herbs, spices, garlic, etc. Generally used to coat very lightly the components of a salad especially leaves, but occasionally to bind the ingredients together

salade *France* Lettuce, green salad

salade composée *France* A substantial mixed salad with a selection of bacon, poached egg, offal, deep-fried cheese and the like. **Salade niçoise** is an example of a salade composée.

salade des fruits *France* Fruit salad

salade de zalouk *North Africa* A type of spicy ratatouille from Tunisia made from cubed aubergine, garlic, courgettes, chilli pepper and tomatoes, sautéed, then cooked together in that order until most of the liquid has evaporated. Served cold.

salade niçoise *France* A typical Provençal salad made of a selection of most of tomatoes, cucumbers, skinned raw broad beans, cooked French beans, hard-boiled eggs, anchovy fillets, tuna, black olives, basil and parsley dressed with a garlic-flavoured vinaigrette

salade panachée *France* Mixed or layered salad

salade russe *France* Russian salad

salade simple *France* Plain salad

salade tiède *France* A lukewarm salad achieved by using a relatively hot salad dressing

salade verte *France* Green salad

salad flowers The principal flowers used in salads are bergamot, borage, chives, nasturtium, marigold, primrose, rose petals, sweet rocket and violet

salad greens The various green leaves that can be used in salads

salad herbs The principal herbs used in salads are (leaves only): alexanders, angelica, basil, bistort, borage, caraway, chervil, chicory, Chinese chives, coriander, corn salad, dill, fennel, lemon balm, lovage, marjoram, mint, mustard, nasturtium, orach, parsley, salad burnet, salad rocket, savory, sorrel, summer purslane, sweet cicely, tarragon, thyme, watercress, wild celery and winter purslane. See also **salad flowers**

saladier *France* Salad bowl

salado *Spain* Salted or salty

salad onion See **spring onion**

salad patta *South Asia* Lettuce

salad rape The light green leaves of a small annual plant, *Brassica napus*, of the rape and swede family used as a salad leaf, or when older, may be cooked as a vegetable

salad rocket See **rocket**

salaison *France* **1.** The process of salting meats, cheeses, etc. **2.** Salted meat or fish used as a hors d'oeuvres

salak *Indonesia, Malaysia* Snake fruit

salam *Switzerland* A type of cervelas or **Brühwurst**

salamander 1. A commercial high intensity grill used in restaurant kitchens **2.** A small circular metal block on the end of a metal rod with a wooden handle, heated to red heat on a fire or stove then held over the food surface to have the same effect as an overhead grill, nowadays a gas operated blow torch is often used for the same effect

salamandre *France* Salamander

salambo *France* An open topped tart filled with a kirsch-flavoured pastry cream and topped with caramel

salame *Italy* A type of cased sausage named after Salamis which was a city of the Roman empire in Cyprus. The plural in Italian is **salami**, which is the English word for the sausage of that name. Salame is variable in composition and texture although with few exceptions it is 100% meat and flavourings and is usually known by a district name in Italy. Also called **salami**

salame alla friulana *Italy* Sautéed slices of salami with vinegar eaten with polenta

salame calabrese *Italy* A short thick salami made of pure pork embedded with chunks of white fat weighing about 250 g. It has a strong peppery flavour and is linked and tied with string.

salame casalingo *Italy* Home-made salami

salame cotto *Italy* Cotto

salame di Cremone *Italy* A large coarse-textured salami similar in composition to salame milanese

salame di fegato *Italy* Liver sausage

salame di felino *Italy* A succulent salami of pure pork meat moistened with white wine, flavoured with garlic and whole peppercorns in a rather uneven shape

salame di porco *Italy* Brawn

salame di Sorrento *Italy* A garlic free salami from Sorrento containing 80% pork and 20% beef

salame fabriano *Italy* A salami made of equal parts of pork and vittelone

salame finocchione *Italy* A large salami made with pork containing some large chunks of lean meat as well as fat and flavoured with fennel

salame fiorentino *Italy* The most famous of the Tuscan salami made of pork containing chunks of fat and lean which give them a mottled appearance when cut. About 10 cm in diameter.

salame genovese *Italy* A salami made of roughly equal parts of vitellone and fatty pork. Very popular in the USA.

salame iola *Italy* A pure pork salami from Sicily flavoured with garlic

salamella di cinghiale *Italy* Wild boar sausage

salame milanese *Italy* A salami made in large quantities containing 50% lean pork, 20% fat pork and 30% beef or vitellone, all coarsely chopped, seasoned and flavoured with garlic and whole white peppercorns. Dextrose is added to encourage lactic fermentation and it is air-dried and matured for 2 to 3 months.

salame napoletano *Italy* A long thin salami from Naples made of pork and beef seasoned with a lot of ground pepper and with a very strong flavour

salame sardo *Italy* A salami from Sardinia highly flavoured and with red pepper

salame ungherese *Italy* A Hungarian salami made in Italy from finely chopped pork, pork fat, beef and garlic, seasoned, moistened with white wine and flavoured with paprika

salame Valdostana *Italy* A small soft sausage made of pork and beef and flavoured with garlic

salami 1. *England, France* A hard sausage with excellent keeping qualities, variously made from fine or coarse chopped pork, beef or veal and mild or spicy often with peppercorns. Normally brined and smoked. Used for antipasto, hors d'oeuvres and sandwiches. **2.** *Poland* A hard cows' milk cheese with a close-textured paste containing many small holes

salamin d'la duja *Italy* A soft mild type of salami preserved in fat in a special pot called a duja

salamine di cinghiale *Italy* A strong-flavoured sausage made of wild boar meat and preserved in brine or oil

salamini *Italy* Small salami (pl.)

salamoia *Italy* Pickling liquid, brine

salat *Denmark, Russia* Salad

Salat *Germany* Salad, lettuce

salata *Greece* Salad of raw fresh vegetables

salată de vinete *Romania* The flesh of baked aubergines, finely chopped, seasoned and mixed with lemon juice and grated onion then blended with oil to form a purée which is served cold as an appetizer

salatagurker *Norway* Dill pickles

salatah arabiyeh *Middle East* Arabic salad generally of chopped or sliced sweet green pepper, onion, tomato, radish and garlic with crushed coriander seeds, dried mint, chopped parsley and seasoning and usually dressed with olive oil and vinegar

salatah-bi-laban *Middle East* Salad ingredients as **salatah arabiyeh** with a yoghurt salad dressing

salatah-bi-taheenah *Middle East* Salad ingredients as **salatah arabiyeh** with a tahini salad dressing

salatina *Italy* Fresh salad leaves

salato *Italy* Salted, savoury, especially of meats

salat olivier *Russia* A salad of julienned chicken meat with chopped hard-boiled eggs, slices of waxy new potatoes, peas and chopped gherkins mounded on a serving dish decorated with slices of hard-boiled egg each with half an olive and topped with a mixture of mayonnaise and sour cream flavoured with Worcestershire sauce

salat po-karabakhsky *Russia* A salad from the Caucasus made from sliced radishes, deseeded and peeled cucumber and spring onions, dressed with olive oil, lemon juice, chopped fresh mint and served with a feta type of cheese

Salatsosse *Germany* Salad dressing

Salbei *Germany* Sage

Salber *Germany* Salt pork

salceson włoski *Poland* A hard unsmoked pork sausage in a natural casing popular throughout the country

salchicha *Spain* Dark coarse-textured fresh sausage with a delicate flavour made from various meats. May be eaten raw or cooked.

salchichas estremeñas *Spain* Salchichas containing equal parts of pork belly, lean pork meat and liver

salchichón *Spain* A large sausage made from lean pork meat and pork belly, seasoned, spiced, dry-salted and lightly smoked

salciccia napoletana *Italy* A pork and beef sausage strongly spiced with powdered sweet red pepper

salcraute *Italy* Sauerkraut

sale *Italy* Salt

salé(e) *France* **1.** Salted, also corned, as of beef **2.** Savoury, as opposed to sweet

saleem *Thailand* Salim

sale grosso *Italy* Coarse salt

salema *England, Spain* A small round seawater fish, *Boops salpa*, with a grey skin and regularly spaced yellow horizontal lines weighing to around 1 kg. Treat as sea bream.

sale marino *Italy* Sea salt

salep *England, France* A starch preparation from the dried tubers of various Middle Eastern orchids used as a thickening agent

saleratus *United States* Potassium and/or sodium bicarbonate used as a raising agent or as an ingredient of baking powder (NOTE: From the Latin *sal aeratus*.)

salers *France* A type of cheese with a red-streaked rind. See also **Cantal**

sa leung geung *China* Lesser galangal

salgado *Portugal* Salted

salgam *Nepal, South Asia* Turnip

salicine plum See **Japanese plum**

Salicornia europaea *Botanical name* Samphire (marsh samphire or glasswort)

salim *Thailand* A dessert made from thin tapioca noodles in a coconut milk and jaggery sauce. Also called **saleem**

Salisbury steak *United States* A grilled seasoned beef patty rather like a hamburger without the bun

sallad *Sweden* Mixed salads made with a variety of salad ingredients including preserved fish, shellfish, pickled beetroot, apples and cold potato

salladsås *Sweden* Salad dressing

Sally Lunn A plain teacake made from a white yeast dough enriched with eggs and butter and baked in various size tins. Served hot, split and buttered, or cold, topped with glacé icing.

Salm *Germany* Salmon

salmagundi *England* A type of old English salad consisting of diced meats, hard-boiled eggs, anchovies, pickles and beetroot, all diced and arranged in a pleasing pattern on a bed of salad leaves. Also called **salmagundy**

salmagundy See **salmagundi**

salmi, in *Italy* In a rich wine sauce, especially game

salmigondis *France* Hotchpotch

salmis *England, France* A dish made from game birds by roasting in the usual way for about half the usual time, removing and reserving the breasts and finishing these off in a salmis sauce made with the remains of the bird, e.g. salmis of grouse, salmis de canard

salmis, sauce *England, France* A **mirepoix** of vegetables browned in butter, chopped game carcasses and white wine added and reduced, **demi-glace** sauce and stock added, simmered and skimmed until reduced to a thick consistency, then strained and finished with mushroom essence and truffle essence. Served with game.

salmistrato *Italy* Pickled, cured in brine

salmon 1. A large, round, oily seawater fish, *Salmo salar*, with a silvery skin and pink flesh, which spends the first two years of its life in a river and returns to the same river to spawn. Found throughout the North Pacific and Atlantic oceans, it is now extensively farmed in Scotland and Norway. The farmed variety may be distinguished from the wild by their intact tails and fins. They normally weigh from 3 to 13 kg and are often cooked whole and served cold and decorated at buffets and banquets. May be cooked in any way and smoked. **2.** *Australia* The Australian salmon, *Arripis trutta*, the eastern variety, and *A. truttaceus*, the western variety, which are not true salmon but are more closely related to perch. The ranges of the two species overlap in Victoria and they are also found in the coastal waters of New Zealand. They are not of great commercial value, although an excellent sport fish, and are generally canned. Also called **bay trout**, **black back salmon**

salmón *Spain* Salmon

salmón ahumado *Spain* Smoked salmon

salmon and onions *Wales* Cleaned salmon boiled in seawater or brine (35 g of salt per litre) for 3 minutes, skin and bones removed, the fish flaked and then fried with finely chopped onions in bacon fat

salmon bass See **bass**

salmon caviar See **ikura**

salmon dace See **bass**

salmone *Italy* Salmon

salmone affumicato *Italy* Smoked salmon

Salmonella enteritidis A food poisoning bacterium found in up to 75% of chickens

salmonete *Portugal, Spain* Red mullet, *Mullus surmuletus*

salmon pie See **laxgryta**

salmon trout 1. A variety of trout, *Salmo trutta*, which spends a season or more in the open sea, where the diet of small crustaceans gives its flesh a pink colour. The flesh is coarser and less succulent than salmon. The salmon trout can be distinguished from the salmon by the jaw line which extends beyond the eye. Also called **pink trout**, **sea trout 2.** Name given to various similar fishes in Australia and North America

salmorejo *Spain* A thick, smoothly blended sauce of **tomato concassée**, garlic, oil, vinegar and salt in which charcoal-grilled fresh chicken, rabbit or fish is placed when hot and left to cool and marinate for at least 6 hours

salmuera *Spain* Pickling brine

saloio *Portugal* A fresh and creamy cows' milk cheese from the countryside near Lisbon (NOTE: Literally 'peasant'.)

salpa *Italy* Salema, the fish

salpicão *Portugal* A fine sausage made with pork fillet, seasoned, spiced and smoked

salpicó de mariscos *Catalonia* A cold shellfish salad with sweet peppers and onions

salpicon *England, France* A mixture of chopped (traditionally 0.5 cm dice) or minced fish, meat or vegetables with flavourings and bound with a sauce. Used for stuffings, canapés, croquettes, vol-au-vents, etc. or similar mixtures of chopped raw or cooked fruits sweetened and flavoured as appropriate for use as fillings.

sal prunella Saltpetre cast in cakes. Because of the method of manufacture it contains potassium nitrite as an impurity and thus imparts a pink colour to meat products. Used for curing meat.

salsa 1. *Italy, Portugal, Spain* Sauce, gravy, ketchup **2.** *Portugal* Parsley

salsa alla pizzaiola *Italy* A tomato sauce well-flavoured with garlic, basil or oregano and chopped parsley. Served with meat, poultry and pasta.

salsa borracha *Mexico* A cold sauce made from a processed mixture of raw onions, pasilla chillies, orange juice and tequila or pulque

salsa comun *Italy* One of the earliest known recipes for a spice mixture from Ruperto de Nola, cook to the King of Naples, consisting of 3 parts cinnamon, 2 parts cloves, 1 part pepper and 1 part ginger with a little ground coriander seed and saffron if so wished

salsa de chile chipotle *Mexico* A sauce made from smoked green chillies (**chipotle chillies**), garlic, oil, water and salsa para enchiladas (tomato sauce); used in Mexican cooking

salsa de tomate *Spain* Tomato ketchup or sauce

salsa di noci *Italy* Skinned walnuts, processed with moistened bread, parsley, salt, oil and a little garlic, let down with cream or curds and served with ravioli

salsa di soia *Italy* Soya sauce

salsa francesa *Spain* French dressing

salsa inglesa *Spain* Worcestershire sauce

salsa roja *Caribbean* A savoury Cuban sauce made by sautéeing peeled tomatoes until soft then simmering them with chopped garlic, sugar, cayenne pepper and finely chopped basil and oregano until thick and finishing with vinegar and pepper

salsa rossa *Italy* A thick sauce made from chopped shallots sweated in butter and olive oil, **tomato concassée**, finely chopped carrots, roasted, skinned and chopped sweet red peppers, seasoning and a little chilli powder, simmered until all tender and amalgamated

salsa verde *Italy* An oil and vinegar mixture flavoured with crushed garlic, anchovy essence or chopped salted anchovies, chopped parsley and capers. Served with salads, cold meats and hard-boiled eggs. Also called **green sauce**

salsetta *Italy* Salad dressing, light sauce

salsicce alla romagnola *Italy* Sausages fried with sage and tomato sauce

salsicce e fagioli *Italy* A Tuscan dish of cannellino beans and coarse-textured sausage with garlic, tomatoes, olive oil and sage

salsiccia *Italy* A small fresh or dried sausage

salsiccia bolognese *Italy* A sausage containing minced heart and lungs

salsiccia di Bologna *Italy* A smoked slicing sausage from Bologna, made from various ingredients mainly finely ground pork with spices and seasonings but also veal, beef, tripe, pistachio nuts, onion, tongue, etc. cooked in wine and stuffed into beef bungs then simmered. Similar to Mortadella. Some are smoked. Also called **polony, bolony, poloney**

salsiccia di fegato *Italy* A sausage made with liver and flavoured with pepper and fennel seeds

salsiccia di nicosia *Italy* A pork and rabbit meat sausage mixture

salsiccia fresca *Italy* A small pure pork-based sausage flavoured with Parmesan cheese. See also **luganega**

salsiccia matta *Italy* A sausage made with giblets and spleen

salsiccia salamella *Italy* A thicker fresh sausage divided into links with looped string

salsiccia salamella vaniglia *Italy* A sausage flavoured with vanilla

salsiccia secca *Italy* Dried salsiccia

salsiccia toscana *Italy* A salsiccia flavoured with garlic, pepper and aniseed

salsiccie alla romagna *Italy* Poached sausages, dried, fried until brown in butter and oil, covered with half their weight of **tomato concassée** and simmered for 15 minutes

salsichas *Portugal* The Portuguese version of salchichas

salsifí *Spain* Salsify

salsifis *France* Salsify

salsify A long narrow root of a hardy biennial plant, *Tragopogon porrifolius,* originating from Spain with an oyster-like flavour. Can be boiled, fried or eaten raw. Similar to scorzonera. Also called **oyster plant, vegetable oyster**

salsitxa *Catalonia* A thin raw sausage

Salsiz *Switzerland* A **Rohwurst** made from a mixture of lean pork meat, beef and pork fat, air-dried and smoked

salt 1. The general chemical name for the compound formed when an acid reacts with a base (usually an alkali) as e.g. sodium acetate, which is formed by the reaction of acetic acid with the corrosive alkali sodium hydroxide or with sodium bicarbonate which is itself the salt of a weaker acid. The common example is sodium chloride, formed from the highly corrosive hydrochloric acid and it has appropriated the name salt to itself. See also **acid, alkali 2.** *Denmark, England, Norway, Sweden* Sodium chloride is used extensively in food processing and cooking as a taste item, to extract plant juices in fermented vegetables, e.g. sauerkraut, to solubilize proteins in meat, to assist emulsification, e.g. frankfurters, and to act as a preservative in e.g. salted fish and meat

salt, to To preserve food by immersing it in brine or covering it with dry salt. This replaces the water in the tissues with salt or a strong solution of salt, in which bacteria and other food degrading organisms cannot grow. See also **cure, to**

saltato *Italy* Sautéed

salt beef A joint of beef, usually brisket, cured in a spiced brine. Usually boiled and served hot or cold, usually in rye bread to make a sandwich.

salt cod Filleted cod layered in coarse salt and allowed to dry out. Used throughout southern Europe and the Caribbean as a cheap source of fish protein.

salt duck *Wales* A large fat duck rubbed inside and out with coarse dry sea salt and left in a cool place for 2 to 3 days, it is then rinsed and simmered slowly in stock or water with a bouquet garni, preferably in a double boiler until thoroughly cooked. Usually served with onion sauce.

salted almonds See **amigdala alatismena**

salted duck eggs Duck eggs packed in tubs and covered with a mixture of finely ground charcoal in brine. After 6 weeks to 3 months, the yolk becomes firm and the white becomes salty as the salt diffuses in. They are cooked by cleaning and boiling for 10 minutes. Used in curries and as hors d'oeuvres. The yolks are used in Chinese moon cakes. Common in China and Southeast Asia. See also **Chinese preserved eggs**

salted water A cooking liquor for poached and boiled fish consisting of 15 g of salt per litre of water used for sea perch, mullet, etc.

saltfish and akee *Caribbean* A mixture of diced salt pork fried in its own fat and reserved, chopped onion, sweet peppers, chillies, spring onions and tomatoes fried in the same fat with a sprig of thyme and all combined and heated with deskinned, deboned and flaked poached saltfish plus the creamy parts of akee which have been boiled in the saltfish poaching liquor for 15 minutes

saltfiskur *Iceland* Salted and dried cod

salt grinder A small mill like a pepper mill which is used to reduce large crystals of sea salt or similar to a small enough size to put on food

salt herrings Gutted herrings preserved between layers of salt, often in wooden casks

saltimbocca *Italy* A meat dish made from thin slices of veal and ham sandwiched together with sage and seasoning, formed into rolls, fried in butter and simmered in wine for 15 minutes

saltimbocca alla marchigiana *Italy* As **saltimbocca**, but made with beef, bacon and ham

saltimbocca alla partenopea *Italy* As **saltimbocca**, but with veal, ham and cheese and cooked in a tomato sauce

saltine biscuits Thin cracker biscuits sprinkled with coarse salt crystals before baking

salt-kind *Caribbean* Either dry or brine-salted meat, including trotters, tails, ears etc. used for making soup or for cooking with beans

salto, in *Italy* Turned over and fried as in sautéing

saltpetre E252, potassium nitrate, a chemical used in mixtures for curing meat and fish. Also a constituent of gunpowder. Also called **nitrate of potash, Prague powder, sal prunella**

salt pork Fat pork cured and preserved in salt or brine

salt potato *United States* A small new potato which has been soaked in brine, from Syracuse N.Y.

saltsa avgolemono *Greece* Avgolemono

saltsa domata *Greece* Tomato sauce

salts of hartshorn Ammonium bicarbonate, once obtained from the antlers of deer, now produced synthetically for use as a raising agent saltspring lamb *Canada* Baby lamb raised on salt marshes in British Columbia, similar to the French pré-salé lamb

salt stick *Pretzel*

saltwater fish Fish which live in the open sea

salume *Italy* Salt pork

salumeria *Italy* Delicatessen, grocer's shop

salumi *Italy* Salted meats

salva *Portugal* Sage

salvado *Spain* Bran

salvastrella *Spain* Salad burnet

salvia *Italy, Spain* Sage

Salvia lavandulifolia *Botanical name* Spanish sage

Salvia officinalis *Botanical name* Sage

Salvia officinalis 'Purpurascens' *Botanical name* Purple sage

Salvia sclarea *Botanical name* Clary sage

salxitxó *Catalonia* A type of cured sausage

Salz *Germany* Salt

Salzburger Nockerln *Austria* Soufflé omelettes baked in three's on a large dish and served with sweetened strawberry flavoured cream or jam sauce. Also called **Austrian pancakes**

Salzburgerwurst *Austria* A non-keeping sausage made with a mixture of beef, pork and bacon, lightly smoked and scalded. Grilled or fried.

Salzgebäck *Germany* Pretzels or crackers sprinkled with coarse salt before baking

Salzgurken *Germany* Dill pickles

Salzkartoffeln *Germany* Plain boiled parsley potatoes

Salzlake *Germany* Pickling brine

Salzwasser *Germany* Brine

samaki wa kupaka *East Africa* Whole firm fish, cleaned, scaled and prepared for barbecueing, slashed along either side and the whole of the surface and cavities covered with a paste of ground ginger, garlic, chilli pepper and salt and left for two hours. The fish is then half cooked on the grill (or in the oven) then basted with a previously made sauce of coconut milk, tamarind, curry powder, salt and cayenne pepper each time it is turned over until cooked.

samaki wa nazi *East Africa* A fish curry from Tanzania prepared in the usual way with firm fish, onions, garlic, tomato paste, chillies, lemon juice and curry powder which are all fried then simmered in coconut milk

samak mahshi beroz *Middle East, North Africa* A dish of Syrian origin consisting of whole white fish, stuffed with rice, pine nuts and almonds, baked and served with a tamarind sauce

samak quwarmah *Persian Gulf* A fish curry flavoured with fried onions, fresh ginger root, garlic, **baharat**, turmeric, a whole **loomi** and cinnamon stick and simmered for about 15 minutes. The loomi and cinnamon are removed before serving with **muhammar**.

sambaar *South Asia* A highly flavoured split pea and vegetable stew containing a lot of chillies, too hot for most Western tastes

sambal 1. *Indonesia, South Asia* Paste-like mixtures of various flavouring agents served separately in small dishes at the table 2. Various cold vegetables and fruits such as chopped tomatoes, sliced sweet peppers, sliced bananas, etc. often sprinkled with grated coconut and served in individual dishes as accompaniments to Indian food, especially curries 3. Side dishes of various meats, vegetables, etc. served with Southeast Asian meals

sambal asem A spice paste similar to sambal trassi with added sugar and tamarind concentrate

sambal bajak *Indonesia* A paste of red chillies, onions, garlic, trassi, candlenuts, tamarind, galangal, oil, salt, soft brown sugar, makrut lime leaves and coconut cream ground together. Used as a relish.

sambal goreng sotong *Malaysia* A side dish of fried squid flavoured with chilli

sambal kemiri A spice paste similar to sambal trassi with added ground dry-roasted candlenuts

sambal manis *Indonesia* A fairly mild dark brown condiment sambal made from mixed herbs, onions and brown sugar

sambal oelek *Indonesia* Dry-roasted fresh red chillies, salt and soft brown sugar processed together to make a paste which is used as a relish and served at the table in a separate dish. Also called **sambal ulek**

sambal trassi A spiced highly flavoured paste made from cooked **terasi** (180°C for a few minutes), red and green chillies, salt, lemon juice and soft brown sugar pounded together. Widely used in East Asia.

sambal ulek *Indonesia* Sambal oelek

sambar masala *South Asia* A spice mix used in the south with a thin vegetable curry comprising urad dal, coriander, cumin and fenugreek seeds and black peppercorns, all dry-roasted and ground. Sometimes contains in addition mustard seeds, dried curry leaves and dried chillies.

sambola *Sri Lanka* Sambal-like side dishes

samboosa holwah *Persian Gulf* Deep-fried filo pastry triangles with a filling of ground cashew nuts and walnuts, caster sugar and ground cardamom seeds, made from 4 cm by 20 cm rectangular strips. By repeated folding of the triangle all the edges are sealed.

sambosay goshti *Central Asia* Deep-fried triangular turnovers made from 9 cm squares of enriched pastry filled with a spiced mixture of minced cooked lamb and onion

samfaina *Spain* Pisto

samla mchou banle *Cambodia* Seafood, grilled and served with, or poached in, an aromatic herby stock with lemon juice and lemon grass

samlet Parr

samna *Middle East* Clarified butter

samong-saba *Burma* Fennel

samoosa *South Asia* Samosa

samosa *South Asia* A triangular pastry turnover containing a savoury filling, deep-fried and eaten as a snack. Also called **samoosa**

samouli *Persian Gulf* A long white bread stick similar to a French baguette, glazed and sprinkled with sea salt, sesame seeds or caraway seeds

samp *South Africa* Coarsely crushed maize often cooked with beans as a staple food for most South Africans

sam palok *Philippines* Tamarind

samphire 1. The annual salt marsh plant, *Salicornia europaea*, whose fleshy stems are cooked like asparagus. The fleshy part is stripped away from the hard core using the teeth. Because of its high proportion of silica it was once used in glassmaking. The succulent young leaves and shoots may be used in salads. Also called **glasswort**, **marsh samphire 2.** A bushy member of the carrot family with fleshy green leaves which grows on sea cliffs and in rocky coastal districts. The fleshy leaves and stems have a strong flavour and may be cooked as a vegetable or pickled. Also called **rock samphire**, **sea fennel**

samsa *Russia* Pasties made with an unleavened dough of creamed Greek-style yoghurt and butter with flour, rolled out and cut into 10 cm circles and each filled with a spiced and flavoured meat mixture, sealed, egg-washed and baked at 200°C for 15 minutes until golden

Samsø *Denmark* A semi-hard, scalded-curd cows' milk cheese cast in 15 kg cylinders. The paste has a few irregular holes and a delicate nutty flavour which develops as it matures. Not normally cooked.

sanbai-zu *Japan* A vinegar-based dressing for sunomono consisting of a mixture of rice vinegar, soya sauce and a little **mirin**

sanbusak *Turkey* A turnover made with a yeasted dough filled with a mixture of minced meat and onions with pine nuts and cinnamon

sancele *Italy* A black pudding from Sicily made with pig's blood, raisins, sugar and spices. Usually sliced and fried with onions.

sanchal *South Asia* A blackish rock salt with a good flavour due to other mineral contaminants

sancoche *Caribbean* A thick broth made from salt pork, salt beef, fresh meat, tropical vegetables, green figs, yellow split peas and coconut. Served with dumplings. A much simpler version from Trinidad is a lentil soup flavoured with a pig's tail.

sancocho *South America* A meat and vegetable stew similar to cocido from Columbia

Sandaal *Germany* Sand eel

sand biscuits Sablé biscuits

sand cake A rich sponge cake made with corn flour, ground rice or **fécule**. Also called **sandkage**

sand crab See **blue crab**

sand dab See **American plaice**

sand eel Various small thin long fishes of the *Ammodytidae* or *Hypotychidae* families which bury themselves in the sand at low tide. Used as bait and an important food for sea birds, They may be substituted for elvers in the appropriate dishes. Referred to and used as whitebait in the USA. Also called **sand lance**

sand flathead *Australia* See **flathead**

sandía *Spain* Water melon

sandkage *Denmark* Sand cake

sand lance *United States* Sand eel

sand lobster A general name for various species of small lobster-like crustaceans with similar quality meat known variously as bay lobster, bay bug, shovel-nosed lobster, rudder-nosed lobster, similar to slipper lobsters. Some bay bugs (*Moreton Bay bug and Balmain bug*) are fished commercially in Australia.

sandre *France* Pike-perch

sand smelt A thin round oily seawater fish, *Atherina presbyter*, up to 15 cm long found in the Mediterranean. It has a translucent green skin and a silver line along each side. Fried or grilled. Also called **silverside**, **European sand smelt**

sand sole A flatfish, *Pegusa lascarisk*, smaller than the Dover sole and with a speckled brown upper surface, found in shallow waters around the Mediterranean and the English Channel. The flesh is not as fine as

Dover sole but may be cooked in the same way.

Sandspierling *Germany* Sand eel

sand sugar *United States* Light brown sugar

sanduiche *Portugal* Sandwich

sandwich Two slices of bread enclosing a filling. The bread is coated on the inside with butter or similar to prevent the filling soaking into the bread. See also **open sandwich, smørrebrød, double-decker sandwich, casse-croûte**

sandwich cake See **layer cake, sponge sandwich**

sanfaina *Catalonia* A sauce made from sweet peppers, tomatoes, garlic, courgettes and aubergines, all sweated together until soft then sieved and seasoned

sang *France* Blood

sang chau *China* Light soya sauce

sang chow bow *China* A stir fry of diced pigeon meat, **lap cheong** and spices wrapped in bite-sized parcels of lettuce leaf

sang keong *China* Ginger

sanglier *France* Wild boar

sangrando *Spain* Rare, underdone, as of meat

sangre *Spain* Blood

sangre, con *Spain* Rare, or underdone (of meat, steak, etc.)

sangre con cebolla *Spain* A fried mixture of sliced onions, garlic, finely chopped fennel, cooked potatoes and pieces of baked coagulated blood

sangre con pimientos *Spain* As sangre con cebolla, but including sweet pepper and less onion

sangue *Italy, Portugal* Blood

sangue, al *Italy* Rare, underdone, as of meat

sangue, em *Portugal* Rare, underdone, as of meat

sanguinaccio *Italy* The Italian version of black pudding (**boudin noir**)

sanguinaccio alla fiorentina *Italy* Pig's blood mixed with a variety of nuts, spices, dried vine fruits, honey, etc. and baked in a tart or fried as a flat cake. See also **migliaccio**

Sanguisorba minor *Botanical name* Salad burnet

sangyak *Central Asia* The same bread as **nane lavash** but shaped in an oval and baked on a dish of oiled pebbles about 1 to 2 cm in diameter so as to give an indented effect. The bread is pressed onto the pebbles after 1 minute and again when turned over.

sanitize, to To reduce the number of microorganisms on a surface by treatment with a biocide, usually using a spray and cloth

San Maurin *Italy* A soft cheese from Piedmont with a lactic goaty flavour made from naturally soured goats' milk and cast in small elongated cylinders

San Pedro *Spain* John Dory, the fish

Sanroch *Italy* A somewhat sharp soft goats' milk cheese made in small elongated cylinders

sansho One of the few spices used in Japanese cooking. It is the berry corresponding to anise pepper from the variety of *Xanthoxylum piperitum* cultivated in Japan. Used as a condiment.

sansho sauce *Japan* Equal quantities of soya sauce and sake mixed with soft brown sugar, thinly sliced spring onions and a small amount of ground sansho

San Simón *Spain* A pear-shaped (up to 2 kg) cows' milk cheese from Galicia. It is ripened in hot whey and often smoked.

Santa Claus melon *United States* Christmas melon

santan *Indonesia, Malaysia* Coconut milk

santara *South Asia* Mandarin orange

santola *Portugal* Edible crab

santoreggia *Italy* Savory

sanwa Japanese millet

sa-nwin *Burma* Turmeric

saor, in *Italy* Soused, pickled

sap *Netherlands* Juice

saparot *Philippines* Pineapple

sapin-sapin *Philippines* A layered dessert made from galapong or rice flour mixed with sweetened coconut milk. Each layer is separately coloured and the whole is steamed.

sapodilla The fruit of the evergreen tree *Achras sapota* from Central America now grown in Southeast Asia and Sri Lanka, which is also the source of chewing gum base. The fruits are 5 to 7.5 cm in diameter and when ripe, the skin is brown, rough and sticky, the seeds are inedible and the flesh is pasty, sweet and tastes of burnt sugar. Used as a dessert. Also called **chiko, chiku, chikku, naseberry, neeseberry, tree potato, zapote, sapodilla plum**

sapodilla plum See **sapodilla**

saponins Chemical compounds found in many plants and especially in legumes such as chick peas, soya beans and navy beans thought to have important blood cholesterol lowering effects

sapore *Italy* Taste, flavour

saporoso *Italy* A relish

sapota *Italy* Sapodilla

sapote The fruit of a deciduous Central American tree *Calocarpum mammosum*. It is

sapotiglia

oval, up to 15 cm long and has a brown rough skin enclosing a sweet spicy flesh with a large central seed. May be eaten as a dessert, used in fruit salads or made into jam.

sapotiglia *Italy* Sapodilla

Sapotiglis *Germany* Sapodilla

sapotille *France* Sapodilla

SAPP Sodium acid pyrophosphate, used to prevent blackening in potatoes

Sapsago A very hard grating cheese from Switzerland made from cows' milk and shaped like a truncated cone, weighing from 50 to 200 g. It is flavoured with a local herb, *Melilotus caerulea*, which gives it a green tinge. Contains 37% water, 15% fat and 41% protein. Also called **Schabzieger, Ziger, Glarnerschabziger, Krauterkäse, green cheese**

sapsis *United States* A type of porridge made from beans

sapucaya nut Paradise nut

saracen corn Buckwheat

saraceno *Italy* Buckwheat

sarago *Italy* Sea bream

sarang burung *Malaysia* Bird's nest

sarapatel *Portugal* A type of haggis, hodgepodge

sarashi-an *Japan* Ground adzuki bean flour used for making desserts

Saratoga potatoes *United States* Potato chips, named after the town where they were first introduced

sar bo *China* A terracotta cooking pot glazed or unglazed on the inside that can be placed directly on a heat source. The clay from which it is made contains a high proportion of sand.

sarcelle *France* Teal, the wild duck

sard *Catalonia* Sea bream

sarda *Italy* Sardine

sarde, à la In the Sardinian style, i.e. garnished with rice, tomatoes, stuffed cucumber and possibly mushrooms. Used of roasts.

sardeles sto fourno *Greece* Cleaned and prepared sardines baked in a shallow dish at 190°C for 15 minutes with a dressing of latholemono. Served with chopped marjoram.

sardella *Italy* Sardine

Sardelle *Germany* Sardine

sardenaira *Italy* Pissaladeira

sardin *Sweden* Sardine

sardina *Italy, Spain* Sardine

sardine *England, France* A young **pilchard**. Also used for the young of other oily fish such

as sprats and herring. Grilled or available in cans.

Sardine *Germany* Sardine

sardiner *Denmark, Norway, Sweden* Sardines

sardines escabetxades *Catalonia* Pickled sardines

sardineta *Spain* Sprat

sárgarépa *Hungary* Carrot

sargo *Italy* Sea bream

sarma *Balkans* Sarmale

sarmale *Romania* Cabbage rolls filled with a mixture of minced beef and pork, chopped onion, boiled rice, garlic and seasoning, placed in a baking dish between 2 layers of sauerkraut with a layer of fried sliced onions at the base, covered with tomato sauce mixed with juice from the sauerkraut and braised in the oven until cooked through. Served with thick sour cream.

sarmale în foi de spanac *Romania* As sarmale but in spinach leaves and without the sauerkraut

sarmale în foi de viţă *Romania* As sarmale but in vine leaves and without the sauerkraut

sarmie *South Africa* Sandwich, probably misspelling of sarnie or vice versa

sarnie *United Kingdom* Sandwich (*colloquial; North West*)

sarpa *Italy* Sea bream

sarrasin *France* Buckwheat

sarriette *France* Savory, the herb

sarsaparilla A flavouring made from the dried roots of a tropical climbing plant, *Smilax officinalis*, used mainly for soft drinks. Also called **sarsparilla**

sarson *South Asia* Mustard greens

sarson ka tel *South Asia* Mustard oil

sarsparilla See **sarsaparilla**

sarsuela *Catalonia* A spicy fish and shellfish stew with a large variety of species. Similar to the Spanish zarzuela.

Sarusø *Denmark* A semi-hard cows' milk cheese made in squat cylinders to 14 kg. It has a dry golden brown rind and a firm, mild and sweet paste with pea-sized holes.

sås *Sweden* Sauce

sasafrás *Spain* Sassafras

sasage *Japan* Asparagus bean

sasami *Japan* The two small muscles in a chicken breast closest to the carcass and breast bone, often called the mignons. They are readily detached from the complete chicken breasts.

sashimi *Japan* Raw, very fresh seafood of contrasting textures and colour, sliced very thin and arranged decoratively on a bed of salad or grated mooli or rolled with contrasting colours, etc. Served with **wasabi**

and a dipping sauce based on flavoured soya sauce. See also **ito-zukuri**, **hira-zukuri**, **kaku-zukuri**, **usu-zukuri**

sashimi bocho *Japan* A knife with a long thin blade for cutting fish fillets

saslik *Turkey* Kebab

sassafras The tree, *Sassafras albidum*, whose dried leaves are used to make filé powder. A spicy, lemon-scented oil used as a flavouring for confectionery and ice cream is extracted from the leaves, bark and roots.

Sassafras *Germany* Sassafras

Sassafras albidum *Botanical name* Sassafras

sassefrica *Italy* Salsify

Sassenage *France* Bleu de Sassenage

sassermaet *Scotland* A Shetland speciality of minced beef preserved by mixing it with 50 g of salt per kg of meat plus ground pepper, cloves and cinnamon to taste. This mixture will keep for several weeks in a refrigerator or cool larder.

sassofrasso *Italy* Sassafras

saster *Scotland* A sausage made with pork shoulder meat containing about 25% fat, seasoned, flavoured with cloves, packed into casings, linked and air-dried

sås till grönsaker *Sweden* Mousseline sauce

sa-taw *Thailand* Parkia

satay *Southeast Asia* Cubes of meat, poultry or seafood marinated in a highly spiced mixture threaded on skewers and grilled until cooked. Usually served with a sweet or peppery hot peanut sauce. Also called **saté**

saté See **satay**

sato *Russia* Dried pork fat eaten on bread with mustard

sato imo *Japan* Field yam

sa tong *China* Granulated sugar

satsivi *Southwest Asia* A classic Georgian sauce of shelled walnuts processed with garlic and chopped onions, sweated in chicken fat and simmered in chicken stock with a bay leaf for 15 minutes until thick. The bay leaf is removed, and the mixture is flavoured with vinegar, ground coriander, turmeric, cloves, cayenne pepper and seasoning, finished with chopped tarragon and parsley and chilled for 2 hours, before being served with chicken. Also called **Circassian sauce**

satsuma A variety of mandarin, *Citrus unshiu*, which arose as a sport. It is slightly flattened and seedless with a well developed orange colour and sweet flavour, sometimes with a navel at the tip. It is grown extensively in Japan and Spain since both have cold winters. Also called **unshiu**, **mikan**

satsuma-imo *Japan* Sweet potato

saturated fat Hard fats in which all the carbon atoms are attached to the maximum number of other atoms, usually two carbon and two hydrogen atoms. Unsaturated soft fats and oils are converted to harder fats by hydrogenation, a process which can produce the trans fatty acids which some suspect to be harmful for pregnant and nursing mothers. Saturated fats are said to be unhealthy but fashions in health change from time to time. Small amounts of natural saturated fats (suet, lard, butter, etc.) are probably beneficial.

saturated solution A solution containing the maximum amount of solid (solute) that can be dissolved in and remain in solution in a liquid solvent at a particular temperature. The amount of solute dissolved depends upon and usually increases with temperature. A supersaturated solution may be obtained by cooling a saturated solution but this is unstable and any shock will cause solid to crystallize out.

Satureja hortensis *Botanical name* Summer savory

Satureja montana *Botanical name* Winter savory

Saubohnen *Germany* Broad beans

sauce *England, France* A liquid thickened by a roux, starch, **beurre manié**, egg yolks or blood, made by adding cream and/or butter or oil to a reduced cooking liquor or other liquid, or consisting of puréed vegetables or fruit. Sauce should have a smooth glossy appearance in most cases and a definite taste and light texture. It is used to flavour, coat or accompany a dish or to bind ingredients together. Savoury sauces are usually based on stock, milk, wine or juices extracted from vegetables; sweet sauces on milk, fruit juice or puréed fruits. Emulsion sauces are emulsions of fat or oil with vinegar or acid, and a few sauces are made by compounding butter with flavourings, by combining herbs and spices with vinegar and/or oil or from a variety of puréed beans, fermented products, nuts and the like.

sauce, to To nap with sauce, to place sauce on a plate either to stop food sticking to the plate and/or to contribute to the decorative effect

sauce abricot *France* Apricot sauce

sauce airelles *France* Cranberry sauce

sauce Allemande *France* White velouté sauce thickened with egg yolks. Also called **sauce Parisienne**

sauce boat An oval shallow wide-mouthed jug standing on an oval plate. Used to serve sauces usually with a small ladle.

saucepan Once restricted to a small pan for making sauces, now used for cylindrical pans of all sizes

saucer scallop A large variety of scallop, *Amusium balloti*, common in Australia

sauce soja *France* Soya sauce

sauce ti-malice *Caribbean* Finely chopped onions and chives marinated in lime juice for 2 hours then all cooked with finely chopped garlic and chilli pepper and olive oil. Served cold.

saucière *France* Sauce boat, gravy boat

saucijzebroodje *Netherlands* Sausage roll, a pastry roll filled with sausage meat

saucijzen *Netherlands* Sausages

saucisse *France* Sausage, especially the smaller types of fresh sausage made with chopped lean pork shoulder, seasoned and minced, packed into 2 to 3 cm casings and linked. Normally grilled or fried. See also **saucisson**

saucisse à la catalane *France* A ring of sausage (e.g. Cumberland) fried in fat until brown then simmered for 30 minutes in a sauce consisting of a roux made with pan residues, white wine, stock, tomato purée, a bouquet garni, orange peel and a large number of garlic cloves

saucisse au champagne *France* A gourmet sausage made from very fresh, preferably just killed, trimmed meat from a leg of pork and back fat, chopped and mixed with egg, sugar, quatre-épices and seasoning, moistened with Champagne and left to marinate for 12 hours, chopped truffles mixed in and all packed into sheep casings and linked, allowed to mature for a further 12 hours and deep-fried before serving

saucisse au fenouil *France* Very small sausages flavoured with fennel and poached then grilled as a kebab

saucisse au paprika *France* A kind of short Frankfurter flavoured with paprika and cooked in the same way

saucisse bretonne *France* Chopped fat pork meat mixed with chopped parsley, chives, quatre-épices and seasoning, packed into casings and linked

saucisse d'Ajoie *Switzerland* A smoked sausage from the Jura made with seasoned chopped pork. It can be boiled and eaten hot, or air-dried and eaten cold. Also called **Jurawurst**

saucisse d'Alsace-Lorraine *France* A sausage made from 2 parts of lean pork to 1 part pork fat mixed with saltpetre, seasoning and flavoured with quatre-épices and ginger, packed into hog casings and linked. Sometimes decorated for the Christmas season and eaten at the Réveillon celebratory meal either fried or heated in stock.

saucisse d'Auvergne *France* A small saucisson sec

saucisse de campagne *France* A common air-dried sausage made from a mixture of seasoned lean pork and fat bacon, moistened with red wine and flavoured with any of allspice, savory, marjoram, thyme, bay or coriander, packed into beef runners and sometimes lightly smoked

saucisse de Dole *France* Saucisse de Montbéliard

saucisse de Montbéliard *France* A lightly smoked sausage made of pork only. It is cooked by placing in cold water, bringing to the simmering point. Served with lentil purée or sauerkraut. Also called **saucisse de Dole**, **saucisse de Thann**

saucisse de Strasbourg *France* A thin sausage made of lean pork, possibly salted, and two thirds its weight of pork back fat, seasoned and flavoured with coriander and mace or similar, mixed with a little saltpetre, all minced at least twice to make a fine paste, packed into thin casings, tied off into 15 to 20 cm lengths, air-dried and then cold-smoked for 8 hours

saucisse de Thann *France* Saucisse de Montbéliard

saucisse de Toulouse *France* A sausage made from 3 parts coarsely chopped lean pork to 1 part pork back fat with sugar and saltpetre, seasoned and packed into 3 to 4 cm casings and either linked or left as a continuous length

saucisse du Périgord *France* A sausage made from lean pork plus three quarters as much pork back fat, minced, mixed with a little saltpetre, flavoured with shaved truffles and quatre-épices, seasoned, moistened with white wine and left to mature for a day before being packed in casings

saucisse en brioche *France* A good quality sausage baked in a brioche paste rather like a large sausage roll. Served warm and sliced as a starter.

saucisse espagnole *France* A sausage made of equal parts of seasoned lean pork and pork back fat mixed with raisins and flavoured with quatre-épices and allspice

saucisse juives *France* A sausage similar to the merguez but whose meat content is entirely calves' liver

saucisse madrilène *France* A sausage made from chopped veal, pork fat and filleted sardines in oil, seasoned, packed into beef runners and tied in rings, poached in veal stock, cooled and fried in butter

saucisses à la languedocienne *France* Sausage (e.g. saucisse de Toulouse) sweated in goose fat with chopped garlic and a bouquet garni for 20 minutes and served with a sauce made with the pan residues, **demi-glace** sauce, tomato purée, wine vinegar and capers and finished with chopped parsley

saucisses au gruau *France* Grützewurst

saucisses d'Arosa *Switzerland* Sausages made from two parts of chopped pork to one part **viande de boeuf blitzée**. Eaten hot. Also called **Aroserli**, **saucisses de Davos**, **saucisses de Schaffhouse**

saucisses de Davos *Switzerland* Saucisses d'Arosa

saucisses de Francfort *France* Frankfurter

saucisses de Schaffhouse *Switzerland* Saucisses d'Arosa

saucisse sèche *France* Small coarse-textured sausage, partially dried and sometimes lightly smoked and usually cooked further before consumption

saucisse soudjouk *Middle East* A highly spiced beef sausage served as a hors d'oeuvre

saucisse viennoise *France* An expensive sausage from Vienne made of equal parts of finely minced lean pork, veal and fillet steak with saltpetre, seasoning, cayenne pepper and coriander, moistened with a little water, packed in casings and lightly smoked

saucisson *France* A normally large sausage, either boiled like Cervelas, dried to make saucisson sec or smoked to make saucisson fumé (NOTE: Named after either a district or some component of the contents)

saucisson au foie de porc *France* Equal parts of pork liver, pork back fat and lean pork, separately chopped and combined with chopped onions sweated in lard, seasoning, quatre-épices, cayenne pepper and kirsch, rechopped, packed into hog casings, tied or knotted to make 10 to 15 cm lengths, air-dried for a day, simmered in water until cooked and served cold

saucisson au poivre vert *France* A sausage made of 100% pork flavoured with green peppercorns

saucisson-cervelas *France* A sausage filled with various mixtures of meat and bacon, sometimes pork only together with saltpetre, garlic, shallots and other spices, packed into beef runners, linked or looped, possibly brined and lightly smoked

saucisson chasseur *France* A small air-dried sausage consisting mainly of pork, for snacking

saucisson cuit au madère *France* A sausage made with 2 parts of seasoned pork fillet and 1 part pork back fat, flavoured with quatre-épices and Madeira wine, mixed with truffle shavings and/or blanched pistachio nuts, packed in 5 cm diameter casings and simmered until cooked

saucisson d'Arles *France* A mixture of coarsely chopped seasoned pork, pork fat and ground lean beef, flavoured with garlic, paprika, peppercorns and quatre-épices. May have saltpetre, sugar (for lactic fermentation) and red wine added, then packed into large casings and air-dried for some considerable time.

saucisson de Bourgogne *France* 2 parts of finely minced seasoned pork mixed with 1 part of coarsely chopped pork back fat and some sugar, flavoured with quatre-épices and brandy or kirsch, packed into beef middles and air-dried for at least 6 months

saucisson de campagne *France* A sausage made in the same way as saucisson de Bourgogne but with the addition of garlic and with the brandy or kirsch left out. May be smoked. Also called **saucisson de ménage**

saucisson de cheval *France* A pork sausage containing approximately 25% horse meat

saucisson de jambon *France* A ham sausage from Strasbourg

saucisson de lièvre *France* A sausage from Savoie made with hare meat

saucisson de Lyon *France* A saucisson sec made as saucisson lorrain but with 4 parts of lean pork leg meat to 1 part of pork back fat (salted pork or bacon)

saucisson de ménage *France* Saucisson de campagne

saucisson de montagne *France* A coarsely chopped pork sausage, air-dried

saucisson de Paris *France* A small sausage made of coarsely chopped lean pork with little fat, seasoned, flavoured and packed in casings. Normally boiled.

saucisson d'Italie *France* Minced seasoned lean pork and veal with about one fifth of the combined weight of pork back fat, flavoured with nutmeg, cinnamon and ginger, moistened with pigs' blood and white wine, packed into a pig's bladder, air-dried, smoked with juniper berries added to the wood, and coated with olive oil

saucisson gris *France* Saucisson lorrain

saucisson lorrain *France* A saucisson sec made of 2 parts of lean pork, 1 part of soft pork fat and 1 part lean beef, all chopped finely and mixed with saltpetre, quatre-épices and chopped and crushed garlic, packed tightly into hog casings, tied and strung in 40 to 50 cm links, air-dried for up to 6 months, packing down the filling as needed and keeping the sausage straight. Also called **saucisson gris**

saucisson provençal *France* A sausage made from pork from the leg or shoulder with little fat, containing saltpetre, peppercorns, quatre-épices and seasoning. Air-dried for several days and lightly smoked.

saucisson sec *France* Cured and dried sausages similar to some salami, normally eaten without further cooking

saucisson sec aux herbes *France* Coarse-textured dried pork sausage coated with herbs from Provence

saucisson vaudois *France* An air-dried and smoked sausage made with chopped pork and cured pork back fat

Sauerampfer *Germany* Sorrel

Sauerbraten *Germany* Beef, marinated in boiling red wine vinegar and water (1:2) with chopped onion, herbs and spices for 2 days, dried, browned and baked in a covered dish with the onions and half the marinade at 250°C for 1.5 hours. Served with the strained thickened pan juices. Sometimes ginger biscuits or ginger cakes are added to the cooking liquor.

Sauerkraut *Germany* Salted cabbage which has been subjected to a lactic fermentation. Widely used in central European cooking. Available canned. It may be made from cleaned, washed and finely shredded white cabbage mixed with 1.5% by weight of salt, placed in a straight sided, sterilized tub and covered with a sterilized muslin cloth, droplid and weight. After a day liquid should cover the lid and the sauerkraut is ready in 3 weeks, The liquid is skimmed off and the sauerkraut is used from the tub as required, always covering it with a sterilized cloth.

Sauermilch *Germany* Sour milk

Sauermilchkäse *Germany* Handkäse

säuern *Germany* To leaven or raise with yeast or a chemical raising agent

Sauerteig *Germany* Sourdough starter

sauge *France* Sage

saumon *France* Salmon

saumon blanc *France* Hake, the fish

saumon fumé *France* Smoked salmon

saumure *France* Pickling brine

saumuré Pickled or marinated in brine

saunf *South Asia* Aniseed or fennel

saupe *France* Salema, the fish

saupiquet *France* A sharp spicy wine-based sauce or stew. The sauce sometimes served with roast hare.

saur *France* Salted and smoked, usually of herring

saure Kartoffeln *Germany* Sliced peeled potatoes boiled until tender and served in a sauce which is made from a brunoise of bacon fried until crisp, flour added and cooked to a roux, potato cooking liquor added, seasoned and soured with vinegar at 65 ml per litre

saure Rahmsauce *Germany* Sour cream, salad dressing

saure Sahne *Germany* Sour cream

saure Sahnensosse *Germany* Sour cream sauce

sauro *Italy* Sorrel

saursuppe *Italy* Tripe soup from the north

saury pike A long seawater fish, *Scomberesox saurus*, found in temperate waters

saus *Netherlands, Norway* Sauce

sausage Chopped or minced meat, seasoned, possibly mixed with spices, herbs, flavouring agents, extenders and binders, all stuffed into a casing usually of cleaned intestines, may then be boiled, scalded, cured, dried, smoked or any combination of these before sale. The name probably derived from the Latin salsisium, meaning salted, i.e. preserved.

sausage maker A hollow long tapered cylinder that fits over the outlet of a mincing machine. The casing with one end tied in a knot is placed over the cylinder like a wrinkled stocking and as it is filled with the mixture extruded from the machine is allowed to slip off the cylinder. The long sausage may then be linked or divided as required.

sausage meat A meat mixture similar to that for stuffing sausages, used for pies, rolls, turnovers, meat loaf, etc. In the UK, a revolting paste of ground meat scraps, drinde, MRM, rusk, etc. See also **English sausage**

sausage roll Sausage meat or similar meat mixture wrapped in puff or shortcrust pastry to form a small roll, egg-washed and baked in the oven

sauté, to To shallow fry food in hot fat or oil whilst shaking or tossing the ingredients so as to cook it and/or brown the surface (NOTE: From the French *sauter*, 'to jump', from the jumping of the food as it is tossed around the pan.)

sauté de boeuf et rognons en croûte *France* Steak and kidney pudding

sauté pan See **plat à sauter**

sauter, faire *France* To sauté or to fry

sautoir *France* Sauté pan, plat à sauter

sauvage *France* Wild, undomesticated, usually of animals

savarin *England, France* A rich yeast mixture similar to a baba, baked in a ring mould and demoulded. Sometimes soaked in spirit or liqueur-flavoured sugar syrup and may be filled or decorated, sometimes cut in slices as a basis for other desserts such as croûte aux fruits. Often incorrectly used to describe a sweet or savoury mousse set in a ring mould, demoulded and garnished or sauced. (NOTE: Named after Brillat-Savarin.)

savarino *Italy* Savarin

Savaron *France* A semi-hard mild-flavoured cows' milk cheese from the Auvergne with a thick covering of mould on the rind. Similar to Saint Paulin.

savelha *Portugal* Shad, the fish

saveloy Cervelas

savenna *Spain* Venus shell clam

savijaca od jabuka *Balkans* The original apple strudel from Croatia which eventually found its way to Hungary and Austria

savoiardi *Italy* Sponge fingers

savore *Italy* Savory, the herb

savory A perennial herb similar to thyme which comes in two main forms, **summer savory** and **winter savory**. Traditionally used to flavour beans.

savoureux *France* Tasty, flavoursome

savoury 1. With a pleasant meaty, salty, piquant, herby or spiced flavour, the opposite of sweet 2. A small savoury item of food usually presented on a small piece of toast for eating with the fingers 3. A savoury tasting dish, once served in small quantities after the sweet at very formal multi-course dinners. Nowadays a substantial savoury-tasting dish used as a main course at a lunch, supper or snack meal.

savoury butter A compound butter with a savoury flavour, e.g. anchovy butter

savoury duck *Wales, England* Faggot

savoyarde, à la In the Savoie style, i.e. containing potatoes and a local cheese

savoy biscuit A small dry sponge finger biscuit made by the creaming method with whipped egg whites folded in at the end. Used for lining moulds or as the base of desserts made from setting mixtures such as charlottes. See also **sponge fingers**

savoy cabbage A winter ball type cabbage with dark green crinkly leaves surrounding a tight ball of similar but light green leaves. Excellent boiled, braised or steamed, then wrung out, chopped, buttered, seasoned

and reheated. The finest cabbage commonly available.

savu *Finland* Smoked

savulohi *Finland* Smoked salmon

saw A serrated-edge steel blade with sharp, ground, alternately offset to right and left, teeth used for cutting bones and frozen food, shaped like a hacksaw or conventional saw or made as a continuous power driven loop (bandsaw) for cutting up animal carcasses

sawara *Japan* Mackerel

saw knife See **bread knife**

saya endo *Japan* Mangetout peas

sayori *Japan* A very thin fish, *Hyporhamphus sajori*, similar to the garfish, It is cleaned very thoroughly and served as a double fillet in sushimi or can be used in tempura, shioyaki or sunomono (NOTE: Literally 'half beak'.)

sayote *Philippines* Choko

sayur *Indonesia* A dish of crisp cooked vegetables in a thin coconut milk sauce

sayur salat *Malaysia* Lettuce

sayyadiya *Middle East* A fish, onion and rice stew popular in the Arabian gulf, especially Kuwait

sbattere *Italy* To whip or whisk

Sbrinz *Switzerland* A hard, dark-yellow grating cheese made from unpasteurized cows' milk. A lactic whey starter is used and the curd is hard cooked, gathered in cheesecloths, moulded in up to 25 kg lots, pressed and brined for 3 weeks then matured for 6 to 12 months. It is also made in Germany, France and Italy. Also called **Spalenkäse**

sbrisolona *Italy* A flat crisp cake made with a mixture of wheat flour and cornmeal and incorporating chopped almonds

scabbard fish A long thin edible seawater fish, *Lepidopus caudatus*, with a smooth silvery skin

scad Horse mackerel

scads *United Kingdom* Fish (*colloquial*; *Scilly isles*)

scalcione *Italy* Focaccia del venerdi santo

scald A sinistral flatfish, *Arnoglossus laterna*, similar to the lemon sole but of inferior quality

scald, to 1. To pour boiling water over something or immerse in steam for a few moments so as to cook a thin outer layer without affecting the inner part. Used to remove skin from tomatoes or to loosen hair on animal skin. 2. To heat milk to just below boiling point and then immediately cool 3. To clean cooking utensils by immersing in boiling water 4. To seal in flavour by bringing food in water to a temperature which coagulates surface proteins, usually 80°C

scalded cheese Cheese which has been made from curds which have been heated to between 40 and 48°C, soft cheeses at the lower temperature

scalded curd Curd for making cheese, which has been heated to a temperature between 40 and 48°C

scalded sausages Brühwurst

scale, to To remove the **scales** from fish

scales 1. A device for measuring weight **2.** The outer protective coat of fish consisting of overlapping tile-like sheets of a tough substance (chitin) about 3 to 6 mm in diameter attached at one edge. Removed by scraping against the free side with the back of a knife or similar.

scalibada *Catalonia* **1.** A dish of vegetables grilled over charcoal or on a barbecue **2.** Roasted aubergines, onions and sweet peppers dressed with olive oil

scallion 1. See **spring onion 2.** The name often given in Chinese and Southeast Asian cooking to the **Welsh onion**

scallop A bivalve mollusc of the *Pectinidae* family with an almost circular white to brown shell with a distinctive straight hinge varying in diameter from 7.5 to 20 cm. After scrubbing and washing they are baked at 150°C for 10 minutes to open the shell. After opening and detaching from the rounded upper shell, the beard is removed, the scallop separated from the lower shell and the black intestinal sac removed. The shell and flesh with the orange roe are well washed to remove all traces of sand. Usually served on the shell and have a delectable flavour and soft texture. They must not be overcooked. There are over 400 species worldwide. Also called **scollop, coquille St-Jacques**. See also **great scallop, queen scallop, bay scallop, saucer scallop, pilgrim scallop, Atlantic deep sea scallop, Iceland scallop, variegated scallop**

scallop, to 1. *United Kingdom* To decorate and seal the edge of a double-crust pastry pie by making small radial incisions in from the edge and half turning over the pastry with the back edge of the knife to give a scalloped effect. A similar effect may be obtained with the forefinger of the left hand and the thumb and forefinger of the right hand or vice versa. **2.** *United States* To cover with sauce and breadcrumbs and bake in a casserole

scalloped Cooked in a scallop shell

scalloped potatoes *United States* Raw sliced potatoes, baked in a dish with butter, milk and seasoning

scallops 1. The pieces of meat and hard tissue left after rendering down fat into lard. Also called **greaves 2.** *United Kingdom* Slices of potato fried like potato chips (*colloquial*)

scallop squash Patty pan squash

scalogni *Italy* Shallots

scaloppina *Italy* A schnitzel of veal or pork fillet, either panéed and fried or floured and fried, often finished with Marsala and/or cream and served with tomato sauce

scaloppina alla milanese *Italy* A plain Wiener Schnitzel garnished only with lemon wedges

scaly custard apple Sweet sop

Scamorza *Italy* A soft spun-curd cows' milk cheese similar to but somewhat firmer than Mozzarella. A lactic starter is used followed by rennet and the curds are hot kneaded and shaped into teardrops (up to 250 g) which are tied with raffia at the top. They are then cooled, briefly brined and sold young. Contains 51% water, 24% fat and 23% protein.

scampi 1. *United Kingdom* The tail meat of the Dublin bay prawn. Many restaurants substitute pieces of monkfish tail if they can get away with it. **2.** *Italy* Dublin bay prawns (singular scampo), strictly only those caught in the Bay of Naples

Scandinavian sweet mustard sauce See **gravlax sauce**

scapece, a *Italy* Soused, fried then marinated in oil and vinegar with garlic and herbs, used of fish

Scappi's spice mix A mixture of cloves, dried ginger, nutmeg, grains of paradise, saffron and soft brown sugar from Bartolomeo Scappi's cook book 'Opera dell' Arte del Cucinare'

scarlet runner bean See **runner bean**

Scarlett O'Hara herb *United States* Lemon verbena

scarola *Italy* Batavian endive

scarole *France* Batavian endive

scaup A wild duck, *Aythya marlo*, shot for the table in the UK

scaveccio alla grossetana *Italy* Eel, marinated in oil, vinegar and pepper

scelta, a *Italy* According to choice, as preferred

scented geraniums Tender evergreen perennials of the genus *Pelargonium*, growing to 1 m with various scented leaves which may be used for flavouring or crystallized for decoration. The flowers may be used in salads. See under *Pelargonium* for particular scents and uses.

schaaldieren *Netherlands* Shellfish

Schabzieger *United States* Sapsago

Schafmilckkäse *Germany* A slicing cheese made from ewes' milk

Schafsragout Emmentaler Art *Switzerland* A blanquette of lamb or mutton, coloured with saffron and containing diced root vegetables

Schalotten *Germany* Shallots

Schaltiere *Germany* Shellfish

schapevlees *Netherlands* Mutton

Schaum *Germany* Mousse or foam

Schaumrollen *Germany* Puff pastry rolls filled with whipped cream

schaum torte *Denmark* A dessert made with almonds and egg white, sometimes incorporating crushed fruit

schav A Jewish soup made from spinach or sorrel, lemon juice, eggs, sugar and soured cream. Served chilled.

Schellfisch *Germany* Haddock

schelvis *Netherlands* Haddock

Schenkeli *Switzerland* Small oval rolls, fried in butter (NOTE: Literally 'little thigh'.)

schiacciata *Italy* A very thin flattened yeast-raised bread incorporating olive oil and sometimes herbs, chopped onions or olives

schiacciato *Italy* Crushed, flattened

schidionata *Italy* Spit-roasted

Schildkröte *Germany* Turtle

Schildkrötensuppe *Germany* Turtle soup

Schinken *Germany* Ham

Schinkenbrötchen *Germany* Ham sandwich

Schinkenkipferl *Austria* A yeasted dough made from mashed potatoes, flour, eggs, egg yolks and milk, proved, rolled out thinly, filled with a mixture of chopped boiled ham, butter, egg yolks and grated Parmesan cheese, formed into croissants, proved, egg-washed and baked. Served hot or cold.

Schinkenkipper *Austria* A croissant with a ham filling

Schinkenplockwurst *Germany* A somewhat firmer sausage than Schinkenwurst containing large pieces of fat

Schinkenwurst *Germany* A speciality slicing sausage from Westphalia made with flaked ham and smoked over beech and ash with juniper berries. Best chilled before slicing to prevent it disintegrating.

schinus molle The aromatic dried red berries of a tree *Schinus molle* often sold as a pink peppercorn. They have a brittle outer shell enclosing a small seed.

schiumare *Italy* To skim

Schlachtplatte *Germany* A plate of sliced cold meat and sausages

Schlackwurst *Germany* A dark red-coloured beef and pork sausage similar to cervelat

Schlag- *Germany* With cream

schlagen *Germany* To whip or whisk

Schlagobers *Austria* Whipped cream

Schlagsahne *Germany* Whipped cream

Schlegel *Germany* Drumstick (of poultry), leg (of veal)

Schlehe *Germany* Sloe

Schleie *Germany* Tench, the fish

Schlemmer-Topf *Germany* Chicken brick

Schlesisches Himmelreich *Germany* A dish from Silesia of pork chops cooked with dried apples, pears, apricots and prunes, alternatively roast pork or goose with potato dumplings or with sauerkraut and purée of peas

Schlosskäse *Austria* A cows' milk cheese similar to, but milder than **Limburger**

Schlumperweck *Germany* A pie filled with grated apple and baked

Schlupfkuchen *Germany* A chemically raised sponge cake flavoured with lemon zest made by the creaming method, 3 mm slices of apple inserted in to the dough and all sprinkled with a cinnamon and sugar mixture before baking at 175°C

Schmalz *Germany* Melted or rendered down fat, dripping, lard, etc., more specifically a description of chicken fat rendered down with onion. See also **chicken fat**

Schmalzgebackenes *Germany* Fried food

Schmand *Germany* Sour cream

Schmankertorte *Austria* Pastry

Schmelz *Germany* Processed cheese

Schmorbraten *Germany* A pot roast of beef with mushrooms, gherkins and vegetables

schmoren *Germany* To braise or stew

Schmorfleisch *Germany* Spiced meat, meat for pot-roasting or stewing

Schmorgurken *Germany* Peeled and seeded cucumbers, halved and cut into 3 cm pieces, poached in a type of béchamel made with browned chopped onion and a brown roux, served with sour cream and chopped dill

Schnäpel *Germany* Houting, the fish

Schnecken *Germany* 1. Snails 2. Sweet cinnamon-flavoured rolls

Schneeballen *Austria* Strips of sugared pastry twisted into large constructions

Schneeklösschen *Austria* A wine- and egg-based soup

Schnepfe *Germany* Woodcock

Schnitt *Germany* A slice of food, or a food which can easily be cut into slices

Schnitte *Germany* Chop, steak, slice of meat, fillet of fish, etc.

Schnittlauch *Germany* Chives

Schnittlauchsosse *Austria* Chive sauce. An emulsion sauce made with milk soaked white bread, hard-boiled and raw egg yolks pounded together with oil added as for mayonnaise, finished with vinegar, seasoning and chopped chives.

Schnitzel *Austria, England, Germany* A piece of tender meat beaten out to a large thin sheet using a cutlet bat, then panéed, shallow-fried and garnished. Usually pork or veal.

Schokolade *Germany* Chocolate

Schokoladeneis *Germany* Chocolate ice cream

Schokoladenpudding *Germany* A type of chocolate mousse made from plain chocolate, butter. separated eggs and blanched almonds (2:2:5:2) and a little strong coffee. The chocolate is melted with the coffee (6:1), the butter and sugar are creamed, the egg yolks whisked in followed by the cooled chocolate and almonds and finally the whipped egg white (soft peak) are folded in. The mixture is cooked in a covered mould in a simmering bain-marie for 1 hour, demoulded and served with Chantilly cream whilst still hot.

schol *Netherlands* Plaice

Scholle *Germany* Plaice

school prawn *Australia* A type of prawn, *Metapenaeus macleayi*, intermediate in size between the deepwater and king prawn found in river estuaries and bays

Schöpsenschlegel *Germany* Roast leg of lamb

schorseneer *Netherlands* Scorzonera

Schotensuppe *Germany* Fresh green pea soup

schotisches Moorhuhn *Germany* Grouse

schrod *United States* Baby halibut under 1 kg, popular on the northeast coast of North America. See also **scrod**

Schrotbrot *Germany* Wholewheat bread

Schübling *Austria, Switzerland* A small smoked sausage containing beef, pork, bacon, diced bacon, seasoning and spices. Eaten hot.

Schulter *Germany* Shoulder

Schupfnudeln *Germany* Thick and heavy noodles

Schutzauf *Austria* A cream cheese cake

Schwäbische Wurst *Germany* A mixture of two thirds lean pork and one third fat pork, seasoned, flavoured with garlic, packed into casings, boiled then smoked

Schwamm *Germany* Mushroom

Schwärtelbraten *Germany* Roast leg of pork usually accompanied with sauerkraut, dumplings and sour cream

schwartenmagen *France* A type of short black pudding from Alsace made with minced lean pork and pigs' blood. Also called **Blut Schwartenmagen**

Schwarzbrot *Germany* Brown or rye bread, coloured with molasses or treacle

schwarze Johannisbeere *Germany* Black currant

Schwarzkümmel *Germany* Nigella

Schwarzsauer *Germany* Goose giblets stewed with dried apples, pears and prunes and thickened with goose blood

Schwarzwälder Eierküchlein *Germany* Pancake batter flavoured with kirsch, cooked very thin. rolled around a filling of butter cream with sugar mixed with chopped and drained morello cherries flavoured with kirsch. Flamed with kirsch when served.

Schwarzwälder Kirschtorte *Germany* Black Forest gateau

Schwarzwurst *France, Germany* A highly spiced black pudding from Alsace and adjoining Germany, made from minced lean pork, fat, breadcrumbs and garlic, mixed with pig's blood, seasoned, flavoured with cloves, packed into casings, linked, boiled, air-dried and smoked. Sometimes flavoured with onions.

Schwarzwurzeln *Germany* Salsify

Schwein *Germany* Pig

Schweinebauch *Germany* Belly pork

Schweinebraten *Germany* Roast pork, often browned and then covered and baked at 250°C

Schweinefett *Germany* Lard

Schweinekeule *Germany* Hind leg of pork

Schweinekotelett *Germany* Pork chop

Schweineohren *Germany* Crisp and very thin sweet pastry (NOTE: Literally 'pigs' ears'.)

Schweinepfeffer *Germany* Highly seasoned cooked pork with pepper

Schweinepökelfleisch *Germany* Salt pork

Schweinerippchen *Germany* Pork spare ribs or cutlets

Schweinerücken *Germany* Pork fillet (**tenderloin**)

Schweineschenkel *Germany* Leg of pork

Schweinesülze *Germany* Jellied pork, brawn

Schweinfleisch *Germany* Pork

Schweinshaxe *Germany* Leg of pork

Schweinsjungfernbraten *Germany* The back meat of the pig after removing the eye of the loin and fillet, roasted until the skin is crisp

Schweinskarre *Germany* Smoked pork chops

Schweinskopfwurst *Austria* A sausage made from 4 parts of pork head meat mixed with 1 part of beef, all minced, seasoned, moistened with water, bound with **fécule** and packed into casings

Schweinswurst *Germany* Pork sausage from Bavaria flavoured with marjoram and scalded before sale

Schweizerkäse *Germany* Swiss cheese

Schweizer Leberspiessli *Switzerland* Bacon-wrapped liver kebabs, brushed with molten butter, seasoned, flavoured with chopped sage and wrapped in pig's caul before grilling

Schwertfisch *Germany* Swordfish

sciarrano *Italy* Sea perch

sciatti *Italy* Pancakes filled with a mixture of molten Bitto cheese and grappa and served hot (NOTE: Literally 'sloppy'.)

sciroppato *Italy* Sweetened in syrup

sciroppo *Italy* Syrup

sciroppo d'acera *Italy* Maple syrup

sciroppo di zucchero *Italy* Treacle

scissors Two pivoted opposing blades with handles arranged to close together and overlap. Used for a variety of cutting tasks in the kitchen. The two blades are differently ground and sharpened, one being the cutter with the oblong finger hold and rounded tip, the other being the anvil blade with the round finger hole and the sharp tip. The cutter blade is usually on top of the work and does the actual cutting.

scoiattolo *Italy* Squirrel

scollop See **scallop**

Scolymus ardunculus *Botanical name* Cardoon

scone An eggless plain cake made with self-raising flour, butter and sugar (4:1:1) and added baking powder (50g per kg flour) using the rubbing in method, gathered into a paste with milk possibly with added sultanas, cut into small rounds or a quartered larger circle and baked at 200°C for 15 to 20 minutes. Must be eaten fresh, usually split and buttered or with jam and whipped cream. Also called **English scone**, **hot biscuit** (NOTE: Named after the original oatmeal and sour milk cake made in Scone, Scotland.)

scone round A large round scone scored in wedges before baking. The separate wedges are usually split open and eaten with a savoury or sweet filling.

scoop A type of spoon with a hemispherical or deeper bowl. Used for ice cream and for dispensing powders.

score, to To make shallow cuts (1 to 4 mm) in the surface of food using the point of an office knife, to assist marinating, or skinning, or in the case of skin on the surface of meat to assist the rendering of the subcutaneous fat and to prevent the shrinking of the skin from distorting the shape of the meat, or to make indentations in a cake, biscuit or scone, etc. to assist portioning

scorfano di fondale *Italy* Bluemouth, the fish

scorfano rosso *Italy* Scorpion fish

scorpion fish A very ugly fish, *Scorpaena scrofa*, with a rough red mottled skin and weighing up to 1 kg. Used in bouillabaisse and similar soups and stews. Found in Mediterranean and similar climates.

scorthalia Skorthalia

scorza *Italy* Skin, rind or peel, e.g. of citrus fruit

scorzonera *England, Italy* The long black root of a member of the daisy family, *Scorzonera hispanica,* originating from Spain and used as a vegetable or in salads. Also called **black salsify** (NOTE: Literally 'black serpent'.)

Scorzonera hispanica *Botanical name* The scorzonera plant

Scotch barley Pot barley

Scotch bean Broad bean

Scotch black bun See **black bun**

Scotch bonnets The common Caribbean name for a rounded version of the sweet pepper which comes in a wide range of colours

Scotch broth Washed barley simmered in white beef stock until tender, brunoise of carrot turnip, leek, celery and onion and a bouquet garni added, simmered until tender, skimmed, bouquet garni removed, seasoned and served with chopped parsley

Scotch bun See **black bun**

Scotch egg A hard-boiled egg completely covered in sausage meat, panéed and deep-fried at 185°C, halved and served hot with tomato sauce or cold with salad

Scotch egg sauce *United Kingdom* As egg sauce but the yolks of the hard-boiled eggs passed through a coarse sieve and the whites diced. Served with salt cod.

Scotch grouse See **grouse**

Scotch haddock pudding *Scotland* A type of soufflé using mashed potatoes flavoured with celery salt, lemon juice and tabasco sauce instead of the flour-based panada. Flaked cooked haddock is added to the mixture of egg yolks and potatoes before folding in the stiffly beaten egg whites. Baked at 180°C for half an hour in a rather shallow layer.

Scotch kale *Scotland* A thick broth from Scotland containing shredded cabbage similar to the soup part of pot-au-feu

Scotch oats *Scotland* Pinhead oatmeal

Scotch pancake Drop scone

Scotch pie *Scotland* A raised pie made with a beef dripping hot water pastry, (flour, water and dripping (8:5:2)). The sides stand up to 1.5 cm above the top and the filling which is made with minced lean mutton and chopped onion browned in lard and simmered with water, parsley and seasoning and thickened with flour for about 20 minutes. The round pies, which are about 8 cm diameter and 5 cm deep, are baked at 180°C for 45 minutes. It used to be the custom to fill the top with vegetables to make a complete meal. Always served hot.

Scotch woodcock A savoury made of buttered toast variously covered with a thick butter sauce containing anchovy purée and capers then gratinated and grilled or lightly scrambled eggs decorated with fillets of anchovy and capers or similar, served hot

scoter duck A large dark-coloured diving duck genus *Melanitta* or *Oidemia* which lives in coastal seas

scottadito *Italy* Small cutlets eaten with the fingers whilst hot (NOTE: Literally 'burning fingers'.)

scottare *Italy* To scald

scottiglia *Italy* A rich stew from Tuscany made with veal, poultry, pork and game

Scottish black pudding *Scotland* Salted and sieved fresh pig's blood mixed with milk (4:1), one third the combined weight of suet, minced onions, seasoning and a small quantity of lightly toasted oatmeal, filled into beef runners leaving room for expansion, tied, simmered for 2 hours pricking to prevent splitting, then dried. Served hot either boiled or fried.

Scottish ginger cake *Scotland* As gingerbread with a little oatmeal, sultanas, chopped stem ginger and mixed peel

Scottish grouse Red grouse

Scottish hare A hare, *Lepus timidus scoticus*, found in the Alps, Scotland, Ireland and Scandinavia. It has a smaller body, shorter ears, a larger head and longer legs than the common hare and its fur turns white in winter. See also **hare**. Also called **varying hare**, **blue hare**, **alpine hare**

Scottish lovage A plant, *Ligusticum scoticum*, very similar to lovage which grows wild on rocky coasts. Used in salads and as a pot herb.

Scottish pancake Drop scone

Scottish shortbread See **shortbread**

scouse See **lobscouse**

scrag end of lamb *United Kingdom* The neck of the lamb extending to the ribs from the head end. Used for stewing. Occasionally the longitudinal muscle is dissected out and sold as neck fillet.

scrag of veal *United Kingdom* The neck and neck vertebrae of veal used for stewing and stock. Usually boned out for stewing.

scram *United Kingdom* Food in its cooked form (*colloquial; navy*)

scramble, to To stir beaten eggs continuously over heat scraping solid egg off the base of the pan until all is set to the required consistency

scrambled eggs Seasoned beaten eggs mixed with milk or cream and scrambled with a little butter in the pan. It should look moist and creamy and not be overcooked.

Scrapple 1. *Germany* Pork scraps and offal, boiled and chopped, seasoned, mixed with cornmeal or other cereal and flavoured with sage, cooked like a meat loaf, cooled, sliced and fried **2.** *United States* As the German Scrapple but made with better quality meat

scratchings *United Kingdom* Crisp fried pieces of pork skin, eaten as a bar snack. Also called **pork scratchings**

screwpine The fragrant leaves of the palm-like screwpine, *Pandanus odaratissimus* and *P. amaryllifolius*, from tropical swamps in Southeast Asia, used as a flavouring in Malay, Thai and Indonesian dishes, and as a source of kewra essence. Also called **pandanus leaf**

scrigno di venere *Italy* Large stuffed pasta shells

scrod *United States* Young cod under 1 kg in weight, popular on the northeast coast of North America. See also **schrod**

scum The layers of greyish, foamy, coagulated protein and dirt which rise to the top of a simmering liquid. Must be skimmed off or the liquid will lack clarity.

scungilli *Italy* Conches, the gastropod mollusc

scup *United States* Sea bream

sea anemone A primitive flower-like polyp consisting of a digestive sac with a ring of tentacles around the opening and attached to the rocks at the base by a foot, common in European waters. They are prepared by removing the tentacles, turning inside out and cleaning thoroughly. The **beadlet** (also called 'tomate de mer') and **oplet** are eaten in France.

sea bass A seawater bass, genus *Centropristus*, which feeds mainly on shellfish and crustaceans and has a delicately flavoured firm white flesh. Found off the coast of North America.

sea beet A species of wild beet, *Beta vulgaris* subspecies *maritima*, with a sprawling habit which grows on the seashore and sea walls. The leaves are cooked like spinach. Also called **sea spinach**

sea biscuit Hardtack

sea bream Various blunt-nosed medium oily seawater fish of the *Pagellus* and *Spondyliosoma* families, principally *Pagrus pagrus* and *P. vulgaris*, with deep, red to pink bodies ranging in length from 20 cm to 1 m. The flesh is pink or white and may be cooked in any way. See also **bream**. Also called **porgy, red porgy, scup**

sea burbot Ling

Seabutt *Germany* Brill, the fish

sea cat Catfish

sea celery *Australia* A low growing herb, *Apium prostratum*, with a slight celery flavour. It grows near sea or fresh water estuaries and swamps etc. The leaves are used in salads and the stems may be braised like celery.

sea cucumber A slow-moving worm-like sea grub, *Isostichopus fuscus*, related to the star fish, between 3 and 9 cm in length, which processes sea sediments to extract nutrients. The dried flesh is much prized in Asia and is used to thicken and flavour soups. The flesh is firm and gelatinous with a slight fishy flavour. The dried variety most commonly available must be soaked for several days before cooking. To prepare from fresh, wash and clean, soak overnight, blanch 5 minutes, cut open and gut, then simmer for 4 hours. Also called **bêche de mer, sea slug, sea rat**

sea date A tiny bivalve mollusc, *Lithophaga lithophaga*, from the Mediterranean which is the same shape, colour and size as a date, usually eaten raw. Also called **date shell, date mussel**

sea drum A deep bodied seawater fish, *Pogonias cromis*, of the drum group up to 4 kg in weight and 1 m long. The lean flesh may be cooked in any way. Also called **black drum**

sea ear Abalone

sea fennel *United States* Samphire

seafood Any edible marine animal, fish, shellfish, and various other species which inhabit the sea bottom or are free floating or swimming

seafood in puff pastry Bouchées de fruits de mer

sea girdle A variety of brown kelp, *Laminaria digitata*, similar to kombu and found in shallow water of the North Atlantic. Also called **tangle, sea tangle, finger kombu**

sea kail See **seakale**

seakale A seashore plant, *Crambe maritima*, of the cabbage family prevalent in northern Europe whose stems are blanched and served like asparagus with melted butter. Also called **sea kail**

seakale beet Swiss chard

seal, to To briefly expose the surface of meat to intense heat which is supposed to form an impermeable seal to prevent loss of juices on further cooking

sea laver 1. See **sea lettuce 2.** Nori

sea lettuce 1. A pale green seaweed, *Ulva lactuca*, resembling lettuce leaves, found around the shores of the UK and sometimes used as a vegetable. Also called **sea laver, green laver, lettuce laver, ulva 2.** Carragheen

sea mullet *Australia* One of the most common edible Australian fishes, *Mugil cephalus*, is plentiful in all the states except Tasmania. It is olive green above with silvery sides and grows to 3 kg. It has an oily flesh which is good to eat, especially if grilled or smoked. Also called **poddy mullet**

sea oak *United States* Arame

sea ormer Abalone

sea owl Lumpfish

sea perch Comber

sea pie 1. *United Kingdom* A beef stew partially cooked in a casserole, a layer of suet crust pastry rested on top of the stew, the lid replaced and cooking continued until the meat is tender. Served from the casserole. **2.** *United States* A veal, pork or chicken stew with dried dessert apples, molasses and dumplings from New England

seapuss *Caribbean* Octopus

sear, to To brown food, especially meat, in a very little hot fat or oil before grilling, roasting, braising or stewing

sea rat Sea cucumber

sea robin Gurnard

sea salt Salt produced by the artificial evaporation of cleaned and filtered seawater. Usually large crystals up to 5 mm.

sea slug Sea cucumber

season, to To add salt and ground pepper to taste

seasoned flour Flour mixed with salt and ground pepper used for coating food (esp. surface damp food) before frying

seasoned salt *United States* A mixture of salt, MSG, spices and vegetable salts, used as a general seasoning

seasoning Salt and ground pepper

sea spinach Sea beet

sea tangle *United Kingdom* Sea girdle

sea trout See **salmon trout**

sea urchin A spherical-spine covered animal, *Paracentrotus lividus* and other species, up to 8 cm in diameter which lives on rocky coasts in all oceans and seas. The spines require careful handling. They are opened when alive and the orange-coloured ovaries are removed and either eaten raw or used as a garnish. Must be live when purchased and consumed as soon as possible. See also **edible sea urchin**, **green sea urchin**

sea vegetables Edible seaweed, i.e. plants of the algae family which grow in seawater and may be green (shallow water), brown, or red (deep water). Usually dried. See also **sea lettuce**, **laver**, **dulse**, **kombu**, **nori**, **wakame**. Also called **seaweed**

seawater This contains 35 g of salt per litre. Fish and shellfish should be boiled in a similar concentration of salt in water to avoid making the flesh soft and watery.

seaweed See **sea vegetables**

seaweed gelatine Agar-agar

seaweed jelly Agar-agar

sea wing Fan mussel

sea wolf Catfish

sebo *Spain* Suet

sec *France* **1.** Dry **2.** Dried (NOTE: The feminine form is *sèche*.)

secchielli *Italy* Dried chestnuts

secco *Italy* Dry, dried

sèche See **sec**

séco *Portugal* Dried, dry

seconda portata *Italy* The main dish or course of a meal

second bamboo See **bean curd sticks**

second feather duck A duck which is not killed until it has replaced its first set of feathers at about 3 months of age. Usually free-range and with a fuller and more mature flavour.

secondi *Italy* The main courses of a meal as displayed on a menu

secondo grandezza *Italy* S.G.

section waiter See **station waiter**

sedani *Italy* Ridged macaroni (NOTE: Literally 'sticks of celery'.)

sedani corti Short pieces of sedani, the classical pasta for minestrone

sedano *Italy* Celery

sedano di verona *Italy* Celeriac

sedano rapa *Italy* Celeriac

Sedgemoor Easter cake *England* A thin crisp biscuit from the southwest containing currants and flavoured with brandy

sediment Unwanted solid particles which settle out at the bottom of liquids

sedlo olenia, sedlo olenya *Russia* Saddle of venison marinated 24 hours, barded with bacon and roasted with the marinade at 230°C for 30 minutes, reducing to 180°C until tender. Served with reduced pan juices mixed with cream and horseradish.

Sedum rosea *Botanical name* Roseroot

Seeanemone *Germany* Sea anemone

Seebarsch *Germany* Bass, the fish

see byan *Burma* The stage in making a curry at which the oil or fat separates. This occurs when most of the water has evaporated and the dish is then considered to be correctly cooked.

seed The structure containing an embryo, stored food and a seed coat derived from the fertilized ovule of a flowering plant or tree from which a new plant will arise if it germinates successfully. Variously known as grains, cereals, pips, nuts, stones, kernels, etc.

Seedattel *Germany* Sea date

seed cake A type of Madeira cake flavoured with caraway seeds and possibly lemon and/or vanilla

seedless Without seeds

seedy cake *England* A West Country victoria sponge flavoured with caraway seeds. The cake is made by the creaming method but incorporating the egg yolks in the usual way and folding in the stiffly beaten egg whites. No baking powder is used. Baked at 200°C for 30 to 45 minutes.

Seehecht *Germany* Hake

Seeigel *Germany* Sea urchin

Seekarpfen *Germany* Black bream

seek kabab *South Asia* Minced meat croquettes shaped with the hand over a steel or iron skewer the thickness of a pencil and grilled over or under a fierce heat. The meat should be free of fat and gristle and may contain aromatics and herbs. It is bound with an egg.

Seekrabben *Germany* Crabs

seeng *South Asia* Drumstick vegetable

Seeohr *Germany* Abalone

Seepolyp *Germany* Octopus

seer *South Asia* A unit of weight equal to 4 powas or 20 chattaks, approximately 900 g or 2 lb

Seespinne *Germany* Spider crab

Seeteufel *Germany* Monkfish

seet gnee *China* White fungus

seethe, to To simmer

see yau *China* Light soya sauce

Seezunge *Germany* Dover sole

seffa *North Africa* Sweetened couscous from Morocco flavoured with cinnamon. Sometimes prunes, raisins and almonds are added.

segala *Italy* Rye, rye bread

segedínsky gulás *Czech Republic* Selny gulás

seiche *France* Cuttlefish

seigle *France* Rye

seiro *Japan* Mushi-ki

seiron-nikkei *Japan* Cinnamon

seitan Wheat gluten obtained by washing the starch out of flour dough. It is marinated in soya sauce with various flavourings and used in vegetarian meals as a protein source and flavouring agent.

seitó (*plural* **seitons**) *Catalonia* See **anchovy**

sekar pala *Indonesia* Mace

seker geker *Turkey* Sugar

seki han *Japan* Boiled rice mixed towards the end of the cooking with cooked adzuki beans and cooked a further 5 minutes, then flavoured with a little sake and soya sauce. The rice is cooked in the liquor from the cooked adzuki beans made up with extra water as required.

sel *France* Salt

selasih *Indonesia* A wild basil with a very mild flavour

Selchfleisch *Germany* Smoked pork

Selchwurst *Austria* A sausage similar to **Burgenländisch Hauswürstel**

sel'd *Russia* Herring

sel de mer *France* Sea salt

selderie *Netherlands* Celery

self-raising flour A wheat flour which incorporates a chemical raising agent, usually sodium bicarbonate plus an acid salt for reaction and completed liberation of all the available carbon dioxide. 30 g of baking powder per kg of plain flour may be substituted (9 teaspoons per kg or 4 teaspoons per lb).

self rising flour *United States* Self-raising flour

self-service A type of service of food where the customers go to a counter where food is laid out and usually help themselves to cold items and sometimes to hot items. The food is then taken to a cash receiving point, if to be paid for, where the cost is computed and paid. Cutlery, napkins, seasonings and condiments are usually collected after payment.

selha chawal *South Asia* Converted rice

selino *Greece* Celery

Selkirk bannock *Scotland* A yeast-raised sweetened dough enriched with butter and sultanas, baked and glazed to a golden brown (NOTE: From the Scottish border country and traditionally served at Hogmanay. It weighs about 0.5 kg)

sella *Italy* Saddle (of lamb or veal)

sell-by date Date shown on packaged food to aid stock control, usually for food with a short shelf life. Food may well remain edible after this date but should be consumed quickly or stored appropriately.

selle *France* Saddle, e.g. of lamb or venison

selleri 1. *Denmark* Celery **2.** *Sweden* Celeriac, not celery

Sellerie *Germany* **1.** Celeriac, not celery **2.** Celery

Selles-sur-Cher *France* A soft, mild-flavoured goats' milk cheese from Loire et Cher, whose rind is dusted with powdered charcoal. Protected by appellation d' origine status. Also called **Romorantin**

sellou *North Africa* A dryish sweet made with sugar, butter and ground almonds

selodka *Russia* Russian salt herrings, made by covering whole herrings, not gutted, with a mixture of coarse salt, coarsely ground pepper and bay leaves for 3 days in a cool larder. They are then removed, the salt brushed off and the fish covered in a marinade made from water boiled with a large amount of chopped garlic and bay leaves mixed with some of the liquor from the herrings and a few tablespoons of the salt. To serve they are rinsed, gutted, deboned and laid on a bed of bay leaves and crushed peppercorns.

selon grandeur *France* S.G.

selshcaree Trimmed loin of pork cured in spiced brine and lightly smoked. Popular in Northern Europe boiled with sauerkraut.

Selva *Spain* A soft cows' milk cheese made in small cylinders (up to 2 kg) with a delicate slightly salty taste which develops after ripening for 3 to 6 weeks

selvaggina *Italy* Game, venison

selvatico *Italy* Wild, uncultivated

sem *South Asia* Green beans

semangka *Indonesia, Malaysia* Water melon

sembei *Japan* A small crisp rice cracker

sementare *Italy* Very small eels, elvers

semi *Italy* **1.** Seeds **2.** Half

semi-cos lettuce A type of lettuce with sweet crunchy leaves shorter than the cos

semi di papavero *Italy* Poppy seeds

semidure *Italy* Soft-boiled, of eggs

semi-fino *Italy* A grade of rice requiring about 15 minutes cooking time

semifreddo *Italy* A chilled mousse type dessert or ice cream on a crushed biscuit base

semifrío *Spain* A chilled dessert

semi-hard cheese A fairly rigid cheese with normally a moisture content between 40 and 45%

semini *Italy* Small seed-shaped pasta

semi-skimmed milk *United Kingdom* Milk with a butterfat content between 1.5 and 1.8%. Sold in bottles with a silver and red striped top.

semi-soft Holding its shape but easily cut with a knife

semi-sweet Lightly sweetened

semlor *Sweden* Light sweetened yeast-raised buns flavoured with spice and filled with almond paste. Served as a dessert floating in bowls of hot milk on Shrove Tuesday. Also called **Shrove Tuesday bun**

semmel *United States* A breakfast roll introduced by German immigrants, i.e. the Pennsylvania Dutch (from 'Deutsch')

Semmelkloss *Germany* Bread dumpling

sémola *Spain* Semolina

semolina 1. A technical term for the large pieces of endosperm from wheat which are made by the fluted rolls used to separate the bran from the semolina **2.** The culinary term for a particular type of semolina made from durum wheat. The particle size varies according to the use to which it is going to be put. Fine semolina is used for pasta, coarser varieties are used to make a boiled milk pudding.

semolina pudding *United Kingdom* A pudding made by boiling milk and sprinkling in semolina at the rate of 70g per litre, simmering for 20 minutes then adding sugar and butter at the rate of 100g and 20g per litre of milk respectively. It may be browned under the grill.

Semolino *Italy* Semolina, from durum wheat

semoule *France* Semolina

Sempervivum tectorum *Botanical name* House leek

semplice, alla *Italy* Simply cooked

senap *Sweden* Mustard

senape *Italy* Mustard

senape di digione *Italy* Dijon mustard

senapssås *Sweden* Mustard sauce made with a fish velouté with dry mustard added equal in weight to one sixth of the flour used in the roux. Finished with cream.

sendai-miso *Japan* Inaka-miso

Senf *Germany* Mustard

Senf Kartoffeln *Germany* Sliced cooked potatoes in a mustard sauce

Senfkohl *Germany* Rocket, the plant

sen-giri *Japan* A very fine **julienne** vegetable cut. Also called **hari-giri**, **hari-kiri**. See also **needle cut**

sen leck *Thailand* Medium-sized rice noodles

sen mee *Thailand* Small rice noodles similar to vermicelli

senmen-giri *Japan* A cucumber fan used as a garnish

sennep *Denmark, Norway* Mustard

sen yai *Thailand* Rice sticks

separate, to To take one part of a substance away from the whole, as for instance in separating egg yolks from whole eggs or cream from whole milk

sepia *Spain* Cuttlefish

sèpia amb pèsols *Catalonia* Cuttlefish with peas

seppia *Italy* Cuttlefish

sera *South Asia* Lemon grass

serai *Malaysia* Lemon grass

serai powder Sereh powder

serbal *Spain* Rowanberry

serbuk perasa *Malaysia* Monosodium glutamate

sereh *Indonesia, Malaysia* Lemon grass

sereh powder Dried and ground lemon grass used for flavouring. Also called **serai powder**

Serena *Spain* A hard vegetarian cows' milk cheese with a dry rind and dense hole-free yellow paste cast in cylinders (up to 1.5 kg). The curd is moulded in esparto grass containers and is ripened for 50 days. Contains 40% water, 30% fat and 26% protein.

serendipity berry *Central Africa, West Africa* An edible red berry from a tropical tree, *Dioscoreophyllum cumminsii*, which has an extremely sweet taste

sériole *France* Amberjack

Serpa *Portugal* A ewes' milk cheese eaten fresh when soft and buttery or ripened for 1 to 2 years in caves where it is regularly cleaned and wiped with a paste of olive oil and paprika. It has a dry texture and nutty flavour.

serpenyös rostélyos *Hungary* Sirloin steak flattened and browned in lard with chopped onions and garlic, well dusted with paprika and flour, and braised in water with crushed caraway seeds, marjoram, tomato purée and chopped sweet green peppers, adding thick slices of parboiled potatoes towards the end

Serra *Portugal* Queijo da Serra

serrano chilli A variety of hot chilli pepper from Mexico, usually sold green. They are plumpish (4 cm by 1.5 cm) with a strong rich flavour.

serrated knife See **bread knife**

serruda *North Africa* A Moroccan dish of mashed chickpeas served with onion, butter and saffron

seru ndeng *Indonesia* A condiment made from fried shredded coconut mixed with peanuts and brown sugar. Served with rice.

service 1. A full set of crockery for a specific meal for several persons (usually 4, 6 or 12), as in tea service, dinner service **2.** The attendance given to customers in a restaurant by waiters and staff

serviceberry Juneberry

service charge The charge added to a restaurant bill, usually as a percentage of the total to cover the cost of providing waiters. It originated in the times when waiters were paid only this percentage for their labour. This archaic and demeaning practice dies out as society develops.

service compris *France* Service included. Used on a restaurant bill.

serviço incluido *Portugal* Service included. Used on a restaurant bill.

Serviettenklösse *Germany* Bread dumplings cooked in a cloth to hold their shape. Usually served with cooked pears, bacon and French beans in a sweet-and-sour sauce.

serving A single portion of food or drink. See also **serving: fish and shellfish**, **serving: healthy eating**, **serving: meat**, **serving: soups and sauces**, **serving: vegetables, grains and pulses**

serving: fish and shellfish Main course servings are 300 g fish per portion on the bone, 125 g fish boned and skinned, 250 g or half lobster in the shell, half a litre of mussels in the shell

serving: healthy eating Nutritionists state that an adequate diet should contain 5 servings per day of fruit or vegetables each approximately 80 g (3 oz). Typical servings are, a medium-sized apple or orange, half a grapefruit, 2 to 3 tablespoons (50 ml) of peas or beans or other vegetables, 200 ml of salad, 100 ml of fruit juice.

serving: meat Main course servings are meat off a piece, 100 g off the bone, 150 g on the bone, individual steak or chop, 2 to 3 lamb cutlets or two lamb kidneys

serving: soups and sauces Soup as starter 100 to 150 ml, sauce with meat or fish 50 to 75 ml, sauce as accompaniment e.g. mint, cranberry, apple, 20 to 40 ml

serving spoon A spoon with a large oval bowl end which may or may not be slotted

serving: vegetables, grains and pulses Cooked vegetables 80 to 100 g, mushrooms 50 g, old potatoes in skin 170 g, new potatoes in skin 125 g, rice and other dried starch staples 25 to 50 g, pulses and beans as main course 60 g

servizio *Italy* Service charge in a restaurant

sésame *France* Sesame

sesame butter See **tahini**

sesame chilli oil Red chillies fried in sesame seed oil to give the oil a red colour and hot flavour. Used as a seasoning and condiment.

sesame salt Gomasio

sesame seed Cream to black oval seeds from the seed pods of an annual plant, *Sesamum indicum*, mainly grown in China, Central America and South West USA. After dry-roasting they have a pleasant nutty taste and contain about 50% oil. Used in bread and cakes, to make tahini and to add texture to other foods. See also **black sesame seeds**, **white sesame seeds**, **tahini**. Also called **benne seed**

sesame seed oil Oil extracted from sesame seeds, sometimes toasted, with a pronounced flavour and good colour. Used for stir-frying, to add flavour to other dishes and added to deep-frying oil (1 part in 10). Also called **oriental sesame oil**

sesame seed paste See **tahini**

sesamo *Italy* Sesame

sésamo *Spain* Sesame

Sesamum indicum *Botanical name* Sesame

sesos *Spain* Brains

set, to 1. To lay out crockery, cutlery and glassware on a table **2.** To leave jellies and other thickened mixtures to go solid usually by cooling **3.** To freeze ice cream, sorbets, etc.

seta *Spain* Fungus

Setaria italica *Botanical name* Foxtail millet

seui gwa *China* Loofah

sevastopolskoe pechenye *Russia* An almond tart from the Crimea made in a square blind-baked case, the pastry made from flour, sugar, butter and eggs (8:3:5:3), filled with a mixture of egg white and light brown sugar (7:10) mixed with flaked almonds and flavoured with cinnamon and lemon zest, the mixture slightly thickened over a low heat, then baked until brown. Served cut in 5 cm squares.

seven minute frosting *United States* Egg whites, granulated sugar, boiling water, cream of tartar and flavouring beaten briskly for 7 minutes over hot water until of a meringue-like consistency. Used for icing and as a cake filling.

sevian *South Asia* Baked vermicelli-type noodles in a creamy sugar syrup flavoured with rose water

seviche *South America* A dish of marinated white fish. See also **ceviche**

Seville orange The round orange-coloured fruit of the original orange tree of the Mediterranean, *Citrus aurantium*, about 7 cm in diameter, which is now only cultivated around Seville and Malaga. It is harvested in January and used for marmalade manufacture and as a substitute for lemon. Also called **sour orange**, **bitter orange**

sevruga sturgeon The smallest of the sturgeon, *Acipenser stellatus*, up to 10 kg in weight, which produces about 1.5 to 2 kg of fine-flavoured, dark grey to black caviar which has the same name

sew, to To close a pocket of meat or the abdominal cavity of a bird or fish by sewing with thick thread so as to prevent a stuffing from leaking out during cooking

sewin *Wales* Salmon trout

sfenj *North Africa* Doughnuts

sfenzh *North Africa* Deep-fried Moroccan doughnuts

sfilatino *Italy* A bread from Tuscany

sfilato *Italy* Boned or jointed, as applied to small game animals (NOTE: Literally 'unthreaded'.)

sfincione *Italy* A Sicilian pizza with a thick soft base topped with tomato, cheese, anchovies and olives

sfingi *Italy* Sweet biscuits

sfoglia *Italy* A sheet of pasta dough

sfogliata *Italy* **1.** Flaky pastry **2.** A type of Napoleon cake sometimes filled with ricotta cheese, spices and candied fruit

sfogliatelle *Italy* A Neapolitan speciality cake

sformata *Italy* Moulded food, timbales, etc.

S.G. 1. *France, Italy* Selon grandeur (French) or secondo grandezza (Italian), i.e. according to size. Used e.g. for pricing fish in restaurants according to the weight of the fresh fish to be cooked. **2.** See **specific gravity**

S-Gebäck *Germany* 'S'-shaped biscuits flavoured with lemon zest made from flour, butter sugar and egg yolk (4:2:2:1) by the creaming method. The dough is refrigerated, rolled out into 1 cm by 10 cm sticks, formed into flattened S shapes on the baking tray, brushed with egg white, sprinkled with crushed sugar lumps and baked at 200°C until firm.

sgombro *Italy* Mackerel

shabu shabu *Japan* A one-pot meat and vegetables dish cooked at the table in boiling stock. Served with sesame-flavoured sauce. Similar to sukiyaki.

sha cha jiang *China* A slightly coarse-textured sauce made from peanuts, dried fish, dried shrimp, chillies, garlic and various spices such as five spices and coriander. Used in Cantonese cooking. Also called **sha zha chiang**

shad A white, seawater fish of the genus *Alosa*, belonging to the herring family, which migrates from the sea to rivers to spawn. There are several varieties, e.g. Allis shad, *Alosa alosa*, and the slightly smaller twaite shad, *Alosa fallax*, ranging from 30 cm to 1 m in length. Its oily delicate flesh is often marinated in acid or cooked with acidic leaves to loosen or dissolve the bones. It is generally grilled, fried or baked, and is also used raw in sushi. Also called **alose**, **gizzard shad**

shaddock Pummelo

shadow bennie sauce *Caribbean* Chadon bennie, sauce

shaggy cap Shaggy ink cap

shaggy ink cap An edible fungus, *Coprinus comatus*, with a dark shaggy cap on top of a short stem, paler when young. Also called **ink cap**, **shaggy cap**

shaggy parasol An edible mushroom, *Lepiota rhacodes*, similar to the parasol mushroom, with a rough light brown cap on an off-white stem. Skinned before cooking.

sha gou dou fu *China* Casseroled bean curd stew

sha he *China* A noodle made from rice flour which puffs up when deep-fried

sha jeera *South Asia* Caraway seed

sha jen *China* Cardamom

shakarkandi *South Asia* Sweet potato

shake *United States* Milk shake

shakkar *South Asia* Raw sugar (NOTE: The Sanskrit origin of the English word *sugar*.)

shako *Japan* **1.** A giant clam, *Hippopus hippopus*, to 1 m high. The flesh near the shell is the most flavoursome and the adductor muscle is dried and used as a flavouring or in other dishes. **2.** The mantis shrimp, *Oratosquilla oratorio*, which grows to 15 cm long. When boiled, and removed from its shell with some difficulty, it has a purplish skin and white flesh. Used as a topping for **nigiri-zushi** or for **tempura**.

shallot 1. A small hard onion, *Allium cepa* Aggregatum Group which grows in clusters, usually stronger-flavoured than the onion. The green leaves may be harvested for use as a flavouring. **2.** *Australia* same as **spring onion**

shallot butter See **beurre d'échalotes**

shallow-fry, to To cook food in a small amount of hot oil and/or fat in a frying pan or plat à sauter, the aim being to complete the cooking of the centre of the food at the same time as the outside is brown and crisp

shallow-frying, fish Skinned and filleted or whole fish washed and drained, passed through seasoned flour, fried in a small amount of hot clarified butter presentation side first, placed on a dish, covered with **beurre noisette** and garnished with a slice of lemon

shallow-poaching, fish A method of cooking cuts of fish by placing presentation side up on sweated chopped onions or shallots in a pan, adding cooking liquor to half way up the fish, bringing to the boil, placing a cartouche over then placing the pan in the oven at 160°C to 180°C for 3 to 10 minutes. The fish is removed and kept warm while the cooking liquor is made into a sauce. See also **poached white fish**

shama millet A slightly smaller seed than normal from a millet, *Echinochloa colona*, used in the same way as Japanese millet

shami kabab *South Asia* Small croquettes made with minced meat and soaked yellow split peas (4:1), cooked in water with flavourings such as garlic, coriander, cumin, mint, ginger, minced onion or the like until soft and all liquid absorbed. The mixture is then processed to a smooth paste, formed into small flat circular croquettes and fried in clarified butter on both sides, taking care not to break them.

shami kebab *South Asia* Deep-fried meatballs made from lamb, onion, garlic, yellow split peas, ground black cumin, chilli powder, cashew nuts, garam masala, salt and chopped coriander leaves blended together and bound with egg and lemon juice

shamouti *Middle East* A variety of common orange which occurred by mutation in a Palestinian orchard in 1844. It is easily peeled without releasing much oil and is virtually seedless and has a good flavour. It is not suitable for processing owing to delayed bitterness (like the navel orange). Grown in Cyprus, Turkey and Swaziland. Also called **Jaffa**, **Cyprus oval**

Shanghai cooking A cosmopolitan style of Chinese cooking influenced by many of the provinces of China

Shanghai hairy crab A small square-bodied crab with a covering of dark hair on the legs and edge of the top shell. It is found on the Chinese coast around Shanghai and the meat and the roe are highly prized.

Shanghai noodles Round fresh egg or white wheat flour noodles from Shanghai which are thicker than Italian spaghetti. Generally served with sauce in the same way as spaghetti.

Shanghai nuts Roasted peanuts with a crisp savoury coating. Eaten as a snack.

shank 1. Part of the leg of any animal, usually including the knuckle **2.** *United Kingdom* Beef from the lower muscular part of the foreleg, with more gristle than shin beef and generally used for consommé and stock **3.** The Welsh term for leg of lamb

shank end of lamb *United Kingdom* The lower half of a hind leg of lamb

shan na *China* Lily bulb

Shantung cabbage Chinese leaves

shan yao *China* Chinese yam

shao *China* Braising

Shaohsing rice wine See **red girl wine**

shao mai *China* Steamed pork dumplings

sharbat billooz *North Africa* A popular Moroccan drink made from whole blanched almonds liquidized with milk, water, sugar and rose water or orange flower water, strained and served chilled

shariyya *North Africa* Very fine Moroccan noodles

shark A group of fish ranging from 70 g to 20 tonnes characterized by their lack of mineralized bones, the skeleton being of very flexible cartilage-like material. Many of the smaller varieties are edible and traded. Because of their unusual physiology they tend to smell of ammonia but this can be counteracted by cooking at high temperatures e.g. deep fat frying. Varieties include tope, guitar fish, angel fish, dogfish, skate, porbeagle, hammerhead and mako.

shark-ray Angel fish

shark's fin The fin of a species of shark found in the Indian Ocean. It requires lengthy preparation to clean and soften it and it may be converted into chips or strands. It is always cooked in a rich stock of poultry bones and pork shank, possibly supplemented with dried oyster and **con poy**. Whole cleaned fins are slow- cooked and eaten for their taste and texture, usually without any accompaniment save perhaps a little vinegar.

shark's fin soup A soup made with prepared shark's fin (chips or strands) cooked in clarified and seasoned chicken stock with strips of chicken meat and Chinese mushrooms. May be thickened with corn flour and garnished with a **julienne** of ham.

shark's skin Dried shark's skin is used as a flavouring agent. It has to be softened by repeated long simmering and refreshing.

shark's stomach The dried stomachs of sharks are treated in the same way as shark's fin

sharlotka *Russia* Charlotte Russe

sharmoola *North Africa* A processed mixture of finely chopped onion, garlic, parsley, and other herbs and spices. See also **chermoula**

sharon fruit A seedless variety of persimmon, not as astringent as the true persimmon, with a thin edible orange skin grown in and exported from Israel. It should be eaten when hard and may be used in fruit salads, stuffed or sliced as a decoration or garnish.

sharp 1. With a pungent, tart or acid flavour **2.** With a finely ground and honed edge. A really sharp knife should easily cut a ripe tomato without deformation using only a slight downward pressure.

shashlik *Southwest Asia* The Georgian term for kebabs, usually cubes of lamb marinated in wine and lemon juice with garlic, parsley, dill and seasonings, skewered with sweet red pepper and button onions and grilled

shauk-nu, shauk-waing *Burma* Makrut lime

shaurabat adas *Persian Gulf* Lentil soup made with red lentils, fried onions, garlic and tomatoes and flavoured with **baharat** and **loomi**

sha zha chiang *China* Sha cha jiang

shchi *Russia* Cabbage soup made with beef stock, tomatoes, onions, butter and herbs accompanied by soured cream. Also called **shtchi**

shea butter An edible solid fat obtained from the shea nut. Also used for soap- and candle-making.

shea nuts The seeds of the tropical shea tree, *Butyrospermum parkii*, used for their fat content

shebbakia *North Africa* Pastry formed into knots, deep-fried and dipped in honey

she-crab soup *United States* A soup from South Carolina made from the roe and the meat of the female blue crab flavoured with Worcestershire sauce and sherry and finished with cream

sheep casings The cleaned and scraped intestines of sheep ranging from 16 to 24 mm in diameter Classified as narrow, medium, wide and extra wide. Used for thin sausages such as chipolatas and frankfurters.

sheepshead fish *United States* **1.** A deep-bodied seawater fish, *Archosargus probatocephalus*, caught off the south-east coast with white firm flesh similar to the sea bream. It weighs from 2.5 to 4.5 kg and its back is silvery blue with seven dark vertical bars on the back and each side. Poach, bake or grill. Also called **fathead 2.** Freshwater drum

sheer *South Asia* A dessert based on rice cooked in milk. See also **kheer**

sheftalia *Cyprus* A **crépinette** with a filling of seasoned fatty pork mixed with an equal quantity of veal or lamb, all minced with grated onion

sheh paan *China* Garoupa, the fish

shelf life The length of time a foodstuff will stay fresh and palatable when stored as indicated by the supplier or manufacturer

shellac The strained resin exuded by various lac insects which live on the bark of some Eastern trees. Used to coat apples to give them a glossy appearance. See also **E904**

shell bean Broad bean

shellfish The collective name for a group of generally sea-dwelling creatures comprising molluscs, cephalopods and crustaceans. Oysters, squid and lobsters are typical examples. The only freshwater shellfish is the **crayfish** which is a crustacean.

shell mould Pee tee

shell steak *United States* A boneless steak cut from the fleshy part of the sirloin of beef

shemis *Scotland* A wild lovage, *Levisticum scoticum*, one of the greens (**kail**) eaten by the poor in the olden days

sheng tsai *China* Lettuce

shepherd's pie *United Kingdom* A dish made in the same way as cottage pie and often confused with it. However, the meat used is lamb or mutton. See also **cottage pie**

shepherd's purse A common weed, *Capsella bursa-pastoris*, which was once eaten as a green vegetable (NOTE: So called from the shape of the seed capsule)

sherbet *United States* A frozen dessert made from sweetened fruit juice or purée or other flavoured syrups with added beaten egg white and/or cream

sherry sauce As Madeira sauce but substituting dry sherry. Also called **xérès, sauce**

Sherwood A double Gloucester cheese flavoured with chives and onions

Shetland sheep *Scotland* A breed of sheep from the Shetland Isles which feed on grass, heather and seaweed to produce a tender lamb with a gamey flavour

Shetland sparls *Scotland* A type of sausage made with seasoned minced beef flavoured with allspice, cloves, mace, ginger and cinnamon, wrapped in wide sheep casings and smoked

sheto *West Africa* Shitor din

sheung moy cheung *China* Plum sauce

shia jeera *South Asia* Caraway seed

shiba-kuri *Japan* Small firm sweet chestnuts

shichcheta *Bulgaria* Spicy lamb kebabs

shichimi *Japan* Shichimi togarishi

shichimi togarashi *Japan* A blend of seven flavouring agents, white and black sesame seeds, sansho, nori, dried tangerine peel, togarashi and white poppy seeds, ground together and used as a condiment and to flavour soups, noodles and grilled meats. Some formulations include black hemp seeds. Also called **shichimi**

shiitake mushroom A variety of fungus fruiting body, *Lentinus edodes*, from East Asia where it is grown on tree trunks, now grown in Europe on wheat straw. They have a white stem, a brown flattish cap and white ruffled gills. They are high in protein and keep their shape when cooked. The flavour intensifies on drying and they become darker. Often sold dried in Chinese shops as winter mushrooms. Also called **Chinese dried black mushroom**, **black forest mushroom**, **fragrant mushroom**, **oak mushroom** (NOTE: Literally 'tree mushroom'.)

shikar korma *South Asia* A pork korma made with loin of pork cut in pieces, fried with honey and ghee until browned, salted water added and all simmered until cooked and dry. Grated shallots, turmeric, black pepper, orange and lemon peel are added and the whole cooked until the butter fat separates, yoghurt added and again cooked until the fat separates, crushed garlic, ground cardamom and cinnamon added and cooked 1 minute, a little mace added and all left in a slow oven with a tight fitting lid on the dish for 15 minutes.

shiltong *Nepal* Rice bean

shimeji *Indonesia, Japan, Malaysia* Oyster mushroom

shin beef *United Kingdom* The lower muscular part of the rear leg of beef. It contains a lot of connective tissue and being well used is tough but of excellent flavour. Used for making consommé, beef tea and for long stewing.

shingala *South Asia* Catfish

shinmai rice *Japan* Freshly harvested rice with moist, tender and sweet grains which do not require as much water for cooking as most rice types

shinshu-miso *Japan* A light thin yellowish miso in which rice is the added grain

shio *Japan* Salt

shiogame *Japan* A heavy earthenware platter used for grilling or roasting food. Usually covered with a layer of coarse salt on which the food rests.

shioyaki *Japan* Grilled in salt, a method of cooking fish

ship biscuit *United States* Hardtack

ship caviar *United States* The caviar from a hybrid of the osciotre and sevruga sturgeon

shiraita kombu The thin membrane left after shaving off the fleshy part of kombu to make oboru and tororo kombu. Used as a food wrapping.

shirasu ae *Japan* Cooked vegetables, e.g. dried beans, mushrooms, aubergines, courgettes containing as little moisture as possible, combined with a sesame seed sauce made from dry-roasted white sesame seeds pounded with sugar, vinegar, **mirin**, salt and bean curd which has been boiled for 3 minutes and wrung out in a cloth. The sauce should be smooth and sticky.

shirataki noodles Very fine noodles made from the glutinous tuber of the snake palm plant. They soften immediately on contact with hot food and require no other cooking. Often stored in cold water in the same way as cooked spaghetti is stored in commercial kitchens.

shiratamako *Japan* Glutinous rice flour

shirauo *Japan* Whitebait

shirazi *Iran* West Indian lime

shirini polo See **shirin polo**

shirin polo *Middle East* A rice and chicken dish flavoured with almonds, saffron and candied orange peel. Also called **shirini polo**

shiro-goma *Japan* White unhulled sesame seeds

shiro-kikurage *Japan* White fungus

shiro-miso *Japan* A very light-coloured, almost sweet, miso suitable for making salad dressings

shirona *Japan* See **hakusai**

shiro wat *East Africa* A vegetable stew from Ethiopia made from onions fried with berbere or chopped chillies and simmered with a variety of vegetables in a ground peanut and water liquor for the appropriate times. Sometimes thickened with egg. Served with injera especially on fasting days.

shirr, to To bake food, especially eggs, in small shallow containers or dishes in the oven

shirred eggs Shelled eggs baked in a shallow tray in the oven. Alternatively stiffly beaten egg white spread in a buttered shallow tray, depressions made for individual yolks and all baked in the oven at 180°C for 10 minutes. See also **oeufs sur le plat**

shirumono *Japan* Technically a thick soup but the thickness is only relative when compared with suimono and usually comes from the higher proportion of vegetables, tofu, mushrooms, etc. in the soup

shishi-to, shishi-togarashi *Japan* A small green sweet or sometimes hot pepper

shish kebab A kebab made with cubes of lamb and possibly pieces of tomato, onion and sweet pepper

shiso *Japan* A member of the mint family, *Perilla argus*, which comes in both green and red leaved forms and is used as a garnish or a vegetable. See also **green shiso, red shiso, mejiso, hojiso, perilla, beefsteak plant**

shitor *West Africa* A hot chilli sauce used to add flavour to bland carbohydrate foods in Ghana. All contain chopped chillies or chilli powder and variously onions, tomatoes, garlic, ginger, shrimp paste etc.

shitor din *West Africa* A relish rather like the Mexican salsa, very common in Ghana. The fresh version is made from deseeded fresh chilli peppers, onions and tomatoes processed with some salt and allowed to mature. The oil-based version is made by cooking dried shrimps with dried chilli flakes in oil with salt prior to bottling. Also called **sheto**

shi zi *China* Persimmon

shi zi tou *China* Large meatballs of minced pork

shoestring potatoes *United States* Very thin deep-fried strips of potatoes like pommes pailles

shoga *Japan* Ginger

shoga sembei *Japan* Small crisp rice crackers coated with a mixture of ground ginger and sugar

shole zard *Iran* An Iranian dessert made from soft cooked rice, sugar and crushed almonds, flavoured with rose water, saffron and cinnamon

shoofly pie *United States* A sweet treacle or molasses pie with a crumble topping. Served cold or warm with cream or ice cream.

shoppe kebab *Bulgaria* A beef stew with tomatoes, onions, paprika, butter, marjoram and chillies thickened with eggs, yoghurt and flour, finished with vinegar and garnished with chopped parsley

shopska *Bulgaria* A salad of cucumber, dried tomatoes and ewes' milk cheese dressed with vinaigrette and garnished with chopped parsley

shore crab A small green shelled crab, *Carcinus maenus* and *C. mediterraneus*, sometimes with yellow spots and up to 7 cm across. Popular in Venice just after they have shed their shell where they are known as moleche. If the shell has hardened they are used in soups and stocks. Also called **green crab, green swimming crab**

shore dinner *United States* A seafood dinner

shortbread *Scotland* A Scottish crisp biscuit made of butter, caster sugar and flour or flour plus fine semolina mixed (2:1:3), baked at 150°C, usually prescored in thick rectangles. Also called **Scottish shortbread**

shortcake *United States* Two rounds of a baked rich scone mixture sandwiched together with a filling of fruit and cream

shortcrust pastry The commonest pastry made of soft flour, lard or vegetable shortening and butter (4:1:1). It is mixed by the rubbing in method and brought together with sufficient chilled water. The paste should not be kneaded, rolling will compact the mixture. It improves if rested for 30 minutes after forming. Baked at 200 to 220°C until light brown. Also called **short pastry, pâte à foncer, pâte brisée, piecrust pastry**

shortening The fat used in pastry, biscuit and cake making. See also **shortening power**

shortening power The ability of a fat to allow air bubbles to become trapped in a mixture and therefore lighten the texture of the resulting baked item. This is achieved by adding soft unsaturated fats or oils to harder ones to increase their plasticity or by adding emulsifying agents such as glycerol monostearate to the fat. Such a superglycerinated fat prevents the development of gluten network structures in the dough and also aids the incorporation of more liquid and hence sugar in the mix.

short-grain rice A rice with a low length to diameter ratio, generally sticky when cooked

short loin *United States* The front half of a sirloin of beef including the fillet

shortnin' bread *United States* A chemically raised sweet bread from the Southern states made with butter or lard

short pastry See **shortcrust pastry**

short plate *United States* The lower part of the centre of the beef animal extending from halfway down the body including the ends of the ribs, the English plate and part of the thin flank. Used for braising.

short ribs *United States* Part of the ribs of beef excluding the large longitudinal muscles beside the vertebrae, i.e. between the rib roast and the plate

shorva *South Asia* Soup

shot pepper Mignonette pepper

shou de *China* Lean, as of meat, without fat

shoulder The top of the foreleg of an animal including the shoulder blade and surrounding muscles but not the vertebrae and ribs and the longitudinal muscles associated with them. The methods of cooking depend upon the amount of work the muscles have done, e.g. lamb, pork and veal may be roasted, older beef and mutton shoulder is usually stewed or braised.

shoulder of veal *United Kingdom, United States* The shoulder blade, the upper bone of the leg and the surrounding tissues excluding the rib sheet. Similar to shoulder of lamb and used for braising and stewing.

shovel-nosed lobster Sand lobster

shoyu *Japan* A naturally fermented light soya sauce made from soya beans and grains such as wheat or barley

shpinatnyi shchi *Russia* Spinach and sorrel soup made with beef stock with added onions and root vegetables, served with hard-boiled eggs and soured cream. Also called **zelonye shchi**

shprota (*plural* **shproti**) *Russia* Sprats

shred, to To cut food into very thin pieces or strips

shredded wheat A crisp breakfast cereal made from a cooked wheat flour paste extruded in a rectangular multitude of fine (0.5 to 1 mm) threads, partly dried, chopped transversally into rectangular biscuits, dried and browned

shred pie Mince pie

Shrewsbury biscuit *England* A traditional English biscuit about 13 cm diameter, made from a basic biscuit paste flavoured variously with citrus rind, mixed spice, dried vine fruits or cocoa, rolled and cut into shape

Shrewsbury Eastertide biscuit *England* A rich crisp biscuit made with brown sugar and flavoured with caraway seeds, vanilla and sherry. Also called **Shrewsbury Eastertide cake**

Shrewsbury Eastertide cake *England* Shrewsbury Eastertide biscuit

shrimp 1. Small white transparent to grey brown crustaceans generally much smaller than prawns and cooked as soon as caught. Used fresh cooked and shelled in potted shrimps and shrimp salads and also either shelled or unshelled as a snack food. They are also salted and dried for use in Chinese cooking. See also **brown shrimp, pink shrimp 2.** *United States* A general term used for assorted species of prawns and shrimps

shrimp butter Beurre de crevette

shrimp eggs The roe of shrimps and prawns usually dried and salted. They are very expensive and used as a garnish in Chinese cuisine.

shrimp floss Dried shrimp

shrimp paste A paste of ground, salted and partially fermented shrimps, dried and compressed into blocks. See also **blachan, bagoong**

shrimp powder Dried shrimps ground to a fluffy powder and used as a condiment on salads, vegetables, rice dishes, etc.

shrimp pudding *England* Equal parts of minced shrimp or prawn meat and chopped cold chicken, veal or sweetbreads, bound with egg yolks, breadcrumbs and cream, packed into casings and served fried in butter

shrimp sauce See **crevettes, sauce aux**

shrinkage The reduction in size of baked items or roast meat and poultry due to loss of water. Generally less when cooked at lower temperatures.

Shropshire blue See **blue Shropshire**

Shrove Tuesday bun See **semlor**

shtchi *Russia* Shchi

shuan yang rou *China* Mongolian fire-pot with lamb. See also **flying lamb slices**

shuck, to To open and prepare bivalve shellfish or to remove husks, shells or pods from seeds and nuts, etc.

shui dian fen The suspension of corn flour or other starch in water (1:2) always kept together with oil and stock beside the wok where the Chinese restaurant cook prepares food

shui dou fu *China* Silk bean curd

shui guo *China* Fruit

shui guo zhi *China* Fruit juice

shui jiao *China* Boiled dumpling

shungiku *Japan* Leaves of the garland chrysanthemum which impart a subtle flavour to soups and other dishes

shwa *North Africa* A barbecued whole sheep from Morocco, served with salt and cumin

Siamese ginger Greater galangal

sianliha *Finland* Pork

siba *Portugal* Cuttlefish

Siberian millet Foxtail millet

Siberian salmon A salmon, *Oncorhynchus keta*, found in the Siberian and western Canadian rivers which drain into the Pacific. The source of ketovaia and ikura. Also called **dog salmon, chum salmon**

Siberian sturgeon A variety of sturgeon, *Acipenser baeri*, found in the Siberian rivers that drain into the Pacific Ocean

Sichuan *China* A province of China famous for its cooking. Also called **Szechuan** (NOTE: The words tend to be interchanged at random)

Sichuan dumplings *China* Ground seasoned pork fillet mixed with finely chopped pork fat, chopped garlic or garlic chives, bound with a little sesame seed oil, corn flour and egg white, divided amongst won ton wrappers, formed into purses, poached in simmering water for 5 minutes and served with a spicy sauce

Sichuan hot bean paste See **chilli bean paste**

Sichuan pepper Anise pepper

Sichuan pepper oil Vegetable oil flavoured with finely ground anise pepper

siciliana, alla *Italy* In the Sicilian style, i.e. with anchovies, pine nuts, sultanas and vinegar. Used especially of fish and vegetables.

Siciliano A semi-hard scalded-curd Sicilian cheese. See also **Canestrato**

side dish An accompaniment to a main food dish such as a salad, a bowl of rice or pasta or vegetables

side of meat One half of an animal carcass split lengthways along the centre of the backbone, generally without the head

Siebling *Germany* Arctic char

sieden *Germany* To boil or simmer

sieni *Finland* Mushroom

sienimunakas *Finland* Mushroom omelette

sienisalaatti *Finland* Mushroom salad

sien ts'ai *China* Kale

siero di latte *Italy* Buttermilk or whey

sierra *South America* The local name for **snoek** caught off the coast of Chile

sieva bean A variety of **butter bean**

sieve A fine stainless steel wire, plastic or other stranded fine mesh either stretched in a flat circle on a metal or wooden former or made into the shape of a half sphere or inverted cone. Used for separating large from fine particles, for straining liquids or for reducing soft foods to a purée.

sieve, to To pass dry powder, e.g. flour or icing sugar, through a sieve to remove large particles or foreign bodies and to aerate it, or to pass a liquid through it to remove solid particles

si-ew *Thailand* Light soya sauce

sift, to To pass dry ingredients through a sieve either to clean or aerate them or to spread them evenly over a food

sifter A closed cylindrical container with a sieve or perforated top at one end for sprinkling flour, sugar or other powders over food items

sigarilla *Philippines* Goa bean

sigir *Turkey* Beef

signal crayfish A large fast-growing crayfish farmed in the UK for the restaurant trade. It has now escaped into the wild where it is supplanting the native species.

sigtebrød *Denmark* Light rye bread

sigui *Eastern Europe* A fish found in the Baltic with flesh similar to the shad

siikas ja munakokkelia *Finland* White fish with scrambled egg

sik *Sweden* Whitefish

sikbadj *North Africa* A Moroccan stew with aubergines, dried dates and dried apricots, flavoured with cinnamon and allspice. The aubergines are added after the lamb is tender and the fruit after a further 20 minutes and all cooked until the fruits are soft. Garnished with toasted almonds and sesame seeds.

si-klok *Thailand* A sausage made of 3 parts of minced pork mixed with 2 parts of crabmeat, chopped onion, coriander leaves and roasted peanuts, flavoured with red curry paste, moistened with equal parts of nuoc mam and coconut milk, filled into casings and coiled like a Cumberland sausage

sikuk *North Africa* Moroccan couscous eaten without vegetables but with butter, milk and steamed fava beans

silakka *Finland* Baltic herring

silba *Balkans* A cows' milk cheese resembling **Port-Salut**

sild 1. *England, Norway* A small type of herring once found in huge quantities off the Norwegian coast and canned in the same way as sardines **2.** *Denmark* Baltic herring

sildeboller *Norway* Herring fish balls

sildesalat *Norway* Herring salad

silgochu *Korea* Finely shredded dried chillies used as a seasoning and condiment instead of powdered or whole chillies

silicon dioxide See **E551**

silk bean curd A very smooth soft bean curd made by straining the coagulated bean curd through fine mesh and allowing the strained curds to settle under gravity without pressing

silke cepts *Lithuania* A dish of herring fillets in a mustard and onion sauce

sill *Sweden* Herring

sillabub See **syllabub**

sillgratäng *Sweden* Gratinated herrings made with sliced matjes herring fillets, sliced boiled potatoes and sweated onion rings layered alternately in a greased dish with potatoes on top, gratinated with toasted breadcrumbs and possibly cheese, heated in the oven or under the grill and buttered

silli *Finland* Herring

sill med brynt smör *Sweden* Herrings in brown butter made from matjes herrings or soaked cleaned and filleted salt herrings covered with a mixture of dried dill weed and equal parts of diced hard-boiled egg and chopped onion and served covered with **beurre noisette**

sill med gräslök och gräddfil *Sweden* Herring with sour cream and finely chopped chives

sillpudding *Sweden* As laxpudding but using salt herring or matjes herring fillets instead of salmon

sillsalad *Sweden* Finely chopped salt herrings mixed with chopped cooked potatoes, pickled beetroot, pickled cucumber, chopped dessert apple and onion, bound with a little of the beetroot vinegar, packed in a mould, chilled, demoulded, garnished with hard-boiled eggs and picked parsley and served with soured cream which can be coloured pink with beetroot vinegar

silotakia tiganita *Greece* Small pieces of fried chicken liver or calf liver dipped in lemon juice and speared on cocktail sticks for use as a snack or appetizer

silsi *East Africa* A peppery fried tomato and onion sauce from Eritrea eaten at breakfast

Silter *Italy* A hard, scalded-curd skimmed cows' milk cheese from Brescia. It has a close-textured curd with a few cracks and holes.

silvano *Italy* Chocolate meringue tart

silver E174, a precious metal sometimes used in very thin films as a food decoration

silver balls Small silver-coloured sugar balls, 2 to 4 mm in diameter used for cake decoration

silver beet *Australia, United States* Swiss chard

silverbeet *United States* Swiss chard

silver fungus White fungus

silver hake A seawater fish, *Merluccius bilinearis*, of the cod family with a silvery skin, weighing about 400 g found off the North American Atlantic coast. It has a white moist flesh which softens rapidly if not frozen and it may be cooked in any way. Also called **whiting**

silver leaf E174 as gold leaf but made with silver. Used for decorating Indian festive dishes. Also called **varak**

silver salmon Coho salmon

silverside *United Kingdom* The inside cut from the top of the rear leg of beef. It is virtually fat-free and traditionally is pickled in brine and boiled, but now sometimes sold, wrapped in a layer of fat, as a cheap roasting joint.

silverside (fish) 1. See **Atlantic silverside 2.** Sand smelt

silversides *United States* Any small silver-coloured fish such as whitebait, anchovies, sardines, etc.

silverskin onion A very small variety of onion, less than 2 cm in diameter, with a silver skin and white flesh. Used for pickling, or, in a sweet pickle, as a cocktail onion for use with drinks and snacks, etc.

silver smelt See **smelt**

silver sprouts Mung bean sprouts which have had the root and leaf removed to leave a thin white stalk. Used as a garnish or vegetable in expensive Chinese dishes.

silver threads *United States* Cellophane noodles

silver top Full cream milk

sima *East Africa* Ugali

simi *Nepal* French bean

simla mirich *South Asia* Sweet pepper

simmer, to To keep a liquid at a temperature just below boiling point around 95 to 97°C for pure water, but around 87°C for meat. The heat input necessary to maintain this temperature with a heat source under the pan will cause slight movement of the surface of the liquid but no evolution of steam bubbles. The lower temperature is best for extracting the maximum flavour from meat, bones and vegetables as in making stock, but speed of extraction is increased with temperature. Also called **seethe, to**

simmuledda alla foggiana *Italy* Potato and fennel soup thickened with buckwheat flour

simnel cake *England* A spiced Easter fruit cake with a layer of marzipan baked in the centre. Sometimes covered with marzipan and decorated.

sim-sim *East Africa* Sesame seed

sinaasappel *Netherlands* Orange, the fruit

sinaasappelen *Netherlands* Oranges

sinappi *Finland* Mustard

sindootan *Indonesia* Parkia

síndria *Catalonia* Watermelon

sin gaun *Burma* Sea urchin

singe, to To use a flame (blowtorch or lighted taper) to remove hairs from pork skin or pin feathers etc. from poultry and game birds

singhara nut *South Asia* The fruit of an aquatic plant, *Trapa bispinosa*, similar to **water caltrop**, but it may have either 1 or 2 projecting horns. It is extensively grown in Kashmir and either eaten raw or cooked as a kind of porridge.

singing hinny *England* A Northumberland cake, made from a currant scone mix, cooked on a griddle and eaten hot. The name comes from the sound of the steam being released when it is cooked on the griddle.

singkong *Indonesia* Cassava

single-acting baking powder Baking powder that releases carbon dioxide only on contacting water

single cream Cream with a minimum butterfat content of 18%. Not suitable for whipping.

single-crust Describes a pie or food dish with a single layer of pastry below the filling, and none above

single Gloucester A hard, mild Cheddar-like white farmhouse cheese made in the form of a squat cylinder from the skimmed cows' milk of an early season day's milking. Also called **haymaking cheese**

single loin of lamb See **loin of lamb**

sinigang *Philippines* A thin stew of meat or fish with vegetables, simmered in a cooking liquor soured with some of lime, lemon, tamarind or unripe tomatoes, seasoned and flavoured with fish sauce or soya sauce

sinistral Describes a flatfish in which the eye on the right of the juvenile form moves to join that on the left which becomes the uppermost side of the adult fish

sink tidy A triangular metal or plastic dish with perforations in the base and sides used to strain off vegetable peelings and the like

sinn *China* Eel

Sint Jakobsschelp *Netherlands* same as **coquille Saint Jacques**

sipoli merce *Latvia* A dish of herring fillets coated in a mixture of German mustard, French mustard, egg yolks and cream, covered and left overnight in the refrigerator, passed through rye flour and pan fried in butter. Served with onion rings and lemon wedges.

sippet A small right-angled isosceles triangle of toast about 2 cm on the side (12 per slice of English bread). Several are served in a sauce boat as an accompaniment to soup. See also **croûtons**

sipuli *Finland* Onion and the onion family generally

sipulipihvi *Finland* Steak and onions

sir *Eastern Europe* The generic name for cheese in Balkan and some Slav countries

siracha *Thailand* A thin red chilli sauce in which individual flakes of chilli pepper can be seen

sirap *Sweden* Syrup

Sirene *Bulgaria* A firm white salty and crumbly white cheese similar to Greek feta

sirka *South Asia* Vinegar

sirloin *United States* A cut of beef from the upper part of the loin just in front of the round, including some of the English rump and the rear part of the English sirloin, the rear half of the whole loin

sirloin of beef Part of a loin of beef, comprising about 6 full vertebrae. Sometimes roasted on the bone, boned out and reassembled on the bone or boned and rolled. Also used as steaks.

sirloin steak 1. *United Kingdom* A slice about 1.5 to 2 cm thick cut from a boned out sirloin of beef. Also called **entrecôte steak 2.** *United States* Steak cut from the sirloin usually including bone and the outer layer of fat. They are designated by the shape of the vertebra and its extension as pinbone, flatbone and wedgebone or, if without bone, as boneless.

sirop *France* Syrup

sirop d'érable *France* Maple syrup

sirsak *Indonesia, Malaysia* Soursop

Sirup *Germany* Molasses

sishi salad *Netherlands* A dark bluish brown sprouted seed grown like mustard and cress as a decoration

sis kebap *Turkey* A shish kebab consisting of cubes of meat, pieces of tomato and pieces of sweet pepper grilled on separate skewers, removed from the skewers on to the plate and served with a rice pilav

sis köfte *Turkey* Meatballs of lamb threaded on and/or formed around a skewer as a flattened rectangle, grilled and served off the skewer with a rice pilav

sissay yassa *West Africa* Joints of chicken marinated in lemon juice and oil with onions, garlic, ginger and chilli, fried and served with rice. A Gambian speciality.

sitaw *Philippines* Long bean

sitron *Norway* Lemon

sitruuna *Finland* Lemon

sitruunakohokas *Finland* Lemon soufflé

sitruunankuori *Finland* Lemon zest

sitsaro *Philippines* Mangetout peas

sitsaron *Philippines* A dry snack made from pork crackling or fried chitterlings. Also called **chitcharon**

siu choy *China* Chinese leaves

siu mai *China* Dumplings made from won ton wrappers filled with a paste made from lean pork and prawn meat, chopped water chestnuts, reconstituted black mushrooms, spring onions, fresh ginger, salt, sugar and soya sauce. The wrappers are circular and made into a cup shape as they are filled, left open at the top, sprinkled with grated carrots and the dumplings placed in an oiled steamer basket and steamed for 12 minutes.

Sium sisarum *Botanical name* Skirret

siwalan *Indonesia* Palm nut

sjokolade *Norway* Chocolate

sjokoladefarget *Norway* Covered in chocolate

sjömansbiff *Sweden* A casserole of alternate layers of fried slices of rump or sirloin beef, sliced onions with seasoning and thyme and sliced potatoes, starting and finishing with potatoes, simmered in water, lager or stout (NOTE: Literally 'seaman's beef'.)

sjøørret *Norway* Sea trout

sjötunga *Sweden* Dover sole

sjøtunge *Norway* Dover sole

skaba puta *Latvia* A cold soup made from a duxelle of mushrooms and onions brought to the boil with tomato purée, lemon juice and chicken stock, barley added and simmered until tender, cooled, mixed with 10% buttermilk and 10% sour cream and chopped dill. Served cold garnished with chopped hard-boiled eggs and gherkins.

skalddyr *Denmark* Shellfish

skaldjur *Sweden* Shellfish

skalldyr *Norway* Shellfish

skånsk kålsoppa *Sweden* Cabbage soup from Skåne, made from diced lean pork simmered in water, skimmed, sliced cabbage, swede, carrots and potatoes added with salt, peppercorns and a bay leaf, simmered until all tender, seasoning adjusted and served with a chopped parsley garnish

skånsk potatis *Sweden* Diced potatoes browned in butter and reserved. Chopped onion fried in the same fat, potatoes added back, seasoned and the whole mixed with double cream. Served with a chopped parsley garnish.

skärbönor *Sweden* French beans

skarpsås *Sweden* A sharp sauce made with equal parts of mashed hard-boiled and raw egg yolk, with a little vinegar and French mustard into which oil is emulsified as in mayonnaise production, seasoned with salt and cayenne pepper, mixed with an amount of double cream equal to the oil and finished with chopped dill. Often served with baked fish.

skate A flat triangular-shaped seawater fish, *Rajus batis*, of the shark family, with eyes on the upper side and mouth and gills on the lower side. The upper surface is greenish brown with spots and they can be up to 2 m wide. The white medium oily flesh from the skinned sides (wings) cut into pieces and nuggets of flesh cut from under the body are cooked in any way. See also **common skate**, **thornback ray**, **guitar fish**. Also called **ray**

skewer Variously sized wooden or metal rods resembling knitting needles with a handle, loop or enlargement at one end. Used for trussing joints of meat, birds and poultry or for holding meat, fish or pieces of vegetables for grilling.

skewer, to To hold the edges of joints of meat together, to hold the limbs of poultry and birds against the body using skewers or to thread pieces of meat or vegetable on a skewer

skillet *United States* Frying pan, sometimes with a lid

skim, to To remove surface layers of fat, froth and scum from a simmering stock, sauce, soup, stew or jam, using a ladle, spoon or skimmer. Occasionally adsorbent kitchen paper is used especially to remove the last traces of fat from a consommé.

skimmed milk Milk with a butterfat content of 0.3% or less. Tends to burn on heating. Sold in bottles with a silver and blue checked top.

skimmed milk quark Magerquark

skin 1. The outer protective covering of an animal, fruit or vegetable **2.** The hard dryish film which forms on top of soups, sauces and jams when cooled and left. Prevented by using a cartouche or other means to avoid evaporation.

skin, to To remove the skin from food items such as fish, fruit, meat, vegetables, etc.

skinka *Sweden* Ham

skinkbullar *Sweden* Ham and potato balls

skinke *Denmark, Norway* Ham

skinkestek *Norway* Roast ham

skinkfärs *Sweden* A mousse made with finely ground ham

skinklåda *Sweden* Ham omelette cooked in the oven

skink of beef *Scotland* A Scottish term used for leg or shin of beef. Also called **hough of beef**

skipjack tuna A cheap species of tuna fish, *Katsuwonus pelamis*, often substituted for the more expensive yellow fin or the rare blue fin. Also called **Pacific bonito**, **California bonito**, **oceanic bonito**

skirlie *Scotland* A Scottish accompaniment to grouse consisting of finely chopped onion fried slowly until coloured in butter or pork dripping, then enough medium oatmeal added to absorb the fat, crisped and seasoned

skirret A hardy herbaceous perennial, *Sium sisarum*, growing to 1 m with small clusters of tiny fragrant flowers, narrow leaves and aromatic tuberous roots. The young shoots may be steamed or stir-fried. The roots, which should be cooked in their skins to preserve the flavour, are steamed, boiled or pickled and are eaten in Germany with new potatoes. The hard inner core of the root is removed.

skirt *United Kingdom* A fairly tough cut of beef from the extreme bottom of the belly of the animal and the diaphragm, divided into thick, thin and body skirt. Thick skirt is part of the inner muscle of the belly wall attached to the rump, whilst thin skirt and body skirt are part of the diaphragm. It must either be braised very slowly or cooked fast on a high heat and served rare. Also called **thin flank**

sköldpadda *Sweden* Turtle

sköldpaddsoppa *Sweden* Turtle soup

skordalia *Greece* Skorthalia

skorpor *Sweden* Rusks

skorthalia *Greece* Mayonnaise flavoured with raw garlic, ground almonds and lemon juice or vinegar, thickened with pounded bread and sometimes with the addition of chopped walnuts or pine nuts. Used as a general cold sauce or condiment. Also called **skordalia**

skull cap Preformed cooked pieces of puff pastry used to cover sweet or savoury dishes of food. The pastry is rolled to 3 mm, cut to the shape of the bowl, edges dampened and placed on bowls full of warm water and baked in the oven at 220°C for 12 minutes.

skyr *Iceland* **1.** Curds **2.** A soft cultured and very smooth cheese made from rennet-curdled skimmed milk similar to fromage frais or a strong-flavoured yoghurt

Skyros *Greece* A cheese from the island of the same name similar to Kefalotiri

sla *Netherlands* Salad, lettuce

sladkoe pechenye iz gryetskikh orekhov po-uzbeksky *Central Asia* Uzbekistan walnut brittle

slagroom *Netherlands* Whipped cream

slake, to To mix a powder with a small amount of water or other liquid to a creamy lump-free consistency

slaked lime Lime (calcium hydroxide)

släpärter *Sweden* Peas in the pod

slapjack *United States* A large flat pancake

slata *North Africa* Salad

slatka *Balkans* Preserved fruits from Serbia served as an afternoon snack with strong coffee and cold water

slatur *Iceland* **1.** Butcher's meat **2.** Sheep's pluck **3.** A version of haggis

slätvar *Sweden* Brill, the fish

slaughterhouse See **abattoir**

slaw See **coleslaw**

slice, to To cut into thin sheets

sliced beef *United States* Dried beef

slicing knife A knife with a long thin blade (30 cm by 2 to 3 cm) with a rounded end used for slicing, usually cooked food

slicing machine A machine with a motor-driven circular knife blade together with a tray which holds a solid food item and is moved by hand or mechanically so as to cut the food in slices of a predetermined thickness. Also called **food slicer**

slip *Australia* Baking tray

Slipcote *England* A small soft cheese produced in Kent which is placed between cabbage leaves to ripen for 1 to 2 weeks. When ripe its skin becomes loose.

slipper lobster A small lobster, *Scyllarus arctus* or *Scyllarides squammosis*, with a flat slipper-shaped tail which is the part used. The Mediterranean variety *S. arctus* (up to 13 cm) has little meat and is usually used in soups. The tail of the larger variety *S. squammosis* which is fished off the coast of Queensland in Australia, is eaten as a dish in its own right. Also called **flat lobster**

sliver A thin narrow strip of a foodstuff, e.g. of almonds, cheese and the like

sloe The small black sour fruit of the blackthorn bush *Prunus spinosa* about 1 cm in diameter and with a central stone. May be used in jam, as a souring agent or to make sloe gin.

sloke Laver

slokum Laver

sloppy joe *United States* A split bread bun filled with a thinnish mixture of seasoned and cooked minced beef mixed with tomato sauce

slot *Wales* A thick oatcake without fat, crushed and served with cold buttermilk poured over it

slott *Scotland* A Shetland dish of cod roe, beaten with flour and seasoning until smooth and creamy, dropped in spoonfuls into boiling seawater or brine (35 g salt per litre) and eaten either hot or left to cool, sliced and fried

slotted spoon A large long-handled spoon with holes in the bowl end used for removing large solids from a liquid

slottsstek *Sweden* Roast sirloin of beef generally served with braised onions, roast potatoes and jus rôti, More traditionally a boned sirloin was seasoned, browned then braised in a covered dish with stock, onion, anchovy, bay, white vinegar, sugar and peppercorns. Served with a jus lié thickened with **beurre manié** and finished with cream, accompanied with boiled potatoes, cucumber salad and redcurrant or cranberry jelly.

slouk Laver

slow cook, to To cook at a low temperature in the range 80 to 95°C

slow cooker A thermostatically controlled electrically heated deep metal container into which a lidded earthenware or glass, deep and well fitting pot is placed. Used for slow cooking food at or below simmering temperature for long periods of time.

Slow Food Society *Italy* The Arcigola slow food society of Cuneo, Italy was formed in 1986 to promote slow eating and has since flourished. Their logo is a snail shape and appears in restaurant guides, the most well known of which is the Osteria d'Italia, a guide to Italy's family-run restaurants.

slugane *Ireland* Laver

slumgullion *United States* Disgusting food (*colloquial*)

slump *United States* A dessert made of stewed fruit topped with a dumpling-like pastry and served with cream

sly cake *England* See **Cornish sly cake**

småbröd *Sweden* Small cakes and biscuits

småkage *Denmark* Biscuits

småkakor *Sweden* Biscuit

små köttbullar *Sweden* Small meatballs

småländsk ostkaka *Sweden* A type of cheesecake from Småland

smallage Wild celery

small calorie The scientific calorie written with a lower case c, equal to the one thousandth part of the calorie (kilocalorie) used in nutrition. See also **calorie**

small eats *United Kingdom* Savouries, canapés, etc. served with drinks (*colloquial*; *a naval term*)

small thread stage See **sugar cooking**

Smältost *Sweden* A mild runny cooking cheese

småsill *Sweden* Pilchards

smatana Smetana

småvarmt *Sweden* Hot dishes served at the smörgåsbord, traditionally filled omelette, sautéed kidneys, chipolata sausages or items in a thick cream sauce

smedovska lukanka *Bulgaria* A smoked sausage made with two thirds pork and one third beef, chopped, mixed with sugar, seasoning and caraway seed and packed into ox middles

smell See **odour**

smelt Various small round oily silver-coloured seawater fish of the genus *Osmerus*, with a flavour similar to trout. Gutted by squeezing out the entrails through an incision made below the gills and deep-fried or baked.

smen *North Africa* A type of clarified butter with the flavour of cheese, which may be flavoured with herbs and kept for years to mature

smeriglio *Italy* Porbeagle shark

smetana A soured low-fat cream (12% butterfat) originating in Russia and Eastern Europe, now made in the West from a mixture of skimmed milk and single cream. The original Russian version was made by mixing sweet double cream and sour cream and had a much higher fat content than nowadays. Also called **smatana**, **smitane**, **smytana**

Smilax officinalis *Botanical name* Sarsaparilla

sminuzzato *Italy* Brawn

smitaine sauce See **smitane, sauce**

smitane Smetana

smitane, sauce *England, France* Chopped onions, sweated in butter, white wine added and reduced, sour cream added and reduced, strained, seasoned and finished with lemon juice. Also called **smitaine sauce**

Smithfield ham *United States* Ham from pigs traditionally fattened in the woods on hickory nuts, beechnuts and acorns, finished before slaughter on peanuts, obtained by rooting in the fields after the peanut harvest, followed by maize. The hams are dry salt-cured, spiced and smoked. Also called **Virginia ham** (NOTE: From the town of the same name)

Smith tangerine Honey tangerine

smoke, to To expose food, usually hung on racks, to the dense smoke from slowly smouldering sawdust or wood chips. Usually fish, meat and occasionally cheese are smoked but most of the latter so described is flavoured with a synthetic mix of chemicals which mimic the real thing. Meat and fish will be partially cooked and dried which helps to preserve them and the flavour will be improved. See also **cold-smoke, to, hot-smoke, to**

smoked bacon Bacon which is smoked after curing

smoked beef *United States* Dried beef

smoked cheese See **Räucherkäse**

smoked cod Brined cod fillets, naturally smoked to a pale straw colour or more often dyed a deep yellow and then smoked or sprayed with a smoke flavour

smoked cod's roe Salted and smoked cod roes usually separated from the tough enclosing membrane and used for savouries, canapés and hors d'oeuvres

smoked eel Lightly brined eel, smoked then cut in slices. Served in the same manner as smoked salmon and equally regarded as a delicacy.

smoked egg Shelled hard-boiled eggs marinated then smoked and served as a hors d'oeuvre

smoked fillet *Scotland* Aberdeen fillet

smoked fillets See **golden fillets**

smoked haddock Unskinned haddock fillets or small whole haddock, brined then smoked as cod. Sometimes dyed. Finnan haddock is the superior version.

smoked haddock creams *United Kingdom* A processed mixture of smoked haddock, egg and egg yolk, curd cheese or yoghurt with seasoning and Tabasco sauce, filled into ramekins, cooked in a bain-marie, cooled and demoulded

smoked mackerel A popular prepared fish usually filleted and cold- or hot-smoked. Often coated with crushed peppercorns. Eaten cold as purchased or hot.

smoked mussels Cooked mussels, brined (250 g salt per litre) for 5 minutes, oiled, smoked at 82°C for 30 minutes packed in jars with oil and retorted at 121°C for about 15 minutes

smoked oysters Oysters removed from the shell, steamed to set them, brined, smoked and generally canned or packed in oil. Used for savouries, canapés or as an appetizer.

smoked salmon Fillets of salmon still on the skin, cold-smoked for a long period of time and considered by some to be a delicacy. Usually cut very thin on the slant and served with brown bread and butter and garnished with lemon slices or wedges.

smoked salmon butter A compound butter made from smoked salmon pounded with 2.5 times its weight in butter and sieved

smoked sprats Lightly brined and smoked sprats which keep their silvery appearance. Eaten without further cooking as a savoury or as a hors d'oeuvre. Sometimes canned in oil.

smokehouse A well-sealed chamber in which food is hung on racks for smoking with provision for the generation of smoke from smouldering wood, for temperature control and for the removal of smoke. Such a chamber may range in size from a small box up to a large room.

smoke point The minimum temperature at which oils and fats begin to decompose and produce smoke, usually above 160°C

smoke-roast, to *United States* To smoke meat such as spare ribs or steaks at a temperature between 97 and 107°C without prior salting or cold smoking. Such meat requires cooking.

smokie *Scotland* Hot-smoked, gutted and deheaded haddock or whiting tied together in pairs by the tails. See also **Arbroath smokie**

smolt A 2- to 3-year-old salmon about 12 to 14 cm long which is leaving the river where it hatched for the open sea. Not caught or eaten at this stage.

smoored chicken *Scotland* A young chicken, split in half down the backbone, flattened with a cutlet bat, seasoned and basted with molten butter before grilling either side for 5 minutes. The flesh side is coated with a milk and mustard mixture and grilled slowly or cooked in a covered pan for 25 minutes then finished by sprinkling with breadcrumbs and briefly grilling to form a crust. (NOTE: Literally 'smothered chicken'.)

smoorsnoek *South Africa* A lightly curried stew of snoek and onions

smoorvis *South Africa* A dish made from onions cooked in oil and butter until caramelized, diced parboiled potatoes, tomatoes and finely chopped chillies added and cooked until the potatoes brown, cooked rice, flaked smoked fish and sultanas added and all cooked through. Lemon juice and chopped parsley are added before service and it is traditionally served with black grape jam or acar and brown bread.

smooth hound A large, long and thin, edible sea fish, *Mustelus mustelus*, with a brown skin, very prominent fins and a fairly well-flavoured flesh

smooth venus clam Venus shell clam

smör *Sweden* Butter

smør *Denmark, Norway* Butter

smørbrød *Norway* Open sandwiches similar to smörrebröd

smörgås *Sweden* Sandwich

smörgåsbord *Sweden* A buffet meal of various hot and cold fish, meat and egg dishes with vegetables, salads, etc., always starting with herring, bread and butter and boiled potatoes followed by a succession of more or less elaborately presented foods and finally cheese and coffee, all eaten separately in small portions

smørrebrød *Denmark* Open sandwiches consisting of a rectangular slice of buttered bread topped with cold savoury items, meats, fish, salads, etc. usually eaten with a knife and fork at informal or snack meals. Also called **Danish open sandwich**

smother, to *United States* To braise in a covered pot with gravy or sauce

smothered beef *United States* Étouffe of beef

smultringer *Norway* Doughnuts

smultron *Sweden* Wild strawberry

Smyrnium olusatrum *Botanical name* Alexanders

smytana Smetana

snack A small amount of food, often savoury, usually eaten between meals, but sometimes as a replacement for a meal

snail Various edible gastropod molluscs of the genus *Helix*, found in the wild on land and in both fresh and seawater and sometimes cultivated. Prepared by starving for at least 24 hours, cleaning and boiling or frying for 5 minutes. The flesh is then removed from the shells, degutted and cooked as appropriate. Sometimes returned to the shell for service.

snail butter Butter mixed with finely chopped shallots, garlic paste, chopped parsley and seasoning. Put in an empty snail shell before inserting the cooked snail.

snake bean Long bean

snake fruit *Indonesia, Malaysia* The small fruit of a low palm with little or no trunk, *Salacea edulis*. The fruit is triangular with a coarse red peel like snakeskin and the flesh is firm and crunchy with a slightly sweet flavour. Also called **snakeskin fruit**

snake gourd The narrow cylindrical fruit of an annual climber from Africa, Asia, Australia, and India, *Trichosanthes anguina* and *T. cucumerina*, which can grow to 2 m long in a spiral shape. Picked when immature and treated like a courgette save that the central core of seeds should be discarded and the skin rubbed with salt to remove the down.

snakelocks Oplet

snake palm plant A plant, *Amorphophallus konjac*, with a glutinous starchy tuber used to make shirataki noodles and black bean curd. Also called **devil's tongue**, **arum root**

snakeskin fruit See **snake fruit**

snap *England* Food taken to work in a lunchbox, especially by the once numerous coal miners (*colloquial*)

snap, to To break a brittle foodstuff with a clean break

snap bean *United States* French bean

snapdoodle *United States* A New England chocolate-coated cake

snapper An inshore fish, *Chrysophrys auratus*, of the red snapper type found in New Zealand and the Arabian gulf

sneeuwballen *Netherlands* A cream puff pastry

sneeze guard See **counter guard**

snickerdoodle *United States* A New England sweet biscuit flavoured with cinnamon and possibly containing dried vine fruits and nuts

snijbonen *Netherlands* Haricot or kidney beans

snip, to To cut into small pieces or cut a small portion off something with scissors

snipe A game bird, *Gallinago gallinago*, with a long bill and striped plumage weighing about 110 g and requiring two per person. Cooked as plover by roasting at 190°C for 15 to 20 minutes. Shooting season in the UK is 12th August to the 31st of January. Young ones can be eaten fresh but skinned if they smell fishy, older ones can be hung for 3 to 4 days.

Snir *Middle East* A semi-soft cows' milk cheese from Israel similar to Bel Paese

snitbønner *Denmark* French beans

snoek 1. A seawater fish, *Thyristes atun*, related to the mackerel, tuna and swordfish found in the southern hemisphere warm waters only. It may weigh up to 8 kg and be up to 1.2 m long and has a delicious flesh. Also called **Australian barracuda**, **sierra**, **barracouta 2.** *Netherlands* Pike

snoekbaars *Netherlands* Pike-perch

snook Robalo

snöripa *Sweden* Ptarmigan

snow A mixture of sweetened puréed fruit and egg white whisked to a peak. Used as a dessert either as a topping or served on its own with biscuits or sponge fingers.

snow crab *Canada* A cold water crab, *Chionoecetes opilio*, from the coast of Canada, with long thin claws which contain a fine-tasting meat

Snowdon pudding *Wales* A boiled pudding made from suet, fresh breadcrumbs, brown sugar, lemon marmalade and ground rice (6:6:4:4:1) and lemon zest well mixed, to which is added beaten eggs equal to twice the weight of the sugar. This mixture is poured into a thickly buttered pudding basin lined with raisins, covered and boiled for about 90 minutes. Also called **pwdin eryri**

snow eggs *United States* Iles flottantes

snow fungus White fungus

snow pea Mangetout

snow pear Asian pear

so *Vietnam* Scallops

soak, to To immerse a foodstuff in water either to rehydrate it or to dissolve out excessive salt used in its preservation, or undesirable constituents e.g. alkaloids, prussic acid, etc. so as to make it suitable for cooking

Soay lamb *Scotland* Lamb from sheep raised on the Scottish islands with an excellent flavour

soba *Japan* Thin brown noodles with a square cross section made from buckwheat flour or a mixture of buckwheat and wheat flour. Popular in Tokyo.

Sobado *Spain* A semi-hard, sharp-tasting cheese. See also **Armada**

sobbollire *Italy* To simmer

soboro *Japan* A chicken and rice dish made from chicken breasts and petit pois, simmered in soya sauce, sake and sugar until cooked, the chicken sliced and arranged with the peas over the top of boiled rice and in turn covered with sliced, reconstituted and cooked shiitake mushroom caps and strips of Japanese omelette

sobrasada *Spain* Chorizo sausage mix but minced much finer and with extra red peppers

sobrasada mallorquina *Spain* A milder version of sobrasada from Majorca with the filling ground to a paste-like consistency

sobremesa *Portugal* Dessert

sobretto al frutto *Italy* Fruit sherbet

socker *Sweden* Sugar

sockerkaka *Sweden* Sponge cake

sockeye salmon One of the Pacific salmon, *Oncorhynchus nerka*, caught off the northwest coast of North America weighing up to 2.5 kg. The deep red flesh is oily with small flakes. Cooked in any way but usually available in Europe as canned red salmon. Also called **red salmon**

sock mai jai *China* Miniature corn

socle A bed of rice, vegetables or similar on which the main component of a dish is raised above a flat for presentation to the customer. Alternatively a base or ornamental stand on which a food item is raised above the rest especially in buffet presentation.

sød *Denmark* Sweet

soda 1. A general name for alkaline sodium compounds such as caustic soda, bicarbonate of soda, washing soda and soda ash. They are not interchangeable. **2.** *United States* Bicarbonate of soda

soda ash The dry powdered anhydrous form of sodium carbonate used for cleaning floors and absorbing dangerous spilt, especially acid, liquids

soda bread *Ireland* A bread made with soured milk or buttermilk and using bicarbonate of soda instead of yeast as the raising agent. It may be made with white or brown flour, if brown, cream of tartar is also added. Also called **Irish soda bread**

soda cake *England* A light spicy fruit cake from Somerset raised with bicarbonate of soda and an acid, usually sour milk (lactic acid) or vinegar. Also called **Somerset soda cake**

soda water See **carbonated water**

sode *Italy* Hard-boiled, of eggs

søn frugtsuppe *Denmark* A sweet fruit soup

sodium 5'-ribonucleotide See **E627**

sodium acid pyrophosphate A compound used in 2% water solution in the USA to treat potato chips before deep-frying to prevent blackening

sodium aluminium phosphate See **E541**

sodium bicarbonate See **bicarbonate of soda**, **E500**

sodium carbonate A mild alkali used for cleaning purposes. See also **E500**. Also called **washing soda**, **soda ash**

sodium carboxymethyl cellulose E466, the sodium salt of a derivative of cellulose used as a thickener and bulking agent

sodium caseinate A food additive made from milk protein used to maintain colour in sausages and other processed meats

sodium chloride The common salt used as a seasoning and preservative

sodium diphenyl-2yl-oxide E232, a synthetic derivative of diphenyl (E230) used in the same way as a fungicide

sodium ferrocyanide See **E535**

sodium formate E237, the sodium salt of formic acid used in the same way as the acid

sodium gluconate See **E576**

sodium glutamate See **monosodium glutamate**

sodium guanylate See **E627**

sodium heptonate A sequestering agent used in edible oils

sodium hydrogen diacetate E262, a sodium salt of acetic acid used as a preservative and firming agent

sodium hydrogen L-glutamate See **E621**

sodium hydroxide The strongest alkali available for domestic or general industrial use. It should be handled with extreme care with all bare skin and eyes protected. Used for dissolving fats from drains, etc. by converting them to soaps and for removing the bitterness from unripe olives. Also called **caustic soda**. See also **E524**

sodium inosinate See **E631**

sodium lactate See **E325**

sodium nitrate E251, the sodium salt of nitric acid used for curing and preserving meat

sodium nitrite E250, the sodium salt of nitrous acid which is used in curing salts to preserve meat and maintain a pink colour by its reaction with haemoglobin. Banned in some countries because of fears that it might induce stomach cancers.

sodium orthophenylphenate See **E232**

sodium phosphate An emulsifier used to assist in the incorporation of water into various processed foods such as sausage, luncheon meats, etc.

sodium polyphosphate A chemical used to increase the water uptake of poultry and of other meats and bacon so as to increase their weight. All of this water is lost on cooking and can cause problems e.g. when frying bacon.

sodium saccharin A sodium salt of saccharin used in the same way as saccharin

sodium sesquicarbonate See **E501**

sodium stearoyl-2-lactate E481, the sodium salt of a stearic acid ester with the lactate of lactic acid used to stabilize doughs and emulsions and to improve the mixing properties of flour and the whipping and baking properties of dried egg white

sodium sulphate See **E514**

soep *Netherlands* Soup

soezen *Netherlands* A large cream puff

soffiato *Italy* Soufflé

soffrito *Italy, Spain* Sofrito

soffrito calabrese *Italy* Lamb's offal cooked to a paste with tomatoes, herbs and seasoning and spread on bread. Also called **suffritu**

sofregit *Catalonia* A sauce made from onion, garlic, tomatoes and sweet peppers, sweated in oil until very soft and then sieved

sofrito 1. *Italy, Spain* A condiment and flavouring made by slowly cooking until tender a mixture of chopped onions, garlic, green sweet peppers, ham, salt pork, tomatoes, herbs and seasoning. Also popular in the Caribbean, Central and South America. Also called **soffrito 2.** Floured and seasoned stewing steak, browned in oil then simmered in equal parts of vinegar and water with garlic, herbs and tomato purée until tender, seasoned and finished with chopped parsley

soft ball stage See **sugar cooking**

soft-boil, to To boil an egg in the shell for roughly 3 to 4 minutes so that the white is just set but the yolk remains runny

soft cheese A cheese made with the retention of much of the whey so it has a high water content. The limits of water content are 80% for low-fat (2 to 10% butterfat), 70% for medium-fat (10 to 20% butterfat) and 60% for full-fat (greater than 20% butterfat) soft cheeses.

soft corn See **squaw corn**

soft dough *United States* A thick flour water mixture suitable for biscuits and bread, roughly 1.5 parts of flour per part of water. The proportions depend on the flour.

soft drop batter *United States* A soft flour water mixture suitable for cakes and muffins with roughly equal parts of flour and water. The proportions depend on the flour.

soften, to 1. To allow hard fats or frozen foods to become soft by raising their temperature **2.** To sweat chopped vegetables in a little oil or fat to make them soft

soft flour Flour made from soft wheat consisting of unbroken starch granules, mostly used for cakes, biscuits and general thickening and coating. Much cheaper than strong flour.

soft fruit Summer fruits such as berries and currants which are easily damaged

soft red winter wheat flour *United States* A good low gluten pastry flour

soft roe The sperm of male fish which is soft and creamy and forms a long packet within the abdominal cavity. Usually floured and fried, steamed or poached. Also called **milt**

soft roe butter Beurre de laitance (Fr)

soft-shell clam A large, grey- to fawn-coloured clam, *Mya arenaria*, up to 15 cm diameter with a thin brittle shell. They are often gritty and need thorough cleaning. Found throughout the Atlantic Ocean. Also called **long neck clam**, **steamer clam**

soft-shelled crab A crab eaten just after it has shed the hard shell it has grown out of before its new shell has had time to harden. Usually applied to the American blue crab.

soft sugar Light brown sugar

soft wheat A wheat in which the starch granules are loosely bound with voids between. This is thought to be caused by the protein triabolin which is only found in soft wheats. The endosperm is brittle and when ground tends to give intact granules since the cracks pass around them. Not necessarily, but often with a low protein content.

so fun *China* Rice vermicelli

soggy Of a cake, damp and heavy in the centre due to excess of moisture, lack of raising agent or incorrect baking temperature

sogi-giri *Japan* A diagonal cut of long thin vegetables such as leeks, carrots, etc.

sogliola *Italy* Dover sole

sogliola limanda *Italy* Lemon sole

soia *Italy* Soya

soissonaise, à la *France* Garnished with or including white cooked haricot beans

soissonaise, purée *France* As **purée Saint Germain** but with soaked haricot beans substituted for the peas. Also called **haricot bean soup**

soja *France, Spain* Soya

Sojabohne *Germany* Soya bean

Sojasosse *Germany* Soya sauce

sokeri *Finland* Sugar

Solanum melongena *Botanical name* Aubergine

Solanum torvum *Botanical name* Pea aubergine

Solanum tuberosum *Botanical name* Potato

Solanum x Burbankii *Botanical name* Wonderberry

sole *England, France* The name given to several types of flatfish, in particular Dover sole, lemon sole and witch or Torbay sole. Also called **flounder**

sole Albert Whole soles skinned and cleaned, one side dipped in melted butter and stale white breadcrumbs, put crumb side up in a buttered baking tin with the base covered with 3 parts dry vermouth to 1 part water, seasoned and sprinkled with chopped shallots and parsley and baked in a hot oven so that the bottom is steamed and the top browned. The fish is removed carefully and served with the strained and reduced cooking liquor with butter (**monté au beurre**).

sole Bercy *England, France* Bercy, fish

sole bonne femme *England, France* Bonne femme, fish

sole Colbert *England, France* Whole sole skinned, gutted, eyes and gills removed, fins trimmed, fillets on one side cut from centre to within 1 cm of the edge and folded back, back bone broken in 3 places, the whole panéed and deep-fried with fillets open, bone removed exposing white flesh in the centre which is piped with parsley butter. The whole served with lemon wedges or pigtails.

sole dieppoise *France* Sole poached in white wine and mussel liquor, garnished à la dieppoise and napped with sauce vin blanc made with the poaching liquor

sole Dugléré *England, France* Dugléré, fish

sole limande *France* Lemon sole

sole normande *France* Poached sole coated with a truffle-scented cream sauce and garnished with oysters, mussels and other seafood

soles in coffins *England* Baked potatoes with a lid cut off, scooped out, filled with poached paupiettes of sole napped with a suitable sauce, lids replaced and the coffins baked at 200°C for 10 minutes

sole Walewska *England, France* Walewska, fish

Solferino, crème *France* Equal parts of crème de tomates and purée parmentier

Solferino, sauce *England, France* The juice from very ripe tomatoes reduced, mixed with meat glaze, lemon juice and a little cayenne pepper, finished with **beurre maître d'hôtel**, pounded shallots and chopped tarragon

solferino cutter A sharp-edged scoop-shaped implement for cutting out small pea shaped balls of e.g. carrot, turnip, cucumber

sôlha *Portugal* Plaice

solianka *Australia* Fish fillets covered in a thick, sieved, tomato, onion and cucumber sauce, all poached in fish stock and served garnished with chopped olives and capers

solidified cooking oil Decolorized and deodorized vegetable oil, hardened by hydrogenation and used for frying and baking

sollo *Spain* Pike

solöga *Sweden* A dish consisting of concentric rings starting from the centre of chopped anchovies, chopped onions, capers and chopped pickled beetroot. A raw egg yolk is placed in the centre just before serving and the ingredients are mixed at the table and either fried in butter and spread on toast or spread on buttered bread and grilled. (NOTE: Literally 'eye of the sun'.)

solomillo *Spain* 1. Loin of pork 2. Sirloin

solomillo a la sevillana *Spain* Loin of pork with boiled potatoes, artichoke hearts, stuffed olives and tomato sauce

solomon gundy *Canada* Chopped salt herrings and onions pickled in spiced vinegar with sugar for several days and served as an appetizer (NOTE: From Nova Scotia)

soluble fibre Various non-metabolizeable soluble polysaccharides such as pectin, gums and related compounds found in vegetable matter, seeds, nuts, grains, etc. said to reduce blood cholesterol and low density lipoprotein levels and to be essential for good health

sølvkake *Norway* A light coconut- and lemon-flavoured cake

solyanka *Russia* A thick fish soup or thin stew made with salmon, chopped pickled cucumbers, olives, capers, onions, etc., butter and seasoning

som *Thailand* Orange

somen *Japan* 1. A thin white noodle resembling vermicelli, made from wheat flour 2. Cooked, refreshed, drained and chilled somen noodles served on a bed of ice with a platter of decoratively arranged hard-boiled eggs, cucumber and ham sprinkled with strips of mint leaves and served with a dipping sauce made with chopped reconstituted shiitake mushrooms, **dashi**, soya sauce, sugar and sake, all boiled together then cooled

Somerset apple cake *England* Cake, sauce

Somerset chicken *England* Chicken portions roasted until cooked, then added to a roux-thickened sauce with sweated onions, milk and cider. The mixture is finished with grated Cheddar cheese and mustard, the top gratinated with more cheese and browned under the grill.

Somerset cider cake *England* Wholewheat flour, butter, sugar and eggs (2:1:1:1) made up by the creaming method, with 2 dsp of bicarbonate of soda per kg of flour and a large amount of grated nutmeg, then brought to a soft dropping consistency with dry cider and baked in the oven for 60 to 75 minutes at 190°C until the top browns and the sides shrink away from the tin

Somerset cider Cheddar *England* A mild Cheddar cheese flavoured with cider

Somerset fish casserole *England* Deboned and skinned white fish cut in chunks, passed through seasoned flour, briefly fried with previously sweated chopped onion and mixed with a sauce made from pan residues, butter, flour, cider, anchovy essence, lemon juice and seasoning then baked at 180°C for 20 minutes. Garnished with apple rings fried in butter and chopped parsley.

Somerset soda cake *England* Soda cake

som khay *Laos* A delicate-coloured dip made from the roe of the **pa boeuk**. Also called **Laotian caviar**

sommacco *Italy* Sumac

sommargryta med korv *Sweden* A summer casserole of fresh spring vegetables simmered with good quality pork sausages

sommelier *France* Wine waiter

som mu *Laos* A pungent flavouring ingredient made from powdered pork and fermented rice

som-o *Thailand* Pummelo

som pa *Laos* A pungent flavouring ingredient made from pounded fish and fermented rice

som saa *Thailand* Citron

son *France* Bran

soncaya A particularly large custard apple, *Anona purpurea*, from Mexico and Central America

sone ka warq *South Asia* Gold leaf used for decorating food

song tse *China* Mulberry

song zi huang yu *China* Yellow croaker fish garnished with pine nuts

Sonnenbarsch *Germany* See **butterfish 3**

Sonnenblume *Germany* Sunflower

sonth *South Asia* Soondth

soo hoon *Malaysia* Cellophane noodles

soojo *South Asia* Semolina

sookha dhania *South Asia* Coriander seeds

soondth *South Asia* Dried powdered ginger root. Also called **sonth**

soonf *South Asia* Fennel seed

soon geung *China* Pickled ginger

soong hwa dan *China* Chinese preserved eggs

so' o-yosopy *South America* Sopa de carne

sop Hard bread soaked in a hot liquid such as milk or soup

sopa 1. *Catalonia* Soup **2.** *Spain* A breakfast dish of hot coffee and milk poured over toasted bread from the previous day

sopa a la mallorquina *Spain* A fish soup with tomatoes and onions

sopa blanca *Spain* A cold soup from Andalusia made from equal parts of blanched and skinned almonds and cooked broad beans processed with garlic and oil and let down with lemon juice and water, seasoned, chilled and served over cubes of bread

sopa burgalesa *Spain* Lamb and crayfish soup

sopa coada *Italy* A bread-thickened soup made from roast pigeon flesh

sopa cuarto de hora *Spain* Quick soup made by adding leftovers to stock

sopa de aguacate *Mexico* Soup made from defatted seasoned chicken stock with mashed avocado and chopped parsley and coriander leaf. Served lukewarm or chilled. Also called **avocado soup**

sopa de almejas *South America* A clam and white fish soup with vegetables (from Colombia)

sopa de batata e agrião *Portugal* Potato and watercress soup

sopa de camarão e mexilhão *Portugal* A soup of mussels and shrimps

sopa de carne *South America* A beef and vegetable soup with rice or vermicelli (from Paraguay). Served with grated Parmesan cheese. Also called **so' o-yosopy**

sopa de feijão *Portugal* Bean soup

sopa de legumbres *Spain* Vegetable soup

sopa de moni *South America* A peanut and potato soup finished with cream (from Ecuador)

sopa de pescado *Spain* Fish soup

sopaipilla *Malaysia* A flat bread which is fried and puffs up

sopar *Catalonia* Dinner

sopari *South Asia* Betel nut

sopa seca *Portugal* Shredded left-over meat layered in a large oven-proof pot with sliced boiled potatoes and carrots, bread and chopped mint, covered with boiling stock and dried in a hot oven (NOTE: Literally 'dry soup'.)

sope *Mexico* A filled turnover made with tortilla dough. See also **garnacha**

sopp *Norway* Mushroom

soppa *Sweden* Soup

soppressa *Italy* A Veronese salami made from pork and beef

soppressa del pasubio *Italy* A firm textured pork sausage with potatoes and chestnuts

soppressate *Italy* A large sausage from the southwest, oval in cross-section, well-seasoned and flavoured with ginger, sometimes preserved in olive oil

soprafino *Italy* Superfine olive oil

sopressa *Italy* Coppa

sorb Rowanberry

Sorbais *France* Maroilles cheese

sorb apple A close relative, *Sorbus domestica*, of the rowanberry, native to southern Europe. It is cultivated for the small green apple- or pear-shaped fruit which may be eaten as a fruit or used to make a type of cider.

sorbates Salts of sorbic acid used as permitted food preservatives, the sodium salt is E201, the potassium E202 and calcium sorbate is E203

sorbet A soft water ice rather like a soft snow made by freezing a sweetened fruit juice or liqueur-flavoured light syrup mixed with whipped egg white, whisking vigorously at intervals to inhibit ice crystal formation and to incorporate air. Used as a dessert.

sorbet colonel *South Asia* An Anglo-Indian dessert of lemon sorbet with a sprig of mint floating in a coupe of spirituous liquor, e.g. vodka

sorbetto *Italy* Sorbet

sorbic acid A permitted preservative, E200, for use in baked and fruit products. May be obtained from berries of the mountain ash but is now synthesized and is a mould and yeast inhibitor.

sorbier des oiseaux *France* Rowanberry

sorbitol A compound found in many fruits and berries but now synthesized from glucose for use as a humectant and as a sweetening agent for diabetics. Available as a water solution E420(ii). See also **E420(i)**

Sorbus americana *Botanical name* See mountain ash 2

Sorbus aucuparia *Botanical name* Rowan tree (rowanberries)

Sorbus domestica *Botanical name* Sorb apple

Sorbus scopulina *Botanical name* See mountain ash 2

sorgho *France* Sorghum

sorghum A very important plant, *Sorghum vulgare*, which grows in semi-arid tropical and subtropical regions. It has the general appearance of the maize plant with thinner leaves and a top terminal spike of small seeds. Some varieties produce white seeds which are preferred for eating, the red seeded type is more bitter and used for brewing beer. There is also a variety whose stems are crushed like sugar cane to produce a syrup used for sweetening, mainly in the USA. Sorghum grain is used for human consumption where grown and is only traded for compounding animal feeds. See also **sweet sorghum**, **great millet**, **kaffir corn**. Also called **Guinea corn**

sorghum flour Ground sorghum or milo maize occasionally used to thicken soups

sorghum syrup The juice of the sweet sorghum evaporated to produce a slightly acid molasses-like syrup

Sorghum vulgare *Botanical name* Sorghum, great millet

sorpresine *Italy* Tiny pasta shapes used in soups

sorrel A hardy perennial plant, *Rumex acetosa*, with pointed oval, sour leaves used in salads, soups, etc., cooked with fish or used as a spinach-like vegetable. The variety grown in France is less acid than that which grows wild in the UK. The leaves may be blanched before final cooking to reduce the acidity. Also called **broad leaf sorrel**, **sourgrass**

sorsa *Finland* Wild duck

sorsapaisti *Finland* Roast wild duck

sorvete *Portugal* Ice cream

sosaties *South Africa* Mutton kebabs

sose *Finland* Purée, sauce, stewed and mashed, mash

sosiska *Russia* Sausage, usually pork and smoked. May be cooked or eaten as a snack.

sospiri *Italy* Small custards with a cheese and egg filling

Sosse *Germany* 1. Sauce 2. Gravy

söt, sött *Sweden* Sweet

søt *Norway* Sweet

sotánghon *Philippines* Cellophane noodles

sot-l'y-laisse *France* Oyster (2), part of chicken

sotong *Malaysia* Squid

sotong karang *Malaysia* Cuttlefish

søtsuppe *Norway* A sweet fruit soup

sottaceti *Italy* Pickles, pickled vegetables

sottaceto *Italy* Pickled

sotto *Italy* Under, as in *sottaceto*, under vinegar

søtunge *Denmark* Sole, the fish

Soubise, sauce *England, France* An onion sauce boiled with more onion to extract the onion flavour or a béchamel with a large quantity of onion purée added, passed through a chinois, seasoned and flavoured with nutmeg. Used for roast meats.

souchet *France* A type of wild duck

souchet, sauce *France* The poaching liquor from fish, reduced, mixed with sauce aux vin blanc, consistency corrected if necessary with **beurre manié** and garnished with julienned carrot, leek and celery which has been sweated in butter and drained

souci *France* Marigold

soudzoukakia *Greece, Middle East* A variety of frying sausage made from seasoned and minced pork or veal, breadcrumbs and onions, flavoured with garlic, salt, parsley and ground cumin and bound with egg

soufflé *England, France* An air-raised fluffy sweet or savoury baked dish made from a flavoured starch-based mixture (a thick white **panada** or crème pâtissière) into which stiffly beaten egg whites are folded, this poured into a buttered and floured soufflé dish and baked for about 25 minutes at 200°C. The soufflé should rise well above the rim of the dish and be served immediately. See also **cold soufflé**

soufflé dish A straight sided ovenproof dish in which soufflés are baked

soufflé omelette Whisked sweetened or seasoned egg whites, folded into slightly stirred egg yolks, a little water added, rewhisked then cooked as an omelette, often with a sweet filling

soulie *Ireland* Sugar dissolved in hot vinegar used as a salad dressing

Soumaintrain *France* A strong-flavoured surface-ripened cows' milk cheese from Burgundy cast in the form of a disc. The rind is reddish brown and the paste has a slightly spicy flavour.

so-un *Indonesia* Cellophane noodles

soup A flavoured liquid based on meat and/or vegetable extracts in water, milk or occasionally water only, with added ingredients. Derived from the old English 'sop', a term applied to hard bread dipped into water or wine to make it palatable. There are 7 classical types of soup: consommé, potage, broth, purée, cream, velouté and bisque plus a few specials, often cold, based on fruit or tomato juice, wine and the like. See also **basic soup**

soupa *Greece* Soup

soupa faki *Greece* A brown lentil soup made from blanched and refreshed lentils simmered in water (1:3 on dried lentils) for 45 minutes in a closed pan with finely sliced onions, garlic, celery and carrots, olive oil, tomato purée, **tomato concassée** and a faggot of herbs, the herbs removed and the soup finished with a little vinegar and chopped thyme or parsley

soupe *France* Soup, tends to be more substantial than **potage**

soupe à l'ail *France* Garlic soup

soupe à l'oignon *France* See **brown onion soup**

soupe au pistou *France* A country-style vegetable soup accompanied with a **pistou** The soup is made from shredded white of leek and brunoise-cut carrots and turnips sweated in butter, mixed with cooked haricot beans, chopped green beans, broad beans, **tomato concassée**, tomato purée, macaroni, seasoning and vegetable stock simmered until all tender

soupe aux légumes *France* Vegetable soup

soupe aux rognons *France* Kidney soup

soupe de poisson *France* Saffron-flavoured and coloured fish soup, usually passed through a chinois to remove all large pieces of fish and bones. Served in the south of France with rouille, toast and grated cheese.

soupe germou *Caribbean* A vegetable soup with pumpkin, onions, celery and garlic thickened with a roux and served hot or cold

soup herbs The principal herbs used in soup are basil, bay, borage, caraway, chervil, chives, dill, juniper, lemon balm, lovage, marjoram, mint, parsley, rosemary, summer savory, sorrel, tarragon, thyme, wild celery and winter savory

soup spoon A large oval-bowled (France) or round-bowled (UK) spoon, used to drink soup

sour, to To add a souring agent such as acid or acid fruits to a foodstuff to give it a sour taste

sour cherry Acid cherry

sour cream Cream allowed to sour by a lactic fermentation either naturally or more usually with the addition of a starter culture which may be cottage cheese. See also **acidulated cream**

sour cream sauce A chicken or game velouté flavoured with vinegar, sweated chopped shallots, white wine and soured cream. A simple version of smitane sauce.

sourdough bread Bread which uses in place of yeast, dough from a previous batch which has been allowed to ferment with a little warm water and sugar overnight or longer.

About 10% of a batch is reserved as starter for the next equal-sized batch. Less will require a longer time to prove. The method is simple and the taste of the bread is thought by some to be superior.

soured cream Made by adding a souring culture of *Lactobacillus* to homogenized single cream

sour finger carambola Belimbing

sourgrass Sorrel

souring agent Any edible substance containing a reasonable concentration of acid such as vinegar, lemon juice, tamarind, etc.

sour milk Milk which has naturally curdled or been deliberately exposed to some acid-producing organism and thus curdled at around 30 to 35°C. UHT milk should not be soured. Useful in baking where bicarbonate of soda is used as double the amount of carbon dioxide will be liberated.

sour milk cheese 1. Handkäse **2.** The curd separated from naturally soured milk by straining through muslin. Commonly made in the home before refrigerators.

sour orange See **Seville orange**

sour skons *Scotland* An unusually flavoured scone made from oatmeal, buttermilk, flour and caster sugar (3:3:3:1) with 4 tsp of bicarbonate of soda and 4 dsp of caraway seeds per litre of buttermilk. The oatmeal is mixed with the buttermilk and left in a cool place for 2 to 3 days before blending with all the other ingredients to make a soft elastic dough, adding more buttermilk if necessary. The dough is shaped into large rounds about 2 cm thick, each cut in quarters and baked on a hot griddle for 5 to 10 minutes, then wrapped in a cloth to cool.

sour sop A type of custard apple from a tree, *Anona muricata*, which has large 15 to 23 cm long heart-shaped fruits with a green spiny skin. They are more acid-tasting than most custard apples and the texture of the juicy flesh is not as good. Suitable for drinks and desserts. Also called **prickly custard apple**

sous-chef *France* Under chef, assistant chef

souse *Caribbean* Pigs' trotters and tails possibly chickens' feet and/or pork meat boiled until soft, rinsed and drained then marinated overnight in lime juice and water (1:2) with chilli peppers and cucumbers, garnished with parsley and served cold often with black pudding and sliced boiled breadfruit

souse, to To pickle in vinegar or brine especially of herrings

soused herrings *United Kingdom* Herring fillets, rolled and secured with a sliver of wood, briefly cooked in a non-metallic covered dish with vinegar, water, onions, sugar, herbs, spices and seasoning and allowed to cool in the cooking liquor. Eaten cold.

soused mackerel *United Kingdom* As soused herring but substituting small mackerel fillets for the herring

sous-noix *France* Undercushion of veal

South American oyster An oyster, *Crassostrea chilensis*, found off the coasts of central and south America

southern bean *United States* Cow pea

southern bluefin tuna A common variety of tuna, *Thunnus macoyii*, from the southern hemisphere. The catch is worth half a billion pounds a year but is in danger of being fished out.

southern blue whiting A deep-water fish from New Zealand

southern bream *Australia* Australian black bream

southern calamari *Australia* A variety of squid, *Sepioteuthis australis*, found from the south of Western Australia to southern New South Wales. It is extensively fished for human consumption although once was considered only fit for bait.

southern cornpone *United States* Corn pone

southern fried chicken *United States* Jointed portions of chicken passed through seasoned flour and fried until crisp on the outside and just cooked through. Sometimes served with a béchamel-based sauce and mashed potatoes.

southern lobster See **spiny lobster**

southern rock lobster A type of spiny lobster, *Jasus novahollandiae*, coloured yellow, orange and purple, found in Southern Australia and shipped to the USA as rock lobster. Also called **crayfish (seawater)**

southern sea garfish *Australia* A long slender fish, *Hyporhamphus melanochir* and *H. australis*, with a characteristic beak-like elongation of the lower jaw, found mainly in South Australia and Victoria with some in Western Australia and Tasmania. The flesh has a sweet taste and firm texture but the fish is small and has many fine bones. It is generally cooked whole with the beak pushed into the tail end and grilled or barbecued or in chunks. It is a very gelatinous fish and makes excellent soup. Also called **beakie**

southern stone crab *United States* A greyish crab, *Menippe mercenaria*, up to 12 cm across and with very large claws, one of which is bigger than the other. It lives in deep holes in mud or rock piles around the coast from Texas to the Carolinas. Only the claw meat is edible and often only the claws are traded.

soutribbetjie *South Africa* Ribs of lamb or mutton lightly brined, hung up to dry then cooked on a barbecue

Souvaroff, à la *France* (*of a casserole of poultry or game birds*) Containing brandy, foie gras and truffles

souvlakia *Greece* Kebabs of lamb, veal or pork, cooked on a griddle or over a barbecue and sprinkled with lemon juice during cooking. Served with lemon wedges, onions and sliced tomatoes.

sovs *Denmark* Sauce

sowa *South Asia* Dill

sowbelly *United States* Salted fat belly pork or streaky bacon

sow cabbage See **jiu la choy**

soya batter *Japan* A batter sometimes used for tempura made from water, egg and soya sauce (13:3:1) whisked together lightly then mixed with half its combined weight of flour to give a lumpy consistency

soya bean The seeds of an erect bushy plant, *Glycine max*, of the pea family, originating in China but now a major crop grown worldwide in frost-free, warm summer climates and containing about 20% oil and 35% protein on a dry weight basis. The pods contain between 2 and 4 seeds which may be green, brown, yellow or black. A common food in China and Southeast Asia and an important animal feed. Used as a source of bean sprouts, oil, flour, milk, protein curds, vegetable protein and meat analogues and sauce as well as being an important food pulse in its whole state. The beans, especially the oil, are rich in compounds which behave like weak oestrogens and dilute the effect of the body's own oestrogens, thus reducing the risk of breast cancer, but evidence has been reported that raw soya flour fed to rats produced pancreatic cancer. See also **black soya bean**, **yellow soya bean**, **bean curd**

soya bean cheese See **bean curd cheese**

soya bean condiment See **yellow bean sauce**

soya bean curd See **bean curd**

soya bean flour Ground lightly-roasted soya beans containing a high percentage of fat from the beans

soya bean oil See **soya oil**

soya bean paste Ground fermented black soya beans mixed with flour, salt and water to give a thick paste used in Chinese cooking

soya bean sprouts Long (up to 13 cm) yellow sprouts from soya beans, used as a vegetable

soya flour Flour produced from soya beans with a high fat and protein content, used together with wheat flour in baking and in ice creams and other manufactured foods

soya milk A substitute for cows' milk used by vegetarians and vegans made by boiling ground soya beans with water for long periods of time and filtering off the sediment

soya noodles See **bean curd noodles**

soya oil Oil extracted from soya beans used as a cooking oil, for salad dressings and for the manufacture of margarine containing only about 10% of saturated fat. Said to have protective effects against breast cancer. Also called **soy bean oil**

soya sauce A highly flavoured liquid which is obtained by long fermentation of soya beans and various cereal grains. It is produced in 3 stages. In the first, polished rice is fermented with *Aspergillus oryzae*. This is then mashed with boiled soya beans and crushed roasted grains of wheat, incubated at 30°C for 3 days, diluted with brine then fermented with *Pediococcus halophilus* to reduce the pH. In the third stage the mixture is fermented slowly for between 1 and 3 years with *Saccharomyces rouxii*. Both light and dark varieties are produced with varying amounts of salt added. Also called **soy sauce**

soya vermicelli See **bean curd noodles**

soy bean See **soya bean**

soy bean oil See **soya oil**

soy sauce See **soya sauce**

Spaetzle *Germany* See **Spätzle 1**

spag bol *United Kingdom* Spaghetti Bolognese (*colloquial*)

spagetti *Sweden* Spaghetti

spaghetti *England, Italy* Thin solid pasta made by extruding a pasta paste though circular holes about 2 to 3 mm in diameter, either cooked immediately or cut into lengths (up to 40 cm) and dried for future use

spaghetti al aglio e olio *Italy* The basic dish of spaghetti with chopped garlic and olive oil

spaghetti al burro *Italy* Spaghetti with butter

spaghetti alla Bellini *Italy* Spaghetti with tomatoes, aubergines and ricotta cheese (NOTE: Named after the composer.)

spaghetti alla bolognese *Italy* Spaghetti with a tomato and minced meat (Bolognaise) sauce

spaghetti alla carbonara *Italy* Freshly cooked spaghetti tossed with crisply fried bacon chopped in small pieces, cream and sometimes beaten egg. Served with a sprinkling of grated Parmesan.

spaghetti alla carrettiera *Italy* Spaghetti with tuna fish, mushrooms and **tomato concassée** or purée

spaghetti alla marinara *Italy* Spaghetti with clams, mussels, garlic, tomatoes and onions

spaghetti all'amatriciana *Italy* Spaghetti with a tomato sauce flavoured with chopped onions and pieces of salt pork or bacon and sprinkled with grated Pecorino cheese

spaghetti alla napoletana *Italy* Spaghetti with mushrooms, tongue and tomatoes

spaghetti alla pommarola *Italy* Spaghetti with tomatoes, garlic and basil

spaghetti alla puttanesca *Italy* Spaghetti with capers, black olives, parsley, garlic and olive oil

spaghetti alle vongole *Italy* A classic spaghetti dish with a sauce made from chopped tomatoes and courgettes, sweated in olive oil, warty venus clams put in a minimum of cold water and heated until all the clams open, clams reserved, cooking liquor added to the vegetables and all reduced, the reserved clams added just before serving

spaghetti al pesto *Italy* Spaghetti with a pesto sauce

spaghetti marrow See **vegetable spaghetti**

spaghettini *Italy* A thin version of spaghetti

spaghetti squash See **vegetable spaghetti**

spalla *Italy* **1.** Shoulder of lamb, veal, etc. **2.** Cured and pressed shoulder of pork forced into a rectangular mould

spam *United States* A canned pork and ham meat loaf imported in large quantities into the UK during World War II (NOTE: Spam is short for Spiced Pork And Ham.)

spanakopita *Greece* Cheese and spinach pie

spandauer *Denmark, Sweden* A cake made from squares of unproved Danish pastry each with a blob of apple purée, almond paste, conserve, crème pâtissière or similar in the centre, the four corners folded in towards the centre and pressed down, proved 30 minutes then baked at 230°C for 10 minutes and glazed with icing after cooking

Spanferkel *Germany* Sucking pig

spanischer Pfeffer *Germany* Sweet pepper, capsicum

spanische Windtorte *Germany* A decorative meringue shell filled with cooked berry fruit and topped with whipped cream

Spanish *United Kingdom* Liquorice

Spanish bayonet *United States* See **yucca 2**

Spanish black radish A round radish the size of an orange with a black skin, eaten raw or cooked

Spanish chestnut See **chestnut**

Spanish dagger *United States* See **yucca 2**

Spanish garlic Giant garlic

Spanish lime A small round fruit like a grape. See also **genip**

Spanish ling A fish related to the ling found in the western Mediterranean and the Bay of Biscay

Spanish omelette Tortilla

Spanish onion A large delicately flavoured onion with a brown or red skin favoured by professional chefs for its ease of handling and suitability for frying. Grown in most countries. May be served raw.

Spanish peanut A variety of peanut with an upright habit and 2 light brown seeds per pod

Spanish pepper Sweet pepper

Spanish rice *United States* A mixture of rice, chopped onion, chopped green sweet pepper and chopped tomatoes, all cooked separately with herbs and seasoning. Served as an accompaniment to a meat course.

Spanish sage A narrow-leaved sage, *Salvia lavandulifolia*, with a slightly balsamic flavour. Also called **narrow leaf sage**

Spanish salami A salami very similar to the Italian but with a milder flavour

Spanish sauce See **espagnole, sauce**

spanner crab *Australia* A deep red-coloured frog-like crab, *Ranina ranina*, with claws that resemble spanners. It is found along the coasts of Queensland and northern New South Wales. The white meat is particularly fine.

spanocchi *Italy* Large prawns

spanspek *South Africa* Cantaloupe melon

sparaglione *Italy* Small sea bream

spare rib of pork *United Kingdom* The cutlets, i.e. rib bones, vertebrae and longitudinal muscles equivalent to middle neck of lamb, which are hidden behind the shoulder. They may be roasted whole, chopped into cutlets for grilling or the meat used for pies, etc.

spare ribs *United Kingdom* A sheet of skinned and partially defatted lower part of the rib bones of pork cooked either as a whole sheet or in separate ribs, often marinated in a spicy sauce, and barbecued or fried. Served as a starter or appetizer. Not to be confused with spare rib.

Spargel *Germany* Asparagus

Spargelfest *Germany* A country festival held annually in the spring for the sole purpose of eating white asparagus

Spargelkohl *Germany* Broccoli

sparl *United Kingdom* A broad sheep casing

sparling *United States* Smelt

sparris *Sweden* Asparagus

sparrow grass Asparagus

spatchcock A chicken prepared by removing the wish bone, severing the leg sinews, cutting horizontally from below the rear point of the breast over the tops of the legs down to the wing joints without removing the breasts, bending the breasts towards the neck end and snapping the backbone so that the point of the breast extends forward, flattening and neatening the whole chicken. When placed skin side up it should resemble a toad. It is then seasoned, brushed with oil and cooked under the grill for approximately 15 minutes per side. Also called **chicken spatchcock**, **poulet à la crapaudine** (NOTE: So called because it can be cooked in a hurry, i.e. with dispatch)

spatula 1. A flexible plastic or rubber scraper, rectangular in shape with a curve on one side, used for removing all the contents of bowls and pans which would otherwise stick to the sides. Some have a handle. **2.** A long thin flexible rectangular metal blade on a handle used for spreading and smoothing icing and fillings and for handling long fillets of fish

spatule *France* Spatula

Spätze *Germany* A type of gnocchi made with seasoned flour and beaten eggs (2:1) made into a soft dough with water if necessary, teaspoonfuls poached in boiling salted water for 6 to 10 minutes, drained and served with molten butter and fried bread crumbs

spätzele *France* Short lengths of cooked pasta lightly browned in the oven or fried until golden. Also called **spetzli** (NOTE: From the Alsace region of France)

Spätzle *Germany* **1.** A batter of flour, milk, eggs, salt and nutmeg made into noodles by pouring through one or more small holes into fiercely boiling water. Served tossed or fried in butter. (NOTE: From the southern and Alsace regions) **2.** A type of gnocchi made with seasoned flour and beaten eggs (2:1), made into a soft dough with water if necessary, teaspoonfuls poached in boiling salted water for 6 to 10 minutes, drained and served with molten butter and fried bread crumbs

spaul of beef *Scotland* A Scottish term for chuck and blade steak of beef

spear A young pointed cylindrical plant sprout, especially of asparagus

spearmint A type of mint, *Mentha spicata*, with closely set toothed leaves and a clean spearmint flavour. Used for drinks and for flavouring and can be crystallized for decoration. Also called **Moroccan spearmint**

specialité *France* Speciality, e.g. of the house, de la maison, etc.

specific gravity The ratio of the density of a substance to the density of water at the same temperature. It has no units and substances with a specific gravity greater than 1 will sink in water, whilst if less than 1 they will float. Sugar solutions and brines have a specific gravity greater than 1, oils and fats less than 1. Also called **SG**, **relative density**

Speck *Germany* Bacon or the mildly cured and smoked pork fat used in traditional cooking

Speckblutwurst *Germany* A large-diameter sausage made with seasoned and minced lean pork mixed with diced speck and pigs' blood

Speckknödel *Austria* Bread and onion dumplings mixed with diced bacon and Speck from the Tyrol

Speckkuchen *Germany* A flat cake containing diced bacon

Specklinsen *Germany* Lentils cooked with a piece of bacon, a whole onion and root vegetables until soft, bacon and vegetables removed, strained and the lentils bound with a **demi-glace** sauce and sprinkled with crisply fried finely diced bacon

speculaas *Netherlands* Spiced biscuits made for the feast of St Nicholas and the rest of the Christmas season

spegepølse *Denmark* A type of salami made with a mixture of various minced or chopped meats, seasoned. sugar and saltpetre added, packed into ox runners, dry-salted then air-dried and smoked.

speilegg *Norway* Fried egg

Speiseeis *Germany* Ice cream

Speisekarte *Germany* Menu

Speisequark *Germany* Quark

spejleæg *Denmark* Fried egg

spekemat *Norway* Cured meat

spekepølse *Norway* A mutton sausage, lightly smoked

spekeskinke *Norway* Cured ham eaten raw

Spekulatius *Germany* A sweet almond biscuit. Eaten during the Christmas season.

spelt flour Flour made from an ancient variety of wheat which has a hard husk making it difficult to mill. It has a high gluten content which makes it very suitable for making bread.

spenat *Sweden* Spinach

spenatsoppa *Sweden* Spinach soup based on roux-thickened beef stock finished with double cream

spencer *Ireland* Ulster roll

spencer steak *United States* Delmonico steak

spermaceti A low melting point wax obtained from the whale's buoyancy aid, used as a releasing agent

sperm oil The oil rendered from the blubber of the sperm whale used as a releasing agent

spettekaka *Sweden* A tall cake baked on a spit

spetzli *France* Spätzele

spezie *Italy* Spices

spezzatino *Italy* A light stew usually of tender meat, sautéed and finished with a sauce. Also called **spezzato**

spezzato *Italy* Spezzatino

spicchi, in *Italy* In segments or sections

spicchio *Italy* Clove, e.g. of garlic

spice One or other of various strongly flavoured aromatic substances of vegetable origin obtained from tropical plants, particularly dried roots, seeds, buds, berries, fruits and bark

spice bread See **Yorkshire spice bread**

spiced beef *United Kingdom* Salted and rolled silverside, soaked, simmered with onions, carrots and turnips for 4 hours, left to cool in the cooking liquor, drained, stuck with cloves, covered with dark muscovado sugar, mustard powder, ground cinnamon and lemon juice and baked at 180°C for one hour

spiced salt *China* A mixture of salt and anise pepper heated in a heavy frying pan until the anise pepper darkens, cooled and ground. Used in China as a dip for raw or deep-fried vegetables, roast meat and poultry.

spice Parisienne *United States* Épices composés

spicken sill *Sweden* Top-quality plain salt herrings, soaked 12 hours, rinsed, dried, deboned and skinned. Two fillets formed into a whole herring and cut into 2 cm slices, garnished with fresh dill and accompanied by potatoes boiled in their skins, chives and soured cream.

spicken sill med sur grädde *Sweden* Pieces of pickled herring dressed with a mixture of soured cream and mayonnaise flavoured with chopped dill weed or chives

Spickgans *Germany* Smoked breast of goose

spider A shallow circle of steel mesh with the appearance of a spider's web about 20 cm in diameter with a metal handle used for collecting deep-fried food, especially fritters and any food in batter, from the oil or fat

spider crab A round-bodied leggy crustacean, *Maia squinado*, from Spain, also found in the English Channel. It has an oval shell to 20 cm across and is brown to reddish-orange with prickly spines. It has a fine flavour and is usually poached and served in its shell. Also called **spiny crab**

spiedino *Italy* Skewered or spitted, usually meat or prawns

spiedo, alla *Italy* Grilled over charcoal

Spiegelei *Germany* Fried egg

Spiessbraten *Germany* Spit-roasted meat

spigola *Italy* Bass

spijskaart *Netherlands* Menu

spinace *Italy* Spinach

spinach A fast-growing annual plant, *Spinacia oleracea*, which grows as a loose cluster of leaves to a height of 15 to 20 cm and a spread of 15 cm. Used as a vegetable and puréed as a base for other food. Very popular in Italian cooking as a colouring for pasta and as a constituent of fillings.

spinach beet A variety of beet, *Beta vulgaris* Cicla Group, grown for its leaves which resemble spinach. Grows well in northern climates.

spinach mustard Komatsuna

spinaci *Italy* Spinach, the vegetable

spinaci alla milanese *Italy* Spinach finished with pine nuts and butter and served with scrambled eggs

spinaci alla piemontese *Italy* Spinach finished with garlic and anchovies

spinaci alla romana *Italy* Spinach finished with garlic, ham, pine nuts and raisins

Spinacia oleracea *Botanical name* Spinach

spinaci in padella alla trasteverina *Italy* Spinach cooked in fat in a frying pan with raisins and pine nuts

spinacio *Italy* Spinach, the plant

spinarola *Italy* Rock salmon

spinat *Denmark, Norway* Spinach

Spinat *Germany* Spinach

spinazie *Netherlands* Spinach

spineless amaranth Chinese spinach

spinkrab *Netherlands* Spider crab

spinola *Italy* Sea bass

spiny bitter gourd A close relative, *Momordica cochiniensis*, of the bitter gourd but more rounded in shape with pointed warts on the skin

spiny cockle A large variety of cockle, *Acanthocardia aculeata*, growing up to 10 cm in diameter

spiny crab See **spider crab**

spiny dogfish Rock salmon

spiny lobster A seawater crustacean, *Palinurus elephas* var. *vulgaris*, resembling a lobster in taste and texture but without the large claws. They are reddish brown with yellow and white markings and may be up to 50 cm long, but taste better when smaller.

They are found around the coasts of Britain, Spain, France and the Mediterranean, but now rare. Often called crayfish especially in Australia and the USA. Cooked as lobster. Also called **crawfish**, **rock lobster**, **southern lobster**

spiral peel A continuous strip of apple or citrus peel about 6 to 9mm wide, used for decoration

spisekart *Norway* Menu

spit A substantial metal rod on which meat is impaled for roasting in front of, over, or under a source of radiant heat, or in an oven. It usually has attachments which clamp to the rod and engage the meat so that it turns as the rod is turned giving even cooking on all sides. The term often includes the supporting structure and the mechanism for turning the spit.

spitchcock A split eel, grilled or fried

spit-roast, to To roast meat whilst it is being turned on a spit

spitskool *Netherlands* Chinese cabbage

spleen A soft red pulpy organ near the stomach of an animal which is used for recycling the iron from dead or damaged red blood cells. Used in offal-based dishes or for stuffings.

split almonds Blanched and dehusked almonds split into their two halves

split pea Dehusked dried peas split into two equal hemispheres along the natural dividing line

split tin loaf *England* A bread loaf baked in a tin in which the top of the dough has been cut along the centre to allow outward expansion as the dough rises and more crust area

spoileensmall *Ireland* A joint of meat

spongada *Italy* A type of sherbet made with stiffly beaten egg whites

sponge cake A light chemical or air raised cake generally made by the creaming or whisking methods. Varieties include Genoese or Victoria sponge.

sponge finger biscuits See **sponge fingers**

sponge fingers Thin fingers of sponge made from creamed egg yolks and caster sugar (3 per 100 g of sugar) mixed with sifted flour equal in weight to the sugar, the stiffly beaten egg whites and salt folded in to the mixture progressively and then baked for 12 minutes at 160°C either in sponge finger tins or after piping onto a baking tray

sponge flan A circular flan case made with a sponge cake mixture in place of pastry. After baking and cooling, the centre is filled with fruit, whipped cream, mousse or the like and decorated.

sponge gourd Loofah

sponge pudding A hot, baked or steamed pudding made from a Victoria sponge mixture possibly with added fruits which is cooked in a pudding basin, sometimes with jam, golden syrup or treacle in the base. Served hot with a sweet sauce.

sponge sandwich A victoria sponge or genoese sponge sliced horizontally in half using a serrated knife, and filled with jam and/or whipped cream or butter cream, the top dusted with icing sugar. Also called **sandwich cake**

spoom *France* A dessert made from fruit juice, champagne or fortified wine, frozen then mixed with Italian meringue

spoon An implement with a shallow, oval or round bowl at one end of a handle, constructed of metal, plastic, ceramic, wood or other natural materials or a combination of these. Wooden spoons are often used in mixing and stirring so as not to leave scratches on the container. Spoons used for eating are either small (around 5 ml capacity) called teaspoons, medium (around 10 ml capacity) called dessert spoons or large (around 15 ml capacity) called tablespoons. Larger ones may be used for serving. The Chinese ceramic spoon is around 20 ml capacity. See also **measuring spoon**, **slotted spoon**, **ladle**

spoon bread *United States* Batter bread

spore The inactive form of a bacterium which is very resistant to heat or chemical treatment. It will, however, start to grow and divide again, given the appropriate environmental conditions.

sport coconut Makapuno

sposi *Italy* A small soft cream cheese

spot prawn *Canada* The most important prawn, *Pandalus platyceros*, found on the west coast of Canada

spotted dick *England* A steamed pudding made from a sweetened, egg-enriched suet pastry mix with dried vine fruits and a raising agent cooked in a pudding basin or cloth for several hours and served with cream or English custard. An alternative uses fresh breadcrumbs, self-raising flour, shredded suet, caster sugar and currants in the proportions 4:3:3:2:6, flavoured with grated lemon zest and brought together with milk. Also called **spotted dog**

spotted dog *England* Spotted dick

spotted whiting *Australia* King George whiting

sprængt oksekød *Denmark* Corned beef

sprag *United States* A large codfish

sprängd *Denmark, Sweden* Salt-cured e.g. of meat

sprat *England, France* A small, round-bodied member of the herring family, *Sprattus sprattus*, up to 14 cm long and with a bluish-green back. Found on the northeastern shores of the Atlantic. Baked, fried or grilled. Also called **brisling, Swedish anchovy**

spratto *Italy* Sprat. Also called **papalina**

spray-drying A method of drying solutions of foods or other soluble materials in liquid by spraying the liquid into a warm atmosphere and collecting the solid powder. Used for coffee extracts, milk and egg white.

spread A semi-solid savoury paste spread on bread for sandwiches or on toast for canapés, also any soft food item which can easily be spread

spread, to To smear out a semi-solid food to form a uniform thin layer using a knife or a spatula as with butter on bread, whipped cream or icing on a cake or a savoury spread on toast

spremuto *Italy* Squeezed, of citrus fruit, etc.

spring cabbage An early-season cabbage, mainly leaf with no heart, planted in the autumn, overwintered and harvested in spring. See also **spring greens**

spring chicken A chicken weighing a round 1.5 kg and 3 to 4 months old

Springerle *Germany* Aniseed-flavoured biscuits stamped with various designs before cooking for the Christmas season

spring-form cake tin A cake tin with a flexible side which can be tightened around or loosened from the circular base by means of a latch mechanism, thus making the release of the cooked cake easy

spring greens Individual leaves of the brassicas, especially cabbage, picked early in the season before the plants have hearted

spring lamb Milk-fed lamb between 6 weeks and 4 months old

spring onion A variety of onion, *Allium cepa*, which initially grows with a long white leek-like stem (up to 1 cm diameter) before forming a bulb. When young has a mild flavour and the whole stem including part of the green leaves is used in salads, as a garnish, and in many Chinese dishes. Also called **salad onion, shallot**

spring roll A thin rectangle of pastry made with eggs instead of water, wrapped securely around a cylinder of filling and deep-fried until crisp and golden. The filling consists of various mixtures of cooked chopped meat, poultry, shellfish or vegetables. Also called **pancake roll**

spring salmon See **chinook salmon**

sprinkle, to To scatter small or large particles or liquid drops over the surface of food as e.g. icing sugar over cakes, grated cheese over soup or a fish dish, flour over bread or vinegar over a salad. See also **drizzle, to**

spritärter *Sweden* Green peas

spritsar *Sweden* Almond butter biscuits

spritz biscuits Biscuits made by piping or squirting a biscuit mixture in zigzag shapes onto a tray then baking at 175°C until crisp and brown. A typical mixture might be flour, butter, sugar, ground nuts and eggs (2:2:2:1:1) made by the creaming method. Popular in Holland and Belgium.

Spritzgebäck *Germany* Spritz biscuits

sproal *Ireland* A joint of meat

Sprotten *Germany* Sprats, whitebait

sprout 1. The initial growth from a seed, usually very delicate and crisp, e.g. bean sprouts 2. See **Brussels sprouts**

sprout, to To keep seeds, beans or grains in warm damp conditions after soaking in water so that they germinate and begin to grow and generally convert starch and protein into sugars and plant tissue. Many seeds become more palatable and digestible after this process.

sprouting broccoli Large, very hardy biennial plants *Brassica oleracea* Italica Group growing to 90 cm, with many flowering shoots which develop in spring and are cooked as a vegetable. Both purple and white forms are available.

sprue Thin shoots of asparagus

spruitjes *Netherlands* Brussels sprouts

spruzzare *Italy* To baste or sprinkle with a liquid

spuma *Italy* Mousse

spun curd cheese Cheese in which the curd had been extruded through small holes or otherwise drawn and kneaded to make cheeses like Mozzarella

spun sugar Sugar syrup cooked to the hard ball stage (121°C) which is spun or pulled into fine threads when sufficiently cool and used to make cake and dessert decorations

spur dog Rock salmon

spurtle *Scotland* A carved wooden stick used in Scotland to stir porridge

squab 1. *United Kingdom* A young pigeon 2. *United States* A small single-portion chicken

squab pie *England* See **Devonshire squab pie**

squadro *Italy* Angel fish

squash The Native American derived name for various members of the *Cucurbitaceae* family, a vine crop originating in North America now grown worldwide. See also **summer squash, winter squash**

squash blossom Courgette flowers

squash melon Tinda

squaw corn A soft mealy variety of maize preferred by Native North and South Americans. Also called **soft corn**, **flour corn**

squid A widely distributed member of the cephalopod group of molluscs, genus *Loligo*, varying from small to over 60 cm in length with a torpedo-shaped body, eight arms and two long tentacles growing from around the central mouth parts at the rear of the body. It is semi-transparent with a reddish spot but can change colour and is opaque when cooked. May be cooked in any way. It has an inner shell. See also **flying squid**, **southern calamari**. Also called **inkfish**

squidgy chocolate roll *England* A fatless, flourless type of Swiss roll made from eggs, caster sugar, milk and cocoa powder (8:4:5:1). The egg yolk and sugar are creamed and mixed with milk and cocoa powder, the stiffly beaten egg whites folded in, all baked in a Swiss roll tin at 180°C, rolled, cooled, filled with whipped cream and decorated.

squille *France* Mantis shrimp

squirrel A bushy tailed tree climbing rodent of the family *Sciuridae*, eaten in many parts of the world. Well known in Cajun cookery, probably the grey squirrel, *Sciurus carolinensis*.

squirrel cut A method of preparing fish for frying by cutting at an angle to the vertical in a cross hatch pattern from skin to bone for whole fish or from fish to skin for fillets so that it looks like a pine cone. The cuts are opened out with the fingers and dusted with corn flour to prevent them closing up.

srikhand *South Asia* A dessert made from drained yoghurt with sugar, nuts and saffron

srpska proja *Balkans* Serbian bread made from maize flour

stabburpølse *Norway* Black pudding

stabilizers Food additives used to prevent food constituents separating out from a mixture. Emulsifiers are usually considered to be under this classification.

stable emulsion An emulsion which will not separate into its components under the conditions for which it was made

Stachelbeere *Germany* Gooseberry

stachys Chinese artichoke

Stachys sieboldii *Botanical name* Chinese artichoke plant

Staffordshire beef steaks *England* Slices of braising steak flattened, dipped in seasoned flour and fried with sliced onion until brown, simmered in beef stock until the meat is tender and finished with walnut ketchup

Staffordshire yeomanry pudding *England* A double-crust tart made with sugar pastry, the base layered with raspberry jam and the filling made from butter, caster sugar, beaten eggs and ground almonds (4:4:3:1) by the creaming method and flavoured with almond essence. Baked at 180°C for 40 minutes with a foil covering placed over the tart as soon as the pastry starts browning.

stag chicken *United States* An old male chicken with a good strong flavour

staghorn endive See **endive**

staghorn fungus Bamboo fungus

stagionata *Italy* Ripe or mature, of cheese

stagione *Italy* Season, of the year, as in pizza quattro stagione

stainless steel A high chromium and nickel iron alloy which is corrosion-proof and does not tarnish. Used for basins and cooking utensils.

stake Laver

staling The process that occurs when foods such as bread or cooked potatoes are stored. It is caused by the crystallization of amylose in starch gels.

stalker's pie A type of shepherd's pie made with finely diced cooked venison and chopped onion bound with gravy, topped with mashed potatoes and root vegetables, coated with butter and baked at 200°C, covered whilst warming through then uncovered to brown the top

stallina, alla *Italy* In the style of the stable, i.e. pasta with bacon and garlic

stambecco *Italy* Wild goat

stamp and go *Caribbean* Small pieces of salt cod coated in a batter flavoured with chillies, spring onions and thyme, deep-fried and eaten as a hot snack

stampinjong *Norway* Mushroom

stamppot *Netherlands* Hotpot

standard beef *United States* A tough grade of beef from low-quality young animals with no marbling and a bland flavour

standing rib of beef *United Kingdom, United States* The fore rib of beef, a term used in the northwest of England and North America

standing rump *United States* The top of the round of beef including the bone. Used for roasting.

Stangen *Germany* Long rectangular sweet or savoury pastries

Stangenkäse *Austria* A soft cows' milk cheese cast in bricks and resembling **Tilsit**

Stangensellerie *Germany* Celery

stångkorv *Sweden* A sausage packed with beef, pork, liver, kidney and boiled pearl barley. Usually fried.

stanislas *France* A cake filled with almond cream

Staphylococcus aureus A food poisoning bacterium whose toxins are not destroyed by cooking. It is found in meat pies and meat products containing salt and in confectionery. The incubation period is 2 to 6 hours and the duration of the illness 6 to 24 hours. The symptoms are nausea, vomiting, diarrhoea, and abdominal pain without fever. There may be collapse and dehydration in severe cases.

Staphylococcus carnosus Bacteria used as a starter culture for lactic fermentation in meat products such as salami and in vegetables such as cucumbers

staple crops Food plants which provide the major source of energy and/or protein for most of the world's population. The five most important are rice, wheat, corn (maize), cassava (energy only) and beans.

star anise The dried fruit of a Chinese tree, *Illicium verum*, which has the appearance of an eight-pointed star, each point containing one seed. It has a sweetish aniseed/liquorice flavour and is used in Chinese and Vietnamese cooking.

star apple The fruit of a subtropical tree, *Chrysophyllum cainito*, about 7.5 cm diameter with a white to purple, sticky, inedible skin, a white sweet pulp containing inedible black seeds in a star-shaped core rather like an apple core. Eaten on its own or in fruit salad.

starch An odourless and tasteless polysaccharide which is the principal carbohydrate store in plant tissues, tubers and seeds and is an important constituent of the human, herbivore and omnivore diet

star fruit See **carambola**, **babaco**

star gazey pie *England* A fish pie from Cornwall made with whole pilchards cooked beneath a crust of pastry with their heads poking up through the pastry around the rim of the dish. The pie also contains a sauce flavoured with onion, bacon, parsley, vinegar or cider and seasoning, which is thickened with breadcrumbs and eggs.

starjerska kisela corba *Balkans* A soup from Slovenia made with pigs' tails and trotters, vegetables, garlic, seasoning and a little vinegar and thickened with flour

stark senap *Sweden* Hot (English) mustard

starna *Italy* Grey partridge

starna di montagna *Italy* Grouse

star ruby A highly pigmented grapefruit variety developed by an artificially induced mutation using ionizing radiation

starter 1. The first course of a meal **2.** A bacterial or fungal culture used to initiate fermentation, and thus flavour development,

in fermented foods, e.g. *Lactobacillus* in milk to make yoghurt, *Rhizopus oligosporus* in **tempeh** or the lactic cultures used to replace the microorganisms and enzymes lost during milk pasteurization preparatory to making cheese

station waiter A waiter in charge of a certain number of tables in a restaurant

steak 1. *England, France* A piece or slice of meat or fish up to 2.5 cm thick usually cut across the muscle fibres and sufficiently tender to be grilled or fried **2.** A general name for lean muscle from animals used for braising, stewing, grilling or frying depending on the muscle concerned

steak and kidney pie *United Kingdom* Pieces of cheek of beef marinated in red wine, dried, fried in oil and butter, dusted with flour, simmered until tender in clarified marinade and beef stock, lightly fried pieces of veal or beef kidney added, poached oysters and mushrooms added if required, cooking liquor reduced and all combined in a bowl and precooked tops (skullcaps) of puff pastry placed over. Served piping hot. A simpler version is made from precooked steak and kidney stew baked quickly between a top and bottom crust of pastry.

steak and kidney pudding *United Kingdom* A pudding basin lined with suet crust pastry, filled with diced stewing beef and kidney, onions, seasoning and thickened stock, covered and sealed with more pastry, vents cut in the top, covered with cooking foil and boiled or steamed for 3 to 3.5 hours. Served from the basin or, less formally, turned out on a plate.

steak au poivre *France* Pepper steak

steak diane Tail end of fillet of beef, batted out, sautéed in butter, flambéed with brandy and served with a sauce made from pan juices, sliced mushrooms, Dijon mustard, double cream and **demi-glace**

steak haché *France* Hamburger steak

steak tartare Chopped (not minced) tail end of fillet of beef, mixed with chopped onions, gherkins and capers, shaped on the plate like a steak and served with a raw egg in a depression on top of the steak. Mixed at the table by the customer and eaten raw.

steam, to To cook in the vapour from boiling water. See also **steamer**, **atmospheric steamer**, **pressure cooker**

steamboat *Southeast Asia* An implement for cooking at the table consisting of an annular vessel containing cooking liquor (stock) around a circular chimney at the base of which is a source of heat. Prepared food is cooked by diners using fondue forks, chop sticks or wire mesh baskets. Various dips are usually supplied and the stock is often consumed after all the solid food has been cooked and eaten. See also **Mongolian hot pot**

steamed pudding Puddings based on sweetened suet pastry or a cake sponge mixture with additions and flavourings, cooked in a pudding basin, in a cloth or in a special hinged closed container using either steam or boiling water. Usually served with a sweet sauce which may be cooked as an integral part of the pudding.

steamed pudding mixture *United Kingdom* Made from self-raising flour, shredded beef suet or softened butter, caster sugar and beaten egg (6:3:2:2), the flour, fat and sugar combined with a little salt, then brought together with the beaten egg and sufficient milk to produce a soft dropping consistency

steamed rice See **absorption method**

steamer A double or triple saucepan with a top lid in which the compartments above the bottom pan are perforated so that steam generated at the bottom can circulate around the food items in the upper compartments

steamer clam Soft-shell clam

steam table A stainless steel table or counter with openings to take food containers heated by steam or hot water. Used to keep food hot prior to service. See also **bain-marie**

stearic acid One of the main saturated fatty acids in hard beef and lamb fats, responsible when esterified with glycerine for the hardness of the fat

stearyl tartrate An ester of stearyl alcohol and tartaric acid with the same uses as sodium stearoyl-2-lactylate

stecche, al *Italy* On a skewer

stecchi *Italy* Attereaux

Steckerfisch *Germany* Fish on a stick

steel A tapering rod either of hardened steel with very small longitudinal sharp edged grooves, carborundum stone or diamond dust coated metal, used to put a sharp edge on knife blades. The knife blade is stroked across and down the steel at an angle of about 45° or less on either side removing a small amount of metal from the edge. After considerable sharpening on a steel a knife needs to be reground professionally.

steel-cut oatmeal See **pinhead oatmeal**

steep, to To macerate

steer A castrated male of the bovine species, 2 to 4 years old

steg *Denmark* Steak

stegt *Denmark* Roasted. Also called **stægt**

stegtgås gylat med svedsker *Denmark* Roast goose stuffed with prunes

stegt kylling *Denmark* Braised chicken

stegt svinekam *Denmark* Roast pork with red cabbage

Steinbuscher *Germany* A soft cheese made with whole or partially skimmed cows' milk. It is brick-shaped and has a smooth buttery paste with a few holes. It comes from from the east of the country and is similar to Romadur. Contains 52% water, 21% fat and 24% protein.

Steinbutt *Germany* Turbot

Steingut *Germany* Earthenware

Steinpilz *Germany* Cep

stekt *Norway, Sweden* Fried or roasted

stekt ägg *Sweden* Fried egg

stekt and *Sweden* Roast duck, usually stuffed with apple, prunes and the chopped up liver and heart

stekt fläsk med löksås *Sweden* Fried strips of fresh or salt pork served with onion sauce (**löksås**)

stekt gås *Sweden* Roast goose, the cavity stuffed with parboiled prunes and cored, peeled and sliced apples sprinkled with ground ginger, basted with stock from time to time and accompanied with jus lié made from the defatted pan juices. Served with roast potatoes, chestnut purée and red cabbage.

stekt kalvbräss *Sweden* Calves' sweetbreads prepared as for **kalvbräss-stuvning**, sliced, panéed and fried in oil and butter. Served with petit pois.

stekt potatis *Sweden* Fried potato slices

stekt rödspätta *Sweden* Fried plaice usually skinned whole, panéed and fried slowly in butter

stekt salt sill med lök *Sweden* Fried salt herring which have been soaked, filleted and coated with flour and toasted breadcrumbs. Served with sliced onions which have been fried until brown in the butter in which the fish is later fried and the pan residues deglazed with thin cream. A traditional Monday lunch.

stekt salt sill papper *Sweden* Filleted salt herrings soaked, dried and baked or fried **en papillote** with the usual additions (butter, dill, parsley, chives, etc.)

stekt sjötunga *Sweden* Fried sole usually prepared as stekt rödspätta

stekt vildand *Sweden* Wild duck usually pot-roasted for 45 minutes with soured cream and milk after seasoning and browning the bird and its liver. Served with a jus lié made from the roux thickened cooking liquor finished with double cream and a little blackcurrant jelly.

Stellaria media *Botanical name* Chickweed

stellette *Italy* Very small pasta stars used in soup. Also called **stelline**

stellina odorosa *Italy* Sweet woodruff

stelline *Italy* Stellette

stem ginger Peeled ginger rhizome, macerated and preserved in a sugar syrup to give a soft translucent confection

stem lettuce *United States* Celtuce

Stephanie Cremetorte *Austria* An over-the-top sweet dessert invented for Crown Princess Stephanie who complained of the 'coarseness' of Viennese cooking, consisting of chocolate and hazelnuts plus layers of raspberry, hazelnut and chocolate cream

Stepnoi *Russia* Steppe

Stepnoj Steppe

Stepnoy Steppe

Steppe A strong-flavoured cows' milk cheese similar to **Tilsit** and sometimes flavoured with caraway made in Germany, Austria, Scandinavia, Russia and Canada. Also called **Stepnoi, Stepnoj, Steppen, Stepnoy**

Steppen Steppe

sterilize, to To heat food to between 115 and 140°C depending on the type of food and the time at the high temperature. This kills all pathogenic organisms and most microorganisms and spores. See also **ultra-heat treated**

sterilized cream Tinned cream sterilized at about 120°C. It has a slight caramel flavour and cannot be whipped.

sterilized milk Milk heated to 120°C for a few minutes or to just over 100°C for 20 to 30 minutes and aseptically sealed in a narrow necked bottle with a crown cork. This process kills all pathogenic and most other microorganisms and spores and the milk will keep for 1 to 2 years. The milk is off white in colour and has a characteristic caramel, boiled milk taste which is not to everyone's liking.

sterlet A small and very rare sturgeon, *Acipenser ruthenus*, found in the Volga river and Caspian Sea and famed for its golden caviar, the caviar of the Tsar. The fish, which is ugly and eel-like, is served baked with vegetables.

sterlyad *Russia* Sterlet

steur *Netherlands* Sturgeon

stew A mixture of meat, usually tough and cut into small pieces, cooked slowly with vegetables, cooking liquor and flavourings on top of the heat source until tender, a process which can take many hours

stew, to To simmer meat and poultry with cooking liquor and vegetables in a heavy pan with a tight fitting lid or to cook fruit in water until soft, possibly with the addition of a sweetening agent

Stewart cheese *Scotland* A mild cheese which comes in both a white and a blue variety. The white is saltier than the blue and is an acquired taste.

stewed fruit Fruit simmered in sweetened water until soft

stick bean See **runner bean**

sticking piece *England* Clod (of beef)

sticky bun *United Kingdom* A sweet yeast-raised bun often flavoured with cinnamon and coated with a soft icing

sticky rice See **glutinous rice**

stifado *Greece* A stew based on meat, poultry, octopus or squid with oil, onions, garlic, tomatoes, shallots, wine, wine vinegar, herbs and seasoning

stiff dough *United States* A very stiff mixture of 2 parts flour to one part water. The exact proportions depend on the flour used.

stiffen, to To briefly cook flesh in water or fat until it stiffens but is not coloured

stifle *United States* A salt pork and vegetable stew from New England

Stilton *England* An uncooked curd, blue-veined, semi-soft cows' milk cheese with a creamy yellow paste made only in Leicestershire, Derbyshire, Nottinghamshire and Rutland. The blue variety is inoculated with *Penicillium roquefortii* spores and the edges of the cheese are hand-rubbed to exclude air, slow down development and give the characteristic hard greyish-brown rind. The cheeses are needled after 10 weeks to encourage veining and may be sold after 12 weeks. Often sold in small earthenware pots and prized as a dessert cheese.

Stilton pears *England* A starter made from cored but not skinned Comice pears stuffed with a mixture of Stilton and curd cheese, refrigerated, halved and fanned on individual plates, covered in seasoned mayonnaise thinned with oil and lemon juice and flavoured with mustard

stinco *Italy* Shank of veal

stinging nettle See **nettle**

stink bean Parkia

Stint *Germany* Smelt, the fish

stir, to To agitate a liquid, semi-solid, or powder mixture with a spoon or spatula to bring to a uniform consistency or a liquid mixture to prevent sticking or burning during heating

stirabout 1. An oatmeal or maize porridge made with water or milk, originally from

Ireland **2.** *England* Chopped or small whole fruits mixed with a coating consistency batter enriched with sugar and butter and baked for about 30 minutes at 220°C

stir-fry, to To cook small thin pieces of meat or vegetables very rapidly using hot oil in a wok by continuously moving them and turning them over. Used extensively in preparing Chinese food.

stivaletti *Italy* Small pasta shapes (NOTE: Literally 'small boots'.)

stoccafisso *Italy* Stockfish

stock Water flavoured with extracts from herbs, spices, vegetables and/or bones by long simmering

stock cube A mixture of salt, MSG, vegetable and/or meat extracts and various flavourings pressed into soft crumbly cubes or blocks each individually wrapped. One stock cube will usually make 0.4 litres (0.75 pints) of stock. The salt and fat content and their flavour make them unsuitable for the finest cooking. See also **bouillon**. Also called **bouillon cube**

Stockfisch *Germany* Stockfish

stockfish Air-dried cod from Norway which is very popular in Italy. Requires prolonged soaking in water.

stock pot A large cylindrical vessel with a draw off tap between 2 and 5 cm from the base in which stock is prepared and into which all the suitable trimmings of a professional kitchen together with the usual stock ingredients are put, and stock drawn off as required. It is usually kept simmering all the time and cleaned out and replenished on a regular basis.

stock syrup A basic sugar solution with many uses containing 0.3 kg of granulated sugar and 0.1 kg of glucose per litre of water. Often 0.4 kg of granulated sugar with no glucose is used, but it may tend to cause crystallization.

stodge Heavy starchy solid food such as overcooked stews, suet puddings and the like (*colloquial*)

stoemp *Belgium* A dish similar to **colcannon** made with mashed potatoes and vegetables

stoke Laver

Stokenchurch pie *England* A Buckinghamshire baked pie filled with minced meat in a sauce mixed with macaroni

stokkfisk *Norway* Stockfish

Stollen *Germany* A sweetened enriched yeast dough rolled in a rectangle, filled with dried vine fruits, nuts and sometimes marzipan, folded or rolled, baked, brushed with molten butter and dredged with icing sugar. Eaten during the Christmas season. Also called **Christollen**

stomna kebab *Bulgaria* A lamb stew with butter, tomatoes, spring onions, herbs and seasonings, thickened with flour and cooked in an earthenware pot

stone The hard central seed of fruits such as cherry, peach, mango, plum, olive, etc., usually with a hard woody shell enclosing a soft kernel. Also called **pit**

stone, to To remove the central stone from a fruit. Also called **pit, to**, **destone, to**

stone crab *United States* A large edible crab, *Menippe mercenaria*, with very large claws, from the coast of Florida

stone cream *England* A very old Buckinghamshire dish which is a gelatine-stabilised mixture of milk combined with lightly whipped cream and egg whites, sweetened with vanilla sugar and poured before setting into glasses with jam on the base. Approximately equal quantities of milk and cream are used and gelatine is required at the rate of 40 to 50 g per litre of liquid.

stoneground flour Flour which has been ground between a stationary and a rotating stone as opposed to rollers which are used to grind most flour nowadays. The slight frictional heating modifies the flavour of the flour.

stone plover Plover

stoneware Coarse ceramic dishes, pots and jugs etc. which are often only glazed on the inside

stör *Sweden* Sturgeon

Stör *Germany* Sturgeon

storage temperatures Recommended storage temperatures for food are precooked, –3°C for up to 5 days; chilled, less than 5°C; eggs in shell, –10 to-16°C for up to 1 month; bakery produce, –18 to –40°C, blanched vegetables, less than –18°C; apples and pears, –1 to +4°C

store A designated room, cupboard, refrigerator or freezer where foods are kept in their purchased or partially processed condition prior to use

Störe *Germany* Sturgeon

store to To keep foods and articles for future use, either in a dry store, vegetable store, refrigerator or freezer

storione *Italy* Sturgeon

stortini *Italy* Small pasta crescents used in soup

stove, to *Scotland* A Scottish term dating from the 17th century derived from the French étouffer, meaning to cook in a closed pot, generally in the oven at around 150°C, e.g. stoved chicken

stoved chicken *Scotland* A dish of chicken pieces sealed and casseroled in a closed pot with bacon, potatoes, onions, thyme, seasoning and chicken stock at 150°C in the oven

stovies *Scotland* Boiled potatoes (*colloquial*)

stoviglie *Italy* Earthenware

straccetti *Italy* Thin slices

Stracchino *Italy* A soft cows' milk cheese from the north cultured with *Streptococcus thermophilus*, coagulated with rennet, the curd then heated to 80°C for 6 to 10 hours in square 20 cm moulds, salted in brine and matured for 7 to 10 days. Also called **crescenza** (NOTE: Originally made in the autumn from the milk of cows' brought down from Alpine pasture, from *stracche* meaning 'tired')

Stracchino di Gorgonzola *Italy* The original Gorgonzola made from an evening's and the following morning's milking of cows being brought down from mountain pasture and resting at the town of Gorgonzola. The evening curd which cooled overnight was mixed with the next morning's curd and gave a heterogeneous mixture which encouraged mould growth.

stracciata *Italy* Chiffonade of e.g. lettuce

stracciate *Italy* A flat cake

stracciatella *Italy* A beef or chicken broth into which a mixture of beaten eggs, semolina and grated Parmesan is whisked to give solid ragged-looking strands

stracciato *Italy* Scrambled, of eggs

stracci di antrodoco *Italy* Pancakes layered with cheese, meat and vegetables

Strachur haddock *Scotland* Finnan haddock poached for 4 minutes then skinned, deboned and flaked, placed in a buttered ovenproof dish, covered with double cream, peppered, baked for 10 minutes at 180°C then flashed under the grill (NOTE: After the Scottish village of Strachur, which lies on the eastern shore of Loch Fyne, in the Firth of Clyde)

stracotto *Italy* A very slowly cooked pot roast or meat stew

straight neck squash A summer squash common in the US

strain, to To pass a mixture of solid particles and liquid through a strainer, colander, sieve, chinois, muslin cloth, etc. to separate the solid and liquid either of which may be the desired product

strain O157:H7 A strain of the gut bacteria, *Escherichia coli*, found in hamburger-type minced beef which has picked up toxin-producing genes from *Shigella*. These toxins can destroy gut and kidney cells, leading to diarrhoea and kidney failure. The incubation period is 3 to 4 days. Common in the USA, and has occurred in Europe, Africa, Australia and Japan. The organism is killed by a temperature of 70°C for 2 minutes.

strainer General name for colander, sieve or chinois

straining bag A cloth bag used to filter liquids

Strandkohl *Germany* Sea kale

Strandkrabbe *Germany* Shore crab

strangolapreti *Italy* Small dumplings similar to strozzapreti and for the same purpose, i.e. to strangle, figuratively, the priest. There are many local spellings all beginning with *strang-* for what was obviously a widespread problem.

strapazzato *Italy* Scrambled, e.g. of eggs

strasbourgeoise, à la *France* In the Strasbourg style, i.e. cooked with sauerkraut, bacon and foie gras

Strasburg sausage *Australia* A manufactured slicing sausage rather like garlic sausage

strascinati *Italy* Baked ravioli with sauce

Strassburger Truffelleberwurst *Germany* A liver sausage flavoured with truffles

stravecchio *Italy* Very old, mature. Used of cheese or other food items which might improve with age.

strawberries Romanoff *United States* Strawberries steeped in an orange-flavoured liqueur and served with crème chantilly

strawberry The sweet, flavoursome and decorative fruit of a ground-creeping perennial plant, *Fragaria x ananasa*, generally conical, up to 5 cm long and consisting of a cluster of small fleshy globules, each of which has a single seed on the outer surface, around a central fleshy stem, with the remains of the calyx at the broad end. Eaten on their own with cream and possibly caster sugar or in made-up desserts, tarts, cakes and jams. See also **wild strawberry, alpine strawberry**

strawberry beets *United States* Very small beetroots used for pickling or in salads

strawberry guava A smaller and sweeter version of the guava, *Psidium cattleianum*, from Brazil with small reddish-purple fruit. Also called **cattley**

strawberry shortcake *United States* A large scone-like cake split whilst warm, buttered and made into a sandwich with whipped cream and sliced strawberries as a filling

straw chips See **straw potatoes**

straw mushroom A globular, stemless edible mushroom, *Volvariella volvacea*, grown on beds of straw in China. Available canned, but not dried, for use in Chinese and Japanese dishes. It is fawn when young but becomes grey-black and gelatinous as it matures. Also called **grass mushroom**, **yellow mushroom**, **paddy straw mushroom**

straw potatoes Well-washed and drained julienne potatoes deep-fried at 185°C until golden brown and crisp, drained and lightly salted and used as a garnish for grilled meat. Also called **pommes pailles**, **straw chips**

straws See **cheese straws**

streaky bacon Bacon from the rib cage and belly of the pig which when sliced shows alternate strips of lean and fat. Often used to line terrines and pâté dishes.

Streckrübe *Germany* Swede

Streichwurst *Germany* The generic name for any paste-like spreading sausage

Streptococcus A genus of bacteria used for the production of lactic acid in the manufacture of cheese and sauerkraut. Some of the species are pathogenic.

Streptococcus lactis ssp. cremoris One of the microorganisms used in the starter cultures for soured cream, buttermilk and English cheeses

Streptococcus lactis ssp. diacetilicos As *S. lactis* ssp. *cremoris*.

Streptococcus lactis ssp. lactis As *S. lactis* ssp. *cremoris*.

Streptococcus thermophilus One of the microorganisms used in starter cultures for yoghurt and continental cheeses

Stretford black pudding *England* Black pudding flavoured with ground marjoram, mint and pennyroyal

streusel *United States* A mixture of flour or breadcrumbs with sugar, butter and spices used as a crumble topping on baked goods

streusel cake A slightly sweet yeasted cake with a crumble topping of sugar flavoured with cinnamon or mixed spice from Central and Northern Europe

Streuselkuchen *Germany* Streusel cake

string bean 1. *United States* French bean **2.** *United Kingdom* Runner bean

string cheese *United States* A cows' milk cheese similar to Mozzarella which originated in Armenia and Georgia and is shaped as a small cylinder. Sometimes flavoured with caraway. Also called **braid cheese**

string hoppers *Sri Lanka* A thin pouring **appa** batter poured into hot fat through a moving funnel to give long threads of cooked dough. Also called **hoppers**

striped bass A medium-oily seawater fish, *Morone saxatilus* and *Roccus saxatilus*, which spawns in fresh water and is found off the coasts of North America. It has a deep olive-green body with longitudinal stripes

and weighs up to 2.5 kg. The flesh is white and flaky and it may be cooked in any way. Also called **rockfish**

striped bream A small seawater bream, *Lithognathus mormyrus*, with transverse dark grey stripes on a silvery background

striped mullet *United States* A species of mullet, *Mugil cephalus*, with longitudinal lines of dark grey on a silvery grey background

strip loin 1. *Australia* The fillet steak usually of lamb or pork, i.e. the longitudinal muscle that runs along the backbone between the inside of the ribs and the vertebrae. Usually sold as the long muscle. **2.** *United States* The round longitudinal muscle from the back of the beef equivalent to the eye of a lamb loin, boneless and trimmed and usually cut in steaks

strip steak *United States* A beef steak cut from a boneless short loin and sirloin after the fillet has been removed. Popular in New York.

stroganoff See **beef Stroganoff**, **bef stroganov**

strömming *Sweden* High-quality herring and sprats found only in the Baltic and commanding a premium price

strömming à la Operakällaren *Sweden* Cleaned and rinsed herrings and sprats with fins and tails removed, salted, marinated in a mixture of whipped egg and double cream (2:5) for at least an hour, removed, coated in wholemeal flour and shallow-fried in butter until well browned. Served with a simple parsley and lemon wedge garnish.

strömmingslada *Sweden* Young herrings filleted kipper-style (from the back), bones removed as far as possible, seasoned, placed in a buttered baking dish and gratinated with grated Parmesan cheese and breadcrumbs in the oven until browned

strong flour Flour of any type made from a hard wheat, usually containing between 11 and 12% protein which is mostly gluten. Used mainly for bread and puff and choux pastry.

stroop *Netherlands* Syrup or molasses

strozzapreti *Italy* Flour- and egg-based dumplings or gnocchi flavoured with spinach, basil, nutmeg and grated cheese, poached and served with a tomato sauce (NOTE: Literally 'choke the priest', allegedly to fill up the priest when he called on his parishioners.)

struccoli *Italy* Sweet pastry rolls filled with fruit or cream cheese

strudel, Strudel *Austria, Italy* A generic name for a rectangle of strudel pastry spread with a sweet or savoury filling, layered or rolled up like a Swiss roll and, after further proving and egg-washing, baked at 190°C for approximately 1 hour

strudel pastry A wafer-thin pastry common in Austria and Hungary but originating in the Middle East and brought to Europe in the Ottoman invasions of the 15th century. Made from strong white bread flour, beaten egg, melted butter (4:1:1), vinegar and salt, all mixed to a silky dough, rested, rolled out and stretched until thin, then layered to build up thickness. Other formulations omit the vinegar and include milk, sugar and lemon zest and use yeast to raise the dough as in bread dough production. See also **filo pastry**

struffoli *Italy* A pasty filled with cooked sliced onion

strutto *Italy* Lard

Stück *Germany* **1.** Steak **2.** A piece

stucolo *Italy* A north Italian version of strudel, usually layered rather than rolled

stud, to To insert small items such as cloves, sprigs of herbs or slivers of garlic or the like regularly at intervals over the surface of a food item such as an onion or a joint of meat. Also called **piqué, to**

stuet *Norway* Creamed

stufatino *Italy* Stufato

stufato *Italy* Beef braised in red wine with onions, tomatoes, celery, garlic and ham. Also called **stufatino**

stuff, to To fill the central abdominal cavity of animals or fish or of hollowed out vegetables or fruit with a sweet or savoury stuffing or forcemeat

stuffau *Italy* A beef stew from Sardinia. See also **ghisau**

stuffed derma Kishka

stuffed olive A green preserved olive which has been destoned and the central cavity filled with a small piece of anchovy, a piece of sweet red pepper, a caper or the like

stuffing A sweet or savoury mixture or forcemeat used to fill the cavity of animals, fish or hollowed out vegetables or of fruits prior to cooking. See also **forcemeat**

stump *England* A northern vegetable purée made from a combination of carrots, swedes and potatoes mashed with milk, butter and seasoning

sturgeon A medium to large anadromous fish found in the rivers that flow into the Caspian Sea, Black Sea, the western Pacific and the eastern Atlantic oceans. It has a firm white to pink flesh which may be baked, fried, grilled or smoked. They have armour-plated bodies and an elongated snout with a dark grey-green back. The females, which are caught in the estuaries of the rivers to which they return to spawn, are the source of caviar which may amount to 22 kg from a single fish. There are about 24 species but the important ones in order of size are the sterlet and the sevruga, osciotre, common and beluga sturgeon.

stuvad *Sweden* Creamed

stuvad kalvbräss *Sweden* Kalvbräss-stuvning

stuvas potatis *Sweden* Diced potatoes, sweated in butter, boiled with minimum milk and salt until tender, seasoning adjusted and flavoured with chopped herbs

stuvet *Denmark* Creamed

stuvet oksekød *Denmark* Stewed beef

stuvning *Sweden* Stew

su 1. *Japan* Rice vinegar **2.** *Turkey* Water

sua *Vietnam* Milk

sua bhati *South Asia* Dill seed

suacia *Italy* Scald, the fish

su-age *Japan* Deep-frying of food without any coating

suan *China* Preliminary boiling of large cuts of meat prior to other forms of cooking

suan la tang *China* Hot and sour soup from Canton

suan mei jiang *China* Hoisin sauce

suan niu nai *China* Yoghurt

suave *Mexico* Mildly and subtly flavoured

sub *United States* Hoagie

sub gum geung *China* Chow chow preserve

submarine *United States* Hoagie

subo benachin *West Africa* A stew from Gambia made with beef, lamb or fish together with onions, chillies, tomatoes, rice and seasoning

subrics *France* Croquettes sautéed without being panéed or coated

subtilisin A protease obtained from various Bacillus strains of bacteria, used for flavour production from soya bean and milk protein (**casein**)

succari orange *Egypt* A variety of acidless orange with a highly adhering skin and a large number of seeds, very sweet but without the familiar orange flavour

succinic acid See **E363**

succo *Italy* Juice

succory Belgian chicory

succotash *United States* A Native North American dish taken over and adapted by the Pilgrim Fathers, consisting of cooked lima beans and sweetcorn kernels heated together with cream and seasoning. Often served at Thanksgiving.

succu tundu *Italy* Fregula

suck cream *England* A Cornish dessert made from cream and egg yolks (2 yolks per litre) which are mixed with lemon juice and zest and sugar to taste and heated over a double boiler until thick. The mixture is then poured into glasses and eaten cold with long pieces of toast off which it is sucked.

sucker *United States* Various freshwater fishes of the *Catostomidae* family, with a thick-lipped mouth adapted for sucking, most with sweet white flesh

suckling A young unweaned animal

suckling pig, sucking pig A small unweaned baby pig 3 to 6 weeks old which is usually roasted

suco *Portugal* Juice

suco de laranja *Portugal* Orange juice

sucre *Catalonia, France* Sugar

sucré(e) *France* Sweetened or sweet (as opposed to savoury)

sucre cristallisé *France* Granulated or caster sugar. See also **sucre en poudre**, **sucre semoule**

sucre d'orge *France* Barley sugar

sucre en morceaux *France* Lump or cube sugar

sucre en poudre *France* Castor sugar

sucre filé *France* Spun sugar

sucre glace *France* Icing sugar

sucre semoule *France* Granulated sugar

sucrose A disaccharide composed of a glucose and a fructose unit which is the normal commercial variety found in cane and beet sugar

sucuk *Turkey* Sausage flavoured with garlic and herbs

sudachi *Japan* A small citrus fruit, *Citrus sudachi*, similar to **kabosu** but only about one third of its weight. Used in the same way.

sudako *Japan* Octopus pickled in vinegar

Sudanese pepper A dried and ground hot chilli pepper from the Middle East

sudare *Japan* Makisu

sudulunu *Sri Lanka* Garlic

suduru *Sri Lanka* Cumin

suédoise *France* A dessert of sugared fruit and jelly

suédoise, sauce *France* Mayonnaise mixed with apple purée and grated horseradish

suen *China* Bamboo shoots

suen tau *China* Garlic

suer, faire *France* To sweat

suero *Spain* Whey

suet The hard fat surrounding kidneys which has very good cooking properties. Used for suet pastry and puddings and in sweet mincemeat fillings. Commercial suet is granulated and coated with up to 15% flour or starch to prevent sticking.

suet crust pastry See **suet pastry**

suet pastry Self-raising flour and shredded beef suet (2:1) with a little salt brought together with water, kneaded slightly and rested. Also called **suet crust pastry**

suet pudding *United Kingdom* A traditional pudding made from chopped or granulated suet, breadcrumbs, flour, sugar, eggs, milk and flavourings, steamed or boiled in a covered pudding basin and served with a sweet sauce

sufed kaddu *South Asia* Wax gourd

suffle *Italy* Soufflé

Suffolk ham *England* Ham cured in beer and sugar or molasses. It has a deep golden skin and a rich red-brown meat with a blue bloom.

Suffolk sausage *England* A meaty pork sausage flavoured with herbs

suffritu *Italy* Soffrito calabrese

sugar The sweet-tasting water-soluble monosaccharides and disaccharides crystallized from plant juices (sucrose, fructose) or obtained, usually as syrups, by breaking down starch (glucose, maltose). See also **jaggery**, **palm sugar**, **brown sugar**, **lump sugar**

sugar apple Sweet sop

sugar batter biscuit method A method of making biscuits, e.g. langues de chat, by creaming butter and sugar, mixing in eggs to form a stable emulsion, then blending in the dry ingredients

sugar beet A variety of beet, *Beta vulgaris*, whose roots when mature contain a high concentration of sucrose which is extracted using water and crystallized from the solution

sugar cane The thick bamboo-like canes of a tropical grass, *Saccharum officinarum*, about 2 m long by 4 to 5 cm diameter Sometimes sold in pieces as a sweet for children to chew, but usually chopped and crushed to a give a liquid from which sucrose is crystallized

sugar cooking The process of modifying sugar (pure granulated sucrose) by dissolving it in a little water then heating it without stirring to various temperatures to produce various non-crystalline consistencies until finally there is caramelization which changes its flavour and chemical composition. The stages are: small thread (103°C), large thread (107°C), soft ball (115°C), hard ball (121°C), hard crack (157°C), and caramel (182°C). With practice these stages can be judged by the behaviour of the sugar between the fingers or when dropped into cold water or on a cold plate. In the USA the stages recognized are thread

(110°C), soft ball (112°C), firm ball (118°C), soft crack (132°C), hard crack (149°C) and caramel (154 to 170°C). The differences may be due to differences in the sugar. In France and Europe generally, the density of the sugar water mixture in °Be is often used but is rather inconvenient. Many names for the various stages exist and the above are not exclusive. Also called **sugar boiling**

sugar crust pastry *United States* Sugar pastry

sugared almond A large Spanish almond coated with a layer of amorphous coloured and flavoured sugar. Also called **Jordan almond**

sugar loaf A brick- or cone-shaped mass of refined sugar made by pouring wet sugar crystals into moulds to dry. Sugar used to be sold in this form.

sugar loaf chicory A green leaved chicory, *Cichorium intybus*, which forms a conical head rather like cos lettuce. The leaves may be harvested separately or the whole head cut when mature. The inner leaves are naturally blanched and are less bitter than the outer leaves.

sugar lump See **cube sugar**

sugar maple tree A variety of maple, *Acer saccharum*, found in North America. The spring sap obtained by boring a hole in the trunk contains 1% to 4% saccharose and is used to prepare maple syrup and maple sugar.

sugar orange See **acidless orange**

sugar palm A large palm tree, *Arenga saccharifera* or *A. pinnata*, which grows to over 15 m. The sugary sap is obtained by beating the feathery immature male flower spike for 14 days, then as soon as the flowers open the spike is cut off at the base of the flowers and the sap collected. The beating and slicing off of a little more of the flower stem continues until the flow of sap stops.

sugar pastry Pastry made from soft flour, butter, eggs and sugar (8:5:2:2) with a little salt using the creaming or rubbing in method. Used for flans and fruit tartlets. Also called **sugar crust pastry**

sugar pea Mangetout

sugar-snap pea Mangetout

sugar sorghum Sweet sorghum

sugar substitutes See **artificial sweeteners**

sugar syrup A solution of sugar in water. See also **syrup**, **light syrup**

sugar thermometer A thermometer used to measure the temperature of boiling sugar syrups, usually calibrated from 50 to 200°C, sometimes marked with the stages of **sugar cooking**

sugna *Italy* Lard

sugo *Italy* Gravy, juice, sauce

sugo, al *Italy* Served with any sauce

sugo di carne *Italy* Meat gravy

suif *France* Mutton fat or suet

suiker *Netherlands* Sugar

suimono *Japan* A delicate clear soup served in a fine lacquered bowl with traditionally three additional ingredients, a few pieces of fish, shellfish or chicken, a few decorative vegetables, mushrooms or pieces of seaweed and a piquant or fragrant addition such as ginger juice, lemon peel or yuzu. Often accompanied by sashimi.

suino *Italy* Pig, pork

suisse *France* An unsalted soft fresh cheese made from cows' milk enriched with cream. The mixture is curdled with a small quantity of rennet and left to stand for 1 to 2 days. The soft curd is then collected and packed into 60 g pots for immediate consumption. Served with fruit, desserts, etc. See also **petit-suisse**, **demi-suisse**

suji *South Asia* Semolina

suka *Philippines* A low acidity (1 to 3% acetic acid) vinegar with a pleasant aroma made from coconut sap

sukade *Netherlands* Candied peel

sukat *Norway* Candied lemon peel

sukha bhoona *South Asia* Sautéing in Indian cooking. See also **bhoona**

sukiyaki *Japan* Very thin slices of beef fried at the table in oil, soya sauce, rice wine, sugar and water added followed by squares of bean curd and sliced vegetables, the whole cooked for a few minutes, then taken by guests, dipped in beaten raw egg followed by a dipping sauce and eaten with rice (NOTE: Literally 'broiled on a ploughshare'.)

sukiyakinabe *Japan* A shallow iron pan used for cooking sukiyaki

sukker *Denmark, Norway* Sugar

sukkererter *Norway* Petit pois, sugar peas

sukkerkavring *Norway* Sweet biscuit

suklaa *Finland* Chocolate

suklaakuorrute *Finland* Chocolate icing

sukuma wiki *East Africa* A Kenyan dish made by simmering left-over chunks of cooked meat with onions, tomatoes and sweet peppers and a large amount of green leaf vegetable (NOTE: Literally 'push the weak', i.e. for the time when there is nothing better to eat.)

Sulperknochen *Germany* Pickled pork boiled with sauerkraut

sulphites Salts of sulphurous acid which is formed when sulphur dioxide is dissolved in excess water, used as food preservative.

Common in the food industry are sodium sulphite E221 and calcium sulphite E226.

sulphur dioxide E220, a pungent and irritating gas which dissolves in water to form sulphurous acid or its salts the sulphites, hydrogen sulphites and metabisulphites, all of which liberate the gas in solution. It is one of the most common preservatives used in foods.

sulphuric acid See **E513**

sultanas Dried seedless white grapes kept light-coloured by treatment with sulphur dioxide

sultanina *Italy* Sultana

Sultanine *Germany* Sultana

Suluguni *Southwest Asia* A Georgian cheese rather like haloumi

sülün *Turkey* Pheasant

-sülze *Germany* In aspic

Sülzwurst *Germany* A type of brawn made with large pieces of cooked pork from the head and leg, sometimes with sliced mushrooms, in a wine-flavoured aspic jelly. Usually sliced and served with French dressing.

sumac *England, France* The dried red berries of a Middle Eastern bush, *Rhus coriaria*, containing several small brown seeds with a sour flavour. Commonly used in Middle Eastern cooking.

Sumach *Germany* Sumac

suman *Philippines* Glutinous rice or other starchy material possibly mixed with coconut cream and sweetened, wrapped in young banana leaves, boiled and served with grated coconut as a dessert

sumibiyaki *Japan* Charcoal grilling. Often done at the table, especially in **ryotei**.

summer flounder *United States* A large flatfish, *Paralichthys dentatus*, related to plaice but up to 1 m long with a dark grey to brown spotted skin, found all along the east coast of North America. It is mainly caught in summer when it moves to shallow waters. The flesh is firm, white and non-oily and may be cooked in any way. Also called **northern fluke**

summer melon Fuzzy melon

summer pudding *United Kingdom* A uncooked pudding of soft fruits and bread made from a sauce of sieved raspberries, icing sugar and liqueur, which after warming slightly is mixed with a variety of soft fruits. White crustless bread soaked in the juice from this mixture is used to line a mould, the fruits are packed into the lined mould which is covered with more sauce-soaked bread and the whole left under pressure and

chilled. When firm the pudding is demoulded onto a plate and garnished as appropriate.

summer purslane A half-hardy low-growing plant, *Portulaca oleracea*, with slightly succulent leaves used in salads or as a vegetable. There are two varieties, green leaved with the better flavour and the yellow or garden type which looks better in salads. The leaves may be cut regularly during the summer. Also called **pigweed**, **portulaca**, **common purslane**, **green purslane**

summer sausage *United States* The general term for keeping sausages made with cured pork and beef, similar to cervelat. Sometimes dried and smoked.

summer savory An annual herb, *Satureja hortensis*, with a taste like a mixture of rosemary and thyme with a hint of pepper. It has slightly larger and more rounded leaves than the winter variety and a sparser habit. Used in the same way as winter savory.

summer squash Various fruits of the genus *Cucurbita*, which are normally harvested when immature before the skin hardens, and the whole fruit used as a vegetable. The most common is the vegetable marrow, the juvenile version of which is the courgette. Examples of USA squashes are crookneck, straight neck, scallop or patty pan, cocozelle, beinz and vegetable spaghetti.

sumo domoda *West Africa* A meat or fish stew from Gambia containing fried onions, tomato purée, peanut butter, chillies and seasoning

Sumpfmyrte *Germany* Bog myrtle

su mui jeong *China* Plum sauce

sunberry 1. Wonderberry **2.** A hybrid blackberry of the genus *Rubus*

sunchoke *United States* Jerusalem artichoke

sundae An elaborate decorated dessert made with ice cream, whipped cream, fruit or chocolate sauces and chopped nuts

sunflower A tender annual, *Helianthus annuus*, which grows up to 3 m high with a large yellow daisy type of flower. The seeds are a major source of vegetable oil and are often eaten raw or roasted especially as a snack. The flower buds may be steamed and served like globe artichokes.

sunflower (seed) oil One of the commonest European vegetable oils extracted from sunflower seeds. Suitable for all culinary uses and used to make margarine. Can be heated to high temperatures without burning.

sunflower seeds The seeds of the **sunflower**, eaten raw or roasted as a snack or used in salads

sunfruit A citrus hybrid grown in Swaziland which is very similar to the New Zealand grapefruit

sung kha ya *Thailand* An egg custard made with sweetened coconut milk flavoured with jasmine essence or orange-flower water and baked in the shells of young coconuts

sunnyside up *United States* Describes a fried egg with the yolk uppermost on a plate, which has not been turned over in the frying pan to set the yolk

sunomono *Japan* A variety of salad-type dishes (poultry, seafood, vegetables, etc.) dressed with variously flavoured vinegar-based sauces and served either in tiny portions as an appetizer or as a separate dish or course in a meal

sunset yellow FCF A synthetic yellow food colouring. See also **E110**

sun tsui *China* Sweet pepper

suola *Finland* Salt

suomalainen lammamuhennos *Finland* A mutton stew with potatoes, onions, carrots and turnips (NOTE: Literally 'Finnish lamb stew'.)

suomolaisleipä *Finland* Yeasted bread (NOTE: Literally 'Finnish bread'.)

suong *Vietnam* Chop or rib of meat

sup *Russia* Soup

supa kangya *West Africa* A Gambian dish of fried fish and onions simmered in stock with tomato purée, garlic, spinach, okra and palm oil

supa khlebova *Eastern Europe* A Ukrainian black bread soup made from mixed vegetables e.g. carrot, leek, celery, onion, parsnip and broad beans, a little stale black bread and beef stock, simmered until tender, puréed, seasoned, thickened with egg yolk and finished with 10% buttermilk and 10% milk. Served with croûtons fried in bacon fat.

super chill storage Storage of food at –5°C

superfine olive oil The second cold pressing (higher pressure) of the olives with a 1.5% maximum oleic acid content

superfine sugar *United States* Icing sugar

superfino *Italy* The finest grade of rice with large long grains, of which arborio is the well-known example. It requires 18 minutes cooking time and is used for the best-quality risotto.

superglycinerated fat Fat with only one or two, as opposed to the normal three, fatty acid residues per molecule of glycerol. They are good emulsifiers.

superkanja *West Africa* A soup/stew from the Gambia made with meat, palm oil, onion, sweet red pepper, chilli pepper, smoked or dried fish, fresh fish, greens and okra, all cooked in water for about two hours. Meat, if used, is first fried in palm oil, as is the onion and sweet pepper. Also called **kanjadaa**

sup iz syra i kartofelya *Russia* A potato and cheese soup from Moldavia made from chopped onions and carrots sautéed in butter until golden, simmered with chopped potatoes, seasoning, paprika, cayenne pepper and parsley in chicken stock, puréed, consistency adjusted and hard ewes' milk cheese (Brynza, Ektori or equivalent, 50 to 100 g per litre) dissolved in over a low heat

sup iz yogurta *Russia* A cold soup made from Greek-style yoghurt and soda water (2:1), seasoned and flavoured with chopped tarragon and dill. Chopped walnuts, dried apricots or other ingredients may be added.

supparod *Thailand* Pineapple

suppe *Denmark, Norway* Soup

Suppe *Germany* Soup

Suppenbrühe *Germany* Stock

supper Either a light meal or snack taken after the main evening meal before retiring or an alternative name for the main evening meal

supper herrings *Wales* Filleted herrings spread with mustard and rolled up. The herring rolls are placed on a layered bed of sliced potatoes, sliced onions and sliced apples in that order, covered with more sliced potatoes, butter and seasoning and the dish half filled with cider then covered and baked at 180°C for 45 minutes, uncovered and browned for a further 30 minutes. Also called **swper sgadan**

suppli *Italy* Croquettes made from a mixture of boiled risotto rice mixed with butter, Parmesan, eggs and pepper wrapped around a filling of ham and cheese or tomato and chicken liver, panéed and deep-fried. Eaten as a snack.

suprême The best or most delicate cut. See also **suprême de volaille**

suprême, sauce *England, France* A velouté sauce made from chicken stock flavoured with mushroom trimmings, strained, reboiled, a liaison added to the sauce off the heat and finished with lemon juice

Suprême des Ducs *France* A soft surface-ripened cheese made from whole cows' milk and cast in small ovals. The smooth creamy paste becomes stronger tasting as it ages.

suprême de volaille *France* The breast and wing to the first joint from one side of a chicken, turkey or other bird

suprême of fish A piece of fish cut diagonally from a fillet of fish

supuya papai *East Africa* A soup from Tanzania made by sweating onions and unripe papaya in butter, then boiling with stock until tender

suquet *Catalonia* A fish and seafood stew with saffron, wine, tomatoes and potatoes

suquet de peix *Catalonia* The traditional fish dish of Catalonia made with a variety of very fresh fish, fried and served in a sauce of onions, garlic and parsley sweated in olive oil together with tomatoes, sweet peppers and potatoes

sur 1. *Norway* Milk several months old **2.** *Norway, Sweden* Sour

suram Elephant's foot

surati panir *South Asia* A white cheese produced in Gujarat from buffalo milk. It develops a sharp pungent flavour as it is matured in whey.

surface-ripened cheese Cheeses ripened by the growth of moulds (Camembert or Brie types) or bacteria (Pont l'Evêque or Munster types) on the surface of the cheese

surf clam *Southeast Asia, United States* A very abundant clam, *Spisula solidissima*, up to 15 cm across, found in deep water off the eastern coasts. It is triangular in shape with dark brown zigzag markings on a yellowish shell. The flesh is usually cooked in other made-up dishes. Also called **bar clam**, **eastern surf clam**

surf 'n' turf *United States* Seafood and meat served together

surgelato *Italy* Deep-frozen

surgelé(e) *France* Deep-frozen

sur grädde *Sweden* Sour cream

suribachi *Japan* A serrated porcelain mortar with a wooden pestle (**surikogi**). Traditionally used for puréeing miso and vegetables and for grinding seeds, The serrated ribs prevent the seeds moving around.

surikogi *Japan* A wooden pestle used with a ceramic mortar (**suribachi**)

surimi 1. *Japan* Minced fish **2.** Processed white fish flavoured and coloured, used for making imitation crab sticks and fish cakes (**kamaboko**)

surimi-ika *Japan* See **ika no surimi**

surimi soup *Japan* An unthickened fish soup based on fish stock simmered with surimi, sliced mushrooms and cucumber and finished with soya sauce and chopped celery leaves

Surinam amaranth See **amaranth 1**

Surinam cherry The fruit of a shrub, *Eugenia uniflora*, of the myrtle family which grows in tropical or subtropical areas. The fruit is like a large red, turning to black, cherry with eight clefts starting at the stem end. The red flesh is soft and juicy and may be eaten raw or cooked. Also called **jambos**

süri rüewe *France* Smoked blade bone and knuckle of beef stewed with turnips and onions in white wine (NOTE: From the Alsace region of France)

surkål *Norway, Sweden* Sauerkraut

suro *Italy* Horse mackerel

Surrey lamb pie *England* Trimmed lamb or mutton chops, dipped in seasoned flour and browned in butter, arranged in a pie dish with sliced onions and lamb kidneys, flavoured with rosemary, just covered with lamb stock which has been used to deglaze the frying pan and covered with a thick layer of sliced mushrooms brushed with butter. Baked in a 180°C oven. It can be topped with pastry if desired.

surstek *Sweden* Sirloin, marinated for 5 to 10 days in red wine, vinegar and oil with chopped sweated shallots, thyme, cloves, bay, crushed peppercorns and juniper berries, sugar and salt. It is then dried, larded, seasoned, browned and roasted at a low temperature until tender. (NOTE: Literally 'sour roast'.)

surströmming *Sweden* Fermented Baltic herring (**strömming**) from the north of Sweden

surtidos *Spain* An assortment

sushi *Japan* Small rolls of cooked rice flavoured with rice vinegar, sugar and salt, topped with a variety of sliced or shaved raw seafood, pieces of sweet omelette or shredded vegetables, wrapped in **nori** and sliced, or alternatively moulded to form a decorative bite-sized package. Served with **wasabi**, beni-shoga and a soya sauce dip. See also **sushi meshi, chirashi-zushi, fukusa-zushi, maki-sushi, nigiri-zushi, oshi-zushi** (NOTE: Sushi was invented to fulfil the same need as the sandwich, i.e. for keen gamblers who wished to eat whilst playing.)

sushi meshi *Japan* The rice used in sushi made by cooking short-grain rice in water with kombu, draining, removing the kombu and tossing with a mixture of rice vinegar, salt and sugar whilst still hot. Prepared as needed.

sushi-su *Japan* Seasoned rice wine vinegar for sushi

sushoga *Japan* Pink-coloured, wafer-thin slices of pickled ginger rhizome used as an accompaniment to Japanese dishes especially sushi

susina damaschina *Italy* Damson

susine *Italy* Plums

susino selvatico *Italy* Bullace, the fruit

susis *North Africa* Morrocan dried sausage

süss *Germany* Sweet

Süssespiesen *Germany* Sweet desserts

Sussex bacon pudding *England* Bacon, wholewheat flour, finely chopped onion and shredded suet (4:2:2:1) mixed with chopped herbs and seasoning with 4 tbsp of baking powder per kg of flour, all brought together with beaten eggs and a little milk if necessary to a soft dropping consistency and steamed in a covered pudding basin for 90 minutes

Sussex churdles *England* Shortcrust pasties with a liver, bacon, onion and mushroom filling which has been fried in lard

Sussex dumpling *England* A dumpling made only of flour, salt and water. Also called **hard dumpling**, **Sussex swimmer**

Sussex heavies *England* Scones

Sussex plum heavies *England* A cake made from self-raising flour, butter, currants and caster sugar (8:6:3:1). One third of the butter is rubbed into the flour and currants to make a dough, which is rolled into a rectangle and the remaining butter is used to make two three-fold turns (see **puff pastry**). This is formed into a cake shape, glazed with milk and baked at 200°C for 30 minutes.

Sussex pond pudding A suet pudding made by lining a pudding basin with suet pastry and filling with brown sugar, currants and butter with a pricked lemon in the centre, covering the top with pastry and foil, boiling for 3 hours and turning out on a plate, when a pond is formed around the pudding

Sussex shepherd's pie *England* Chump chops of lamb are seasoned and floured then laid on a bed of chopped onion and lentils in a casserole dish, packed with small peeled potatoes, sprinkled with flour and brown sugar and covered with stock. The dish (with lid) is then put in an oven at 160°C for 3 hours with the lid removed for the last 20 minutes to brown the potatoes.

Sussex swimmer *England* See **Sussex dumpling**, **swimmers**

Sussex tartlets *England* Single-crust tarts made with shortcrust pastry which is filled with grated apple mixed with lightly beaten eggs, lemon zest and juice, caster sugar and cinnamon. Baked at 190°C for 15 to 20 minutes.

Süssholz *Germany* Liquorice

Süssigkeiten *Germany* Sweet desserts

süss-sauer *Germany* Sweet-and-sour

susumber 1. Pea aubergine 2. Drumstick pod

süt *Turkey* Milk

su tang *China* A rectangle of gluten dough rolled up like a Swiss roll then cut across in slices and cooked in stir-fried and braised dishes

sutari *South Asia* Rice bean

sütlaç *Turkey* Rice pudding made on top of the stove and served with ice cream

suya *West Africa* Nigerian kebabs made with cubes of beef, chicken or veal. The meat is marinaded in and thoroughly coated with a spice mixture made with ground roasted peanuts, cayenne pepper, paprika, salt and other dried flavourings according to the vendor's taste. Cooked on a spit over an open fire or in a hot oven. The meat is often alternated on the skewer with pieces of onion, sweet pepper and/or tomato.

suyo *Japan* A variety of Japanese cucumber

Suzette See **crêpes Suzette**

suzuki *Japan* Sea bass

svamp *Sweden* Mushrooms. Also called **champinjoner**

svampfylld kalkon *Sweden* Turkey, seasoned and rubbed with lemon, stuffed with cold creamed mushrooms (**svampstuvning**) mixed with the chopped heart and liver plus butter, barded with bacon and roasted whilst basting with water. Served with jus rôti and redcurrant jelly.

svampstuvning *Sweden* Creamed mushrooms made from seasoned and chopped onions and mushrooms sweated in butter, to which flour is added, cooked and followed by cream, then all boiled for about 20 minutes

svariati *Italy* Assorted, varied

svarta vinbär *Sweden* Black currant

svartsoppa *Sweden* A very elaborate soup garnished with slices of apple and prunes boiled in water, goose liver sausage and giblets, served at the goose feast on the 11th of November. It is made from a strained veal and goose giblet stock, thickened with flour, cooked out and removed from the heat to which 20% of strained goose blood is added with vigorous stirring whilst the soup is brought back to boiling point. It is again removed from the heat and 3% red wine, 2% Madeira, 1% brandy and 1% sugar syrup (all percentages on original stock) added plus water from cooking the apples and prunes. The whole is seasoned and flavoured with cinnamon, ginger and cloves. The flavour improves with ageing up to 24 hours.

Sveciaost *Sweden* A hard cows' milk cheese made in very large blocks and varying in taste from mild to strong depending on maturity. It has a few medium-sized holes.

svedsker *Denmark* Prunes

Svenbo *Denmark* A semi-hard cooked-curd cows' milk cheese with a mild flavour and a few large holes. Contains 43% water, 25% fat and 24% protein.

Svensk panna *Sweden* Slices of veal and pork fillet and calf's kidney blanched, refreshed and boiled in stock with a bouquet garni and sliced onions until half-cooked. Sliced potatoes are added and all cooked until just done. (NOTE: Literally 'Swedish pot'.)

svestkové knedliky *Czech Republic* A plum dumpling formed round a prune, possibly with cottage cheese

svieza desra *Russia* A highly prized pork and beef sausage

svin *Denmark* Pig

svinekjøtt *Norway* Pork

svinekød *Denmark* Pork

svinekotelett *Norway* Pork chop

svine kotelette *Denmark* Pork chops

svine mørbrad *Denmark* Pork fillet

svinestek *Norway* Roast pork

svinina *Russia* Pork

svinoe filye *Russia* Pork loin

svisker *Norway* Prunes

sviskon *Sweden* Prunes

swäbischer Kalbsvogel *Germany* Paupiettes of veal filled with veal forcemeat and bacon, braised on a **mirepoix** with stock and white wine. Served with the reduced cooking liquor mixed with capers and chopped anchovies.

Swaledale *England* A semi-soft, creamy and moist cheese matured for 3 weeks to give it a mild distinctive flavour. It is made from whole Jersey cows' milk in Swaledale, Yorkshire.

swamp cabbage A relative of the sweet potato, *Ipomoea aquatica* and *I. reptans*, which grows in water, hence the botanical name. Grown for its delicate leaves and stems which are used as a vegetable and eaten raw in salads. Originated in Africa but now grown in Australia, USA and Southeast Asia. Also called **water spinach**, **Chinese water spinach**, **swamp spinach**, **water convolvulus**

swamp spinach Swamp cabbage

Swatow mustard cabbage See **daai gaai choy**

sweat, to To cook without colouring in fat over a low heat in a pan with a tightly fitting lid

swede The large swollen spinning-top shaped root of a brassica *Brassica napus* (Napobrassica Group), with purple skin and dense yellow flesh weighing up to 1.5 kg. Used as a vegetable in the same way as carrots and turnips and also as animal feed. Also called **Swedish turnip**

Swedish anchovies See **brisling**, **sprat**

Swedish blood sausage *Sweden* A black pudding made with pig's blood, rye meal and raisins

Swedish hash Pytt i panna

Swedish sauce Mayonnaise mixed with apple purée and grated horseradish served with cold meats, etc.

Swedish turnip Swede

sweet One of the four fundamental tastes, sweet, sour, bitter and dry. See also **sweets**

sweet almond Almond

sweet-and-sour A method of cooking or preserving food in a mixture of vinegar and sugar

sweet-and-sour pork A typical Chinese dish served in Europe of floured pork, deep-fried and served in sweet-and-sour sauce possibly mixed with stir-fried vegetables and fruit

sweet-and-sour sauce A corn flour thickened sauce based on vinegar and sugar with soya sauce, flavourings and rice wine or sherry, possibly with the addition of white stock, chopped pineapple and vegetables

sweet anise *United States* Florence fennel

sweet apple Sweet sop

sweet basil See **basil**

sweet bay See **bay**

sweet bean paste A thick brown sauce made from ground fermented soya beans mixed with sugar and brine. Popular in Taiwan as a condiment or seasoning.

sweetbreads The pancreas and thymus glands from beef cattle, calves and lambs. Usually prepared by washing, blanching, refreshing and trimming then braising with stock on a bed of roots until tender. Served with some of the cooking liquor.

sweet brier Rose

sweet cherry The dessert cherry, *Prunus avium*, used for eating raw or cooking and varying in colour from pale yellow to deep red

sweet chestnut See **chestnut**

sweet cicely A hardy herbaceous perennial, *Myrrhis odorata*, with feathery leaves and long (up to 20 mm) ridged black seeds. The leaves have a pleasant myrrh-like scent and flavour with a hint of aniseed. Both the unripe and ripe seeds have a stronger aniseed flavour. Unripe seeds may be used in salads, ripe seeds as a spice. The leaves may be added to soups, stews, or used to flavour omelettes, salad dressing and cabbage. Also called **myrrh**

sweet clover Melilot

sweet corn A variety of maize, *Zea mays saccharata*, with a higher proportion of sugars in the maturing kernels. Usually boiled or roasted and eaten directly from the cob after being buttered and salted. The kernels are often sold separately either canned or frozen. Unscrupulous suppliers will often sell maize cobs, *Zea mays*, which are less sweet and more chewy. Also called **corn on the cob**

sweet cream butter *United States* Unsalted butter containing at least 80% butterfat

sweet crust pastry Flan pastry

sweet cumin Fennel seed

sweet cure A quick curing fluid containing a high proportion of sugar

sweeten, to To add sugar or artificial sweetener to a dish

sweet flag Calamus

sweet gale Bog myrtle

sweet granadilla The fruit of a variety of passion flower, *Passiflora ligularis*, which has a typical orange-coloured passion fruit skin enclosing a loose packet of grey seeds in a gelatinous pulp, which taste rather like a sweet gooseberry. Also called **orange passion fruit**

sweetgrass buffalo and beer pie *Canada* A stew of buffalo meat with vegetables, sago, herbs, spices, beer and seasoning, cooked then put in a pie dish, covered with pastry and baked (NOTE: From Alberta)

sweet haggis *Scotland* A slow-cooked pudding from Kilmarnock made from a mixture of medium oatmeal, finely chopped suet, flour, soft brown sugar, currants and raisins (3:3:1:1:1:1), with salt, pepper and sufficient water. It is then steamed in a covered pudding basin for 3 to 4 hours. Served as a dessert in slices, but may be fried with bacon.

sweetheart melon A type of canteloupe melon with a bright scarlet flesh

sweetie *Middle East* A pummelo/grapefruit cross extensively grown in Israel. It has a greenish thick rind, a high sugar content and low acidity. As it matures, the rind becomes yellow orange and it is marketed as golden sweetie.

sweet laurel See **bay**

sweet lime A low acid rather insipid lime, *Citrus limettiodes*. It has a smooth yellow rind with a distinctive aroma and a tender flesh with a few seeds. Popular in India and the Middle East. Also called **Indian sweet lime**, **Palestine sweet lime**

sweet maragan *Scotland* Flour, oatmeal, finely chopped suet, sugar and raisins (4:4:2:1:1) mixed with a little chopped onion and seasoning and brought together with minimum water. Packed in a cloth lined pudding basin, covered and steamed for 2 to 3 hours. Served hot or sliced and fried.

sweet marjoram A herb, *Origanum majorana*, with aromatic grey-green leaves from the Mediterranean and western Asia now grown in France, Chile, Peru and California. Used

in Italian cooking and with lamb, chicken and oily fish. Since it has a delicate flavour which is destroyed by cooking it should be added at the last moment. See also **marjoram**. Also called **knotted marjoram**

sweet melon See **melon**

sweet milk *United States* Cows' milk

sweet nim Leaves of a bush similar in appearance to bay but smaller and thinner

sweet orange The common orange of commerce, *Citrus sinensis*, with an easily removed skin, and an excellent, sometimes slightly acid, flavour and few or no seeds. Classified in four groups, Navel, Common (e.g. Valencia), Pigmented (blood orange) and Acidless. It has been cultivated in southern China for several thousand years and was first grown in the Mediterranean around 1450. Modern varieties were introduced by the Portuguese. Also called **orange**

sweet pepper The fruit of an annual bush *Capsicum annuum* Grossum Group which is green when unripe and passes through yellow to red as it becomes riper. Some can be purple or brown. They are generally about 8 – 15 cm long, 6 – 10 cm in diameter, possible tapering with a fleshy outer covered with a tough shiny skin and with small seeds in the mainly hollow interior. Known by their colour (i.e. green, red peppers) or as paprika or bell peppers. Their flavour is due to the compound **capsaicin** which is an irritant in high concentrations. Also called **Spanish pepper**

sweet pickle See **chutney**

sweet pickled pork *England* A leg or hand of pork pickled in a mixture of equal volumes of beer and stout which have been boiled with 150 g of coarse salt, 150 g of bay salt and 25 g of saltpetre per litre. The boiling pickle is poured over the pork, which is then turned in the pickle every day for 2 weeks.

sweet potato A starchy tuber similar to an elongated potato which grows on a tender perennial, *Ipomoea batatus*, with trailing stems usually grown as an annual in tropical and subtropical climates (24 to 26°C). It has a white to purple skin and a dense white to orange flesh with a sweetish perfumed taste. Used as a staple food and cooked like potatoes. The leaves may also be eaten as spinach. Also called **kumara, Louisiana yam, yam, yellow yam**

sweet potato pastry *England* Cooked potatoes, flour and butter (16:4:1) mashed together with 2 tsp of muscovado sugar per kg of potatoes and kneaded until smooth

sweet red bean paste *Japan* Boiled adzuki beans mashed into a paste with oil and sugar and cooked until fairly thick and dry. Used in cakes and desserts. See also **koshi-an**, **tsubushi-an**

sweet rocket A hardy biennial cottage flower, *Hesperis matronalis*, with white to purple four-petalled flowers, now a wild garden escape. The young leaves are more bitter than **rocket** but may be used sparingly in salads.

sweets 1. Confections based mainly on flavoured sugar, caramel and chocolate with sometimes butter, cream and/or milk. Made in small individual bite-sized pieces as comfort food. **2.** A common name for desserts, puddings, etc. being a variety of fruit, cake, pastry, sugar, eggs and cream confections served at or near the end of a meal, before the cheese in the UK and after the cheese in France

sweet sake Mirin

sweet sop A type of **custard apple** from a tree, *Anona squamosa*, cultivated in the tropics. It is about 5 to 7.5 cm in diameter with a green scaly skin and a white flesh with the texture of thick custard containing embedded black inedible seeds. Eaten raw or in made-up dishes and drinks. Also called **sugar apple**, **sweet apple**, **scaly custard apple**

sweet sorghum A variety of sorghum, *Sorghum vulgare* var. *saccharatum*, which is grown for the sugary sap pressed from the stems especially in the USA. This is evaporated to make sorghum syrup which is like a thin and slightly acidic molasses. Also called **sugar sorghum**

sweet soya sauce A dark soya sauce sweetened with sugar and maltose which gives it a malty taste. Used extensively in the eastern coastal provinces of China.

sweet vinegar *China* A dark mild rice vinegar containing sugar and caramel and flavoured with cassia and star anise. Used in relatively large quantities in braised meat dishes.

sweet violet The most highly scented of the violets *Viola odorata*, is a hardy, spreading, perennial growing to 15 cm. The flowers are crystallized for use as a decoration and also used to flavour syrups and vinegar.

sweetwater grape Dessert grape

sweet woodruff A white flowered herb, *Galium odoratum*, with the scent of new mown hay found growing wild in woodland. Used to flavour some wines, apple juice, liqueurs and German white beer as well as the young German wine known as Maibowle.

swells Canned foods where the can bulges because of the gas produced by internal bacterial action. These are always discarded.

swimmers *England* A Norfolk dish of suet and self-raising flour dumplings flavoured with chopped chives and cooked on top of soups or stews (*colloquial*) Also called **Sussex swimmers**

swimming crab A small crab, *Macropipus puber*, to 10 cm across found in the Mediterranean and Atlantic. Eaten in France.

swirl, to To mix one liquid with another or a soluble solid in a liquid by a gentle circular, figure-of-eight or to-and-fro motion

Swiss bun A plain white yeast-raised dough shaped into a long soft roll (up to 15 cm), cooled and covered with glacé icing

Swiss chard A variety of beet, *Beta vulgaris* Cicla Group, grown for its dark crinkly glossy leaves with thick white or red stems which grow in a cluster from the base. The leaves and stems are generally cooked as separate vegetables usually by steaming. Common in the Mediterranean countries and similar to spinach. Also called **chard**, **silver beet**, **white beet**, **leaf beet**, **seakale beet**

Swiss cheese *United States* A hard cooked-curd cows' milk cheese made in large cylinders or blocks (up to 100 kg) to resemble Emmental. The starter culture contains *Lactobacillus bulgaricus*, *Streptococcus thermophilus* and *Propionibacter shermanii* and the milk is curdled with rennet. The pressed curd is brined, stored at high temperature and humidity for 3 to 6 weeks and ripened at low temperatures for 4 to 12 months.

Swiss fondue Fondue

Swiss meringue Meringue suisse

Swiss omelette Eierhaber

Swiss roll A Genoese sponge baked in a shallow rectangular tray about 1.5 cm final thickness on greased paper, turned out onto sugared paper, spread with jam and rolled up whilst still hot leaving the paper to hold its shape until cooled. If to be filled with cream, first rolled hot then unrolled to fill. May be eaten cold as a cake or hot with a suitable sweet sauce.

Swiss steak *United States* **1.** Rump steak, seasoned and stewed with onions, tomatoes, sweet peppers and possibly garlic and flavoured with herbs and spices **2.** Round steak tenderized by breaking down the fibres mechanically with a mallet faced with many points at the same time forcing flour and seasoning into the meat then treating as (1)

sword bean A perennial legume, *Canavalia gladiata*, similar to the jack bean but with curved pods and pink to brown seeds. Used both for the ripe beans, which should be boiled, and for the green pods. Also called **sabre bean**

swordfish A seawater fish, *Xiphias gladius*, which grows to 3 m long with a snout or sword one third its length. It can weigh up to 100 kg and travel at 100 km per hour. It has a dryish firm pink flesh usually sold in steaks and grilled or fried especially in Mediterranean countries. May be smoked and served as smoked salmon.

swper sgadan *Wales* Supper herrings

syau *Nepal* Apple

Sydney rock oyster *Australia* A comparatively cheap and popular variety of farmed oyster, *Saccostrea commercialis*

Sydney salad *Australia* Mixed green leaves (**mesclun**), smoked game meats and croutons of mountain bread, seasoned with salt and lemon myrtle powder and dressed with wild lime and oil vinaigrette

syllabub *England* An old English dessert originally either the froth from a whisked mixture of cream, wine, sugar and lemon zest, or a frothy mixture of milk with wine, cider or ale and sugar, spices and spirits. Nowadays made by mixing whisked egg whites with sweetened whipped cream flavoured with lemon juice and wine or spirits. Also called **sillabub**

sylt *Sweden* Jam

syltede rødbeder *Denmark* Pickled beetroot

syltetøj *Denmark* Jam

syltetøy *Norway* Jam

syltlök *Sweden* Button onion

Symphytum officinale *Botanical name* Comfrey

symposium The second part of a formal meal in ancient Greece given over to drinking and entertainment. See also **deipnon**

synthetic fats E471, E472(a to e), E473, E474, E475 and E477, various esters of fatty acids all derived from natural products for use in place of natural fats and oils in baked goods, desserts, etc. to improve their keeping qualities and to soften and stabilize them

syr *Russia* Cheese

Syrecky *Czech Republic* A strong cows' milk cheese similar to **Handkäse**. See also **Olomoucké syrecky**

syringe A piston and cylinder with provision for attaching piping nozzles, used in cake decorating where the paste or cream is too thick for a piping bag

syrniki *Russia* Curd cheese fritters

syrup A concentrated solution of sugar (sucrose or sucrose with a third its weight of glucose) in water used as an ingredient in many sweet dishes and drinks. Concentrations can be measured in °Beaumé, kg of sugar per litre of solution or kg of sugar per litre of water, the last named being the most convenient. In these last units, a light syrup has between 0.1 and 0.4 kg, a medium syrup between 0.4 and 0.8 kg and a heavy syrup between 0.8 and 3.0 kg of sugar per litre of water. Stock syrup has 0.4 kg of sugar per litre of water.

syrup pudding *United Kingdom* **1.** A **roly-poly pudding** sweetened with golden syrup. Also called **syrup roly-poly 2.** A pudding made from the basic steamed pudding mixture poured into a greased basin whose base has been covered with golden syrup

syrup roly-poly *United Kingdom* Syrup pudding

syrup sauce Stock syrup and lemon juice, thickened with corn flour or arrowroot, cooked out and strained

Syzygium malaccensis *Botanical name* Rose apple

Szechuan *China* A province of China. Also called **Sichuan** (NOTE: The two names are interchanged at random)

Szechuanese cooking The style of cooking from the Chinese province of Szechuan, which is in the west next to the Tibetan border. It is renowned for its peasant-based hot and spicy dishes with a strong emphasis on preserved foods.

Szechuan pepper Anise pepper

sze gwa *China* Angled loofah

székelygulyás *Hungary* A seasoned pork stew with onions fried in lard, sauerkraut and flavoured with caraway, garlic, paprika and chopped dill. Served with soured cream.

szynka sznurowana *Poland* A hard-smoked ham sausage available throughout the country

taai goo choy *China* Chinese flat cabbage

ta'amia *Egypt* Soaked and cooked chickpeas or broad beans minced, mixed with water, egg, seasoning, turmeric, ground cumin, cayenne pepper, chopped garlic and coriander leaves, breadcrumbs and tahini or olive oil to form a soft but firm paste, formed into 2 to 3 cm balls and shallow-fried until golden brown. Traditionally a Coptic Lenten dish but now served throughout the Middle East. See also **falafel**

taapke *Nepal* Frying pan

taart *Netherlands* Layer cake, fancy cake

Tabasco sauce A hot, red-coloured sauce made from particular red chillies grown in Louisiana, USA, ground with vinegar and matured for 3 years in oak barrels

tabbouleh *Middle East* Tabouleh

tabbuli *Middle East* Tabouleh

tabil *North Africa* A Tunisian mixture of coriander seeds, caraway seed, garlic and chilli flakes, dried in a slow oven and ground

table cream *United States* Coffee cream

table d'hôte *England, France* A fixed price menu with a fixed number of courses with possibly some choice of dishes in each course. Sometimes supplements for more expensive dishes are charged.

table queen squash A winter squash common in the USA which varies in colour from pale green to deep orange. It is round with a tough green skin. Also called **acorn squash**

table salt A fine-grained, free-flowing salt suitable for being dispensed at the table from a salt shaker. It is pure sodium chloride with the addition of anti-caking agents, a function which was performed before additives by a few grains of dry rice.

tablespoon 1. A standard volume measure, 15 ml in the UK and USA, 18 ml in Australia. Abbreviated to *tbsp*, sometimes *tbspn*. **2.** A large spoon used for serving food at the table, now standardized as a unit of volume

table water See **carbonated water**

tablier de sapeur *France* Panéed pieces of tripe, fried or grilled and served with snail butter (NOTE: Literally 'sapper's apron'.)

tabouleh *Middle East* A salad made with fine bulgur which has been well washed and drained, mixed with peeled and chopped tomatoes, cucumber, sweet green pepper and onion, chopped mint and parsley, seasoned then dressed with olive oil and lemon juice. Eaten with lettuce or pitta bread. Also called **tabbouleh**, **tabbuli**

tacchina *Italy* Turkey hen

taccula *Italy* Blackbirds trussed and defeathered but not drawn, wrapped in myrtle leaves and braised

taco *Mexico* A small tortilla either fried crisp and eaten immediately or cooked like a pancake, rolled around a stuffing and eaten hot. Served as a snack or a light meal.

tadka *South Asia* A spice-flavoured butter used in cooking

taeng ka *Thailand* Cucumber

Tafelsenf *Germany* Common table mustard

Tafelspitz *Austria* Top rump or other good cut of beef simmered with blanched beef bones, aromatic vegetables, bouquet garni, leeks, onion clouté, garlic, tomato and dried ceps. Served with Apfelkren and Schnittlauchsosse.

Taffel *Austria* A semi-hard cooked-curd cows' milk cheese with a close-textured paste containing a few holes. Contains 45% water, 24% fat and 23% protein.

Tageskarte *Germany* Dish of the day

Tagessuppe *Germany* Soup of the day

tagine *North Africa* **1.** A slowly simmered stew of meat or fish with appropriate vegetables, pulses and fruits, cooked in its own juices in an earthenware pot with a conical lid. Almost anything can go in a tajine. **2.** The pot in which tagine is cooked. Also called **tajine**

tagliarine *Italy* Tagliatelle

tagliatelle *Italy* 5 mm-wide noodles made from an egg-based pasta dough, available fresh or dried. Also called **tagliarine**

tagliatelle alla biellese *Italy* Tagliatelle with milk or cream, butter and grated Parmesan cheese

tagliatelle della duchessa *Italy* Tagliatelle with chicken livers, egg yolk and grated Parmesan cheese

tagliatelle verde *Italy* Green tagliatelle made from egg-based pasta dough coloured with spinach purée

tagliato *Italy* Cut or sliced

tagliolini *Italy* A thin linguine

tahari *South Asia* A dish of rice and peas flavoured with spices and herbs

taheena Tahini

tahina Tahini

tahini A thick paste made from ground, husked or unhusked white sesame seeds mixed with sesame seed oil and of the same texture as peanut butter. The unhusked seeds give a darker and more bitter paste. Used in savoury dishes and as a constituent of hummus. In Asia usually made from toasted seeds. Also called **taheena**, **tahina**, **sesame butter**, **sesame seed paste**

tahini salad dressing Tahini paste, lemon juice and water (2:2:5) mixed until smooth

tahinyeh *Middle East* Tahini paste mixed with lemon juice, milk, finely chopped parsley, crushed garlic, salt, chilli powder and white breadcrumbs to form a thick creamy paste and sprinkled with parsley and cumin. May be used as a dip or in place of mayonnaise.

Tahiti lime Persian lime

taho *Philippines* Bean curd brains or silk bean curd

tahong *Philippines* Asian mussel

tahu 1. *China* Tofu or bean curd **2.** *Indonesia, Malaysia* Bean curd or bean curd cheese

tahure *Philippines* Bean curd

tai *Japan* The prized fish, sea bream e.g. *Pagrus major* used for weddings and other celebrations. Sometimes red snapper is substituted.

taikina *Finland* Dough, batter, pastry

tail The tails of animals or fish. Of the animal tails only oxtail is commonly used. Pigs' tails are occasionally used in some cuisines.

tail cut The tail end of a fillet from a large round fish

tailed pepper Cubeb

tailler *France* To cut

taingang daga *Philippines* Cloud ear fungus

tai tai *China* Seville orange

tajadas *Spain* Slices, of e.g. roast meat

tajine *North Africa* **1.** A slowly simmered stew of meat or fish with appropriate vegetables, pulses and fruits, cooked in its own juices in an earthenware pot with a conical lid. Almost anything can go in a tajine. **2.** The pot in which tajine is cooked. Also called **tagine**

tajine barrogog *North Africa* A lamb tajine with prunes, flavoured with ginger, onion, parsley, cinnamon, orange blossom water and honey. It may be garnished with blanched almonds and sesame seeds.

tajine bel hout *North Africa* A fish tajine containing tomatoes, sweet red pepper, chillies, ginger and saffron

tajine de lapin *North Africa* A tajine of rabbit with vegetables

tajine de poisson *North Africa* A tajine of fish, usually bream or sardines, with tomatoes and herbs

tajine de poulet *North Africa* A tajine of chicken cooked with lemon and olives

tajine de viande *North Africa* A mutton tajine with vegetables or prunes

tajine slaoui *North Africa* A tajine of meatballs with vegetables

take-away 1. A food shop or restaurant which supplies hot food, generally cooked to order, in containers or wrappings for taking away and consuming elsewhere, e.g. fish and chips, Indian and Chinese dishes **2.** The general name for the hot package of food supplied by a take-away

takegushi *Japan* Bamboo skewers used for grilling chicken and tofu

takenoko *Japan* Bamboo shoots

takiawase *Japan* A mixture of firm vegetable pieces, e.g. potatoes, carrots, courgettes, aubergines, each cooked separately in separate pans until al dente, mixed with fried cubes of tofu and flavoured with a light soya sauce

taklia *Egypt* A spice mix of ground coriander fried with either crushed garlic or cumin

tako *Japan* Octopus

tako-kushisashi *Japan* Octopus kebabs

ta krai *Thailand* Lemon grass

takuan *Japan* A pickle made of **mooli**, air-dried for 2 to 3 weeks, salted and immersed in rice bran (the **nuka-zuke** method)

talaba *Philippines* Oyster

talas *Indonesia* Taro

talattouri *Greece* A dip based on finely chopped or grated, deseeded cucumber. See also **tsatsiki**

talawa *South Asia* Deep-frying in exactly the same way as in the West

talawa kabab *South Asia* A kebab of alternate layers of lightly boiled tender pork or lamb dusted with paprika, and mushrooms and onions cut to exactly the same size. The kebab is then coated with **kastha besan** thickened with a little extra **besan** and clotted cream, dusted with flour and coated in beaten egg before deep-frying until golden brown.

talc See **E553(b)**

Taleggio *Italy* A semi-soft, mild cows' milk cheese from Lombardy resembling Camembert. It is produced in 2 kg squares and has a white paste with a few small holes and a pinkish-grey surface mould on the rind. It develops flavour as it matures. Also called **Talfino**

Talfino *Italy* Taleggio

tal ha'emek *Middle East* An Emmental-type cheese from Israel

taliány *Czech Republic* A sausage similar to vurty but with diced fat bacon in the mix

talim num *Philippines* Spinach

tallarines *Spain* Noodles

Talleyrand, à la *France* In the Prince Talleyrand style, i.e. garnished with macaroni, cheese, truffle, foie gras and possibly button mushrooms

tallow A hard coarse fat originally rendered from mutton and used for lighting

talmouse *France* Cheesecake

talong *Philippines* Aubergine

tamaater *Nepal* Tomato

tamago *Japan* Eggs

tamago-hanjuku *Japan* See **hanjuku tamago**

tamago-medamayaki *Japan* Fried eggs

tamago-pochi *Japan* Poached eggs

tamago-yakiki *Japan* A rectangular omelette pan the same shape as a Swiss roll tin used for making rectangular egg or batter sheets which are rolled up or used as a wrapping. Also called **maki-yakinabe**

tamago-yude *Japan* See **yude-tamago**

tamakibi *Japan* Winkle, the shellfish

tamale flour *Mexico* See **masa harina**

tamale pie *United States* Cornmeal porridge with a filling of chopped meats and hot chilli sauce

tamales *Mexico* A thick porridge made from **masa harina**, one serving placed on a banana leaf, maize leaves or foil and topped with a cooked meat and chilli mixture or with cheese, rolled up, steamed and served hot with chilli sauce

tâmara *Portugal* Date

tamari, tamari-joyu *Japan* A thick strong soya sauce

tamarillo A large yellow to red, hard, egg-shaped fruit of an evergreen shrub, *Cyphomandra betacea*, related to the tomato

and kiwi fruit and resembling a giant rosehip, grown in tropical and subtropical climates. The flesh is somewhat acid but high in vitamin C and the seeds are edible. It is blanched and peeled before eating and may be used in fruit salads, for jam-making and has been used for flavouring yoghurt and cheesecake. Also called **tomarillo**, **tree tomato**

tamarin *France* Tamarind

tamarind The long (10 cm) dark-brown pods of a tropical tree, *Tamarindus indica*, usually sold as blocks of mashed pods and pulp or as a concentrated juice. The former is soaked in hot water and the juice squeezed out and used for souring in the same way as lemon juice. Also called **Indian date**

Tamarinde *Germany* Tamarind

Tamarindicus indica *Botanical name* Tamarind

tamarindo *Italy* Tamarind

tamatar *South Asia* Tomato

tambak merah *Malaysia* Snapper or bream

tamba kuri *Japan* Large mealy chestnuts

tambor *South Africa* Ortanique

tambusa *South Asia* Red snapper

Tamié *France* A smooth round cows' milk cheese from Annecy. Also called **Trappiste de Tamié**

tamis *France* Sieve or sifter

tamiser *France* To rub through a tammy cloth, to sieve

tammy cloth A fine-woven woollen cloth used for straining very fine particles from stocks, sauces, juices, etc. Best used after an initial straining through muslin

tampala *South Asia* Chinese spinach

tanaceto *Italy, Spain* Tansy

Tanacetum balsamica *Botanical name* Costmary

Tanacetum vulgare *Botanical name* Tansy

tanaisie *France* Tansy

tanche *France* Tench

tandoor *South Asia* An unglazed barrel-shaped, deep clay pot with a top opening, used as an oven in India. It is heated by charcoal in the base or gas. The food, e.g. nan bread, is either stuck on the inside or put on long skewers which are either rested over the opening or stood with their points at the base propped up against the rim.

tandoori *South Asia* A method of cooking on a greased spit in a clay oven. The oven is often a deep pot and the spits stand vertical from the bottom resting on the rim. It gives a crisp dry finish. See also **tandoor**

tandoori colouring A special food colouring powder formulated to give the orange red colour required in tandoori cooked food. Added to marinades.

tandoori spice mix A selection from cinnamon bark, nutmeg, dried ginger, dried red chillies, paprika, cardamom, dried garlic, cumin and coriander seeds, ground to a fine powder, the colour adjusted to a bright orange with food colourings and used for marinating and coating meat prior to tandoori cooking

tang *China* Soup

tang chi Preserved radish, whole or in slices, usually vacuum packed in the West. Used to add texture and flavour to Southeast Asian dishes.

tang cu li ji *China* Sweet-and-sour boneless pork

tangelo A naturally occurring hybrid of *Citrus* species *mandarin* and *grapefruit*, which occurs as two varieties, Minneola and Orlando

tangerina *Portugal* Tangerine

tangerine See **mandarin**

tangerine peel The dried peel of mandarins (tangerines) which is ground and used as a flavouring in Chinese and Vietnamese food

tangia *North Africa* A casserole of lamb or beef cooked with spices

tang kuei *China* The dried root of a relative of angelica, *Angelica sinensis*. See also **dang gui**

tangle Sea girdle

tangleberry A dark-blue berry with a sweet sharp flavour which grows in the USA. Similar to the blueberry or huckleberry.

tang mien *China* Noodles in soup

tangor *Middle East* Ortanique

tang ya suan tou *China* Pickled shallots

tanmen *Japan* Ramen noodles with fried vegetables

tannia A plant, *Xanthosoma sagittifolium*, which yields heavy (3–5 kg) yam-like tubers and arrow-shaped leaves which are used as a leaf vegetable. Cultivated throughout the tropics. Also called **new cocoyam**, **pomtannia**, **yautia**

tannia fritters *Central America* Boiled and mashed tannia mixed with brunoise onion, finely chopped deseeded chilli pepper, mashed garlic and butter, then deep-fried in oil until crisp. A speciality of the island of Margarita in Venezuela.

tannic acid One of the acids in tannin, used for flavouring and as a clarifying agent in beer, wine and cider and other natural brewed drinks

tannin A mixture of strong astringent acids found in plants, particularly tea leaves, red grape skins and the bark of trees, with the ability to coagulate proteins. Responsible for the keeping qualities of fine red wines.

tannour *Middle East* An oven rather like a large tandoori oven. Glowing charcoal is put in the base with a deep dish on top and the food to be cooked over this.

tanrogan *England* The local name in the Isle of Man for great and queen scallops which are found around its coasts

tansy 1. A hardy perennial and very invasive herb, *Tanacetum vulgare*, with green leaves and yellow flowers and a very strong flavour. Used by the Victorians for flavouring baked goods, sausages, stuffings and some desserts. **2.** A soufflé omelette mixture with fried tart fruit originally flavoured with tansy, nowadays with cloves and cinnamon

Tantallon cakes *Scotland* A type of shortbread made with flour, butter and caster sugar (8:4:1) and lemon zest with roughly 1/20th of the flour replaced with rice flour. All the ingredients are kneaded together to a stiff paste and formed by hand into rounds 4 cm in diameter and 1 cm deep. These are baked on a greased oven tray at 170°C for 25 to 30 minutes and sprinkled with caster sugar while still hot.

tanuki soba *Japan* Brown buckwheat noodles with tempura batter flakes

tanuta *Italy* Black sea bream

tanyet *Burma* Palm sugar

tanzaku-giri *Japan* Thin slender rectangles cut from root vegetables. Also called **poem card cut**

tanzhiyya *North Africa* **1.** A slow-cooked meal of meat, vegetables and spices in water made in a narrow-necked round-bellied earthenware pot of the same name with two handles which is sealed. This is usually taken to the local bakers for cooking on the ashes over an 8-hour period and is called the 'bachelor's dish' as it does not require a stove. A speciality of Marrakesh. **2.** A type of **tagine** from Marrakesh made with a joint of meat (e.g. shoulder of lamb) slowly cooked with vegetables and spices at the cook's discretion

taoco *Indonesia* Yellow bean sauce

tao do *Vietnam* Dried Chinese plums

tao hu *Thailand* Bean curd

tao hu kon *Thailand* Bean curd

tao tanu *Thailand* Turtle

tao zi *China* Peach

tapa *Philippines* Thinly sliced dried and/or cured meat used as a snack (NOTE: From the Spanish *tapas*.)

tapas *Spain* Originally a slice of ham or chorizo sausage placed over the mouth of a wine glass, from tapa to cover, some say to keep out flies, others to increase thirst. Now consists of small portions of any kind of made-up dish or individual snack served in bars with wine.

tapenade A Provençale purée of capers, black olives and anchovies in olive oil. Sometimes other ingredients are added. Used as a dip or spread or to fill hard-boiled eggs or hollowed out cucumber.

tapéno *France* Caper

tapes *Catalonia* Tapas

ta pin *Malaysia* Steamboat

tapioca *England, France, Italy, Spain* An alternative name for **cassava** but also used for the processed starch produced from cassava by cooking, drying and then flaking the starch. It is a useful thickener as it holds its consistency better than corn flour and arrowroot. Sometimes added to other flours to strengthen the dough.

tapioca starch See **tapioca**

Tapioka *Germany* Tapioca

tapulon alla burgomanerese *Italy* Stewed donkey with red wine and cabbage

taquitos *Mexico* Small tacos filled with **picadillo** (2), folded, secured with a skewer and deep-fried,

tara *Japan* Cod

tarako *Japan* Codfish roe, salted and dyed red to resemble caviar

tarama *Greece* The orange-coloured salted and dried roe of the grey mullet, an expensive delicacy used for hors d'oeuvres or in the preparation of authentic taramasalata

taramasalata Taramossalata

taramossalata *Greece* A pounded mixture of tarama, or more usually, smoked cod's roe, soft white breadcrumbs or mashed potatoes, crushed garlic, olive oil and lemon juice, used as a dip or served with bread as part of a **mezze**. More commercial versions, known as taramasalata in the West, are smoother and contain excessive amounts of extenders and fish flavouring, besides being a rather strange pink colour.

tarator *Bulgaria, Hungary* A chilled, dill-flavoured yoghurt and cucumber sauce thickened with ground walnuts; alternatively a chilled soup made with grated cucumber, yoghurt, milk, lemon juice, garlic and parsley

tarator od krastavaca *Balkans* A salad of grated cucumber, green chillies, yoghurt and garlic from the Former Yugoslav Republic of Macedonia

Taraxacum officinale *Botanical name* Dandelion

tarbot *Netherlands* Turbot, the fish

tarbujaa *Nepal* Watermelon

tardno *Italy* Parmesan cheese made between September and November. See also **Parmigiano Reggiano**

targone *Italy* Tarragon

tarhonya *Hungary* Small dried barley-shaped pellets of egg noodle dough. They are fried in lard then cooked in bouillon like a risotto and served with goulash, etc.

tari *South Asia* Gravy

taring scale A weighing scale which can be set to zero with any weight on it. It is conveniently used to weigh ingredients into a bowl by zeroing between the addition of each ingredient.

tarka *South Asia* A style of finishing in Indian cookery involving the fierce searing of precooked food in ghee and seasonings to flavour and coat the surface of the food. Also called **chamak**

tarkaari *Nepal* Vegetable

tarkari *South Asia* Containing vegetables which have been fried in ghee then gently cooked in their own juices

taro A tropical and subtropical plant, *Colocasia esculenta*, brought from Southeast Asia to the Caribbean as a staple food for slaves. The tubers are boiled, baked or roasted. Also called **cocoyam**. See also **eddoe, dasheen**

taronja *Catalonia* Orange

taro starch A greyish flour made by grinding taro chips. Used as a thickener and for making desserts.

tarragon A half hardy perennial herb, *Artemesia dracunculus* (France) and *A. dracunculoides* (Russia), growing to 1 m, whose narrow leaves have a warm, peppery bitter-sweet scent with a note of anise. The Russian variety is milder than the French. It has a wide variety of uses, as a flavouring for vinegar, emulsion sauces and dips, soups, omelettes, chicken, compound butters, etc. One of the constituents of fines herbes. Unlike the Russian, French tarragon does not set seeds and is propagated from cuttings. See also **Russian tarragon**. Also called **French tarragon**

tarragon butter A compound butter made from blanched and drained tarragon leaves squeezed dry, pounded with twice their weight of butter and sieved

tarragon vinegar A white wine vinegar flavoured with tarragon leaves

tart A shallow dish-shaped open pastry case usually shortcrust or flan pastry with a filling which may either be baked with the case e.g. Bakewell tart, or added later to a case which has been baked blind e.g. custard tart and most French fruit tarts. See also **flan**, **pâtisserie 2**

tarta, tarta catalana *Catalonia, Spain* A small, single-crust, open top tart. Usually called **pastís**.

tårta *Sweden* Layer cake

tartafin *France* A potato dish made from slices of waxy potatoes laid over sweated garlic with seasoning, covered with sliced Gruyère cheese and cooked in a closed container over a low heat until done

tartaleta *Spain* Small tart

tartara, alla *Italy* With tartare sauce

tartare 1. *France* A fresh cream cheese made from cows' milk and flavoured with chopped herbs **2.** *England* Steak tartare

tartare, sauce *England, France* **1.** Chopped capers, gherkins and parsley, dried and mixed well with mayonnaise. Served with fried fish. **2.** Mashed hard-boiled egg yolks, seasoned and mixed with vinegar, oil whisked in as in making mayonnaise and finished with a sieved purée of raw spring onions mixed with a little mayonnaise

tartaric acid E334, an acid present in many fruits which is precipitated as crystals in old wine

tartar med æg *Denmark* Steak tartare used as a topping for smørrebrød

tartar sauce *United States* Tartare sauce

tartaruga *Italy* Turtle

tartaruga aquatica *Italy* Terrapin

tarte *France* A single-crust, open top tart

tarte à la crème *France* Custard tart on thin pastry

tarte à l'oignon *France* An open tart filled with onions in a rich cream sauce

tarte au citron *France* A pâte sablée pastry case filled with a whisked egg and sugar mixture to which has been added melted butter, lemon juice and grated lemon zest

tarte au riz *Belgium* An open pastry case filled with a creamy dessert rice mixed with raisins or sultanas, chopped almonds and flavoured with nutmeg

tarteletta *Italy* Tartlet

tartelette *France* Tartlet, small tart

tarte limousine clafoutis *France* A **clafoutis** baked in a blind pastry case

tarte lorraine *France* A tart similar to a quiche filled with well-spiced pork or veal and onions

tarte normande *France* An apple flan

tarte Tatin *France* An upside down apple pie made from sliced dessert apples fried in a baking dish with butter and flavourings, possibly with sugar so as to caramelize, covered with pastry, baked in the oven and

turned out on a serving dish with the apple slices uppermost, hopefully with an attractive appearance

tartina *Italy* Canapé, tartine

tartine *France* A slice of bread and butter, sometimes a small tart or slice of fruit loaf

tartine suisse *France* Puff pastry filled with vanilla-flavoured crème pâtissière

tartrates Salts of tartaric acid used as stabilizers, the principal ones being sodium- E335, potassium- E336 and the potassium sodium mixed salt E337

tartrazine E102, a synthetic dye used as a yellow food colouring, suspected of causing hyperactivity and allergies in some children

tartufato *Italy* With truffles

tartufi di cioccolato *Italy* Chocolate truffles

tartufi tre scalini *Italy* A ball-shaped dessert of chocolate ice cream, cake and whipped cream

tartufo *Italy* Truffle

tartufo di mare *Italy* Warty venus clam

tarwebrood *Netherlands* Wholewheat bread

tasala The traditional cooking pot of Nepal and Kashmir with a round base and a flared neck and rim

Taschenkrebs *Germany* Common crab

Tascherin *Austria* A type of ravioli with either a jam or savoury filling

tashreeb *Middle East* An Iraqi dish of lambs' tripe and feet or shanks which are blanched then simmered with well-soaked chick peas, noomi and a whole unpeeled head of garlic. Sweated chopped onions, chopped tomatoes and **baharat** are then added and all simmered for 2 hours. It is served over flat bread with the meat and tripe on top.

Tasmanian crayfish *Australia* A large crayfish, *Astacopsis gouldi*, which can grow up to 6 kg in weight

tasse *France* Cup

tasse, en *France* Served in a cup, especially of soups

taste powder See **monosodium glutamate**

ta suan li *China* Asian pear

tataki *Japan* **1.** A method of preparing fish by chopping it finely with a knife, together with shiso, negi and ginger. It is served with a soya and grated ginger dipping sauce. **2.** A method used for serving fish or beef steaks. They are lightly grilled so that they are brown on the outside and raw inside. They are then sliced thinly and presented in a fanned layer with the dipping sauce of 1 above.

tate-jio *Japan* A method of treating food with a low concentration brine (30 g per litre) containing some **kombu** flavouring

tatties *Scotland* Potatoes (*colloquial*)

tatws llaeth *Wales* New potatoes cooked in their skins, peeled then served in a bowl with buttermilk

Taube *Germany* Pigeon

taucheo *Malaysia* Yellow bean sauce

tauge *Indonesia* Bean sprouts

tauhu tod *Thailand* Fried bean curd

tau kau *China* Nutmeg

tau ngok *Thailand* Mung bean or bean sprouts

taupe *France* Porbeagle shark

tau sa *Malaysia* Yellow bean sauce

tausi *Philippines* Bean curd cheese

tavola calda *Italy* Snack bar

tavola fredda *Italy* Cold buffet, cold table

tavsan *Turkey* Hare

tawa *South Asia* A circular, slightly dished steel or iron griddle with a handle, used for making Indian breads or, when placed below another dish, to reduce the heat especially on a difficult to control heat source

tawas *Philippines* Alum

tayberry A cross between a blackberry and raspberry species of *Rubus*. It is large and conical, a bright deep purple in colour and with a rich flavour.

tay vi *Vietnam* Star anise

tazhin *North Africa* The Moroccan name for **tagine**

tazza *Italy* Cup or small bowl

tazzina Small cup, coffee cup

tazzine, nella *Italy* Coddled, of eggs

T-bone steak *United States* A steak cut from between the sirloin and short loin of beef (the centre of the sirloin (UK)) including a piece of vertebra in the shape of a capital T and about 5 cm thick. It will feed 2 persons.

tea cake A flat, slightly sweetened yeast-raised round bread bun with currants and mixed peel about 10 cm in diameter. Usually split, toasted and buttered.

tea cream *England* Milk infused with an aromatic tea, thickened with egg yolks, cream and gelatine, whipped egg whites folded in, set in a mould, turned out and decorated

teal A small wild duck, *Anas crecca*, weighing about 400 g and served 1 per person. Roasted at 180 to 190°C for 25 to 30 minutes and served garnished with watercress and lemon wedges. Shooting season 1st September to 31st of January, hanging time 2 to 3 days.

tea leaf egg Egg boiled for 2 to 3 hours in water with tea leaves, star anise and other flavourings. After 20 minutes the shells are cracked to allow penetration of the flavours

and to produce marbling. Served as hors d'oeuvres.

tea loaf *Scotland* A very common chemically raised slicing cake made from flour, sugar, sultanas, butter and eggs (3:2:2:1:1) flavoured with ground cloves and cinnamon and ground caraway seeds. The butter is rubbed in to the flour and the other ingredients mixed in. Raised with bicarbonate of soda at the rate of 1 tbsp per kg of flour and baked at 220°C for 10 minutes then at 190°C for an hour or until cooked.

tea smoking A method of smoking meat or fish using a domestic steamer. The base is lined with foil and equal volumes of brown sugar, uncooked rice and an aromatic tea (e.g. lapsang souchong) are put on the foil; the food is placed on the steaming rack with a tight fitting lid. It is then placed over a high heat for 2 minutes to generate smoke, on a low heat for 10 minutes and then let stand.

teaspoon 1. A standard volume measure, 5 ml in the USA and UK, 6 ml in Australia. Abbreviated to *tsp*, sometimes *tspn*. **2.** A small spoon used for stirring drinks, now standardized as a volume measure

teaterskinka *Sweden* A supper dish of slices of ham marinated in sherry, removed, dried, covered with a mixture of double cream and tomato purée and warmed in the oven (NOTE: Literally 'theatre ham'.)

teba *Japan* Chicken wing

tebrød *Norway* Teacake

technical white oil See **mineral hydrocarbons**

Teegebäck *Germany* Tea cake

tee ma yau *China* Sesame seed oil

teeri *Finland* Black grouse

teething cake See **moh lung ye baw**

Teewurst *Germany* A smooth, pink, spreading sausage made from the finest of pork, beef and spices

teff *Africa* One of the indigenous cereals of Ethiopia, *Eragrostis teff*. The pinhead-sized grain is part of the Ethiopian staple diet and used to make the bread indura. Also called **teff grass**

teff grass See **teff**

tefteli *Russia* Meatballs

teg 2 year old sheep

tegame *Italy* A heavy frying pan or casserole

tegame, al *Italy* Fried or pot-roasted

tegamino, al *Italy* Coddled, of eggs

teglia *Italy* A wide and shallow baking dish or pie dish

Teifi *Wales* A Gouda-like cheese

teifi salmon *Wales* Skinned salmon fillets, cut in slices, or a piece of salmon covered with a sauce made from molten butter blended with one sixth its volume of port, an anchovy fillet or anchovy essence and a little mushroom ketchup. All placed in a covered dish and baked at 190°C for 45 minutes.

Teiggerichte *Germany* Macaroni dishes

teisen gri *Wales* See **Welsh griddle cake**

teisen lap *Wales* An oblong fruit and spice cake eaten when cold as buttered slices

teisennau cocos *Wales* Cockle cakes

teisennau tatws *Wales* Welsh potato cakes

teisen nioned *Wales* Onion cake

teisen resi *Wales* Rice cakes

teishoku *Japan* Set menu

t'ejj *East Africa* An alcoholic drink rather like mead, made from honey and usually taken with Ethiopian raw meat dishes

tej pat In) The leaves of cassia used as a flavouring agent in Indian cooking

tej patta *South Asia* Bay leaf

tekaka *Sweden* Teacake, crumpet

tel *South Asia* Oil

Telemea *Romania* A soft rindless ewes' milk cheese resembling Feta made from uncooked curd which is dried, pressed in square blocks, dry-salted and matured for 30 days in a salted acid whey. It can be stored for a long period in the same whey at 5°C. Contains 50% water, 25% fat and 20% protein.

Teleme Jack *United States* A cooking cheese from California resembling Mozzarella

teliatina, telyatina *Russia* Veal

tel kadayif *Turkey* Noodles cooked in sweetened milk and served with raisin syrup

tellina *Italy* Wedge shell clam

Teltower Rübchen *Germany* A small and well-flavoured variety of turnip grown around Berlin

telur *Indonesia, Malaysia* Egg

telur asin *Indonesia, Malaysia* Salted duck egg

tembikai *Malaysia* Water melon

tempe *Indonesia* A firm substance like cheese made by soaking and boiling soya beans, inoculating them with a fungus *Rhizopus oligosporus*, packing them into thin slabs wrapped in polythene or banana leaves pierced with holes and leaving to ferment. It is an easily digestible and well-flavoured source of protein and is usually shallow-fried. See also **oncom**. Also called **tempeh**

tempeh *Indonesia* Tempe

temper, to To bring to a desired consistency, texture, temperature or other physical condition by blending, mixing, kneading or standing, etc. as in to temper a pancake batter

temperature A measure of the intensity of heat such that heat always flows from a high intensity to a low one. Measured in cooking on the **Fahrenheit scale** or **Celsius scale**.

temperature probe A small pointed rod about 3 to 4 mm diameter which measures the internal temperature of food in which it is inserted. Used to determine the degree of roasting of meats and for checking that microwaved food is heated through.

tempestine *Italy* Tiny pasta shells used in soup

temple *Caribbean* A naturally occurring hybrid of *Citrus* spp

tempura Pieces of fish, shellfish, bundles of noodles and firm vegetables, covered with a thinnish coating of tempura batter, deep-fried and served with a dipping sauce made from **dashi**, **mirin** and light soy sauce, with added grated **daikon** (mooli) and fresh ginger. The technique was introduced to Japan by the Spanish and Portuguese in the late 16th century.

tempura batter *Japan* A lumpy batter made with iced water, sifted flour and egg yolk (12:6:1). The egg yolk and iced water are beaten together and poured over the flour which is stirred lightly.

tempura dipping sauce *Japan* A mixture of **dashi**, light soya sauce and **mirin** (8:3:2), served with separate bowls of minced ginger and **daikon oroshi**

temu putih *Indonesia, Malaysia* Zedoary

tenca *Spain* Tench

tench A small dark-skinned freshwater fish, *Tinca tinca*, of the carp family found in European rivers. It has rather a muddy flavour and is generally soaked in salted water for several hours before frying or grilling.

tender cure, to To quick cure

tenderize, to To break down the connective tissue of meat, octopus tentacles and the like by beating with a spiked mallet, by chemical treatment with acids, proteases or marinades, by hanging meat to allow natural enzymes to break down the fibres and by the correct application of heat at the right temperature

tenderloin *United States* Fillet steak (of beef), pork fillet and occasionally a corresponding muscle in lamb

tenderloin of pork The long inner back muscles equivalent to the fillet of beef, grilled, fried, used for kebabs, stir fries or batted out as escalopes. Also called **pork fillet**

tendon 1. The sinew or strand of strong connective tissue which attaches a muscle to bone. It contains a high proportion of elastin and does not liberate much gelatine on boiling. Usually excised and discarded. **2.** *Japan* Boiled rice with pieces of tempura (deep-fried battered fish, shellfish and vegetables) arranged decoratively on top and dressed with a sauce made from **dashi**, sake, soya sauce, sugar and grated ginger root, then garnished with chopped spring onions

tenero *Italy* Tender, fresh, soft

teneroni di vitello *Italy* Ribs of veal (equivalent to spare ribs of pork or breast of lamb)

tengericsuka *Hungary* Hake

tenok *Malaysia* Barracuda

tentsuyu *Japan* A dipping sauce for tempura

tepary bean A drought resistant bean, *Phaseolus acutifolius*, grown in Mexico and the southern USA for local use

tepeh *Malaysia* Ridged sand clam

tepid The term applied to water at about 50 to 60°C. See also **lukewarm**

tepong pulot *Indonesia, Malaysia* Glutinous rice flour

teppan *Japan* A griddle used to cook food at the table

teppan yaki *Japan* A method of cooking food, usually in front of the diner, either on a hot griddle or over burning charcoal

Teppichmuschel *Germany* Carpet shell

tepung beras *Indonesia, Malaysia* Rice flour

tepung hoen kwe *Indonesia, Malaysia* Mung bean flour

tequila *Mexico* A clear spiritous liquor made by distilling fermented sap from the blue agave. It is produced and bottled only in Jalisco state, Mexico, and originated around the town of Tequila and has denomination of origin status. It has the same relationship to **mescal** as cognac has to brandy and is used in cooking in the same way as brandy. The finest is designated *añejo* ('aged') and is aged in oak barrels for at least a year. See also **mescal**

terasi *Indonesia, Malaysia* Shrimp paste, **blachan**. Also called **trasi**

terbiye *Turkey* A sauce used on vegetables, made from vegetable stock thickened with an egg, water and flour mixture and finished with lemon juice

terbiyéli köfte *Turkey* Flat cakes made from a mixture of minced beef and onions, soaked breadcrumbs, eggs, chopped parsley and seasoning, fried in butter then simmered in stock and served with a sauce made from flour and water enriched with egg yolks and lemon juice, seasoned and flavoured with paprika

tereyagi *Turkey* Butter

teri *Japan* A glaze for meat, vegetables, etc.

teriyaki *Japan* Kebabs, marinated in a soya sauce, sugar, and/or **mirin** mixture and grilled whilst being repeatedly basted with the marinade to give a rich, brown glaze. Alternatively escalopes, tender steaks, chicken breasts, fish, etc. browned then gently cooked in simmering teriyaki sauce until the sauce is reduced to a glaze. Served with a decorative garnish.

teriyaki sauce *Japan* Equal quantities of sake, **mirin** and dark soya sauce with about one twelfth ot the combined weight of sugar and all boiled until the sugar dissolves

Terlaner Weinsuppe *Austria* A South Tyrolean soup made from beef stock and white wine with egg yolk and whipped double cream

termites akoumba *Africa* Pounded fresh termites mixed with palm oil and used as a dip in Malawi and Zaire

ternera *Spain* A rose-coloured veal from calves which have been raised outdoors and are slaughtered between 8 and 12 months

terong *Malaysia* Aubergine

terraglie *Italy* Earthenware

terrapin *United States* A small fresh or brackish water turtle whose flesh is considered a delicacy. Available canned in Europe.

terre cuite *France* Earthenware

terrina *Italy* Terrine

terrine *England, France* **1.** A meat or fish loaf made from coarsely chopped or finely processed meat, chicken or game flesh, liver, fish or shellfish and fat with herbs, spices and flavourings, placed in an oblong earthenware dish lined with streaky bacon, blanched leek leaves or similar, covered and baked in the oven, cooled, demoulded and sliced for use as a hors d'oeuvre **2.** A heat proof earthenware dish with a lid used for baking a terrine

terrine, en *France* Potted

terung *Indonesia* Aubergine

testa *Italy* Head of an animal or cap of a mushroom

testicles The sperm-producing organs of male animals shaped like elongated balls, often cooked as a delicacy. See also **mountain oysters, lamb's fry**

testicoli *Italy* Testicles, lamb's fry

testina *Italy* Testa

testuggine marina *Italy* Turtle

tête *France* Head

Tête de Moine *Switzerland* An alpine semi-hard unpasteurized cows' milk cheese with a pale yellow, mild and creamy paste enclosed in a rough slightly greasy rind. It is made in 0.5 to 2 kg rounds and is cured for 3 to 5 months. Traditionally served in thinly sliced curls with ground pepper and cumin.

tête de nègre *France* A variety of cep. See also **cèpe de vendage**

Tetilla *Spain* A soft white cheese made from cows' milk, the salted curd being placed in pear-shaped moulds and cured for 2 months. It has a slightly sour salty flavour. Contains 50% water, 22% fat and 21% protein. Also called **perilla**

tétine *France* Udder

Tetragonia expansa *Botanical name* New Zealand spinach

Tetragonia tetragonioides *Botanical name* New Zealand spinach

Tetrapanax papyriferum *Botanical name* The tree from which rice paper is made

tétras *France* Grouse

tetrazzini *Italy* Pasta with a creamy cheese sauce and seafood or poultry meat

tette melk *Norway* Cultured milk preserved and flavoured with tette leaves

Teviotdale pie *Scotland* Minced beef or lamb browned in butter for 5 minutes then simmered in a little water with seasoning for about 10 minutes, put in a pie dish which is then topped with a batter made from flour, milk, suet and egg (6:5:3:2) with a dsp of baking powder per kg of flour and all baked at 180°C for 40 minutes. Also called **Benalty pie**

Tewkesbury mustard *England* A pale smooth blend of mustard seed, horseradish, wine vinegar and salt. Used with sausages.

Texas ruby red *United States* A red fleshed grapefruit

Texel *Netherlands* A green ewes' milk cheese

textured vegetable protein Protein extracted from vegetable sources, usually soya beans which is flavoured, solubilized and forced through a multitude of fine holes into a coagulating medium. The numerous fibres are brought together into a thick rope which is then chopped into pieces and dried. Used as a meat substitute. See also **quorn**. Also called **TVP**

teynadam *East Africa* An Ethiopian herb often used in making spice mixes (NOTE: Literally 'Health of Adam'.)

tfaya *North Africa* A Moroccan meat dish in a brown sauce with coriander, saffron, onion and seasoning. Served with roasted almonds and hard-boiled eggs.

Thai fragrant rice See **jasmine fragrant rice**

Thai ginger Greater galangal

Thai jasmine rice See **jasmine fragrant rice**

Thai yellow chilli A pale yellow green chilli with a mild flavour, often stuffed and cooked as a snack

thal *South Asia* A large brass, copper, silver or stainless steel platter with raised edges on which Indian food is served

thala *Sri Lanka* Sesame seed

thali *South Asia* A smaller version of the thal

thambili *Sri Lanka* Milk from the king coconut which is drunk directly from the shell

thaumatin A protein extract from berries, *Thaumatococcus danielli*, which is 3 to 4000 times as sweet as sucrose, used in table top sugar substitutes and yoghurts

thee complet *Netherlands* Afternoon tea with biscuits and cakes

thelele *East Africa* A thickish mixture of onion, okra, garam masala, tomatoes and spinach leaves fried in oil then simmered in a little water for 10 minutes. From Malawi.

Theobroma cacao *Botanical name* Cocoa bean tree

thermidor The method of preparation is only used with lobster. See also **homard thermidor**

thermometer An instrument for measuring temperature, essential for cooking especially for determining when meat is cooked, for oven, freezer, refrigerator, fat and sugar temperatures and for ensuring adequate defrosting and cooking in microwave ovens

thermos flask A double-walled vessel made from silvered glass or stainless steel in which the space between the inner and outer wall is a vacuum, mounted in a protective case and fitted with a closure. The vacuum reduces transfer of heat by convection and the silvering reduces transfer by radiation, thus the contents may be kept hot or cold for a considerable period of time (heat is eventually transferred by conduction). Other types of insulation, e.g. foamed polystyrene or polyurethane, are used for the same purpose especially in larger rectangular containers. Also called **vacuum flask**

thermostat An electrically or mechanically operated instrument which monitors the temperature in an enclosure and if it deviates from a preset value increases or reduces the energy input to or abstracts more or less energy from the space to maintain the preset temperature. Commonly used in gas or electric ovens, refrigerators and freezers, deep fat fryers, slow cookers and the like.

thetchouka *North Africa* See **chakchouka 2**

thiabendazole See **E233**

thiakry *West Africa* A sweet dessert made with couscous. See also **caakiri**

thiamine Vitamin B1

thick batter *United States* Soft drop batter

thicken, to To increase the viscosity or consistency of a liquid by a variety of techniques including reduction, addition of cooked starches, gums, proteins such as white of egg or yolk or gelatine, by emulsifying a discontinuous phase into the liquid or by adding finely ground solids. See also under: roux, liaison, beurre manié, purée, coulis, sabayon, emulsions, etc.

thickened gravy See **jus lié**

thickeners Substances, usually carbohydrates or proteins which may have been chemically modified, used to increase the viscosity or consistency of liquids

thick flank United Kingdom A cut of beef from the front of the rear thigh. It is lean and used for braising and pot-roasting. Often sold as cheap frying steak. Also called **top rump**

thick flank of veal United Kingdom The muscle at the front of the thigh bone of the rear leg of veal, equivalent to thick flank of beef. Used in the same way as cushion of veal.

thick oxtail soup Disjointed oxtail and a **mirepoix** of onion, garlic, carrot and turnip browned in fat, flour added to make a brown roux, tomato purée, a bouquet garni and brown stock added, simmered and skimmed for 4 hours, oxtail and bouquet garni removed, flesh returned, liquidized, strained, seasoned and consistency corrected, finished with sherry and garnished with dice or small balls of carrots and turnips and the tip of the oxtail cut in rounds. Also called **queue de boeuf lié**

thick seam tripe Tripe from the third stomach of the cow or ox. It has the same flavour as blanket tripe or honeycomb tripe.

thick skirt United Kingdom That part of the inner muscles of the belly wall attached to the rump. Also called **goose skirt**

thiebou diene West Africa Braised fish and vegetables served with rice

thiebu djen West Africa A fish dish from Senegal. See also **ceebu jën**

thin Vietnam Thinh

thin batter United States A thin flour liquid mixture (1:2) suitable for crêpes, pancakes, dipping, popovers, cream puffs, etc. The proportions depend upon the flour. Also called **pour batter**

thin flank United Kingdom The better cut of beef from the abdominal cavity equivalent to pork belly. Contains a lot of fat and is used for stewing and manufacturing.

thinh Vietnam Rice dry-fried to a deep golden brown then ground into a coarse powder and used as a flavouring and binder. Also called **thin**

thin skirt United Kingdom The muscular part of the diaphragm of beef cattle

thin soya sauce See **light soya sauce**

thit Vietnam Minced or thinly sliced

thit ba chi Vietnam Bacon

thit bo kno Vietnam Vietnamese stewed beef, usually eaten with French bread

thit-ja-bo-gauk Burma Cinnamon

thon France Tuna fish

thonine France Bonito (2), the fish

thon rouge France Blue fin tuna fish

thornback ray A type of skate, Raja clavata, found in European and Mediterranean waters which grown to about 1 m long

thorny mandarin Mediterranean mandarin

Thousand Island dressing Olives, onion, hard-boiled egg, green sweet pepper and parsley all chopped and combined with mayonnaise and tarragon vinegar or lemon juice

thousand year egg Chinese preserved egg

thread herring A species of herring, Opisthonema oglinum, up to 15 cm long and with a distinctive thread-like ray at the end of the dorsal fin. It is found in the Gulf of Mexico and off the southeast coast of the USA. Used mainly for canning. Also called **Atlantic thread herring**

three-bearded rockling A small, round, pink skinned seawater fish, Gaidropsarus mediterraneus, found in the Mediterranean Sea

throughcut bacon A complete rasher of bacon including the back and the streaky from the middle portion of the pig

thrumenty See **frumenty**

thrush A small brown songbird Turdidae family caught in France and Italy for use in pâtés, pies or terrines

thunder and lightning England Cornish splits eaten with cream and treacle

Thunfisch Germany Tuna fish

Thüringer Blutwurst Germany A blood sausage made with diced parboiled pork belly and finely chopped pork rind, liver and lights plus occasionally other cooked offal. This is mixed with warm pigs' blood, seasoned, flavoured with marjoram, caraway and ground cloves, loosely filled into large casings, boiled, refreshed, dyed red and cold-smoked with juniper berries and sawdust.

Thüringer Rostbratwurst Germany A Bratwurst made of pork or veal from Thuringia

Thüringer Rotwurst Germany A cooked, red-coloured blood sausage from Thuringia

thym France Thyme

thyme A hardy evergreen low growing sub shrub, *Thymus vulgaris*, with tiny aromatic leaves and pale lilac flowers. The stalks with leaves attached are used in bouquet garnis or bundled up with other herbs to make a faggot of herbs. Alternatively the leaves alone are used fresh or dried in stuffings, sauces, soups, stocks and meat dishes. Fresh sprigs may be used to flavour oil or vinegar. Also called **garden thyme**

Thymian *Germany* Thyme

thymus A large gland from the neck of vertebrates important in the immune response. It, together with the pancreas, comprises the sweetbreads.

Thymus pulegioides *Botanical name* Broad leaf thyme

Thymus vulgaris *Botanical name* Thyme

Thymus x citriodorus *Botanical name* Lemon thyme

tian *France* A shallow dish used in Provence, in which food is baked or grilled; alternatively a dish of food made in a tian

tian ya *China* Peking duck

t'ibs *East Africa* Fried meat, usually beef with butter, onions and chilli sauce. From Ethiopia.

tidbid *Denmark* Light snack

tiède *France* Warm, tepid

tiefgefroren *Germany* Deep-frozen

Tiefseegarnele *Germany* Deepwater prawn

tiella *Italy* A large baking dish or the food cooked in it, usually a mixture of vegetables with offal, shellfish, cheese or ham, possibly in pastry case

Tientsin pear A smooth, almost round, yellow fruit with a sweet crisp pear-like texture. Eaten raw after peeling and coring.

tieo *Laos* Chilli paste

tier pans A set of cake tins of several diameters used to make elaborate two- or three- tier cakes such as wedding cakes

tiffin *South Asia* Lunch, light repast (NOTE: From Old English *tiff*, to drink or to lunch.)

tiffin box *South Asia* Stackable stainless steel boxes or tins with lids in which lunch and snacks are delivered to office workers in India

tiganita *Greece* Fried or deep-fried

tiganito sikoti *Greece* Calves' liver cut in 2.5 cm cubes, passed through seasoned flour mixed with powdered dried herbs, fried in hot butter for 1.5 to 2 minutes until brown and served as a starter with salad and bread

tigerella tomato A decorative tomato streaked with green

tiger lily bulb Lily bulb

tiger melon A variety of cantaloupe melon from Turkey with an orange-yellow and black striped skin and a fragrant orange flesh

tiger nut A small wrinkled brown tuber which forms on the roots of a plant, *Cyperus esculentus*, that grows around the Mediterranean. It has a crisp, sweet, nutty-flavoured white flesh and is eaten as is, in ice cream or is ground to make the Spanish drink **horchata**. Also called **chufa**, **galingale**, **earth almond**, **pignut**, **rushnut**

tiger prawn A type of king prawn, *Penaeus esculentus*, with a brown and orange striped shell and a dark-coloured head and tail. It retains the stripes on cooking.

tikka *South Asia* Small pieces of meat or poultry marinated in yoghurt and tandoori spice mix, grilled or roasted and served with Indian bread and salad

tikki channa dal *South Asia* Small croquettes of yellow split peas, cooked until very soft, puréed and mixed with minced parsley, chopped ginger, salt, powdered bay leaf and crushed cumin seeds, then bound with egg and fried

til *South Asia* Sesame seed

tilapia A perch-like member of the *Cichlid* family originating in Africa but now the most widely farmed fish in the tropics. An all-male variety has been genetically developed which grows to 2 kg in 1 year. It is also farmed in temperate climates, where supplies of warm fresh water are available from industrial processes. Also called **St Peter's fish**

tilefish A reddish blue seawater fish, *Lopholatilus chamaeleonticeps*, with small yellow spots on the upper side and fins, found in deep waters off the North American coast. The flesh is very firm and tender and may be substituted for lobster or scallops.

til ka tel *South Asia* Sesame seed oil

Tillamook *United States* A Cheddar-type cows' milk cheese from Oregon

Tilsit *Germany* A semi-hard, cooked curd, slicing cheese made from raw or pasteurized cows' milk inoculated with *Lactobacillus* and curdled with rennet. They are cast in large rounds or loaf shapes, dry-salted and ripened for a month whilst being regularly washed with brine, then matured for 5 months. The paste is creamy-yellow with a mild and delicate flavour and numerous small holes. It is suitable for cooking and melting as well as for slicing. Made in many Central European countries. Contains 45 to 50% water, and 10 to 30% fat. Also called **Tollenser**, **Tilsiter**

Tilsiter *Germany* Tilsit

timbale *England, France* **1.** A cup-shaped mould **2.** A light creamy puréed mixture, baked in a timbale, demoulded and served with a sauce

timballa e'latte *Italy* A baked almond custard from Sardinia. Also called **tumbada**

timballo *Italy* A hot pie or mould much more robust than the English **timbale**

timballo al abbruzzese *Italy* Pancakes layered in a dish with meatballs, chicken livers, cheese and tomato sauce and baked in the oven

timballo di riso alla piemontese *Italy* A mould of rice with chicken livers, kidneys and a meat sauce

tim cheon *China, Malaysia* Plum sauce

tim cheong *Malaysia* A sweet and very dark soya sauce similar to the Chinese sweet soya sauce

timman *Middle East* Steamed basmati rice

timman z'affaran *Middle East* A festive rice dish from Iraq, enriched with sweated chopped onion and minced meat which are fried until dry with **baharat**, sultanas and salt. The rice is first soaked for 30 minutes then simmered in chicken stock with the meat mixture for a further 30 minutes and allowed to rest under a tight-fitting lid. It is served sprinkled with toasted split almonds and rose water and coloured and flavoured with saffron.

timo *Italy* **1.** Thyme **2.** The thymus gland

timpana *Malta* A covered pie made with puff pastry filled with cooked al dente macaroni, fried chicken livers, grated cheese and chopped hard-boiled eggs in a Bolognaise sauce prior to baking at 190°C for 40 minutes

timum balu *Malaysia* Fuzzy melon

timun *Malaysia* Cucumber

timur *Nepal* Anise pepper

tin **1.** Any metal container used for baking, e.g. cake tin, loaf tin, bun tin, etc. or for storing or preserving food **2.** The relatively inert metal used to coat the inside of copper cooking utensils to prevent corrosion in acid solutions

tinamou *South America* A game bird of the *Tinamidae* family resembling a partridge. Sold in France.

tinca *Italy* Tench

tinda *South Asia* A type of squash, *Citrullus vulgaris* var. *fistulosus*, resembling a small green, apple-sized water melon with cream flesh and light-coloured seeds. Used as a summer vegetable. Also called **round gourd**, **squash melon**

tindola Tindoori

tindoori *South Asia* A small elongated oval green squash from a vine, *Trichosanthes dioica*, rather like a cucumber. Important in Indian cooking and may be eaten cooked or raw. Also called **ivy gourd**, **parwal**, **palwal**, **tindola**, **tindori**

tindori See tindoori

ting hsian *China* Cloves

tinker Common skate

tinker's apple cake *Wales* Made from cooking apples, self-raising flour, butter and demerara sugar (3:2:1:1), the flour is rubbed into the butter and made into a thick batter with a little milk, this is mixed with the peeled, cored and chopped cooking apples and baked in a buttered tin for 30 minutes at 200°C. Also called **dinca fala**, **Welsh apple cake**

tinned food Food preserved and sterilized in sealed, tinned or coated steel or aluminium cans

Tintenfisch *Germany* Cuttlefish

tippaleipä *Finland* A spiral-shaped sweetened pastry similar to crullers. Traditionally eaten on May day.

Tippenhaas *Germany* A type of jugged hare

tipsy cake *England* A dome-shaped cake moistened with sherry, studded with dehusked almonds and coated with an egg custard sauce. Served cold as a dessert.

tipsy pudding *United States* An English-style trifle without fruit but well laced with liqueur or sherry

tirakia tiganita *Greece* Stiffly beaten egg whites seasoned with pepper, mixed with finely grated Parmesan or Kefalotiri cheese until firm, deep-fried at 190°C in teaspoonfuls until puffy and brown, drained and served hot on cocktail sticks as an appetizer

tiram *Indonesia* Oyster

tiram batu *Malaysia* Oyster

tiramisú *Italy* A rich dessert from Venice made with sponge fingers dipped in coffee and spirit or liqueur and layered with a creamed egg yolk, sugar and Mascarpone cheese (1:1:5) mixture sprinkled with chopped chocolate, finished with chopped nuts and refrigerated (NOTE: Literally 'pick me up'.)

Tirggel *Switzerland* A heavily spiced Christmas gingerbread biscuit baked in a wooden mould carved with a relief of some ancient or modern design. See also **Basler Leckerli**

Tirolen Eierspeise *Austria* A casserole of hard-boiled eggs, potatoes and anchovies

Tiroler *Austria* An **Extrawurst**-type sausage containing mainly lean cured pork with a little veal and/or beef

Tirolerknödel *Austria* Meatball

Tirolersuppe *Austria* Soup with dumplings

tiropita *Greece* A triangular filo pastry pasty filled with cheese mashed with egg, seasoned and flavoured with nutmeg and chopped parsley. Also called **tiropitakia**

tiropitakia *Greece* Tiropita

titanium dioxide E171, an inert white pigment permitted for use in food. It has no known health benefits.

tit-bits Small items of savoury food, appetizers

Tivoli, à la *France* In the Tivoli style, i.e. garnished with asparagus tips and mushrooms. Used of meat dishes.

tjobek *Indonesia* A ceramic mortar. See also **cobek**

tlacenka *Czech Republic* A large sausage filled with a kind of brawn

tlanochtle *Mexico* A sweet, green skinned fruit with a very high vitamin C content about the size of a tomato from a plant, *Lycianthes moziniana*, once widely cultivated by the Aztecs but now rare, suitable for steep marginal land

t'min, t'meen *Russia* Caraway seed

tô *West Africa* A fufu-like staple from Mali and Burkina Faso made from millet, maize or sorghum flour

toad in the hole *England* Cooked English sausage placed in a shallow tin with a Yorkshire pudding mix and baked

toast Slices of bread browned on both sides either under the grill or in a toaster. See also **French toast**

toast, to To brown bread, marshmallows, cheese and similar items under the grill or in front of a fire, or to brown bread in a toaster

toasted almonds See **toasted seeds**

toasted seeds Seeds, e.g. buckwheat, sesame seeds, almond pieces, which are baked in the oven on an ungreased tray until they are brown

toaster An implement consisting of a spring loaded carrier for a slice of bread moving in a vertical slot with electrically heated elements on either side. The bread is placed in the carrier which when depressed, automatically switches on the elements and a timer which after a preset time releases the catch which holds the carrier down thus releasing the toast and switching off the elements.

toastie A sandwich which has been fried or toasted between two electrically heated grill plates which are pressed together. Depressions moulded in the grill plates hold the sandwich and give it a distinctive cushion shape.

tobiko *Japan* Orange/red flying fish roe with a crisp crunchy texture. Used with sushi and as a garnish.

tocană cu mămăligă *Romania* Boned and cubed shoulder pork, browned in lard and braised with sliced onions browned in the same fat, stock and white wine flavoured with thyme. Served with mămăligă.

tocino *Spain* Salted pork belly or other fat pork often covered in crystalline salt (NOTE: (Note – not bacon))

tocino de cielo *Spain* A thick crème caramel

tocmchams *Iran* Apricots

tocopherols A group of natural substances with vitamin E activity used as antioxidants. Individual tocopherols now synthesized are alpha-tocopherol E307, gamma-tocopherol E308 and delta-tocopherol E309. See also **E306**

tod *Thailand* Deep-fried

toddy Coconut wine

toespijs *Netherlands* Sweet, dessert, side dish

toey *Thailand* Screwpine

tofeja canavesana *Italy* A stew of pork offal, sausages and beans

tofu See **bean curd**

tofujiru *Japan* A tofu soup made with **dashi** flavoured with a little soya sauce, **mirin** and reconstituted shiitake mushroom caps, boiled and thickened with corn flour, simmered for 15 minutes, diced tofu added, simmered a further 5 minutes and served

tofu no miso shiru *Japan* A very simple soup made from **dashi** mixed with diced bean curd and miso (20:5:1 by volume) and garnished with chopped spring onions

togan *Japan* Wax gourd

togarashi *Japan* A small intensely hot chilli, usually flaked, used as a flavouring and in shichimi, also used of the dried chilli powder made from the same

Toggenburger *Switzerland* A semi-hard white cheese made from naturally soured skimmed cows' milk which is shaped into cubes and matured for 6 months

Toggenburger Ploderkäse *Switzerland* Ploderkäse

togue *Philippines* Bean sprouts

toheroa *New Zealand* A rare shellfish, *Amphidesma ventricosum*, found on only a few beaches and used to make a highly prized green soup (NOTE: Literally 'long tongue'.)

toi *Vietnam* Garlic

tokány *Hungary* A thick beef stew with tomatoes, green peppers, onions, garlic, sliced mushrooms and paprika. Served with soured cream and accompanied with rice or pasta.

Tokyo hotchpot *Japan* See **oden**

tola *South Asia* A unit of weight based on the old rupee coin equal to 0.4 oz or approximately 11 g

tolee molee *Burma* Condiments including fish sauces and other pungent mixtures and pastes

Tollenser Tilsit

Toll House cookie *United States* A biscuit made with brown sugar, nuts and chocolate chips in the paste (NOTE: Named after the Toll House inn in Massachusetts)

töltött káposzta *Hungary* Cabbage rolls filled with a mixture of chopped onions, boiled rice, eggs, garlic, marjoram, paprika and seasonings, braised in a covered dish, between two layers of sauerkraut which have been sprinkled with flour and paprika. Sour cream is added when the dish is half cooked.

tom *Thailand* Boiled or simmered in water

Toma *Italy* A hard cheese made from whole or partially skimmed cows' milk and cast in thick discs (up to 4kg). The curd is moulded, dry-salted or brined and ripened for at least 30 days. The rind is rough and the dense paste has a sharp salty taste.

tomaat *Netherlands* Tomato

tomalley The liver of the lobster which is yellow green in colour and a delicacy. Used like the coral in sauces. Also used of crab eggs and ovaries.

Tomar *Portugal* A very small ewes' milk cheese from Tomar north of Lisbon. It may be smoked.

tomarillo Tamarillo

tomat *Denmark, Norway, Sweden* Tomato

tomate *France, Portugal, Spain* Tomato

tomate, sauce *France* Tomato sauce

Tomate *Germany* Tomato

tomate con cáscara *Mexico* Tomate verde. lit. tomato with a husk.

tomate de mer *France* Beadlet, a sea anemone

tomates, crème de *France* Tomato soup finished with milk or cream in the proportions of 1 to 4. Also called **cream of tomato soup**

tomates farcies *Belgium* Skinned tomatoes, stuffed with shrimps in mayonnaise

tomate verde *France, Mexico* The fruit of a plant, *Physalis ixocarpa*, a relative of the cape gooseberry, resembling a green tomato with a papery husk. Used extensively in Mexican cookery and in the production of salsa verde. It develops flavour when boiled and is an essential ingredient of genuine

guacamole. Also called **tomate con cáscara, jamberry, ground tomato, tomatillo**

tomatillo Tomate verde

tomato The fruit of an annual plant (in temperate climates) or short-lived perennial (in warm climates), *Lycopersicon esculentum*, of which some varieties grow to over 2.5 m high whilst others are low bushes. Although technically a fruit they are used exclusively as a salad or cooking vegetable or as a flavouring and thickener for a range of soups, sauces and other cooked dishes. The fruits are from 1 cm to over 10 cm in diameter, slightly flattened spheres with a yellow to red fleshy pulp divided internally in hollow segments each containing a slack pulp with embedded seeds. They are easily skinned by blanching for 10 to 20 seconds in boiling water and are used skinned and unskinned, raw, cooked and sometimes deseeded in a wide variety of dishes. Most tomatoes of commerce are picked green and ripened in the box. Vine ripened tomatoes found in warmer climates generally have a superior flavour. See also **cherry tomato, plum tomato, beef tomato, Marmande, tigerella tomato, yellow pear tomato**

tomato concassée Finely chopped skinned and deseeded tomato pulp used in a variety of sauces and soups. The juice from the seeds may be strained off and added to the chopped pulp.

tomato paste See **tomato purée**

tomato purée Partially dehydrated sieved tomato pulp with a deep red colour and spreadable consistency used for flavouring. Sold in collapsible tubes, tins and jars. Also called **tomato paste**

tomato sauce A **mirepoix** of onion, carrot, celery, bay leaf and thyme browned with bacon scraps in butter, flour added and cooked to a slight colour, tomato purée and white stock added, boiled than simmered with garlic, strained and seasoned. Also called **tomate, sauce**

tomato sausage *England* An English sausage containing about 10% tomato, popular in the Midlands

tomato soup A **mirepoix** of bacon, onion and carrot browned in butter, flour added and cooked out, tomato purée or fresh tomatoes, stock and a bouquet garni added off heat, simmered and skimmed for 1 hour, passed through a chinois, seasoned, consistency adjusted and served hot with croûtons. Also called **potage de tomates**

tomatsaft *Norway* Tomato juice

tomatsoppa *Sweden* Tomato soup

tom bac ga *Vietnam* **1.** Shrimp **2.** Prawn

tombarello *Italy* See **bonito** 1

tomber à glace *France* To reduce a stock to a thick sticky glaze

tomillo *Spain* Thyme

Tomino *Italy* A soft cows' milk cheese shaped in 2 to 3 cm elongated cylinders which are consumed as soon as they have been salted. A lactic starter is used which gives the fresh white paste its characteristic flavour. Used for dessert or as a hors d'oeuvre.

Tomme *France* The general name of a variety of small cheeses produced in Savoie, being the name for the container in which the cheese is made

Tomme au raisin *France* A small round cheese made from skimmed milk and ripened in a coating of grape pips. Also called **fondu au marc, fromage fondu, fondu au raisin, grape cheese**

Tomme d'Annot *France* A goats' or ewes' milk cheese from the Haut-Alpes

Tomme de Cantal *France* A cooking cheese from the Dordogne made from cows' milk or occasionally from goats' milk

Tomme de Saint Marcellin *France* A soft cows' milk cheese from Savoie made from various milks and formed into thin discs (up to 80 g) which are ripened for 2 weeks to give a hole-free paste and a delicate rind covered in greenish blue mould

Tomme de Savoie *France, Switzerland* A semi-hard skimmed cows' milk cheese formed into a squat cylinder (up to 1.5 kg). It has a pleasant aromatic and lactic flavour and a firm texture resembling Saint Paulin.

Tomme du Mont-Ventoux *France* A fresh and slightly salty ewes' milk cheese from Provence

Tomme vaudoise *Switzerland* A soft surface-ripened cows' milk cheese made in small cylinders or oblongs (up to 100 g). The taste varies from mild to savoury and fragrant after 10 days ripening.

tom su *Vietnam* 1. Shrimp 2. Prawn.

tom yam gung *Thailand* A spicy prawn soup flavoured with herbs and lemon juice

tom yam kung *Thailand* A spicy brown soup

Tonbridge biscuit *England* A thin sweet biscuit glazed with egg white and sprinkled with caraway seeds before baking

tonfisk *Sweden* Tuna fish

tonfisksallad *Sweden* Tuna salad, normally tinned tuna, mixed with diced hard-boiled eggs, chopped onions and celery and arranged on lettuce. Generally served on the smörgåsbord.

tong *Netherlands* Dover sole

tongs A scissor-shaped implement made of metal or wood, with blunt ends and no cutting edges used for handling hot or delicate foods

tongue The tongues of cattle and lambs usually soaked, cleaned, simmered with a bouquet garni and aromatic vegetables until tender, skinned and the meat pressed in a basin to cool and set in the natural jelly. Sliced and eaten as a cold meat or julienned for use as a garnish.

ton hom *Thailand* Scallion

tonijn *Netherlands* Tuna fish

tonka bean The leguminous seeds of various trees of the genus *Dipteryx*. They contain coumarin, a chemical responsible for the smell of new mown hay, and are used as a flavouring.

tonkatsu *Japan* Slices of pork fillet, panéed with large toasted breadcrumbs (**panko**), deep-fried, sliced in strips and served on a chiffonade of lettuce garnished with lemon wedges and served with tonkatsu sauce

tonkatsu sauce *Japan* A type of barbecue sauce served with tonkatsu. A typical recipe might contain tomato ketchup, dark soya sauce, sake, Worcestershire sauce and mustard.

tonnato *Italy* With tuna fish or a tuna fish sauce

tonnetto *Italy* Little tunny, the fish

tonnino *Italy* Tuna fish

tonno *Italy* Tuna fish

tonyina *Catalonia* Tuna fish

tooa lisong *Thailand* Peanut

toogbei *West Africa* Deep-fried dough balls similar to chinchin (NOTE: Literally 'sheep's balls'.)

toon *Thailand* To steam or steaming

toonhaai *Netherlands* Smooth hound, the fish. Also called **gladde hai**

toor dal Pigeon pea

top and tail, to To remove either end of a fruit or vegetable, as in removing the stalk and tip of a French bean

topaz *Middle East* Ortanique

tope A type of shark, *Galeorhinus galeus*, taken as a game fish in the Atlantic. The fresh fish has a strong smell of ammonia which disappears on cooking.

Topf *Germany* Pot

Topfen *Austria* Curd or cottage cheese made from skimmed milk

Topfenknödel *Austria* A sweet dumpling flavoured with curd cheese

topfenpalatschinken *Hungary* Large thin pancakes spread with a mixture of strained cottage cheese, sugar, egg yolks, currants and grated lemon zest into which the stiffly beaten egg whites are folded. These are rolled, cut in pieces, placed in a greased dish, filled with a sweet egg custard, baked in the oven and finished with a dusting of icing sugar glazed under the grill.

Töpferware *Germany* Earthenware, crockery

topinambour *France* Jerusalem artichoke (NOTE: Said to be named after a group of Brazilian natives of the Topinambous tribe brought to Paris at the same time as the tuber was introduced.)

topinambur *Italy* Jerusalem artichoke

topinky *Czech Republic* Fried bread with garlic

topping Any covering such as breadcrumbs, grated cheese, sweet or savoury sauces, cream, etc. placed on the surface of a prepared dish as a garnish or decoration or as an integral part of the dish

top round steak *United States* Steak cut from the upper part of a round of beef below the rump. It is more tender than round steak.

top rump *United Kingdom* Thick flank

top shell Winkle, the shellfish

topside *United Kingdom* A lean boneless beef joint from the rear inside of the hind leg. It is inclined to be dry and fine grained with no marbling and is used for braising, stewing and second class roasting.

toranja *Portugal* Grapefruit

Torbay sole Witch sole

torch ginger The pink-tinged **ginger bud** and the tender part of the pink stem

torciolo *Italy* Pancreas gland of veal or beef. Together with the thymus makes up the sweetbreads.

tordi *Italy* 1. Thrushes, the birds 2. Wrasse, the fish

tordi allo spiedo *Italy* Small birds (thrushes), skewered and grilled or barbecued

tori 1. *Japan* Chicken 2. Loofah and angled loofah

toridon *Japan* Chicken donburi

torigai *Japan* A type of cockle

tori motsu *Japan* Chicken giblets, principally the heart, liver and gizzard, grilled, fried or served in nabemono

torinese *Italy* Grissini

toriniku *Japan* Chicken meat

torkad frukt *Sweden* Dried fruits

tørkage *Denmark* Plain cake

torlo *Italy* Yolk, of an egg

toro *Japan* The belly flesh of tuna (**maguro**), much prized for sushi and sashimi

toronja *Spain* Pummelo, grapefruit

tororo kombu *Japan* Shavings from soaked kombu cut with the grain leaving the tough membrane

torrada *Portugal* Toast

torrades *Catalonia* Toasted country bread

tørret fruktsuppe *Norway* A soup made from dried fruits, served hot or cold

tørrfisk *Norway* Stockfish

torrone *Italy* Nougat

torsh *Iran* West Indian lime (NOTE: Literally 'acid'.)

torshi *Middle East* Pickles

torshi betingan *Middle East* Long thin aubergines, incised to a depth of 2 cm down the long side, simmered in water for 10 minutes, drained, the aubergines filled with a mixture of chopped garlic, chilli pepper, celery leaves and stalks and walnuts, then pickled in water and vinegar (4:3) plus salt. Left for 3 weeks before eating after rinsing in cold water.

torshi khiar *Middle East* Gherkins pickled in water and vinegar (3:1) with salt, dill seeds, coriander seeds, black peppercorns and garlic cloves

torsk *Denmark, Norway, Sweden* Cod

torsk-filé à Willy *Sweden* Seasoned cod fillets put in a buttered ovenproof dish with a little water, coated with French mustard and sprinkled with sliced leek, covered and cooked for about 20 minutes in a moderate oven until tender

torsk på Norsk *Sweden* Cod slices, 2.5 to 3 cm thick, boiled vigorously for 5 minutes in a 10% brine, removed immediately and kept warm

torta 1. *Italy* Cake, tart or pie 2. *Mexico* Cake or loaf 3. *Portugal* A rolled and filled cake similar to a Swiss roll 4. *Spain* Pie or tart

torta del Casar *Spain* A soft ewes' milk cheese with a thin soft rind and a white paste with a few small holes. The milk is curdled with vegetable rennet, drained, pressed in flat discs, then salted and ripened for 30 days at low humidity.

torta Gorgonzola *Italy* Torta San Gaudenzio

torta margherita *Italy* A basic sponge cake usually dusted with cocoa powder

torta pasqualina *Italy* An Easter dish of boiled eggs, beetroot and cottage cheese layered with pasta and baked

torta San Gaudenzio *Italy* A cheese built up from alternate layers of Mascarpone and blue-veined Gorgonzola to give a layered effect. Sometimes flavoured with anchovy and caraway seeds. Also called **torta Gorgonzola**

Törtchen *Germany* Small tarts

Torte *Austria, Germany* An open tart or flan with a pastry or rich, dry cake type of lining filled with a variety of sweet ingredients

torteau *France* A sweet cornmeal pancake from Bordeaux

tortellata alla crema *Italy* Cream tart

tortelli *Italy* Variously-shaped ravioli often with unusual fillings

tortelli alla cremasca *Italy* Bow-shaped tortelli filled with a processed mixture of macaroons, sultanas, nutmeg and cheese and served with butter

tortelli di zucca *Italy* Tortelli filled with a mixture of macaroons, vegetable marrow, pickled fruit and cheese

tortellini *Italy* **1.** Small parcels of pasta with a cheese or meat filling available fresh or dried. The meat should be chopped rather than minced and lightly browned in oil before mixing with breadcrumbs and egg. **2.** Small versions of the tortello fritter from the Bologna region

tortellini in brodo *Italy* Tortellini cooked in a well-flavoured broth

tortelli sguazzarotti *Italy* Tortelli filled with a mixture of beans, vegetable marrow and nuts. Served cold with a wine sauce.

tortello *Italy* **1.** A type of doughnut or sweet fritter **2.** A kind of pie

tortelloni Large versions of tortellini (1)

tortera *Spain* Pastry

tortiera *Italy* Cake tin

tortiglione *Italy* **1.** Fusilli **2.** Almond cake

tortilha de mariscos *Portugal* An omelette filled with chopped cooked shellfish

tortilla 1. *Spain* A thick omelette usually consisting of fried sweet onion and potatoes bound together with egg and shallow-fried on both sides. Also called **Spanish omelette 2.** *Mexico* A thin pancake made from a dough of **masa harina** or tortilla flour, shaped and flattened by hand and cooked on both sides on a griddle until dry. May be salted and eaten after rolling in place of bread or filled and rolled as tacos or enchiladas. Not to be confused with the Spanish tortilla.

tortilla chips Small triangles (2 to 4 cm on the side) cut from the Mexican tortilla and deep-fried until crisp. Used as potato chips. Also called **corn chips, topotos, tostaditas**

tortilla de huevo *Mexico, Spain* Omelette

tortilla de pimientos *Spain* The standard Spanish tortilla with the addition of sliced green sweet pepper

tortilla flour Flour made from maize kernels by soaking them in lime water (calcium hydroxide solution) until they are soft enough to pound into flour. This process imparts a special tortilla flavour by breaking down the amino acid tryptophan in the corn to 2-amino acetophenone, and also makes the B vitamin niacin available. Those who use the untreated flour may suffer from vitamin deficiency.

tortina *Italy* Tartlet

tortino *Italy* **1.** Pie **2.** A frittata (Spanish tortilla) baked in the oven and drier than normal

tort iz sushyonykh fruktov i orekhov *Russia* A sweet pastry single-crust tart with a filling of dried apricots and peaches boiled in sweet white wine and honey (3:1) until the liquid is absorbed, mixed to a sloppy consistency with blanched almonds, walnuts, egg, honey, butter and wine and baked at 180°C for 45 minutes. Served with cream whipped with cinnamon and sugar.

tortoni *Italy* Ice cream made from cream and sugar flavoured with Maraschino cherries, chopped almonds and rum

torttu *Finland* French or Danish pastry, cake, tart

torttutaikina *Finland* Pastry or cake dough

tortue *France* Turtle

tortue, sauce *France* Boiling veal stock infused with mixed herbs, mushroom trimmings and crushed peppercorns off the heat, strained and mixed with **demi-glace** and tomato sauce, reduced, strained and finished with Madeira wine, truffle essence and a little cayenne pepper. It should have a definite herby flavour.

tortue claire, soupe *France* Clear turtle soup

tortue d'eau douce *France* Terrapin

tortuga *Spain* Turtle

tortuga de agua dulce *Spain* Terrapin

tor yau yu *China* Squid

tosa soya sauce *Japan* A mixture of light and dark soya sauces with a little **mirin** flavoured with Pacific bonito flakes and kombu, both of which are removed by straining before the sauce is served with sashimi

toscane, à la *France* In the Tuscan style, i.e. garnished with pasta, foie gras and truffles. Used especially of panéed and fried chicken or sweetbreads

toscanello *Italy* A semi-hard scalded-curd ewes' milk cheese from Tuscany and Sardinia made in cylinders (up to 3 kg). The drained and moulded cheeses are brined and ripened for 3 to 4 months to give a yellow to white rind and a dense white, mild to sharp-flavoured paste with a few holes.

toscatårta *Sweden* An almond topped cake

tosin *East Africa* Rosemary

toss, to 1. To turn over food, usually with two spoons, so that it becomes coated with a dressing, e.g. melted butter on vegetables or vinaigrette dressing on salads **2.** To coat pieces of food with a powder such as flour by shaking them together in a bag **3.** To turn over something being cooked in a frying pan by throwing it into the air with a flicking motion of the pan and catching it

tostada *Spain* Toast, rusk

tostadas *Mexico* Medium-sized tortillas, fried until crisp and served with a topping of salad, meat, poultry, fish or cheese with chilli sauce and served as a light meal or snack

tostaditas *Mexico* Tortilla chips

tostato *Italy* Toast, toasted

tostones *Caribbean* Fried plantain chips flavoured with garlic. Served as an appetizer.

totano *Italy* Flying squid

tôt-fait *France* A quickly made sponge cake (NOTE: Literally 'soon made'.)

totopos *Mexico* Tortilla chips

toucinho defumado *Portugal* Smoked bacon in a piece

toulonnaise, à la *France* In the Toulon style, i.e. with a tomato, aubergine and garlic sauce

toulousaine, à la *France* In the Toulouse style, i.e. used of chicken garnished with kidneys, cockscombs, mushrooms, truffles and sauce suprême

Toulouse sausage A fresh French sausage made from pork or chicken

tourangelle, à la *France* In the Touraine style, i.e. garnished with a mixture of flageolet beans and chopped French beans in a velouté sauce

tourin *France* Cream of onion soup thickened with egg yolks and sprinkled with grated cheese

tourné(e) *France* Turned in the sense of shaped like a barrel. See also **turn, to**

tournedos *England, France* Individual steaks cut from the middle part of a trimmed fillet of beef and grilled or shallow-fried. Usually tied before cooking to preserve a round shape.

tournedos Oscar *United States* A tournedos shallow-fried and served on an equal-sized crouton of fried bread garnished with crab meat and asparagus tips or artichoke hearts topped with béarnaise sauce

tournedos Rossini A tournedos shallow-fried in clarified butter and served on an equal-sized croûton of bread, topped with a slice of lightly fried foie gras and a slice of truffle. Served with a Madeira sauce.

tournesol *France* Sunflower

Tournon Saint Pierre *France* A soft strong-smelling cows' milk cheese from Poitou-Charente made in the shape of a cone

touron *France* A type of nougat or almond pastry covered with nuts

tourrée de l'Aubier *France* A large cows' milk cheese with a thin rind and a sweet, nutty-flavoured, velvety paste. Suitable for cooking and as a dessert cheese.

tourte *France* A shallow tart or flan made with puff pastry and with a savoury or sweet filling

tourteau *France* Common crab

tourtière 1. *France* Pie dish, tin or plate **2.** *Canada* A topped pastry pie from Quebec filled with seasoned minced pork and onion flavoured with herbs

toute-épice *France* Allspice

tovaglia *Italy* Tablecloth

tovagliolo *Italy* Napkin, serviette

towel gourd A type of gourd

toxins Poisons produced by bacteria that cause food poisoning, e.g. the nerve poison botulin

toyo *Philippines* Light soya sauce

trace elements Mineral elements, usually metals in various chemical forms, which are needed by the body for optimum health in quantities of less than 50 mg per day. Those currently identified as necessary are, in alphabetical order, chromium, cobalt, copper, fluorine, iodine, iron, manganese, molybdenum, nickel, selenium, silicon, vanadium and zinc. Other minerals required in greater daily quantities and not classed as trace elements are calcium, chlorine, magnesium, phosphorus, potassium and sodium.

tragacanth See **gum tragacanth**

Tragopogon porrifolius *Botanical name* The salsify plant

trail 1. The name given to the entrails of birds and fish which are cooked with the item and considered a delicacy, especially the heart and liver of a woodcock served with the roast bird **2.** The long somewhat ragged piece of muscle which runs the length of fillet steak as it is cut in the UK. Usually removed from the muscle before slicing it into tournedos, filet mignon and chateaubriand steaks. **3.** A stage in the whipping of cream when the cream poured from a spoon onto the whipped cream leaves a distinct trail which persists for several seconds

traiteur *France* An establishment which prepares and sells food for consumption off the premises, both in a shop and as an outside caterer. See also **chef traiteur**

tranche *France* Slice or rasher

tranche de boeuf *France* A beef steak. Also called **bifteck**

tranche grasse *France* Silverside, of beef

tranchelard *France* A long thin carving knife

tranche napolitaine *France* Multiflavoured and layered ice cream

tranche plombières *France* A slice of tutti frutti ice cream

trancher *France* To slice

trancia *Italy* Slice

transmontana, à *Portugal* In the style of Tràs-os-Montes, i.e. with chopped sausage, beans, garlic and onions

transparent icing A very thin icing used to give a professional finish to royal icing after it has been sanded or scraped down until quite smooth

transparent noodles Cellophane noodles

transparent vermicelli Cellophane noodles

Trapa bicornis *Botanical name* Water caltrop

Trapa bispinosa *Botanical name* Singhara nut

Trapa natans *Botanical name* Caltrops

Trappiste *France* A semi-hard cows' milk cheese closely associated with the Trappist monks and made in most countries where they had monasteries. It resembles **Port-Salut** with a smooth close-textured paste containing a few holes covered with a soft rind. Usually cast in 3 kg discs. Contains about 45% water, 25% fat and 22% protein. Also called **Trappisten**

Trappiste de Chambarand *France* A small, creamy, delicately flavoured cheese made by Trappist monks. See also **Chambarand**

Trappiste de Tamié *France* A smooth round cows' milk cheese from Annecy. See also **Tamié**

Trappiste d'Oelenberg *France* A mild-flavoured, cows' milk cheese from Oelenberg monastery. See also **Oelenberg**

Trappisten *Austria, Germany* Trappiste

trasi, trassi *Indonesia, Malaysia* Terasi

trattoria *Italy* A family-run style of restaurant

Traube *Germany* Grape

travailler *France* To work, in the sense of beating or blending

tray service Service where the complete meal is assembled on a tray and taken or given to the consumer, as in hospitals or prisons

treacle The non-crystallizeable impurities in sugar cane juice which remain in liquid form after processing to separate the pure sucrose. It is thick, black, sticky and sweet with a distinctive flavour and used in cakes, tarts and toffees. The similar substance from sugar beet juice is too bitter for human consumption. See also **black treacle**

treacle pudding *United Kingdom* A pudding made from basic steamed pudding mixture poured into a greased basin whose base is covered with treacle or golden syrup, before steaming or baking

treacle tart An open tart made from shortcrust pastry with a filling of golden syrup (not black treacle) and breadcrumbs flavoured with grated lemon zest and mixed spice and covered with a lattice of pastry strips before baking

Trebizond nuts Turkish hazelnuts

Trecce di bufala *Italy* A Mozzarella cheese made with pure buffalo milk. See also **Mozzarella di bufala**

tree ear Cloud ear fungus

tree fungus Cloud ear fungus

tree onion Egyptian onion

tree oyster mushroom See **oyster mushroom**

tree potato Sapodilla

tree tomato Tamarillo

trefoil *United States* Mitsuba

trelleborgsgryta *Sweden* Herring and tomato stew made from rolled herring fillets packed lightly in a greased dish covered with salted water with lemon juice, parboiled small onions and peeled sliced tomatoes placed on top and the whole sprinkled with chopped dill, parsley and ground pepper and small pieces of butter. Simmered for 20 minutes.

trelough duck A modern breed of duck similar to the Gressingham

tremadode See **fluke**

tremella White fungus

Tremella fuciformis *Botanical name* White fungus

trencher 1. A squared up plate made from coarse wholemeal bread four days old, 60 to 75 mm thick, used in medieval times to hold food. Lower classes of person known as trenchermen also ate the trencher. Upper classes didn't. **2.** A wooden serving dish

trencherman A hearty eater and drinker

trenette A small noodle from Genoa similar to tagliatelle and usually eaten with a pesto sauce

Trenton cracker *United States* A light, round, puffy cracker

trepang Sea cucumber

Tresterbrantwein *Germany* The German equivalent of **marc** or **grappa**

trey andeg *Cambodia* Catfish

trey pek chhieu *China* Pomfret, the fish

trey reach *Cambodia* A very large fish caught in the Mekong river. See also **pa boeuk**

triabolin A protein found only on the starch granules of soft wheats and which may be responsible for reducing the adhesion between them

triacetin See **glycerol tri-acetate**

triammonium citrate See **E380**

trianon *France* A garnish of 3 colours

trichinosis A disease of humans caused by eating fresh pork infested with the eggs or cysts of a parasitic worm, *Tricinella spiralis*, which can also reproduce in the human body. It is for this reason that pork is always well cooked and never eaten raw. Curing and smoking raw meat kills any infestation so that hams, bacon, salamis and smoked pork sausages are safe. They are also killed at 75°C and at –15°C for 3 weeks.

Tricholoma gambosum *Botanical name* Saint George's mushroom

Tricholoma matsutake *Botanical name* Matsutake

Tricholoma nuda *Botanical name* Wood blewit

Tricholoma saevum *Botanical name* Blewit

Trichosanthes anguina *Botanical name* Snake gourd

Trichosanthes cucumerina *Botanical name* Snake gourd

Trichosanthes dioica *Botanical name* The tindoori plant

trid *North Africa* A chicken stew with ribbons of warkha pastry

trifle *United Kingdom* A cold dessert made with sherry, fruit juice or liqueur-soaked sponge cake in the base of a large or individual dish, covered with layers of fruit, jelly, custard and whipped cream in various combinations and usually elaborately decorated

trifle sponge Fatless sponge cake or plain Madeira cake used as a base for English trifles

trifolato *Italy* Thinly sliced and sautéed in oil with garlic and parsley and possibly mushrooms and lemon

trifoliate orange Poncirus

triglia *Italy* Red mullet

triglia di fango *Italy* Plain red mullet, *Mullus barbatus*

triglia di scoglio *Italy* Striped red mullet, *Mullus surmuletus*

triglyceride The medical term for fats and oils containing three fatty acid molecules esterified with a glycerol molecule. Often measured in blood analysis.

trigo *Mexico, Spain* Wheat

trigo negro *Spain* Buckwheat

Trigonella foenum-graecum *Botanical name* Fenugreek

trim, to 1. To removed unwanted bits such as fat, gristle, tendons, blood vessels, feet, etc. from meat or poultry or fins from fish **2.** To cut to a pleasing shape

trimmings 1. The discarded parts resulting from trimming food, e.g. small pieces of pastry, bread crusts and the like **2.** Traditional garnishes and accompaniments to a dish as in the phrase 'steak and all the trimmings'

tripa *Portugal* Tripe

tripa a la catalana *Catalonia* Tripe in an onion, garlic, tomatoes and sweet pepper sauce with pine nuts and almonds

tripailles *France* Guts or innards, sometimes tripe

tripe *England, France* The stomach lining of animals, usually cattle (first 3 stomachs), which are cleaned, and in the UK, bleached and parboiled before sale. Various types are available depending on the animal and which stomach it comes from. Normally boiled in salted water until tender then stewed, braised or fried or in the north of England, served cold with vinegar. See also **blanket tripe, honeycomb tripe, thick seam tripe**

tripe and onions *United Kingdom* Pieces of prepared tripe simmered with onions in seasoned and flavoured milk, thickened with flour and simmered a further 10 minutes

tripes à la mode de Caen *France* Pieces of prepared tripe simmered or casseroled until tender with calf's foot, belly pork, carrots, onions, garlic cloves and a bouquet garni in either cider and calvados or dry white wine. The casserole may be covered with thin strips of bacon and thickened if necessary with corn flour.

tripes à l'Djotte *Belgium* A traditional Christmas season sausage made from equal parts of chopped borecole sweated in fat, scallops (from lard making) and finely chopped raw pork, mixed with chopped onion and seasoning, flavoured with grated nutmeg and whole cloves and packed into fat ends prior to tying and cooking

tripoux *France* A dish of sheep's trotters and veal tripe flavoured with herbs and cloves

trippa *Italy* Tripe

trippa alla fiorentina *Italy* Thinly sliced tripe casseroled with meat, tomatoes and stock and served with white beans and grated cheese

trippa alla romana *Italy* Tripe with a cheese sauce

tritato *Italy* Finely chopped or minced

tritello d'avena *Italy* Oat grits, coarse oatmeal

triticale A cross between wheat and rye with a higher protein content than wheat. Not in common use because of poor agricultural yields.

Triticum aestivum *Botanical name* Common wheat

Triticum durum *Botanical name* Durum wheat

Triticum monococcum *Botanical name* Einkorn

Triticum spelta *Botanical name* Spelt

trivet A small metal stand on which hot dishes are kept off the table surface or on which delicate food items may be held in a pan so that they can be removed without damage

Trockenmilch *Germany* Dried milk

Troldkrabbe *Germany* Spider crab

trollod *Wales* Dumplings made from oatmeal and the fat skimmed off the top of stock, cooked in broth when potatoes were scarce in the spring

tron *Vietnam* 1. To mix 2. Mixed

Tronchón A semi-hard, firm cheese made with goats' and/or ewes' milk. See also **Aragón**

tronçon *England, France* A slice of fish at right angles to the backbone of a large flatfish and including the bone. See also **fish steak**

tronçonner *France* To cut into steaks

Tropaeolum majus *Botanical name* Nasturtium

Tropaeolum tuberosum *Botanical name* Ysaño

trosc bake *Ireland* A fish bake made with cod chunks, sliced parboiled potatoes, brunoise onions and sliced mushrooms in a tomato sauce, topped with sliced potatoes and baked in the oven for about 25 minutes

trota *Italy* Trout

trota di torrente *Italy* Brown trout

trota iridea *Italy* Rainbow trout

trota salmonata *Italy* Salmon trout

trotters See **pig's trotters**, **calf's foot**

Trou de Sottai *Belgium* A soft buttery cows' milk cheese made in cylinders (up to 400 g) with a smooth paste and yellow rind

trousser *France* To truss

trout A round, oily fish, *Salmo trutta*, of the salmon family which is found in both fresh and salt water in a variety of forms varying from a few hundred grams to 35 kg (the American lake trout). The flesh is cream to pink depending on diet and the fish may be cooked in any way although they are generally shallow-fried or grilled in Europe. Nowadays extensively farmed as well as being an important game fish.

trout caviar Cured trout eggs which are orange in colour and similar to sturgeon caviar in taste and texture

Troyes *France* Barberey

trucha *Spain* Brown trout

truckle *England* The name of a smaller version of farmhouse Cheddar to 7 kg

truelle à poisson *France* Fish slice for cutting and serving fish

trufas *Portugal, Spain* Truffles

truffade *France* A dish from the Auvergne of potatoes fried with bacon, garlic and cheese

truffe *France* 1. Truffle 2. Chocolate truffle

truffé(e) *France* Garnished with truffle

Trüffel *Germany* Truffle

Trüffel Leberwurst *Germany* A liver sausage flavoured with truffles

truffiat *France* A potato cake from the Loire

truffle 1. A fungus whose fruiting body grows underground as an irregular roundish mass without a distinct stalk. They are always associated with the roots of trees and may have a symbiotic relationship with the tree. The two most highly prized are the **French black** and the **Italian white**. See also **English truffle**, **Chinese truffle** 2. A round soft chocolate-based sweet or confection usually rolled in grated chocolate, cocoa powder or chopped nuts or dipped in chocolate couverture and served with a selection of small cakes or as an after dinner sweet with coffee

truffle butter A compound butter made from diced black truffles with a little **béchamel sauce**, pounded with twice their weight of butter and sieved

truita *Catalonia* Omelette used for tapas

truita espanola *Catalonia* Spanish omelette

truite *France* Trout

truite à la hussarde *France* Trout slit open sideways and stuffed with aubergine

truite arc-en-ciel *France* Rainbow trout

truite de mer *France* Sea trout, salmon trout

truite de rivière *France* River trout

truite saumonée *France* Salmon trout

trumpeter Agami

trumpet gourd Bottle gourd

trung den *China* Chinese preserved egg

trunza di fera *Italy* Red cabbage stewed in oil with vinegar, capers and olives

truss, to To tie or skewer into shape before cooking. Usually applied to poultry, game birds or boned joints of meat.

truta *Portugal* Trout

Truthahn *Germany* Male turkey

Truthenne *Germany* Female turkey

trypsin One of the proteases in the human digestive system which is made in the pancreas. Seeds of some legumes contain trypsin inhibitors which prevent its digestive action.

tsarine, à la *France* In the Tsarina's style, i.e. used of chicken breasts garnished with cucumber cooked in butter and mixed with cream

tsatsiki *Greece* Finely chopped or grated, deseeded cucumber, salted and drained, washed, dried and mixed with yoghurt, chopped garlic and mint, seasoning and possibly oil and vinegar. Used as a dip or constituent of **mezze** and eaten with pitta bread. Also called **talattouri, tzajiki, zatziki, tzatsiki**

tseet gwa *China* Fuzzy melon

tseng dau gok *China* A dark green variety of long bean

tseng gwa *China* Cucumber

tseng loh baak *China* Green oriental radish

tsimmes 1. A thickened Jewish New Year dish of brisket of beef simmered with carrots, onions and potatoes, sweetened with sugar and honey. Also called **tzimmes 2.** The vegetables of tsimmes without the meat often supplied as the vegetable accompaniment to salt beef in a Jewish restaurant

tsim tau sha *China* Shark

tsing kaau *China* Mackerel

tso gwoo *China* Straw mushroom

tsubushi-an *Japan* A crunchy sweet red bean paste in which the beans are only partially crushed

tsukemono *Japan* Pickles, generally served at the end of a meal with rice to clean the palate. Pickling may be in salt or vinegar or in rice bran. See also **nuka-zuke, nukamiso-zuke**

tsukemono-oke *Japan* A large wooden or earthenware vessel used for the production of preserved vegetables

tsuki dashi *Japan* An appetizer, e.g. **aemono.** See also **sakizuke**

tsukune *Japan* Meat or fish balls made from the finely minced flesh bound together with egg

tsuma *Japan* The general name for a wide variety of attractively constructed garnishes of vegetable origin

ts'ung *China* Scallion

ts'ung tau *China* Shallots

tsu ts'ai *China* Nori

tsut sing paan *China* Garoupa, the fish

tua *Thailand* **1.** Bean **2.** Nut

tua ngak *Thailand* Bean sprouts

tua poo *Thailand* Goa bean

tubellini *Italy* Tubetti

tuber The fleshy swollen underground root or root tip of a plant used as a store of carbohydrate for the next generation of the plant which usually sprouts from the tuber. An important source of energy in human nutrition.

Tuber aestivum *Botanical name* English truffle

Tuber himalayense *Botanical name* Chinese truffle

Tuber magnatum *Botanical name* Italian white truffle

Tuber melanosporum *Botanical name* French black truffle

tubero edule *Italy* Arrowroot. Also called **maranta**

tubetti *Italy* Very small pasta tubes used in soup. Also called **tubellini, tubettini**

tubettini *Italy* Tubetti

tub fish See **tub gurnard**

tub gurnard A small round seawater fish, *Trigla lucerna*, with a medium brown skin and two characteristic gill whiskers on either side. Similar to the gurnard. Also called **tub fish**

tuchowska *Poland* A regional sausage

tucker *Australia* Food, usually informally presented (*colloquial*)

tuck shop A shop, usually in a school, which sells snacks to the pupils

tuiles *France* Thin sweet biscuits sometimes covered in almond flakes slightly rounded when still hot to resemble continental tiles

tule potato Arrowhead

tulingan *Philippines* Tuna, bonito

tulipe *France* A circular brandy snap type of biscuit, draped when hot over a cup to cool so as to make an edible bowl in which fruit or desserts might be served

tulsi *South Asia* Hairy or purple basil seeds

tumbada *Italy* A baked almond custard from Sardinia. See also **timballa e'latte**

tumbet *Spain* A vegetarian dish made from alternate layers of sliced potatoes and salted, drained, washed and dried aubergines brushed with oil and browned on both sides, the layers separated by thinly sliced sweet peppers fried in olive oil and a tomato sauce made from finely chopped onions sweated in olive oil to a golden brown, combined with oregano and tomatoes and simmered to a purée. The whole built up in an ovenproof dish and baked at 180°C until cooked through.

tumbler A flat bottomed tall cylindrical drinking glass

tummelberry A hybrid blackberry of the genus *Rubus*

tumpaeng *Cambodia* Bamboo shoot

tuna A large round fish of the genus *Thunnus*, especially *Thunnus thynnus*, weighing up to 600 kg and coming in various forms. The flesh looks almost like beef; some is light and lean and some dark and oily. Baked or grilled when fresh but most consumption in Europe is in canned form. See also **bluefin tuna,**

yellow fin tuna, skipjack tuna, albacore. Also called **tunny**

tuna fig Prickly pear

Tunbridge Wells sausage *England* An English sausage from the town of the same name made to a 100 year old recipe comprising coarsely chopped lean pork, chopped pork fat and yeastless bread rusk (10:5:2), seasoned, flavoured with sage, mace and other herbs, filled into casings and linked

tunfisk *Denmark, Norway* Tuna fish

tunga *Sweden* Tongue

tunge *Denmark, Norway* Tongue

tung sum Bamboo shoots

tung ts'ao *China* Rice paper

Tunisian sweet limetta A small North African lime, *Citrus limetta*, only of local importance. Also called **Mediterranean sweet limetta, Mediterranean sweet lime**

Tunke *Germany* Sauce or gravy

tunny See **tuna**

tuong *Vietnam* A very strong-tasting fermented sauce probably including soya sauce and fermented fish. Also called **Vietnamese soya sauce**

tuong ngot *Vietnam* Hoisin sauce

tuong ot *Vietnam* Yellow bean sauce

tuoni e lampo *Italy* Bits of cooked pasta mixed with cooked chick peas (NOTE: Literally 'thunder and lightning'.)

tuorlo d'uovo *Italy* Egg yolk

tupí *Spain* A spread or flavouring made from finely grated old cheese blended with oil and wine or brandy and left to mature in jars for 2 to 3 months

tur *South Asia* Pigeon pea

turban *France* A ring mould or a method of presenting food in a circle on the plate usually by using a ring mould

turban gourd A type of gourd

turban of cod *England* A large cod fillet, seasoned and brushed with lemon juice, coiled into a turban shape and secured, then placed in a shallow dish and baked at 180°C for 20 to 25 minutes until done. The fish is put on a serving plate and the centre filled with a little **béchamel sauce** which has been flavoured with lemon juice and any fish juices and mixed with chopped hard-boiled eggs. Additional sauce is served separately and the turban is garnished with lemon slices and parsley.

turban squash Turk's cap squash

turbante *Italy* A ring mould of food, e.g. rice, presented in a demoulded ring with a filling in the centre

turbinado sugar *United States* A coarse grained partially refined sugar which is light beige in colour and contains a little adhering molasses

turbot 1. *England, France* A diamond-shaped flatfish, *Psetta maxima*, up to 1 m in length and 15 kg with a spotted sandy back covered in small bumps. Found in the North Atlantic, the Mediterranean and the Black Sea. The fine white flesh is firm and medium oily and can be cooked in any way. The head and bones are a rich source of gelatine and make excellent stock. The turbot found in the East Atlantic is a different species, *Scophthalmus maximus*, but otherwise is similar. **2.** *Canada* See **Greenland halibut**

turbotière *France* A large fish kettle for poaching whole turbot and similar large fish

turbotin A small turbot weighing 1 to 2 kg

turcarri *South Asia* A type of curry. See also **turrcarri**

tureen A large dish with a lid and ladle from which soup is served at the table

turian *Thailand* Durian

turkey A large (up to 15 kg) flightless bird, *Meleagris galopavo*, native to North America but now farmed worldwide for its high-yielding flesh. Popular in the UK at Christmas and in the USA at Thanksgiving but now available throughout the year as one of the cheapest forms of animal protein. Cooked like chicken.

turkey baster *England* Bulb baster

turkey cock A male turkey

turkey roll Boned and cooked turkey meat formed in a tight roll and encased in plastic, sold for slicing

Turkish delight A confection made from sugar boiled with water to the large thread (107°C) stage and thickened with corn flour, lemon juice and gum arabic, cooled until thick, flavoured with rose water and poured into a flat cake moulds which have been liberally dusted with icing sugar or chopped pistachio nuts. When set cut into cubes and rolled and stored in icing sugar.

Turkish hazelnut A smaller and cheaper hazel type of nut, *Corylus colurna*, than hazelnuts or filberts. Also called **Messina cob, Trebizond nut**

Turkish pilaf See **iç pilav**

Turk's cap gourd A type of gourd

Turk's cap squash A decorative thick-skinned winter squash, *Cucurbita maxima*, with a flattened circular base surmounted by a smaller grooved top resembling a turban. It has a firm, slightly sweet orange yellow flesh with a green and white streaked orange skin.

Boiled or baked as a vegetable. Also called **turban squash**

türlü *Turkey* A mixed vegetable stew including a selection from onions, sweet peppers, tomatoes, green beans, courgettes, aubergines, okra, squash, chillies and the like

turmeric The boiled and skinned root of a perennial plant, *Curcuma longa*, which is dried and ground. It originated in India but is now also grown in East Asia and South America. It has a slightly aromatic peppery and musky taste and imparts a deep yellow colour to food. Used in Indian and Asian cooking and as a colouring agent in the west.

Turmerikwurzel *Germany* Turmeric

turn, to 1. To become sour or start to ferment usually by adventitious microorganisms **2.** To rotate some item of food so as to promote even cooking or browning of the surface **3.** To shape solid root vegetables in a barrel or rugby ball shape, or button mushrooms with a series of swirling radial V-shaped cuts. Used to present an attractive appearance.

turn, to cook to a To cook a food so that it is correctly cooked to the degree expected by the consumer

turnedo *Italy* Fillet of beef

turning knife A small pointed knife with a concave-shaped cutting edge used for turning vegetables

turnip 1. A temperate climate biennial plant, *Brassica rapa* (Rapifera Group), grown as an annual for the swollen underground roots which are 2.5 to 7 cm in diameter and round, flat or long and tapering. The hard flesh is white or yellow and the skin white, pink, red or yellow. Young turnips may be eaten raw or pickled, the mature ones are used as a root vegetable. The young leaves are known as turnip tops. **2.** *Scotland, United States* Swede

turnip greens The green leaves from the top of turnips used as a vegetable

turnip rape Broccoli raab

turnip rooted parsley Hamburg parsley

turnip soup Basic soup with turnips. Also called **navets, purée de**

turnip tops The young leaves and flower heads of the turnip plant, *Brassica rapa* Rapifera Group, eaten as spring greens or raw in salads

turnover A circular or square piece of pastry folded over into a sealed half circle or triangle and containing a sweet or savoury filling. See also **apple turnover, jam turnover, Cornish pasty**

turntable 1. A rotating circular platform on a stand onto which a cake may be placed to assist in its icing and decoration **2.** A rotating circular platform on the base of a microwave oven on which the dish of food being cooked is placed to ensure even penetration of microwaves

turrcarri *South Asia* A style of curry making with meat simmered in excess of water (at least 5 cm over the top of the meat) until the meat falls apart. See also **mhaans turcarri khasta, mhaans turcarri sadah, gurdakupura turcarri**

turrcarri molee *South Asia* A meat curry with coconut. The meat is cut in strips, simmered in coconut milk with chopped ginger, coriander, garlic and sliced onion for 45 minutes. The solids are strained and fried in ghee, adding ground fenugreek and poppy seed until all dry and golden. The liquid, plus more coconut milk if required, is added back, and all simmered with lemon or lime leaves until tender. The leaves are removed and lime juice and seasoning added before serving.

turrón *Spain* Praline or a sweetmeat made with almonds resembling halva or sometimes nougat

turtle The aquatic version, *Chelonia mydas*, of the tortoise found worldwide in warm seas. Most varieties have edible flesh. The green turtle was once famed as the basis of turtle soup but has now been hunted almost to extinction. Turtles have long been exploited in Southeast Asia for their meat and as medicine. Turtle eggs are considered an aphrodisiac, the blood is believed to increase a person's energy and the ground-up shells are considered to have medicinal properties. To prepare and cook, decapitate the live turtle, drain the blood, blanch for 3 minutes, scrape off the skin, cut the body from the shell, disembowel, rinse and cut the meat into strips.

turtle herbs A blend of basil, sage, thyme, coriander leaves, marjoram, rosemary, bay leaf and peppercorns used to flavour turtle soup

turtle soup 1. Basic consommé simmered with turtle herbs in muslin for 10 minutes, thickened with arrowroot, seasoned, strained and finished with dry sherry and cooked and diced reconstituted turtle meat. Served with cheese straws and lemon wedges. Also called **tortue claire 2.** Genuine turtle soup for the London Lord Mayor's banquet was made from 80 kg of cleaned female turtles simmered with their shell for 2 days in 450 litres of veal stock flavoured with thyme, marjoram, basil, parsley, 9 litres of sherry and 4.5 litres of sweet white wine, settled, clarified, reduced to 225 litres and finished with sherry and diced gelatinous turtle meat

tuscarora rice Wild rice

tusk A North Atlantic fish, *Bromse bromse*, which resembles hake but is of the cod family. It has lean white flesh and may be cooked in any way. Often substituted for cod in Scandinavian cooking.

tusli *South Asia* Basil

tussa jute *Middle East* A plant related to okra. See also **meloukhia**

Tussilago farfara *Botanical name* Coltsfoot

tutti frutti *England, Italy* Ice cream containing chopped dried or glacé fruits

tuvaram *South Asia* Pigeon pea

tuware Pigeon pea

tu ya ts'ai *China* Bean sprouts

tuyo *Philippines* Small fish, salted and dried then fried or grilled. Served with sliced tomatoes.

tuz *Turkey* Salt

Tvarvsky *Czech Republic* A strong cows' milk cheese similar to **Handkäse**

Tvorog *Russia* Twarog

tvorozhinka *Russia* Cheese dumplings

tvorozhniki *Russia* Thin patties made from sieved curd cheese, flour and egg (9:1:1) with a little sugar, salt, vanilla essence and lemon zest, chilled and rested, floured then fried, with some difficulty, in butter until brown on each side. Served at breakfast.

TVP See **textured vegetable protein**

twaalfuurtje *Netherlands* Lunch

twaite shad See **shad**

Twaróg *Poland* A soft acid curdled cows' milk cheese without rind eaten young. Contains approximately 70% water, 10% fat and 20% protein. Also called **Tvorog**

Tweed kettle *Scotland* Originally a dish of the poor made with boned and skinned salmon cut in small pieces and poached for 4 to 5 minutes in strained stock made with the skin, bones and head of the salmon, together with an equal quantity of white wine plus a few chopped shallots, mace and parsley or dill. Chopped mushrooms fried in butter to prevent them floating are added and the fish stew may be served either hot with mashed potatoes or cold with salad.

Twelfth night cake A rich fruit cake sweetened with brown sugar and black treacle and flavoured with cinnamon and mixed spice eaten on the twelfth night after Christmas. Traditionally some silver charms are baked in it.

twisted cluster bean Parkia

twists napolitani *United States* Gemelli pasta

txangurro al horno A dish of baked spider crabs with tomato, chilli and brandy from the Basque country of northern Spain

Tybo *Denmark* A hard scalded-curd cows' milk cheese with a supple paste containing a few scattered holes and a thin yellow rind cast in bricks (up to 4 kg). Similar to Samsø.

tykmælk *Denmark* Junket dessert

tykvennyi sup z pryanostiami *Southwest Asia* An Armenian soup made from sweated pumpkin flesh, chopped leeks, carrots and currants, puréed with chicken stock and milk flavoured with allspice and simmered until cooked. Finished with yoghurt and dry-roasted pumpkin seeds.

Tyroler Alpenkäse *Austria, Switzerland* A hard cooked-curd cows' milk cheese made in large wheels to 14 kg. It is ripened for 3 months and the paste is mild and slightly sweet and contains a few large holes.

Tyroler Graukäse *Austria, Switzerland* A soft surface-ripened cooked-curd cows' milk cheese curdled with a lactic ferment. It is formed into discs and ripened for 10 to 20 days at high temperatures and humidity.

tyrolienne, à la *France* In the Tyrolean style, i.e. garnished with tomatoes and fried onions

tyrolienne, sauce *England, France* Finely chopped shallots cooked with colour in oil, **tomato concassée** added and cooked until dry, all passed through a fine sieve, cooled and mixed with mayonnaise, chopped parsley, chervil and tarragon. Served with fried fish and cold meats.

tyrolienne à l'ancienne, sauce *France* Finely chopped onion sweated in butter mixed with an equal weight of **tomato concassée** and twice its weight of sauce poivrade and all simmered until cooked

tyttebær *Denmark* Lingonberry

tzatsiki, tzatziki *Greece* A dip based on finely chopped or grated, deseeded cucumber. See also **tsatsiki**

tzimmes See **tsimmes**

U VWXYZA

● ●

ube *Philippines* Yam

ubi *Philippines* Yam

ubi jalar *Indonesia* Sweet potato

ubi manis *Indonesia* Sweet potato

ubod *Philippines* The central pith of trunks of the coconut and other palms. Eaten raw or cooked as a vegetable or salad ingredient.

ubre *Spain* Udder

ubriaco *Italy* Drunk, i.e. cooked in wine

uccelletti *Italy* Small birds

uccelletti alla maremmano *Italy* Small birds, browned in oil then cooked in a vinegar and tomato sauce with anchovies, olives and garlic

uccelletti scappati *Italy* Paupiettes of veal with bacon cooked on a skewer

uccelli *Indonesia* Birds

ucche Kantola

uchepos *Mexico* Fresh corn tamales from Michoácan

udang *Indonesia, Malaysia* **1.** Shrimp **2.** Prawn

udang kering *Indonesia, Malaysia* Dried shrimp

udder The fatty white meat of the mammary glands of milking animals such as cows, sheep and goats which is cooked and sliced. Once popular but now rarely available. Occasionally used as a pasta stuffing. Also called **elder**

udo *Japan* A stalk vegetable with a flavour similar to fennel used raw or blanched and sliced in salads

udon *Japan* A wheat flour noodle from the south of Japan. It is thicker than the soba noodle, is either round or flat and is usually served in soup.

udovolstvie testia *Russia* A highly decorated pickled herring salad where the herring is deboned and skinned and rearranged in a herring shape on a dish. It is then surrounded with chopped vegetables in a vinaigrette sauce thickened with hard-boiled egg yolk, and decorated with slices of hard-boiled eggs, beetroot and chopped spring onions.

Uferschnecke *Germany* Winkle

ugali *East Africa* The Kenyan name for finely ground corn or maize meal porridge generally made with twice its volume of water, sometimes with milk. The yellow variety is considered inferior to the white but is more nutritious.

ugli fruit A naturally occurring hybrid of the grapefruit and mandarin found growing wild in Jamaica in 1914. It has a very rough, uneven and thick peel usually with blemishes. The orange flesh has a soft texture and is very juicy. Usually eaten with a spoon like a grapefruit.

ugnsångad fisk *Sweden* Oven-steamed fish. Cleaned whole fish put in an oven-proof dish which has been rinsed out with water and cooked in the oven at 95°C for between 1 and 4 hours. No other treatment is necessary.

ugnspannkaka *Sweden* A thick pancake baked in the oven

ugnstekt *Sweden* Oven-baked

ugnstekt blomkål med tomat *Sweden* Parboiled cauliflower surrounded with halved tomatoes in a buttered dish, gratinated with cheese and butter and baked in a hot oven until browned

UHT See **ultra-heat treated**

uien *Netherlands* Onions

uitsmijter *Netherlands* An open sandwich with a slice of ham or roast beef topped with two fried eggs and garnished with lettuce, tomato and sliced gherkin, eaten as a snack

ukad *South Asia* Unpolished rice, slightly dusty with a reddish colour and thick grain

ukasi *West Africa* The leaves of a forest plant eaten as a vegetable. See also **afang**

ukha *Russia* A light fish consommé made from enriched fish stock (800 g of white fish bones and trimmings per litre) resimmered with onions, carrots, parsley, bay leaf, cloves, and finely chopped dill before clarifying and straining. A little dry white wine may be added. Often served with **katushki**.

ukoy *Philippines* A fritter of peeled shrimps mixed with chopped spring onions, in a rice or wheat flour batter. Fried and served with vinegar and minced garlic.

Ukraine eggs *Eastern Europe* Very intricately decorated hard-boiled eggs. A peasant art form in the Ukraine dating back to 1000 BC at least.

uleg-uleg *Indonesia* A ceramic pestle that goes with a matching mortar (**cobek**)

ulekan *Indonesia* A small deep granite or other hard rock mortar and pestle

uliva *Italy* Olive

Ulloa *Spain* A semi-hard cows' milk cheese similar to **Tetilla** cast in 1 kg discs

ulluco The pink or yellow tubers of a half hardy perennial yam, *Ullucus tuberosus*, from South America. It can be grown in the UK.

Ullucus tuberosus *Botanical name* Ulluco

Ulster roll *Ireland* A boned bacon joint from Northern Ireland which is cured, dry-salted, soaked in water then dried and smoked. Also called **spencer**

ultracongelado *Spain* Deep-frozen

ultra-heat treated (A liquid) which has been rapidly heated to 132°C, held at this temperature for 1 to 2 seconds (up to 6 minutes for some products), then rapidly cooled, generally in a stainless steel plate heat exchanger through which the liquid flows as a very thin film. This treatment sterilizes the liquid without too much change in its flavour. However the process does not necessarily destroy enzymes which may induce rancidity after several months. Also called **UHT, long life, extended life**

uluhaal *Sri Lanka* Fenugreek

ulutham *South Asia* Black gram

ulva Sea laver

Ulzama *Spain* A semi-hard ewes' milk cheese from Navarra made in cylinders to 2 kg. The white dense paste has a strong flavour and a few holes and is covered in a brown rind.

umani *Japan* Vegetables simmered in **dashi** flavoured with soya sauce, **mirin**, sugar and salt, added to the broth in order of cooking times. Garnished with very fine strands of mooli.

umble pie Humble pie

umbles The edible entrails of deer or other game animals

umbra *Spain* Arctic char

umbra, all' *Italy* In the style of Umbria, i.e. with an anchovy, tomato and truffle sauce

umbrella mushroom Parasol mushroom

ume *Japan* Plum

umeboshi *Japan* Dried plums which are them pickled

umeboshi plum A Japanese apricot, coloured with red **shiso** leaves and pickled in salt. It has a tart salty flavour and is served at the end of a meal as a digestive and is also used in cooking. It may be puréed for use as the souring agent bainiku.

ume shiso zuke *Japan* Tiny pickled plums with **shiso**

umido *Italy* Stew

umido, in *Italy* 1. Braised 2. Stewed.

umngqusho *South Africa* Samp and dry cowpeas or similar (2:1) soaked in water overnight, drained then simmered on a low heat for 1 to 2 hours until all the water is absorbed, adding water as required. Seasoned and served hot. (NOTE: Said to be Nelson Mandela's favourite dish.)

unagi *Japan* Freshwater eel

unbleached flour Flour which has not been treated with a bleaching agent to whiten the colour

unchun *Thailand* A natural blue colour obtained from the petals of a local plant. Often used to colour jicama and water chestnuts for dessert use.

uncooked curd Curd for cheese making which has not been heated to more than 40°C

Undaria pinnatifida *Botanical name* Wakame

undercushion of veal *United Kingdom* The thick longitudinal muscle at the rear outside of a leg of veal equivalent to silverside of beef with the same uses as cushion of veal. Also called **undernut of veal**

underdone Still red or pink in the centre of the meat after cooking. Also called **rare**

undernut of veal *United Kingdom* Undercushion of veal

Ungarische Art *Germany* In the Hungarian style, i.e. with paprika

ung choi *China* Swamp cabbage

ung choy Swamp cabbage

uni *Japan* Sea urchin, often presented in a nori basket as sushi

univalve Gastropod

unleavened Without any natural or chemical raising agent

unleavened bread Bread made from flour, water and salt without using a raising agent or incorporating air

unna coffee *East Africa* The traditional coffee of Ethiopia which is roasted, ground and brewed at the table

unpolished rice Rice from which the bran and most of the germ has been removed. See also **brown rice**

unsaturated fat See **polyunsaturated**

unshu-mikan *Japan* Satsuma

unsweetened chocolate Chocolate containing no sugar, used for baking

uova alla Bela Rosin *Italy* Egg mayonnaise

uova con pancetta *Italy* Bacon and eggs

uova di bufala *Italy* Mozzarella di bufala

uova di pesce *Italy* Hard fish roe

uova strapazzate *Italy* Scrambled eggs

uovo *Italy* Egg

uovo affogato *Italy* Poached egg

uovo al burro *Italy* Fried egg

uovo al tegamino *Italy* Shirred egg

uovo bazzotto *Italy* Lightly boiled (3 minutes) egg

uovo di mare *Italy* See **violet 2**

uovo molle *Italy* Soft-boiled egg

uovo sodo *Italy* Hard-boiled egg

upotettu muna *Finland* Poached egg

upshwa *South Africa* A maize or cassava-based staple porridge from Mozambique. See also **xima**

upside down cake A cake baked in a tin with a decorative layer of fruit on the bottom so that when it is turned out the fruit will be on top

upside down pudding A Victoria sponge pudding made in the same way as upside down cake

urad dal *South Asia* Black gram

urad dal chilke wali *South Asia* Split but unskinned black gram

urad dal dhuli *South Asia* Polished black gram

Urbasa, Urbia A smoked ewes' milk cheese from the Basque country. See also **Idiazabal**

urda A Balkan cheese similar to Ricotta

urd bean *South Asia* Black gram bean

urney pudding *Scotland* A variation of glister pudding using strawberry jam in place of the marmalade

Urtica dioica *Botanical name* Nettle

use-by-date Date mark used on packaged food which is intended to be consumed within 6 weeks. Under UK regulations this date may be changed by the manufacturer after the first date has expired.

usli ghee *South Asia* Ghee

uso di, all' *Italy* In the style of

usuage *Japan* Soya bean pouches. See also **abura-age**

usu-kuchi shoyu *Japan* A particularly light, clear and salty soya sauce

usu-zukuri *Japan* A diagonal cut of thin slices of firm fish fillets for use in sashimi

utaw *Philippines* Soya beans

uthappam *South Asia* A thicker variety of the South Indian dosa, with items such as vegetables, onions, chillies and coriander added to the batter before cooking rather than used as a stuffing afterwards

utility beef *United States* Commercial beef

uunipuuru *Finland* A baked barley or rice porridge

uunissa paistettu hauki *Finland* Baked stuffed pike

uva *Italy, Portugal, Spain* Grape

uva fragola *Italy* Strawberry grape

uva passa *Italy* Raisins and currants

uva secca *Italy* Raisins and currants

uva spina *Italy* Gooseberry

Uzbekistan walnut brittle *Southwest Asia* Light brown sugar and evaporated milk (3:1) flavoured with allspice, ginger and cinnamon, cooked to the soft ball stage (115°C) then mixed with halved walnuts and vanilla essence, cooled and broken up

uzhin 1. *Russia* Supper, a late evening meal varying in style from **zakuski** with unlimited vodka to a more Western three-course meal **2.** See **dill**

uzura no tamago *Japan* Quail egg

uzvar *Eastern Europe* A compote of dried fruits soaked in water overnight then boiled in water or apple juice with a little honey or sugar. It is often served with **kutya** in the Ukraine on Christmas Eve and on feasts of the dead.

V WXYZAB

va *Vietnam* And, used as a linking word in many Vietnamese dish descriptions. See also **Vietnamese names of dishes**

vaca *Portugal, Spain* Meat from old cows, rather tough

vaca cozida *Portugal* Boiled beef

vaca guisada *Portugal* Beef stew

Vaccinium ashei *Botanical name* Blueberry (rabbit eye blueberry)

Vaccinium corymbosum *Botanical name* Blueberry (highbush blueberry)

Vaccinium macrocarpum *Botanical name* Cranberry

Vaccinium vitis-idaea *Botanical name* Cowberry

Vachard *France* A strong-flavoured cows' milk cheese from the Massif Central similar to Saint Nectaire

vacherin *France* 1. Meringue formed in a large or small shell or disc filled with whipped cream, ice cream or fruited ice cream. Served as a dessert or cake. 2. A soft runny cheese from the Jura usually served with cream

Vacherin des Beauges *France* Soft cows' milk cheese cast in large flat discs to 2 kg and wrapped in a strip of spruce bark to give it a resinous flavour. The rind becomes soft and grey or brown after it is ripened in cool damp conditions.

Vacherin fribourgeoise *France* A smaller (up to 12 kg) soft version of Gruyère cheese with golden yellow paste and holes of varying shapes. It is started with a lactic culture, pressed, salted and surface-ripened in high humidity. Considered as a cheese for special occasions. Also called **Freiburger Vacherin**

Vacherin Mont d'Or *Switzerland* A winter cheese made from unpasteurized cows' milk which is sold in thin wooden boxes. The paste is very soft and runny and eaten with a spoon. The rind is rust-coloured.

Vacherol du Port-du-Salut de la Trappe *France* A semi-hard cows' milk cheese made in squat cylinders (up to 5 kg) and similar to Saint Paulin. The paste is yellow with a reddish rind.

vacuum drying A method of drying foods by subjecting them to a vacuum so that the water evaporates at ambient temperatures. May be used with frozen food.

vacuum flask See **thermos flask**

vacuum pack A long-life pack in which food is sealed under vacuum in polythene or other clear plastic pouches. Also known as sous-vide when the contents are cooked or partially cooked food or meals for use in restaurants.

vadelmat *Finland* Raspberries

våfflor *Sweden* Waffles

vafler *Norway* Waffles

vagem *Portugal* Green beans, runner or French. See also **feijão verde**

vainilla *Spain* Vanilla

vaktel *Sweden* Quail

val *South Asia* Hyacinth bean

Valais raclette *France* A semi-hard scalded-curd cows' milk cheese made in 6 to 7 kg wheels from full cream milk. The paste is pale and creamy and very suitable for melting as a **raclette**.

Valdeteja *Spain* A semi-hard goats' milk cheese shaped into long cylinders with a white paste containing a few holes. It is ripened for up to 15 days and the rind is rubbed with olive oil.

Val di Muggio *Switzerland* A cows' milk cheese with a delicate taste and smooth rind

Valençay *France* A pyramid-shaped soft goats' milk cheese from the Loire valley, matured for 4 to 5 weeks and coated in wood ash

valenciano *Mexico* A type of chilli pepper

Valencia orange The most well known of the common (sweet) oranges and probably the most important world orange. Its history can be traced back to the Portuguese but it was popularized by a British nurseryman who recognized its good qualities and shipped it around the world. It has medium to large fruits with a thin and leathery peel, about 2 to 4 seeds per fruit and an excellent flavour, though slightly acid if immature. The rind is often greenish especially if grown in tropical regions.

Valencia peanut A variety of peanut with an upright habit and up to four dark red seeds per pod

Valencia rice A Spanish rice similar to Carolina which swells and becomes tender without releasing starch. Ideal for paella.

valeriana cultivado *Spain* Lamb's lettuce

Valerianella locusta *Botanical name* Lamb's lettuce

valérianelle *France* Lamb's lettuce

valigini mantovani *Italy* Cabbage rolls filled with chicken and potato and cooked in tomato sauce in the usual way

välikyljys *Finland* Entrecôte of beef

valkokaalisalaatti *Finland* Cabbage salad, coleslaw

valnødkage *Denmark* Walnut cake

valnødromkager *Denmark* Walnut and rum-flavoured biscuit

valois, sauce *France* Foyot, sauce

valor *South Asia* Hyacinth bean

vanaspati *South Asia* Hydrogenated vegetable oil used as a butter substitute and for cooking

vand *Denmark* Water

vand melon *Denmark* Watermelon

vaniglia *Italy* Vanilla

vanigliato *Italy* Vanilla-flavoured

vanilje *Norway* Vanilla

vaniljglass *Sweden* Vanilla ice cream

vaniljsås *Sweden* English custard

vanilla The seed pod of a vine, *Vanilla planifolia*, which can grow up to a height of 15 m. The pods are picked when unripe and go through a complex curing process which leaves the best pods narrow, dark brown, supple and long, coated with white crystals of vanillin, but this frosting can be faked. The flavour is mellow and the aroma fragrant and unmistakeable. It is used to flavour desserts and chocolate. Synthetic vanillin is widely available and is used in most manufactured goods. It has a heavier odour and a disagreeable aftertaste.

vanilla bean See **vanilla pod**

vanilla essence An alcoholic extract of the vanilla pod used for flavouring

vanilla flavouring The name usually given to an aqueous solution of artificial vanilla made from the eugenol in clove oil

Vanilla planifolia *Botanical name* Vanilla

vanilla pod The fruit of the vanilla vine. Also called **vanilla bean**

vanilla sugar Sugar flavoured by being kept in contact with a vanilla pod in a closed jar. Used for flavouring other dishes.

vanille *France, Netherlands* Vanilla

Vanille *Germany* Vanilla

Vanille Rahmeis *Germany* Vanilla ice cream

vanillin One of the flavouring components of natural vanilla, now synthesized chemically and used in artificial vanilla flavourings

vann *Norway* Water

vanneau *France* Queen scallop

vannmelon *Norway* Watermelon

vanukas *Finland* Pudding

vapeur, (à la) *France* Steamed. Used especially of potatoes.

vapor, à *Portugal* Steamed

varak *South Asia* Silver leaf

varaq *South Asia* Silver leaf

varié(e) *France* Assorted, as in hors d'oeuvres variés, mixed hors d'oeuvres

variegated scallop A small variety of scallop, *Chlamys varia*, with a firmer and less white muscle than the queen or great scallop

variety meats *United States* Offal

varkenskarbonaden *Netherlands* Fried pork chops

varkenvlees *Netherlands* Pork

värmlandskorv *Sweden* A sausage made from equal parts of finely minced pork, finely minced beef and chopped raw potatoes all reminced with onion, seasoned, flavoured with allspice, moistened with ham stock, packed loosely into casings, linked, dry-salted for a day then cooked and refreshed

varmrätt *Sweden* A hot dish (of food)

vår-primör *Sweden* Smoked salmon served with creamed spinach and poached eggs as an early spring delicacy

varske *Russia* Cottage cheese

vårsoppa *Sweden* Spring vegetable soup based on beef stock with new carrots, cauliflower, asparagus, fresh peas and fresh spinach, chopped as appropriate, boiled in turn until tender and reserved;the stock thickened with a liaison of egg yolks and double cream and the vegetables added back together with chopped parsley and dill and sliced radish. Served hot.

varying hare See **Scottish hare**

vasikanliha *Finland* Veal

vasikanpaisti *Finland* Roast veal

vassoio *Italy* Tray or cheese board

Västerbottenost *Sweden* A hard scalded-curd cows' milk cheese made with a lactic

Västergota

starter followed by rennet. The scalded curds are pressed in moulds, salted and ripened for up to 8 months to give a strong-flavoured firm paste with small holes. Also called **Västergota**

Västergota See **Västerbottenost**

västkustsallad *Sweden* A mixed salad of prawns, lobster meat, cooked and shelled mussels, cooked peas and asparagus, sliced raw mushrooms and tomatoes dressed with a dill-flavoured vinaigrette. Served in individual dishes garnished with dill weed.

vat A large tub used for large-scale processing of cheese, pickles, etc. and for fermenting and ageing wine

vatrushki *Russia* Savoury tartlets made from an egg and sour cream enriched short pastry raised with baking powder and filled with an egg, cottage cheese, sugar, butter and lemon zest filling

vatrushki s tvorogom *Russia* Turnovers made with an unsweetened yeast-raised dough filled with a mixture of cottage cheese, butter, eggs and salt, egg-washed, proved and baked in a hot oven. Served with sour cream.

vatten *Sweden* Water

vattenmelon *Sweden* Watermelon

vaxbönor *Sweden* Wax beans

veado *Portugal* Deer

veal The meat of a young calf 6 to 14 weeks old. Rearing methods range from calves run with their mothers on grass which gives a good-textured, dark pink meat, to those which are removed from their mothers at birth, crated and fed with an iron-deficient reconstituted milk to give an anaemic animal with very pale flesh. This latter was once highly prized but is now gradually going out of fashion.

veal and calf grades Grades in the US are prime, choice, good, standard and utility, in descending order of quality

veal and ham pie *United Kingdom* A raised pie with a filling of diced ham, pork and veal, usually surrounding a hard-boiled egg

veal axoa A veal hash from the Basque country of France made with chopped onions and sweet red peppers fried in olive oil, diced veal added to the frying pan followed by **tomato concassée**, all cooked briskly for 5 minutes then simmered with dry white wine until tender

veal chops Chops cut from the loin of veal

veal cordon bleu An **escalope cordon bleu** made with veal

veal cuts *United States* Cuts of veal generally correspond to beef cuts but because of European, especially Italian influence, there

are many separate cuts such as neck slices, riblets, foreshanks, brisket pieces, etc. confined to particular localities

veal Oscar *United States* A veal cutlet, sautéed, garnished with asparagus tips and crayfish tails and accompanied with a **béarnaise sauce**

veal Parmigiana *United States* Veal chops panéed using breadcrumbs mixed with grated Parmesan cheese as the final coating, baked or fried and served with a tomato sauce

veau *France* 1. Calf 2. Veal

veau de mer *France* Porbeagle shark

veau sous la mère *France* Veal from calves which have been reared outdoors with their mothers until ready for slaughter

vecchia maniera, alla *Italy* In an old fashioned style

vecchio *Italy* Old. Used of cheese or other food items which might improve with age.

vedella *Catalonia* Veal

vegan A person who will not eat the meat or products derived from any animal or once living creature including eggs, milk, fish, etc. Honey is excluded by some

vegemite *Australia* Concentrated yeast extract similar to marmite (2)

vegetable carbon See **carbon black**

vegetable extract A dark brown paste made from hydrolysed vegetable protein and vegetable flavourings, possibly mixed with yeast extract. Used as a flavouring agent especially by vegetarians and vegans.

vegetable gelatine Agar-agar

vegetable marrow The large cylindrical green to yellow fruits of the genus *Curcubita*, known as summer squashes which are harvested in summer. Cooked whole or stuffed or their flesh made into jams or used as a vegetable. Very young vegetable marrows up to 15 cm in length are known as courgettes or zucchini.

vegetable oyster Salsify

vegetable pear Choko

vegetable peeler See **peeler**

vegetable soup A **mirepoix** of mixed vegetables sweated in butter, flour added and cooked out without colour, white stock, a bouquet garni and sliced potatoes added, simmered and skimmed for 1 hour, bouquet garni removed, the remainder liquidized, seasoned, consistency adjusted and served accompanied by croûtons. Also called **légumes, purée de**

vegetable spaghetti A yellow summer squash whose flesh separates into spaghetti-like strands when it is cooked. Also called **spaghetti marrow**

vegetais *Portugal* Vegetables

vegetale *Italy* Vegetable

vegetarian A person who avoids eating the flesh of once living creatures although some will eat animal products such as eggs, milk and milk products and fish. See also **vegan, lacto-vegetarian, lacto-ovo-vegetarian**

vegetarian cheese Cheese made with a curdling agent not derived from animals

veggieburger *United Kingdom* A vegetarian patty shaped like a hamburger, made with a savoury mixture of vegetables and vegetable protein (*colloquial*)

veggies *United Kingdom, United States* Vegetables, as in veggieburger (*colloquial*)

Veilchen *Germany* Violet, the flower

veitchberry A hybrid blackberry

vellay poondoo *South Asia* Garlic

vells The lining of the fourth stomach of an unweaned calf used as a source of rennet

velösleves *Hungary* A soup made from calves' brains and sliced mushrooms sweated in butter with parsley, sprinkled with flour and simmered with seasoned beef stock flavoured with mace until all cooked. Passed through a sieve, reheated and served with croûtons.

velouté *England, France* A type of soup in which a blond roux is combined with stock and vegetables, possibly sweated, herbs and seasonings, simmered and skimmed, then forced through a sieve or liquidized and finished with a liaison of egg yolk and cream (NOTE: Literally 'velvety'.)

velouté sauce A basic white sauce made from a blond roux and a white stock, simmered and skimmed for one hour and strained. (100 g flour per litre).

velutato *Italy* Thickened with egg yolks (NOTE: Literally 'velvety'.)

velvet apple Mabalo

Venaco *France* A soft surface-ripened goats' milk cheese from Corsica made in cylinders (up to 400 g) and ripened for up to 50 days in cool damp caves to give a greyish rind. Only made at certain times of the year.

venado 1. *Spain* Venison **2.** *Mexico* Deer, venison

venaison *France* Venison

venaison, sauce *France* Venison sauce

vendace A small, medium oily, freshwater fish, *Coregonus albula*, smaller than the related lake whitefish. Found in European waters and may be baked or fried.

vendace roe *Finland* The highly prized roe of the local vendace served as caviar, e.g. with chopped onion, sour cream and blini

vending service Service using machines to dispense the food and beverages, which are usually prepacked

Vendôme *France* An unpasteurized cows' milk cheese from the Loire valley cast in 250 g discs. The cheeses are ripened for 1 month either in humid caves so as to blue externally (*Vendôme bleu*) or covered in wood ash from vine shoots to give a brown crust (*Vendôme cendré*). Contains 50% fat based on dry matter.

venison The meat of deer either farmed or caught in the wild. That from the wild is in season from July to the end of February. The meat tends to be tough and is usually hung for 1 to 2 weeks and marinated before use. It has a low proportion of fat and requires special care in cooking. Popular in Germany.

venison salami Lean venison and one quarter its weight of lean pork finely minced and mixed with coarsely minced pork belly and diced pork back fat each equal in weight to the lean pork, seasoned, mixed with saltpetre and brown sugar and flavoured with nutmeg, ginger, peppercorns, garlic and juniper berries, packed tightly into ox middles or bungs and air-dried until mature

venison sauce Poivrade sauce made with game stock and finished with molten redcurrant jelly and cream

venison sausage *Scotland, United States* A sausage of variable composition, roughly 2 parts lean venison to 1 part fatty pork, minced, extended with soaked pinhead oatmeal in Scotland, seasoned and mixed with any of saltpetre, sage, garlic, juniper berries, brown sugar, lemon zest, spices and brandy, moistened with red wine, stock or lemon juice, packed into casings, linked and dried

vénitienne, sauce *France* A reduction of tarragon vinegar, chopped shallots and chopped chervil, strained, mixed with twice the original vinegar volume of sauce vin blanc and finished with green butter, chopped tarragon and vinegar

venkel *Netherlands* Fennel

ventaglio *Italy* Scallop, the shellfish

ventaglio, a *Italy* Scallop- or fan-shaped

ventresca *Italy* Belly of pork or tuna fish

ventresca bollita *Italy* Boiled belly of tuna fish, considered to be the tastiest part

Venushaar *Germany* Maidenhair fern

venus shell clam A shiny red or pink clam, *Callista chione*, up to 9 cm in diameter Found from southern England through to the

Mediterranean. It can be cooked or eaten raw. Also called **smooth venus clam**

verace *Italy* Authentic, fresh, not tinned

verats a la brasa *Catalonia* Mackerel cooked over an open flame

verbena *Italy, Spain, United States* Lemon verbena

Verbena *Germany* Lemon verbena

verde *Italy* Green

verdesca *Italy* A type of shark

verdura *Italy, Spain* Vegetables, greens

vergine *Italy* Virgin olive oil

verigüeto *Spain* Warty venus clam

Veritable Nantais *France* Nantais

verivanukas *Finland* Black pudding

verjuice In England the juice of crab apples, in France the juice of unripe grapes. Used as a souring agent in place of vinegar.

verjus *France* Verjuice

vermicelli *Italy* A very fine thin pasta usually bundled up like a bird's nest and used in soups

vermicellini *Italy* Angel's hair

Vermont *United States* A Cheddar-type cheese from the state of the same name

vermouth A spice, herb and essential oil flavoured wine used as an aperitif and as a flavouring agent

verni *France* Venus shell clam

vero *Italy* Real, authentic

Véron, sauce *France* 3 parts of **sauce normande** mixed with 1 part of **sauce tyrolienne** and finished with a pale meat glaze and anchovy essence

Véronique *France* Garnished with white seedless grapes, used of savoury dishes

Véronique, fish As for **fish Bercy**, glazed and garnished with white grapes, blanched, skinned and depipped

verseworst *Netherlands* Fresh sausage

verte, sauce *England, France* Mayonnaise flavoured and coloured with chopped tarragon or chervil, chives and watercress (NOTE: Literally 'green sauce'.)

vert galant *France* A jam made from blueberries, honey and spices from Béarn (NOTE: Literally 'ladies's man', after the French king Henri IV.)

vert-pré, au *France* Garnished with water cress and straw potatoes or coated with green mayonnaise or a sauce suprême coloured with a green beurre printanier and garnished with bouquets of green vegetables (NOTE: Literally 'like a green meadow'.)

verveine *France* Lemon verbena

Verwurrelt gedanken *Luxembourg* Crisply fried pastries

verza *Italy* Savoy cabbage

verzelata *Italy* Grey mullet

verzini *Italy* Small cooking sausages

vescica *Italy* Bladder, used as a sausage casing

vesi *Finland* Water

vésiga *France* The dried spinal cord of the sturgeon

vesigha *Russia* Dried sturgeon marrow

vesop A concentrated vegetable extract used in Eastern cooking

vetchina *Russia* Ham

vetiver An aromatic grass used in Indian cookery. See also **khas khas**

Vetiveria zizanioides *Botanical name* Khas khas

vetkoek *South Africa* Deep-fried balls of dough

ve tsin *Vietnam* Monosodium glutamate

Vézelay *France* A strong-flavoured goats' milk cheese from Burgundy, shaped like a cone

Vezzena *Italy* A hard scalded-curd cheese made from skimmed cows' milk, curdled with rennet and formed into cylinders (up to 40 kg). These are dry-salted and ripened for 6 months to give a slicing cheese or for 12 months to give a grating cheese.

vi *Catalonia* Wine

vialone rice *Italy* A fino-grade rice with long tapering grains able to absorb large quantities of liquid without losing its structure. Used for risotto.

viande *France* Meat

viande de boeuf blitzée *Switzerland* Beef reduced to a very fine paste or cream using a bowl chopper or possibly a high powered food processor

viande des grisons *France* Cured and dried beef. See also **Bünderfleisch**

viande faisandée *France* Meat kept until it is high, well hung

viande hachée *France* Minced meat

viandes froides *France* Sliced cold meats

viands A formal term for food and provisions. Also called **victuals**, **vittals** (NOTE: From Old English.)

Vibrio parahaemolyticus An infective type of food poisoning bacteria found in shellfish and seafood generally. The incubation period is 2 to 48 hours, usually 12 to 18 hours and the duration of the illness is 2 to 5 days. The symptoms are diarrhoea often leading to dehydration, abdominal pain and fever.

Vichy, à la *France* Garnished with Vichy carrots, or with a sauce containing the red of carrots which has been sweated and puréed

Vichy carrots Young carrots turned or scraped, cooked in (Vichy) water, butter, a little sugar and seasoning until all the liquid has evaporated and the carrots are tender and glazed

Vichyssoise A cold version of the homely French leek and potato soup, **potage bonne femme**, which has been finished with cream (NOTE: Invented by Louis Diat, chef at the New York Ritz Carlton, in a fit of nostalgia for his Vichy boyhood.)

Vichy water A natural mineral water bottled in Vichy, France

Vicia faba *Botanical name* Broad bean or horse bean

vickning *Sweden* Food offered to guests just before they are about to leave, e.g. Jansson's temptation. Sometimes called **nattmat**, night food, but this refers more to solitary midnight snacks.

Victoria, à la *France* In the Victoria style, i.e. garnished with tomatoes, macaroni, lettuce, potatoes and sometimes artichokes

Victoria plum *England* A large oval red skinned dessert plum with sweet juicy flesh. Often eaten raw but may be cooked.

victoria sandwich A victoria sponge mixture baked in two shallow cake tins, turned out, cooled, trimmed and sandwiched together with a filling of whipped cream and/or jam and the tops dusted with icing sugar

victoria sponge mixture Equal parts by weight of flour, butter, caster sugar, and eggs with 2 level teaspoons of baking powder per 4 oz of flour (60 g per kg flour) made up using the creaming method

victuals See **viands**

Vidalia onion *United States* A particularly sweet onion which may only be grown in a limited area near Glenville, South Georgia. One of the few restricted area foods in the USA.

vider *France* 1. To empty 2. To draw poultry, to disembowel or eviscerate

Vienna bread See **Vienna loaf**

Vienna coffee A particular blend of coffee beans favoured in Vienna

Vienna loaf A short oval-shaped white bread about 30 cm long often with several diagonal slashes and with a fairly crisp brown crust. The inspiration for French baguettes and other similar breads. Also called **Vienna bread**

Vienna sausage 1. A small Frankfurter 2. *United States* Frankfurter sausage

Viennese coffee *Austria* 1. A mocha coffee 2. Ground coffee mixed with dried figs

viennois, pain *France* An oval soft-crumbed crusty loaf of bread

viennoise, à la *France* In the Viennese style, i.e. used of roasts garnished with noodles,

spinach, celery and potatoes. Also used of escalopes garnished with a lemon slice plus some of anchovy fillets, chopped hard-boiled egg white and yolk, chopped capers or chopped parsley arranged in a pleasing pattern.

viennoiserie *France* The generic name for French pastries, croissants, pain au chocolate, Danish pastries, brioche, pain au raisins, etc.

vierge, beurre *France* Softened butter whipped with seasoning and lemon juice, used to dress boiled vegetables

Vietnamese mint A herb of the genus *Polygonum* with long slender deep green leaves and with an intense flavour of basil and mint. Used to flavour fish and noodle dishes in Malaysia and salads in Vietnam. (NOTE: So called because of its introduction into Australia by Vietnamese migrants.)

Vietnamese names of dishes *Vietnam* Apart from one of two names left over from the French occupation, Vietnamese dishes rarely have names in the Western style such as cottage pie, boeuf bourguignonne and the like. Rather they list the ingredients and the cooking methods using the linking words *voi* (with) and *va* (and). For example (thit ga) (tron) voi (buoi) is (sliced chicken) (mixed) with (grapefruit), and (rau thom) va (xa) is (mint) and lemon grass.

Vietnamese peanut sauce Roasted peanuts, deseeded red chillies, garlic, mint and lemon juice, processed to a fine paste then thinned down with a 4:1 mixture of thin coconut milk and fish sauce

Vietnamese soya sauce See **tuong**

Vigna catjang *Botanical name* Black-eyed pea

vignarola *Italy* Chopped leeks, quartered artichokes, mint, seasoning, shelled broad beans and peas added progressively to heated olive oil and cooked until soft and all liquid disappeared

Vigna sesquipedalis *Botanical name* Long bean

Vigna unguiculata *Botanical name* Cow pea

vigneronne, à la *France* In the wine grower's style, i.e. with a wine sauce and garnished with grapes

viili *Finland* A soured milk, curds, junket, yoghurt

viinimarjakiisseli *Finland* Redcurrant sauce

viinirypäle *Finland* Grape

vijg *Netherlands* Fig

vild hönsfågel *Sweden* Grouse. Also called **ripa**

villageoise, sauce *France* A mixture of veal stock, mushroom essence, velouté sauce and soubise sauce, reduced, strained and thickened with egg yolks and cream and finished with butter. Used for white meat.

Villalón *Spain* An even-textured, soft, mild and rindless ewes' milk cheese from Valladolid. The paste is made from scalded curds and has lots of small holes. It is moulded in the shape of a long cylinder with rounded ends and an oval cross section. Also called **pata de mulo**

Villeroi, sauce *France* **Sauce Allemande** mixed with ham **fumet** and truffle essence, reduced until very thick. Used for coating items of food which are then panéed and deep-fried.

Villeroi Soubise, sauce *France* **Villeroi sauce** with one part soubise sauce added to 2.5 parts of sauce allemande at the initial stage

Villeroi tomatée, sauce *France* **Villeroi sauce** with 1 part fresh tomato purée added to 3 parts of sauce allemande at the initial stage

viltfågel *Sweden* Game

viltsuppe *Norway* Game or venison soup

vin *Denmark, France, Norway, Sweden* Wine

vinäger *Sweden* Vinegar

vinagre *Portugal, Spain* Vinegar

vinaigre *France* Vinegar (NOTE: Literally 'sour wine'.)

vinaigrette *England, France* 1. A mixture of oil and vinegar seasoned with salt and pepper, possibly with mustard and sugar, then shaken together but not so as to make a stable emulsion. Used to dress salads or as a dip. Also called **French dressing 2.** See **ravigote, sauce**

vinbär *Sweden* Currant

vin blanc, au *France* With white wine

vin blanc, fish As for **fish Bercy**, but sauce finished only with butter and cream and not glazed. Garnished with fleurons.

vin blanc, sauce *France* Boiling fish velouté mixed with white wine, cooled, butter and cream added, seasoned, lemon juice added then strained through a tammy cloth. Used for fish. Also called **white wine sauce**

Vincent, sauce *France* Equal parts of green sauce and tartare sauce well mixed

vincisgrassi maceratese *Italy* An 18th-century pasta dish consisting of lasagne layered with ceps, cream and parma ham, topped with Parmesan cheese and white truffle shavings. Also called **pincisgrassi** (NOTE: Named after the Austrian Prince Windischgratz.)

vindaloo *South Asia* A particularly hot Indian stew (from chillies). The name is a corruption of *vinho de alhos* ('wine and garlic marinade') introduced to the Portuguese colony of Goa. Other authorities derive the name from 'vinegar' and *aloo* (the Indian word for 'potato'). See also **pork vindaloo**

vindaloo paste A spice paste used to make vindaloo consisting of dried red chillies, coriander, cumin and fenugreek seeds and peppercorns, all dry-roasted then processed with turmeric, salt, vinegar, tamarind, garlic, fresh ginger root and plenty of raw onion

vindrue *Norway* Grape

vindruvor *Sweden* Grapes

vine fruits See **dried vine fruits**

vinegar A dilute solution (4 to 6%) of acetic acid made by biological oxidation of alcoholic liquids such as ale, cider or wine. Known by its source i.e. malt vinegar (from ale), cider vinegar or red or white wine vinegar. Occasionally a cheap solution is made from chemically produced acetic acid which is known as spirit vinegar. Many flavourings are added to vinegar e.g. tarragon or garlic. Extensively used as a preservative and flavouring agent in all cuisines. Vinegar can be made by allowing a 15% sugar solution to ferment, open to the air, for about 6 months using yeast and/or bread as a starter if mother of vinegar is not available.

vinegar cake *England* An eggless fruit cake made with plain flour, mixed dried fruit, butter and soft brown sugar (2:2:1:1) using the rubbing in method and brought together with a foaming mixture of milk with bicarbonate of soda and vinegar (60:1:9), baked at 200°C for 30 minutes then at 170°C until cooked

vinegar herbs The principal herbs used for flavouring vinegars are basil, bay, chervil, dill, fennel, lemon balm, marjoram, mint, rosemary, savory, tarragon and thyme

vine leaves The young leaves of grape vines sold fresh, canned or pickled in brine. Served in salads or used as a wrapping for various stuffings, e.g. for dolmades.

vine spinach Ceylon spinach

vinha d'alhos *Portugal* Fish fillets or pork steaks marinated in wine with garlic, cloves, pepper and bay leaf, then fried, alternatively, the marinade

vino *Italy, Spain* Wine

vinous grape Dessert grape

vin rouge, au *France* With red wine

vin rouge, sauce *France* A fine **mirepoix** of vegetables lightly browned in butter, red wine added and reduced by half, crushed garlic and **espagnole sauce** added, simmered, skimmed, strained and finished with butter, anchovy essence and a little cayenne pepper. Served with fish.

vinsuppe *Norway* Wine soup

viola mammola *Italy* Sweet violet

Viola odorata *Botanical name* Sweet violet

Viola tricolor *Botanical name* Pansy

violaxanthin See **E161(e)**

violet 1. A small wild flower of the genus *Viola* which looks like a very small pansy and whose mauve flowers are crystallized for use as cake or dessert decoration. The petals of the sweet violet, *V. odorata*, are used for their flavour by steeping them in vinegar. See also **sweet violet 2.** *England, France* A Mediterranean sea creature, *Microcosmus sulcatus*, like a soft sac enclosed in a rubbery skin similar to the sea squirt and attached to deep rocks. The raw soft insides are relished by some who like the sour iodine taste. An acquired taste.

violet apricot Plumcot

violetta, alla *Italy* With crystallized violets

violette odorante *France* Sweet violet

violon *France* Guitar fish

vipérine *France* Viper's bugloss

viperino *Italy* Viper's bugloss

viper's bugloss A hairy biennial plant, *Echium vulgare*, similar to borage which grows on chalky and sandy soils to a height of 60 cm to 1 m. The flowers are edible and can be crystallized and used for decoration or in salads.

Virginia ham *United States* Smithfield ham

Virginia peanut A less common variety of peanut with two dark brown seeds per pod

virgin oil Oil which has not been treated after being pressed from the fruit or seed and thus has a more distinctive flavour and higher vitamin content. Not to be confused with extra virgin or virgin as applied to olive oil.

virgin olive oil Oil produced by the next pressing of the heated olive pulp after fine olive oil has been removed. The free oleic acid content must not exceed 4%. This oil is referred to as refined.

virgin pastry Puff pastry after it is first made, which must be used for vol-au-vents, bouchées and items which require an even rise or lift. Cuttings which are rerolled are only suitable for pies, palmiers, etc.

Viroflay, à la *France* In the style of Viroflay, near Paris, i.e. garnished with spinach, artichokes, potatoes, parsley and occasionally Mornay sauce. Used especially of roast lamb.

vis *Netherlands* Fish

viscera See **innards**

viscosity That quality of a liquid which determines its flow properties: the higher the viscosity the less well it flows. Thus, golden syrup is more viscous than cream, which in turn has a higher viscosity than water.

viskoekjes *Netherlands* Fish cakes

visniski *Russia* A chopped fish ball seasoned with fennel, covered with dough and deep-fried

vispgrädde *Sweden* Whipping cream

vispi puuro *Finland* The juice from summer berries cooked with sugar and semolina to a paste then whipped off the heat until light and frothy. Served cold with milk and sugar. (NOTE: Literally 'whipped porridge'.)

vit *Vietnam* Duck

vit, vitt *Sweden* White

vitamin A naturally occurring substance required by the human body for optimum health usually in small milligram quantities but sometimes gram quantities may be beneficial. Complete lack of any vitamin usually causes disease or birth defects in foetuses. Recommended daily amounts (RDAs) avoid these diseases but some advocate taking greater amounts especially of antioxidants. All vitamins are listed under either alphabetical names such as Vitamin A, B, C, etc., or under chemical names such as bioflavonoids, biotin, choline, folic acid, inositol, lipoic acid, orotic acid, PABA. Whether all the chemical names listed are true vitamins is constantly being reassessed and new vitamins are discovered at intervals. See also **trace elements**

vitamin A A long-chain fat-soluble alcohol which exist in various forms of which the most active is retinol which is found in animal tissues. Precursors of the vitamin are widely distributed in vegetables as **carotenes** which are transformed in the intestinal wall into Vitamin A. It is concerned with the integrity of epithelial tissues (skin and mucous membranes) and of the retina, especially for low light conditions, and is also needed for the correct functioning of many body cells. Major food sources are fish and animal livers, eggs and milk. It is possible to overdose.

vitamin B1 A water-soluble vitamin which must be taken daily. It maintains normal carbohydrate metabolism and nervous system function and is found in high concentration in yeast and the outer layers and germ of cereals. Other major sources are beef, pork and pulses. It has no known toxicity but colours the urine a bright yellow. Lack of vitamin B1 causes beri-beri, the first deficiency disease to be recognized which led to the discovery of vitamins. Also called **aneurin, thiamine**

vitamin B2 A water-soluble vitamin (**riboflavin**), essential for metabolic processes and for cell maintenance and repair. It is stored in the liver, kidneys and heart muscles. It is widely distributed in all leafy vegetables, in eggs, milk and the flesh of warm blooded animals. Lack of vitamin B2 causes soreness of the lips, mouth, tongue and eyelids. It has no known toxicity.

vitamin B3 A water-soluble vitamin which occurs in three forms, niacin, nicotinic acid and nicotinamide. The first two can cause skin flushing and should only be taken by diabetics and persons with peptic ulcers under strict medical supervision. Both niacin and nicotinamide forms are essential for bodily health. They are widely distributed in foodstuffs. Meat, fish, wholemeal flour and peanuts are major sources. Maize contains the vitamin in a non-absorbable form and it is for this reason that it is treated with lime which makes the vitamin available as well as improving the taste. Lack of the vitamin causes pellagra summarized as diarrhoea, dermatitis and dementia. It can also cause severe lesions when the skin is exposed to light.

vitamin B5 A water-soluble vitamin (pantothenic acid) destroyed by boiling, found in all animal and plant tissues, especially poultry, liver, fish, eggs, potatoes and whole grains. It is converted to co-enzyme A in the body and as such is involved in all metabolic processes. There is no known toxicity. Lack of the vitamin can cause headaches, fatigue, impaired motor coordination, muscle cramps and gastrointestinal disturbance. Severe deficiency caused the burning feet syndrome observed in prisoners of war in East Asia during World War II.

vitamin B6 A water-soluble vitamin which consists of three compounds, pyridoxal, pyridoxol (also called pyridoxine) and pyridoxamine, each with a different function. They are found in low concentration in all animal and plant tissues especially fish, eggs and wholemeal flour. They are involved in protein, fat and carbohydrate metabolism and in brain function. Lack of the vitamin can cause lesions around the eyes, nose and mouth, peripheral neuritis and, in infants, convulsions. It is not recommended that supplements exceed 300 mg per day.

vitamin B12 A cobalt-containing water-soluble vitamin (cobalamin) which together with folic acid has a vital role in metabolic processes and in the formation of red blood cells. It is responsible for the general feeling of well-being in healthy individuals. It is normally found only in animal products, particularly ox kidney and liver and oily fish. Vegetarians and vegans should take supplements which are produced by a fermentation process. Lack of vitamin B12 which may be due to its absence in the diet or poor absorption in the gut can cause a form of anaemia (Addison's pernicious anaemia). It is normally prescribed together with folic acid.

vitamin Bc See **folic acid**

vitamin B complex The whole complement of B vitamins plus biotin and folic acid. They are all water-soluble and tend to be found together in natural foodstuffs. Most are prone to destruction by excessive temperatures and sunlight. Some authorities include choline, inositol and PABA in this grouping.

vitamin C A water-soluble vitamin (**ascorbic acid**) which is synthesized in the bodies of most animals except humans, primates and guinea pigs who have to obtain it from vegetables and fruit. It is essential for good health, wound repair, the effectiveness of the immune system and is thought by some to play a role in the prevention of cancer. Vitamin C deficiency results in scurvy, a disease still found in the poor and the old. Large amounts (up to 8 g daily) are recommended by some doctors and more famously by Linus Pauling, the chemistry Nobel prize winner. It has no known toxicity.

vitamin D A fat-soluble vitamin (calciferol) whose main function is regulating calcium and phosphate metabolism (bone formation and repair). It is not normally present in nature but its precursors or provitamins, vitamin D2 and D3 are found in milk, cheese, eggs, butter, margarine (fortified) and especially oily sea fish. These provitamins are converted in the body to vitamin D by the action of sunlight. Lack of vitamin D causes rickets (deformation of the bones) in children and liability to fracture in adults. The vitamin is toxic in excess, 30,000 IU for adults and 2,000 IU for children.

vitamin D2 A precursor of vitamin D. Also called **ergocalciferol**

vitamin D3 A precursor of vitamin D. Also called **cholecalciferol**

vitamin E A fat-soluble vitamin (**tocopherol**) found in small quantities in soya beans, other seeds, butter, margarine (fortified), vegetables, whole grains, eggs and liver. It exists in several forms indicated by a Greek prefix, the alpha form being the most potent. It is a very powerful antioxidant and is vital for normal procreation and for cell processes. There is some evidence that it has anti-cancer activity. Natural sources are the best and though it has no known toxicity it may affect some medical conditions and supplements should only be taken on medical advice. Deficiency diseases in otherwise normal humans have not been reported.

vitamin F An obsolete term for essential fatty acids

vitamin H See **biotin**

vitamin K This vitamin relates to a group of chemical quinones, some fat-soluble and others water-soluble, which are synthesized by human gut microorganisms and are found in abundance in brassicas and spinach and in moderate concentration in tomatoes and pig's liver. Lack of the vitamin causes haemorrhages especially in new born infants. It is usually only administered under medical supervision.

vitamin M See **folic acid**

vitela *Portugal* Veal

vitello *Italy* **1.** Veal from milk-fed calves **2.** Calf

vitello alla genovese *Italy* Thin slices of veal cooked with wine and artichokes

vitello alla sarda *Italy* Veal, larded with anchovies and braised with tomato and olives

vitello di lette *Italy* Sucking calf

vitello di mare *Italy* Dogfish

vitellone *Italy* Meat from up to 3 year old beef cattle, darker than normal veal but lighter than beef

vitello tonnato *Italy* Cold roast veal coated with a sauce made from canned tuna, mayonnaise and lemon juice processed to a smooth mixture, the whole garnished with lemon wedges

vitelotte *France* A firm waxy variety of potato

Vitis labrusca *Botanical name* American fox grape

Vitis rotundifolia *Botanical name* American muscadine grape

Vitis vinifera *Botanical name* European grape

vitkålsoppa med kroppkakor Cabbage soup with dumplings

vitling *Sweden* Whiting, the fish

vitlök *Sweden* Garlic

vitreous endosperm A wheat endosperm with a very dense structure

vitrified china Porcelain

vit sås *Sweden* Béchamel sauce

vittals See **viands** (*colloquial*)

vitt bröd *Sweden* White bread

Vivaro *Italy* A semi-hard scalded-curd cows' milk cheese very similar to Montasio. The pale yellow paste has a few holes, a mild

pleasant taste and is covered with a hard smooth brown rind.

viveiro de mariscos *Portugal* A shellfish stew

viveur en tasse *France* A strong-flavoured bouillon or consommé, often with cayenne pepper, served in a cup

vla *Netherlands* Custard, flan, tart

vlees *Netherlands* Meat

vleesnat *Netherlands* Gravy

voi 1. *Finland* Butter **2.** *Vietnam* With, used as a linking word in many Vietnamese dish descriptions. See also **Vietnamese names of dishes**

volaille *France* Poultry, chicken

volaille, crème de *France* Cream of chicken soup

vol-au-vent *England, France* A round or oval puff pastry case filled with a cooked savoury mixture. It is made by rolling the pastry to 6 to 8 mm thick cutting out the shape, then half cutting a smaller shape in the centre. When baked the centre is removed and the crisp top replaced over the filling.

vol-au-vent à la toulousaine *France* A vol-au-vent with sweetbreads, mushroom and truffle filling

vol-au-vent régence *France* An oval vol-au-vent with a foie gras, mushroom, truffle and chicken quenelle filling

voleipä *Finland* Sandwich

voleipäpöytä *Finland* Hors d'oeuvres, smörgåsbord

volière, en *France* (Game) decorated with their own plumage

volpallière *France* Small chicken fillets, larded, braised and served with a truffle sauce

volume measure A convenient method of measuring ingredients by volume, reasonably accurate in the case of liquids but less so for solids. Volumes are measured in millilitres (ml) and litres (l) in the metric system used in most countries and in fluid ounces (fl oz), pints (pt) and gallons (gal) in the old imperial system taken over with different sizes in the USA. Other measures of volume are in use, e.g. cup measure, can measure and market measure. The disadvantages of volume measure are the variation in density (weight per unit volume) of any solid commodity with particle size and moisture content and the inaccuracy of dispensing from common measuring jugs, etc. Volume measures also include the standard teaspoon, dessertspoon and tablespoon. See also **liquid measure, dry measure, cup measure, can measure, market measure**

Volvariella volvacea *Botanical name* Straw mushroom

vongola *Italy* Clam, especially the warty venus clam used in a pasta sauce such as in **spaghetti alle vongole**

vongola grigia *Italy* Golden carpet shell

vongola nera *Italy* Carpet shell clam

vongola verace *Italy* Carpet shell clam

voorgerechten *Netherlands* Canapés, appetizers

voorjaarssla *Netherlands* Spring salad

vorschmack *Finland* Minced mutton, beef and salt herring cooked with onions and garlic

Vorspeisen *Germany* Hors d'oeuvres, first course, starters

vörtbröd *Sweden* Malt bread

vørterkake *Norway* Spice cake

vrai(e) *France* True, real, as in *vraie tortue*, real turtle

vrilles de vigne *France* Young shoots or tendrils of grape vines, usually blanched and either dressed with vinaigrette or cooked in olive oil

vrucht *Netherlands* Fruit

vruchtengelei *Netherlands* Jam

Vulscombe cheese *England* A goats' milk cheese from Devon

vurty *Czech Republic* A short fat sausage

WXYZABC

Wachholder *Germany* Juniper

Wachsbohnen *Germany* Wax beans, butter beans, yellow beans

Wachtel *Germany* Quail

wafer A thin, crisp, unsweetened biscuit with a papery texture made by cooking a batter between hot plates, served with ice cream and sometimes sandwiched together in several layers with a sweet or savoury cream filling to form a wafer biscuit

wafer biscuit See **wafer**

Waffel *Germany* 1. Waffle 2. Wafer

waffle A crisp golden brown pancake made by cooking a batter between two metal waffle irons which have corresponding indentations and protrusions so that the waffle when cooked has a series of indentations on both sides. Usually served hot with butter or maple syrup or cold with whipped cream or ice cream.

waffle iron Two thick metal plates hinged along one edge with handles at the opposite edge and with heated indented mating surfaces which give waffles their characteristic appearance

wah-bho-hmyit *Burma* Bamboo shoot

Wähe *Switzerland* An open-faced large pie or tart filled with fruit, vegetables or cheese

waiter, waitress A male, female person who serves the customers in a restaurant and is usually responsible for laying up and clearing the tables, making the coffee and presenting the desserts and gateaux on a trolley. In some case waiters carve meat at a side table or in expensive establishments prepare food such as tournedos, beef stroganoff or steak tartare and flambé dishes in front of the customers.

wajan *Indonesia* A type of wok but deeper than the Chinese and with straighter sides

wakame *Japan* A type of curly leaved brown alga, *Undaria pinnatifida*, found in coastal waters, with a mild vegetable taste and a soft texture. It is blanched in the whole leaf form and either sold undried in Japan or exported in dried form. The fresh and, after soaking, the dried form can be used in salads or as a vegetable after boiling for 10 minutes. Also called **curly algae, curly seaweed, lobe leaf seaweed**

wakegi *Japan* Scallion

wal *South Asia* Hyacinth bean pods

Waldmeister *Germany* Sweet woodruff

Waldorf salad A salad of chopped apple, walnut and celeriac or celery, dressed on lettuce leaves with mayonnaise let down with lemon juice

Waldschnepfe *Germany* Woodcock

Walewska, à la *France* In the style of Comtesse Walewska (Napoleon's mistress), i.e. garnished with lobster, truffles and a Mornay sauce

Walewska, fish As **fish Mornay**, but with a slice of cooked lobster and sliced truffles placed on the fish before coating with sauce

wali *East Africa* A Kenyan staple of rice with added fat and spices

wali wa nazi *East Africa* A Swahili dish of long-grain rice cooked with salt and twice its volume of coconut milk, half thin for the initial cooking and half thick to finish. Served with stews and curries.

wallenbergare *Sweden* Triple minced trimmed fillet of veal, seasoned, cooled, mixed with cooled egg yolks and double cream, made into egg-shaped balls, rolled in breadcrumbs and fried carefully in butter. Served with petit pois, creamed potatoes and cranberry sauce. (NOTE: Named after the Wallenberg family.)

walleye pike *United States* A freshwater pike with a firm, fine textured flesh found in the great lakes of North America

walleye pollack See **Alaska pollack**

walleye pollock See **Alaska pollack**

wallies *United Kingdom* Pickled cucumbers (*colloquial*)

Walliser Raclette *Germany, Switzerland* The general name for the semi-hard scalded-curd cows' milk cheeses made in the Valais region and used as melting cheeses and for raclette

Walliskäse *Switzerland* A hard, cooked-curd cows' milk cheese suitable for slicing or grating. See also **Saanenkäse**

walnoot *Netherlands* Walnut

Walnuss *Germany* Walnut

walnut The brown nut from the fruit of the walnut tree, *Juglans regia* and *J. nigra*, which when ripe has a crinkly brain-like appearance and is enclosed in a hard relatively smooth brown shell up to 4 cm in diameter. The nut has a distinctive flavour and is used in both savoury and sweet dishes. The unripe nuts and shells are often pickled in vinegar or preserved in syrup. Also called **hickory nut**, **butternut**

walnut oil A fine nutty-flavoured oil extracted from walnuts. Used as a flavouring.

walu jepan *Indonesia* Choko

wan dou *China* Peas

wansuey *Philippines* Coriander leaves

wappato Arrowhead

warabi *Japan* A fern sprout used in salads or as a vegetable

wara einab *Middle East* Salted vine leaves wrapped around a mixture of cooked rice, pine nuts and raisins and served cold as an appetizer. Also called **waraq ainab**

waraq ainab *Middle East* Wara einab

waribashi *Japan* Disposable chopsticks

warishita *Japan* The mixture of soya sauce, sugar and **mirin** added to sukiyaki

warka *North Africa* Warqa pastry

warkha pastry *North Africa* A type of flaky pastry

warm, to To heat slowly to around 50 to 80°C

Warmbier *Germany* A soup made with beer

warm-water octopus A small species of octopus, *Octopus macropus*, up to 1.2 m maximum length with thin tentacles found in warm waters throughout the world. The quality is not as good as the common octopus.

warq *South Asia* Silver leaf used for decoration of foods

warqa pastry *North Africa* Very thin filo-type leaves of pastry made from a gluey dough. Requires great skill to make.

Warrigal greens *Australia* One of the first plants, *Tetragonia tetragonoides*, to be found by Joseph Banks when the *Endeavour* came into Botany Bay in 1770. The arrow-shaped leaves are like spinach but firmer and they need to be blanched before use to remove some of the oxalic acid. The young leaves have the best flavour. Also called **Botany Bay greens**, **native spinach**, **New Zealand spinach** (NOTE: *Warrigal* comes from an Aboriginal word meaning 'dingo')

warsche *Scotland* Lacking salt (*colloquial*)

Warszawski *Poland* A ewes' milk cheese similar to **Kashkaval**

warty venus clam A plump, grey to brown-coloured clam, *Venus verrucosa*, with raised rows of wart-like projections on the shell, up to 7 cm in diameter. Found from southern England to the Mediterranean. Used in vongole sauce.

Wartzige Venusmuschel *Germany* Warty venus clam

wasabi The edible root of a plant, *Wasabia japonica*, which only grows in Japan. The skinned, pale green root has a fierce flavour rather like horseradish. It is grated and served like this or made into a paste for use with sashimi or in sushi. It can also be dried to a pale brown powder. Also called **Japanese horseradish**, **mountain hollyhock**, **wasebi**

Wasabia japonica *Botanical name* Wasabi

wasa-vasi *Sri Lanka* Mace

wasebi See **wasabi**

washed curd Milk curds which have been separated from the whey then steeped in cold water one or more times. This lowers the acid content of the curds and gives a coarser cheese.

washed-rind cheese A surface-ripened cheese which relies on bacteria on the surface to develop the flavour. They are frequently washed to discourage mould growth and to encourage the growth of bacteria and usually have an orange-red rind and a pungent smell although the paste tends to be sweet to the taste. They are normally small to give a high surface to volume ratio. Pont l'Evêque and Munster are typical examples.

washing soda The crystalline hydrated form of sodium carbonate

Washington The original navel orange from which most navel varieties have been developed. Also called **Bahia**

Washington, à la *France* In the Washington style, i.e. garnished with sweetcorn kernels in a cream sauce

Washington clam Giant west coast clam

Wasser *Germany* Water

Wasserkresse *Germany* Watercress

Wassermelone *Germany* Watermelon

wastle cake *Scotland* A type of griddle cake

wat A traditional Ethiopian stew spiced with berbere or a similar mix of long pepper, black peppercorns, nutmeg and cloves, all dry-roasted and ground to a fine powder with turmeric. The meat is usually beef or chicken but goat or mutton is also used. Very few vegetables are cooked with the meat. See also **zegeni**

water activity A measure of the effective water content (from the point of view of a microorganism) of a food, not necessarily related to the actual water content (% by weight). It is defined as the ratio of the pressure exerted by water vapour in equilibrium with the food to the pressure exerted by water vapour in equilibrium with pure water at the same temperature as the food. (Both increase with temperature but the ratio remains roughly constant.) A food containing no water has a water activity of zero and pure water has a value of 1.0. Freezing reduces water activity by turning liquid water into ice.

water apple A type of rose apple, *Eugenia aqua*, which is smaller, juicier and a deeper pink colour. It may be eaten as a fruit or the juice extracted. Also called **watery rose apple**

water biscuit A thin crisp plain biscuit made of flour, salt and water only, similar to a cream cracker and usually eaten with cheese

water-blommetjie bredie *South Africa* A Cape province stew made with waterlily stems

water caltrop The fruit of an aquatic plant, *Trapa bicornis*, with a shiny brown to black skin and two projecting horns. It has been used for food since neolithic times and is still grown and eaten in China, Korea and Japan. It has a semi-sweet potato-like flesh and must be boiled for an hour to destroy parasites. It is used in various dishes and preserved in honey or syrup. Unfortunately it is often misnamed water chestnut and a flour made from it is called water chestnut starch.

water chestnut The bulbous corm of the plants *Eleocharis dulcis* and *E. tuberosa*, types of sedge. It is used in Chinese and Thai cooking and can be purchased fresh or canned and eaten raw or cooked. It is used as a vegetable in the West but more usually to make desserts and drinks in Southeast Asia and used for its crunchy texture in Chinese cooking. Also called **Chinese water chestnut**. See also **caltrops, water caltrop**

water chestnut starch A grey starch made from the water caltrop. Considered to be very good for making crisp batters and coatings and for producing a good gloss in sauces.

water concentrations The highest water concentrations (% by weight) at which microbial spoilage will not occur are approximately 13 to 15% for wheat flour, 14 to 20% for dehydrated vegetables, 10 to 11% for dehydrated whole egg and 15% for fat-free meat. See also **water activity**

water convolvulus Swamp cabbage

watercress A hardy aquatic perennial, *Rorippa nasturtium-aquaticum,* also called *Nasturtium officinale,* with a round, sharply flavoured green leaf, generally grown in slightly alkaline running water. Used principally as a garnish for roasts and grills, in salads and in soups. It was introduced to Asia by the British and is used in salads in Southeast Asia, as a garnish in Japan and is boiled in soup in China. (NOTE: **Watercress** is called **winter rocket** in the US)

waterfisch *Netherlands* **1.** Freshwater fish **2.** Fish sauce made from vegetables and Seville orange, cooked in fish stock, seasoned, flavoured with mustard and strained

water ice Fruit or liqueur-flavoured sugar syrup, frozen with continuous stirring to make a frozen dessert similar to sorbet

water icing See **glacé icing**

waterleaf *West Africa* A spinach-like plant, *Talinum triangulare,* grown throughout the tropics, similar to purslane. Also called **bologi**

water lemon Yellow granadilla

waterless cooking *United States* A style of cooking using very low heat, a pot or pan with a very tight fitting lid and not more than 1 tablespoon of water

water melon The large round or oval fruit of an annual warm climate trailing plant, *Citrullus lanatus*, and *C. vulgaris* with a thick dark green, possibly yellow striped, skin enclosing a watery crisp, pink/red and slightly sweet flesh with embedded black seeds. Eaten raw as a thirst quencher. The seeds which are oily and nutritious can be eaten as a snack food.

water souchet *United States* The North American equivalent of waterzoetje

water spinach Swamp cabbage

water wolf Pike

watery rose apple See **water apple**

waterzoetje *Netherlands* Waterzooi

waterzoie Waterzooi

waterzooi *Belgium* **1.** A local Brussels dish of boiled chicken in a stock and white-wine-based cream sauce with julienned vegetables **2.** A thin stew or thick soup made with mixed fish and julienned vegetables. Also called **waterzoetje**

wattleseed *Australia* The seeds of various Acacia species. The green pods can be eaten as a vegetable but generally the seeds are dried and ground and taste like a mixture of chocolate, hazelnut and coffee. It may be used as a beverage or a flavouring. Not all species are edible. An extract is also available.

waved whelk See **whelk**

wax bean A type of French bean with yellow waxy pods. Also called **waxpod bean**

wax gourd A very large (up to 45 kg) marrow-type vegetable, *Benincasa hispida*, from China with a thin hard waxy green skin, resembling a water melon in appearance. The flesh is cooked by steaming, braising or simmering. Cubes of the flesh are slit, stuffed and steamed as **dim sum**. The flesh and skin may also be candied or pickled. The skin lends itself to the carving of elaborate patterns. See also **petha**, **dong gwa jong**. Also called **winter gourd**, **white gourd**, **winter melon**, **Chinese vegetable marrow**, **ash gourd**

wax palm Carnauba

waxpod bean See **wax bean**

wazan *South Asia* A master chef of Kashmir

weakfish *United States* One of the drum family of fish, *Cynoscium regalis*, very similar to trout. Fished both for game and food off the Atlantic coast.

weasand The lining of a pigs gullet used for casing sausages. Rather rare.

Webb's lettuce A common crisphead lettuce

Weckewerk *Germany* Pork and pigskin boiled with white bread and flavourings

wedding breakfast The celebratory meal after a marriage ceremony which has taken place in the morning, much more elaborate than a breakfast

wedding cake A celebratory cake served at a wedding feast. In the UK it is a rich fruit cake covered with almond paste and royal icing elaborately sculpted. In France it is a conical heap of profiteroles, held together with caramel.

wedge A triangular cut from the circumference to the centre point of a round cake, cheese, pie, etc. Between 4 and 12 wedges are normally cut from a circle

wedgebone steak *United States* A steak cut from the sirloin

wedger A special tool that cuts tomatoes, lemons etc. into wedges

wedge shell clam A small white, brown or purple clam, *Donax trunculus*, up to 4 cm diameter, which is plentiful in the Mediterranean. Related to the American bean clam.

Wedmore *England* A semi-hard cheese from Somerset made with unpasteurized cows' milk and with a band of chopped chives running through the centre

weever fish Various edible seawater fish of the genus *Trachinus* with upward-looking eyes and very sharp spines on the back and gill covers

Wegerich *Germany* Plantain

wei *China* Braising food in its own juice. See also **dun**

Weichkäse *Germany* The generic name for various fresh tasting soft cows' milk cheeses with high water content, close-textured pastes and white bloom covered rinds

weight measure The most accurate method of measuring ingredients using the gravitational force exerted on the material to deflect a calibrated spring or by balancing the weight of the ingredient against a known weight using a lever. Weights are measured in grams (g) and kilograms (kg) and tonnes (1000 kg) in the metric system used in most countries and in ounces (oz) and pounds (lb) in the imperial system still in use in the USA. Other cultures, especially in country districts, still use local measures. See also **volume measure**

Weihnachtsbäckerei *Austria, Germany* Small pastries and biscuits specially baked for Christmas

Weihnachtstollen *Germany* An enriched almond-flavoured bread popular at Christmas. See also **Stollen**

Wein *Germany* Wine

Weinbergschnecken *Germany* Snails

Weinkraut *Germany* **1.** Sauerkraut heated with bacon fat, then simmered in reduced white wine for 10 minutes, seedless green grapes or peeled apple pieces added and simmered a further 5 minutes **2.** Rue, the herb

Weinschaum sauce A German version of Zabaglione sauce often served with vanilla-flavoured blancmange

Weintrauben *Germany* Grapes

weiss *Germany* White

Weissbrot *Germany* White bread

weisse Bohnen *Germany* Butter beans

Weissfisch *Germany* Whiting

Weissfleisch *Germany* White meat

Weisskäse *Germany* Cottage cheese

Weisskohl *Germany* White cabbage

Weisslacher Bierkäse *Germany* Weisslacker

Weisslacker *Germany* A rectangular-shaped sharp-tasting semi-hard cows' milk cheese with a very white heavily salted paste made from uncooked curd and weighing about 4 kg. The surface is covered in moulds which ripen the cheese from the outside. Also called **Bierkäse, Weisslacher Bierkäse**

Weissrüben *Germany* Turnips

Weisswurst *Germany* A mild-flavoured white sausage made from pork and veal with flavourings, similar to Münchener Weisswurst. Usually heated in water then fried and served with mustard and bread.

Weizen *Germany* Wheat

Weizenbrot *Germany* Brown bread

well done *United Kingdom* Cooked so that no trace of pinkness or free juice exists in the centre of the meat

Wellhornschnecke *Germany* Whelk

well hung (Meat or game) which has been hung sufficiently long to develop flavour and tenderness. The classic description is – hang two pheasants by their necks, when one drops off, cook the other.

wels A very large freshwater catfish, *Silurus gianis*, found throughout Central Asia and Central Europe

welscher Kohl *Germany* Savoy cabbage

Welsh apple cake *Wales* Tinker's apple cake

Welsh blood pudding *Wales* See **pwdin gwaed, pwdin gwaed gwyddau**

Welsh cake *Wales* A drop scone mixture containing currants, cooked by shallow frying

Welsh cawl *Wales* A mutton stew with potatoes, cabbage and carrots

Welsh chicken *Wales* Diced bacon and carrots are sweated in butter in a large pan. Flour is added and cooked to a brown roux and one of two boiling fowl and a shredded cabbage are placed on top. Chopped leeks, herbs, dripping or butter, stock and seasoning are added and all simmered for 2 to 3 hours. Serve the chickens on a bed of cabbage, garnished with the other vegetables and with the thickened cooking liquor poured over.

Welsh curd cakes *Wales* An open pie lined with shortcrust pastry and filled with a mixture of curds or cottage cheese, butter, egg yolks, sugar, cake crumbs and currants (8:4:3:1:1:1) plus lemon zest, brandy and a pinch of salt combined by the creaming method. Baked at 180 to 200°C for about 20 minutes.

Welsh faggot *Wales* As faggot but using oatmeal and never breadcrumbs

Welsh griddle cake *Wales* The normal drop scone mixture but often with dried vine fruits added, sometimes brought together with buttermilk. Also called **teisen gri**

Welsh onion A very hardy perennial, *Allium fistulosum*, with hollow leaves to 45 cm tall and 1 cm in diameter, which grows in clumps like chives with thickened leaves below ground level. Either the leaves or parts of the clump are used, especially as a winter vegetable. Also called **ciboule, European Welsh onion** (NOTE: The Welsh onion is not from Wales: the name probably derived from the German *welsch* meaning 'foreign'.)

Welsh pancake *Wales* Pancakes but made with buttermilk instead of milk and cooked thicker than normal. Served hot and buttered or may be filled with leftovers or specially prepared meat or fish fillings. Also called **crempog**

Welsh parsley pie *Wales* A type of quiche made with an egg custard containing a little flour and sugar and a good amount of chopped bacon and parsley. Baked at 205°C until cooked and the custard set. Also called **pastai persli**

Welsh potato cakes *Wales* A yeast raised potato cake made from milk, flour, boiled potatoes and butter (10:6:4:1). Yeast (1:12) on flour is mixed with the warmed milk and butter and made into a dough with the flour and potatoes, kneaded then proved for an hour, shaped into cakes and baked at 200°C until golden brown. Also called **teisennau tatws**

Welsh pudding *Wales* Butter, sugar, egg white and egg yolk (4:3;:2:2) made into a filling by melting the butter, beating in the egg yolks and then the sugar and folding in the stiffly beaten egg whites. Lemon zest is added and the mixture poured into a pie tin lined with puff pastry then baked at 180°C until cooked, about 1 hour. Also called **pwdin cymreig**

Welsh punchnep *Wales* Equal quantities of potatoes and turnips cooked and mashed separately with butter then combined and seasoned, placed in a dish, several depression made in the surface and covered with cream before serving

Welsh rabbit See **Welsh rarebit**

Welsh rarebit *United Kingdom* A piece of buttered toast covered with a thick cheese sauce made from a white roux, milk, possibly ale, French mustard, Worcestershire sauce and seasoning mixed with an equal weight of grated Cheddar until smooth, and the whole browned under the grill. The sauce may be kept in a refrigerator until needed. Also called **Welsh rabbit**

Wensleydale cheese *England* A hard cows' milk cheese from Yorkshire, made from milk inoculated with a small amount of fermenting whey but not allowed to become acid. The curd is uncooked and cast in 3 to 4 kg discs. The white paste matures rapidly in 3 to 4

weeks to a mellow honey-like taste. It should not be yellow or sour. A blue-veined version is produced which is matured for 4 to 6 months and is similar to Stilton.

wentelteefjes *Netherlands* French toast, pain perdu

western *United States* Western sandwich

western king prawn A greyish king prawn, *Penaeus latisulcatus*

western rock lobster *Australia* A type of spiny lobster, *Panulirus cygnus*, found in Western Australia. It varies in colour from pink to deep reddish brown and is of excellent quality. Also called **crayfish (seawater)**

western sandwich *United States* A scrambled egg or omelette sandwich with sautéed ham, sweet peppers and onions. Also called **Denver sandwich**, **western**

westfälische Blindhunde *Germany* Soaked haricot beans simmered with pieces of bacon until nearly tender, diced peeled and cored apples, French beans, carrots and potatoes added, seasoned and simmered a further 30 minutes until all tender

westfälische Bohnensuppe *Germany* Puréed kidney beans let down with white stock and garnished with blanched **julienne** of celeriac, carrots, leeks and potatoes and sliced Bologna sausage

westfälische Kartoffeln *Germany* Mashed potatoes, mixed with mashed cooking apples and butter, covered with breadcrumbs and butter and browned under the grill

westfälischer Schinken *Germany* Westphalia ham

West Indian cherry Acerola

West Indian curry powder A ground spice mix introduced to the Caribbean by Indian migrants consisting of coriander seeds, aniseed, cumin seed, black mustard seeds, fenugreek seeds, black peppercorns and cinnamon, all dry-roasted, plus dry ginger and turmeric

West Indian lime The original true lime, *Citrus aurantifolia*, originating in or around Malaysia, now grown worldwide. It is a small round lime picked either green or yellow and it has a very acid light greenish yellow flesh with many seeds. Used to make lime juice. Also called **Mexican lime**, **key lime**, **Galego lime**

Westmorland pepper cake *England* A chemically-raised basic cake mixture with added fruit and flavoured with ground ginger, cloves and black pepper but with half the normal quantity of eggs. Made by the melting method and baked at 180°C until cooked.

Westphalia ham *Germany* A brine-cured boneless ham made from pigs fed on acorns. They are well rested before slaughter and completely desanguinated by massaging the meat. The pork is dry-salted for 2 weeks, immersed in a 20% brine for a further 2 weeks and cold-smoked over ash and beech wood with juniper berries for up to 5 weeks. Served raw in very thin slices.

Westphalian sausage *Germany* A sausage made from lean pork and fat pork (3:1) from the forequarter, minced, seasoned, flavoured with ground cloves, packed in casings and air-dried until yellow

Westralian jewfish *Australia* An outstanding deep-bodied table fish, *Glaucosoma hebraicum*, from Western Australia which commands high prices and appears only in the more expensive restaurants. It is silvery blue fading to light blue on the belly and is striped longitudinally. It can grow to more than 1 metre in length and should not be confused with the jewfish (**mulloway**) which, though similar in size, is not striped.

wet fish Fresh uncooked fish, hopefully so fresh that it is still twitching

wetha see pyan *Burma* Pork curry flavoured with lemon, turmeric, garlic and ginger served with boiled rice

wether A castrated male sheep. The flesh is considered to be less fine than a comparable young ewe.

wether gammon Leg of mutton

wet nellie *United Kingdom* A doughnut with jam in the centre (*colloquial*; *North of England*)

whale Animal of the largest mammal order *Cetacea* which, although it breathes air, lives in the sea. There are various species ranging in weight from 2 to 120 tonnes, although dolphins and porpoises which are the same family may be considerably smaller than this. They are hunted for their subcutaneous fat (blubber) which is further processed into whale oil, and the flesh which finds a ready sale in Japan and East Asia. Once a major food source for the inhabitants of Arctic and northern latitudes.

whale oil Oil rendered from whale blubber used after deodorization for margarine and soap manufacture

wheat The seed of a plant, *Triticum aestivum*, which is the most important food grain of the developed world. Used, when ground into flour and processed, to make bread, pastry and cakes, as a thickening agent and for a multitude of other uses. Also used as an animal feedstuff. Alternatively it can be cooked whole, dried and cracked to form another food staple. It contains roughly 85% endosperm, 13% bran and 2% wheat germ. Also called **corn**

wheat classification Wheats are classified either as hard vitreous, hard mealy, soft vitreous or soft mealy. See also **vitreous endosperm**, **soft wheat**, **hard wheat**

wheat composition Protein 8 to 15% and fat around 2%. It is the protein type and not the percentage composition which is the underlying cause of hardness in wheat.

wheat duck *United States* A type of wild duck similar to widgeon

wheatear A small buff and grey European game bird, *Oenanthe oenanthe*, with a white rump (NOTE: From 'white arse'.)

wheat flakes Partially boiled cracked wheat crushed between rollers then dried, lightly toasted and used in muesli and as a breakfast cereal

wheat germ The embryo of the wheat grain which is removed from white flour. It constitutes about 2% of the total weight of the grain, consists mainly of fat and protein and contains most of the B and E vitamins. Often sold separately as a food supplement.

wheat germ flour *United States* The pulverized germ of wheat usually dry-fried or roasted before use

wheat germ oil The oil extracted from wheat germ used as a health supplement and high in vitamin E, which is destroyed by heating

wheat hardness A measure of the ease of grinding of wheat into flour determined either by standard milling tests (time to grind to a particular size in standard apparatus), by biting the wheat seed (miller's test) or by measuring the force necessary to penetrate the wheat with a sharp point (micro penetration test)

wheatmeal flour See **brown flour**

wheat starch A gluten free wheat flour consisting mainly of starch. It is used as a thickener and is mixed with tapioca starch (2:1) to make a boiling water dough suitable, after kneading and rolling or flattening, for wrapping small parcels of food such as **dim sum**. See also **wheat starch dough**

wheat starch dough A dough suitable for food wrappers made from 2 parts wheat starch, 1 part tapioca starch and a little salt, briskly mixed with 4 parts of boiling water and a little oil, kept warm whilst resting then kneaded to a silky soft dough. Small chestnut-sized pieces can be rolled out or pressed out with the fingers or back of a knife.

whelk A large (up to 4 cm across) carnivorous gastropod mollusc, *Buccinum undatum*, with a grey/brown snail-like shell. They are usually boiled at the place of landing and checked for toxicity. They may be sold shelled or unshelled and are poached, baked or grilled. They are rather tasteless and therefore often served with vinegar. Also called **waved whelk**

whetstone cakes *United Kingdom* Hard round cakes made with flour, sugar and egg whites and flavoured with caraway seed. Baked in a cool oven until hard.

whey The translucent liquid which is formed when coagulated milk separates into a semi-solid portion (curds) and a liquid portion (whey). It contains most of the lactose of the milk and a small amount of protein and fat. Usually a waste product but sometimes boiled or acidified to separate more solids from which a kind of cheese is made.

whey cream Any cream or fat still remaining in whey after the curds have been separated in cheese making

whey of butter Buttermilk

whiff Megrim

whig Sour milk, whey, buttermilk

whimberry Bilberry

whim wham *England* An 18th-century dessert of sponge fingers soaked in muscatel or sweet sherry with brandy, orange juice and grated orange zest, topped with whipped cream and sprinkled with almond praline

whip A dessert to which whipped cream or whipped egg white is added, often containing gelatine and with a light texture

whip, to To beat one or a mixture of ingredients with a whisk, rotary beater or electrically-operated mixer to incorporate air and in some cases to form emulsions or to change the phase relationships in emulsions e.g. from oil in water to water in oil. Also called **whisk, to**

whipkull *Scotland* A Yuletide drink from Shetland made from egg yolks, sugar and rum (4:2:1). The egg yolks and sugar are beaten to a cream over hot water and the rum added drop by drop whilst still beating. Poured into glasses and drunk whilst warm or eaten as a dessert when cold.

whipped butter Softened butter whipped to incorporated air so as to make it easy to spread

whipped cream Cream containing between 35 and 40% butterfat which is whipped to incorporate air and to begin linking up the fat globules to make it a semi-solid. If whipping is carried on for too long the fat will become the continuous phase and it will turn to butter. For this reason, food processors must be carefully watched when being used to whip cream.

whipping cream *United Kingdom* Cream containing a minimum butterfat content of 35%. See also **light whipping cream**, **heavy whipping cream**

whip topping *United States* A non milk fat substitute for whipping cream

whisk An implement used for hand whisking, which can be a balloon whisk, a coiled wire whisk or a rotary whisk

whisk, to To whip

whisking method for cakes A method of making cakes by following the procedure for fatless whisking, then at the end folding in molten clarified or whole butter very gently (e.g. by simultaneously throwing in the fat while switching the machine off), used for making e.g. Genoese sponge

whistle pig *United States* Woodchuck

white asparagus Asparagus shoots cut below ground level when the tips protrude at most 5 cm into the light

white aubergine A very light green aubergine used in central China

whitebait Young sprats, herring and possibly other fish under 5 cm long, generally deep-fried whole à l'anglaise and seasoned with salt and cayenne pepper. See also **anglaise, fish à l'**, **sand eel**

white beef stock Beef bones with fat and marrow removed, blanched and refreshed, simmered with aromatic vegetables and a bouquet garni for 8 hours, skimming continuously then strained. Proportions 4 bone, 1 vegetables and 10 water. Also called **fond blanc**, **fond de marmite**

white beet Chard

white bordelaise sauce See **bonnefoy, sauce**

white bread Bread made from a white flour dough

white butter fish Pomfret

white butter sauce See **beurre blanc**

white cabbage A spherical cabbage consisting of a tightly-packed ball of rather thick white leaves with a few green leaves surrounding it. Used for making coleslaw and sauerkraut and in the UK for institutional boiled cabbage.

white cake *United States* A cake made with all white ingredients, i.e. with no egg yolk or coloured fats, etc.

white chicken stock As for white beef stock but substituting chicken bones and carcasses for the defatted beef bones. Also called **fond blanc de volaille**

white chocolate A white, chocolate-tasting confectionery item made from bleached cocoa butter and white sugar

white cinnamon The inner bark of wild cinnamon

white crystal sugar *United States* Granulated sugar

white cumin Cumin, the common brown variety

white currant A variety of redcurrant which lacks the gene for the colouring matter

white curry *Sri Lanka* A mild curry based on coconut milk

white fish 1. A general name for any type of fish with white flesh and less than 6% fat in the flesh, such as haddock, whiting, cod, plaice, etc. **2.** *United States* A small freshwater fish related to the salmon and trout. It is often smoked and the roe processed into a caviar substitute.

white flour Wheat flour from which the bran and wheat germ have been removed leaving between 72 and 74% of the original dehusked grain. Sometimes bleached chemically to enhance the white colour.

white fungus A white to golden-coloured crinkly and rather tasteless fungus, *Tremella fuciformis*, similar to cloud ear fungus and resembling a ball of sponge, normally available in dried form. Also called **snow fungus**, **silver fungus**, **tremella**

white gourd Wax gourd

white ladies pudding *Central Asia* A type of bread and butter pudding in which a well-buttered pie dish is sprinkled with desiccated coconut and filled with triangles of buttered crustless white bread over which is poured a light vanilla-flavoured custard, milk, eggs and sugar (8:2:1). This is then baked in a bain-marie at 160°C for about 90 minutes until set, turned out and eaten hot or cold. (NOTE: The name comes from the village of White Ladies Aston where there used to be a Cistercian convent whose nuns wore white habits)

white long-grain rice A polished long-grain rice with the bran and outer coating removed giving separate fluffy grains when cooked. Requires about 15 minutes boiling to cook.

white meat Term used for the breast flesh of poultry to distinguish it from the dark meat of the legs. Also used of pork and veal.

white mugwort A hardy deciduous shrub, *Artemesia lactiflora*, whose aromatic green leaves are used in stuffings for roast goose

white mustard The pale yellow or fawn, pungent seed of an annual plant *Brassica hirta* or *Sinapsis alba* native to Southern Europe. This mild form of mustard is combined with brown mustard, a more aromatic variety, in various proportions to give the variety of mustard-based condiments available.

white mutton stock As white beef stock but substituting mutton or lamb bones for beef bones. Also called **fond blanc de mouton**

white octopus Curled octopus

white of egg See **egg, egg white**

white onion A variety of onion with a similar shape to the globe but with a silvery white skin. They have a mild sweet flavour and are usually served raw.

white onion soup Basic soup with onions. Also called **oignons, purée d'**

white pepper The dried dehusked berries of a vine, *Piper nigrum*, sold either as whole berries or ground to a fine fawn powder. Used in white sauces where the dark specks from the husks of black peppercorns would detract from the appearance. See also **peppercorn**

white pomfret The silvery-skinned variety of **pomfret** with the finer flavour

white pork *United States* The flesh of completely desanguinated young pigs

whitepot *England* A Devonshire custard made with eggs, flour, milk and cream

white pudding 1. *Scotland* **Skirlie**, packed into hog casings. Also called **mealie pudding 2.** A general name for sausages made from light-coloured offal and meats such as brains, tongue, lights, etc. mixed with whitish cooked grains such as pearl barley, oatmeal, etc., seasoned, flavoured and packed into off-white casings. Generally fried and eaten hot.

white radish Mooli

white roux Equal quantities of plain soft flour and butter, cooked together to a sandy texture for a few minutes without colouring. Used for **béchamel sauce**.

white sapote *United States* A type of baseball-sized custard apple with a green, shading to yellow, edible skin and soft flesh

white sauce See **béchamel, sauce**

white sesame seeds The white variety of sesame seeds used to make tahini. Used as a garnish in Asia and crushed for use in sauces and coatings. In Asia they are dry-fried or roasted to release flavour.

white skate A variety of skate, *Raja marginata*, with a fawny red upper skin and white underside. Used as skate.

white sprouting broccoli See **sprouting broccoli**

white stew A stew made from poultry or veal with onions in a white sauce. See also **blanquette**

white Stilton A semi-hard, crumbly, slightly acid, whitish cheese which is young Stilton before the veining has started. It is matured for about 4 weeks, has little crust and does not keep. May be used as a substitute for Feta.

white sturgeon Osetrina sturgeon

white sugar Fully refined sugar, either granulated, caster or icing

whitetail A name for various game birds with white tails, e.g. wheatear

white tuna fish A variety of tuna with very pale flesh

white turmeric See **zedoary**

white veal stock As for white beef stock but substituting veal bones for beef bones. Also called **fond blanc de veau**

white vegetable stock Chopped aromatic vegetables simmered in water for 1 hour and strained. Proportions 1 vegetables, 4 water.

white vinegar A colourless transparent vinegar either spirit vinegar or a decolorized malt vinegar. Often used for pickling.

white wine court bouillon Equal quantities of white wine and water with 120 g of onion and 12 g of salt per litre together with parsley stalks, a little thyme and bayleaf and peppercorns added. Used for trout, eel, pike and most fish.

white wine sauce See **vin blanc, sauce**

white yam A most important species of yam, *Dioscorea rotundata*, which is grown in the high rainfall zone of West Africa where it is a staple food

whiting 1. A round bodied seawater fish, *Merlangus merlangus* of the cod family found generally in the North Atlantic and weighing about 400 g. The upper skin is grey to dark green or blue and the flesh is lean, white and delicate and may be cooked in any way. See also **King George whiting 2.** *United States* Silver hake

Whitstable oyster *England* A fine native oyster

wholegrain wheat Dehusked wheat grains

wholemeal bread Bread made from wholemeal flour. Also called **Graham bread**

wholemeal flour A flour produced from dehusked wheat grains containing both the bran and the wheat germ. Also called **wholewheat flour**

whole milk 1. *United Kingdom* Full cream milk **2.** *United States* Cows' milk with a least 3.25% butterfat and 8.25% non fat solids

wholewheat flour See **wholemeal flour**

whortleberry Bilberry

wiankowa *Poland* A hard sausage made from lean pork and pork fat, formed into the shape of a horseshoe. Also called **wiejska**

wichity grub See **witchetty grub**

wickenin' *England* Yeast

widgeon A small wild duck, *Anas penelope* which is normally plucked, drawn and trussed and roasted at 220°C for 20 to 25 minutes, garnished with watercress and lemon and served with an orange salad and a jus lié flavoured with redcurrant jelly or port wine. The shooting season is the 1st of September to the 31st of January. Hanging time 2 to 3 days. Also called **wigeon**

wiejska *Poland* Wiankowa

wiener *United States* Frankfurter sausage

Wiener Backhendl *Austria* Deep-fried panéed chicken meat possibly beaten out to escalope thickness

wienerbrød *Denmark* Danish pastry (NOTE: Literally 'Vienna bread'.)

wienerlängd *Sweden* A cake made from a rolled out sheet of Danish pastry 40 by 15 cm. Crème pâtissière laid lengthways along the centre, the 2 sides folded in over part of the filling and pressed down, proved 40 minutes, baked at 230°C for 20 minutes, cooled, iced and cut across into individual pastries.

Wiener Schnitzel *Austria, Germany* A veal escalope or cutlet, panéed (sometimes olive oil in the egg) and fried in butter. Served with a wedge of lemon.

Wiener Schnitzel Holstein *Austria* A Wiener schnitzel topped with a fried egg

Wienerwurst *Austria, United States* A coarse sausage similar in shape to the Frankfurter made from veal or beef and pork lightly cured in sugar, salt and saltpetre, chopped separately, the pork finer than the veal or beef, mixed, seasoned, flavoured with coriander, garlic and grated shallots, filled into narrow sheep casings, lightly smoked, boiled until they rise to the surface, then air-dried. Also called **wienie**, **Würstel**

wienie *United States* Wienerwurst

Wiesenschaumkraut *Germany* Lady's smock

wig *England* A small one-portion cake or bun

wigeon See **widgeon**

wijen *Indonesia* Sesame seeds

wijn *Netherlands* Wine

Wild *Germany* Game

wildappel *Netherlands* Crab apple

wild boar The original ancestor of the domesticated pig, sometimes hunted but now farmed in enclosed woodland. They grow slowly and the flesh is red and tastier than ordinary pig. Generally killed at 14 to 18 months.

wildbraad *Netherlands* Game

Wildbret *Germany* Venison, game

Wildbret Pastete *Germany* Venison pie

wild celery A biennial plant, *Apium graveolens*, whose ground brown seeds are a constituent of celery salt. The chopped leaves may be used in salads, as a garnish or as an aromatic flavouring. Also called **smallage**

wild duck See **mallard**

wilde eend *Netherlands* Wild duck

Wildegeflügel *Germany* Game birds

Wildente *Germany* Wild duck

wildfowl Game birds such as partridge, wild duck, etc.

wild goose Either pinkfoot or greylag. Shooting season 1st September to the 31st of January. Hanging time 2 to 9 days.

wild lime *Australia* The fruits of this true citrus, *Eremocitrus glauca*, are about 1 cm in diameter and have a thin porous skin. They are bitter and very acidic and are used in the same way as limes. Ten wild limes are the equivalent of one ordinary lime. Other similar limes are the finger lime, the round lime and the Russell river lime, some of which are larger.

wild marjoram Oregano

wild plum *Australia* Kakadu plum

wild raspberry *Australia* There are various wild raspberries, varying in size, colour and flavour. The Atherton raspberry is one that is commercially available.

wild rice A black and white seed of a rush plant, *Zizania aquatica,* which is grown in China, Japan and the USA. It is not a rice in spite of its name. It is now cultivated as well as being gathered in the wild. Cooked like rice, but requires about 45 minutes boiling. Also called **Indian rice**, **tuscarora rice**

wild rice shoot The young shoots of the wild rice plant, *Zizania aquatica*, used as a vegetable. They are up to 25 cm long and may be steamed, boiled, baked or stir-fried.

wild rose See **rose**

wild rosella *Australia* The edible, magenta-coloured flower covering (**calyx**) of a naturalized hibiscus, *Hibiscus sabdariffa*, from the north. It has a sharp raspberry and rhubarb flavour and is available fresh in Queensland and frozen elsewhere. It makes excellent jams, sauces and relishes.

Wildschwein *Germany* Wild boar

wild spinach *United States* Pig weed

wild strawberry A hardy evergreen plant, *Fragaria vesca*, whose small fruits have a very fine flavour. Also called **wood strawberry** (NOTE: The cultivated strawberry was bred from imports, *F. virginiana* and *F. chiloensis*, in the 16th and 18th centuries.)

wild thyme *Australia* This low-growing herb, *Ocimum tenuiflorum*, is a member of the basil family and has the same leaf structure and flavour as thyme but more intense and with hints of tarragon and rosemary. It is used sparingly in the same way as thyme. Also called **native thyme**

wild yeast A yeast which grows naturally on ripe fruit and will cause fermentation. Often a mixture of yeasts and bacteria especially in hot countries.

willick *Ireland* Winkle (*colloquial*)

willow grouse A member of the grouse family, *Lagopus lagopus*, widely spread throughout Scandinavia, northern Russia and the north of North America. It goes completely white in winter. Cooked as grouse.

willowleaf mandarin *Mediterranean* mandarin

willow partridge Ptarmigan

Wiltshire cure *England* The principal method of curing bacon in which the curing solution is injected under pressure into a whole side of pork through multiple hollow needles. The sides are then steeped in brine for 2 to 3 days and matured in a cold room for 7 days. At this stage it is known as green bacon. The sides may then be cold-smoked to give smoked bacon.

Wiltshire sausage *England* A sausage made from freshly killed lean pork, fat pork and rusk (7:3:1), minced, seasoned, flavoured with mace, ginger and sage, packed into hog casings and linked

windberry Bilberry

Windbeutel *Germany* A large hollow-centred choux pastry ball filled with whipped cream

wind-blown whiting *Scotland* Blawn whiting

wind egg An imperfectly formed egg with a soft shell

Windermere char *England* The British version of the freshwater Arctic char from the lake of the same name

windfall Fruit which has fallen off trees and is usually bruised or damaged

Windsor bean Broad bean

Windsor red cheese *England* A mature Cheddar cheese flavoured and coloured with a red fruit wine to give a veined appearance

wine 1. The juice of red or white grapes, fermented on or off the skins and matured for varying periods of time depending on quality. Used as a constituent of many sauces especially when reduced to concentrate the flavour, as a cooking liquor and as a constituent of a marinade. **2.** Alcoholic drink made from various sources: palm wine, rice wine, barley wine, elderberry wine, etc.

wine ball A mixed culture of yeasts and fungi formed into small balls used for making Chinese alcoholic beverages and fermented red rice. Also called **wine cube**

wineberry The sweet and juicy fruit of a prickly shrub, *Rubus phoenicolasius*, rather like a conical red blackberry. It may be used as blackberries or raspberries. Also called **Japanese wineberry**

wine cube See wine ball

wine jelly A jelly made with wine, gelatine and flavourings. May be eaten as a dessert or as an accompaniment to meat and game.

wine plant *United States* Rhubarb (*colloquial*)

wine sauce *Scotland* Sweet white wine, thickened with 55 g of corn flour per litre then butter and brown sugar added both at the rate of 100g per litre and finally finely grated lemon zest to flavour. Served hot.

wine vinegar Wine in which the alcohol has been biologically oxidized to acetic acid. The normal concentration is 3 to 4 percent of acetic acid.

wing The feathered front limbs of a bird used for flying or fast ground running. Usually only the bone nearest the body is used, the remainder going into the stockpot. If very meaty the two bones may be used and are often marinated and grilled.

winged bean Asparagus pea

winged pea Asparagus pea

winged yam Asiatic yam

wing kelp *United States* Alaria

wing rib of beef *United Kingdom* The last three ribs of beef closest to the sirloin and the choicest roasting joint. The wing rib with possibly some of the fore ribs is used for the traditional roast beef of England.

winkle A small herbivorous gastropod mollusc, *Littorina littorea*, up to 2.5 cm long found in most coastal waters and usually sold cooked either shelled or still in its shell. They have to be extracted with a long pin or winkle pick. Rather tasteless and usually eaten with vinegar. Also called **periwinkle**, **willick**

winkle pick A straight pin, 4 to 5 cm in length, used for extracting winkles from their shells

winter artichoke See **Jerusalem artichoke**

Winterbergminze *Germany* Winter savory

winter cress *United States* A wild cress, *Barbarea vulgaris*, with somewhat spicy bitter leaves which may be used in salads. Can be cultivated throughout the winter under protection. Also called **yellow rocket**

winter flounder A flatfish, *Pseudopleuronectes americanus*, similar to a large plaice. It is found off the eastern coast of Canada and northern USA and moves towards the coast in winter. It weighs about 2 to 3 kg and averages 45 cm long. The upper skin is reddish brown. Cook as plaice. Also called **common flounder**, **George's bank flounder**

winter frisée See **endive**

winter gourd Wax gourd

wintergreen *United States* A native evergreen plant, *Gaultheria procumbens*, with deep green aromatic leaves and edible spicy berries used as a flavouring. Also called **checkerberry**

Winterkohl *Germany* Kale

winter melon A variety of sweet melon, *Cucumis melo*, with smooth yellow or yellow and green striped skin, weighing up to 1 kg and with a sweet juicy white to orange and green flesh. The melon is ripe when the skin gives slightly at the stalk end when pressed. Also called **casaba melon** (NOTE: The name is also used confusingly for the wax gourd)

winter mushroom Shiitake mushroom

winter purslane A hardy invasive annual plant, *Montia perfoliata*, with mild-flavoured, heart-shaped leaves and small flowering shoots, all of which are cut continuously for use in salads. Also called **miner's lettuce**, **claytonia**

winter radish Varieties of radish which can be left in the ground throughout the winter

winter rape Rape

winter rocket *United States* Watercress

winter savory A perennial herb, *Satureja montana*, with small narrow pointed and folded leaves rather like thyme which is slightly milder than the summer variety. Used in bean and cheese dishes, on roast duck, to flavour vinegar, chopped to garnish soups and sauces and to flavour salami.

winter squash Various fruits of the genus *Curcubita*, e.g. *Curcubita maxima* or *C. moschata*, which are used when fully ripe and the rind has hardened. They are peeled and the seeds removed before cooking. Used for pumpkin pie and soup. Examples are Hubbard, table queen or acorn, golden delicious, butter cup, butternut, turk's cap, etc. They all have much the same flavour. They are often added to curries in India and used tempura-style in Japan. They may also be pickled or made into chutney. The salted

and dry-roasted seeds are eaten as a snack food.

winter wheat Wheat planted in the autumn. The young plants overwinter and growth recommences in spring. Harvested slightly earlier than spring wheat.

wishbone A thin V-shaped bone found in birds which connects the centre of the breast bone to the wing joints, equivalent to the collar bone of humans. It should always be removed from chickens and turkeys to aid carving and jointing.

witchetty grub *Australia* The large white larva of the Australian longicorn beetle about 6 to 10 cm long eaten after frying by the aboriginal population and becoming more generally popular. It tastes like fish cooked in cream. Also called **wichity grub**, **witjuities**

witch sole A small long deepwater flatfish, *Glyptocephalus cynoglossus*, from north Atlantic European waters, up to 50 cm long and with a brown to grey upper skin.Somewhat thinner than the similar winter flounder. Cook as sole. Also called **Torbay sole**, **pole dab**

witherslacks *England* A Lake District term for damsons (*colloquial*)

witjuites *Australia* Witchetty grub

witlof *Netherlands* Belgian chicory

witloof chicory Belgian chicory

wittebonen *Netherlands* White butter beans

wittegoud *Netherlands* The thick white asparagus much liked by the Dutch and in season during May and June (NOTE: Literally 'white gold'.)

wittekool *Netherlands* Cabbage

Wittling *Germany* Whiting

wohlriechende Süssdolde *Germany* Sweet cicely

wok *China* A thin steel pan with one or two handles made in the form of a section of a sphere which is used for very fast Chinese stir-frying. The wok is placed over a very intense heat source and different ingredients may be added to hot oil in order of cooking time. Cooked and part cooked food is often kept on the shallow sloping sides of the wok. Toward the end of the cooking process stock and sauces may be added to complete the whole dish of food. The wok is also used for rapid stir-frying of a single vegetable or item of food, for deep-frying and it can be used for steaming using bamboo nested steamers.

wok lok wuat *China* Cardamom

Wolfbarsch *Germany* Bass, the fish

wolfberry The seed of the matrimony vine which turns a bright red when cooked. It is used as a flavouring and as a tonic in Chinese medicine.

wolf fish Catfish

wolke *England* The Old English term for rolled or kneaded dough

Wollwurst *Germany* A finely minced and ground veal sausage from Bavaria. Normally fried in butter.

wonderberry A tropical and subtropical annual plant, *Solanum x burbankii*, which grows to 1 m and has oval light green leaves and clusters of purple berries each berry up to 1 cm diameter The young leaves and shoots are cooked as spinach. The ripe berries must be thoroughly cooked. Unripe berries contain a poisonous alkaloid. Also called **sunberry**

wong bok *China* Chinese leaves

wong geung *China* Turmeric

wong gwa *China* Cucumber

wong keung *China* Turmeric

wong nga baak *China* Chinese leaves

wong paan *China* Garoupa, the fish

won ton *China* A type of ravioli made with very thin 8 cm squares of noodle pastry with a small amount of a savoury mixture of meat, fish or vegetables placed in the centre, the pastry is then folded into a triangle, sealed and the two acute angles brought together and the right angle folded outwards. They are either deep-fried and served as an appetizer, boiled in a soup or poached until they float.

won ton skin See **won ton wrapper**

won ton wrapper Egg pasta or egg noodle dough rolled out as thinly as possible, cut into 8 cm squares and dusted with corn flour. Also called **won ton skin**

won yee *China* Cloud ear fungus

woo chak *China* Cuttlefish

wood apple An edible fruit indigenous to the Indian sub-continent about the size of an orange. It is eaten raw or mashed with sugar and water and made into jellies or sherberts. Occasionally available in cans. Also called **aegletree fruit, elephant apple**

wood blewit A variety of edible fungus, *Tricholoma nudum*, with a relatively long cylindrical stem and a 5 to 14 cm diameter smooth cap, deep purple to brownish purple in damp conditions and beige brown during drought and when mature. The flesh has a pleasant scent and they grow in clusters on forest floors. See also **blewit**

woodchuck *United States* A North American burrowing rodent, *Marmota monax*, weighing around 2.5 kg in March to 4.5 kg in September prior to hibernation. The flesh when young resemble pork. Also called **groundhog, whistle pig**

woodcock 1. A small squat wild bird, *Scolopax rusticola*, from boggy land with mottled plumage, a long bill and large eyes. It weighs about 280 gram and forms one portion. Roasted with the head on, barded with bacon and without drawing the bird, at 190°C for 20 to 30 minutes. The trail (liver and heart) is spooned onto the bread on which they are served and the whole garnished with watercress and lemon and accompanied with a **jus lié** and cranberry sauce. The shooting season is the 1st of October to the 31st of January in England, 1st of September to the 31st of January in Scotland. Hanging time 1 to 3 days. **2.** *United States* A slightly smaller relative, *Philobela minor*, of the woodcock found in Europe and Asia

wood dove See **pigeon**

wood duck Carolina duck

wood ear Cloud ear fungus

wood fungus Cloud ear fungus

wood grouse Capercaillie

wood hedgehog *United States* A type of wild mushroom with a near white flesh and a bitter flavour

wood pigeon The wild pigeon, *Columba palumbus* recognized by its large feet. Young ones are barded with bacon and stuffed with shallots before roasting at 200°C for 30 to 40 minutes; older birds may be casseroled or stewed. There is no close season (May to October best) and no hanging time is required, although 2 to 3 days are recommended by some authorities.

woodruff See **sweet woodruff**

wood sorrel One of the sorrel family with small heart-shaped sour leaves used for flavouring and in salads and soups

wood strawberry Wild strawberry

wooi heung *China* Fennel

woolly pyrol *Caribbean* Black gram. Sometimes grown as green manure.

woo lo gwa *China* Bottle gourd

woon sen *China* Cellophane noodles

woo tau *China* Taro

wop salad *United States* Lettuce with olives, anchovies, oregano, capers, and garlic dressed with olive oil (NOTE: A politically incorrect name and probably soon obsolete.)

worcesterberry An intermediate-sized blue-black hybrid of the North American gooseberry and the blackcurrant. May be used instead of blackcurrants or blueberries.

Worcester sauce *England* A misspelling of Worcestershire sauce

Worcestershire sauce *England* A thin strong-flavoured sauce usually used to add flavour to sauces and cooked dishes. Made commercially from vinegar, molasses, sugar, salt, anchovies, tamarind, shallots, garlic and spices. It is said to have originated when a barrel of vinegar and spices made up for a customer with Indian connections by the pharmacist's shop, Lea and Perrins, in the early 19th century was not collected and bottled for sale by the pharmacist. Also called **Lea and Perrins' sauce**, **Worcester sauce**

work, to 1. To mix or knead dough with a steady motion **2.** During the process of fermentation, the liquid or paste is said to work

workseed Epazote

wormseed Certain types of fennel used to make a herb tea

wors *South Africa* Boerewors

worst *Netherlands* Sausage

worteltje *Netherlands* Carrot, root vegetable

wot *Africa* A hot curry-like meat stew from East Africa

wrasse A very bony fish usually used as bait in the UK but used in other countries to add flavour to soups and stews

wreckfish *United States* A name given to various different types of fish

wu kwok *China* A **dim sum** made by deep-frying a meat filling surrounded by mashed taro. The taro beomes crisp and lacy.

wun sen *Thailand* Clear transparent noodles

Würfelzucker *Germany* Sugar lumps, cubes

Wurmkraut *Germany* Tansy

Wurst *Germany* Sausage

Würstchen *Germany* Small sausages made from lean pork, veal and pork from the throat, seasoned, flavoured with allspice and cardamom, moistened with wine, filled into casings, tied in bundles, boiled 3 minutes in salted water then dried and grilled

Wurste *Germany* Cold cuts of meat

Würstel 1. *Austria* Sausage **2.** *Austria* Wienerwurst **3.** *Italy* Frankfurter sausage

Würstelbraten *Austria* A large joint of beef, larded with sausages, slowly braised in the oven with a little stock, sliced across the sausages and served with a sauce made from the pan juices thickened with cream

Wursteplatte *Germany* A plate of assorted sliced sausages

Wurst in Teig *Germany* A sausage wrapped in dough and baked

Wurstspeisen *Germany* Pork products (charcuterie)

Wurst von Kalbsgekrüse *Germany* A sausage made from finely chopped calf mesentery, seasoned, flavoured with nutmeg, bound with eggs and cream, packed into hog casings and linked

Würze *Germany* Seasoning, spice or condiment

Wurzelsellerie *Germany* Celeriac

Würzfleisch *Germany* A spicy beef stew containing sour cream, served with dumplings or potatoes

X YZABCD

xa *Vietnam* Lemon grass

xacutti masala *South Asia* A spice mix from Goa consisting of desiccated coconut, dried Kashmiri chillies, coriander, cumin and fenugreek seeds and black peppercorns, all dry-roasted and ground

xai *Catalonia* Lamb

xa-lach xon *Vietnam* Watercress

xanthan gum E414. A gum produced from a bacterium, *Xanthomonas campestris*, by commercial fermentation used as a thickener or gelling agent.

xanthophyll See **E161(b)**

Xanthosoma sagittifolium *Botanical name* The tannia plant

xanthoxylum Anise pepper

Xanthoxylum piperitum *Botanical name* Anise pepper and sansho

xao *Vietnam* Stir-fried, to fry

xarope *Portugal* Syrup

xató 1. *Spain* A vinaigrette sauce flavoured with chopped red chilli peppers and garlic used to dress a salad of endive and almonds. Usually served in winter. **2.** *Catalonia* A variation on a normal salad including some or all of salt cod, tuna, anchovies or almonds

Xaviersuppe *Germany* Consommé garnished with small cheese dumplings

xérès, sauce *France* Sherry sauce

xia *China* Shrimp

xiang gu *China* Shiitake mushroom

xiang tsai *China* Coriander

xiang you *China* Sesame seed oil

xian su ya *China* Crisp roasted or grilled duck

xiao long bao Small steamed buns

xi dau *Vietnam* Light soya sauce

xie *China* Crab

xie rou dou fu *China* Fresh crab meat mixed with soya bean paste

xi gua *China* Watermelon

xi hong shi *China* Tomatoes

xima *South Africa* A maize- or cassava-based staple porridge from Mozambique, usually served with beans, vegetables or fish. Also called **upshwa**

xing zi *China* Apricot

xin xiang de *China* Fresh

xiu *China* A method of cooking in which ingredients are first fried or steamed, then simmered and finally heated uncovered over a high heat to reduce the cooking liquor to a thick sauce

xocolata *Catalonia* Chocolate

xoconostle *Mexico* Green prickly pear

xoi nep *Vietnam* Cooked glutinous rice served at breakfast or dinner in place of plain boiled white rice, but never at lunch

xooñ *West Africa* The crust which forms on the bottom of the pan when rice is cooked in just the right amount of water

xoriço *Catalonia* A spicy red-coloured sausage (**chorizo**) flavoured with paprika

xoxo Choko

xua *Vietnam* Jellyfish

xylitol A polyhydroxy alcohol somewhat sweeter than sugar used in sugar free chewing gum

ya *China* Duck

yabbie *Australia* A freshwater crayfish, *Cherax destructor*, widely distributed in Australian waters and growing to a maximum length of 30 cm but generally caught at a smaller size. They have a slightly muddy flavour and may be brown, green or purple.

yabloko *Russia* Apple

yablonnik *Russia* See **iablonnik**

yachmennyi khleb *Russia* See **iachmennyi khleb**

yachmyen *Russia* Iachmen

Yachtwurst *United States* A coarse-textured sausage made with beef, pork and pistachio nuts

ya dan *China* Duck egg

ya gan *China* Duck liver

yahni *Turkey* Leg of mutton on the bone, browned in mutton fat with sliced onions, then pot-roasted with a little water and seasoning in a well sealed fireproof dish

yahniya ot spanak *Bulgaria* Stewed lamb with spinach

yahourt Yoghurt

yair choy *China* Cauliflower

yaitsa po-russki *Russia* See **iaitsa po-russki**

yak A domesticated animal from Tibet mainly reared for its butter

yak butter A very strong-smelling butter made from yak milk and invariably used in Tibetan tea

yakhnee *Middle East* See **yakhni 2**

yakhni 1. *South Asia* Stock made from meat, bones and vegetables as in the West, simmered 12 to 14 hours in a sealed pan, the vegetables being removed after 3 hours. It may be reduced to a glace de viande when it is known as garhi yakhni. Also called **yakni 2.** *Middle East* Stew, with potatoes as the main ingredient. Also called **yakhnee**

yaki *Japan* Grilled. See also **yakimono, yakitori**

yaki fu *Japan* Large cubes of gluten cake roasted until brown

yakimono *Japan* The term used for foods which are rapidly grilled, barbecued or fried to give a crisp exterior and only a lightly cooked interior. The food is usually supported on one or more thin skewers depending on the size of the food. Abbreviated in recipes to yaki.

yaki myoban *Japan* See **myoban**

yakinasu *Japan* Grilled aubergine

yakitori *Japan* Grilled chicken, chicken livers, onion or Asian leek and sweet pepper kebabs brushed with yakitori sauce during the cooking and sprinkled with sansho or shichimi to garnish

yakitori sauce *Japan* Dark soya sauce, sake, **mirin**, rock sugar and light soya sauce (12:8:5:5:4), simmered for 15 minutes then cooled and refrigerated

yaki zakana *Japan* **1.** Grilled fish **2.** Fish wrapped in foil parcels with onion slices, quarters of sweet green pepper, sliced mushrooms, sake, seasoning and a slice of lemon, baked in a 220°C oven for 15 to 20 minutes and served immediately

yakju *Korea* Rice wine

yakni *South Asia* See **yakhni 1**

yam 1. A generally large tuberous root of one of the genus *Dioscorea*, with dense flesh, used as a starch staple and ranging from less than 0.5 kg to 25 kg in size. They must be cooked and are treated like potatoes. Varieties are found in all tropical and subtropical areas and a few in temperate regions. Typical are cush cush yam, Chinese yam, aerial yam, winged yam, guinea yam and Asiatic yam. **2.** *Thailand* The decorative salads of Thailand which are an art form in their own right **3.** The name sometimes incorrectly given to the sweet potato grown in the USA

yamabukusu *Japan* A sweetened vinegar used for seasoning rice as in sushi. A reasonable substitute is vinegar, sugar and salt (15:2:1) with a pinch of MSG.

yamadon An oil obtained from yellow nutmeg

yamaimo *Japan* Yam

yam bean 1. Jicama **2.** An edible tuber of a plant, *Sphenostyllis stenocarpa*, similar to the **jicama** grown in West Africa

yamo no imo *Japan* See **mountain yam** (NOTE: Literally 'long potato'.)

yang-baechu gimchi *Korea* Pickled cabbage leaves wrapped around a filling of white radish and spring onions flavoured with ginger, garlic, chillies, anchovies and salt

yang-hoe *Korea* Raw minced beef mixed with sesame seed oil, sesame seeds, ginger, garlic, onions and sugar, formed into mounds, topped with a raw egg yolk, sprinkled with chopped pine nuts and garnished with strips of peeled pear

yan grou *China* Lamb or mutton

yankee bean Navy bean

yan kok *China* Aniseed

yan wo *China* Bird's nest

yao dou *China* Cashew nut

yao gou ji ding *China* Diced chicken with cashew nuts

yao horn *Cambodia* A type of **fondue chinoise** in which thin slices of beef, chicken and seafood are poached at the table in stock and dipped in raw egg and peanut sauce after cooking and before eating

yaourt *France* Yoghurt

yaout *Bulgaria, Russia* Yoghurt

ya pi *China* Duck skin

yapon *United States* A plant similar to holly. The leaves are used by Native Americans to make the tea, yaupon.

yaprak dolmasi *Turkey* Vine leaves wrapped around a filling of rice, raisins, chopped onions, pine nuts, chopped parsley or dill and seasoning, baked in the oven and served cold

yard bean Asparagus bean

yard long bean See **long bean**, **asparagus bean**

yari-ika *Japan* A variety of squid

Yarmouth bloater *England* A slightly salted and smoked herring from Yarmouth

yarpakh dolmasy *Russia* See **iarpakh dolmasy**

yarrow A hardy wild perennial, *Achillea millefolium*, with clusters of small flowers and feathery leaves. The slightly bitter and peppery young leaves may be chopped and used in moderation for salads, to flavour dips and as a garnish.

yasai-ryori *Japan* A vegetable dish

yasawa A fried meatball made with chicken from the South Pacific islands

yassa au poulet *West Africa* Chicken fried with onions then simmered in a marinade

yau char koay *Malaysia* Crullers

yau jaar gai *China* Crullers

yaupon *United States* Tea made by Native Americans from yapon leaves

yautia See **tannia**

yau yu *China* Squid

ya xin *China* Duck hearts

ya you *China* Duck fat, often used to add a finish to Chinese food

ya zhang *China* Duck feet

ya zhen *China* Duck gizzards

yeaning *United States* A young lamb or kid

yeanling *England* A young lamb or kid

yearling A year old domesticated animal. It might be any age under 2 years.

yearn, to *United States* To coagulate or curdle milk

yearning *United States* Rennet

yeast A microorganism (strictly speaking a fungus) which reproduces by budding from the parent microorganism. The most important in cooking is *Saccharomyces cerevisiae* which has a multitude of variants used principally for converting sugars to alcohol or water and carbon dioxide as in beer, wine, and bread production. Yeasts can also excrete some enzymes which break down polysaccharides into simple sugars. Yeasts work best around 30 to 35°C and are killed above 60°C.

yeast buns *Wales* A traditional Pembrokeshire New Year bun which is basically an egg, butter, sugar and dried vine fruit enriched, yeast-raised bread with about 75 g of each enriching agent per kg of flour. After kneading and proving, the dough is rolled and cut into rounds, proved again then baked at 220°C for 15 – 20 minutes. Also called **migiod**

yeasted goods Flour- and starch-based mixtures which are treated with yeast to produce a multitude of carbon dioxide bubbles within the mixture prior to baking

yeast extract A dark brown thick glossy semi-solid made by hydrolysing disrupted yeast cells to form a complex mixture of amino acids, peptides, nucleic acids and their reaction products together with vitamins and fragments of other cell contents and concentrating the solution. It has an intense flavour and is used by vegetarians and others for flavouring savoury dishes, as a vitamin supplement and as a sandwich spread.

yee raa *Thailand* Cumin

ye-khu *Burma* Sea urchin

yellow bean paste A strong-flavoured Chinese paste made from fermented soya beans. Sold in jars as a flavouring.

yellow bean sauce Fermented yellow soya beans let down with brine. Used in Sichuan and Hunan cuisines and generally in Southeast Asia. Also called **brown bean sauce**, **soya bean condiment**

yellow cake *United States* Cake in which egg yolks but not egg whites are used

yellow chilli A smooth waxy-skinned chilli slightly larger than a jalapeño and very hot. Also called **yellow wax chilli**

yellow chive Chinese chives whose leaves have been blanched by growing in the dark and which have a mild flavour

yellow crookneck squash An important commercial squash grown in southeastern USA. One of the first plants to be genetically engineered to be resistant to mosaic viruses.

yellow cucumber A coarse yellow variety of cucumber grown in China. It has a rough skin and a melon-like taste. It is often peeled, shredded and preserved in honey, sometimes with ginger. Also pickled in soya sauce.

yellow dal *South Asia* An Indian variety of yellow pea, *Pisum sativum*, allowed to mature and dry on the vine. Normally dehusked and split. Often used as a snack food after dry-roasting with spices (e.g. in Bombay mix). Also called **yellow lentil**, **yellow split pea**

yellow eel *United States* Ocean pout, one of the eelpout family with a sweet white flesh

yellow eye mullet *Australia* A fish, *Aldrichetta fosteri*, that is abundant in the bays, inlets and sheltered coastal waters of southern Australia. It sometimes has an earthy taste which can be removed by soaking in milk for an hour prior to cooking. Skinning the fillets will remove the small amount of oil found in the fish. Best for barbecueing.

yellow fin tuna A variety of tuna fish, *Thunnus albacares*, more expensive than skipjack

yellow granadilla A type of passion fruit, *Passiflora laurifolia*. Also called **water lemon**

yellow gurnard Gurnard

yellow lentil See **yellow dal**

yellow passion fruit The fruit of a vine, *Passiflora edulis* f. *flavicarpa,* with a hard smooth golden-yellow skin mottled with red and a pulpy yellow flesh with a mass of embedded seeds. Slightly larger than the standard purple passion fruit. Also called **golden passion fruit**, **granadilla**, **grenadilla**

yellow pear tomato A tiny pear-shaped yellow tomato used for garnishing and decoration

yellow pea soup See **égyptienne, purée**

yellow rice wine See **red girl wine**

yellow rock See **lump sugar 3**

yellow rocket Winter cress

yellows Light brown sugar

yellow soya bean The dried yellow beans are the common soya bean of commerce. Used for making soya derivatives and the variety which is sold cooked and canned in the west.

yellow split pea See **yellow dal**

yellow squash Crookneck squash

yellowtail dab See **yellowtail flounder**

yellowtail flounder A flatfish, *Limanda ferruginea*, up to 40 cm long and 500 g in weight with an olive-brown upper skin with reddish-brown spots and a yellowish tail. It is found on the northeast coast of North America. Cook as flounder. Also called **yellowtail dab**

yellow wax chilli See **yellow chilli**

yellow wine See **red girl wine**

yellow yam Guinea yam

yelt *United States* A young sow

yemas de San Leandro *Spain* Egg yolk threads cooked in hot sugar syrup. See also **golden threads**

yemek listesi *Turkey* Menu

yemesirkik *East Africa* A vegetarian stew from Ethiopia made from chopped onion browned in oil with berbere paste and garlic, mixed with mashed cooked lentils, water and more oil added and all cooked with a little salt. Served warm or cold with injera.

yen wo *China* Bird's nest

yerba *Spain* Herb

yerba buena *Mexico, United States* A strongly aromatic wild mint used as a flavouring

Yersinia enterocolitica Food poisoning bacteria related to the plague organism. It is found in pork and raw milk and will grow at temperatures below 10°C. The incubation period is not known, the duration is 3 plus days and the symptoms are abdominal pain, fever, headache, malaise, vomiting, nausea and chills. Common in Scandinavia and the USA.

ye som megeb *East Africa* A selection of different vegetable dishes served in Ethiopia on fast days, called **nai tsom** in Eritrea

Yetholm bannock *Scotland* A rich festive shortbread from the border country. The paste, which is made with a little baking powder, is enriched with ground ginger, flaked almonds, chopped candied peel, lemon zest and vanilla essence. It is rolled into two rectangles which are sandwiched with chopped crystallized ginger as the filling and the edges scalloped. The top is brushed with egg yolk and milk and sprinkled with flaked almonds and sugar, then all baked at 170°C for 45 minutes. It may be scored and cut.

yeung choy *China* Watercress

yeung chung *China* Onion

ye zi *China* Coconut

yiaourti *Greece* Yoghurt, traditionally made with goats' milk

yield The number of servings or portions obtained from a given recipe or amount of food

yiner *China* White fungus

ying-shu *China* Poppy seed

yin wor *China* Bird's nest

yiouvetsi *Greece* Pasta

yira *Thailand* Cumin or fennel

yi tong *China* Malt extract or maltose

yiu gor *China* Cashew nut

yod nam mali *Thailand* Jasmine oil

yoghoort See **yoghurt**

yoghourt See **yoghurt**

yoghurt *Denmark, England, Italy, Netherlands, Norway* A fermented product made from any milk treated with a culture of *Lactobacillus bulgaricus* and possibly *Streptococcus thermophilus* at a temperature of 37 to 44°C. The fermentation is stopped by cooling to below 5°C after 4 to 6 hours when the liquid will have developed a lactic acid flavour and will be more or less thick, possibly even a gel. Different cultures of the microorganisms and the different milks lead to country-specific textures and flavours. The raw natural yoghurt so obtained may be further pasteurized, sweetened, flavoured, thickened with gums or starches, have fruit added or be treated in a variety of other ways to satisfy Western tastes. Also called **natural yoghurt**, **plain yoghurt**, **yahourt**, **yoghoort**, **yoghourt**, **yogurt**

yoghurt salad dressing Natural yoghurt mixed with ground coriander seeds, dried mint and seasoning with possibly olive oil and lemon juice

yogur *Spain* Yoghurt

yogurt *Italy, United States* Yoghurt

yok kai sake *Japan* Thinly sliced strips of fresh salmon marinated for an hour in a mixture of sake, soya sauce with chopped ginger root, garlic, spring onions, sugar and salt and served with decorative garnishes

yolk See **egg**, **egg yolk**

York cheese *England* A rich creamy soft cheese made from raw or unpasteurized cows' milk. Also called **Cambridge cheese**

York ham *England* A ham cured with dry salt, lightly oak smoked and matured for 3 to 4 months prior to being boiled. The meat is pale with a mild delicate flavour. One of the classic hams now made all over the world and considered to be the best cooked ham for serving cold.

Yorkshire black pudding *England* Black pudding flavoured with marjoram, thyme, lemon thyme and savory

Yorkshire cheese cake *England* An open shortcrust pastry tart filled with a mixture of curd (or sieved cottage) cheese, butter, currants, eggs, sugar, grated lemon zest and nutmeg before baking. Also called **Yorkshire curd tart**

Yorkshire curd tart See **Yorkshire cheese cake**

Yorkshire parkin *England* A type of gingerbread made with fine or medium oatmeal

Yorkshire pie A galantine of meat

Yorkshire pudding A savoury batter nowadays baked in the oven in a large flat tin or individual patty tins together with a roast of beef, and used as an accompaniment to it. Originally the tin of batter was placed beneath a joint of beef roasting on a spit to catch the juices. The batter would cook with the heat from the fire.

Yorkshire sauce *England* A **julienne** of orange zest cooked gently in port, reserved, the port thickened with equal parts of **espagnole sauce** and redcurrant jelly flavoured with cinnamon and cayenne pepper, reduced, strained and finished with orange juice and the **julienne** of orange zest. Served with braised duck or ham.

Yorkshire spice bread A heavily spiced fruit loaf raised with yeast or baking powder

yosenabe *Japan* Poached chicken breast meat and shellfish served in **dashi**

you ga li *China* Curry-flavoured oil

you men sun *China* Braised bamboo shoots

youngberry A hybrid of the loganberry and dewberry from the south of the USA. Use as blackberry.

you yu *China* Squid or cuttlefish

ysaño A South American knobbly yellow tuber from a perennial climbing plant, *Tropaeolum tuberosum*, related to the nasturtium. It is eaten in Bolivia after freezing. Also called **añu**

Ysop *Germany* Hyssop

yu *China* 1. Fish 2. Pummelo

yuba *Japan* 1. The skin that forms on bean curd 2. Bean curd sticks

yuca Cassava

yucca 1. Cassava **2.** A wild cactus-like plant, *Yucca gloriosa*, and related species with long fleshy leaves ending in a spike. The young stalks may be cooked like asparagus and fruits may be roasted. Also called **Spanish bayonet, Spanish dagger, Adam's needle, bear grass, Eve's darning needle**

Yucca gloriosa Botanical name See **yucca 2**

yu chee *China* Shark's fin

yu chiap *China* A fermented fish sauce

yu choy *China* Broccoli rape

yu choy sin *China* Heart of rape

yudebutaniku no nikomo *Japan* Boneless pork loin simmered in water until tender and most of the water has evaporated, cooled, cut in 2 cm cubes and simmered for 10 minutes in soya sauce, sake, sugar and sliced ginger root and a little water, more soya sauce and sugar added and all evaporated to dryness. Served with minced spring onions.

yude-tamago *Japan* Hard-boiled eggs

yueh shih huo kwo *China* Steamboat

yuen sai *China* Coriander leaves

yufka *Turkey* Filo pastry

yule cake See **Christmas cake**

yule log Chocolate log

yu lu *China* A fermented fish sauce

yum *Thailand* See **yam 2**

yum cha *China* Sweet cakes and savouries served with tea during the late morning

yumurta *Turkey* Egg

yun er *China* Cloud ear fungus

Yunnan A hand made goats' milk cheese from the mountainous southwest province of the same name in China

yu pei *China* Shark's skin

yuri-ne *Japan* Lily bulb

yu ts'ai *China* Broccoli rape

yu tu *China* Fish maw

yu xian rou si *China* Shredded spiced pork

yuzu *Japan* A small yellow-coloured citrus fruit, *Citrus junos*, grown mainly for its rind which is used as a garnish and flavouring for soups and vinegars

ZABCDEF

zabade See **zabady**

zabady The Arabic for yoghurt. Also called **zabade, roba, rob**

zabaglione *Italy* A warm dessert made from Marsala, egg yolks and sugar. Also called **zabaione**

zabaglione sauce A sauce made from Marsala, whipped eggs and sugar served warm with fruit desserts or from white wine and whipped eggs as a savoury sauce

zabaione See **zabaglione**

zabalin *Burma* Lemon grass

zaboca *Caribbean* Avocado

zachte eiren *Netherlands* Soft-boiled eggs

zádélávané drstky *Czech Republic* Thin strips of parboiled tripe sautéed in butter with chopped onions and garlic, flour added to make a roux, stock added with chopped ham and parsley and all simmered until cooked

zafferano *Italy* Saffron

zafferanone *Italy* Safflower

zaffran *South Asia* Saffron

zafraan *South Asia* Saffron

Zahnbrasse *Germany* Dentex, the fish

zahtar 1. *North Africa* A spice mixture of 2 parts dry-roasted sesame seeds, 1 part sumac and 1 part dried thyme, ground together and used as a condiment, dip or mixed with olive oil and used as a bread glaze **2.** *Middle East* Similar to the north African zahtar, it is dry mixture of dry-roasted sesame seeds, coriander seeds, walnuts and cooked and dried chick peas, all crushed but not pulverized, with ground cumin, seasoning, cinnamon powder, dried marjoram and sumac powder. Served with a separate dish of olive oil into which bread is dipped prior to its being dipped into the zahtar. Also called **dukkah**

zakuski, zakouski *France, Russia* **1.** Hors d'oeuvres **2.** In Russia, a table of cold meats, fish, small appetizers and hors d'oeuvres, traditionally, and in wealthy households, made available for casual guests between late afternoon and dinner but now often including hot dishes and served as a first course or like smörgåsbord

Zakussotchnyï, Zakoussotchnyï *Russia* A Camembert-type cheese made from pasteurized cows' milk

zalm *Netherlands* Salmon

zamia A type of palm tree from the pith of which a starch is extracted

zampe *Italy* Feet, trotters

zampetto *Italy* Pig's leg

zampone di Modena *Italy* A sausage made of a mixture of lean and fat pork, seasoned, spiced, moistened with wine and packed into a boned pigs trotter, simmered for an hour and served with potatoes and a sweet sauce (NOTE: From the province of Emilia-Romagna)

zanahorias *Spain* Carrots

Zander *Germany* The freshwater pike-perch caught in European rivers and lakes and considered to be a delicacy. The flesh is firm and white with a stronger flavour than cod. It was introduced into the UK in the 1970s and is in danger of wiping out native species of fish. Also called **Zant**

zanoibe *Italy* A hors d'oeuvres of stuffed pigs' trotters similar to sampone, served hot or cold

Zant *Germany* Pike-perch

zao zi *China* Date

zapote Sapodilla

zarda *South Asia* A sweet rice dessert

zarda palau *Central Asia* An elaborate Afghan dish of boiled rice soaked in a heavy sugar syrup which is flavoured with strips of orange peel. Half the rice covers the base of an ovenproof dish and the remainder surrounds the central pile of meat, which is pieces of chicken breast browned with onions and simmered with water for 20 minutes. The cooking liquor is poured over and the covered dish is casseroled at 150°C for 40 minutes. Finally the dish is decorated with the blanched pieces of orange peel removed from the syrup, browned almond slivers and pistachio nuts, and the rice is coloured with a saffron infusion in water.

zaru *Japan* A strainer made of metal or bamboo

zarzamora *Spain* Blackberry

zarzuela *Spain* A colourful seafood stew mainly of shellfish. A typical zarzuela might consist of cleaned, and prepared as for a stew, mussels, squid, Dublin bay prawns, spiny lobster, hake and eel, added to a mixture of onions, garlic, tomatoes and sweet peppers all chopped and sweated in oil, simmered for 20 minutes with wine, seasoning, saffron and chopped parsley in a casserole dish and finished with stoned olives.

zarzuela de mariscos *Spain* A Catalan seafood dish (NOTE: Literally 'an operetta of seafood'.)

zatore *Middle East* A herb and spice mix used in bread which usually includes sesame seeds, thyme and savory

zatziki *Greece* A dip based on finely chopped or grated, deseeded cucumber. See also **tsatsiki**

zatzizi *Southwest Asia* A Georgian dish of chicken flavoured with herbs and served with mashed walnuts

zavtrak *Russia* Breakfast, traditionally tea, rolls, curd cheese and/or buckwheat porridge and buttermilk

Zea mays *Botanical name* Maize

Zea mays saccharata *Botanical name* Sweet corn

zebda *North Africa* A Moroccan butter made in spring by churning milk which has been left to curdle for 2 to 3 days in an earthenware vessel. It is either used fresh or converted into smen.

zebu A type of domesticated ox, *Bos indicus*, found throughout Africa, India and East Asia

zedoaire *France* Zedoary

zedoaria *Italy* Zedoary

zedoary The dried and ground root of a plant, *Curcuma zedoaria* and *C. zerumbet*, grown and used as a spice in Southeast Asia. It has a pungent gingery flavour with a hint of camphor. The young shoots and leaves of the plant are used in Indonesian cooking. Also called **white turmeric**

zeeduivel *Netherlands* Monkfish

zeekreeft *Netherlands* Lobster

Zeeland oysters Fine oysters from the Zeeland province of the Netherlands

zeelt *Netherlands* Tench

zeepaling *Netherlands* Conger eel

zeera *South Asia* Cumin

zeevis *Netherlands* Seafood

zegeni *North Africa* A spicy meat stew. Also called **wat**

zelná polevká *Czech Republic* Cabbage soup made from beef stock thickened with white roux, seasoned and flavoured with nutmeg, finished with egg yolks and cream and mixed with chopped blanched cabbage

zelny gulás *Czech Republic* A beef goulash flavoured with paprika, caraway seeds and a little vinegar and mixed with shredded white cabbage. Also called **segedinsky gulás**

zelyonyi shchi *Russia* Shpinatie shchi

zemikand *South Asia* Elephant's foot

zensai *Japan* An appetizer, e.g. **aemono**. See also **sakizuke, tsuki dashi**

zenzero *Italy* **1.** Ginger **2.** The Tuscan term for chilli pepper

zephyr 1. *England, France* A very light mousse of Italian origin made with fish or other foodstuff pounded to a smooth paste, mixed with egg white and cream, refrigerated and used to fill small moulds lined with thin fish escalopes or similar, baked in a moderate oven, cooled and demoulded **2.** *United States* A light delicate cornmeal puff served instead of bread rolls with a meal

zeppole *Italy* **1.** Doughnut **2.** Fritter

zest The coloured outer layer of citrus fruit skin which contains the essential oil

zeste *France* Zest

zesté(e) *France* Flavoured with citrus fruit zest

zeste confit *France* Candied peel

zeste d'Italie *France* Candied peel

zester A small very fine toothed metal grater often mounted on a wooden handle for grating the zest of citrus peel

zeytinyagli sebzeler *Turkey* Mixed vegetables, garlic and seasoning simmered slowly with very little water until tender. Served cold with a sprinkling of chopped parsley.

zha *China* Deep-fried

zha cai tang *China* A spicy vegetable soup

zha ge zi *China* Deep-fried pigeon

zhang cha ya *China* Duck, smoked over camphor and tea

zha yu qiu *China* Deep-fried square pieces of fish in a hot and spicy sauce

zheng *China* Steamed

zhi ma yoo *China* A dark-coloured sesame seed oil

zhou *China* A kind of porridge

zhou fan *China* **Congee** rice

zhu *China* Pig

zhug *Middle East* A typical spice mix from the Yemen used as a condiment and containing red peppers, red chillies, coriander leaves and seeds, garlic, green cardamom and lemon juice pounded into a paste

zhu jidan *China* Boiled eggs

zhum *Middle East* Cooked junket

zhu rou *China* Pork meat

zhu sun *China* Bamboo fungus

zhu you *China* Lard

zia, alla *Italy* In the aunt's style, i.e. home cooking

zibet A variety of Asian chive

zibidina *Italy* Pig's ears, chops and calves' feet cooked in chicken stock with salt and liberal pepper then cooled to form a strong jelly

Zichorie *Germany* Chicory

Ziebelwähe *Switzerland* Onion pie

Ziege *Germany* Goat

Ziegen *Germany* Goats' milk cheese

Ziegenkäse *Germany* Goats' milk cheese

Ziegenpfeffer *Germany* Sweet pepper

Ziger *Switzerland* Sapsago

Zigeuner Art *Germany* In the gypsy style. See also **Zingara, à la**

Zigeunerspeck *Germany* Lightly cured and smoked pork fat rolled in paprika and eaten raw

Zigeunerspies *Germany* Meat, pepper and onion kebab grilled on the barbecue or over a fire

zik de venado *Mexico* Shredded cooked venison served with onion, chilli peppers, coriander leaf and Seville orange flesh

zimino *Italy* A soup or stew of fish with white wine, tomatoes, mushrooms and herbs

ziminu *France* As **zimino**, but from Corsica

Zimt *Germany* Cinnamon

Zimtplätzchen *Germany* Cinnamon biscuits

Zingara, à la *France* In the gypsy style, i.e. with ham, tongue, mushrooms and tomatoes

Zingara, sauce *France* A sauce for veal and poultry made to a variety of recipes and little used

Zingiber officinale *Botanical name* Ginger

Zion juice *Caribbean* A Jamaican Rastafarian juice made from raw carrots, boiled water and soya milk (2:2:1) processed to a thick drink then flavoured with coconut cream, nutmeg, rose water, and molasses or raw brown sugar to taste

ziste *France* The white pith on the inner surface of citrus fruit peel (**albedo**). Also called **peau blanche**

zita See **ziti**

zit argan *North Africa* The highly flavoured oil extracted from the fruit of the argan tree used in salads and desserts

ziti *Italy* Long lengths of thick macaroni

ziti mezze *Italy* Long lengths of macaroni slightly thinner than ziti

zitoni *Italy* A very thick version of ziti

zitoni rigati *Italy* A fluted or ridged zitoni

Zitronat *Germany* Candied peel

Zitrone *Germany* Lemon

Zitronenstrauch *Germany* Lemon verbena

zitun *North Africa* Olive

Zitwerwurzel *Germany* Zedoary

zit zitun *North Africa* Olive oil

ziwa *East Africa* Milk

Zizania aquatica *Botanical name* Wild rice

Zizyphus lotus *Botanical name* Lotus jujube

Zizyphus mauritania *Botanical name* Mauritian jujube

Zizyphus mistol *Botanical name* Argentinian jujube

zlabiya *Middle East* A deep-fried sweetened yeast-raised batter from Iraq. The batter is piped directly into the 190°C oil with a 5 mm nozzle to form 10 cm circles with a random and decorative cross filling. These are fried both sides for about 3 minutes, drained and soaked in a flavoured heavy sugar syrup which has been boiled to 108°C.

Z'nuni *Germany* The second breakfast or midmorning snack in Bavaria, traditionally black bread, raw bacon or ham and cherry liqueur

zoetwaterkreeft *Netherlands* Crayfish

zoetzuur *Netherlands* Sweet-and-sour, pickles

zoni *Japan* A New Year celebration soup of mochi, kamaboko, chicken meat and sliced vegetables in **dashi** garnished with yuzu

zoolak A lactic fermented milk product

zosui *Japan* A thick rice soup made from well washed and soaked short-grain rice simmered in boiling **dashi** with grated ginger root until the rice disintegrates, seasoned, petit pois, crumbled crisped **nori** and beaten egg yolk added and all simmered for 10 minutes

zout *Netherlands* Salt

zoutevis *Netherlands* Salt cod

zrazy 1. *Russia* Beef or veal olives filled with sour pickles, hard-boiled eggs and/or vegetables **2.** *Poland* A sirloin steak beaten flat, coated with a mixture of sweated chopped onions, bacon, breadcrumbs, egg and seasoning, rolled and tied, browned in butter then simmered in red wine with chopped onions, diced bacon and a faggot of herbs. Served with the drained cooking liquor thickened with **beurre manié**.

Zsendice *Hungary* A soft, smooth, creamy ewes' milk and whey cheese

zucca *Italy* Marrow, squash

zucca gialla *Italy* Pumpkin

zucchero *Italy* Sugar

zucchetti *Italy* Small courgettes

zucchini *England, Italy* Courgette

zucchini flowers Courgette flowers

Zucker *Germany* Sugar

Zuckererbsen *Germany* Petit pois

Zuckerrübe *Germany* Sugar beet

Zuckerwähe *Germany* A sugar tart

Zuger Kirschtorte *Switzerland* A sponge cake soaked in kirsch-flavoured syrup and covered with pink icing

zulynez *Russia* Sour cream

zulynez gribnoi po-odesski *Russia* Mushrooms in sour cream made by sweating chopped onions in butter, button mushrooms added and softened, a little flour added and cooked to a roux, equal parts of sour cream and double cream added, all well mixed, placed in an ovenproof dish, topped with grated cheese and butter and baked at 180°C until the top colours

zumaque *Spain* Sumac

zumo *Spain* Juice

Zunge *Germany* Tongue

Zungenwurst *Germany* A blood sausage with pieces of cooked tongue and fat embedded in it

zupa *Poland* Soup

zuppa *Italy* A substantial soup either thickened with bread or poured over slices of bread or other farinaceous food

zuppa acida alla bolzanese *Italy* Tripe soup containing cream, sauerkraut and lemon juice, served over polenta

zuppa alla canavesana *Italy* Cabbage, bread and cheese layered in a deep dish, soaked in broth and browned in the oven

zuppa di pesce *Italy* Fish soup

zuppa genovese *Italy* Fish soup thickened with egg yolks and garnished with small fish quenelles

zuppa inglese *Italy* An English-style trifle with a base of macaroons moistened with Marsala, covered with custard and topped with whipped cream and glacé fruit

zuppa pavese *Italy* A dish consisting of a slice of toast topped with a poached egg, sprinkled with grated Parmesan cheese and floated on a clear beef consommé

zuppa rustica *Italy* A country soup containing potatoes, beans and sausages

zur *Poland* A plain soup made from sour rye

Zürchertopf *Switzerland* Beef, macaroni and tomato sauce baked in a casserole

Züritirggel *Switzerland* A honey-flavoured thin biscuit baked in a mould carved with a traditional relief. See also **Basler Leckerli**

zurrette *Italy* A Sardinian dish of lambs' or goats' blood mixed with cheese and steamed until solid then served cold or sliced and grilled

zurruputuna *Spain* Salt cod soup, thickened with bread and flavoured with garlic, paprika and sweet peppers

Zutaten *Germany* Condiments

zuur *Netherlands* Sour

zuurkool *Netherlands* Sauerkraut

zuwai-gani *Japan* Crab

zwaardvis *Netherlands* Swordfish

zweischalig Muscheln *Germany* Bivalve shellfish

Zwetschen *Germany* Zwetschgen

Zwetschgen *Austria, Germany* Plums. Also called **Zwetschen**

Zwetschgendatschi *Austria* Plum cake

Zwieback *France, Germany* A small rusk made from dried and browned breads used as a snack food

Zwiebel *Germany* Onion

Zwiebelgrün *Germany* Spring onion

Zwiebelkuchen *Germany* Onion tart

Zwiebelringe *Germany* Onion rings

Zwiebelrostbraten *Austria* Fried steak and onions with gravy accompanied by fried potatoes and gherkins

Zwiebelsosse *Germany* An onion sauce made with chopped onions, slightly browned in butter, flour added to make a roux, cream whisked in and boiled, seasoned, flavoured with nutmeg, passed though a sieve and the consistency adjusted

Zwischenrippenstück *Germany* Rib steak of beef

zwitsers kaas *Netherlands* Swiss cheese

zwyczajna *Poland* A hard sausage made with coarsely chopped pork, seasoned, packed into casings and knotted in long links. Found throughout the country.

zymase Various enzymes which together induce the alcoholic fermentation of carbohydrates, usually obtained from living yeast but may be added apart from the yeast

zyme Yeast, the origin of the word enzyme, as the first enzymes were extracted from yeast